Collector's Edition

Mobile Suit Gundam
THE ORIGIN

V

—CHAR & SAYLA—

CONTENTS

Humanity had been emigrating excess populations to space for

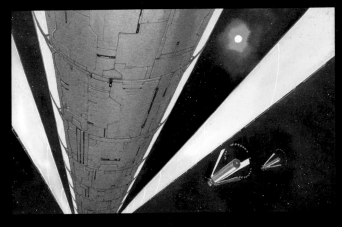

over half a century.

Cosmic cities called space colonies floating near Earth became humanity's second homeland.

Millions of people lived there, had children, and passed on.

The year Universal Century 0079

Under House Zabi and its confederates who touted the superiority of spacenoids, Side 3, the group of colonies farthest from Earth, declared itself the Principality of Zeon

and began to wage a war for independence from the Earth Federation.

In scarcely over a month of fighting, Principality and Federation together slaughtered half of humanity's total population.

All men grew to fear their own deeds.

Having the advantage in a new class of weapon, the mobile suit, the Zeon forces decimated the Federation's military power in space and succeeded in capturing force commander Lieutenant General Revil.

Emboldened, Zeon secured an immense victory at the Battle of Loum and sought thereby to conclude a peace treaty with the Earth Federation government.

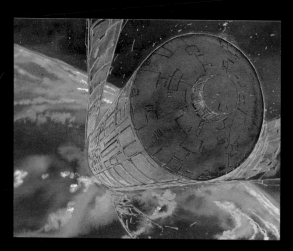

When the Earth Federation Command Center at Jaburo, which had avoided a direct hit by the colonies dropped in Operation British, declared nevertheless that all negotiations would be rejected,

the war entered a stalemate, and eight months went by...

While both sides continued to exhaust their resources, Vice Admiral Dozle Zabi, commander of the Zeon Space Attack Force, sent a Musai cruiser stewarded by Lt. Commander Char Aznable, the famed Red Comet, to the neutral colony of Side 7.

Their objective: to disrupt Operation V, the Federation's top-secret mobile suit development program.

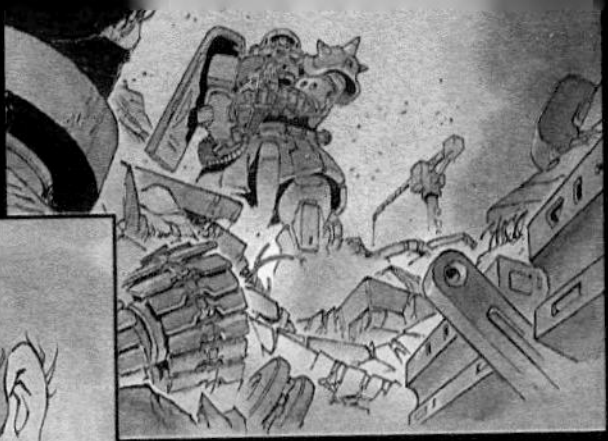

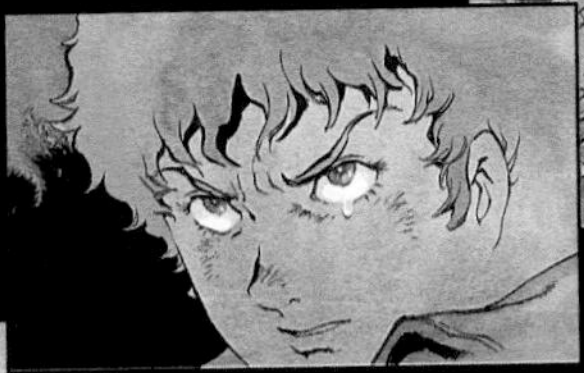

The young Amuro Ray found himself in the midst of combat between the infiltrating Zeon forces and the colony's security details. He climbed into the pilot seat of the "Gundam," a new mobile suit developed by his father, and succeeded in taking out two Zaku units.

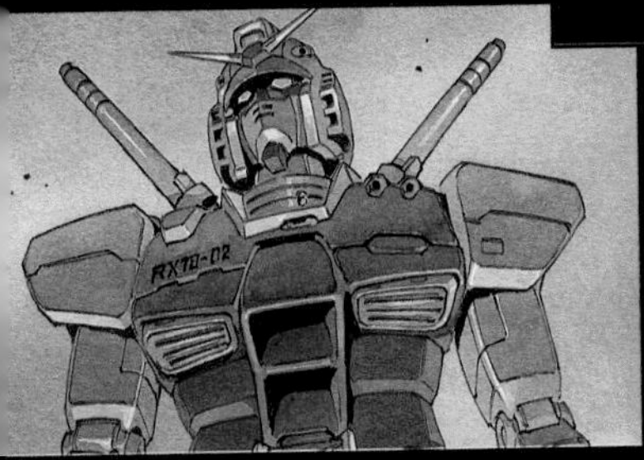
RX78-02

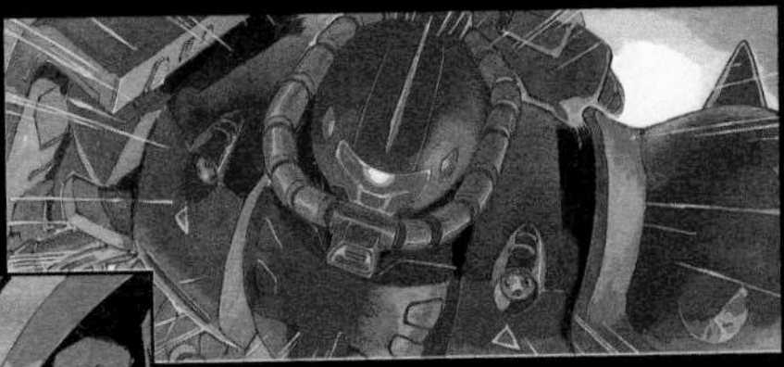

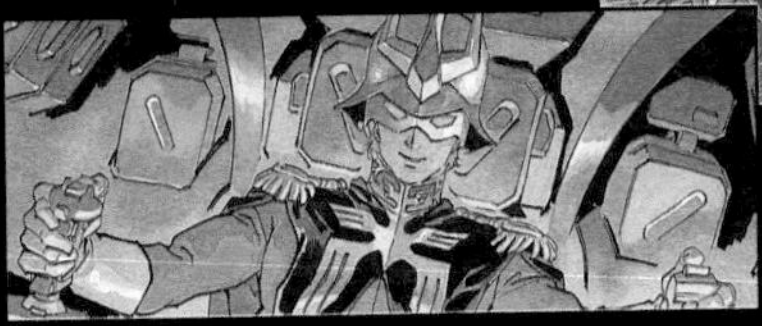

Amuro and others were stowed aboard the new warship *White Base*, along with the Gundam, and after surviving peril after peril finally descended to Earth.

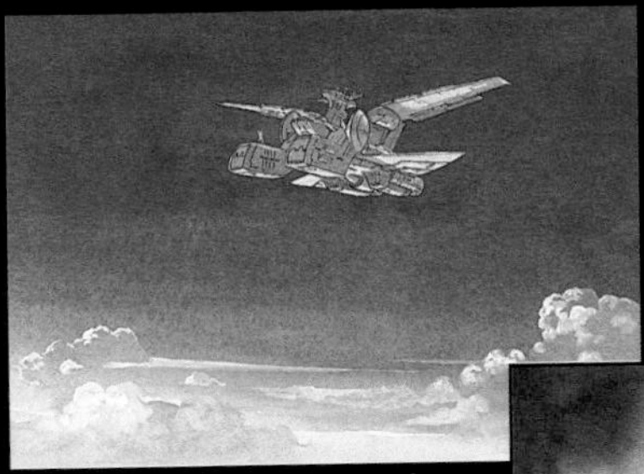

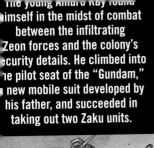

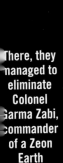

There, they managed to eliminate Colonel Garma Zabi, commander of a Zeon Earth regional force.

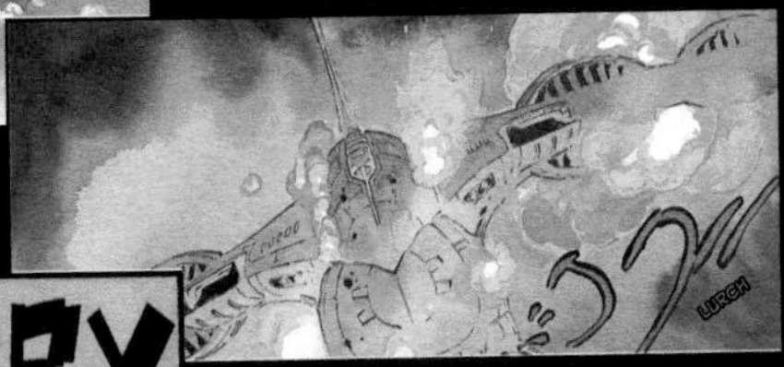

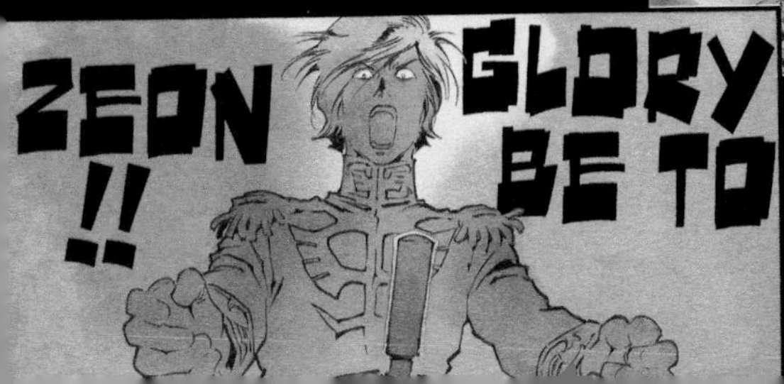
GLORY BE TO ZEON!!

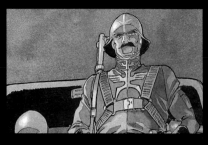

Making it through fierce battles

against Ramba Ral's detachment, sent to seek out and destroy *White Base*, and against Dom heavy mobile suits piloted by the Black Tri-Stars, the best among Zeon's elite troops,

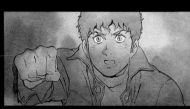

Amuro and company at last reached Jaburo in South America—

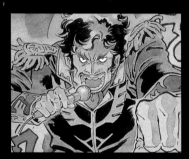

where they were embroiled in a ferocious struggle against the forces of Rear Admiral García Romeo who aimed to capture the Federation Command Center.

The occupation of Jaburo was not to be, and combat ceased without Zeon destroying even those ships and mobile suits the Federation had been constructing for a counteroffensive.

The debacle would come in no small way to sway the course of the war.

At the moment, however, there are no signs that the flames of war will abate. The gears of history go on turning, mercilessly grinding innocent lives in their teeth.

Whether the youths can survive tomorrow,

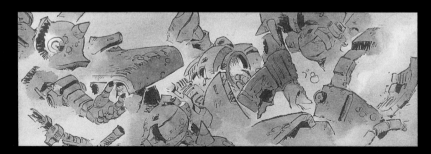

none are given to know.

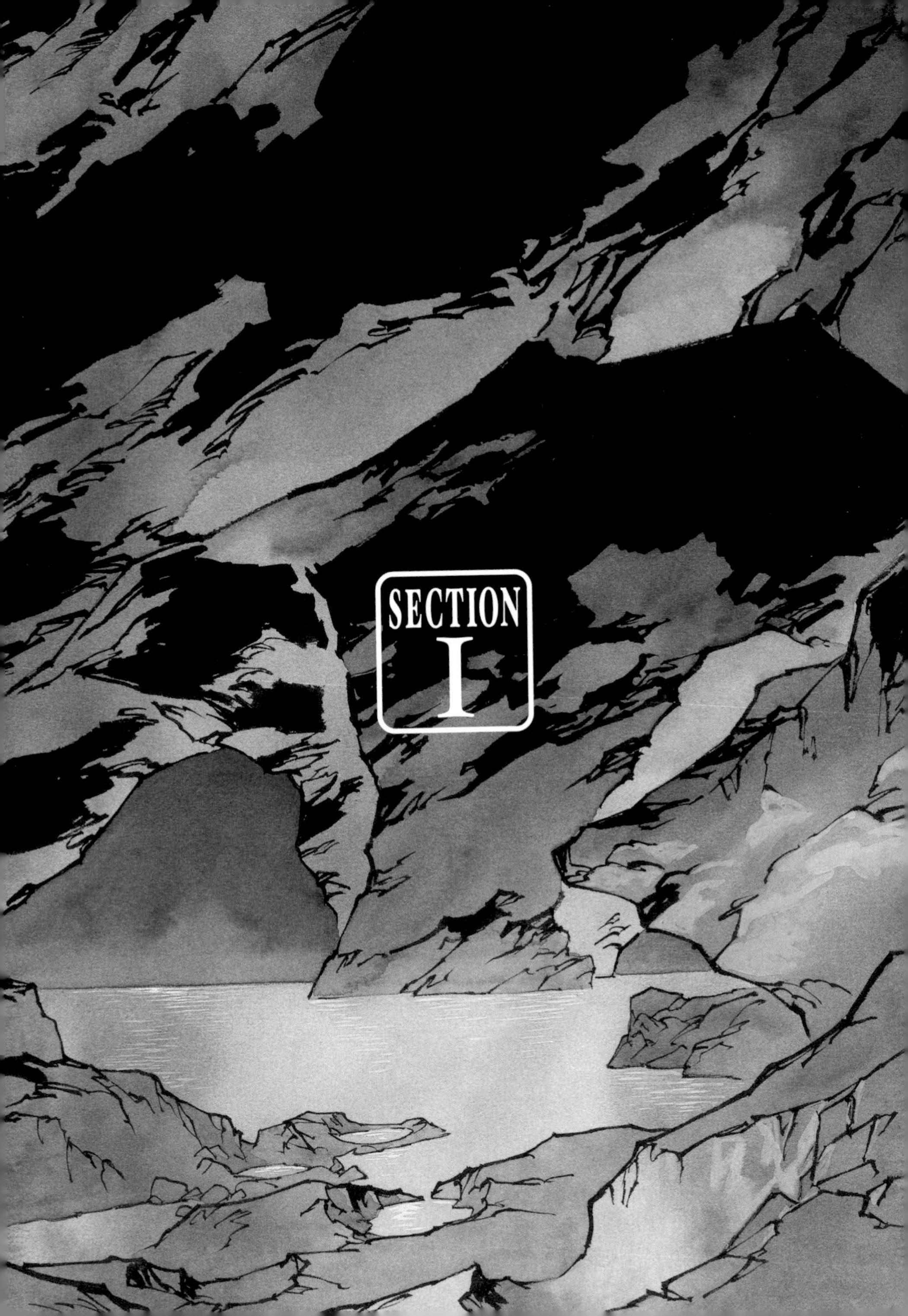
SECTION
I

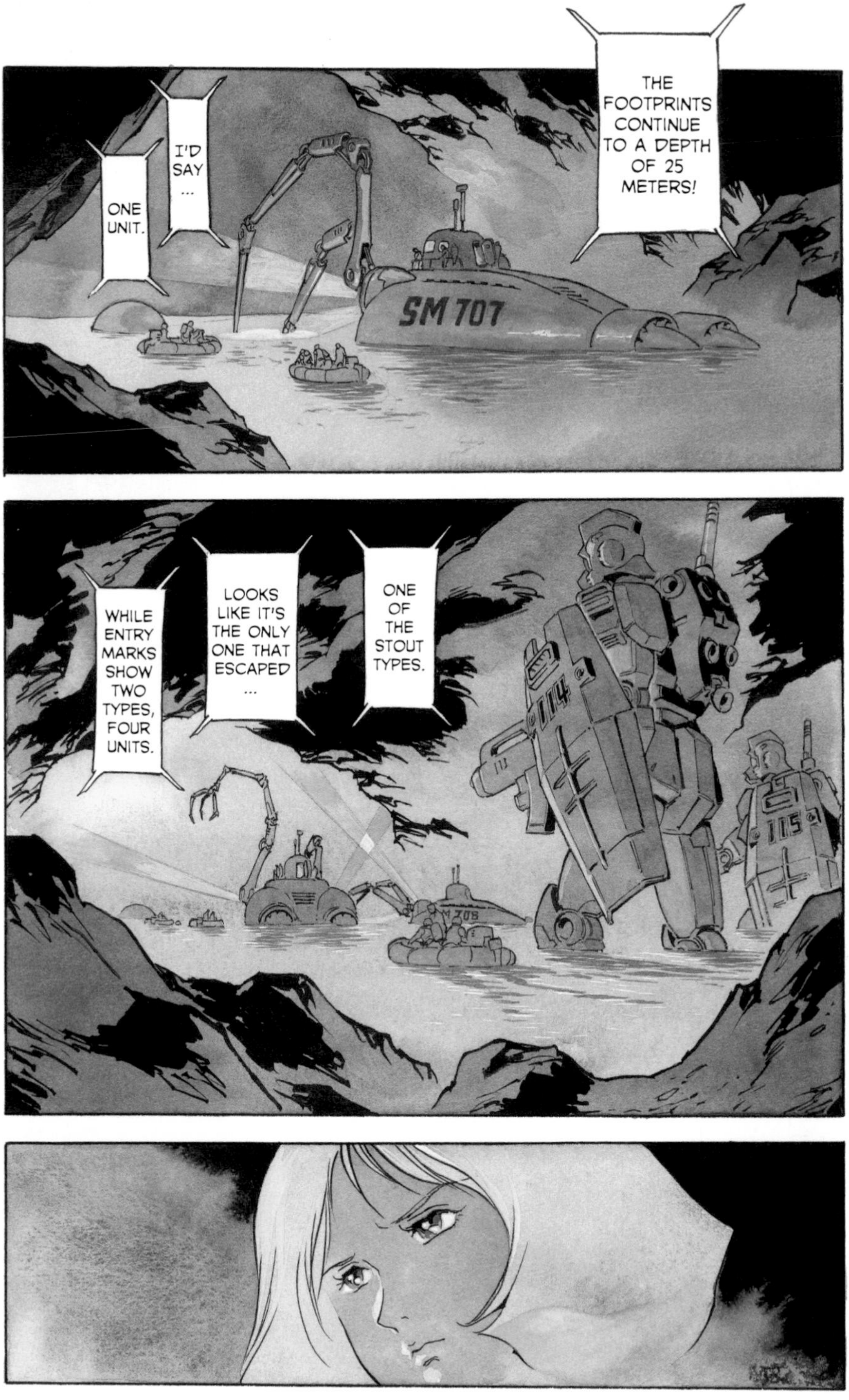
THE FOOTPRINTS CONTINUE TO A DEPTH OF 25 METERS!
SM 707
I'D SAY ...
ONE UNIT.
ONE OF THE STOUT TYPES.
114
115
LOOKS LIKE IT'S THE ONLY ONE THAT ESCAPED ...
WHILE ENTRY MARKS SHOW TWO TYPES, FOUR UNITS.

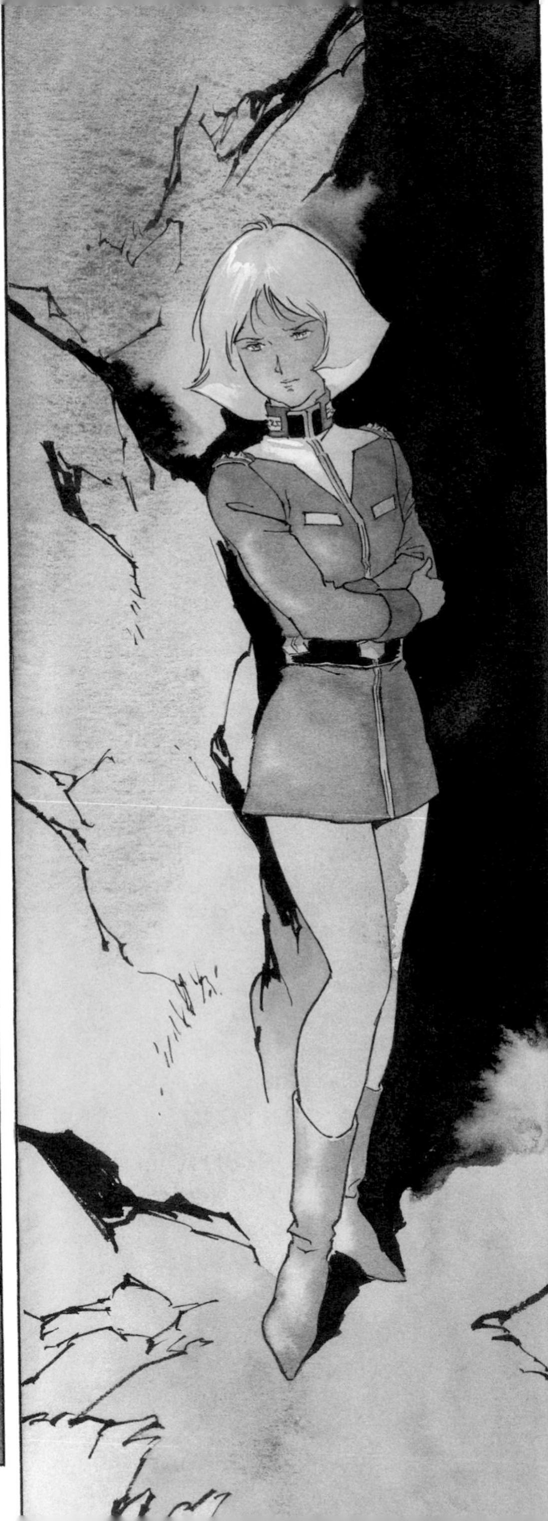

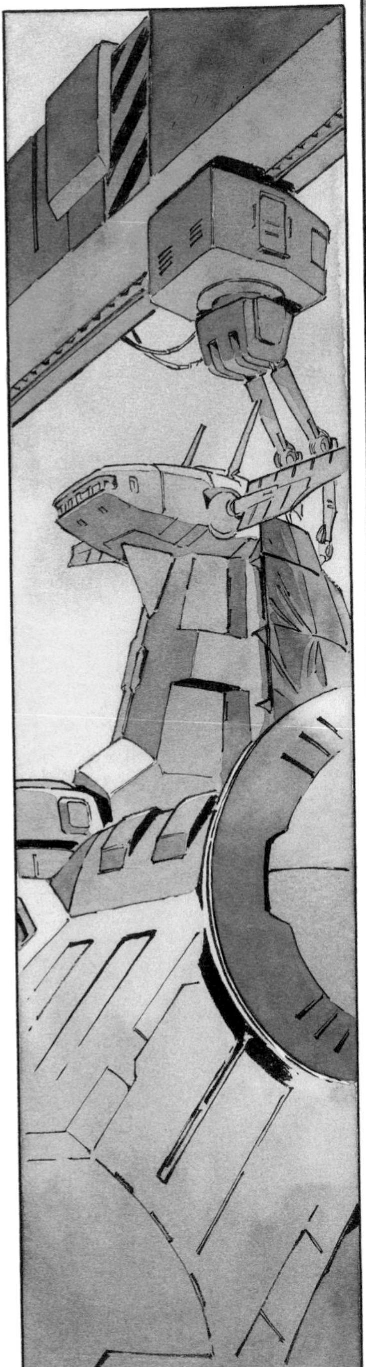

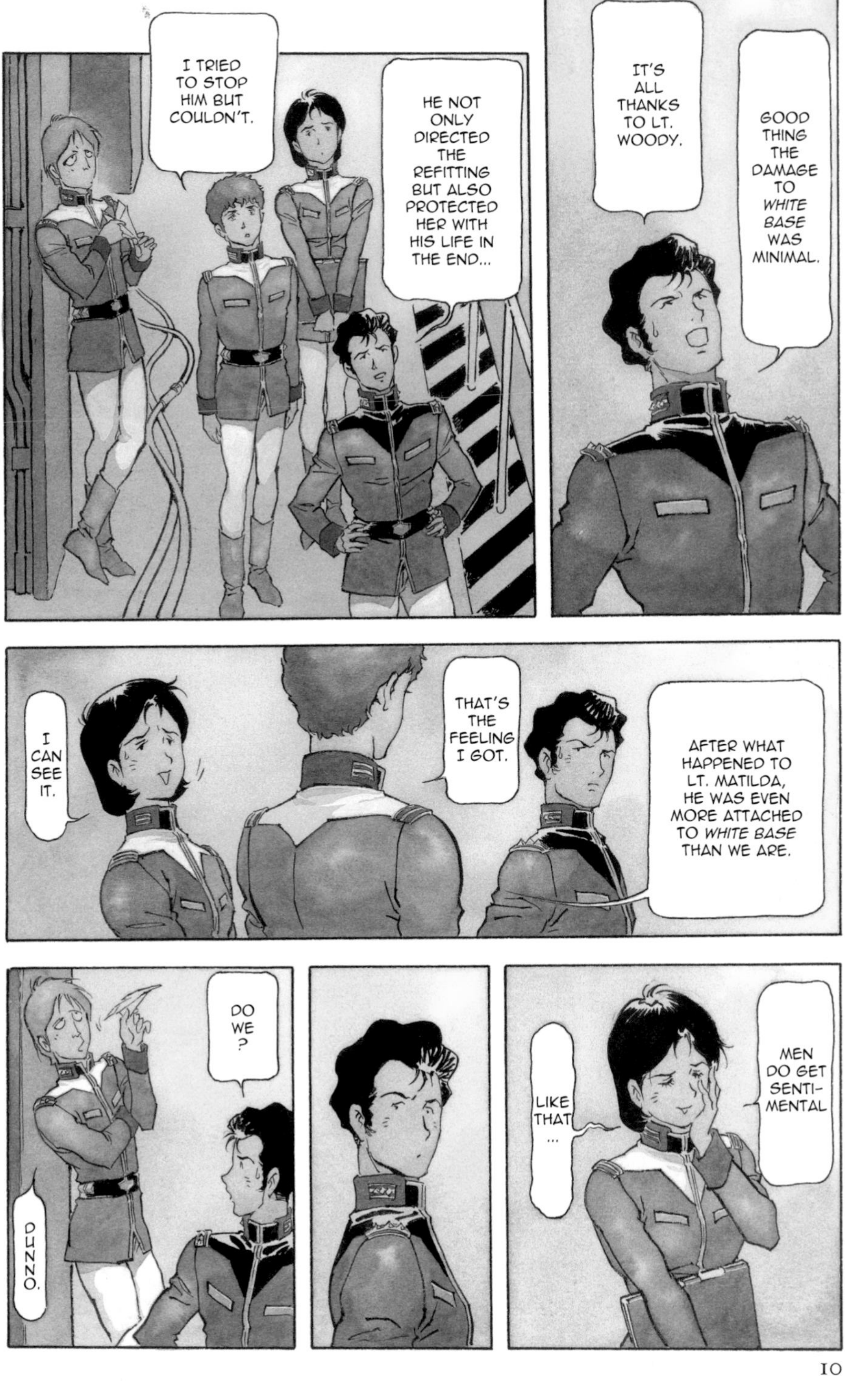
GOOD THING THE DAMAGE TO *WHITE BASE* WAS MINIMAL.
IT'S ALL THANKS TO LT. WOODY.
HE NOT ONLY DIRECTED THE REFITTING BUT ALSO PROTECTED HER WITH HIS LIFE IN THE END...
I TRIED TO STOP HIM BUT COULDN'T.
AFTER WHAT HAPPENED TO LT. MATILDA, HE WAS EVEN MORE ATTACHED TO *WHITE BASE* THAN WE ARE.
THAT'S THE FEELING I GOT.
I CAN SEE IT.
MEN DO GET SENTI-MENTAL
LIKE THAT...
DO WE?
DUNNO.

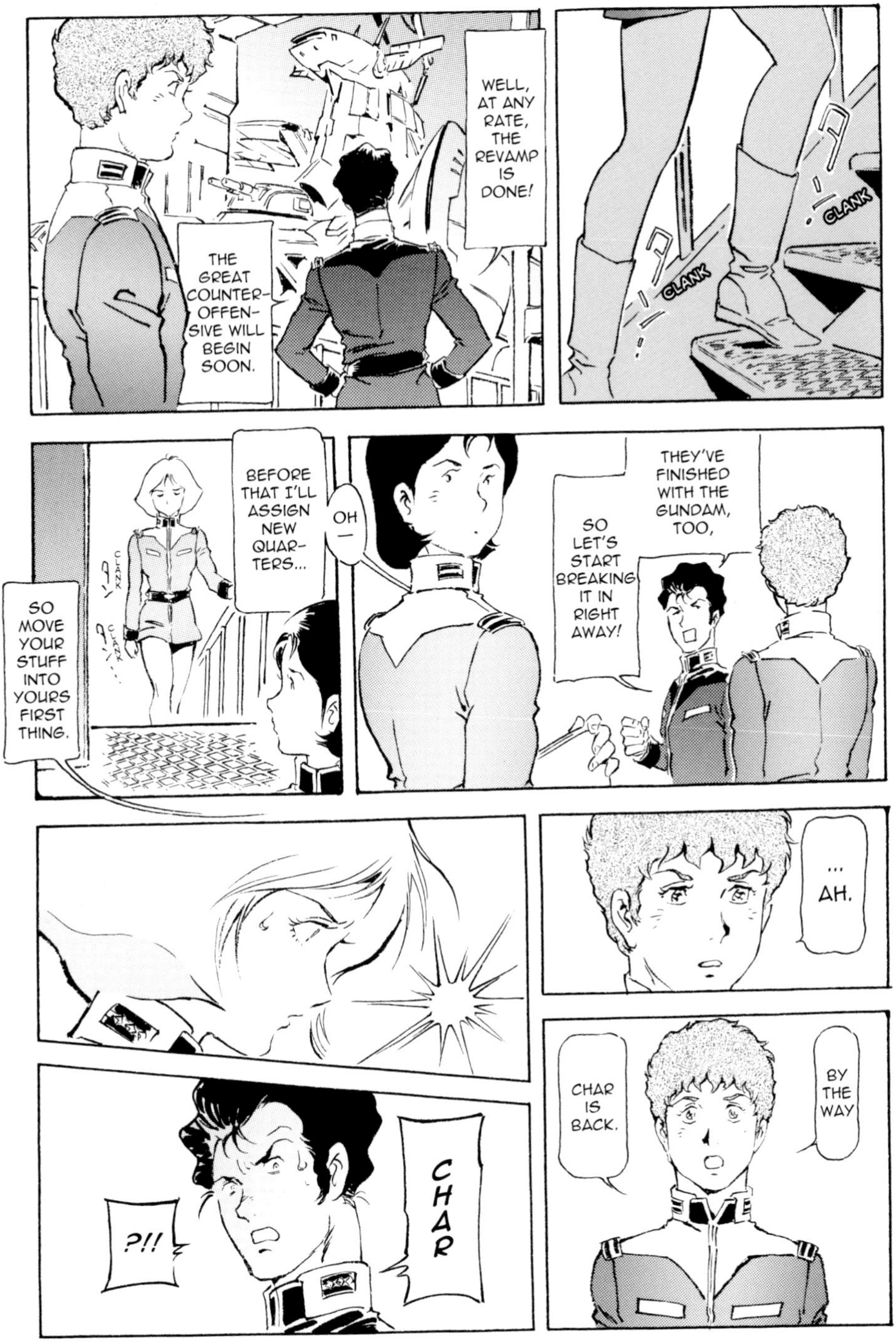
CLANK
CLANK
WELL, AT ANY RATE, THE REVAMP IS DONE!
THE GREAT COUNTER-OFFEN-SIVE WILL BEGIN SOON.
THEY'VE FINISHED WITH THE GUNDAM, TOO,
SO LET'S START BREAKING IT IN RIGHT AWAY!
BEFORE THAT I'LL ASSIGN NEW QUAR-TERS...
OH —
CLANK
CLANK
SO MOVE YOUR STUFF INTO YOURS FIRST THING.
... AH.
BY THE WAY
CHAR IS BACK.
CHAR
?!!

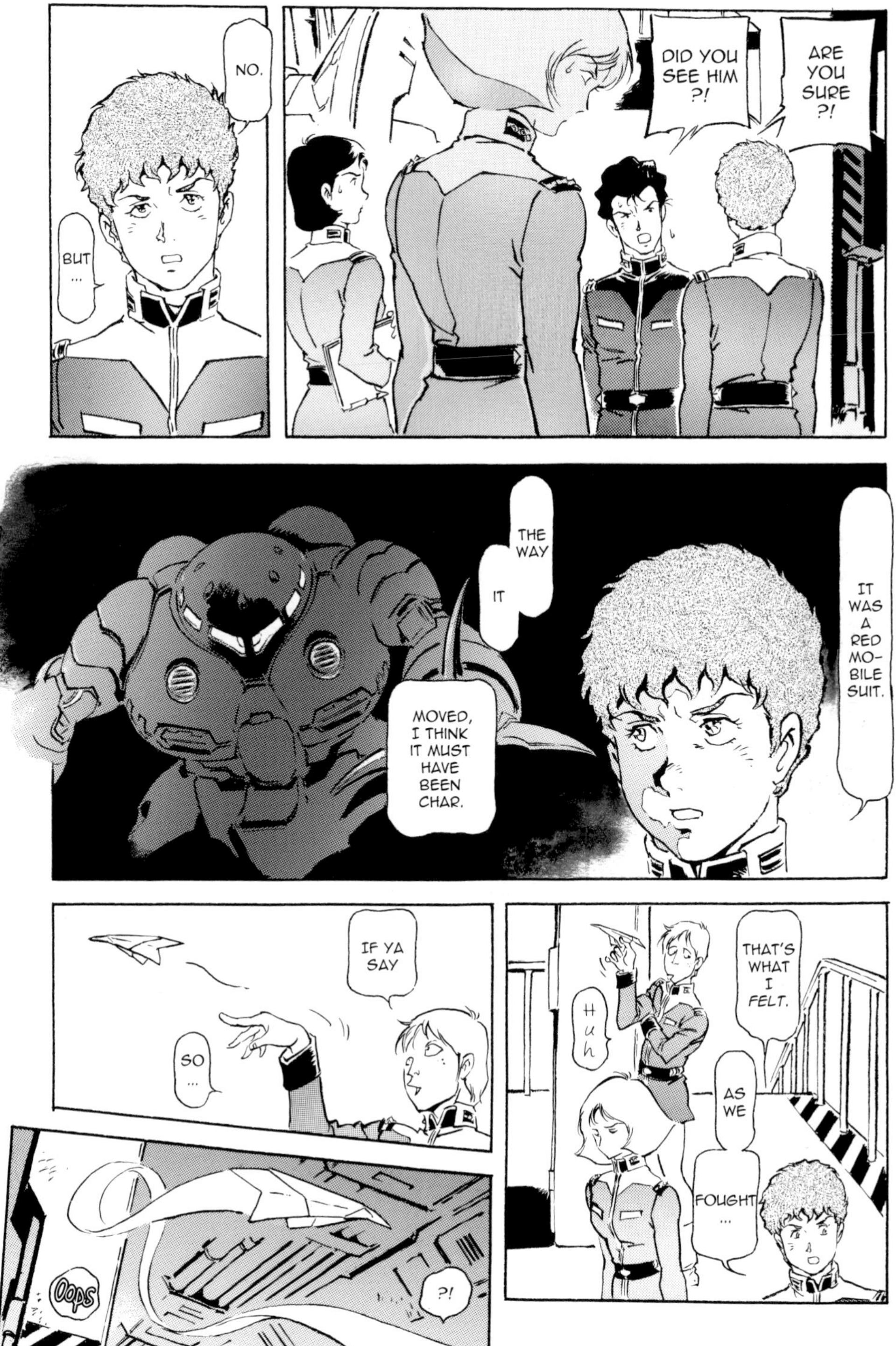
ARE YOU SURE ?!
DID YOU SEE HIM ?!
NO.
BUT ...
IT WAS A RED MO-BILE SUIT.
THE WAY IT
MOVED, I THINK IT MUST HAVE BEEN CHAR.
THAT'S WHAT I FELT.
Huh
AS WE
FOUGHT ...
IF YA SAY
SO ...
?!
Oops

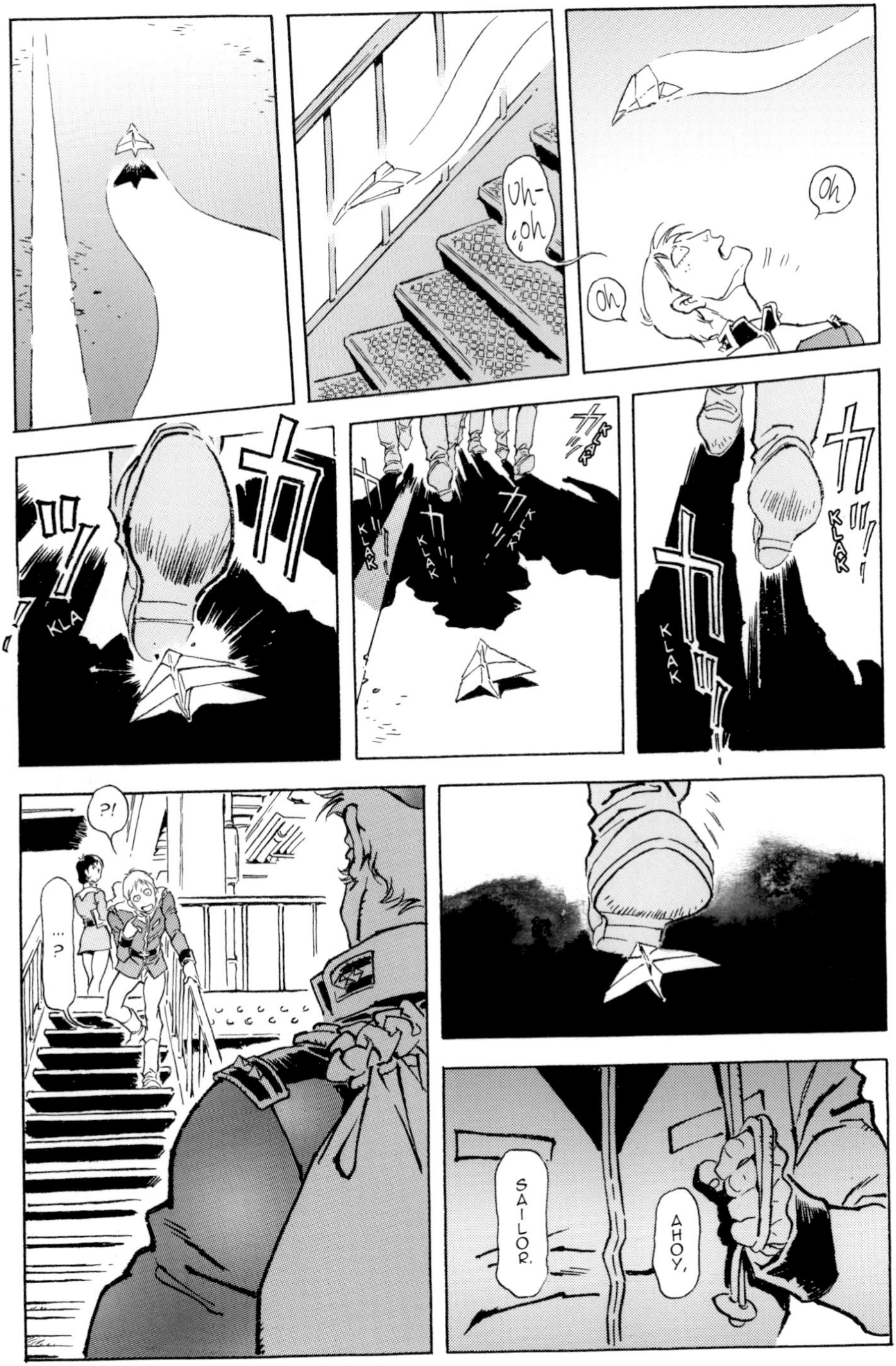
Oh
Oh
Uh-oh
KLAK
KLAK
KLAK
KLAK
KLAK
KLAK
KLA
AHOY,
SAILOR.
?!
...?

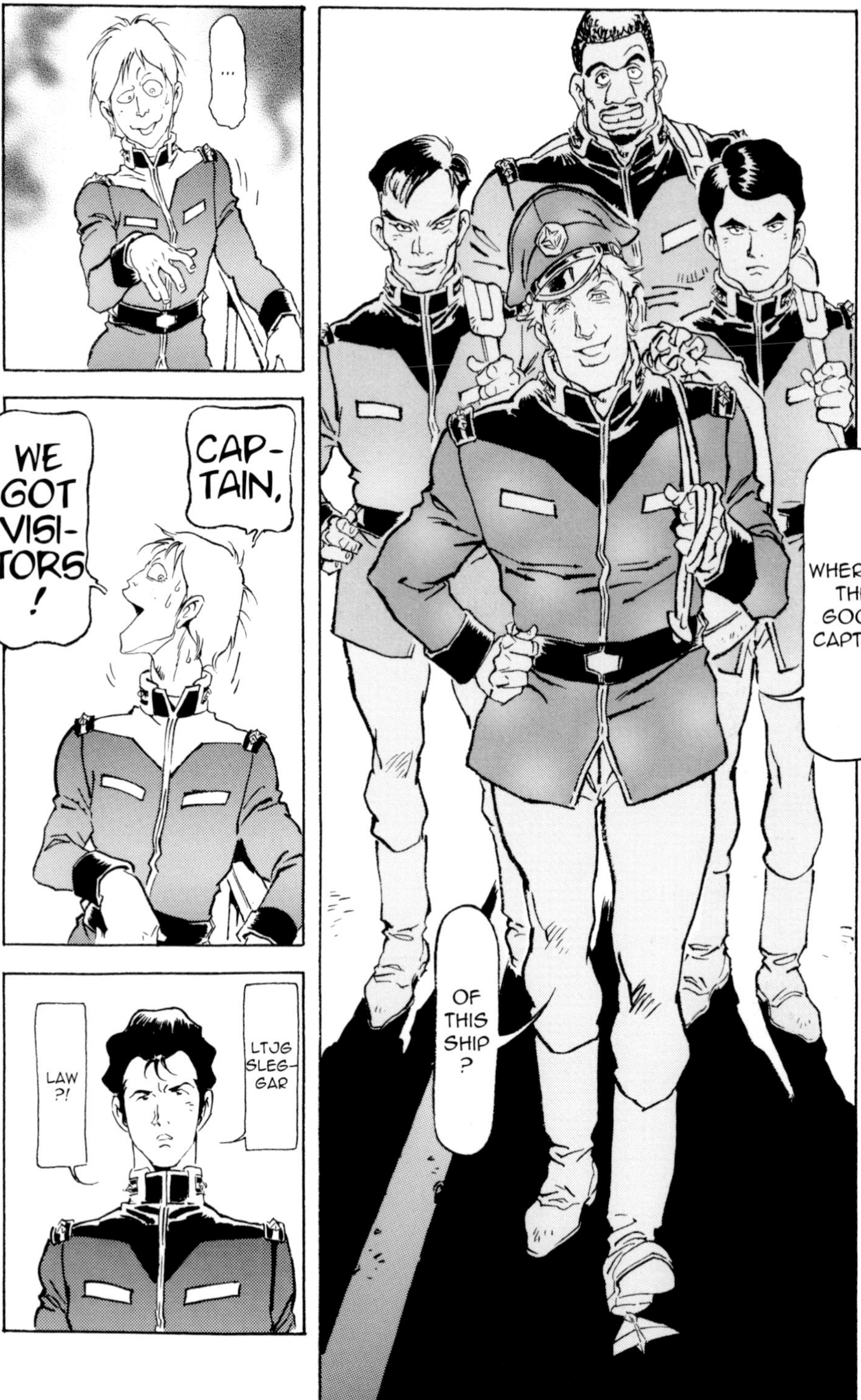
WHERE'S THE GOOD CAPTAIN
OF THIS SHIP?
...
CAP-TAIN,
WE GOT VISI-TORS!
LTJG SLEG-GAR
LAW?!

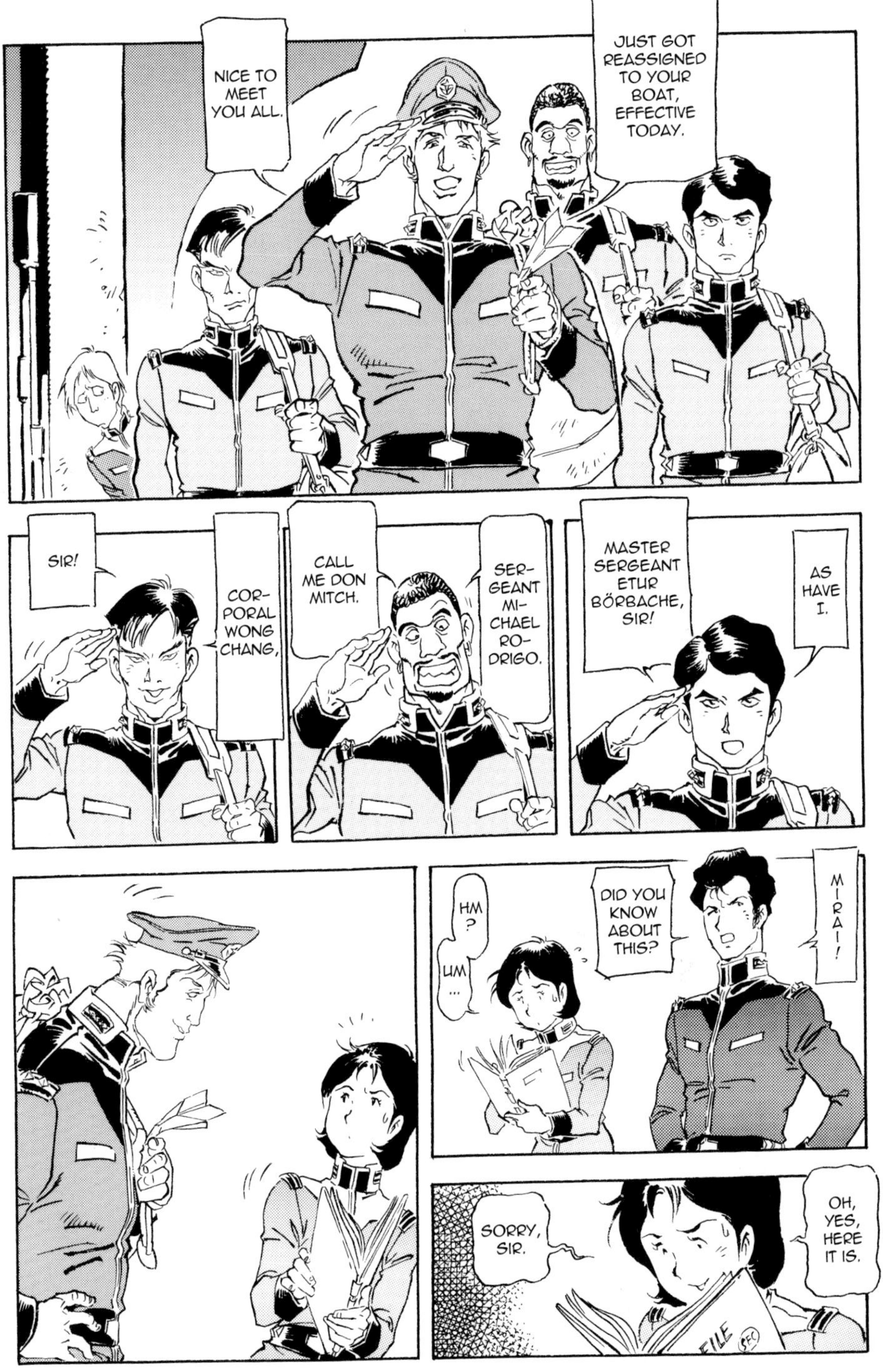
JUST GOT REASSIGNED TO YOUR BOAT, EFFECTIVE TODAY.
NICE TO MEET YOU ALL.
AS HAVE I.
MASTER SERGEANT ETUR BÖRBACHE, SIR!
SER-GEANT MI-CHAEL RO-DRIGO.
CALL ME DON MITCH.
COR-PORAL WONG CHANG,
SIR!
MIRAI!
DID YOU KNOW ABOUT THIS?
HM?
UM...
OH, YES, HERE IT IS.
SORRY, SIR.
FILE

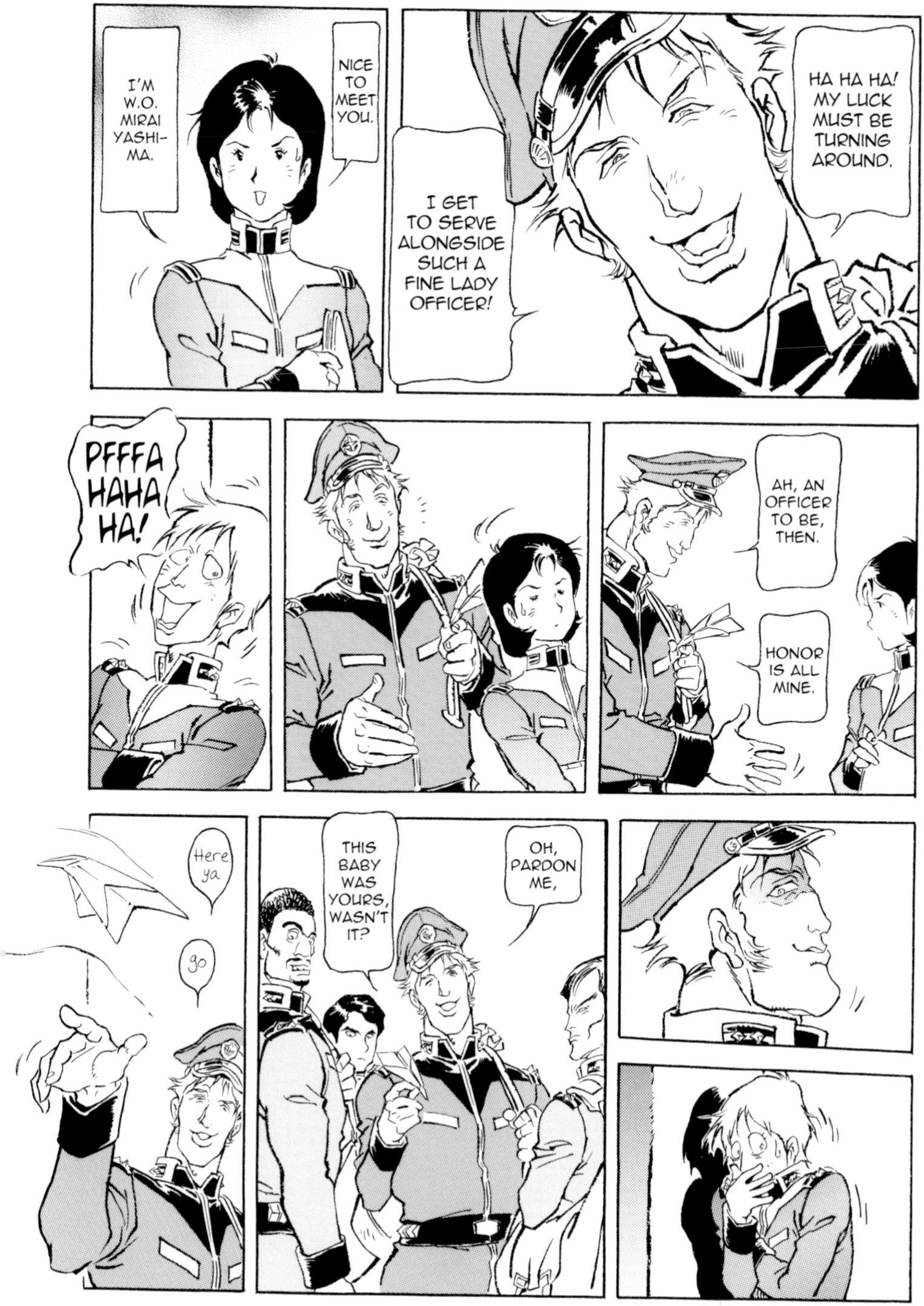
HA HA HA! MY LUCK MUST BE TURNING AROUND.
I GET TO SERVE ALONGSIDE SUCH A FINE LADY OFFICER!
NICE TO MEET YOU.
I'M W.O. MIRAI YASHIMA.
AH, AN OFFICER TO BE, THEN.
HONOR IS ALL MINE.
PFFFA HAHAHA HA!
OH, PARDON ME,
THIS BABY WAS YOURS, WASN'T IT?
Here ya
go

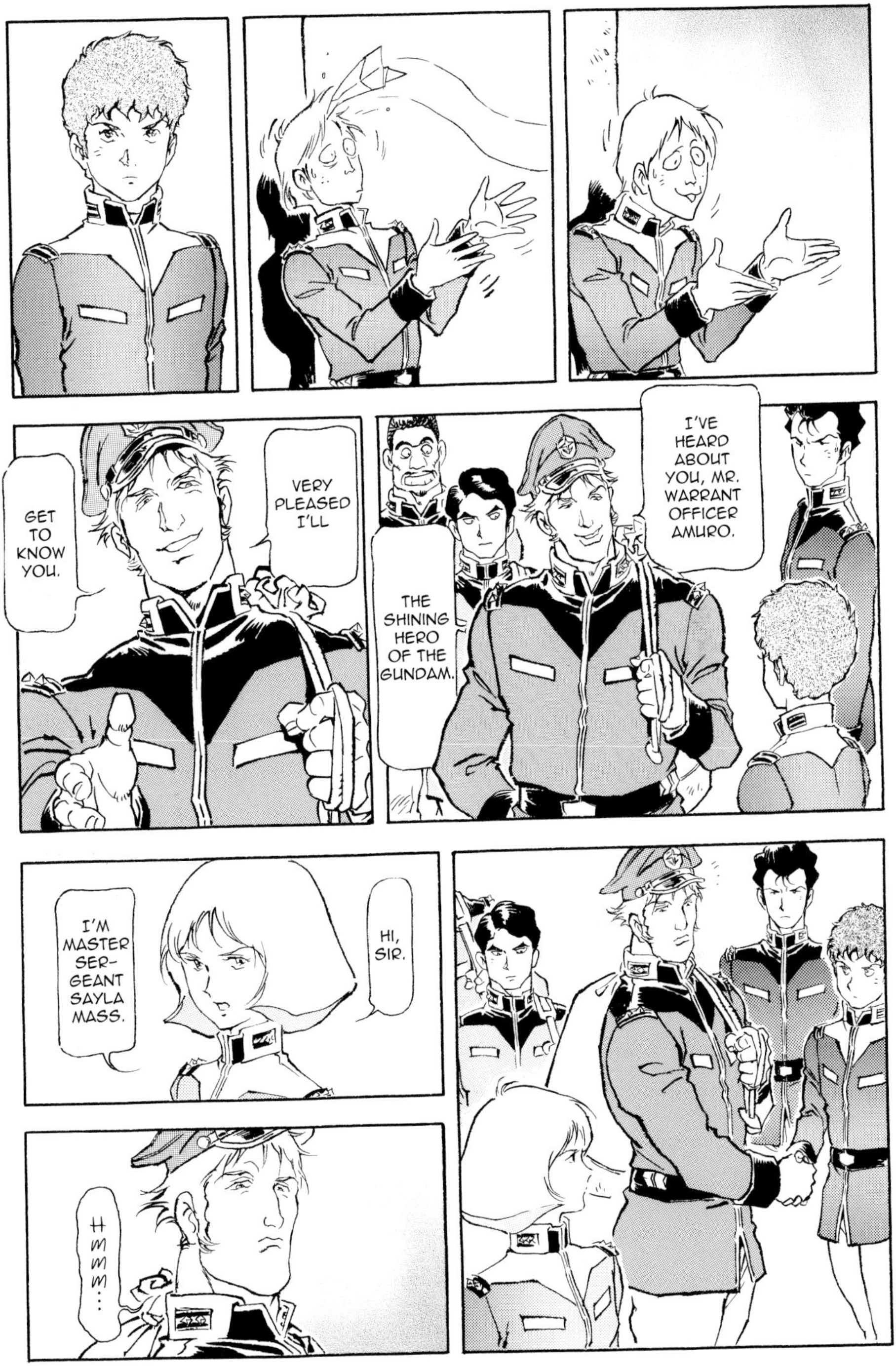
I'VE HEARD ABOUT YOU, MR. WARRANT OFFICER AMURO.
THE SHINING HERO OF THE GUNDAM.
VERY PLEASED I'LL
GET TO KNOW YOU.
HI, SIR.
I'M MASTER SER-GEANT SAYLA MASS.
HMMM...

Ha
Ha
Ha
Ha

YOU

LOOK LIKE YOU'VE GOT A MAN ON YOUR MIND.

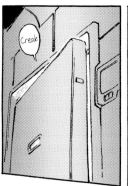
Creak

BUNK HERE?!

SO WHERE ARE WE SUPPOSED TO

HEY!

GO!

ON YOUR MIND...

YOU'VE GOT A MAN

...GET OUT OF THE SERVICE, ARTESIA!

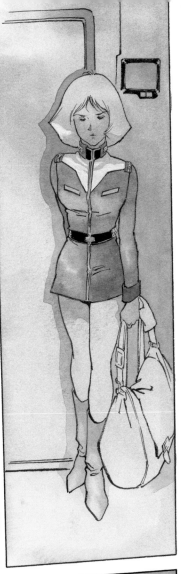

I DON'T WANT TO

KILL YOU.

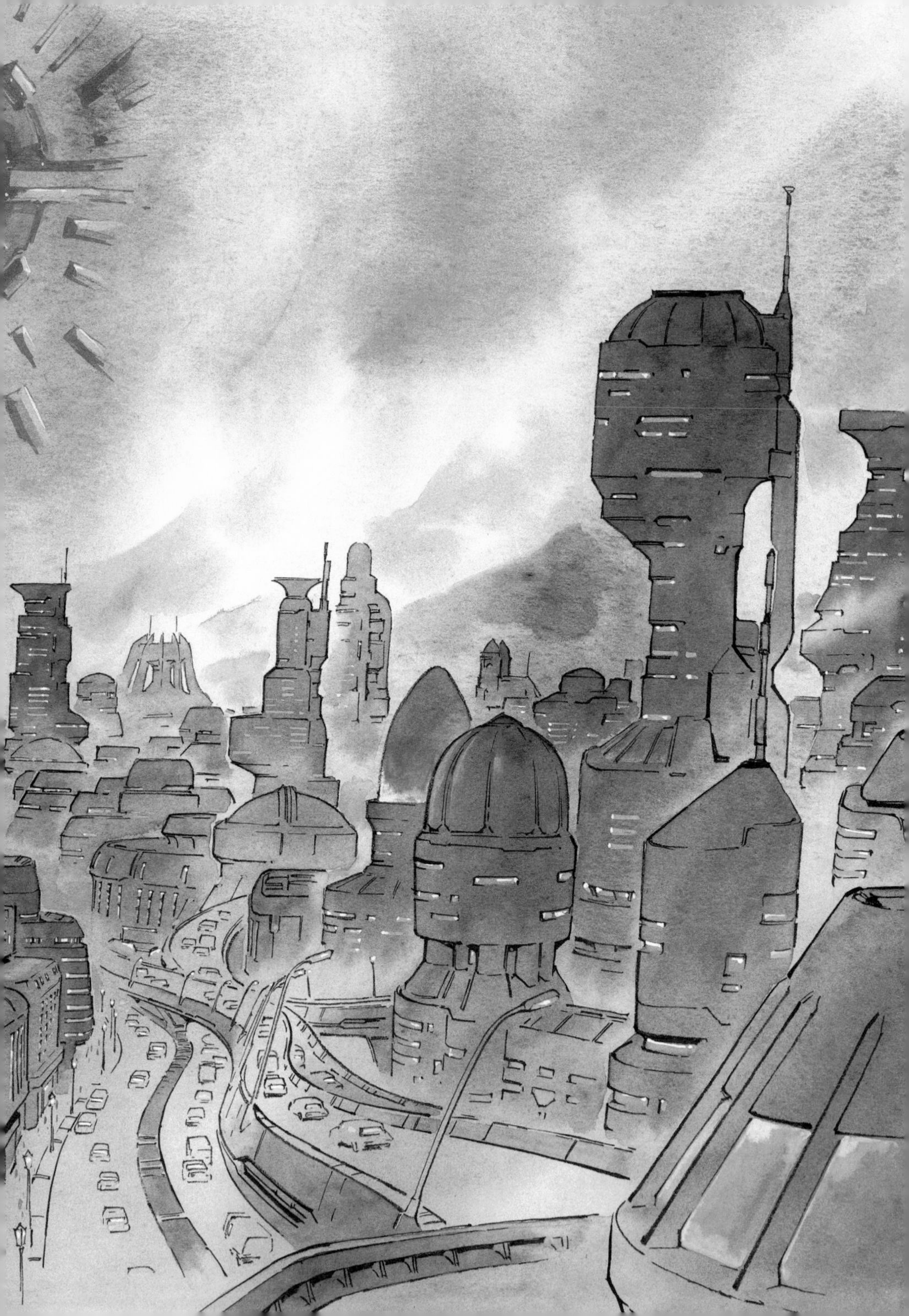

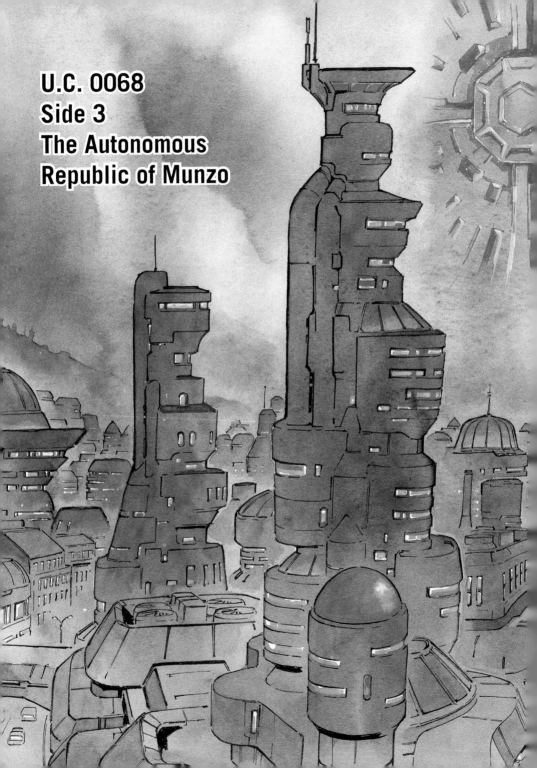

**U.C. 0068
Side 3
The Autonomous
Republic of Munzo**

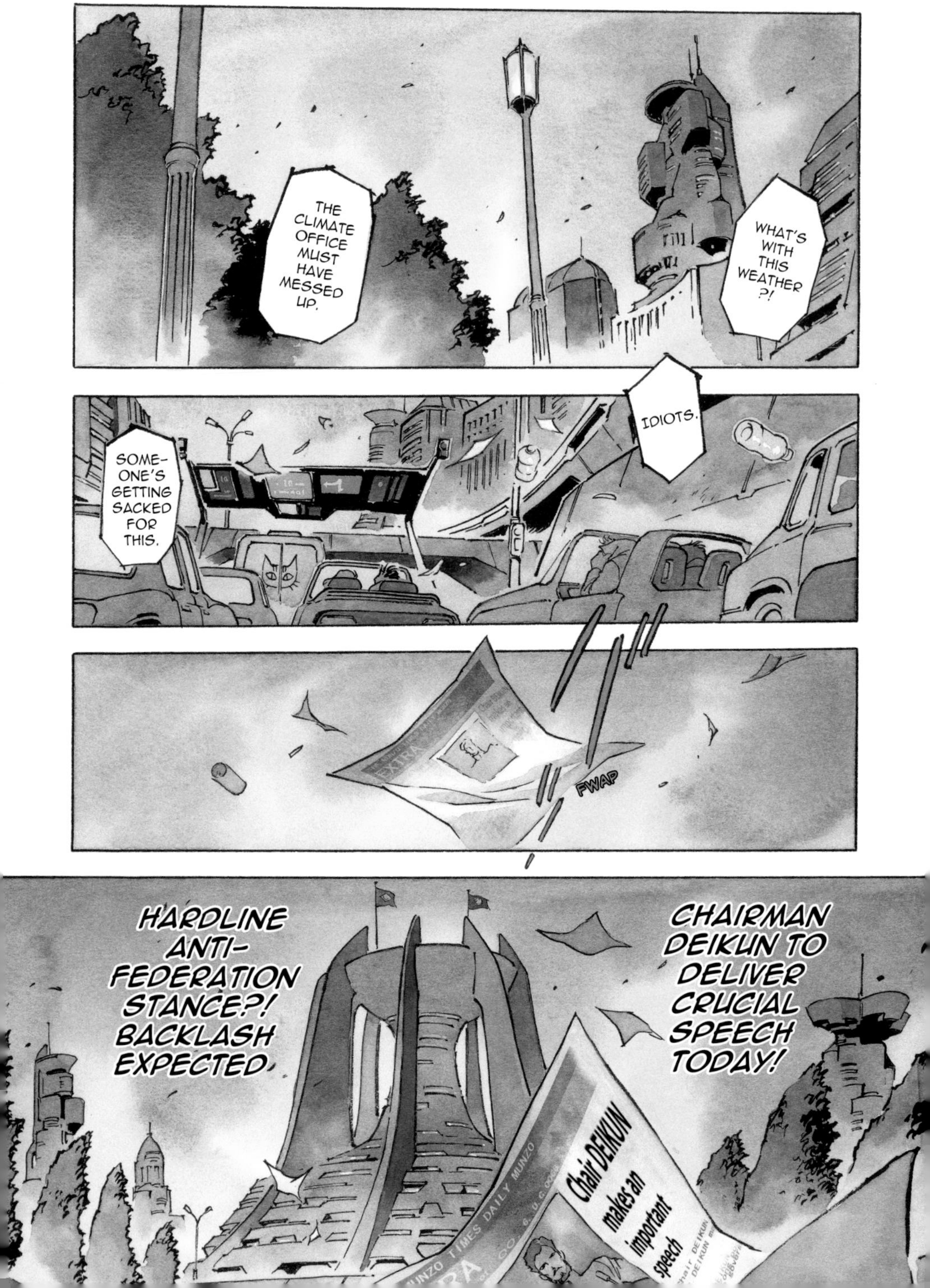
WHAT'S WITH THIS WEATHER?!
THE CLIMATE OFFICE MUST HAVE MESSED UP.
IDIOTS.
SOME-ONE'S GETTING SACKED FOR THIS.
EXTRA
FWAP
CHAIRMAN DEIKUN TO DELIVER CRUCIAL SPEECH TODAY!
HARDLINE ANTI-FEDERATION STANCE?! BACKLASH EXPECTED
Chair DEIKUN makes an important speech
MUNZO TIMES DAILY MUNZO

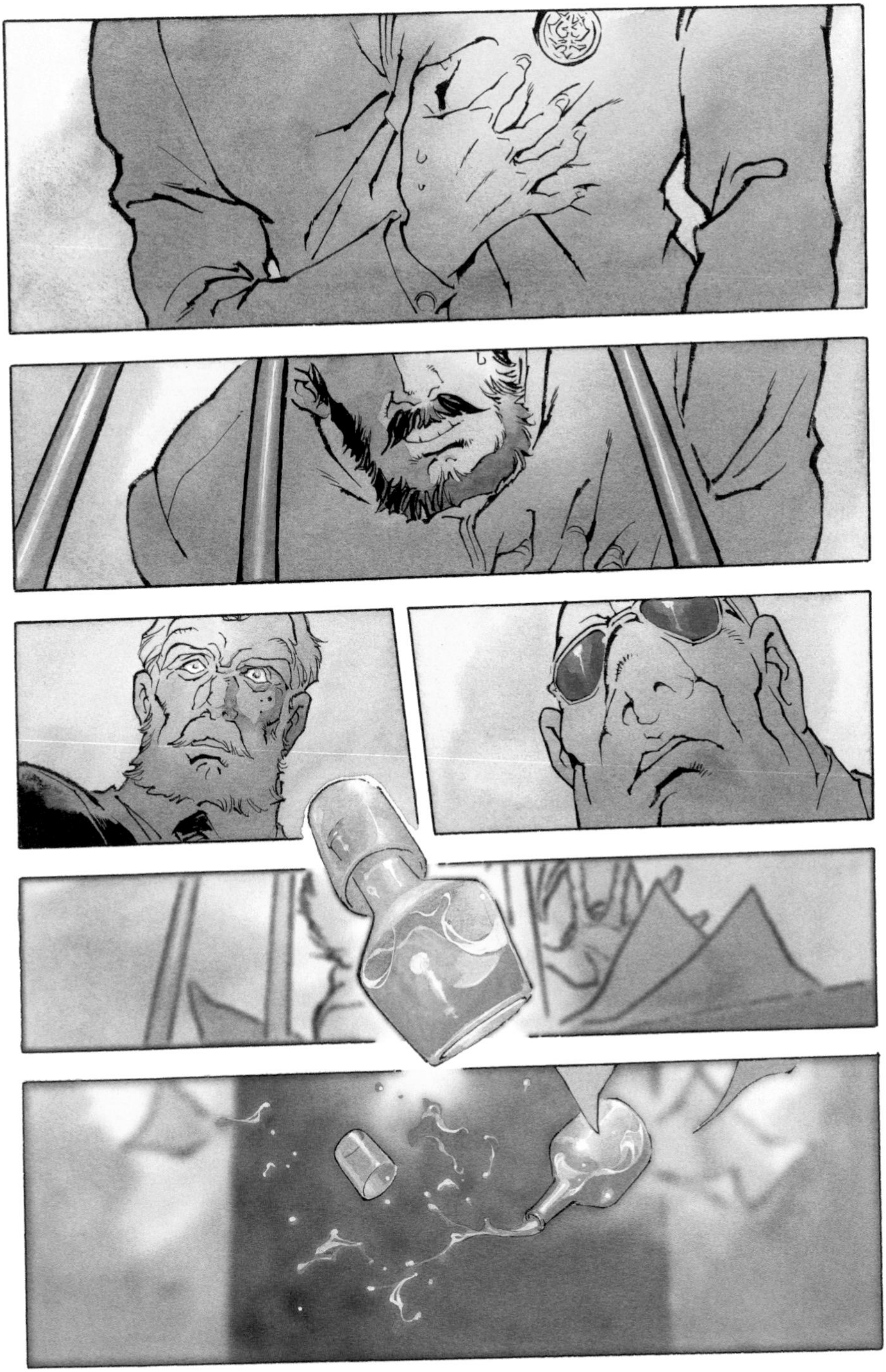

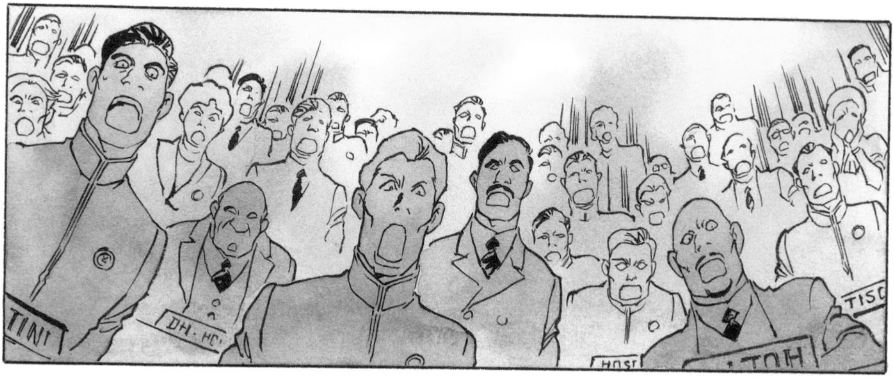

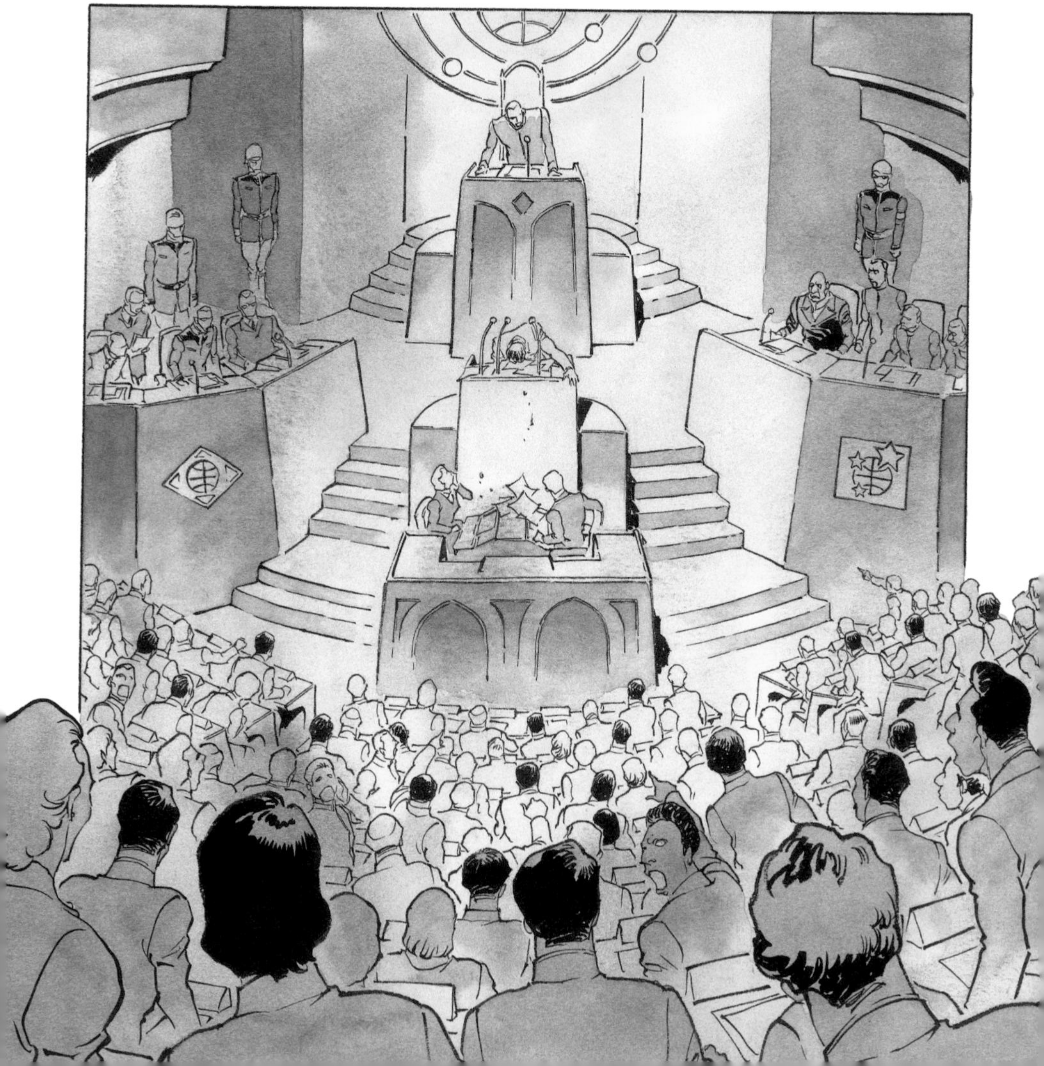

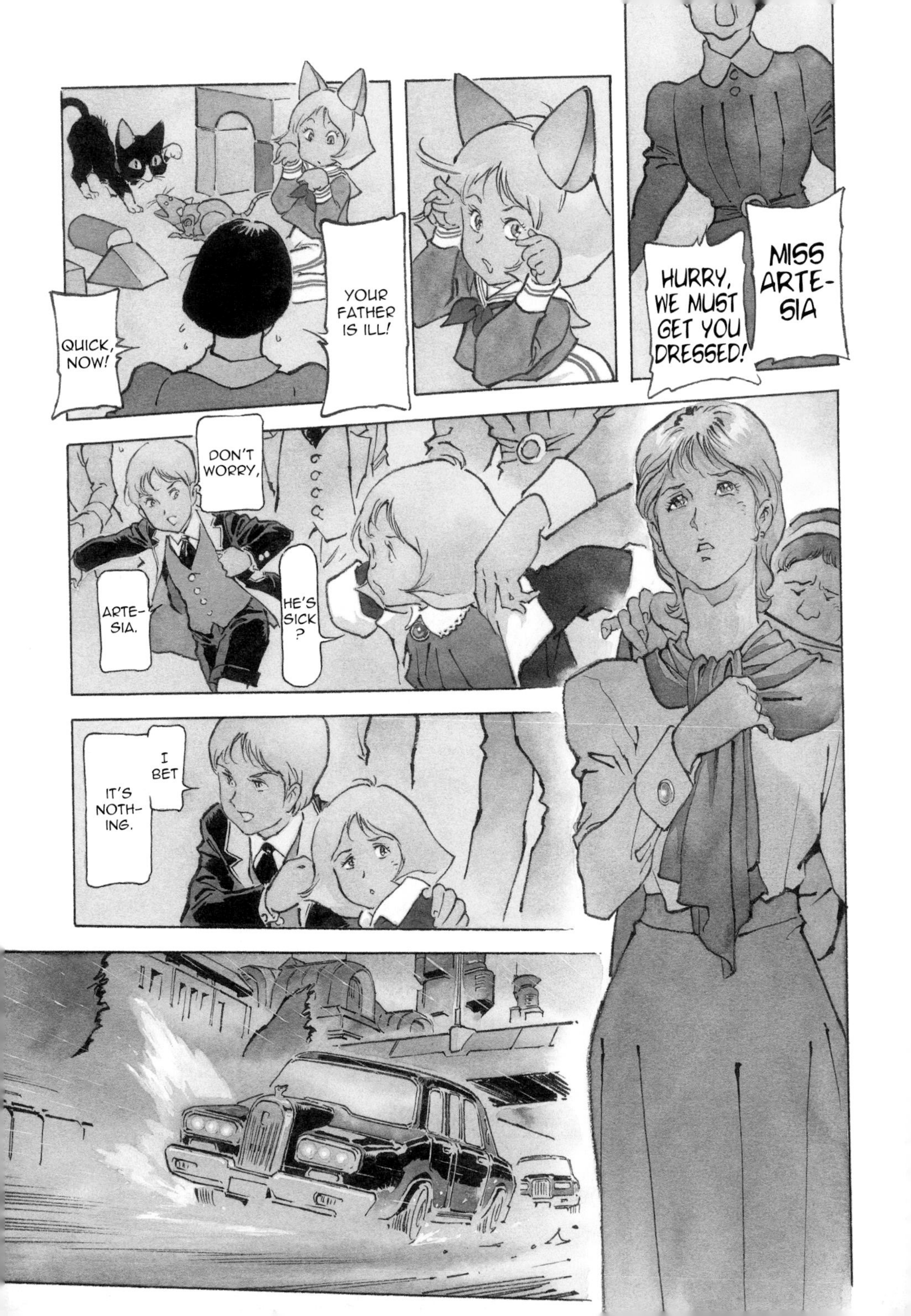
MISS ARTESIA
HURRY, WE MUST GET YOU DRESSED!
YOUR FATHER IS ILL!
QUICK, NOW!
HE'S SICK?
DON'T WORRY,
ARTESIA.
I BET
IT'S NOTHING.

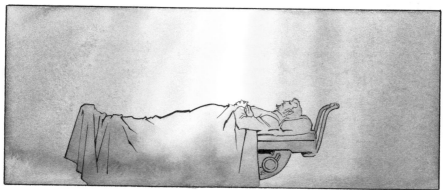

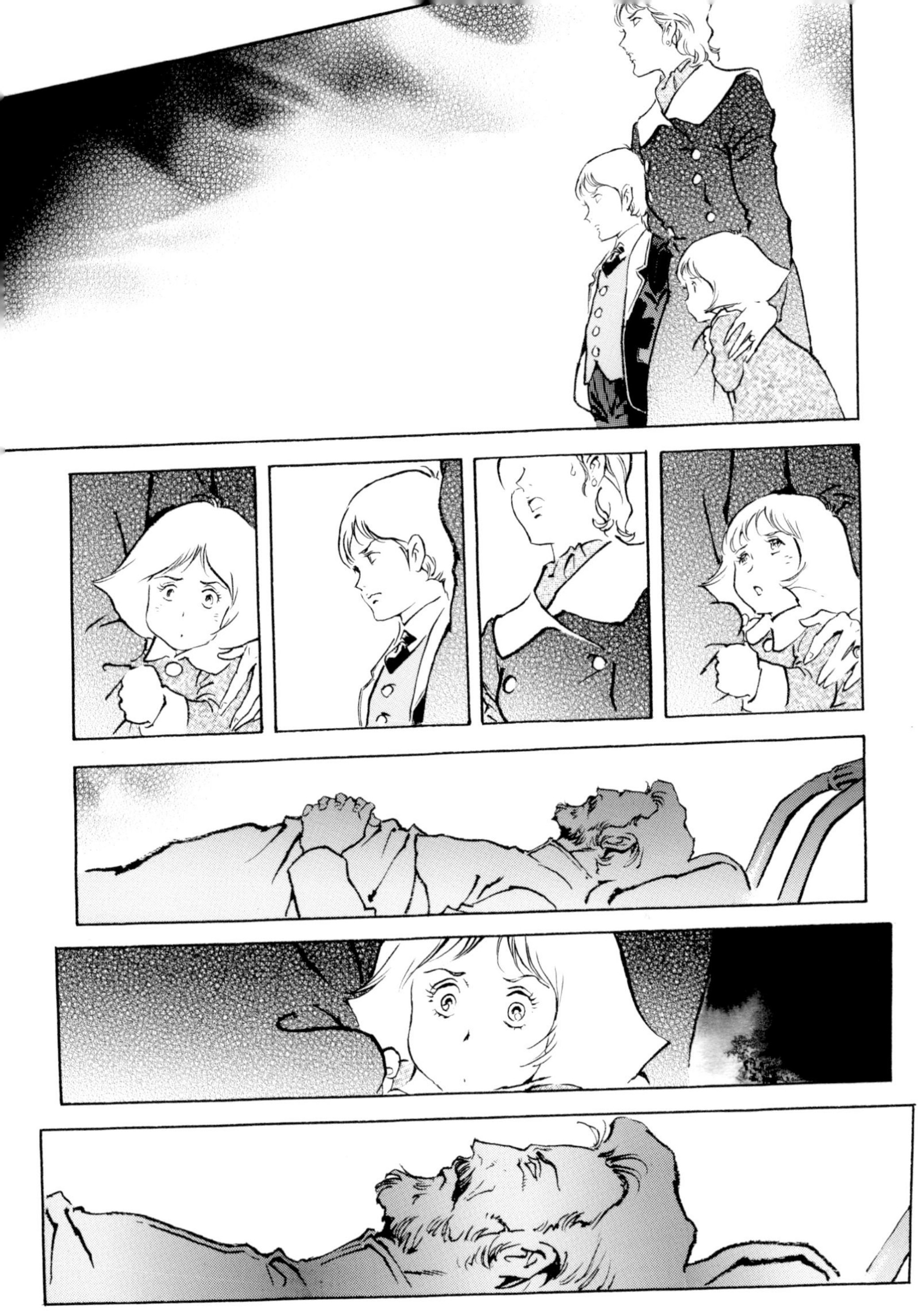

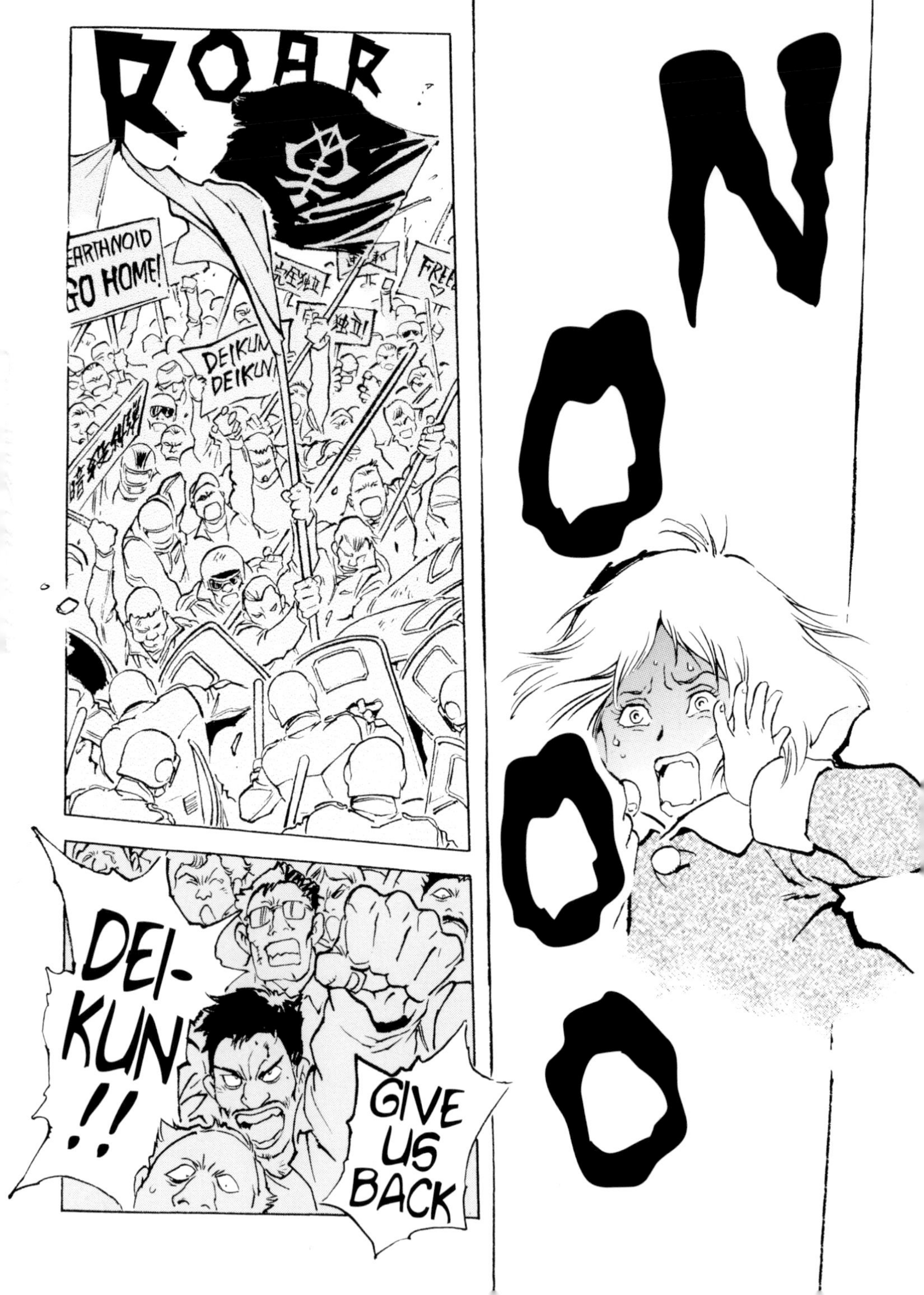
NOOO
ROAR
EARTHNOID GO HOME!
FREE
DEIKUN DEIKUN
GIVE US BACK
DEI-KUN!!

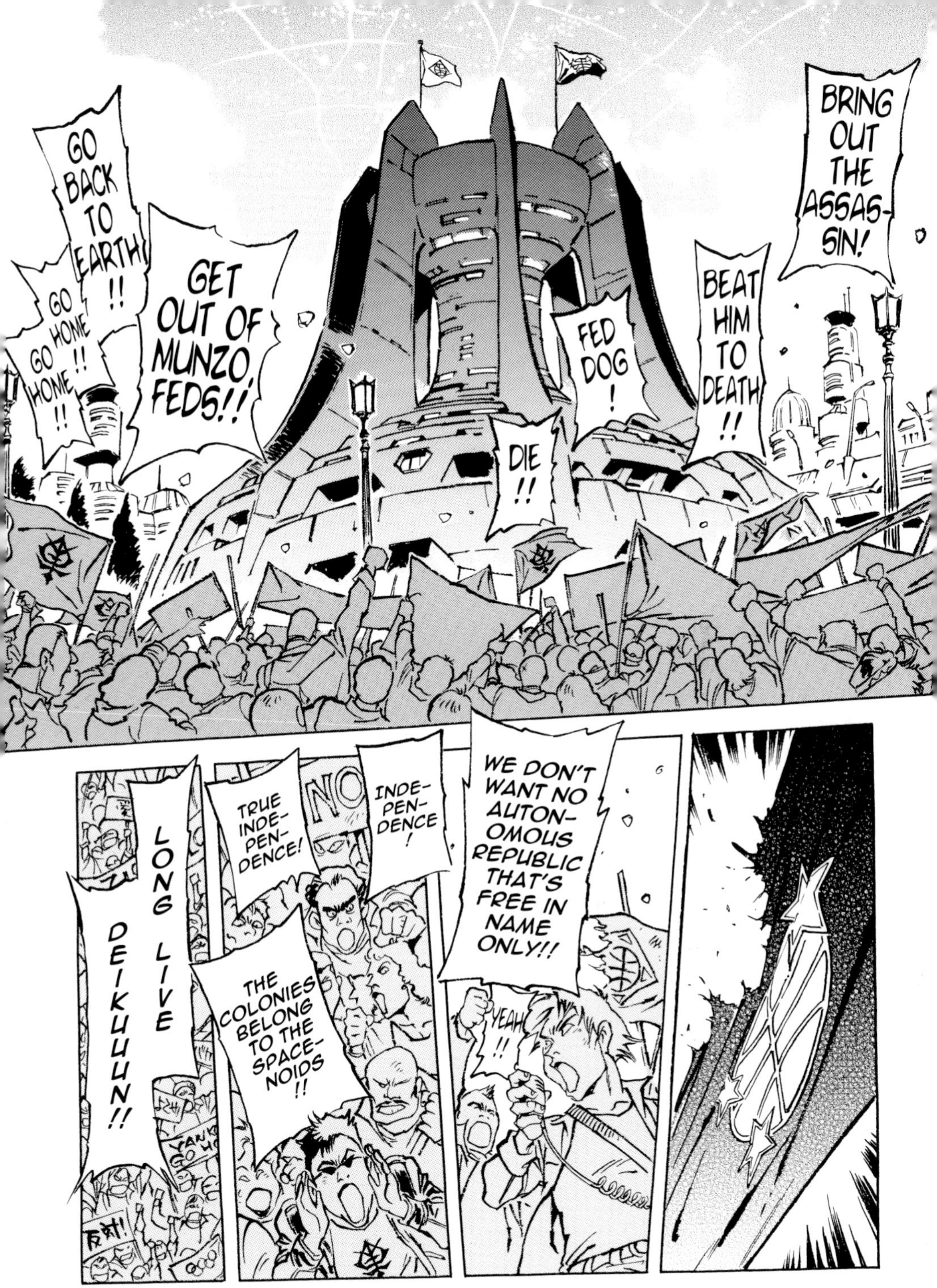
BRING OUT THE ASSASSIN!
BEAT HIM TO DEATH!!
FED DOG!
DIE!!
GET OUT OF MUNZO, FEDS!!
GO BACK TO EARTH!!
GO HOME!! GO HOME!!
WE DON'T WANT NO AUTONOMOUS REPUBLIC THAT'S FREE IN NAME ONLY!!
YEAH!!
INDEPENDENCE!
NO
TRUE INDEPENDENCE!
THE COLONIES BELONG TO THE SPACENOIDS!!
LONG LIVE DEIKUUUUN!!

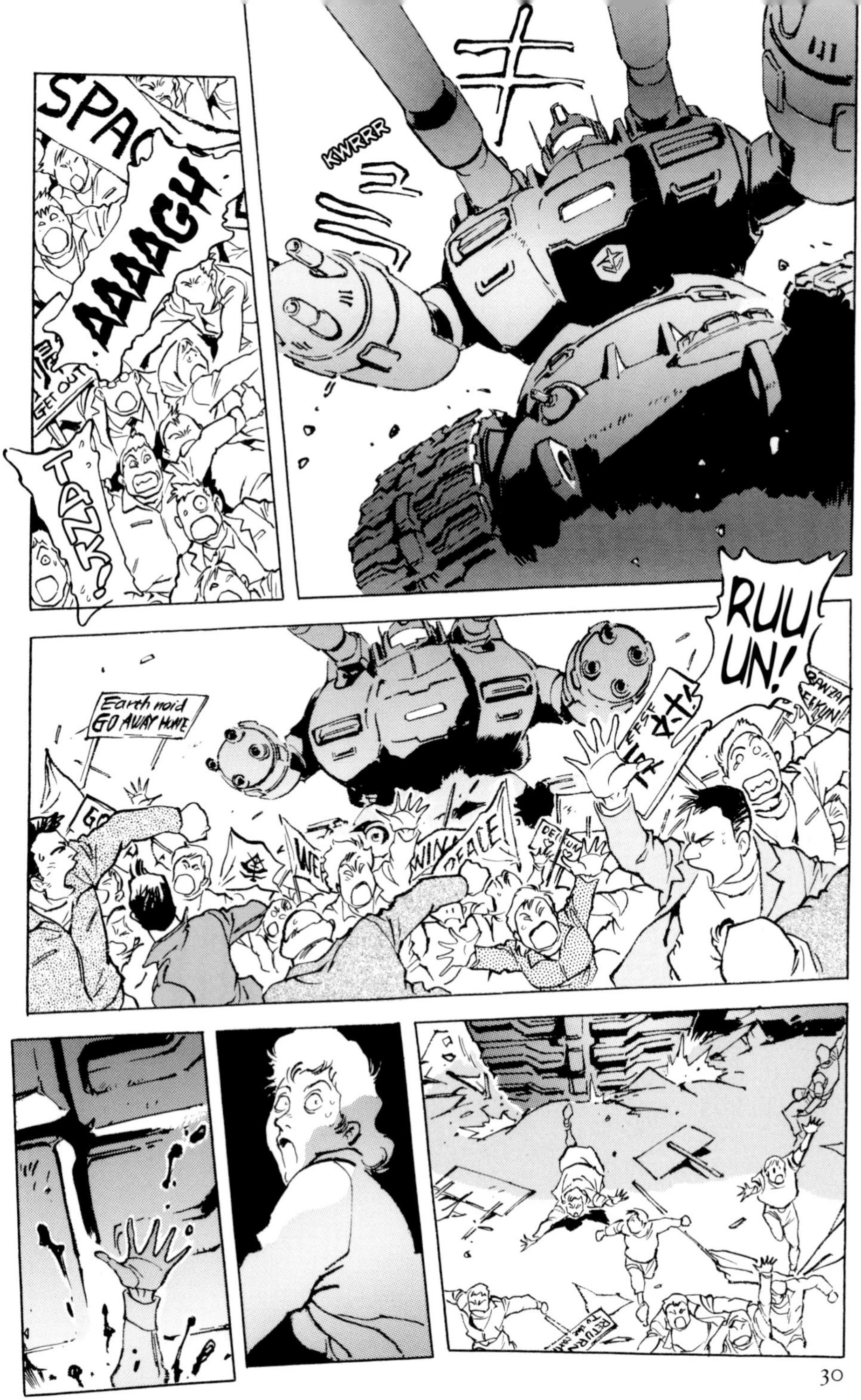
KWRRR
SPAC
AAAGH
GET OUT
TAZK!
RUU UN!
Earth noid GO AWAY HOME
PEACE

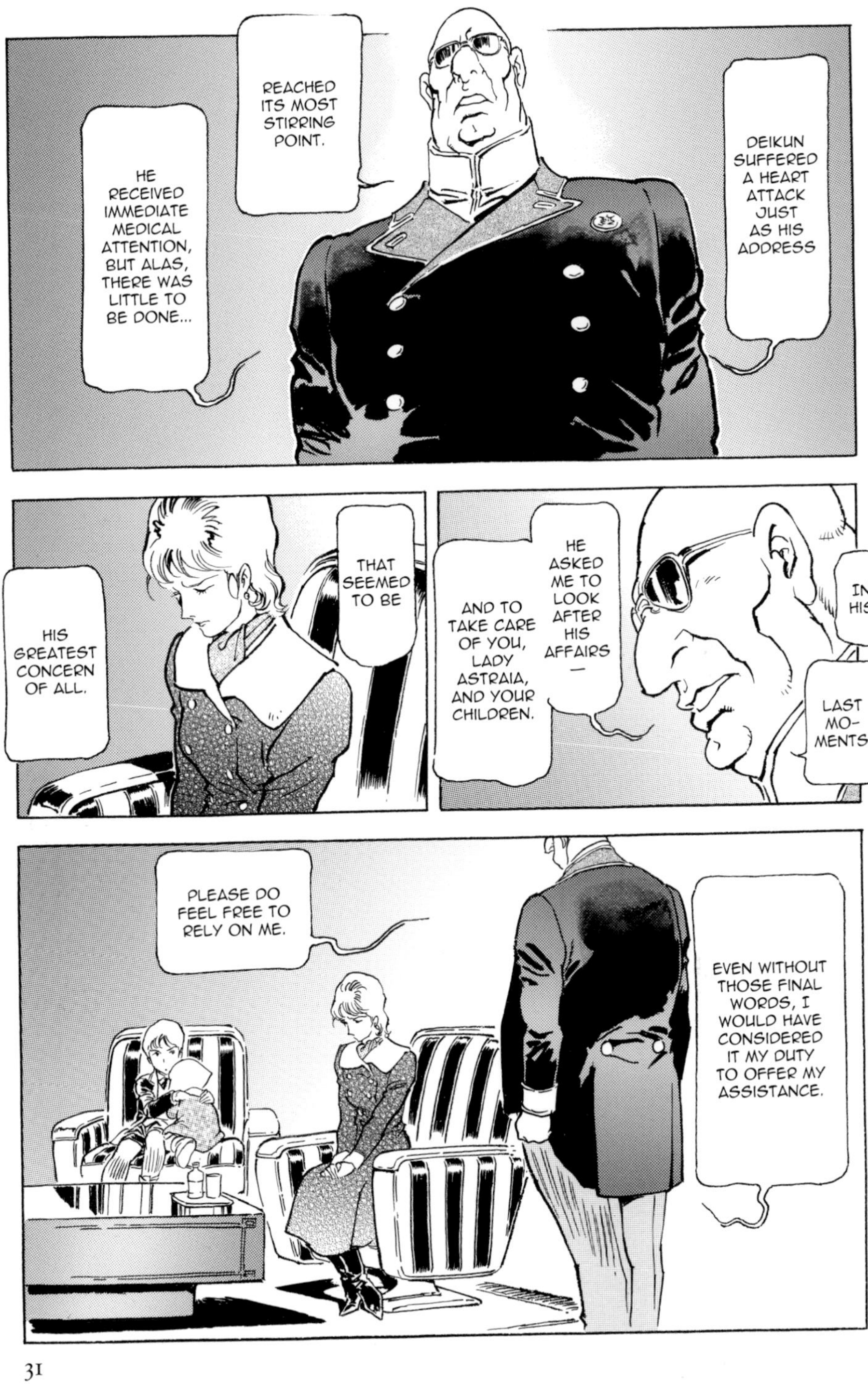
DEIKUN SUFFERED A HEART ATTACK JUST AS HIS ADDRESS
REACHED ITS MOST STIRRING POINT.
HE RECEIVED IMMEDIATE MEDICAL ATTENTION, BUT ALAS, THERE WAS LITTLE TO BE DONE...
IN HIS
LAST MO-MENTS,
HE ASKED ME TO LOOK AFTER HIS AFFAIRS —
AND TO TAKE CARE OF YOU, LADY ASTRAIA, AND YOUR CHILDREN.
THAT SEEMED TO BE
HIS GREATEST CONCERN OF ALL.
EVEN WITHOUT THOSE FINAL WORDS, I WOULD HAVE CONSIDERED IT MY DUTY TO OFFER MY ASSISTANCE.
PLEASE DO FEEL FREE TO RELY ON ME.

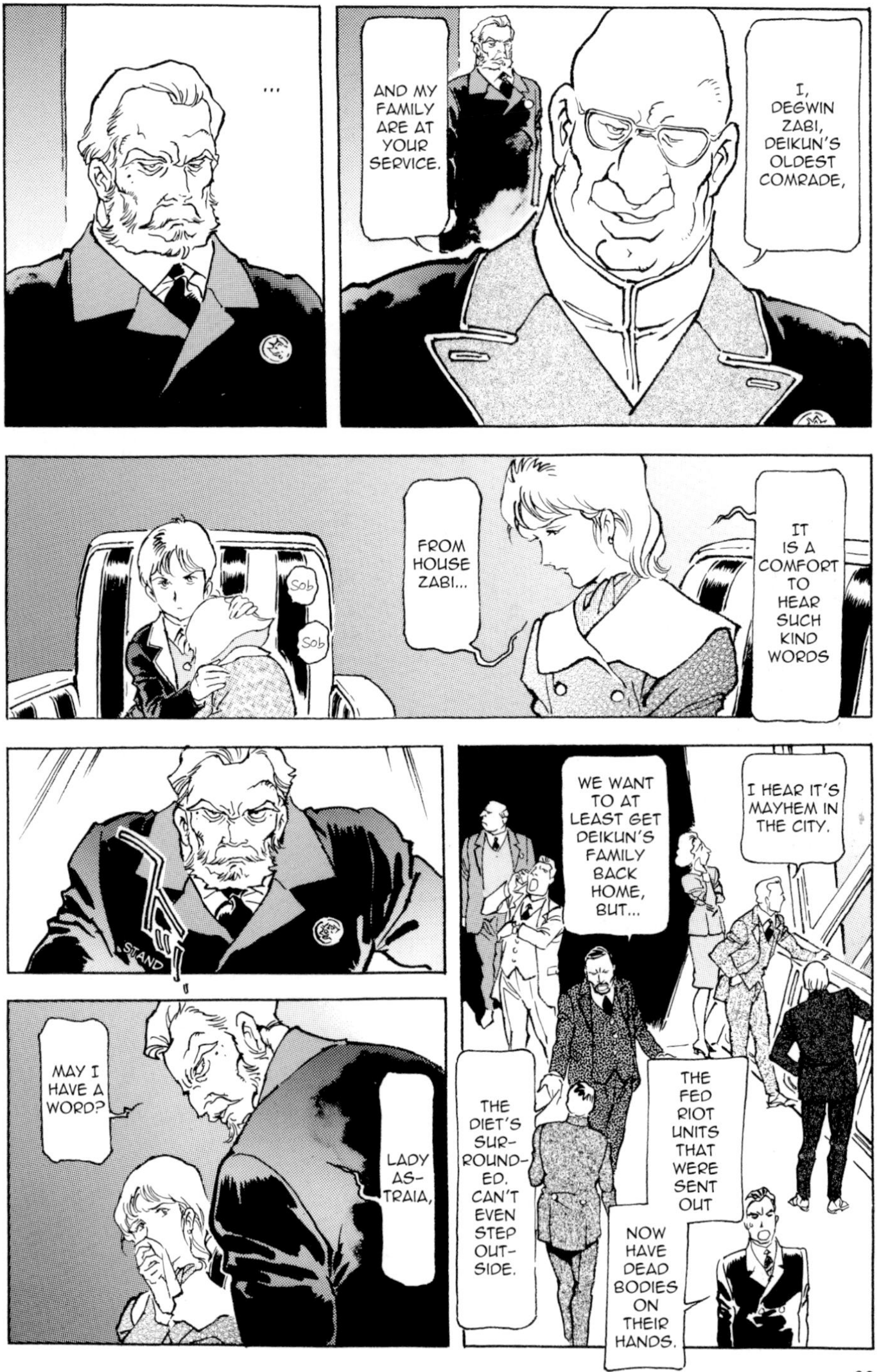
I, DEGWIN ZABI, DEIKUN'S OLDEST COMRADE,
AND MY FAMILY ARE AT YOUR SERVICE.
...
IT IS A COMFORT TO HEAR SUCH KIND WORDS
FROM HOUSE ZABI...
Sob
Sob
I HEAR IT'S MAYHEM IN THE CITY.
WE WANT TO AT LEAST GET DEIKUN'S FAMILY BACK HOME, BUT...
THE FED RIOT UNITS THAT WERE SENT OUT
NOW HAVE DEAD BODIES ON THEIR HANDS.
THE DIET'S SUR-ROUND-ED. CAN'T EVEN STEP OUT-SIDE.
STAND
LADY AS-TRAIA,
MAY I HAVE A WORD?

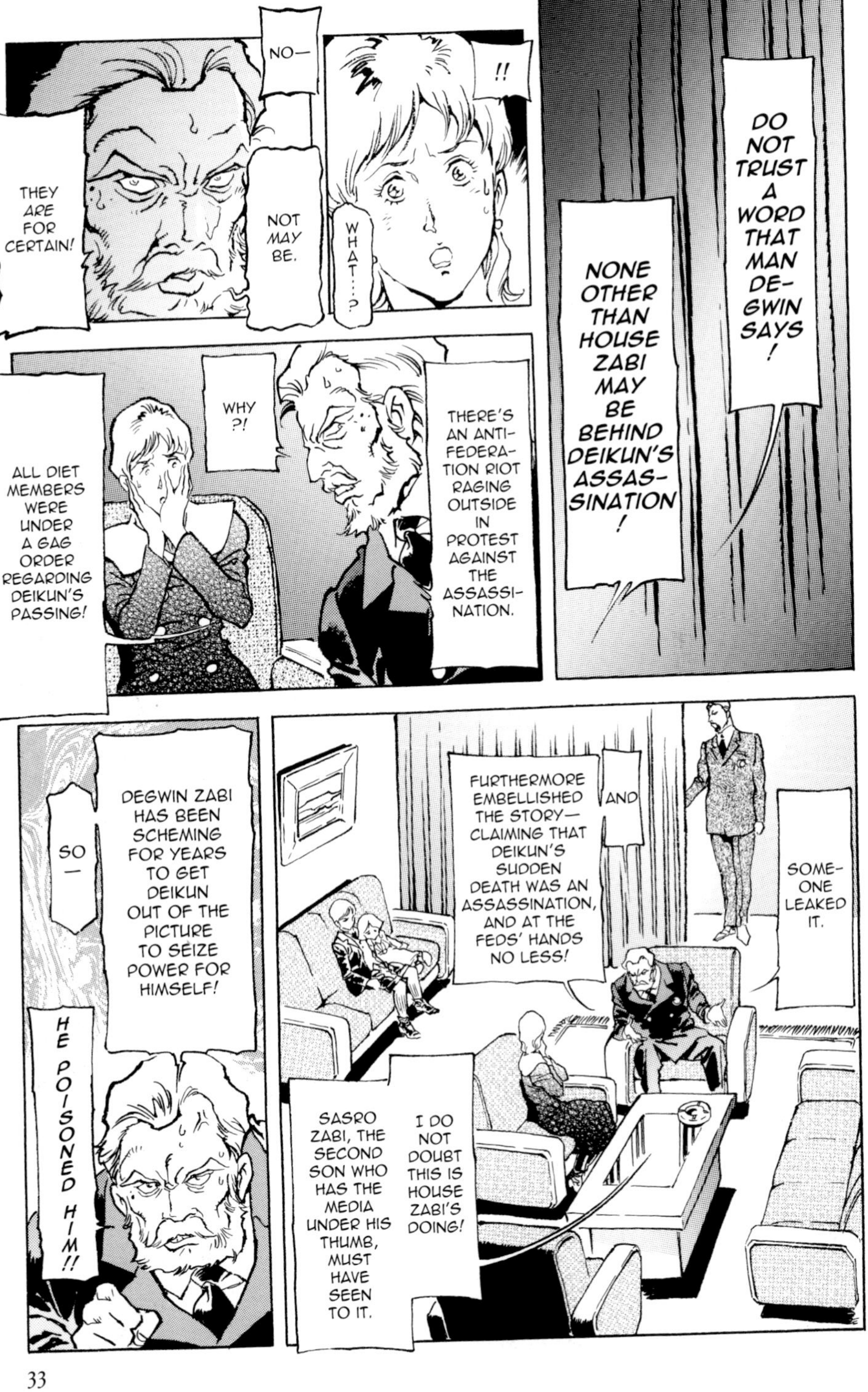
DO NOT TRUST A WORD THAT MAN DEGWIN SAYS!
NONE OTHER THAN HOUSE ZABI MAY BE BEHIND DEIKUN'S ASSASSINATION!
!!
WHAT...?
NO—
NOT MAY BE.
THEY ARE FOR CERTAIN!
THERE'S AN ANTI-FEDERATION RIOT RAGING OUTSIDE IN PROTEST AGAINST THE ASSASSINATION.
WHY?!
ALL DIET MEMBERS WERE UNDER A GAG ORDER REGARDING DEIKUN'S PASSING!
SOMEONE LEAKED IT.
AND
FURTHERMORE EMBELLISHED THE STORY—CLAIMING THAT DEIKUN'S SUDDEN DEATH WAS AN ASSASSINATION, AND AT THE FEDS' HANDS NO LESS!
I DO NOT DOUBT THIS IS HOUSE ZABI'S DOING!
SASRO ZABI, THE SECOND SON WHO HAS THE MEDIA UNDER HIS THUMB, MUST HAVE SEEN TO IT.
SO—
DEGWIN ZABI HAS BEEN SCHEMING FOR YEARS TO GET DEIKUN OUT OF THE PICTURE TO SEIZE POWER FOR HIMSELF!
HE POISONED HIM!!

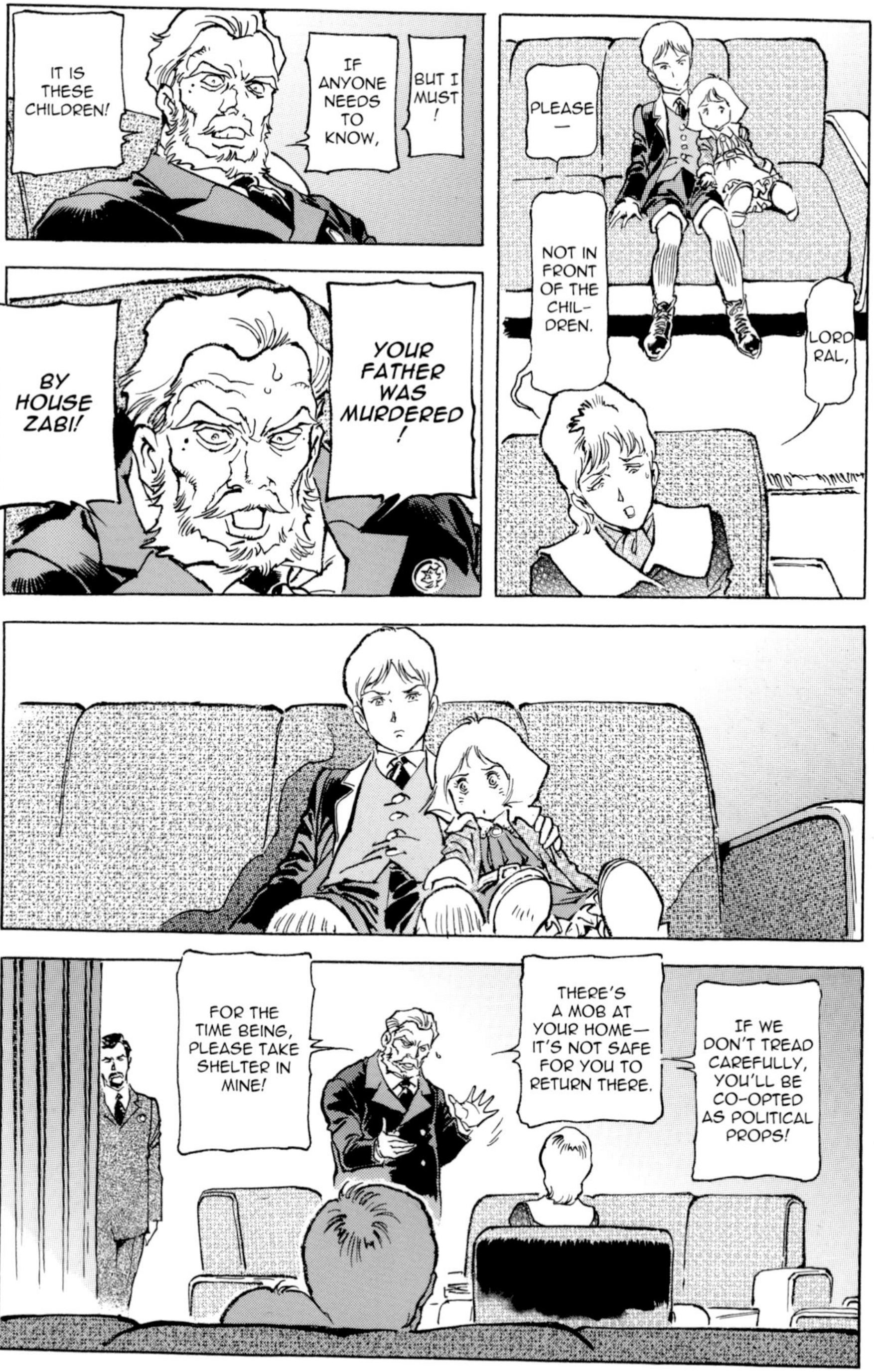
LORD RAL,
PLEASE —
NOT IN FRONT OF THE CHIL-DREN.
BUT I MUST!
IF ANYONE NEEDS TO KNOW,
IT IS THESE CHILDREN!
YOUR FATHER WAS MURDERED!
BY HOUSE ZABI!
IF WE DON'T TREAD CAREFULLY, YOU'LL BE CO-OPTED AS POLITICAL PROPS!
THERE'S A MOB AT YOUR HOME— IT'S NOT SAFE FOR YOU TO RETURN THERE.
FOR THE TIME BEING, PLEASE TAKE SHELTER IN MINE!

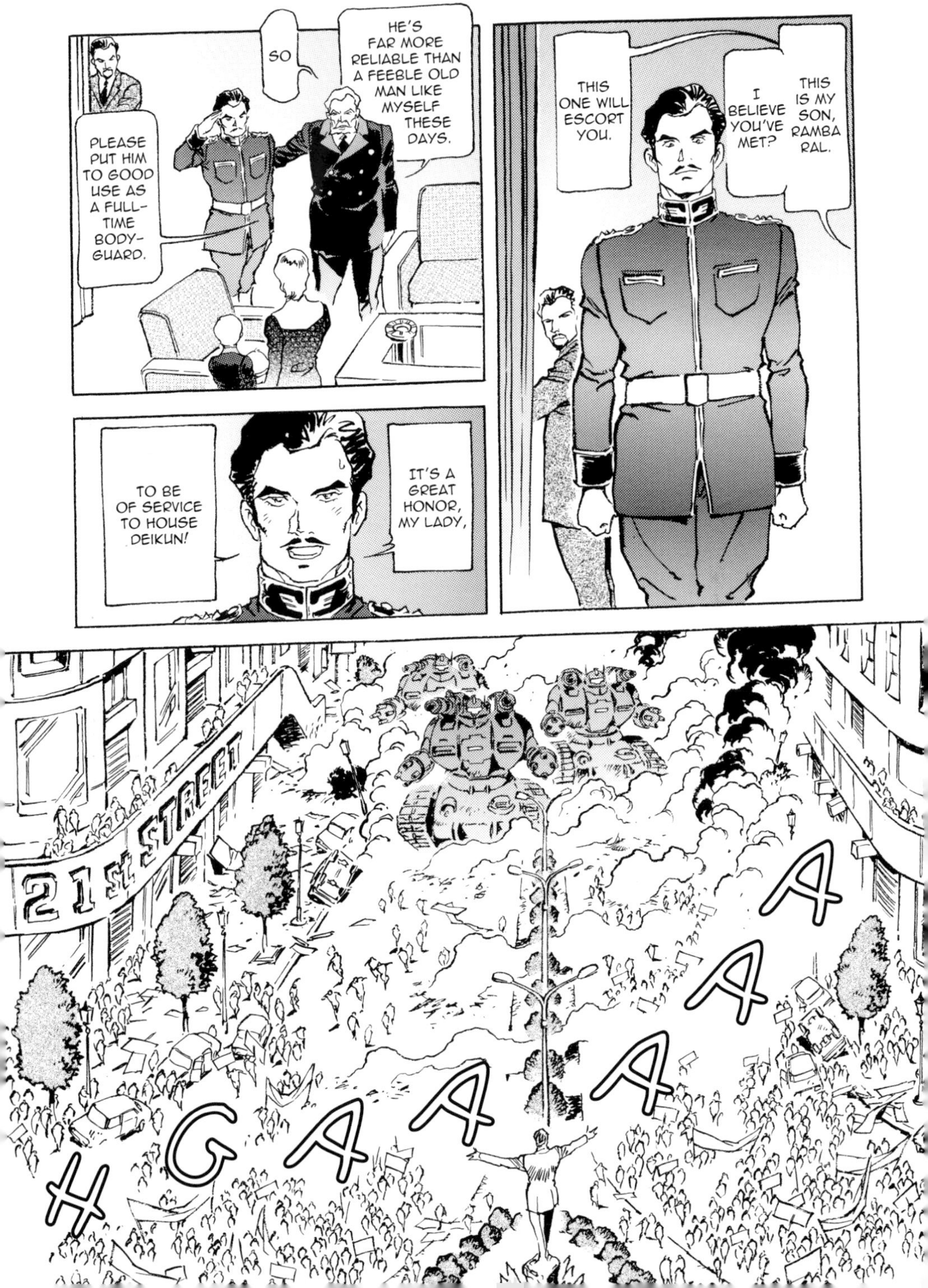
THIS IS MY SON, RAMBA RAL.
I BELIEVE YOU'VE MET?
THIS ONE WILL ESCORT YOU.
HE'S FAR MORE RELIABLE THAN A FEEBLE OLD MAN LIKE MYSELF THESE DAYS.
SO
PLEASE PUT HIM TO GOOD USE AS A FULL-TIME BODY-GUARD.
IT'S A GREAT HONOR, MY LADY,
TO BE OF SERVICE TO HOUSE DEIKUN!
21st STREET
HGAAAAA

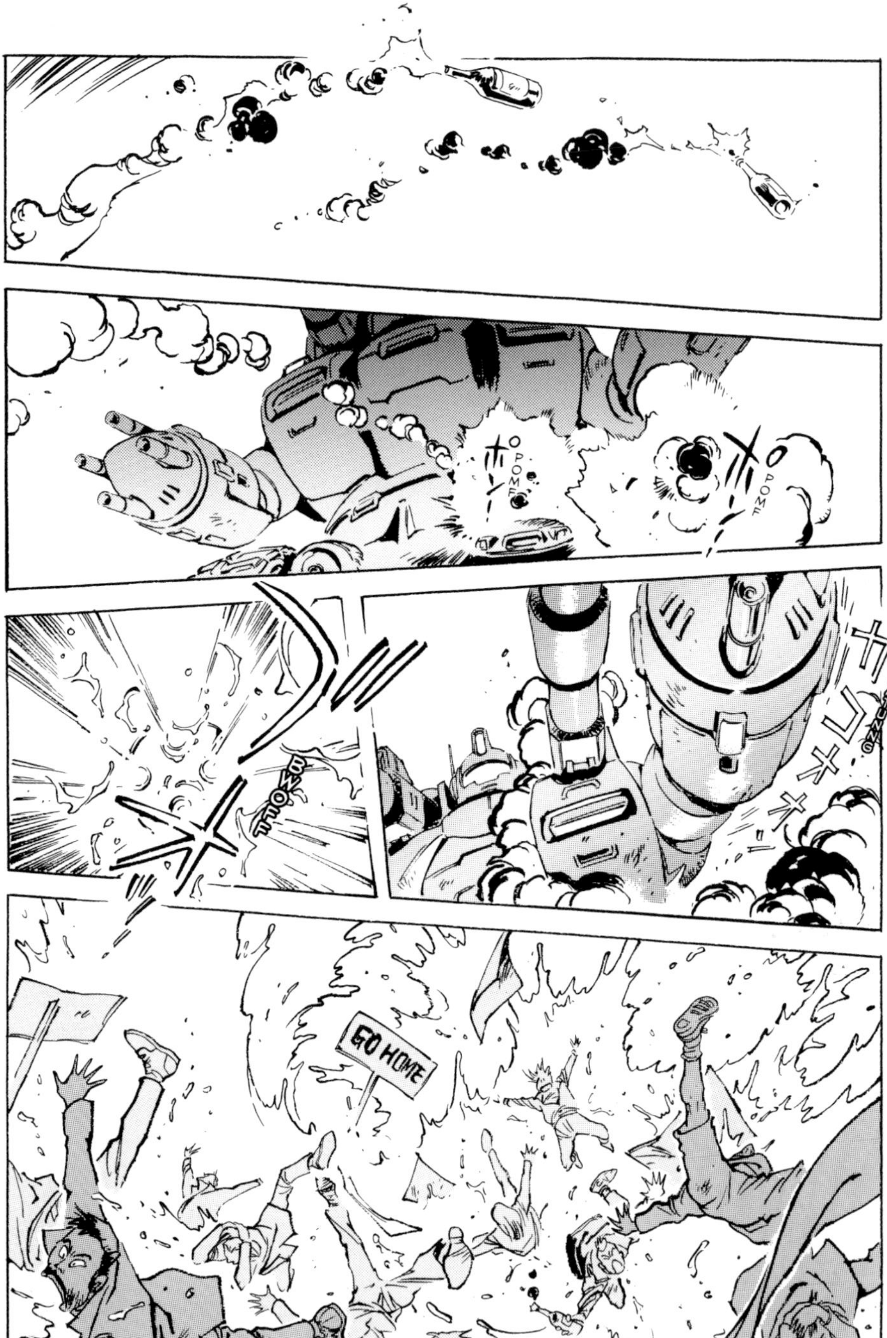
POMF
POMF
GATUNNG
BWOFF
GO HOME

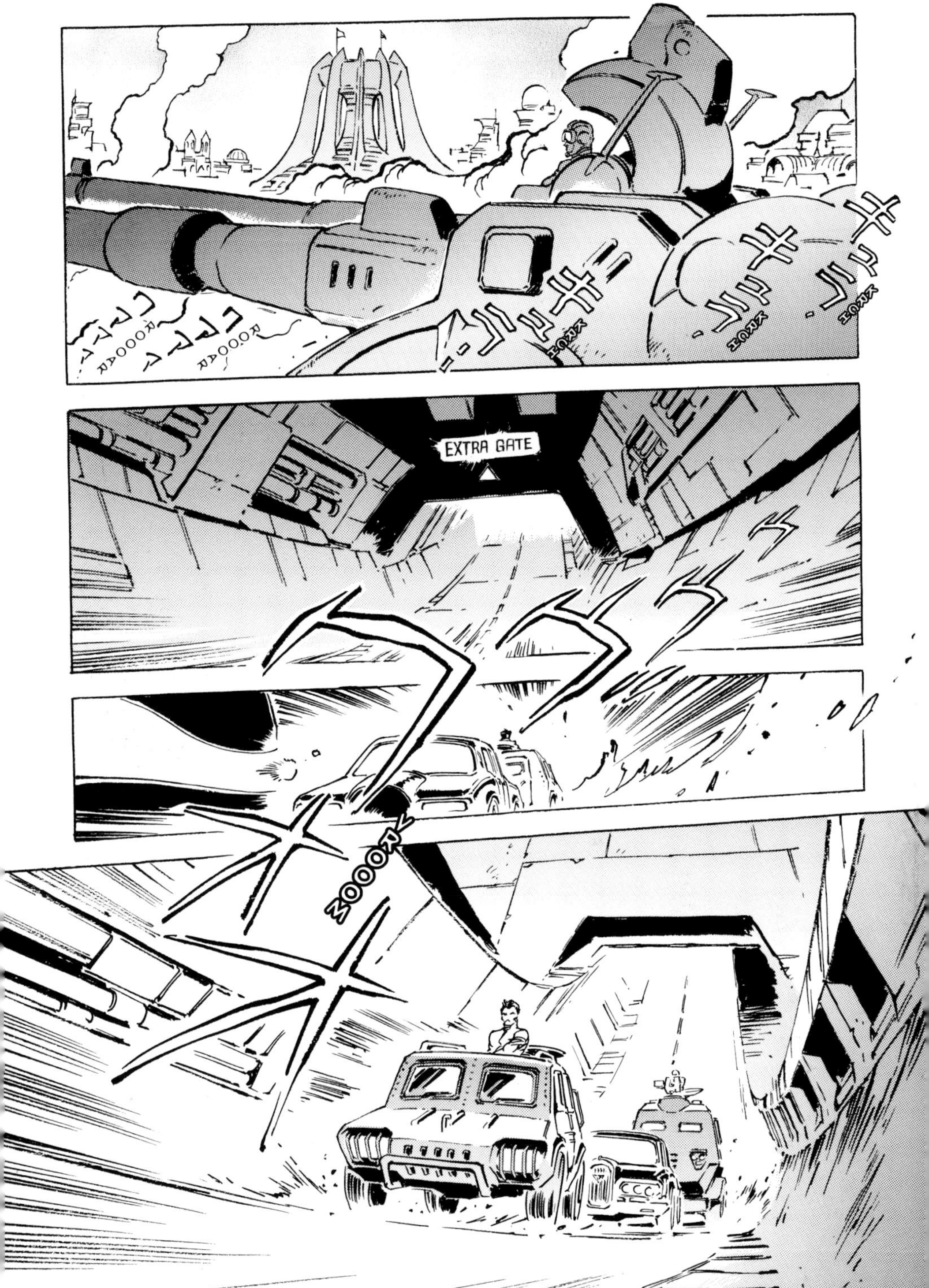
ROOOAR
ROOOAR
EXTRA GATE
VROOOM

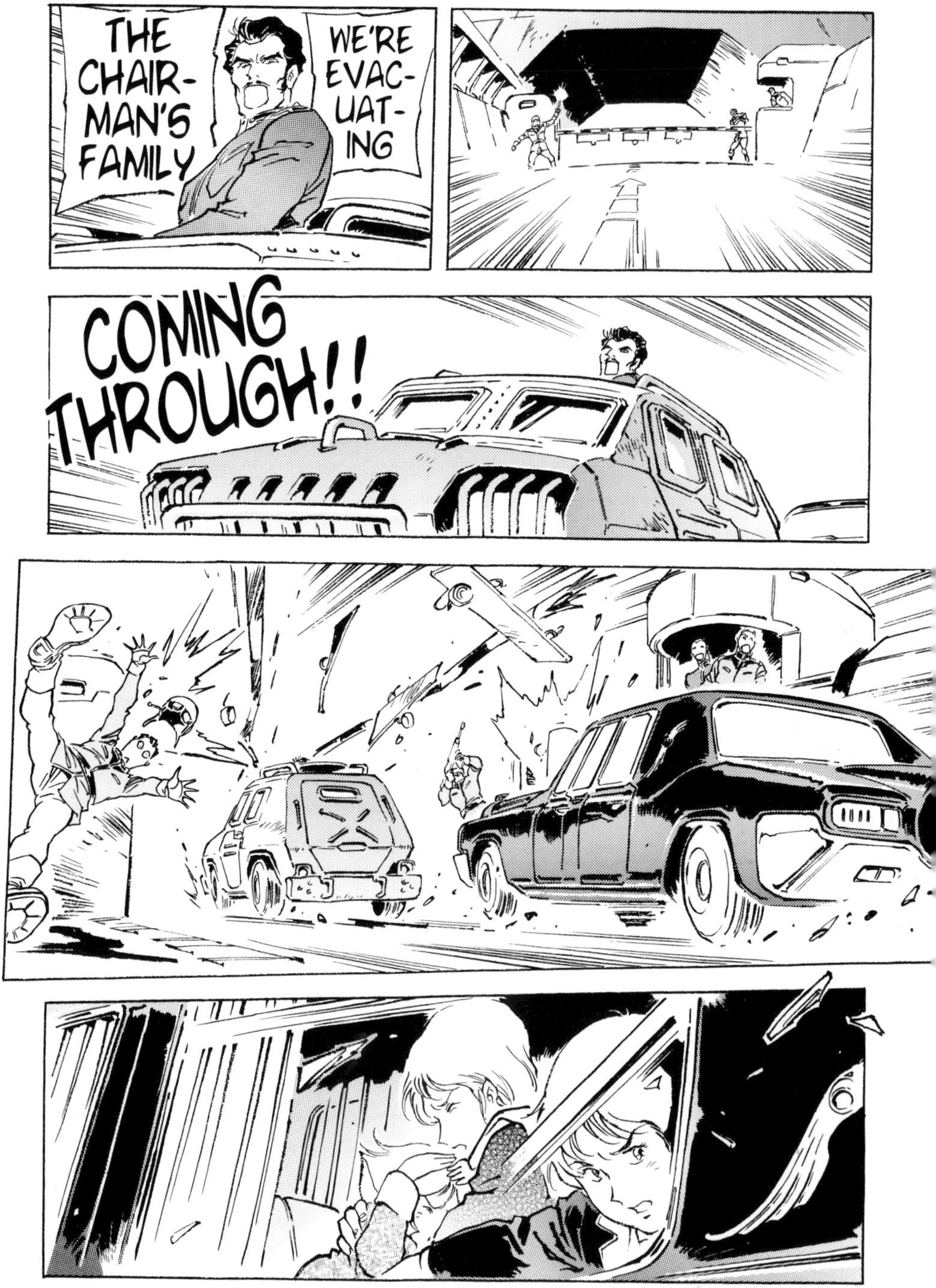
WE'RE EVAC-UAT-ING
THE CHAIR-MAN'S FAMILY
COMING THROUGH!!

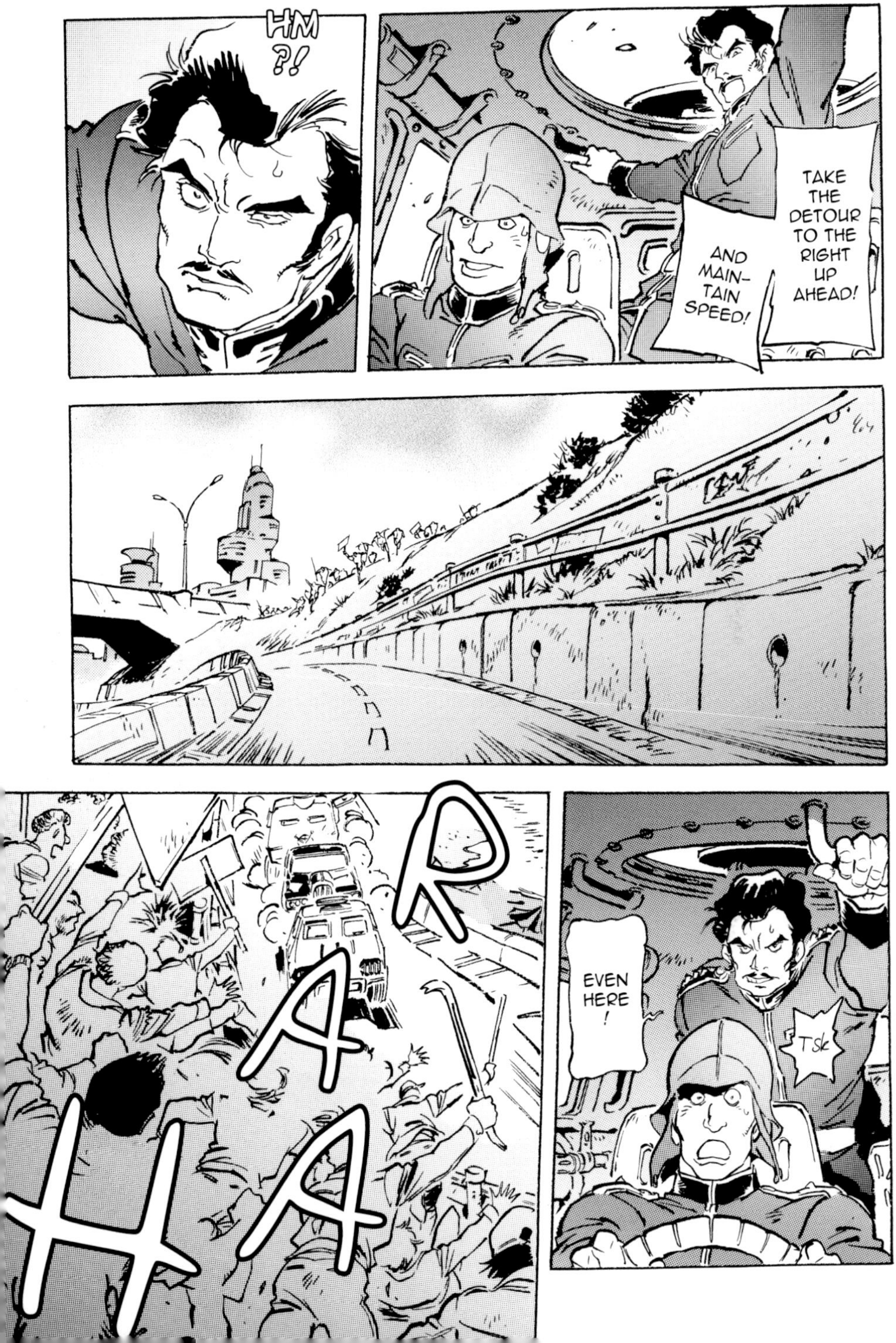
TAKE THE DETOUR TO THE RIGHT UP AHEAD!
AND MAIN-TAIN SPEED!
HM ?!
Tsk
EVEN HERE!
RAAH

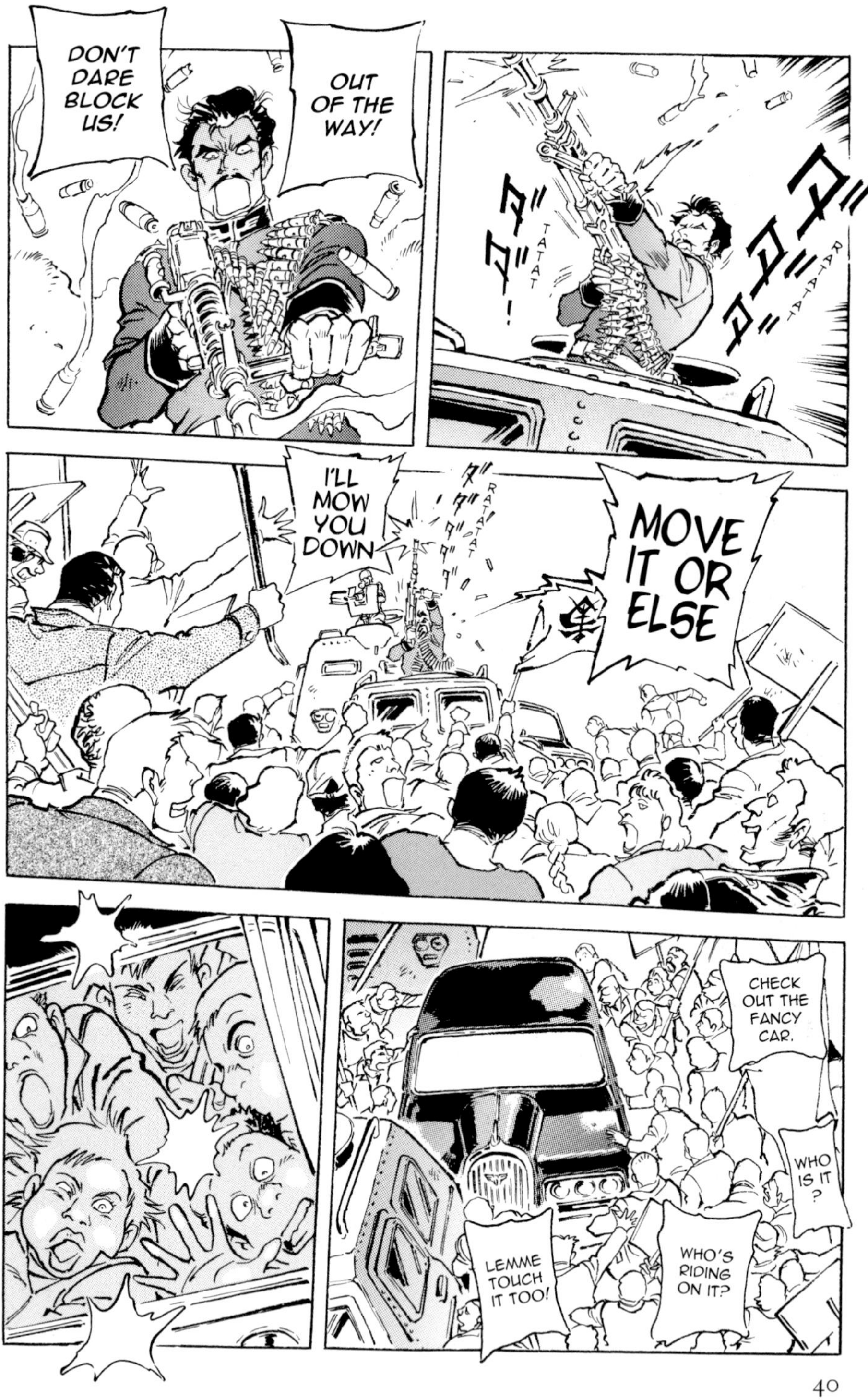
RATATAT
TATAT
OUT OF THE WAY!
DON'T DARE BLOCK US!
MOVE IT OR ELSE
RATATAT
I'LL MOW YOU DOWN
CHECK OUT THE FANCY CAR.
WHO IS IT ?
WHO'S RIDING ON IT?
LEMME TOUCH IT TOO!

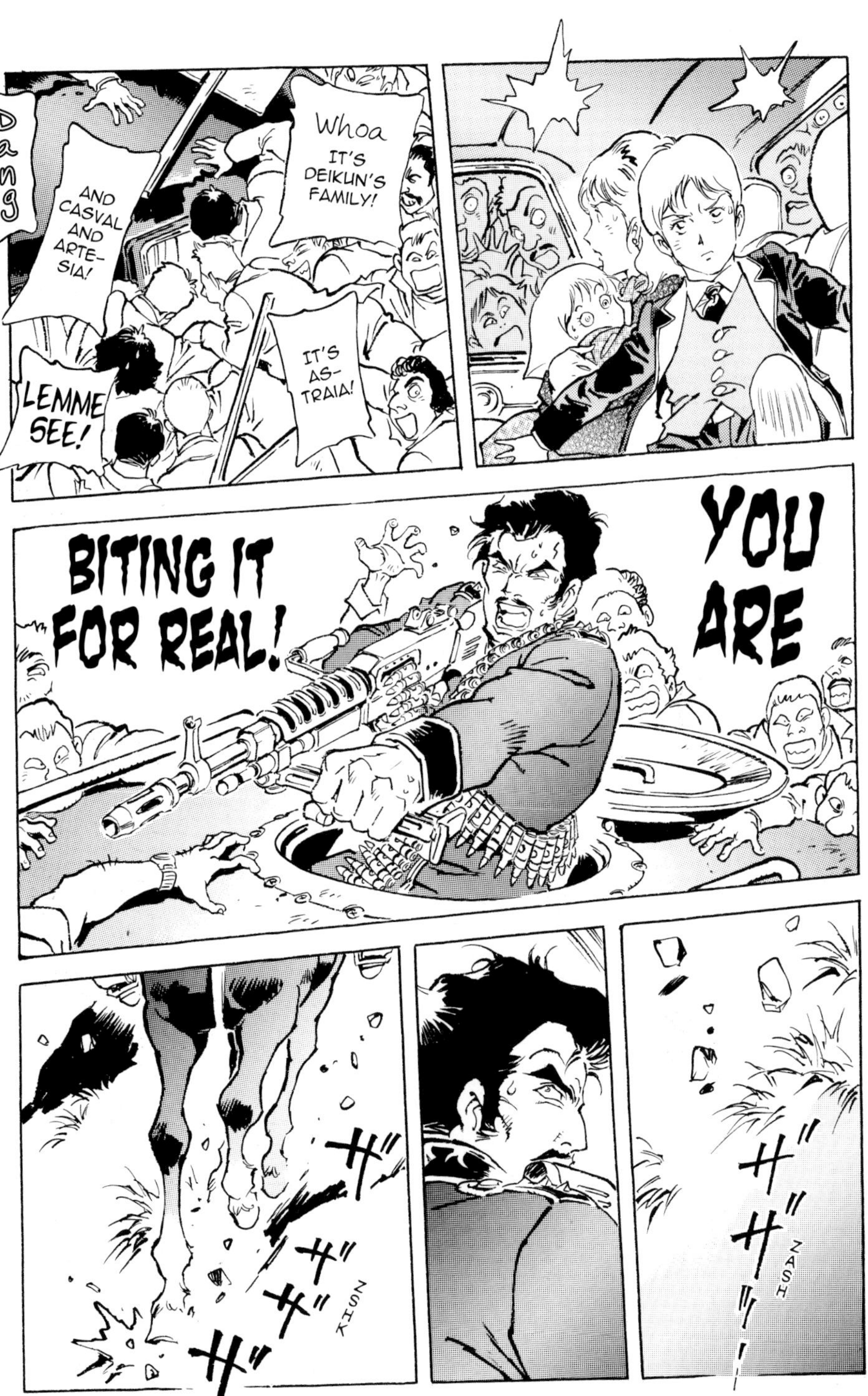

Whoa
IT'S DEIKUN'S FAMILY!
AND CASVAL AND ARTE-SIA!
Dang
IT'S AS-TRAIA!
LEMME SEE!
YOU ARE
BITING IT FOR REAL!
ZASH
ZSHK

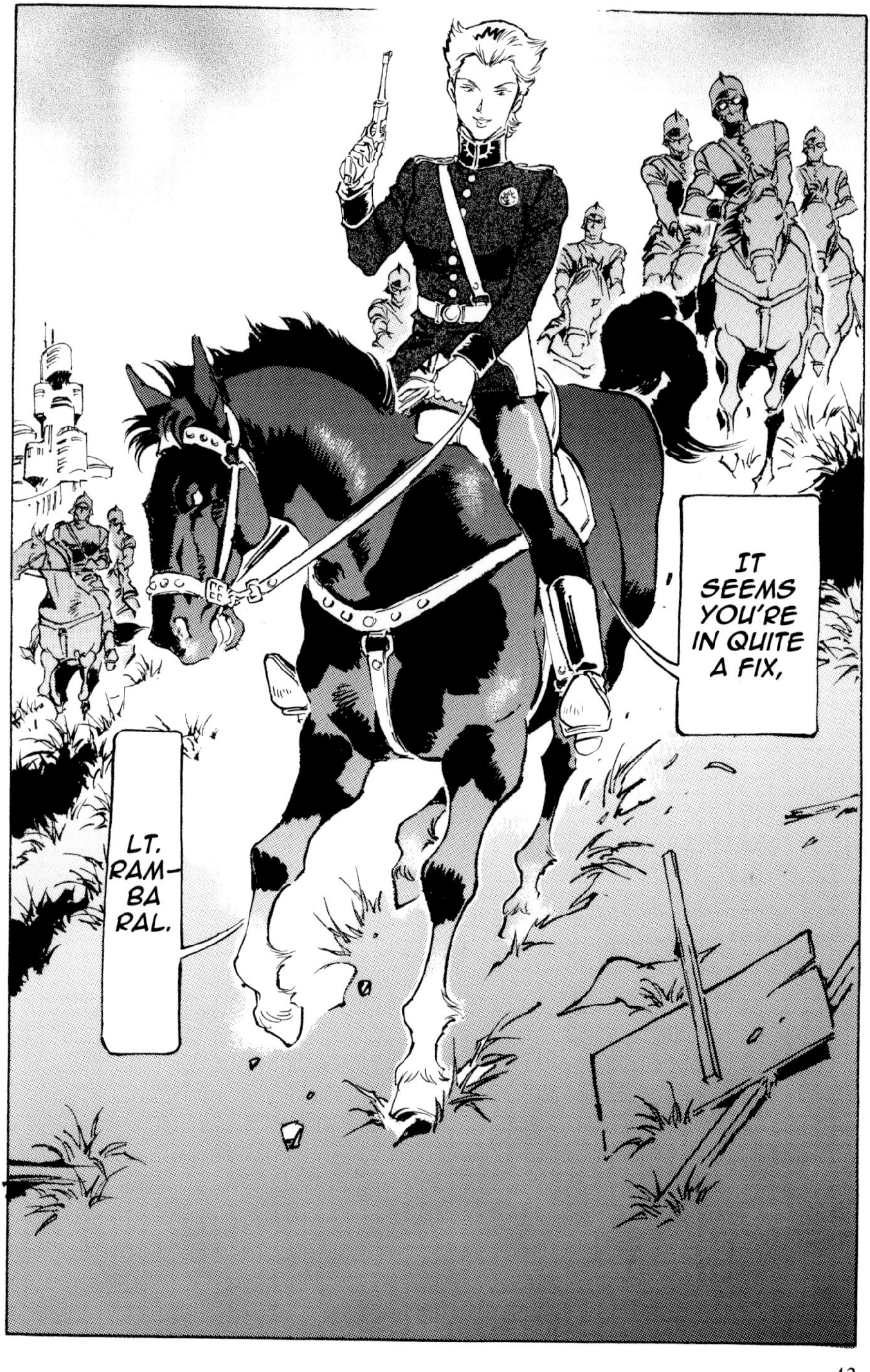
IT SEEMS YOU'RE IN QUITE A FIX,
LT. RAM-BA RAL.

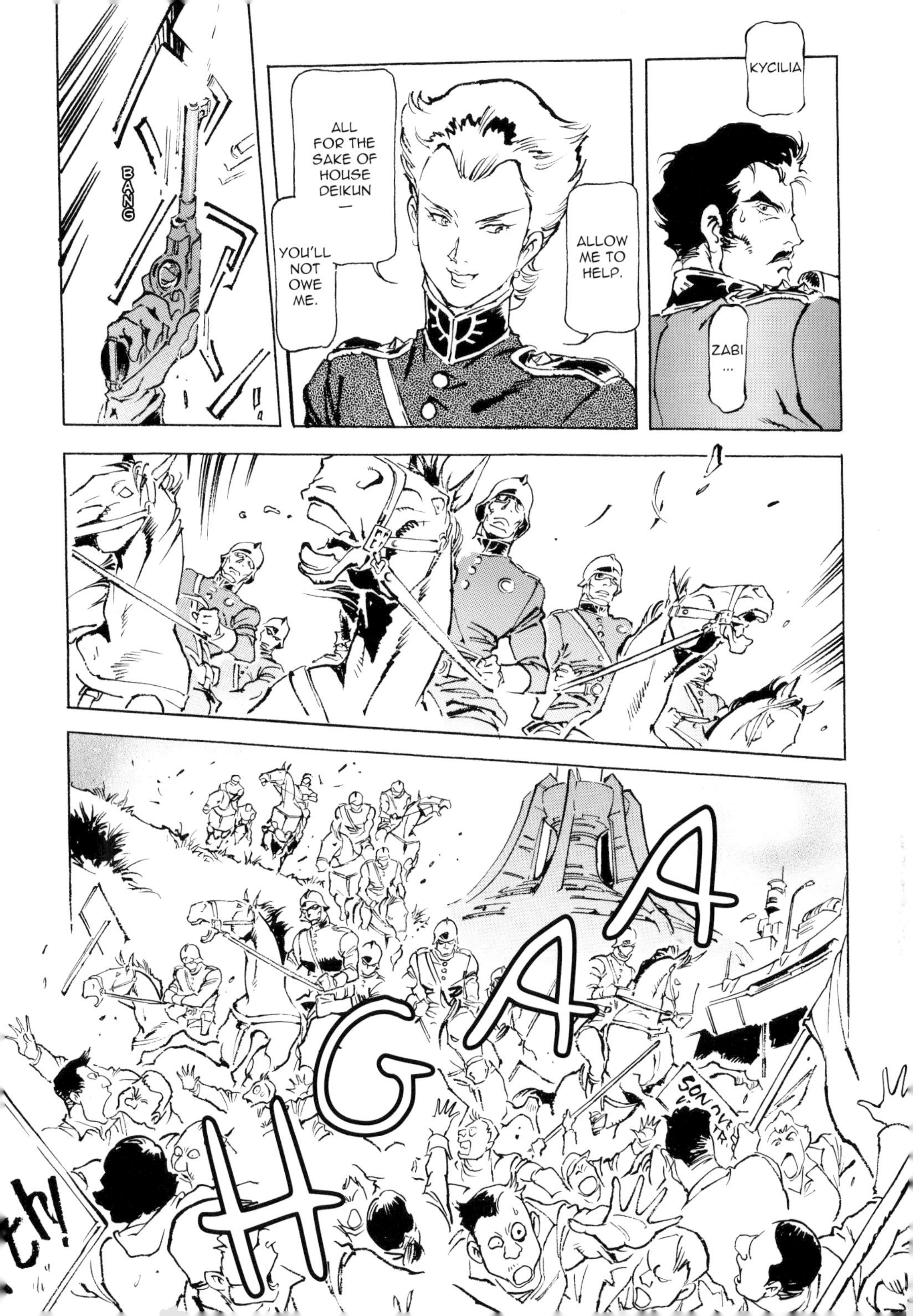
KYCILIA
ZABI ...
ALLOW ME TO HELP.
ALL FOR THE SAKE OF HOUSE DEIKUN —
YOU'LL NOT OWE ME.
BANG
HGAAA

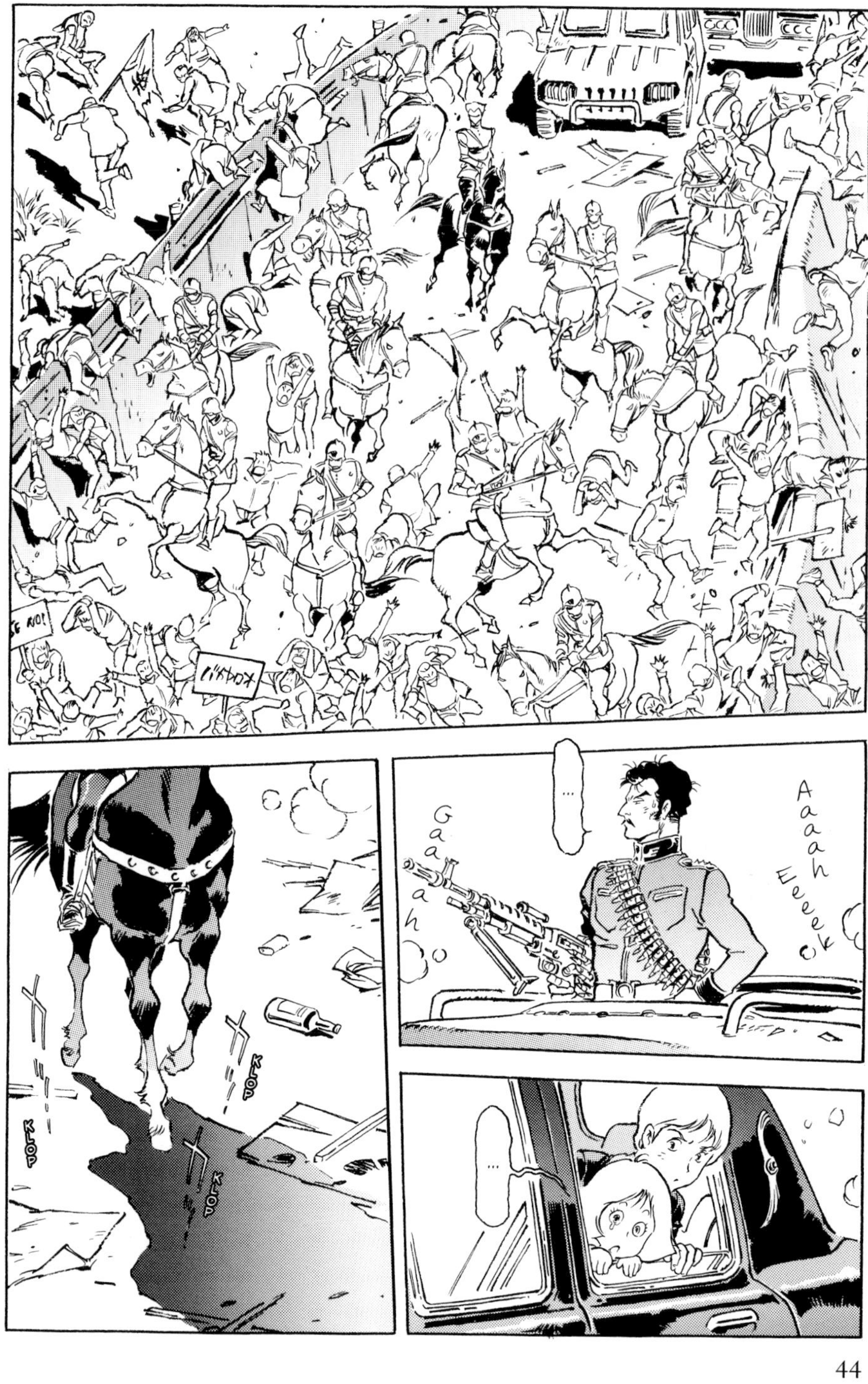
...
Aaaah
Eeeeek
Gaaah
...
KLOP
KLOP
KLOP

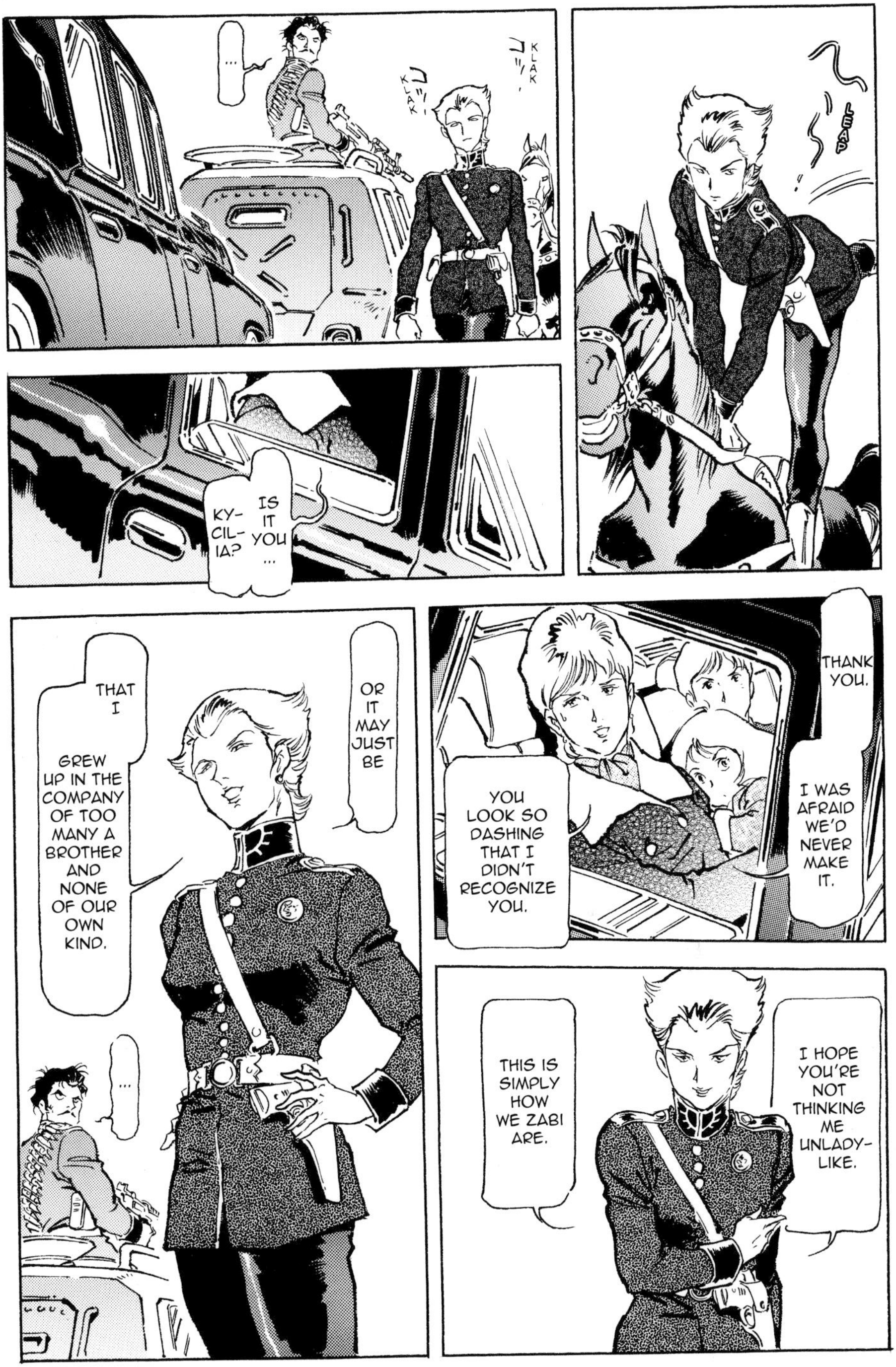
LEAP
KLAK KLAK
...
IS IT YOU ...
KYCILIA?
THANK YOU.
I WAS AFRAID WE'D NEVER MAKE IT.
YOU LOOK SO DASHING THAT I DIDN'T RECOGNIZE YOU.
I HOPE YOU'RE NOT THINKING ME UNLADYLIKE.
THIS IS SIMPLY HOW WE ZABI ARE.
OR IT MAY JUST BE
THAT I GREW UP IN THE COMPANY OF TOO MANY A BROTHER AND NONE OF OUR OWN KIND.
...

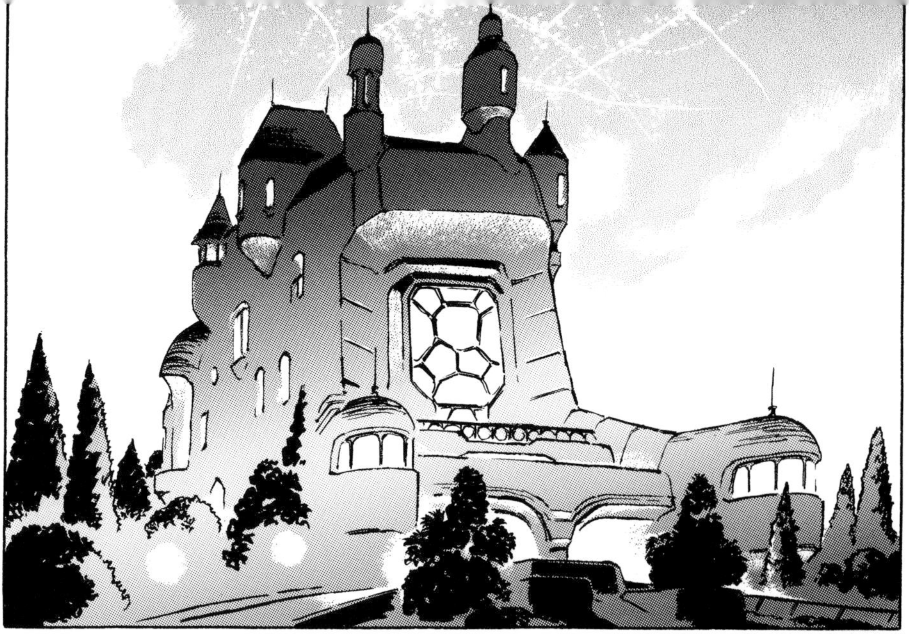

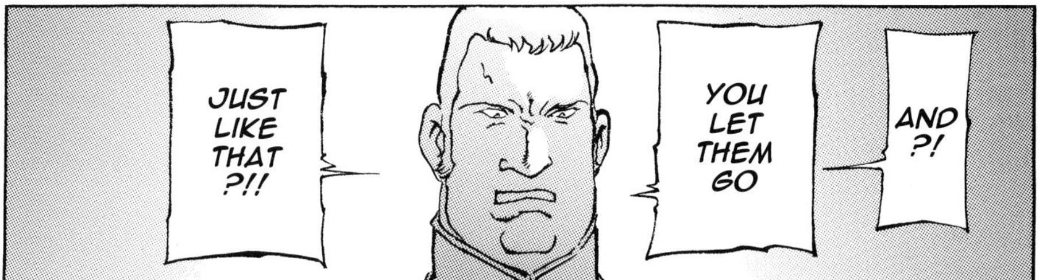
AND ?!
YOU LET THEM GO
JUST LIKE THAT ?!!

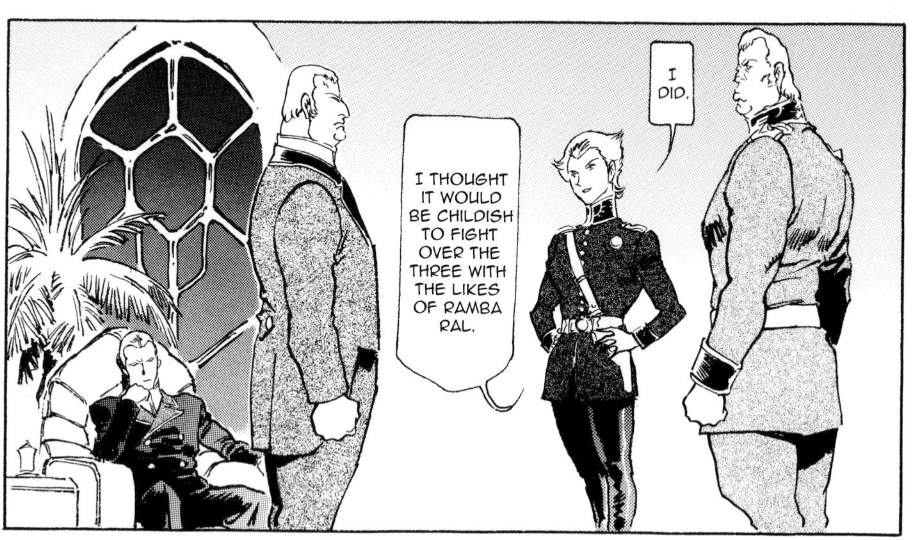
I DID.
I THOUGHT IT WOULD BE CHILDISH TO FIGHT OVER THE THREE WITH THE LIKES OF RAMBA RAL.

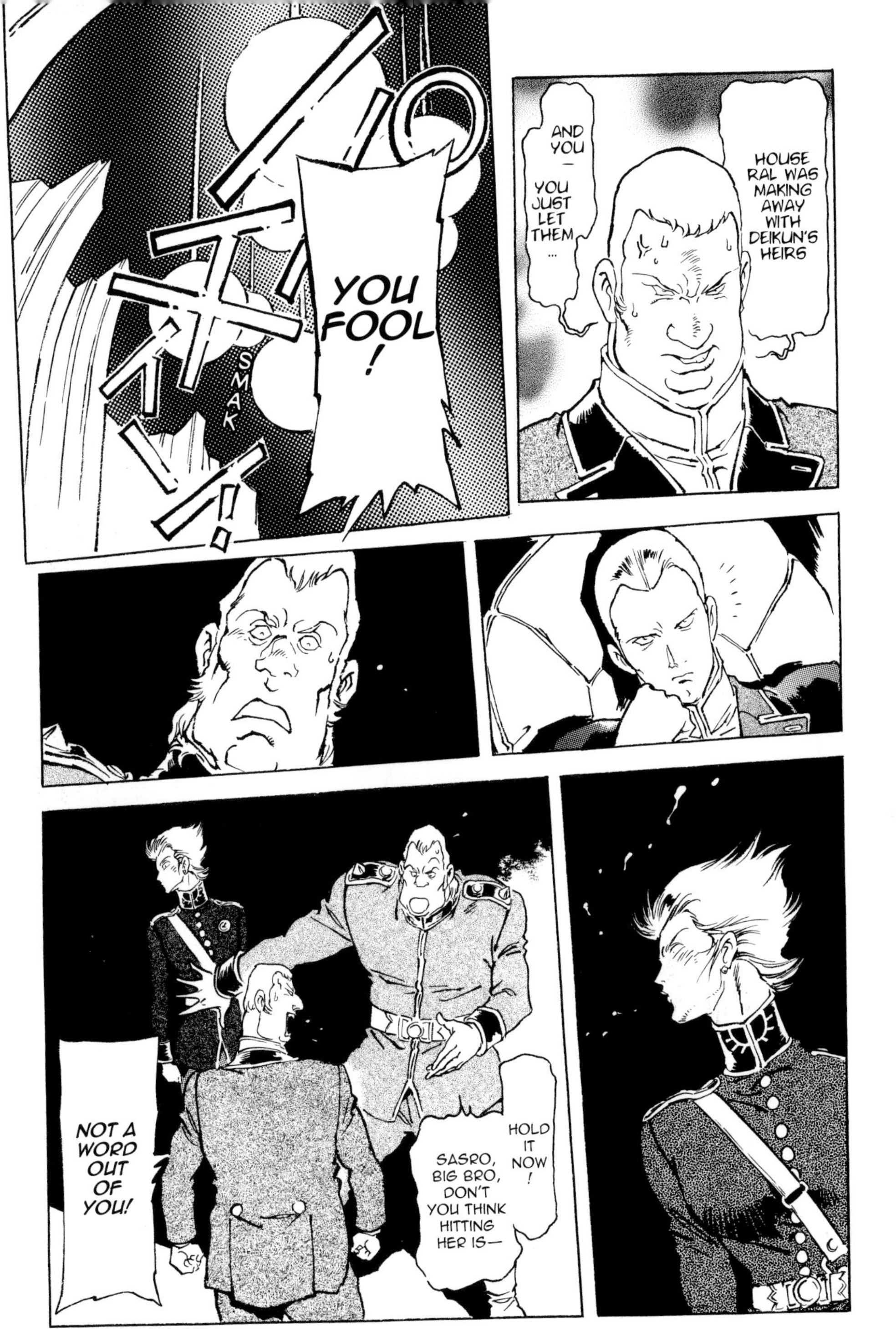
HOUSE RAL WAS MAKING AWAY WITH DEIKUN'S HEIRS
AND YOU — YOU JUST LET THEM ...
YOU FOOL!
SMAK
HOLD IT NOW!
SASRO, BIG BRO, DON'T YOU THINK HITTING HER IS—
NOT A WORD OUT OF YOU!

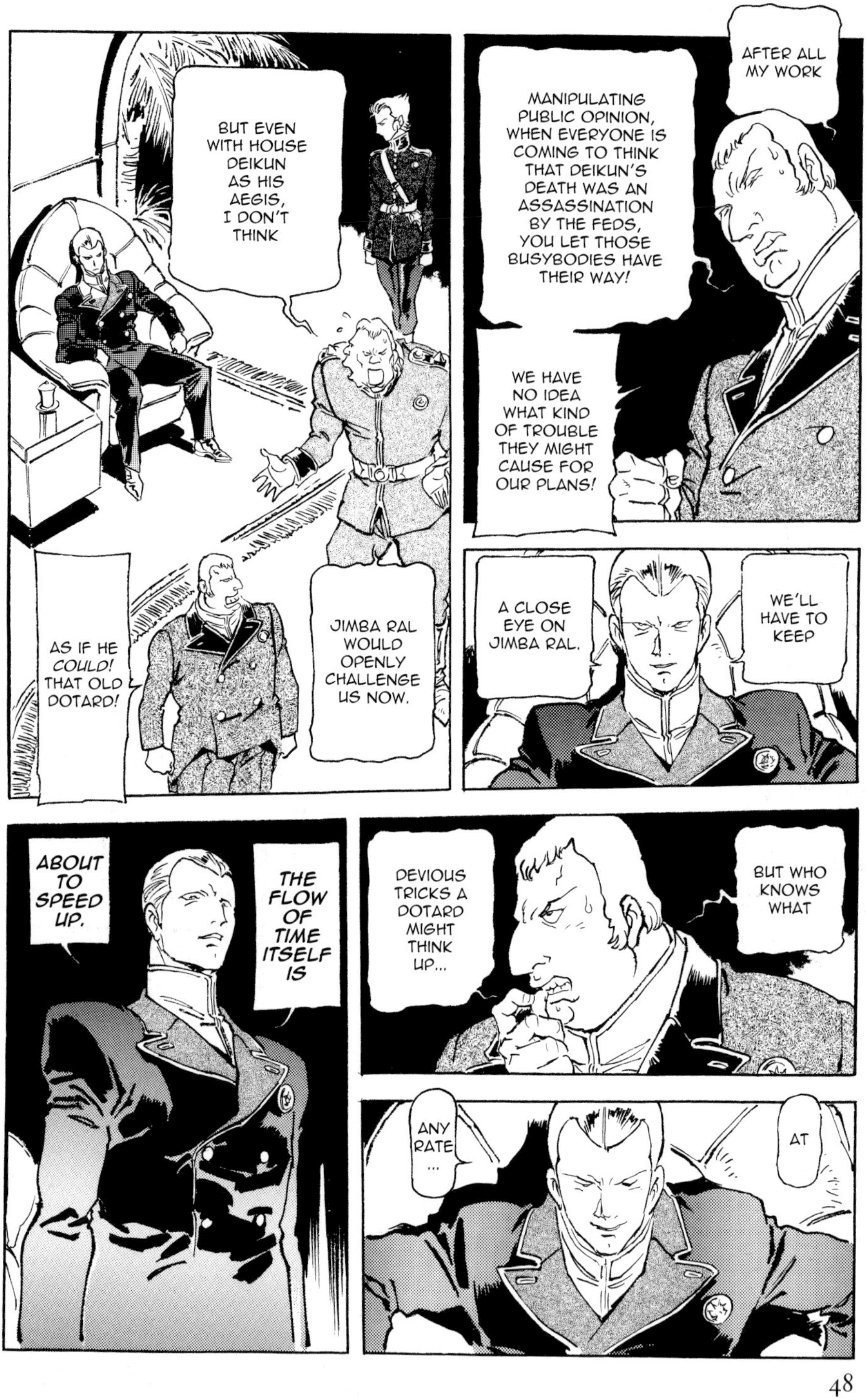
AFTER ALL MY WORK
MANIPULATING PUBLIC OPINION, WHEN EVERYONE IS COMING TO THINK THAT DEIKUN'S DEATH WAS AN ASSASSINATION BY THE FEDS, YOU LET THOSE BUSYBODIES HAVE THEIR WAY!
WE HAVE NO IDEA WHAT KIND OF TROUBLE THEY MIGHT CAUSE FOR OUR PLANS!
WE'LL HAVE TO KEEP
A CLOSE EYE ON JIMBA RAL.
BUT EVEN WITH HOUSE DEIKUN AS HIS AEGIS, I DON'T THINK
JIMBA RAL WOULD OPENLY CHALLENGE US NOW.
AS IF HE *COULD!* THAT OLD DOTARD!
BUT WHO KNOWS WHAT
DEVIOUS TRICKS A DOTARD MIGHT THINK UP...
AT
ANY RATE ...
THE FLOW OF TIME ITSELF IS
ABOUT TO SPEED UP.

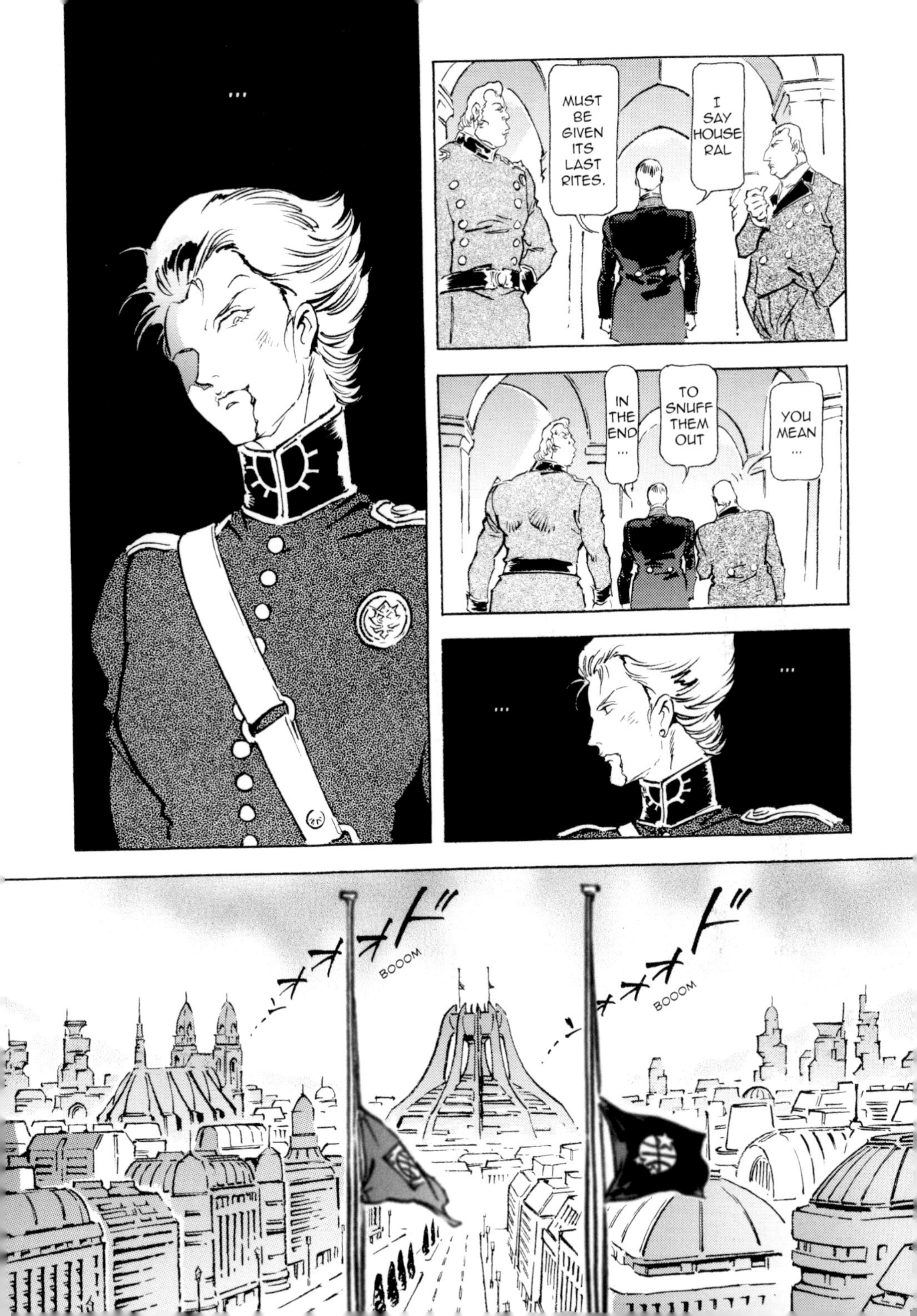
I SAY HOUSE RAL
MUST BE GIVEN ITS LAST RITES.
YOU MEAN ...
TO SNUFF THEM OUT
IN THE END ...
...
...
...
ドオオオン
BOOOM
ドオオオン
BOOOM

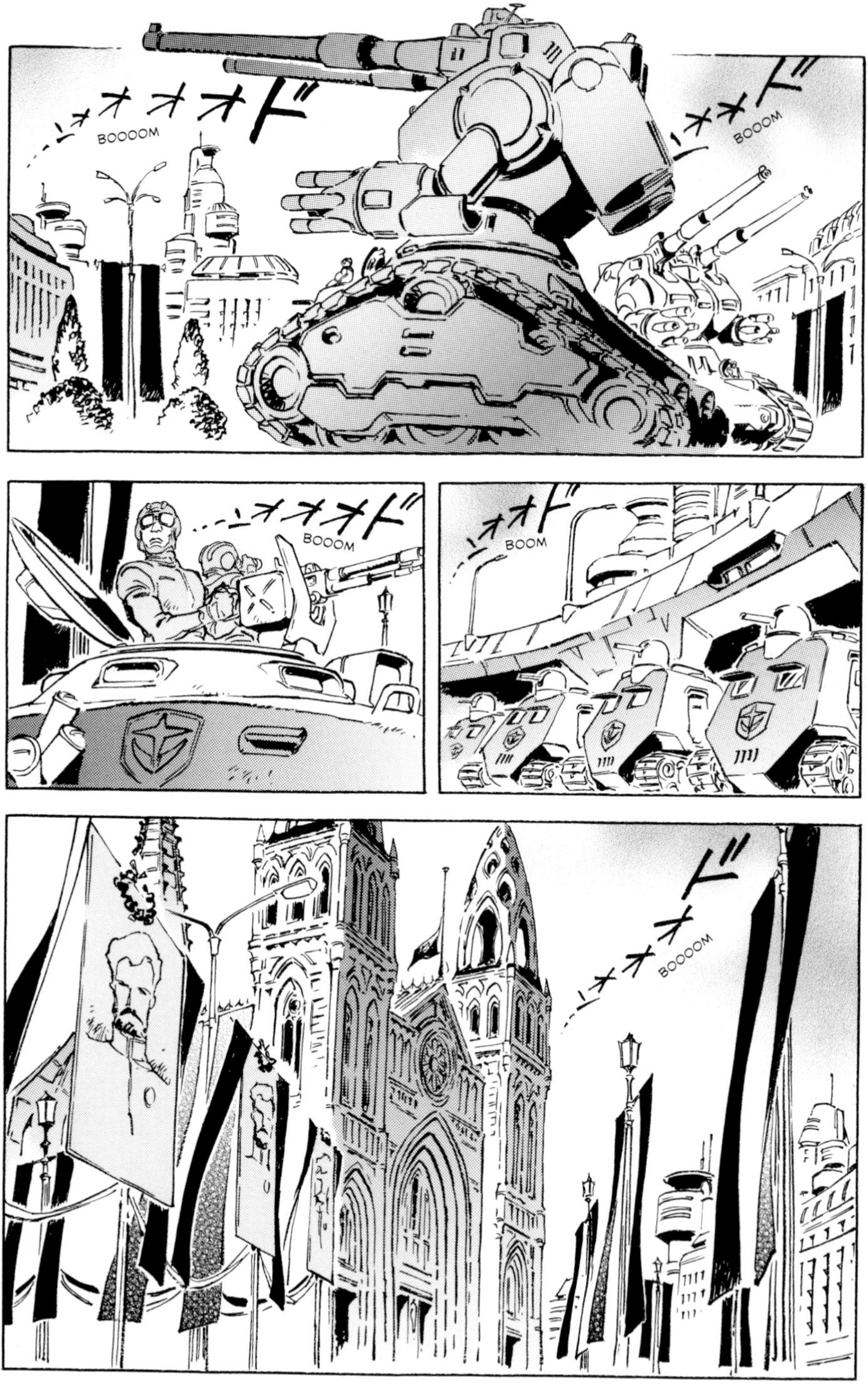
ドオオン
BOOOM
ドオオオォン
BOOOOM
ドオォン
BOOM
ドオオオン
BOOOM
ドオオン
BOOOOM

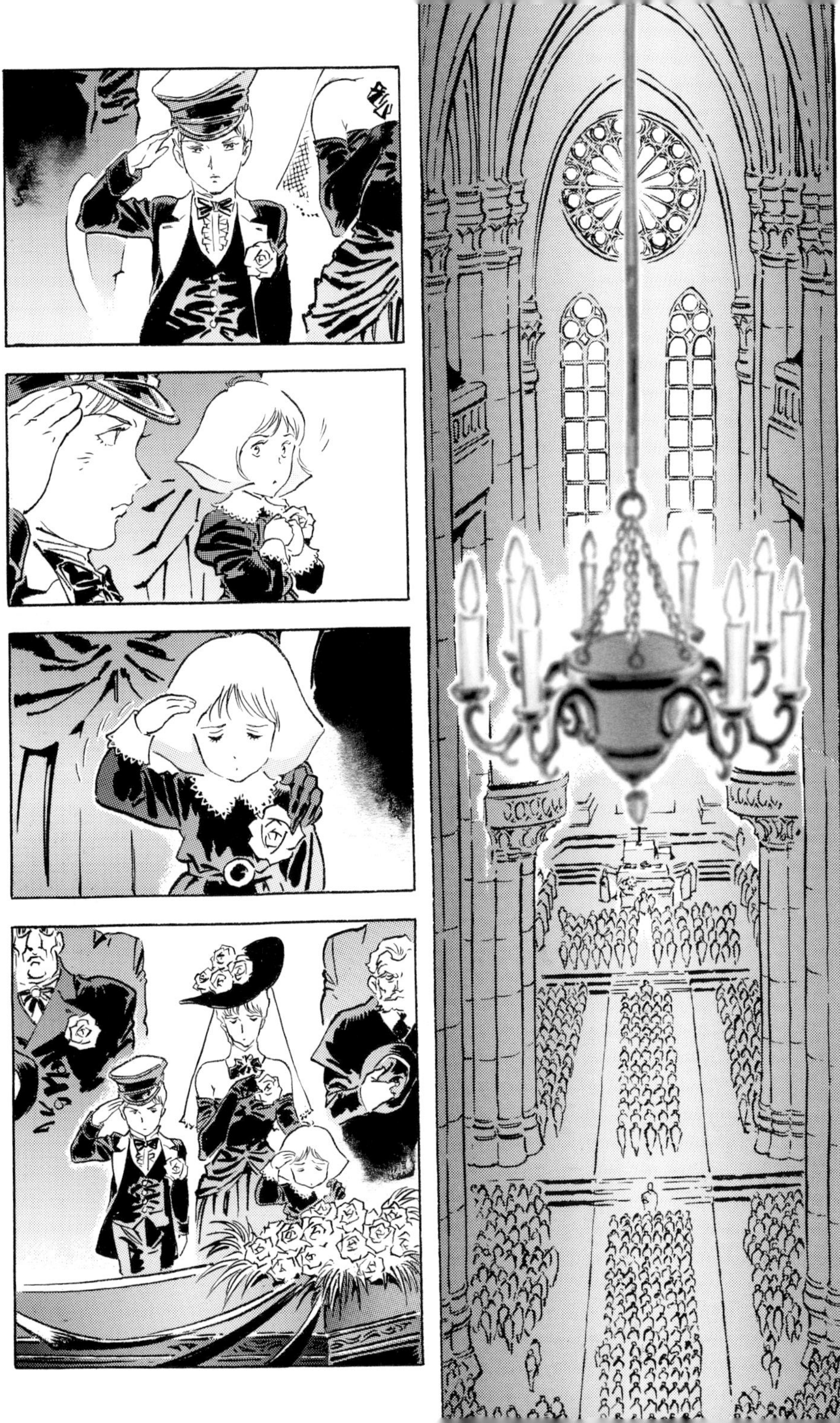

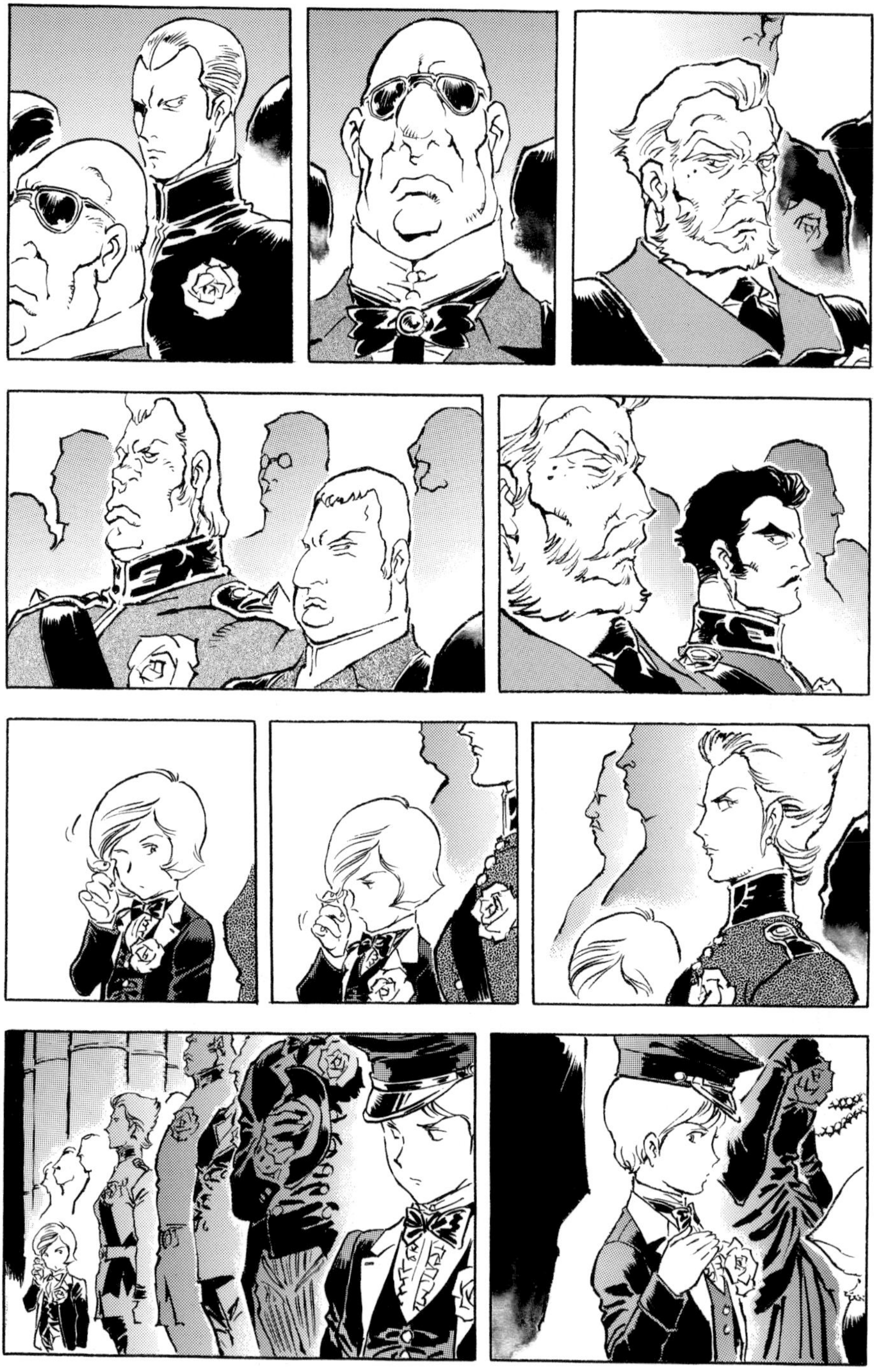

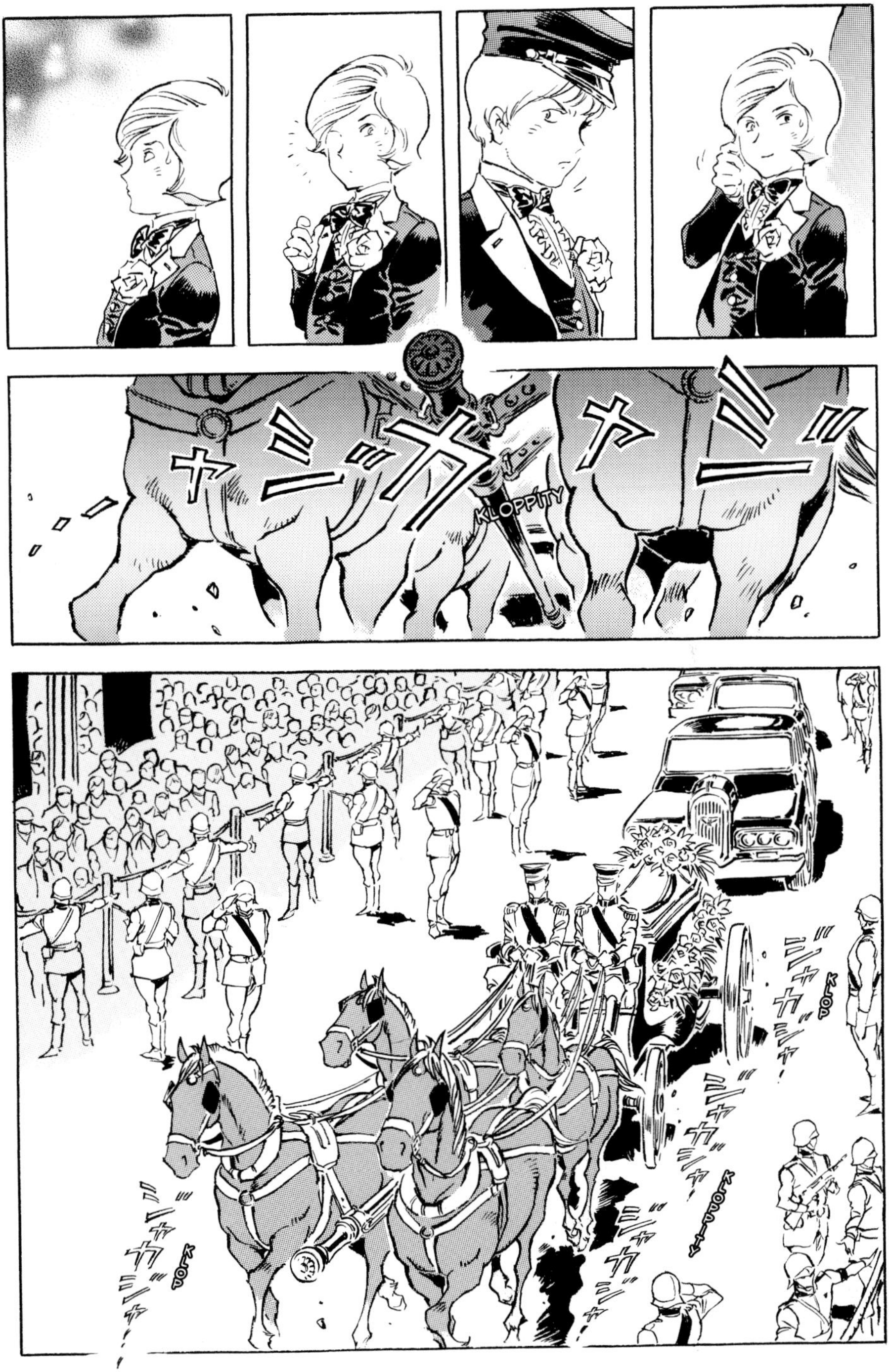
KLOPPITY
ジャカジャカ!
KLOP
ジャカジャカ!
ジャカジャカ…
KLOP

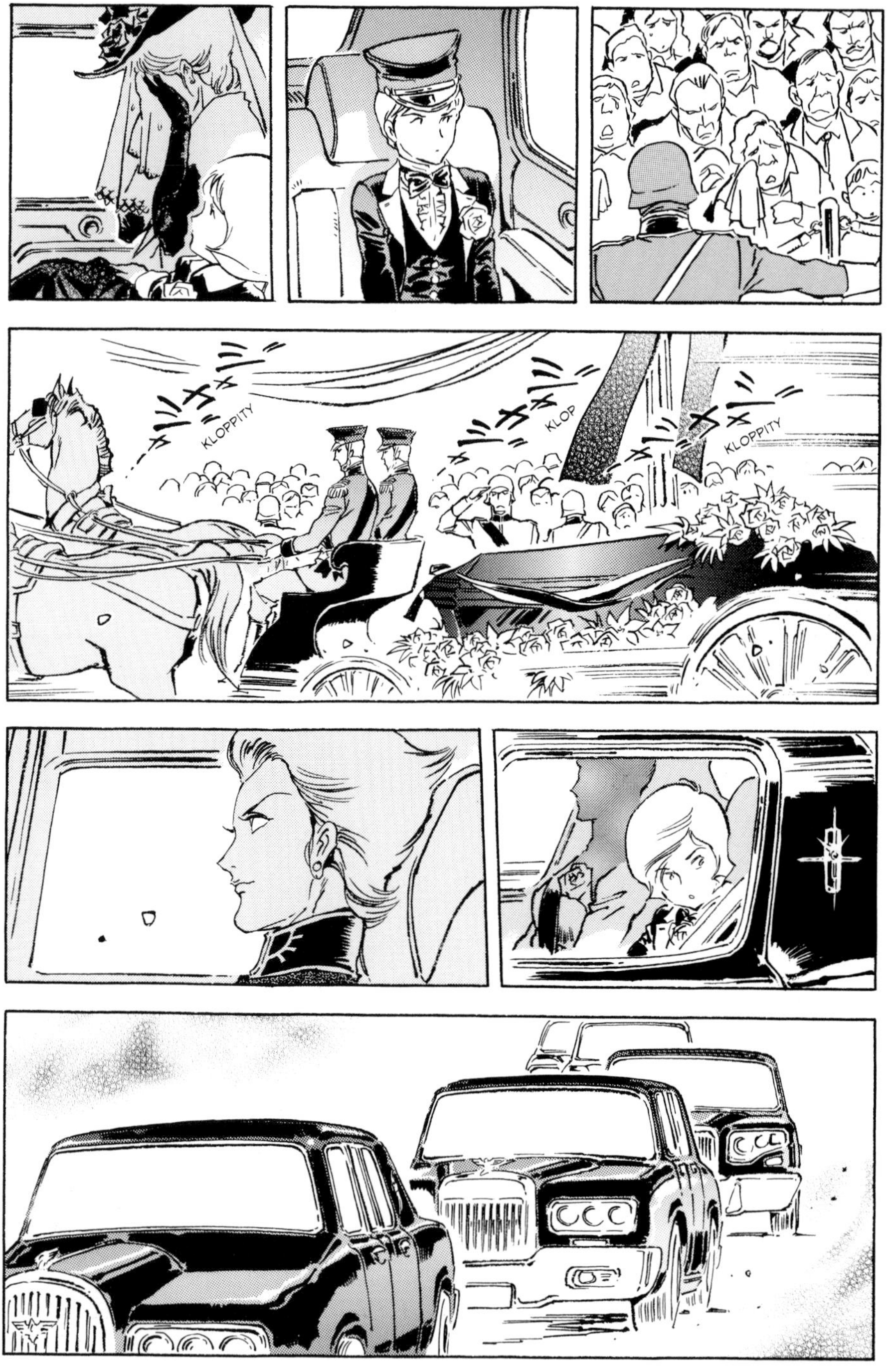
KLOPPITY
KLOP
KLOPPITY

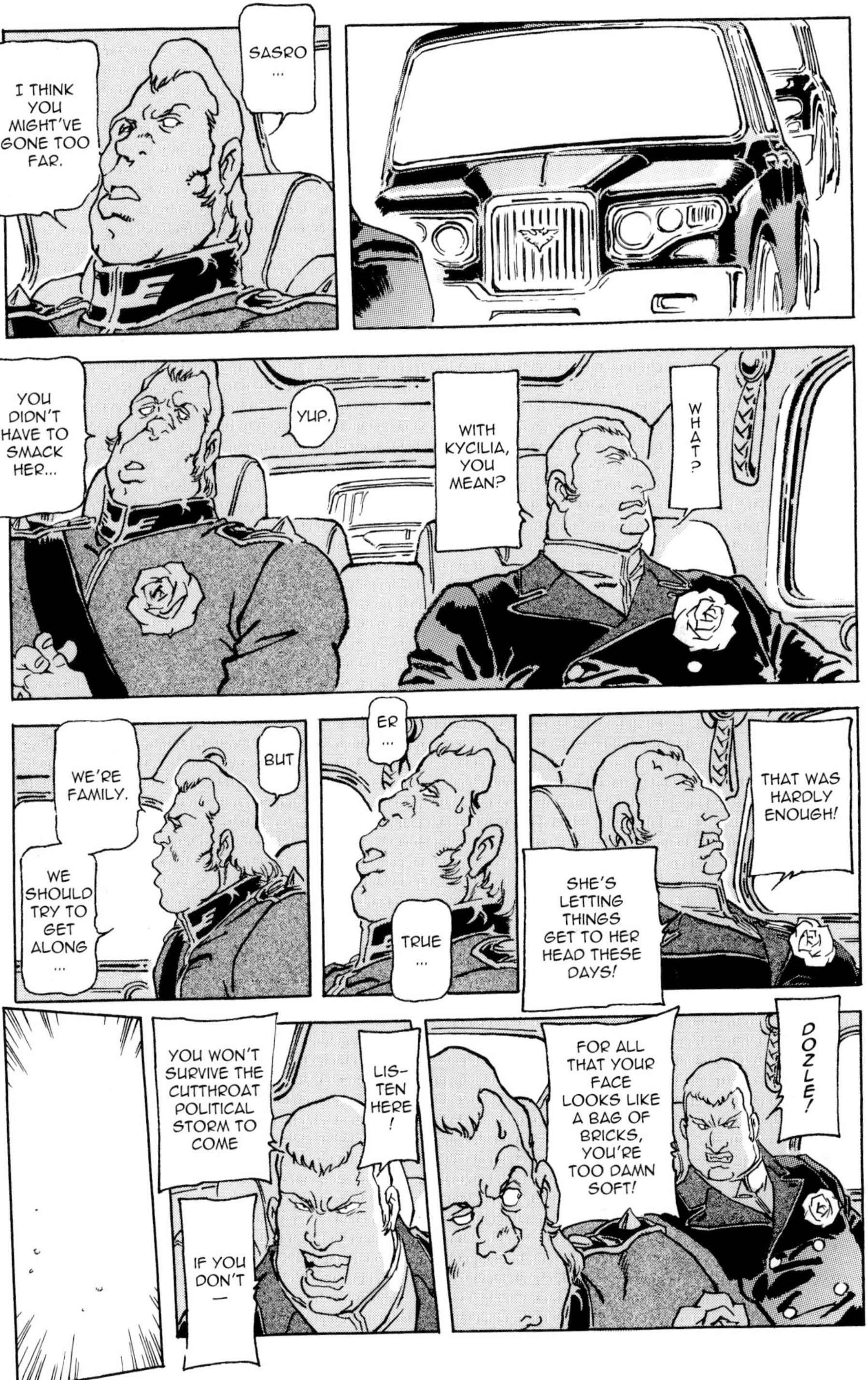
SASRO ...
I THINK YOU MIGHT'VE GONE TOO FAR.
WHAT?
WITH KYCILIA, YOU MEAN?
YUP.
YOU DIDN'T HAVE TO SMACK HER...
THAT WAS HARDLY ENOUGH!
SHE'S LETTING THINGS GET TO HER HEAD THESE DAYS!
ER ...
TRUE ...
BUT
WE'RE FAMILY.
WE SHOULD TRY TO GET ALONG ...
DOZLE!
FOR ALL THAT YOUR FACE LOOKS LIKE A BAG OF BRICKS, YOU'RE TOO DAMN SOFT!
LIS-TEN HERE!
YOU WON'T SURVIVE THE CUTTHROAT POLITICAL STORM TO COME
IF YOU DON'T —

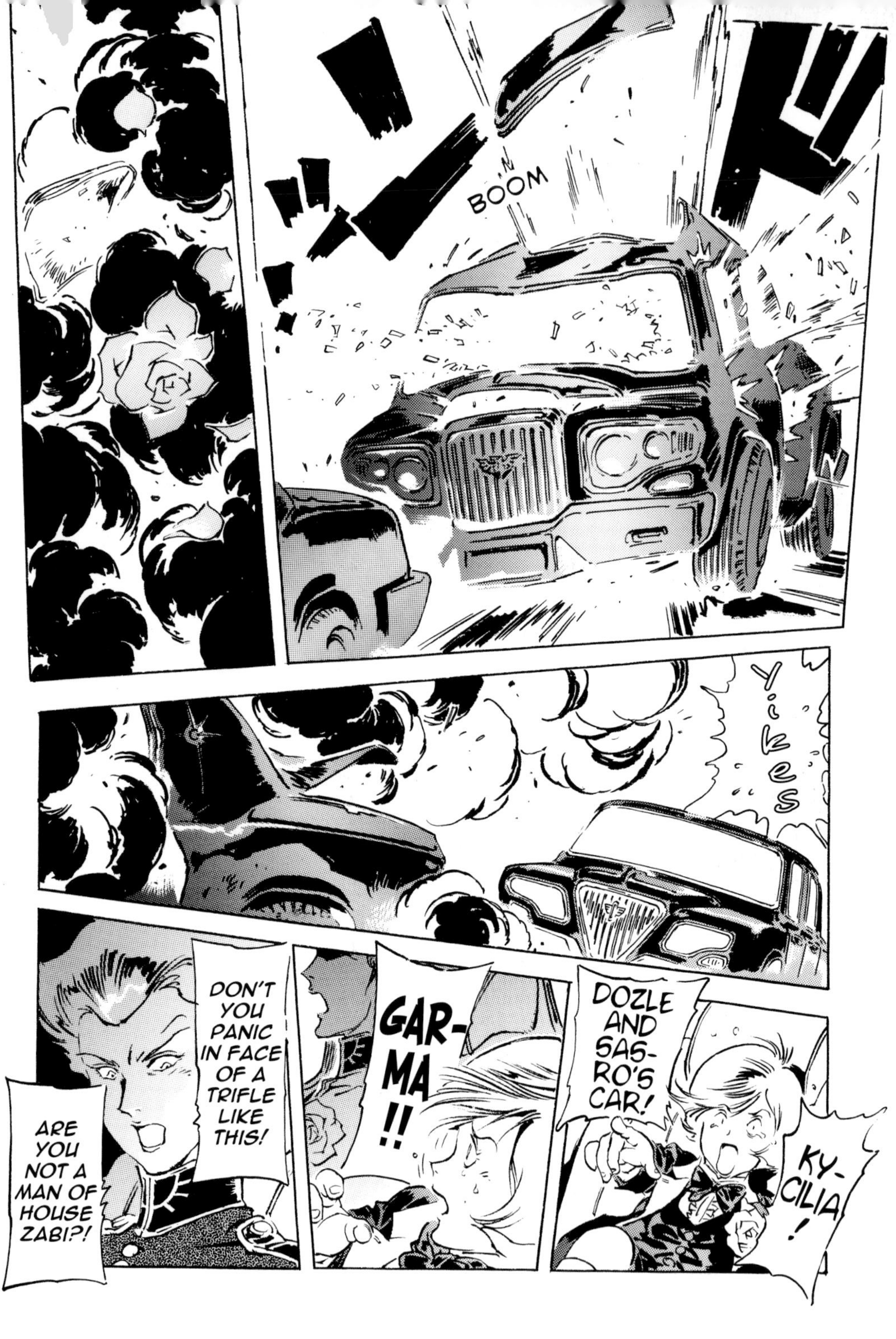
BOOM
Yikes
KY-CILIA!
DOZLE AND SAS-RO'S CAR!
GAR-MA!!
DON'T YOU PANIC IN FACE OF A TRIFLE LIKE THIS!
ARE YOU NOT A MAN OF HOUSE ZABI?!

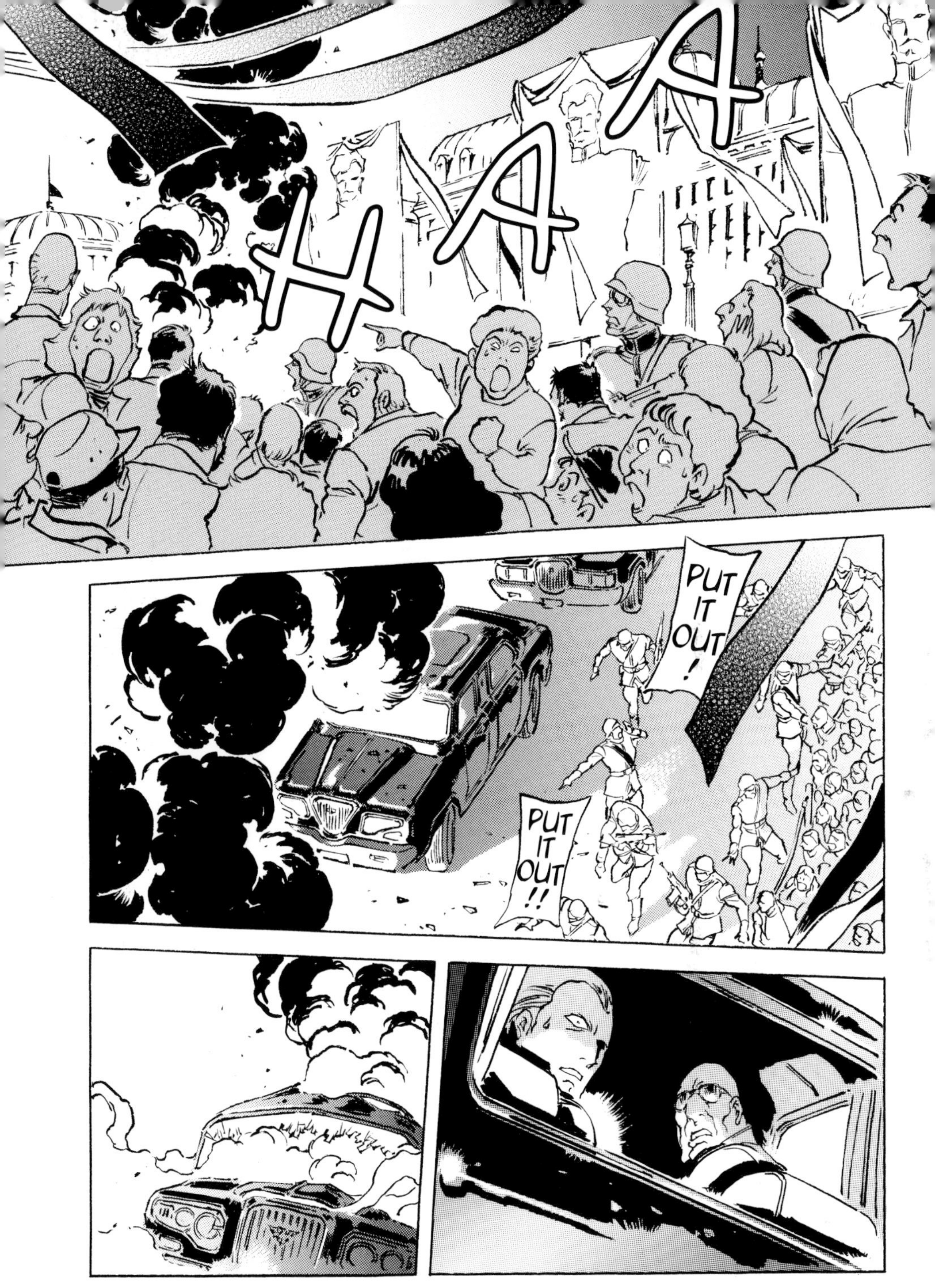
HAAA
PUT IT OUT!
PUT IT OUT!!

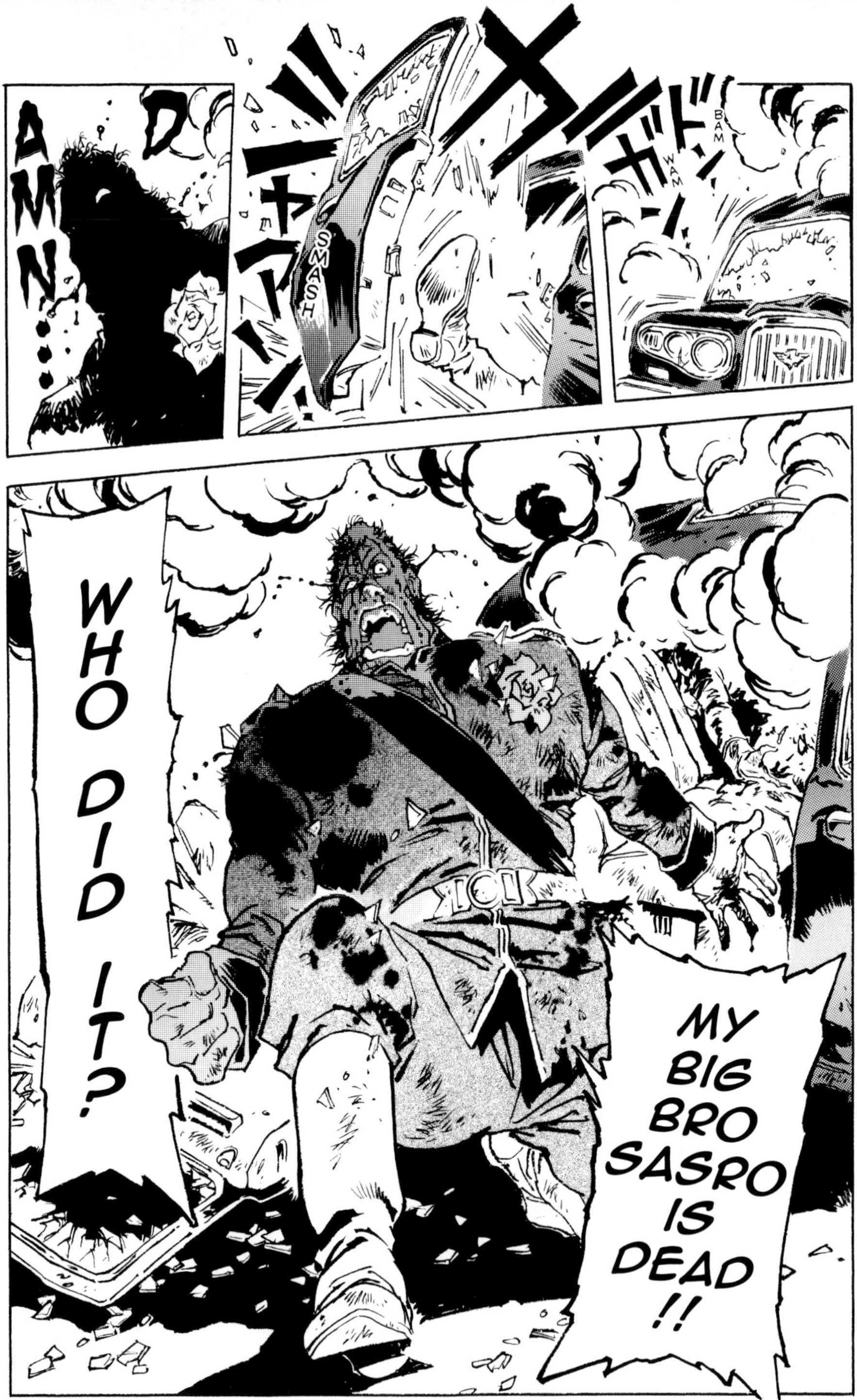
BAM
WAM
SMASH
DAMN...
MY BIG BRO SASRO IS DEAD!!
WHO DID IT?

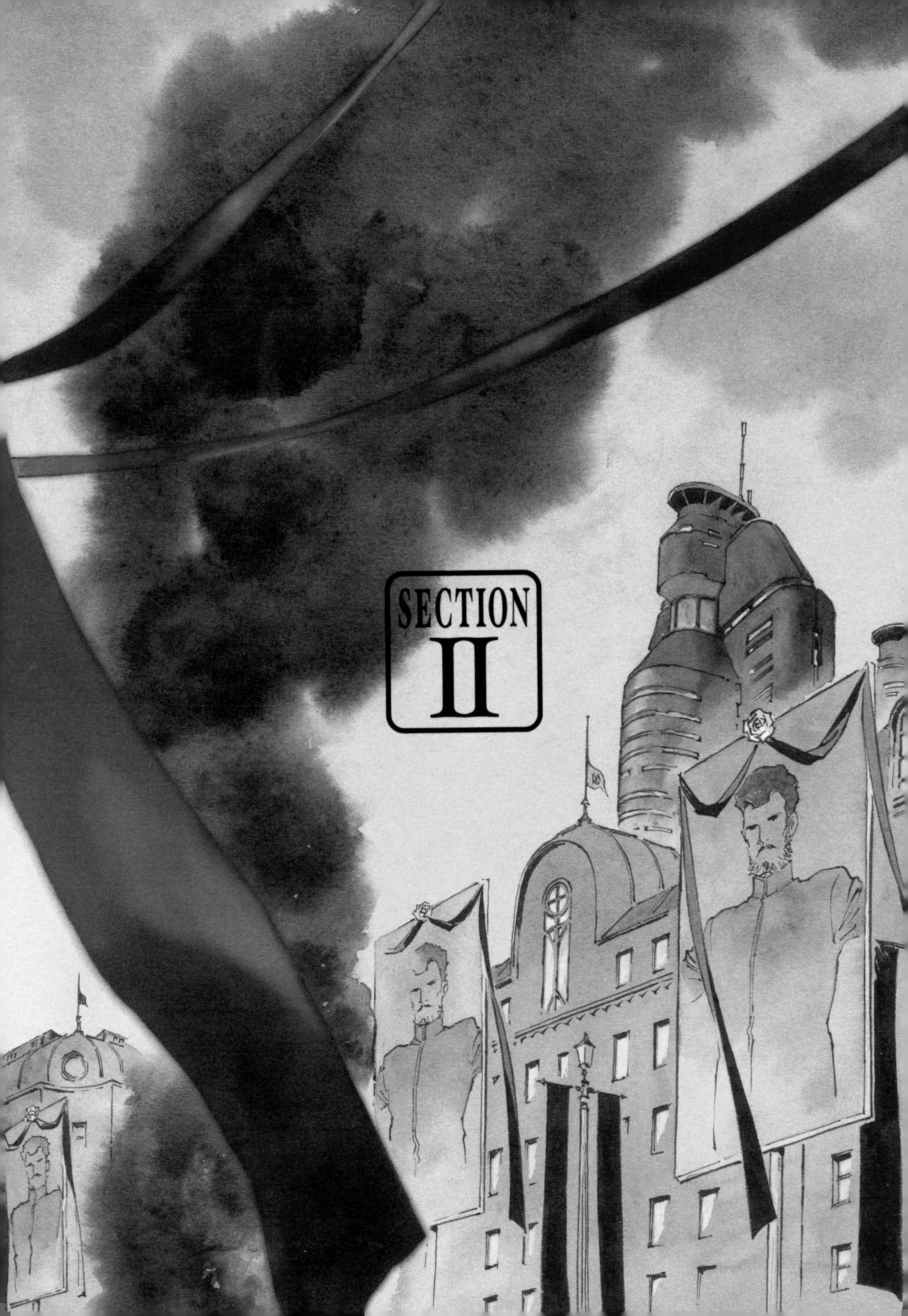
SECTION
II

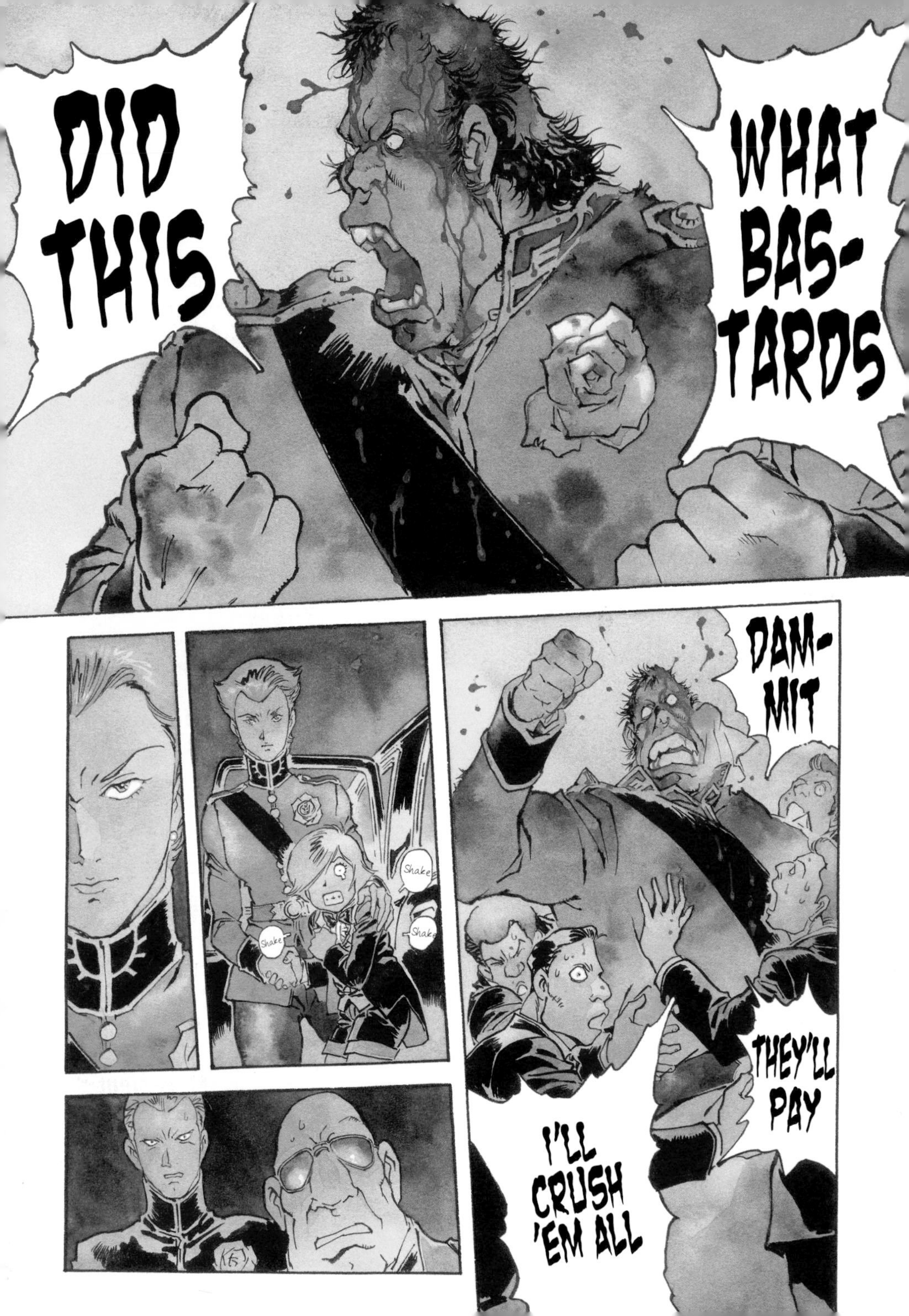
WHAT BASTARDS
DID THIS
DAMMIT
THEY'LL PAY
I'LL CRUSH 'EM ALL
Shake
Shake
Shake

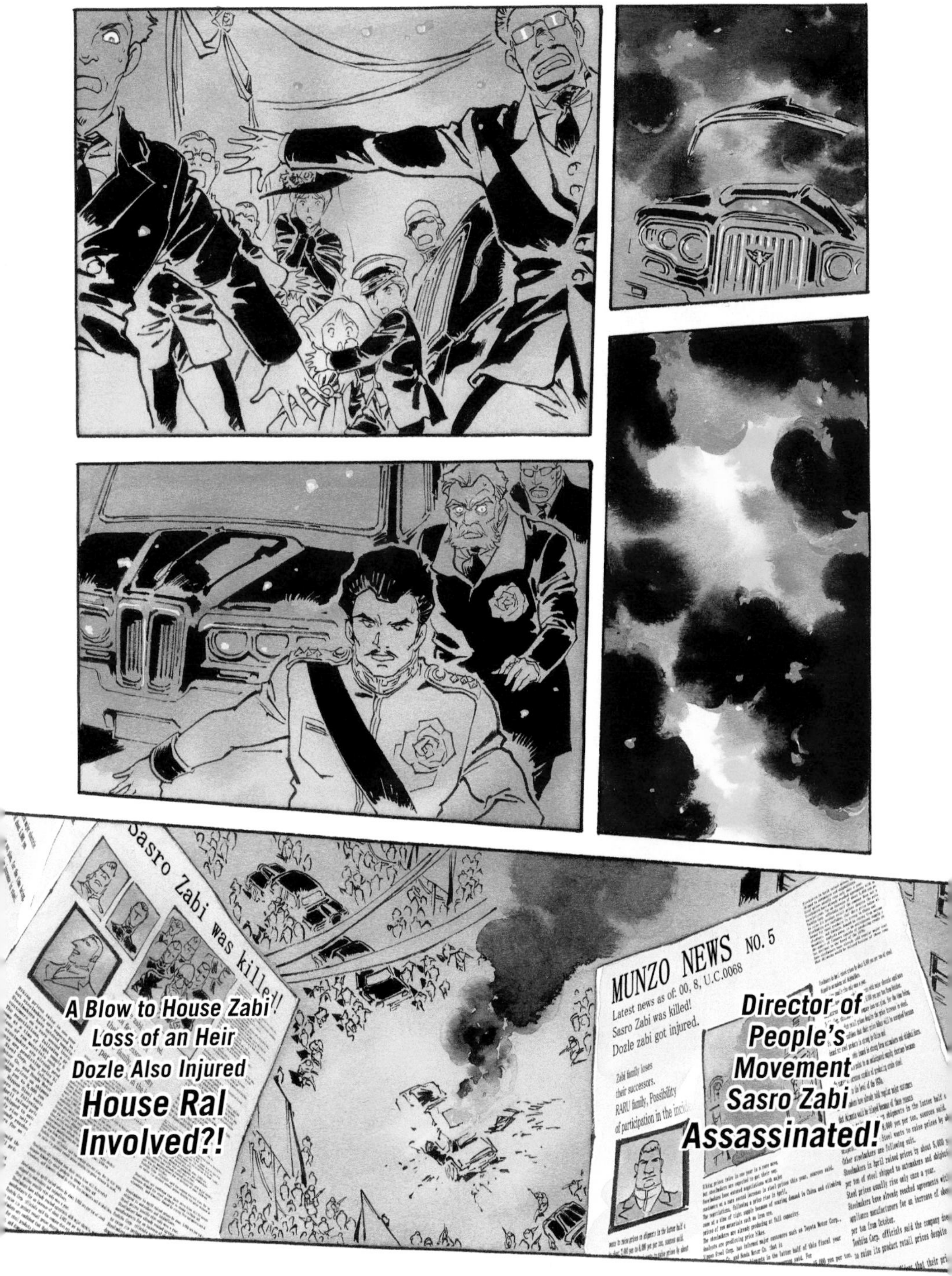
MUNZO NEWS NO. 5
Latest news as of: 00, 8, U.C.0068
Sasro Zabi was killed!
Dozle zabi got injured.
Zabi family loses their successors.
RARU family, Possibility of participation in the incid
Director of People's Movement Sasro Zabi Assassinated!
Sasro Zabi was killed!
A Blow to House Zabi Loss of an Heir Dozle Also Injured
House Ral Involved?!

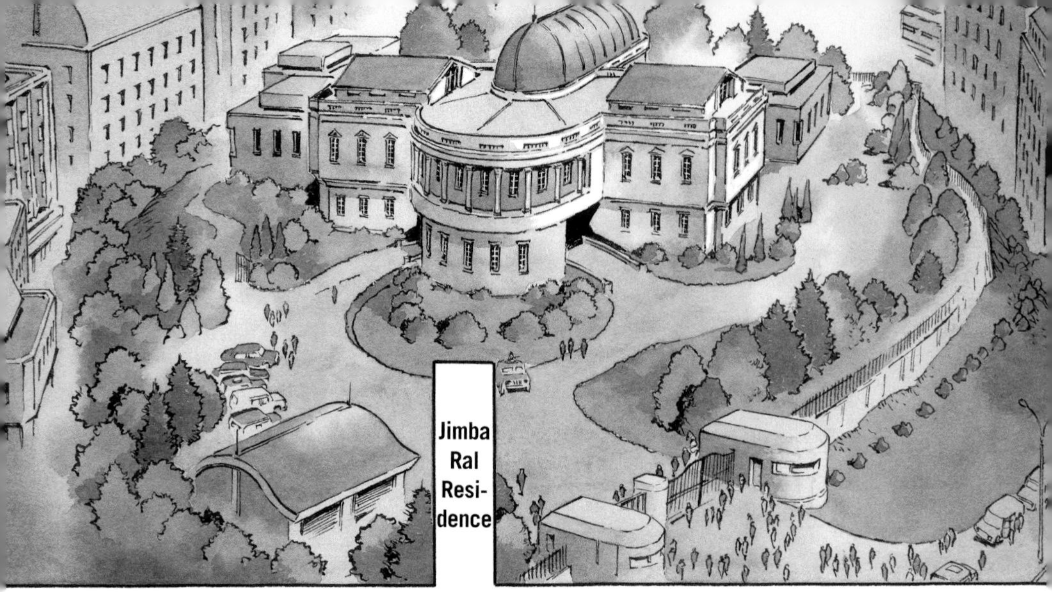
Jimba Ral Residence

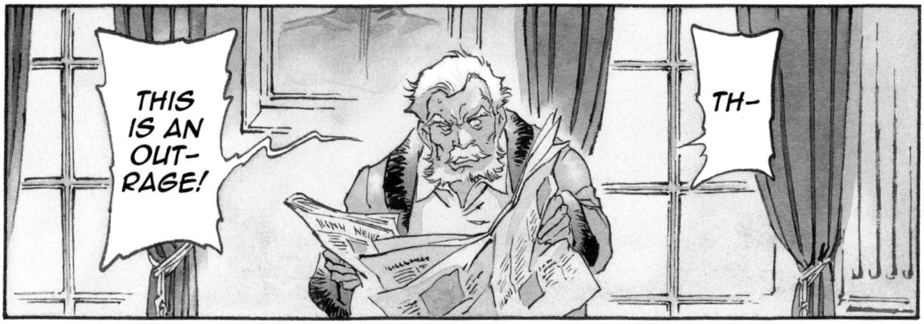
TH-
THIS IS AN OUTRAGE!

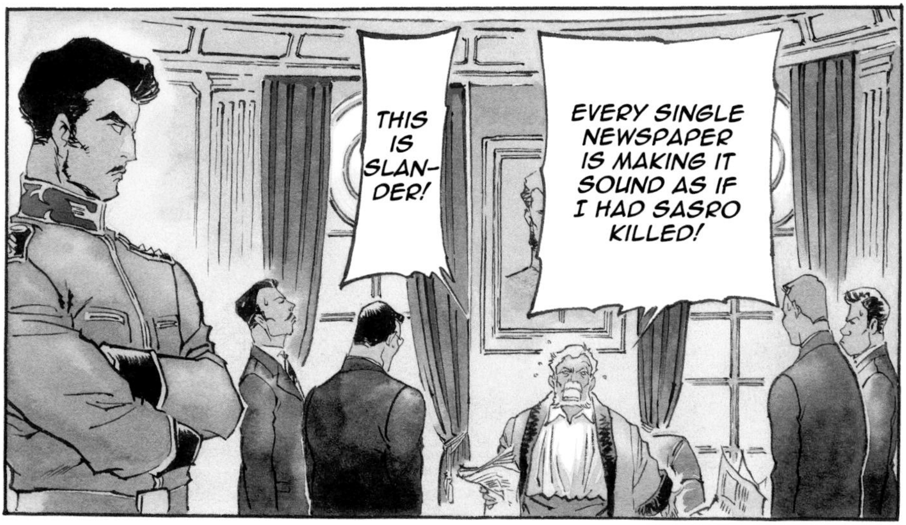
EVERY SINGLE NEWSPAPER IS MAKING IT SOUND AS IF I HAD SASRO KILLED!
THIS IS SLANDER!

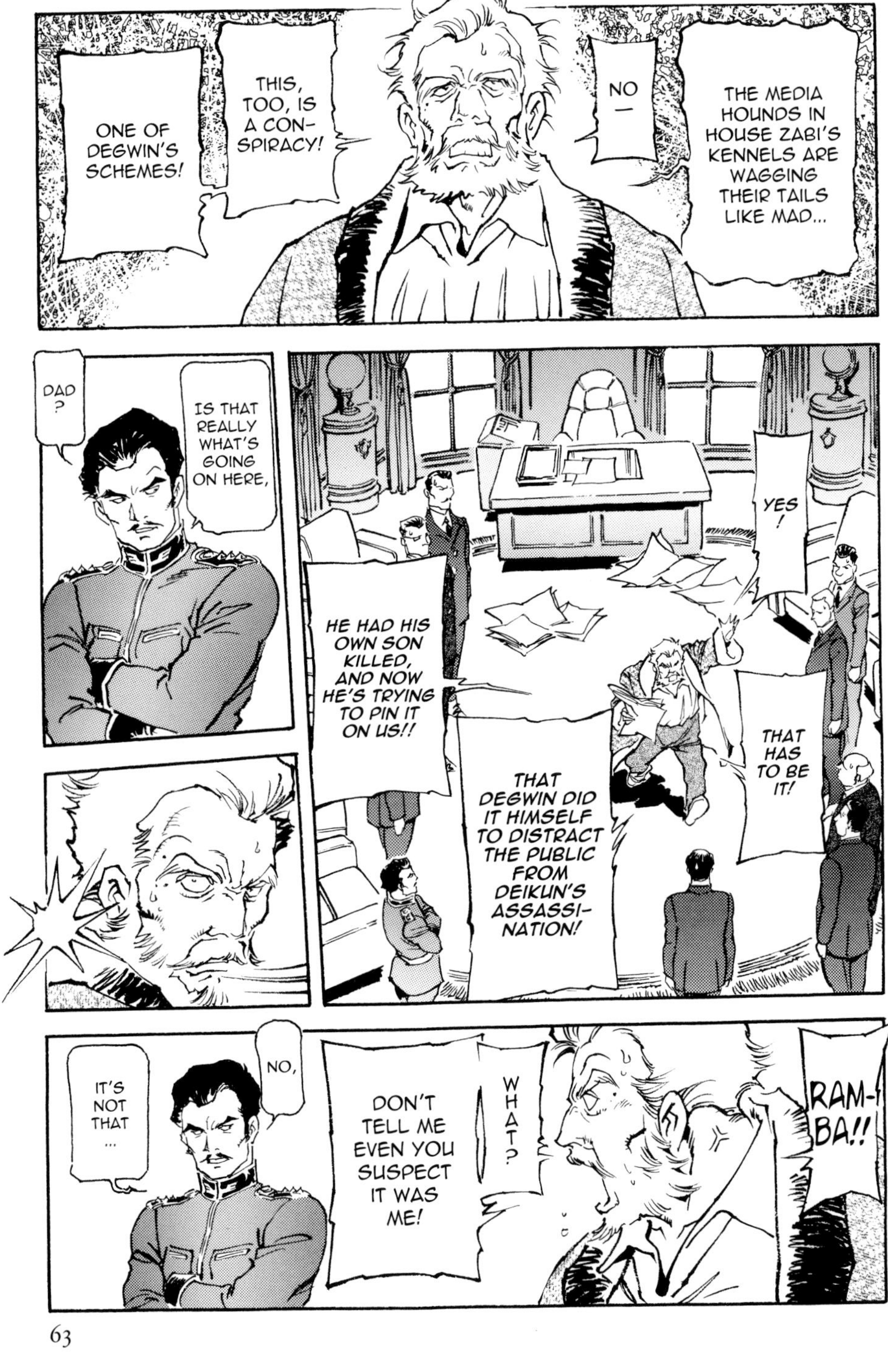
THE MEDIA HOUNDS IN HOUSE ZABI'S KENNELS ARE WAGGING THEIR TAILS LIKE MAD...
NO —
THIS, TOO, IS A CONSPIRACY!
ONE OF DEGWIN'S SCHEMES!
YES!
THAT HAS TO BE IT!
HE HAD HIS OWN SON KILLED, AND NOW HE'S TRYING TO PIN IT ON US!!
THAT DEGWIN DID IT HIMSELF TO DISTRACT THE PUBLIC FROM DEIKUN'S ASSASSINATION!
IS THAT REALLY WHAT'S GOING ON HERE,
DAD?
RAM-BA!!
WHAT?
DON'T TELL ME EVEN YOU SUSPECT IT WAS ME!
NO,
IT'S NOT THAT ...

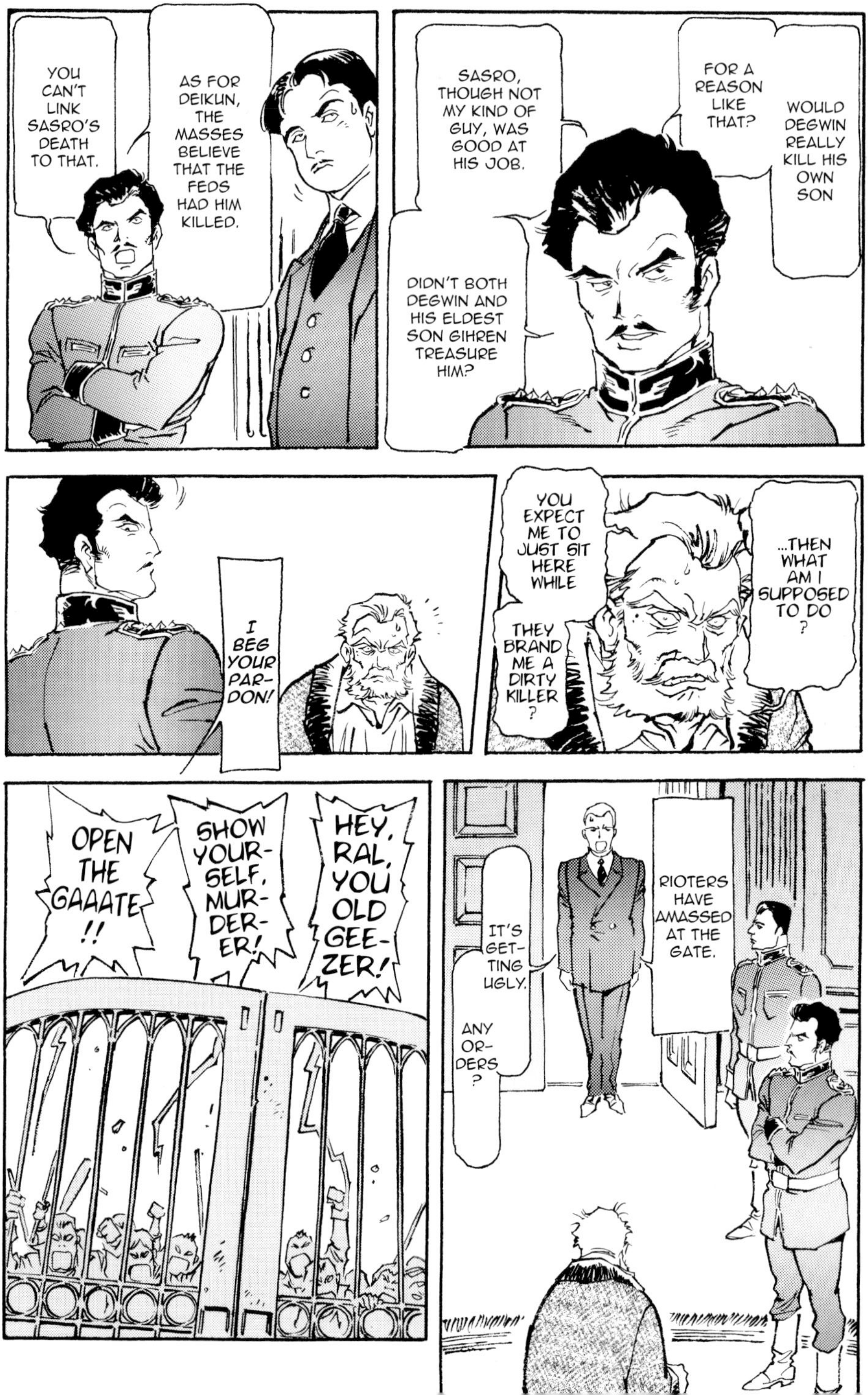
WOULD DEGWIN REALLY KILL HIS OWN SON
FOR A REASON LIKE THAT?
SASRO, THOUGH NOT MY KIND OF GUY, WAS GOOD AT HIS JOB.
DIDN'T BOTH DEGWIN AND HIS ELDEST SON GIHREN TREASURE HIM?
AS FOR DEIKUN, THE MASSES BELIEVE THAT THE FEDS HAD HIM KILLED.
YOU CAN'T LINK SASRO'S DEATH TO THAT.
...THEN WHAT AM I SUPPOSED TO DO?
YOU EXPECT ME TO JUST SIT HERE WHILE
THEY BRAND ME A DIRTY KILLER?
I BEG YOUR PARDON!
RIOTERS HAVE AMASSED AT THE GATE.
IT'S GETTING UGLY.
ANY ORDERS?
HEY, RAL, YOU OLD GEEZER!
SHOW YOURSELF, MURDERER!
OPEN THE GAAATE!!

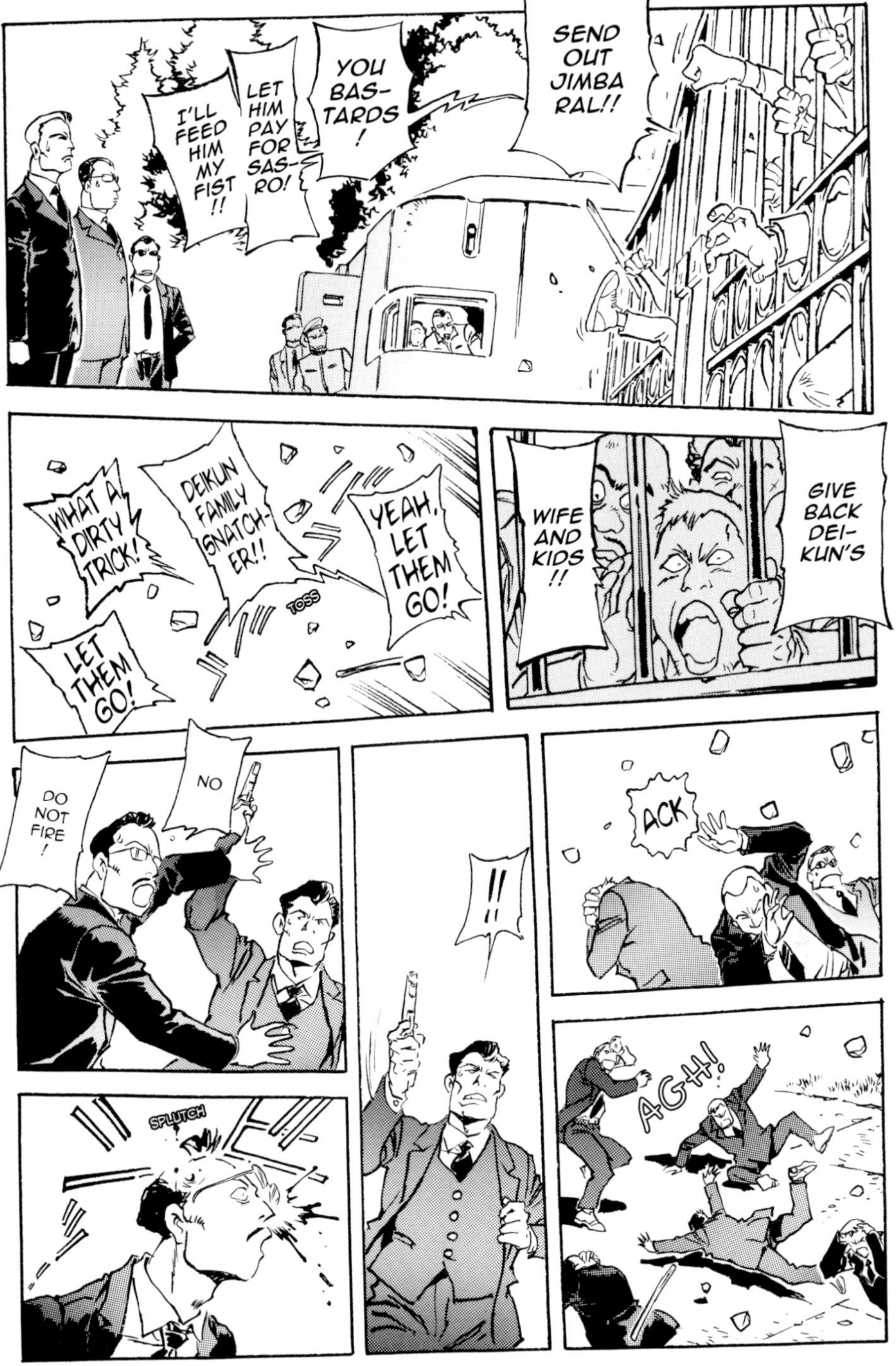
SEND OUT JIMBARAL!!
YOU BASTARDS!
LET HIM PAY FOR SASRO!
I'LL FEED HIM MY FIST!!
GIVE BACK DEIKUN'S
WIFE AND KIDS!!
YEAH, LET THEM GO!
DEIKUN FAMILY SNATCHER!!
TOSS
WHAT A DIRTY TRICK!
LET THEM GO!
ACK
AGH!
!!
NO
DO NOT FIRE!
SPLUTCH

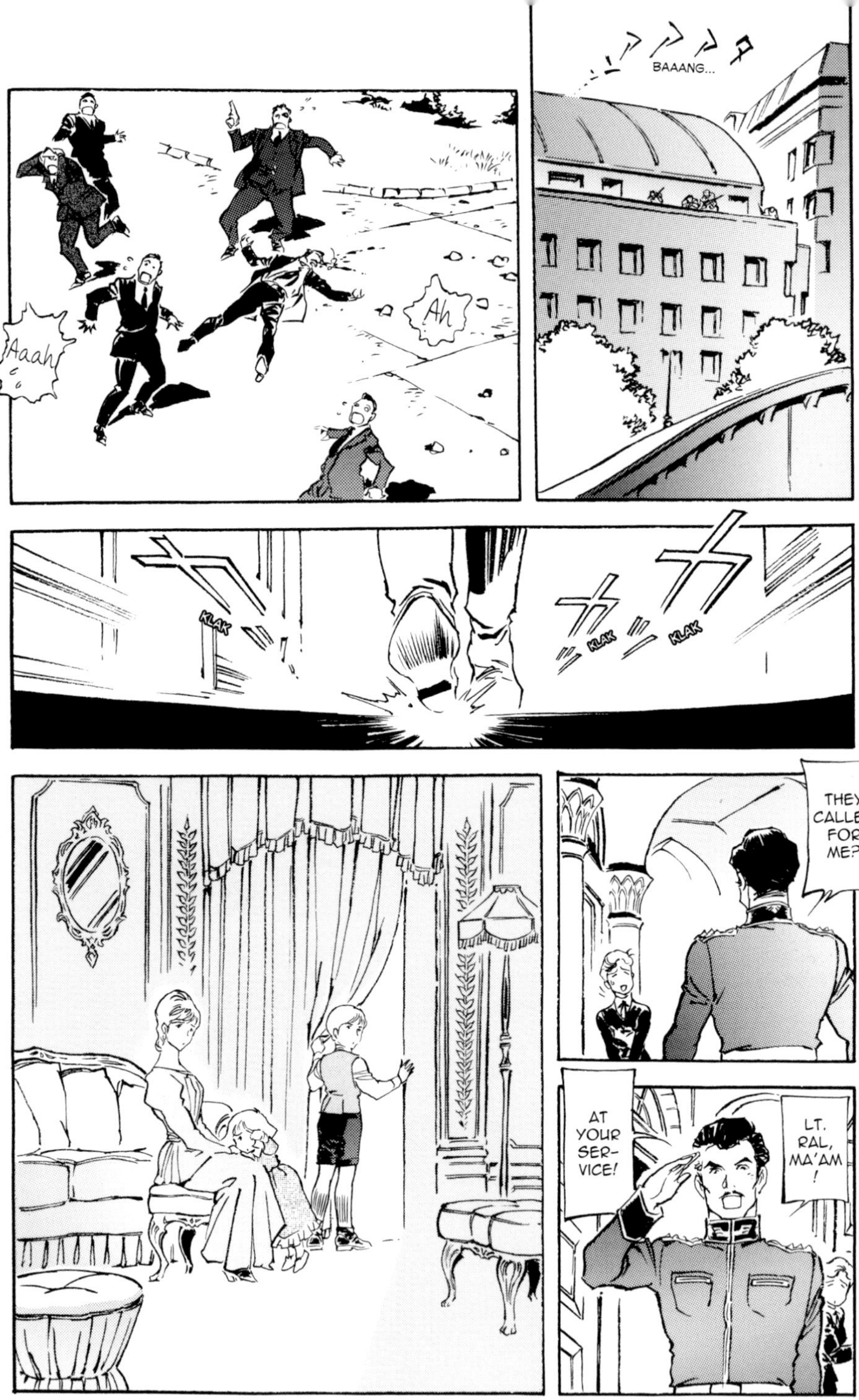
BAAANG...
Ah
Aaah
KLAK
KLAK
KLAK
THEY CALLED FOR ME?
LT. RAL, MA'AM!
AT YOUR SER-VICE!

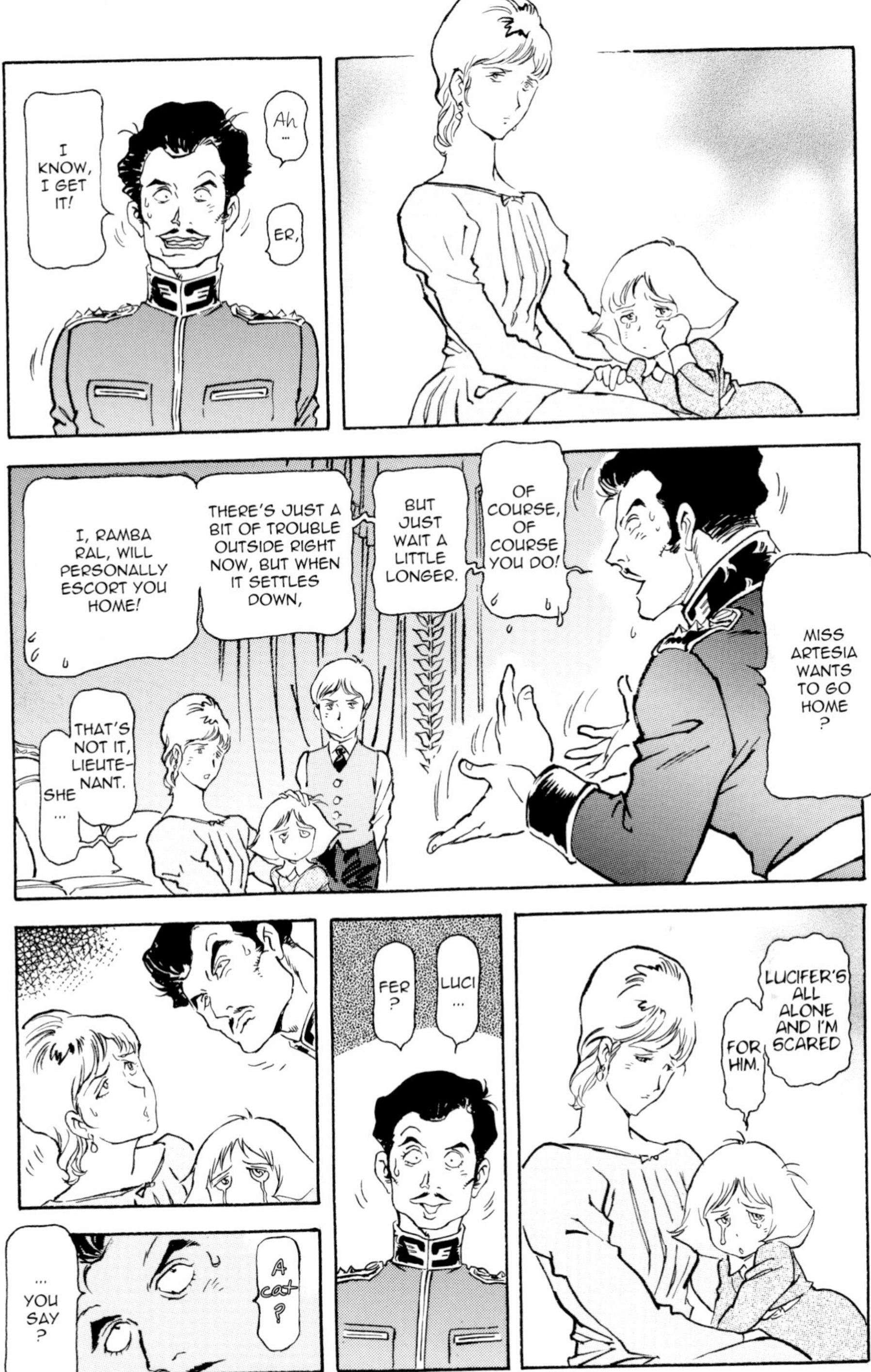
Ah ...
ER,
I KNOW, I GET IT!
MISS ARTESIA WANTS TO GO HOME ?
OF COURSE, OF COURSE YOU DO!
BUT JUST WAIT A LITTLE LONGER.
THERE'S JUST A BIT OF TROUBLE OUTSIDE RIGHT NOW, BUT WHEN IT SETTLES DOWN,
I, RAMBA RAL, WILL PERSONALLY ESCORT YOU HOME!
THAT'S NOT IT, LIEUTENANT.
SHE ...
LUCIFER'S ALL ALONE AND I'M SCARED
FOR HIM.
LUCI ...
FER ?
A cat ?
... YOU SAY ?

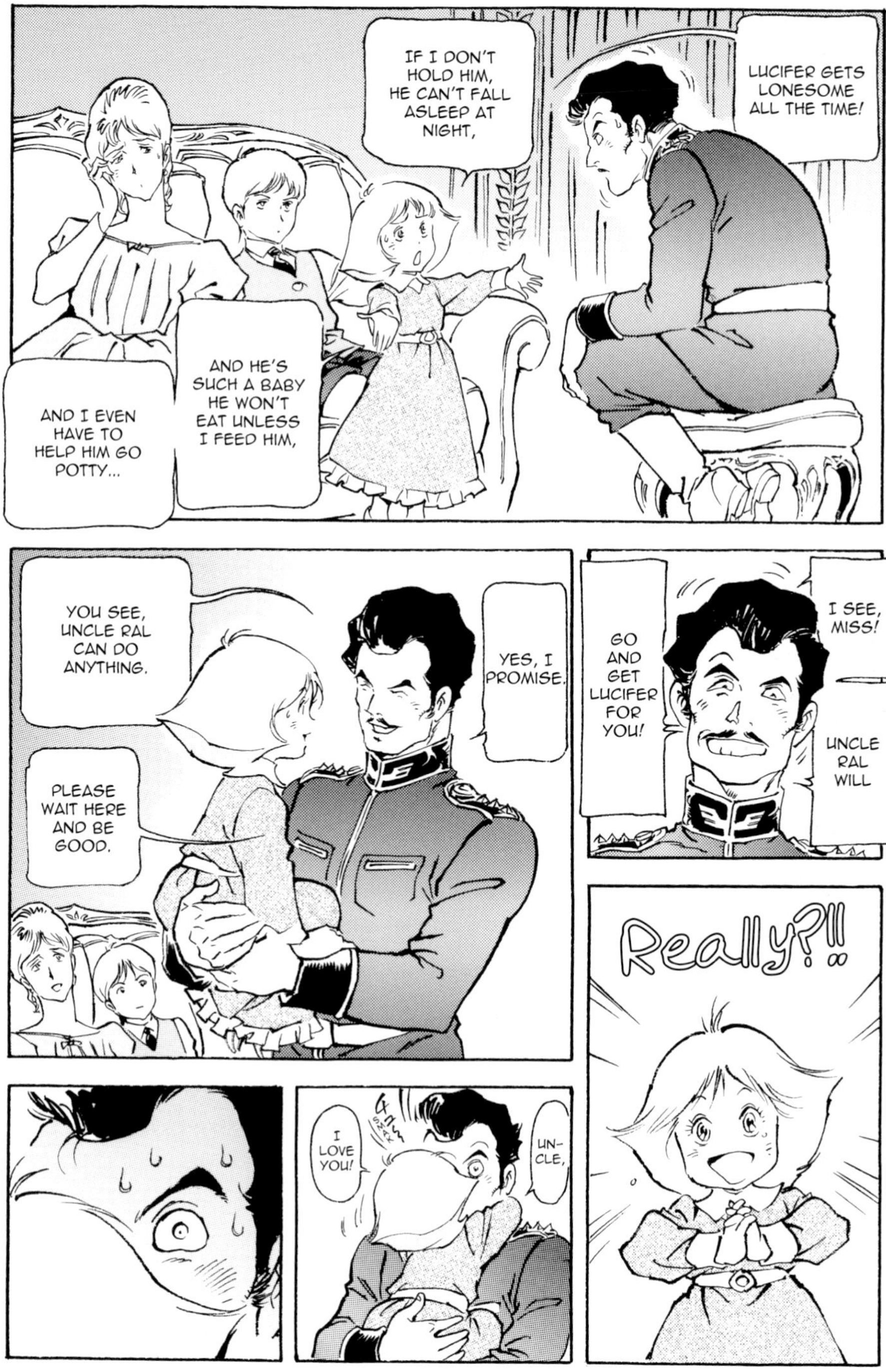
LUCIFER GETS LONESOME ALL THE TIME!
IF I DON'T HOLD HIM, HE CAN'T FALL ASLEEP AT NIGHT,
AND HE'S SUCH A BABY HE WON'T EAT UNLESS I FEED HIM,
AND I EVEN HAVE TO HELP HIM GO POTTY...
I SEE, MISS!
UNCLE RAL WILL
GO AND GET LUCIFER FOR YOU!
Really?!!
YOU SEE, UNCLE RAL CAN DO ANYTHING.
PLEASE WAIT HERE AND BE GOOD.
YES, I PROMISE.
UNCLE,
SMAK
I LOVE YOU!

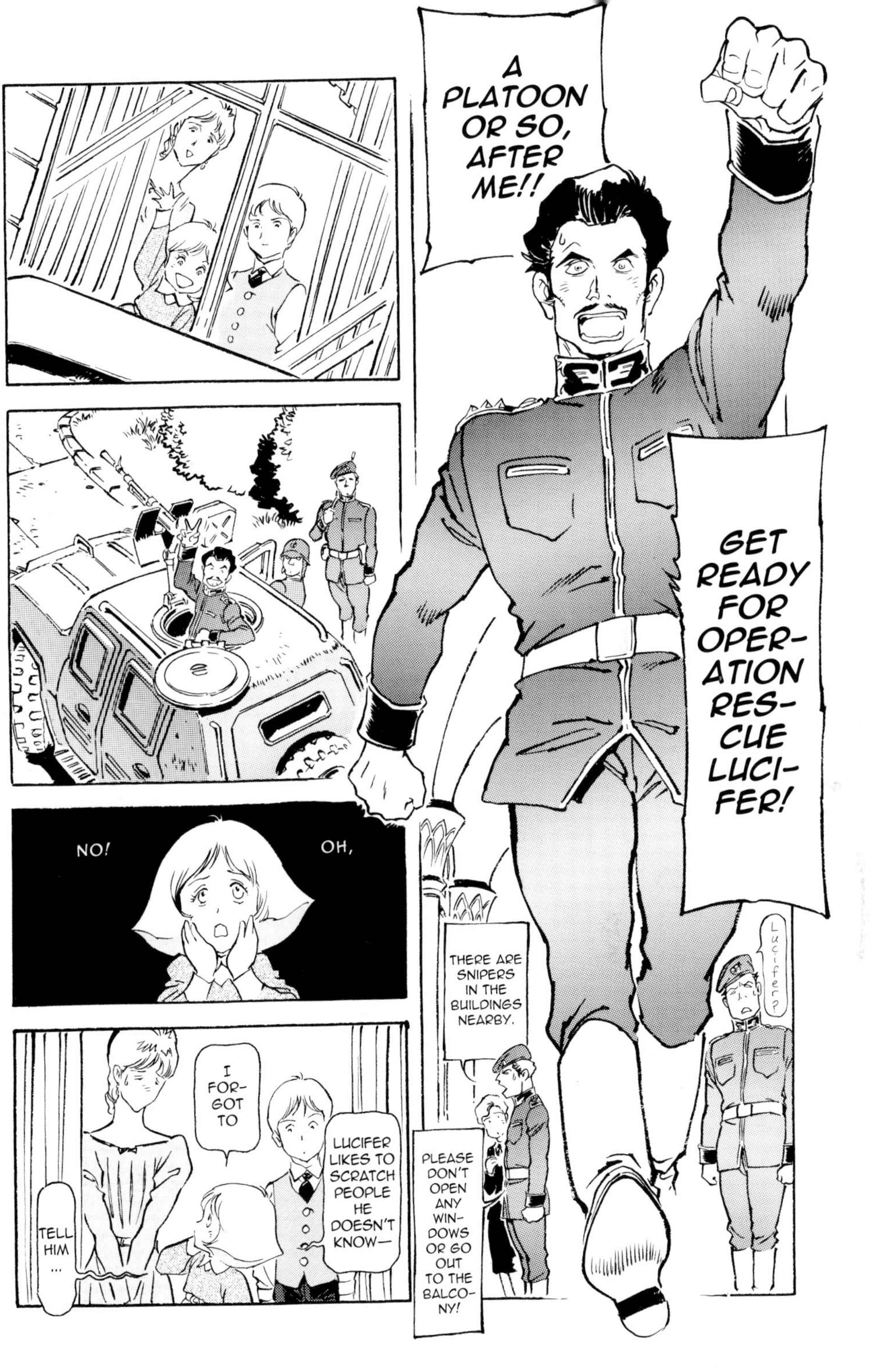
A PLATOON OR SO, AFTER ME!!
GET READY FOR OPERATION RESCUE LUCIFER!
Lucifer?
THERE ARE SNIPERS IN THE BUILDINGS NEARBY.
PLEASE DON'T OPEN ANY WINDOWS OR GO OUT TO THE BALCONY!
OH,
NO!
I FORGOT TO
TELL HIM ...
LUCIFER LIKES TO SCRATCH PEOPLE HE DOESN'T KNOW—

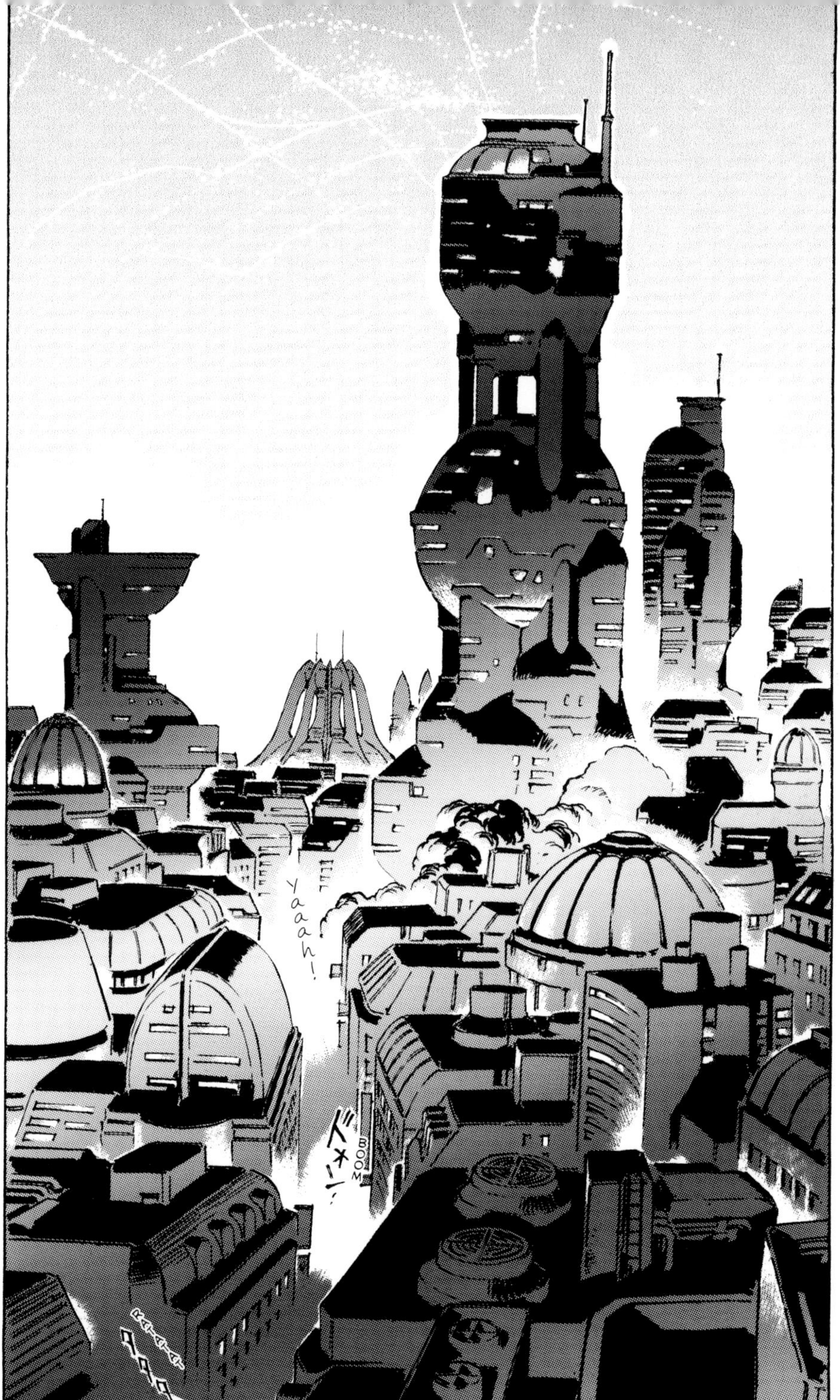
Yaaaah!
ドォン!
BOOM

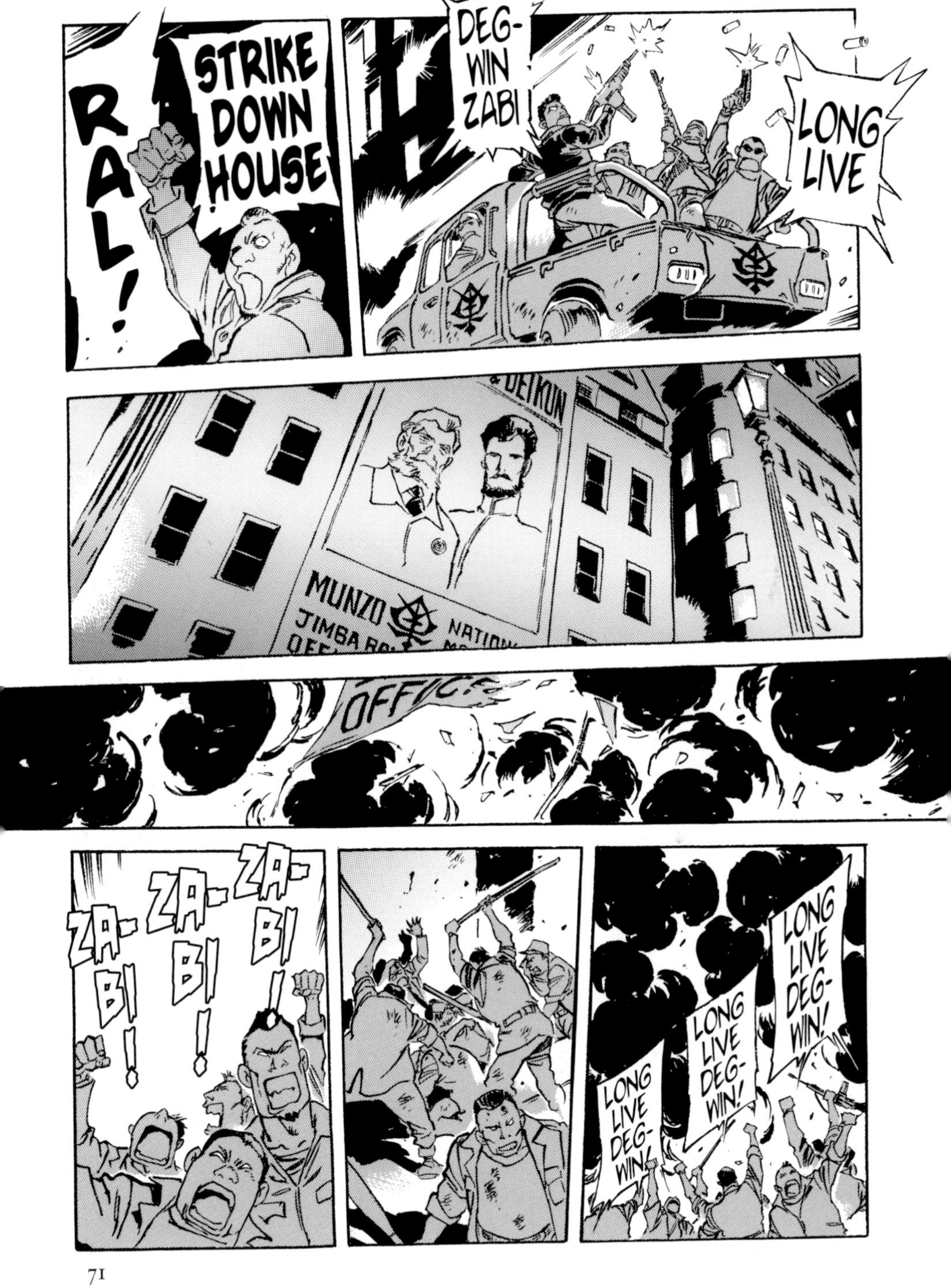
LONG LIVE
DEG-WIN ZABI!
STRIKE DOWN HOUSE
RAL!
& DEIKON
MUNZO
LONG LIVE DEG-WIN!
LONG LIVE DEG-WIN!
LONG LIVE DEG-WIN!
ZA-BI!
ZA-BI!
ZA-BI!

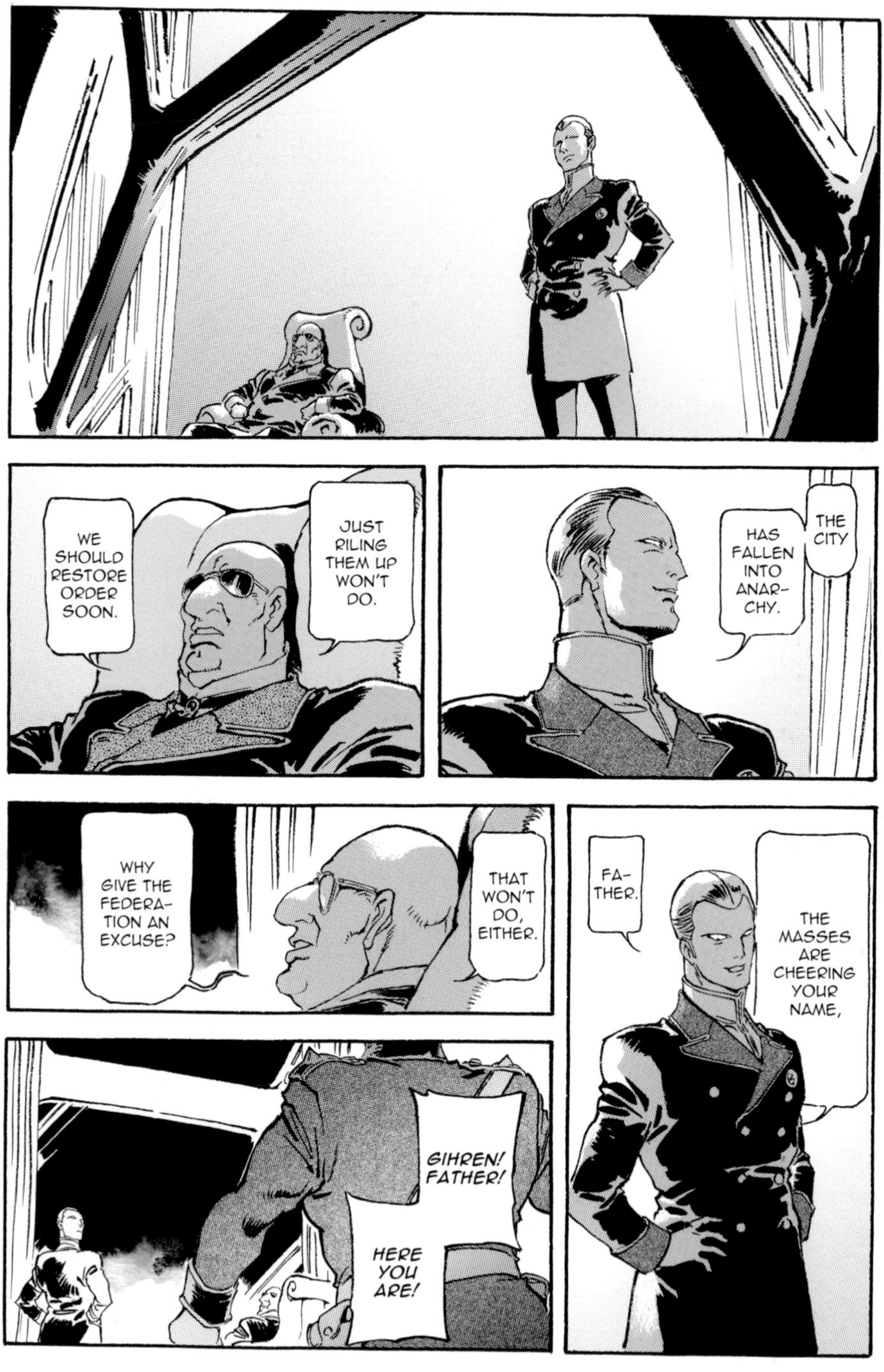
THE CITY
HAS FALLEN INTO ANARCHY.
JUST RILING THEM UP WON'T DO.
WE SHOULD RESTORE ORDER SOON.
THE MASSES ARE CHEERING YOUR NAME,
FATHER.
THAT WON'T DO, EITHER.
WHY GIVE THE FEDERATION AN EXCUSE?
GIHREN! FATHER!
HERE YOU ARE!

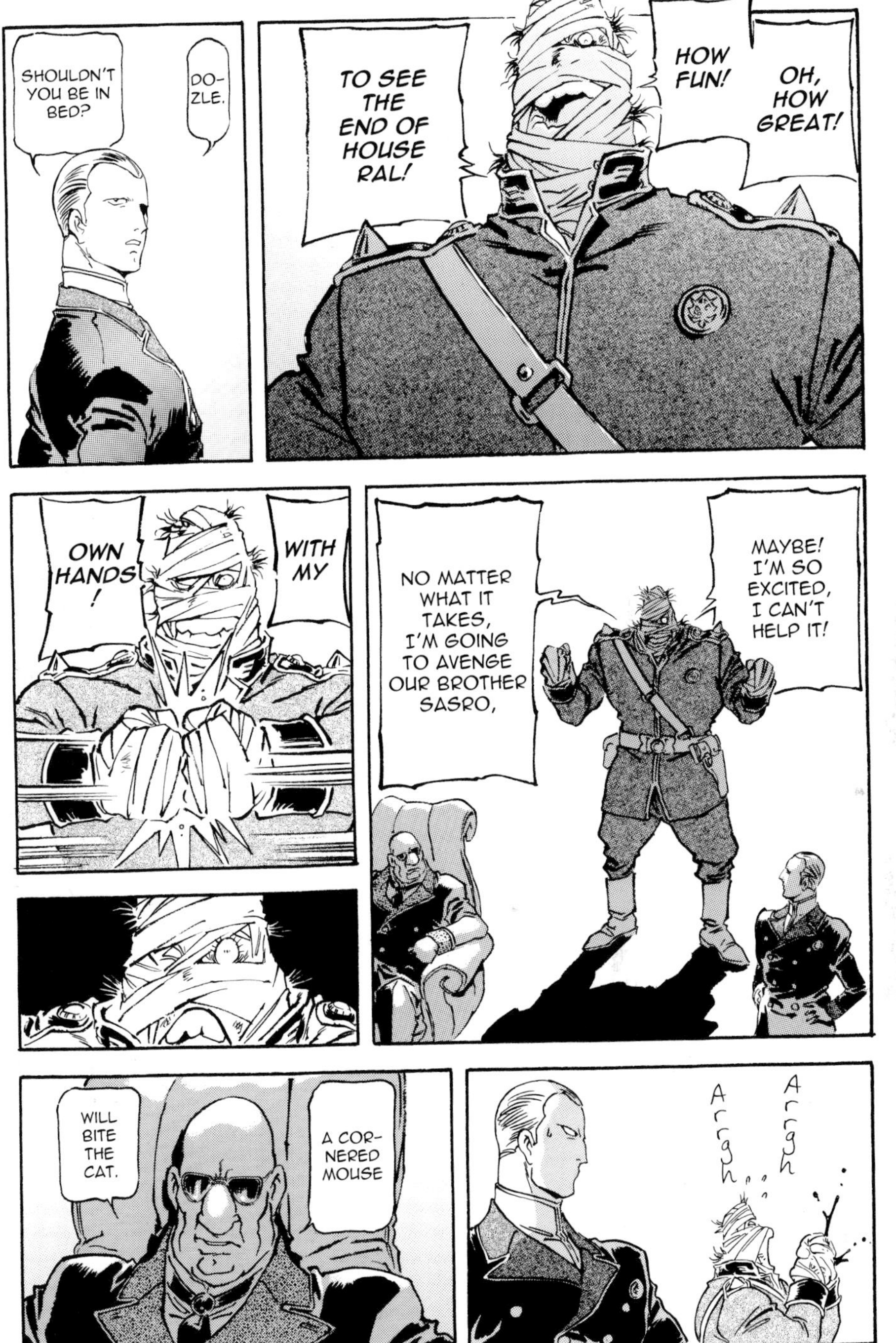
OH, HOW GREAT!
HOW FUN!
TO SEE THE END OF HOUSE RAL!
DO-ZLE.
SHOULDN'T YOU BE IN BED?
MAYBE! I'M SO EXCITED, I CAN'T HELP IT!
NO MATTER WHAT IT TAKES, I'M GOING TO AVENGE OUR BROTHER SASRO,
WITH MY
OWN HANDS!
Arrgh
Arrgh
A COR-NERED MOUSE
WILL BITE THE CAT.

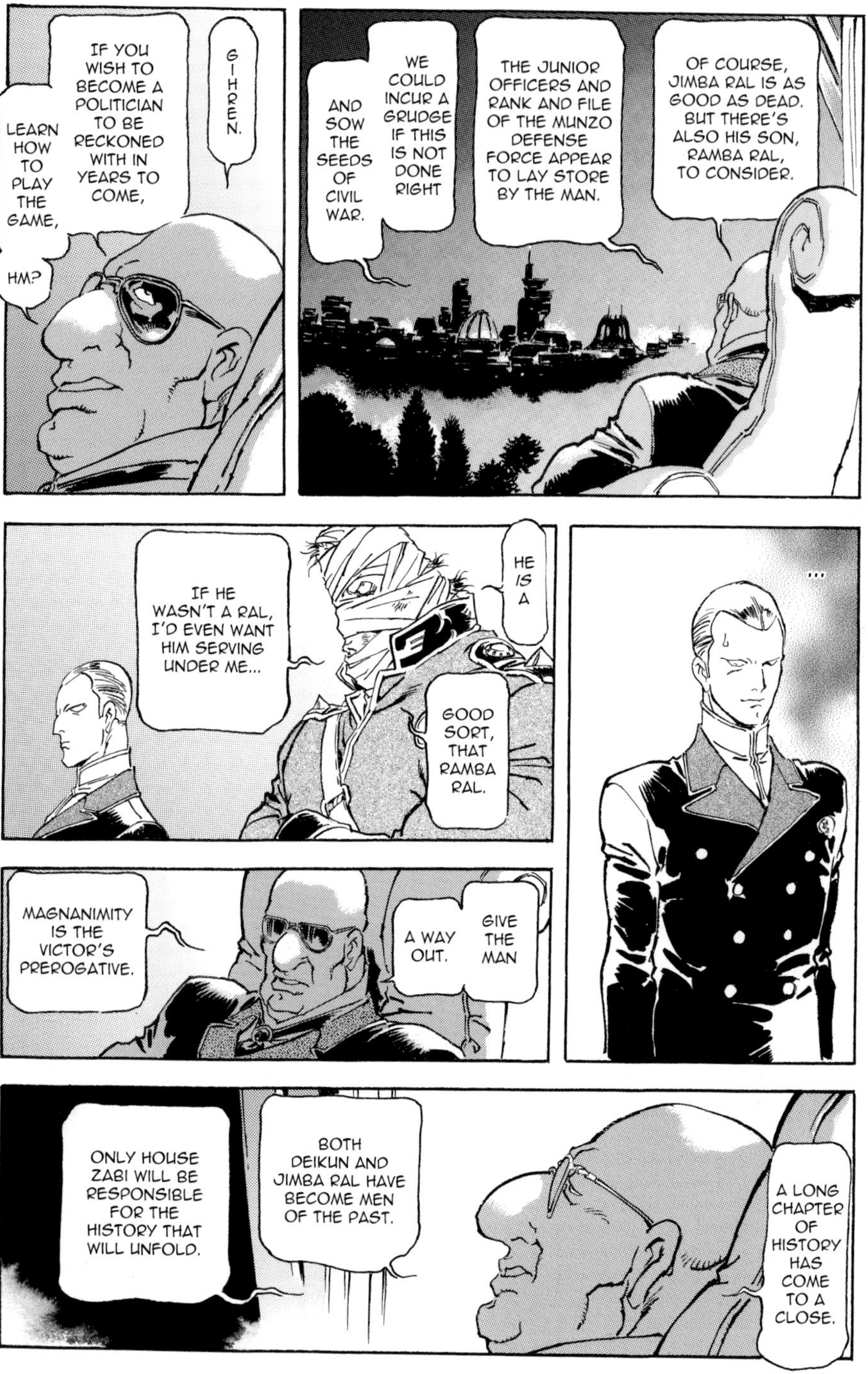
OF COURSE, JIMBA RAL IS AS GOOD AS DEAD. BUT THERE'S ALSO HIS SON, RAMBA RAL, TO CONSIDER.
THE JUNIOR OFFICERS AND RANK AND FILE OF THE MUNZO DEFENSE FORCE APPEAR TO LAY STORE BY THE MAN.
WE COULD INCUR A GRUDGE IF THIS IS NOT DONE RIGHT
AND SOW THE SEEDS OF CIVIL WAR.
GIHREN.
IF YOU WISH TO BECOME A POLITICIAN TO BE RECKONED WITH IN YEARS TO COME,
LEARN HOW TO PLAY THE GAME,
HM?
...
HE IS A
GOOD SORT, THAT RAMBA RAL.
IF HE WASN'T A RAL, I'D EVEN WANT HIM SERVING UNDER ME...
GIVE THE MAN
A WAY OUT.
MAGNANIMITY IS THE VICTOR'S PREROGATIVE.
A LONG CHAPTER OF HISTORY HAS COME TO A CLOSE.
BOTH DEIKUN AND JIMBA RAL HAVE BECOME MEN OF THE PAST.
ONLY HOUSE ZABI WILL BE RESPONSIBLE FOR THE HISTORY THAT WILL UNFOLD.

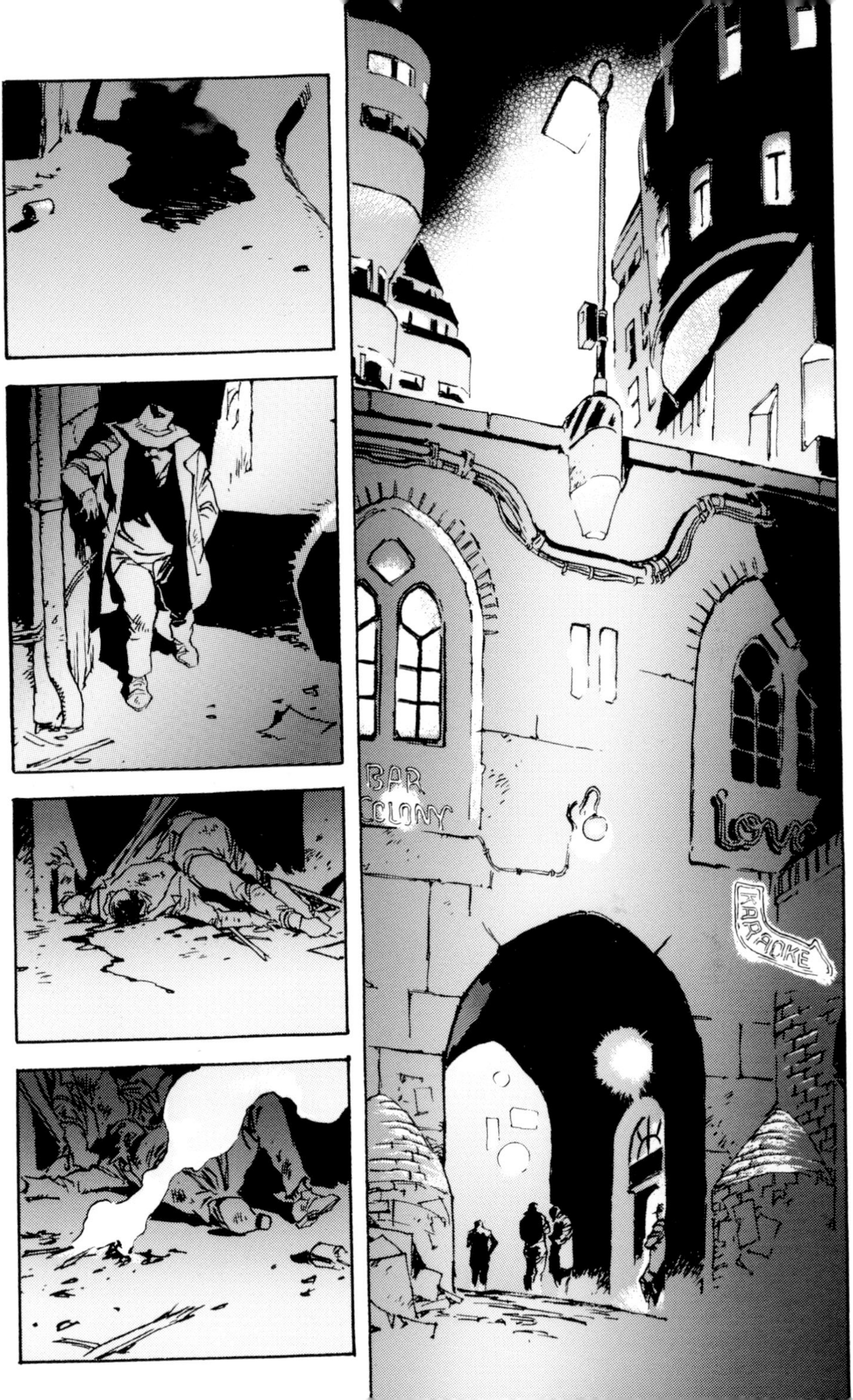
BAR
COLONY
love
KARAOKE

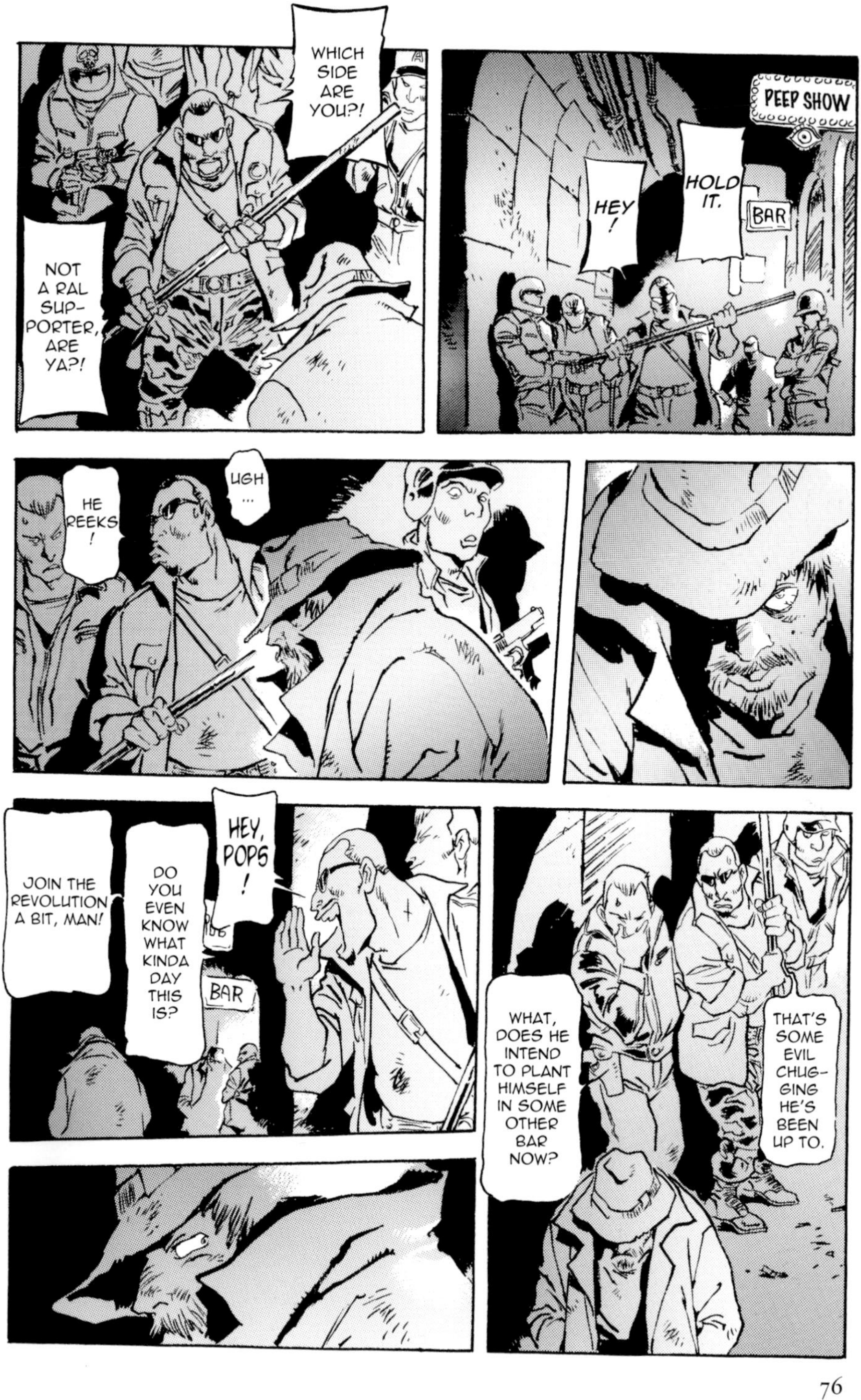
PEEP SHOW
HOLD IT.
HEY!
BAR
WHICH SIDE ARE YOU?!
NOT A RAL SUPPORTER, ARE YA?!
UGH...
HE REEKS!
THAT'S SOME EVIL CHUGGING HE'S BEEN UP TO.
WHAT, DOES HE INTEND TO PLANT HIMSELF IN SOME OTHER BAR NOW?
HEY, POPS!
DO YOU EVEN KNOW WHAT KINDA DAY THIS IS?
JOIN THE REVOLUTION A BIT, MAN!
BAR

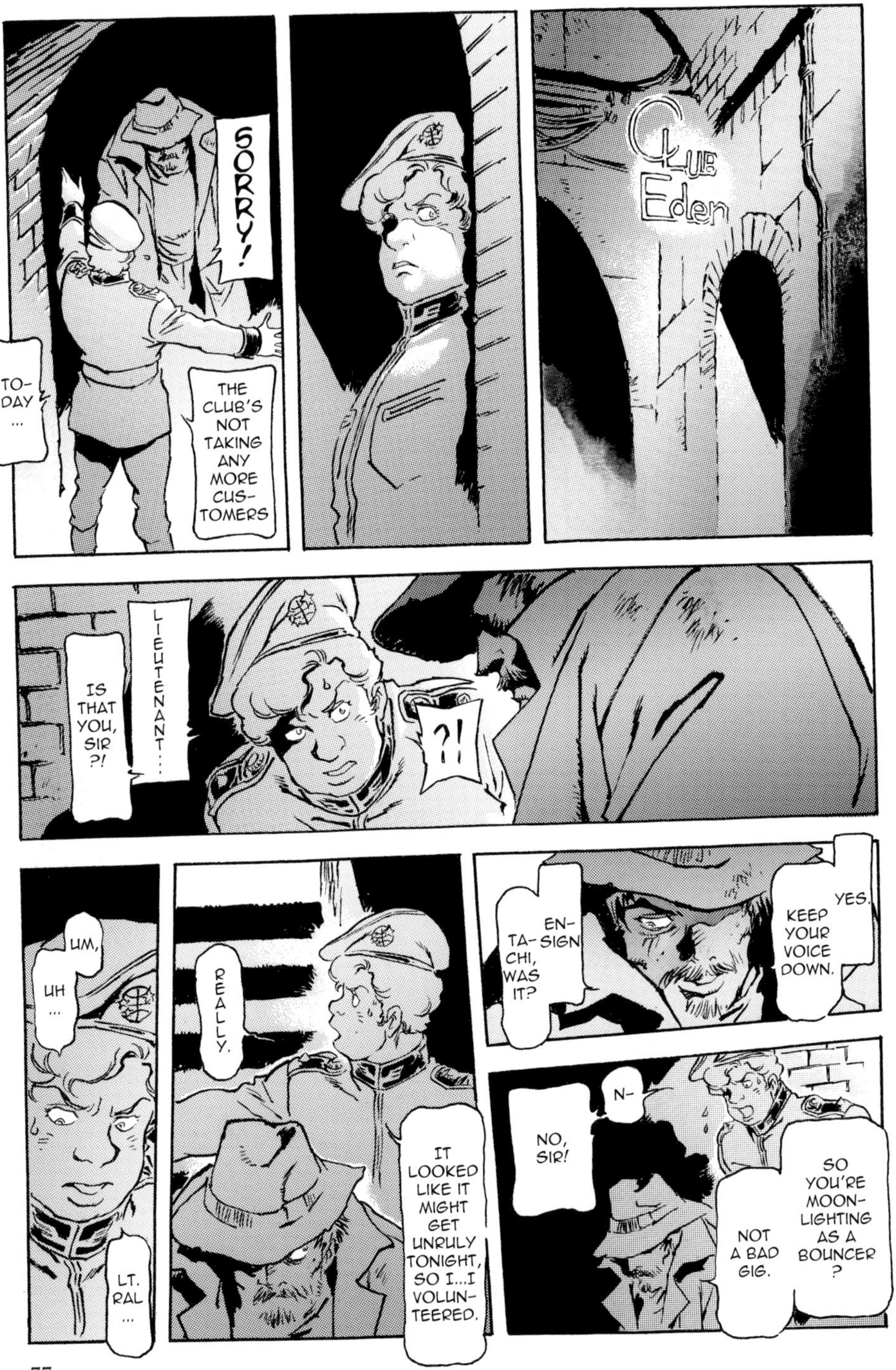
CLUB Eden
SORRY!
THE CLUB'S NOT TAKING ANY MORE CUSTOMERS
TO-DAY...
?!
LIEUTENANT...
IS THAT YOU, SIR?!
YES. KEEP YOUR VOICE DOWN.
EN-SIGN TA-CHI, WAS IT?
SO YOU'RE MOON-LIGHTING AS A BOUNCER?
NOT A BAD GIG.
N-
NO, SIR!
IT LOOKED LIKE IT MIGHT GET UNRULY TONIGHT, SO I...I VOLUN-TEERED.
REALLY.
UM,
UH...
LT. RAL...

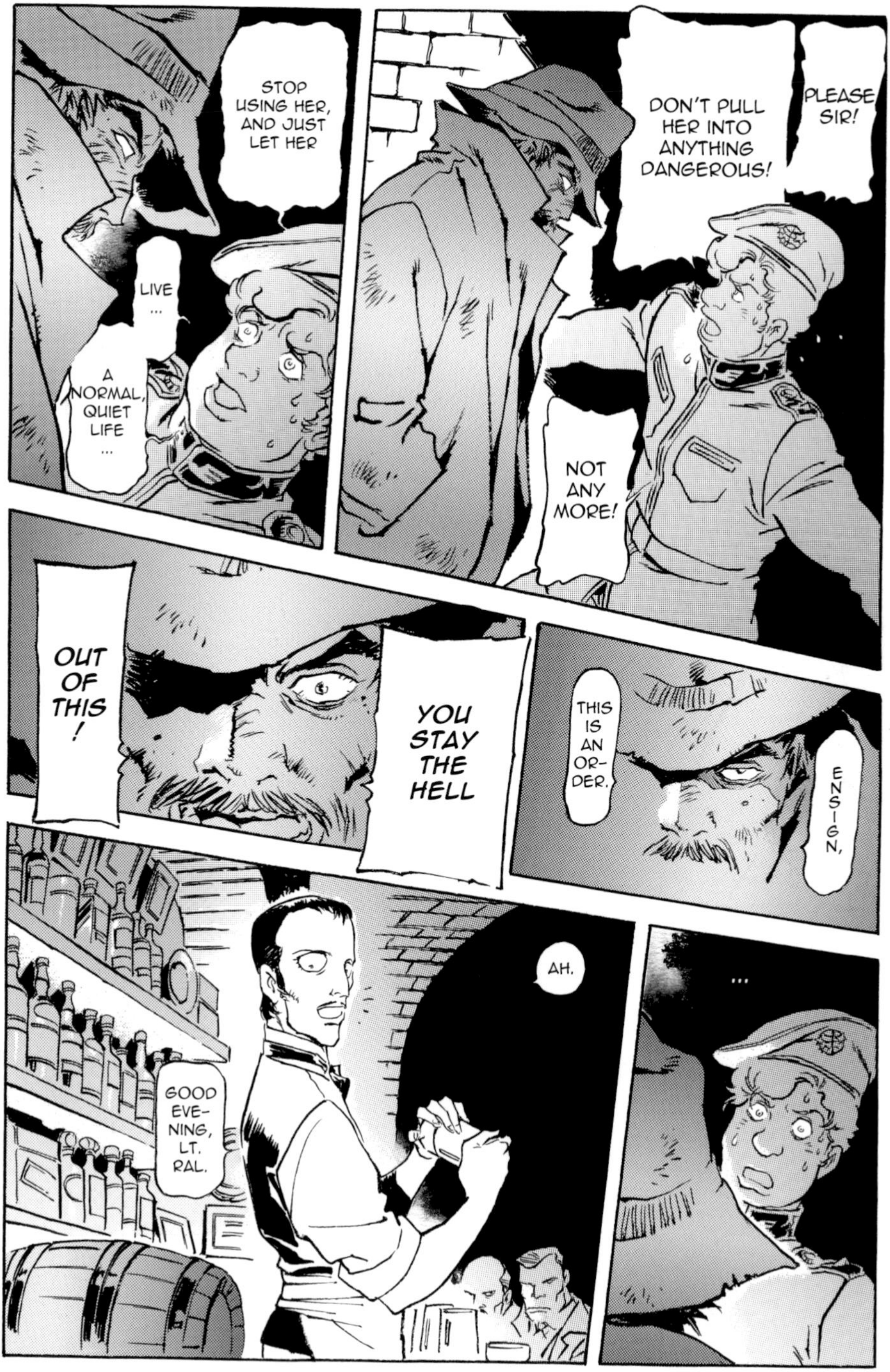
PLEASE SIR!
DON'T PULL HER INTO ANYTHING DANGEROUS!
NOT ANY MORE!
STOP USING HER, AND JUST LET HER
LIVE...
A NORMAL, QUIET LIFE...
ENSIGN,
THIS IS AN ORDER.
YOU STAY THE HELL
OUT OF THIS!
...
AH.
GOOD EVENING, LT. RAL.

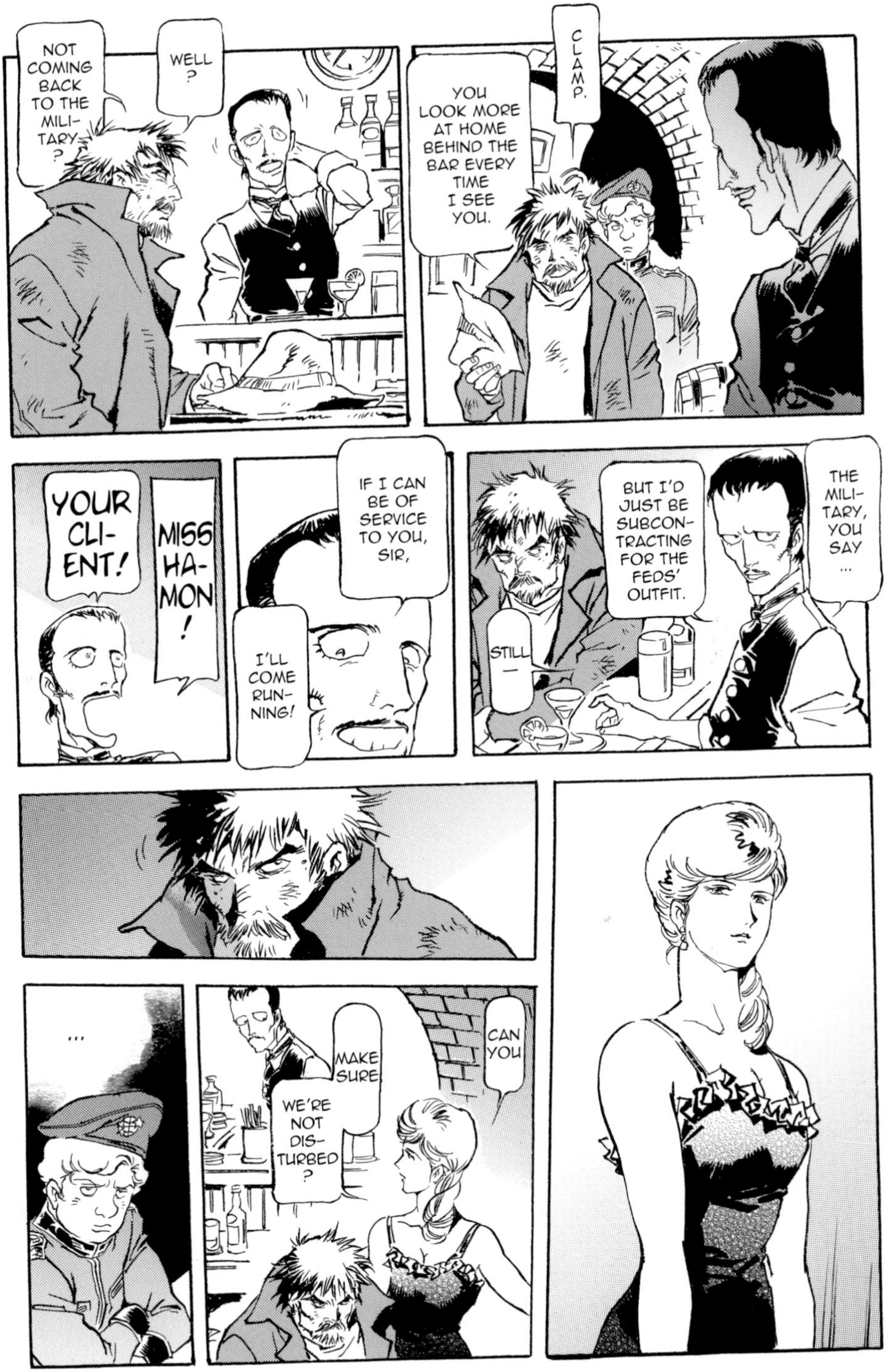
CLAMP.
YOU LOOK MORE AT HOME BEHIND THE BAR EVERY TIME I SEE YOU.
WELL?
NOT COMING BACK TO THE MILITARY?
THE MILITARY, YOU SAY ...
BUT I'D JUST BE SUBCONTRACTING FOR THE FEDS' OUTFIT.
STILL —
IF I CAN BE OF SERVICE TO YOU, SIR,
I'LL COME RUNNING!
MISS HAMON!
YOUR CLIENT!
CAN YOU
MAKE SURE
WE'RE NOT DISTURBED?
...

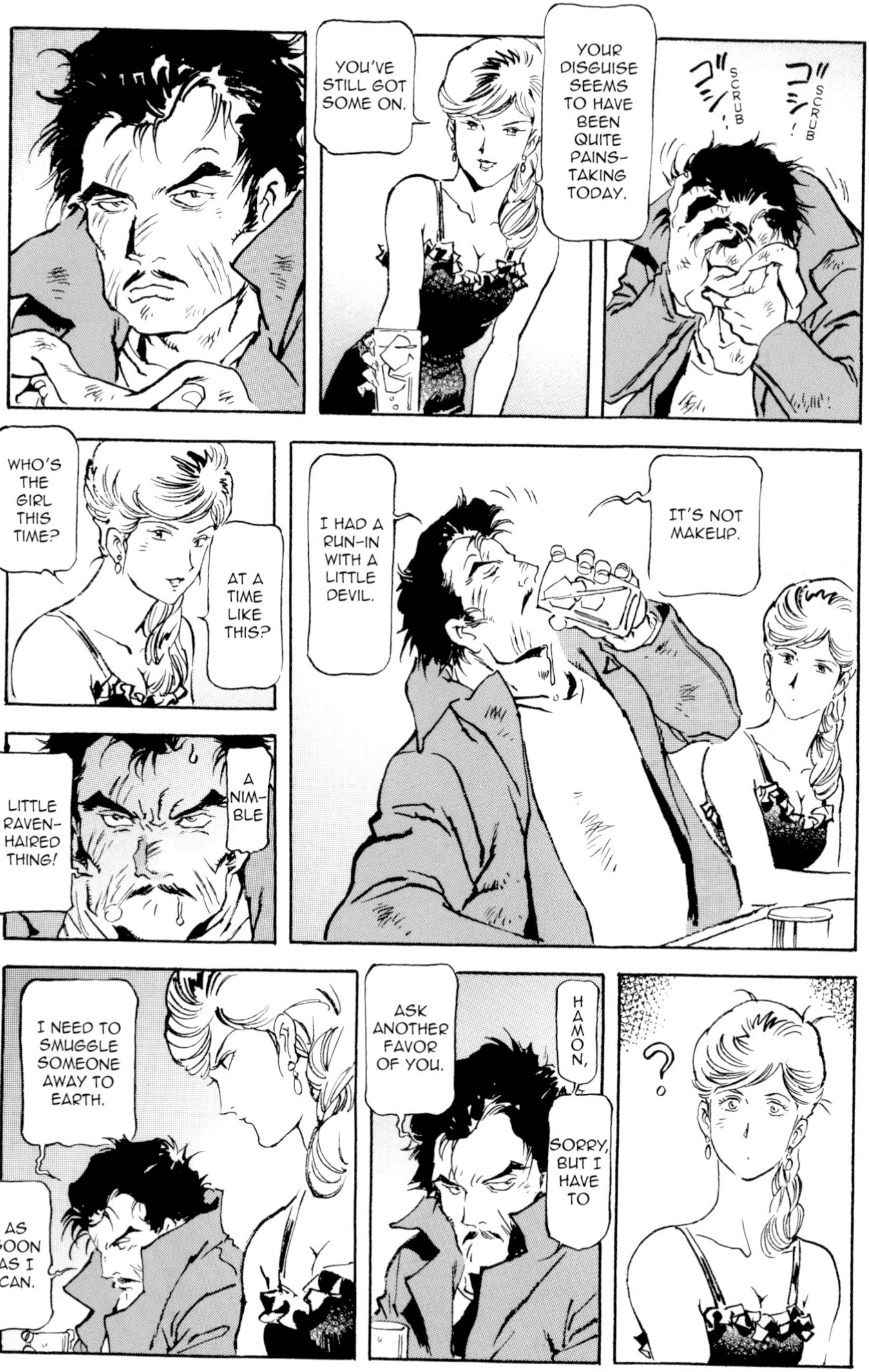
ゴシ SCRUB
ゴシ SCRUB
YOUR DISGUISE SEEMS TO HAVE BEEN QUITE PAINS-TAKING TODAY.
YOU'VE STILL GOT SOME ON.
IT'S NOT MAKEUP.
I HAD A RUN-IN WITH A LITTLE DEVIL.
WHO'S THE GIRL THIS TIME?
AT A TIME LIKE THIS?
A NIMBLE
LITTLE RAVEN-HAIRED THING!
?
HAMON,
SORRY, BUT I HAVE TO
ASK ANOTHER FAVOR OF YOU.
I NEED TO SMUGGLE SOMEONE AWAY TO EARTH.
AS SOON AS I CAN.

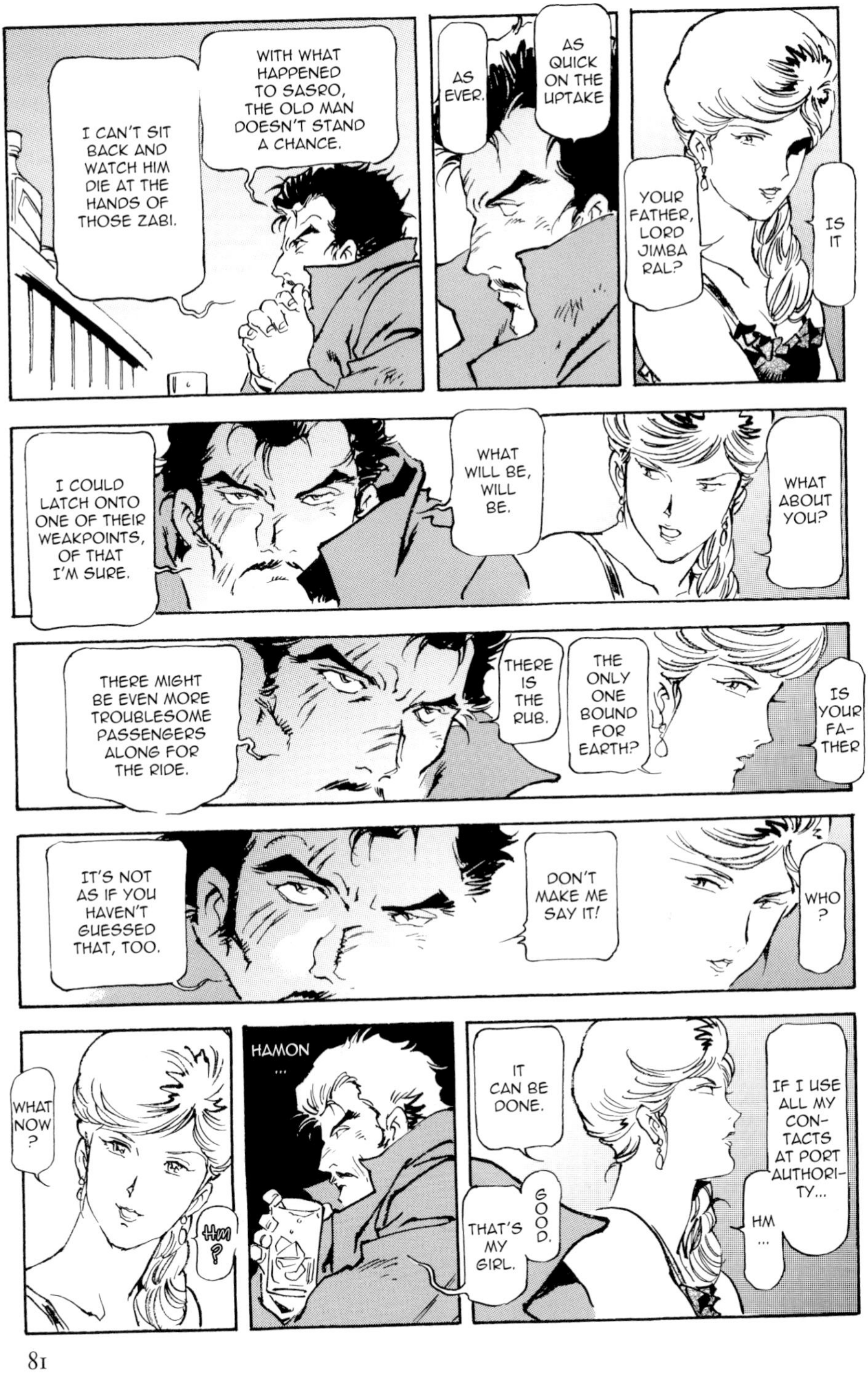
IS IT
YOUR FATHER, LORD JIMBA RAL?
AS QUICK ON THE UPTAKE
AS EVER.
WITH WHAT HAPPENED TO SASRO, THE OLD MAN DOESN'T STAND A CHANCE.
I CAN'T SIT BACK AND WATCH HIM DIE AT THE HANDS OF THOSE ZABI.
WHAT ABOUT YOU?
WHAT WILL BE, WILL BE.
I COULD LATCH ONTO ONE OF THEIR WEAKPOINTS, OF THAT I'M SURE.
IS YOUR FA- THER
THE ONLY ONE BOUND FOR EARTH?
THERE IS THE RUB.
THERE MIGHT BE EVEN MORE TROUBLESOME PASSENGERS ALONG FOR THE RIDE.
WHO?
DON'T MAKE ME SAY IT!
IT'S NOT AS IF YOU HAVEN'T GUESSED THAT, TOO.
IF I USE ALL MY CON- TACTS AT PORT AUTHORI- TY...
IT CAN BE DONE.
HM ...
GOOD.
THAT'S MY GIRL.
HAMON ...
WHAT NOW?
Hm?

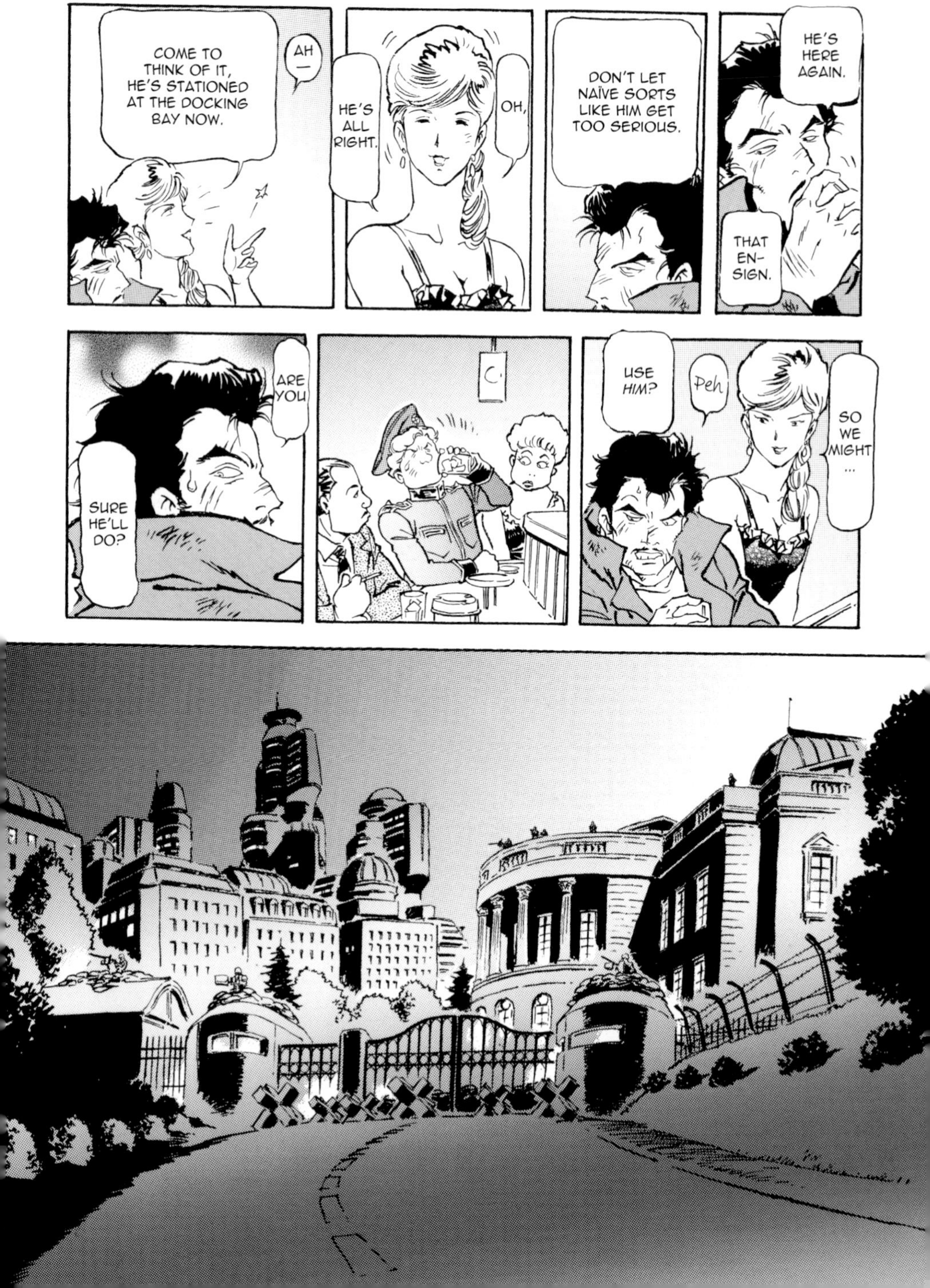
HE'S HERE AGAIN.
THAT EN-SIGN.
DON'T LET NAÏVE SORTS LIKE HIM GET TOO SERIOUS.
OH,
HE'S ALL RIGHT.
AH—
COME TO THINK OF IT, HE'S STATIONED AT THE DOCKING BAY NOW.
SO WE MIGHT ...
Peh
USE HIM?
ARE YOU
SURE HE'LL DO?

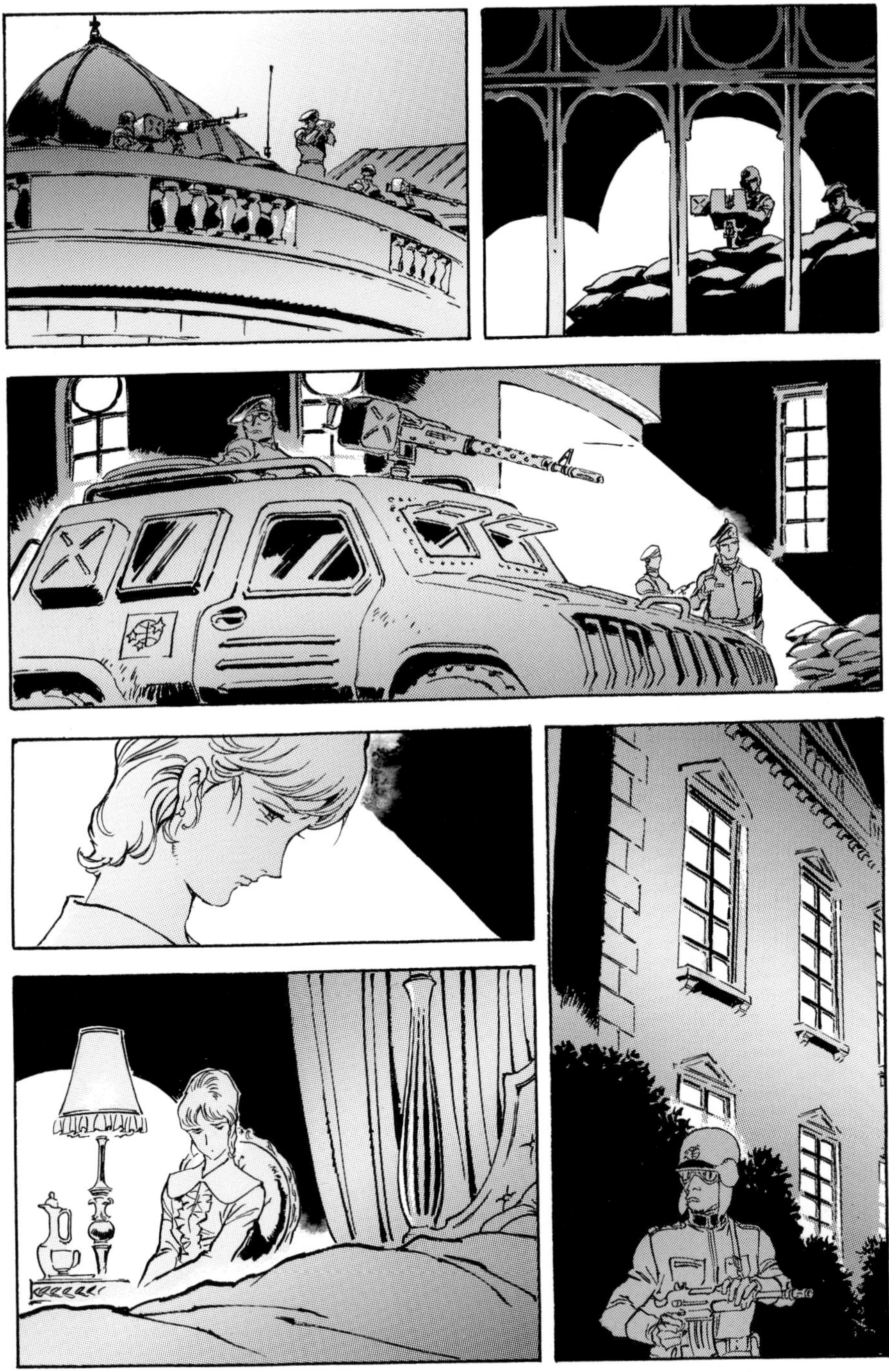

...

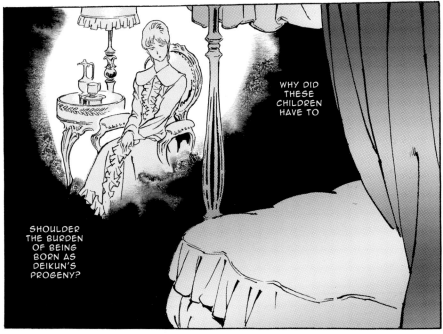

WHY DID THESE CHILDREN HAVE TO

SHOULDER THE BURDEN OF BEING BORN AS DEIKUN'S PROGENY?

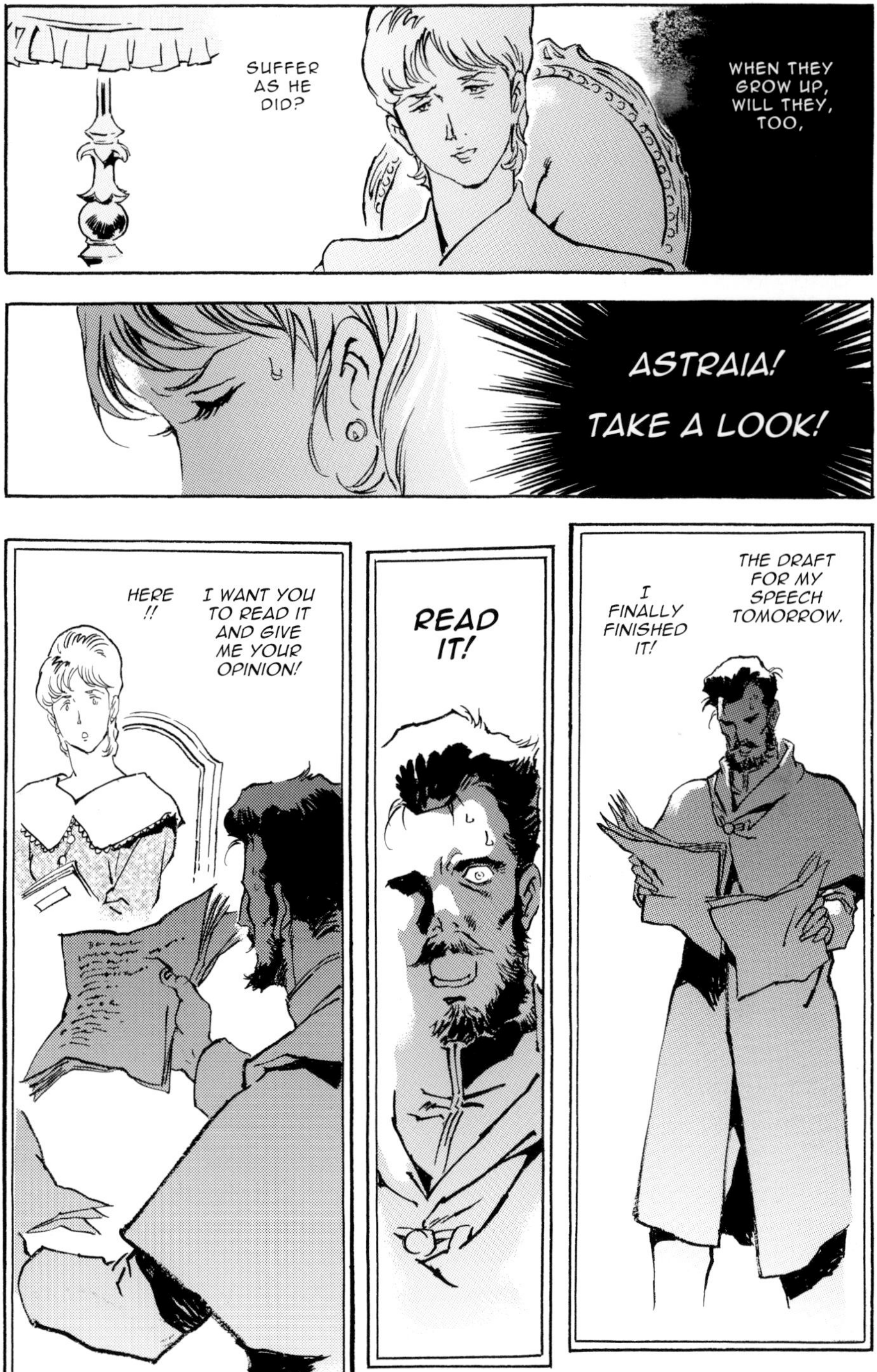
WHEN THEY GROW UP, WILL THEY, TOO,
SUFFER AS HE DID?
ASTRAIA!
TAKE A LOOK!
THE DRAFT FOR MY SPEECH TOMORROW.
I FINALLY FINISHED IT!
READ IT!
I WANT YOU TO READ IT AND GIVE ME YOUR OPINION!
HERE !!

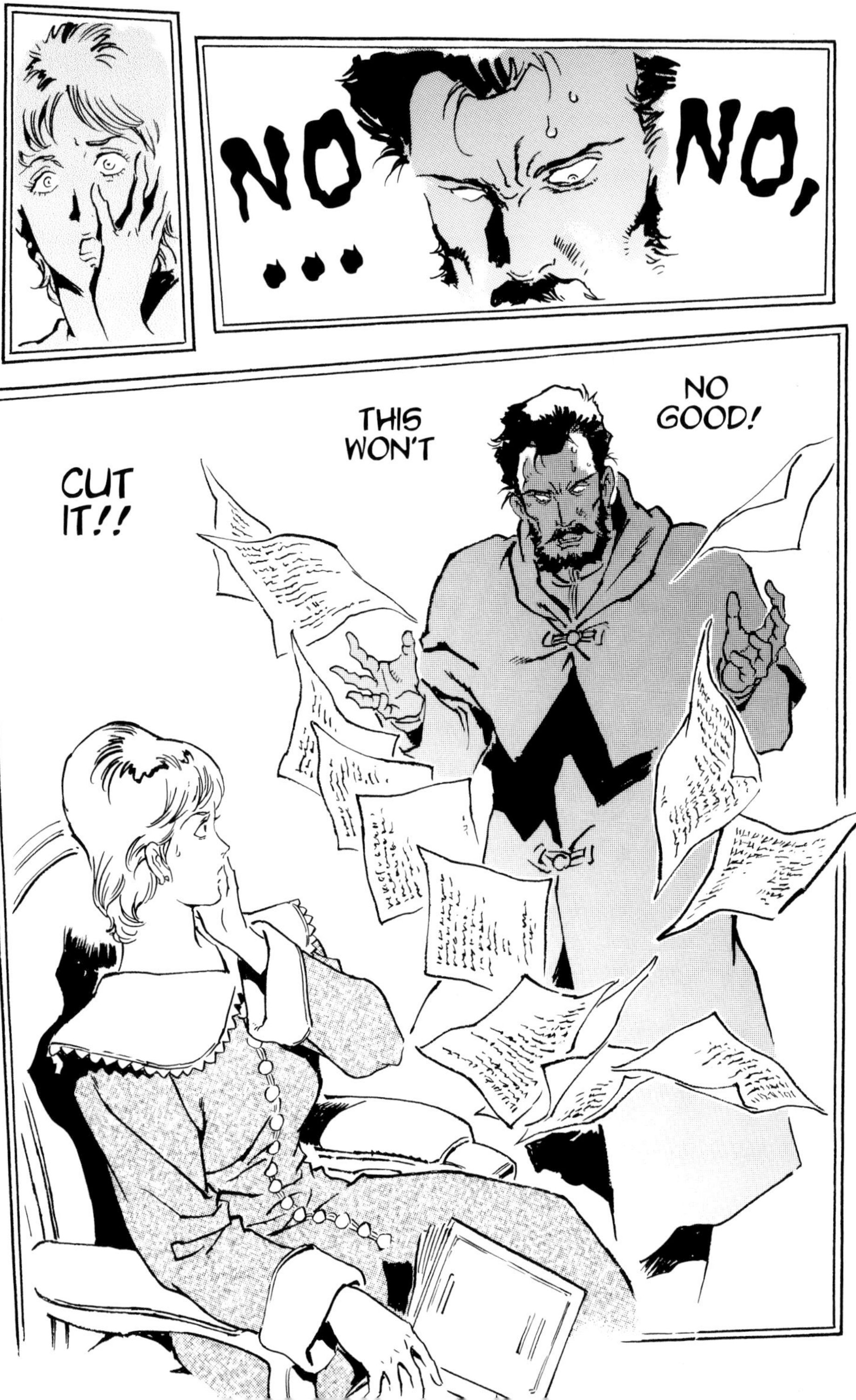
NO,
NO...
NO GOOD!
THIS WON'T
CUT IT!!

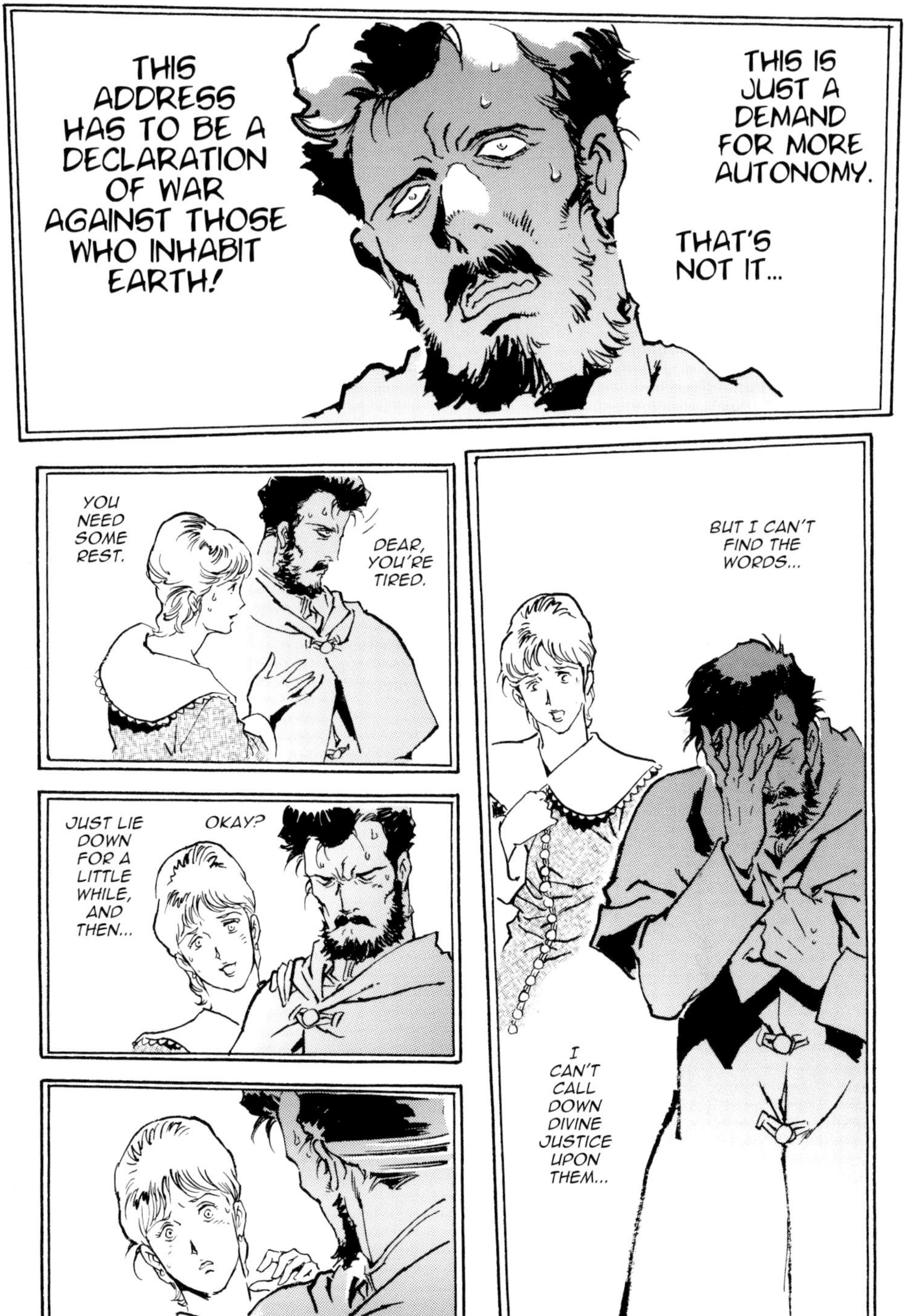
THIS IS JUST A DEMAND FOR MORE AUTONOMY.
THAT'S NOT IT...
THIS ADDRESS HAS TO BE A DECLARATION OF WAR AGAINST THOSE WHO INHABIT EARTH!
BUT I CAN'T FIND THE WORDS...
I CAN'T CALL DOWN DIVINE JUSTICE UPON THEM...
DEAR, YOU'RE TIRED.
YOU NEED SOME REST.
OKAY?
JUST LIE DOWN FOR A LITTLE WHILE, AND THEN...

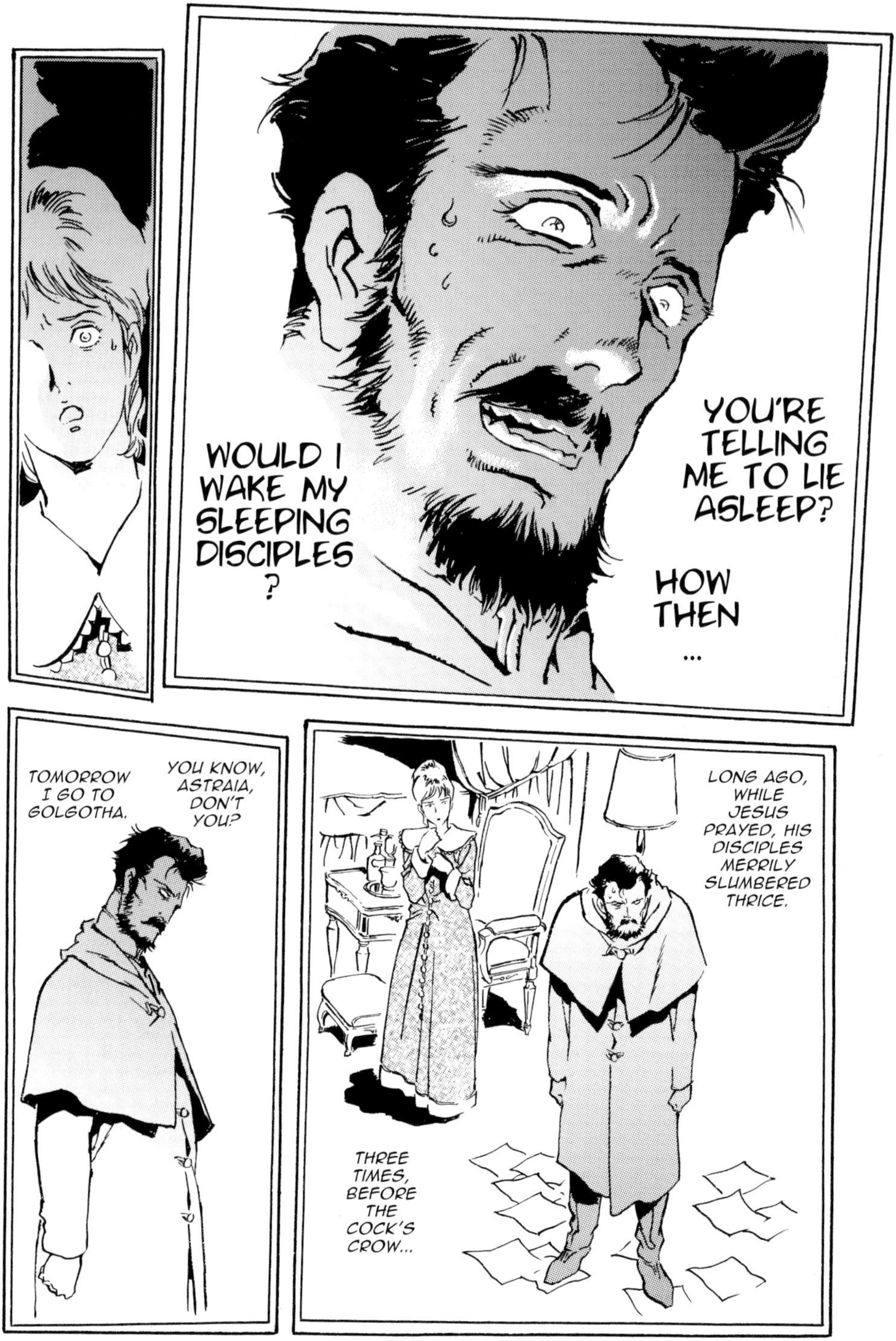
YOU'RE TELLING ME TO LIE ASLEEP?
HOW THEN ...
WOULD I WAKE MY SLEEPING DISCIPLES ?
LONG AGO, WHILE JESUS PRAYED, HIS DISCIPLES MERRILY SLUMBERED THRICE.
THREE TIMES, BEFORE THE COCK'S CROW...
YOU KNOW, ASTRAIA, DON'T YOU?
TOMORROW I GO TO GOLGOTHA.

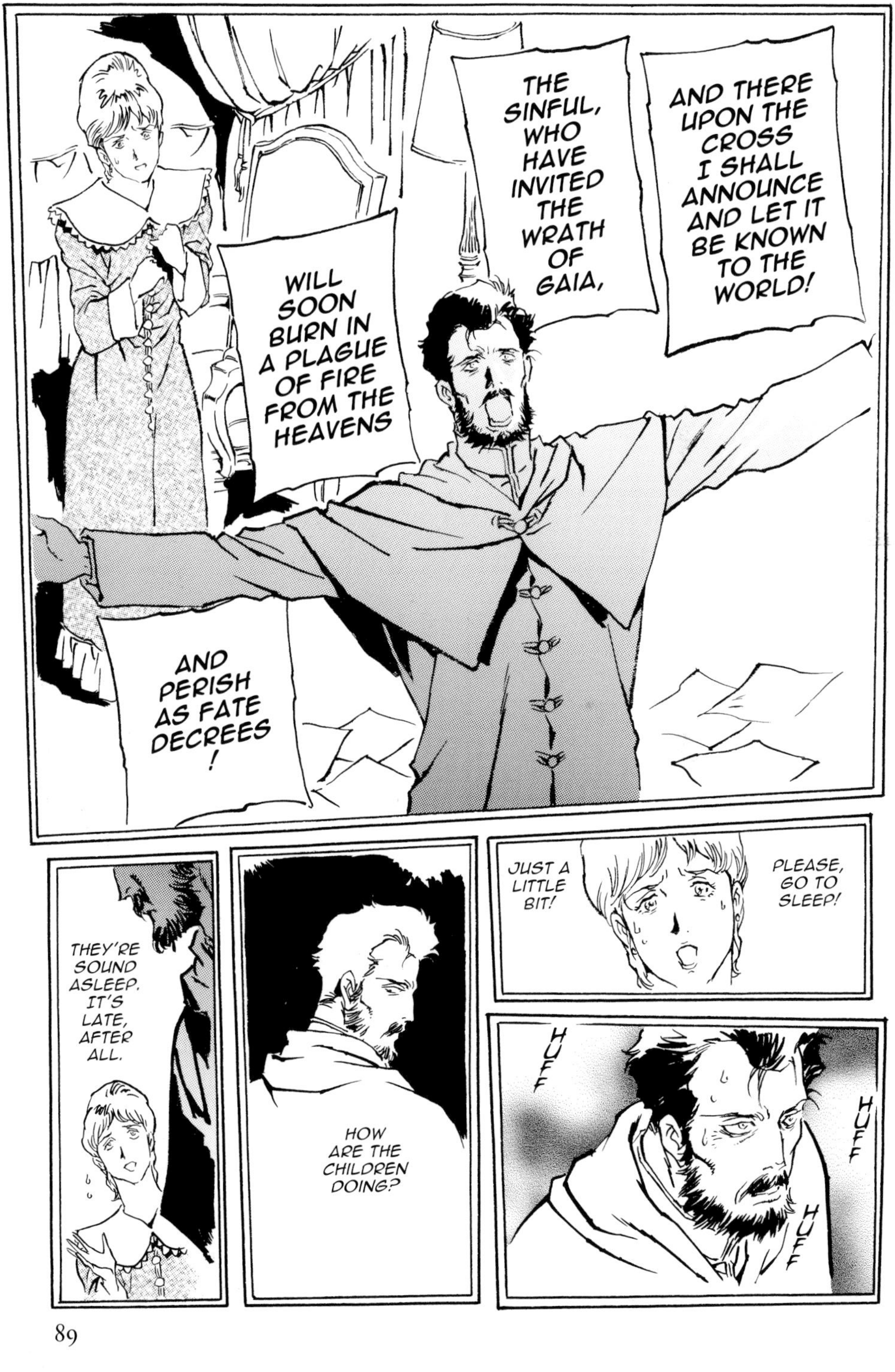
AND THERE UPON THE CROSS I SHALL ANNOUNCE AND LET IT BE KNOWN TO THE WORLD!
THE SINFUL, WHO HAVE INVITED THE WRATH OF GAIA,
WILL SOON BURN IN A PLAGUE OF FIRE FROM THE HEAVENS
AND PERISH AS FATE DECREES!
PLEASE, GO TO SLEEP!
JUST A LITTLE BIT!
HUFF
HUFF
HUFF
HOW ARE THE CHILDREN DOING?
THEY'RE SOUND ASLEEP. IT'S LATE, AFTER ALL.

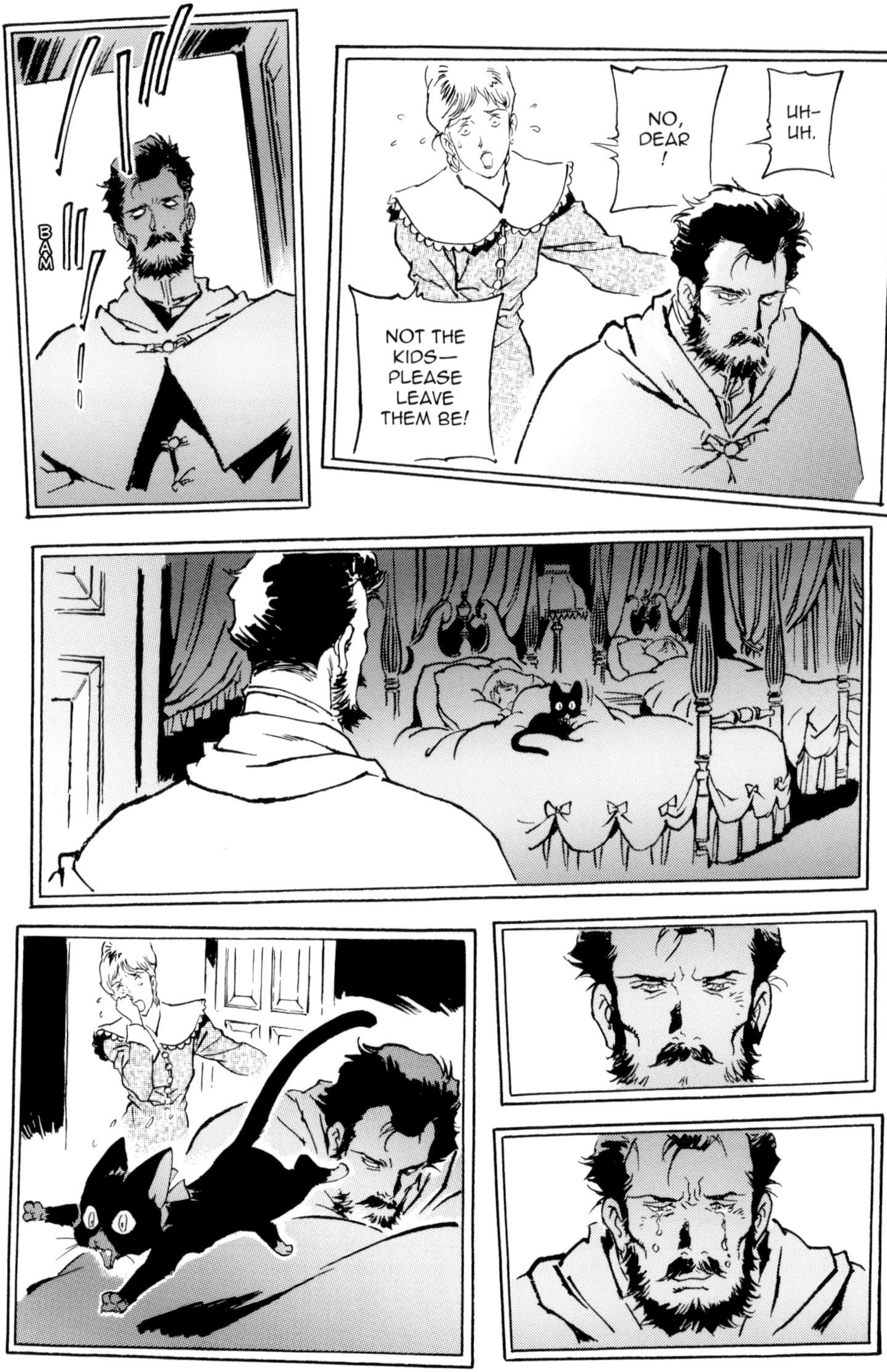
UH-UH.
NO, DEAR!
NOT THE KIDS— PLEASE LEAVE THEM BE!
BAM

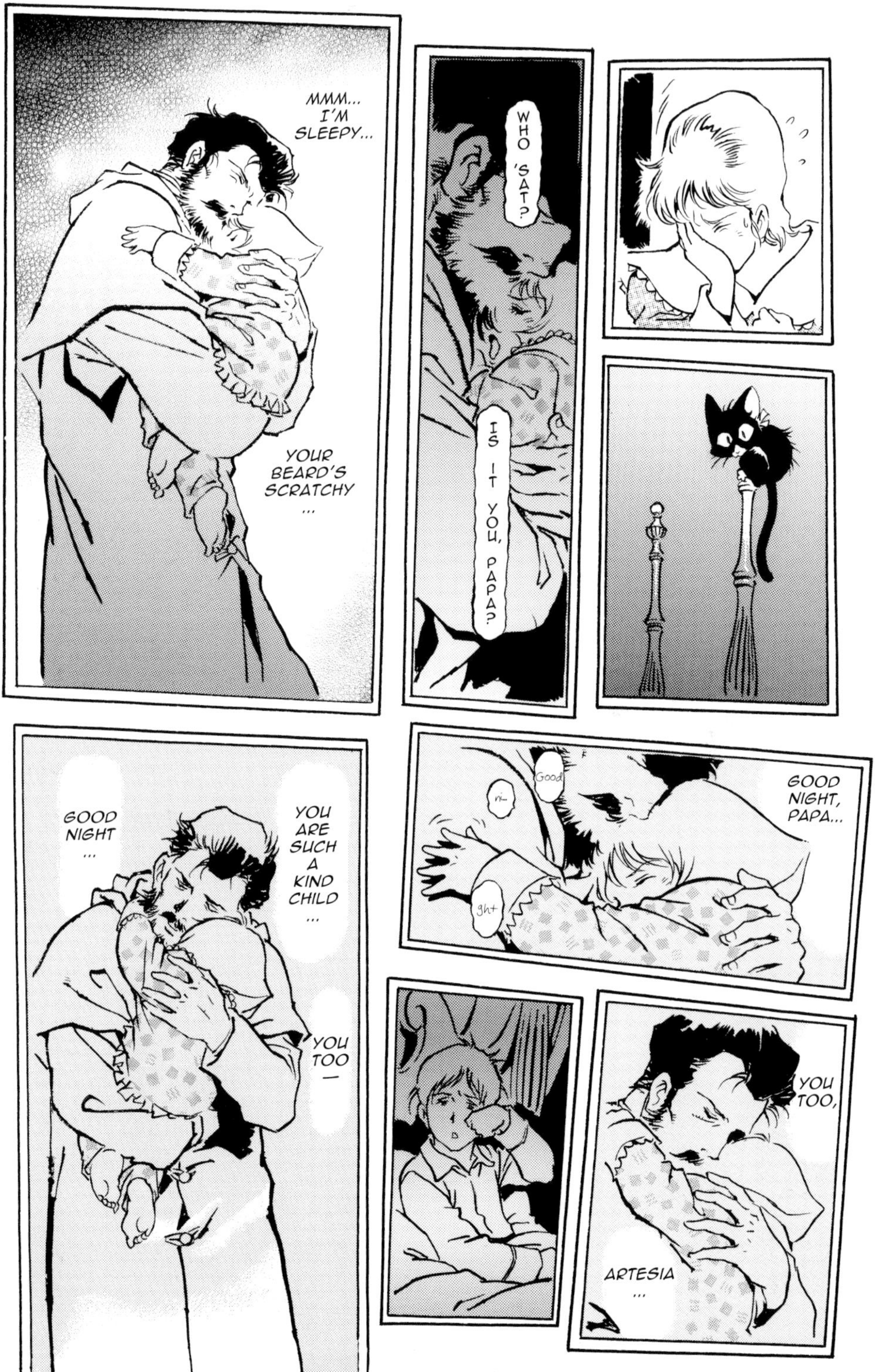
WHO 'SAT?
IS IT YOU, PAPA?
MMM... I'M SLEEPY...
YOUR BEARD'S SCRATCHY ...
GOOD NIGHT, PAPA...
Good
ni...
ght
YOU TOO,
ARTESIA ...
YOU ARE SUCH A KIND CHILD ...
GOOD NIGHT ...
YOU TOO —

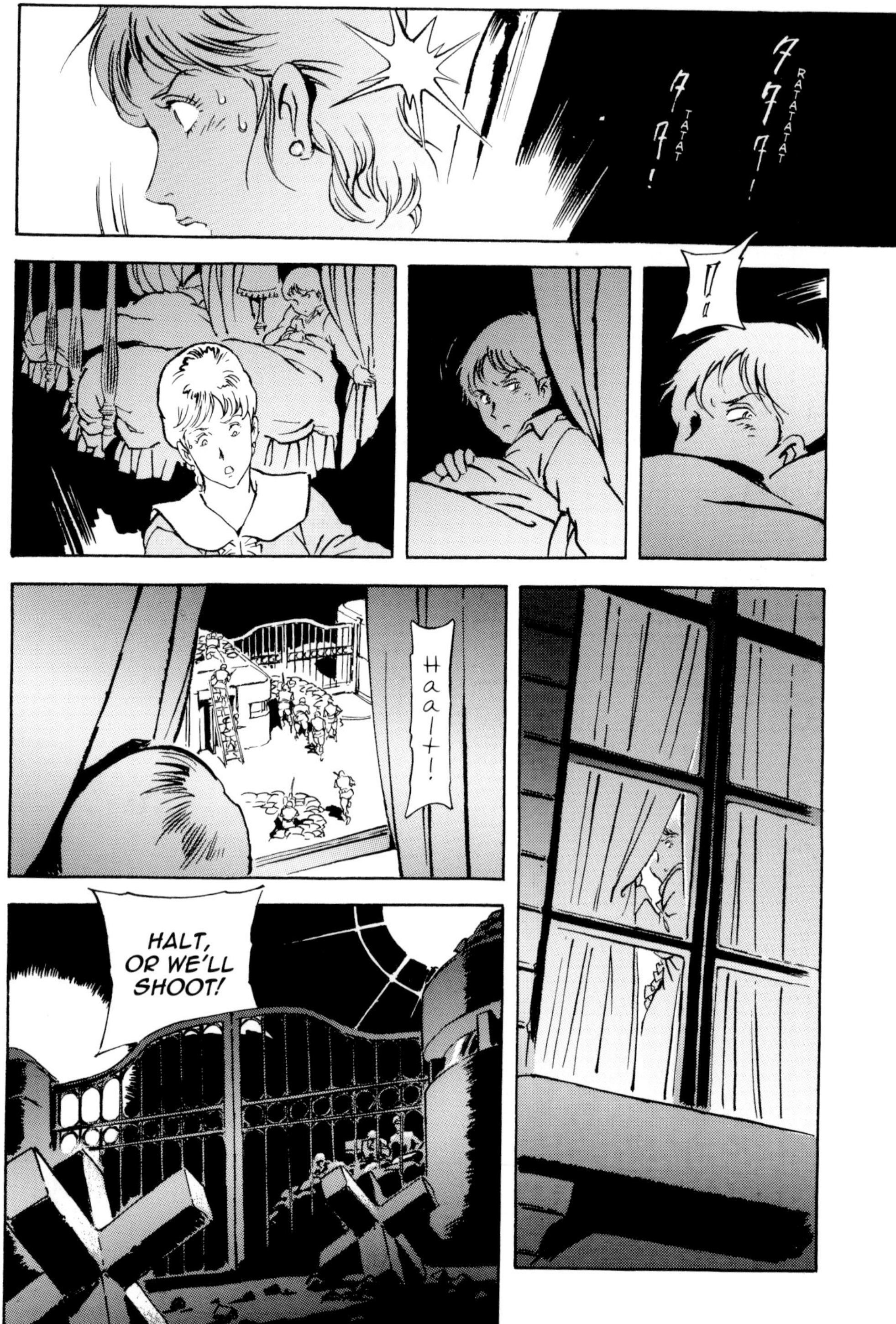
タタタ!
RATATATAT
タタ!
TATAT
!?
Haalt!
HALT, OR WE'LL SHOOT!

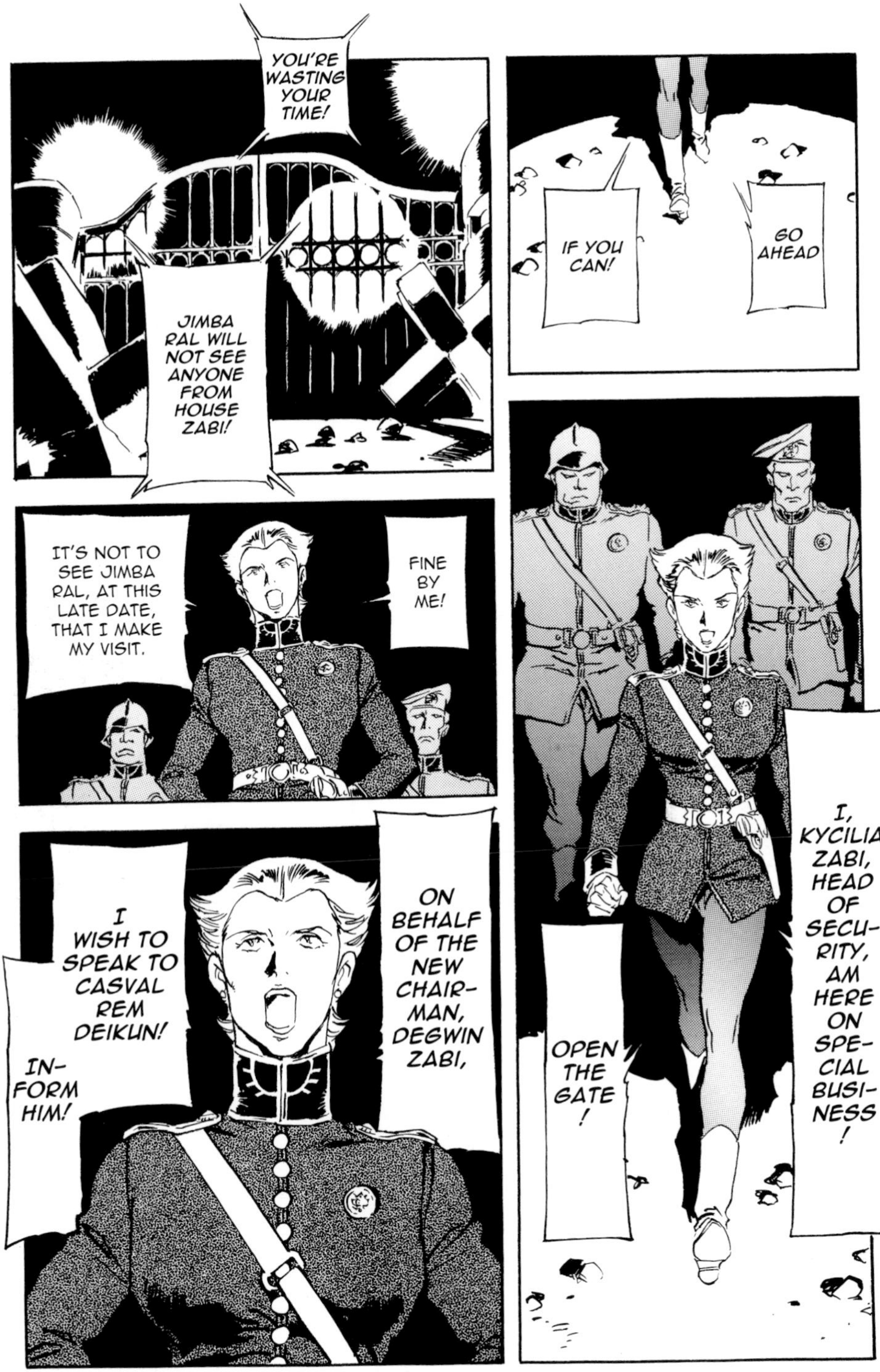
GO AHEAD
IF YOU CAN!
YOU'RE WASTING YOUR TIME!
JIMBA RAL WILL NOT SEE ANYONE FROM HOUSE ZABI!
I, KYCILIA ZABI, HEAD OF SECU-RITY, AM HERE ON SPE-CIAL BUSI-NESS!
OPEN THE GATE!
FINE BY ME!
IT'S NOT TO SEE JIMBA RAL, AT THIS LATE DATE, THAT I MAKE MY VISIT.
ON BEHALF OF THE NEW CHAIR-MAN, DEGWIN ZABI,
I WISH TO SPEAK TO CASVAL REM DEIKUN!
IN-FORM HIM!

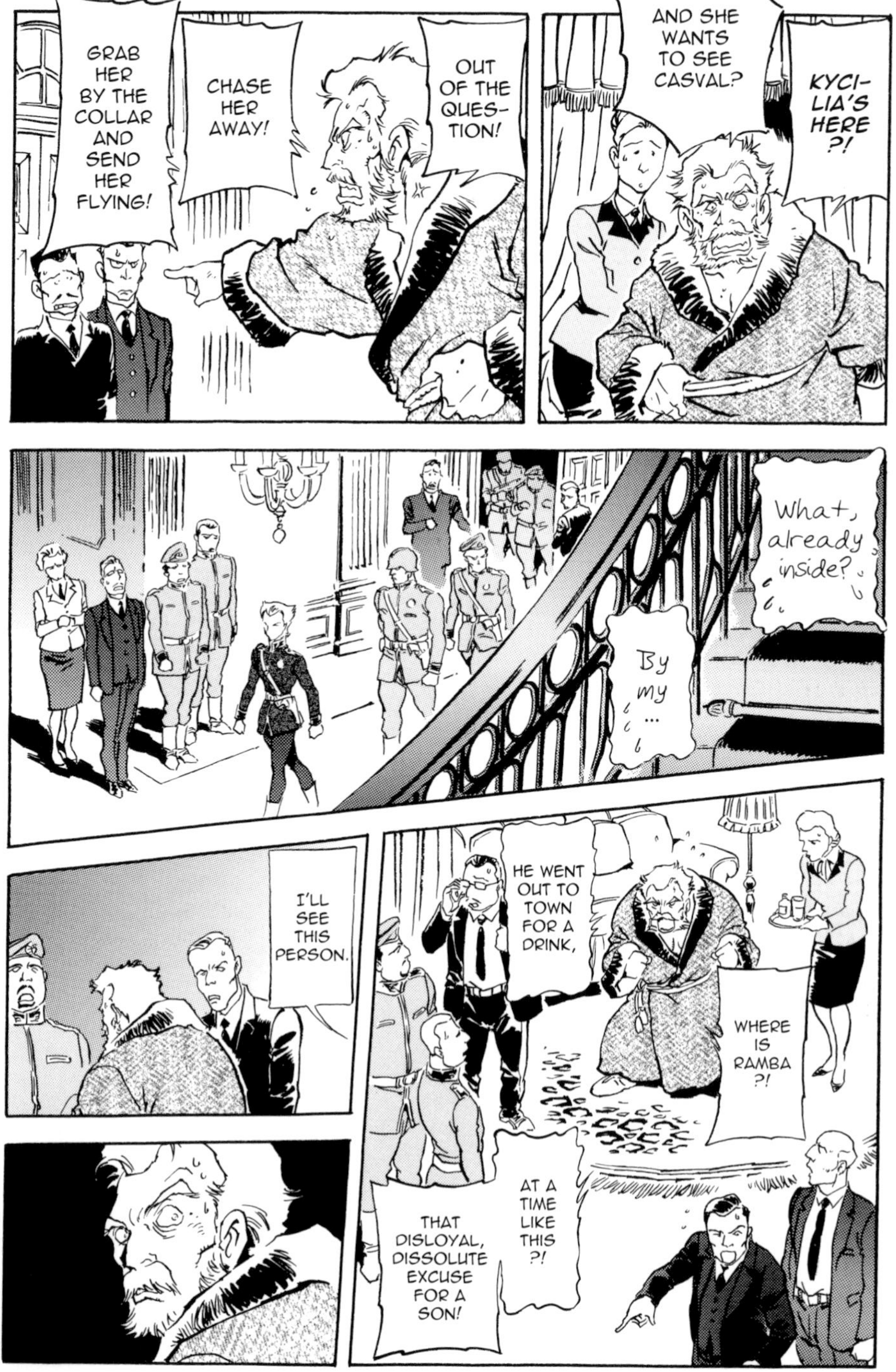
KYCILIA'S HERE?!
AND SHE WANTS TO SEE CASVAL?
OUT OF THE QUESTION!
CHASE HER AWAY!
GRAB HER BY THE COLLAR AND SEND HER FLYING!
What, already inside?
By my ...
WHERE IS RAMBA?!
HE WENT OUT TO TOWN FOR A DRINK,
AT A TIME LIKE THIS?!
THAT DISLOYAL, DISSOLUTE EXCUSE FOR A SON!
I'LL SEE THIS PERSON.

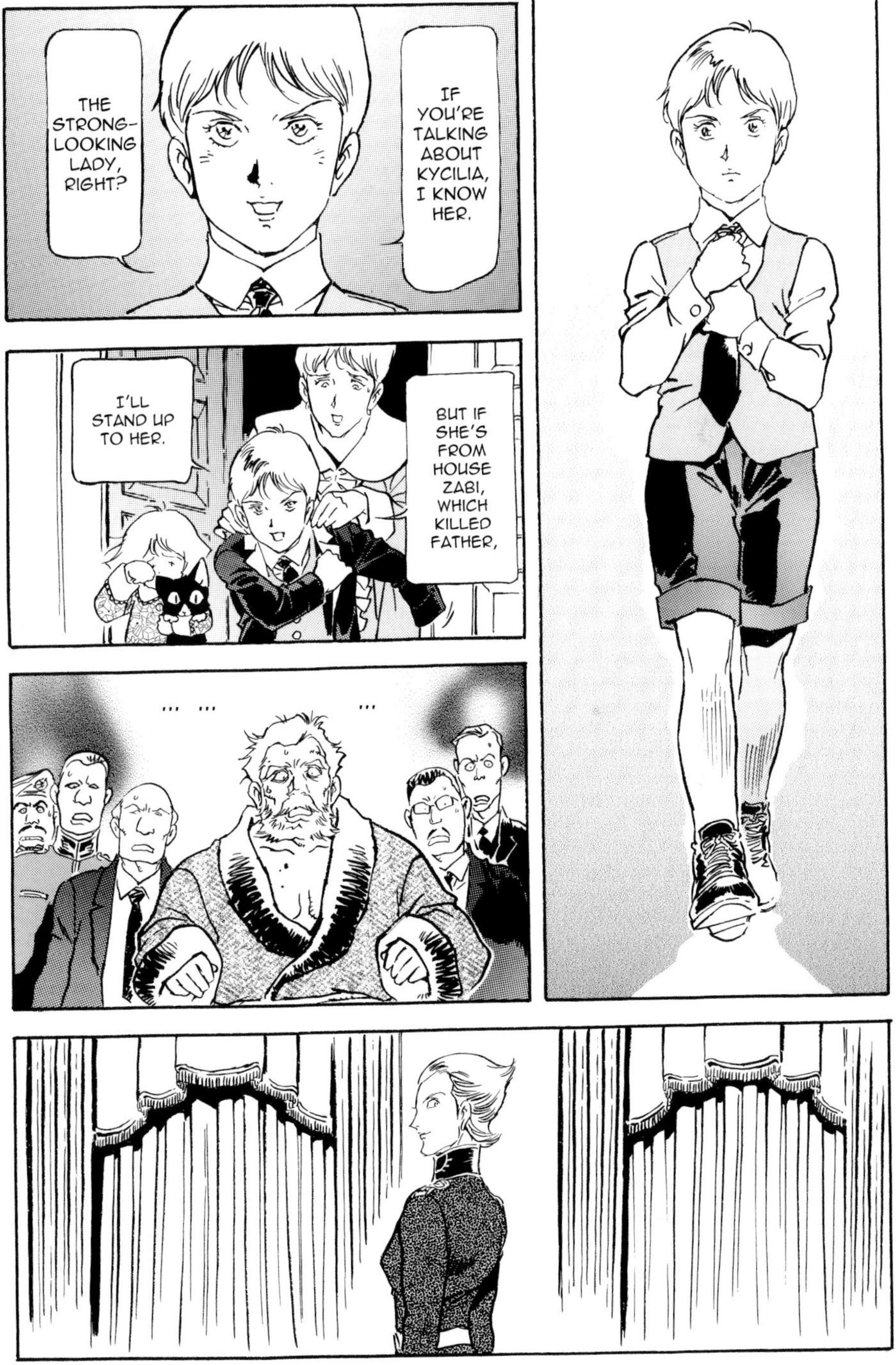
IF YOU'RE TALKING ABOUT KYCILIA, I KNOW HER.
THE STRONG-LOOKING LADY, RIGHT?
BUT IF SHE'S FROM HOUSE ZABI, WHICH KILLED FATHER,
I'LL STAND UP TO HER.
... ...

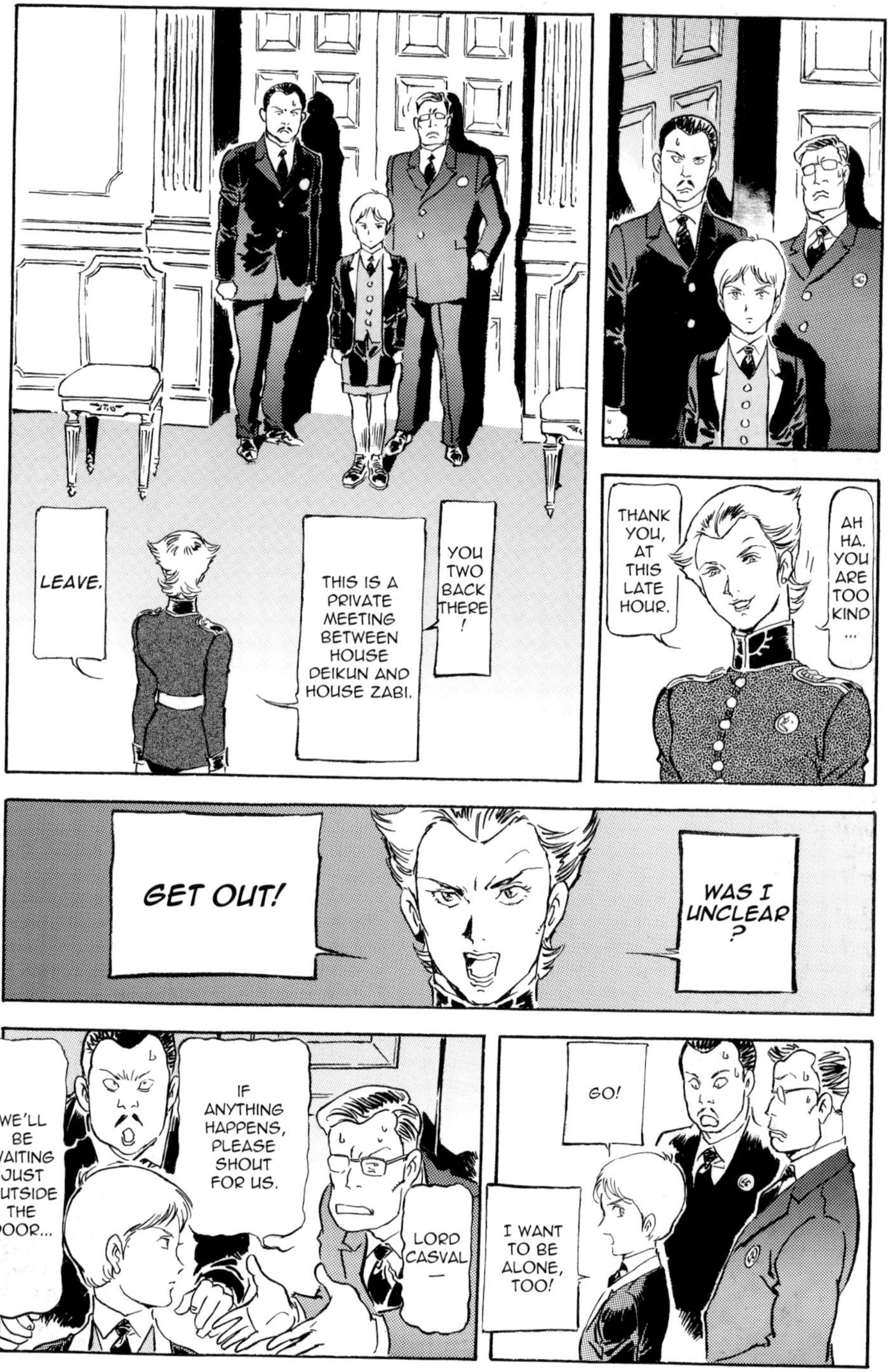
AH HA. YOU ARE TOO KIND ...
THANK YOU, AT THIS LATE HOUR.
YOU TWO BACK THERE!
THIS IS A PRIVATE MEETING BETWEEN HOUSE DEIKUN AND HOUSE ZABI.
LEAVE.
WAS I UNCLEAR?
GET OUT!
GO!
I WANT TO BE ALONE, TOO!
LORD CASVAL—
IF ANYTHING HAPPENS, PLEASE SHOUT FOR US.
WE'LL BE WAITING JUST OUTSIDE THE DOOR...

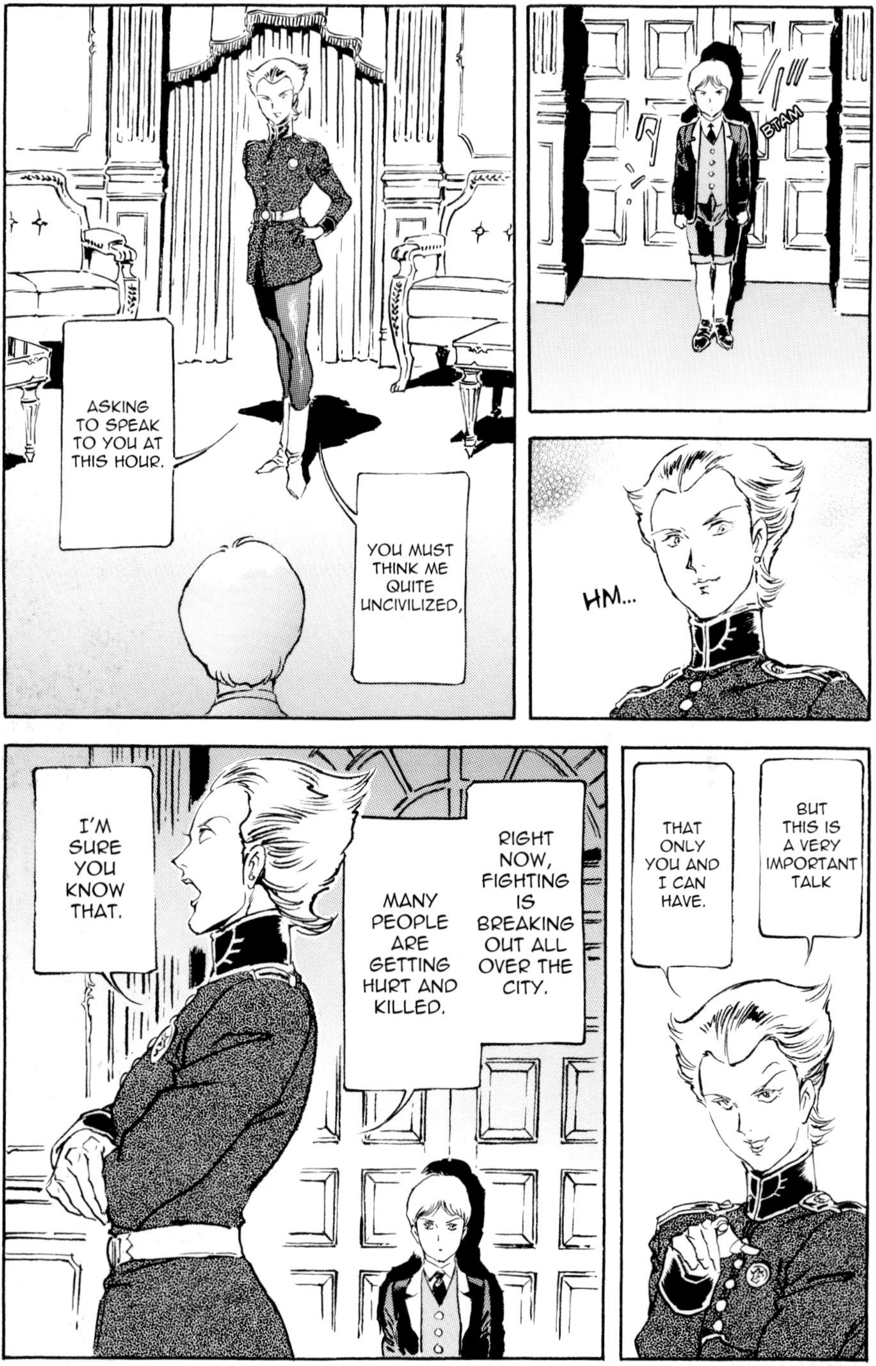
BTAM
HM...
YOU MUST THINK ME QUITE UNCIVILIZED,
ASKING TO SPEAK TO YOU AT THIS HOUR.
BUT THIS IS A VERY IMPORTANT TALK
THAT ONLY YOU AND I CAN HAVE.
RIGHT NOW, FIGHTING IS BREAKING OUT ALL OVER THE CITY.
MANY PEOPLE ARE GETTING HURT AND KILLED.
I'M SURE YOU KNOW THAT.

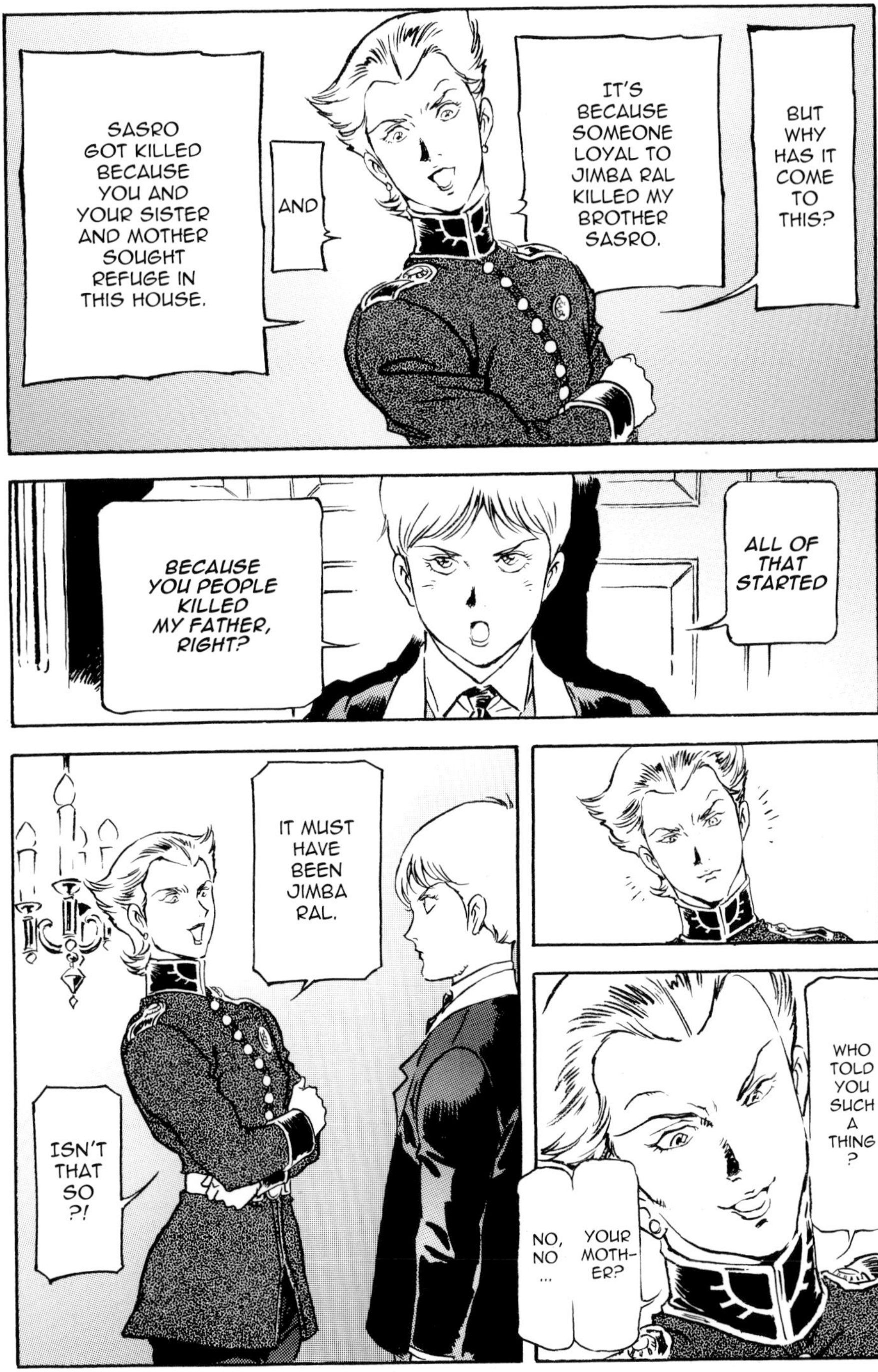
BUT WHY HAS IT COME TO THIS?
IT'S BECAUSE SOMEONE LOYAL TO JIMBA RAL KILLED MY BROTHER SASRO.
AND
SASRO GOT KILLED BECAUSE YOU AND YOUR SISTER AND MOTHER SOUGHT REFUGE IN THIS HOUSE.
ALL OF THAT STARTED
BECAUSE YOU PEOPLE KILLED MY FATHER, RIGHT?
WHO TOLD YOU SUCH A THING?
YOUR MOTHER?
NO, NO ...
IT MUST HAVE BEEN JIMBA RAL.
ISN'T THAT SO?!

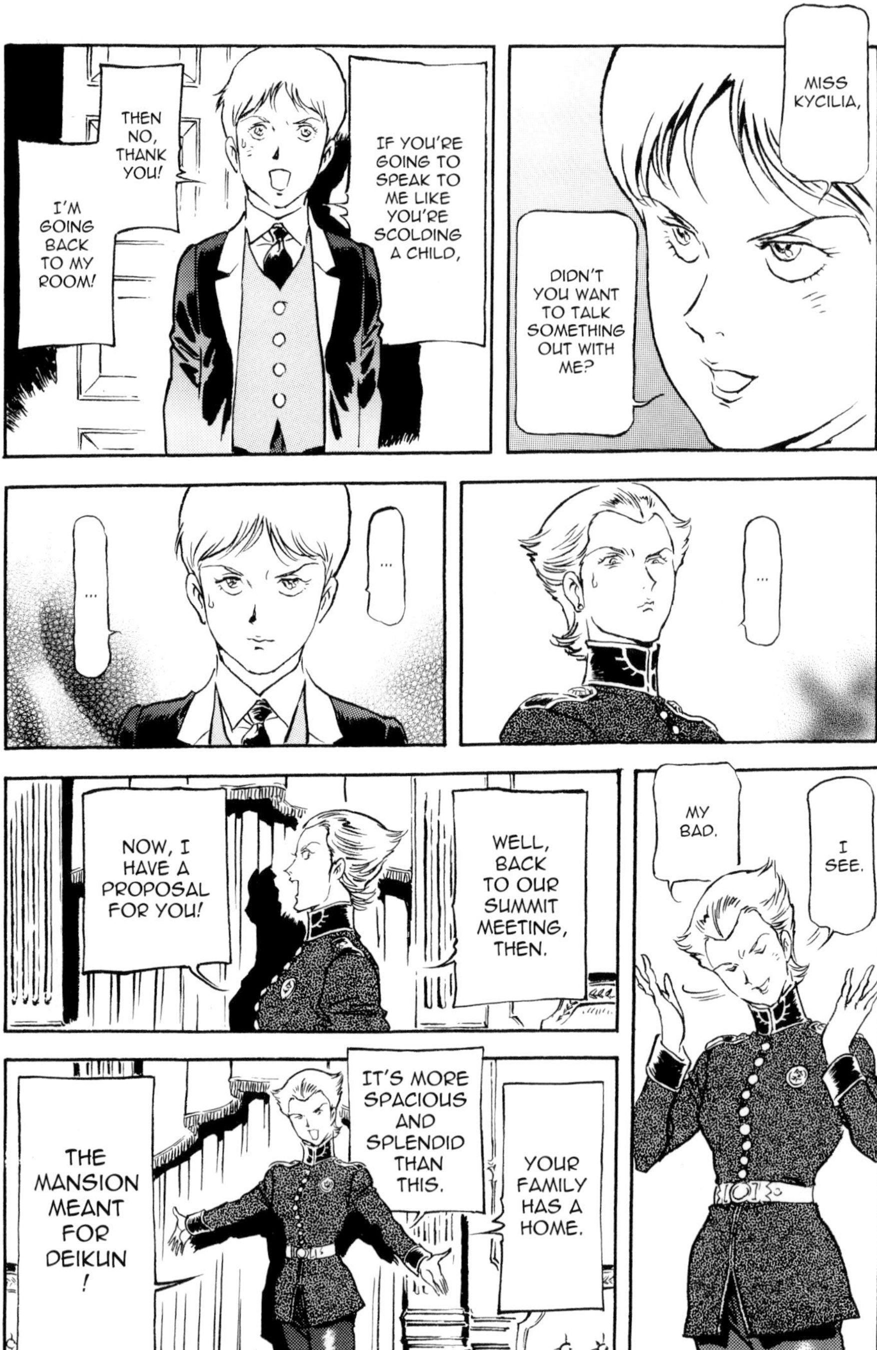
MISS KYCILIA,
DIDN'T YOU WANT TO TALK SOMETHING OUT WITH ME?
IF YOU'RE GOING TO SPEAK TO ME LIKE YOU'RE SCOLDING A CHILD,
THEN NO, THANK YOU!
I'M GOING BACK TO MY ROOM!
...
...
...
I SEE.
MY BAD.
WELL, BACK TO OUR SUMMIT MEETING, THEN.
NOW, I HAVE A PROPOSAL FOR YOU!
YOUR FAMILY HAS A HOME.
IT'S MORE SPACIOUS AND SPLENDID THAN THIS.
THE MANSION MEANT FOR DEIKUN!

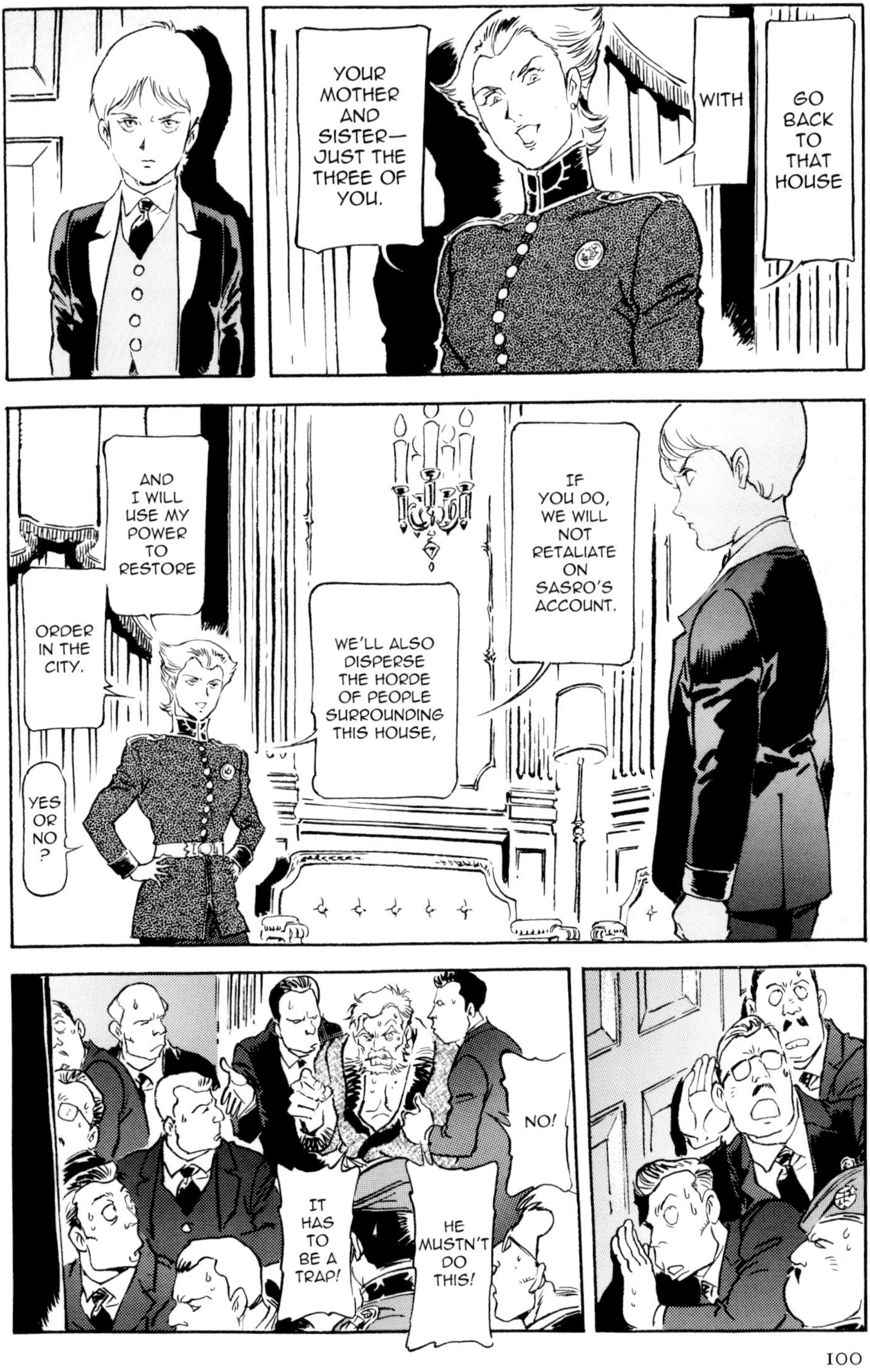
GO BACK TO THAT HOUSE
WITH
YOUR MOTHER AND SISTER— JUST THE THREE OF YOU.
IF YOU DO, WE WILL NOT RETALIATE ON SASRO'S ACCOUNT.
WE'LL ALSO DISPERSE THE HORDE OF PEOPLE SURROUNDING THIS HOUSE,
AND I WILL USE MY POWER TO RESTORE
ORDER IN THE CITY.
YES OR NO?
NO!
HE MUSTN'T DO THIS!
IT HAS TO BE A TRAP!

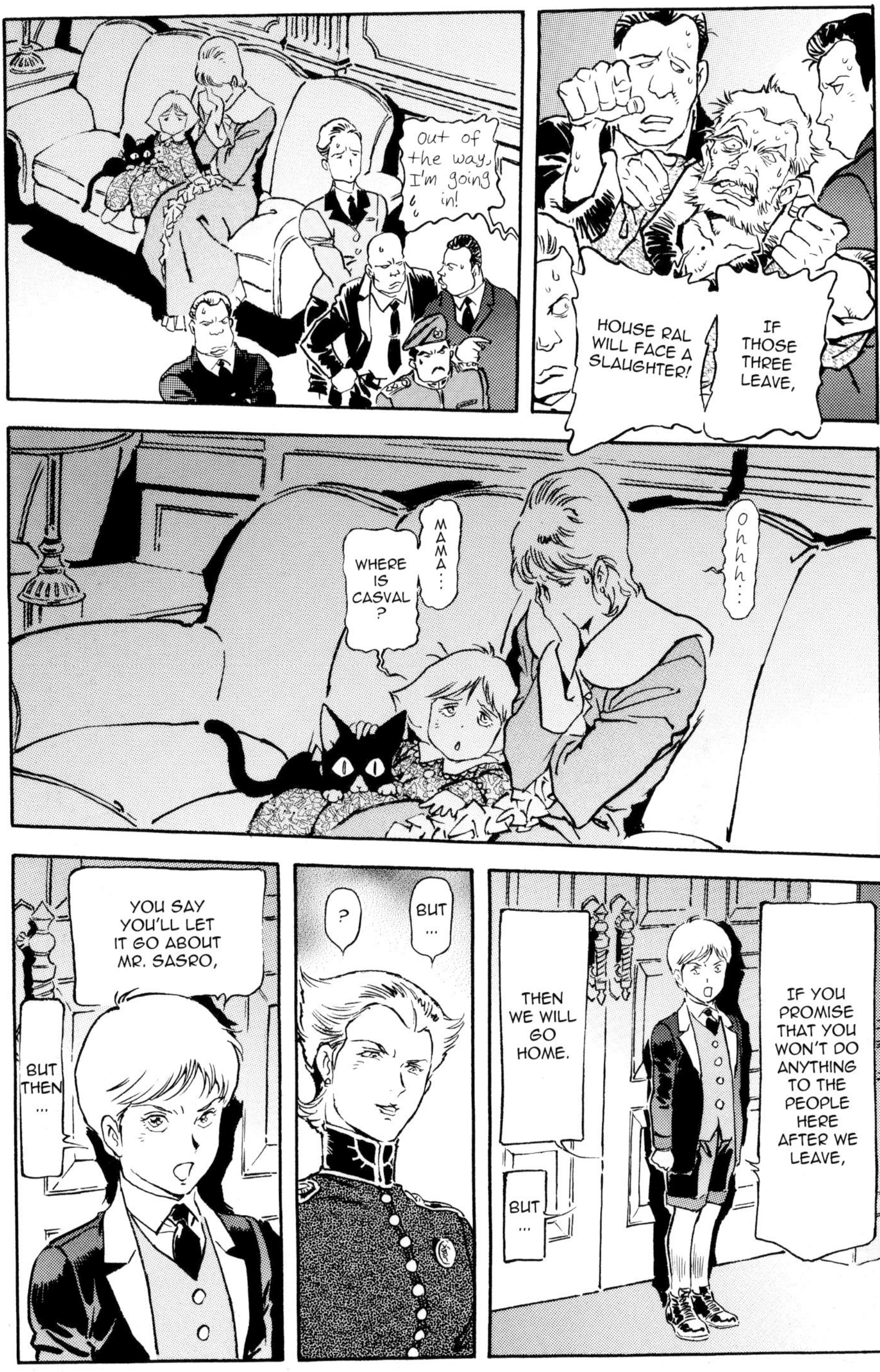
IF THOSE THREE LEAVE,
HOUSE RAL WILL FACE A SLAUGHTER!
out of the way, I'm going in!
Ohhh...
MAMA...
WHERE IS CASVAL?
IF YOU PROMISE THAT YOU WON'T DO ANYTHING TO THE PEOPLE HERE AFTER WE LEAVE,
THEN WE WILL GO HOME.
BUT ...
BUT ...
?
YOU SAY YOU'LL LET IT GO ABOUT MR. SASRO,
BUT THEN ...

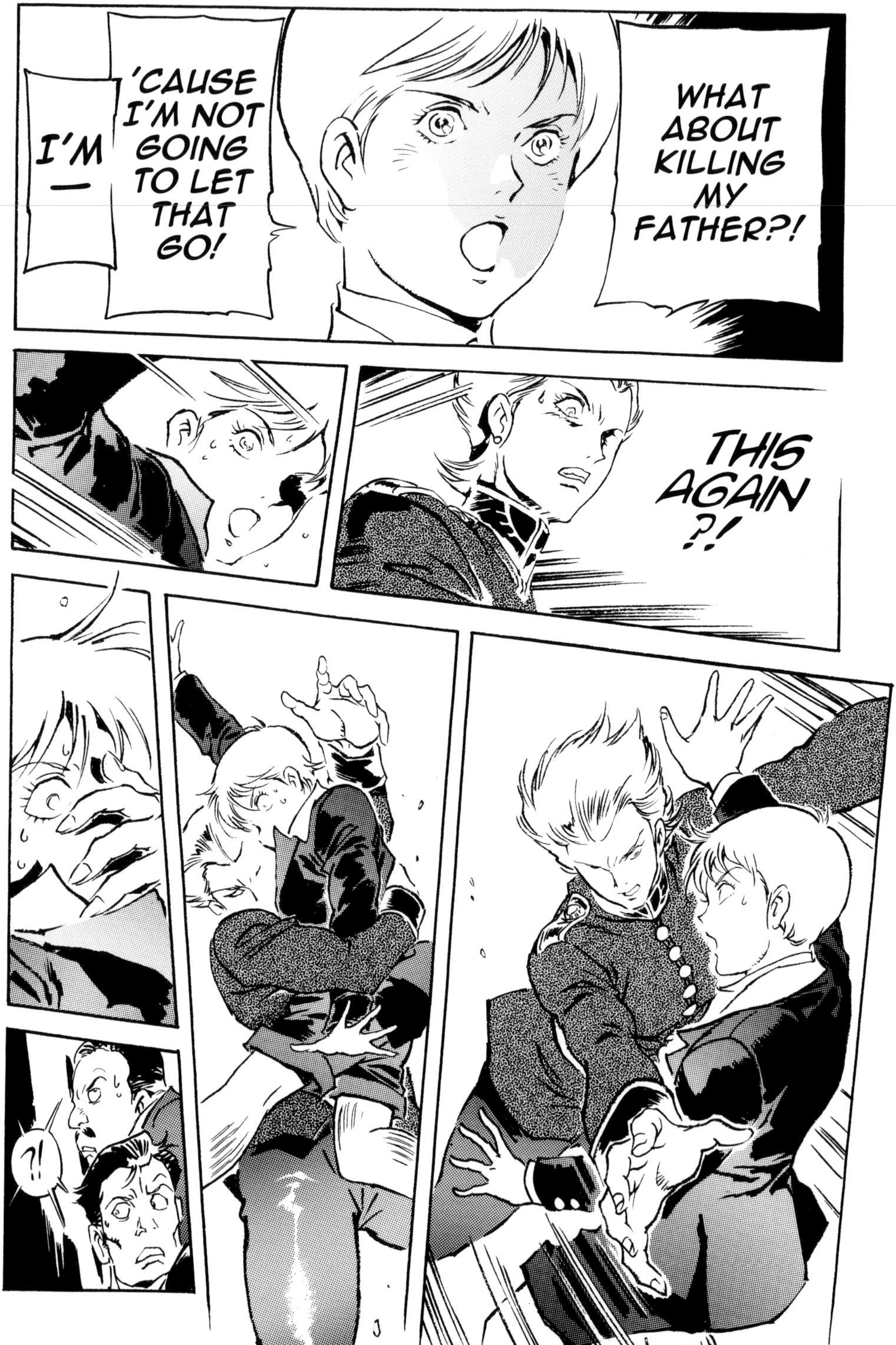
WHAT ABOUT KILLING MY FATHER?!
'CAUSE I'M NOT GOING TO LET THAT GO!
I'M —
THIS AGAIN ?!
?!

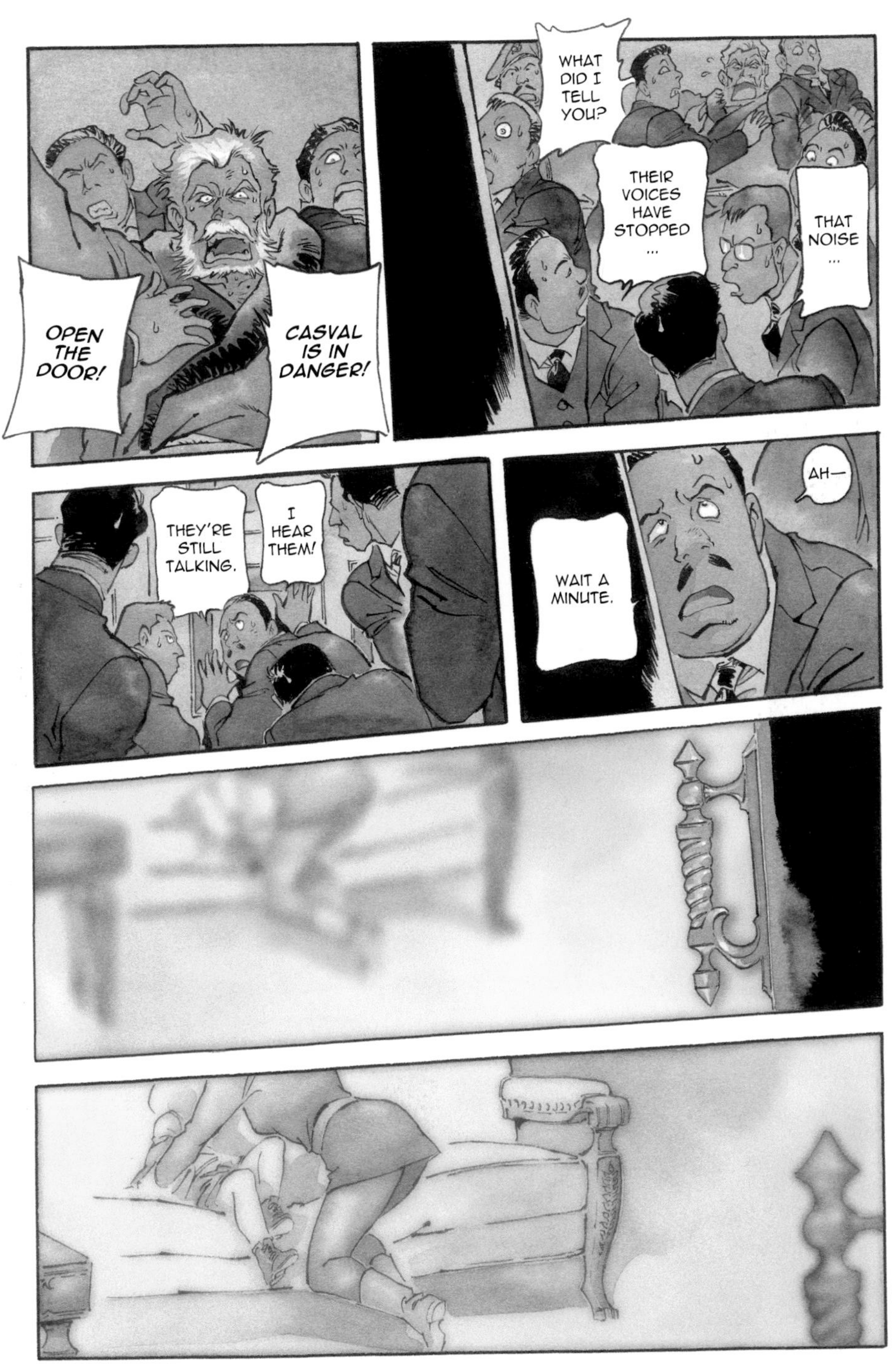
WHAT DID I TELL YOU?
THAT NOISE ...
THEIR VOICES HAVE STOPPED ...
CASVAL IS IN DANGER!
OPEN THE DOOR!
AH—
WAIT A MINUTE.
I HEAR THEM!
THEY'RE STILL TALKING.

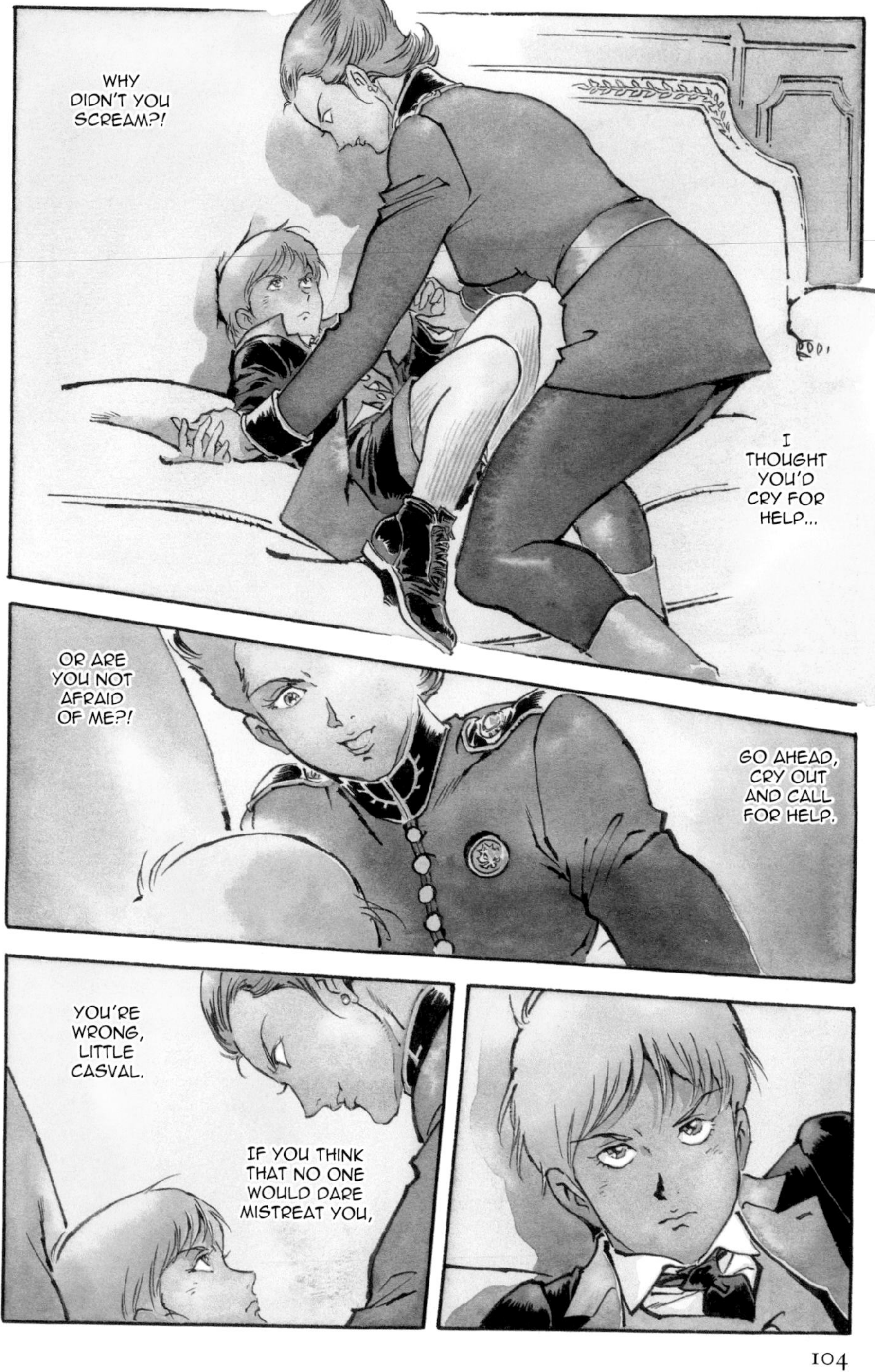
I THOUGHT YOU'D CRY FOR HELP...
WHY DIDN'T YOU SCREAM?!
GO AHEAD, CRY OUT AND CALL FOR HELP.
OR ARE YOU NOT AFRAID OF ME?!
YOU'RE WRONG, LITTLE CASVAL.
IF YOU THINK THAT NO ONE WOULD DARE MISTREAT YOU,

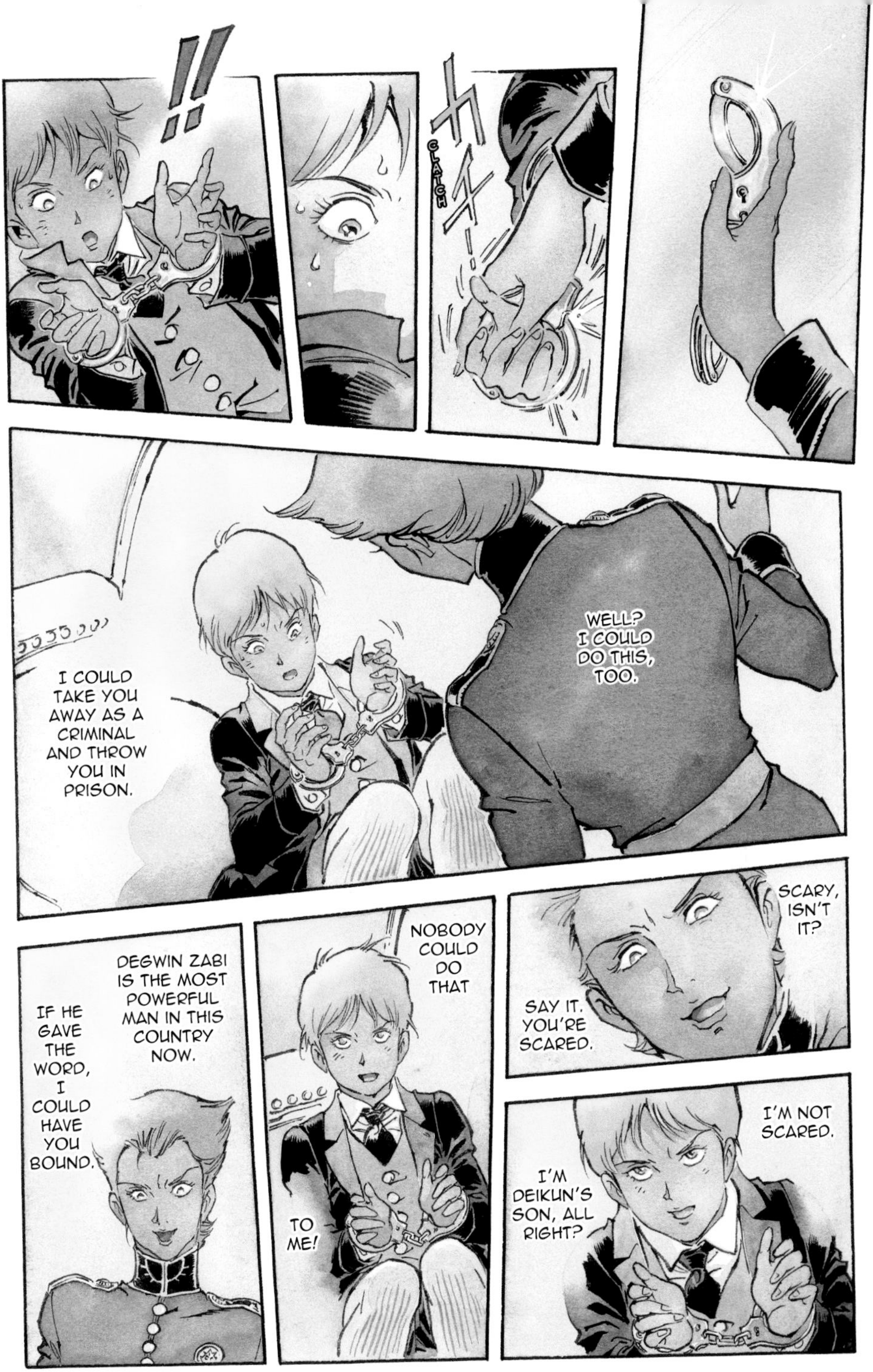
CLATCH
!!
WELL? I COULD DO THIS, TOO.
I COULD TAKE YOU AWAY AS A CRIMINAL AND THROW YOU IN PRISON.
SCARY, ISN'T IT?
SAY IT. YOU'RE SCARED.
I'M NOT SCARED.
I'M DEIKUN'S SON, ALL RIGHT?
NOBODY COULD DO THAT
TO ME!
DEGWIN ZABI IS THE MOST POWERFUL MAN IN THIS COUNTRY NOW.
IF HE GAVE THE WORD, I COULD HAVE YOU BOUND.

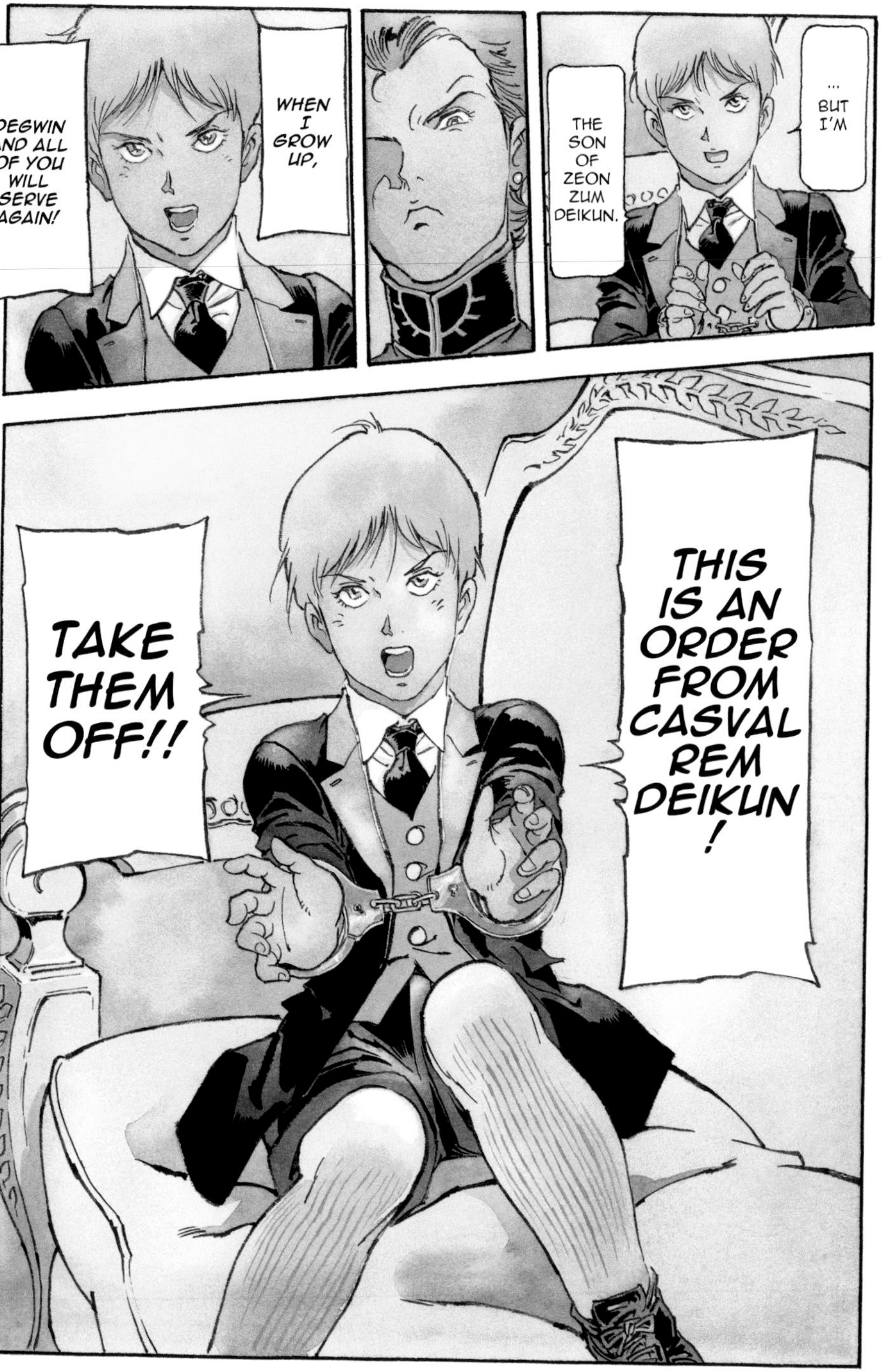
... BUT I'M
THE SON OF ZEON ZUM DEIKUN.
WHEN I GROW UP,
DEGWIN AND ALL OF YOU WILL SERVE AGAIN!
THIS IS AN ORDER FROM CASVAL REM DEIKUN!
TAKE THEM OFF!!

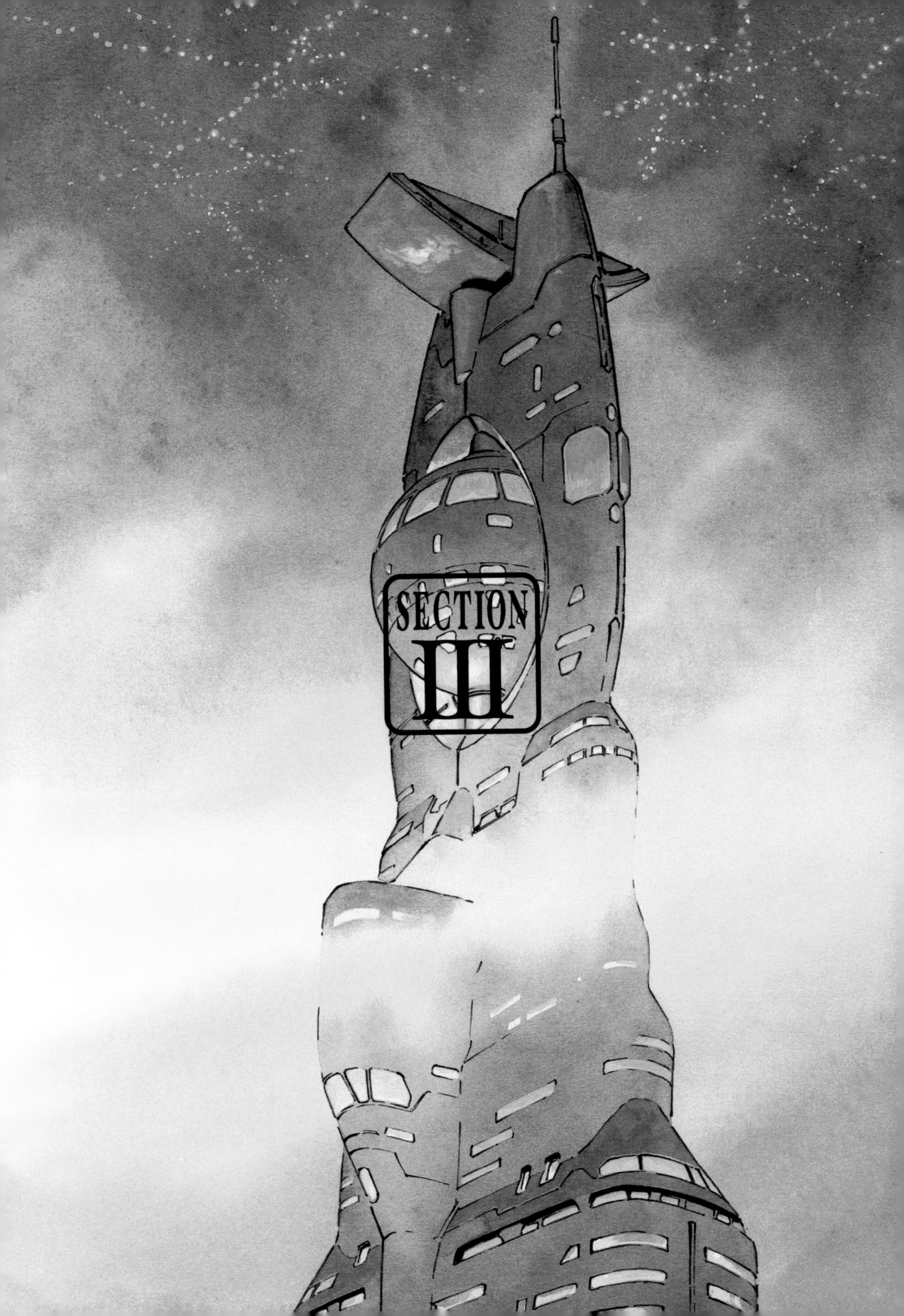
SECTION
III

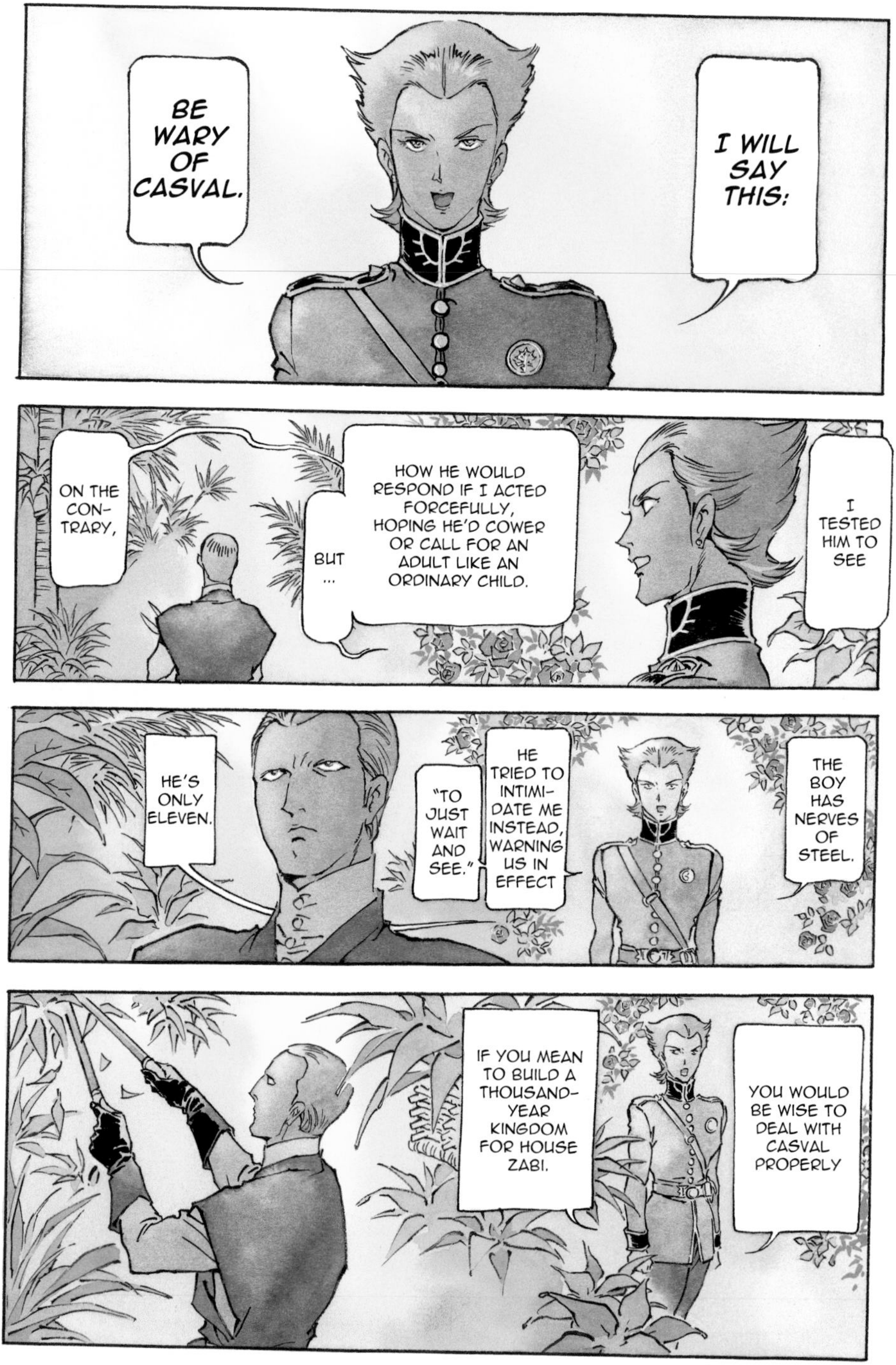
I WILL SAY THIS:
BE WARY OF CASVAL.
I TESTED HIM TO SEE
HOW HE WOULD RESPOND IF I ACTED FORCEFULLY, HOPING HE'D COWER OR CALL FOR AN ADULT LIKE AN ORDINARY CHILD.
BUT ...
ON THE CONTRARY,
THE BOY HAS NERVES OF STEEL.
HE TRIED TO INTIMIDATE ME INSTEAD, WARNING US IN EFFECT
"TO JUST WAIT AND SEE."
HE'S ONLY ELEVEN.
YOU WOULD BE WISE TO DEAL WITH CASVAL PROPERLY
IF YOU MEAN TO BUILD A THOUSAND-YEAR KINGDOM FOR HOUSE ZABI.

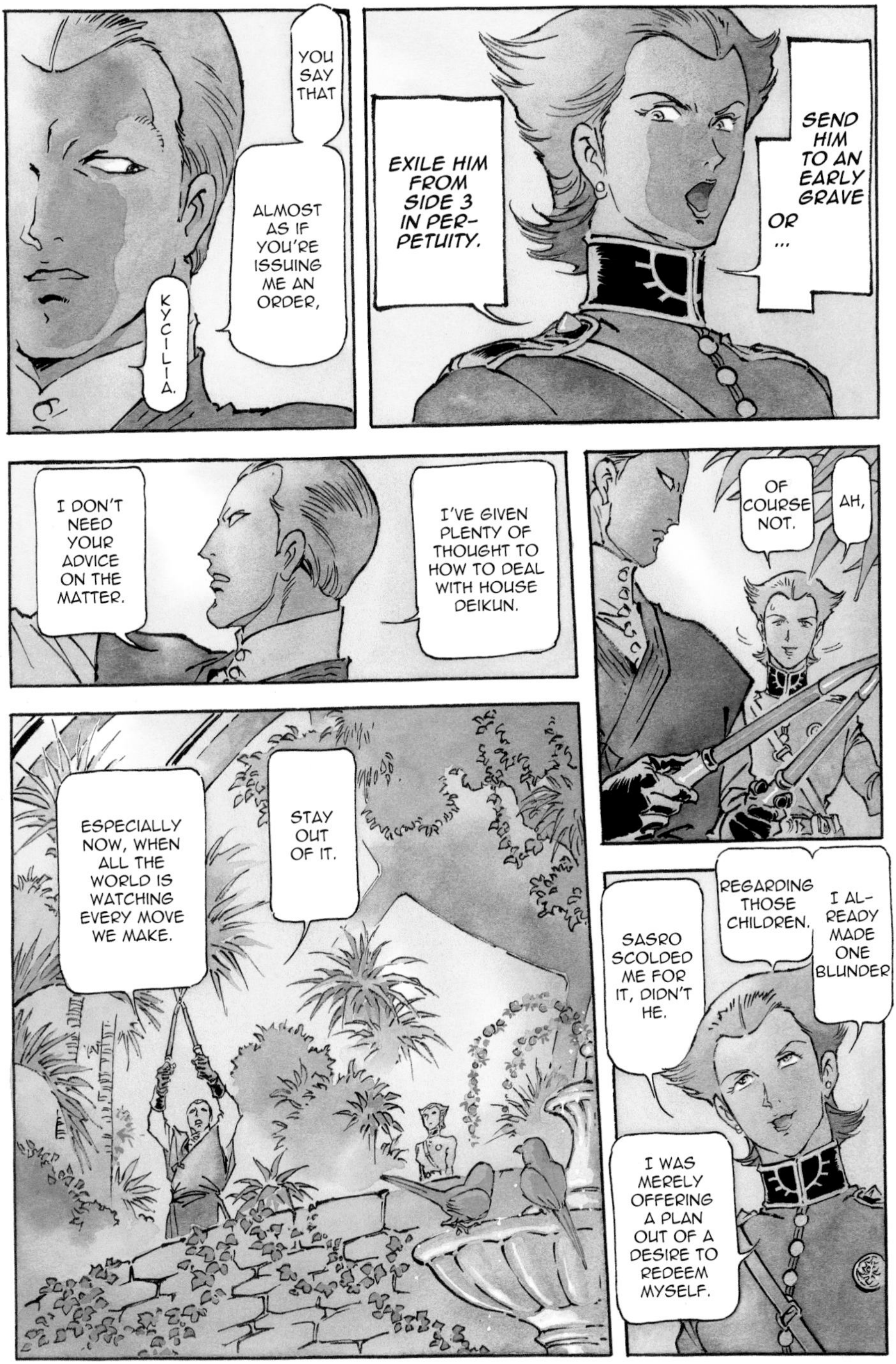
SEND HIM TO AN EARLY GRAVE OR ...
EXILE HIM FROM SIDE 3 IN PERPETUITY.
YOU SAY THAT
ALMOST AS IF YOU'RE ISSUING ME AN ORDER,
KYCILIA.
AH,
OF COURSE NOT.
I ALREADY MADE ONE BLUNDER
REGARDING THOSE CHILDREN.
SASRO SCOLDED ME FOR IT, DIDN'T HE.
I WAS MERELY OFFERING A PLAN OUT OF A DESIRE TO REDEEM MYSELF.
I'VE GIVEN PLENTY OF THOUGHT TO HOW TO DEAL WITH HOUSE DEIKUN.
I DON'T NEED YOUR ADVICE ON THE MATTER.
STAY OUT OF IT.
ESPECIALLY NOW, WHEN ALL THE WORLD IS WATCHING EVERY MOVE WE MAKE.

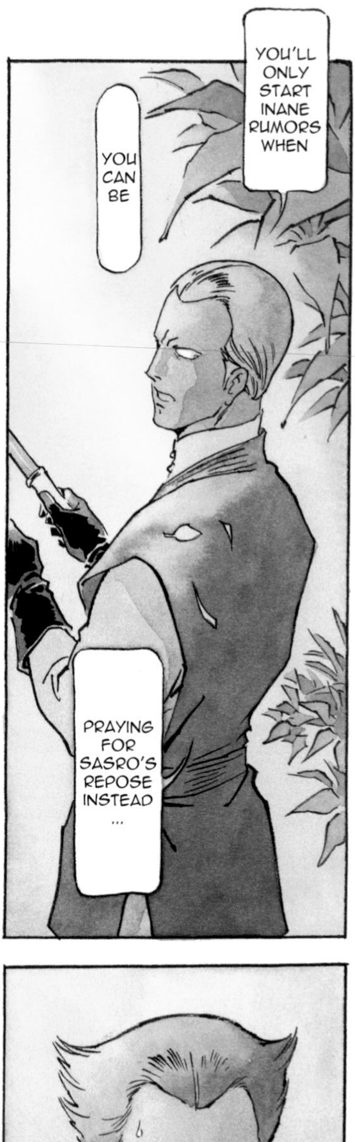
YOU'LL ONLY START INANE RUMORS WHEN
YOU CAN BE
PRAYING FOR SASRO'S REPOSE INSTEAD ...
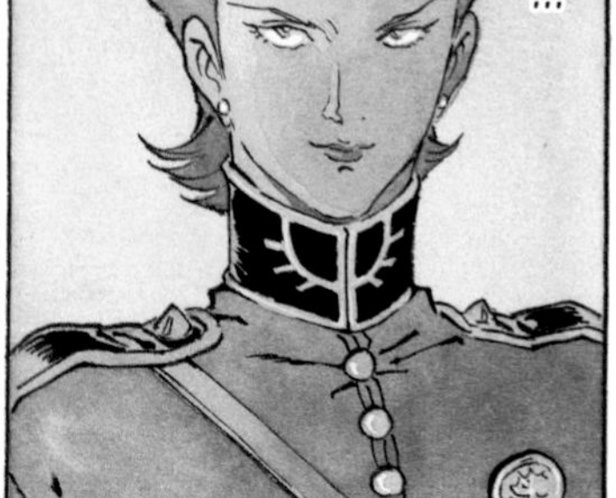
...
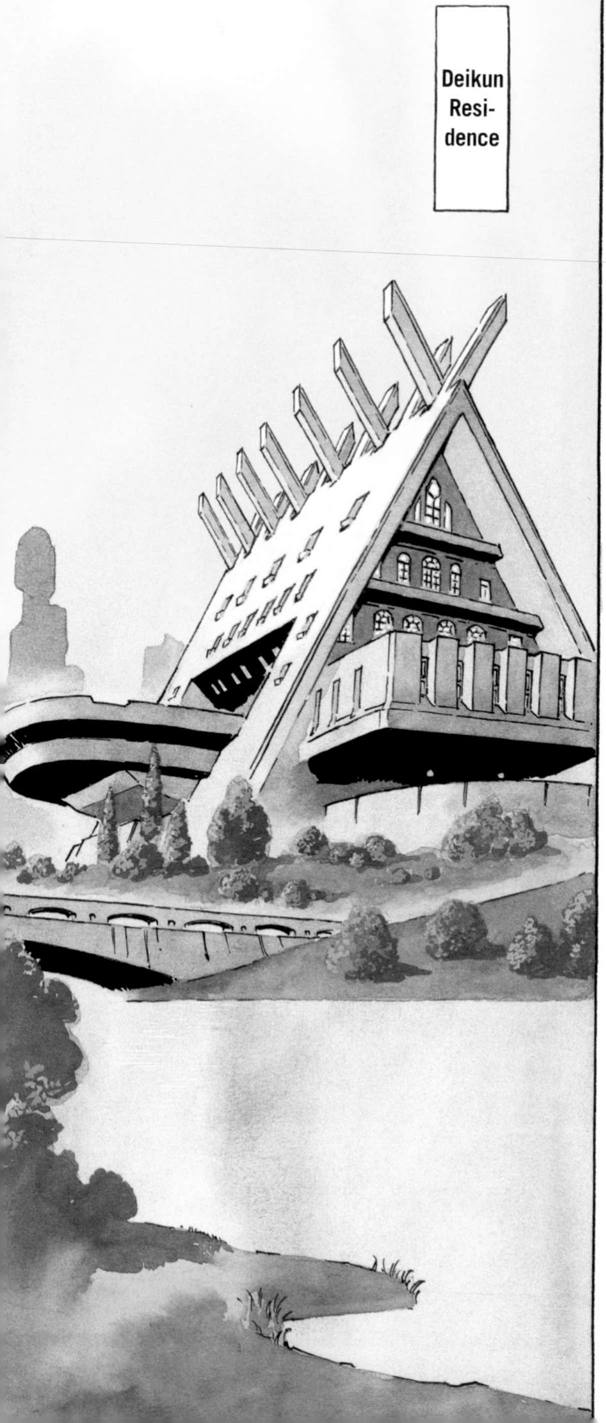
Deikun Resi-dence

WHUPP
WHUPP
WHUPP
WHUPP
WHUPP
WHUPP

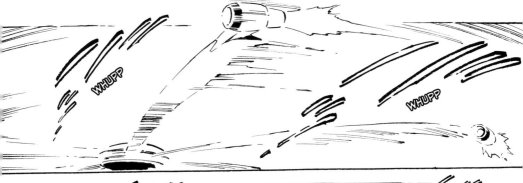

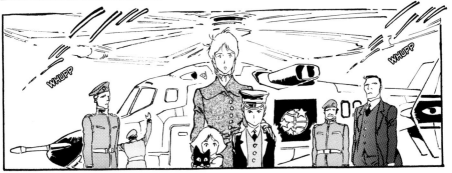

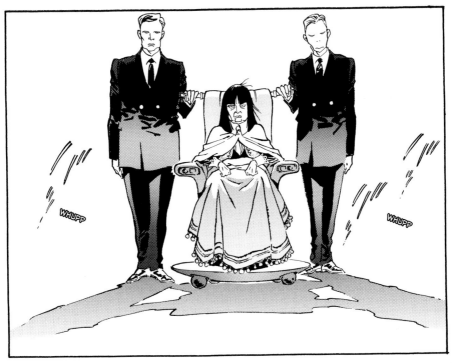

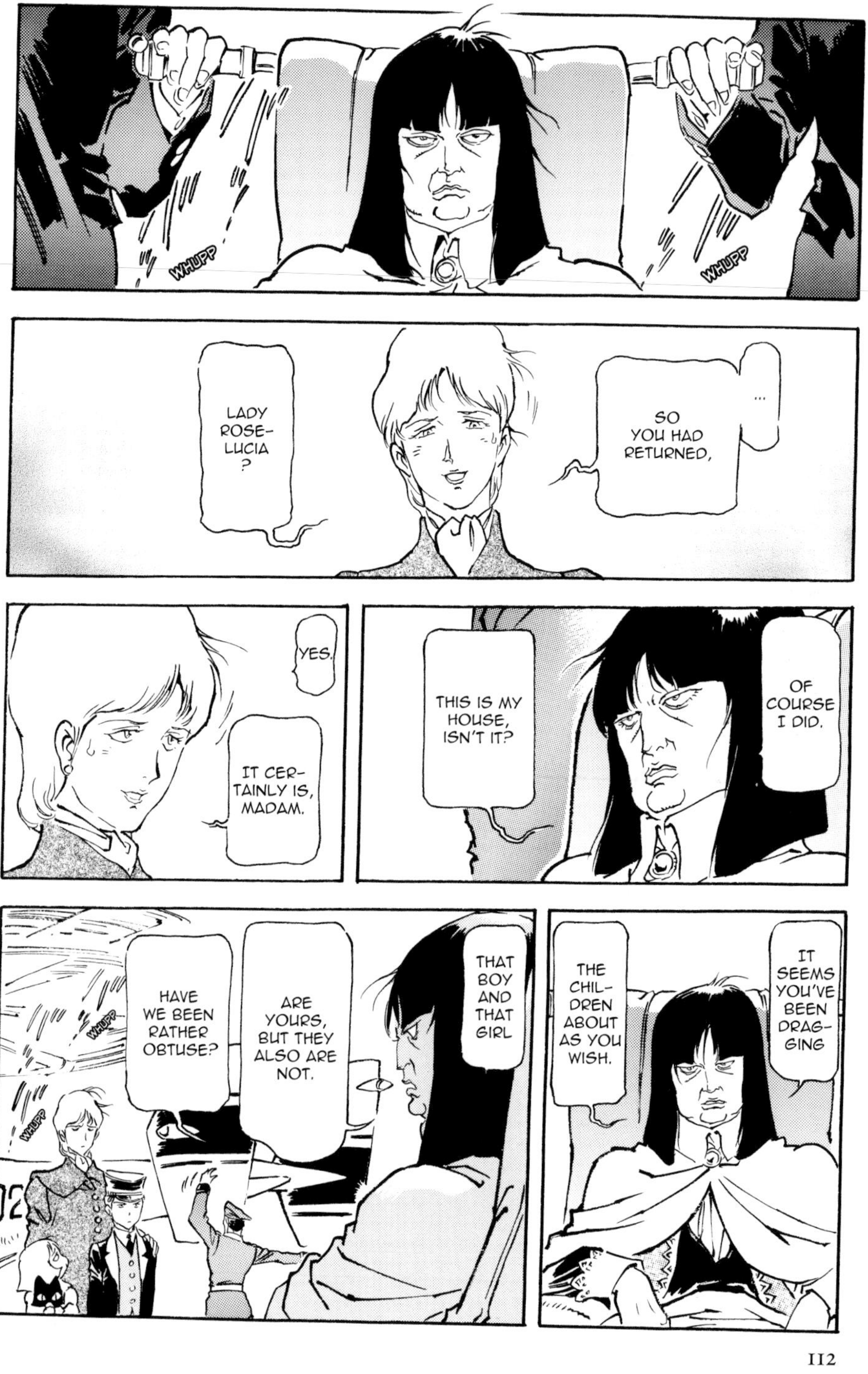
WHUPP
WHUPP
...
SO YOU HAD RETURNED,
LADY ROSE-LUCIA?
OF COURSE I DID.
THIS IS MY HOUSE, ISN'T IT?
YES.
IT CERTAINLY IS, MADAM.
IT SEEMS YOU'VE BEEN DRAGGING
THE CHILDREN ABOUT AS YOU WISH.
THAT BOY AND THAT GIRL
ARE YOURS, BUT THEY ALSO ARE NOT.
HAVE WE BEEN RATHER OBTUSE?
WHUPP
WHUPP

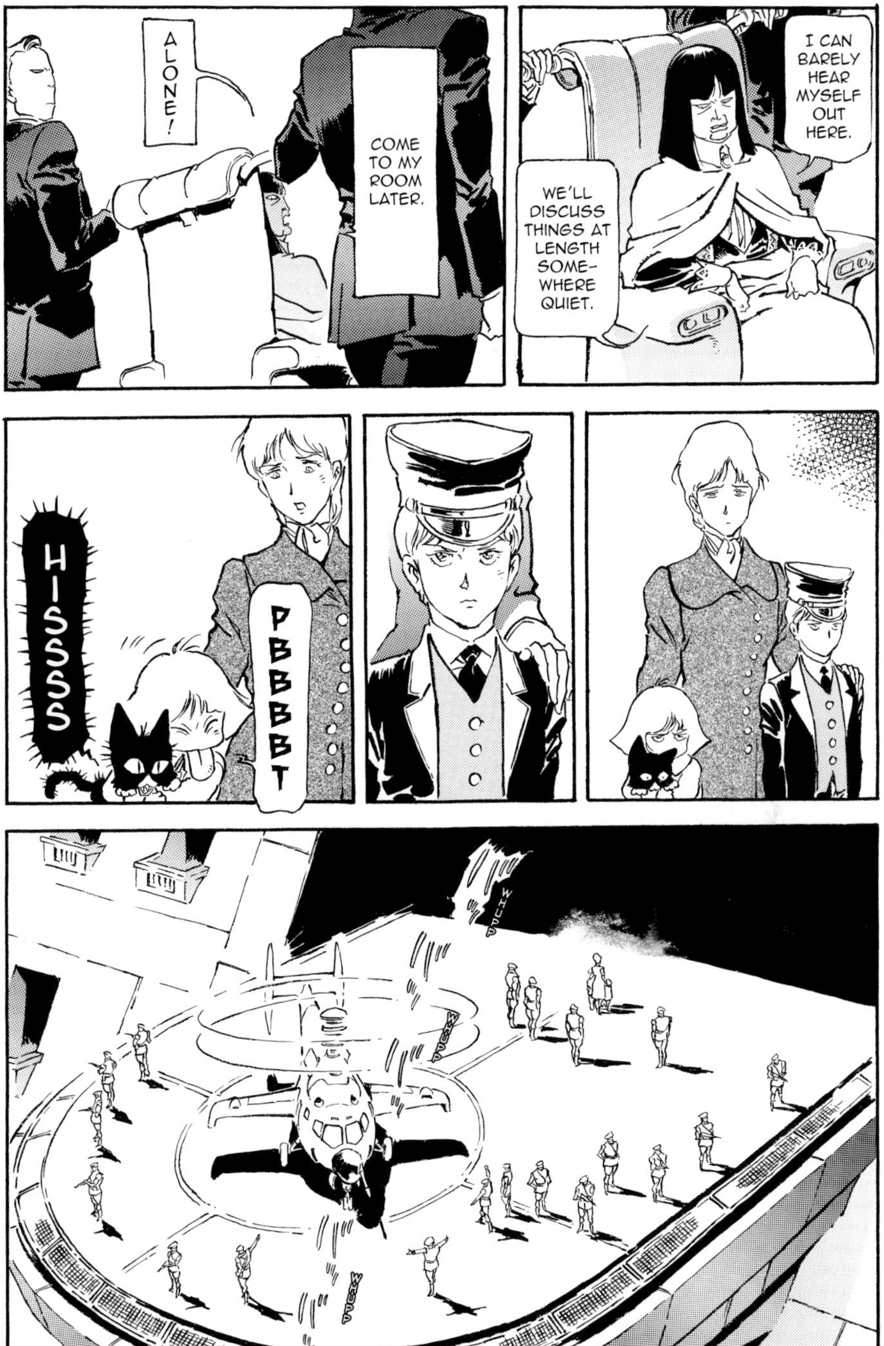
I CAN BARELY HEAR MYSELF OUT HERE.
WE'LL DISCUSS THINGS AT LENGTH SOME-WHERE QUIET.
COME TO MY ROOM LATER.
ALONE!
PBBBBT
HISSSS
WHUPP
WHUPP
WHUPP

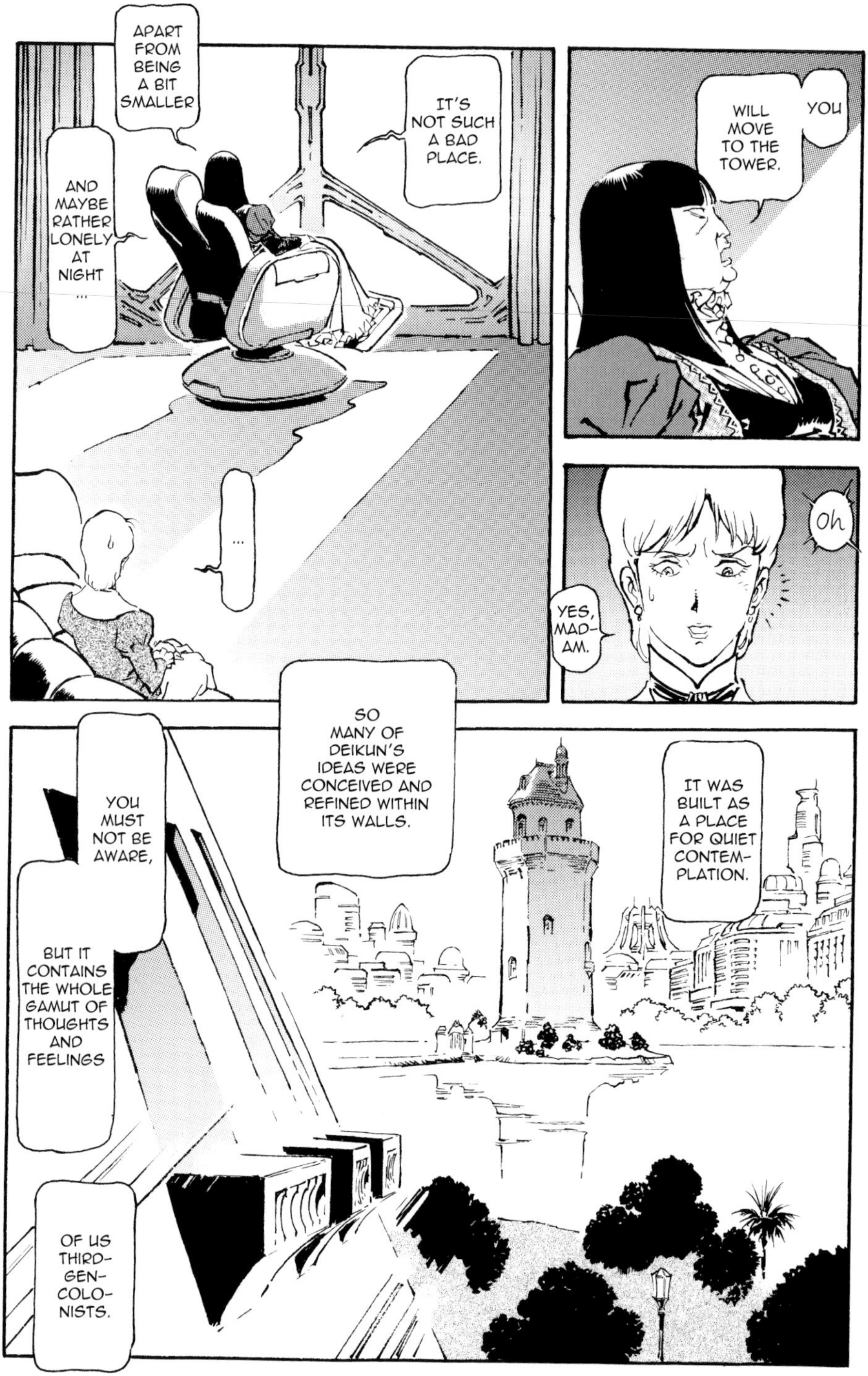
YOU WILL MOVE TO THE TOWER.
APART FROM BEING A BIT SMALLER
IT'S NOT SUCH A BAD PLACE.
AND MAYBE RATHER LONELY AT NIGHT ...
Oh
YES, MAD-AM.
...
IT WAS BUILT AS A PLACE FOR QUIET CONTEM-PLATION.
SO MANY OF DEIKUN'S IDEAS WERE CONCEIVED AND REFINED WITHIN ITS WALLS.
YOU MUST NOT BE AWARE,
BUT IT CONTAINS THE WHOLE GAMUT OF THOUGHTS AND FEELINGS
OF US THIRD-GEN-COLO-NISTS.

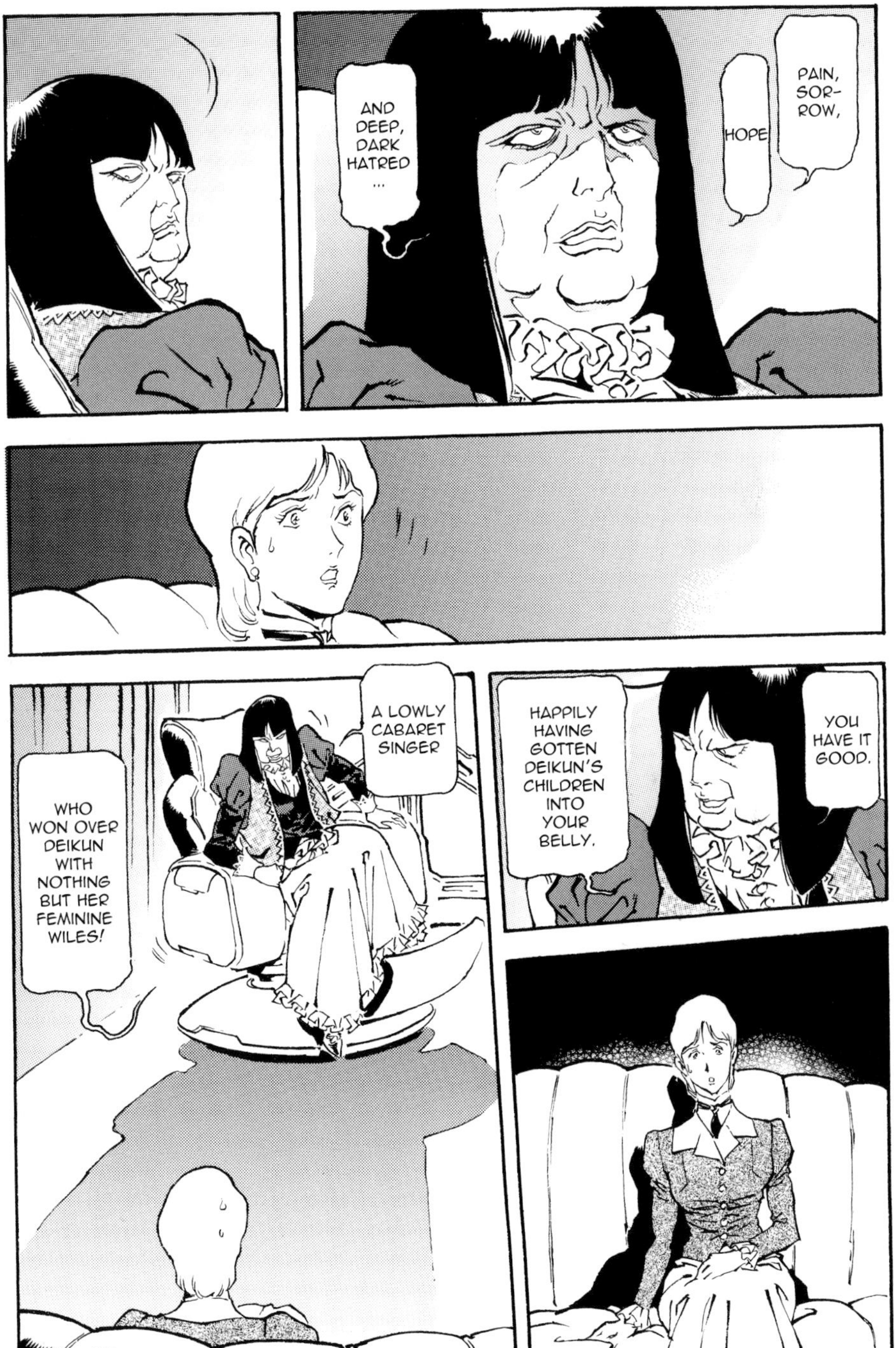
PAIN, SORROW,
HOPE
AND DEEP, DARK HATRED ...
YOU HAVE IT GOOD.
HAPPILY HAVING GOTTEN DEIKUN'S CHILDREN INTO YOUR BELLY.
A LOWLY CABARET SINGER
WHO WON OVER DEIKUN WITH NOTHING BUT HER FEMININE WILES!

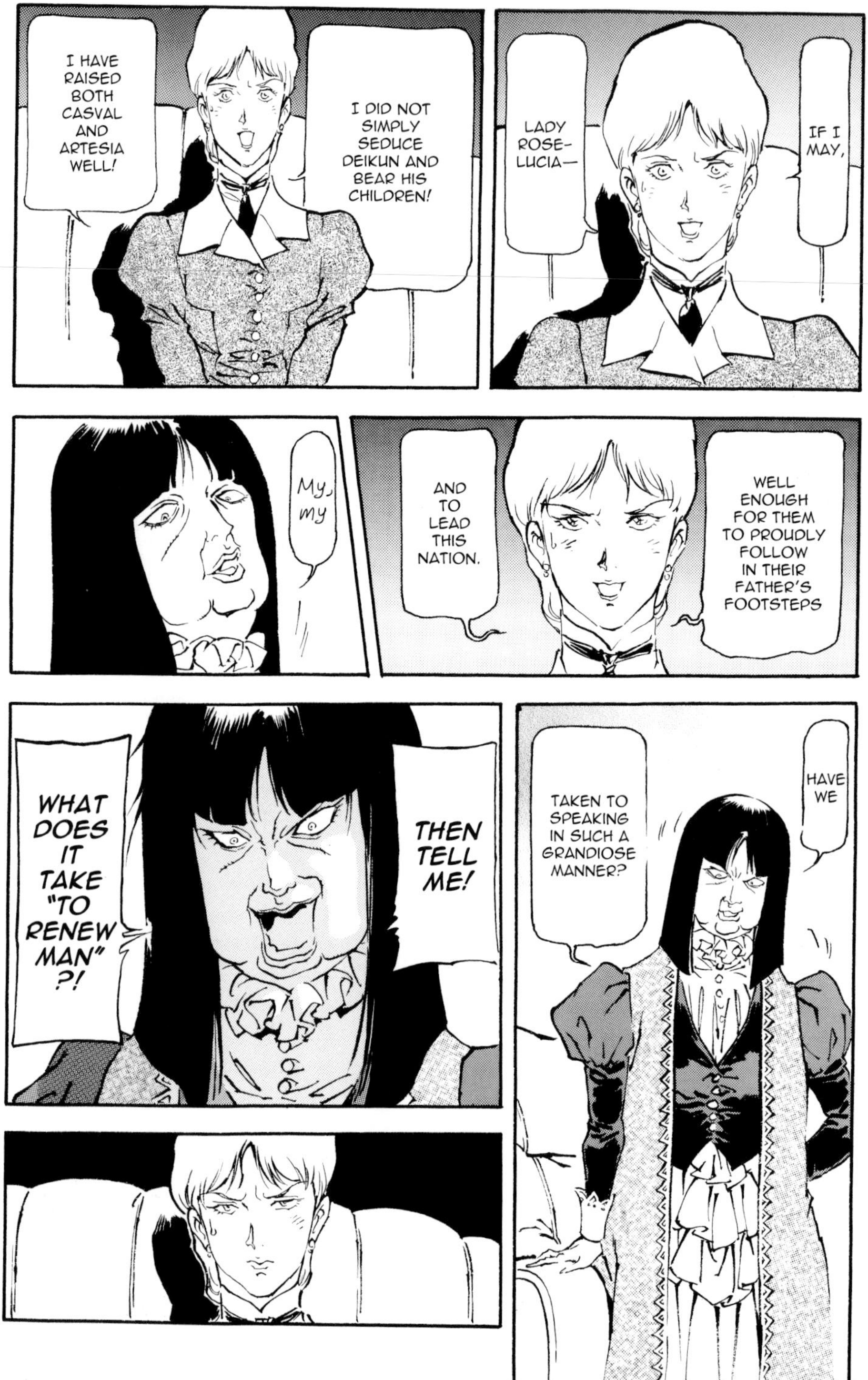
IF I MAY,
LADY ROSE-LUCIA—
I DID NOT SIMPLY SEDUCE DEIKUN AND BEAR HIS CHILDREN!
I HAVE RAISED BOTH CASVAL AND ARTESIA WELL!
WELL ENOUGH FOR THEM TO PROUDLY FOLLOW IN THEIR FATHER'S FOOTSTEPS
AND TO LEAD THIS NATION.
My, my
HAVE WE
TAKEN TO SPEAKING IN SUCH A GRANDIOSE MANNER?
THEN TELL ME!
WHAT DOES IT TAKE "TO RENEW MAN"?!

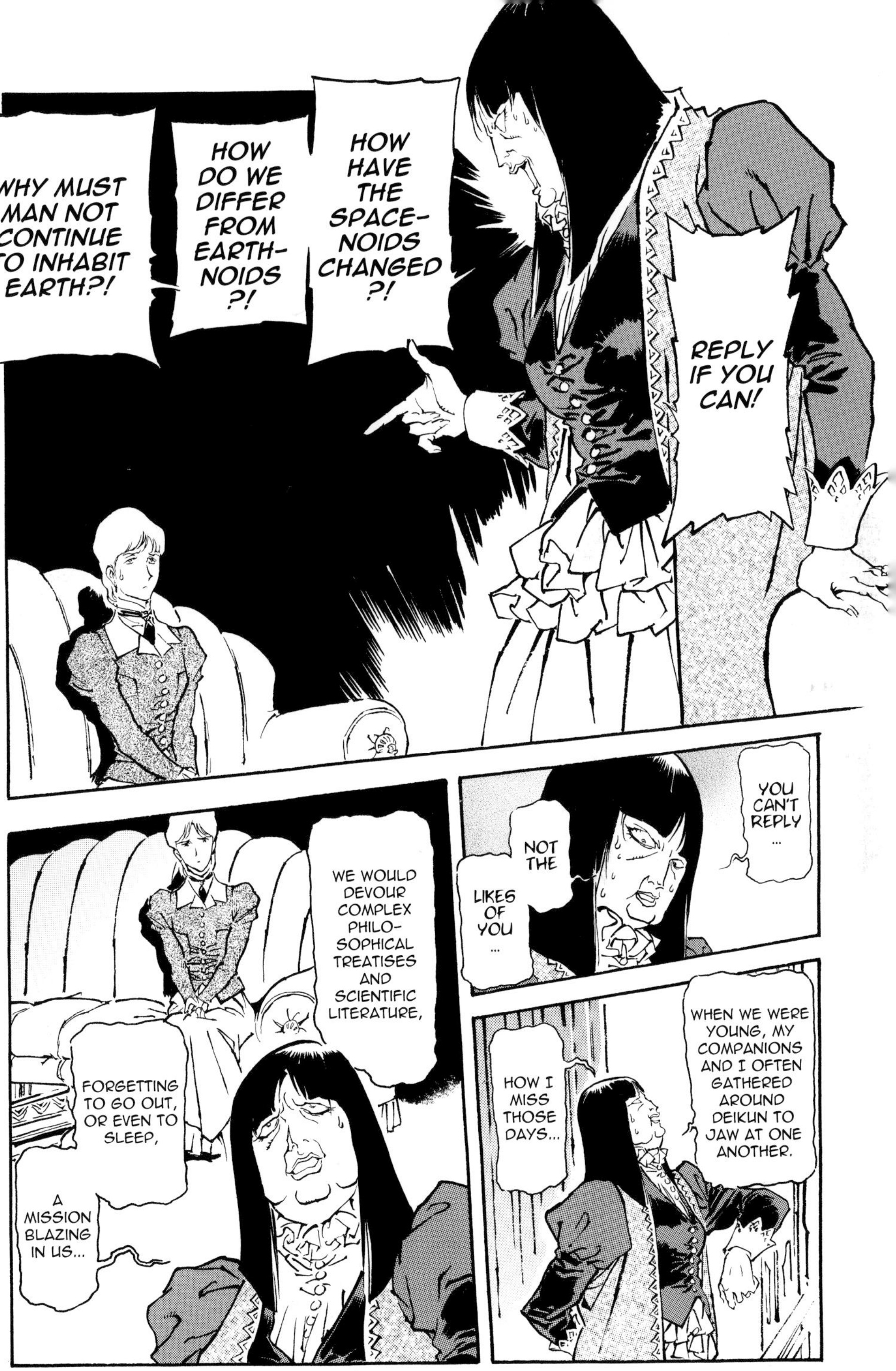
HOW HAVE THE SPACE-NOIDS CHANGED?!
HOW DO WE DIFFER FROM EARTH-NOIDS?!
WHY MUST MAN NOT CONTINUE TO INHABIT EARTH?!
REPLY IF YOU CAN!
YOU CAN'T REPLY...
NOT THE LIKES OF YOU...
WHEN WE WERE YOUNG, MY COMPANIONS AND I OFTEN GATHERED AROUND DEIKUN TO JAW AT ONE ANOTHER.
HOW I MISS THOSE DAYS...
WE WOULD DEVOUR COMPLEX PHILO-SOPHICAL TREATISES AND SCIENTIFIC LITERATURE,
FORGETTING TO GO OUT, OR EVEN TO SLEEP,
A MISSION BLAZING IN US...

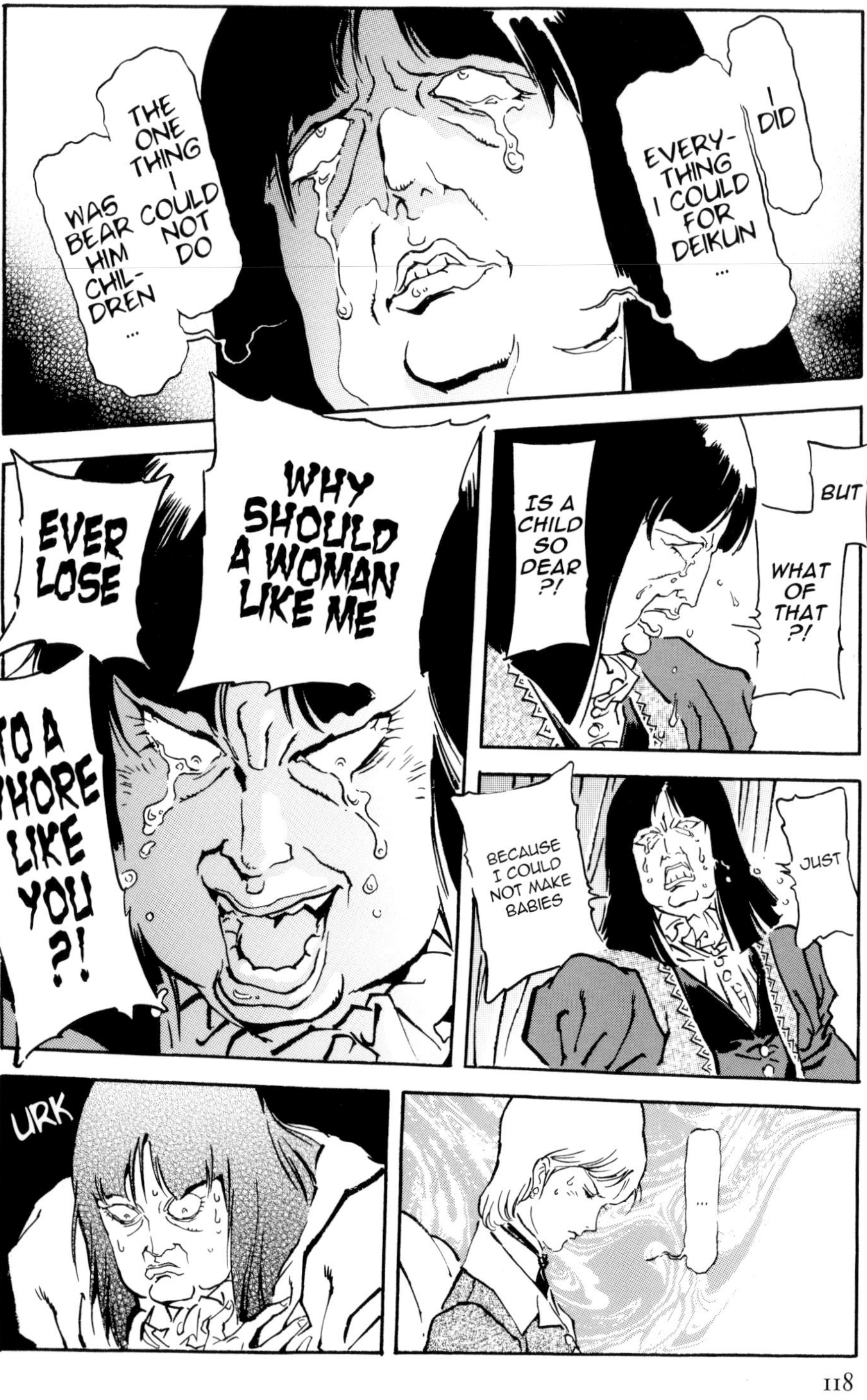
I DID EVERY-THING I COULD FOR DEIKUN ...
THE ONE THING I COULD NOT DO WAS BEAR HIM CHIL-DREN ...
BUT WHAT OF THAT ?!
IS A CHILD SO DEAR ?!
JUST
BECAUSE I COULD NOT MAKE BABIES
WHY SHOULD A WOMAN LIKE ME
EVER LOSE
TO A WHORE LIKE YOU ?!
...
URK

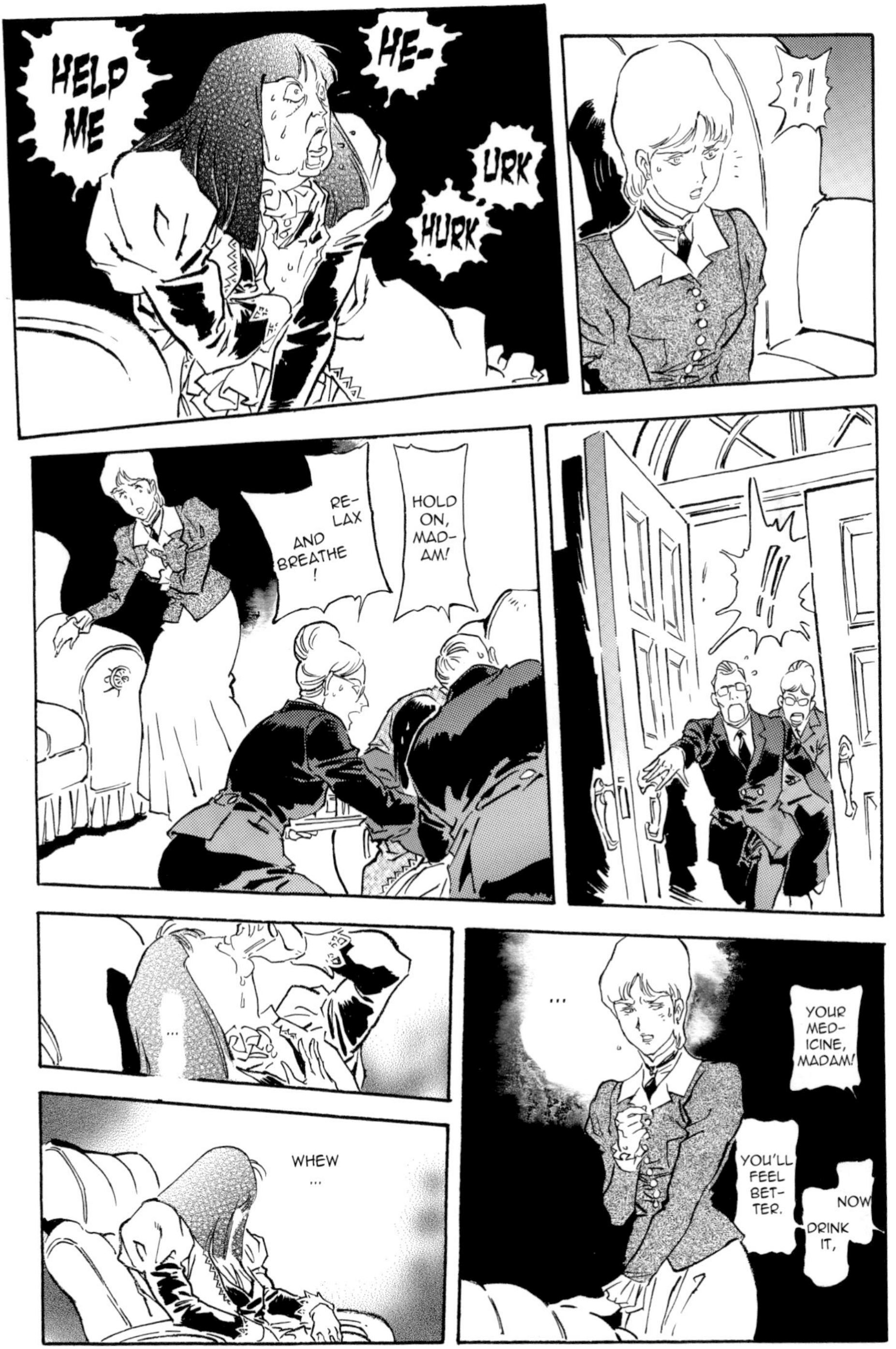
?!
HE-
URK
HURK
HELP ME
!!
HOLD ON, MADAM!
RELAX AND BREATHE!
YOUR MEDICINE, MADAM!
...
NOW DRINK IT,
YOU'LL FEEL BETTER.
...
WHEW ...

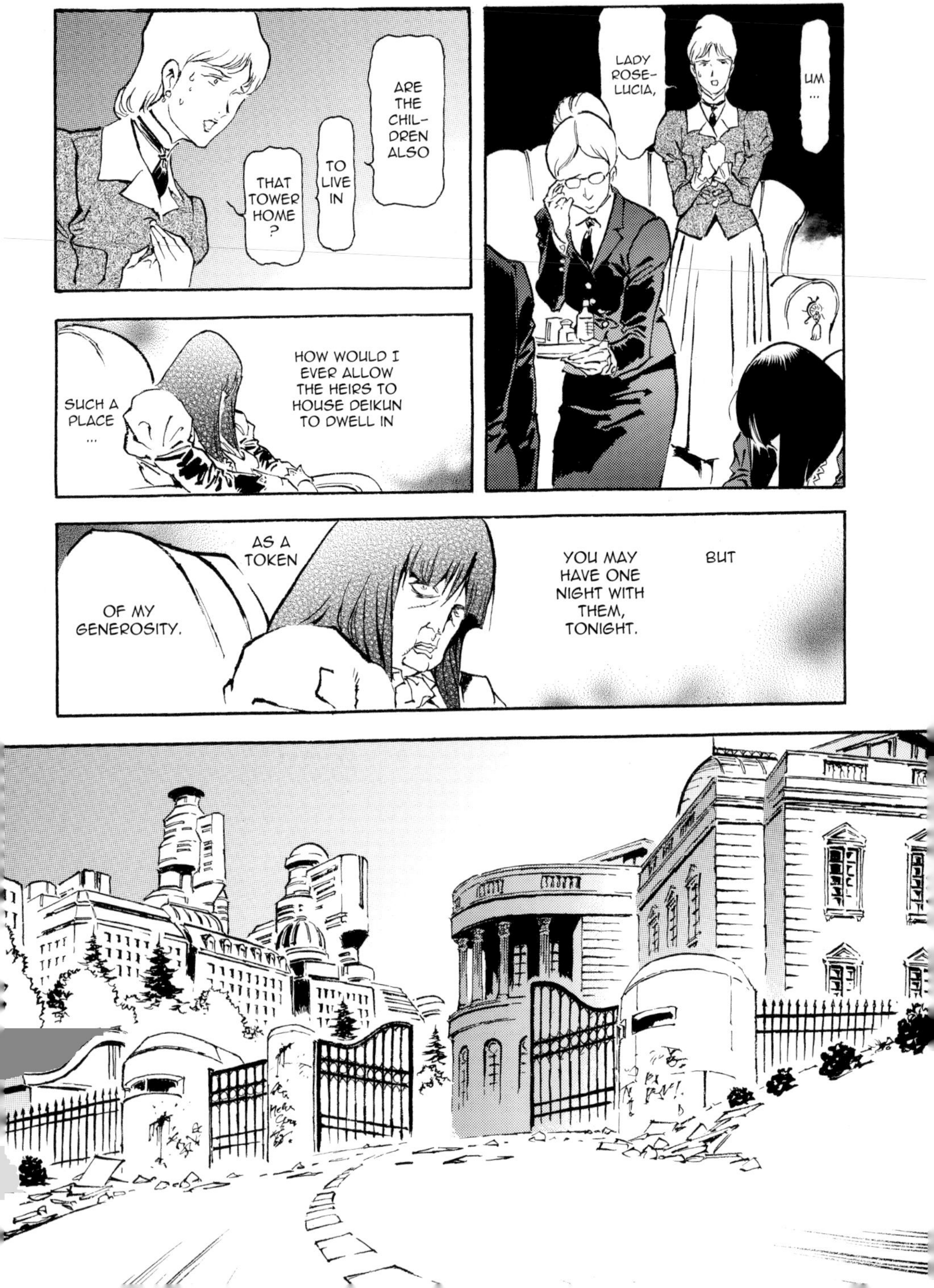
UM ...
LADY ROSE-LUCIA,
ARE THE CHIL-DREN ALSO
TO LIVE IN
THAT TOWER HOME ?
HOW WOULD I EVER ALLOW THE HEIRS TO HOUSE DEIKUN TO DWELL IN
SUCH A PLACE ...
BUT
YOU MAY HAVE ONE NIGHT WITH THEM, TONIGHT.
AS A TOKEN
OF MY GENEROSITY.

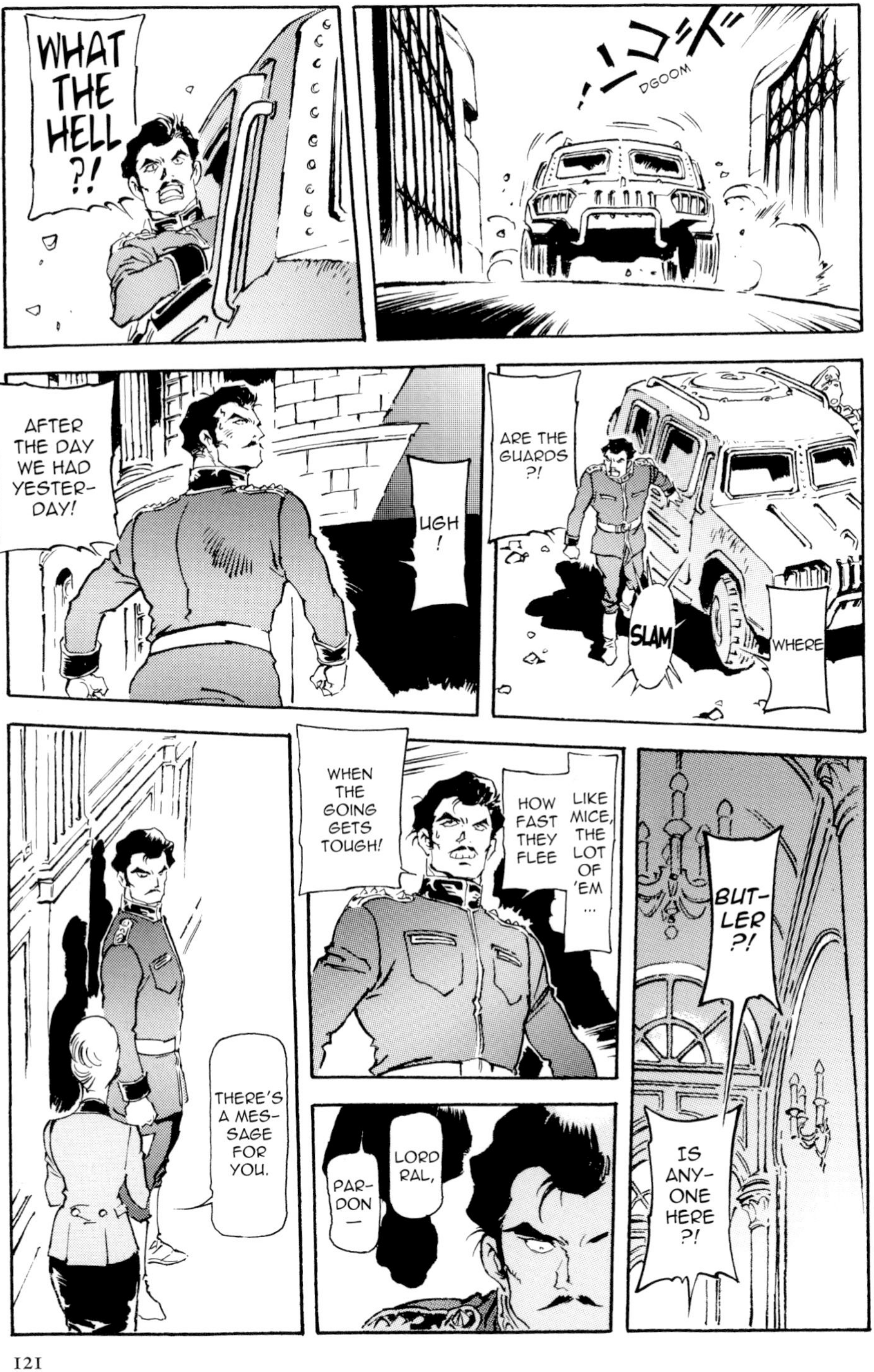
DGOOM
WHAT THE HELL ?!
WHERE
SLAM
ARE THE GUARDS ?!
UGH!
AFTER THE DAY WE HAD YESTER-DAY!
BUT-LER ?!
IS ANY-ONE HERE ?!
LIKE MICE, THE LOT OF 'EM ...
HOW FAST THEY FLEE
WHEN THE GOING GETS TOUGH!
LORD RAL,
PAR-DON —
THERE'S A MES-SAGE FOR YOU.

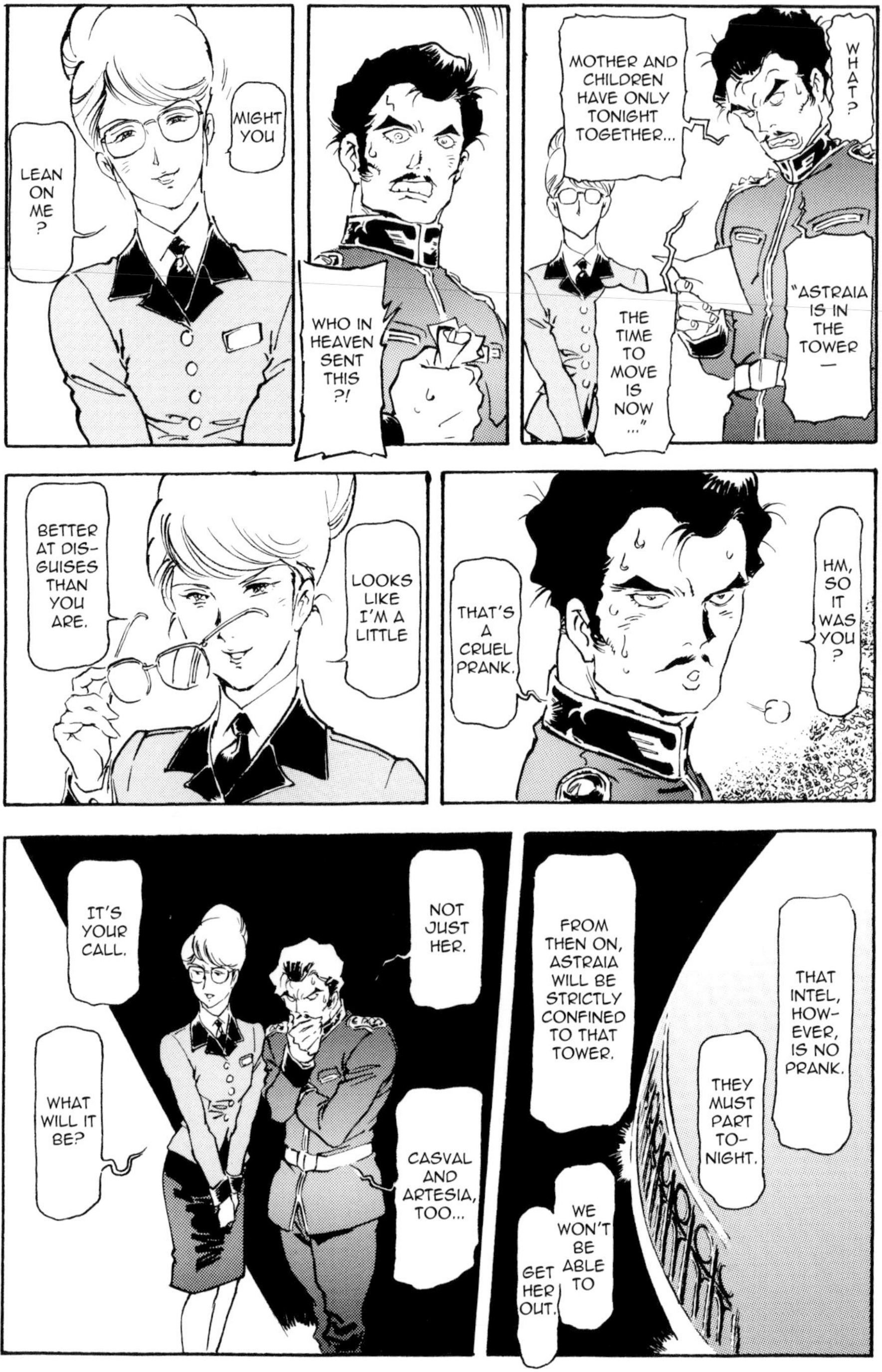
WHAT?
MOTHER AND CHILDREN HAVE ONLY TONIGHT TOGETHER...
"ASTRAIA IS IN THE TOWER—
THE TIME TO MOVE IS NOW..."
WHO IN HEAVEN SENT THIS?!
MIGHT YOU
LEAN ON ME?
HM, SO IT WAS YOU?
THAT'S A CRUEL PRANK.
LOOKS LIKE I'M A LITTLE
BETTER AT DISGUISES THAN YOU ARE.
THAT INTEL, HOWEVER, IS NO PRANK.
THEY MUST PART TO-NIGHT.
FROM THEN ON, ASTRAIA WILL BE STRICTLY CONFINED TO THAT TOWER.
WE WON'T BE ABLE TO
GET HER OUT.
NOT JUST HER.
CASVAL AND ARTESIA, TOO...
IT'S YOUR CALL.
WHAT WILL IT BE?

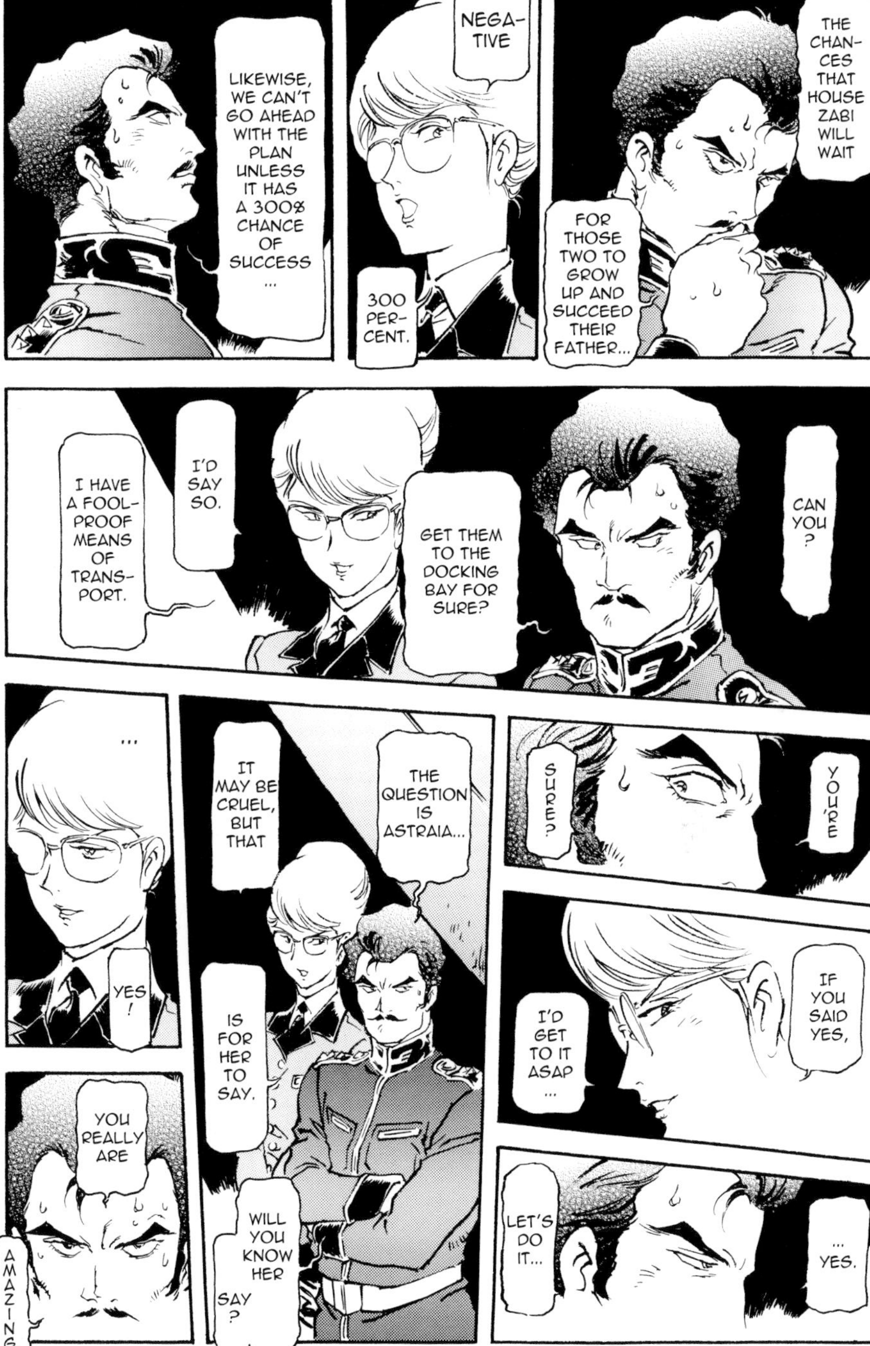
THE CHANCES THAT HOUSE ZABI WILL WAIT
FOR THOSE TWO TO GROW UP AND SUCCEED THEIR FATHER...
NEGATIVE
300 PERCENT.
LIKEWISE, WE CAN'T GO AHEAD WITH THE PLAN UNLESS IT HAS A 300% CHANCE OF SUCCESS ...
CAN YOU ?
GET THEM TO THE DOCKING BAY FOR SURE?
I'D SAY SO.
I HAVE A FOOLPROOF MEANS OF TRANSPORT.
YOU'RE SURE?
IF YOU SAID YES,
I'D GET TO IT ASAP ...
... YES.
LET'S DO IT...
THE QUESTION IS ASTRAIA...
IT MAY BE CRUEL, BUT THAT
IS FOR HER TO SAY.
WILL YOU KNOW HER SAY ?
...
YES!
YOU REALLY ARE
AMAZING.

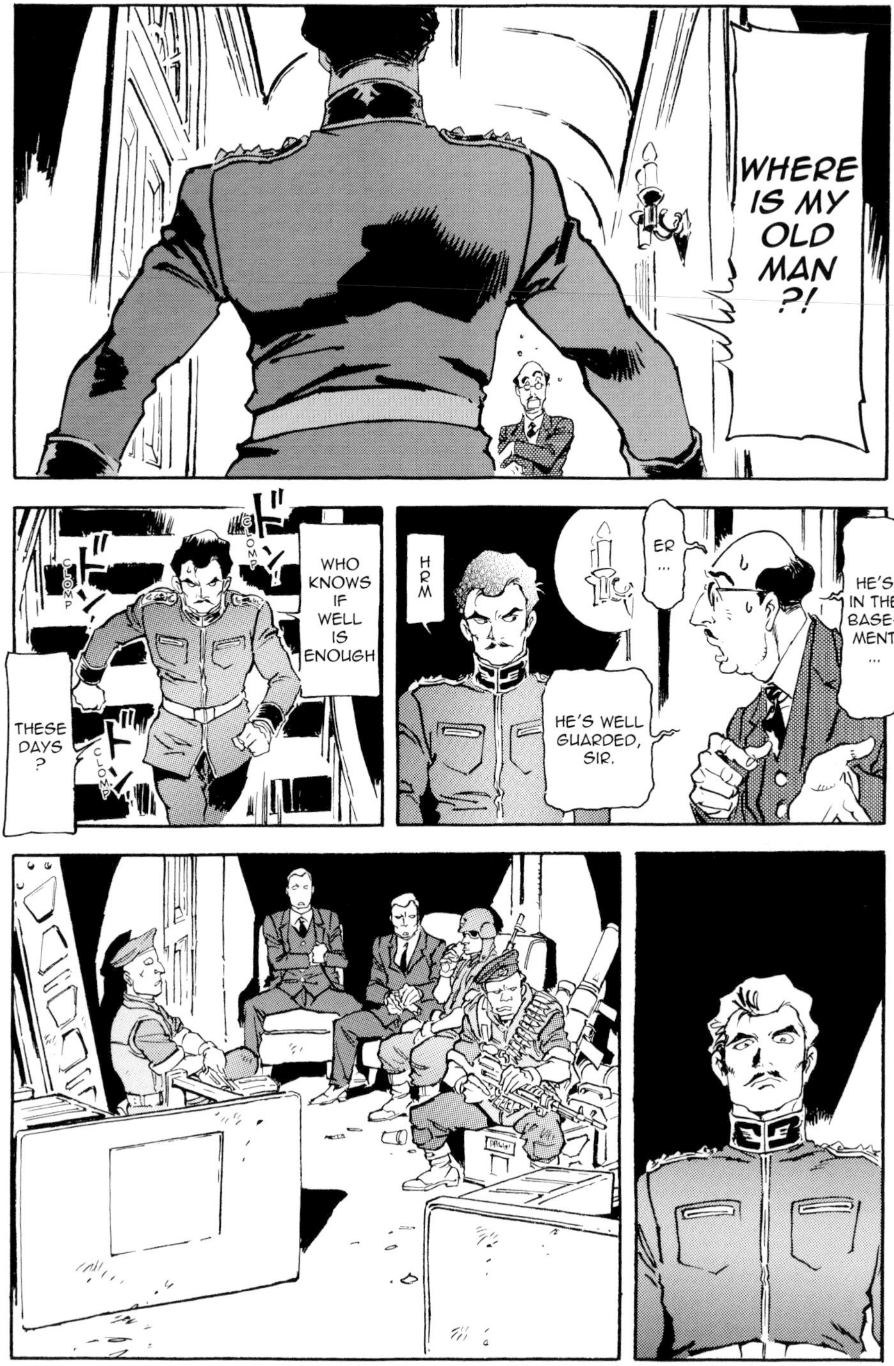
WHERE IS MY OLD MAN ?!
ER ...
HE'S IN THE BASEMENT ...
HRM
HE'S WELL GUARDED, SIR.
CLOMP
CLOMP
WHO KNOWS IF WELL IS ENOUGH
THESE DAYS ?
CLOMP

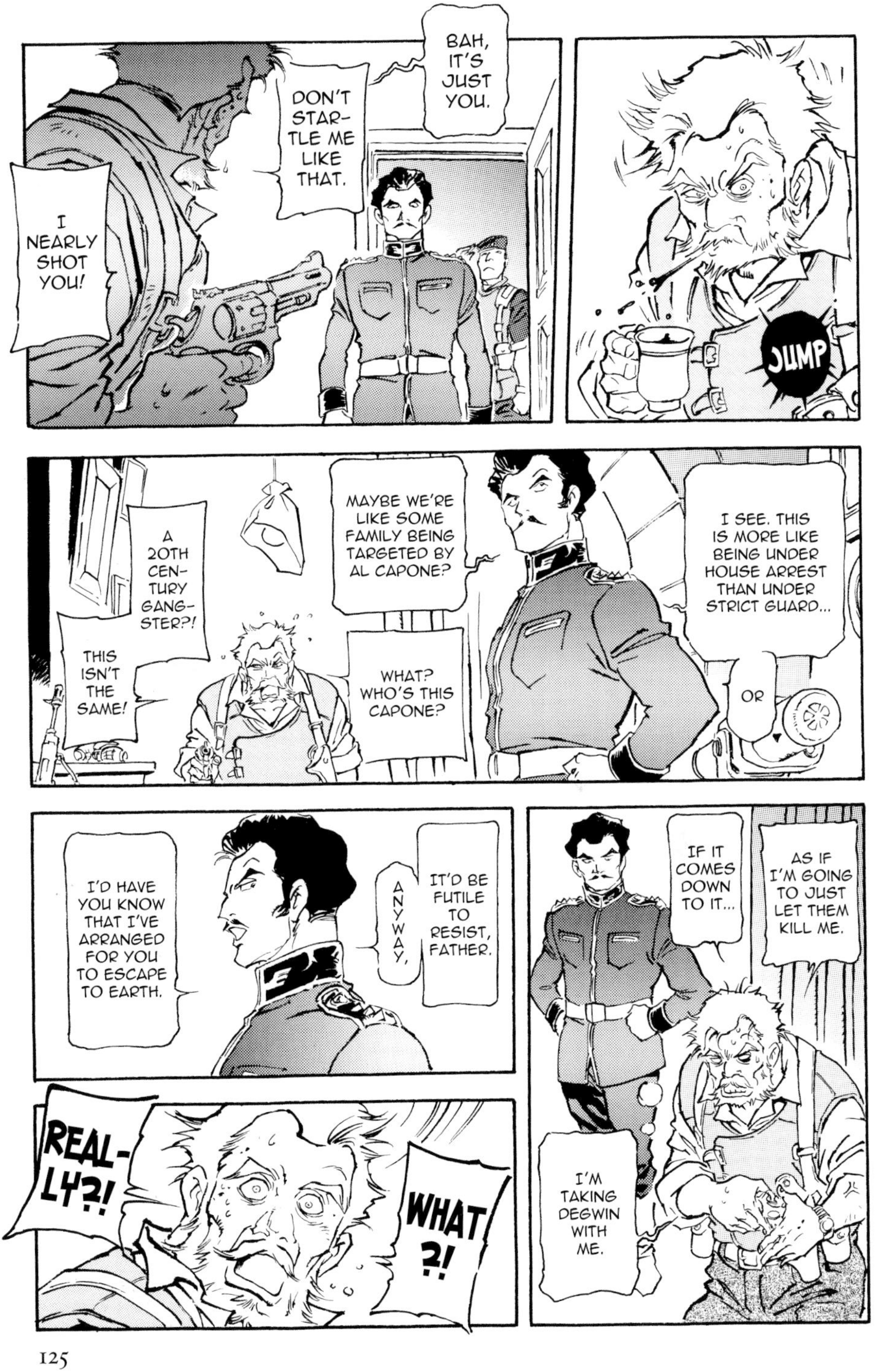
JUMP
BAH, IT'S JUST YOU.
DON'T STARTLE ME LIKE THAT.
I NEARLY SHOT YOU!
I SEE. THIS IS MORE LIKE BEING UNDER HOUSE ARREST THAN UNDER STRICT GUARD...
OR
MAYBE WE'RE LIKE SOME FAMILY BEING TARGETED BY AL CAPONE?
WHAT? WHO'S THIS CAPONE?
A 20TH CENTURY GANGSTER?!
THIS ISN'T THE SAME!
AS IF I'M GOING TO JUST LET THEM KILL ME.
IF IT COMES DOWN TO IT...
I'M TAKING DEGWIN WITH ME.
IT'D BE FUTILE TO RESIST, FATHER.
ANYWAY,
I'D HAVE YOU KNOW THAT I'VE ARRANGED FOR YOU TO ESCAPE TO EARTH.
WHAT?!
REALLY?!

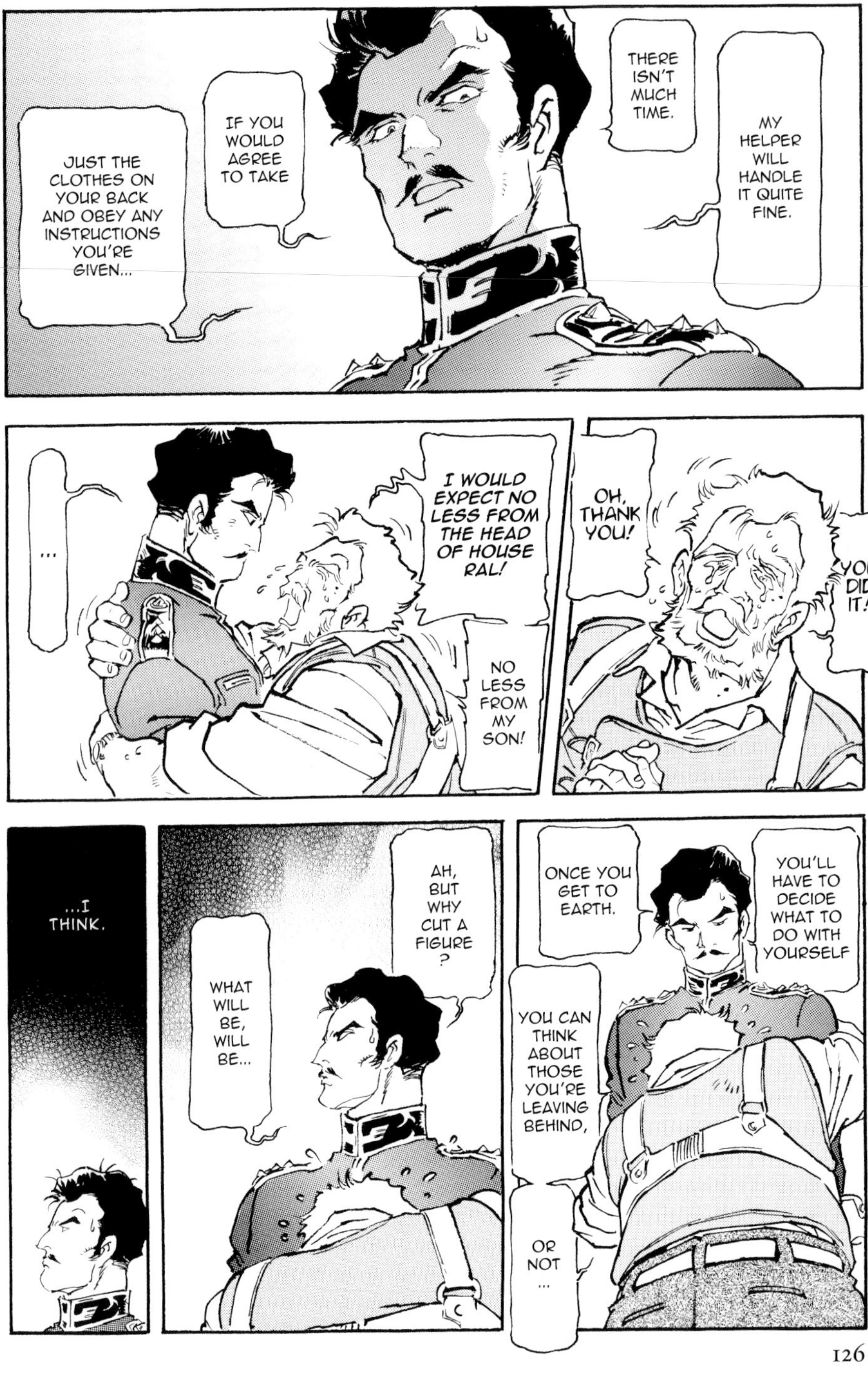
THERE ISN'T MUCH TIME.
MY HELPER WILL HANDLE IT QUITE FINE.
IF YOU WOULD AGREE TO TAKE
JUST THE CLOTHES ON YOUR BACK AND OBEY ANY INSTRUCTIONS YOU'RE GIVEN...
YOU DID IT!
OH, THANK YOU!
I WOULD EXPECT NO LESS FROM THE HEAD OF HOUSE RAL!
NO LESS FROM MY SON!
...
YOU'LL HAVE TO DECIDE WHAT TO DO WITH YOURSELF
ONCE YOU GET TO EARTH.
YOU CAN THINK ABOUT THOSE YOU'RE LEAVING BEHIND,
OR NOT ...
AH, BUT WHY CUT A FIGURE?
WHAT WILL BE, WILL BE...
...I THINK.

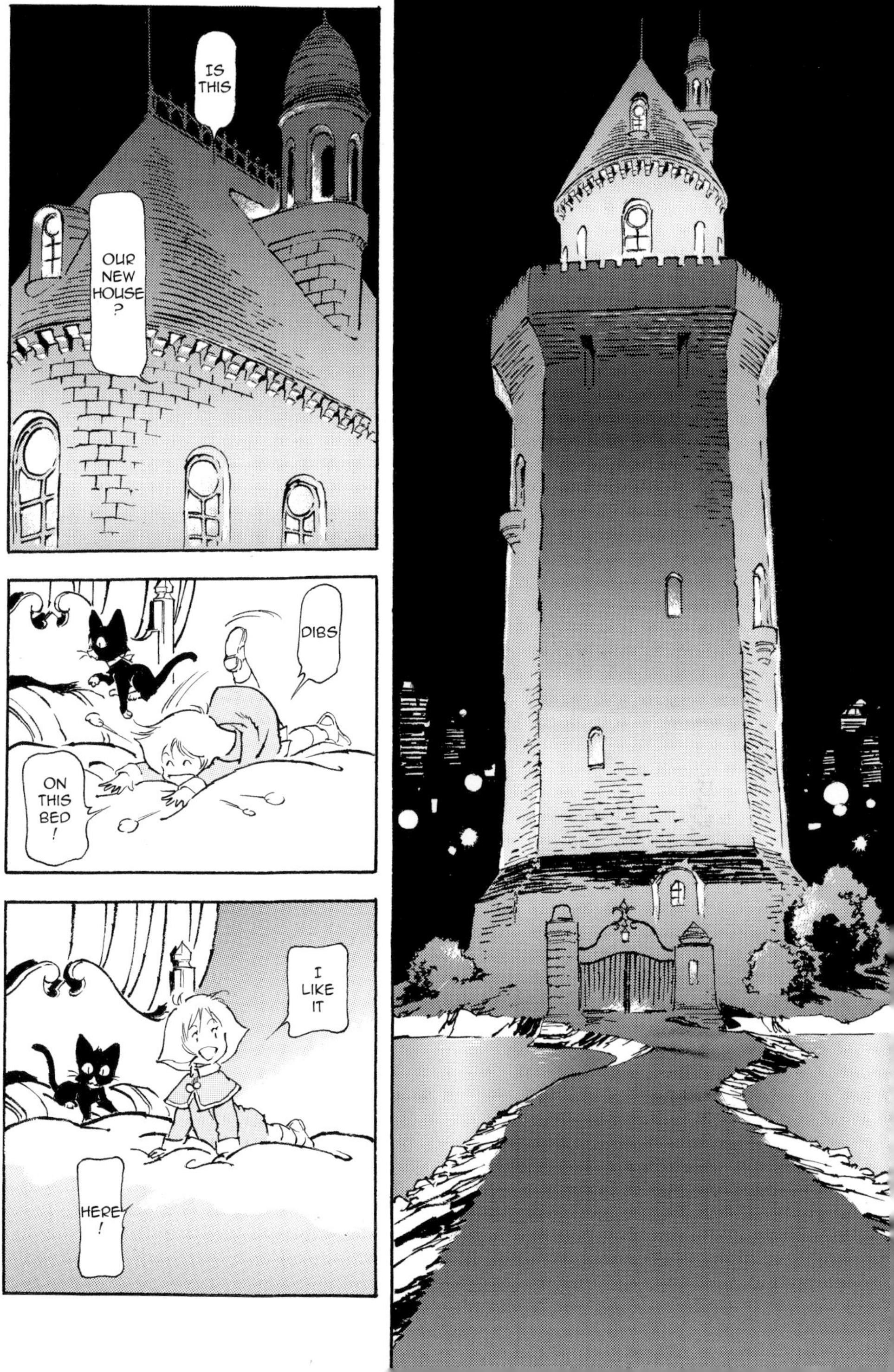
IS THIS
OUR NEW HOUSE?
DIBS
ON THIS BED!
I LIKE IT
HERE!

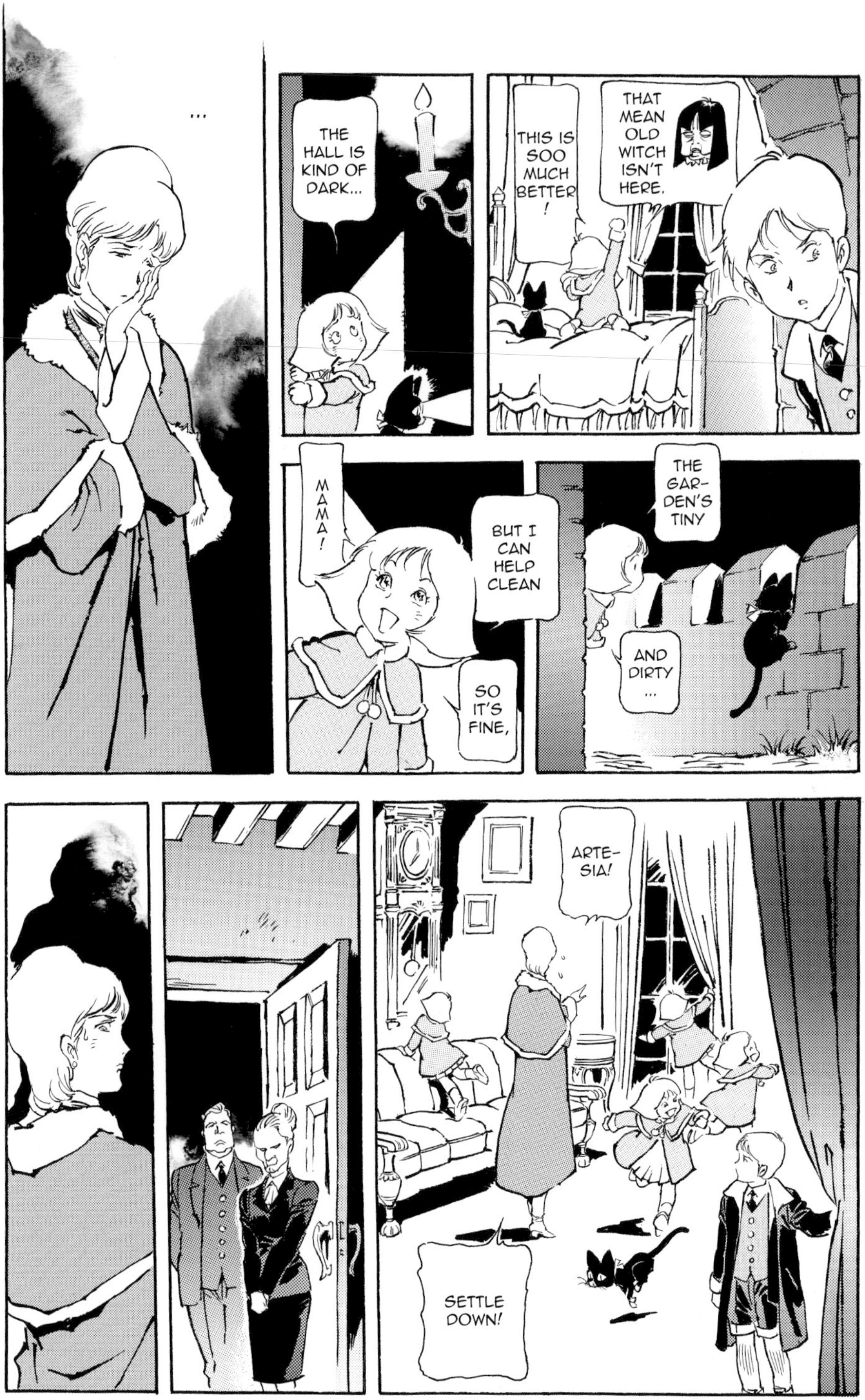
THAT MEAN OLD WITCH ISN'T HERE.
THIS IS SOO MUCH BETTER!
THE HALL IS KIND OF DARK...
THE GAR-DEN'S TINY
AND DIRTY ...
MAMA!
BUT I CAN HELP CLEAN
SO IT'S FINE,
...
ARTE-SIA!
SETTLE DOWN!

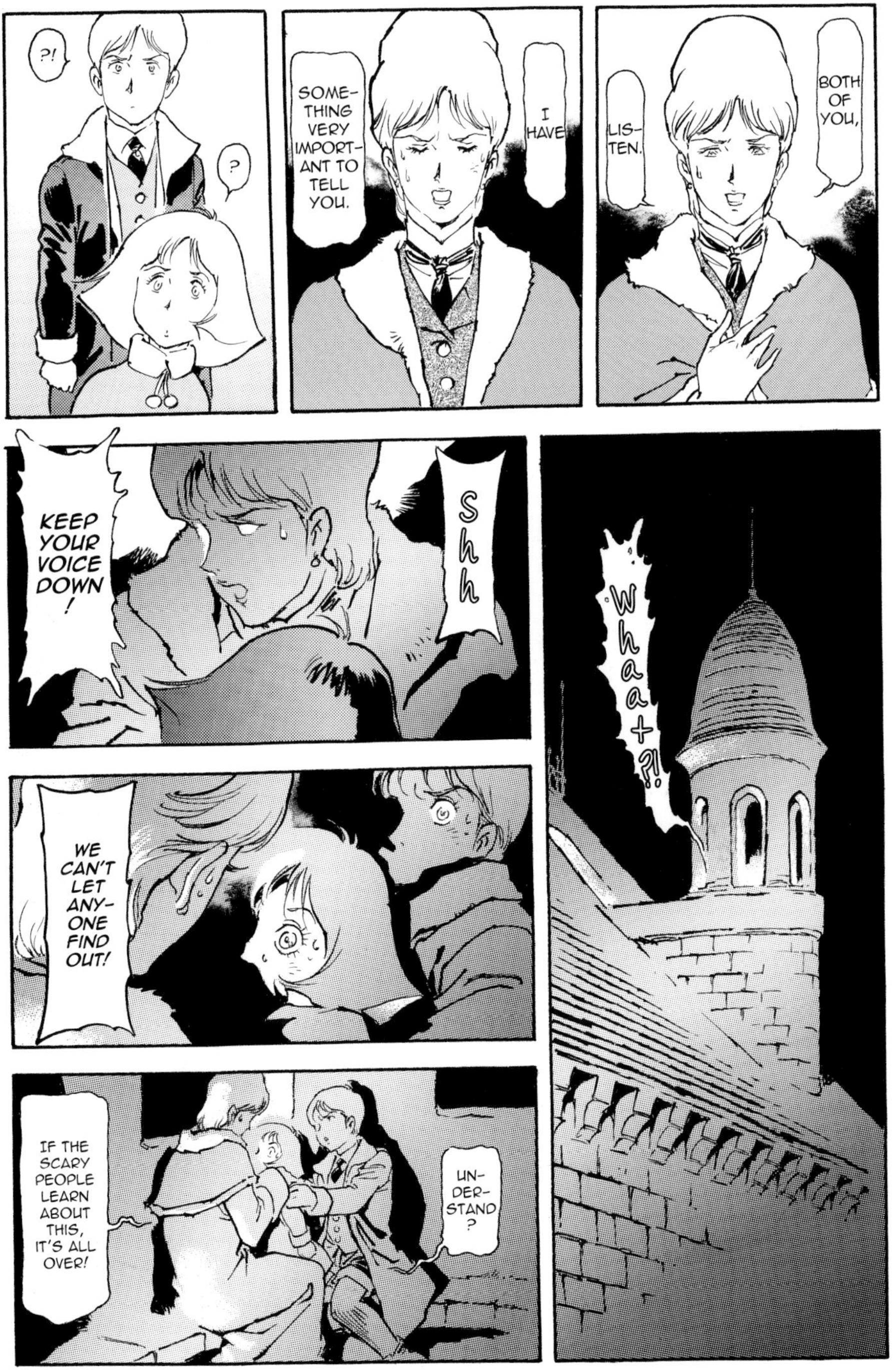
BOTH OF YOU,
LISTEN.
I HAVE
SOMETHING VERY IMPORTANT TO TELL YOU.
?!
?
Whaat?!
Shh
KEEP YOUR VOICE DOWN!
WE CAN'T LET ANYONE FIND OUT!
UNDERSTAND?
IF THE SCARY PEOPLE LEARN ABOUT THIS, IT'S ALL OVER!

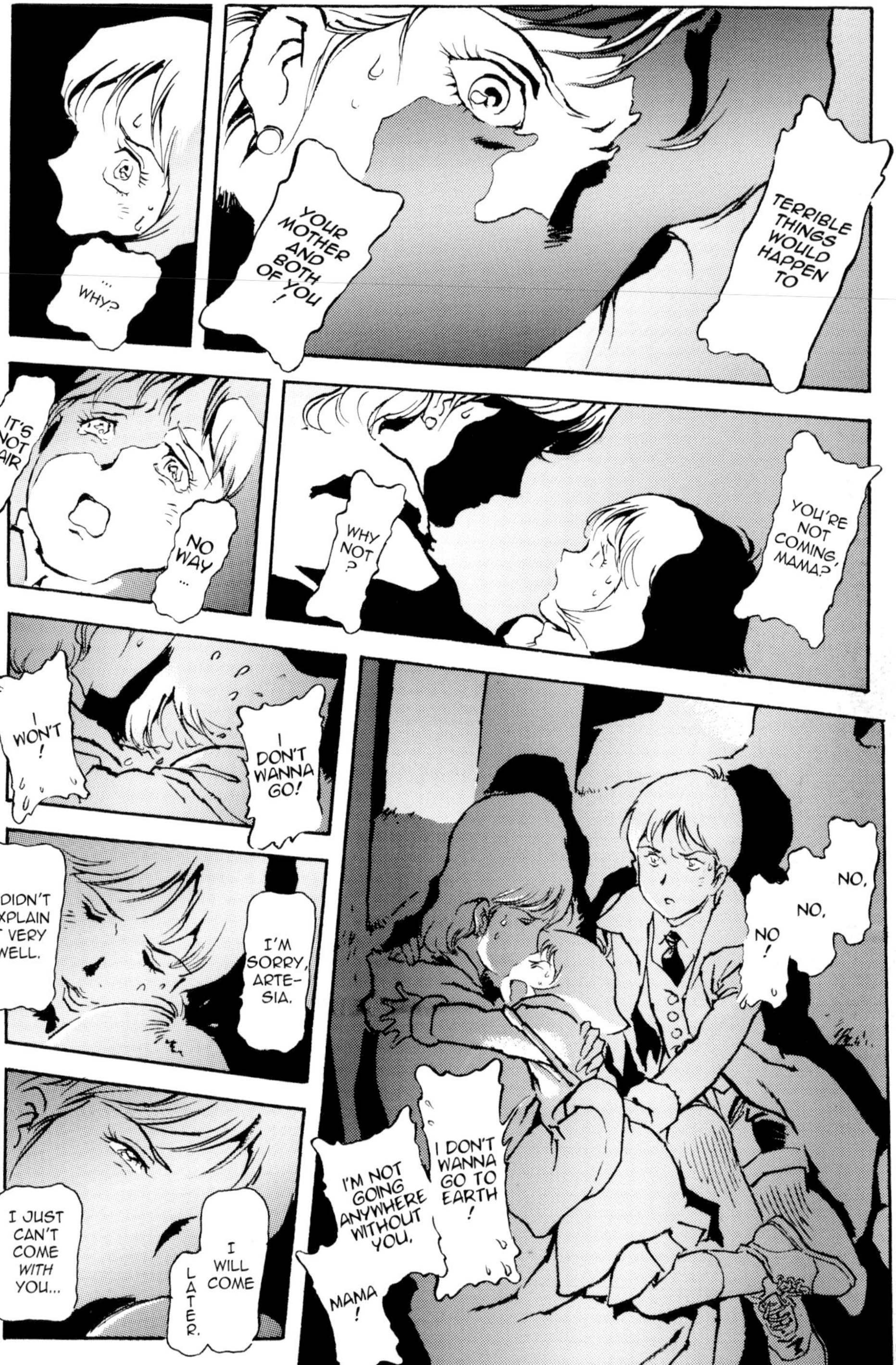
TERRIBLE THINGS WOULD HAPPEN TO
YOUR MOTHER AND BOTH OF YOU!
... WHY?
YOU'RE NOT COMING, MAMA?
WHY NOT?
NO WAY...
IT'S NOT FAIR...
NO, NO, NO!
I DON'T WANNA GO TO EARTH!
I'M NOT GOING ANYWHERE WITHOUT YOU, MAMA!
I DON'T WANNA GO!
I WON'T!
I'M SORRY, ARTESIA.
I DIDN'T EXPLAIN IT VERY WELL.
I WILL COME LATER.
I JUST CAN'T COME WITH YOU...

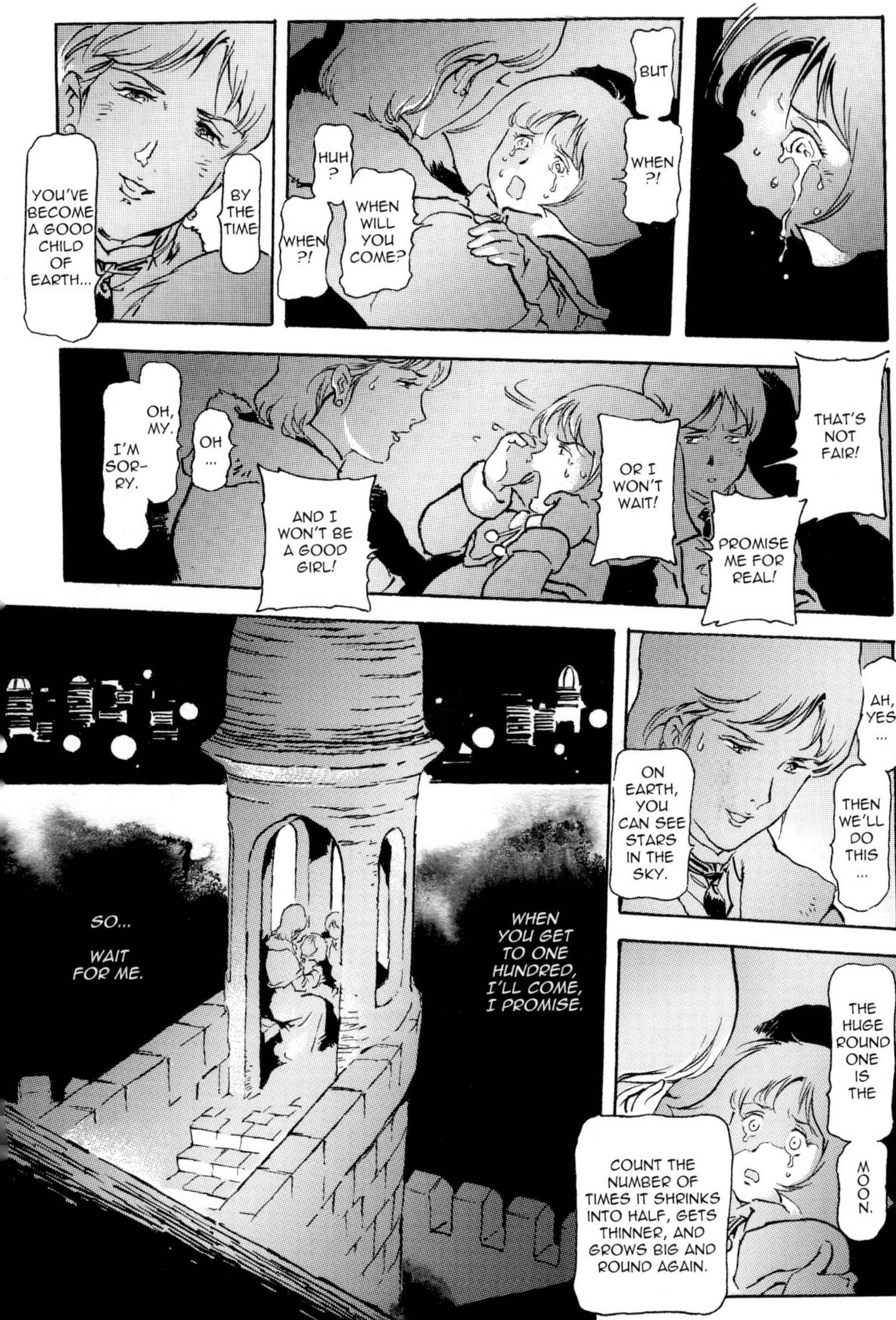
BUT WHEN?!
WHEN WILL YOU COME?
HUH?
WHEN?!
BY THE TIME
YOU'VE BECOME A GOOD CHILD OF EARTH...
THAT'S NOT FAIR!
PROMISE ME FOR REAL!
OR I WON'T WAIT!
AND I WON'T BE A GOOD GIRL!
OH ...
OH, MY. I'M SOR-RY.
AH, YES ...
THEN WE'LL DO THIS ...
ON EARTH, YOU CAN SEE STARS IN THE SKY.
THE HUGE ROUND ONE IS THE MOON.
COUNT THE NUMBER OF TIMES IT SHRINKS INTO HALF, GETS THINNER, AND GROWS BIG AND ROUND AGAIN.
WHEN YOU GET TO ONE HUNDRED, I'LL COME, I PROMISE.
SO...
WAIT FOR ME.

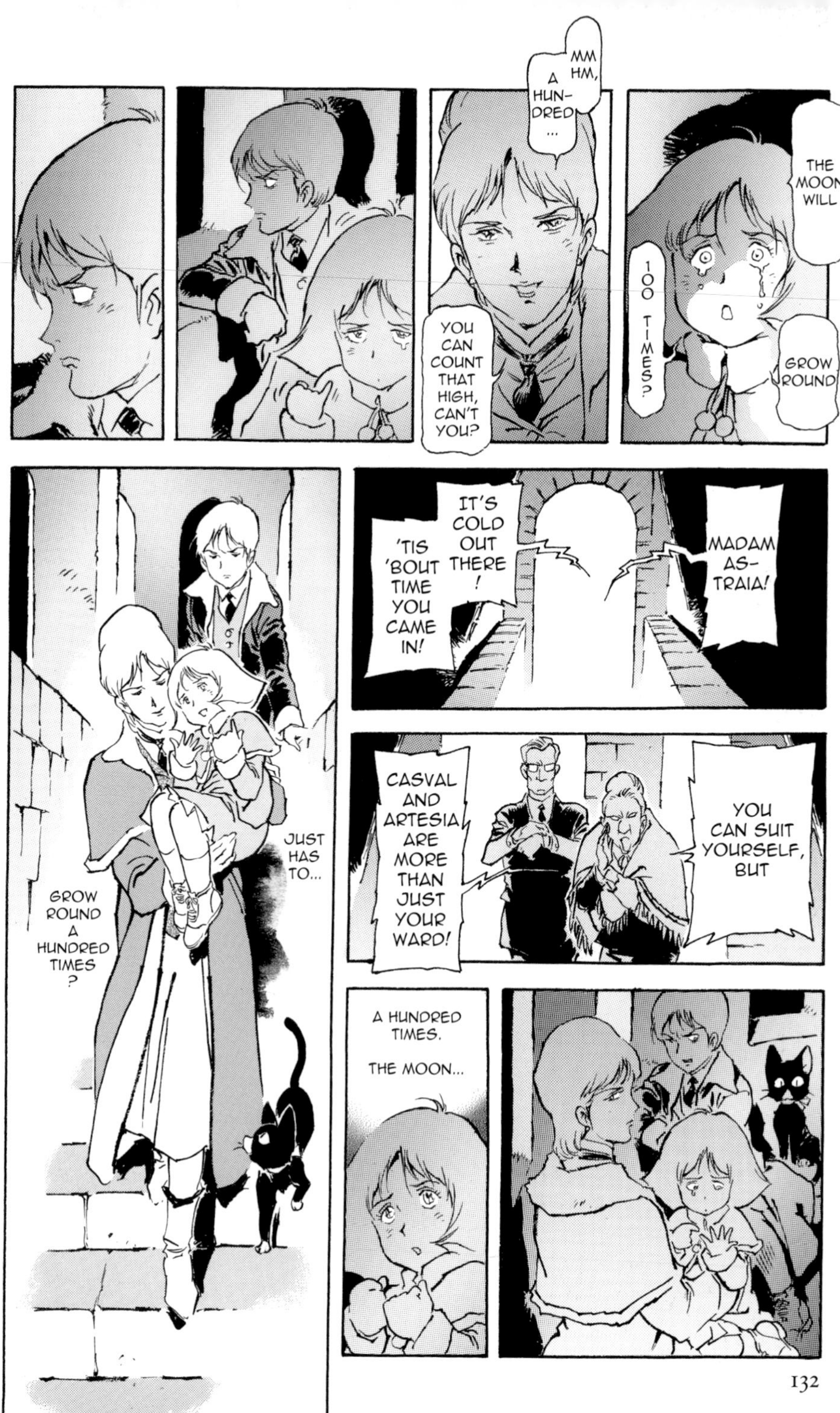
THE MOON WILL
GROW ROUND
100 TIMES?
MM HM, A HUNDRED...
YOU CAN COUNT THAT HIGH, CAN'T YOU?
MADAM AS-TRAIA!
IT'S COLD OUT THERE!
'TIS 'BOUT TIME YOU CAME IN!
YOU CAN SUIT YOURSELF, BUT
CASVAL AND ARTESIA ARE MORE THAN JUST YOUR WARD!
A HUNDRED TIMES.
THE MOON...
JUST HAS TO...
GROW ROUND A HUNDRED TIMES?

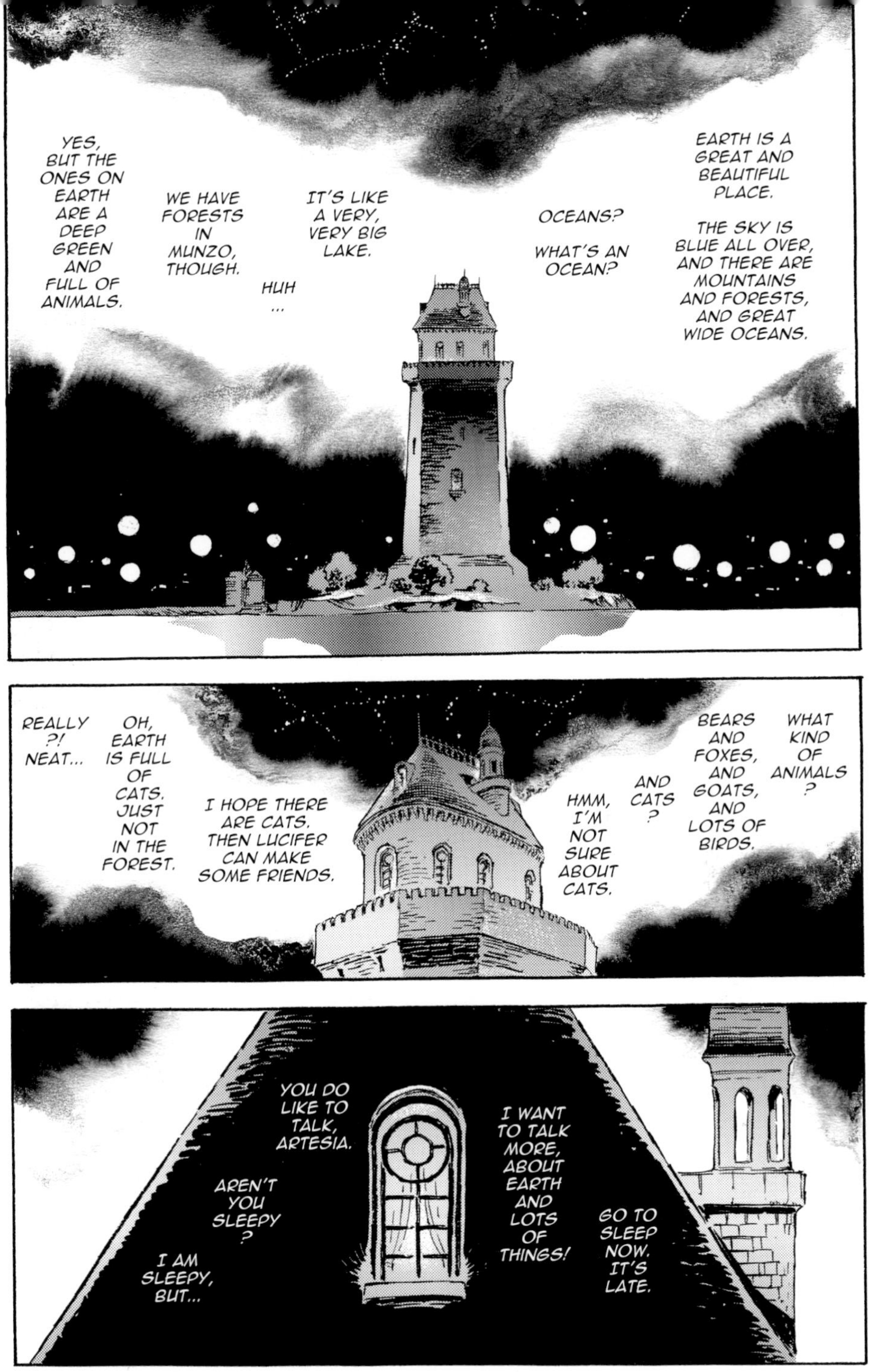
EARTH IS A GREAT AND BEAUTIFUL PLACE.
THE SKY IS BLUE ALL OVER, AND THERE ARE MOUNTAINS AND FORESTS, AND GREAT WIDE OCEANS.
OCEANS?
WHAT'S AN OCEAN?
IT'S LIKE A VERY, VERY BIG LAKE.
HUH ...
WE HAVE FORESTS IN MUNZO, THOUGH.
YES, BUT THE ONES ON EARTH ARE A DEEP GREEN AND FULL OF ANIMALS.
WHAT KIND OF ANIMALS?
BEARS AND FOXES, AND GOATS, AND LOTS OF BIRDS.
AND CATS?
HMM, I'M NOT SURE ABOUT CATS.
I HOPE THERE ARE CATS. THEN LUCIFER CAN MAKE SOME FRIENDS.
OH, EARTH IS FULL OF CATS. JUST NOT IN THE FOREST.
REALLY?! NEAT...
GO TO SLEEP NOW. IT'S LATE.
I WANT TO TALK MORE, ABOUT EARTH AND LOTS OF THINGS!
YOU DO LIKE TO TALK, ARTESIA.
AREN'T YOU SLEEPY?
I AM SLEEPY, BUT...

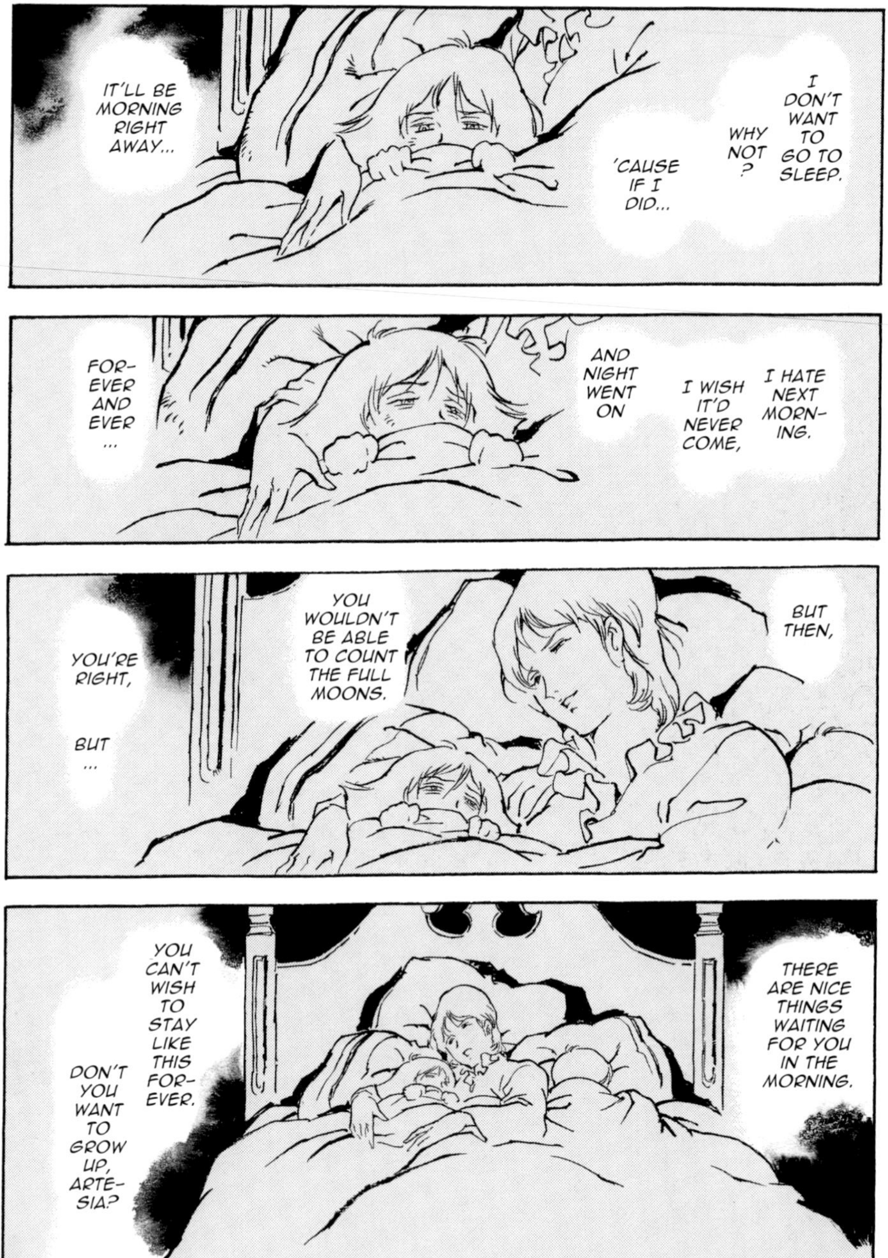
I DON'T WANT TO GO TO SLEEP.
WHY NOT?
'CAUSE IF I DID...
IT'LL BE MORNING RIGHT AWAY...
I HATE NEXT MORNING.
I WISH IT'D NEVER COME,
AND NIGHT WENT ON
FOREVER AND EVER...
BUT THEN,
YOU WOULDN'T BE ABLE TO COUNT THE FULL MOONS.
YOU'RE RIGHT,
BUT...
THERE ARE NICE THINGS WAITING FOR YOU IN THE MORNING.
YOU CAN'T WISH TO STAY LIKE THIS FOREVER.
DON'T YOU WANT TO GROW UP, ARTESIA?

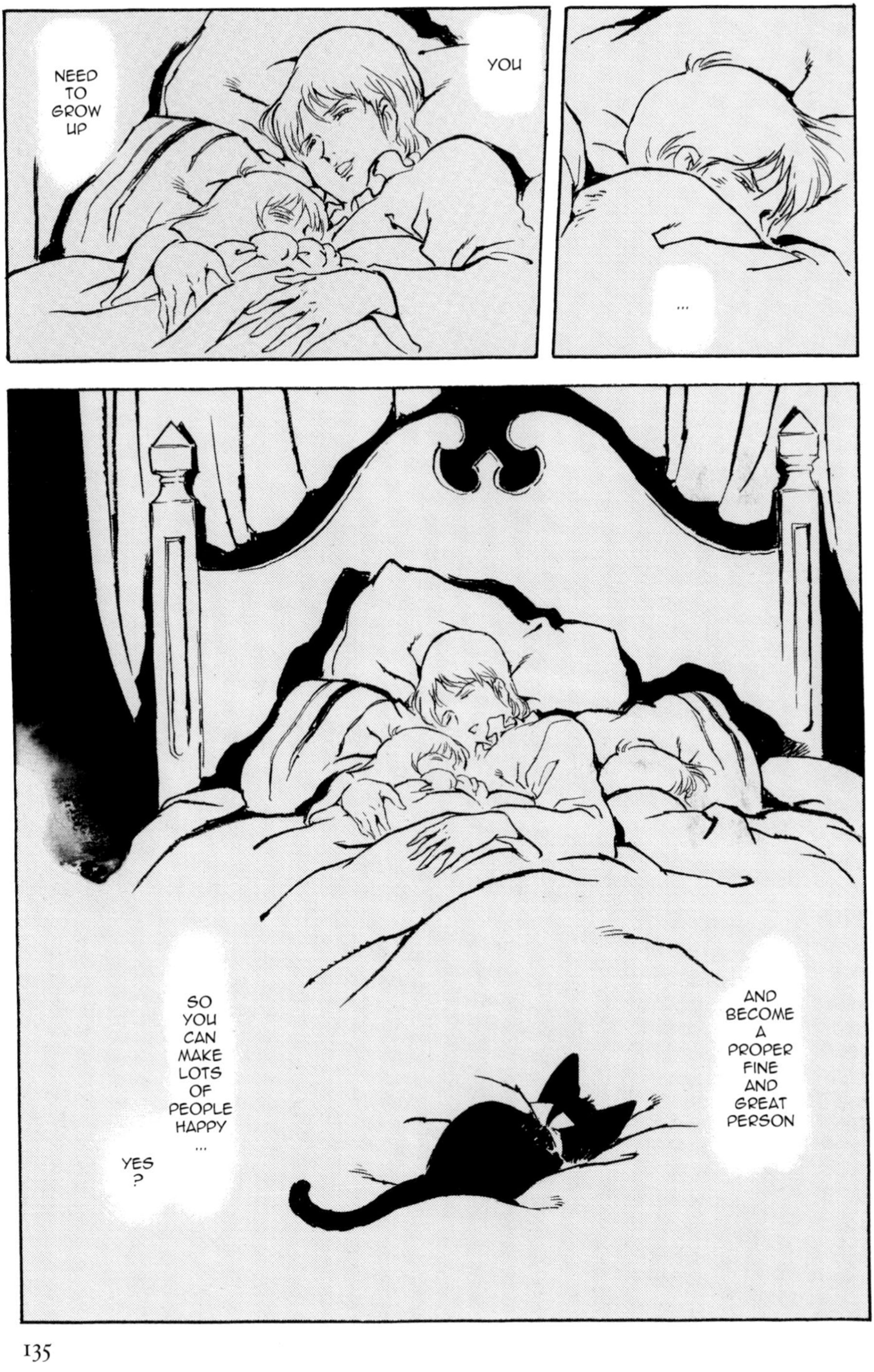
...
YOU
NEED TO GROW UP
AND BECOME A PROPER FINE AND GREAT PERSON
SO YOU CAN MAKE LOTS OF PEOPLE HAPPY ...
YES?

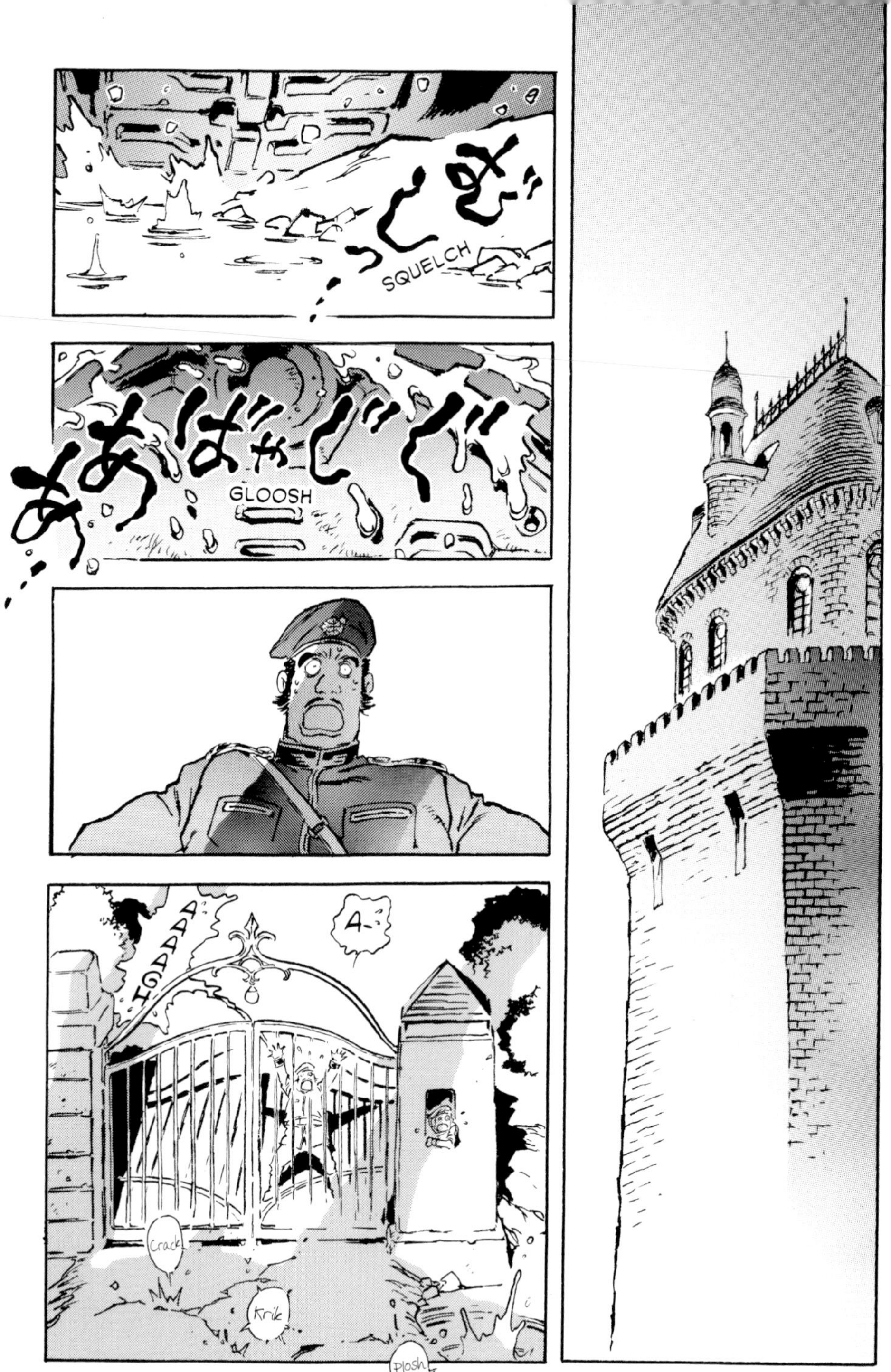
SQUELCH
GLOOSH
AAAAAGH
A-
Crack
Krik
Plosh
...

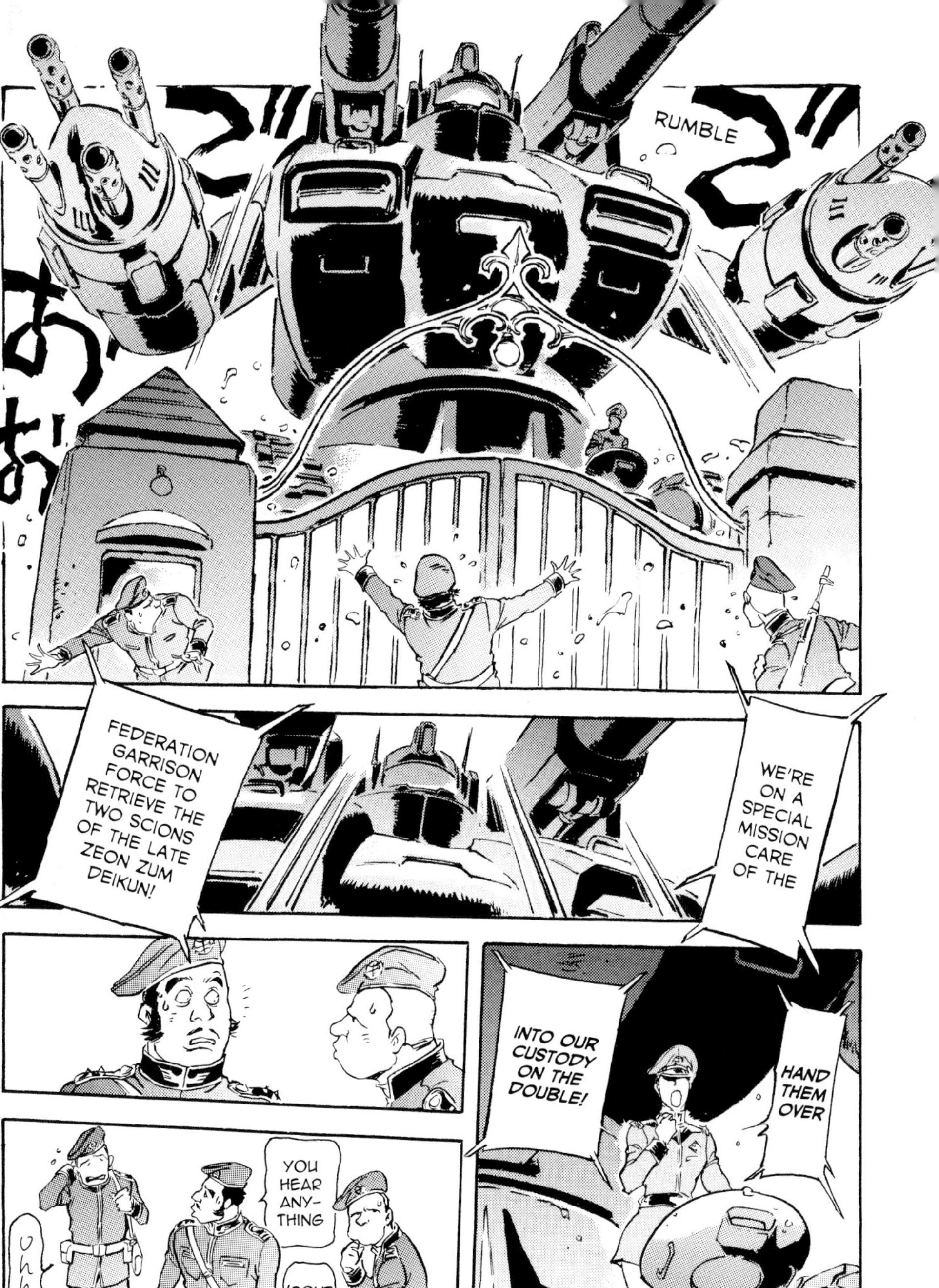
RUMBLE
WE'RE ON A SPECIAL MISSION CARE OF THE
FEDERATION GARRISON FORCE TO RETRIEVE THE TWO SCIONS OF THE LATE ZEON ZUM DEIKUN!
HAND THEM OVER
INTO OUR CUSTODY ON THE DOUBLE!
YOU HEAR ANYTHING
'BOUT THIS?
Uhh

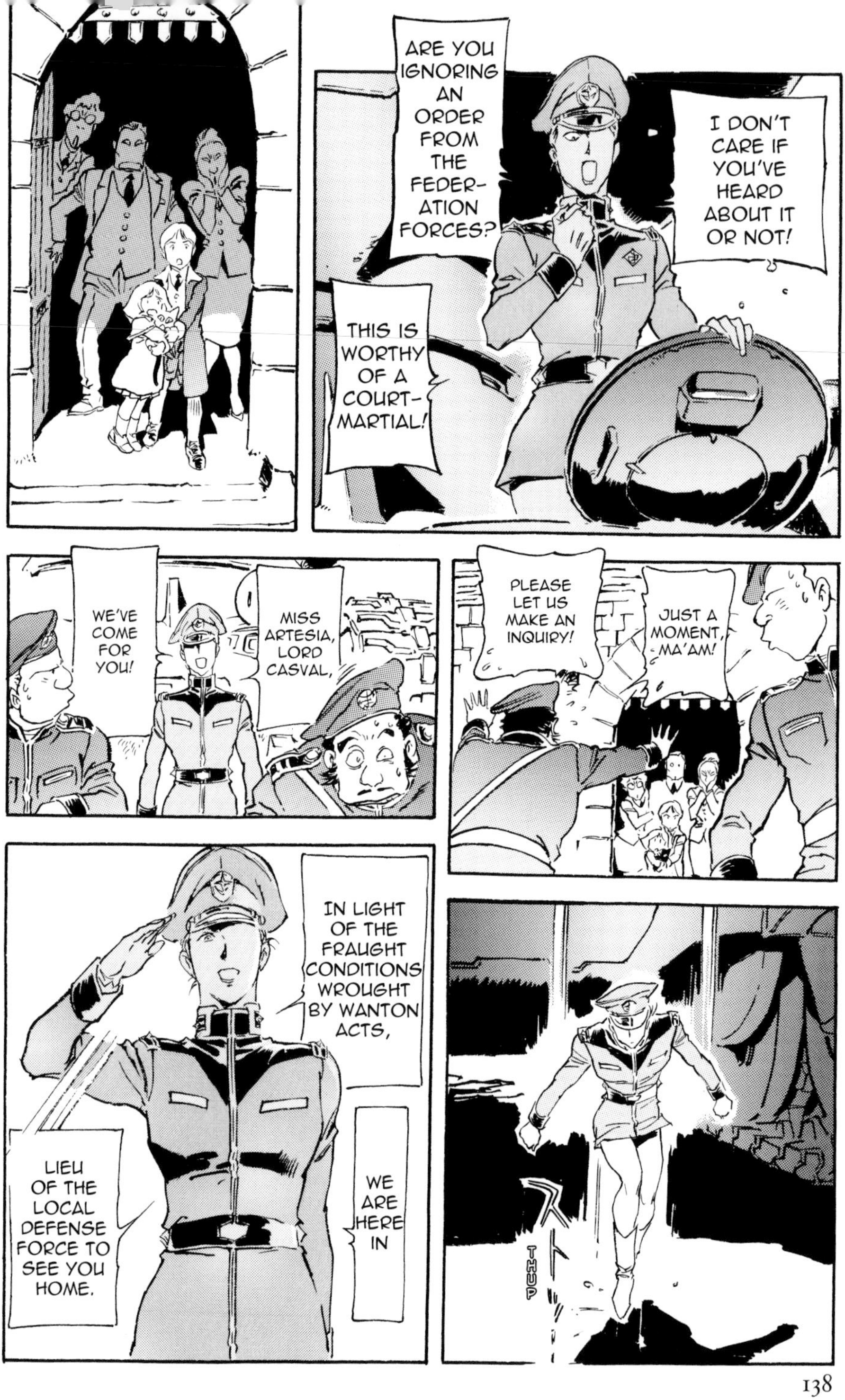
I DON'T CARE IF YOU'VE HEARD ABOUT IT OR NOT!
ARE YOU IGNORING AN ORDER FROM THE FEDER-ATION FORCES?
THIS IS WORTHY OF A COURT-MARTIAL!
JUST A MOMENT, MA'AM!
PLEASE LET US MAKE AN INQUIRY!
MISS ARTESIA, LORD CASVAL,
WE'VE COME FOR YOU!
THUP
IN LIGHT OF THE FRAUGHT CONDITIONS WROUGHT BY WANTON ACTS,
WE ARE HERE IN
LIEU OF THE LOCAL DEFENSE FORCE TO SEE YOU HOME.

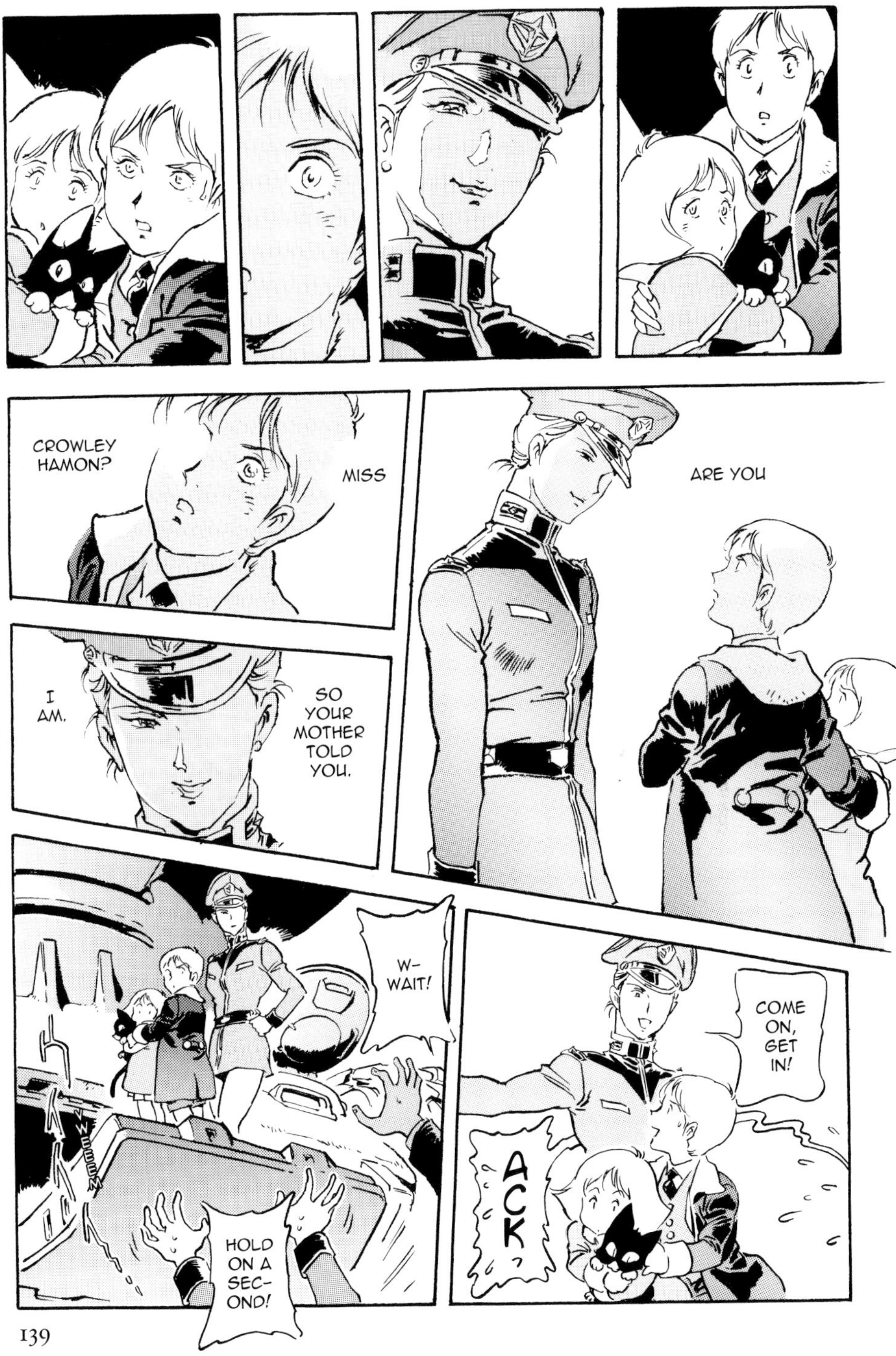
ARE YOU
MISS
CROWLEY HAMON?
SO YOUR MOTHER TOLD YOU.
I AM.
COME ON, GET IN!
ACK
W-WAIT!
HOLD ON A SEC-OND!
WEEEM

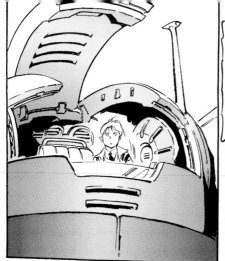

WE'VE GOT A SITUATION HERE!

HELLO?!

WAAAIT!!

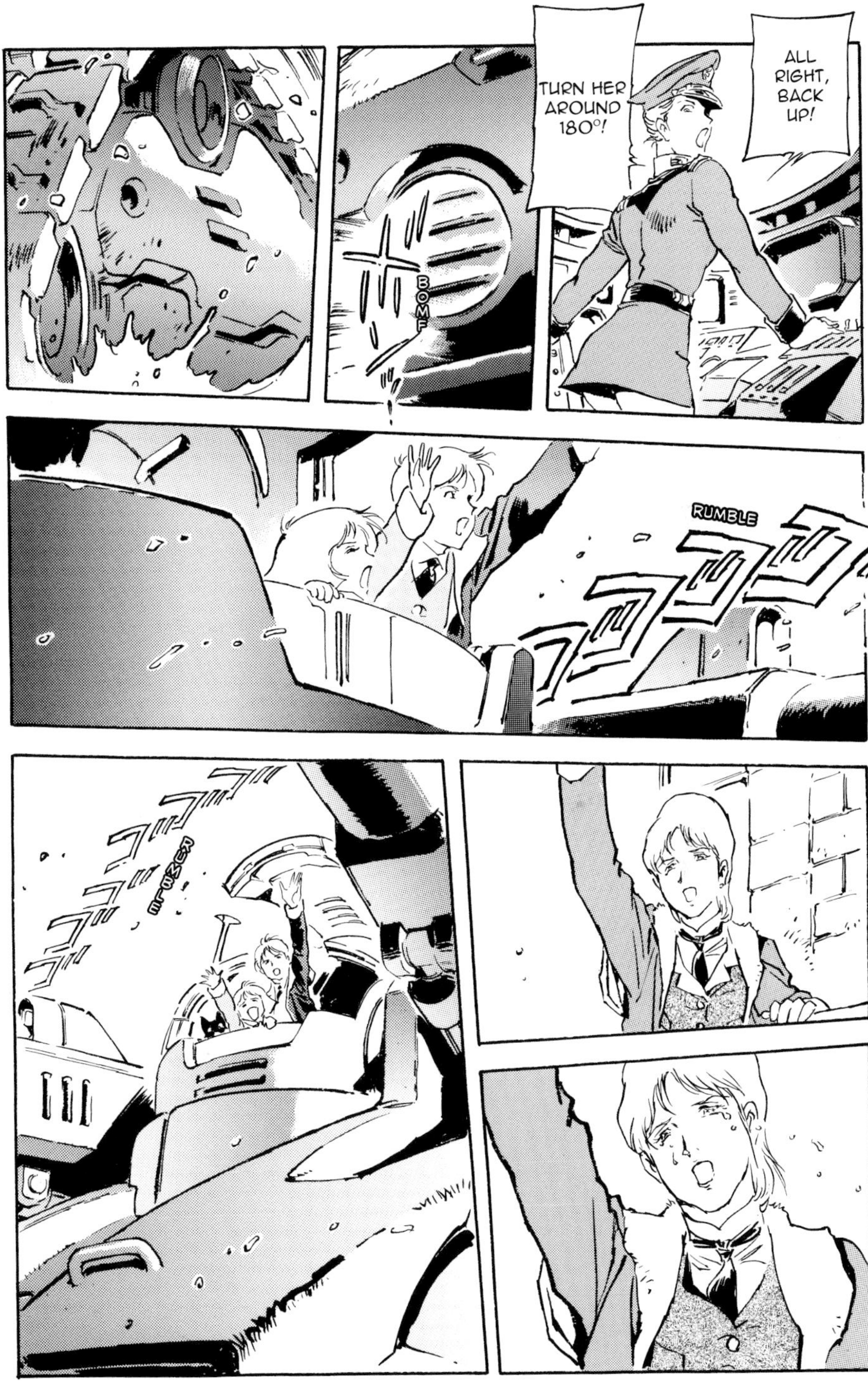
ALL RIGHT, BACK UP!
TURN HER AROUND 180°!
BOMF
RUMBLE
RUMBLE

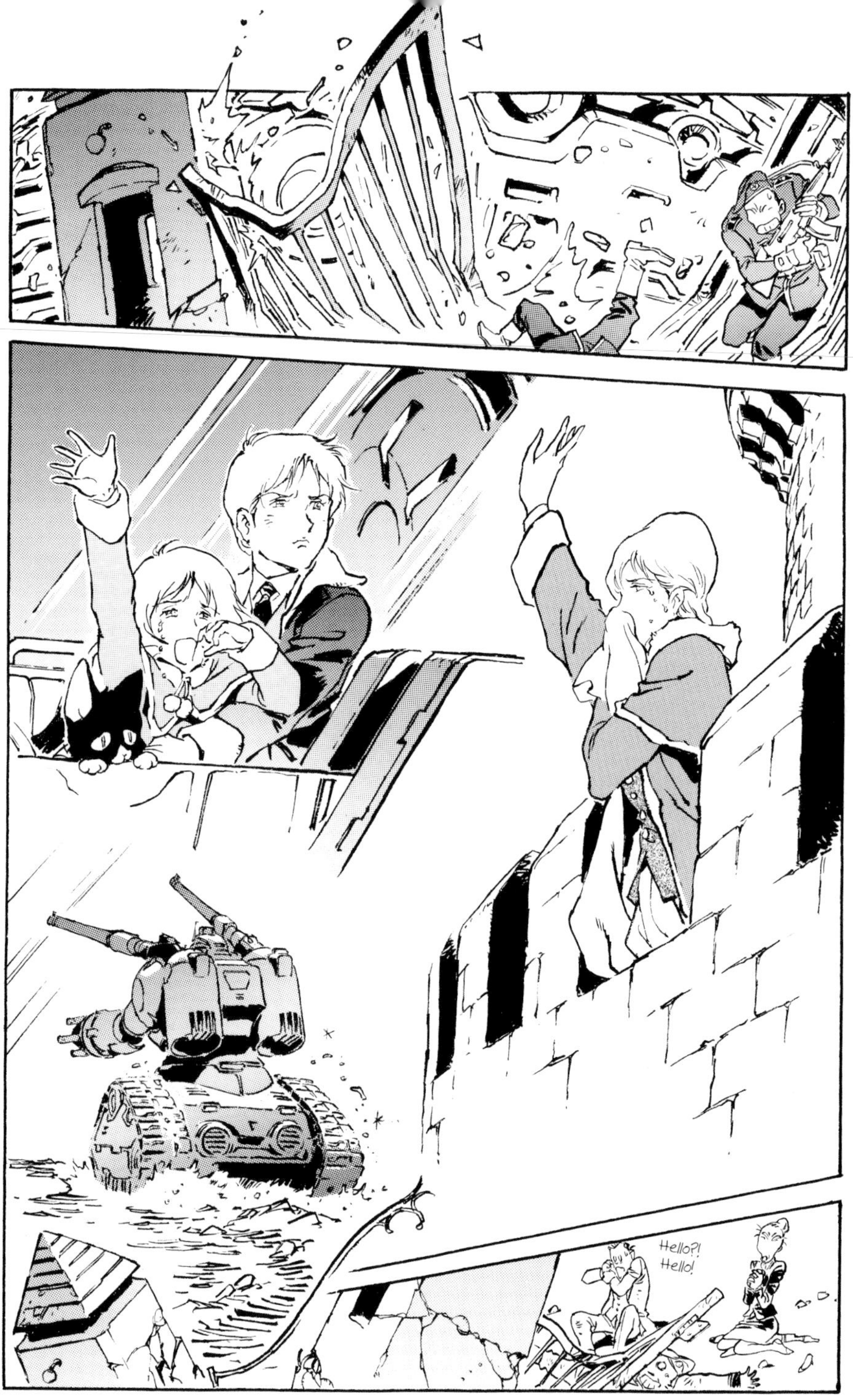
Hello?!
Hello!

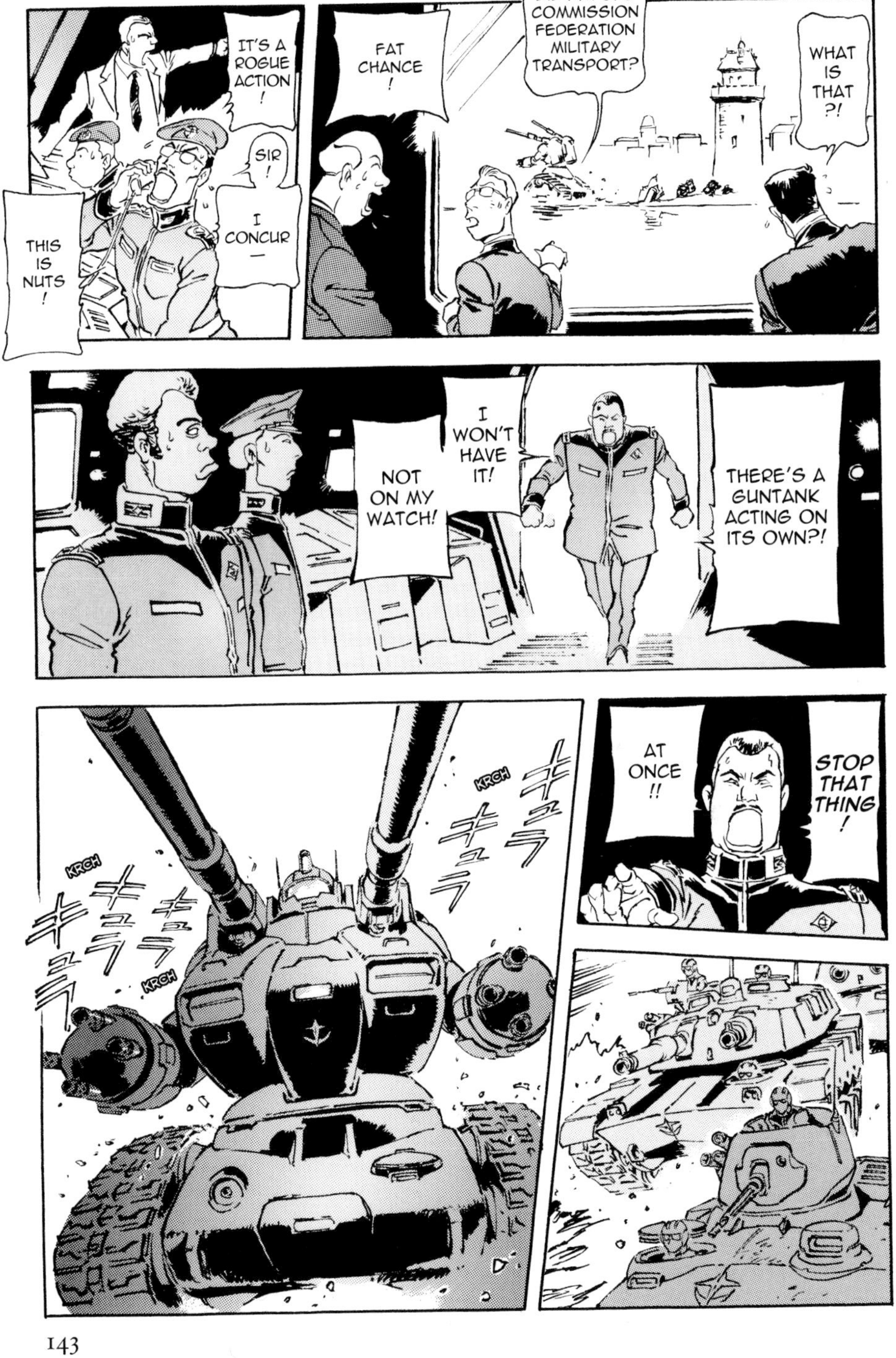
WHAT IS THAT?!
DID ANYONE COMMISSION FEDERATION MILITARY TRANSPORT?
FAT CHANCE!
IT'S A ROGUE ACTION!
SIR!
I CONCUR—
THIS IS NUTS!
THERE'S A GUNTANK ACTING ON ITS OWN?!
I WON'T HAVE IT!
NOT ON MY WATCH!
STOP THAT THING!
AT ONCE!!
KRCH
キュラ
キュラ
KRCH
キュラ
キュラ
キュラ
KRCH

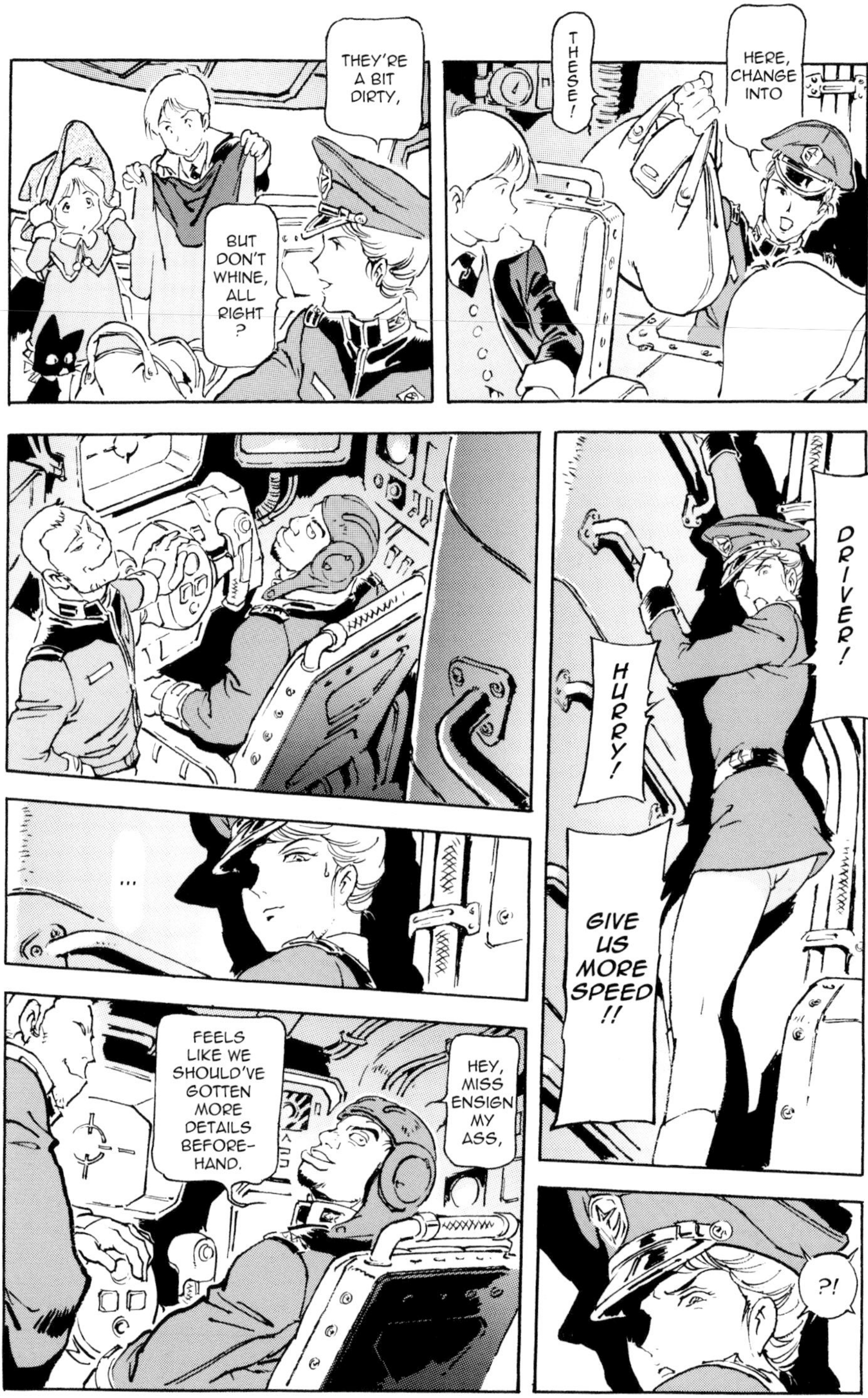
HERE, CHANGE INTO
THESE!
THEY'RE A BIT DIRTY,
BUT DON'T WHINE, ALL RIGHT?
DRIVER!
HURRY!
GIVE US MORE SPEED!!
...
?!
HEY, MISS ENSIGN MY ASS,
FEELS LIKE WE SHOULD'VE GOTTEN MORE DETAILS BEFORE-HAND.

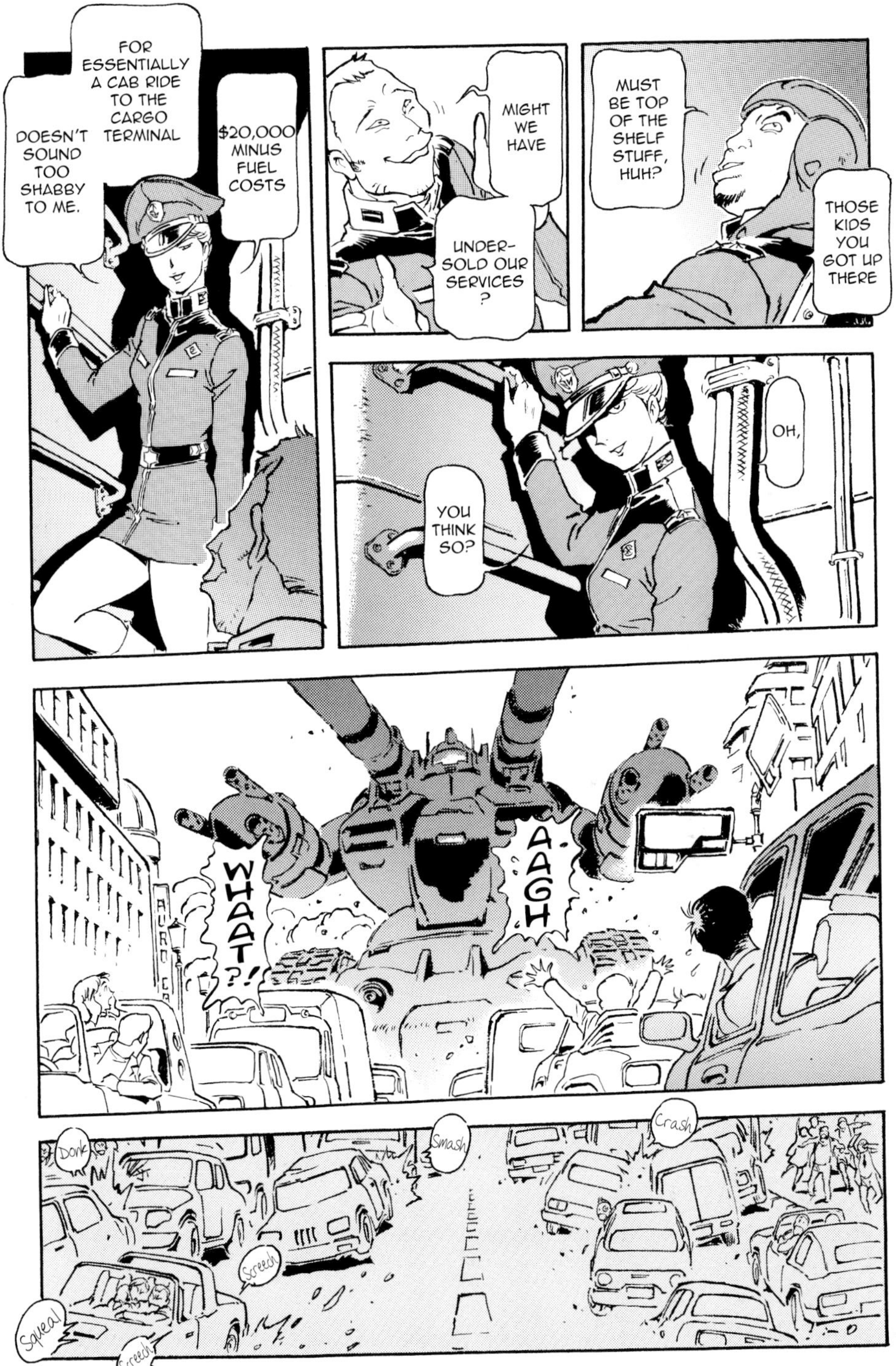
THOSE KIDS YOU GOT UP THERE
MUST BE TOP OF THE SHELF STUFF, HUH?
MIGHT WE HAVE
UNDER-SOLD OUR SERVICES?
OH,
YOU THINK SO?
$20,000 MINUS FUEL COSTS
FOR ESSENTIALLY A CAB RIDE TO THE CARGO TERMINAL
DOESN'T SOUND TOO SHABBY TO ME.
AAGH
WHAAAT?!
Crash
Smash
Donk
Screech
Squeal
Screech

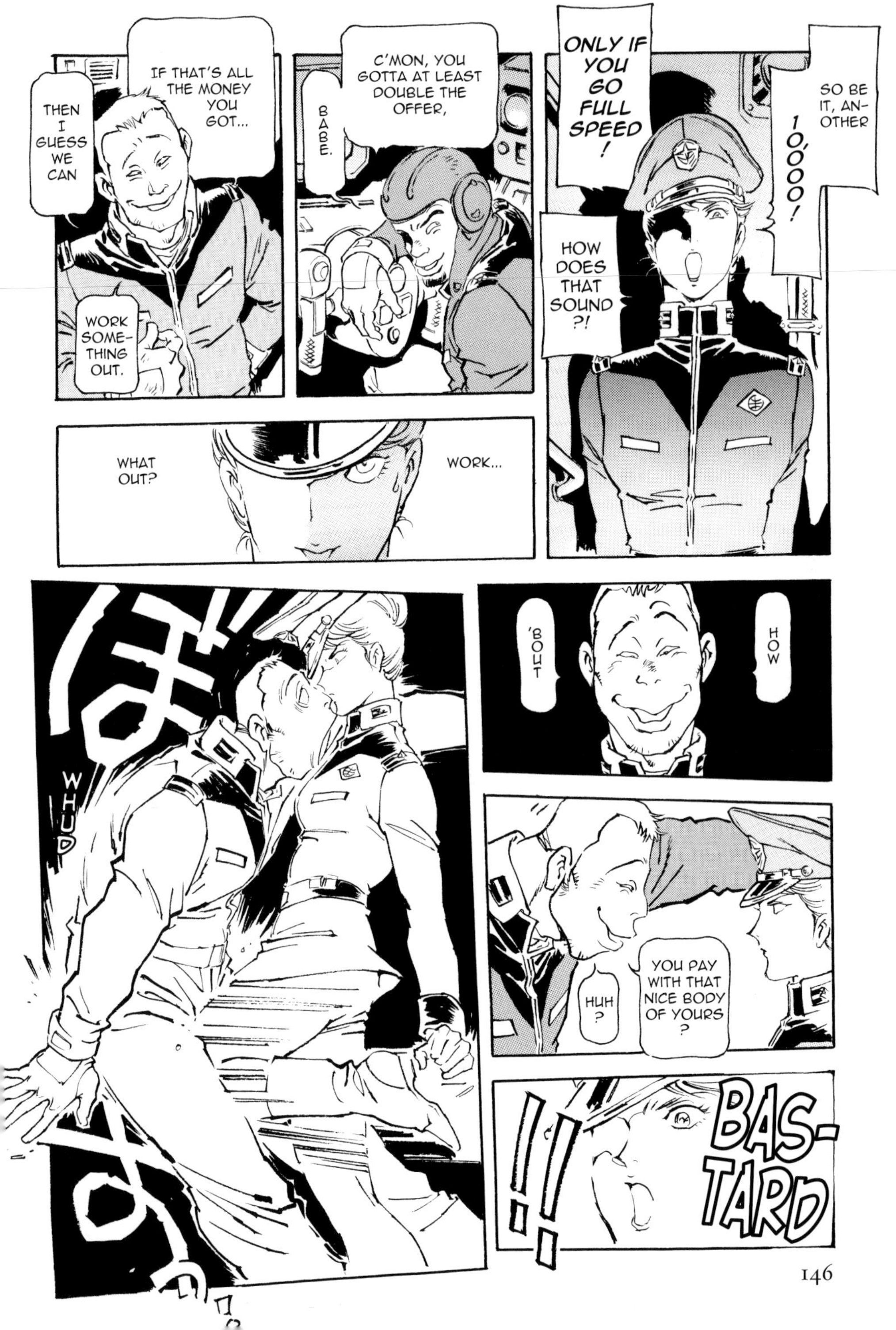
SO BE IT, AN-OTHER
10,000!
ONLY IF YOU GO FULL SPEED!
HOW DOES THAT SOUND?!
C'MON, YOU GOTTA AT LEAST DOUBLE THE OFFER,
BABE.
IF THAT'S ALL THE MONEY YOU GOT...
THEN I GUESS WE CAN
WORK SOMETHING OUT.
WORK...
WHAT OUT?
HOW
'BOUT
YOU PAY WITH THAT NICE BODY OF YOURS?
HUH?
BAS-TARD
!!
WHUD

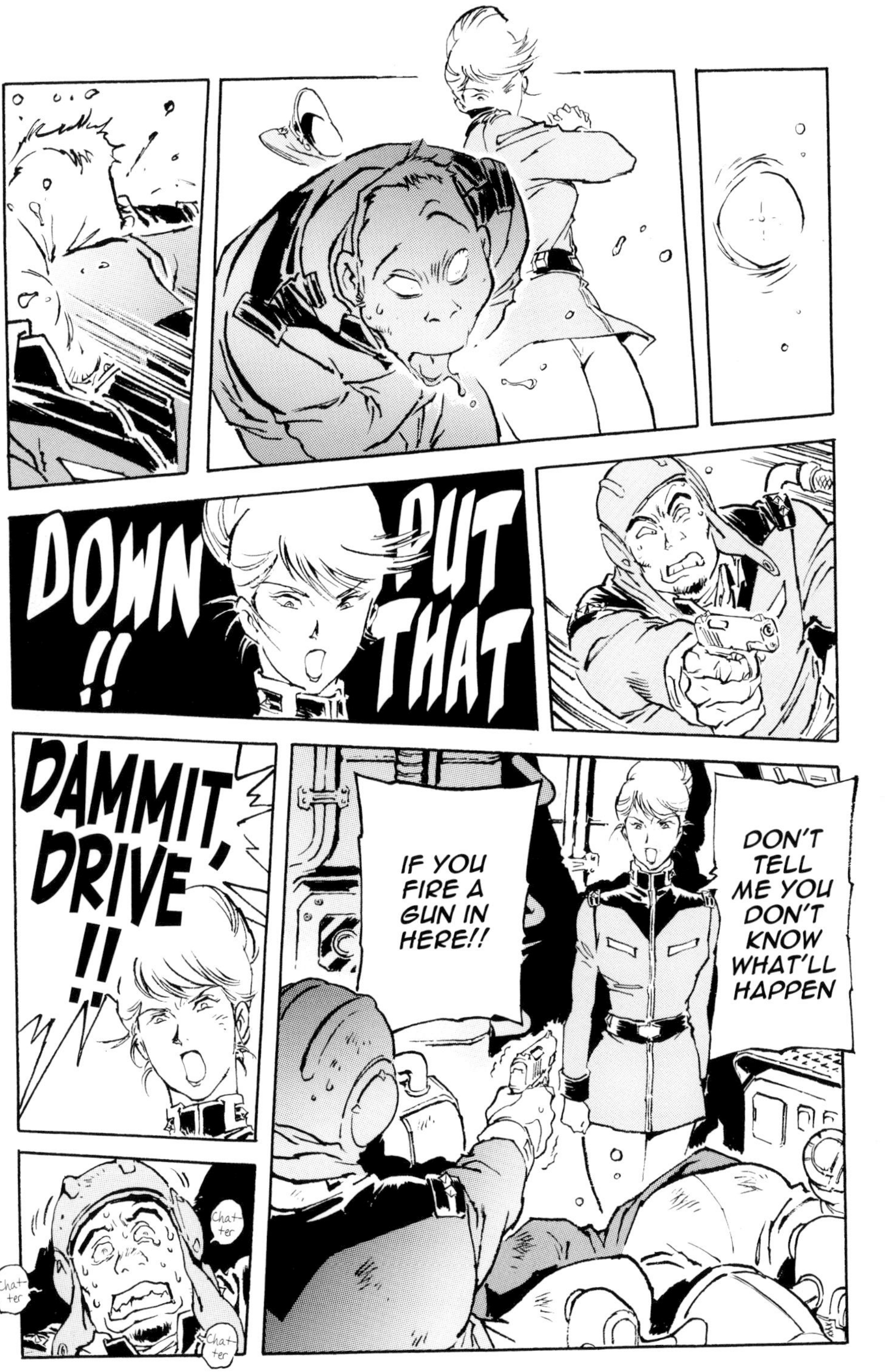
PUT THAT DOWN!!
DON'T TELL ME YOU DON'T KNOW WHAT'LL HAPPEN
IF YOU FIRE A GUN IN HERE!!
DAMMIT, DRIVE!!
Chatter
Chatter
Chatter

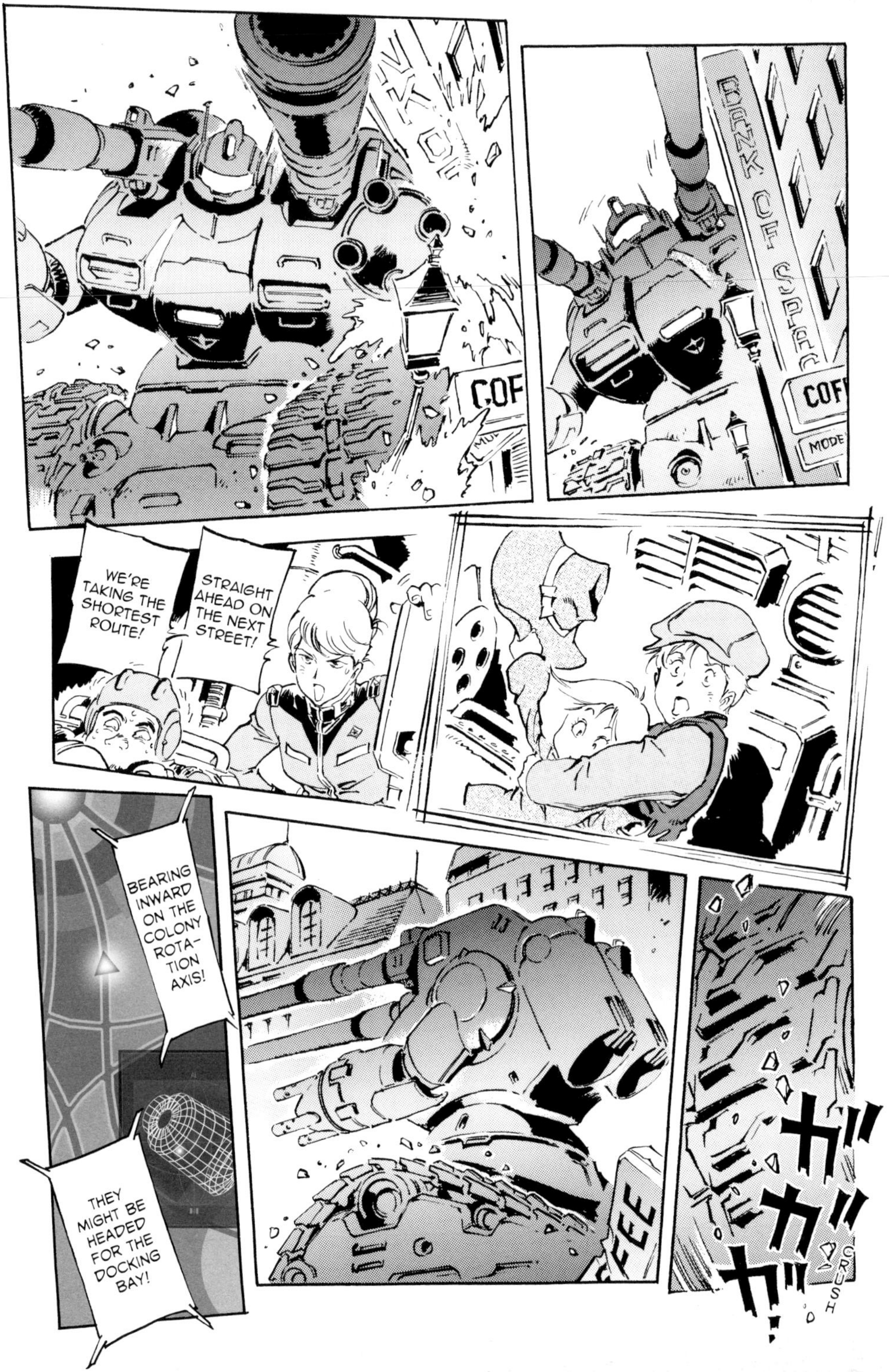
BANK OF SPAC
COFF
MODE
COF
STRAIGHT AHEAD ON THE NEXT STREET!
WE'RE TAKING THE SHORTEST ROUTE!
CRUSH
FEE
BEARING INWARD ON THE COLONY ROTA-TION AXIS!
THEY MIGHT BE HEADED FOR THE DOCKING BAY!

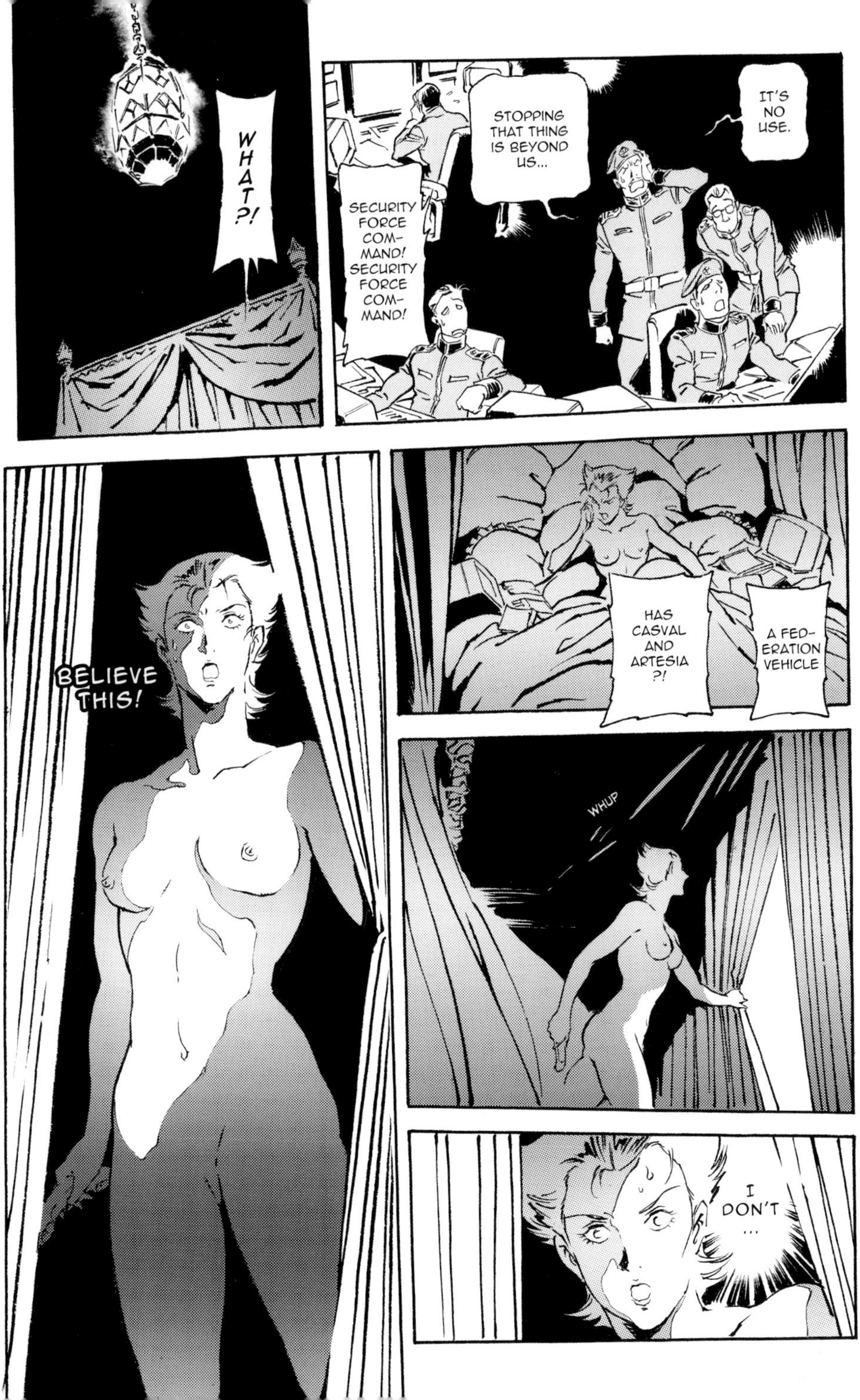
IT'S NO USE.
STOPPING THAT THING IS BEYOND US...
SECURITY FORCE COM-MAND! SECURITY FORCE COM-MAND!
WHAT?!
A FED-ERATION VEHICLE
HAS CASVAL AND ARTESIA ?!
WHUP
I DON'T ...
BELIEVE THIS!

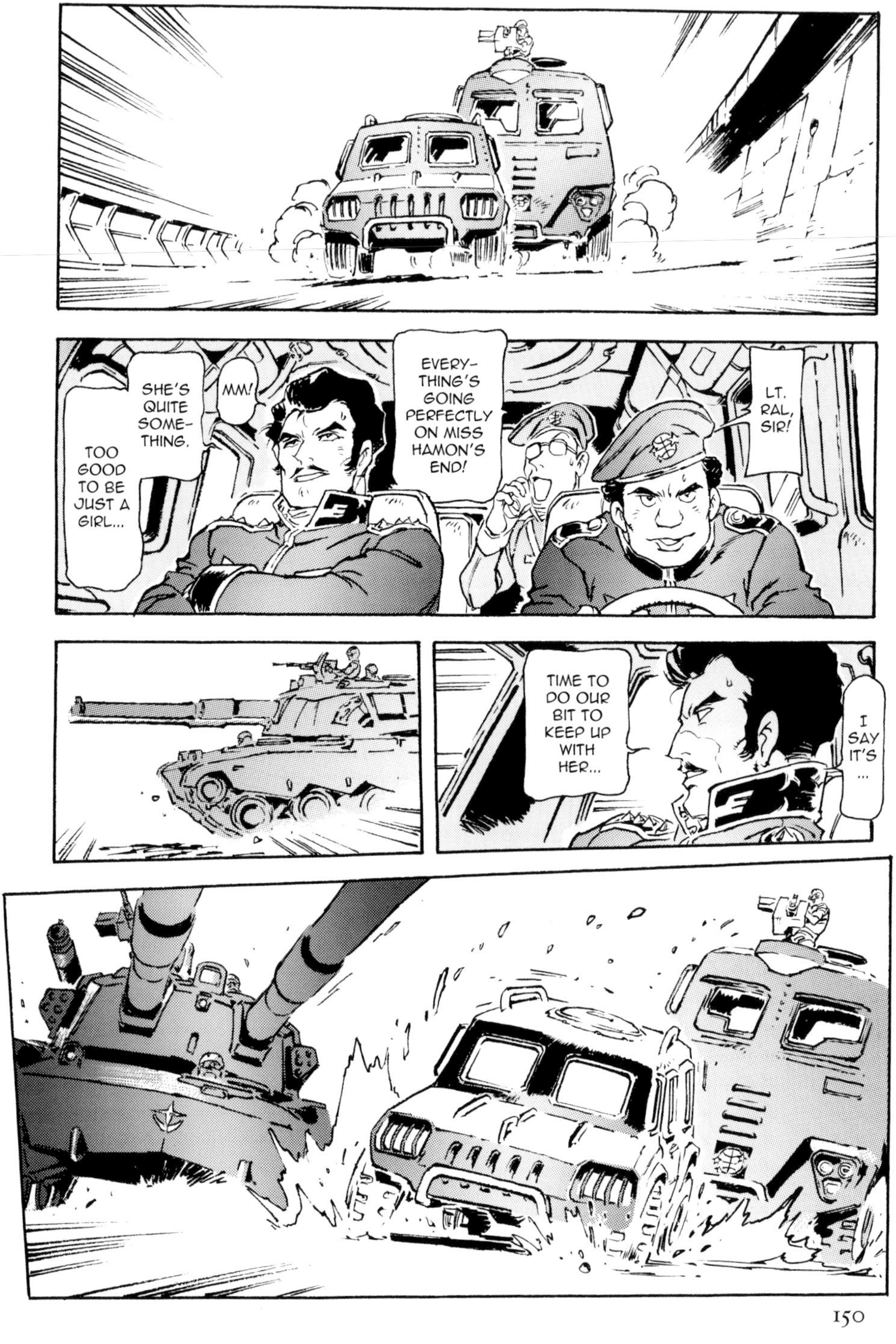
LT. RAL, SIR!
EVERYTHING'S GOING PERFECTLY ON MISS HAMON'S END!
MM!
SHE'S QUITE SOMETHING.
TOO GOOD TO BE JUST A GIRL...
I SAY IT'S ...
TIME TO DO OUR BIT TO KEEP UP WITH HER...

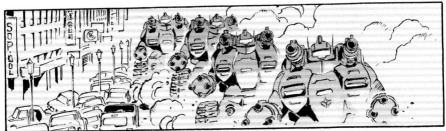

ENE-
MIES
!

WHO
ARE
THEY
?

OUR
ENE-
MY!

MINE,
AND
YOURS,
AND
MOTH-
ER'S—

DESTROY
THEM!

I'M
GONNA

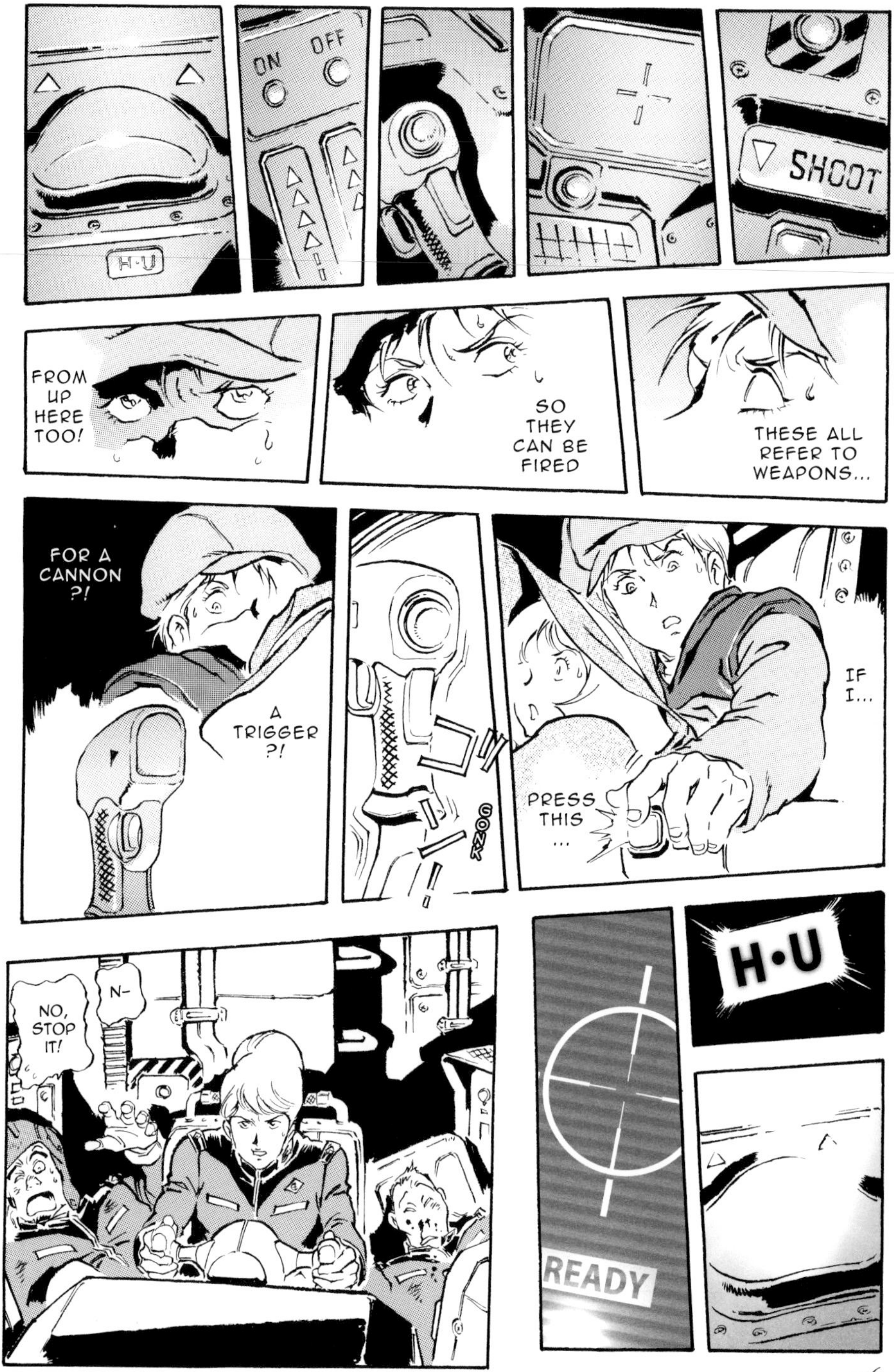
SHOOT
ON
OFF
H·U
THESE ALL REFER TO WEAPONS...
SO THEY CAN BE FIRED
FROM UP HERE TOO!
IF I...
PRESS THIS ...
GONK
FOR A CANNON ?!
A TRIGGER ?!
H•U
READY
N-
NO, STOP IT!

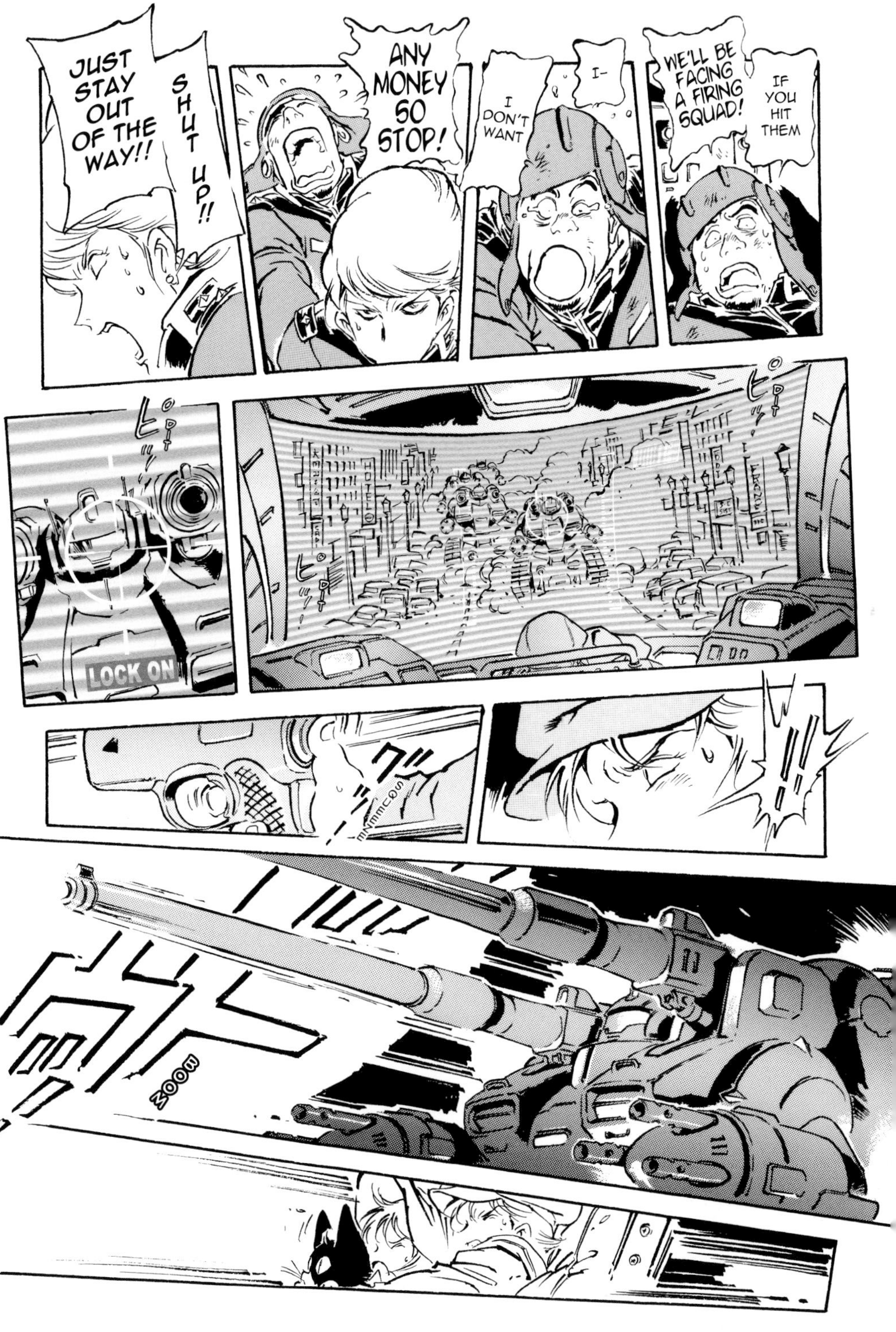
IF YOU HIT THEM
WE'LL BE FACING A FIRING SQUAD!
I-
I DON'T WANT
ANY MONEY SO STOP!
SHUT UP!!
JUST STAY OUT OF THE WAY!!
LOCK ON
ZOOM

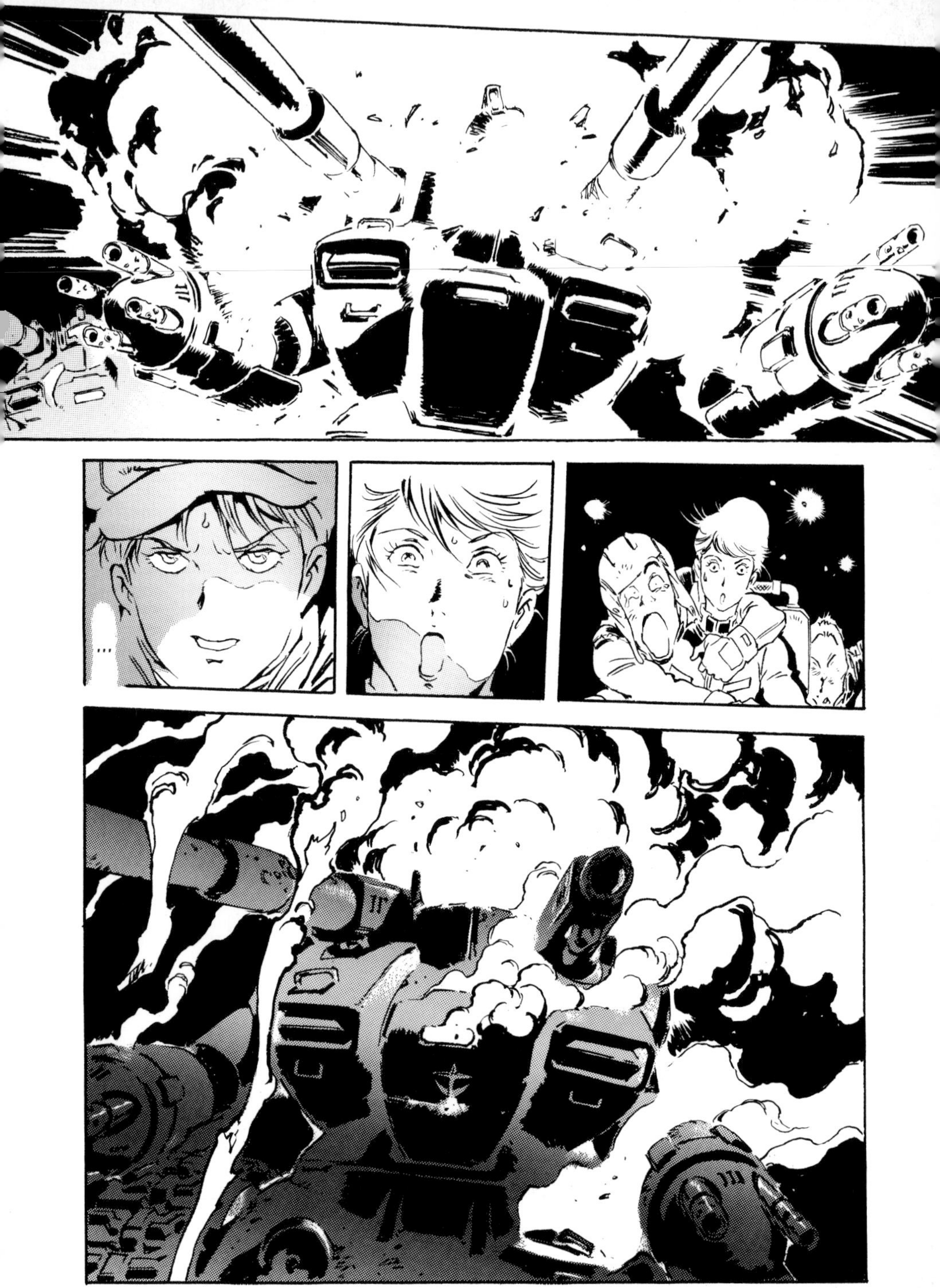
…

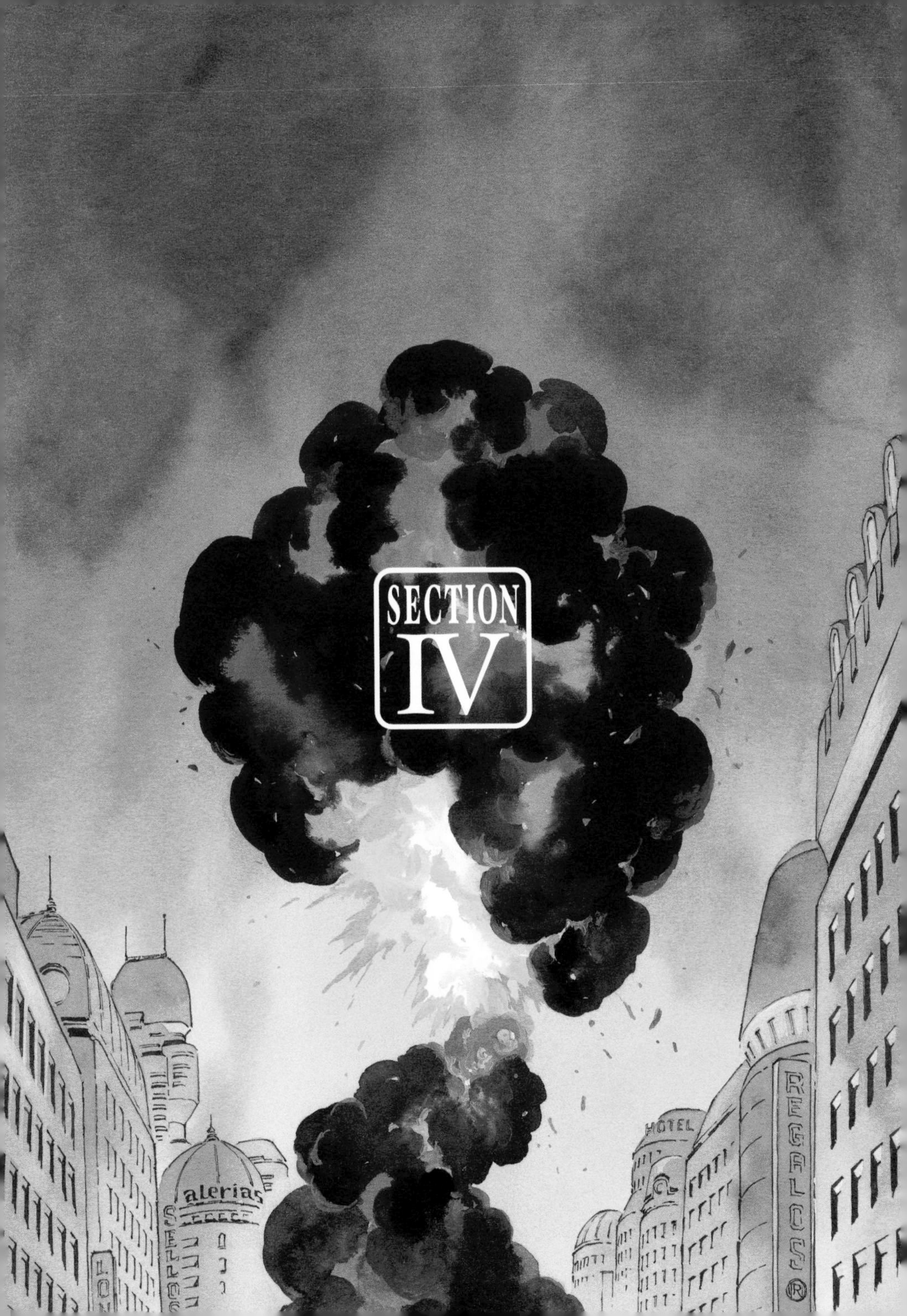
SECTION
IV
alerias
HOTEL
REGALOS

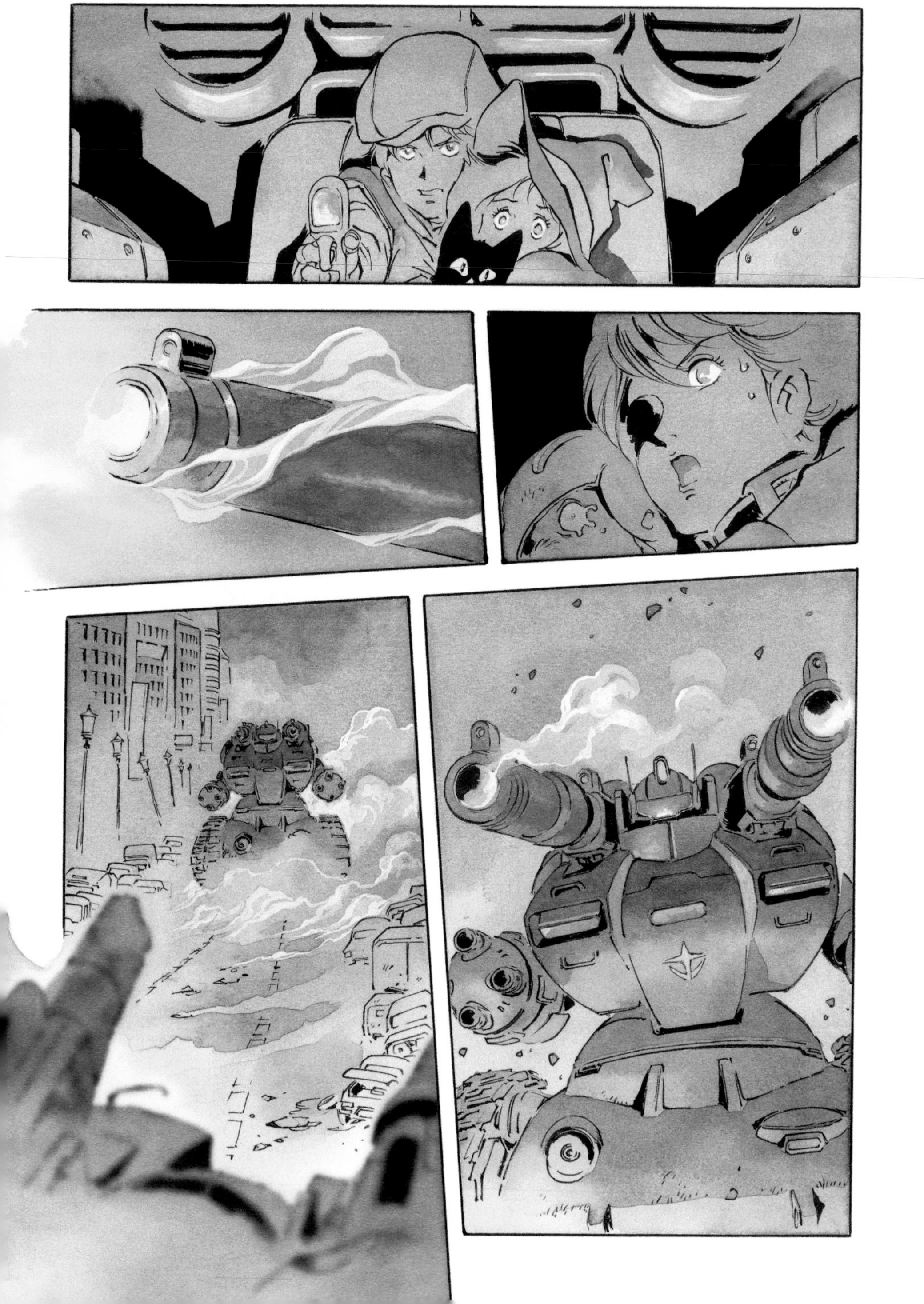

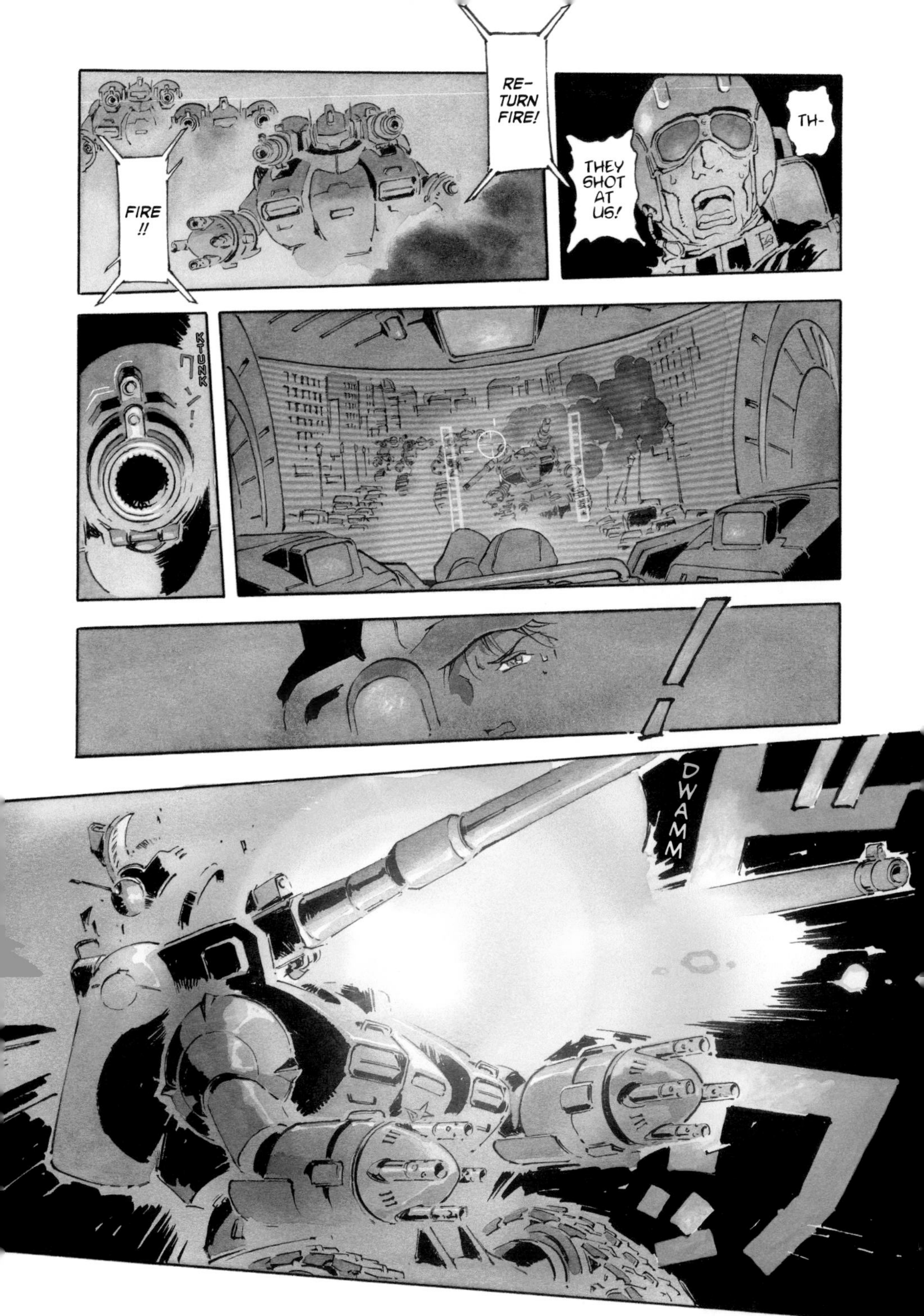
TH-
THEY SHOT AT US!
RE-TURN FIRE!
FIRE !!
KTUNK
DWAMM

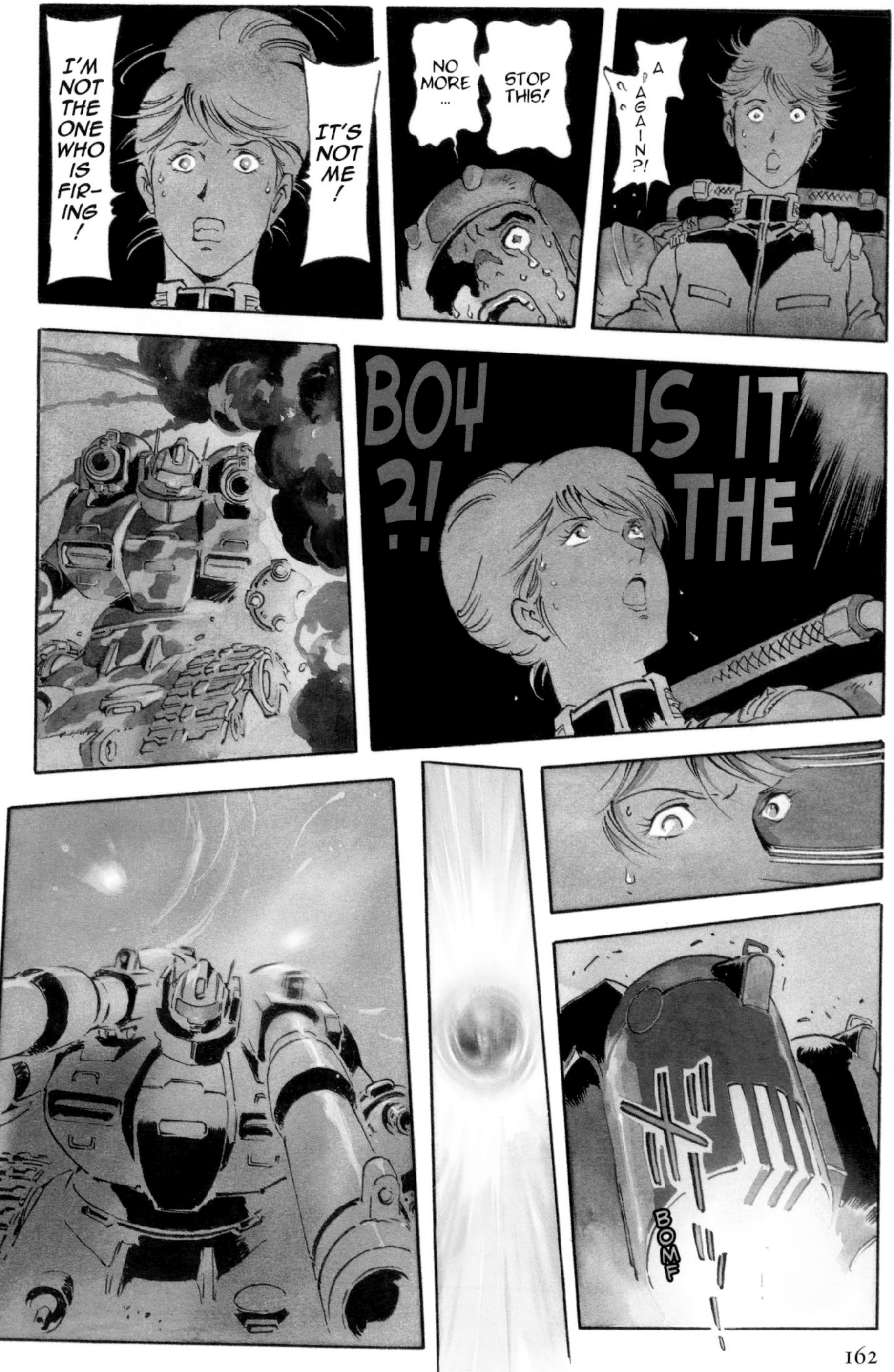
A... AGAIN?!
STOP THIS!
NO MORE...
IT'S NOT ME!
I'M NOT THE ONE WHO IS FIRING!
IS IT THE BOY?!
BOMF

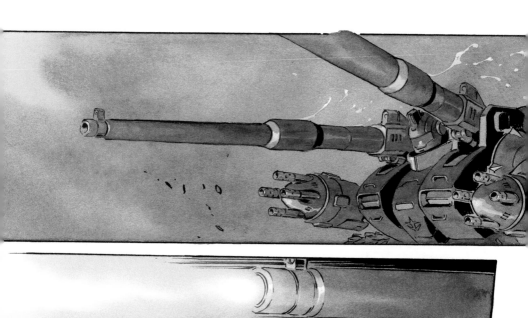

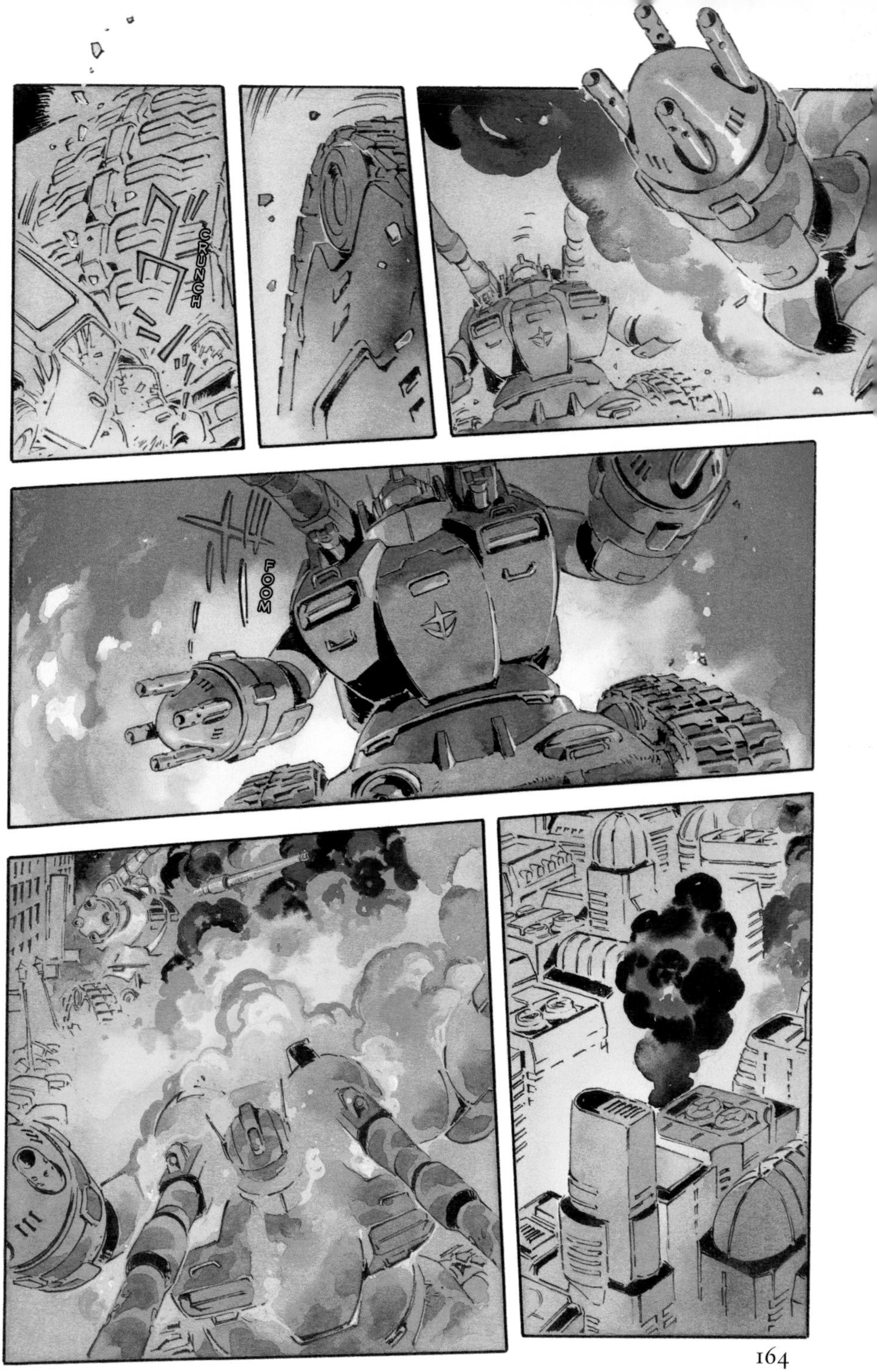
CRUNCH
FOOM

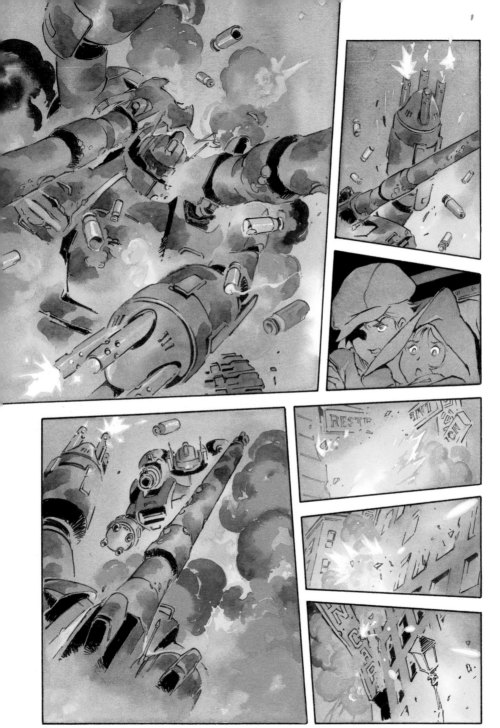

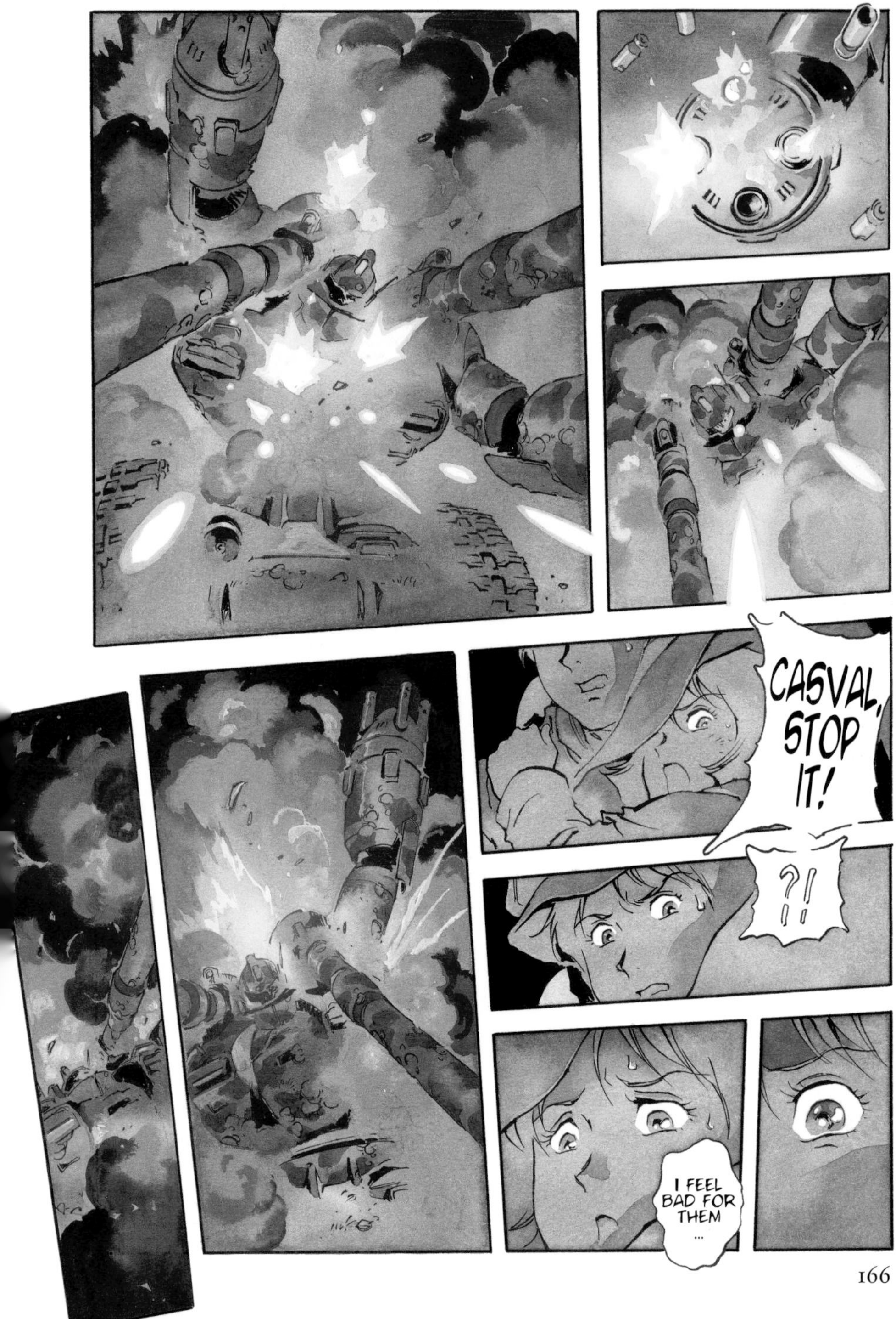
CASVAL, STOP IT!
?!
I FEEL BAD FOR THEM ...

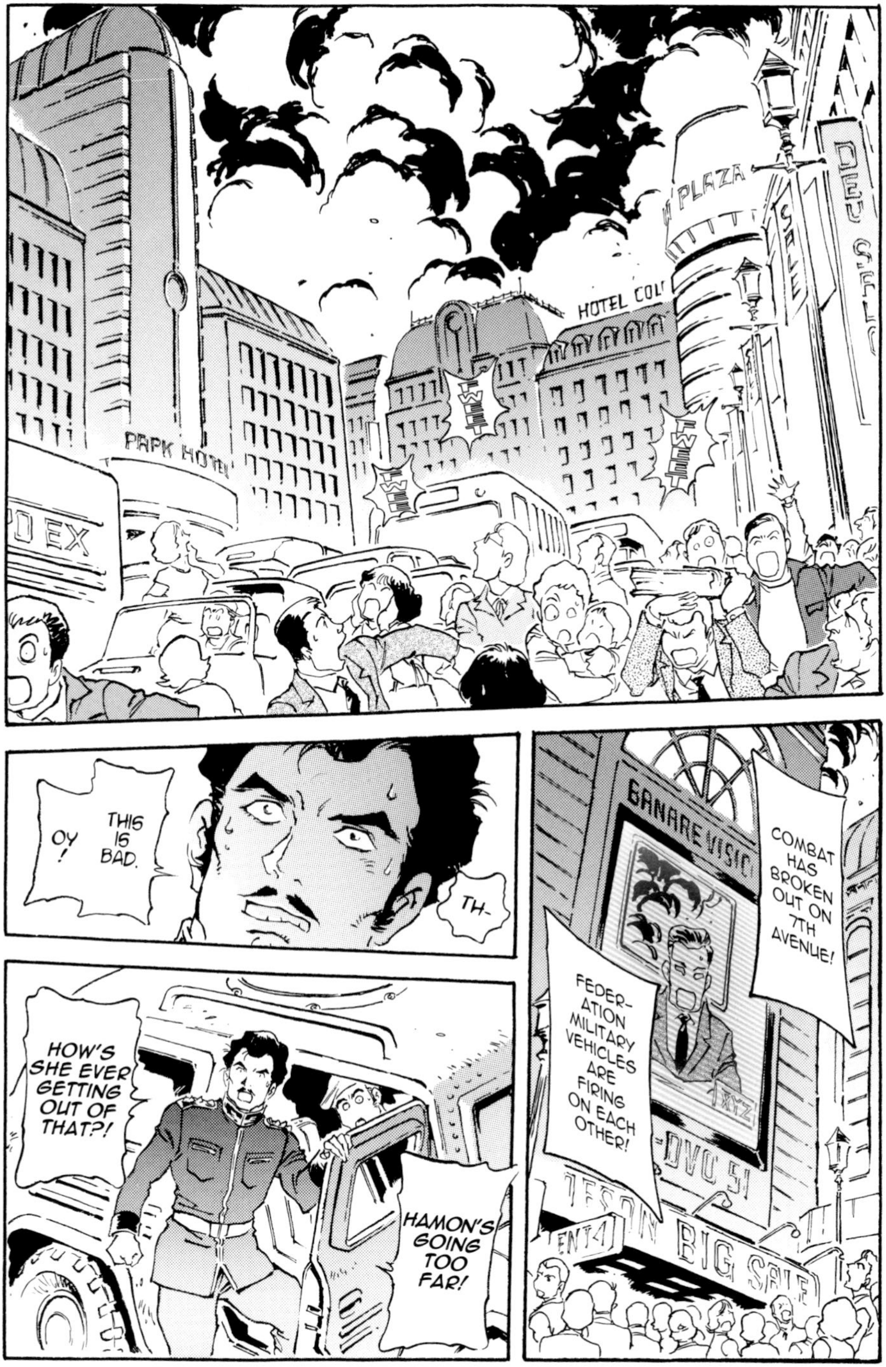
PLAZA
HOTEL COL
PARK HOTEL
FWEET
FWEET
COMBAT HAS BROKEN OUT ON 7TH AVENUE!
FEDERATION MILITARY VEHICLES ARE FIRING ON EACH OTHER!
BIG SALE
TH-
THIS IS BAD.
OY!
HAMON'S GOING TOO FAR!
HOW'S SHE EVER GETTING OUT OF THAT?!

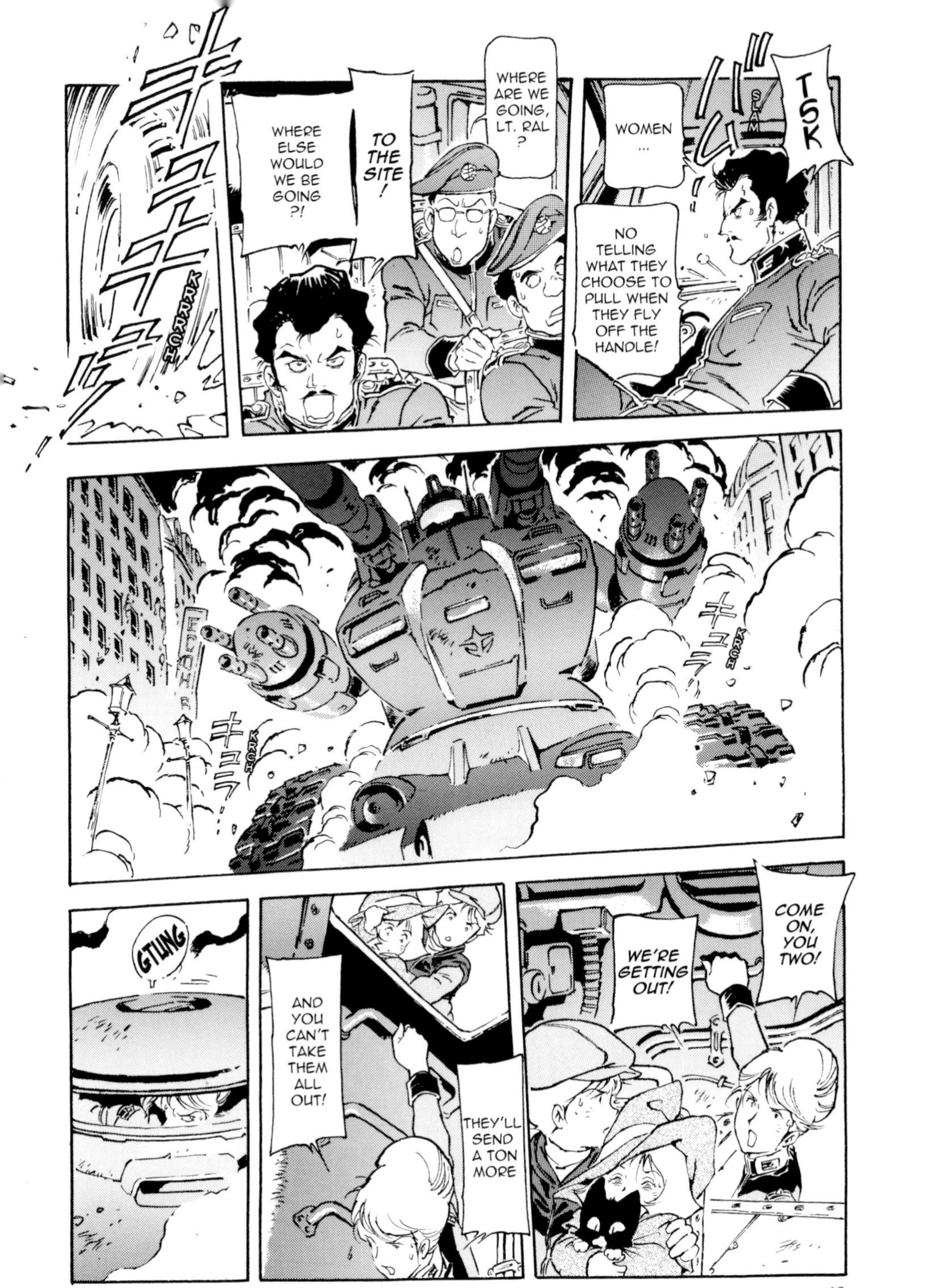
TSK
SLAM
WOMEN ...
NO TELLING WHAT THEY CHOOSE TO PULL WHEN THEY FLY OFF THE HANDLE!
WHERE ARE WE GOING, LT. RAL?
TO THE SITE!
WHERE ELSE WOULD WE BE GOING?!
KRRRCH
KRCH
KRCH
COME ON, YOU TWO!
WE'RE GETTING OUT!
AND YOU CAN'T TAKE THEM ALL OUT!
THEY'LL SEND A TON MORE
GTUNG

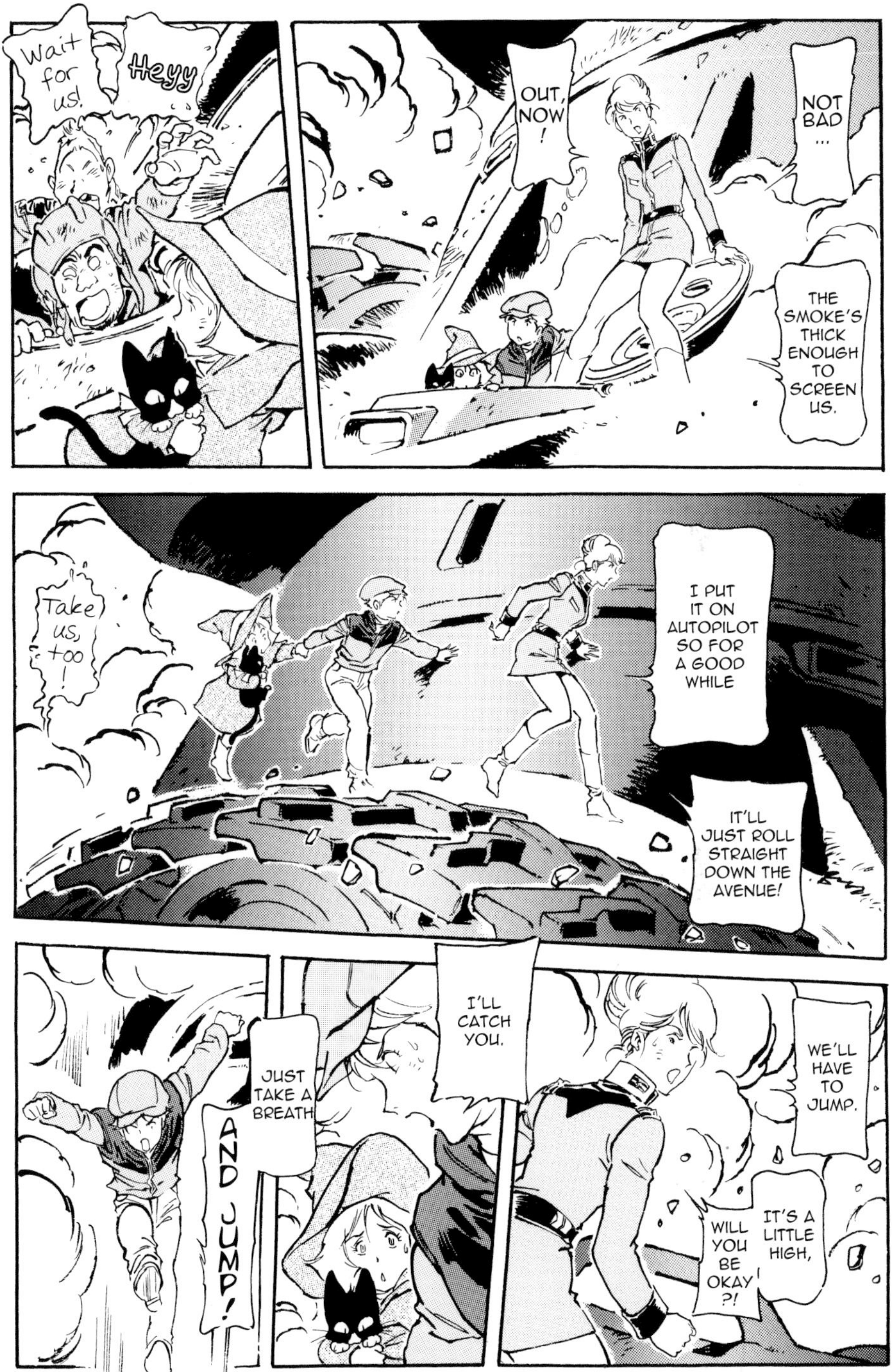
NOT BAD ...
OUT, NOW!
THE SMOKE'S THICK ENOUGH TO SCREEN US.
Heyy
Wait for us!
I PUT IT ON AUTOPILOT SO FOR A GOOD WHILE
IT'LL JUST ROLL STRAIGHT DOWN THE AVENUE!
Take us, too!
WE'LL HAVE TO JUMP.
IT'S A LITTLE HIGH,
WILL YOU BE OKAY?!
I'LL CATCH YOU.
JUST TAKE A BREATH
AND JUMP!

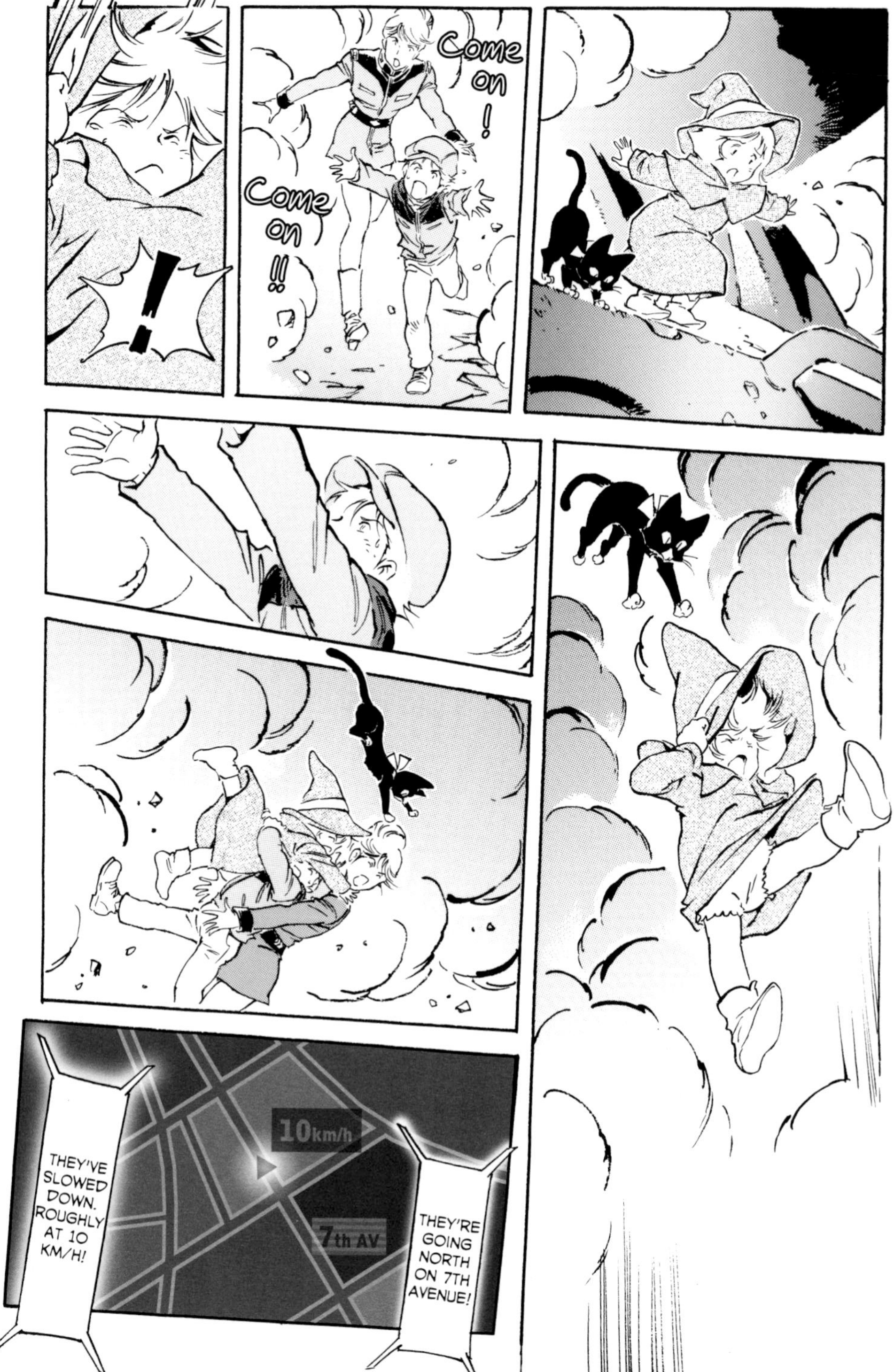
Come on!
Come on!!
!
THEY'VE SLOWED DOWN. ROUGHLY AT 10 KM/H!
10km/h
7th AV
THEY'RE GOING NORTH ON 7TH AVENUE!

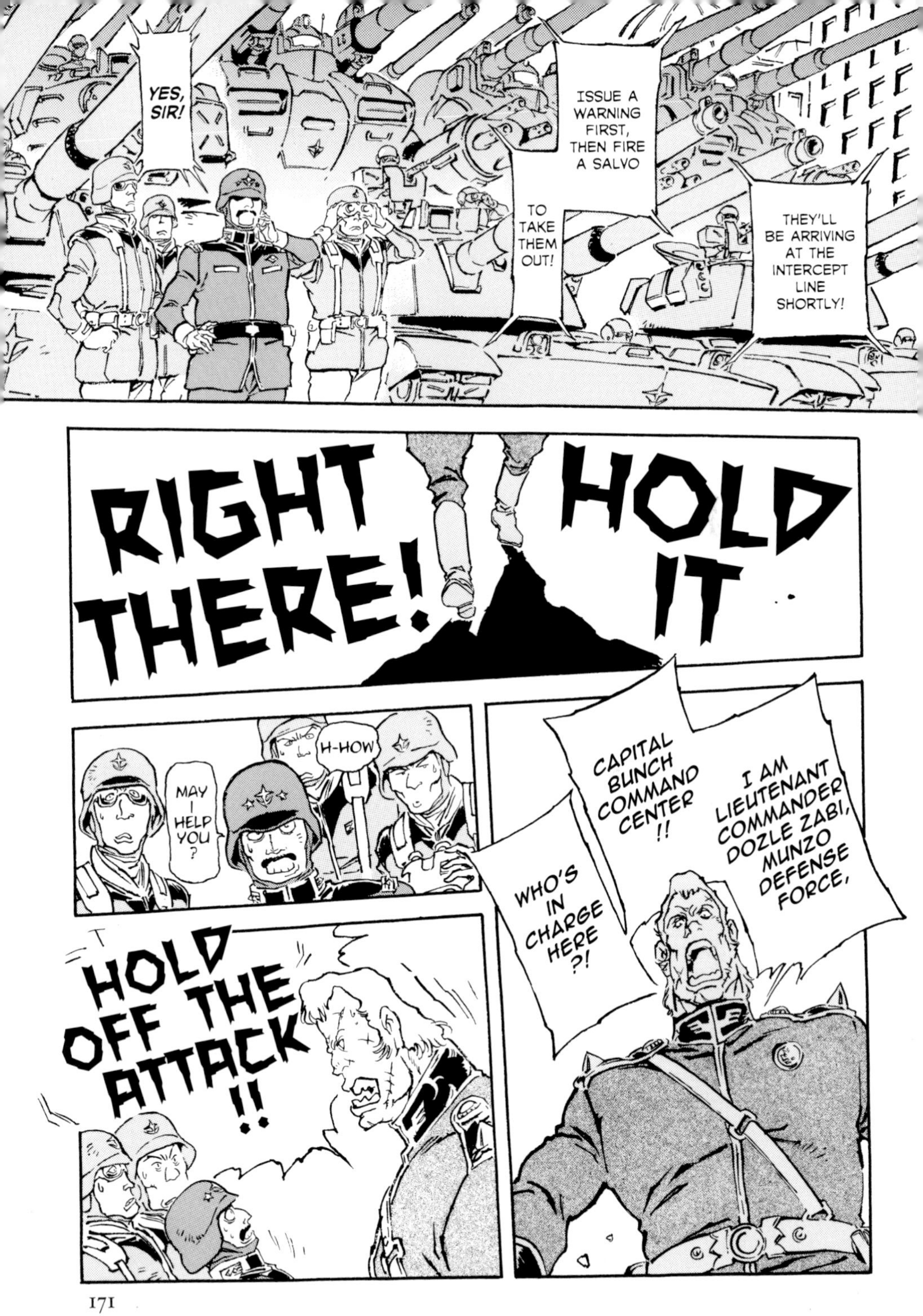
THEY'LL BE ARRIVING AT THE INTERCEPT LINE SHORTLY!
ISSUE A WARNING FIRST, THEN FIRE A SALVO
TO TAKE THEM OUT!
YES, SIR!
HOLD IT
RIGHT THERE!
I AM LIEUTENANT COMMANDER DOZLE ZABI, MUNZO DEFENSE FORCE,
CAPITAL BUNCH COMMAND CENTER !!
WHO'S IN CHARGE HERE ?!
H-HOW
MAY I HELP YOU ?
HOLD OFF THE ATTACK !!

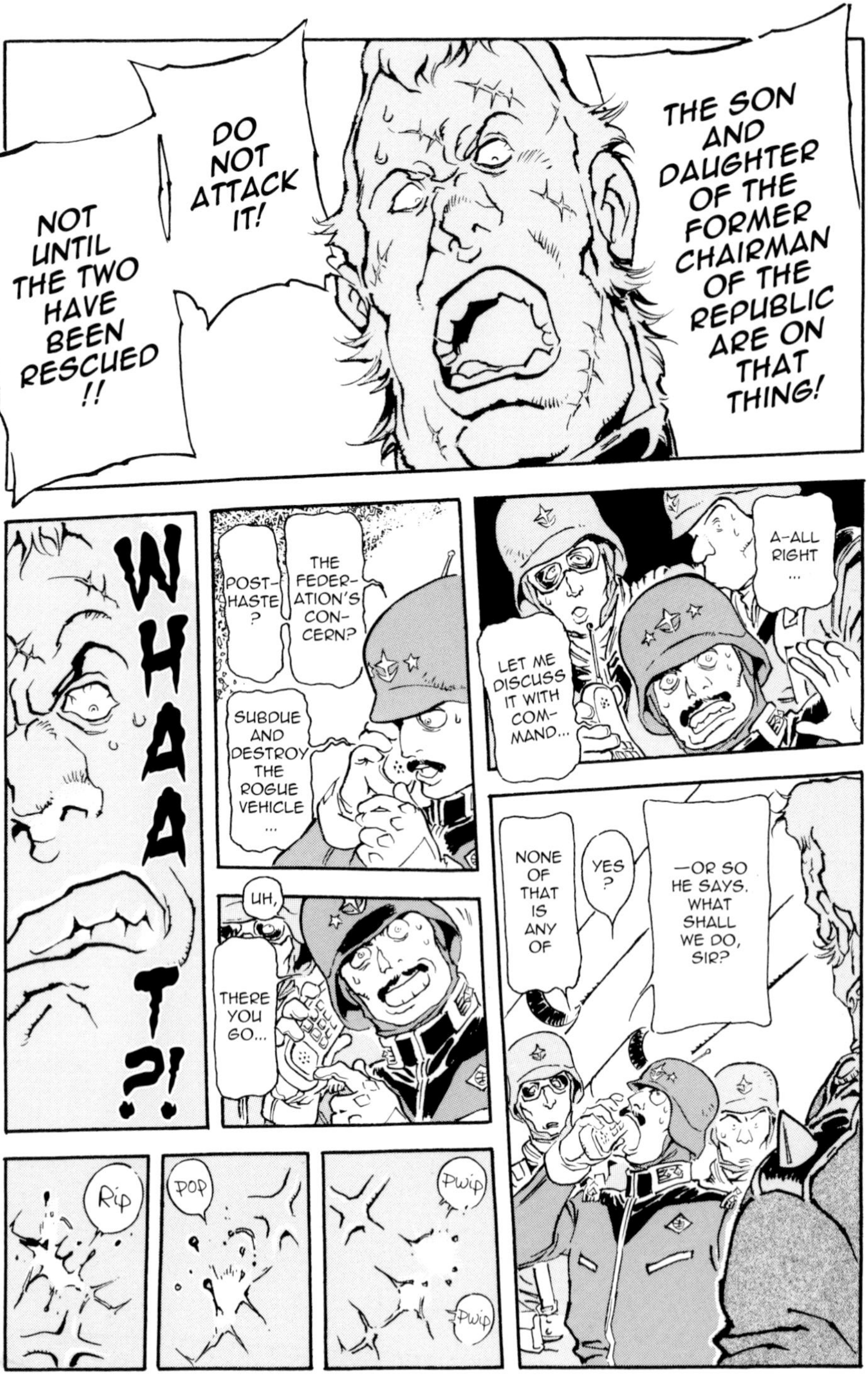
THE SON AND DAUGHTER OF THE FORMER CHAIRMAN OF THE REPUBLIC ARE ON THAT THING!
DO NOT ATTACK IT!
NOT UNTIL THE TWO HAVE BEEN RESCUED!!
A-ALL RIGHT...
LET ME DISCUSS IT WITH COM-MAND...
—OR SO HE SAYS. WHAT SHALL WE DO, SIR?
YES?
NONE OF THAT IS ANY OF
THE FEDER-ATION'S CON-CERN?
POST-HASTE?
SUBDUE AND DESTROY THE ROGUE VEHICLE...
UH,
THERE YOU GO...
WHAT?!
Pwip
Pwip
POP
Rip

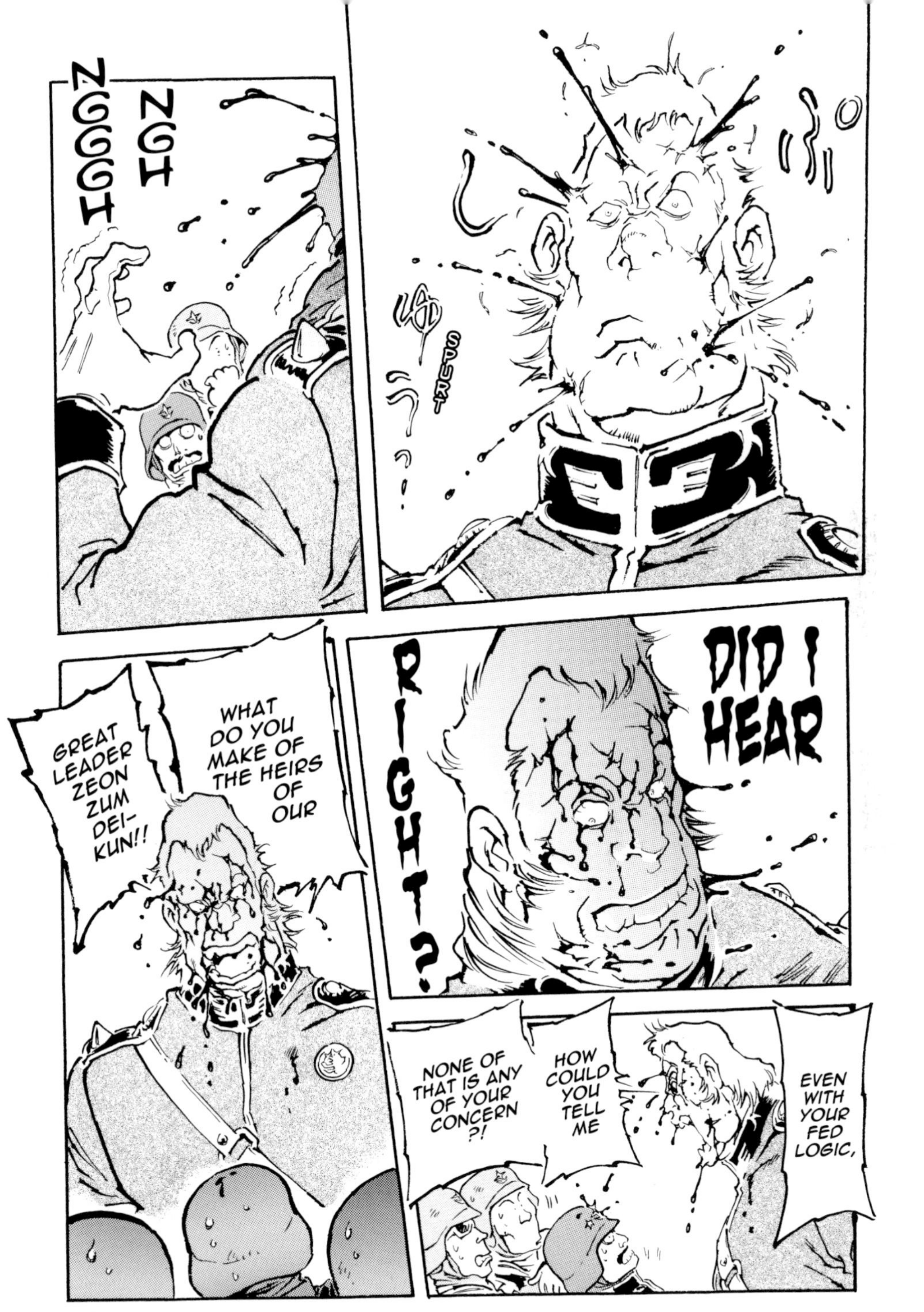
SPURT
NGH
NGGGH
DID I HEAR
RIGHT?
EVEN WITH YOUR FED LOGIC,
HOW COULD YOU TELL ME
NONE OF THAT IS ANY OF YOUR CONCERN ?!
WHAT DO YOU MAKE OF THE HEIRS OF OUR
GREAT LEADER ZEON ZUM DEI-KUN!!

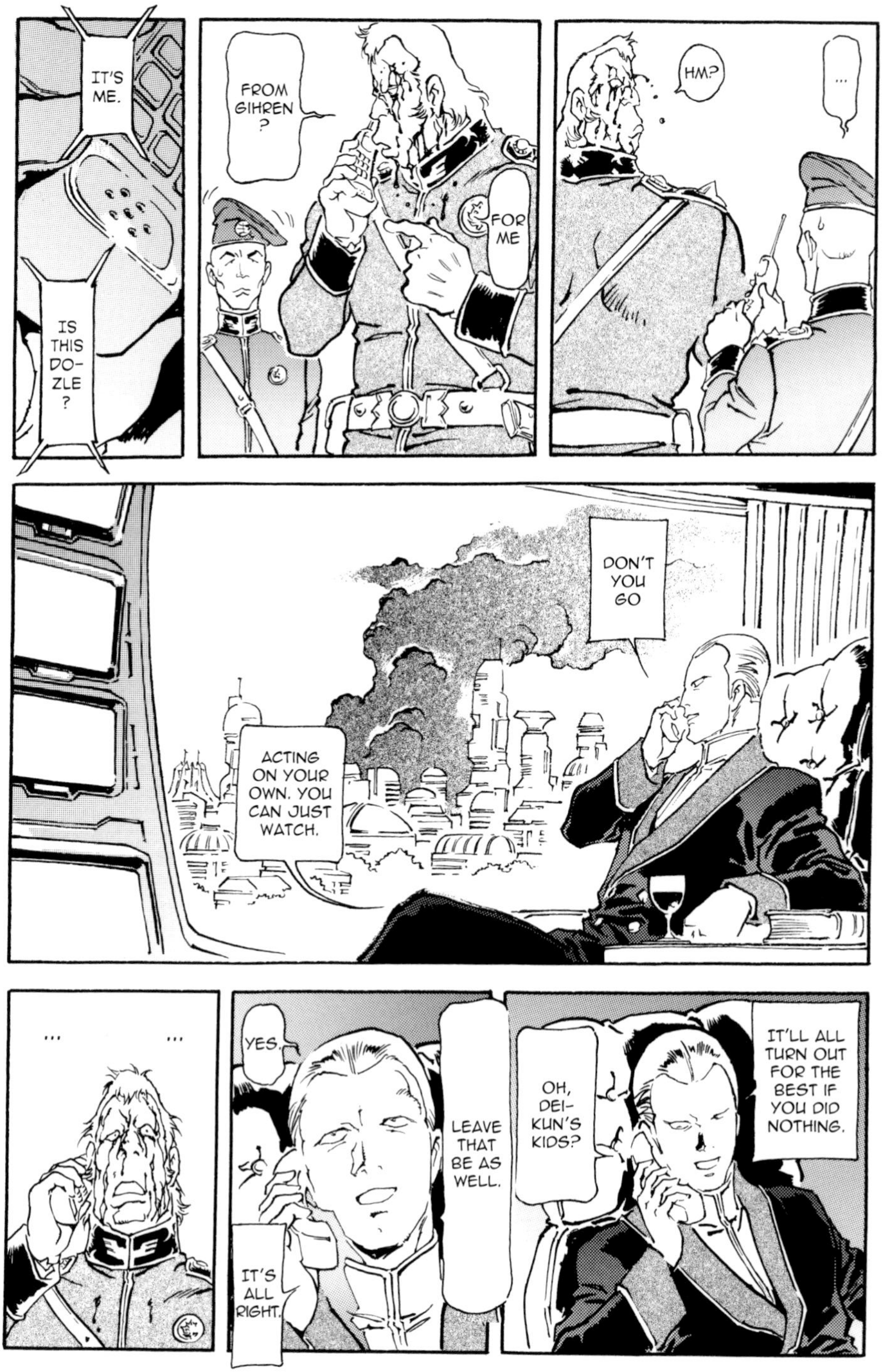
...
HM?
FROM GIHREN?
FOR ME
IT'S ME.
IS THIS DOZLE?
DON'T YOU GO
ACTING ON YOUR OWN. YOU CAN JUST WATCH.
IT'LL ALL TURN OUT FOR THE BEST IF YOU DID NOTHING.
OH, DEIKUN'S KIDS?
LEAVE THAT BE AS WELL.
YES.
IT'S ALL RIGHT.
... ...

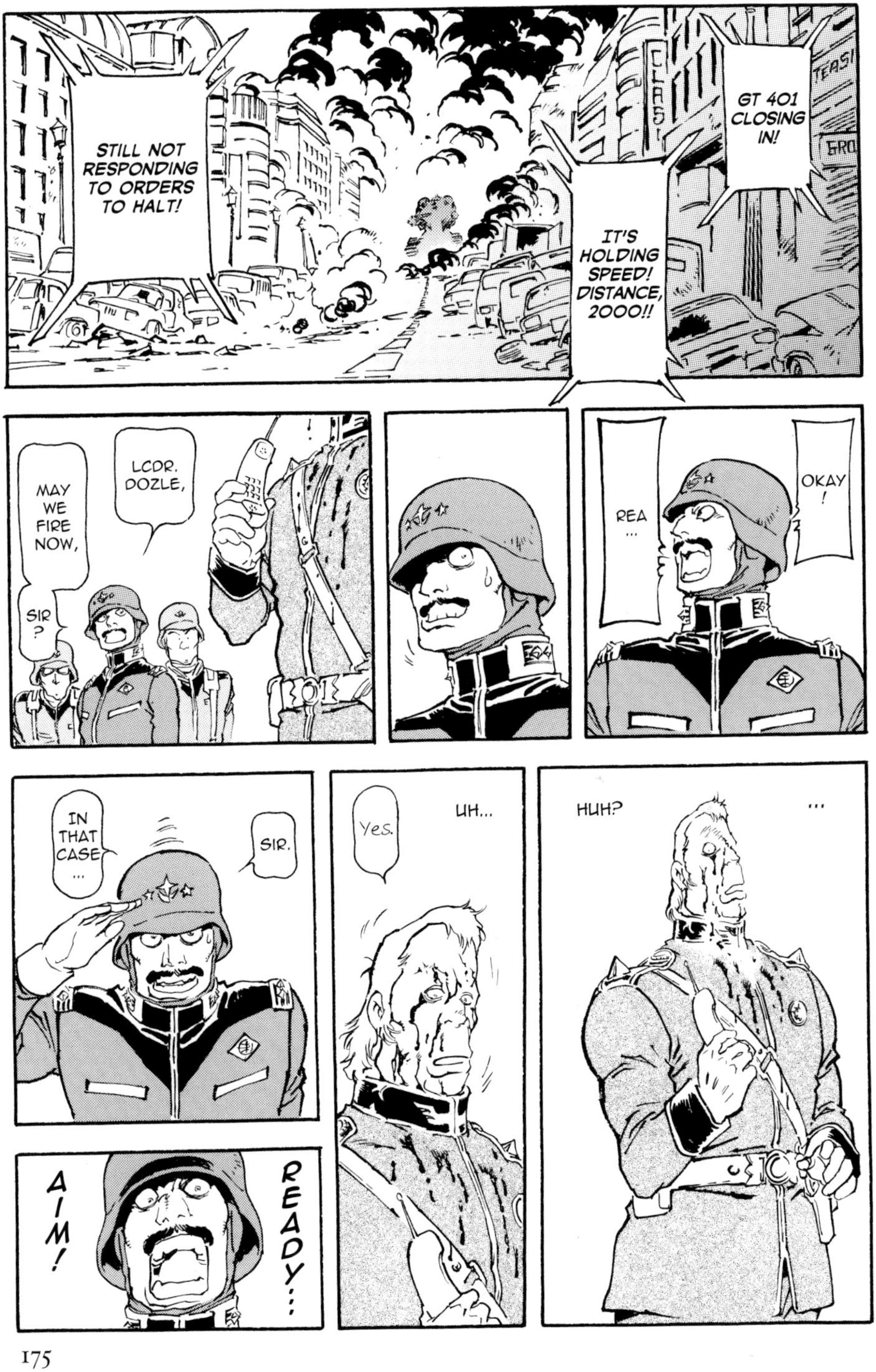
GT 401 CLOSING IN!
IT'S HOLDING SPEED! DISTANCE, 2000!!
STILL NOT RESPONDING TO ORDERS TO HALT!
OKAY!
REA...
LCDR. DOZLE,
MAY WE FIRE NOW,
SIR?
...
HUH?
UH...
Yes.
SIR.
IN THAT CASE...
READY...
AIM!

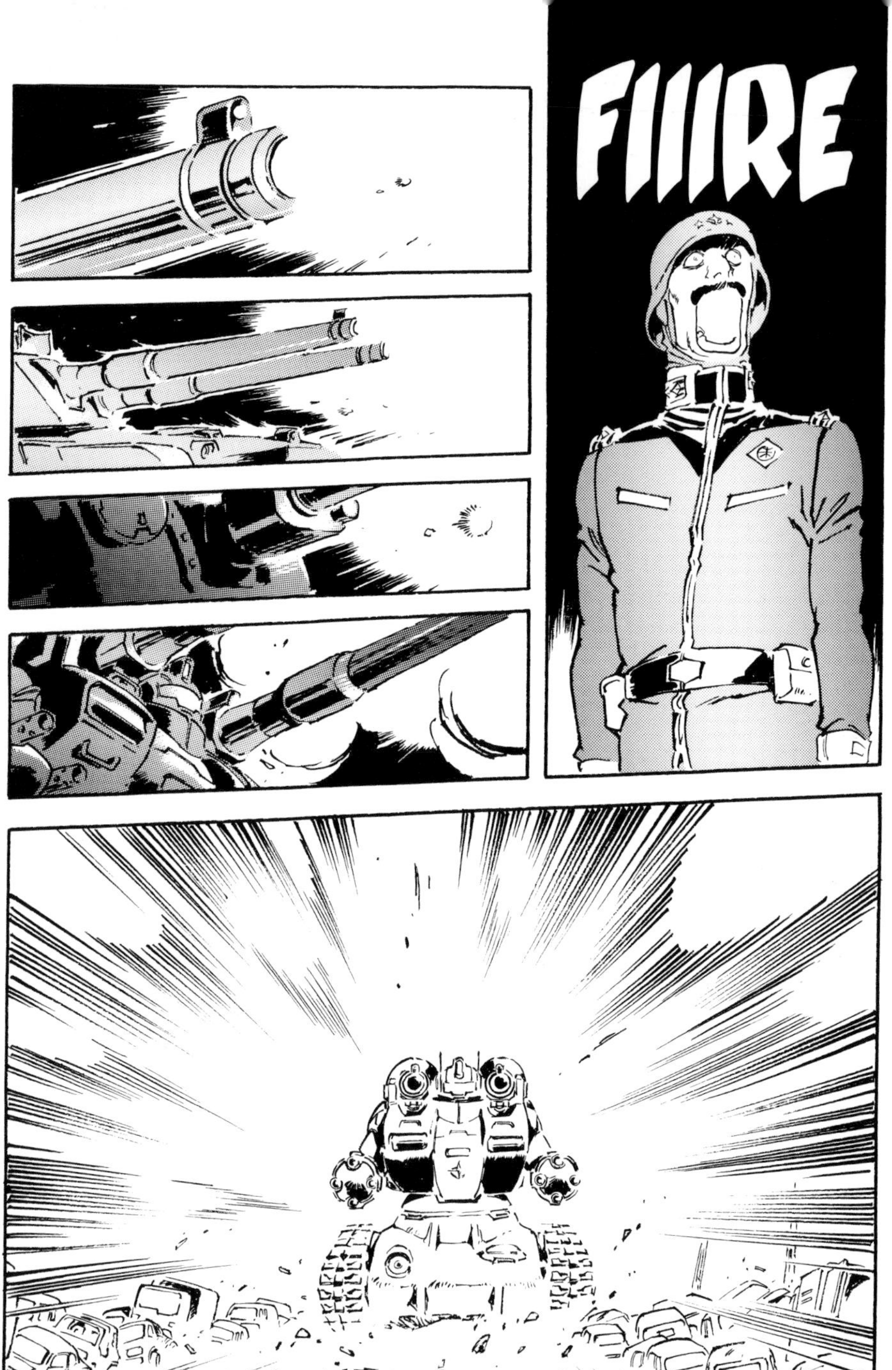
FIIIRE

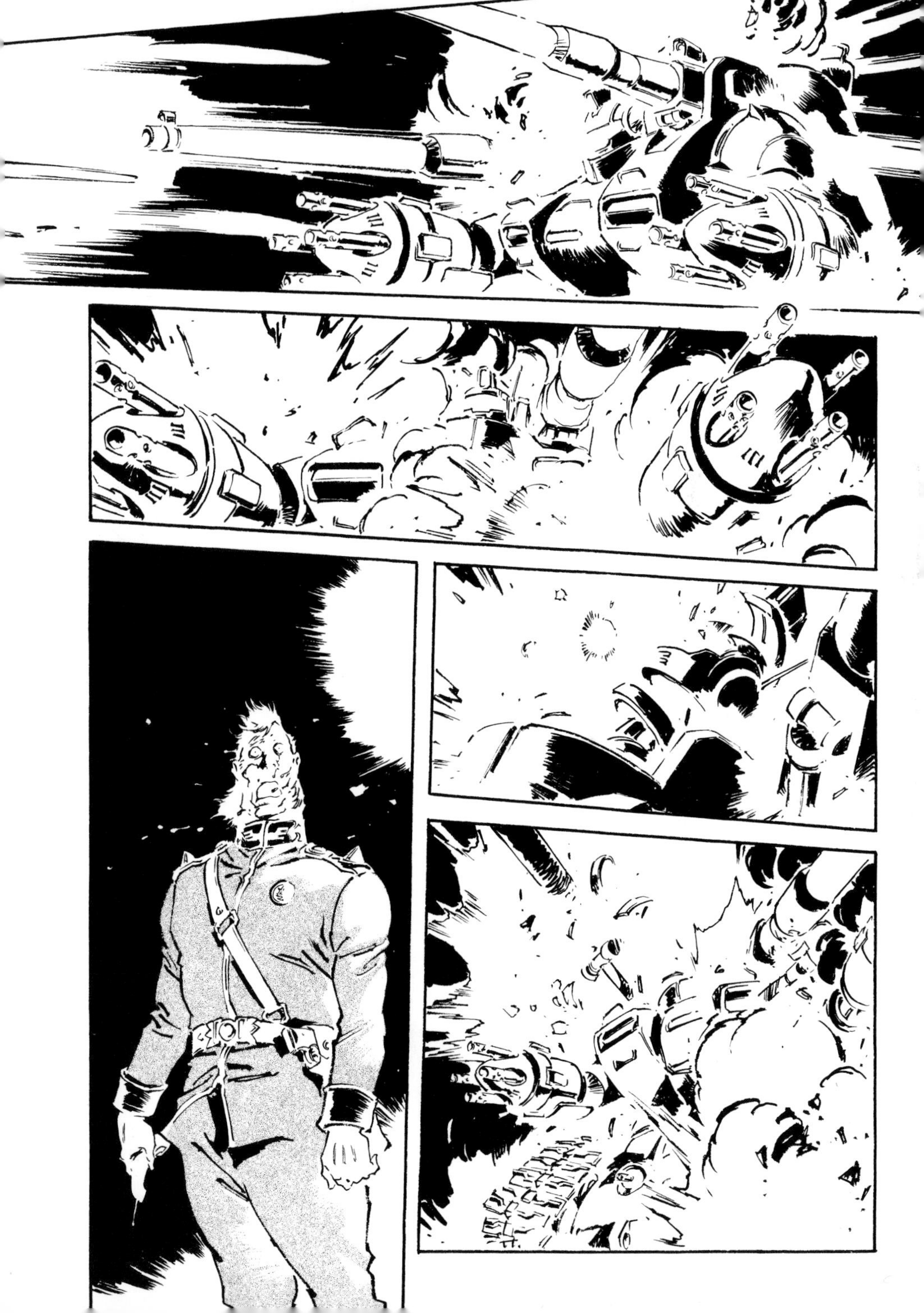

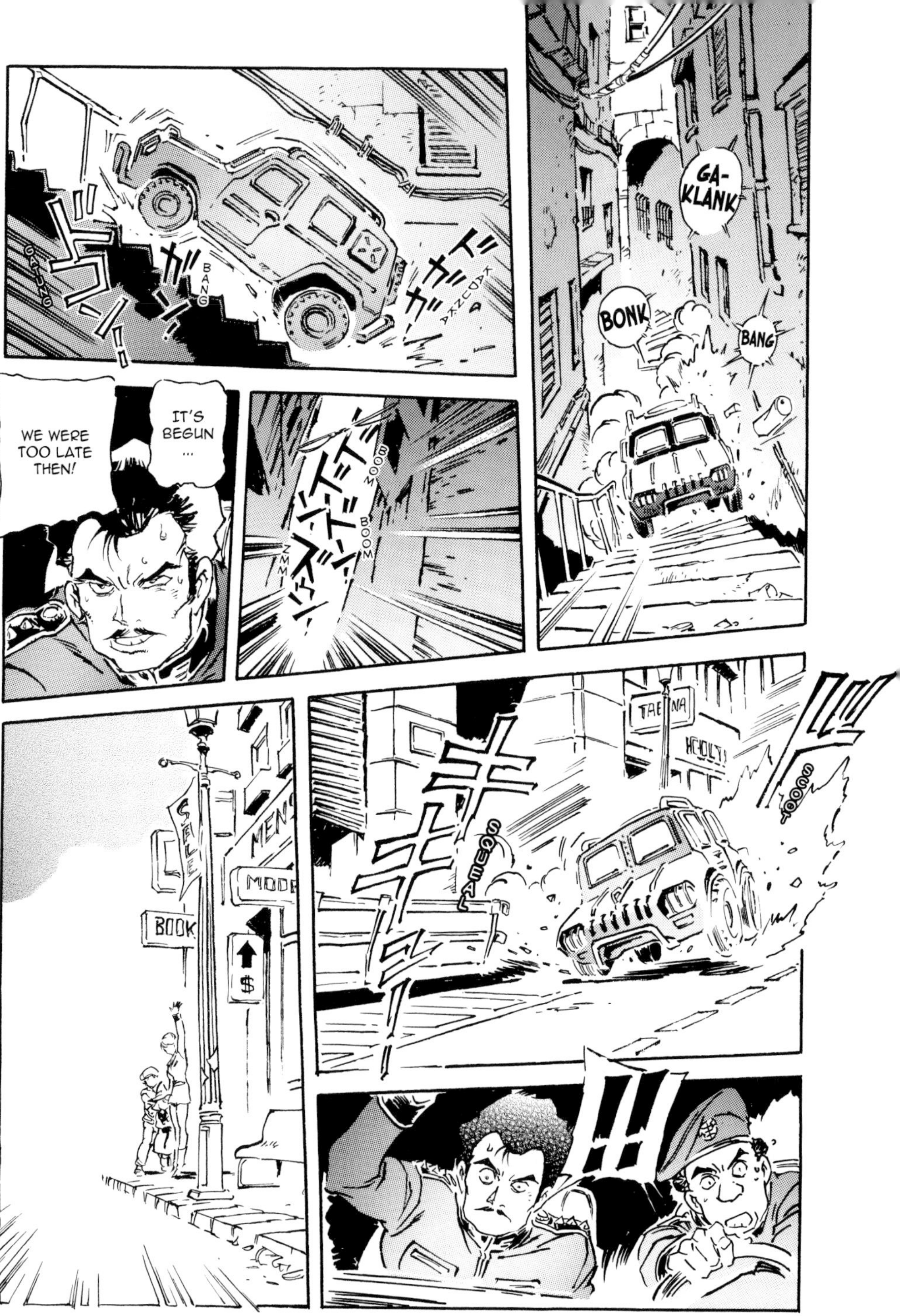

GA-KLANK
BONK
BANG
ドゥッ
KADUNKA
ガガン
BANG
ドンッ
GATUNG
ズドドドッ
BOOM
BOOM
ズズン
ZMM
IT'S BEGUN ...
WE WERE TOO LATE THEN!
TAENA
HOLT
SCOOT
キキキーッ
SQUEAL
MEN'S
MODE
SALE
BOOK
$

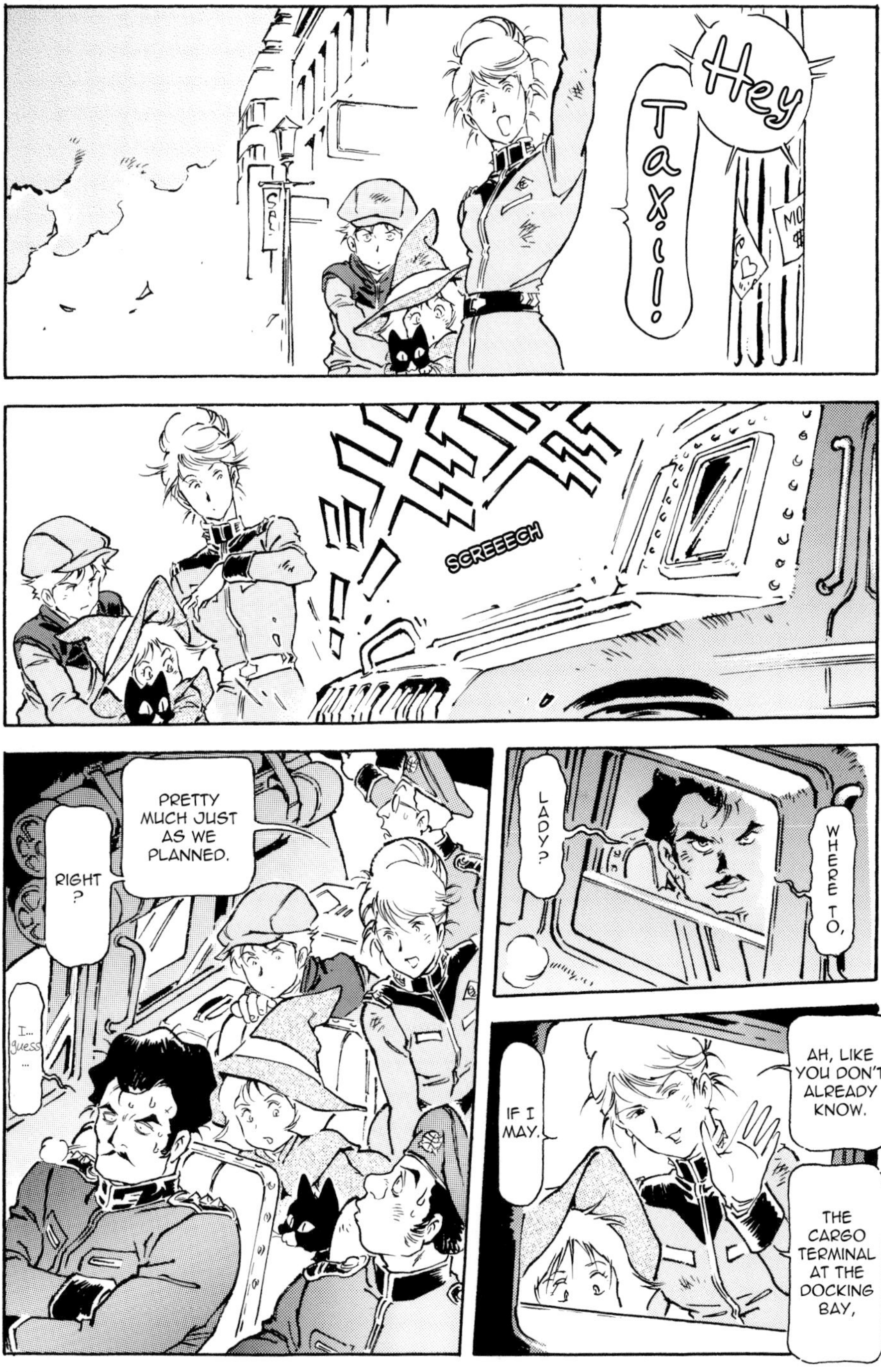
Hey
Taxi!
SCREEECH
Where to,
Lady?
Ah, like you don't already know.
The cargo terminal at the docking bay,
If I may.
Pretty much just as we planned.
Right?
I... guess...

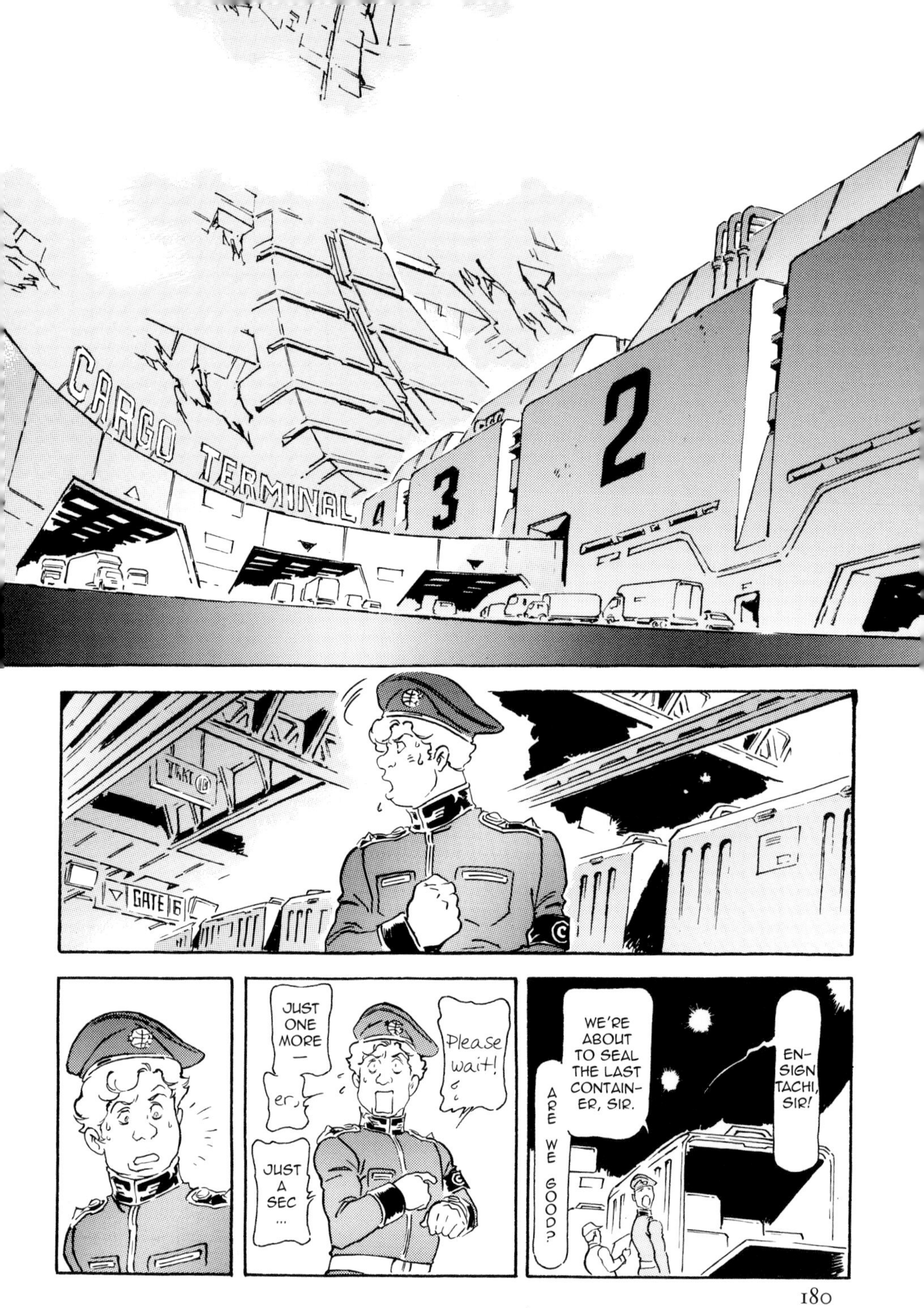
CARGO TERMINAL
3
2
GATE 6
ENSIGN TACHI, SIR!
WE'RE ABOUT TO SEAL THE LAST CONTAINER, SIR.
ARE WE GOOD?
Please wait!
JUST ONE MORE—
er,
JUST A SEC ...

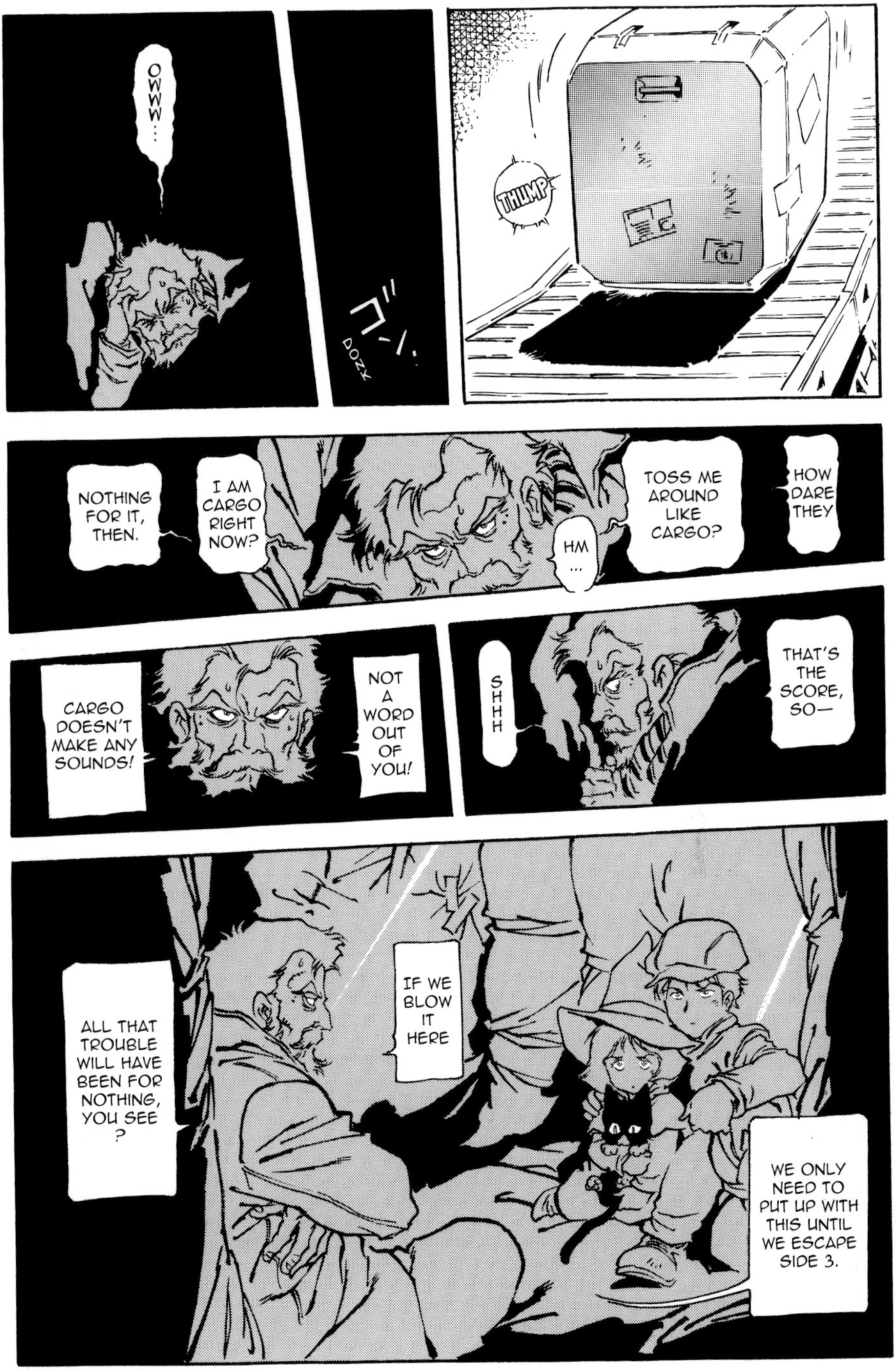
THUMP
ゴン
DONK
OWWW...
HOW DARE THEY
TOSS ME AROUND LIKE CARGO?
HM...
I AM CARGO RIGHT NOW?
NOTHING FOR IT, THEN.
THAT'S THE SCORE, SO—
SHHH
NOT A WORD OUT OF YOU!
CARGO DOESN'T MAKE ANY SOUNDS!
WE ONLY NEED TO PUT UP WITH THIS UNTIL WE ESCAPE SIDE 3.
IF WE BLOW IT HERE
ALL THAT TROUBLE WILL HAVE BEEN FOR NOTHING, YOU SEE?

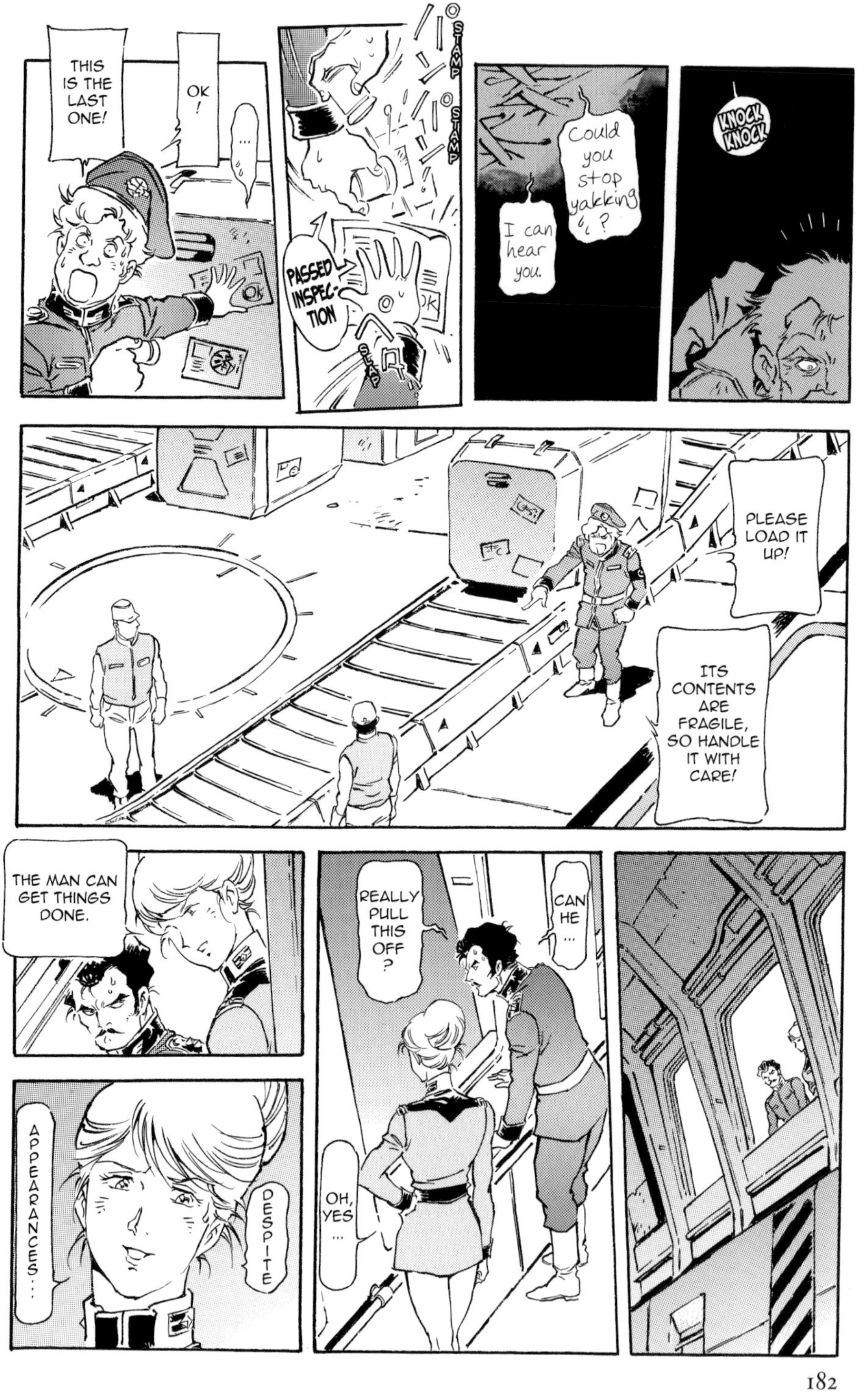
KNOCK KNOCK
Could you stop yakking ¿?
I can hear you.
STAMP
STAMP
PASSED INSPECTION
SLAP
OK!
...
THIS IS THE LAST ONE!
PLEASE LOAD IT UP!
ITS CONTENTS ARE FRAGILE, SO HANDLE IT WITH CARE!
CAN HE ...
REALLY PULL THIS OFF?
OH, YES ...
THE MAN CAN GET THINGS DONE.
DESPITE
APPEARANCES...

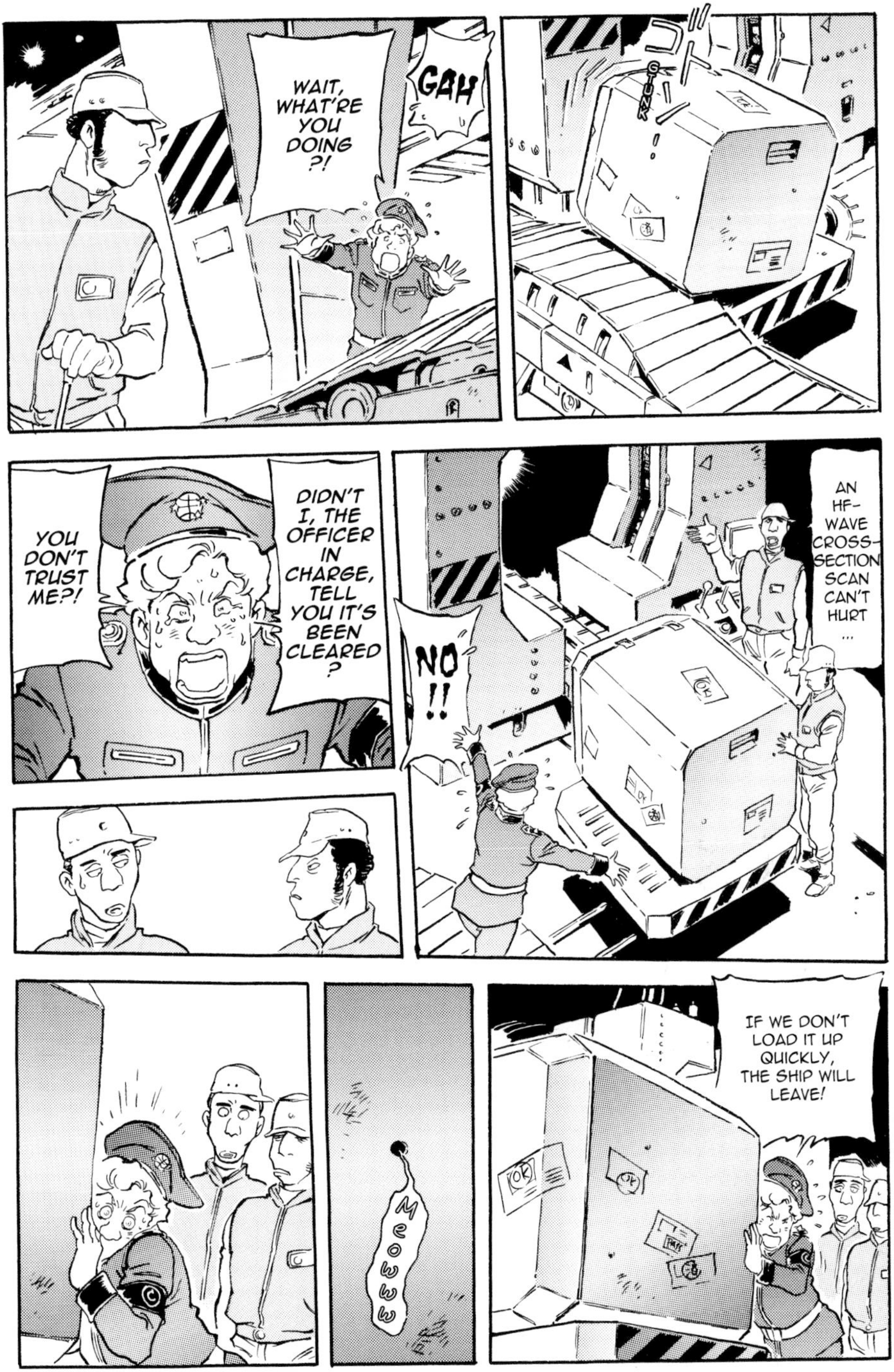
GUNK
GAH
WAIT, WHAT'RE YOU DOING ?!
AN HF-WAVE CROSS-SECTION SCAN CAN'T HURT ...
NO !!
DIDN'T I, THE OFFICER IN CHARGE, TELL YOU IT'S BEEN CLEARED ?
YOU DON'T TRUST ME?!
IF WE DON'T LOAD IT UP QUICKLY, THE SHIP WILL LEAVE!
Meowww

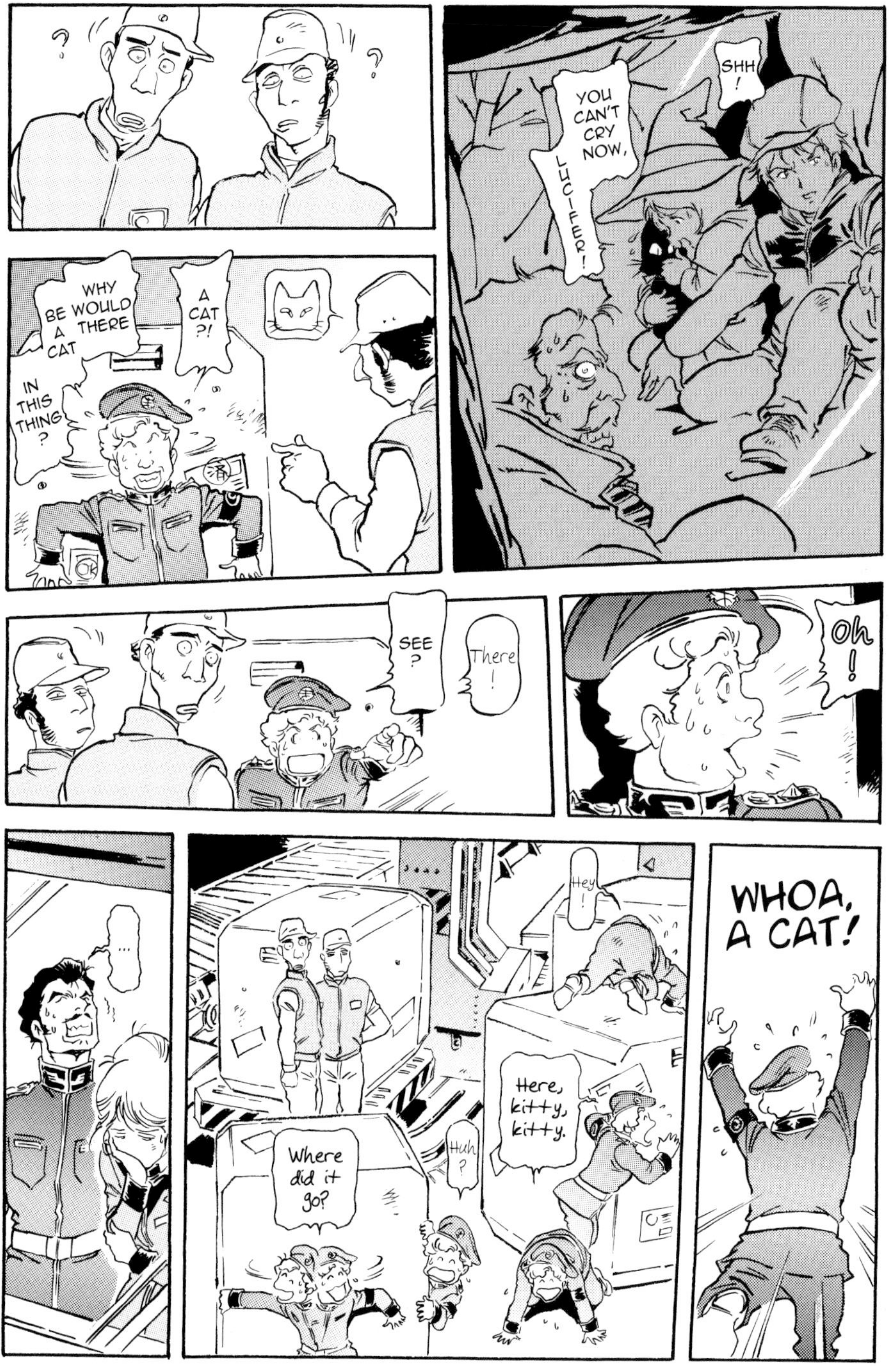
SHH!
YOU CAN'T CRY NOW, LUCIFER!
A CAT?!
WHY WOULD THERE BE A CAT IN THIS THING?
Oh!
There!
SEE?
WHOA, A CAT!
Hey!
Here, kitty, kitty.
Huh?
Where did it go?
...

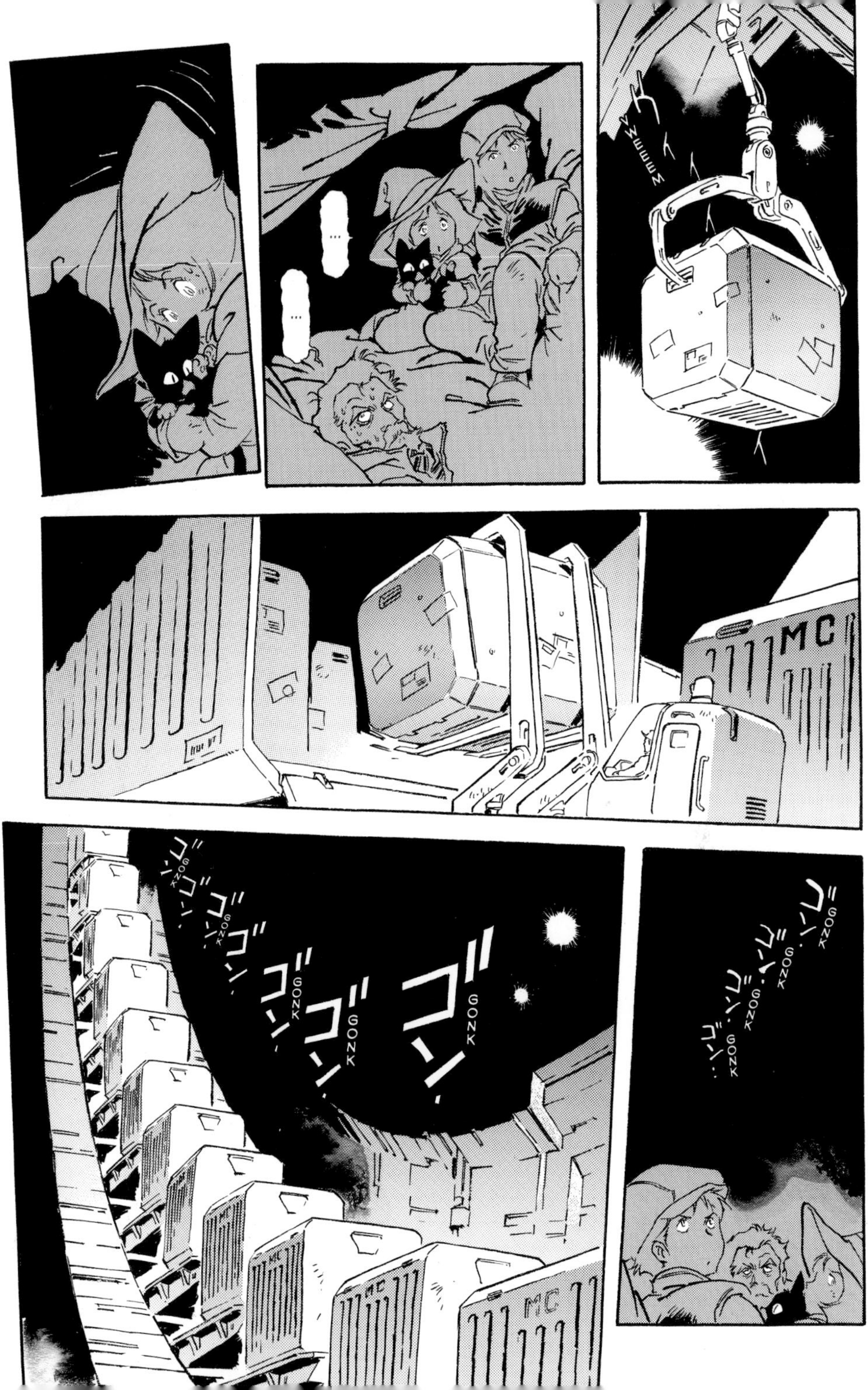

VWEEEM
…
…
ゴン… GONK
ゴン… GONK
ゴン… GONK
ゴン… GONK
ゴン GONK
ゴン GONK
ゴン GONK
ゴン GONK
ゴン GONK
ゴン GONK

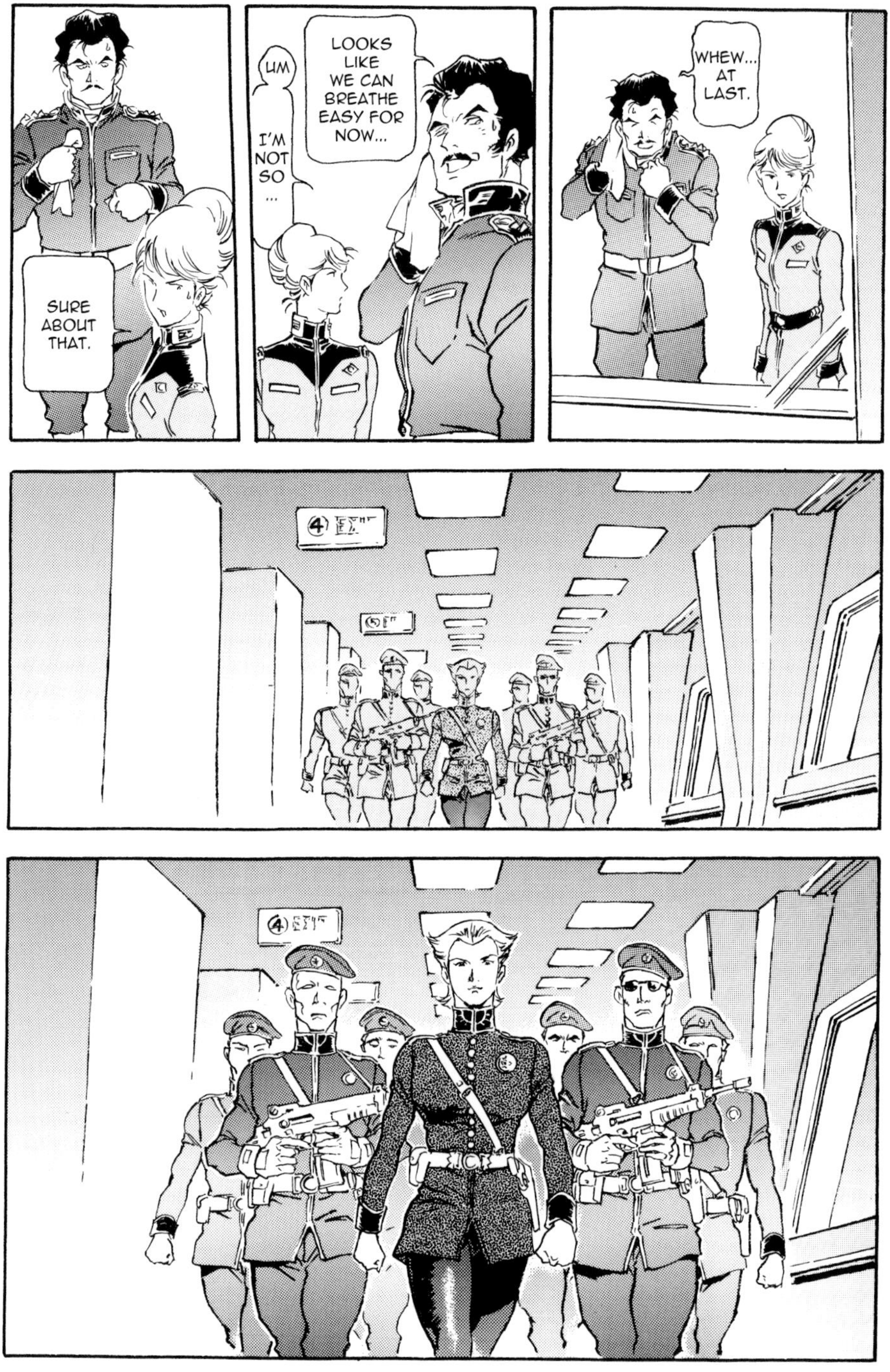
WHEW... AT LAST.
LOOKS LIKE WE CAN BREATHE EASY FOR NOW...
UM
I'M NOT SO ...
SURE ABOUT THAT.

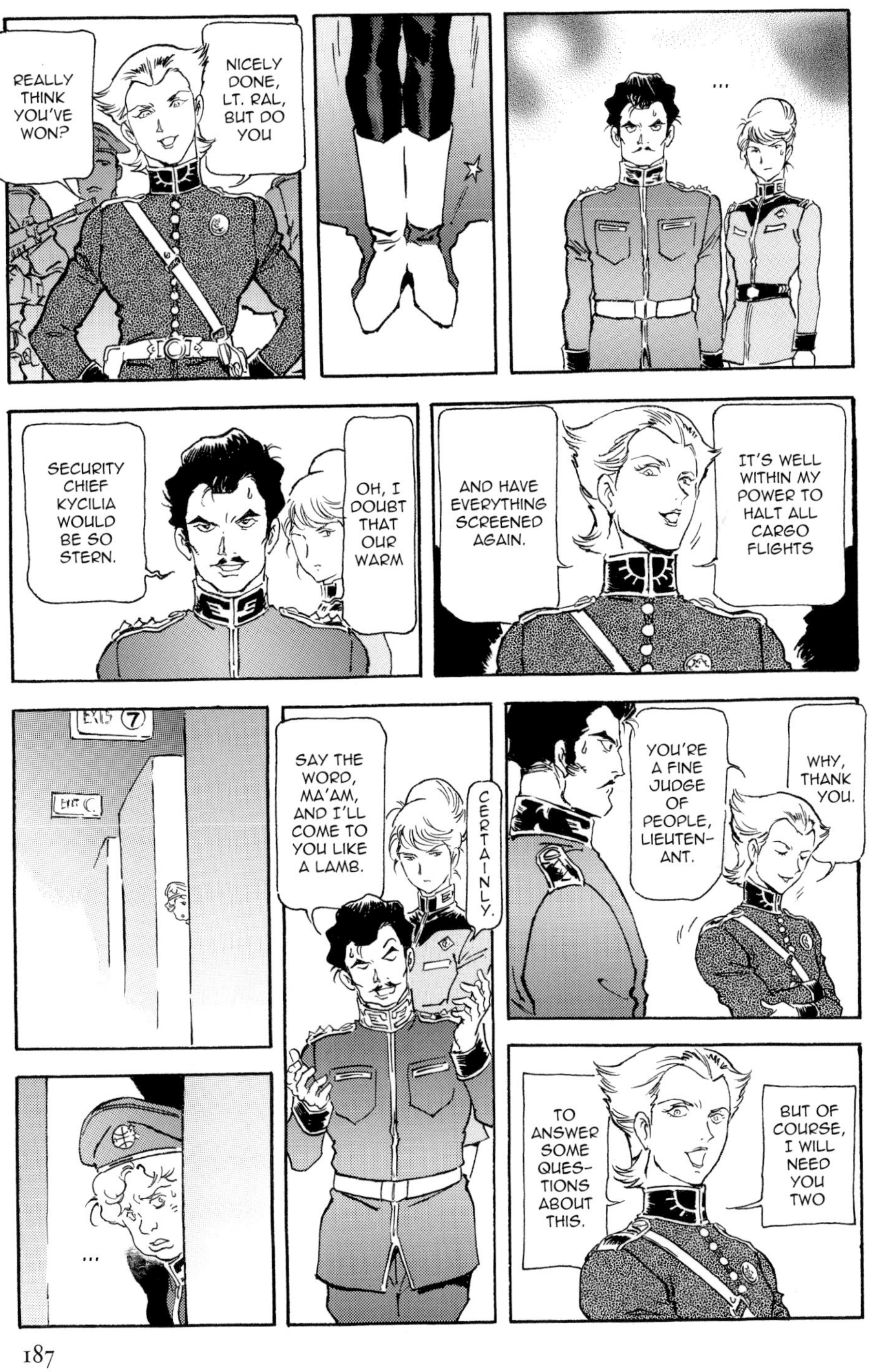
...
NICELY DONE, LT. RAL, BUT DO YOU
REALLY THINK YOU'VE WON?
IT'S WELL WITHIN MY POWER TO HALT ALL CARGO FLIGHTS
AND HAVE EVERYTHING SCREENED AGAIN.
OH, I DOUBT THAT OUR WARM
SECURITY CHIEF KYCILIA WOULD BE SO STERN.
WHY, THANK YOU.
YOU'RE A FINE JUDGE OF PEOPLE, LIEUTEN-ANT.
BUT OF COURSE, I WILL NEED YOU TWO
TO ANSWER SOME QUES-TIONS ABOUT THIS.
CERTAINLY.
SAY THE WORD, MA'AM, AND I'LL COME TO YOU LIKE A LAMB.
EXIT 7
EXIT C
...

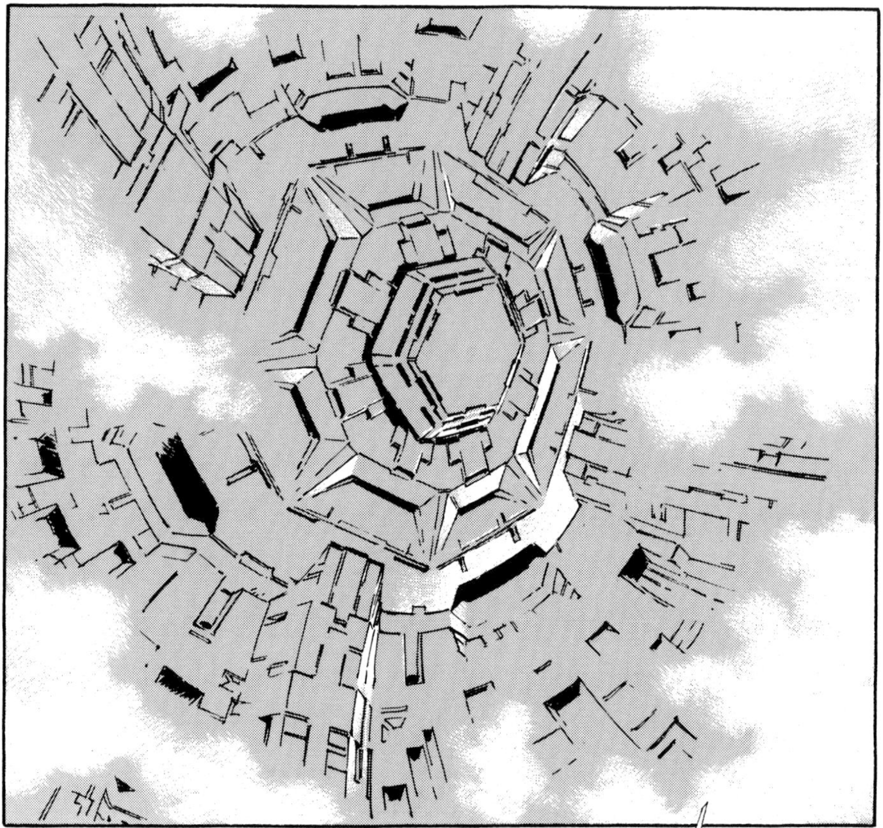

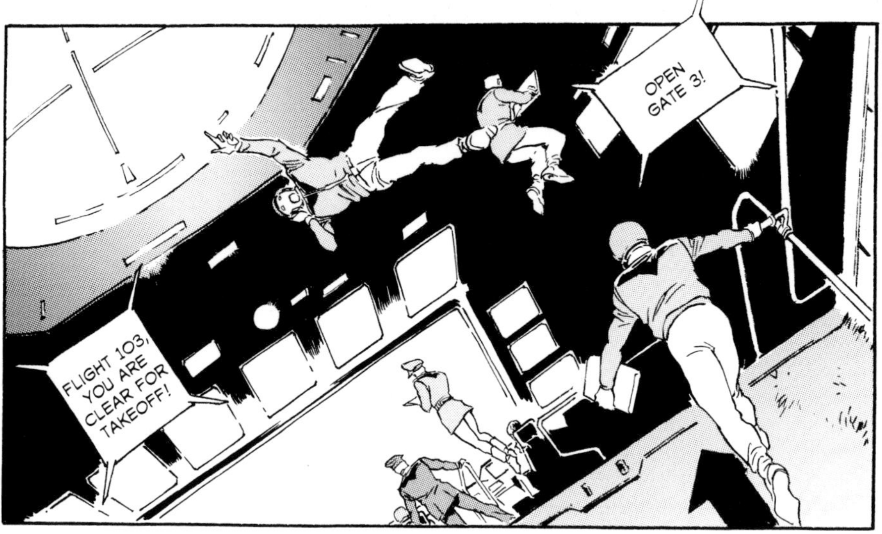
OPEN GATE 3!
FLIGHT 103, YOU ARE CLEAR FOR TAKEOFF!

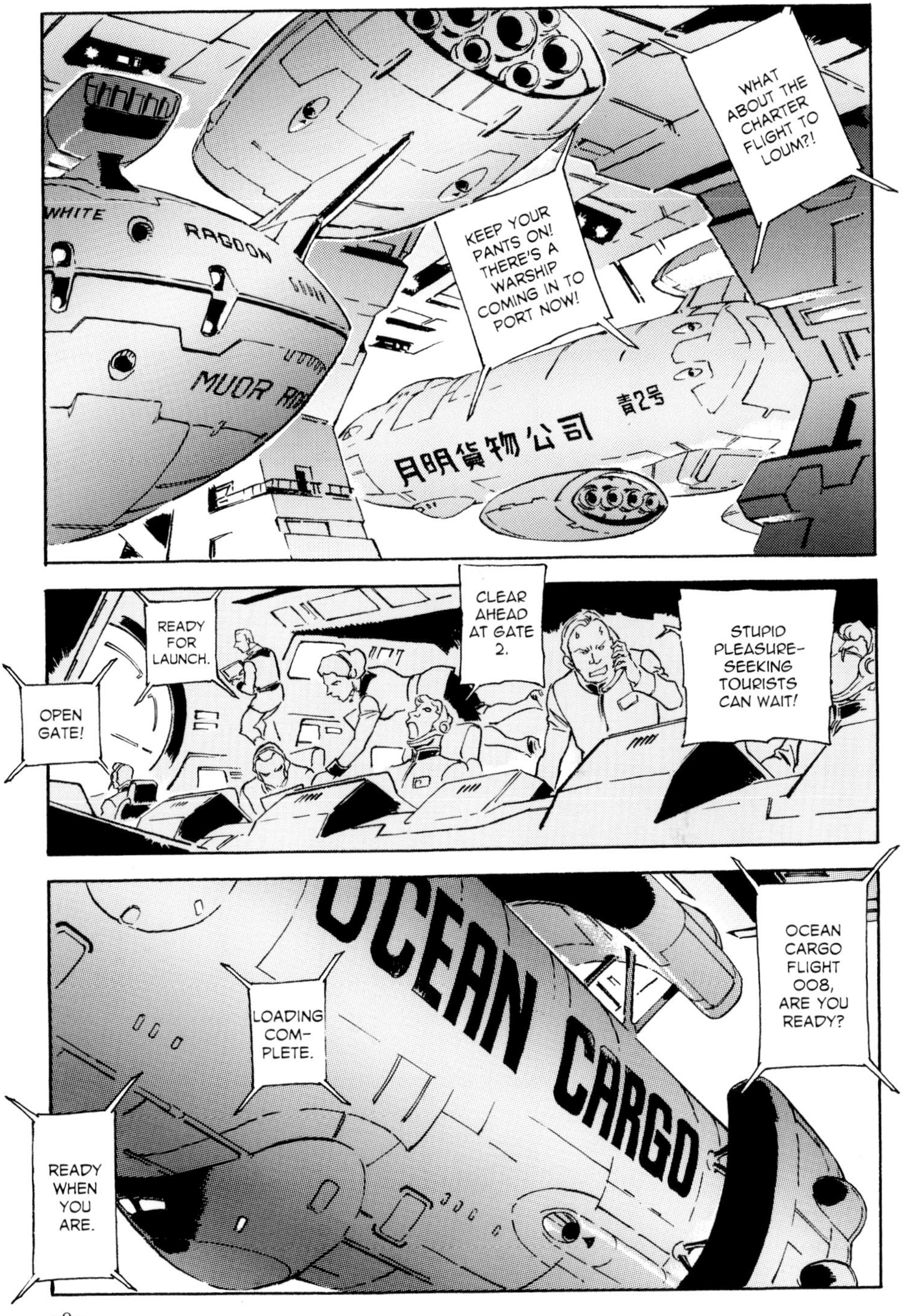
WHAT ABOUT THE CHARTER FLIGHT TO LOUM?!
KEEP YOUR PANTS ON! THERE'S A WARSHIP COMING IN TO PORT NOW!
WHITE
RAGOON
月明貨物公司
青2号
STUPID PLEASURE-SEEKING TOURISTS CAN WAIT!
CLEAR AHEAD AT GATE 2.
READY FOR LAUNCH.
OPEN GATE!
OCEAN CARGO FLIGHT 008, ARE YOU READY?
OCEAN CARGO
LOADING COM-PLETE.
READY WHEN YOU ARE.

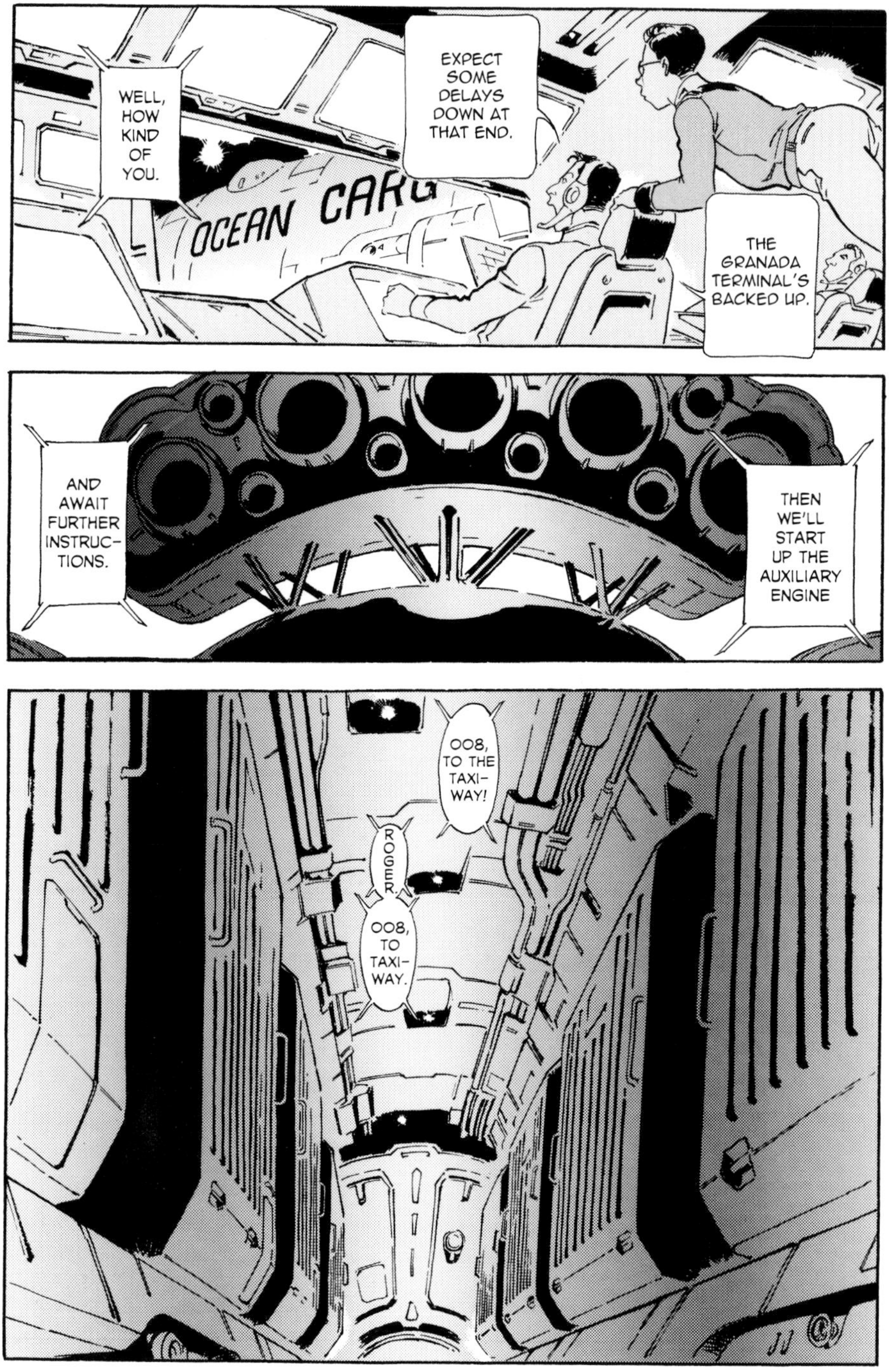
THE GRANADA TERMINAL'S BACKED UP.
EXPECT SOME DELAYS DOWN AT THAT END.
WELL, HOW KIND OF YOU.
THEN WE'LL START UP THE AUXILIARY ENGINE
AND AWAIT FURTHER INSTRUC-TIONS.
008, TO THE TAXI-WAY!
ROGER.
008, TO TAXI-WAY.

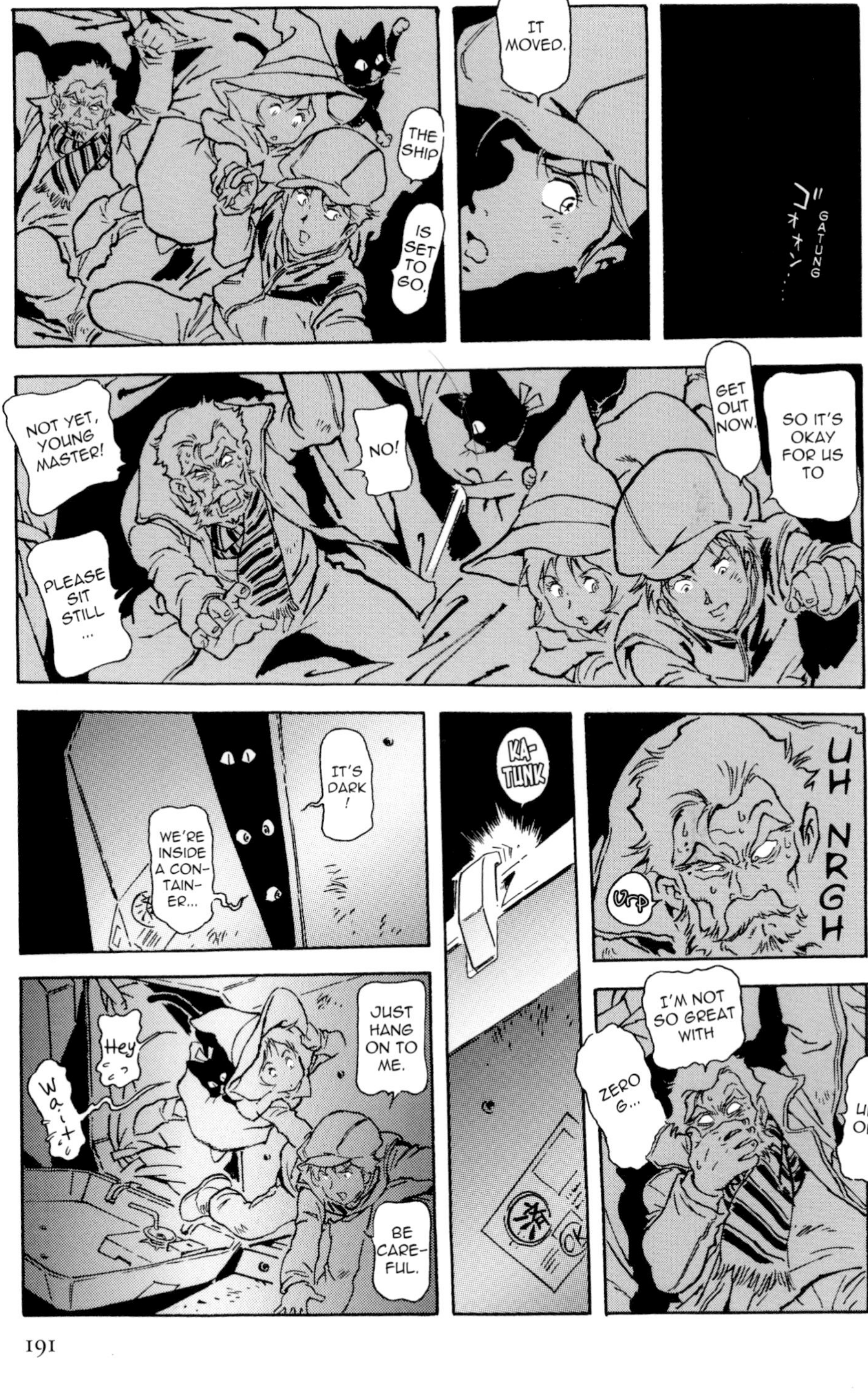
ゴオン…
GATUNG
IT MOVED.
THE SHIP
IS SET TO GO.
SO IT'S OKAY FOR US TO
GET OUT NOW.
NO!
NOT YET, YOUNG MASTER!
PLEASE SIT STILL ...
UH NRGH
Urp
I'M NOT SO GREAT WITH
ZERO G...
UH-OH.
KA-TUNK
IT'S DARK!
WE'RE INSIDE A CONTAINER...
JUST HANG ON TO ME.
BE CAREFUL.
Hey
Wait

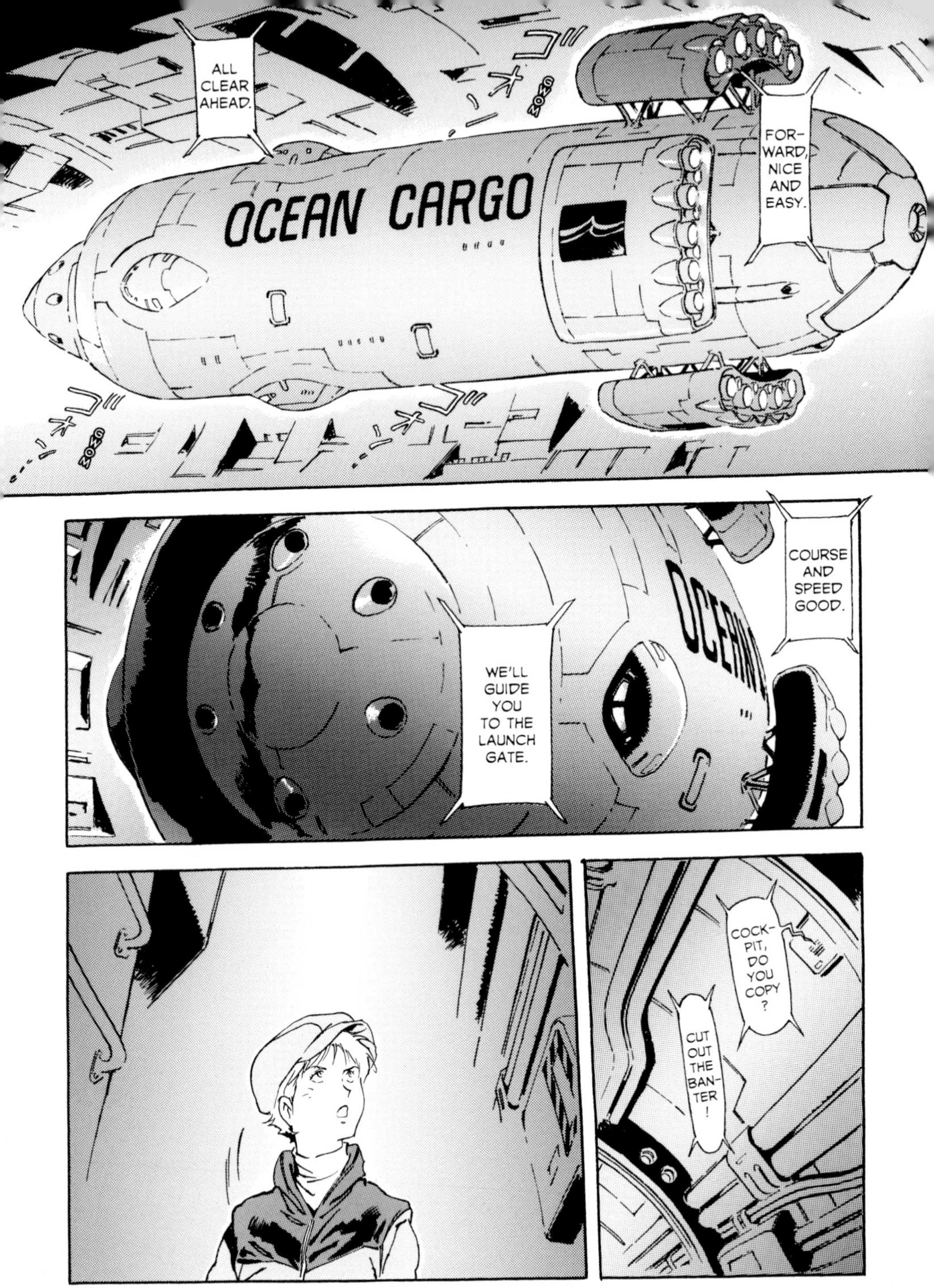
FORWARD, NICE AND EASY.
ALL CLEAR AHEAD.
GWOM
OCEAN CARGO
GWOM
COURSE AND SPEED GOOD.
WE'LL GUIDE YOU TO THE LAUNCH GATE.
COCKPIT, DO YOU COPY?
CUT OUT THE BANTER!

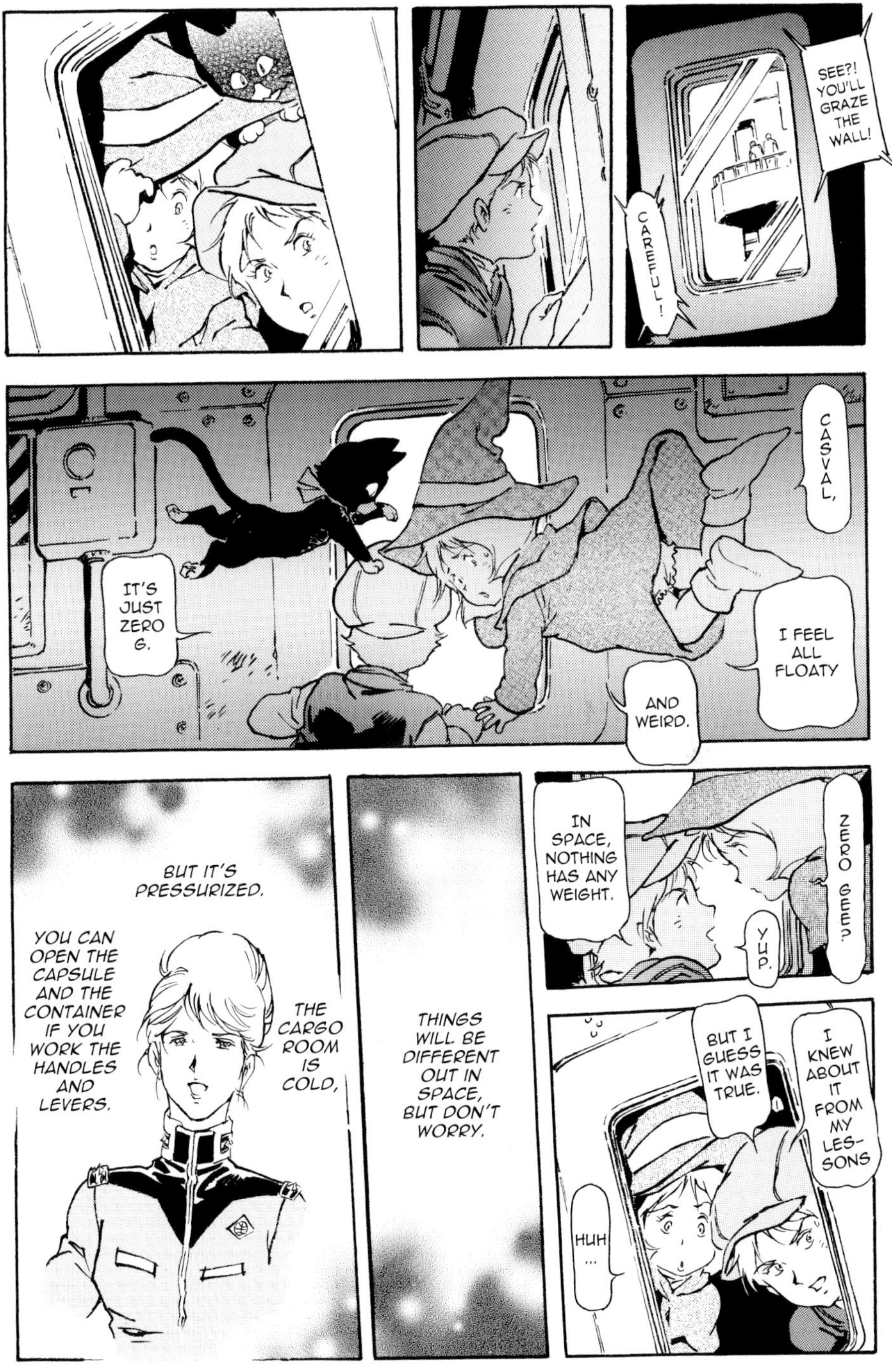
SEE?! YOU'LL GRAZE THE WALL!
CAREFUL!
CASVAL,
I FEEL ALL FLOATY
AND WEIRD.
IT'S JUST ZERO G.
ZERO GEE?
IN SPACE, NOTHING HAS ANY WEIGHT.
YUP.
I KNEW ABOUT IT FROM MY LES-SONS
BUT I GUESS IT WAS TRUE.
HUH ...
THINGS WILL BE DIFFERENT OUT IN SPACE, BUT DON'T WORRY.
THE CARGO ROOM IS COLD,
BUT IT'S PRESSURIZED.
YOU CAN OPEN THE CAPSULE AND THE CONTAINER IF YOU WORK THE HANDLES AND LEVERS.

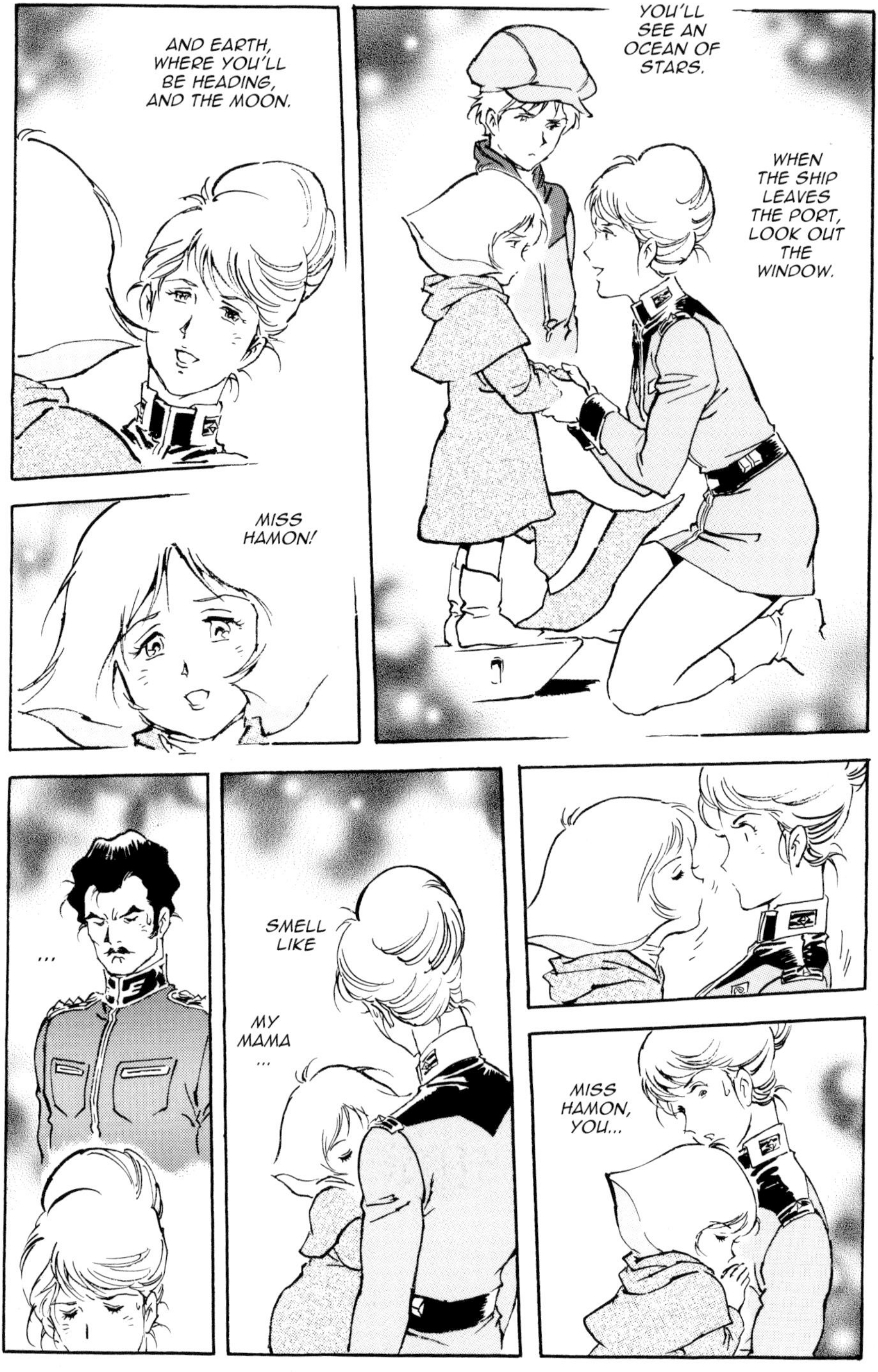
WHEN THE SHIP LEAVES THE PORT, LOOK OUT THE WINDOW.
YOU'LL SEE AN OCEAN OF STARS.
AND EARTH, WHERE YOU'LL BE HEADING, AND THE MOON.
MISS HAMON!
MISS HAMON, YOU...
SMELL LIKE
MY MAMA ...
...

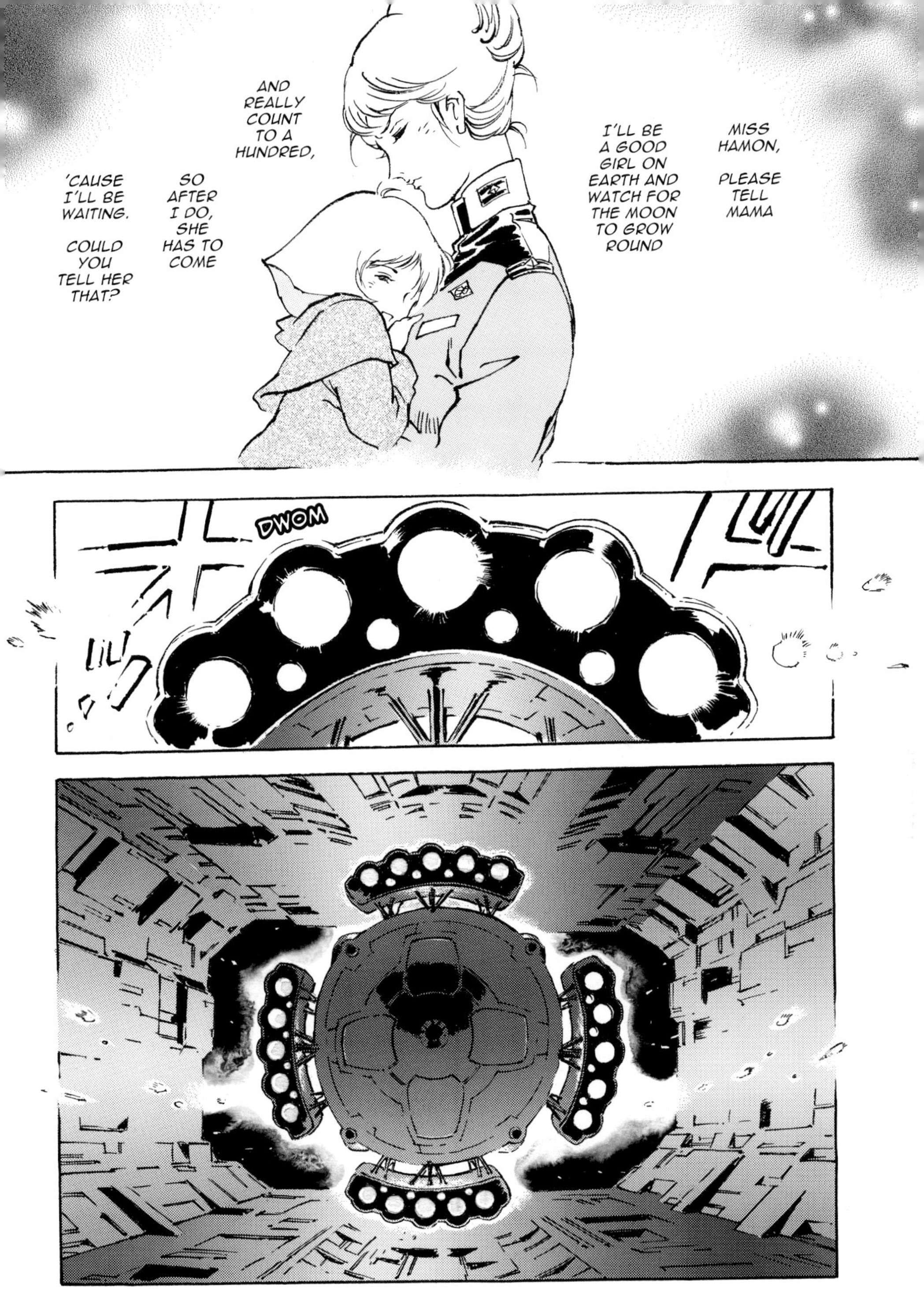
MISS HAMON, PLEASE TELL MAMA
I'LL BE A GOOD GIRL ON EARTH AND WATCH FOR THE MOON TO GROW ROUND
AND REALLY COUNT TO A HUNDRED,
SO AFTER I DO, SHE HAS TO COME
'CAUSE I'LL BE WAITING.
COULD YOU TELL HER THAT?
DWOM

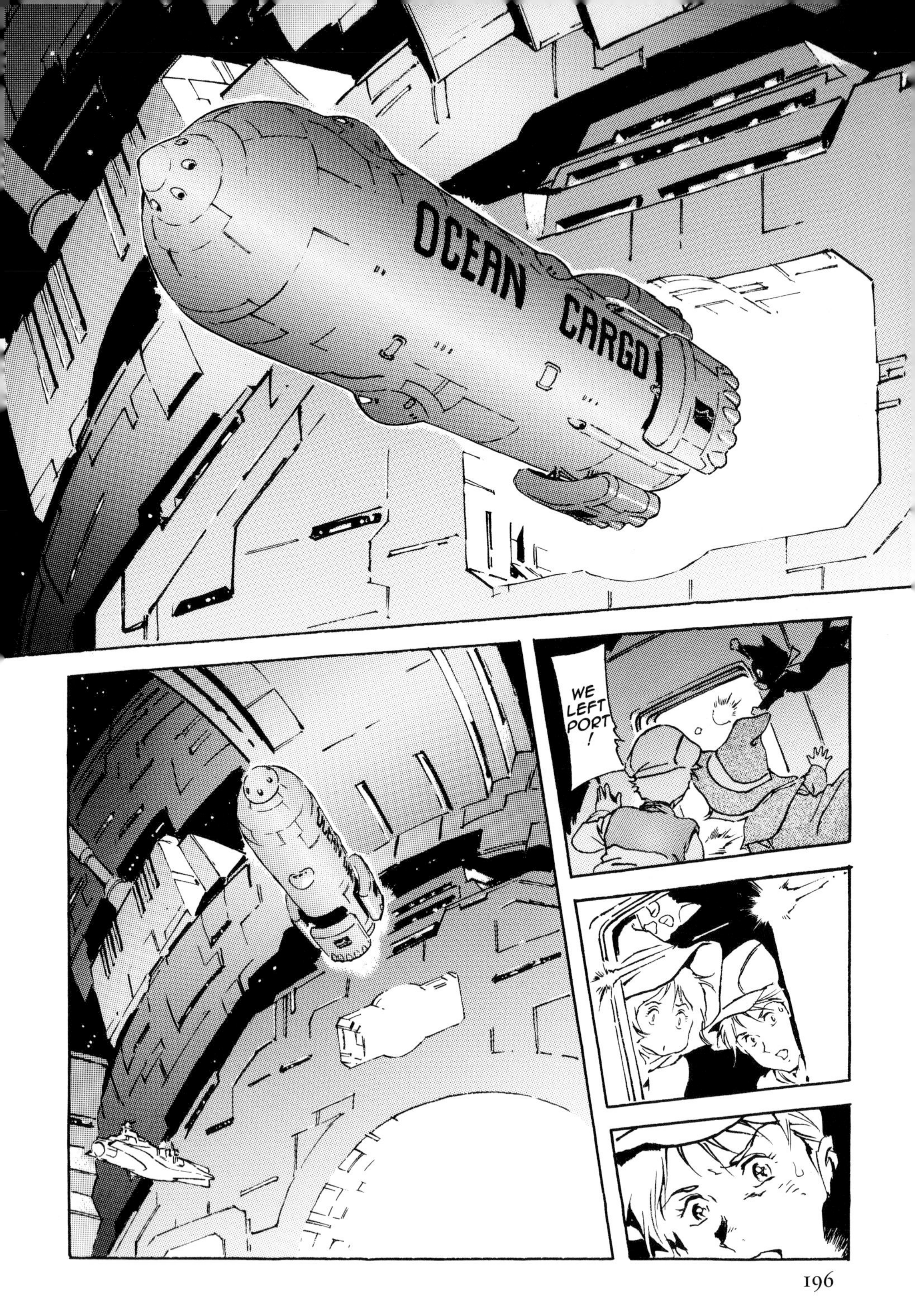
OCEAN CARGO
WE LEFT PORT!

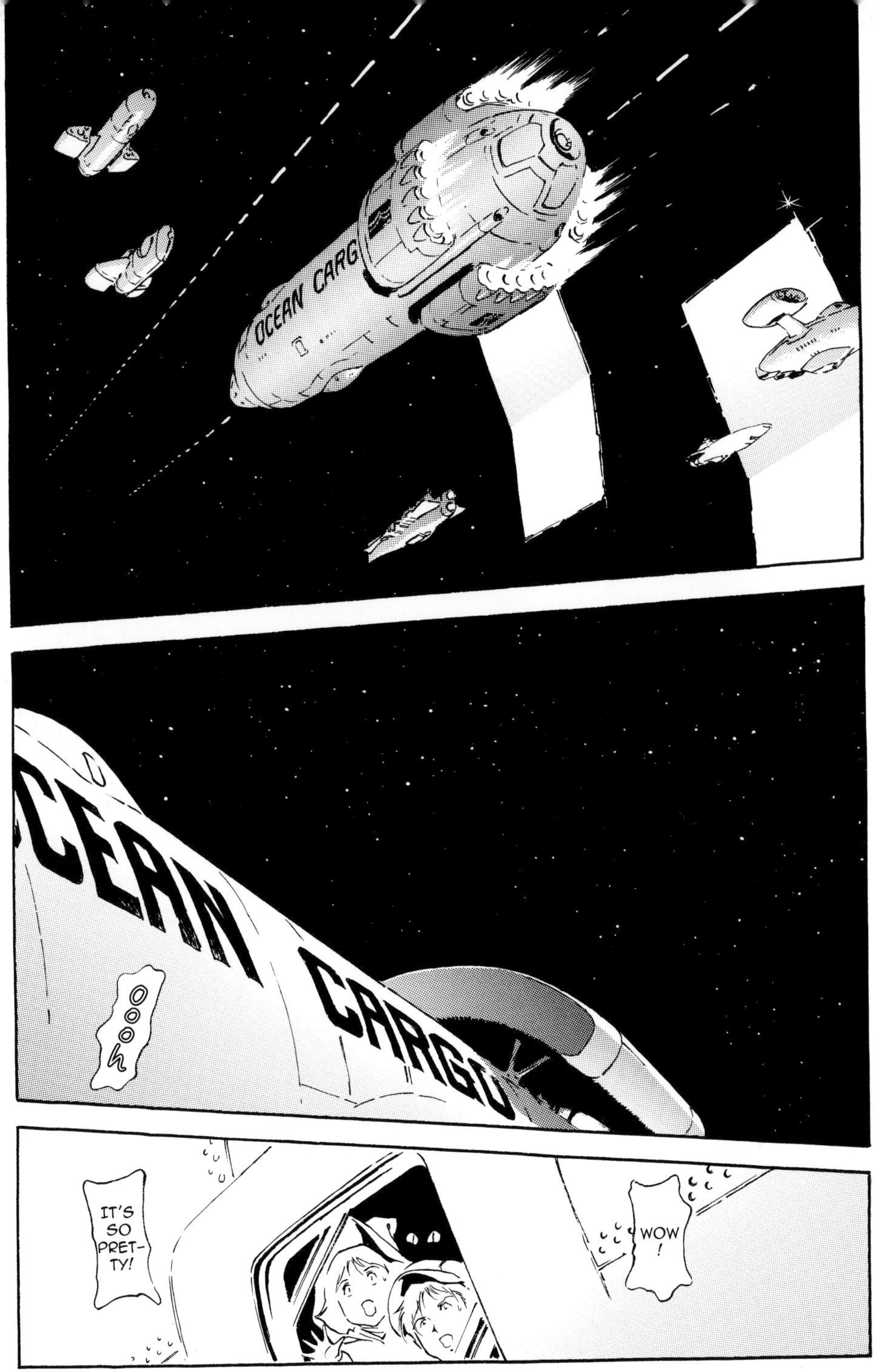
OCEAN CARG
OCEAN CARGO
Oooh
WOW!
IT'S SO PRET-TY!

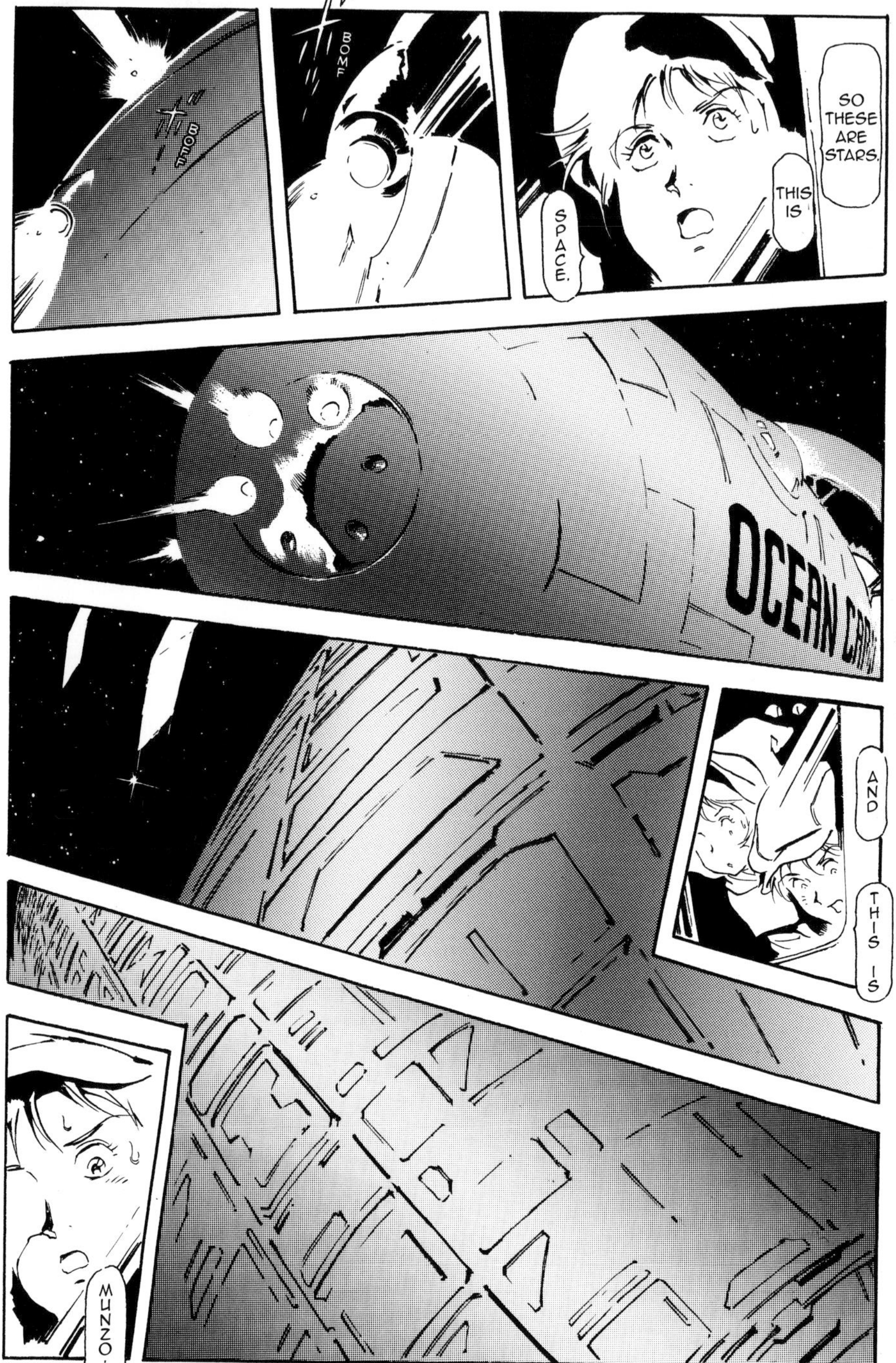
SO THESE ARE STARS.
THIS IS
SPACE.
BOMF
BOFF
OCEAN
AND
THIS IS
MUNZO...

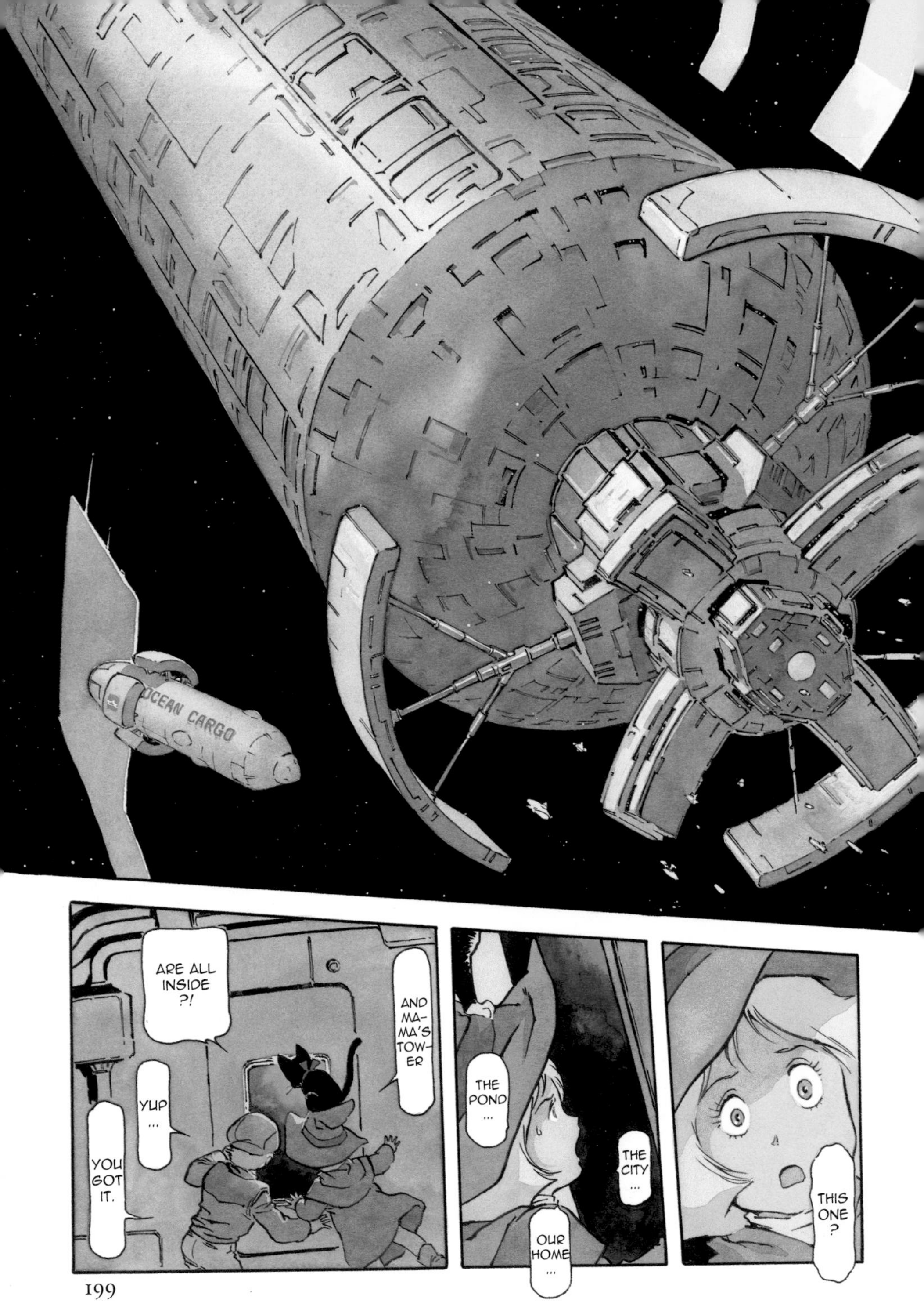
OCEAN CARGO
THIS ONE ?
THE POND ...
THE CITY ...
OUR HOME ...
AND MA-MA'S TOW-ER
ARE ALL INSIDE ?!
YUP ...
YOU GOT IT.

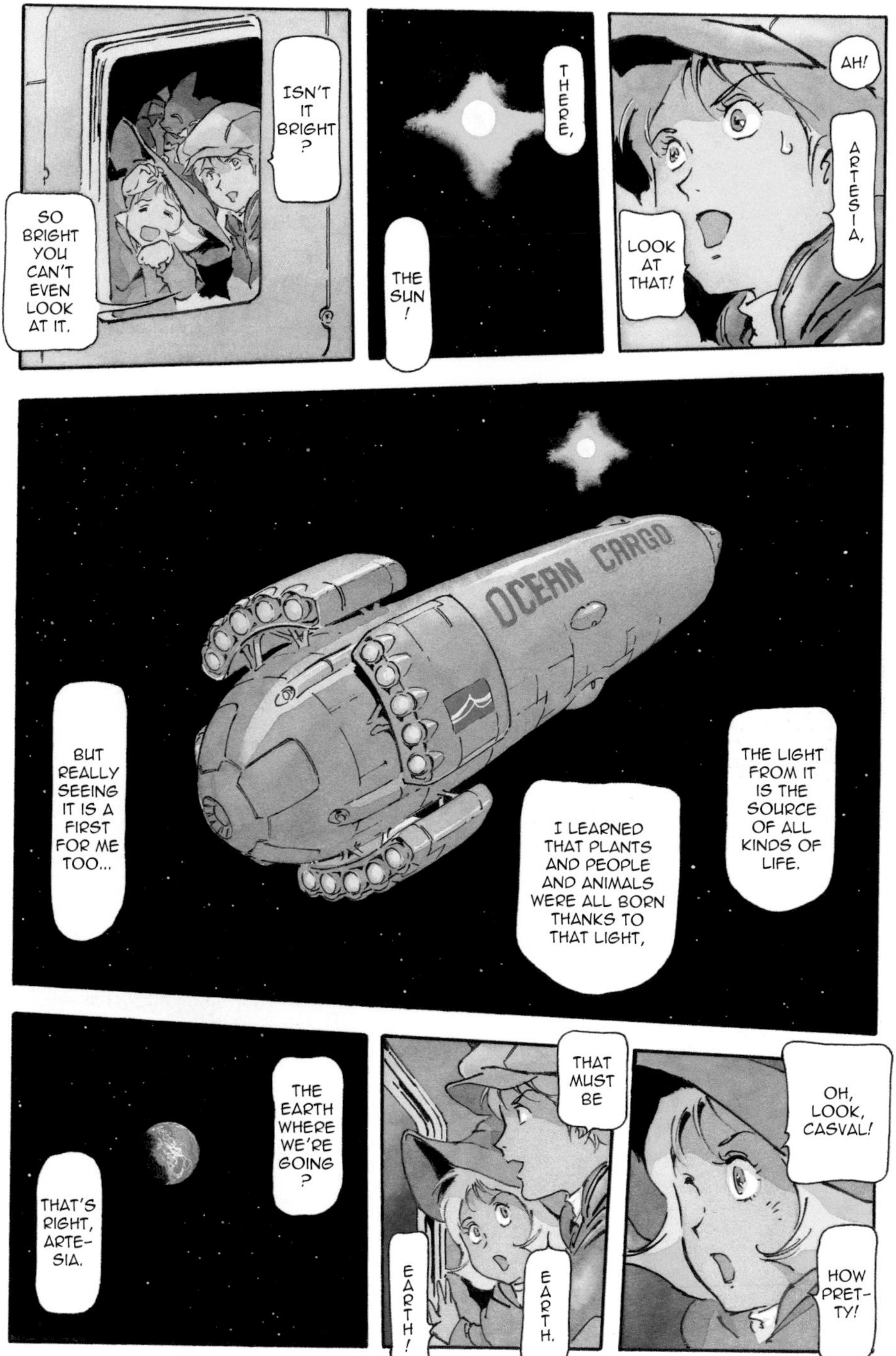
AH!
ARTESIA,
LOOK AT THAT!
THERE,
THE SUN!
ISN'T IT BRIGHT?
SO BRIGHT YOU CAN'T EVEN LOOK AT IT.
OCEAN CARGO
THE LIGHT FROM IT IS THE SOURCE OF ALL KINDS OF LIFE.
I LEARNED THAT PLANTS AND PEOPLE AND ANIMALS WERE ALL BORN THANKS TO THAT LIGHT,
BUT REALLY SEEING IT IS A FIRST FOR ME TOO...
OH, LOOK, CASVAL!
HOW PRETTY!
THAT MUST BE
EARTH.
EARTH!
THE EARTH WHERE WE'RE GOING?
THAT'S RIGHT, ARTESIA.

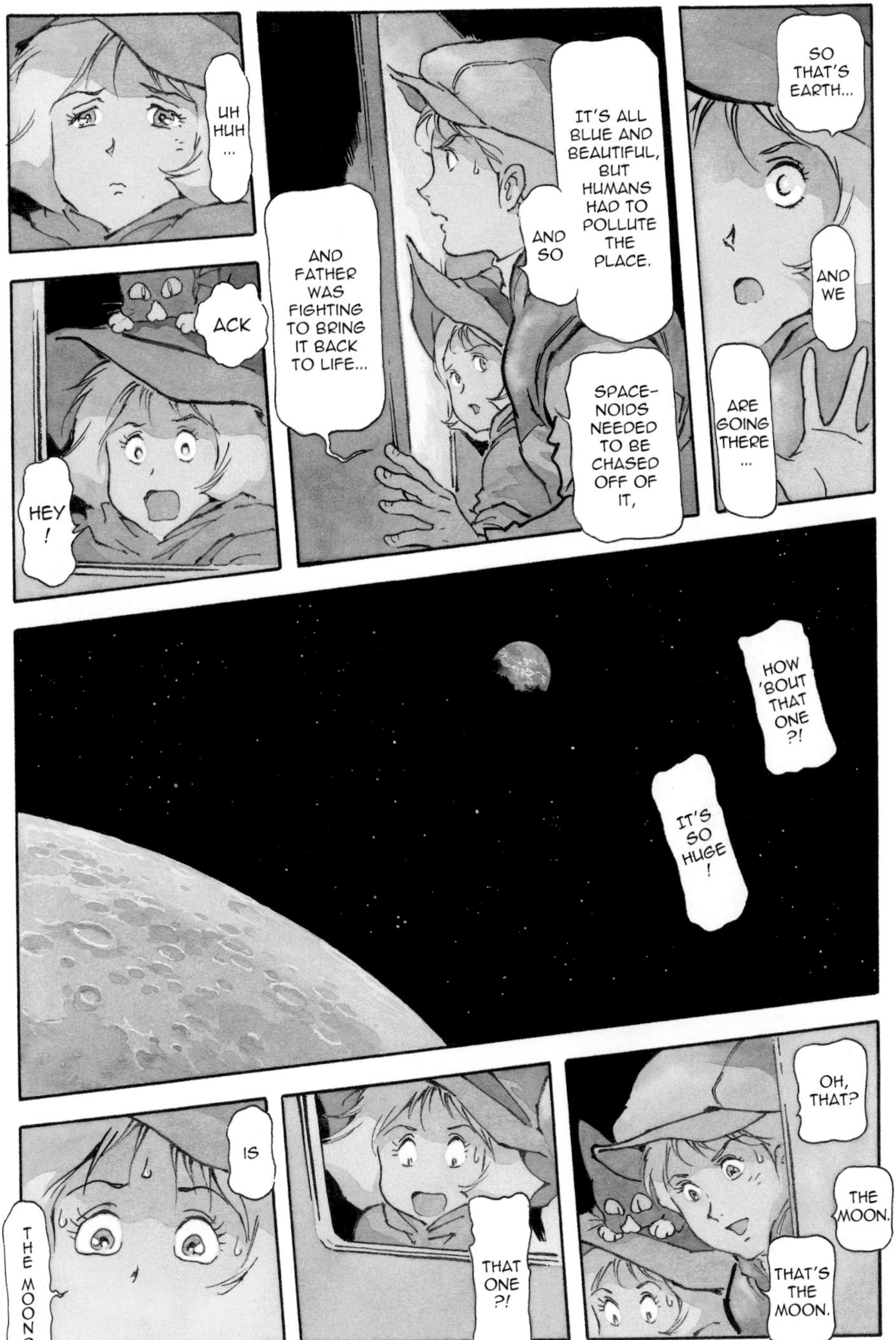
SO THAT'S EARTH...
AND WE
ARE GOING THERE...
IT'S ALL BLUE AND BEAUTIFUL, BUT HUMANS HAD TO POLLUTE THE PLACE.
AND SO
SPACE-NOIDS NEEDED TO BE CHASED OFF OF IT,
AND FATHER WAS FIGHTING TO BRING IT BACK TO LIFE...
UH HUH...
ACK
HEY!
HOW 'BOUT THAT ONE?!
IT'S SO HUGE!
OH, THAT?
THE MOON.
THAT'S THE MOON.
THAT ONE?!
IS
THE MOON?

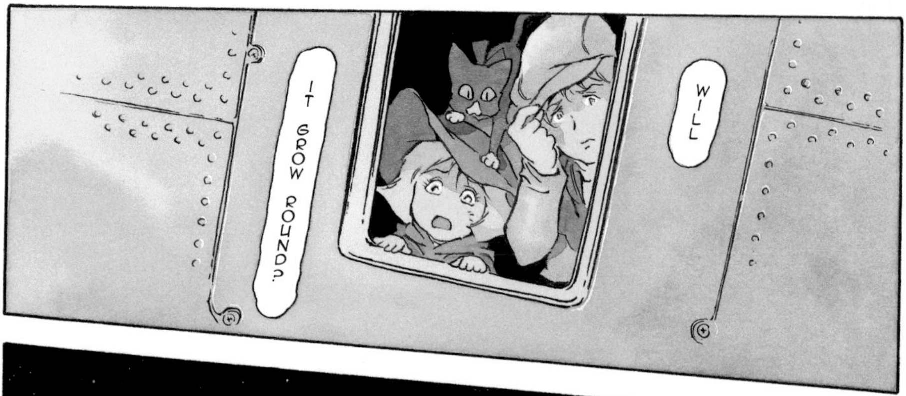
WILL
IT GROW ROUND?
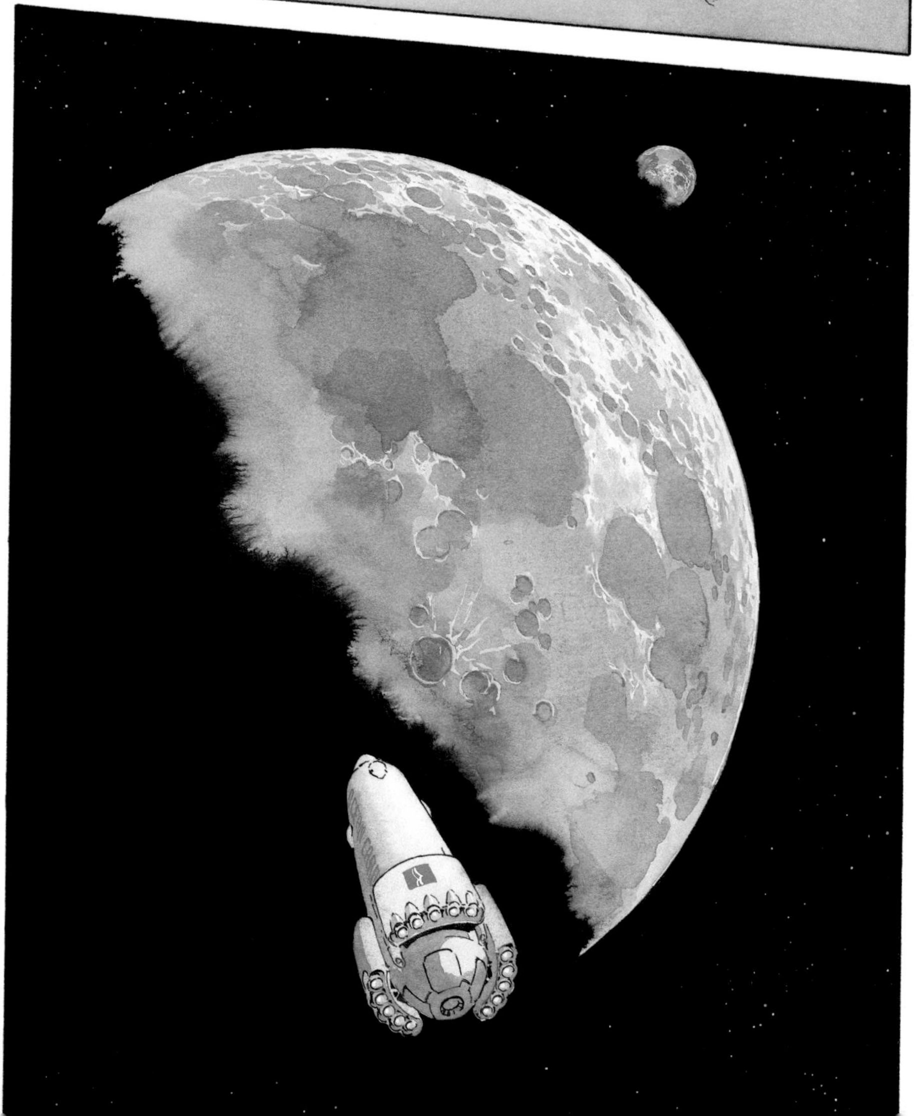

SECTION
V

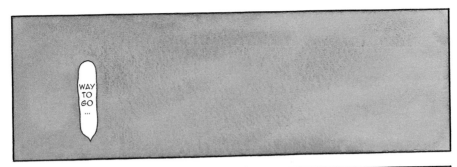

WAY TO GO ...
YOU FROM AROUND HERE, MISS?
HOW OLD ARE YOU?
FOOD
10? NO ...
YOU CAN'T BE.
HOSPITAL
D·P
YOU SEEM SO MATURE.
インスタントラーメン
YOU'LL MAKE
A FINE DOCTOR SOMEDAY ...
GOODNESS.
OH, YOU LIVE THERE?!

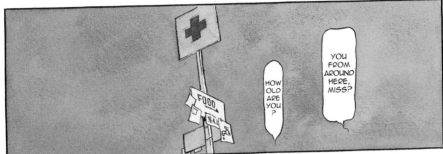

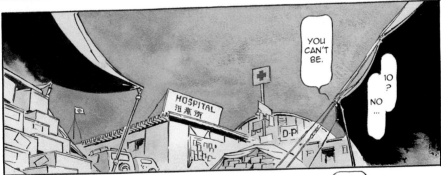

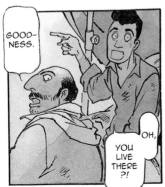

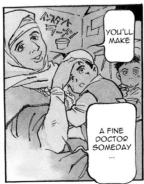

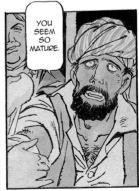

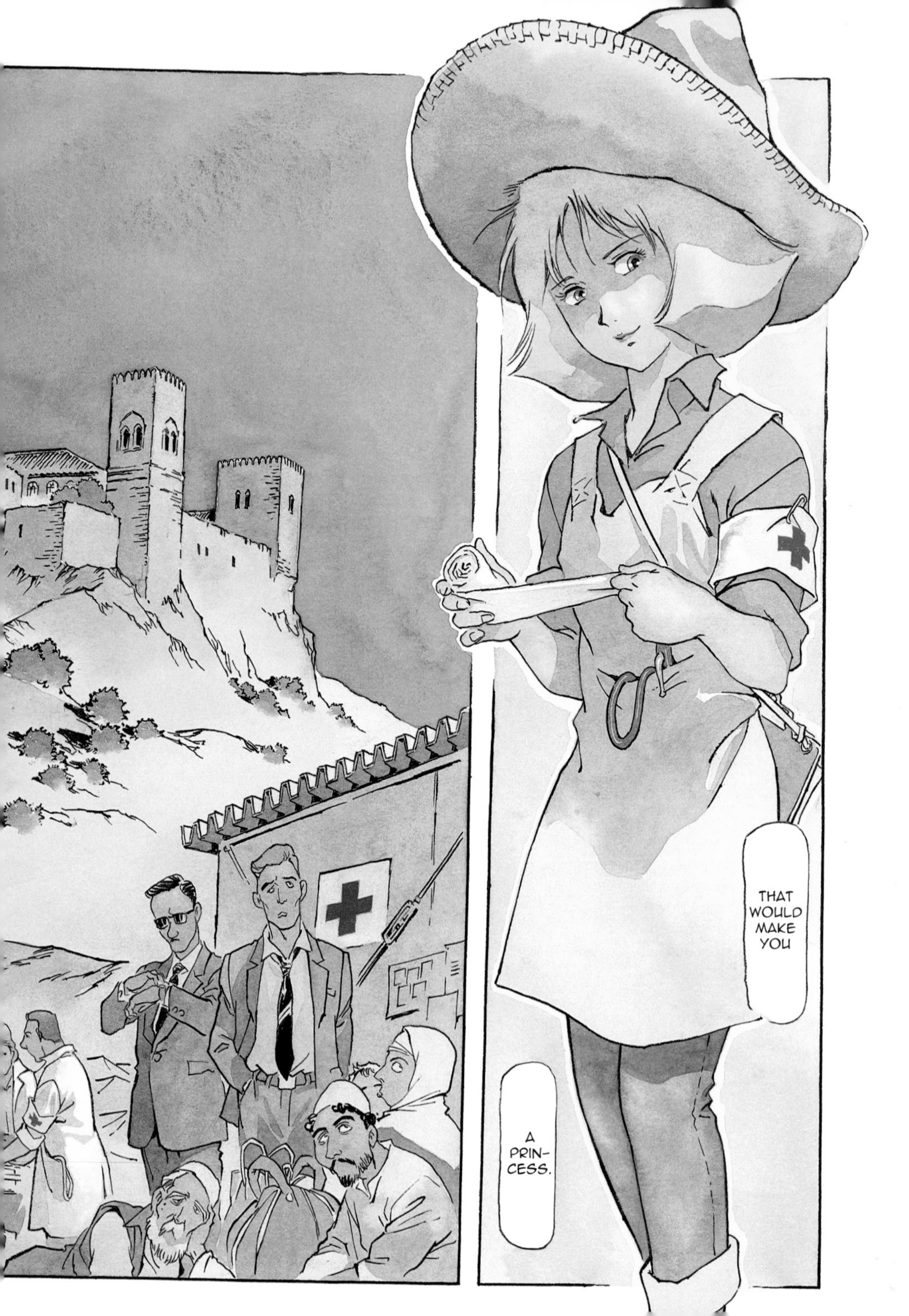
THAT WOULD MAKE YOU
A PRIN-CESS.

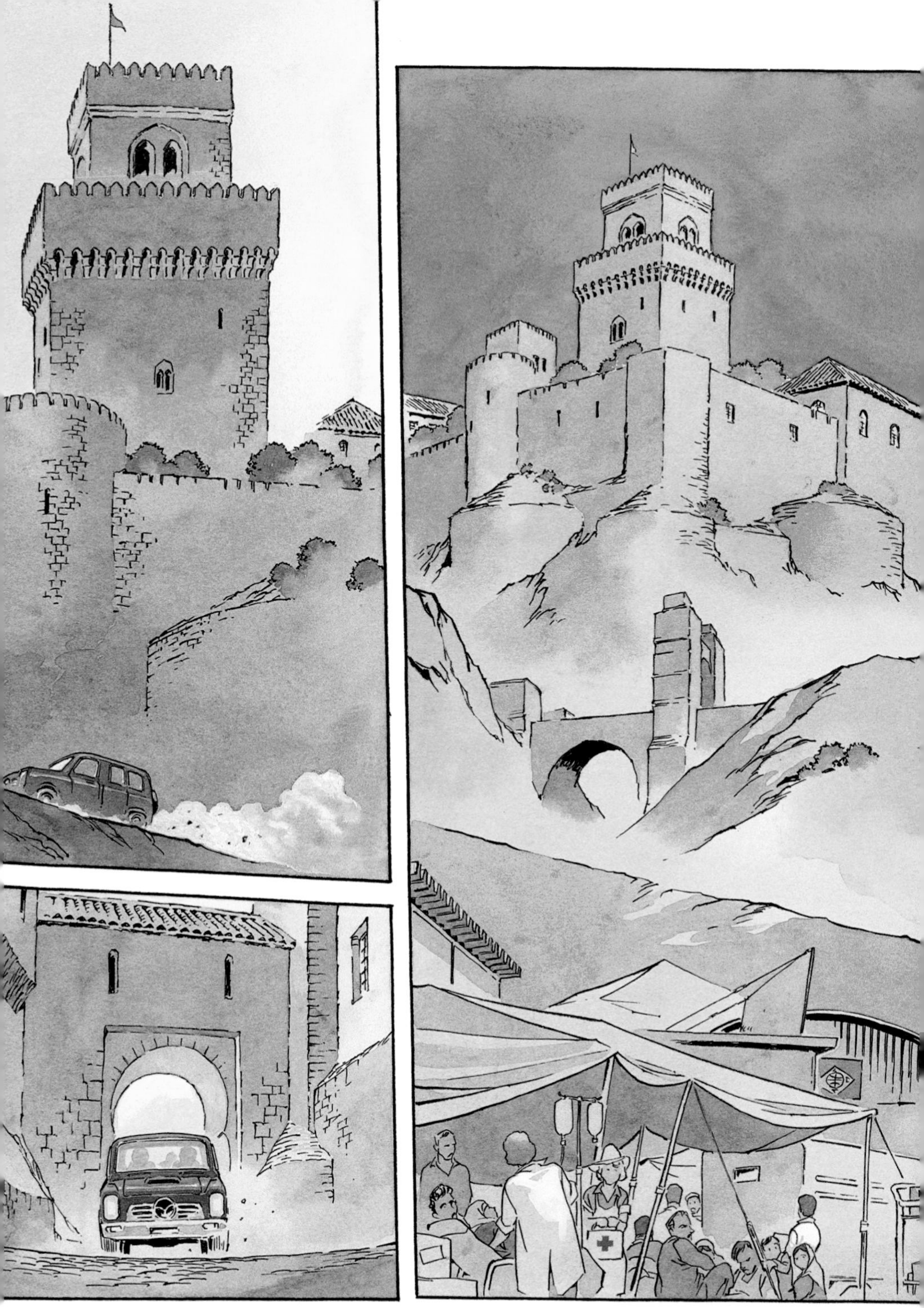

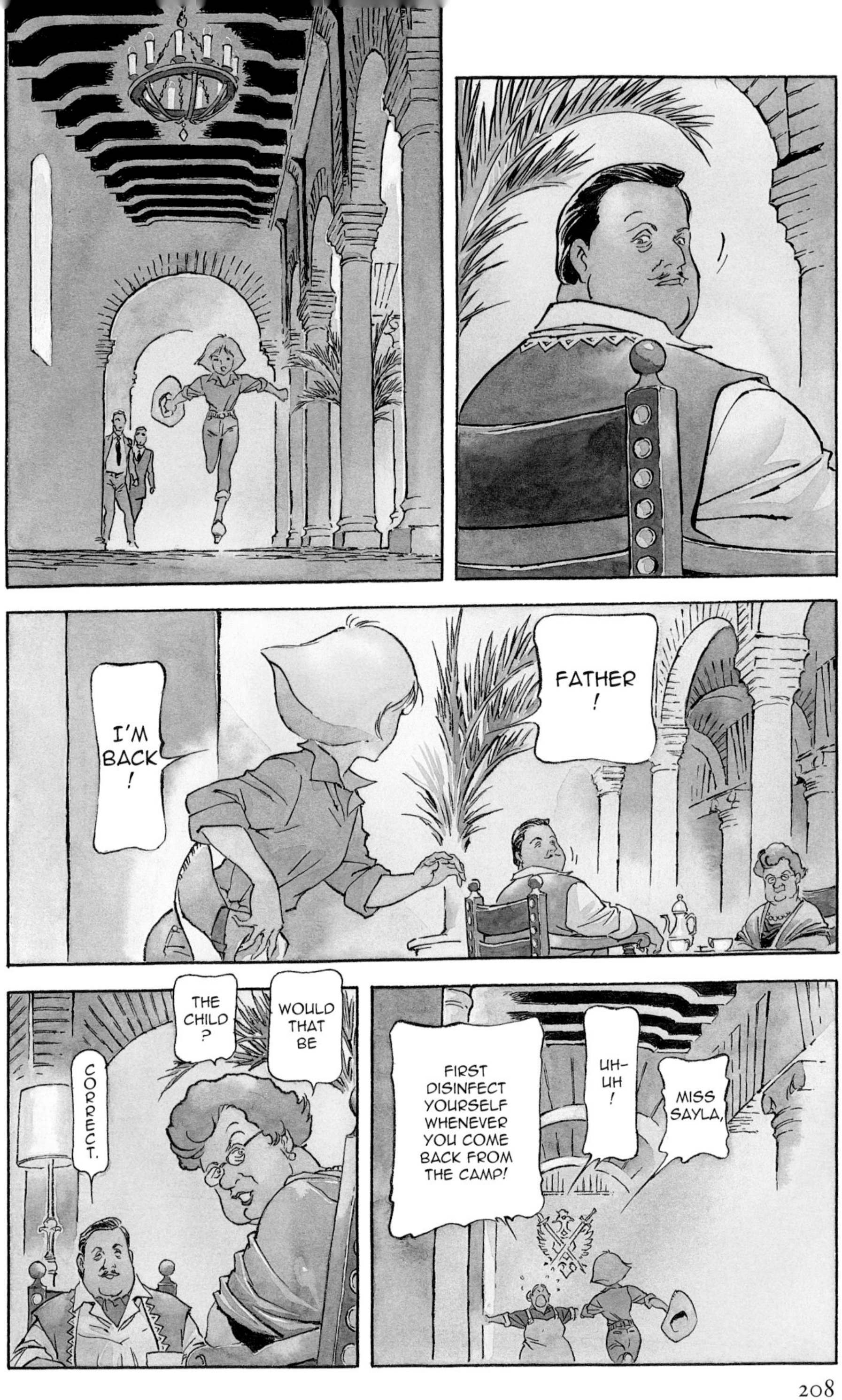
FATHER!
I'M BACK!
MISS SAYLA,
UH-UH!
FIRST DISINFECT YOURSELF WHENEVER YOU COME BACK FROM THE CAMP!
WOULD THAT BE
THE CHILD?
CORRECT.

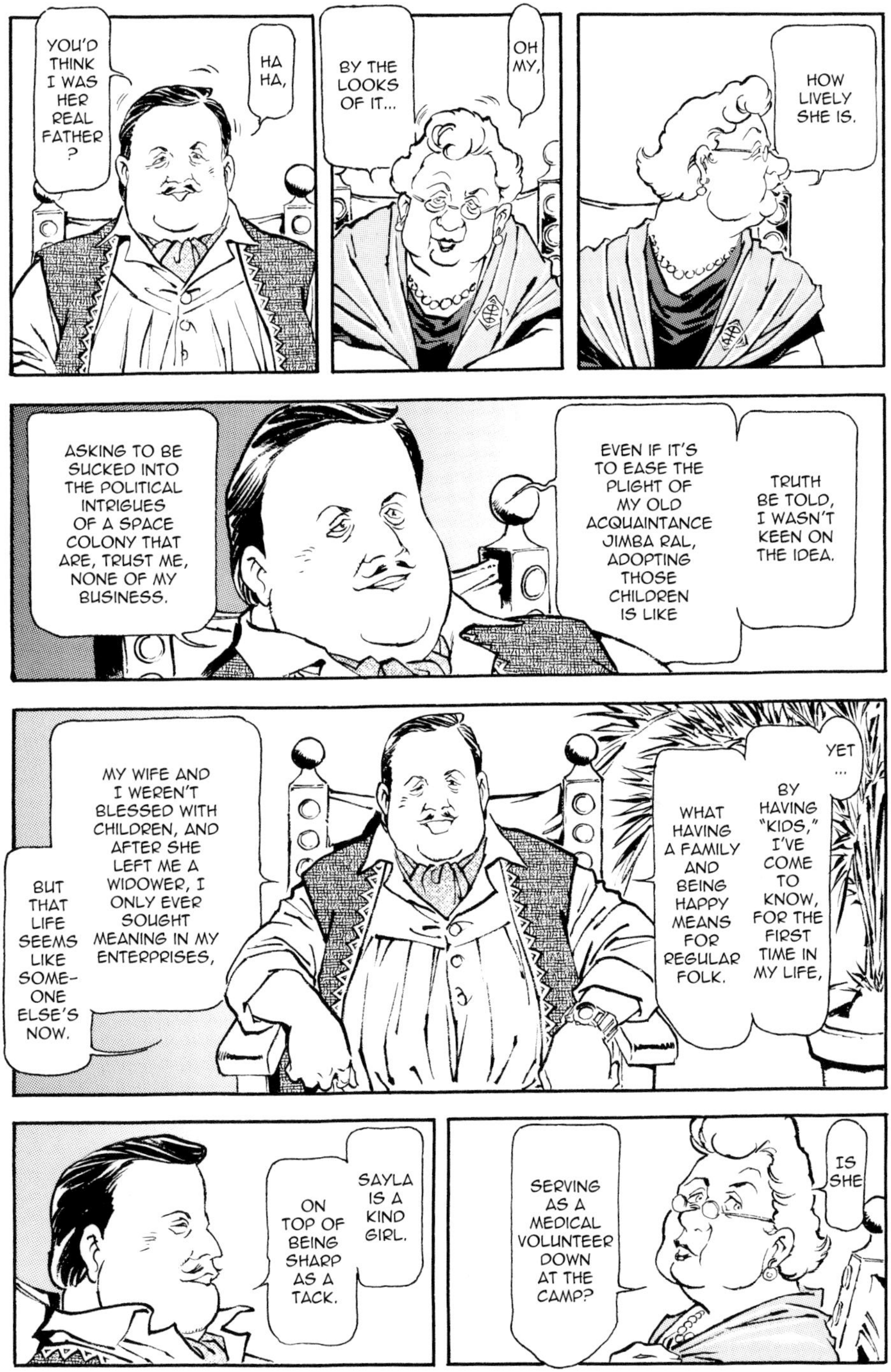
HOW LIVELY SHE IS.
OH MY,
BY THE LOOKS OF IT...
HA HA,
YOU'D THINK I WAS HER REAL FATHER?
TRUTH BE TOLD, I WASN'T KEEN ON THE IDEA.
EVEN IF IT'S TO EASE THE PLIGHT OF MY OLD ACQUAINTANCE JIMBA RAL, ADOPTING THOSE CHILDREN IS LIKE
ASKING TO BE SUCKED INTO THE POLITICAL INTRIGUES OF A SPACE COLONY THAT ARE, TRUST ME, NONE OF MY BUSINESS.
YET ...
BY HAVING "KIDS," I'VE COME TO KNOW, FOR THE FIRST TIME IN MY LIFE,
WHAT HAVING A FAMILY AND BEING HAPPY MEANS FOR REGULAR FOLK.
MY WIFE AND I WEREN'T BLESSED WITH CHILDREN, AND AFTER SHE LEFT ME A WIDOWER, I ONLY EVER SOUGHT MEANING IN MY ENTERPRISES,
BUT THAT LIFE SEEMS LIKE SOME-ONE ELSE'S NOW.
IS SHE
SERVING AS A MEDICAL VOLUNTEER DOWN AT THE CAMP?
SAYLA IS A KIND GIRL.
ON TOP OF BEING SHARP AS A TACK.

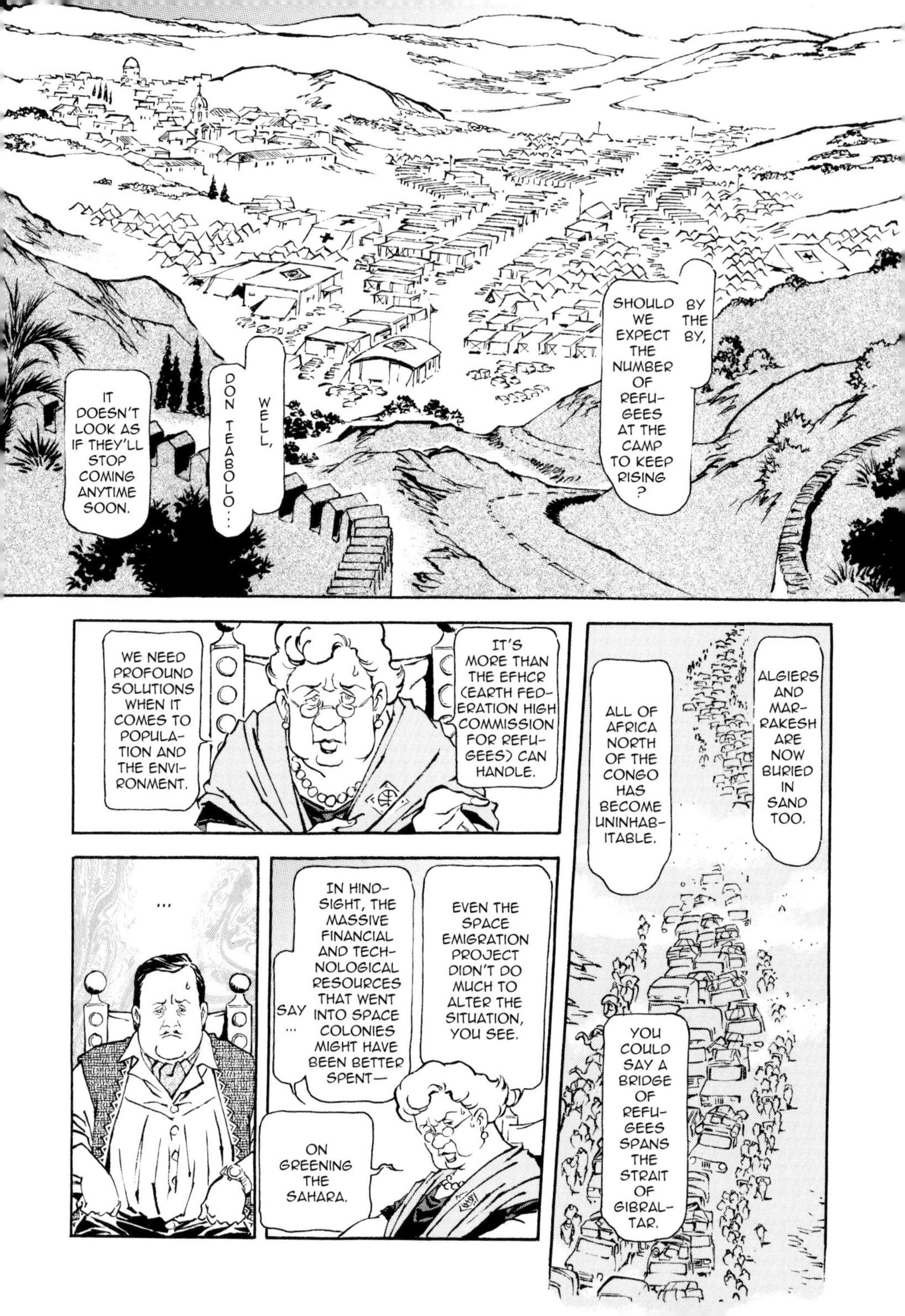
BY THE BY,
SHOULD WE EXPECT THE NUMBER OF REFUGEES AT THE CAMP TO KEEP RISING?
WELL,
DON TEABOLO...
IT DOESN'T LOOK AS IF THEY'LL STOP COMING ANYTIME SOON.
ALGIERS AND MARRAKESH ARE NOW BURIED IN SAND TOO.
ALL OF AFRICA NORTH OF THE CONGO HAS BECOME UNINHABITABLE.
YOU COULD SAY A BRIDGE OF REFUGEES SPANS THE STRAIT OF GIBRALTAR.
IT'S MORE THAN THE EFHCR (EARTH FEDERATION HIGH COMMISSION FOR REFUGEES) CAN HANDLE.
WE NEED PROFOUND SOLUTIONS WHEN IT COMES TO POPULATION AND THE ENVIRONMENT.
EVEN THE SPACE EMIGRATION PROJECT DIDN'T DO MUCH TO ALTER THE SITUATION, YOU SEE.
IN HINDSIGHT, THE MASSIVE FINANCIAL AND TECHNOLOGICAL RESOURCES THAT WENT INTO SPACE COLONIES MIGHT HAVE BEEN BETTER SPENT—
SAY...
ON GREENING THE SAHARA.
...

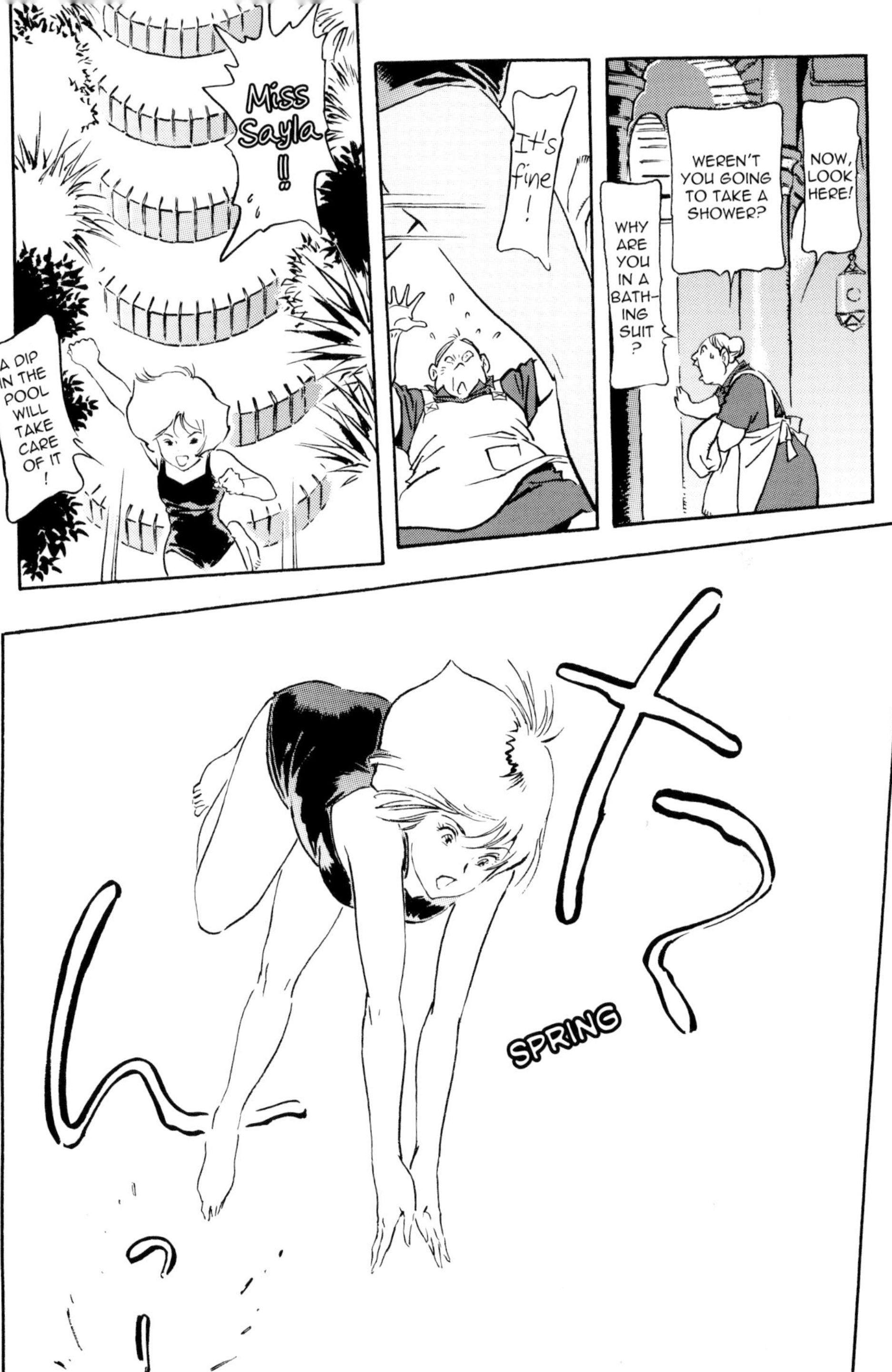
NOW, LOOK HERE!
WEREN'T YOU GOING TO TAKE A SHOWER?
WHY ARE YOU IN A BATHING SUIT?
It's fine!
Miss Sayla!!
A DIP IN THE POOL WILL TAKE CARE OF IT!
SPRING

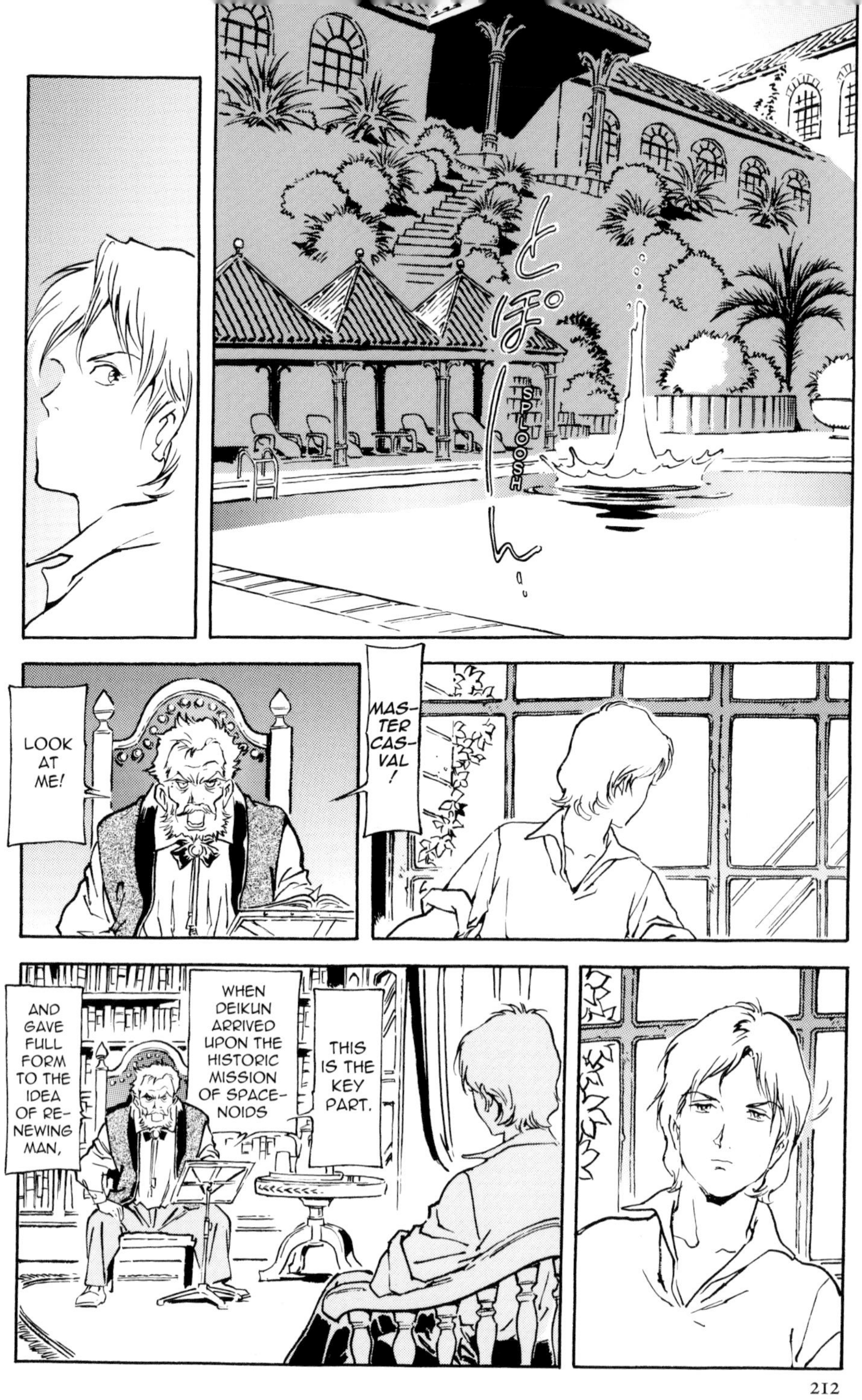
とぽーん
SPLOOSH
MASTER CASVAL!
LOOK AT ME!
THIS IS THE KEY PART.
WHEN DEIKUN ARRIVED UPON THE HISTORIC MISSION OF SPACENOIDS
AND GAVE FULL FORM TO THE IDEA OF RENEWING MAN,

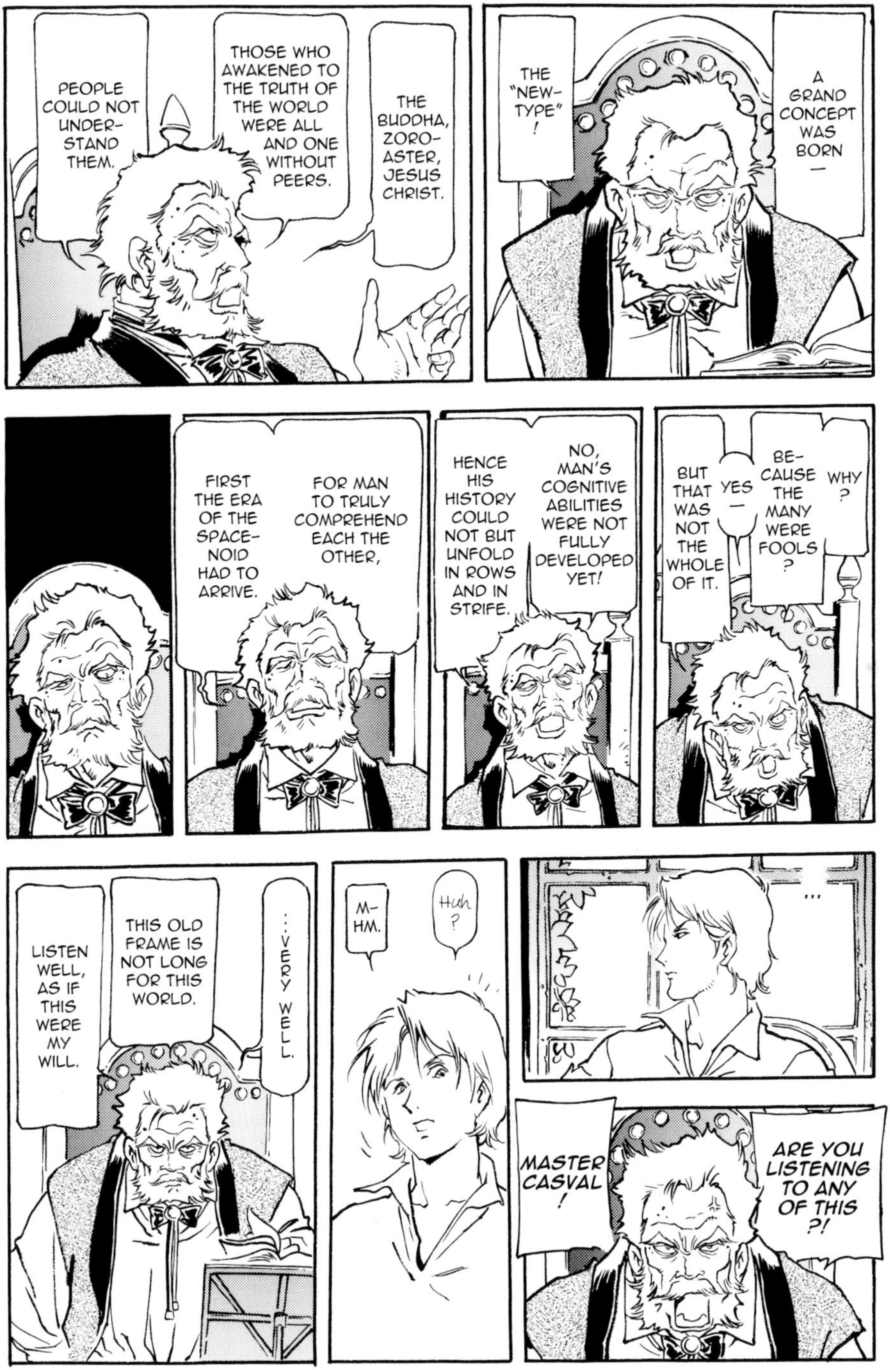
A GRAND CONCEPT WAS BORN —
THE "NEW-TYPE"!
THE BUDDHA, ZOROASTER, JESUS CHRIST.
THOSE WHO AWAKENED TO THE TRUTH OF THE WORLD WERE ALL AND ONE WITHOUT PEERS.
PEOPLE COULD NOT UNDERSTAND THEM.
WHY?
BECAUSE THE MANY WERE FOOLS?
YES —
BUT THAT WAS NOT THE WHOLE OF IT.
NO, MAN'S COGNITIVE ABILITIES WERE NOT FULLY DEVELOPED YET!
HENCE HIS HISTORY COULD NOT BUT UNFOLD IN ROWS AND IN STRIFE.
FOR MAN TO TRULY COMPREHEND EACH THE OTHER,
FIRST THE ERA OF THE SPACENOID HAD TO ARRIVE.
...
ARE YOU LISTENING TO ANY OF THIS?!
MASTER CASVAL!
Huh?
M-HM.
...VERY WELL.
THIS OLD FRAME IS NOT LONG FOR THIS WORLD.
LISTEN WELL, AS IF THIS WERE MY WILL.

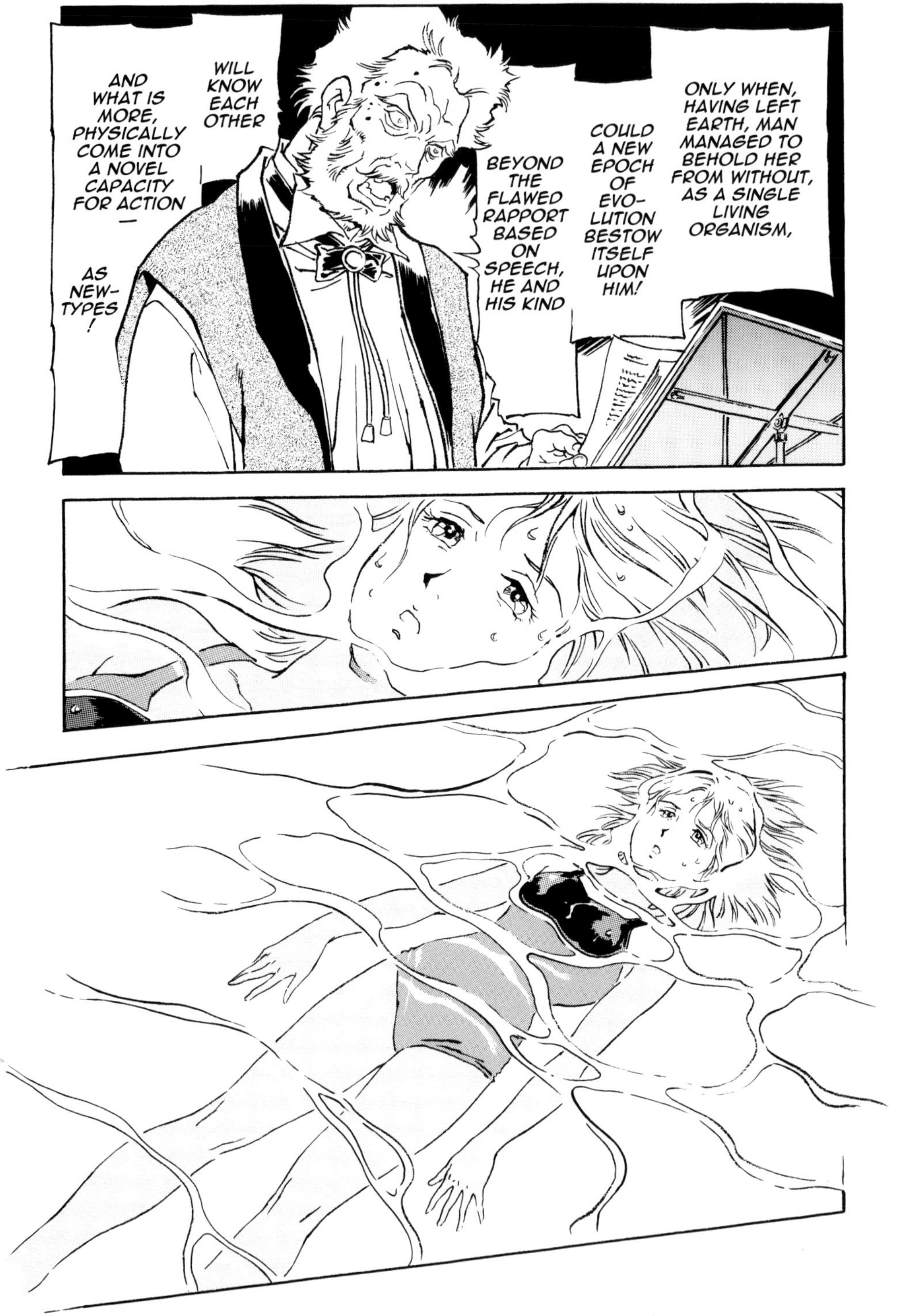
ONLY WHEN, HAVING LEFT EARTH, MAN MANAGED TO BEHOLD HER FROM WITHOUT, AS A SINGLE LIVING ORGANISM,
COULD A NEW EPOCH OF EVO-LUTION BESTOW ITSELF UPON HIM!
BEYOND THE FLAWED RAPPORT BASED ON SPEECH, HE AND HIS KIND
WILL KNOW EACH OTHER
AND WHAT IS MORE, PHYSICALLY COME INTO A NOVEL CAPACITY FOR ACTION —
AS NEW-TYPES!

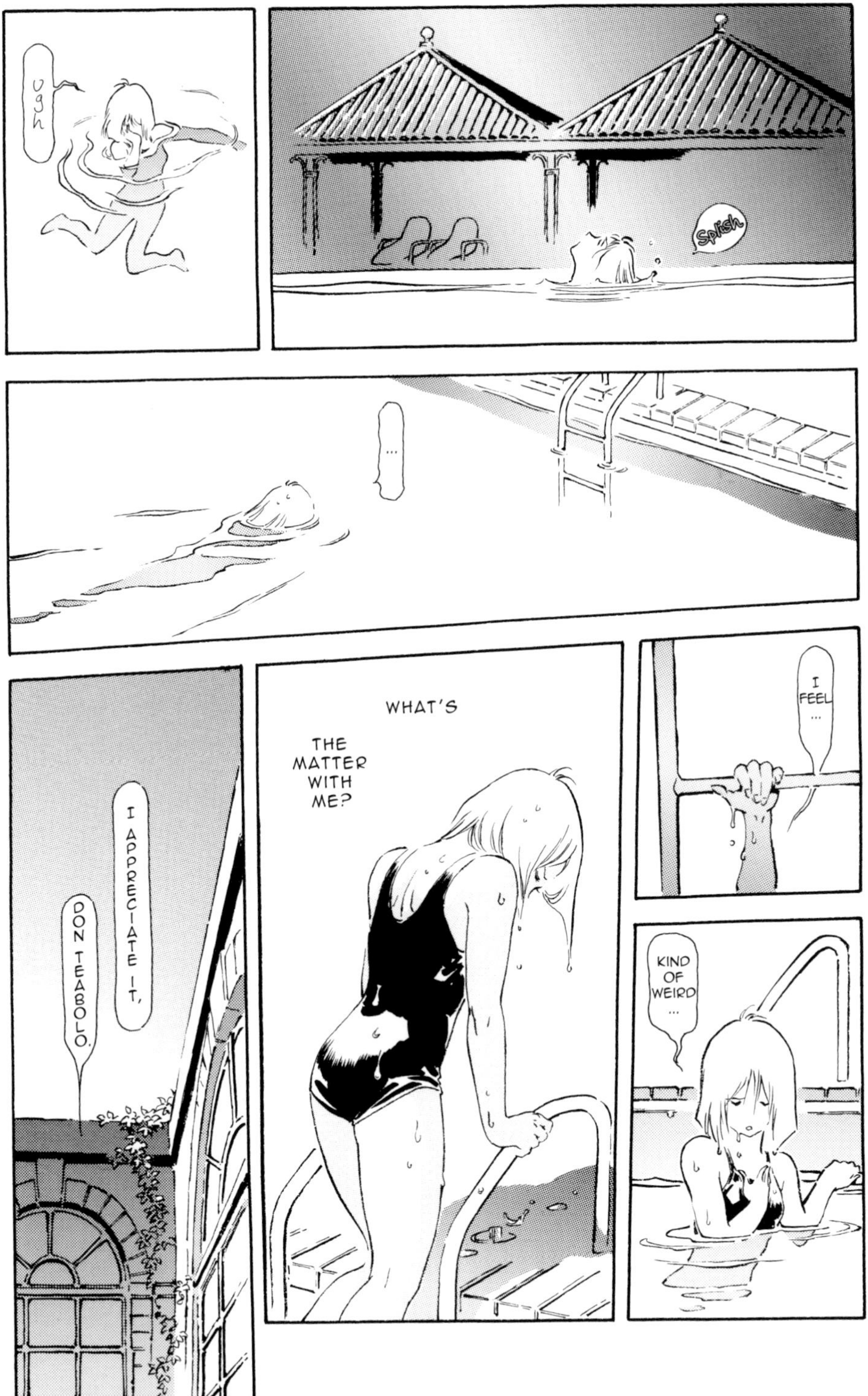
Splish
Ugh
...
I FEEL ...
KIND OF WEIRD ...
WHAT'S THE MATTER WITH ME?
I APPRECIATE IT,
DON TEABOLO.

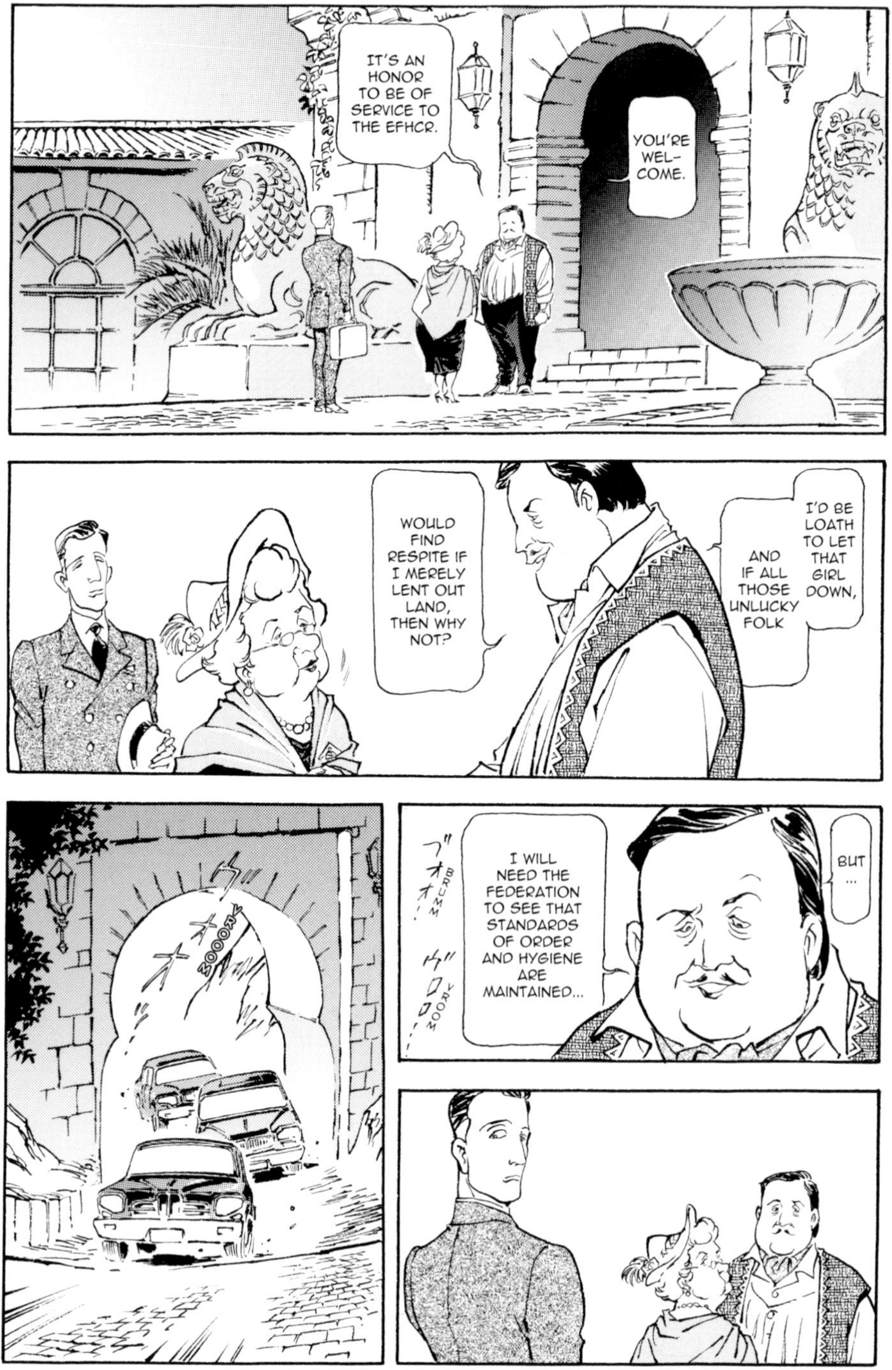
IT'S AN HONOR TO BE OF SERVICE TO THE EFHCR.
YOU'RE WEL- COME.
I'D BE LOATH TO LET THAT GIRL DOWN,
AND IF ALL THOSE UNLUCKY FOLK
WOULD FIND RESPITE IF I MERELY LENT OUT LAND, THEN WHY NOT?
BUT ...
I WILL NEED THE FEDERATION TO SEE THAT STANDARDS OF ORDER AND HYGIENE ARE MAINTAINED...
BRUMM
VROOM
VROOOM

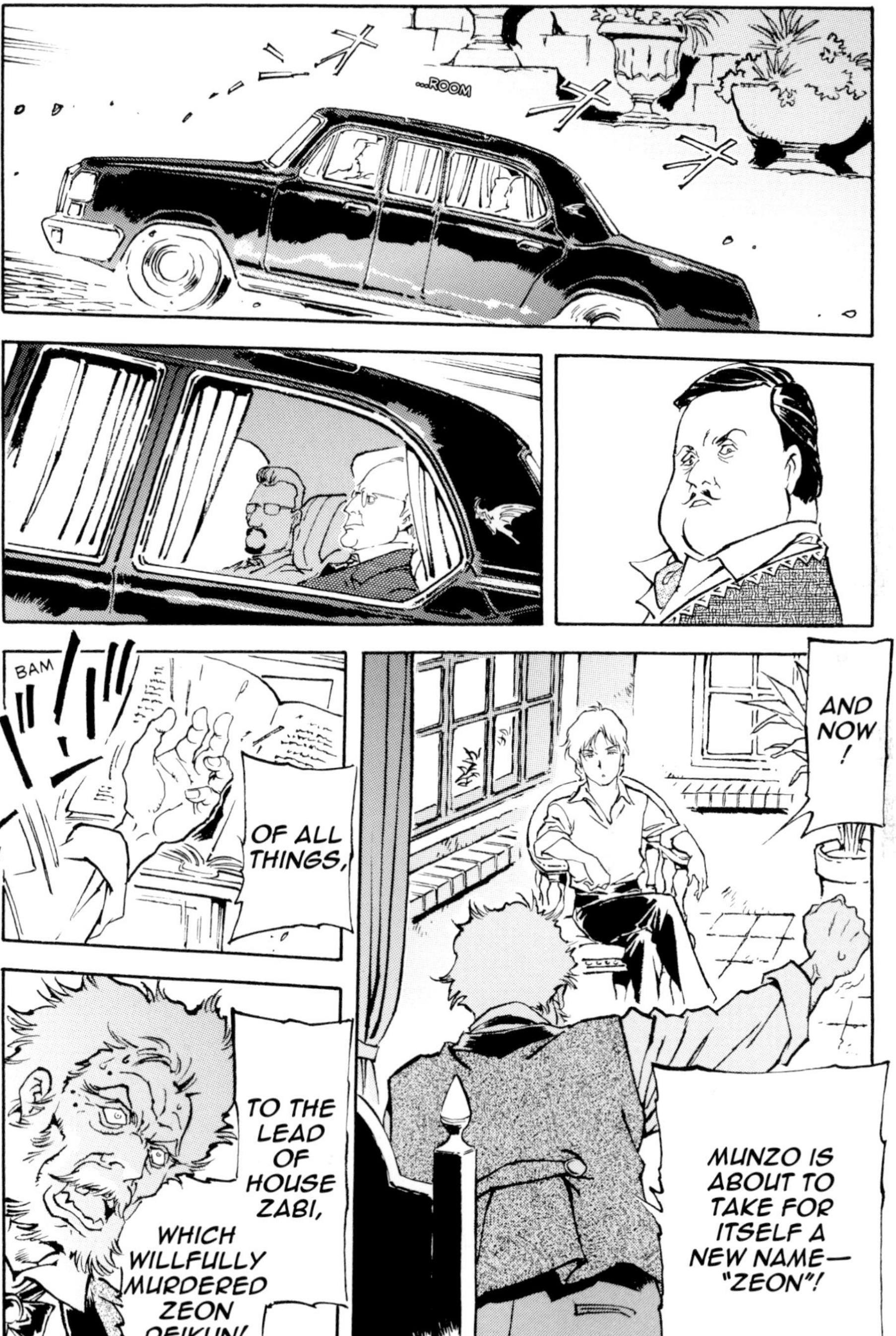
...ROOM
AND NOW!
MUNZO IS ABOUT TO TAKE FOR ITSELF A NEW NAME— "ZEON"!
BAM
BAM
OF ALL THINGS,
TO THE LEAD OF HOUSE ZABI,
WHICH WILLFULLY MURDERED ZEON DEIKUN!

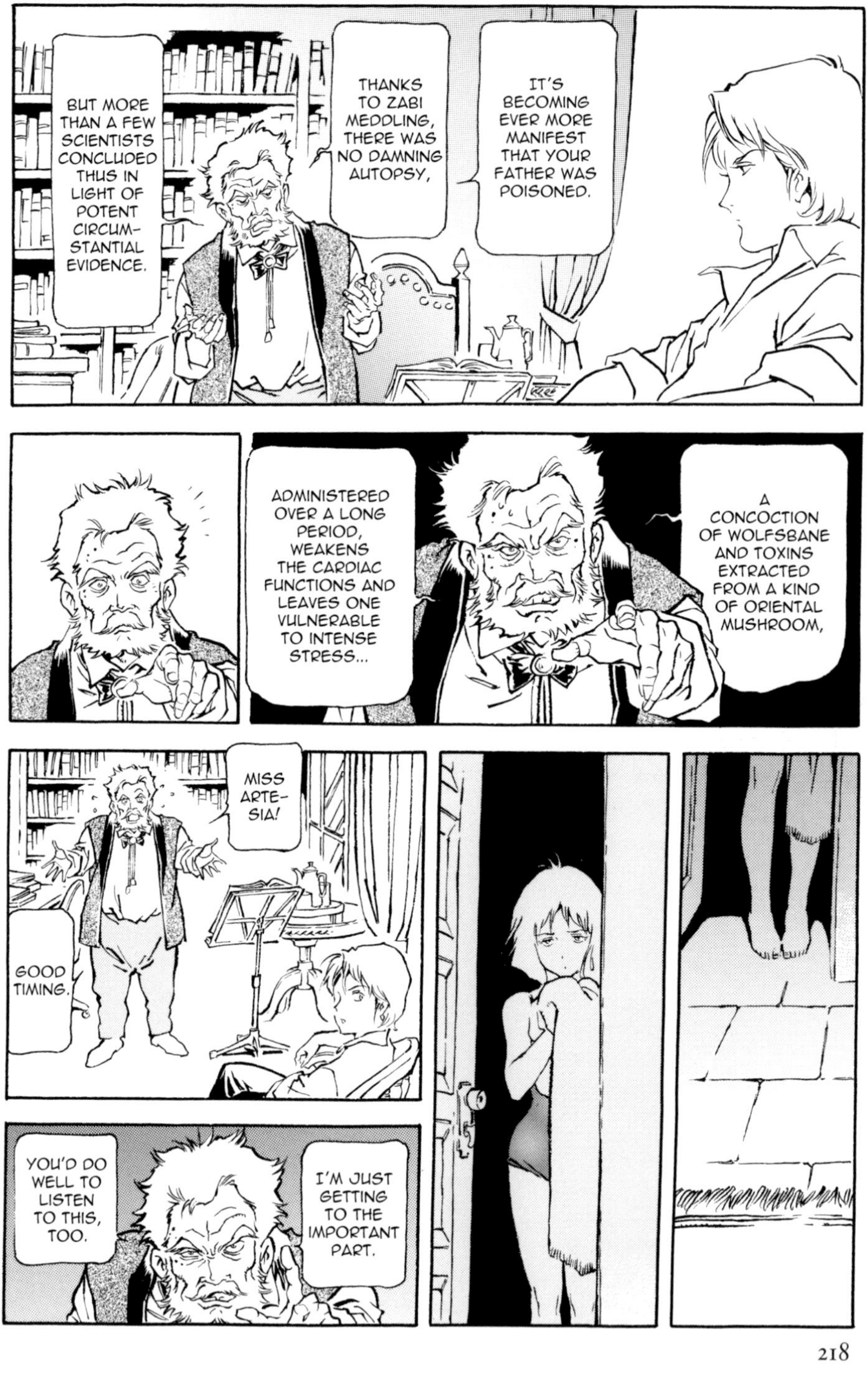
IT'S BECOMING EVER MORE MANIFEST THAT YOUR FATHER WAS POISONED.
THANKS TO ZABI MEDDLING, THERE WAS NO DAMNING AUTOPSY,
BUT MORE THAN A FEW SCIENTISTS CONCLUDED THUS IN LIGHT OF POTENT CIRCUM-STANTIAL EVIDENCE.
A CONCOCTION OF WOLFSBANE AND TOXINS EXTRACTED FROM A KIND OF ORIENTAL MUSHROOM,
ADMINISTERED OVER A LONG PERIOD, WEAKENS THE CARDIAC FUNCTIONS AND LEAVES ONE VULNERABLE TO INTENSE STRESS...
MISS ARTE-SIA!
GOOD TIMING.
I'M JUST GETTING TO THE IMPORTANT PART.
YOU'D DO WELL TO LISTEN TO THIS, TOO.

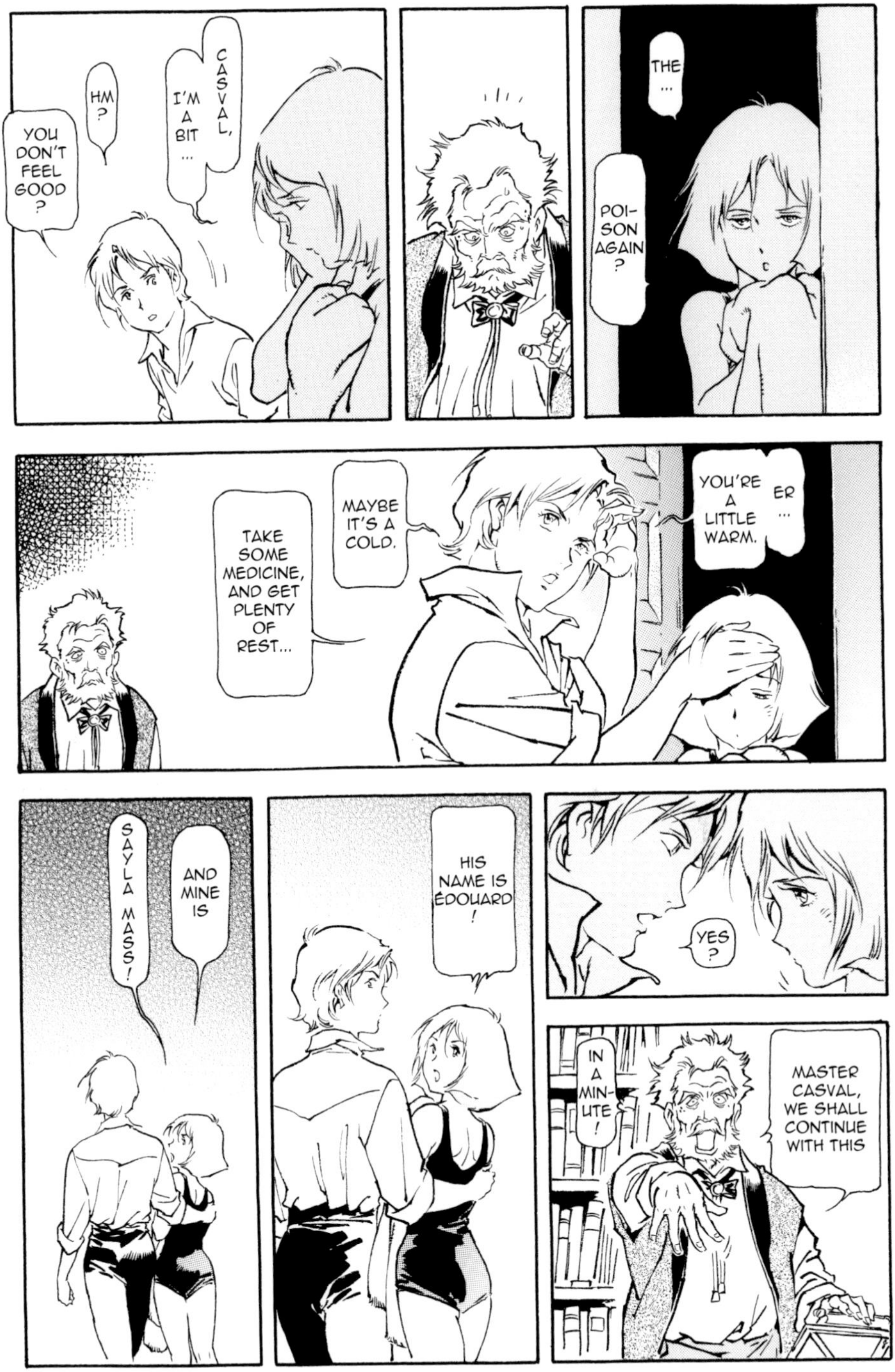
THE ...
POI-SON AGAIN ?
CASVAL,
I'M A BIT ...
HM ?
YOU DON'T FEEL GOOD ?
ER ...
YOU'RE A LITTLE WARM.
MAYBE IT'S A COLD.
TAKE SOME MEDICINE, AND GET PLENTY OF REST...
YES ?
MASTER CASVAL, WE SHALL CONTINUE WITH THIS
IN A MINUTE !
HIS NAME IS ÉDOUARD !
AND MINE IS
SAYLA MASS!

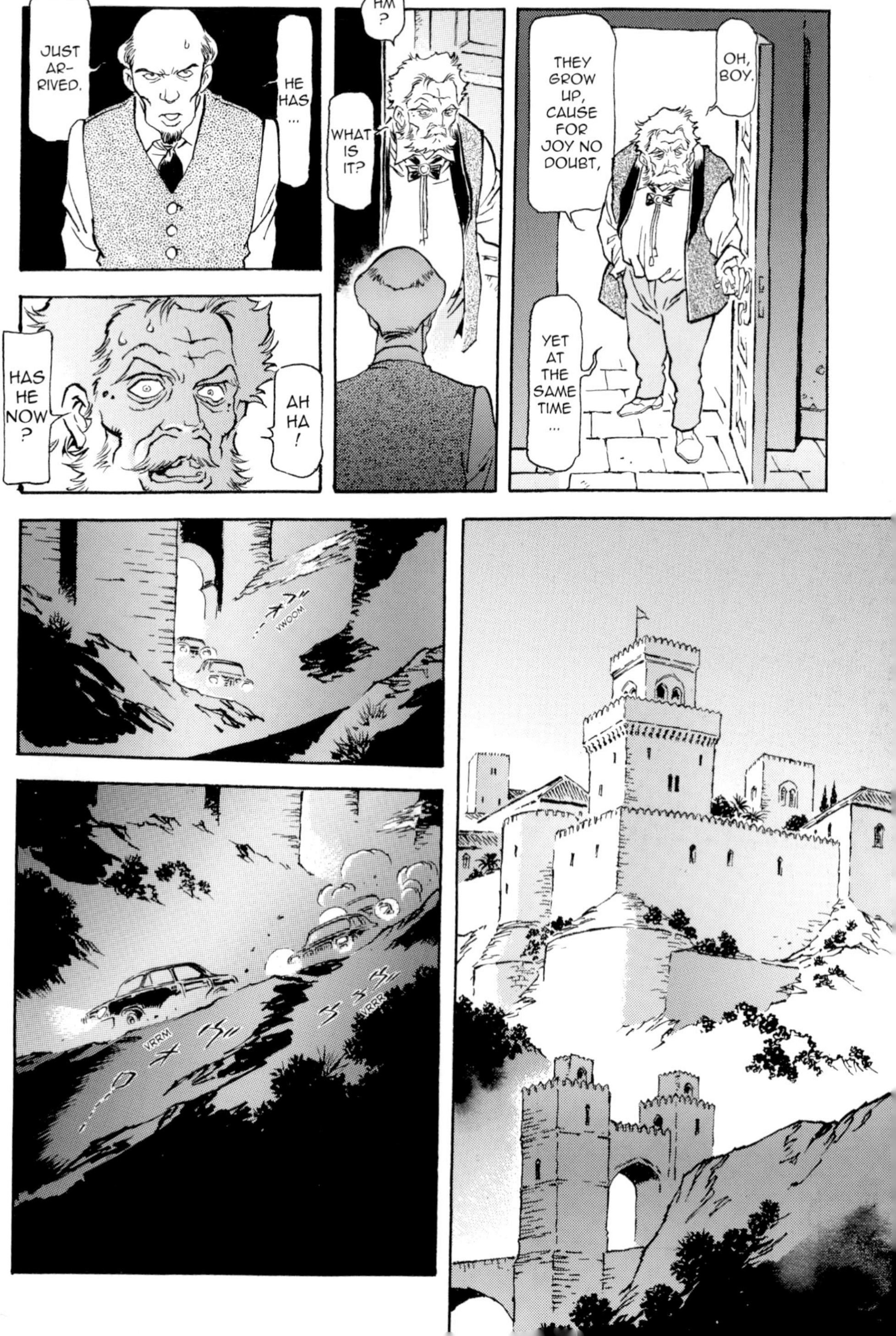

OH, BOY.
THEY GROW UP, CAUSE FOR JOY NO DOUBT,
YET AT THE SAME TIME...
HM?
WHAT IS IT?
HE HAS...
JUST ARRIVED.
AH HA!
HAS HE NOW?
VWOOM
VRRR
VRRM

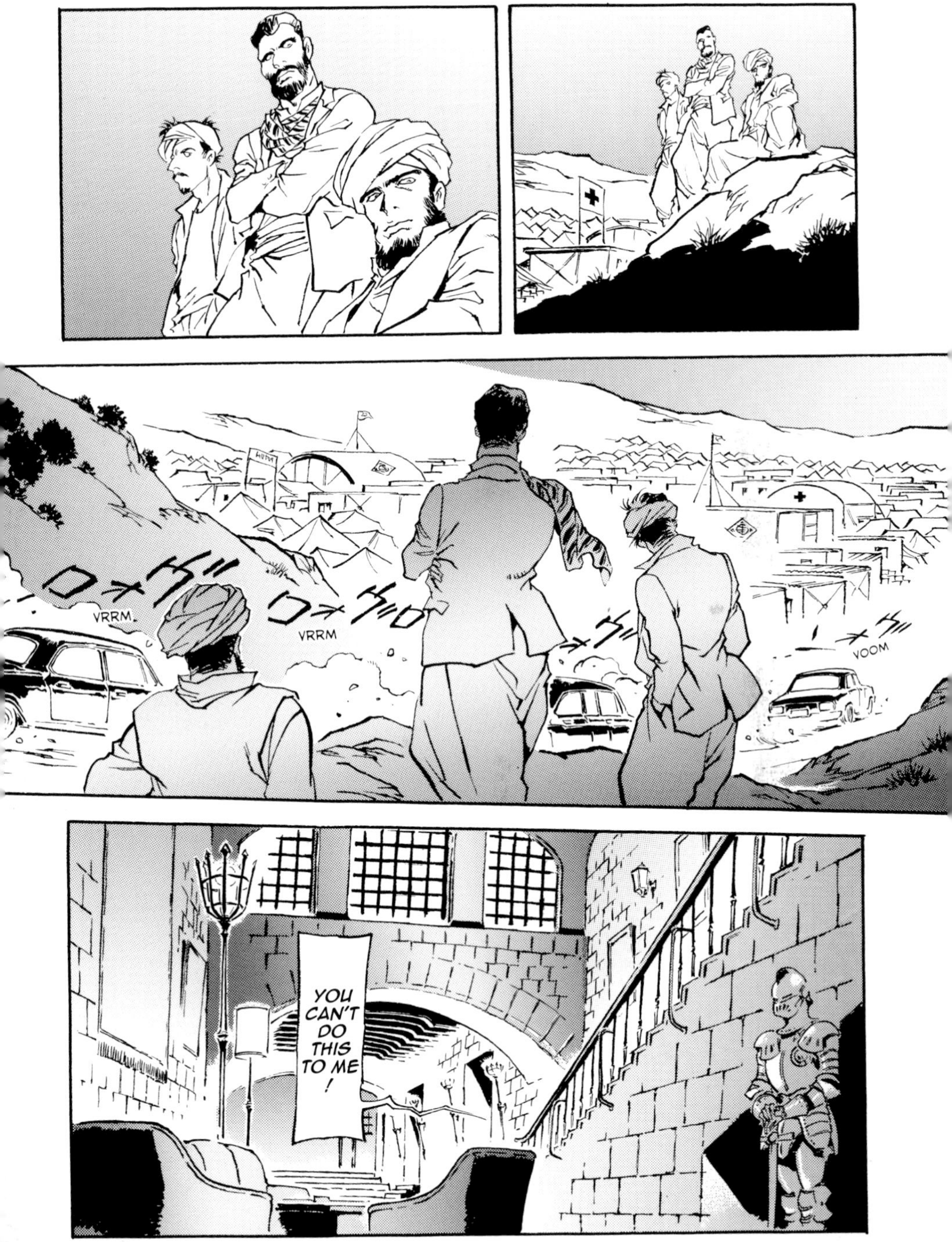
VOOM
VRRM
VRRM
YOU CAN'T DO THIS TO ME!

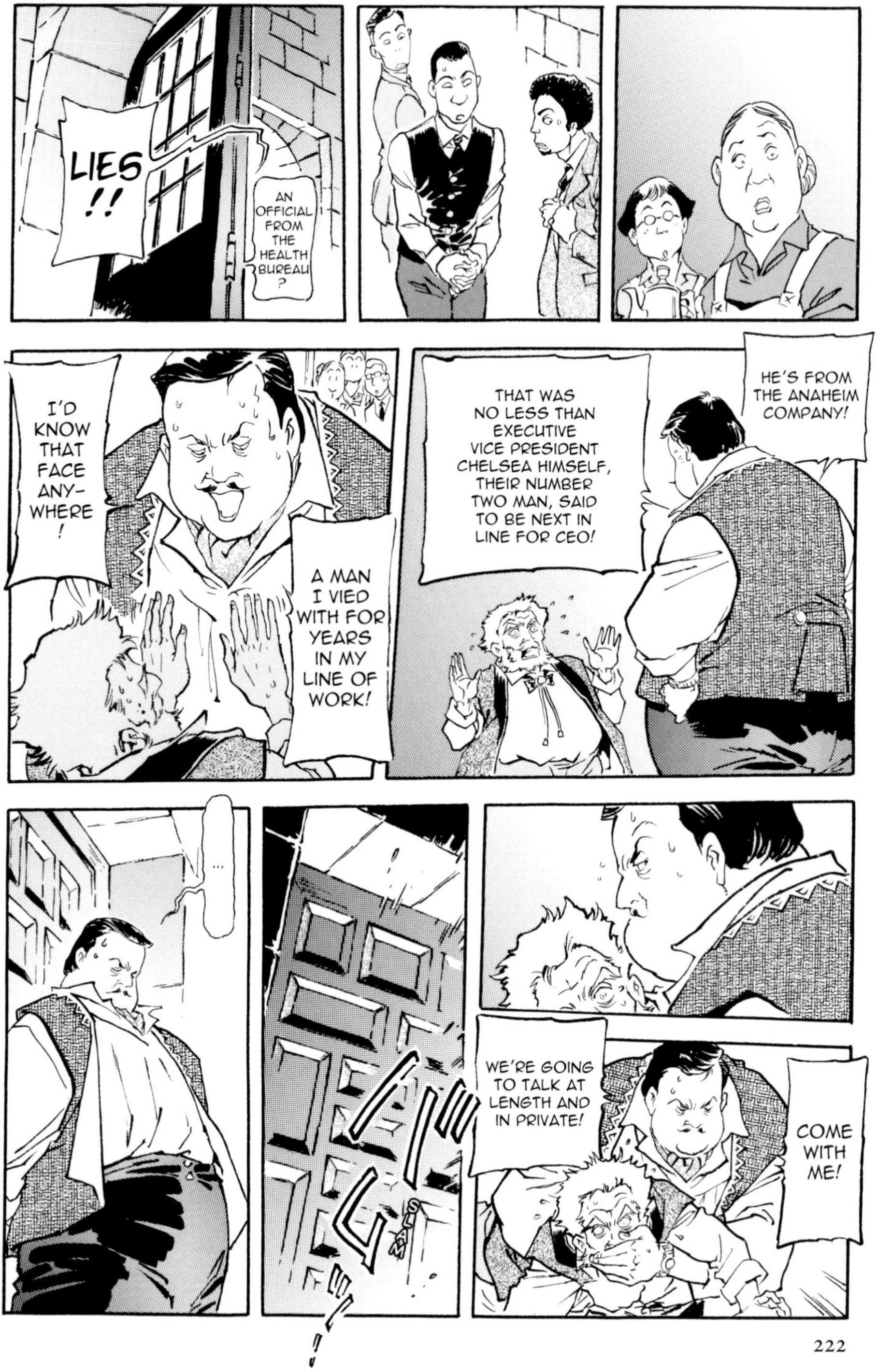
AN OFFICIAL FROM THE HEALTH BUREAU?
LIES!!
HE'S FROM THE ANAHEIM COMPANY!
THAT WAS NO LESS THAN EXECUTIVE VICE PRESIDENT CHELSEA HIMSELF, THEIR NUMBER TWO MAN, SAID TO BE NEXT IN LINE FOR CEO!
I'D KNOW THAT FACE ANY-WHERE!
A MAN I VIED WITH FOR YEARS IN MY LINE OF WORK!
COME WITH ME!
WE'RE GOING TO TALK AT LENGTH AND IN PRIVATE!
SLAM
!!
...

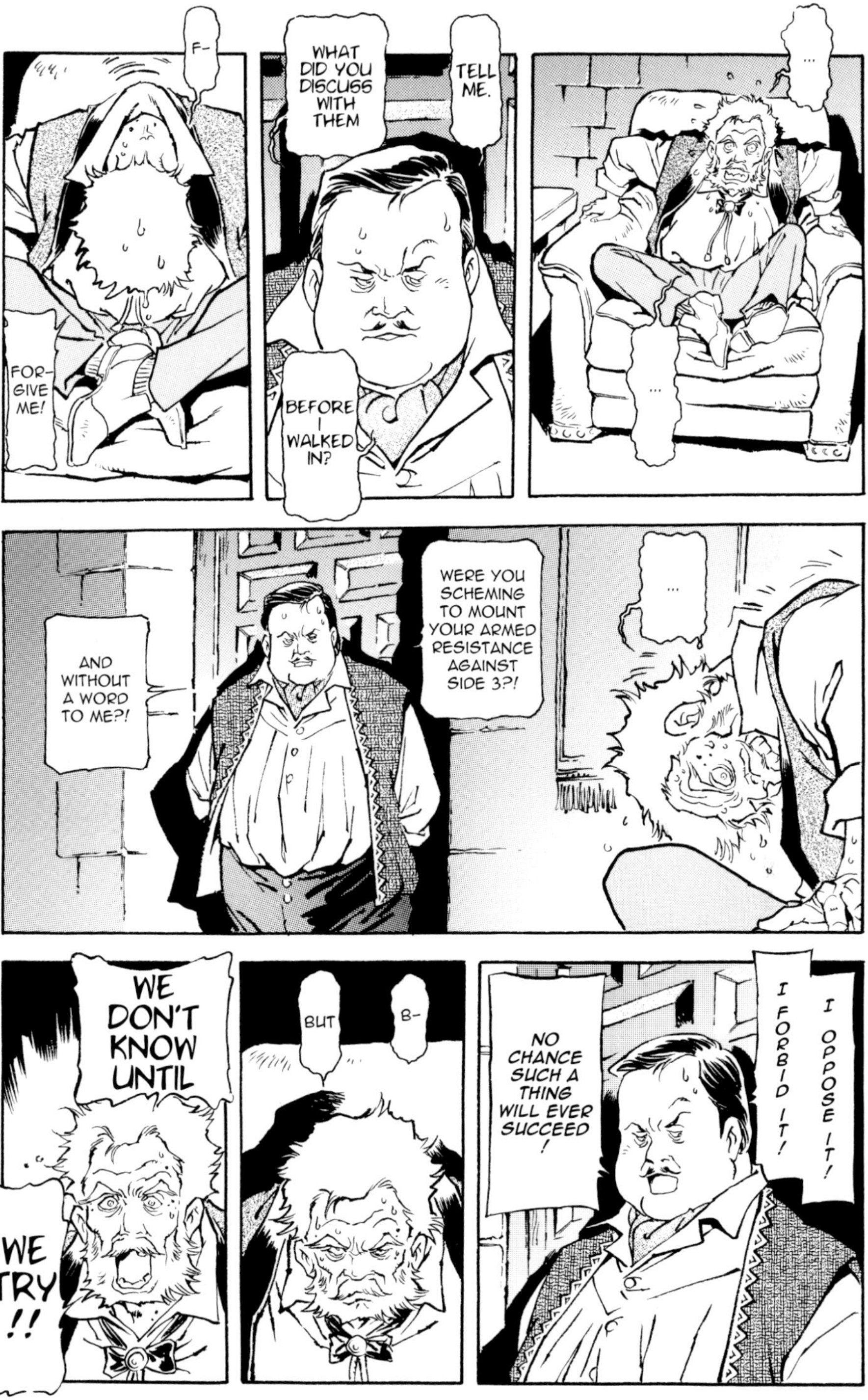
...
...
TELL ME.
WHAT DID YOU DISCUSS WITH THEM
BEFORE I WALKED IN?
F-
FOR-GIVE ME!
...
WERE YOU SCHEMING TO MOUNT YOUR ARMED RESISTANCE AGAINST SIDE 3?!
AND WITHOUT A WORD TO ME?!
I OPPOSE IT!
I FORBID IT!
NO CHANCE SUCH A THING WILL EVER SUCCEED!
B-
BUT
WE DON'T KNOW UNTIL
WE TRY!!

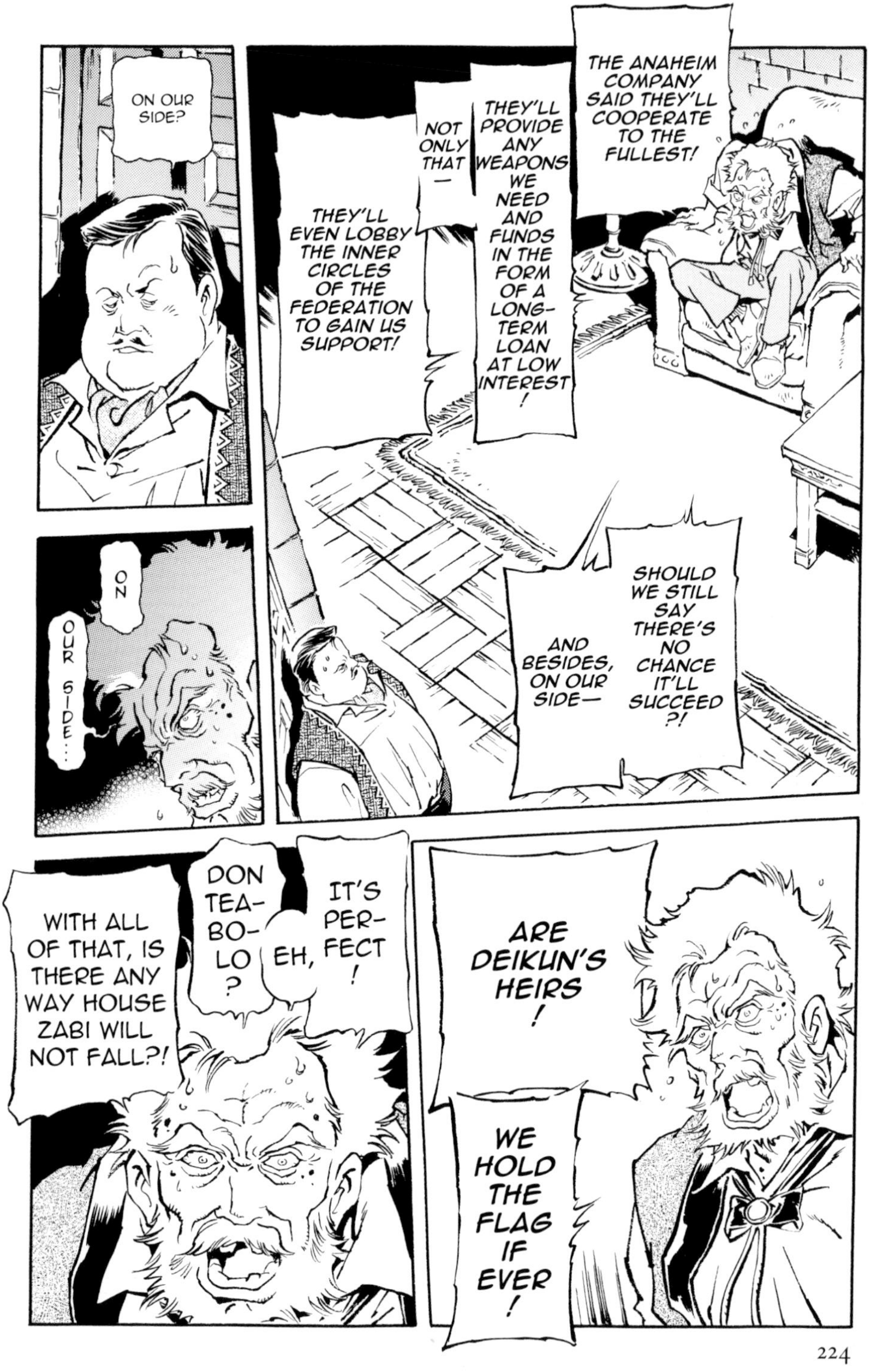
THE ANAHEIM COMPANY SAID THEY'LL COOPERATE TO THE FULLEST!
THEY'LL PROVIDE ANY WEAPONS WE NEED AND FUNDS IN THE FORM OF A LONG-TERM LOAN AT LOW INTEREST!
NOT ONLY THAT—
THEY'LL EVEN LOBBY THE INNER CIRCLES OF THE FEDERATION TO GAIN US SUPPORT!
SHOULD WE STILL SAY THERE'S NO CHANCE IT'LL SUCCEED?!
AND BESIDES, ON OUR SIDE—
ON OUR SIDE?
ON OUR SIDE...
ARE DEIKUN'S HEIRS!
WE HOLD THE FLAG IF EVER!
IT'S PERFECT!
EH,
DON TEABOLO?
WITH ALL OF THAT, IS THERE ANY WAY HOUSE ZABI WILL NOT FALL?!

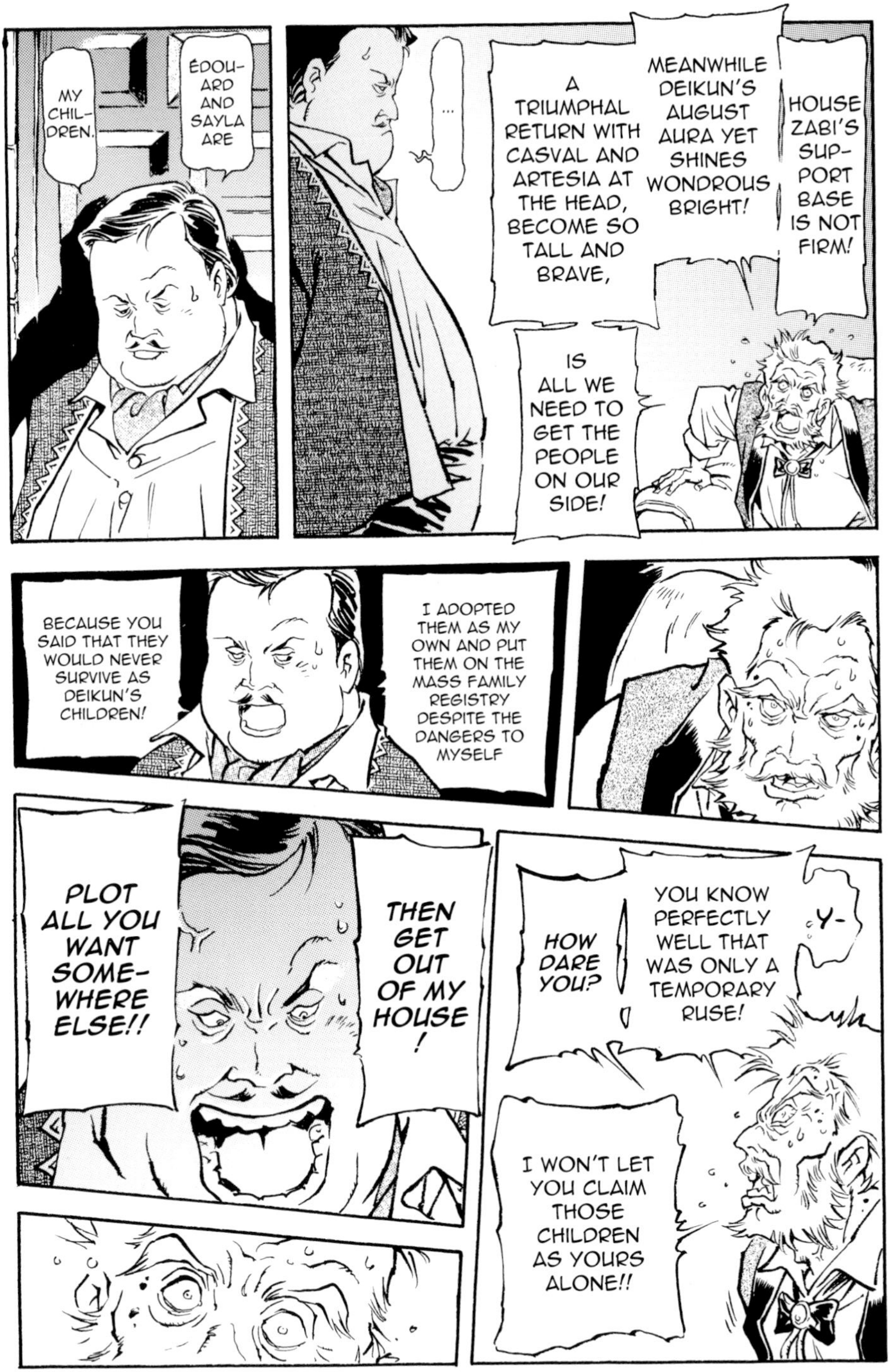
HOUSE ZABI'S SUPPORT BASE IS NOT FIRM!
MEANWHILE DEIKUN'S AUGUST AURA YET SHINES WONDROUS BRIGHT!
A TRIUMPHAL RETURN WITH CASVAL AND ARTESIA AT THE HEAD, BECOME SO TALL AND BRAVE,
IS ALL WE NEED TO GET THE PEOPLE ON OUR SIDE!
...
ÉDOUARD AND SAYLA ARE
MY CHILDREN.
I ADOPTED THEM AS MY OWN AND PUT THEM ON THE MASS FAMILY REGISTRY DESPITE THE DANGERS TO MYSELF
BECAUSE YOU SAID THAT THEY WOULD NEVER SURVIVE AS DEIKUN'S CHILDREN!
Y-
YOU KNOW PERFECTLY WELL THAT WAS ONLY A TEMPORARY RUSE!
HOW DARE YOU?
I WON'T LET YOU CLAIM THOSE CHILDREN AS YOURS ALONE!!
THEN GET OUT OF MY HOUSE!
PLOT ALL YOU WANT SOMEWHERE ELSE!!

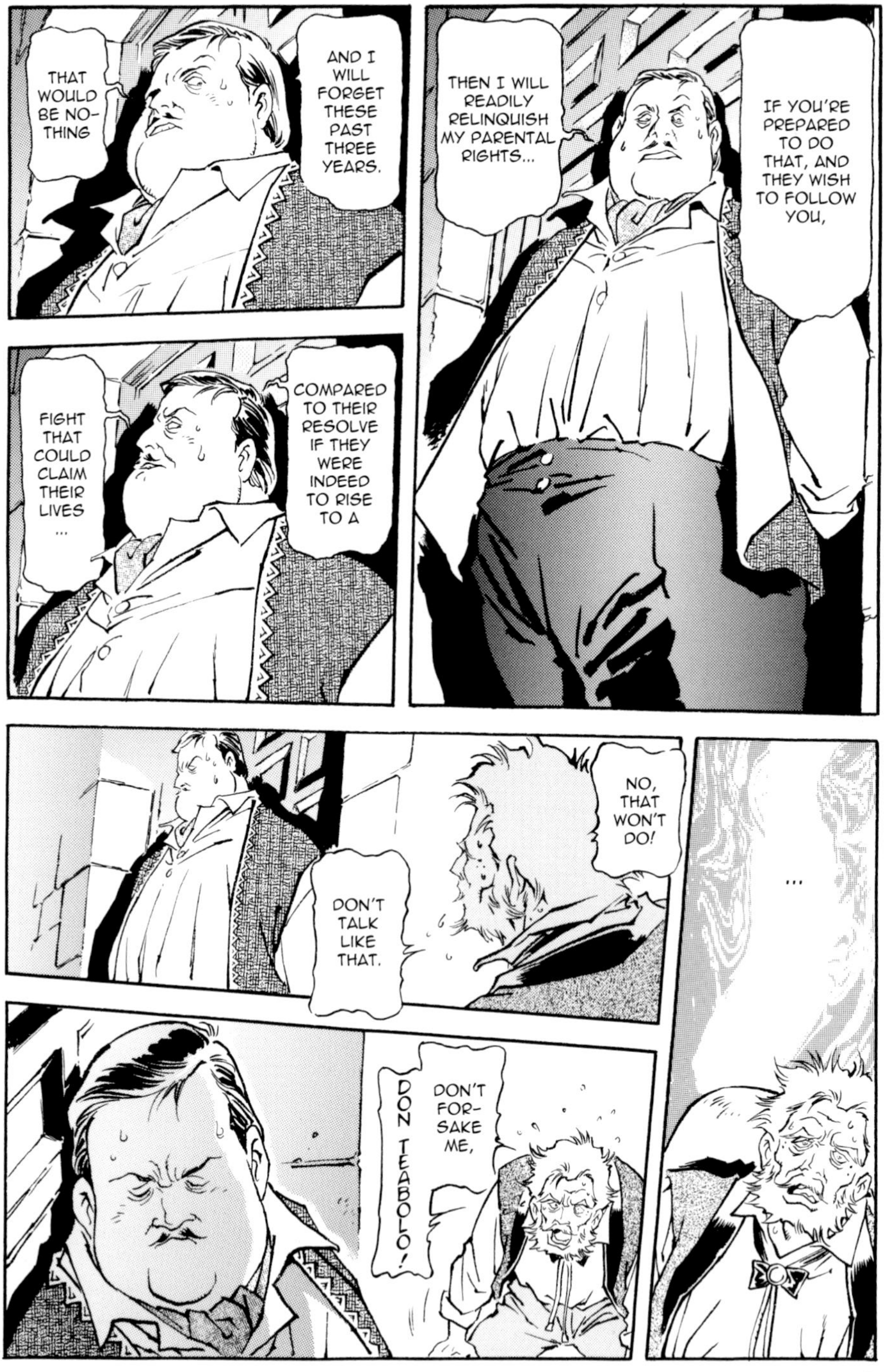
IF YOU'RE PREPARED TO DO THAT, AND THEY WISH TO FOLLOW YOU,
THEN I WILL READILY RELINQUISH MY PARENTAL RIGHTS...
AND I WILL FORGET THESE PAST THREE YEARS.
THAT WOULD BE NO-THING
COMPARED TO THEIR RESOLVE IF THEY WERE INDEED TO RISE TO A
FIGHT THAT COULD CLAIM THEIR LIVES ...
...
NO, THAT WON'T DO!
DON'T TALK LIKE THAT.
DON'T FOR-SAKE ME,
DON TEABOLO!

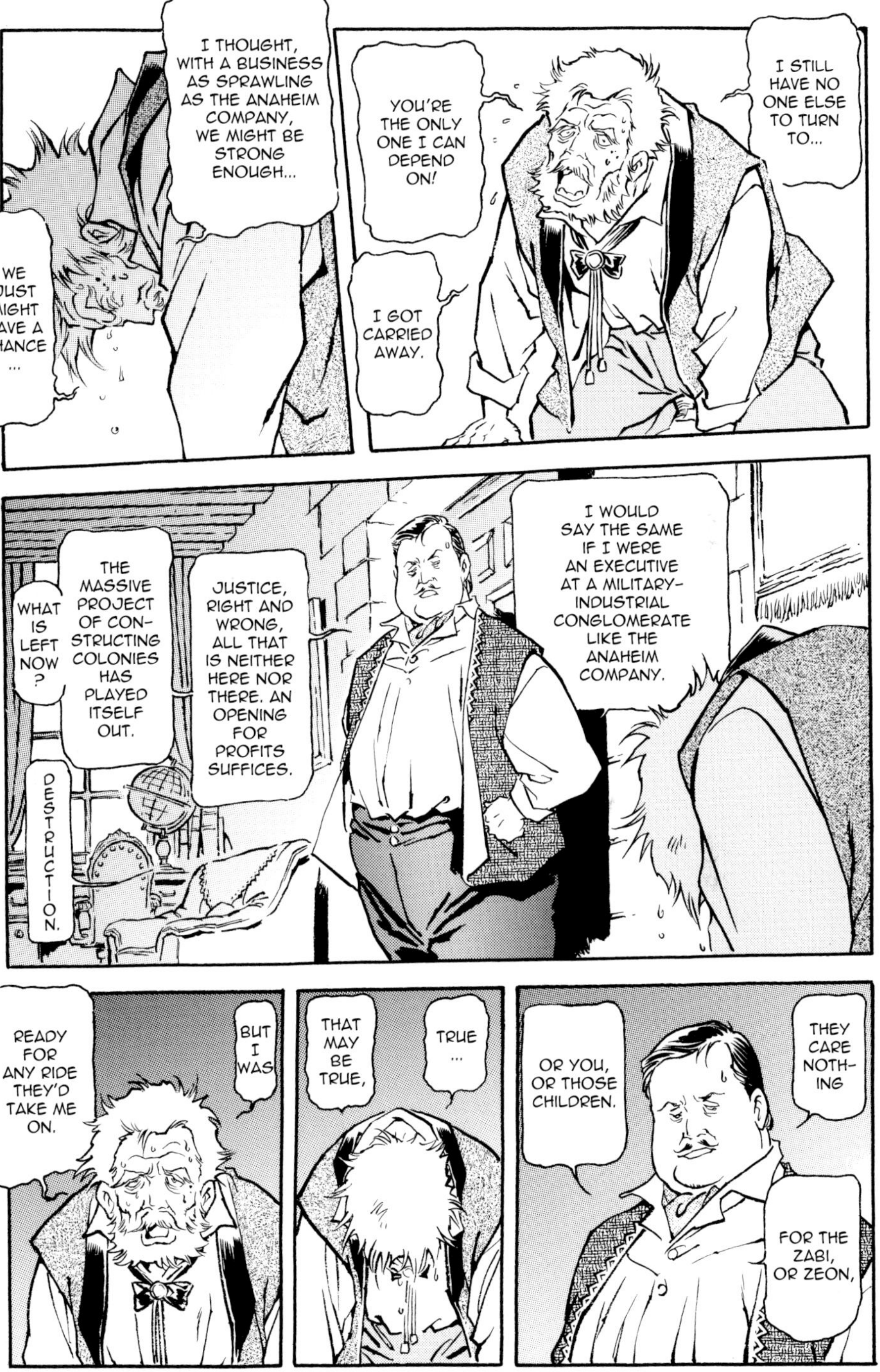
I STILL HAVE NO ONE ELSE TO TURN TO...
YOU'RE THE ONLY ONE I CAN DEPEND ON!
I GOT CARRIED AWAY.
I THOUGHT, WITH A BUSINESS AS SPRAWLING AS THE ANAHEIM COMPANY, WE MIGHT BE STRONG ENOUGH...
WE JUST MIGHT HAVE A CHANCE...
I WOULD SAY THE SAME IF I WERE AN EXECUTIVE AT A MILITARY-INDUSTRIAL CONGLOMERATE LIKE THE ANAHEIM COMPANY.
JUSTICE, RIGHT AND WRONG, ALL THAT IS NEITHER HERE NOR THERE. AN OPENING FOR PROFITS SUFFICES.
THE MASSIVE PROJECT OF CON-STRUCTING COLONIES HAS PLAYED ITSELF OUT.
WHAT IS LEFT NOW?
DESTRUCTION.
THEY CARE NOTH-ING
FOR THE ZABI, OR ZEON,
OR YOU, OR THOSE CHILDREN.
TRUE...
THAT MAY BE TRUE,
BUT I WAS
READY FOR ANY RIDE THEY'D TAKE ME ON.

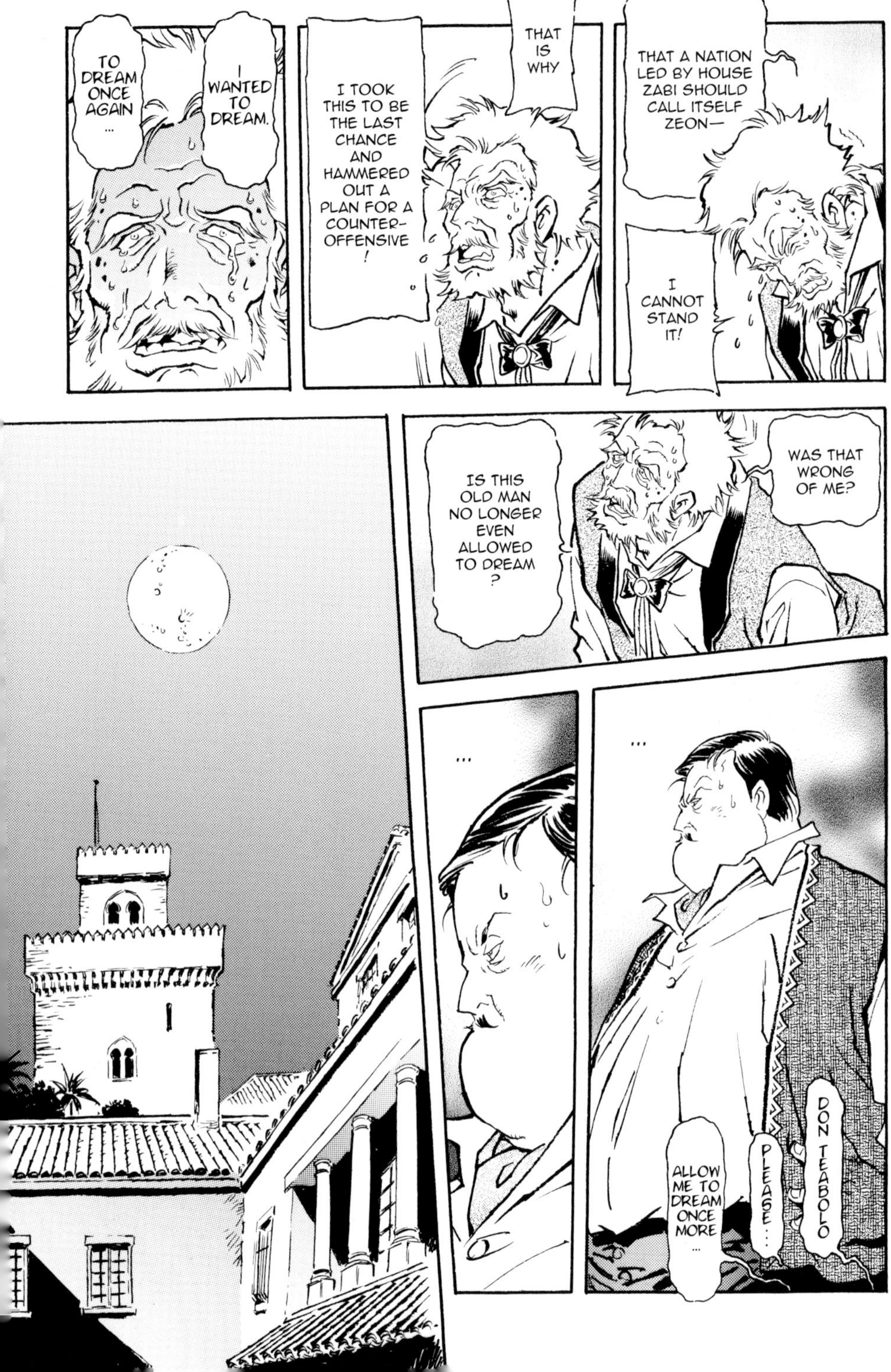
THAT A NATION LED BY HOUSE ZABI SHOULD CALL ITSELF ZEON—
I CANNOT STAND IT!
THAT IS WHY
I TOOK THIS TO BE THE LAST CHANCE AND HAMMERED OUT A PLAN FOR A COUNTER-OFFENSIVE!
I WANTED TO DREAM.
TO DREAM ONCE AGAIN...
WAS THAT WRONG OF ME?
IS THIS OLD MAN NO LONGER EVEN ALLOWED TO DREAM?
...
DON TEABOLO
PLEASE...
ALLOW ME TO DREAM ONCE MORE...
...

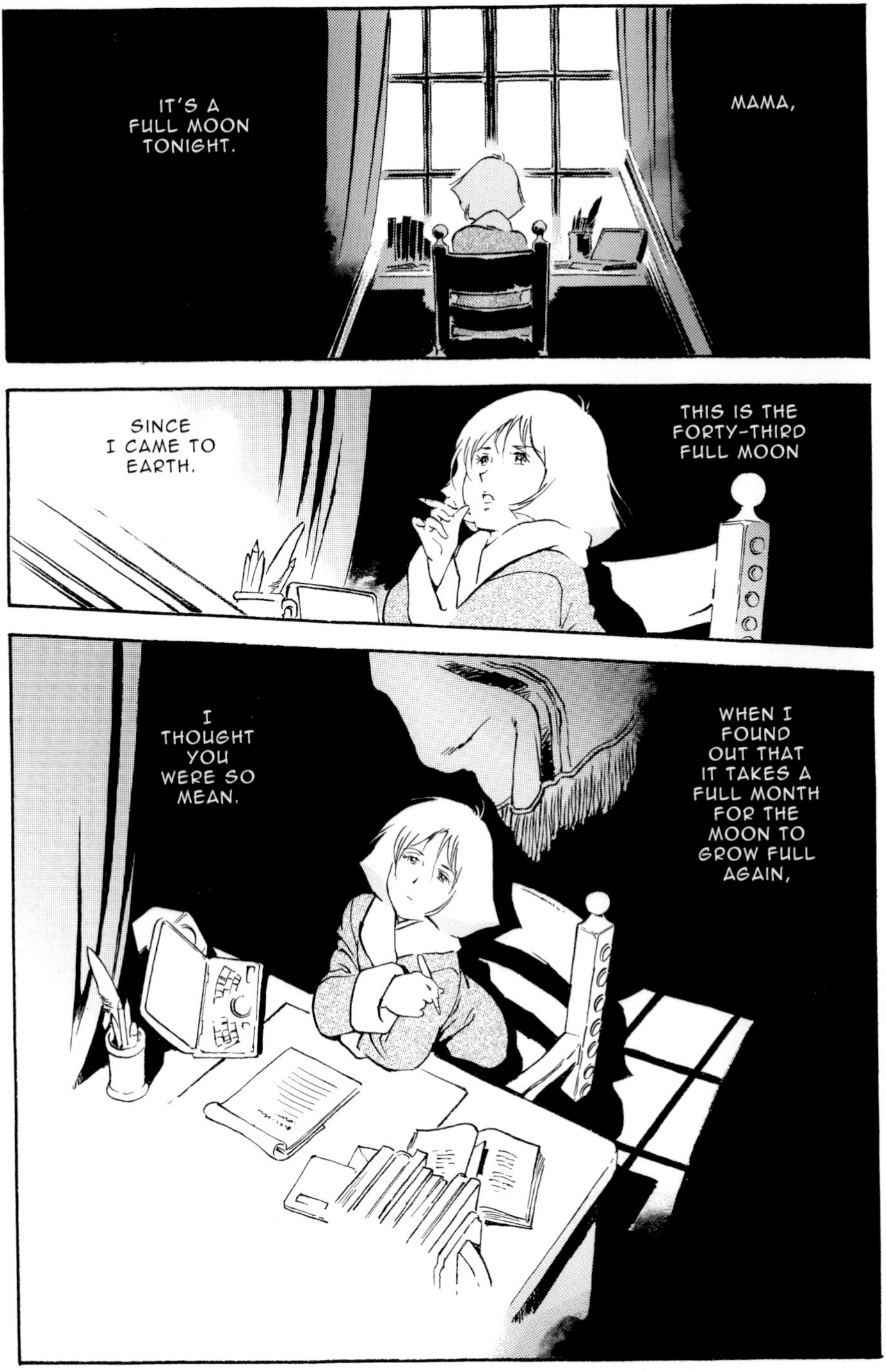
MAMA,
IT'S A FULL MOON TONIGHT.
THIS IS THE FORTY-THIRD FULL MOON
SINCE I CAME TO EARTH.
WHEN I FOUND OUT THAT IT TAKES A FULL MONTH FOR THE MOON TO GROW FULL AGAIN,
I THOUGHT YOU WERE SO MEAN.

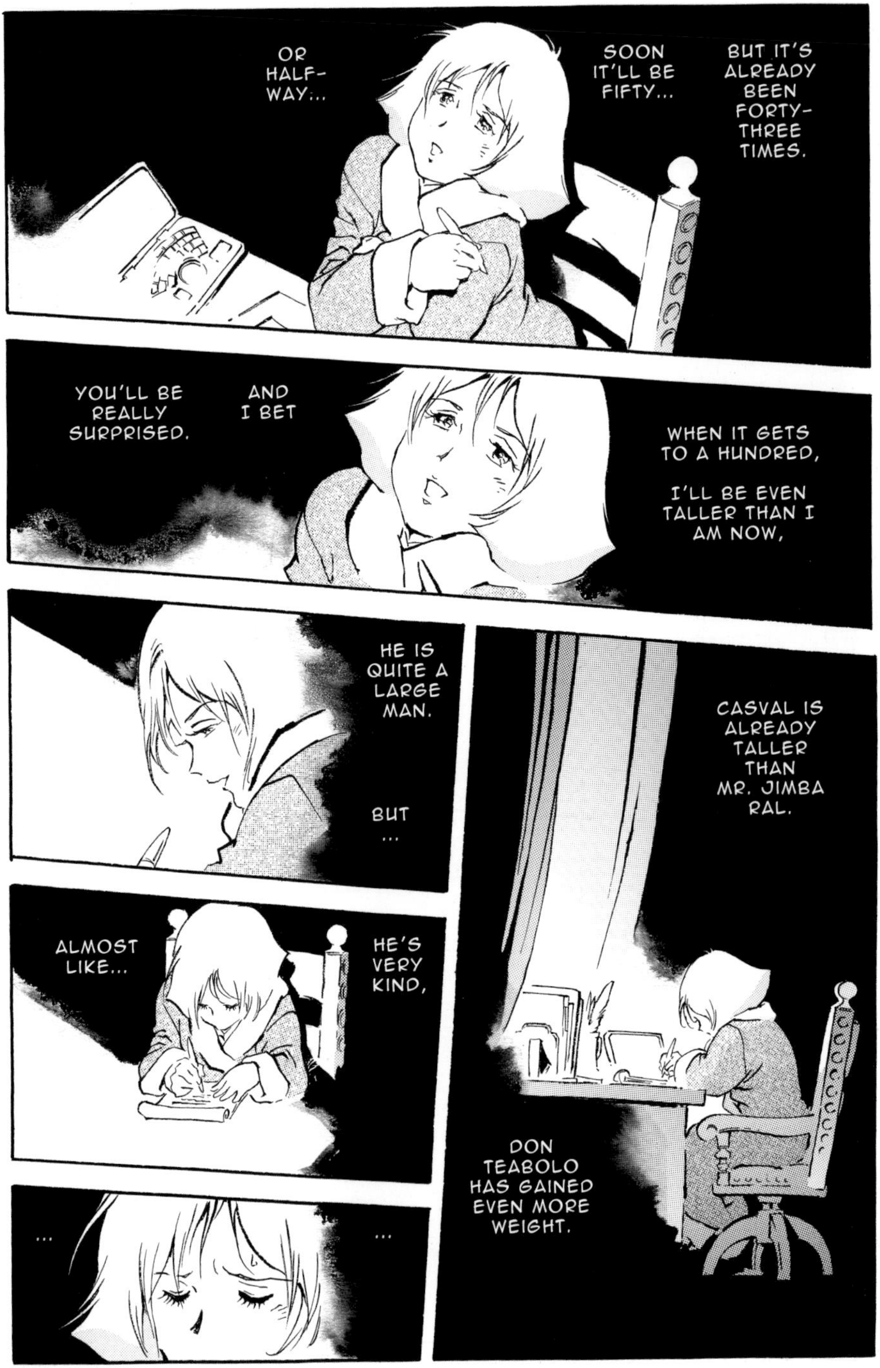
BUT IT'S ALREADY BEEN FORTY-THREE TIMES.
SOON IT'LL BE FIFTY...
OR HALF-WAY...
WHEN IT GETS TO A HUNDRED,
I'LL BE EVEN TALLER THAN I AM NOW,
AND I BET
YOU'LL BE REALLY SURPRISED.
CASVAL IS ALREADY TALLER THAN MR. JIMBA RAL.
DON TEABOLO HAS GAINED EVEN MORE WEIGHT.
HE IS QUITE A LARGE MAN.
BUT ...
HE'S VERY KIND,
ALMOST LIKE...
...
...

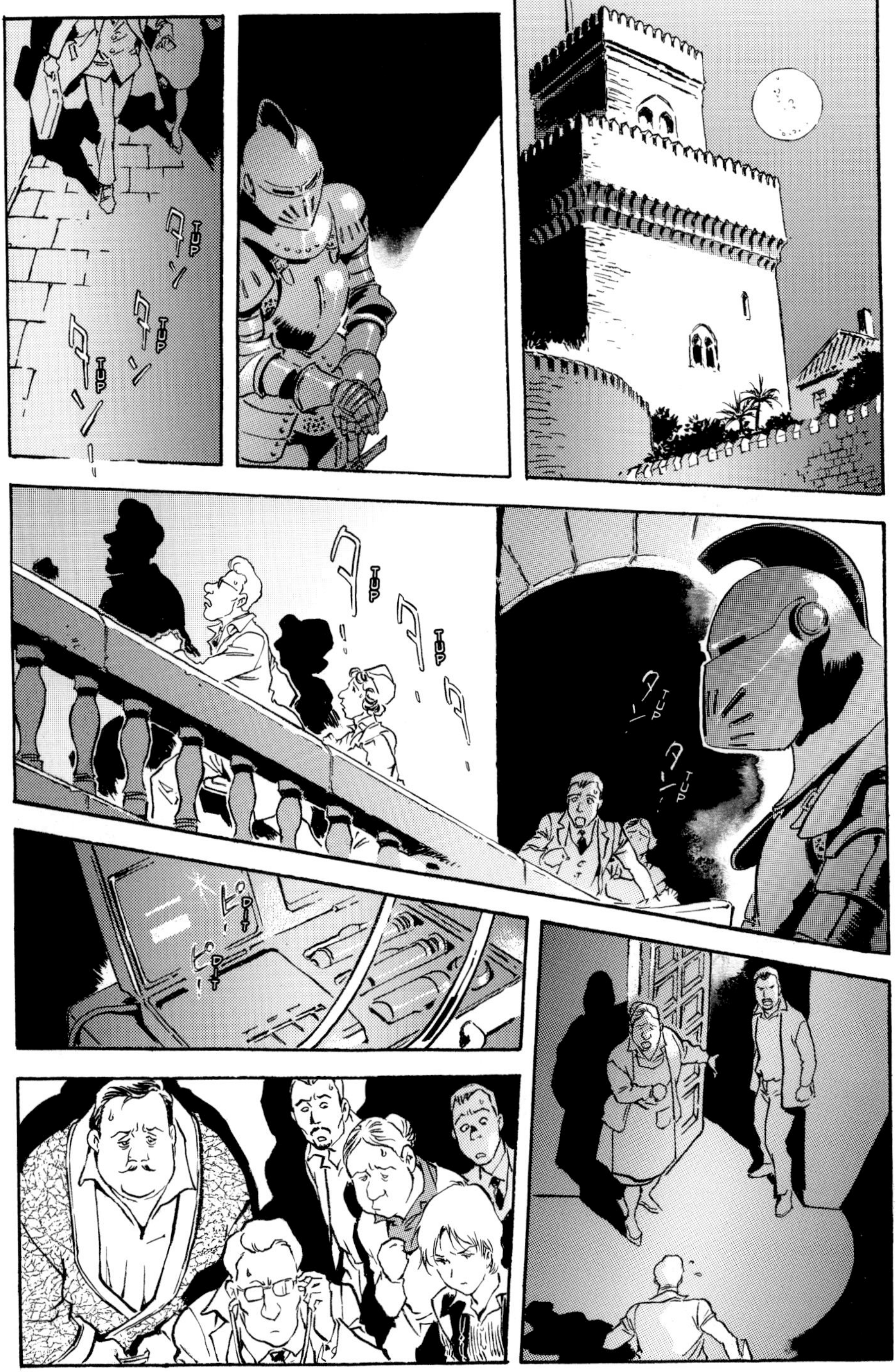
TUP
TUP
TUP
TUP
TUP
TUP
TUP
DIT
DIT

HUFF
HUFF
... HOW
IS SHE?
IT'S PROBABLY JUST A COLD, BUT...
IT'S AN AWFULLY HIGH FEVER, AND I'LL DO WHAT I CAN TO TREAT THAT.
SHE'S HAD A LOT OF CONTACT WITH PATIENTS, SO WE CAN'T DISCOUNT THE POSSIBILITY OF
SAHARA FEVER ...
IT'S EPIDEMIC IN THE CAMPS.
ANYWAY, WE'LL SEE.

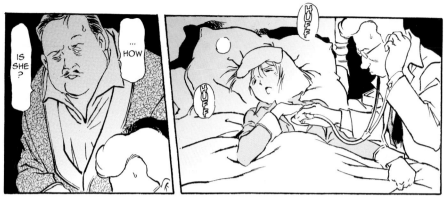

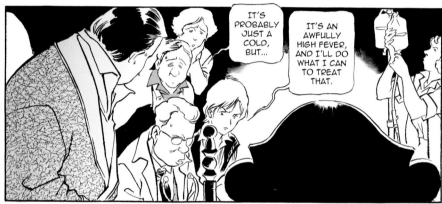

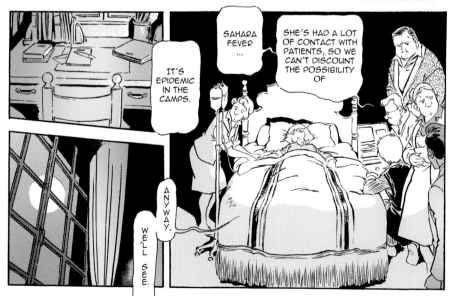

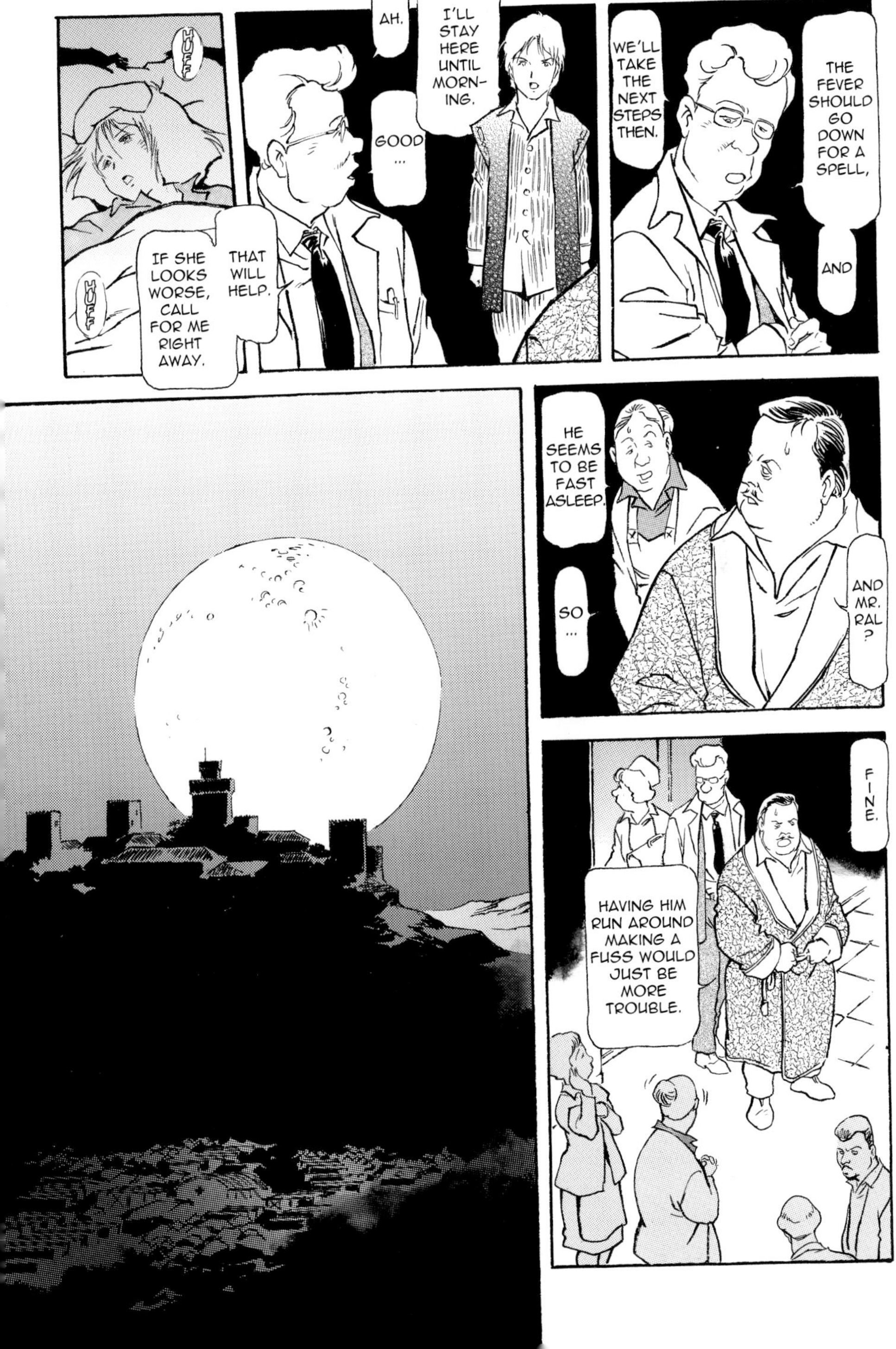
THE FEVER SHOULD GO DOWN FOR A SPELL,
AND
WE'LL TAKE THE NEXT STEPS THEN.
I'LL STAY HERE UNTIL MORNING.
AH.
GOOD ...
HUFF
THAT WILL HELP.
IF SHE LOOKS WORSE, CALL FOR ME RIGHT AWAY.
HUFF
AND MR. RAL?
HE SEEMS TO BE FAST ASLEEP.
SO ...
FINE.
HAVING HIM RUN AROUND MAKING A FUSS WOULD JUST BE MORE TROUBLE.

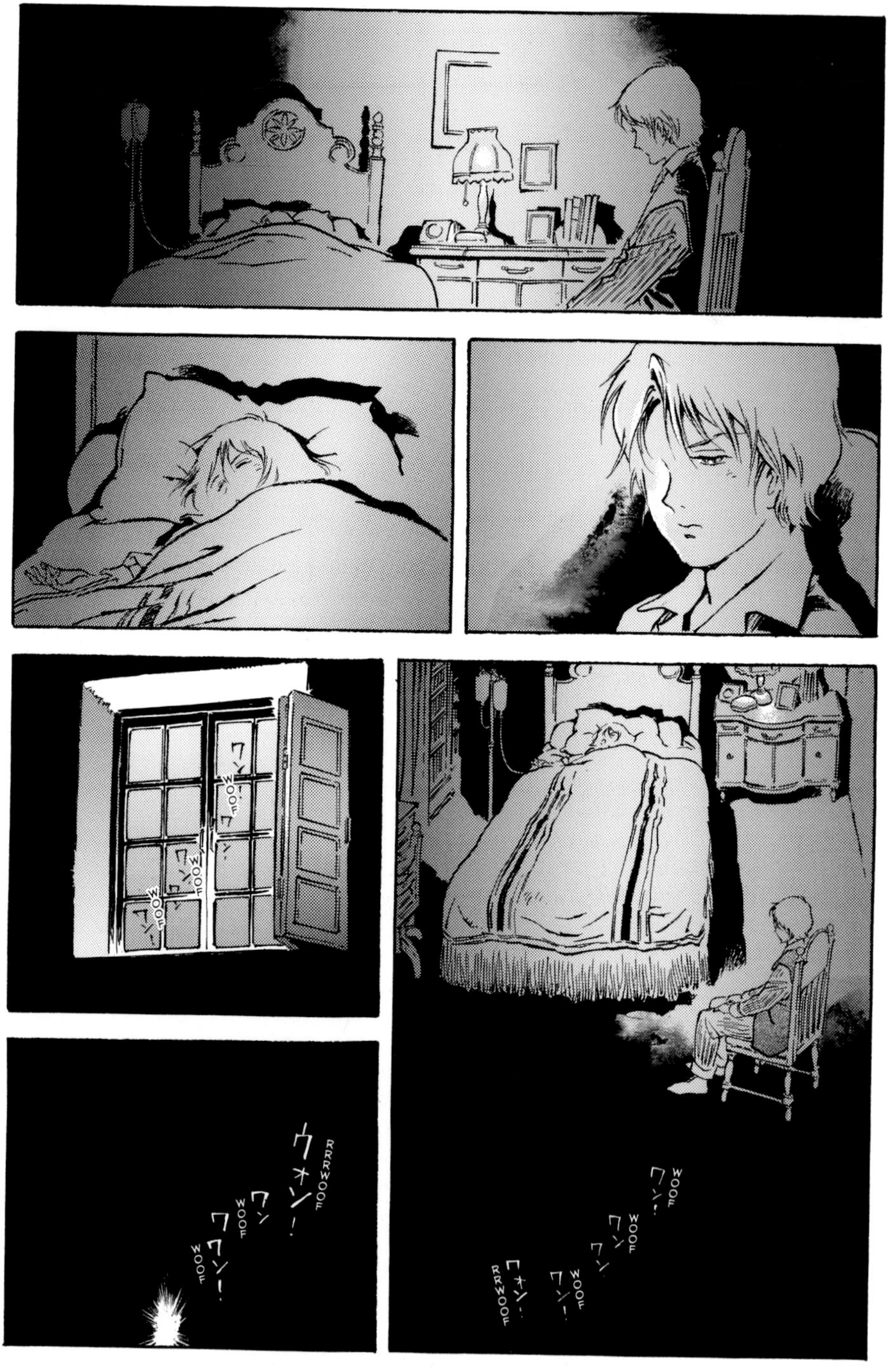
ワン! WOOF
ワン ワン WOOF
ワン! WOOF
ウォン! RRWOOF
ワン! WOOF!
ワン! WOOF
ワン! WOOF
ウォン! RRRWOOF
ワン WOOF
ワワン! WOOF

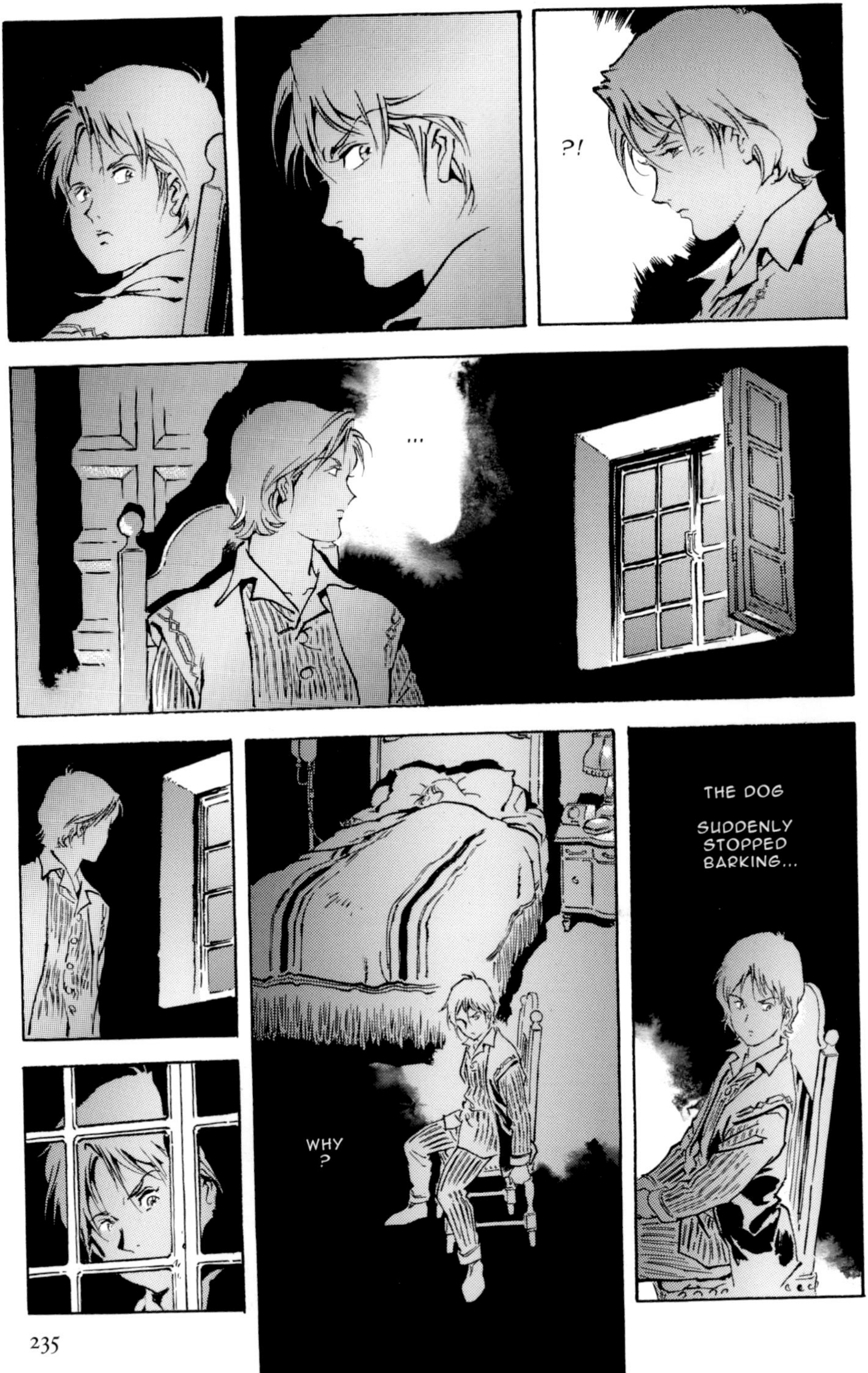
?!
...
THE DOG
SUDDENLY STOPPED BARKING...
WHY ?

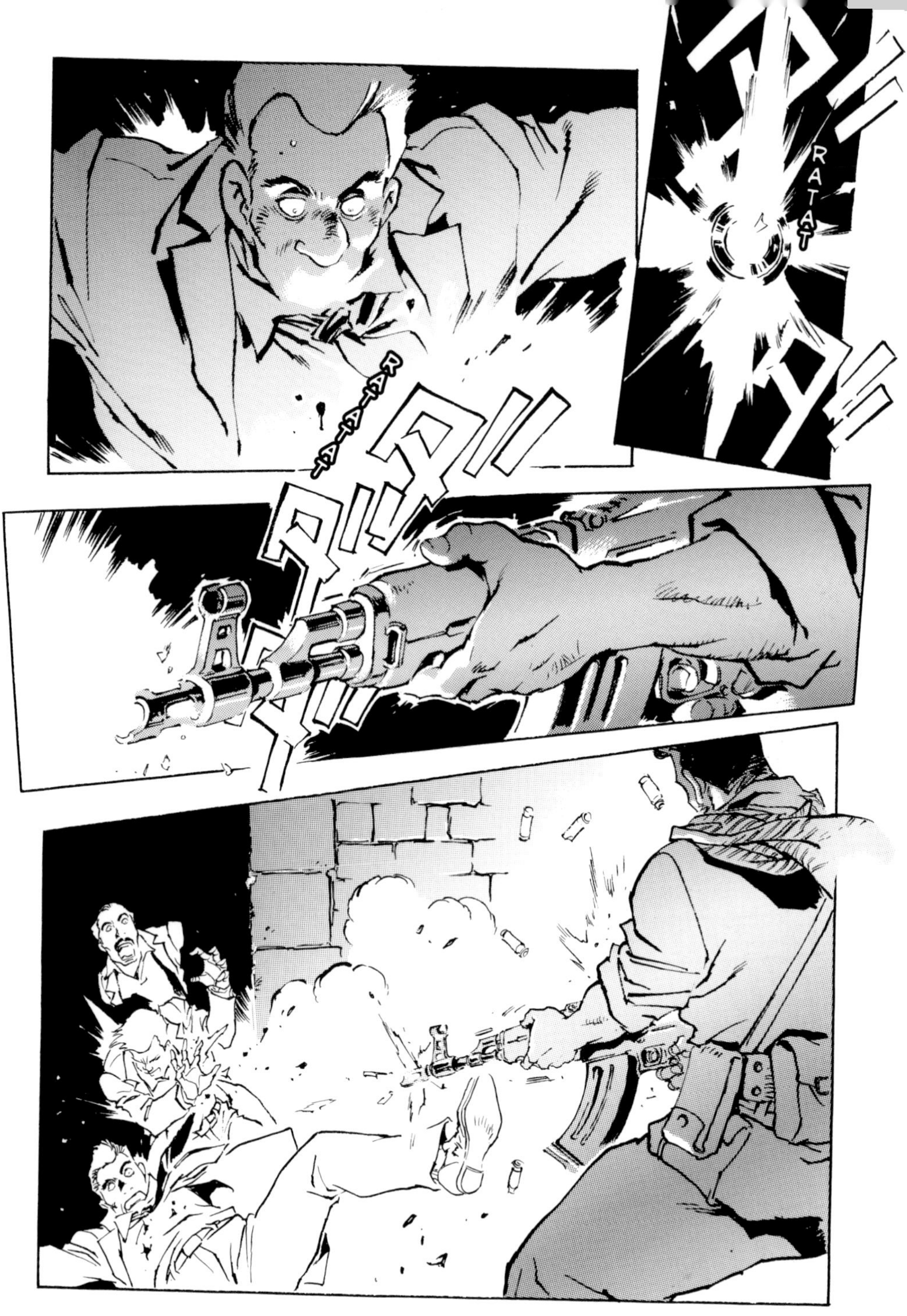
RATAT
RAT-AT-AT-AT

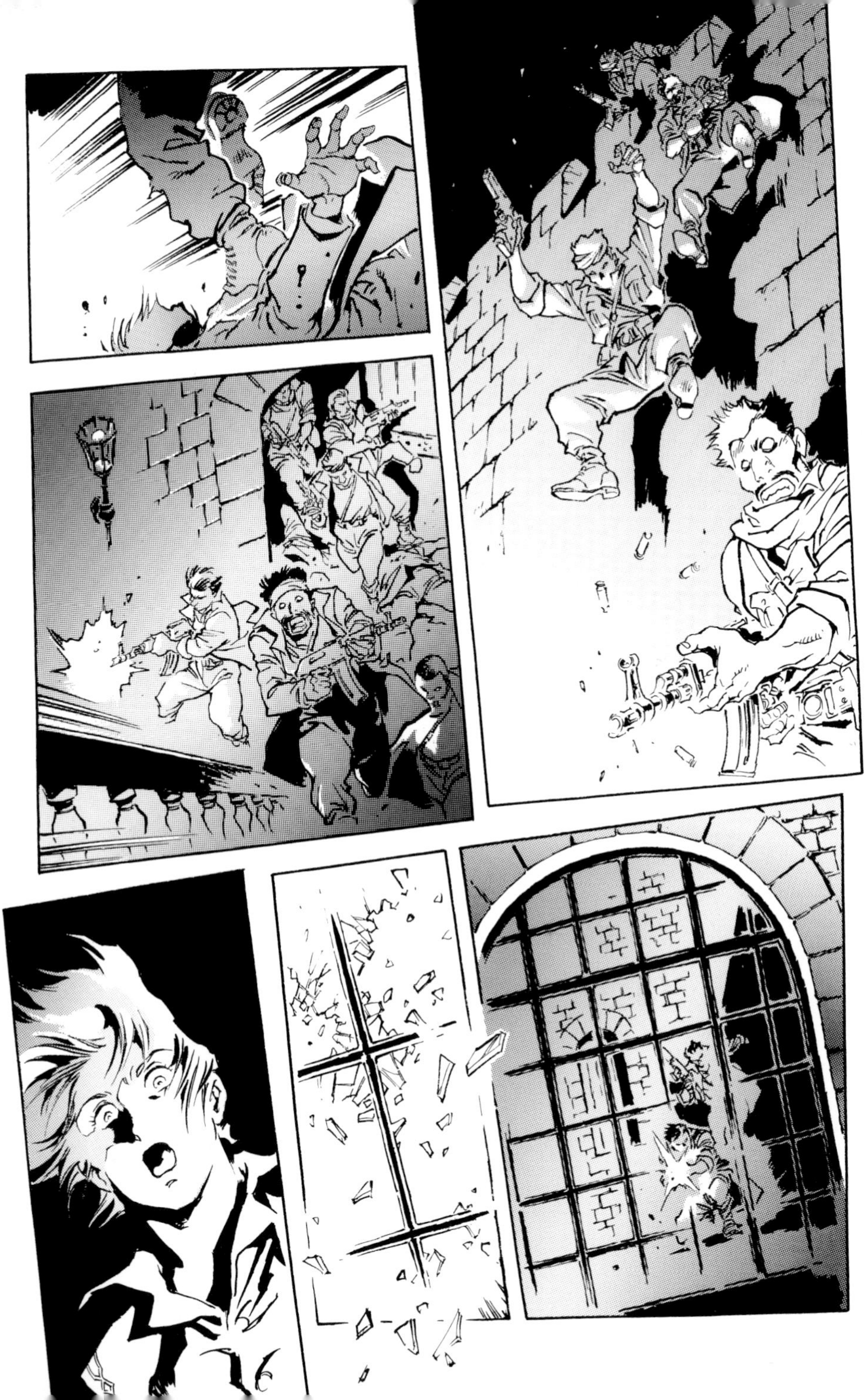

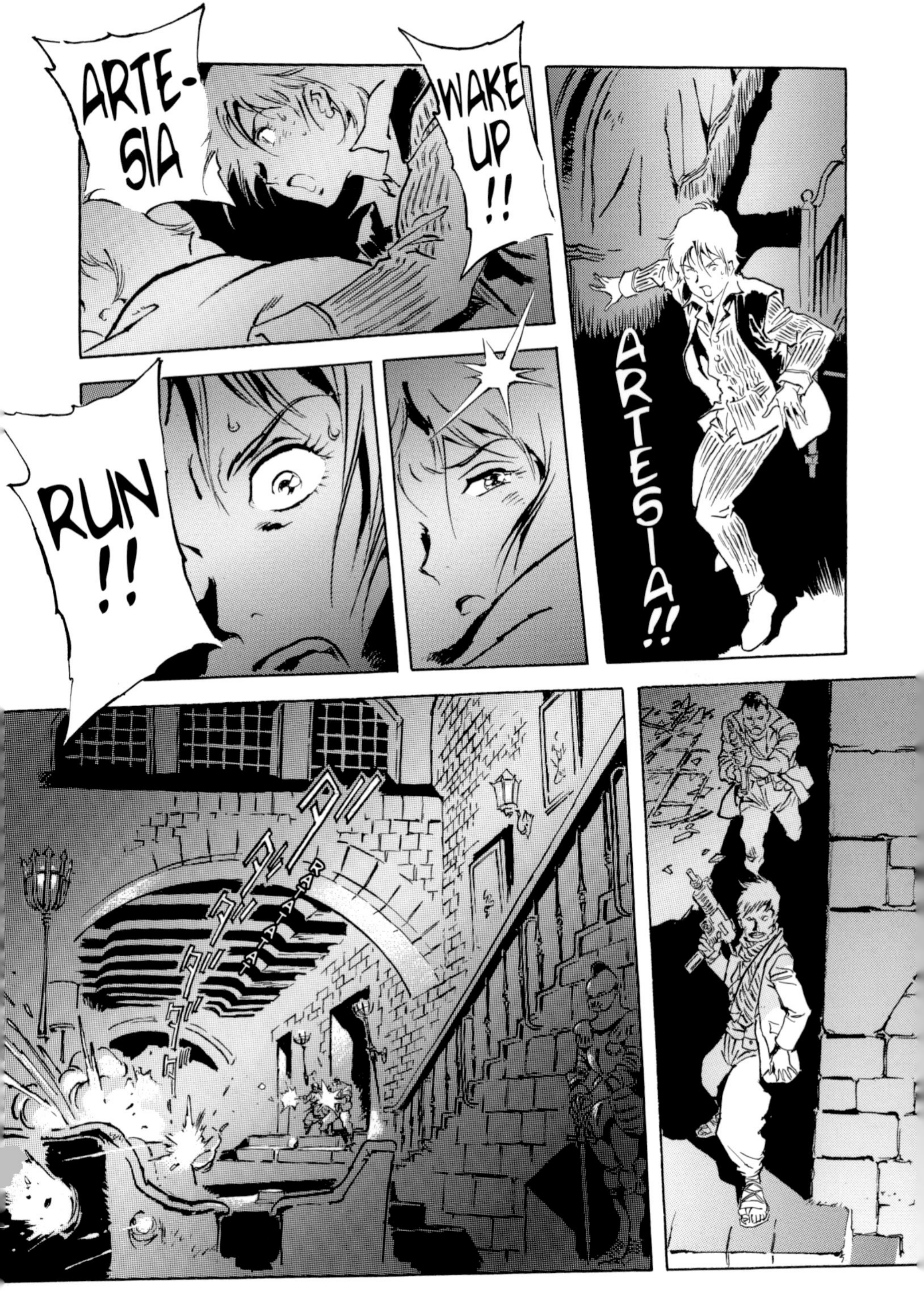
ARTESIA!!
ARTE-
SIA
WAKE
UP
!!
RUN
!!
RATATATAT

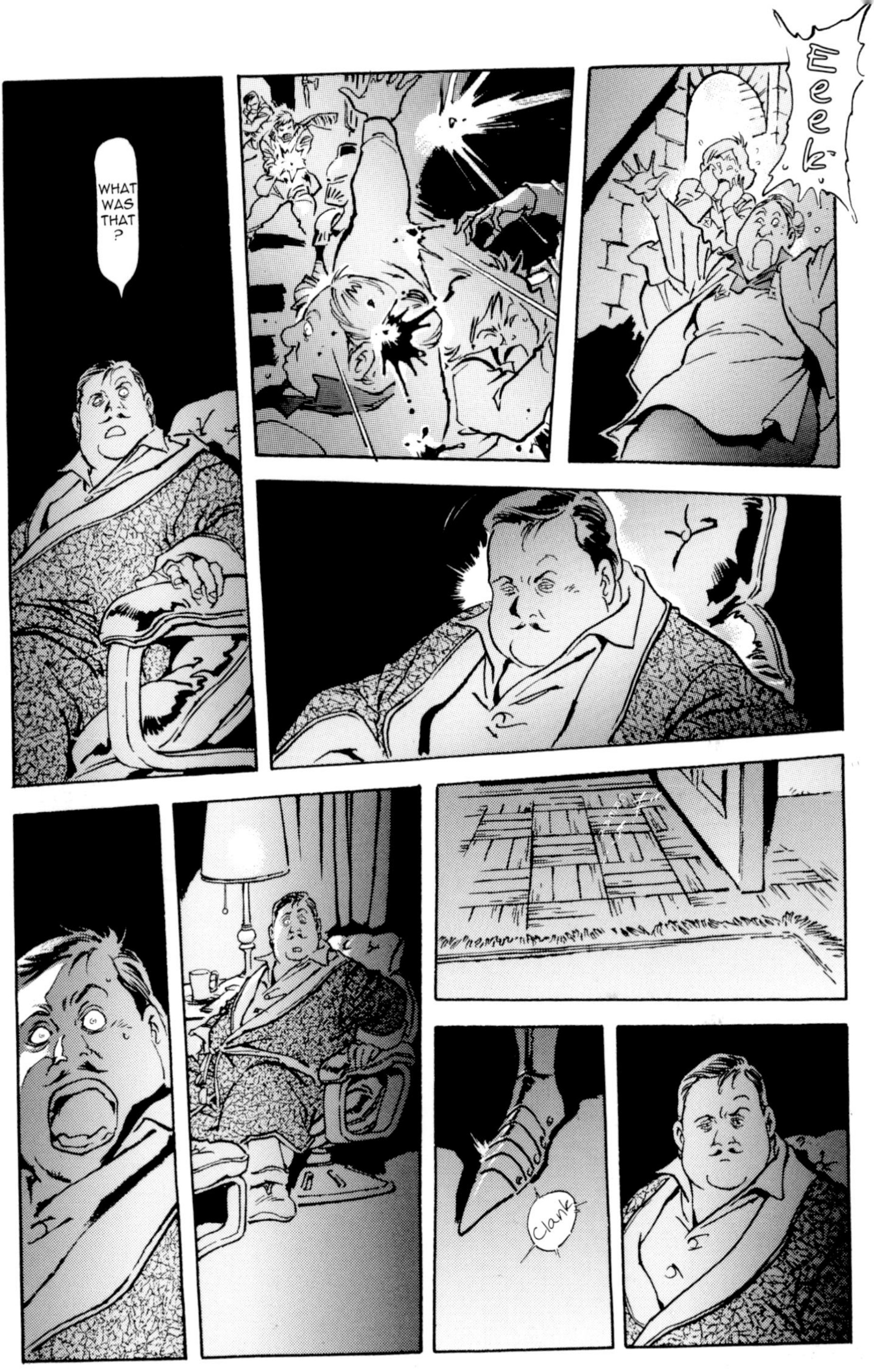
Eeek
WHAT WAS THAT?
Clank

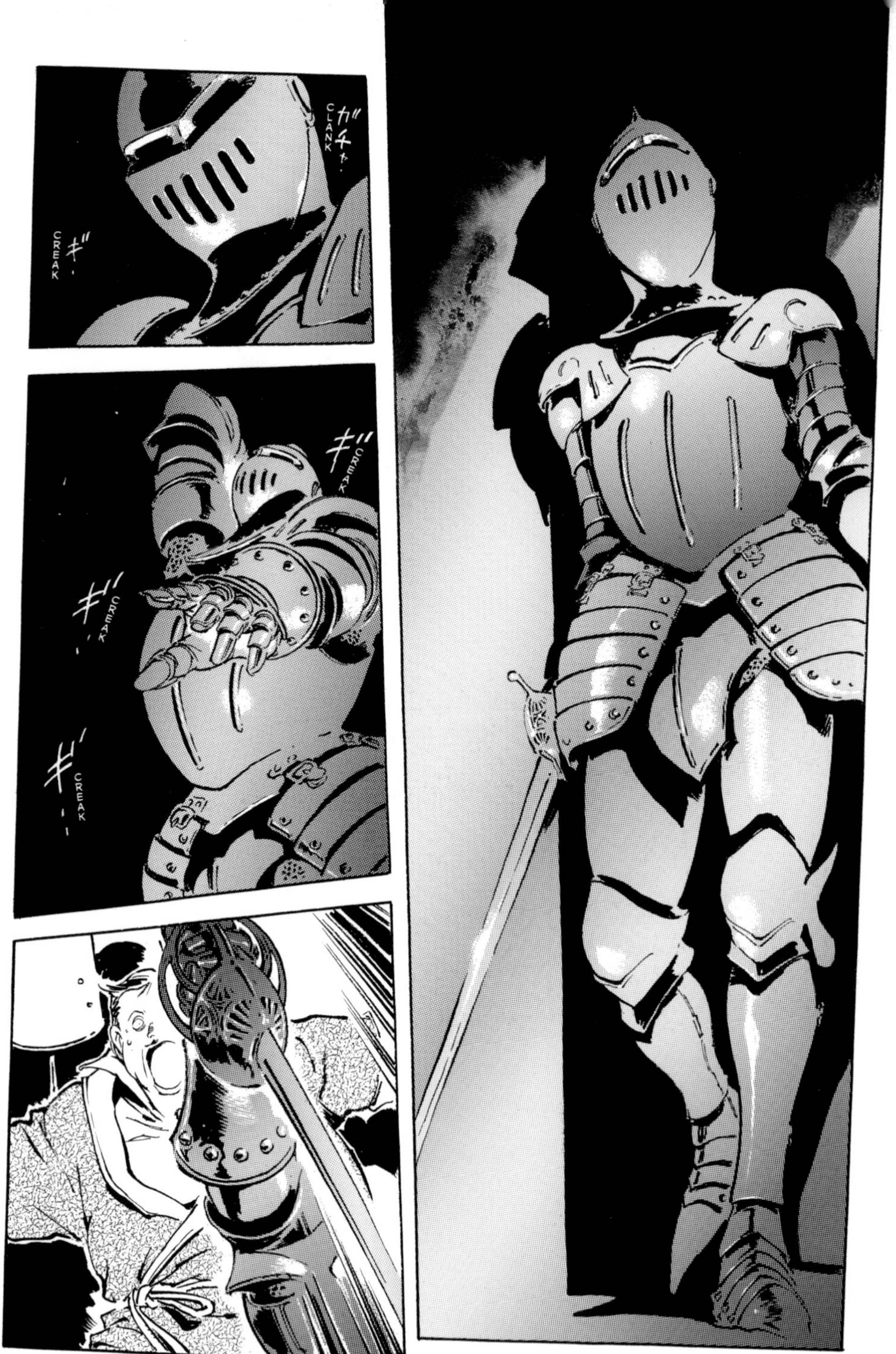
ガチャ CLANK
ギ CREAK
ギ CREAK
ギ CREAK
ギ CREAK

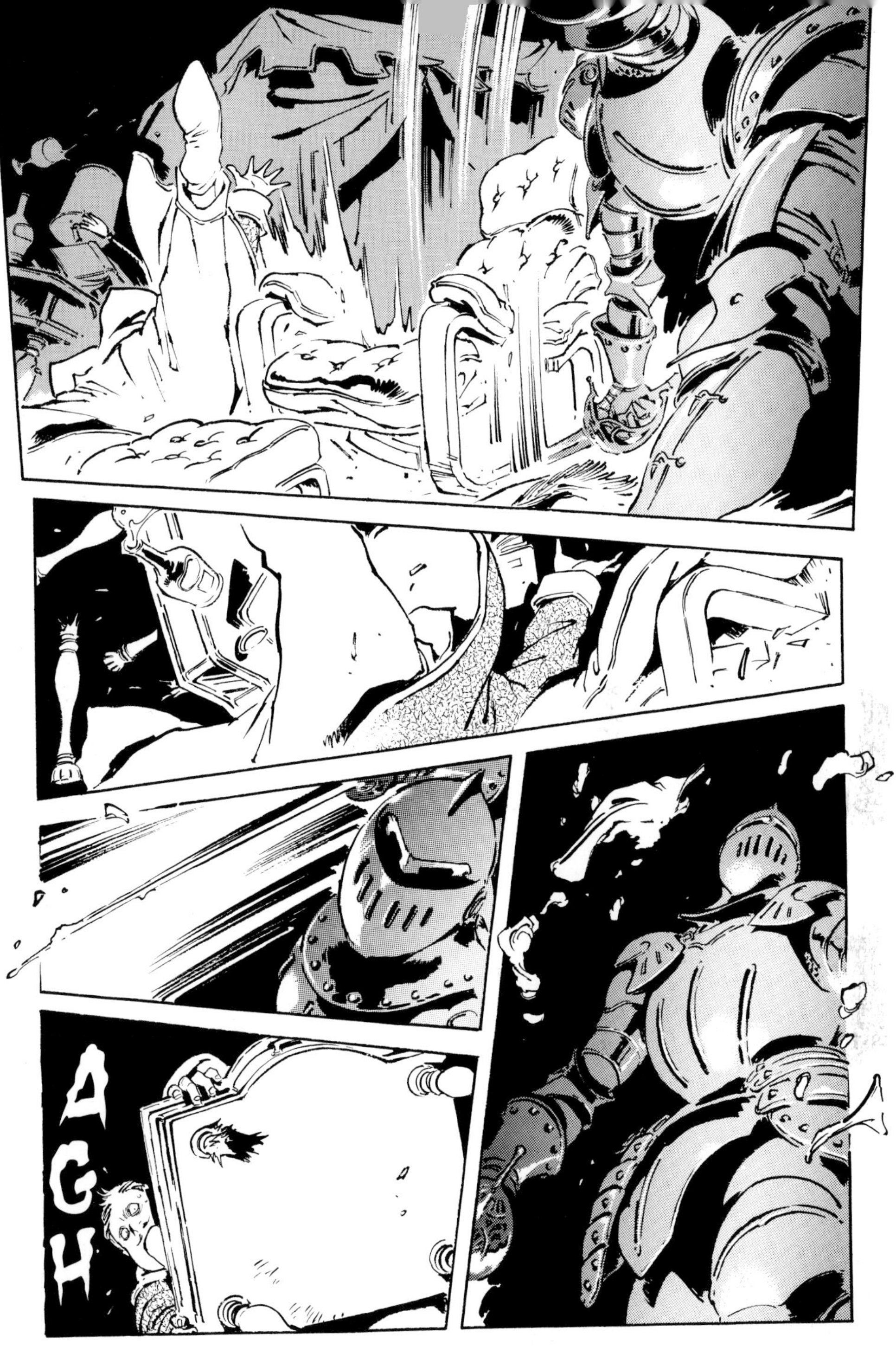
AGH

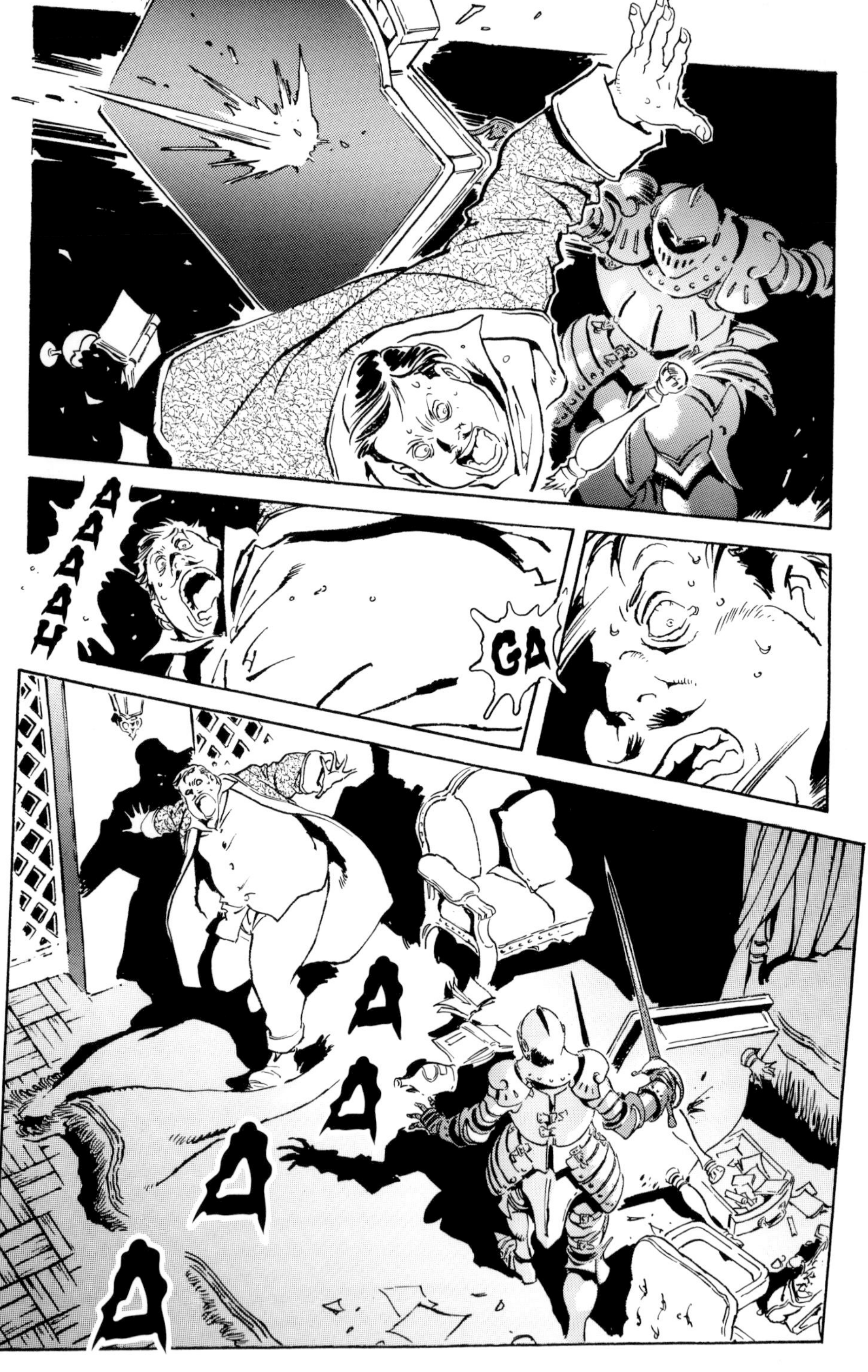
GA
AAAAAH

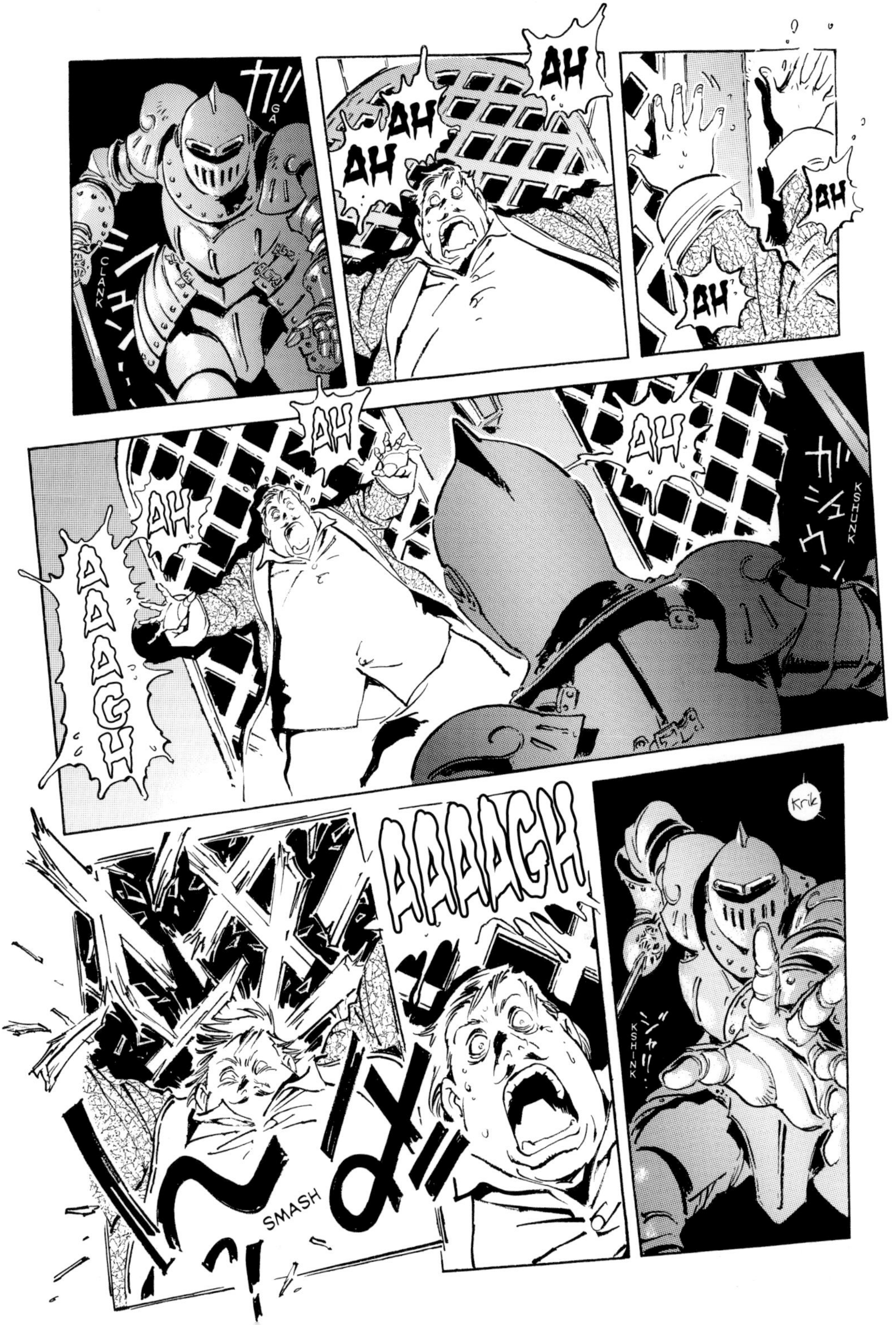
AH
AH
AH
AH
AH
GA
CLANK
KSHUNK
AH
AH
AH
AAAAGH
Krik
KSHINK
AAAAGH
SMASH

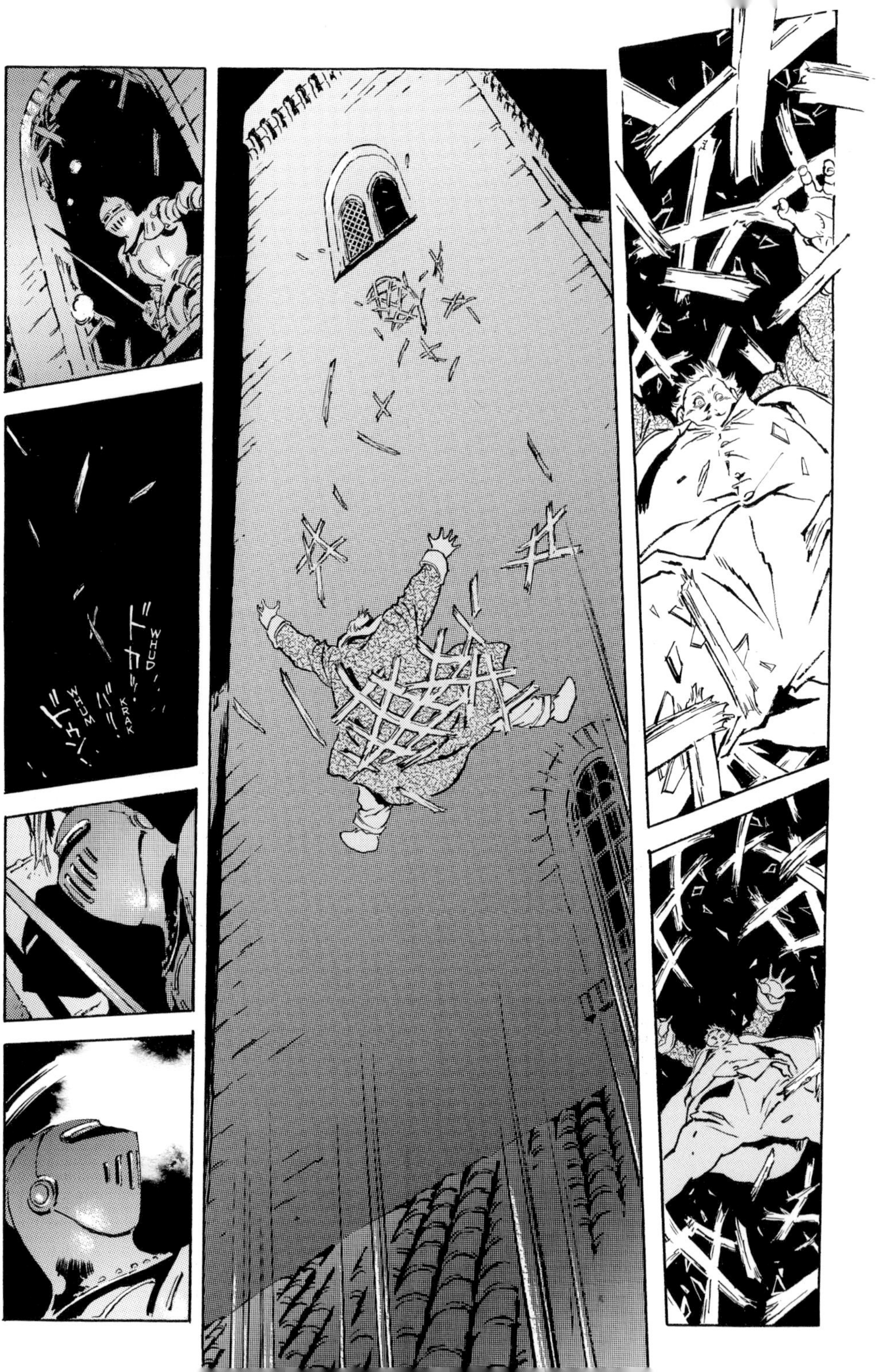
ドカッ!
WHUD!
バリッ!
KRAK
ドゥン!
WHUM

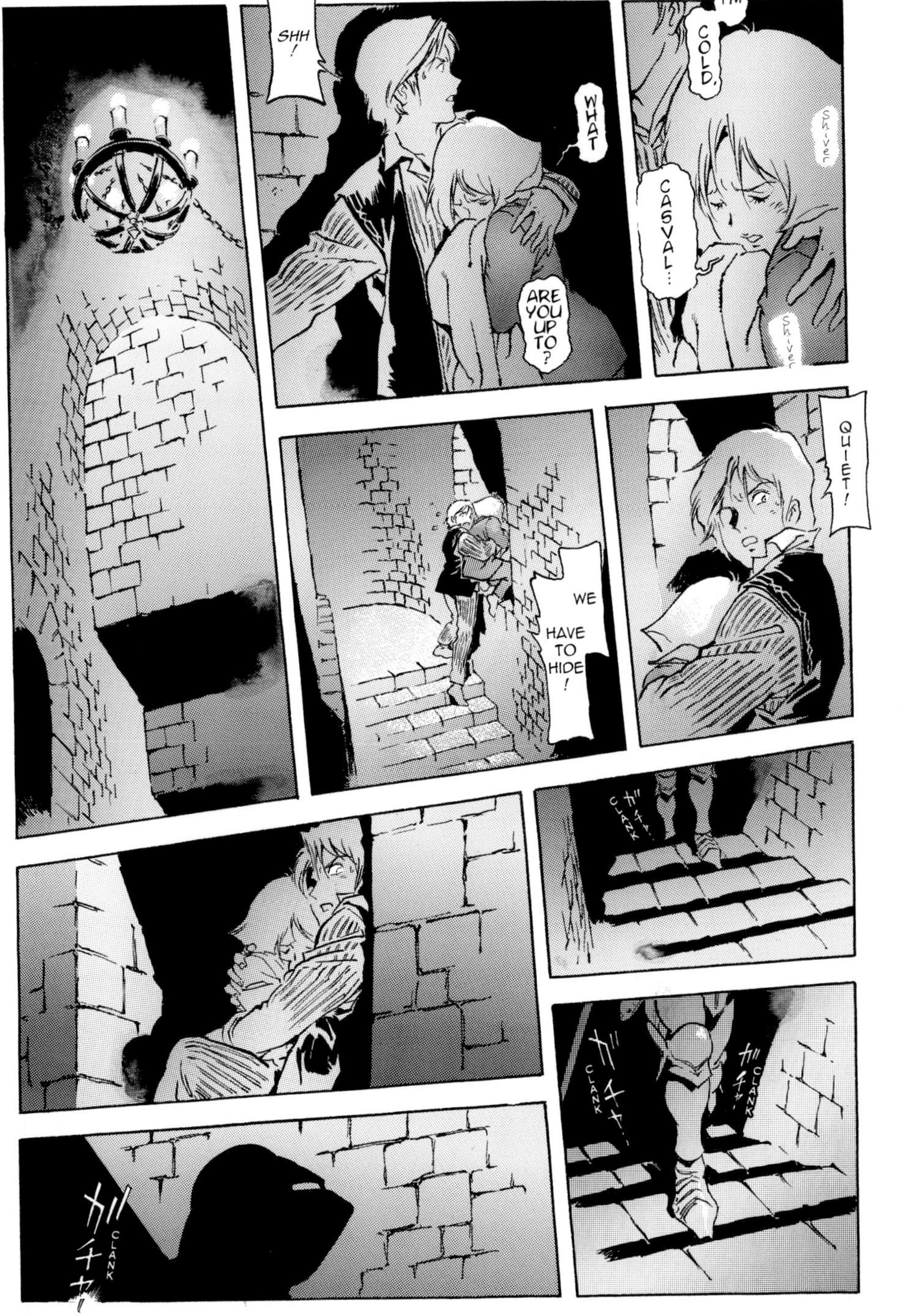
I'M COLD, CASVAL...
Shiver
Shiver
SHH!
WHAT ARE YOU UP TO?
QUIET!
WE HAVE TO HIDE!
CLANK
CLANK
CLANK
CLANK

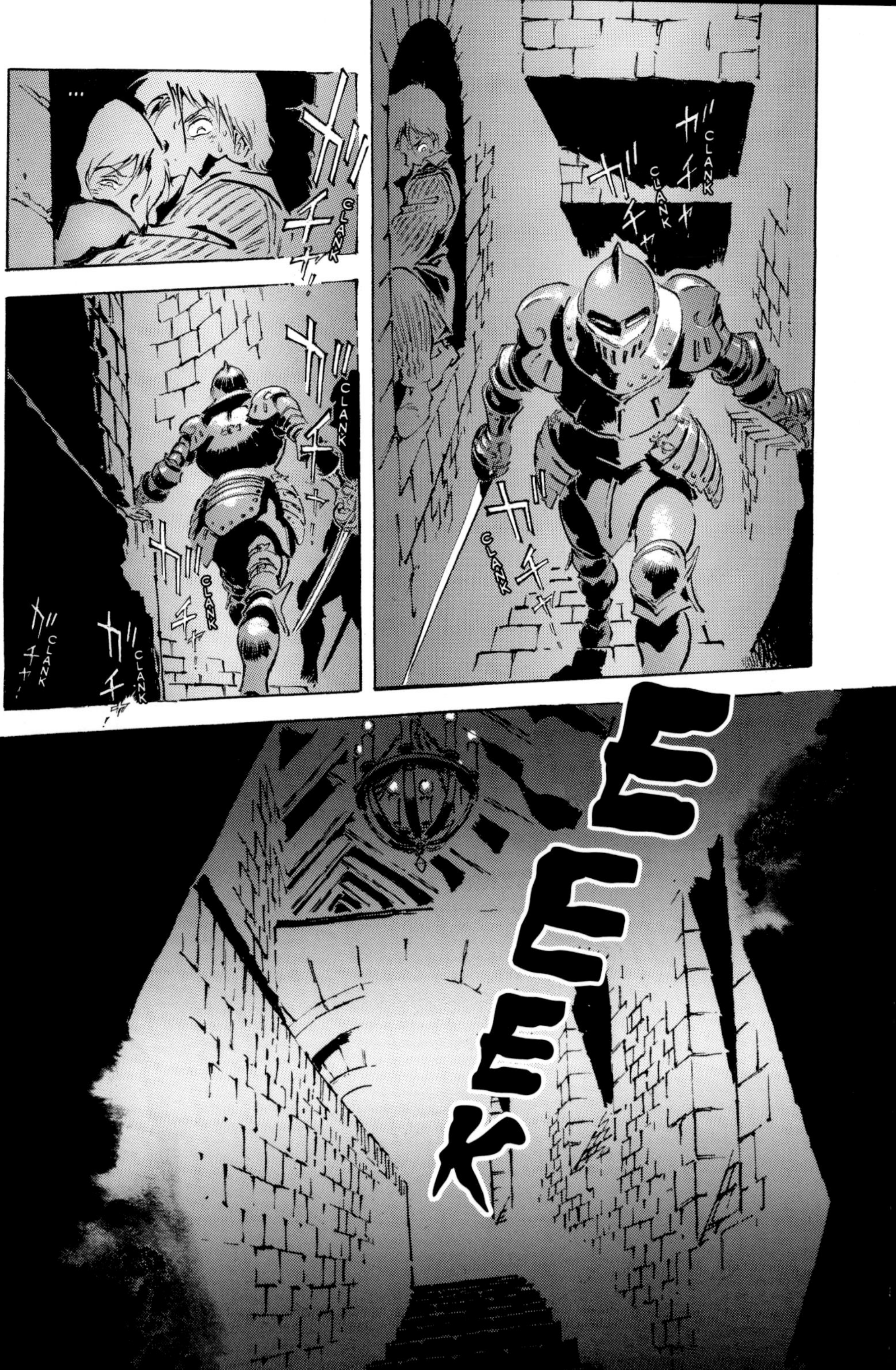
ガチャ CLANK
ガチャ CLANK
ガチャ CLANK
...
ガチャ CLANK
ガチャ CLANK
ガチャ CLANK
ガチャ CLANK
ガチャ CLANK
EEEEK

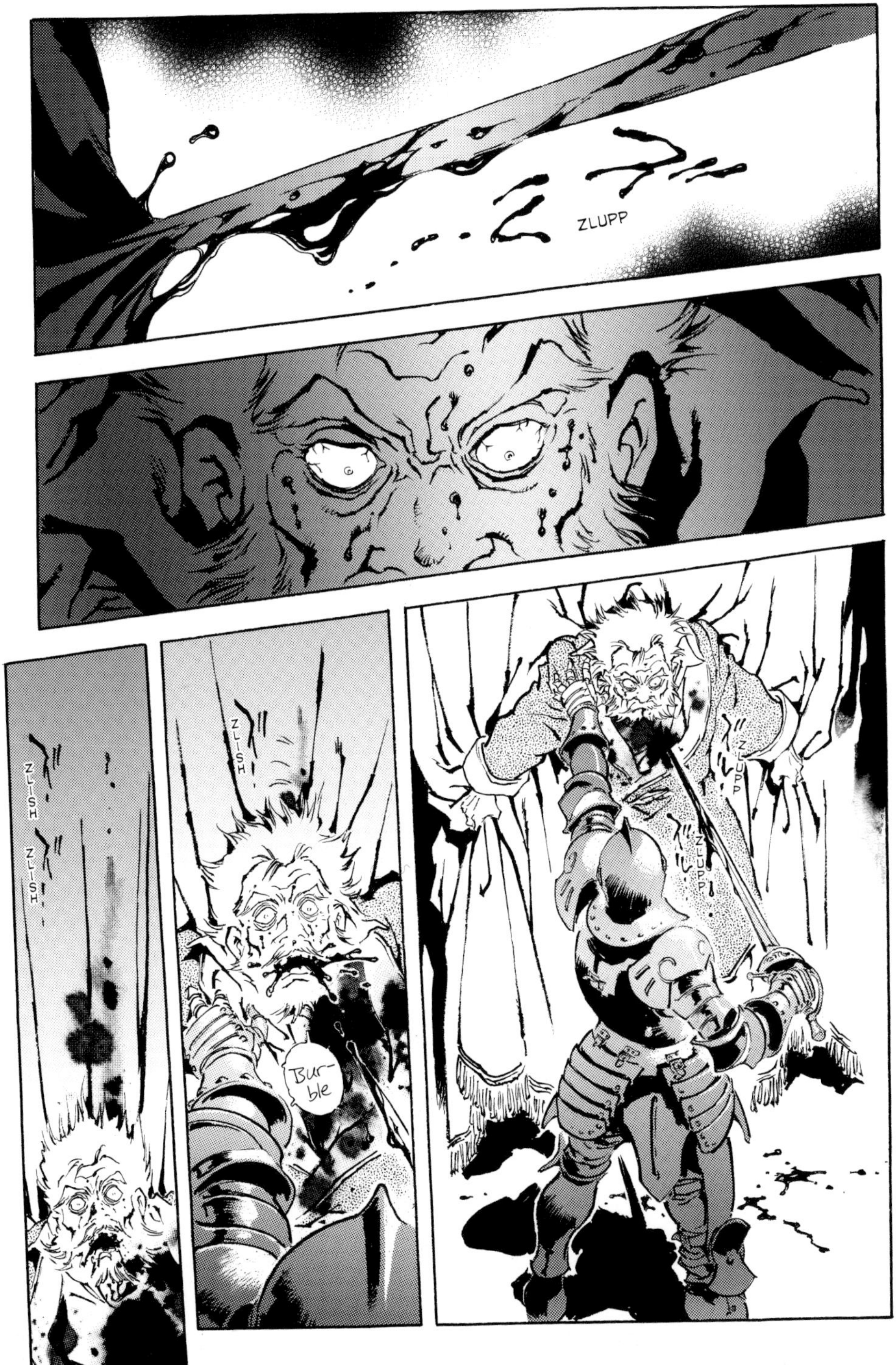
ZLUPP
ZLUPP
ZLUPP
ZLISH
Bur-ble
ZLISH
ZLISH

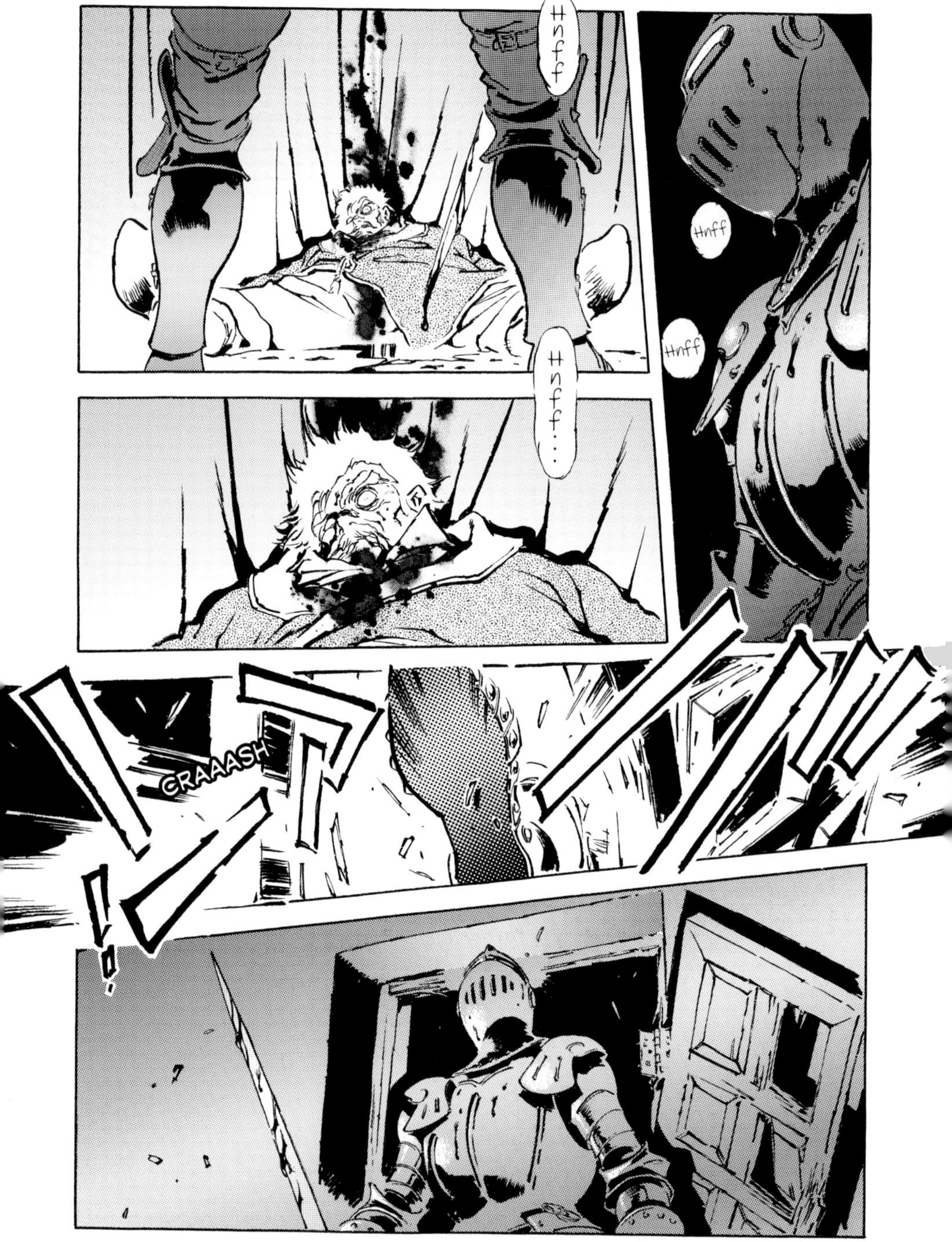
Hnff
Hnff
Hnff
Hnff...
CRAAASH

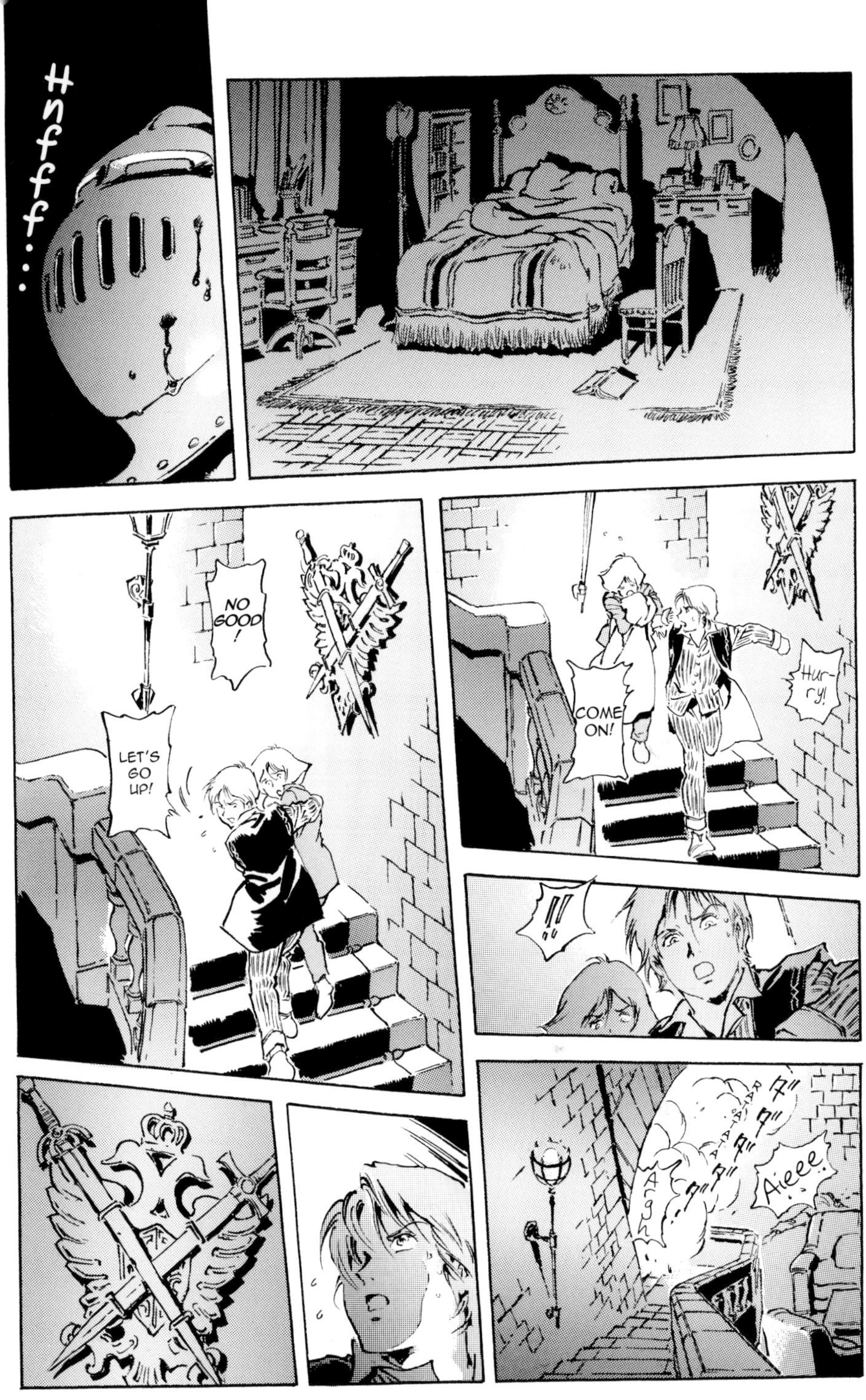
Hnffff...
Hur-ry!
COME ON!
!!
NO GOOD!
LET'S GO UP!
Aieee...
ダダダダダ
RATATATATA
Argh...

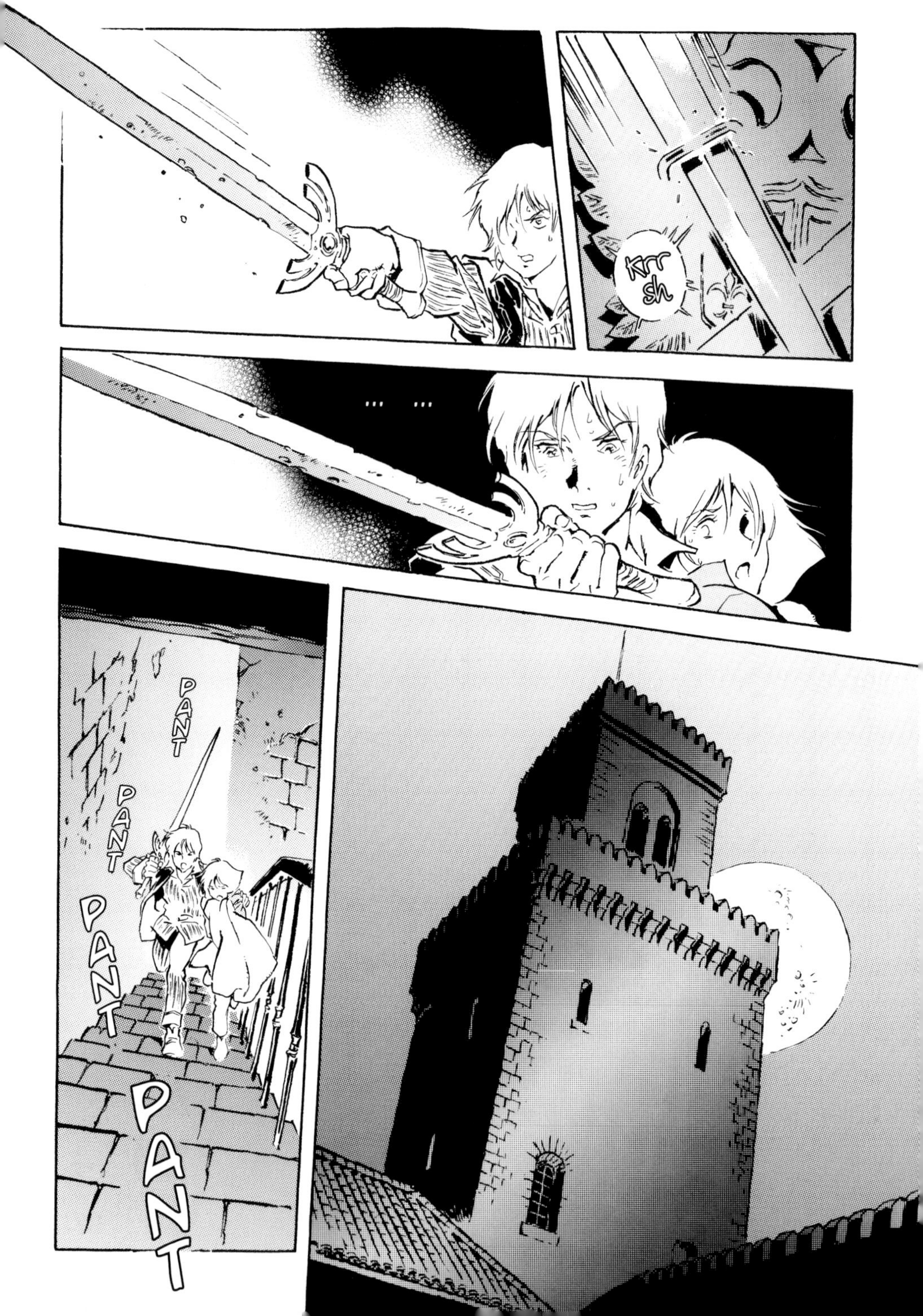
Krr sh
... ...
PANT
PANT
PANT
PANT

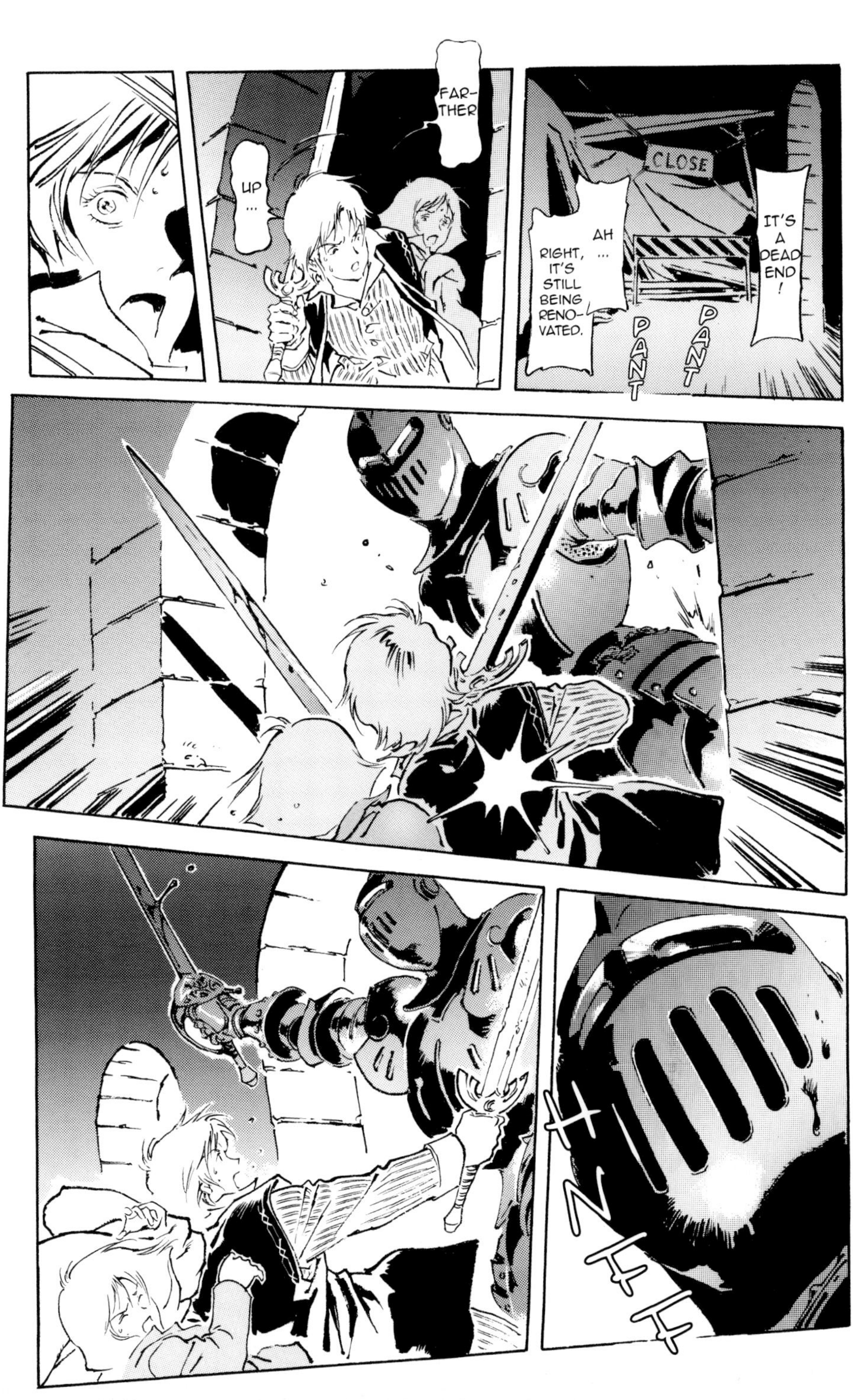
CLOSE
IT'S A DEAD END!
AH ... RIGHT, IT'S STILL BEING RENO-VATED.
PANT
PANT
FAR-THER
UP ...
HNFF

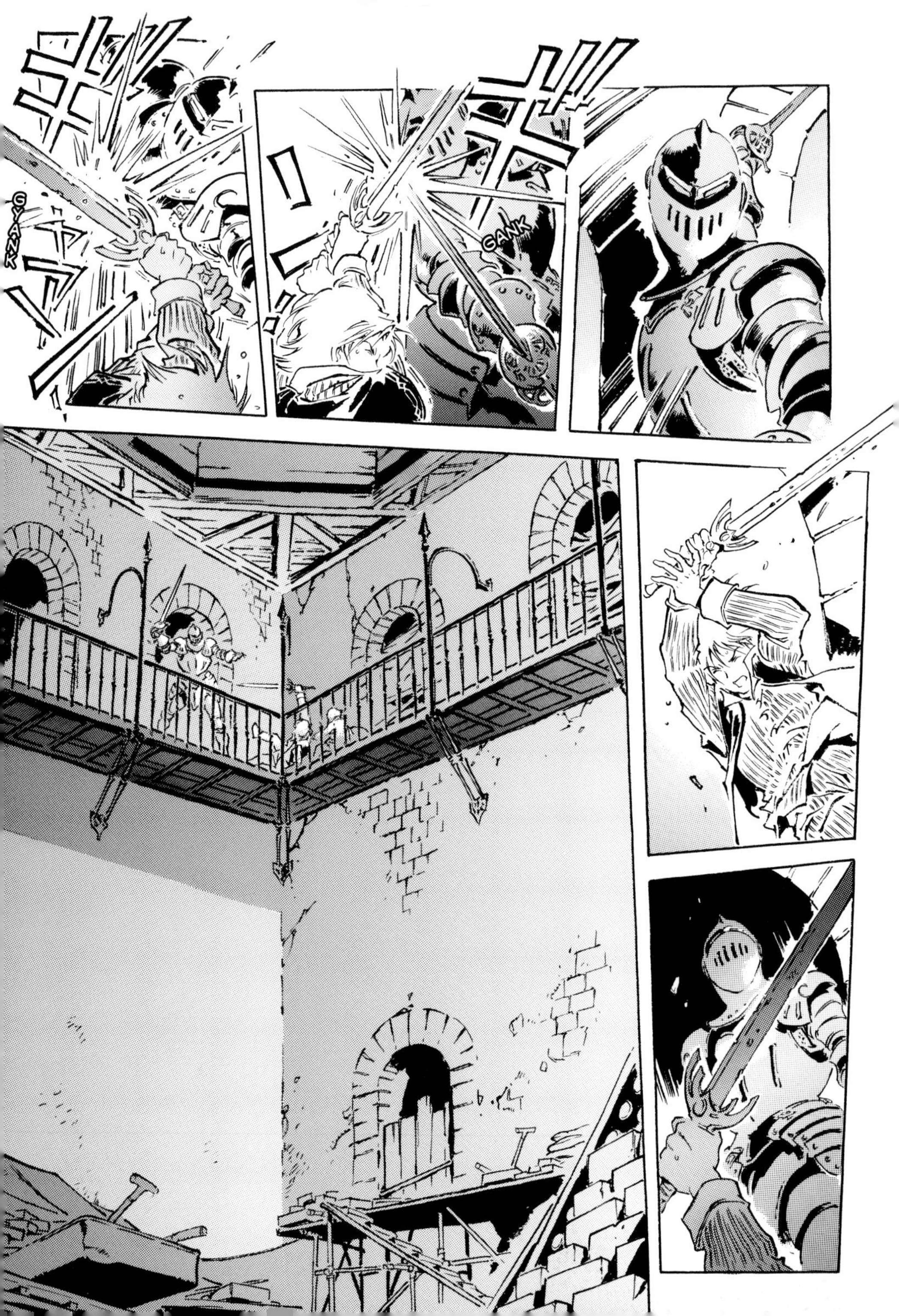
GANK
GYANK

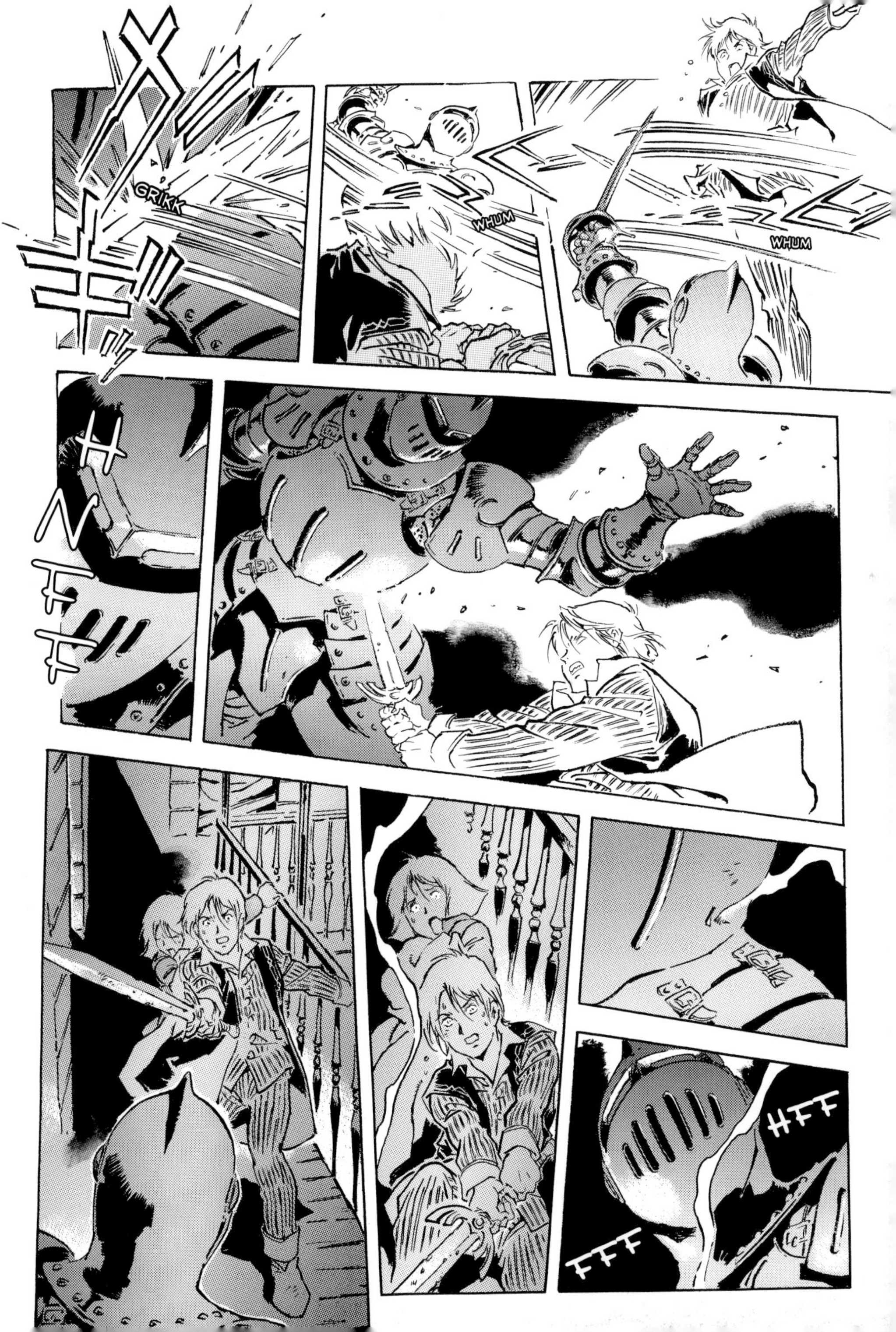
WHUM
WHUM
GRIKK
HNFFF
HFF
FFF

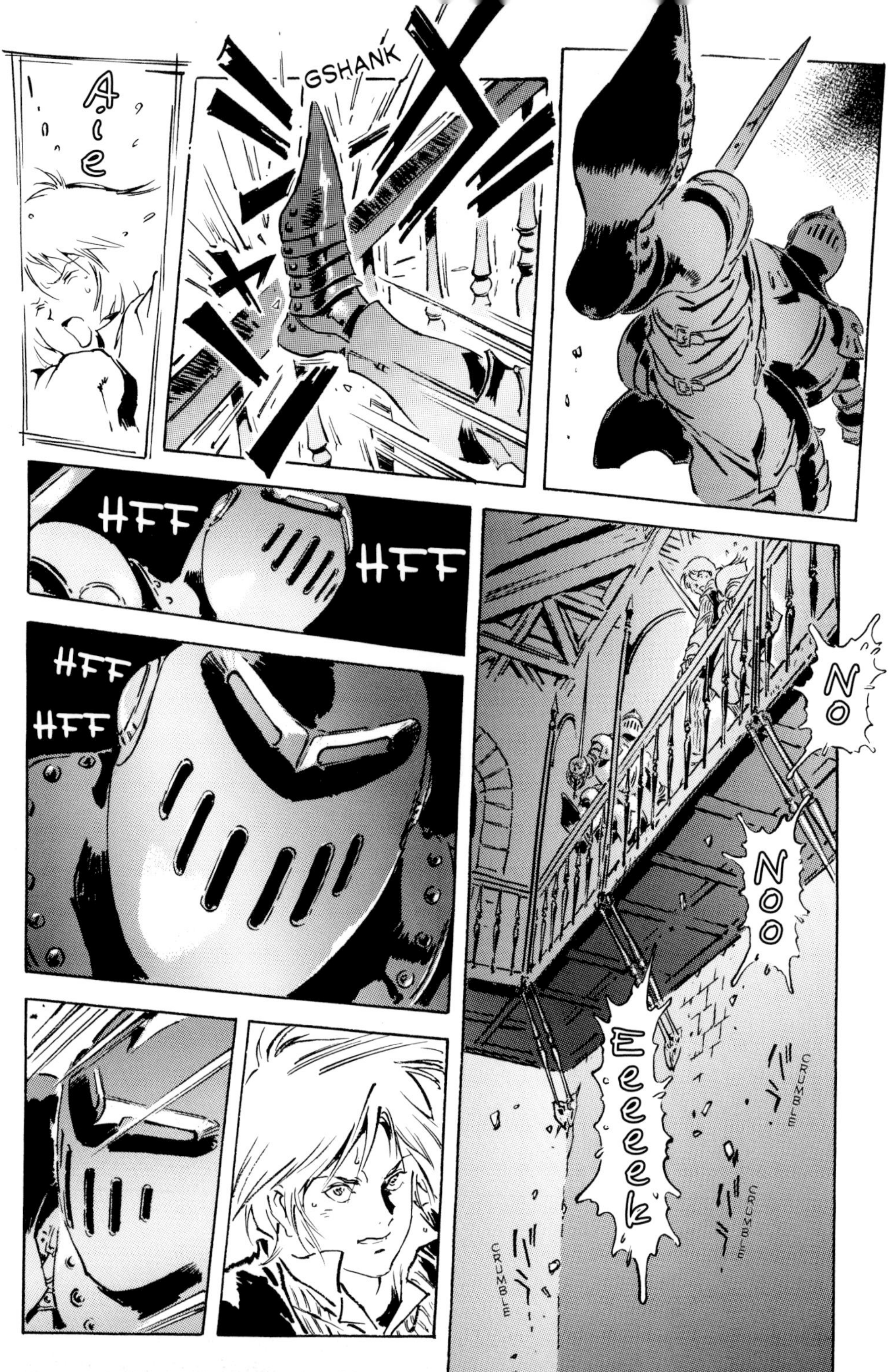
GSHANK
Aie
NO
NOO
Eeeeek
CRUMBLE
CRUMBLE
CRUMBLE
HFF
HFF
HFF
HFF

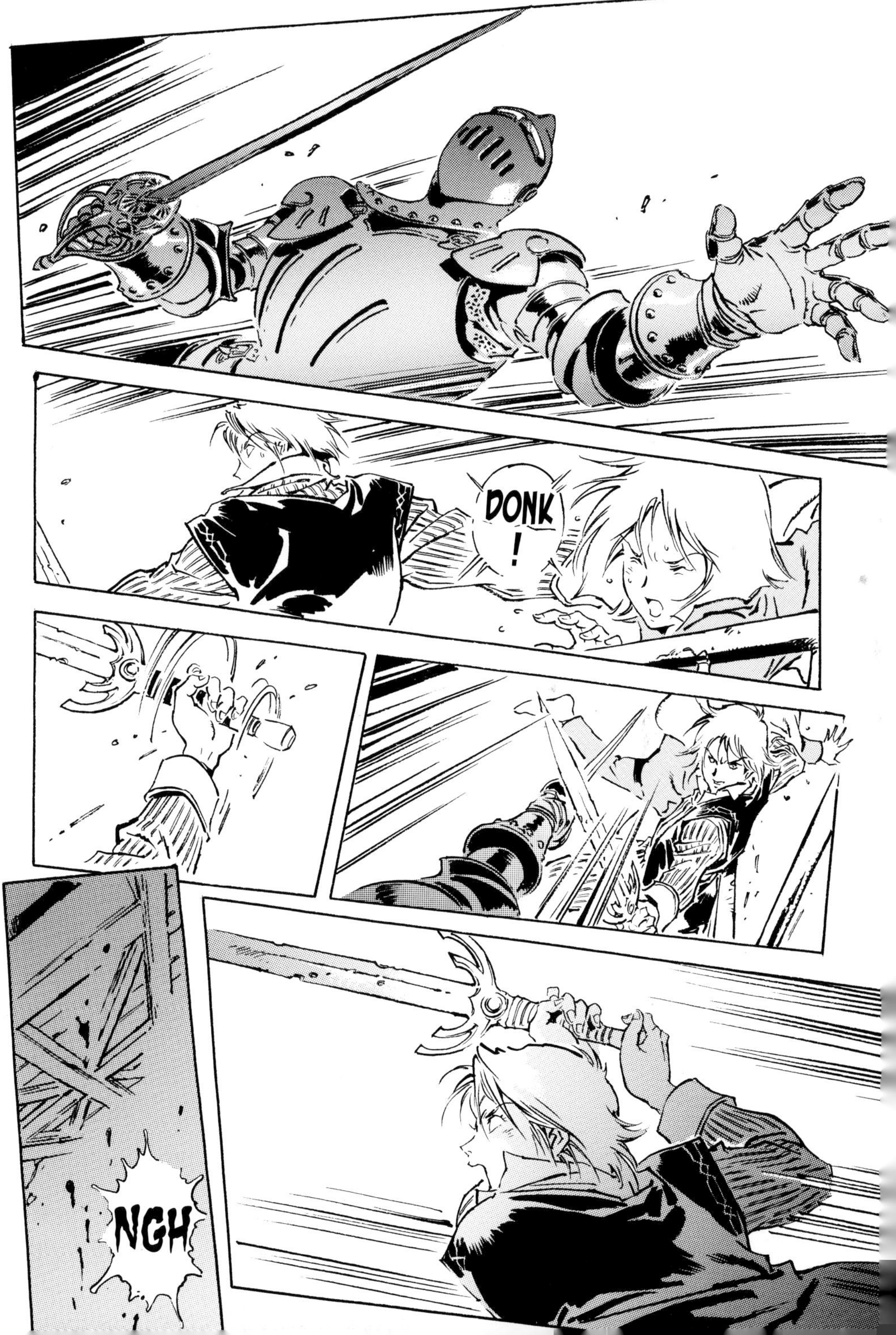
DONK
!
NGH

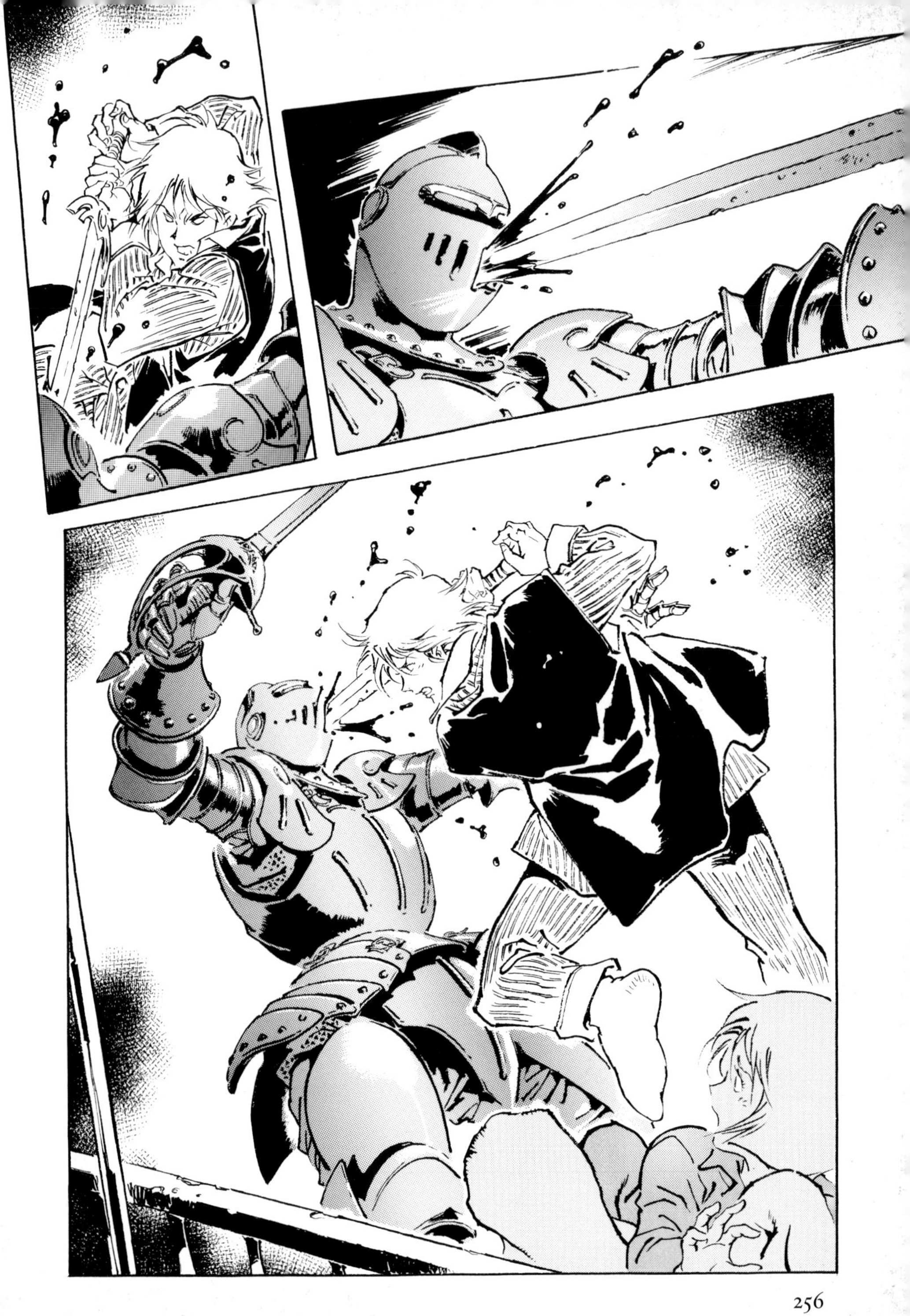

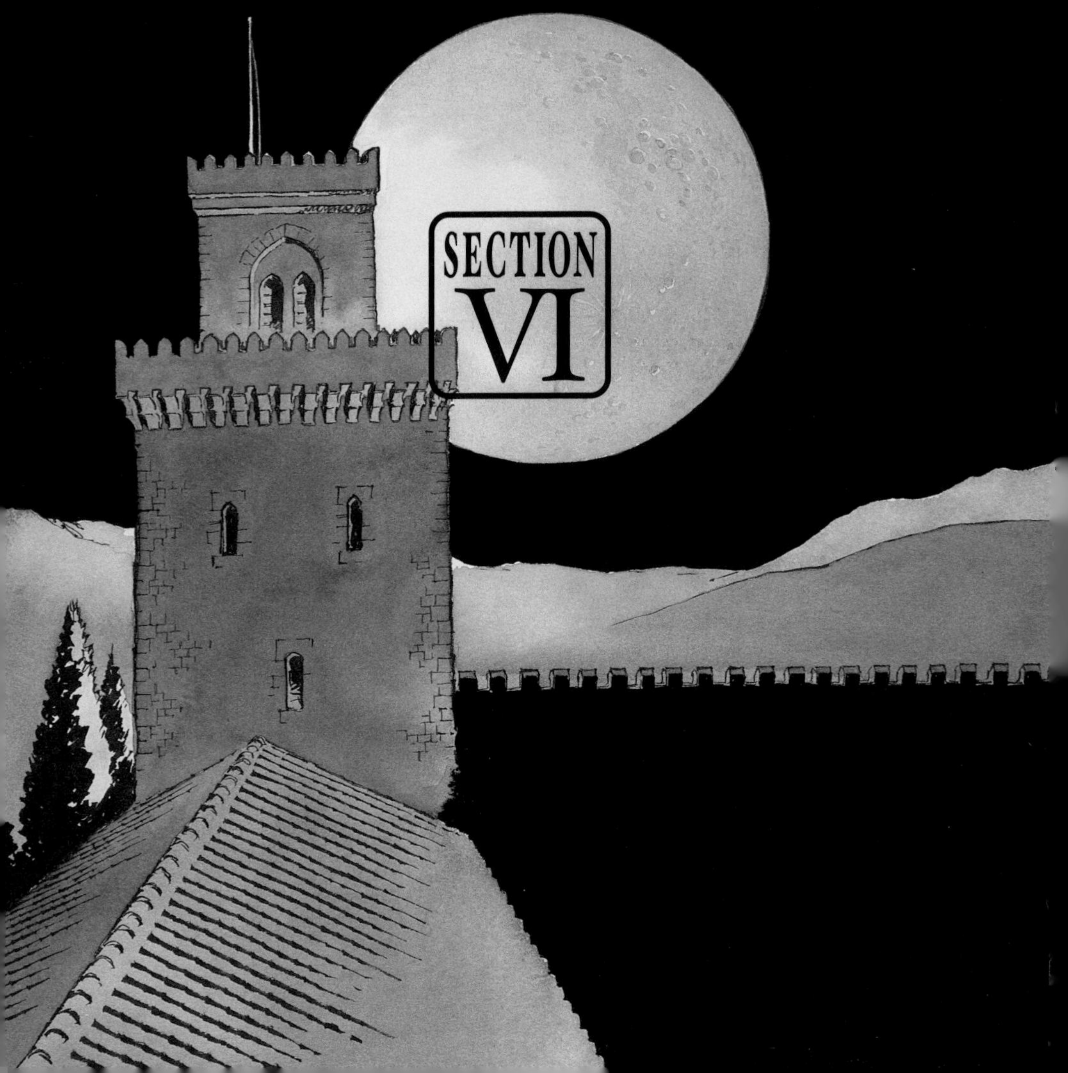
SECTION
VI

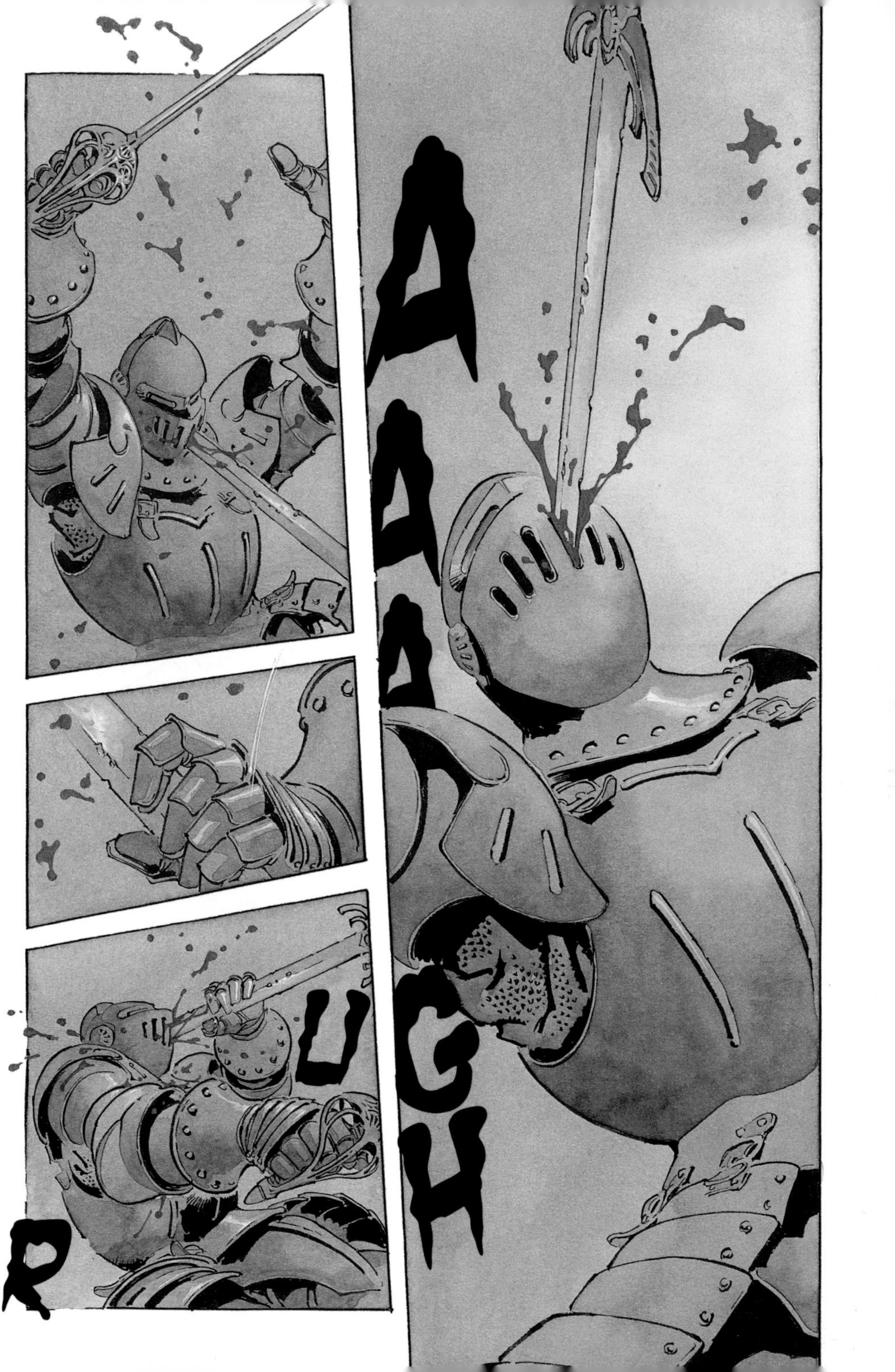
AAA
GH
U
R

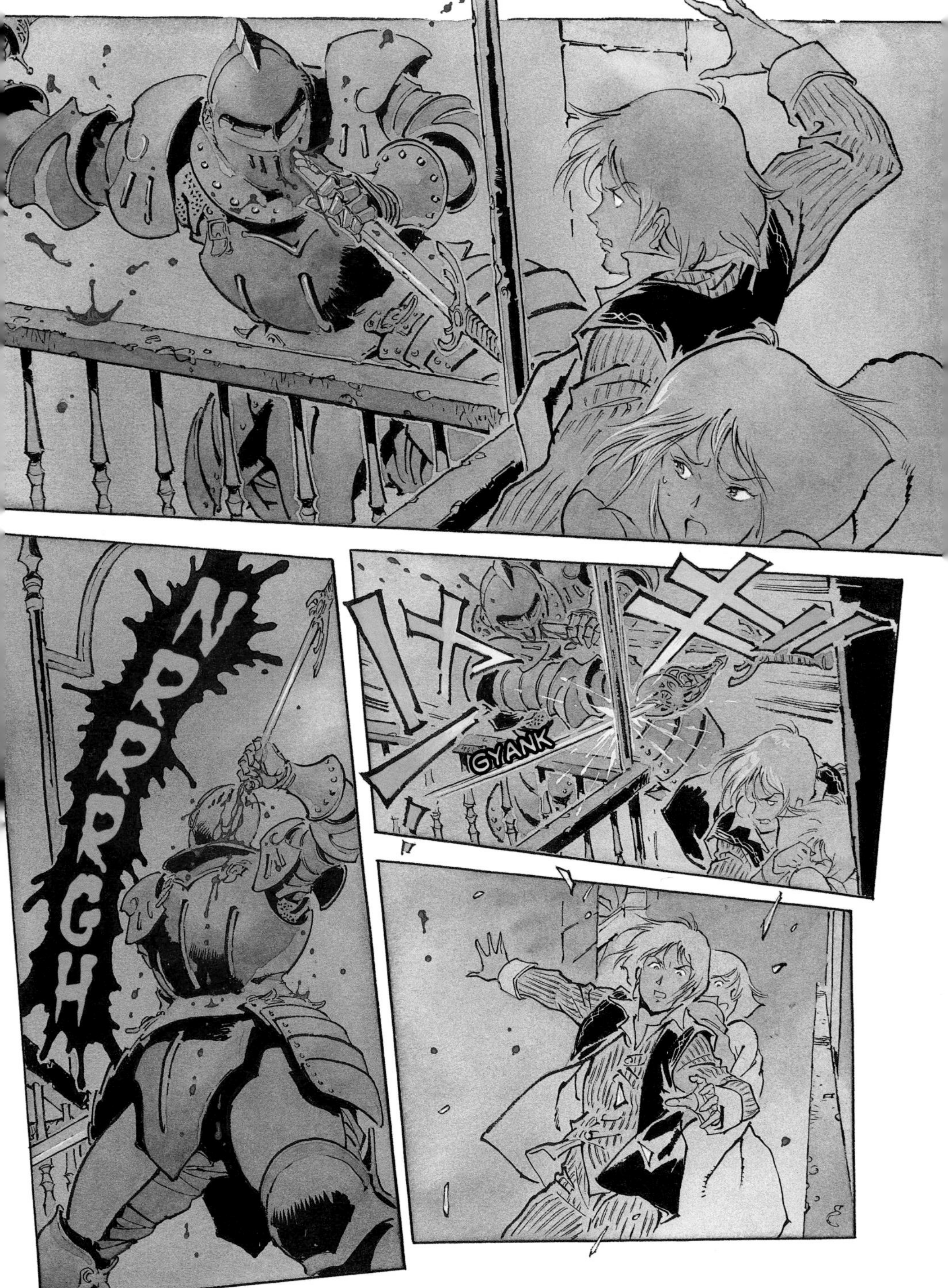
GYANK
NRRRGH

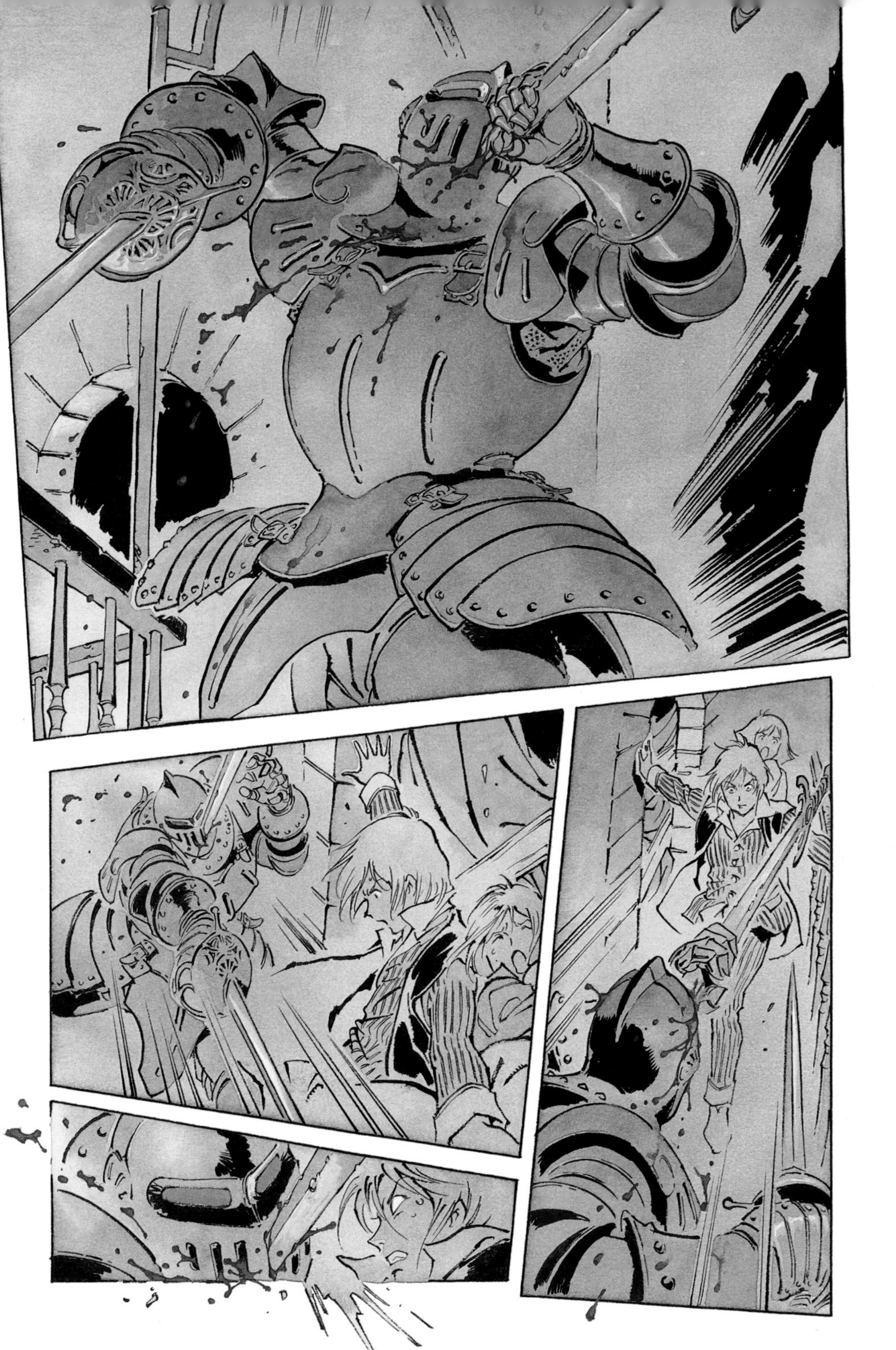

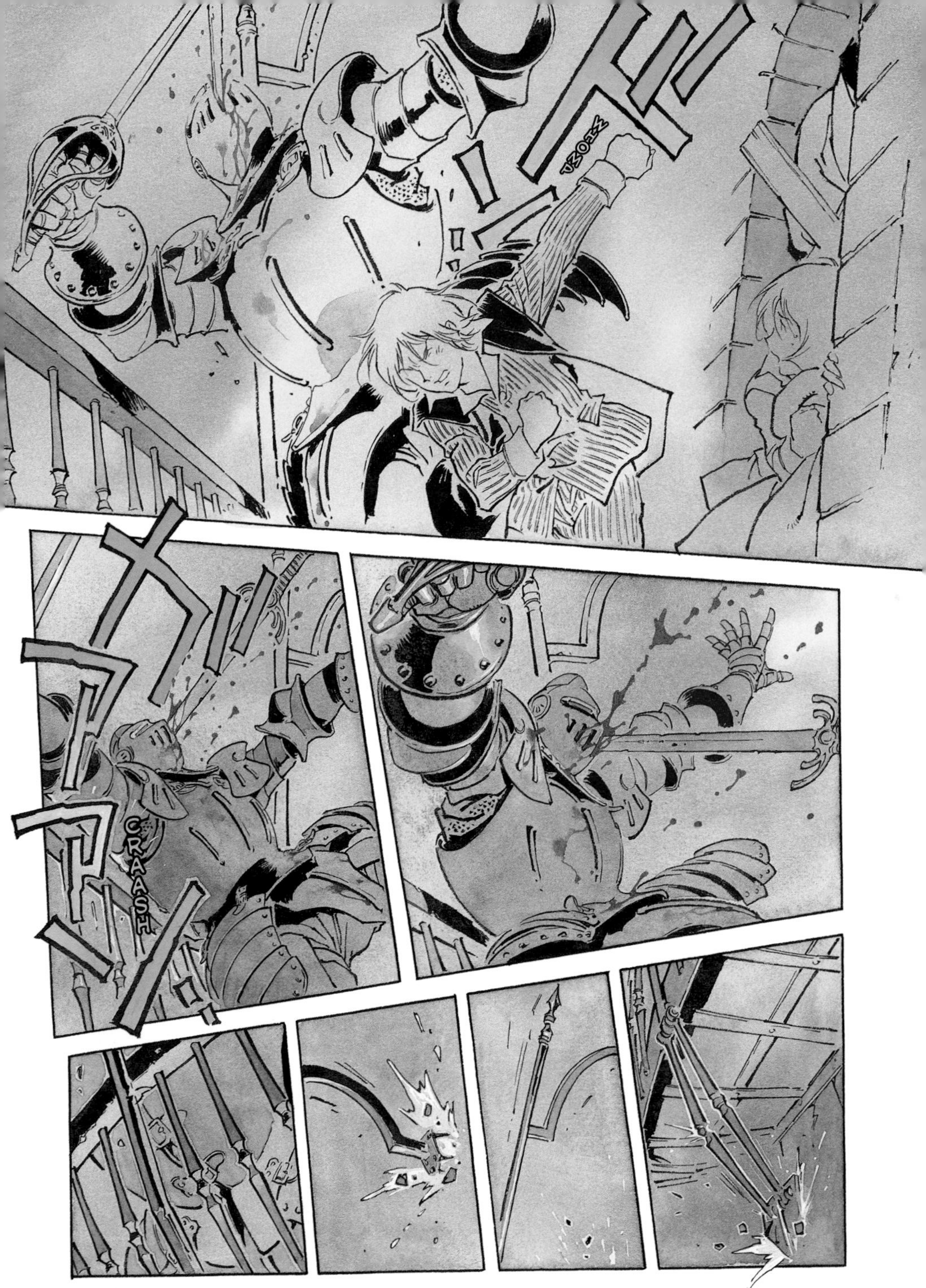

CRAASH

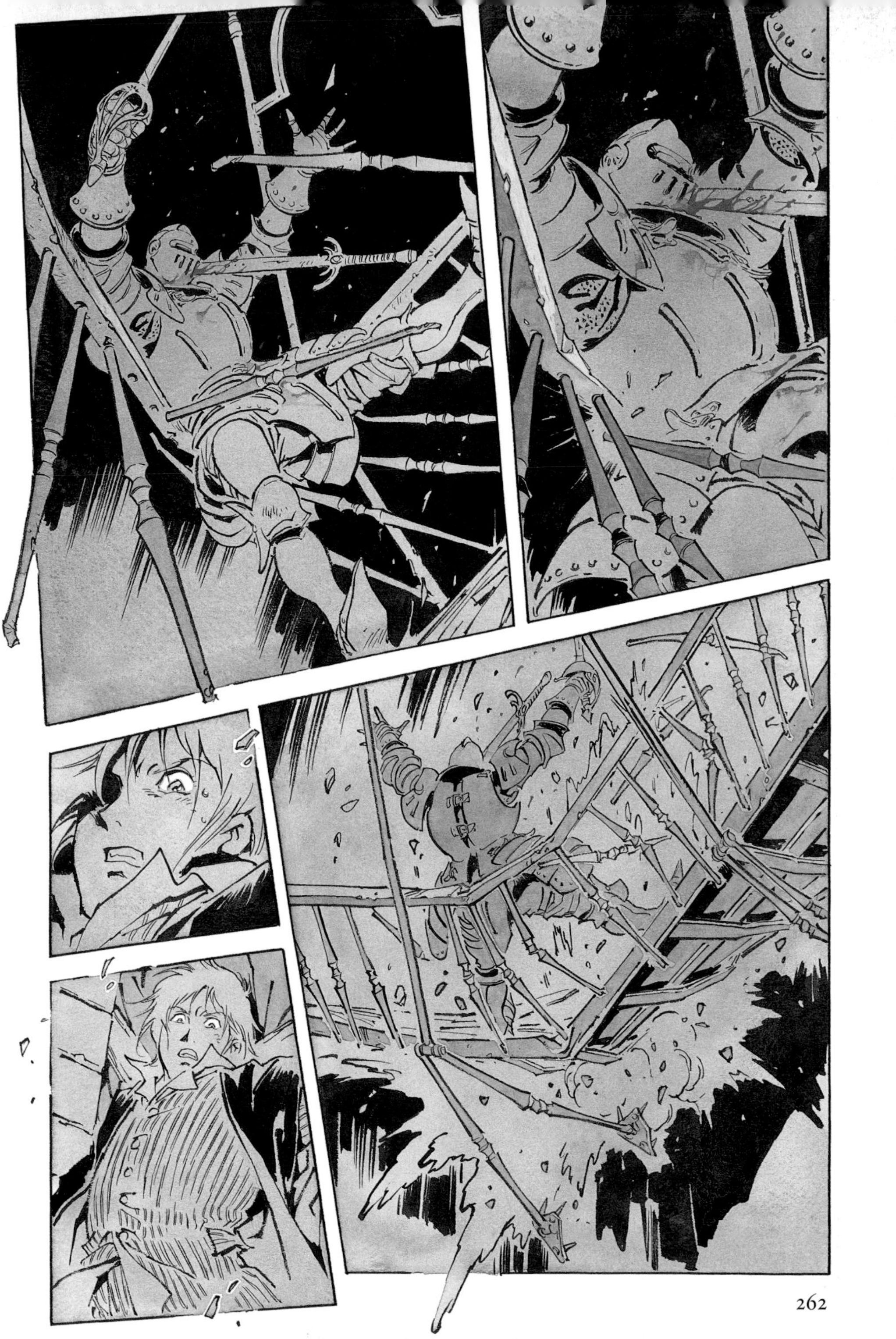

ZMMMM
BLUP

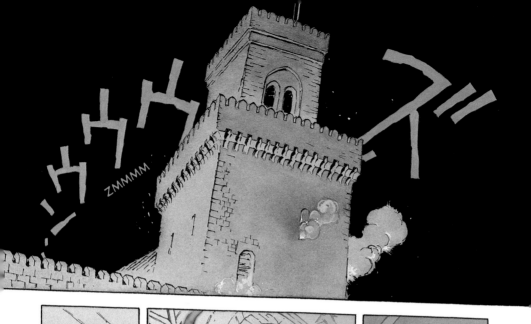

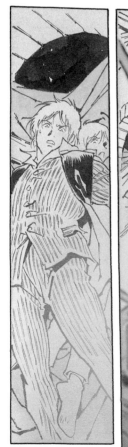

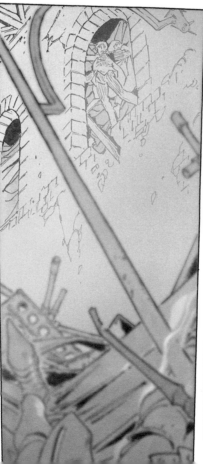

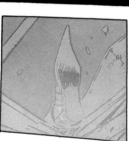

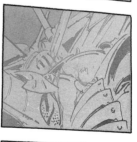

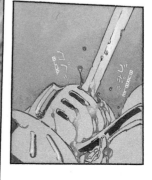

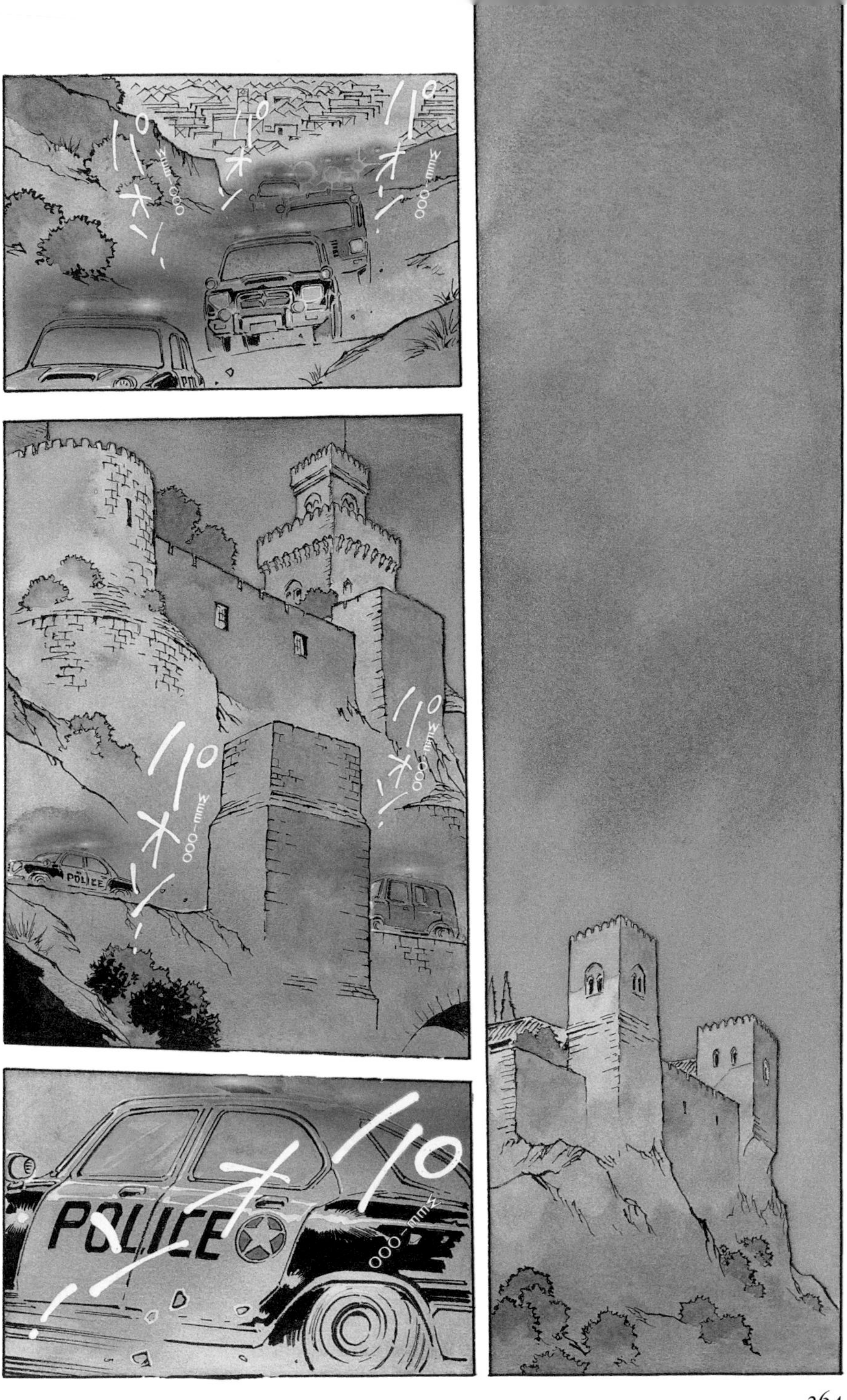
パオン!
WEE-OOO
パオン
パオン、
WEE-OOO
パオン!
WEE-OOO
パオン!
WEE-OOO
パオン!!
WEE-OOO

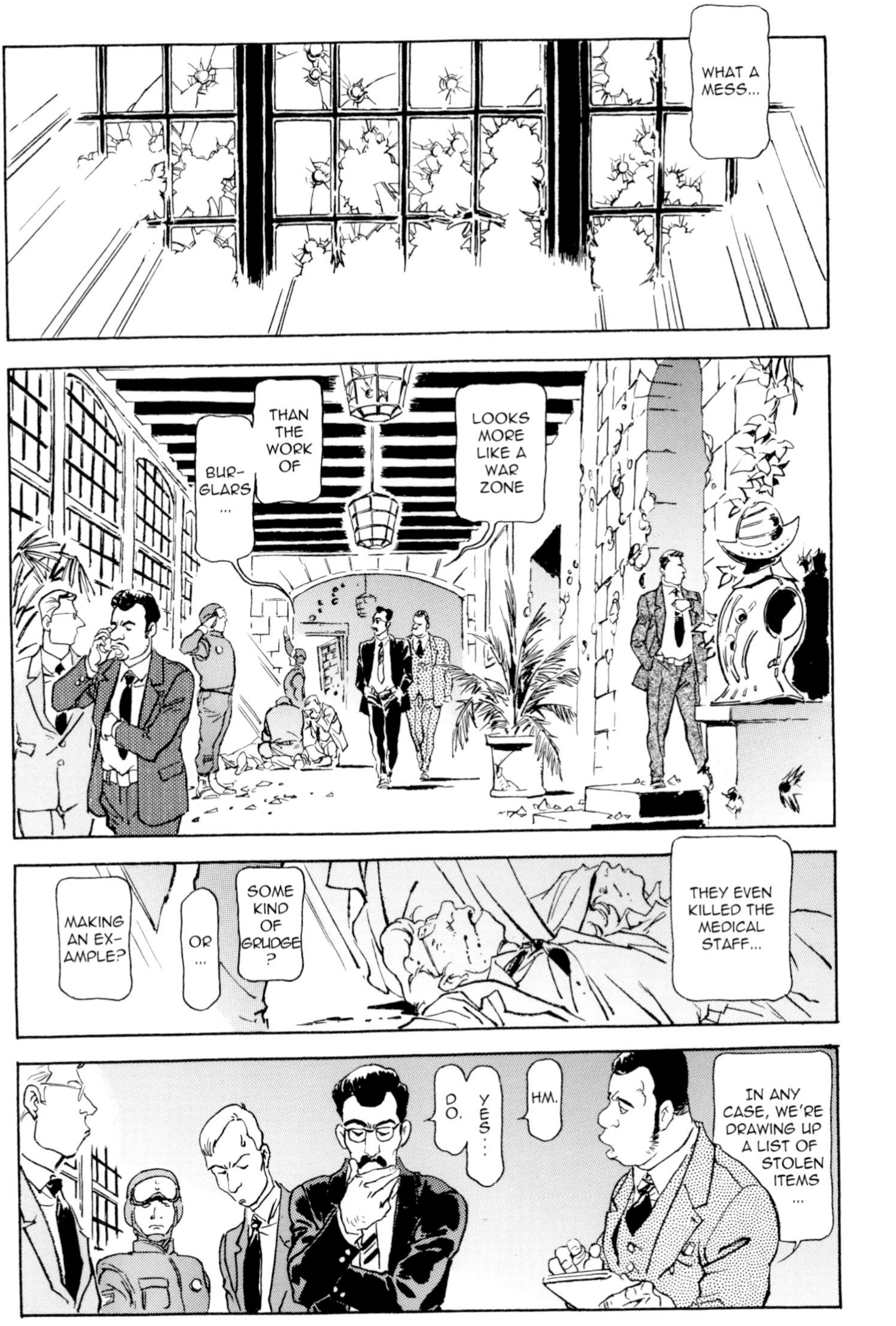
WHAT A MESS...
LOOKS MORE LIKE A WAR ZONE
THAN THE WORK OF
BURGLARS ...
THEY EVEN KILLED THE MEDICAL STAFF...
SOME KIND OF GRUDGE ?
OR ...
MAKING AN EXAMPLE?
IN ANY CASE, WE'RE DRAWING UP A LIST OF STOLEN ITEMS ...
HM.
YES...
D. O.

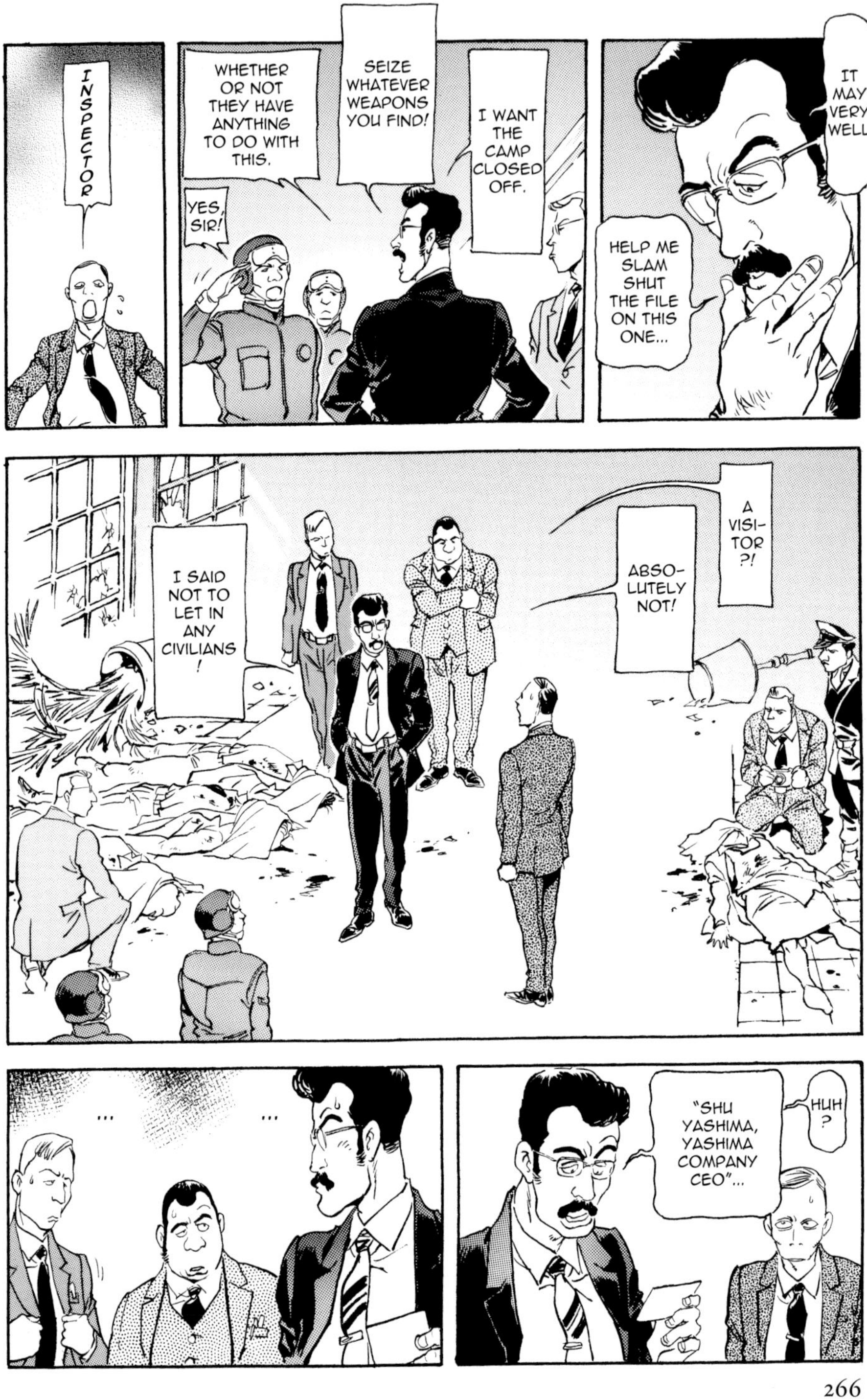
IT MAY VERY WELL
HELP ME SLAM SHUT THE FILE ON THIS ONE...
I WANT THE CAMP CLOSED OFF.
SEIZE WHATEVER WEAPONS YOU FIND!
WHETHER OR NOT THEY HAVE ANYTHING TO DO WITH THIS.
YES, SIR!
INSPECTOR
A VISITOR?!
ABSOLUTELY NOT!
I SAID NOT TO LET IN ANY CIVILIANS!
HUH?
"SHU YASHIMA, YASHIMA COMPANY CEO"...
...
...

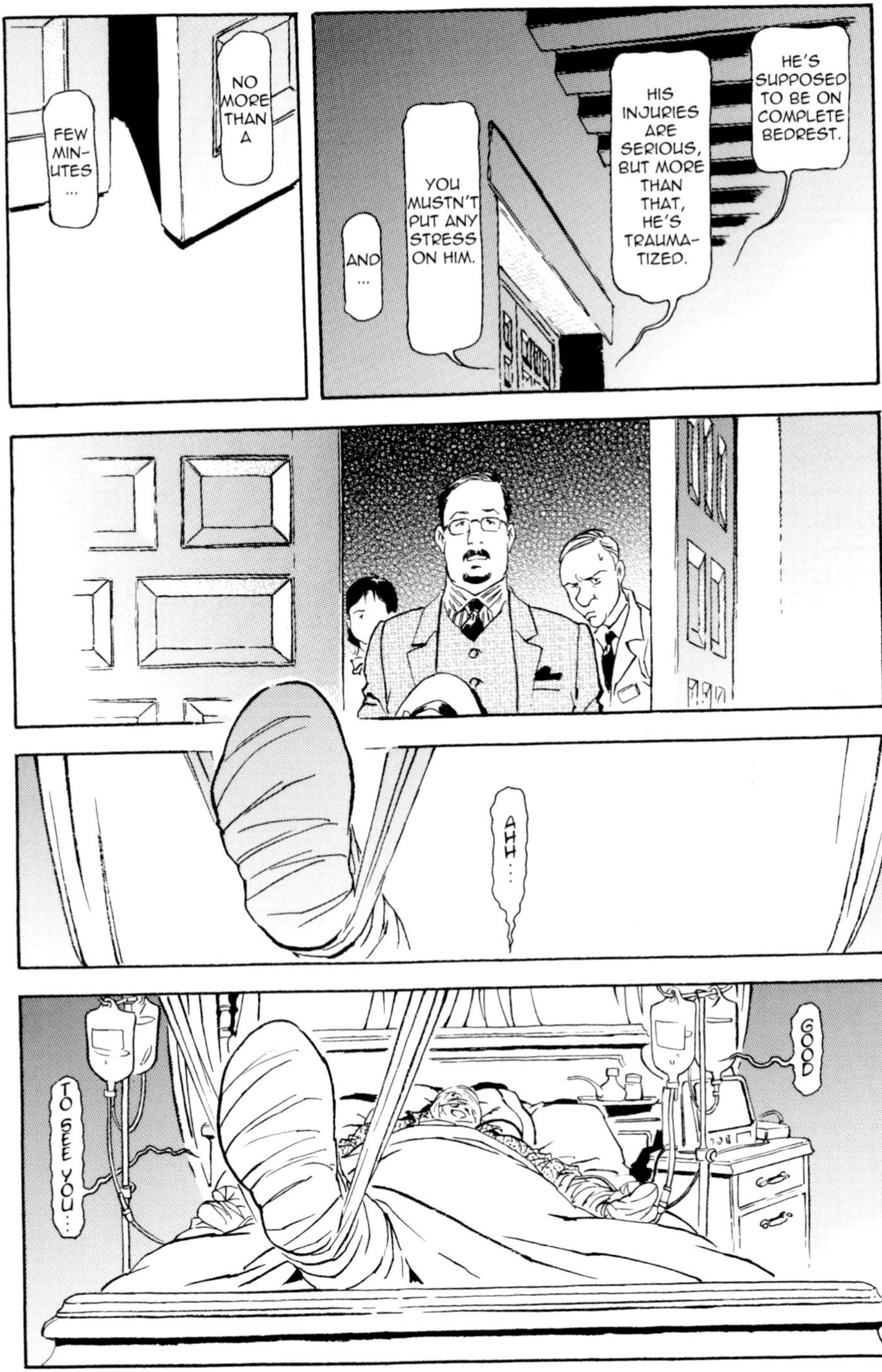
HE'S SUPPOSED TO BE ON COMPLETE BEDREST.
HIS INJURIES ARE SERIOUS, BUT MORE THAN THAT, HE'S TRAUMATIZED.
YOU MUSTN'T PUT ANY STRESS ON HIM.
AND ...
NO MORE THAN A
FEW MINUTES ...
AHH...
GOOD
TO SEE YOU...

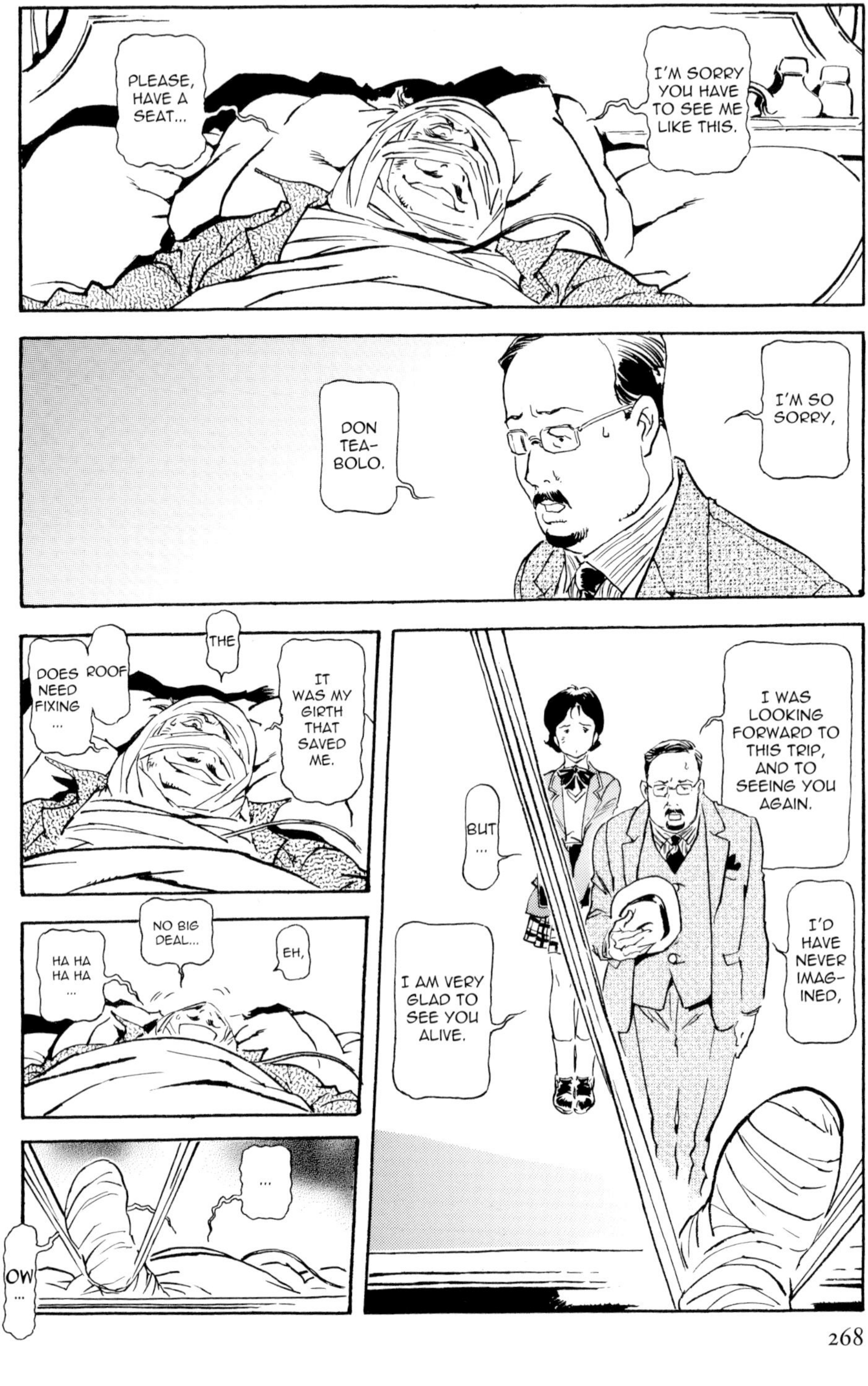
I'M SORRY YOU HAVE TO SEE ME LIKE THIS.
PLEASE, HAVE A SEAT...
I'M SO SORRY,
DON TEA-BOLO.
I WAS LOOKING FORWARD TO THIS TRIP, AND TO SEEING YOU AGAIN.
I'D HAVE NEVER IMAG-INED,
BUT...
I AM VERY GLAD TO SEE YOU ALIVE.
IT WAS MY GIRTH THAT SAVED ME.
THE
ROOF
DOES NEED FIXING...
EH,
NO BIG DEAL...
HA HA HA HA...
...
OW...

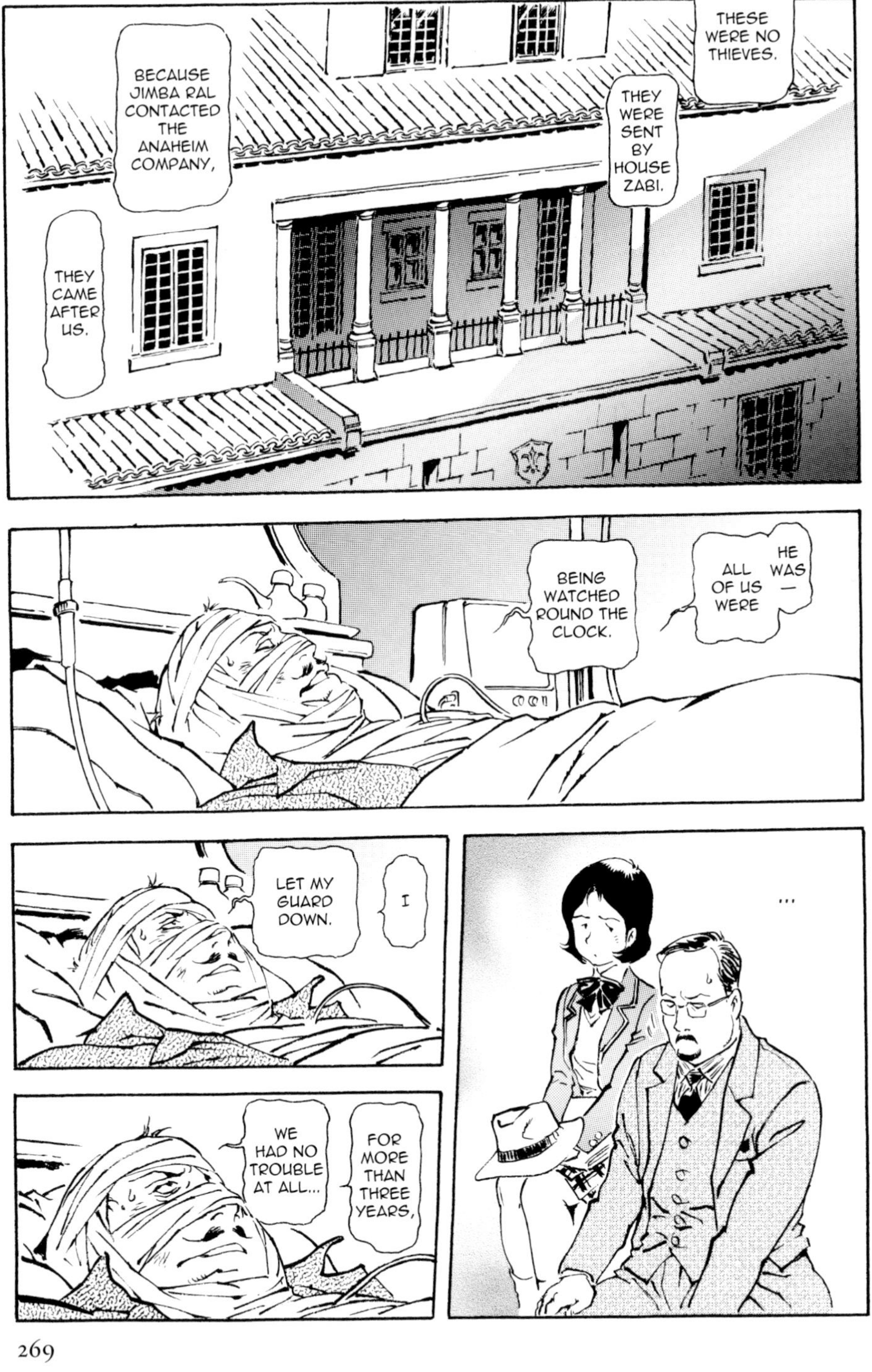
THESE WERE NO THIEVES.
THEY WERE SENT BY HOUSE ZABI.
BECAUSE JIMBA RAL CONTACTED THE ANAHEIM COMPANY,
THEY CAME AFTER US.
HE WAS — ALL OF US WERE
BEING WATCHED ROUND THE CLOCK.
...
I
LET MY GUARD DOWN.
FOR MORE THAN THREE YEARS,
WE HAD NO TROUBLE AT ALL...

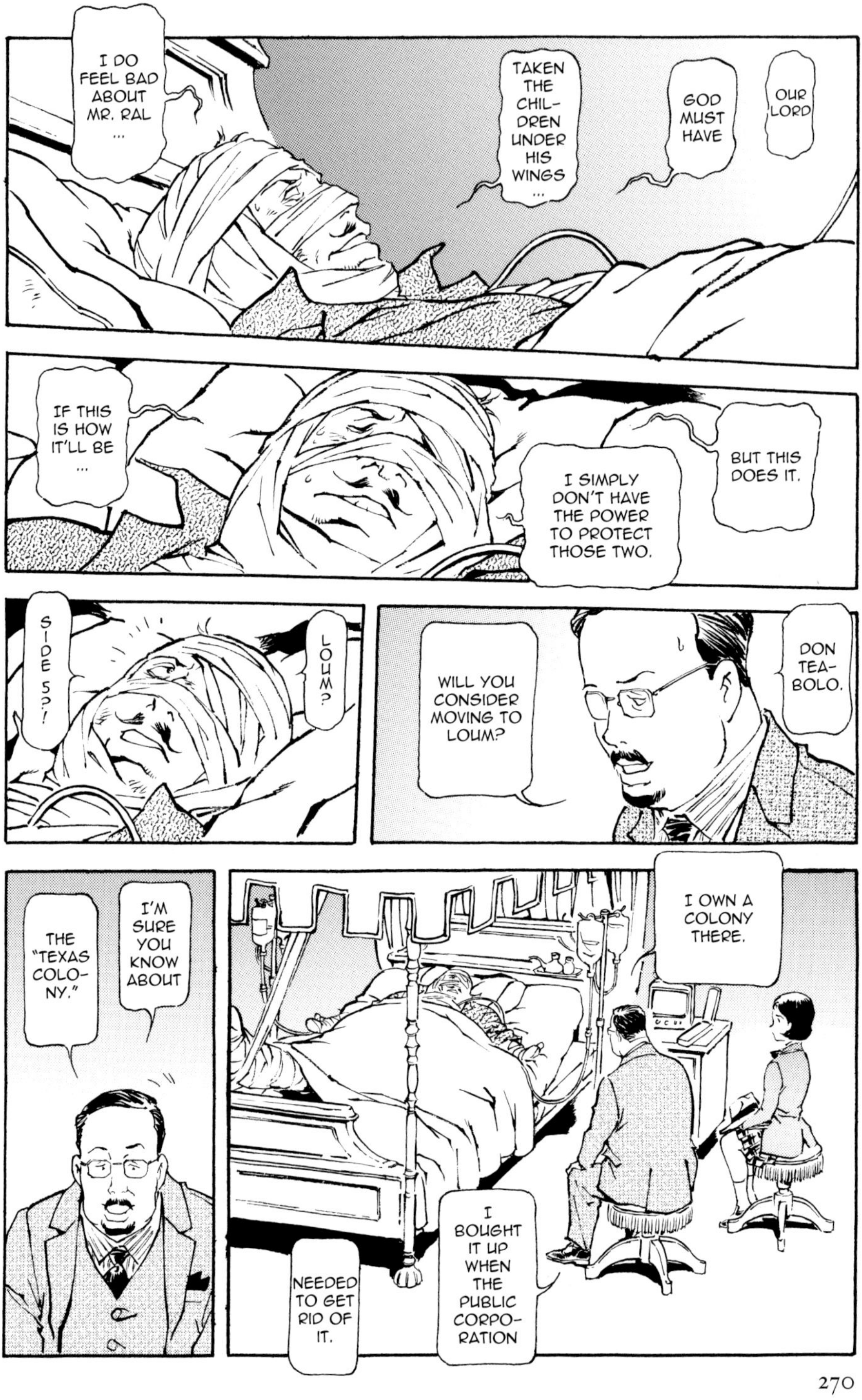
OUR LORD
GOD MUST HAVE
TAKEN THE CHIL-DREN UNDER HIS WINGS ...
I DO FEEL BAD ABOUT MR. RAL ...
BUT THIS DOES IT.
I SIMPLY DON'T HAVE THE POWER TO PROTECT THOSE TWO.
IF THIS IS HOW IT'LL BE ...
DON TEA-BOLO.
WILL YOU CONSIDER MOVING TO LOUM?
LOUM?
SIDE 5?!
I OWN A COLONY THERE.
I BOUGHT IT UP WHEN THE PUBLIC CORPO-RATION
NEEDED TO GET RID OF IT.
I'M SURE YOU KNOW ABOUT
THE "TEXAS COLO-NY."

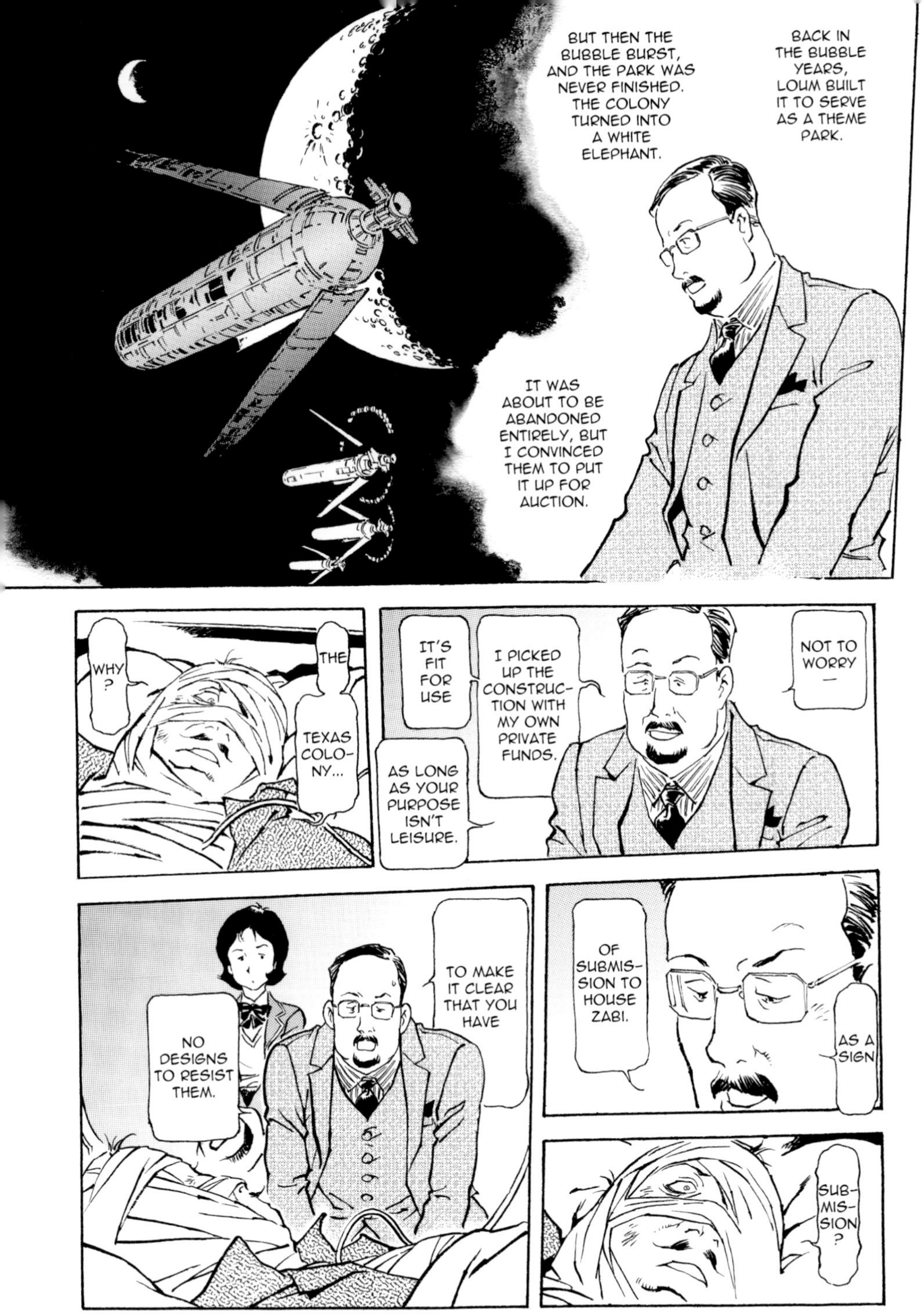
BACK IN THE BUBBLE YEARS, LOUM BUILT IT TO SERVE AS A THEME PARK.
BUT THEN THE BUBBLE BURST, AND THE PARK WAS NEVER FINISHED. THE COLONY TURNED INTO A WHITE ELEPHANT.
IT WAS ABOUT TO BE ABANDONED ENTIRELY, BUT I CONVINCED THEM TO PUT IT UP FOR AUCTION.
NOT TO WORRY —
I PICKED UP THE CONSTRUCTION WITH MY OWN PRIVATE FUNDS.
IT'S FIT FOR USE
AS LONG AS YOUR PURPOSE ISN'T LEISURE.
THE TEXAS COLONY...
WHY?
AS A SIGN
OF SUBMISSION TO HOUSE ZABI.
SUBMISSION?
TO MAKE IT CLEAR THAT YOU HAVE
NO DESIGNS TO RESIST THEM.

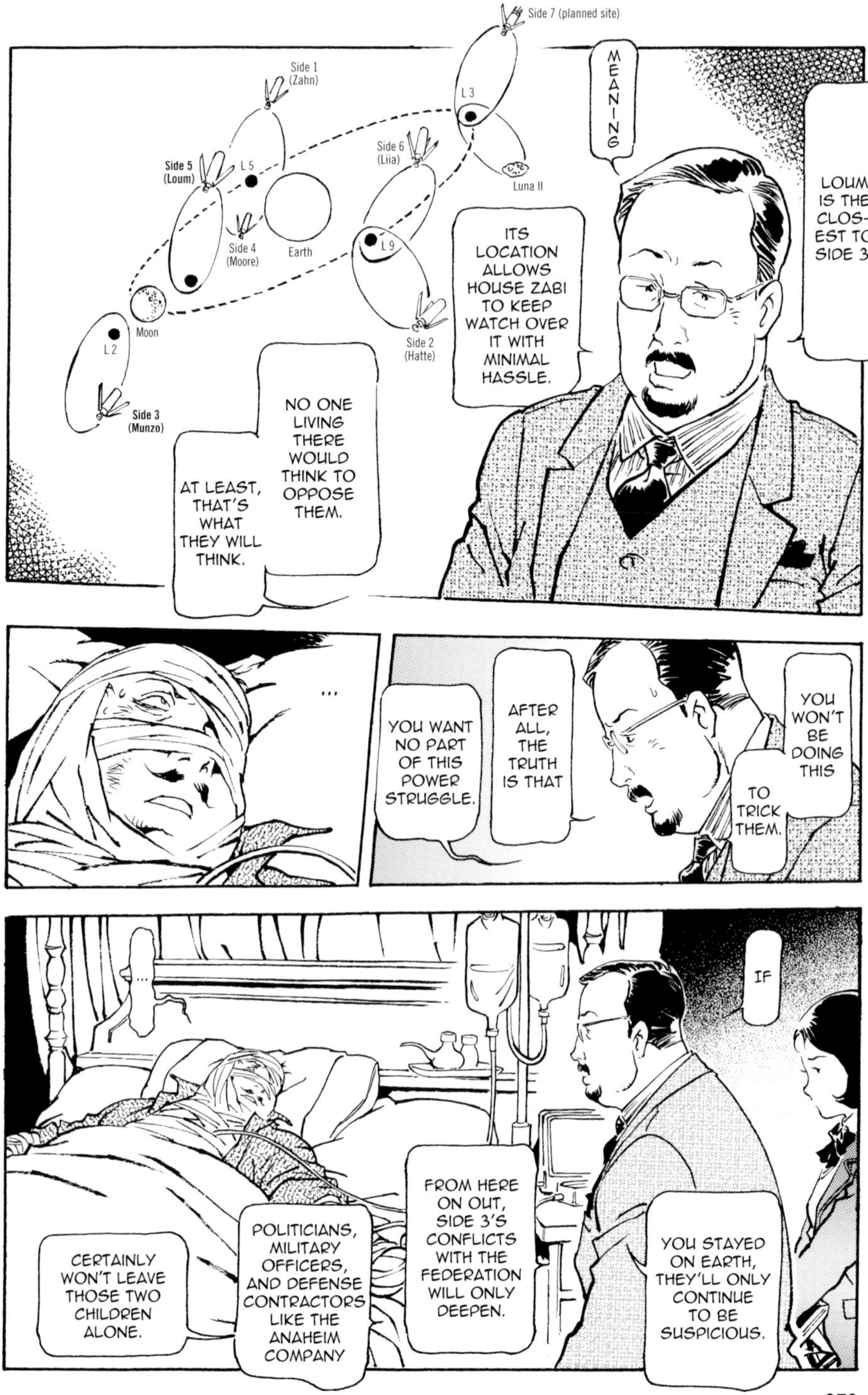
Side 7 (planned site)
Side 1 (Zahn)
L 3
Side 6 (Liia)
Side 5 (Loum)
L 5
Luna II
Side 4 (Moore)
Earth
L 9
Moon
L 2
Side 2 (Hatte)
Side 3 (Munzo)
MEANING
LOUM IS THE CLOSEST TO SIDE 3.
ITS LOCATION ALLOWS HOUSE ZABI TO KEEP WATCH OVER IT WITH MINIMAL HASSLE.
NO ONE LIVING THERE WOULD THINK TO OPPOSE THEM.
AT LEAST, THAT'S WHAT THEY WILL THINK.
YOU WON'T BE DOING THIS
TO TRICK THEM.
AFTER ALL, THE TRUTH IS THAT
YOU WANT NO PART OF THIS POWER STRUGGLE.
...
IF
YOU STAYED ON EARTH, THEY'LL ONLY CONTINUE TO BE SUSPICIOUS.
FROM HERE ON OUT, SIDE 3'S CONFLICTS WITH THE FEDERATION WILL ONLY DEEPEN.
POLITICIANS, MILITARY OFFICERS, AND DEFENSE CONTRACTORS LIKE THE ANAHEIM COMPANY
CERTAINLY WON'T LEAVE THOSE TWO CHILDREN ALONE.
...

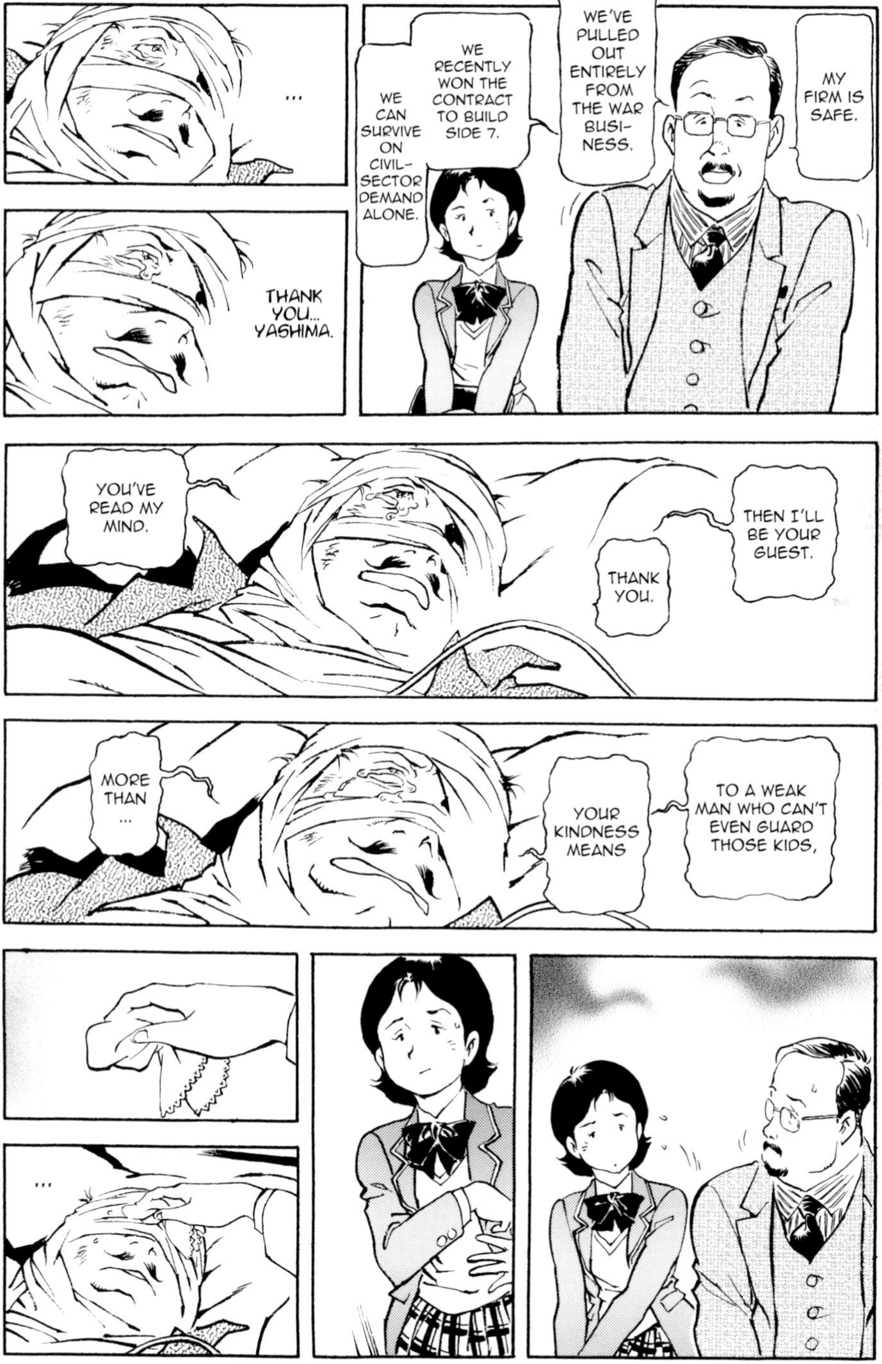
MY FIRM IS SAFE.
WE'VE PULLED OUT ENTIRELY FROM THE WAR BUSINESS.
WE RECENTLY WON THE CONTRACT TO BUILD SIDE 7.
WE CAN SURVIVE ON CIVIL-SECTOR DEMAND ALONE.
...
THANK YOU... YASHIMA.
THEN I'LL BE YOUR GUEST.
THANK YOU.
YOU'VE READ MY MIND.
TO A WEAK MAN WHO CAN'T EVEN GUARD THOSE KIDS,
YOUR KINDNESS MEANS
MORE THAN ...
...

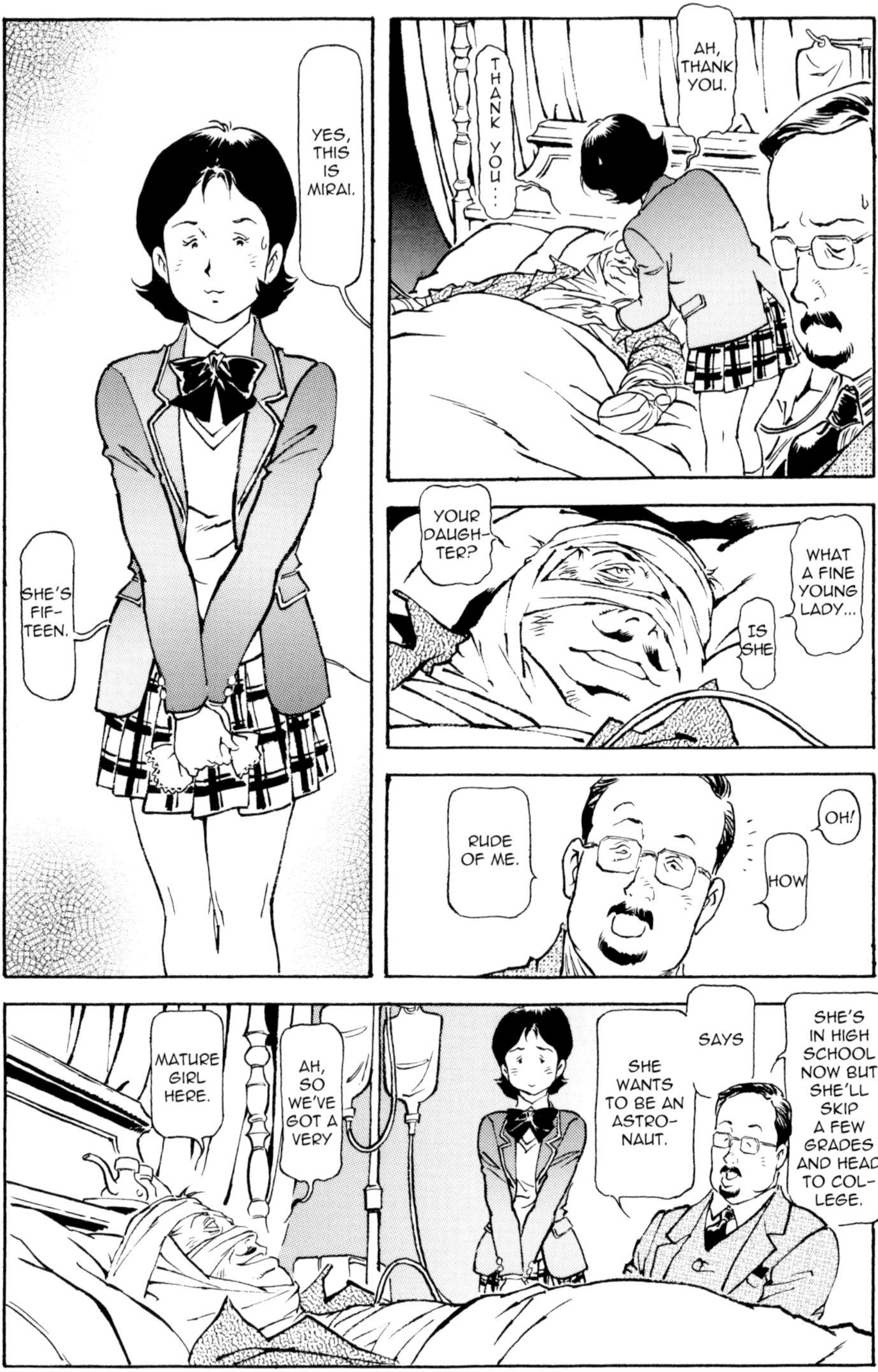
AH, THANK YOU.
THANK YOU...
WHAT A FINE YOUNG LADY...
IS SHE
YOUR DAUGHTER?
OH!
HOW
RUDE OF ME.
YES, THIS IS MIRAI.
SHE'S FIFTEEN.
SHE'S IN HIGH SCHOOL NOW BUT SHE'LL SKIP A FEW GRADES AND HEAD TO COLLEGE.
SAYS
SHE WANTS TO BE AN ASTRONAUT.
AH, SO WE'VE GOT A VERY
MATURE GIRL HERE.

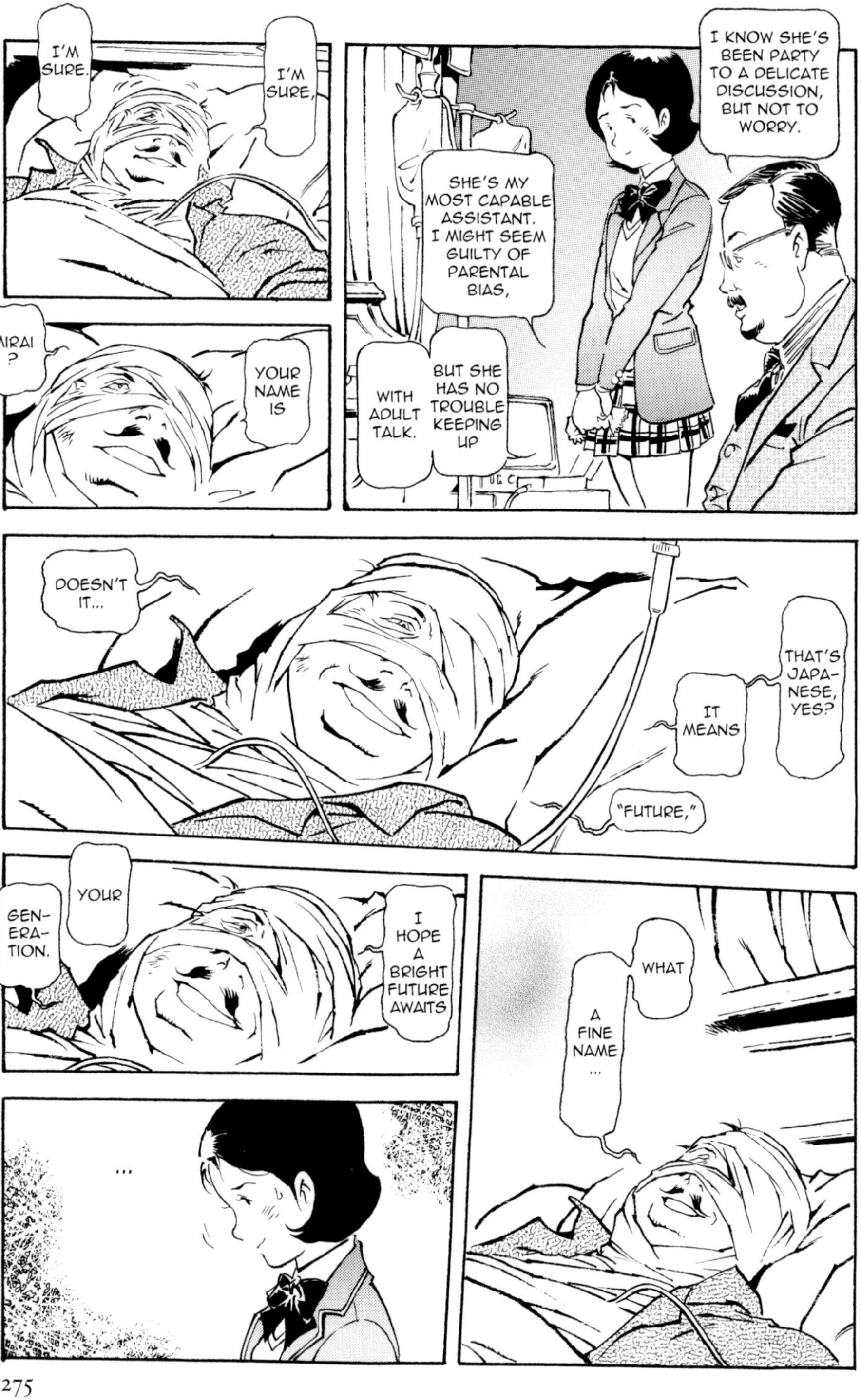

I KNOW SHE'S BEEN PARTY TO A DELICATE DISCUSSION, BUT NOT TO WORRY.
SHE'S MY MOST CAPABLE ASSISTANT. I MIGHT SEEM GUILTY OF PARENTAL BIAS,
BUT SHE HAS NO TROUBLE KEEPING UP
WITH ADULT TALK.
I'M SURE,
I'M SURE.
YOUR NAME IS
MIRAI?
THAT'S JAPA-NESE, YES?
IT MEANS
"FUTURE,"
DOESN'T IT...
WHAT
A FINE NAME ...
I HOPE A BRIGHT FUTURE AWAITS
YOUR
GEN-ERA-TION.
...

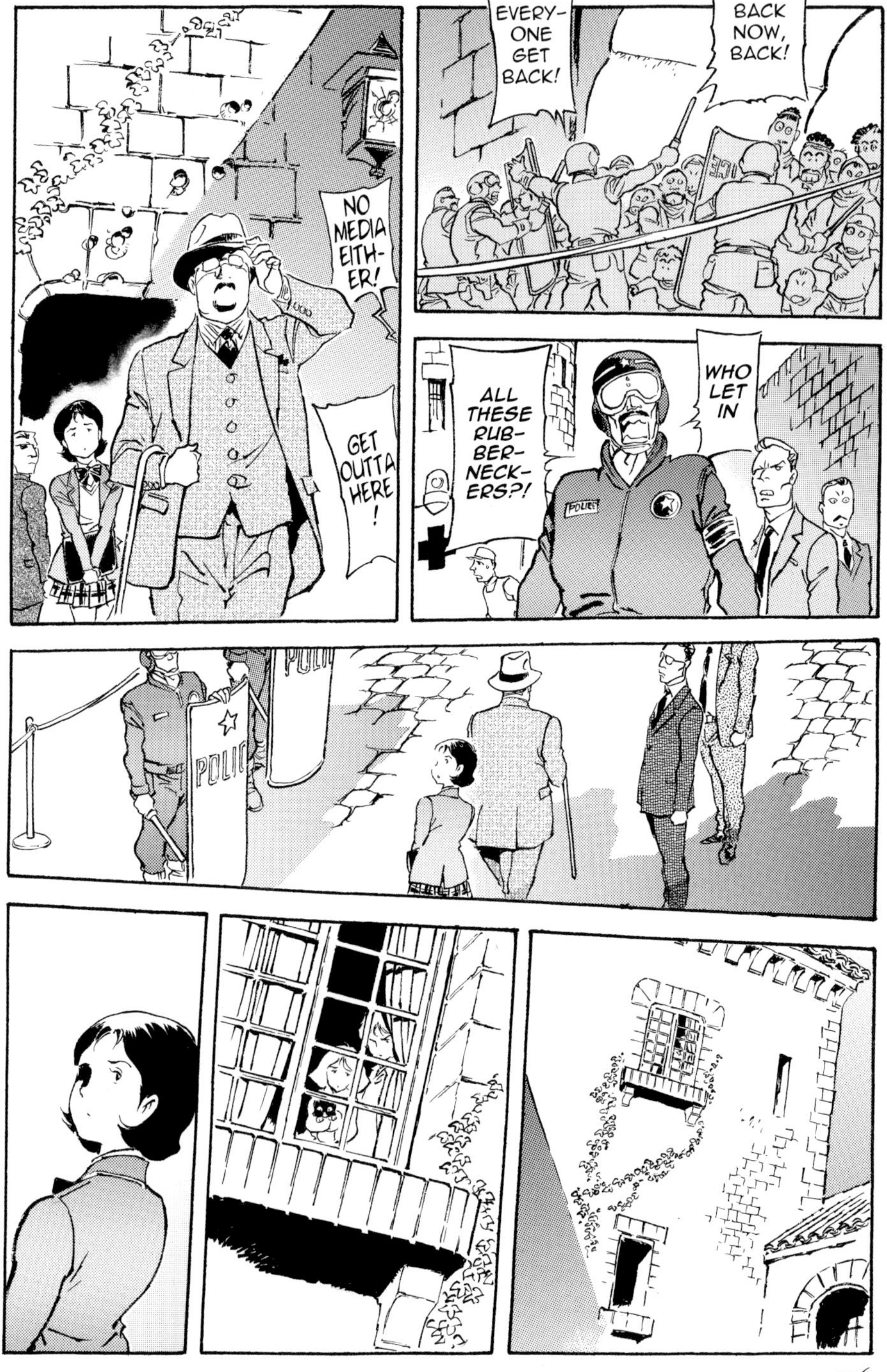
BACK NOW, BACK!
EVERY-ONE GET BACK!
WHO LET IN
ALL THESE RUB-BER-NECK-ERS?!
NO MEDIA EITH-ER!
GET OUTTA HERE!

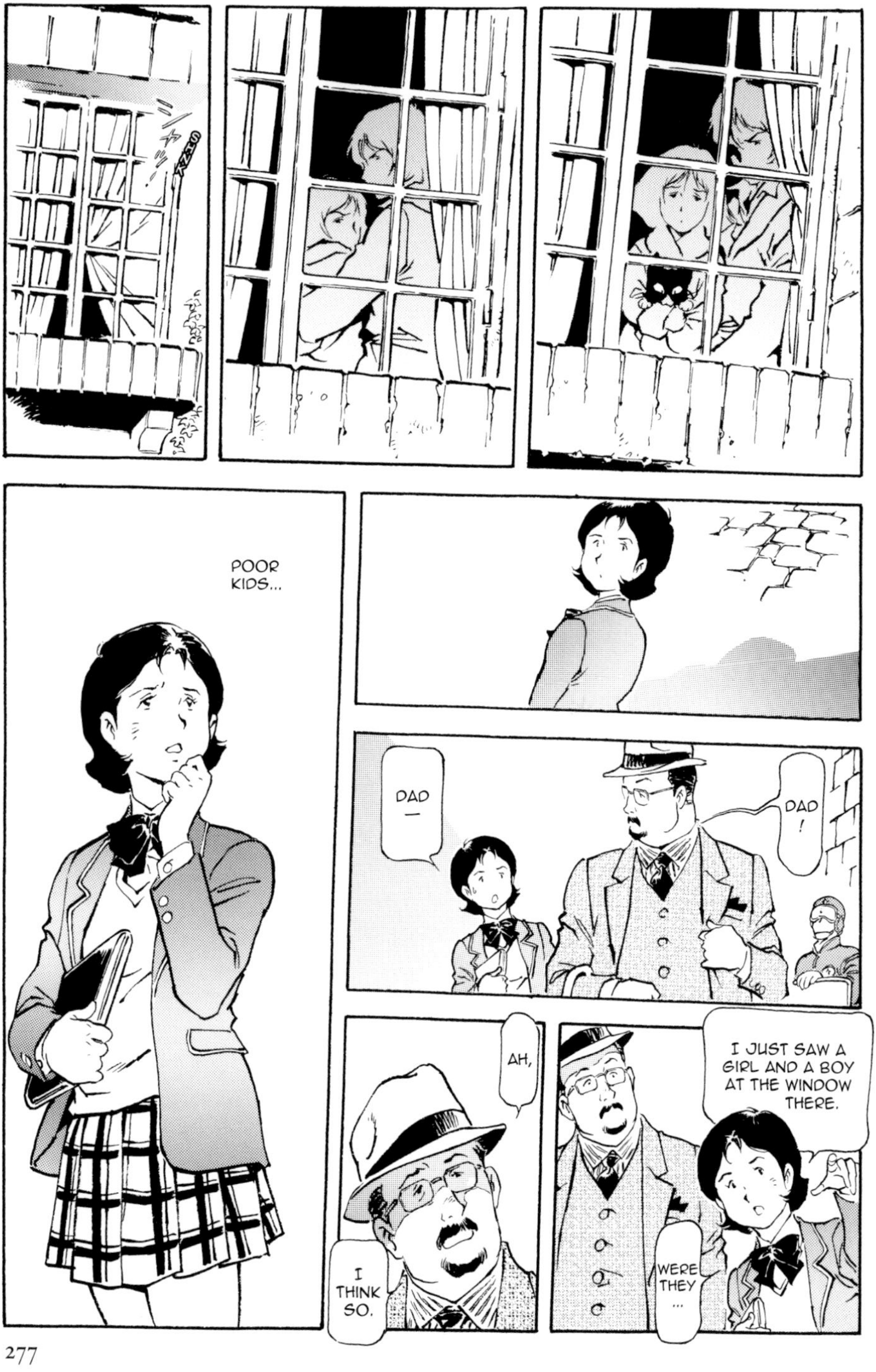
DAD!
DAD—
I JUST SAW A GIRL AND A BOY AT THE WINDOW THERE.
WERE THEY...
AH,
I THINK SO.
POOR KIDS...

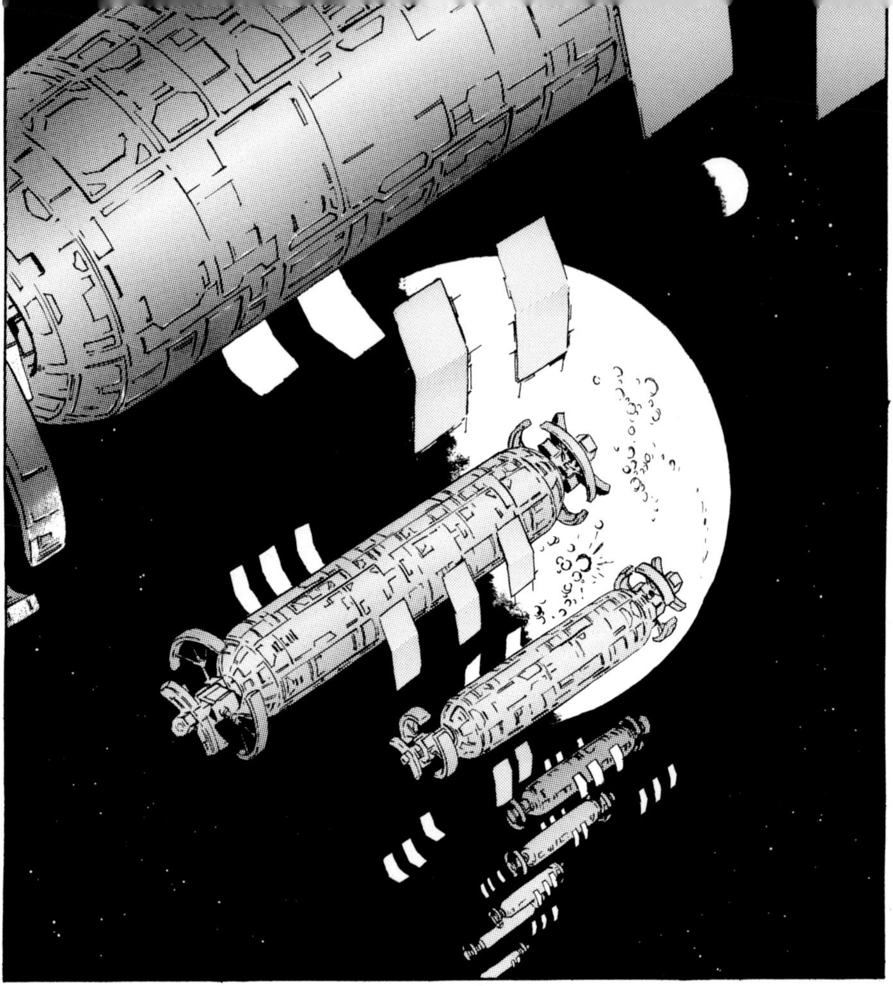
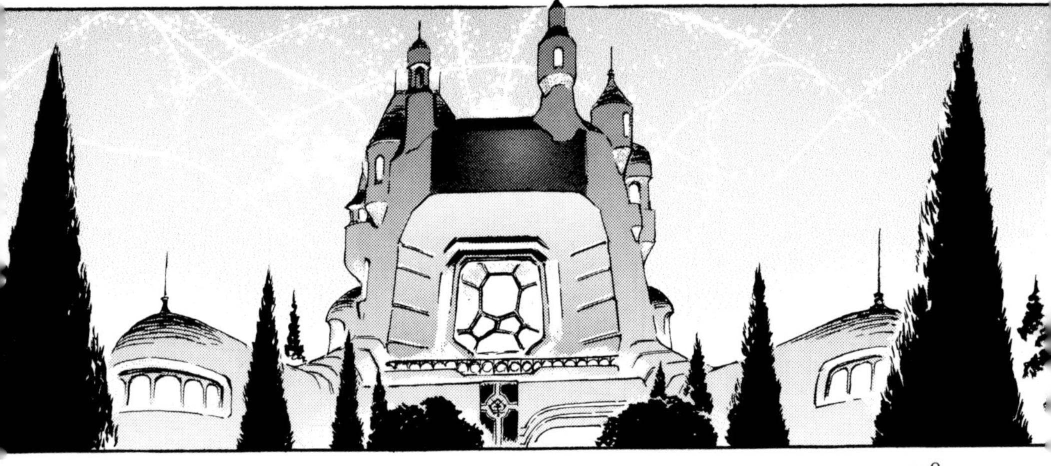

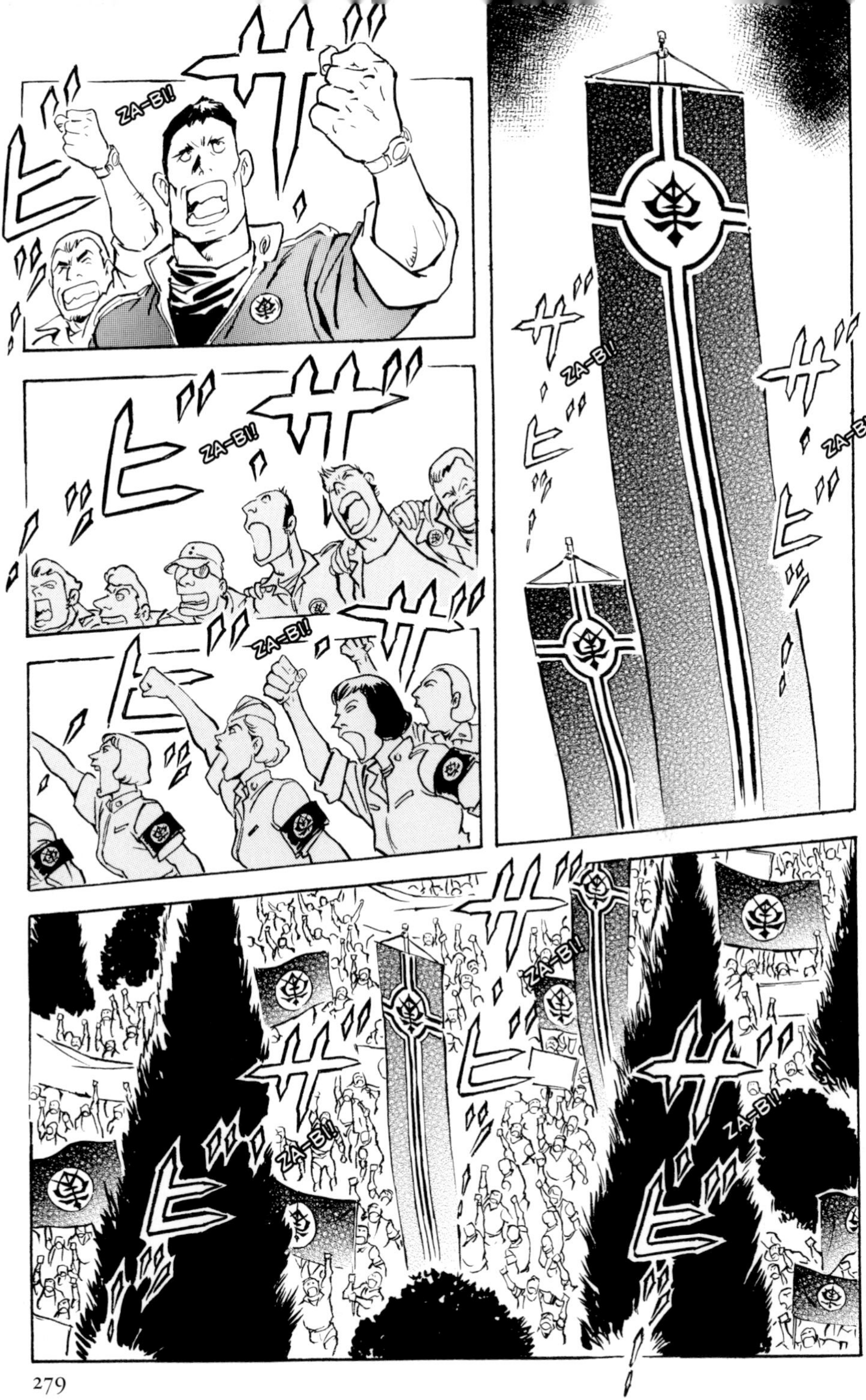
ZA-BI!
ZA-BI!
ZA-BI!
ZA-BI!
ZA-BI!
ZA-BI!
ZA-BI!
ZA-BI!

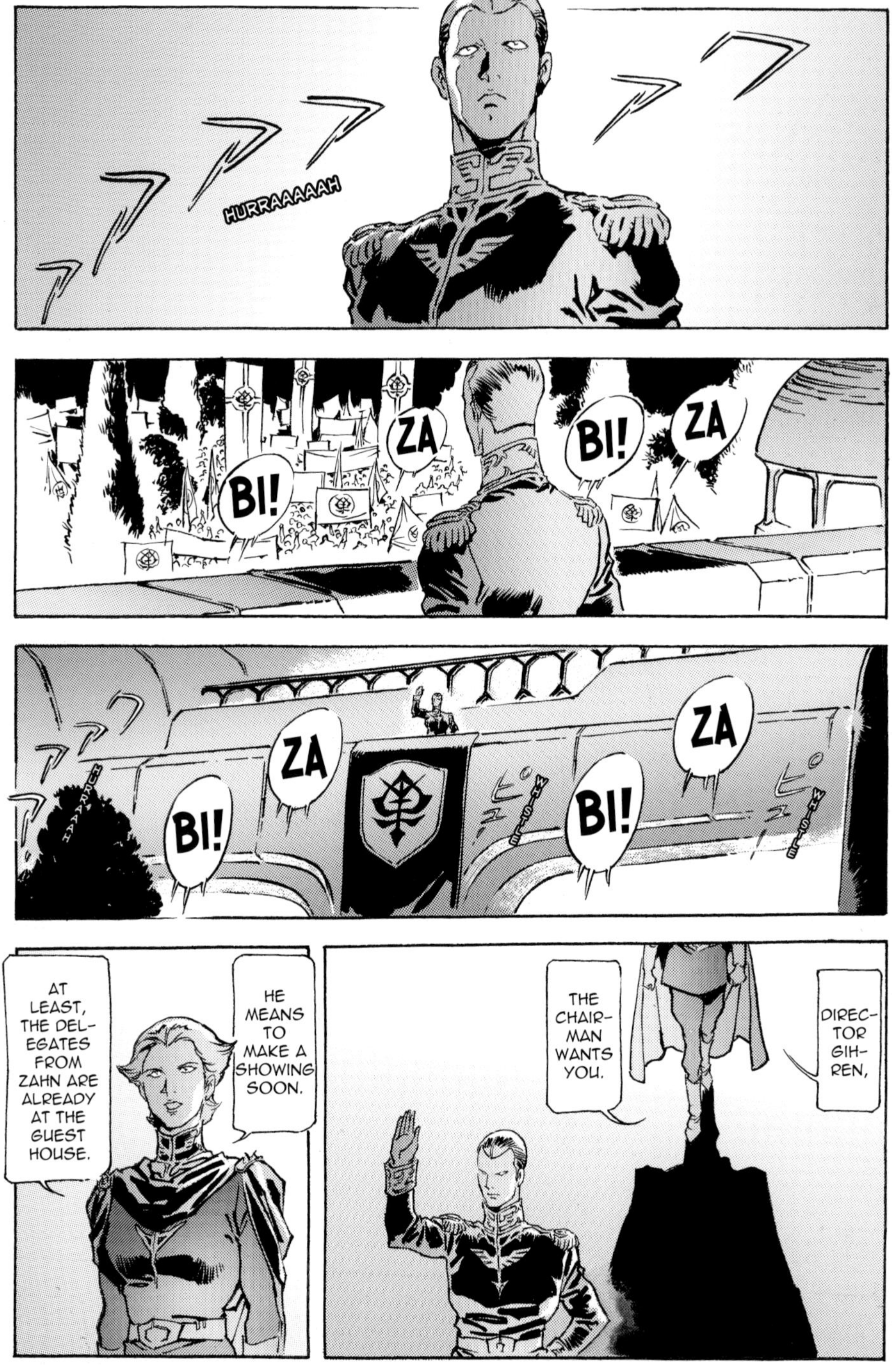
HURRAAAAAH
ZA
BI!
ZA
BI!
ZA
WHISTLE
BI!
WHISTLE
ZA
BI!
HURRAAAH
DIRECTOR GIHREN,
THE CHAIRMAN WANTS YOU.
HE MEANS TO MAKE A SHOWING SOON.
AT LEAST, THE DELEGATES FROM ZAHN ARE ALREADY AT THE GUEST HOUSE.

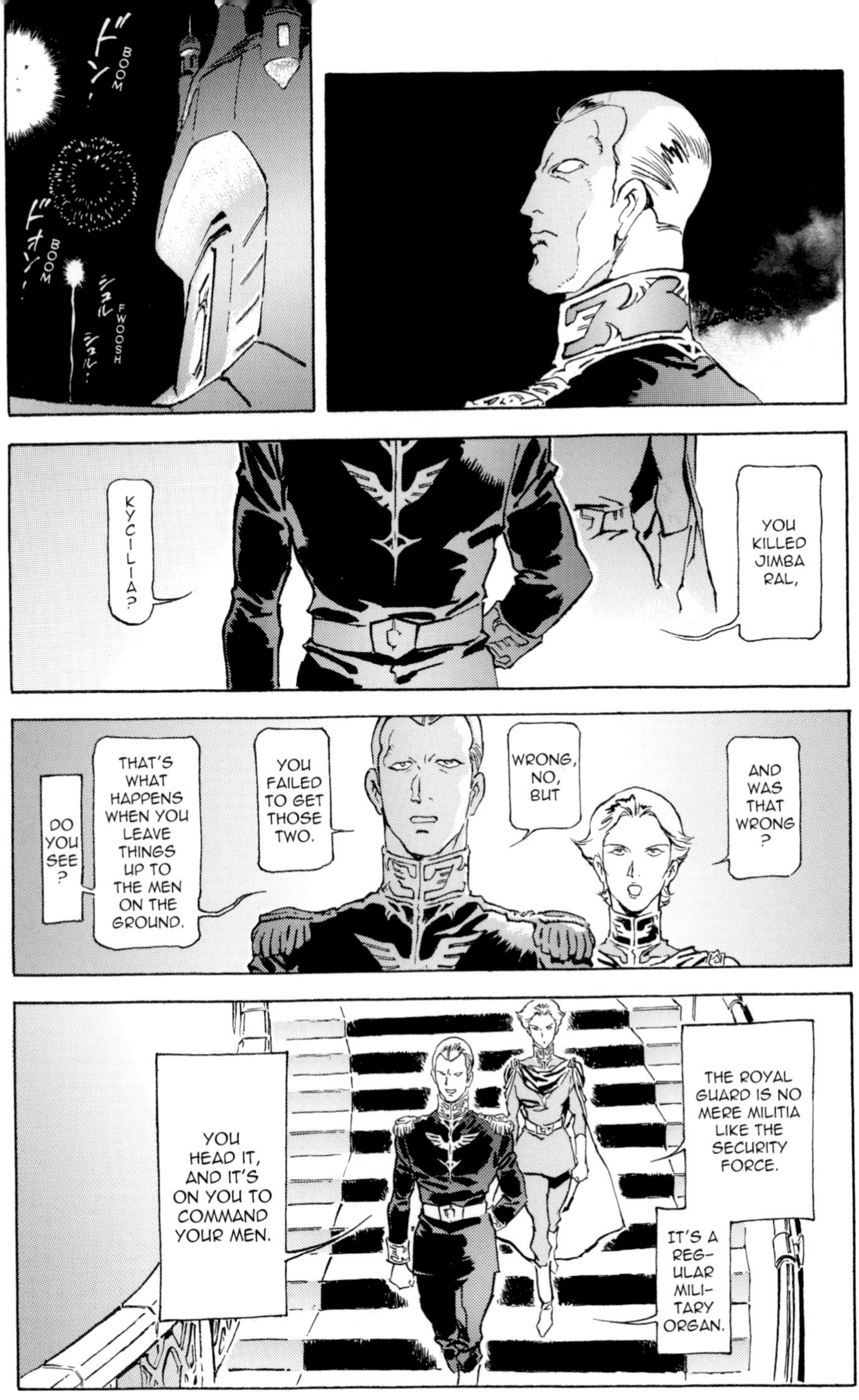
ドン！
BOOM
ドォン！
BOOM
シュル
シュル…
FWOOSH
YOU KILLED JIMBA RAL,
KYCILIA?
AND WAS THAT WRONG?
WRONG, NO, BUT
YOU FAILED TO GET THOSE TWO.
THAT'S WHAT HAPPENS WHEN YOU LEAVE THINGS UP TO THE MEN ON THE GROUND.
DO YOU SEE?
THE ROYAL GUARD IS NO MERE MILITIA LIKE THE SECURITY FORCE.
IT'S A REGULAR MILITARY ORGAN.
YOU HEAD IT, AND IT'S ON YOU TO COMMAND YOUR MEN.

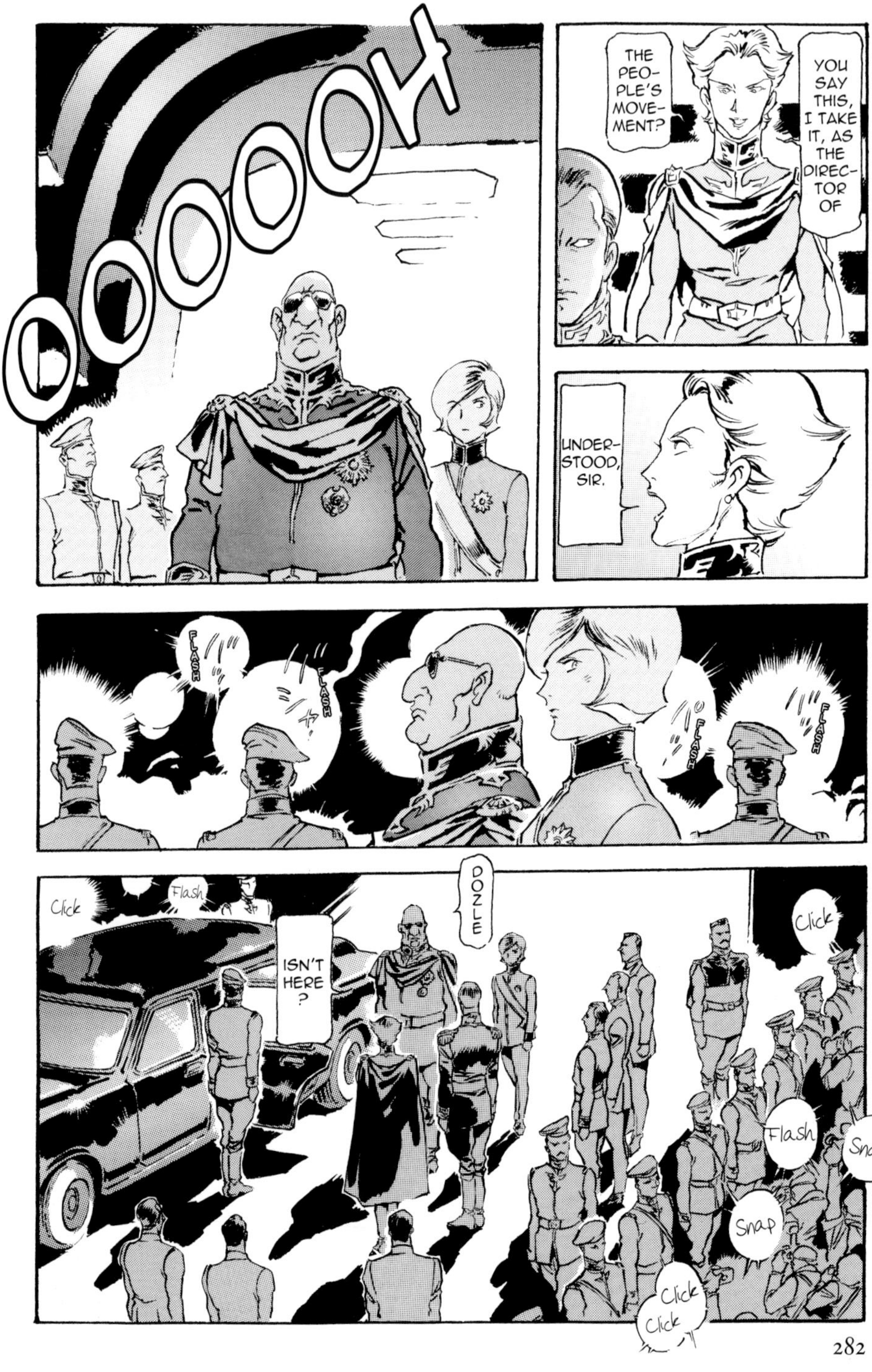
YOU SAY THIS, I TAKE IT, AS THE DIRECTOR OF
THE PEOPLE'S MOVEMENT?
UNDERSTOOD, SIR.
OOOOOOH
FLASH
FLASH
FLASH
FLASH
Click
DOZLE
ISN'T HERE?
Flash
Click
Flash
Snap
Snap
Click
Click

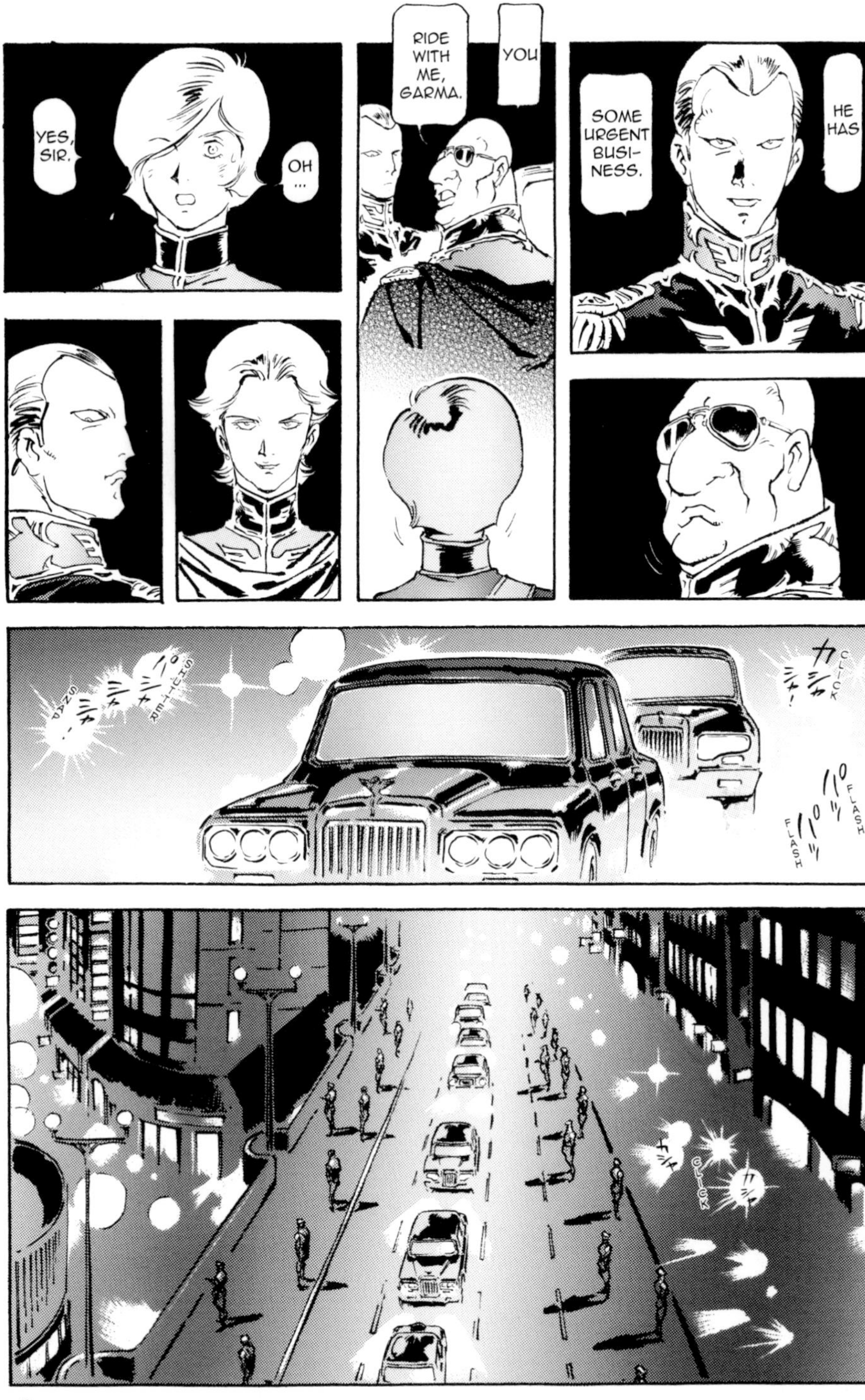
HE HAS
SOME URGENT BUSINESS.
YOU
RIDE WITH ME, GARMA.
OH ...
YES, SIR.
CLICK
FLASH
FLASH
SHUTTER
SNAP
CLICK

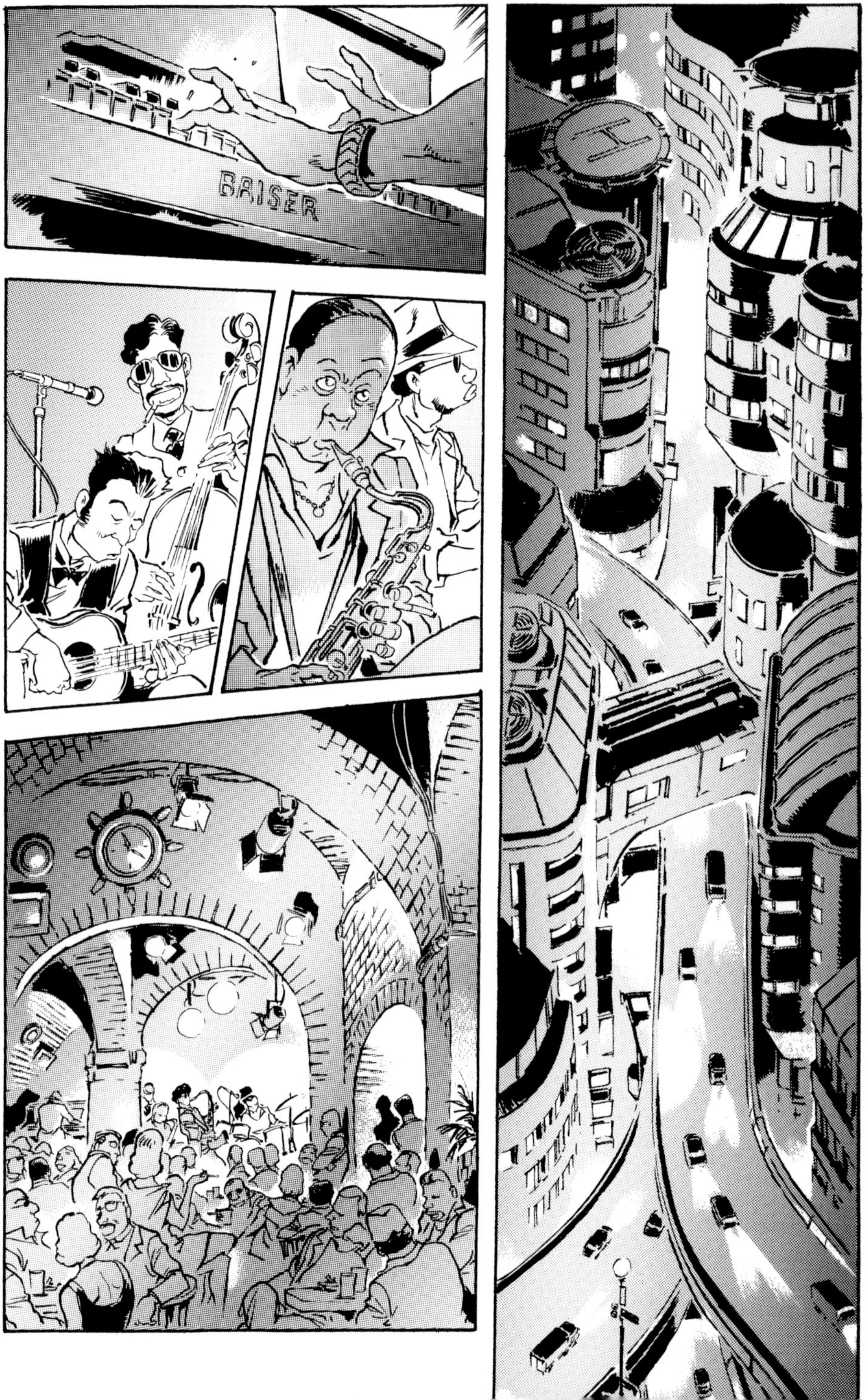
BAISER

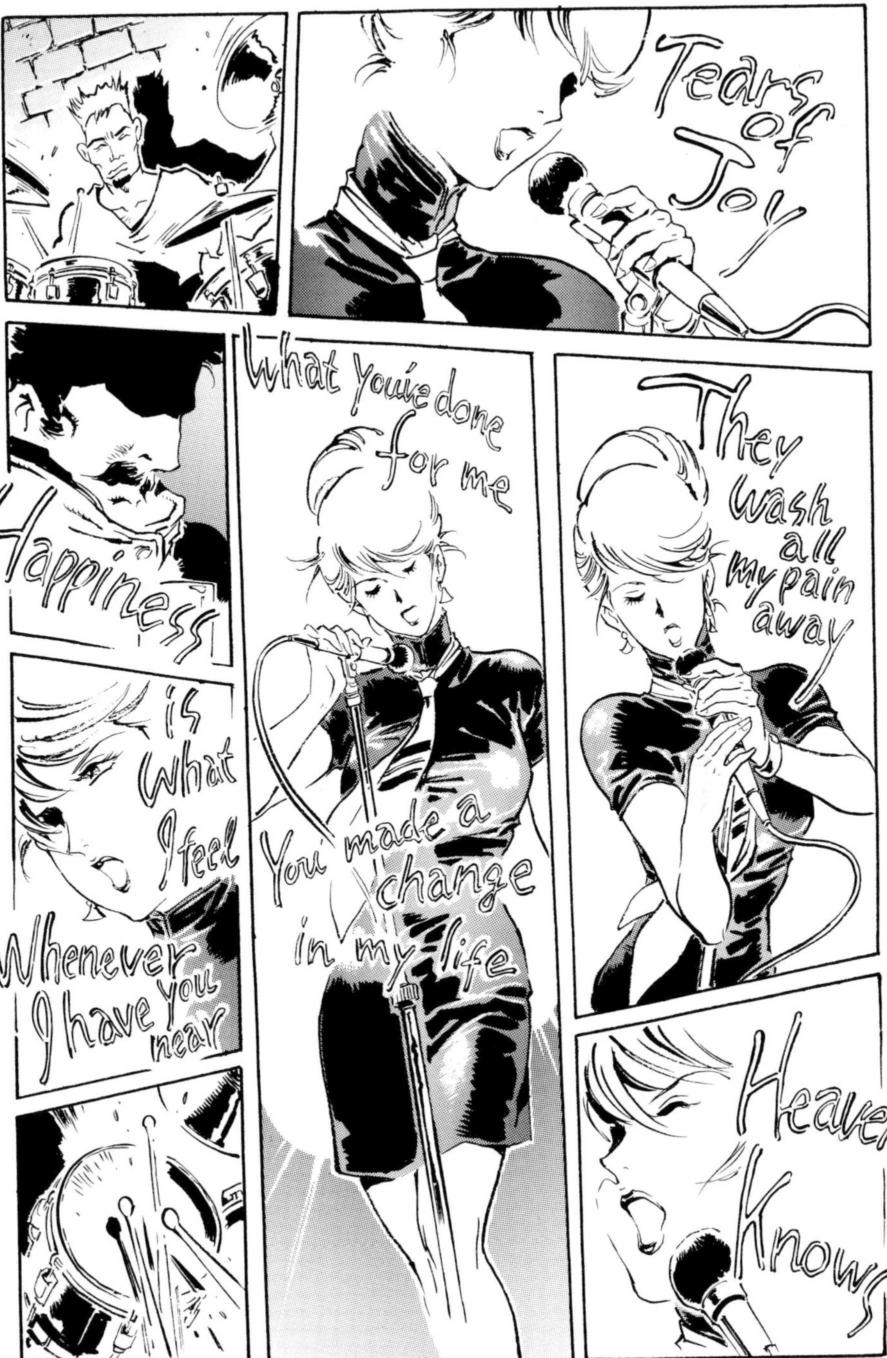

Tears of Joy
They wash all my pain away
Heaven Knows
What you've done for me
You made a change in my life
Happiness
is what I feel
Whenever I have you near

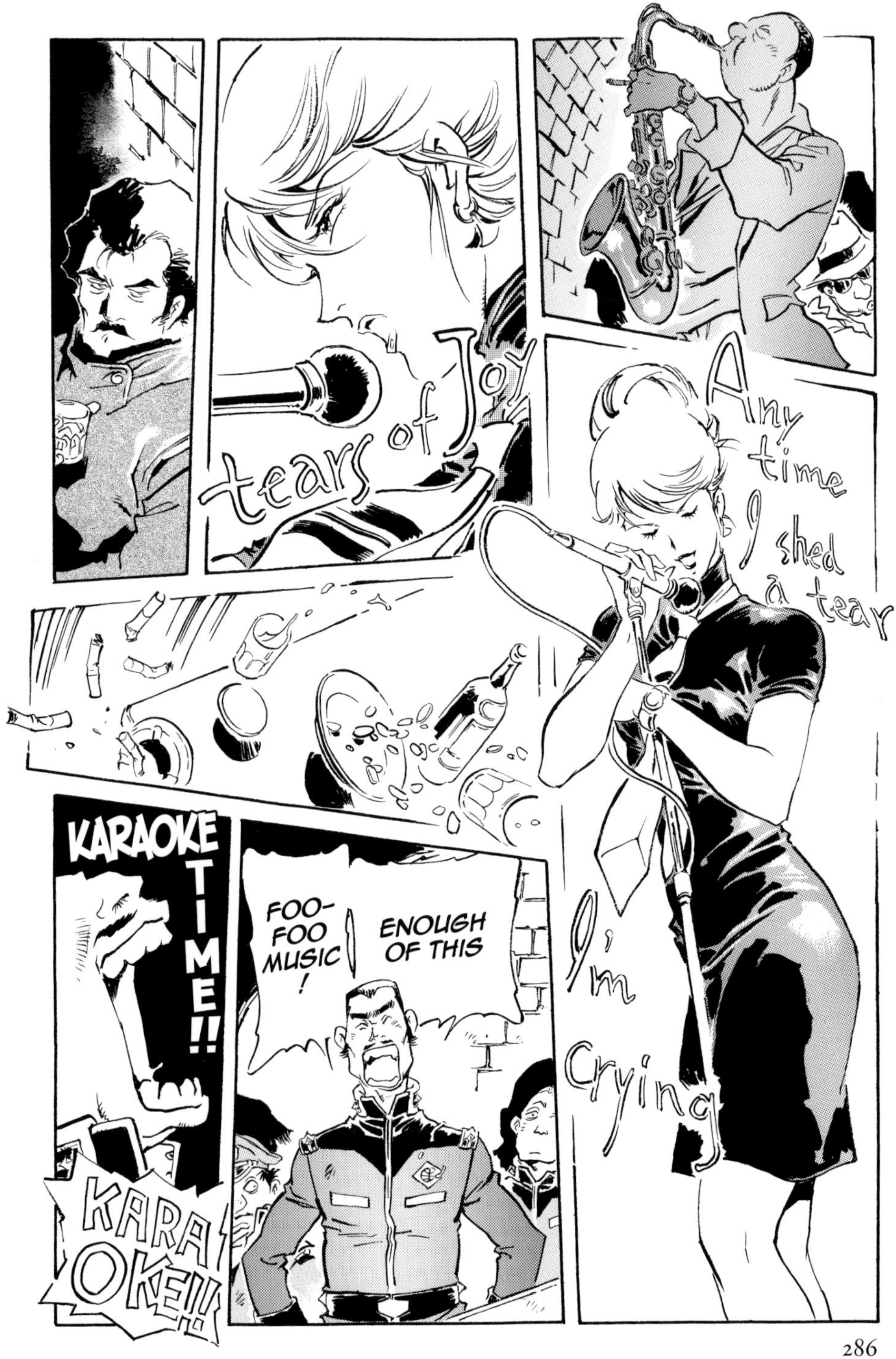
tears of Joy
Any time I shed a tear
I'm crying
ENOUGH OF THIS
FOO-FOO MUSIC!
KARAOKE TIME!!
KARAOKE!!

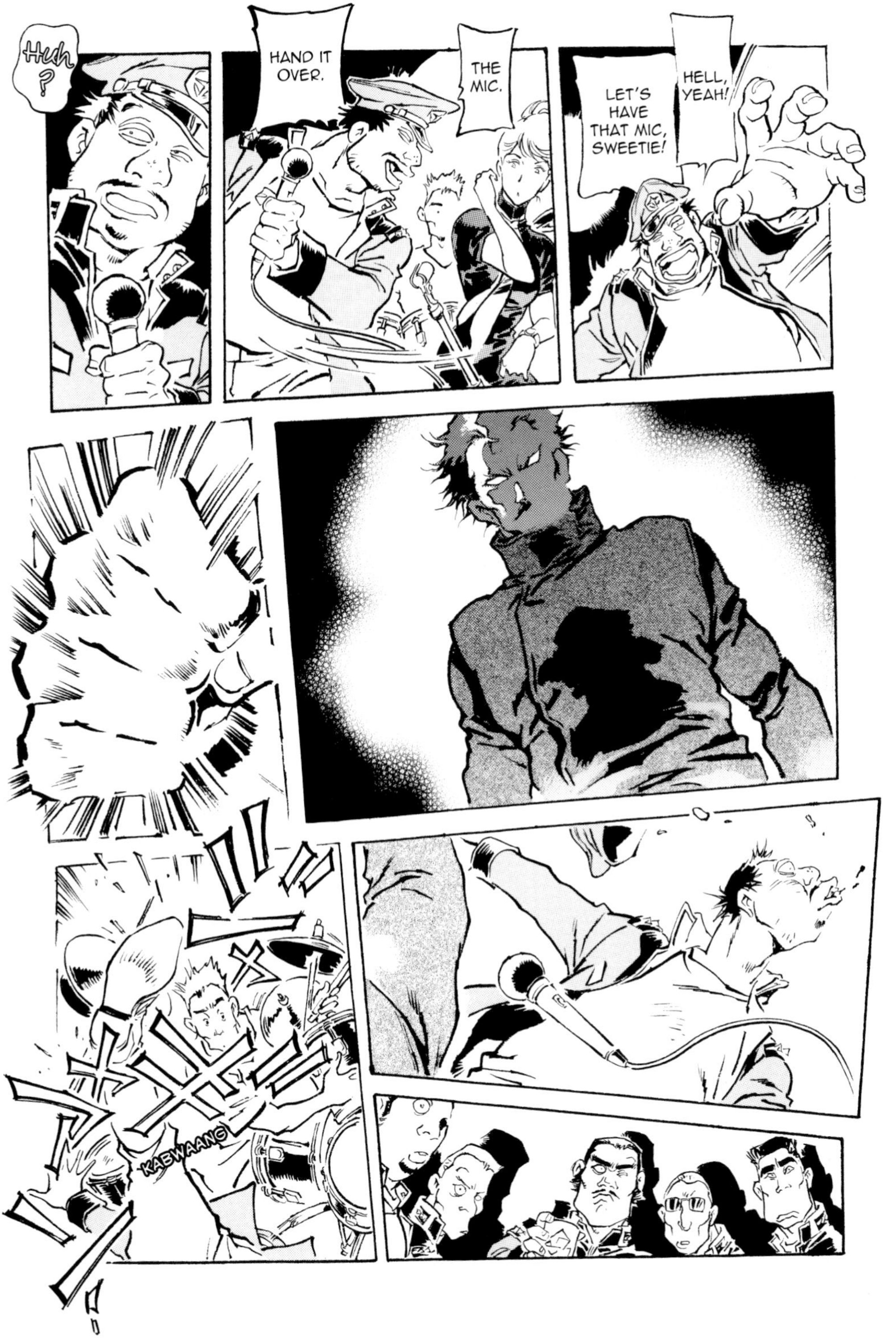
HELL, YEAH!
LET'S HAVE THAT MIC, SWEETIE!
HAND IT OVER.
THE MIC.
Huh?
KABWAANG

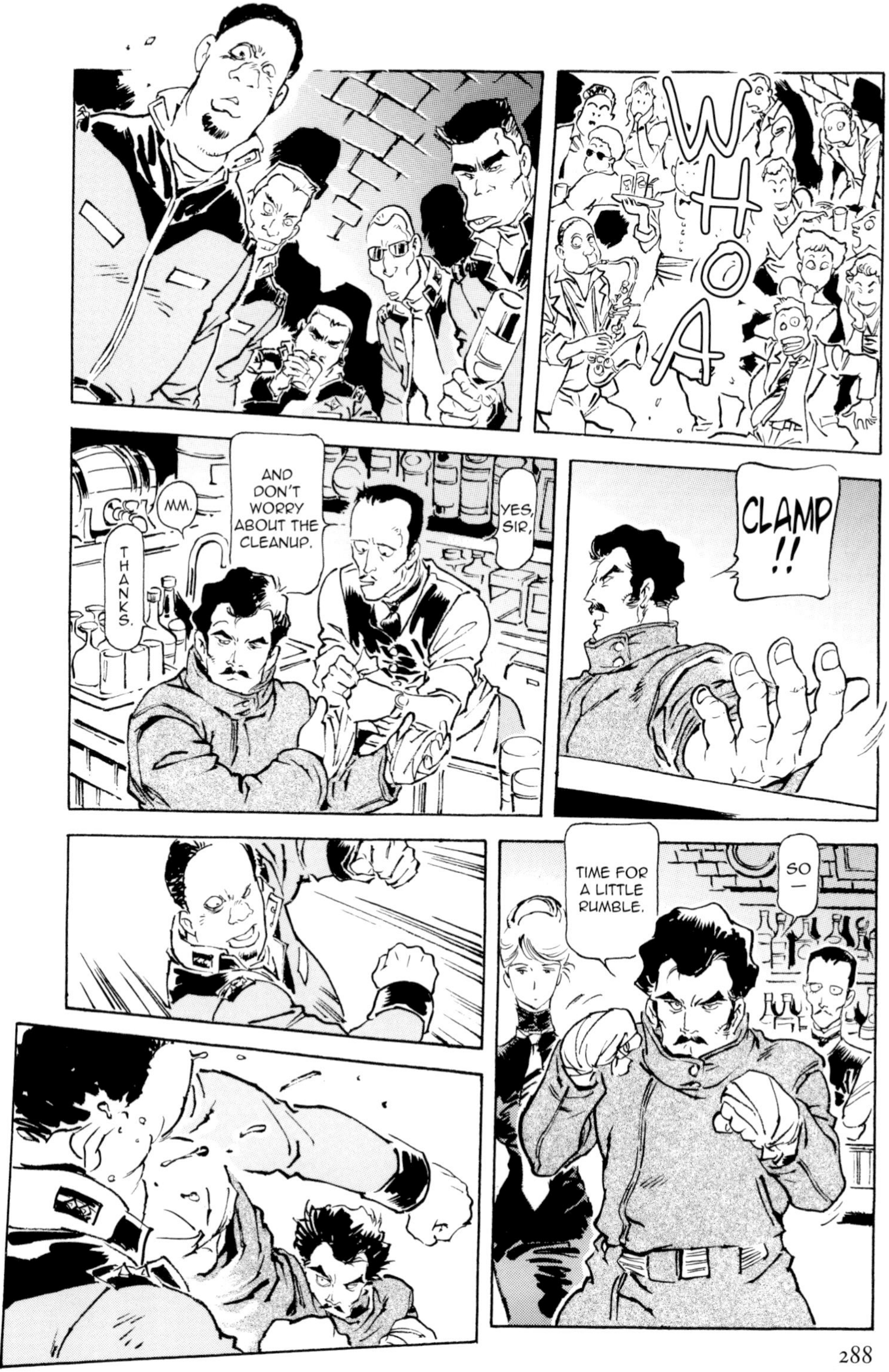
WHOA
CLAMP !!
YES, SIR,
AND DON'T WORRY ABOUT THE CLEANUP.
MM.
THANKS.
SO—
TIME FOR A LITTLE RUMBLE.

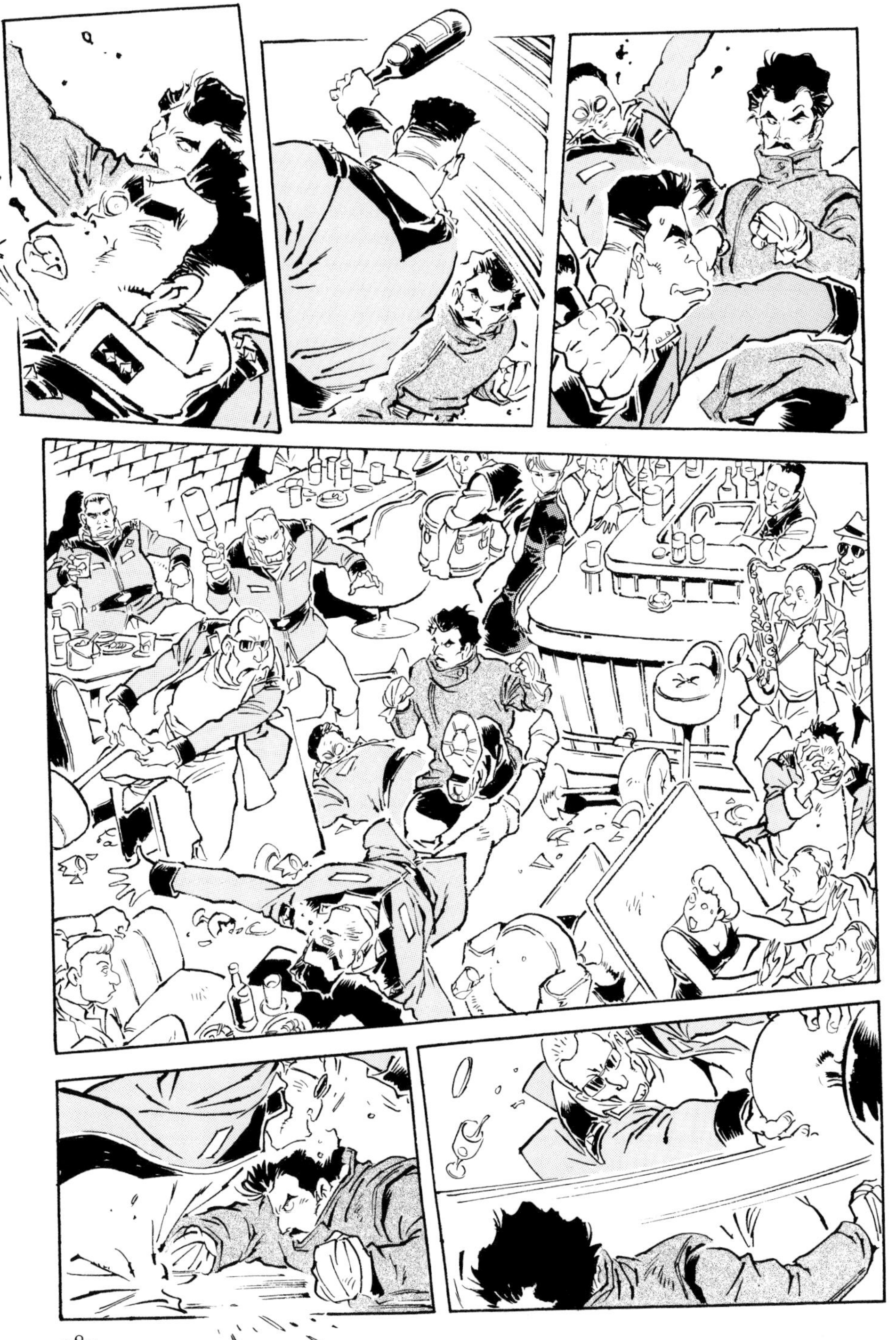

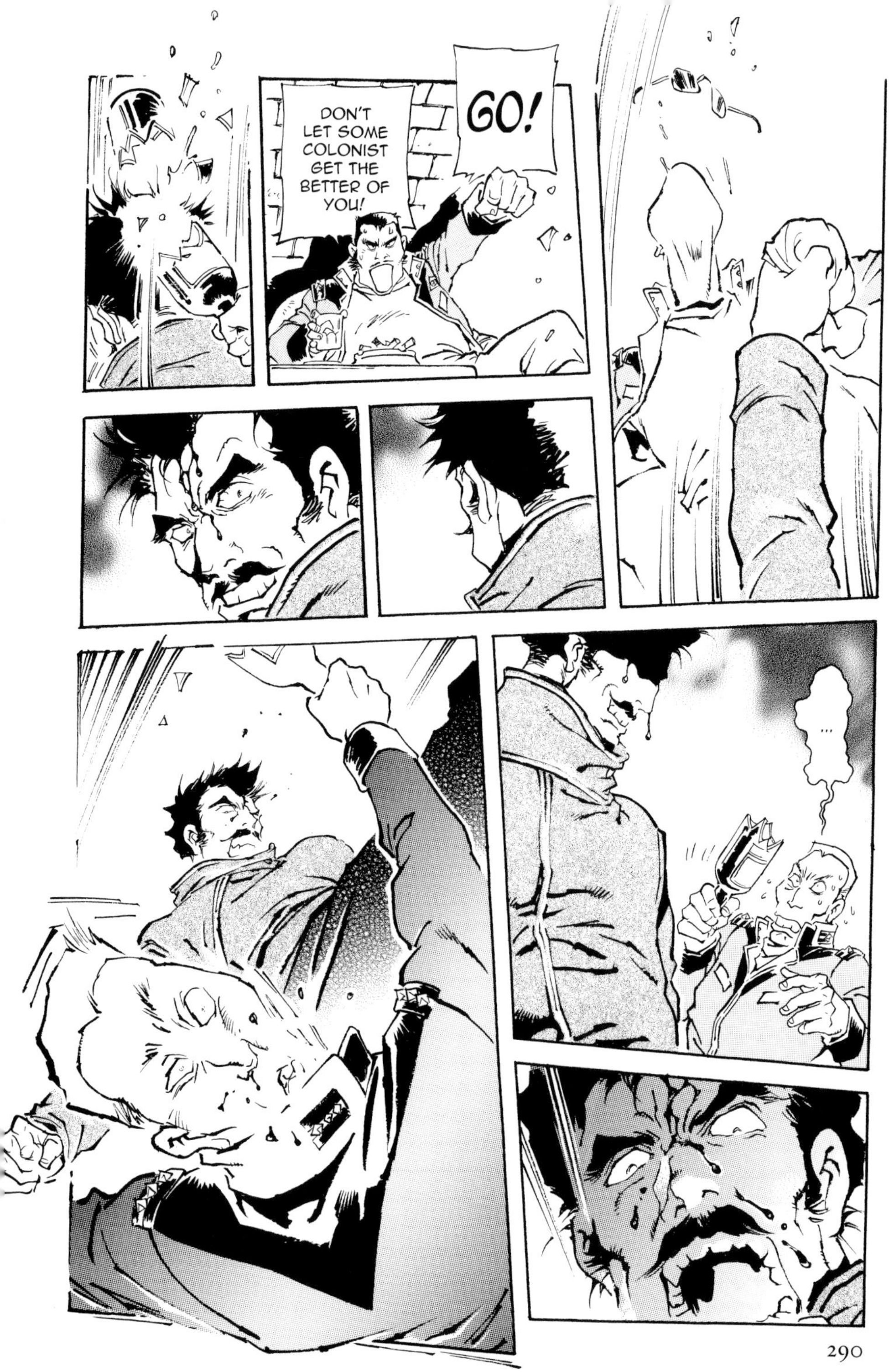
GO!
DON'T LET SOME COLONIST GET THE BETTER OF YOU!
...

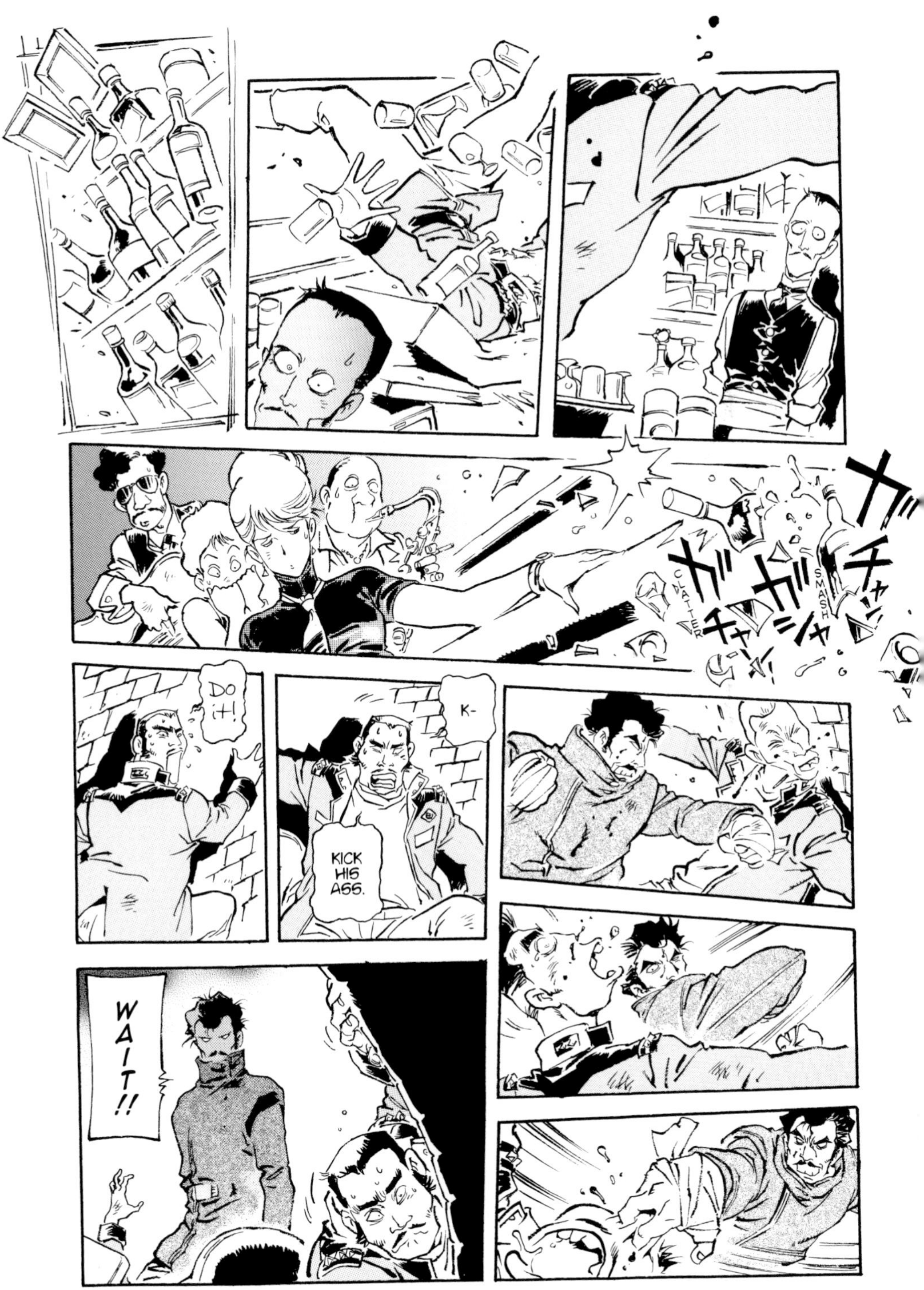
SMASH
CLATTER
K-
KICK HIS ASS.
DO IT!
WAIT!!

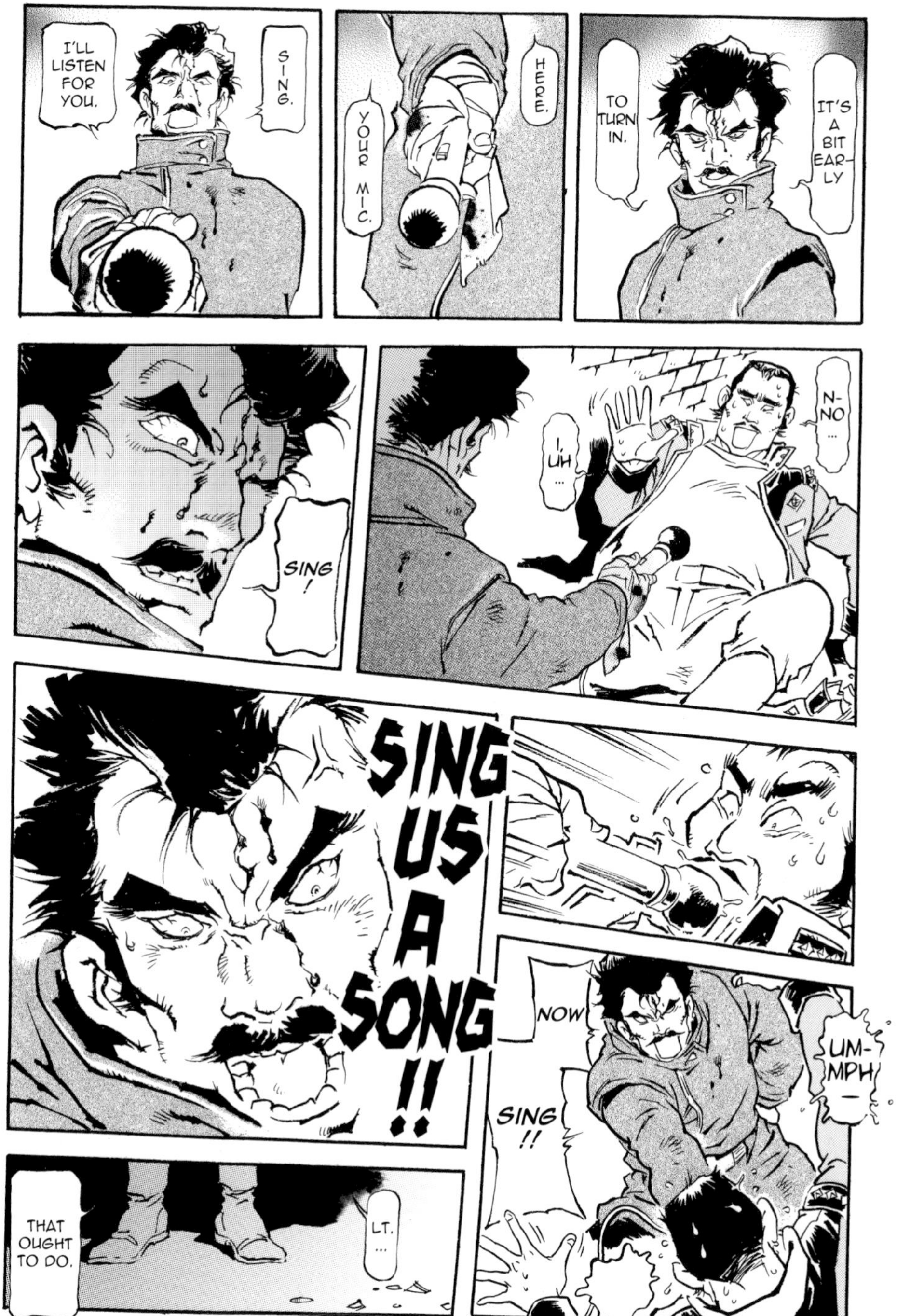
IT'S A BIT EARLY
TO TURN IN.
HERE.
YOUR MIC.
SING.
I'LL LISTEN FOR YOU.
N-NO...
I, UH...
SING!
SING US A SONG!!
UM-MPH—
NOW
SING!!
LT. ...
THAT OUGHT TO DO.

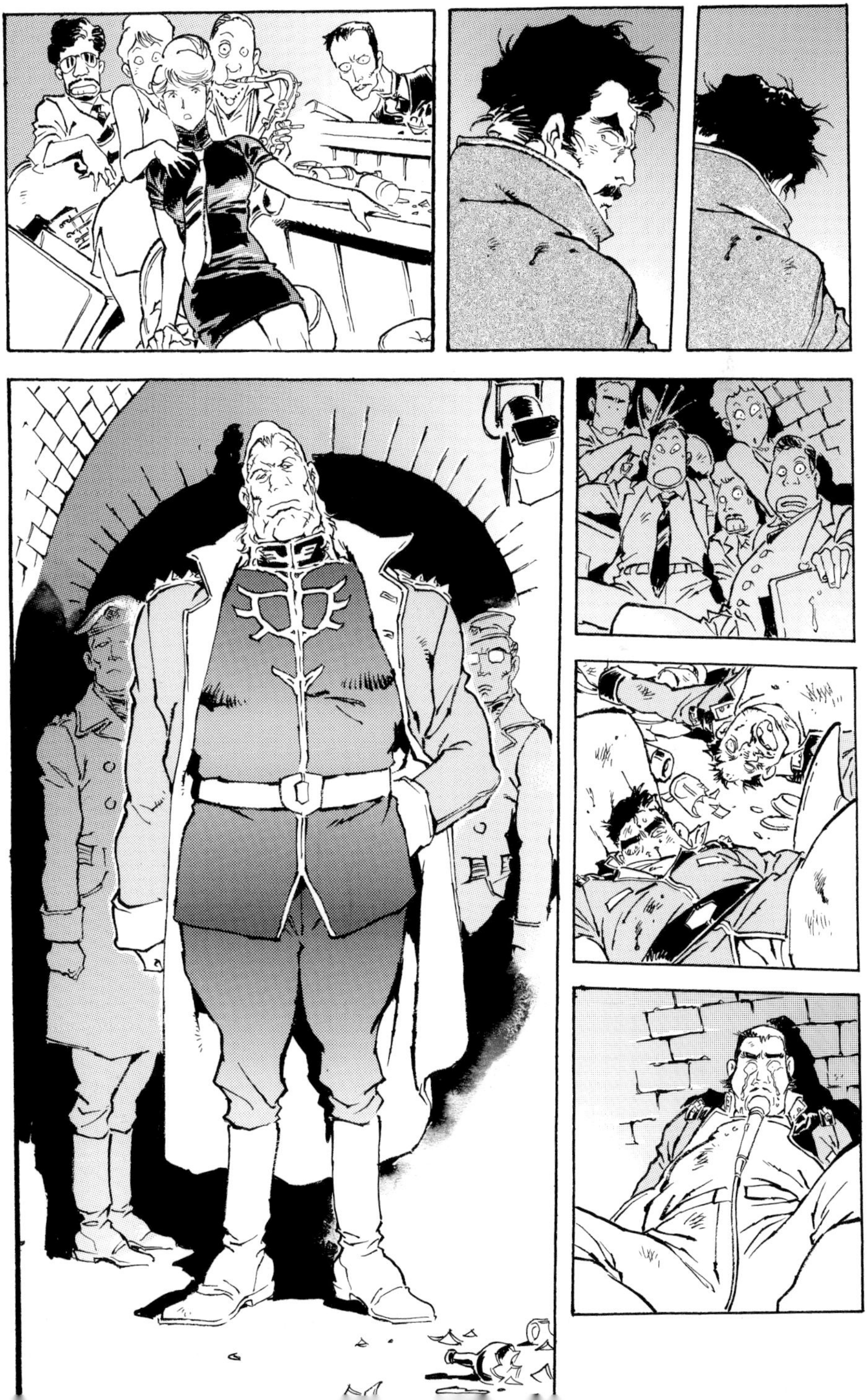

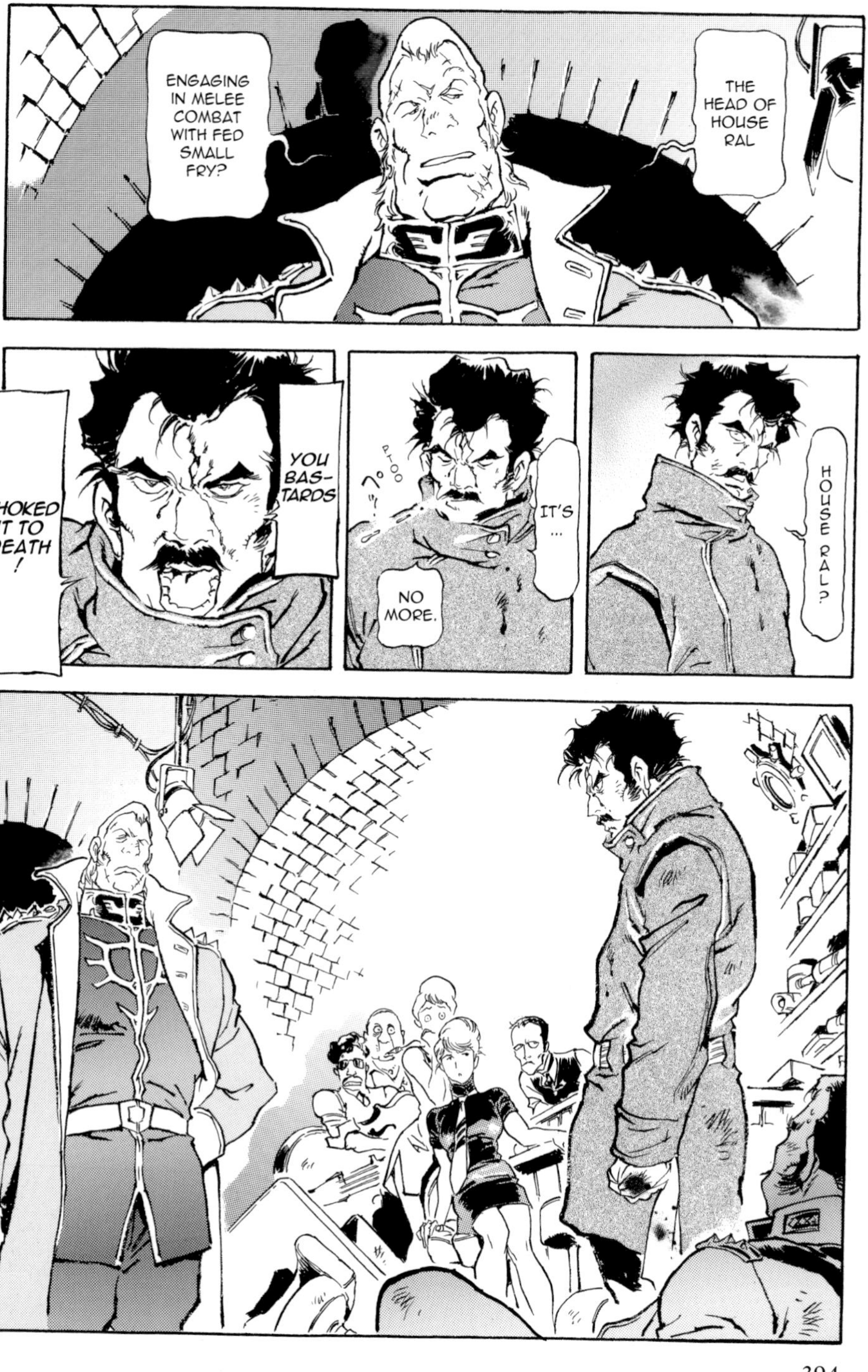
THE HEAD OF HOUSE RAL
ENGAGING IN MELEE COMBAT WITH FED SMALL FRY?
HOUSE RAL?
IT'S ...
NO MORE.
PTOO
YOU BASTARDS
CHOKED IT TO DEATH!

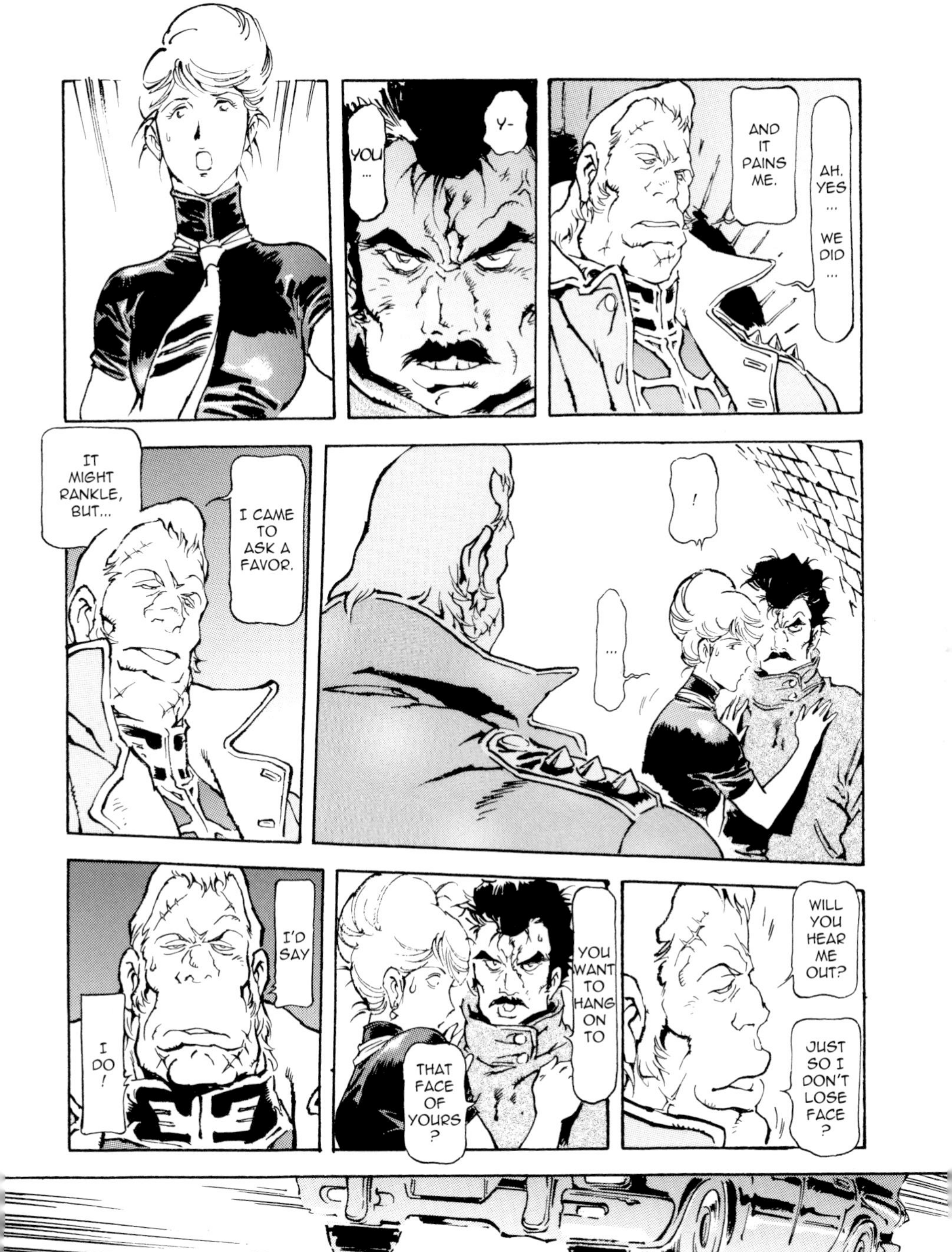
AH. YES ... WE DID ...
AND IT PAINS ME.
Y-
YOU ...
IT MIGHT RANKLE, BUT...
I CAME TO ASK A FAVOR.
!
...
WILL YOU HEAR ME OUT?
JUST SO I DON'T LOSE FACE?
YOU WANT TO HANG ON TO
THAT FACE OF YOURS?
I'D SAY
I DO!

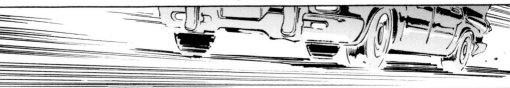

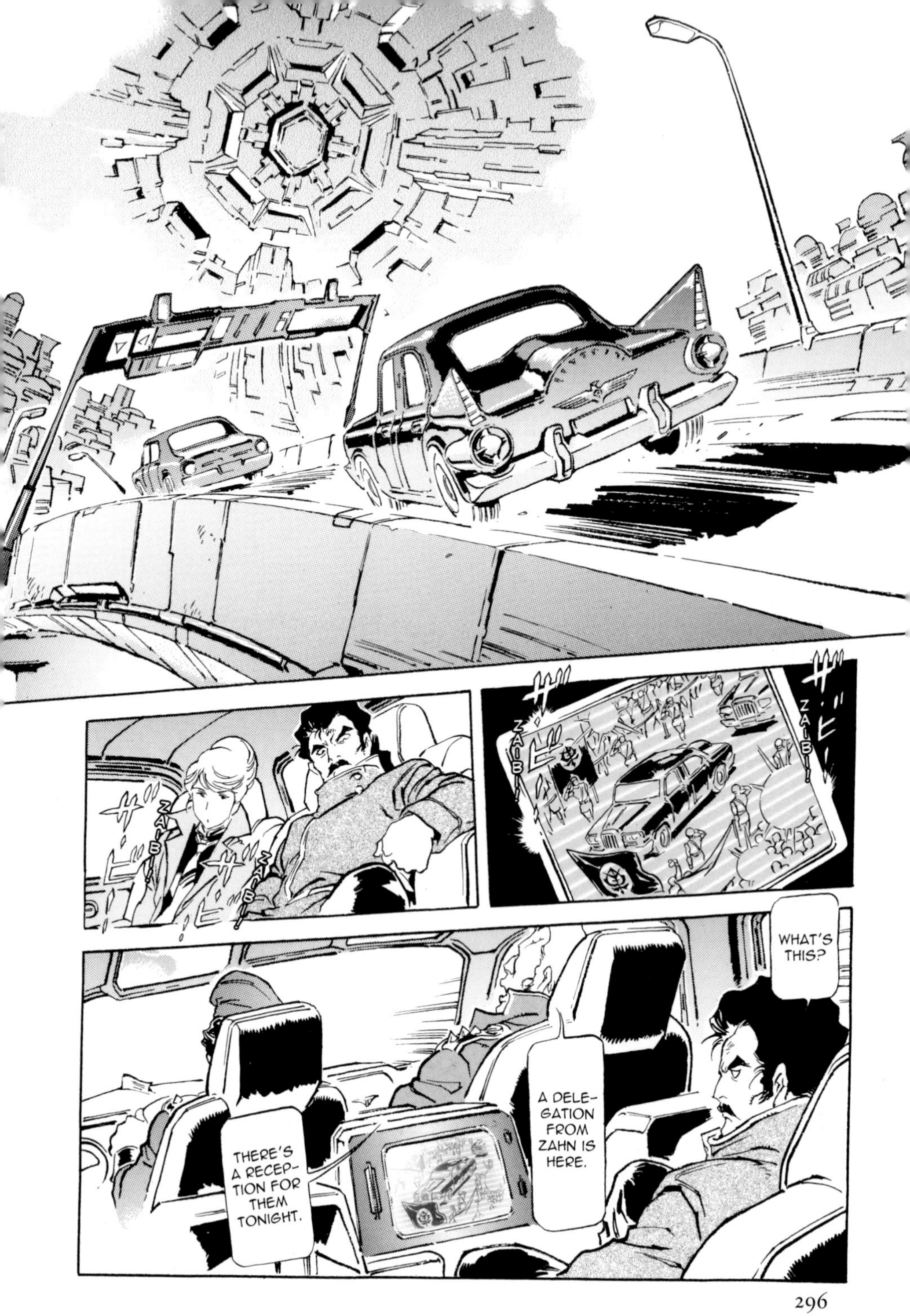
ZAIBI!
ZAIBI!
ZAIBI!
ZAIBI!
WHAT'S THIS?
A DELEGATION FROM ZAHN IS HERE.
THERE'S A RECEPTION FOR THEM TONIGHT.

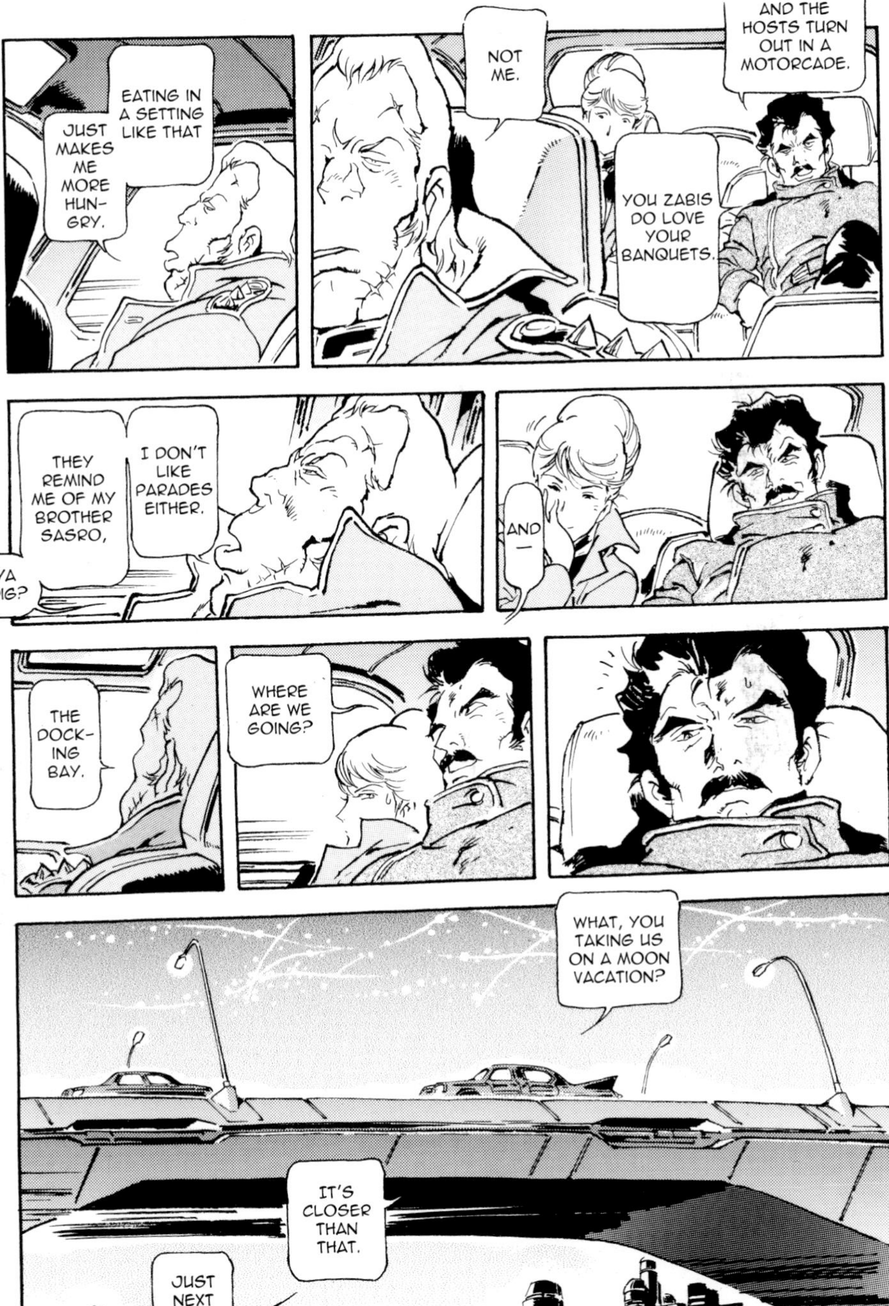
YOU ZABIS DO LOVE YOUR BANQUETS.
AND THE HOSTS TURN OUT IN A MOTORCADE.
NOT ME.
EATING IN A SETTING LIKE THAT
JUST MAKES ME MORE HUN-GRY.
AND—
I DON'T LIKE PARADES EITHER.
THEY REMIND ME OF MY BROTHER SASRO,
YA DIG?
WHERE ARE WE GOING?
THE DOCK-ING BAY.
WHAT, YOU TAKING US ON A MOON VACATION?
IT'S CLOSER THAN THAT.
JUST NEXT DOOR.

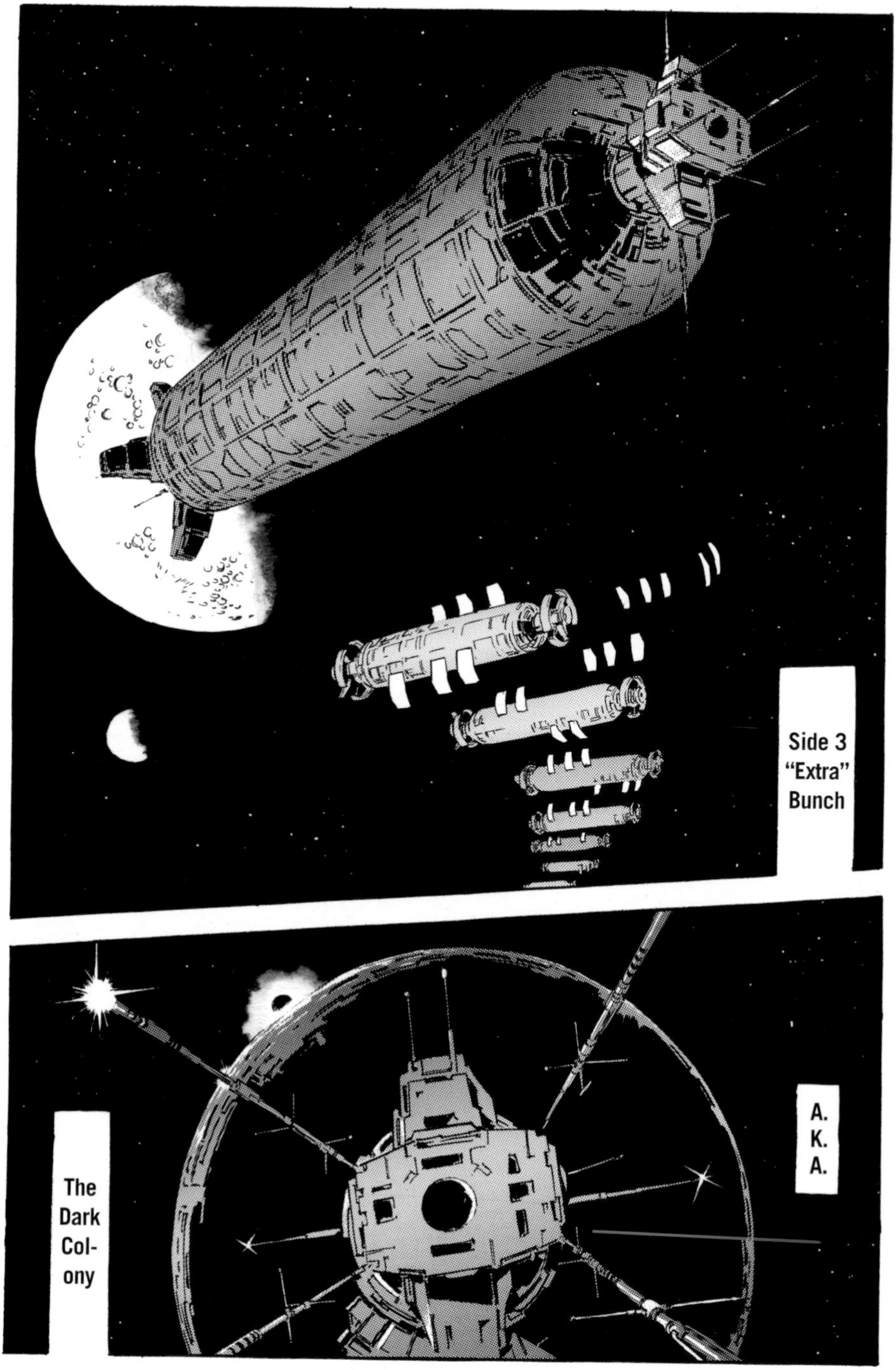
Side 3 "Extra" Bunch
A. K. A.
The Dark Col-ony

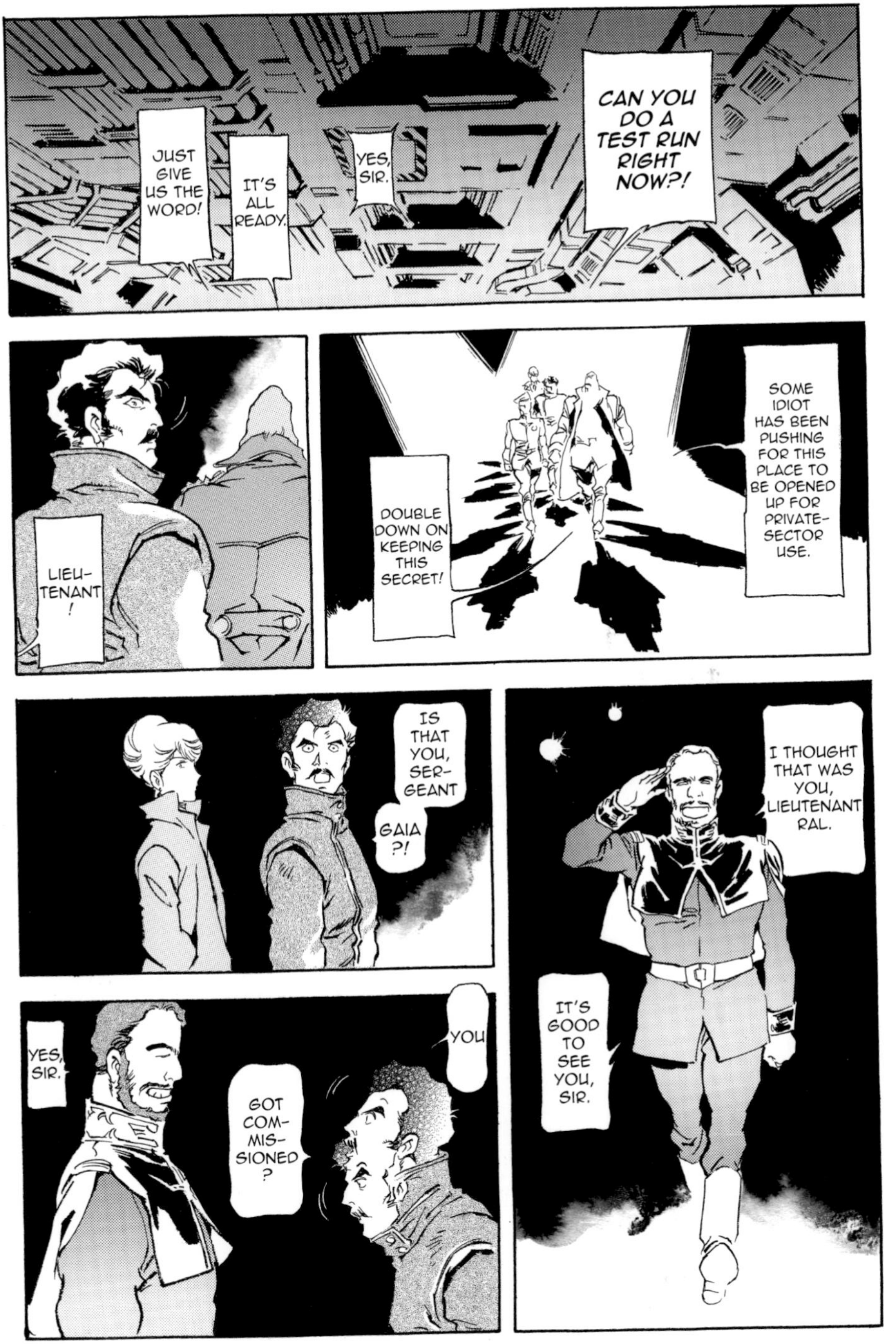

CAN YOU DO A TEST RUN RIGHT NOW?!
YES, SIR.
IT'S ALL READY.
JUST GIVE US THE WORD!
SOME IDIOT HAS BEEN PUSHING FOR THIS PLACE TO BE OPENED UP FOR PRIVATE-SECTOR USE.
DOUBLE DOWN ON KEEPING THIS SECRET!
LIEUTENANT!
I THOUGHT THAT WAS YOU, LIEUTENANT RAL.
IT'S GOOD TO SEE YOU, SIR.
IS THAT YOU, SERGEANT
GAIA?!
YOU
GOT COMMISIONED?
YES, SIR.

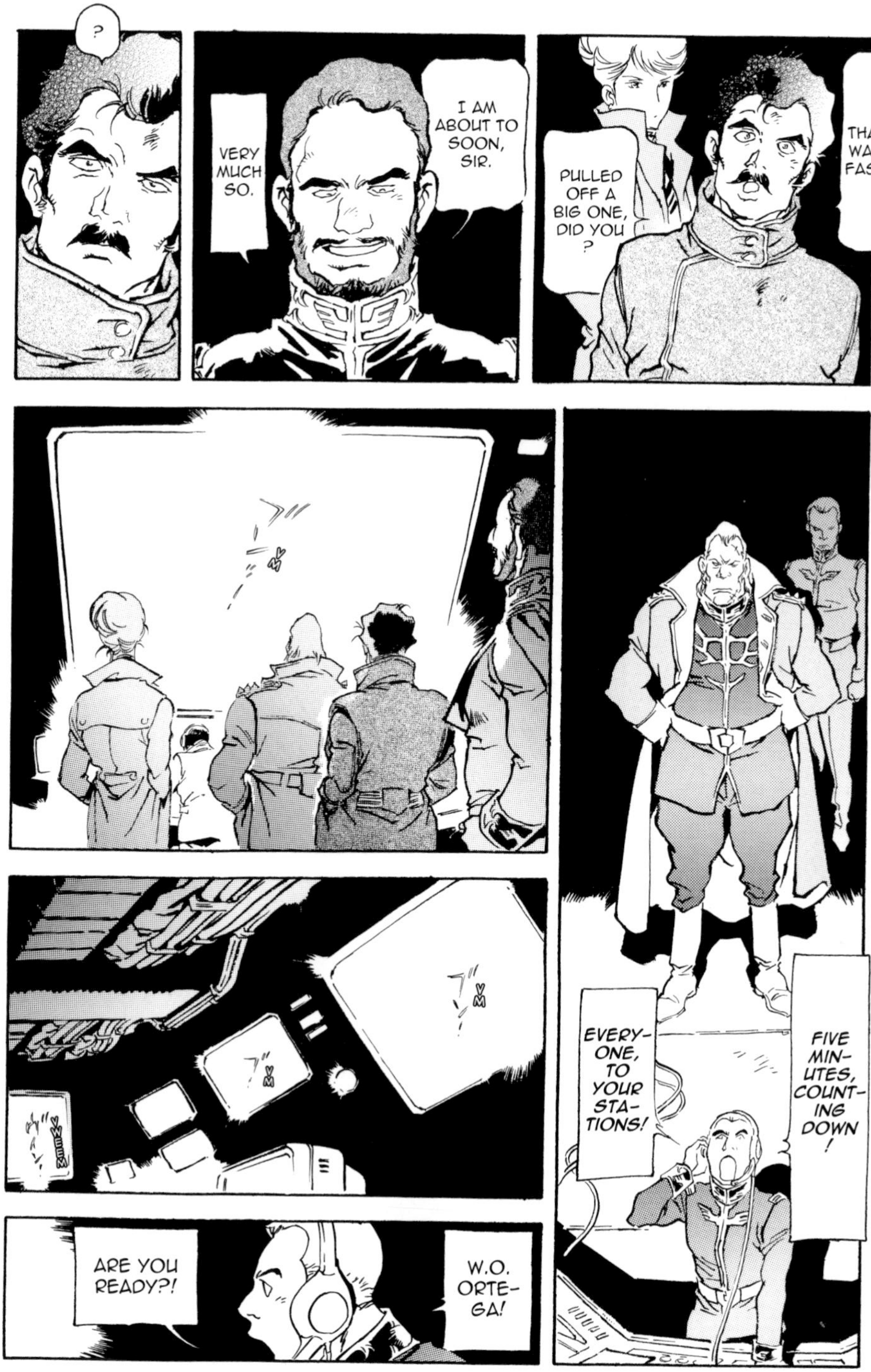
THAT WAS FAST.
PULLED OFF A BIG ONE, DID YOU?
I AM ABOUT TO SOON, SIR.
VERY MUCH SO.
?
FIVE MINUTES, COUNTING DOWN!
EVERYONE, TO YOUR STATIONS!
VM
VM
VM
VVEEM
W.O. ORTEGA!
ARE YOU READY?!

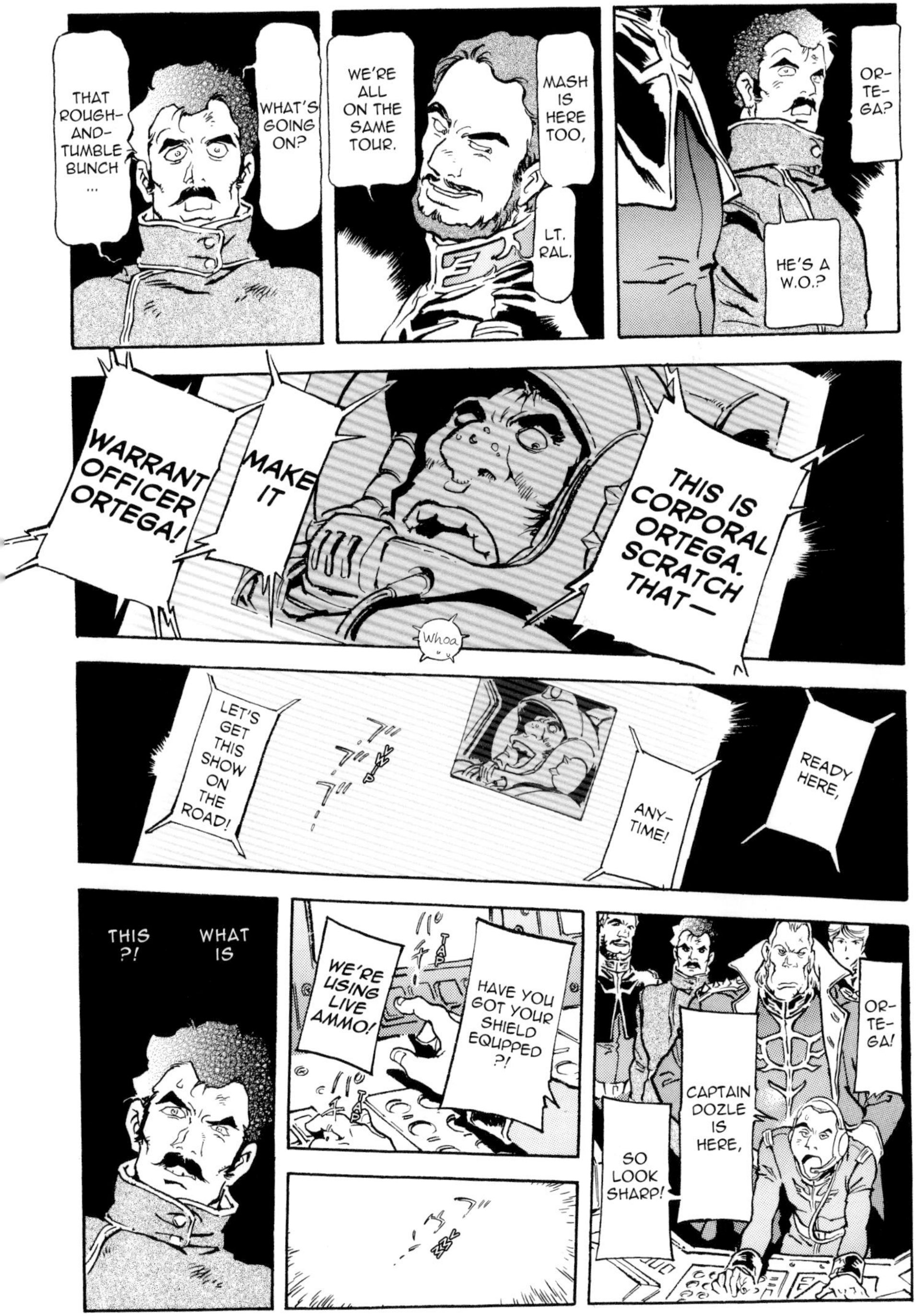
OR-TE-GA?
HE'S A W.O.?
MASH IS HERE TOO,
LT. RAL.
WE'RE ALL ON THE SAME TOUR.
WHAT'S GOING ON?
THAT ROUGH-AND-TUMBLE BUNCH ...
THIS IS CORPORAL ORTEGA. SCRATCH THAT—
MAKE IT
WARRANT OFFICER ORTEGA!
Whoa
READY HERE,
ANY-TIME!
LET'S GET THIS SHOW ON THE ROAD!
OR-TE-GA!
CAPTAIN DOZLE IS HERE,
SO LOOK SHARP!
HAVE YOU GOT YOUR SHIELD EQUPPED ?!
WE'RE USING LIVE AMMO!
WHAT IS THIS ?!

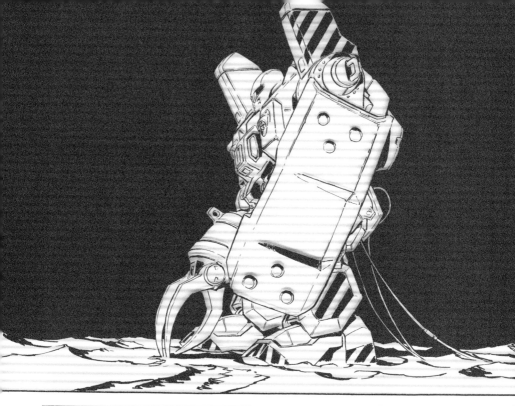

MODEL 01.

THE MOBILE WORKER.

WE WILL CRUSH THE FED-ERATION ...

WITH THIS!

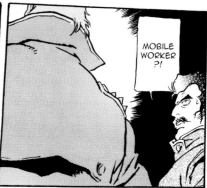

MOBILE WORKER ?!

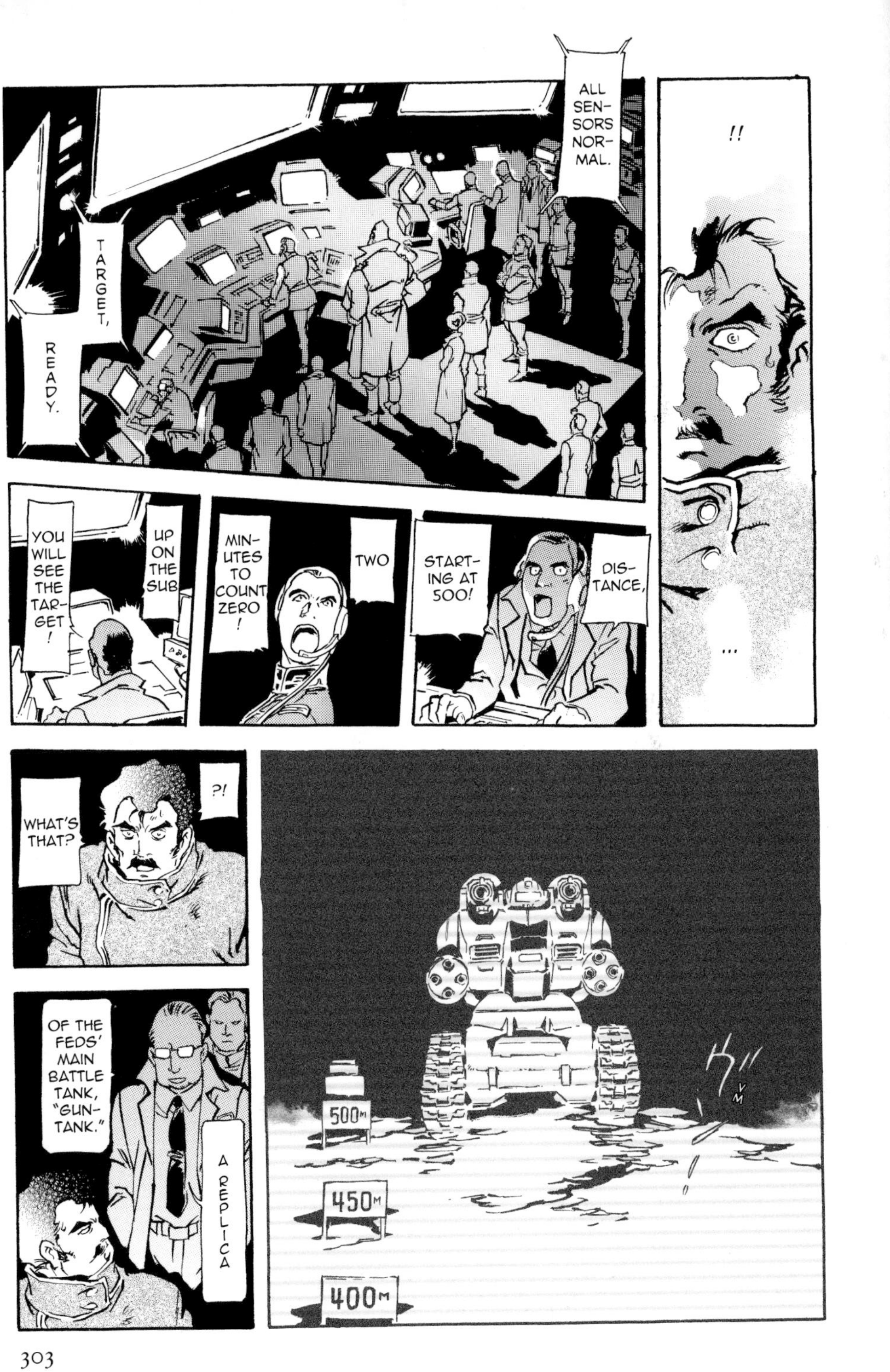
!!
...
ALL SEN-SORS NOR-MAL.
TARGET, READY.
DIS-TANCE,
START-ING AT 500!
TWO
MIN-UTES TO COUNT ZERO!
UP ON THE SUB
YOU WILL SEE THE TAR-GET!
500M
450M
400M
?!
WHAT'S THAT?
A REPLICA
OF THE FEDS' MAIN BATTLE TANK, "GUN-TANK."

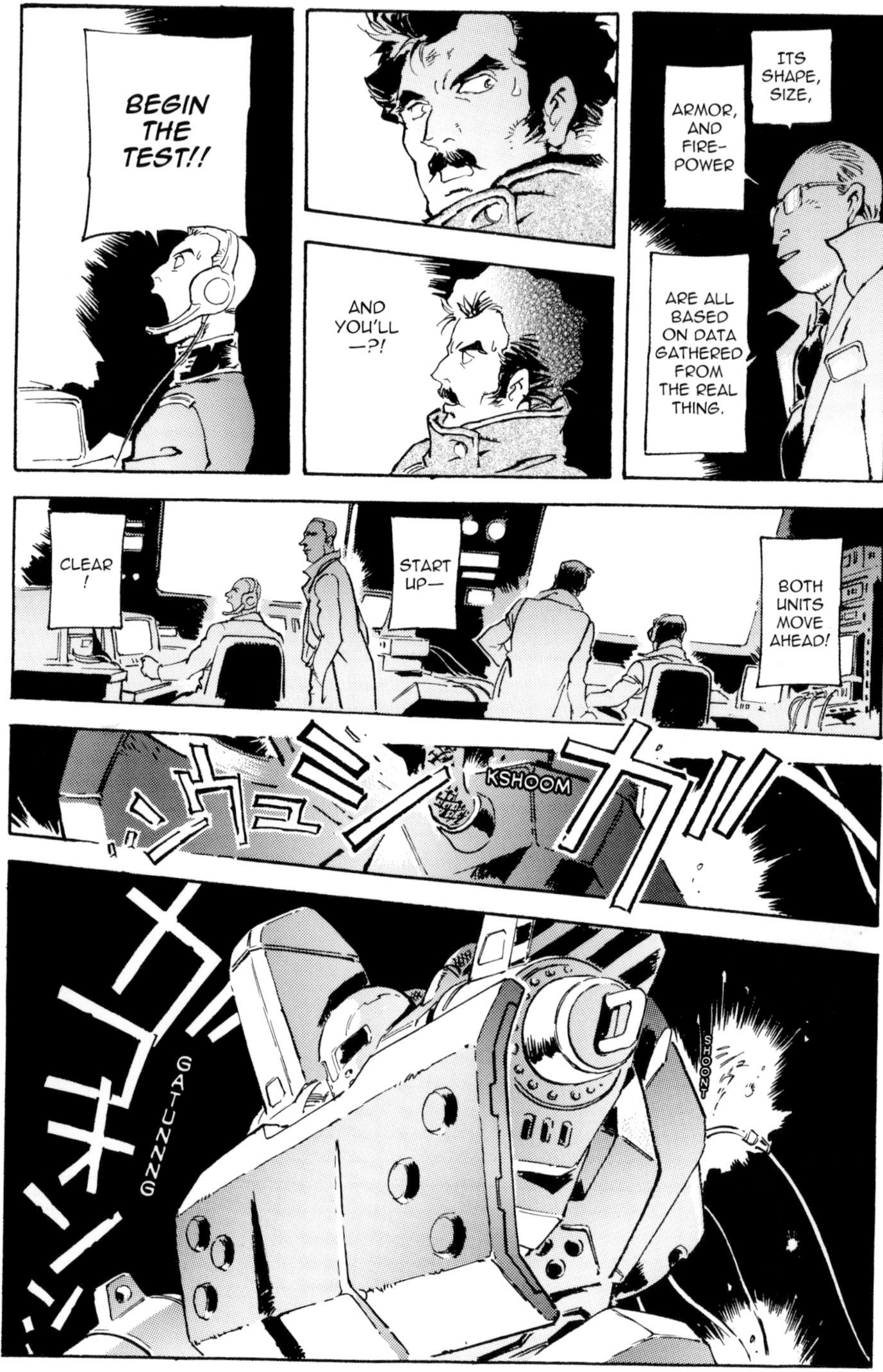
ITS SHAPE, SIZE,
ARMOR, AND FIRE-POWER
ARE ALL BASED ON DATA GATHERED FROM THE REAL THING.
AND YOU'LL —?!
BEGIN THE TEST!!
BOTH UNITS MOVE AHEAD!
START UP—
CLEAR!
KSHOOM
SHOONT
GATUNNNG

BOMF

THIS IS ITS DEFAULT GAIT.

SPEED, 30 KM/H.

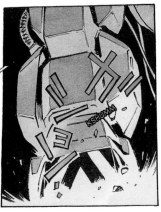

KSHUMM

FIRING VULCANS!

TARGET

DISTANCE 450!

BLAM

BLAM

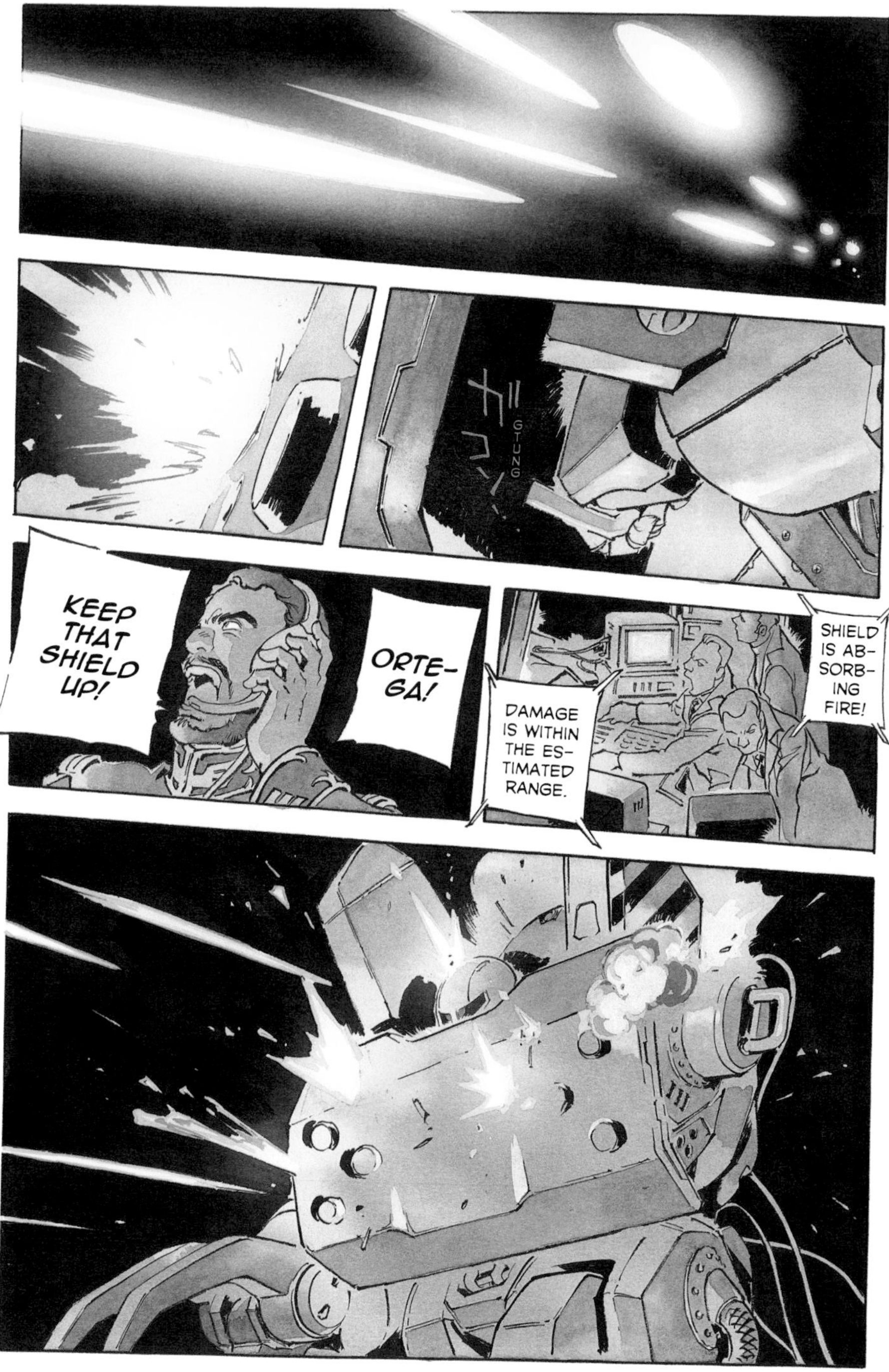
GTUNG
SHIELD IS ABSORBING FIRE!
DAMAGE IS WITHIN THE ESTIMATED RANGE.
ORTEGA!
KEEP THAT SHIELD UP!

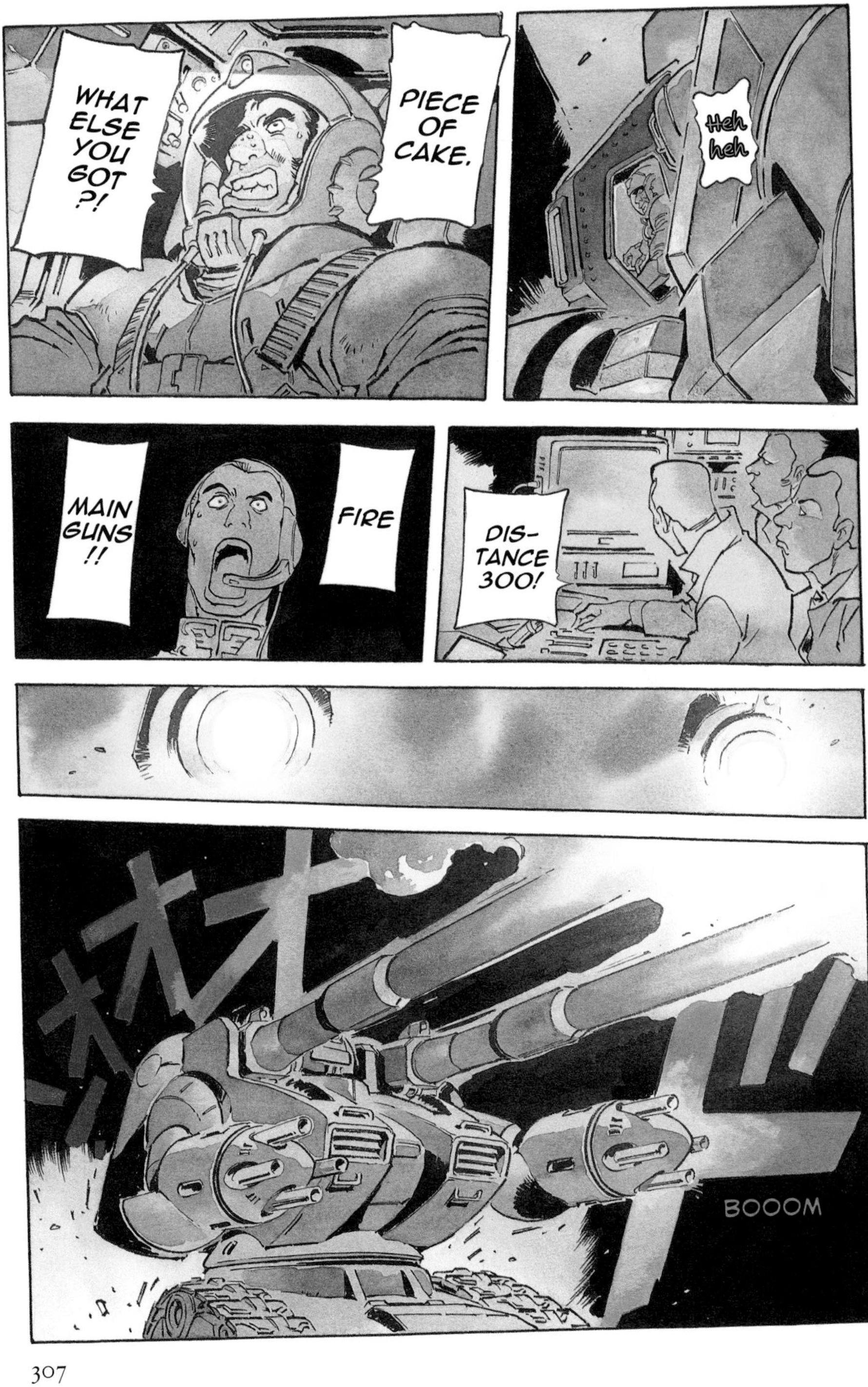
Heh heh
PIECE OF CAKE.
WHAT ELSE YOU GOT?!
DIS-TANCE 300!
FIRE
MAIN GUNS!!
BOOOM

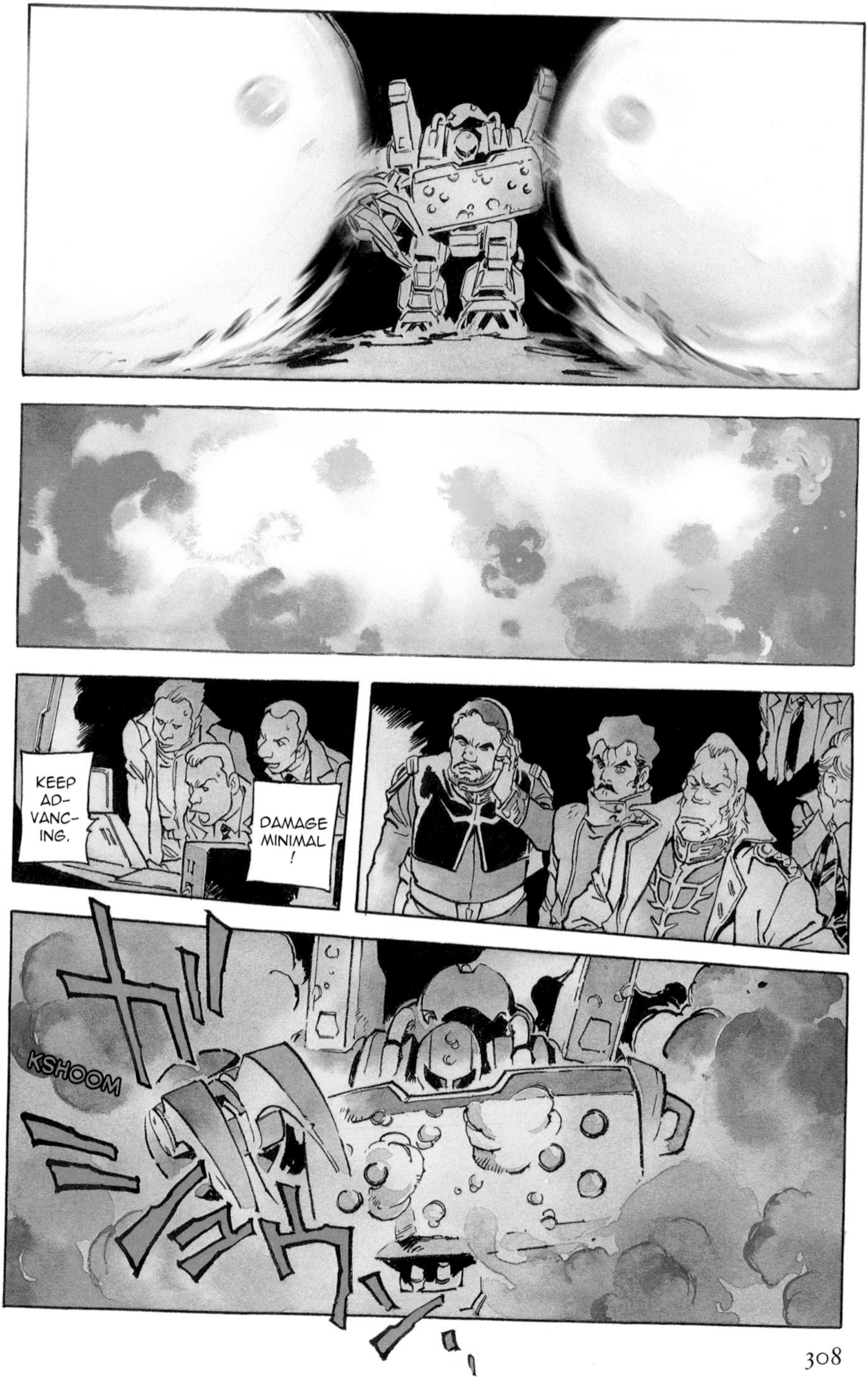
DAMAGE MINIMAL!
KEEP ADVANCING.
KSHOOM

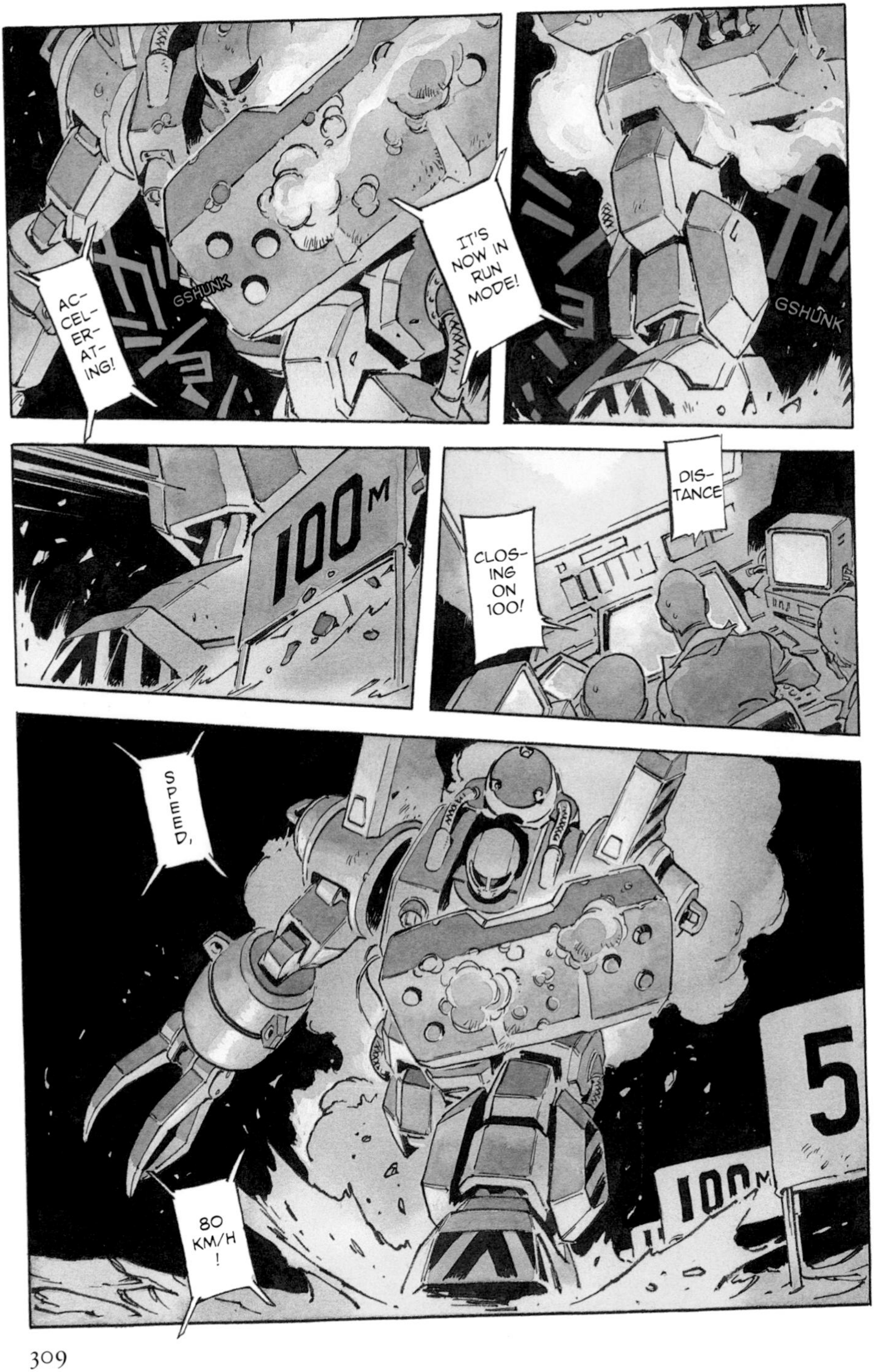
GSHŪNK
IT'S NOW IN RUN MODE!
GSHŪNK
ACCELERATING!
DISTANCE
CLOSING ON 100!
100M
SPEED,
80 KM/H!
5
100M

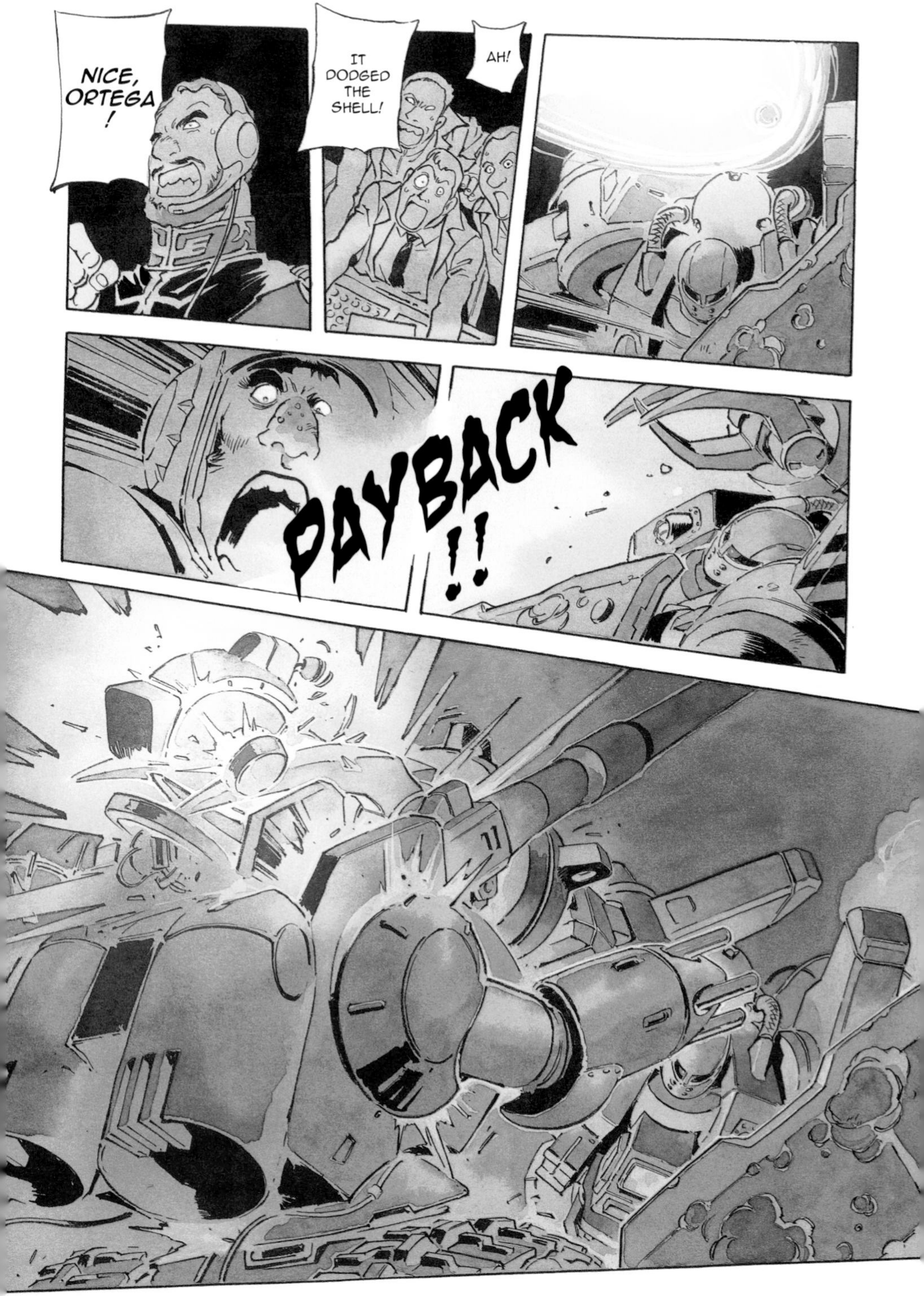
AH!
IT DODGED THE SHELL!
NICE, ORTEGA!
PAYBACK!!

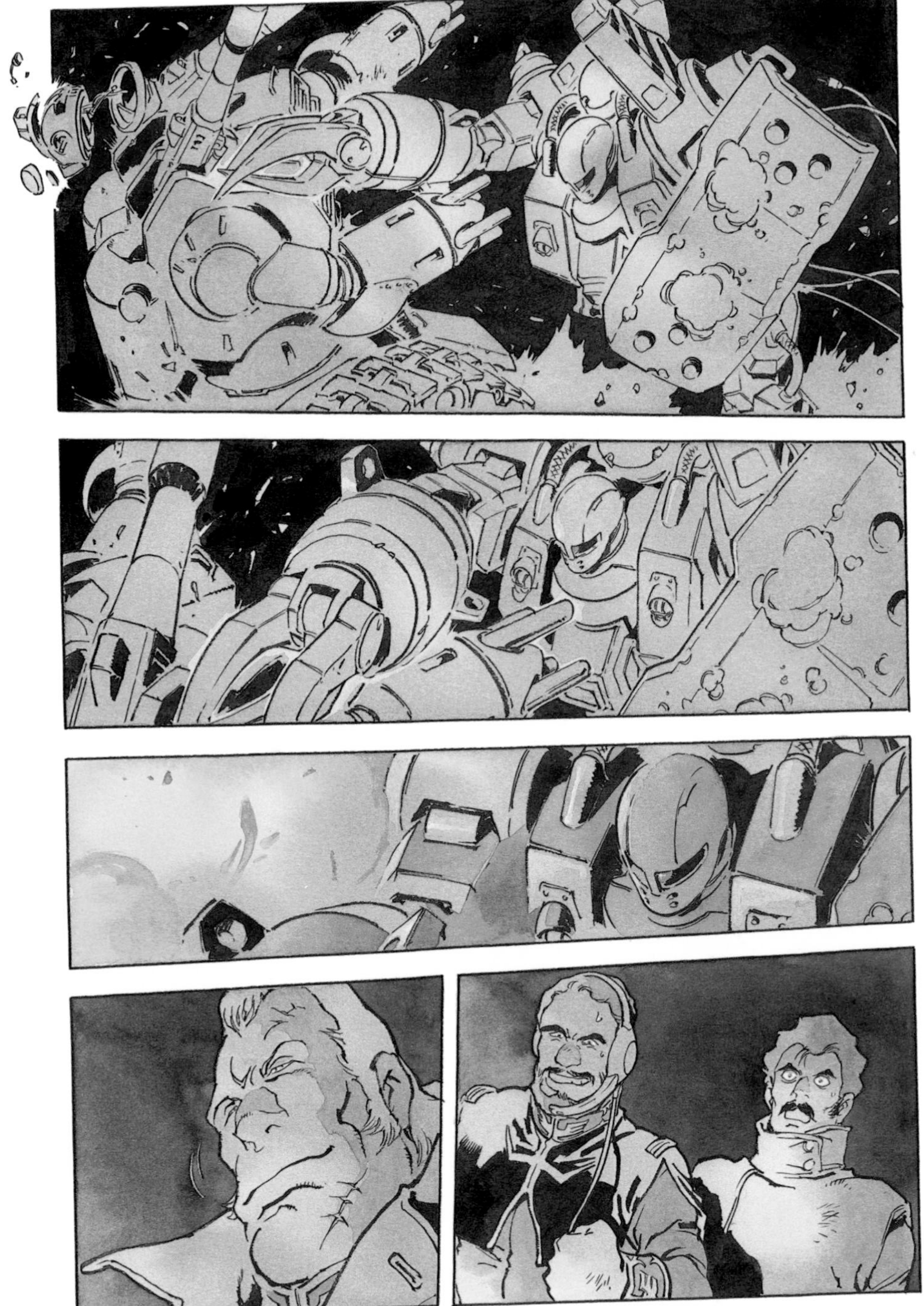

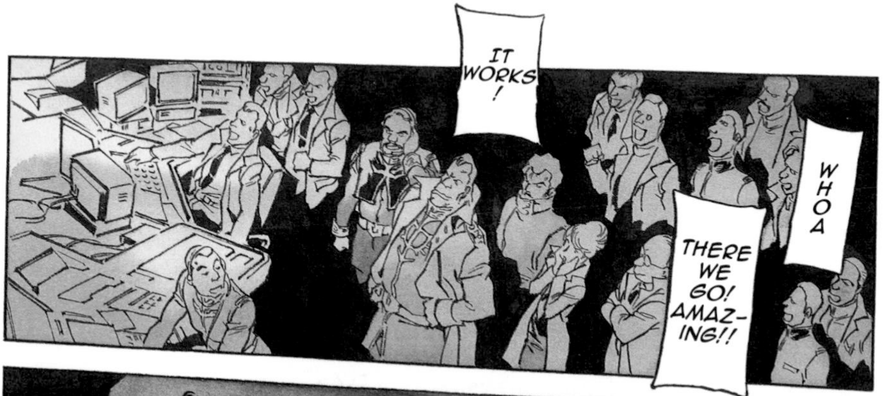
WHOA
THERE WE GO! AMAZ-ING!!
IT WORKS!

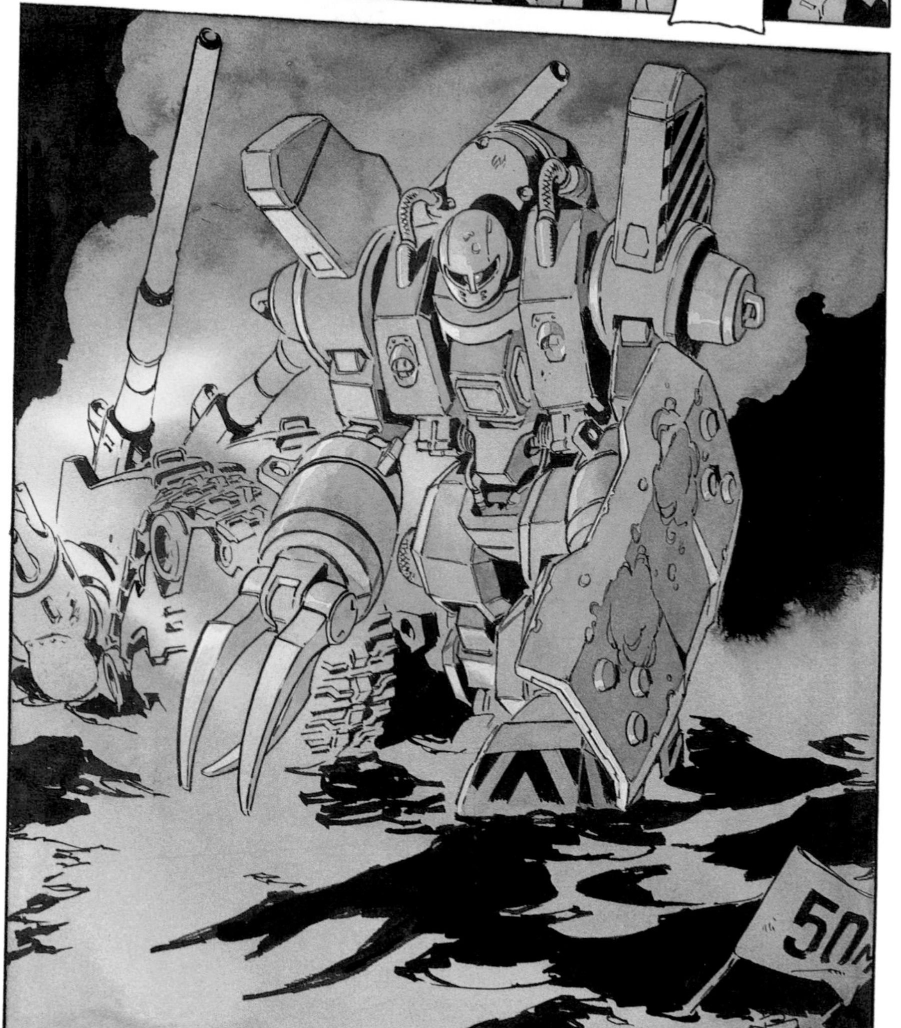

SECTION VII

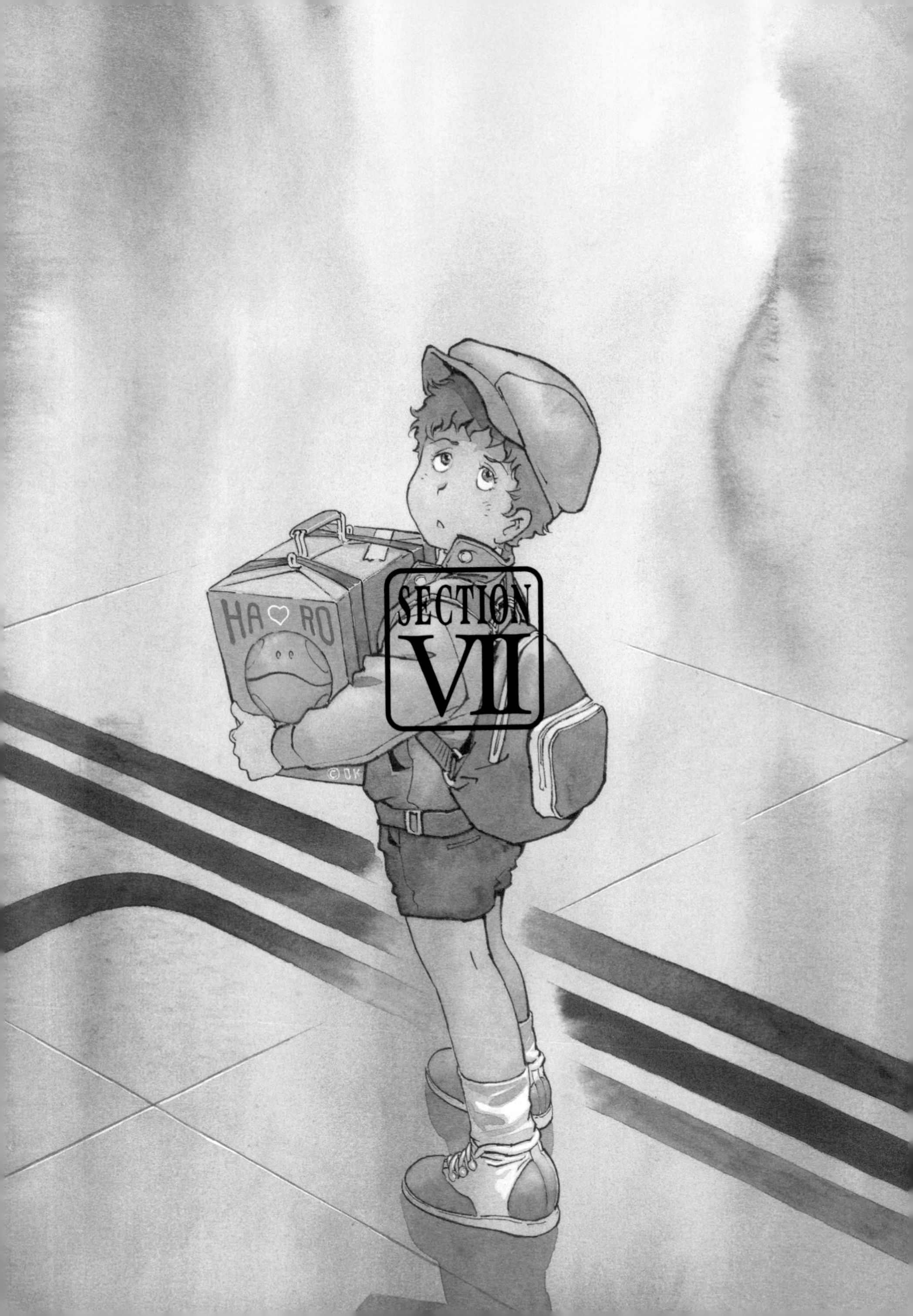
HA♡RO

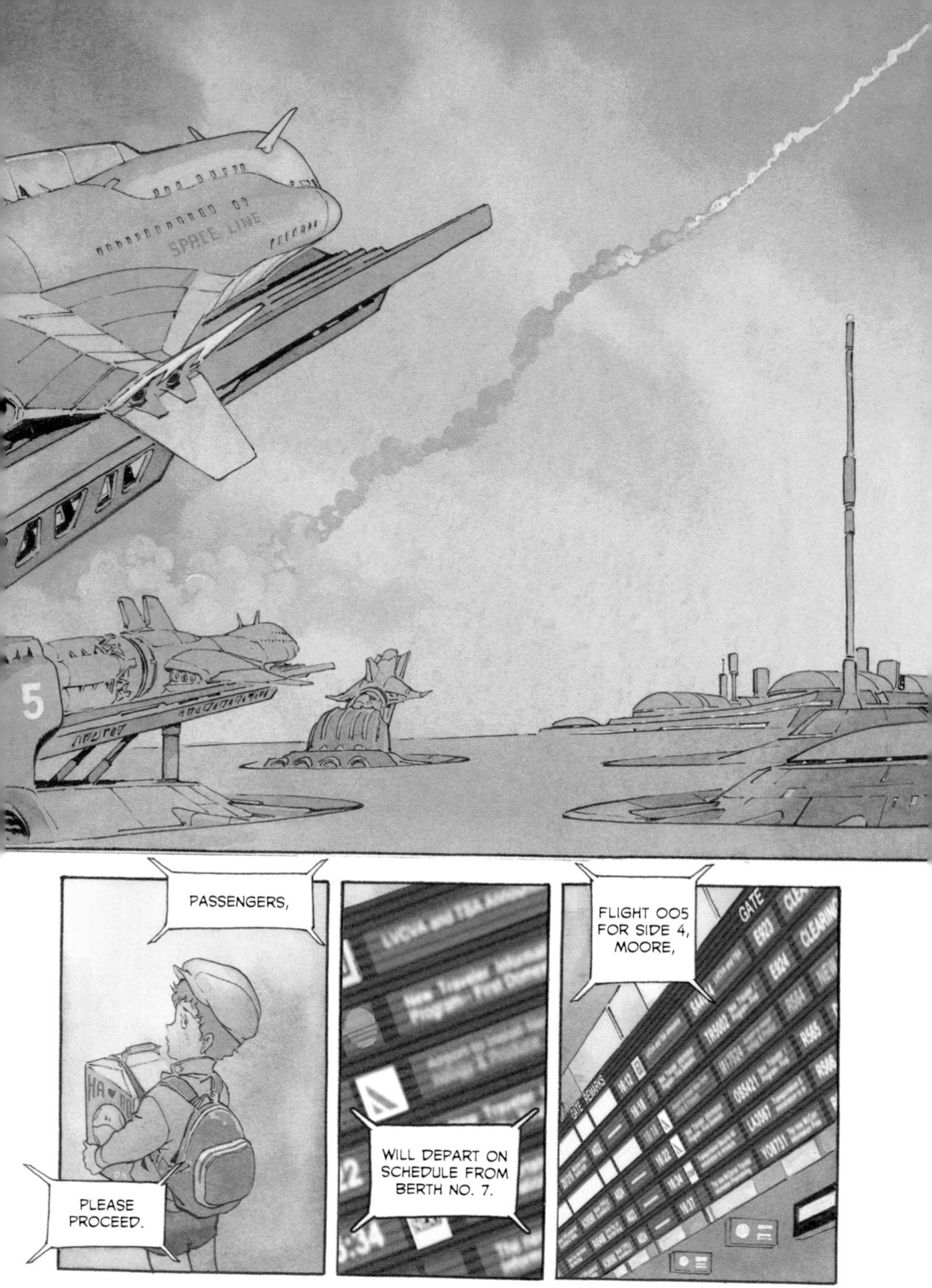
FLIGHT 005 FOR SIDE 4, MOORE,
WILL DEPART ON SCHEDULE FROM BERTH NO. 7.
PASSENGERS,
PLEASE PROCEED.

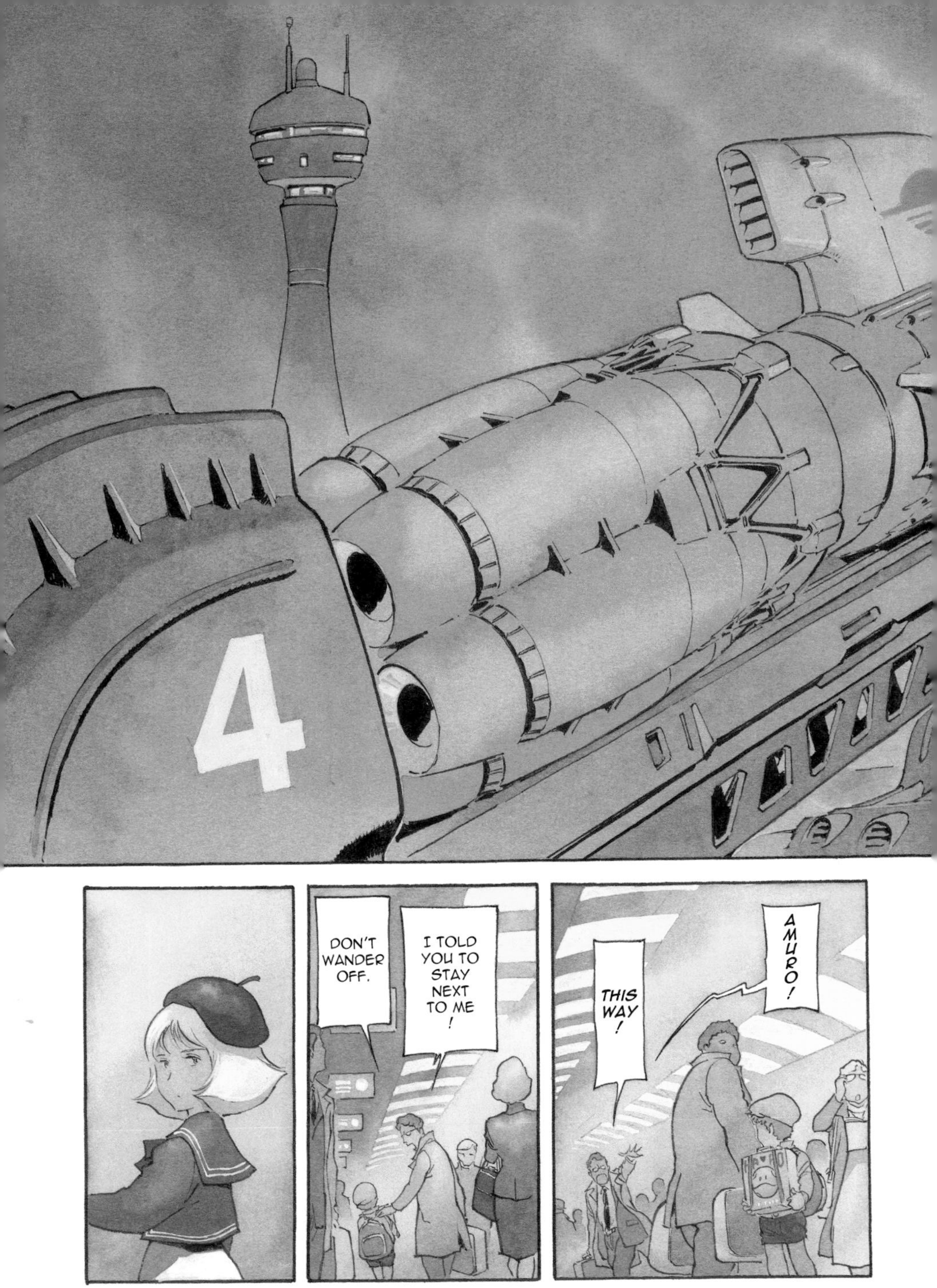
AMURO!
THIS WAY!
I TOLD YOU TO STAY NEXT TO ME!
DON'T WANDER OFF.

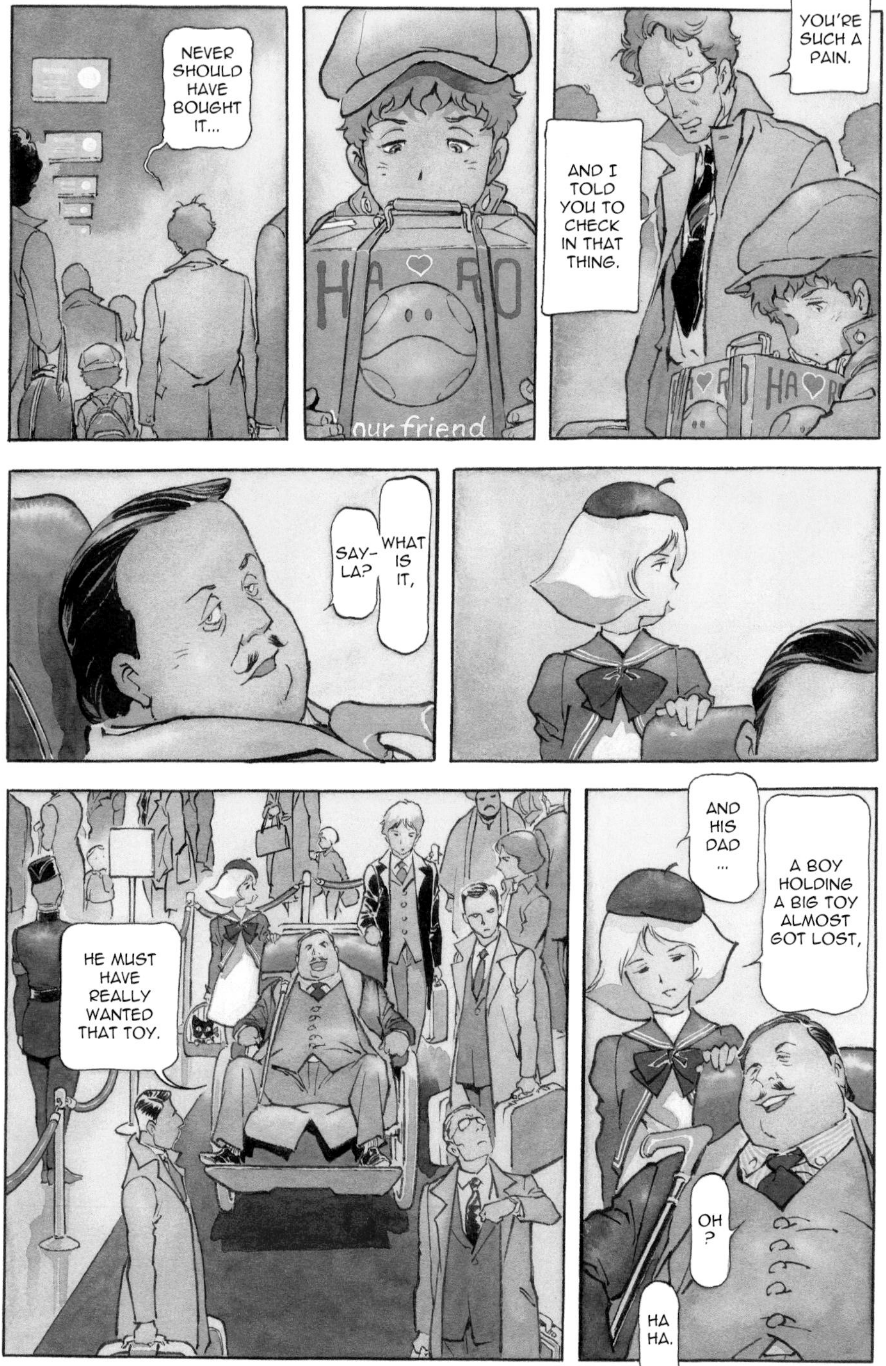
YOU'RE SUCH A PAIN.
AND I TOLD YOU TO CHECK IN THAT THING.
HARO
our friend
NEVER SHOULD HAVE BOUGHT IT...
WHAT IS IT,
SAY-LA?
A BOY HOLDING A BIG TOY ALMOST GOT LOST,
AND HIS DAD...
OH?
HA HA.
HE MUST HAVE REALLY WANTED THAT TOY.

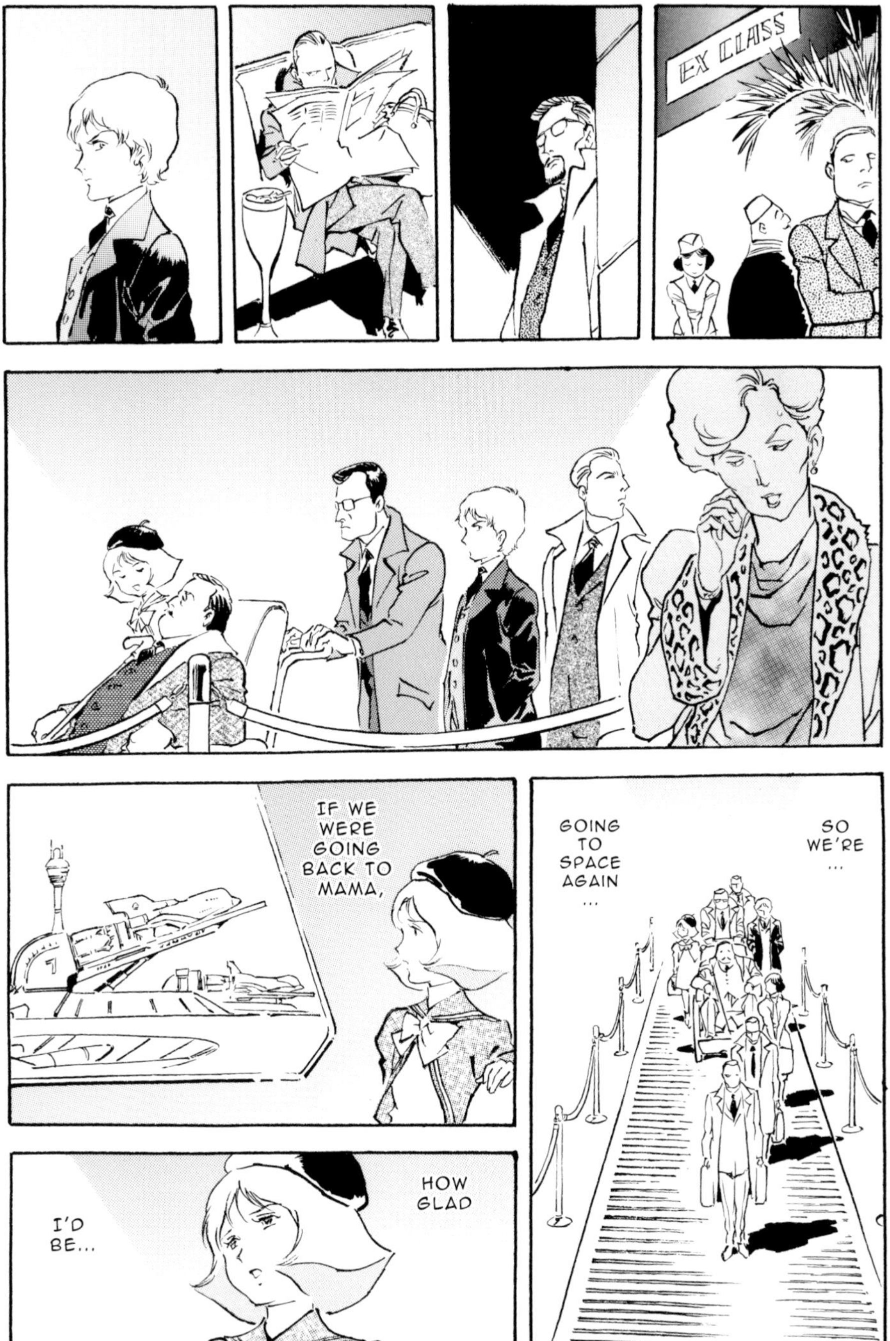
EX CLASS
SO WE'RE ...
GOING TO SPACE AGAIN ...
IF WE WERE GOING BACK TO MAMA,
HOW GLAD
I'D BE...

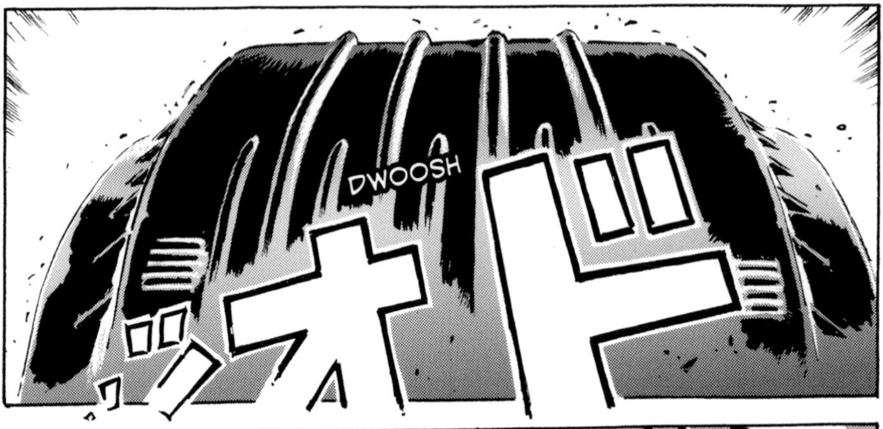
DWOOSH
ドオ
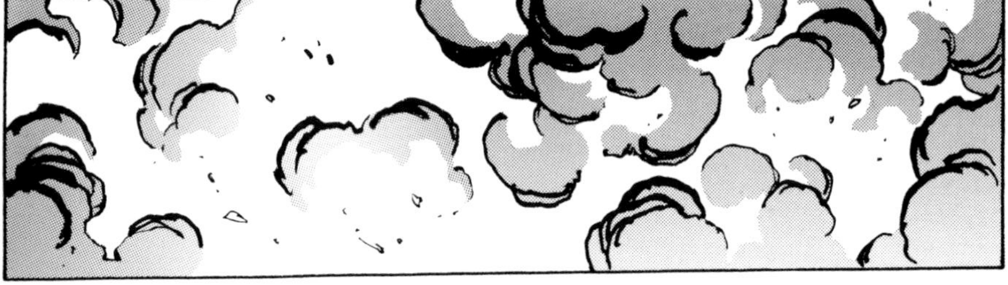
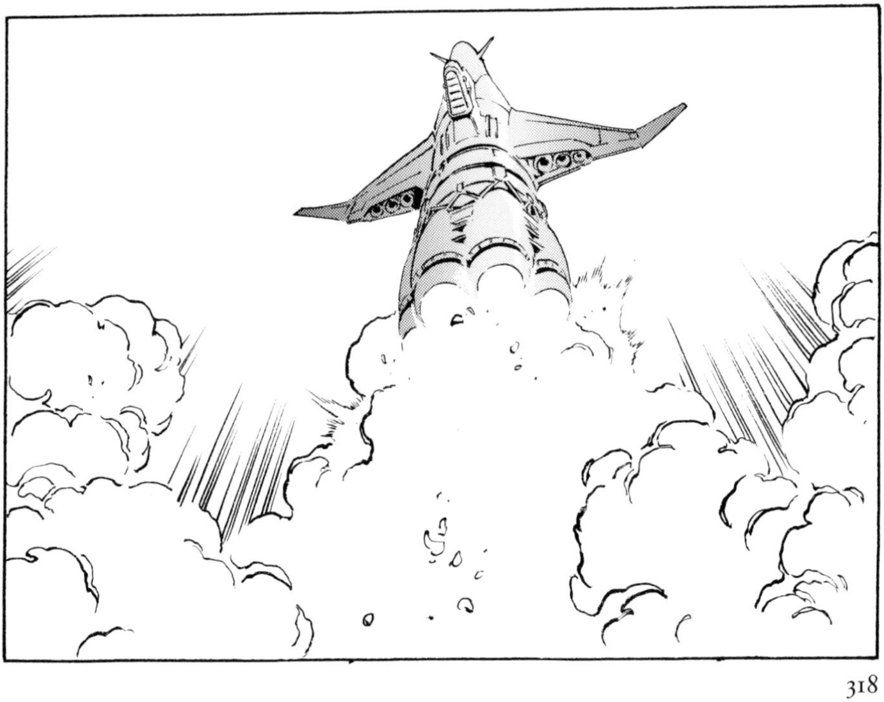

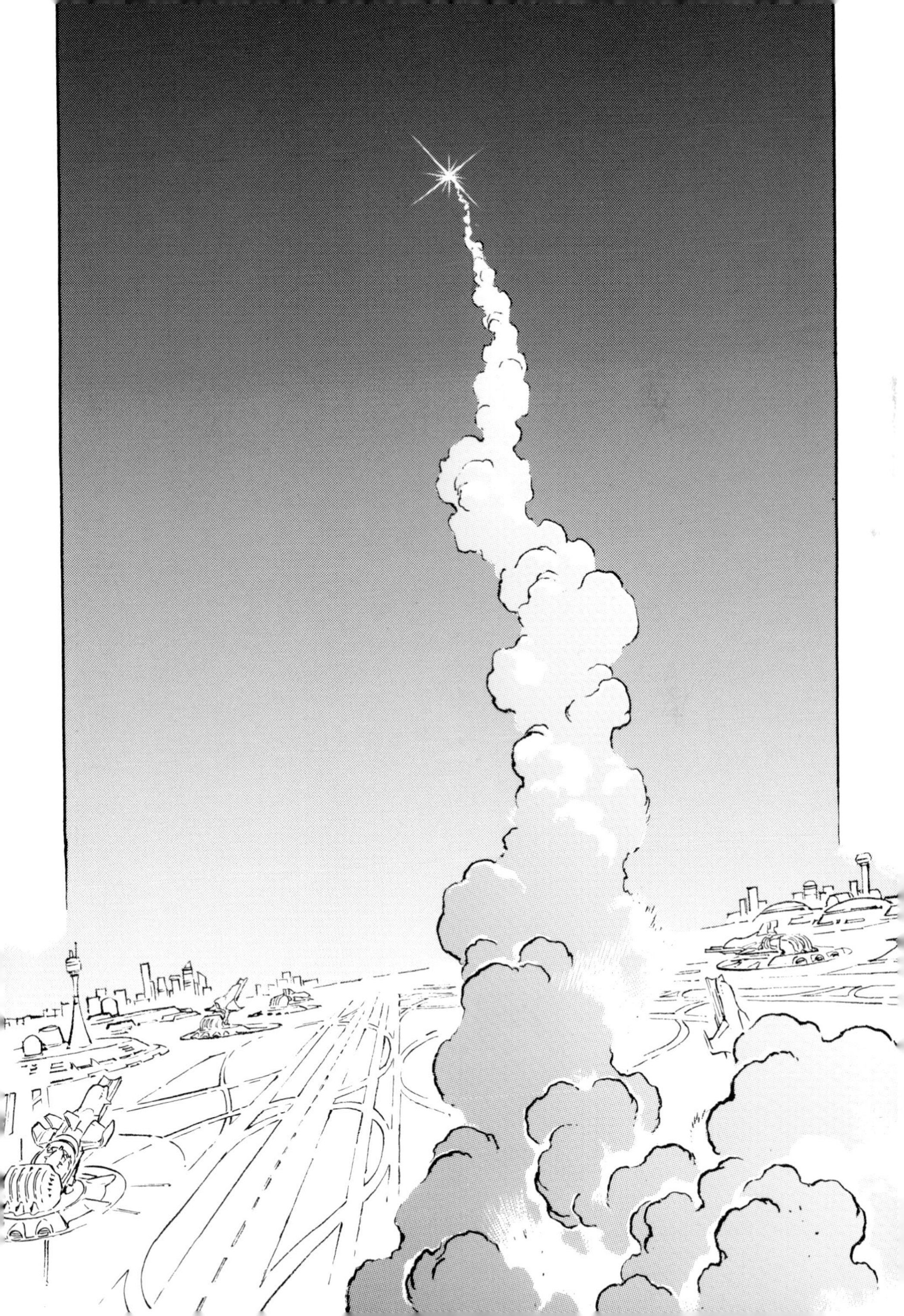

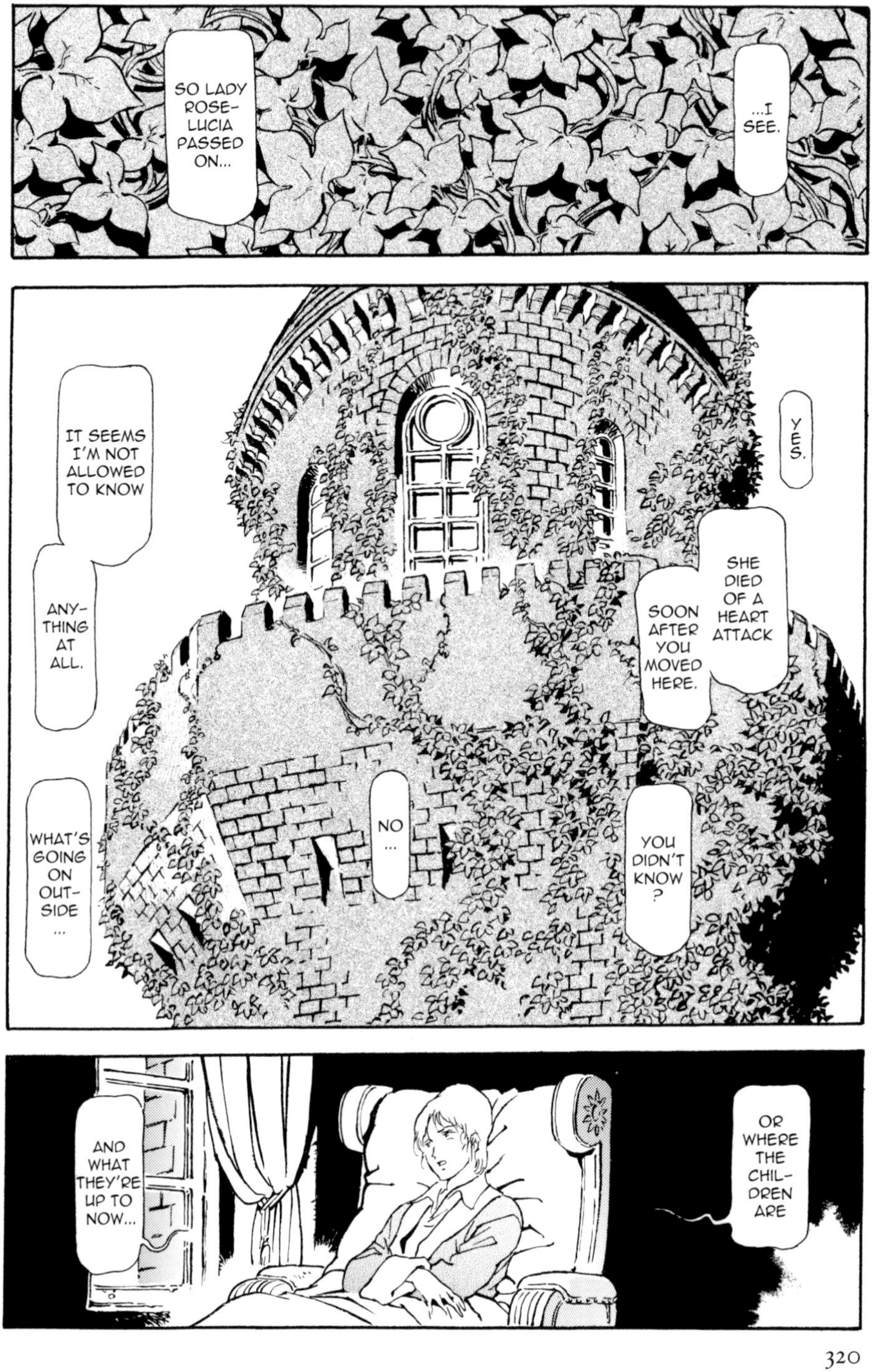
...I SEE.
SO LADY ROSE-LUCIA PASSED ON...
YES.
SHE DIED OF A HEART ATTACK
SOON AFTER YOU MOVED HERE.
YOU DIDN'T KNOW?
NO...
IT SEEMS I'M NOT ALLOWED TO KNOW
ANYTHING AT ALL.
WHAT'S GOING ON OUTSIDE...
OR WHERE THE CHILDREN ARE
AND WHAT THEY'RE UP TO NOW...

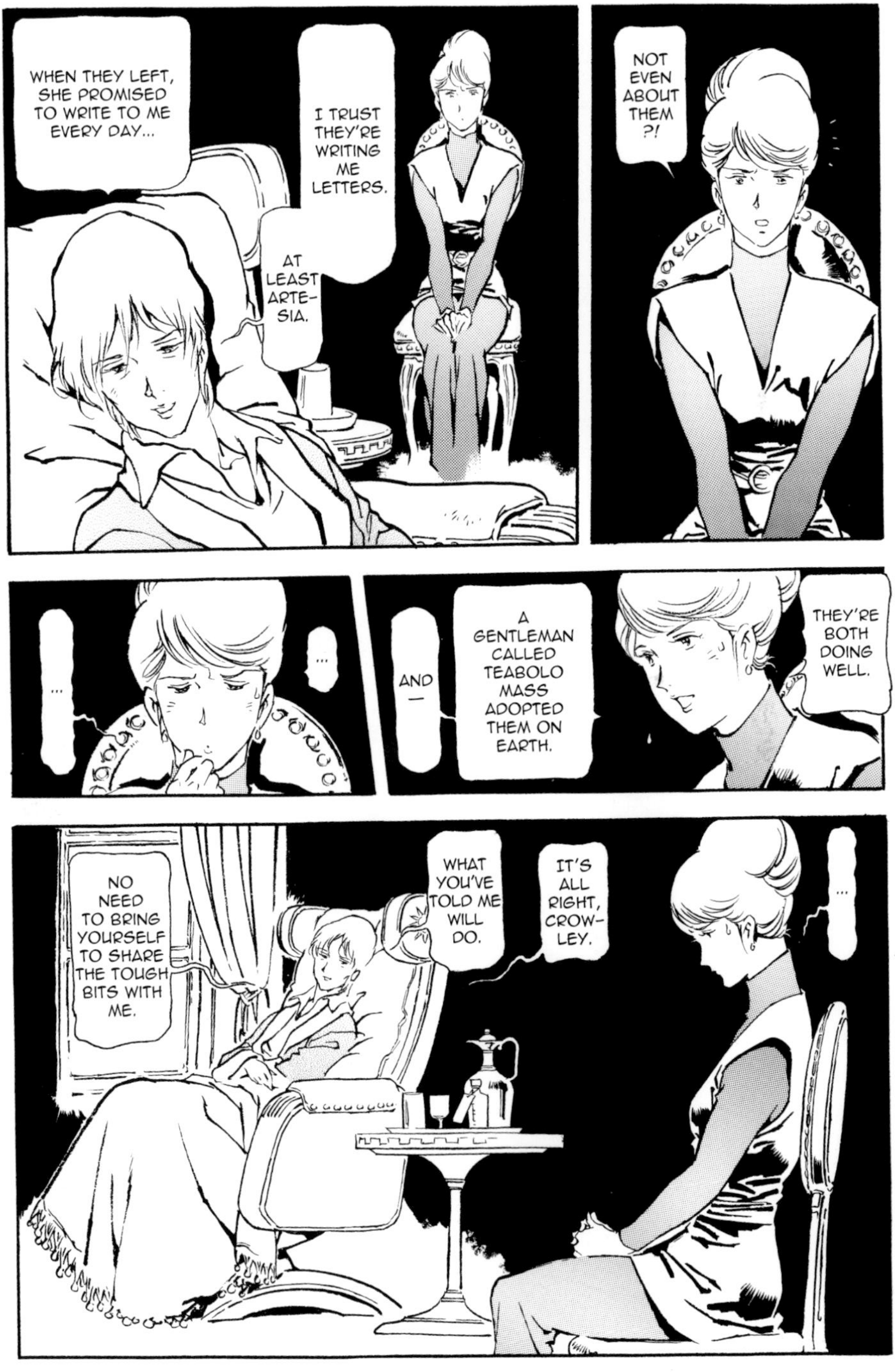

NOT EVEN ABOUT THEM ?!
I TRUST THEY'RE WRITING ME LETTERS.
WHEN THEY LEFT, SHE PROMISED TO WRITE TO ME EVERY DAY...
AT LEAST ARTESIA.
THEY'RE BOTH DOING WELL.
A GENTLEMAN CALLED TEABOLO MASS ADOPTED THEM ON EARTH.
AND —
...
...
...
IT'S ALL RIGHT, CROWLEY.
WHAT YOU'VE TOLD ME WILL DO.
NO NEED TO BRING YOURSELF TO SHARE THE TOUGH BITS WITH ME.

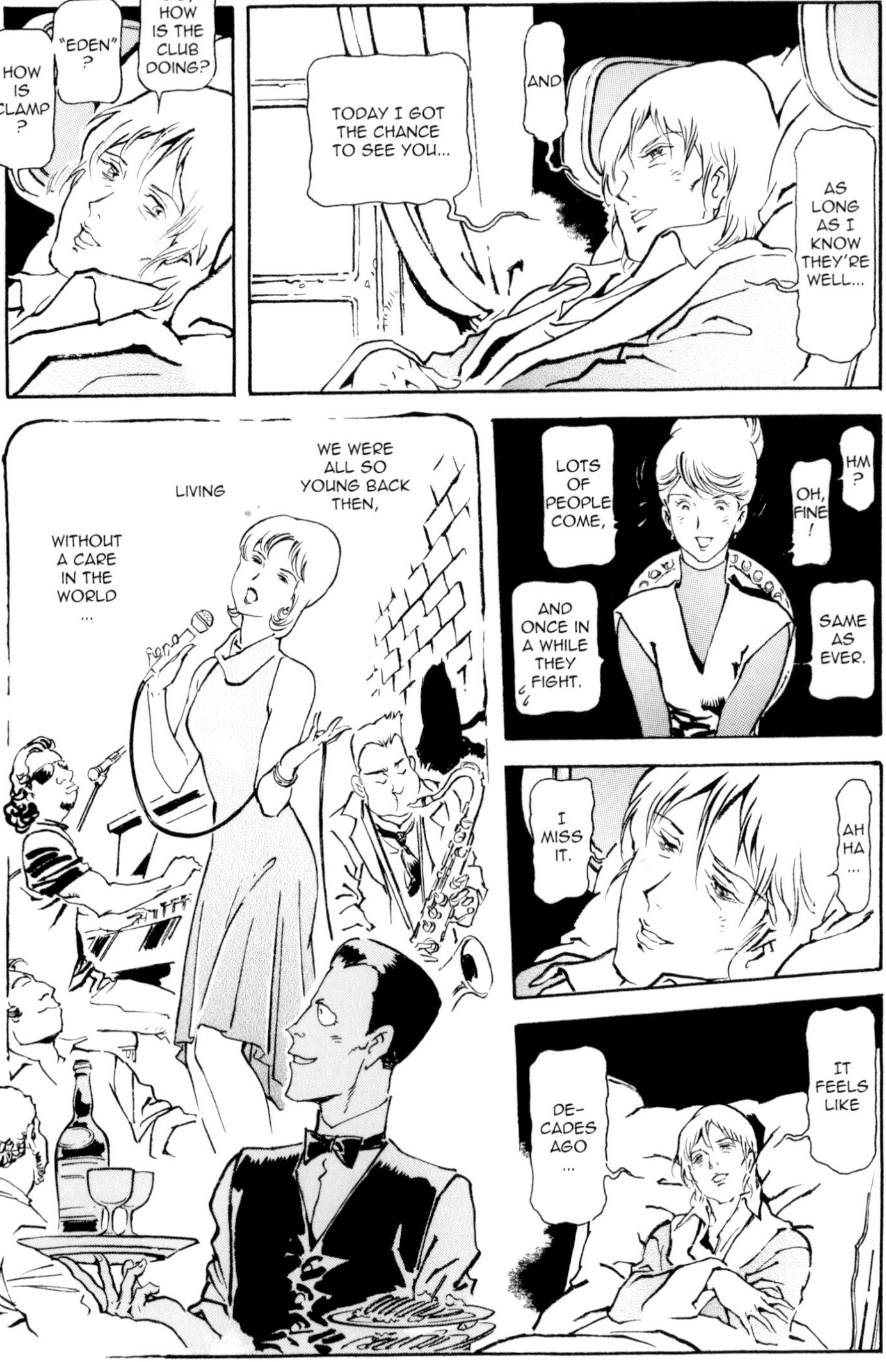
AS LONG AS I KNOW THEY'RE WELL...
AND
TODAY I GOT THE CHANCE TO SEE YOU...
SO, HOW IS THE CLUB DOING?
"EDEN"?
HOW IS CLAMP?
HM?
OH, FINE!
SAME AS EVER.
LOTS OF PEOPLE COME,
AND ONCE IN A WHILE THEY FIGHT.
AH HA...
I MISS IT.
IT FEELS LIKE
DE-CADES AGO...
WE WERE ALL SO YOUNG BACK THEN,
LIVING
WITHOUT A CARE IN THE WORLD...

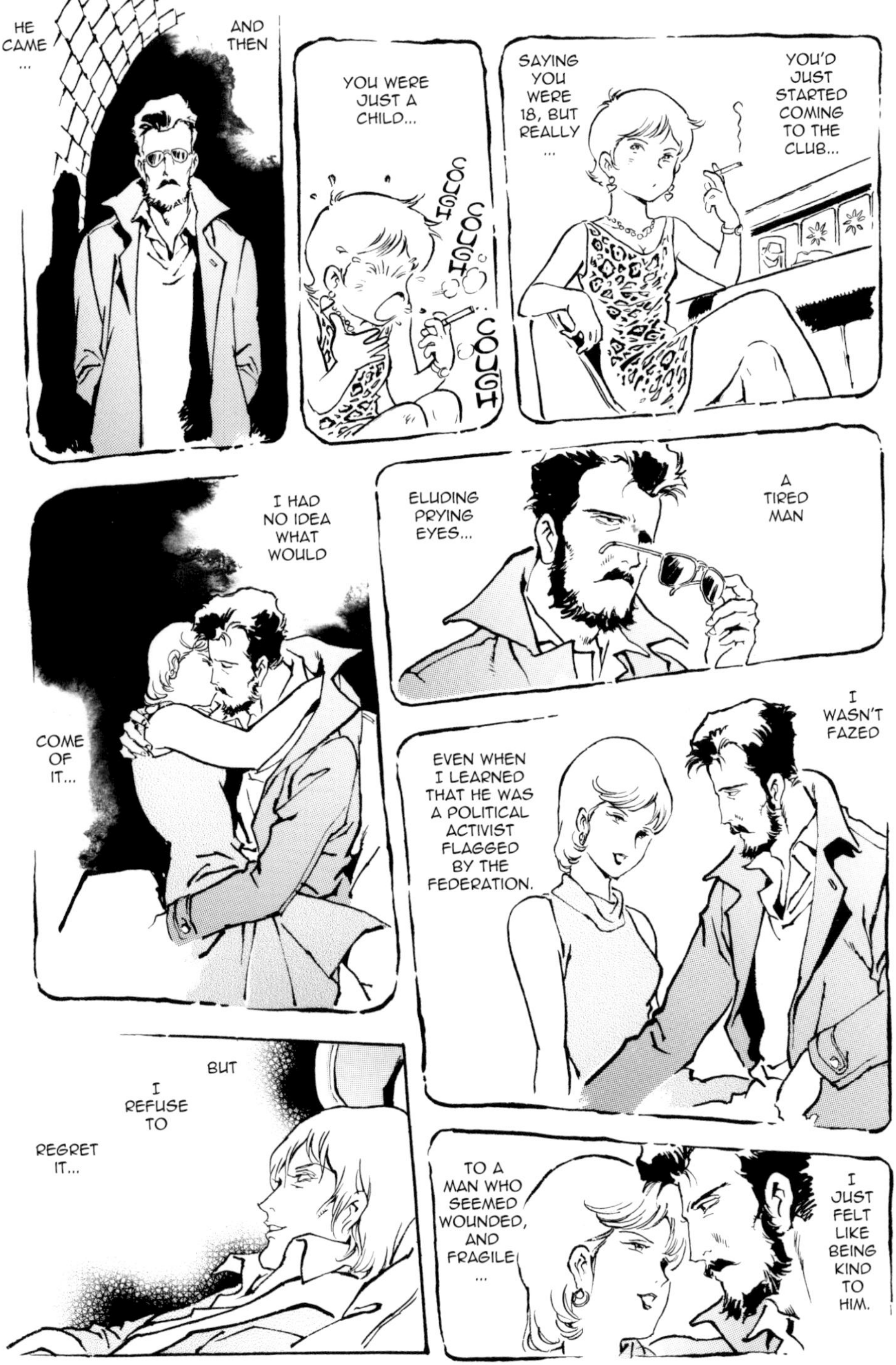
YOU'D JUST STARTED COMING TO THE CLUB...
SAYING YOU WERE 18, BUT REALLY ...
YOU WERE JUST A CHILD...
COUGH
COUGH
COUGH
AND THEN
HE CAME ...
A TIRED MAN
ELUDING PRYING EYES...
I WASN'T FAZED
EVEN WHEN I LEARNED THAT HE WAS A POLITICAL ACTIVIST FLAGGED BY THE FEDERATION.
I HAD NO IDEA WHAT WOULD
COME OF IT...
I JUST FELT LIKE BEING KIND TO HIM.
TO A MAN WHO SEEMED WOUNDED, AND FRAGILE ...
BUT
I REFUSE TO
REGRET IT...

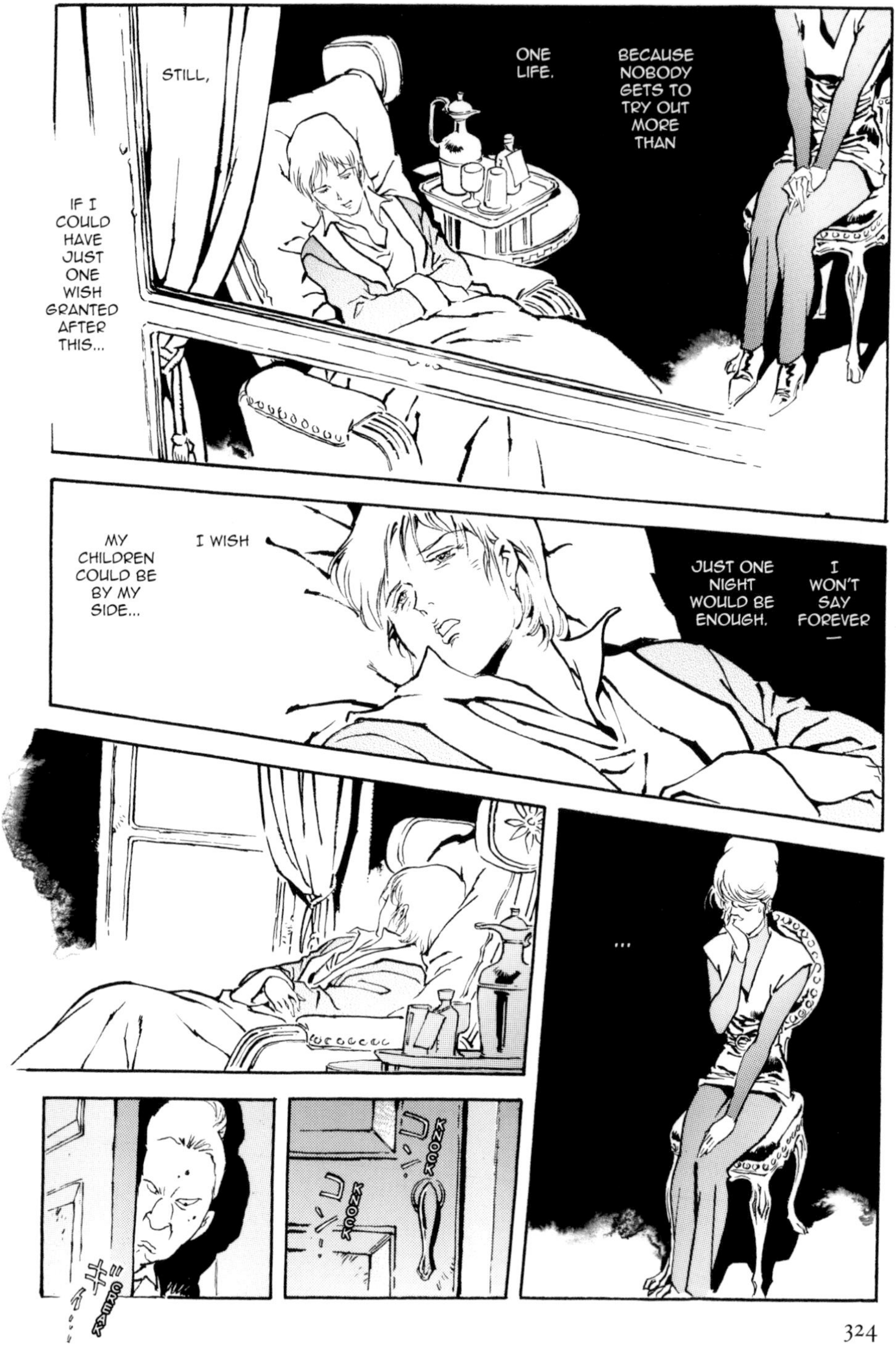
BECAUSE NOBODY GETS TO TRY OUT MORE THAN
ONE LIFE.
STILL,
IF I COULD HAVE JUST ONE WISH GRANTED AFTER THIS...
I WON'T SAY FOREVER —
JUST ONE NIGHT WOULD BE ENOUGH.
I WISH
MY CHILDREN COULD BE BY MY SIDE...
...
KNOCK
KNOCK
CREAK

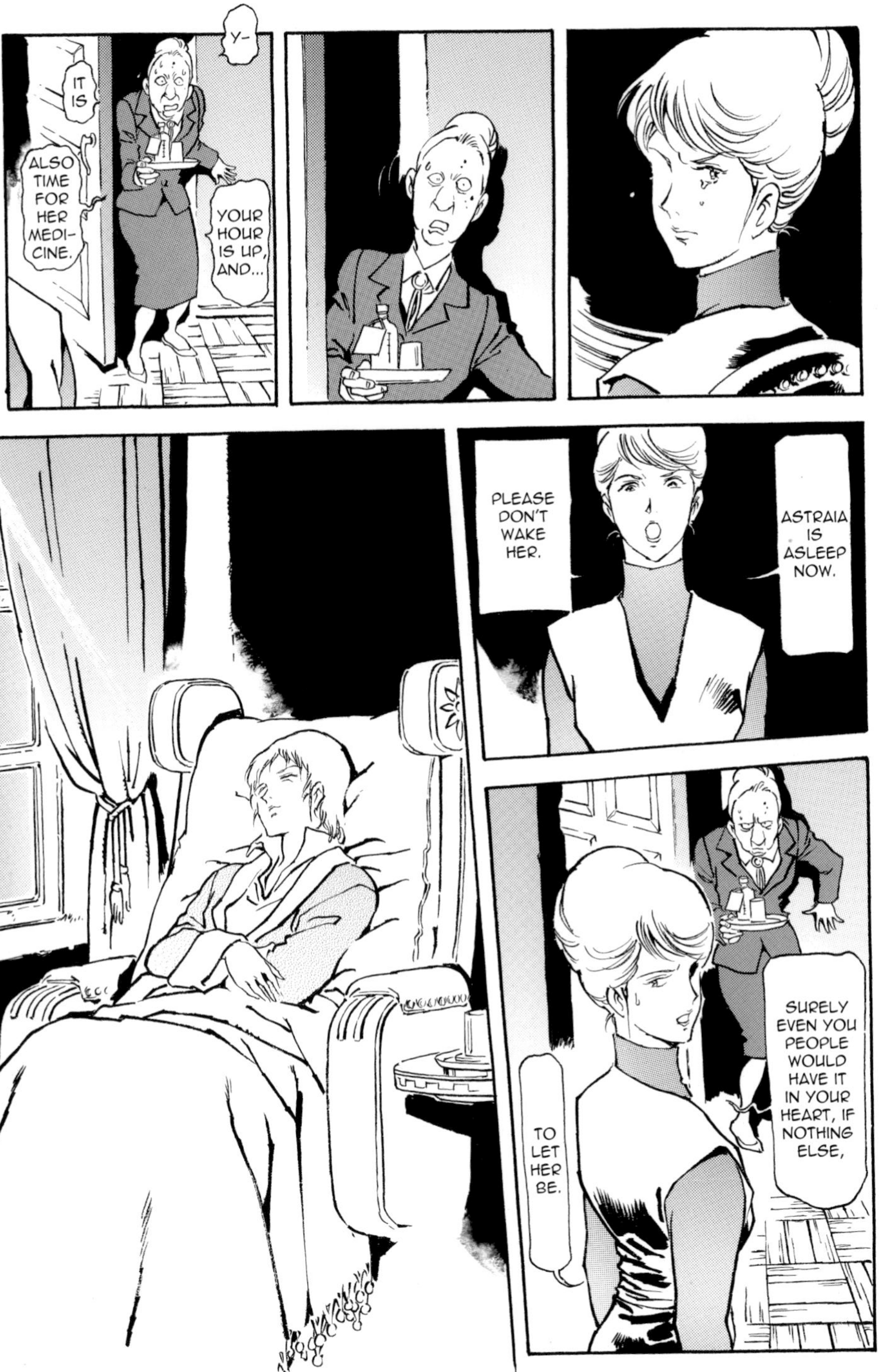
Y-
YOUR HOUR IS UP, AND...
IT IS
ALSO TIME FOR HER MEDICINE.
ASTRAIA IS ASLEEP NOW.
PLEASE DON'T WAKE HER.
SURELY EVEN YOU PEOPLE WOULD HAVE IT IN YOUR HEART, IF NOTHING ELSE,
TO LET HER BE.

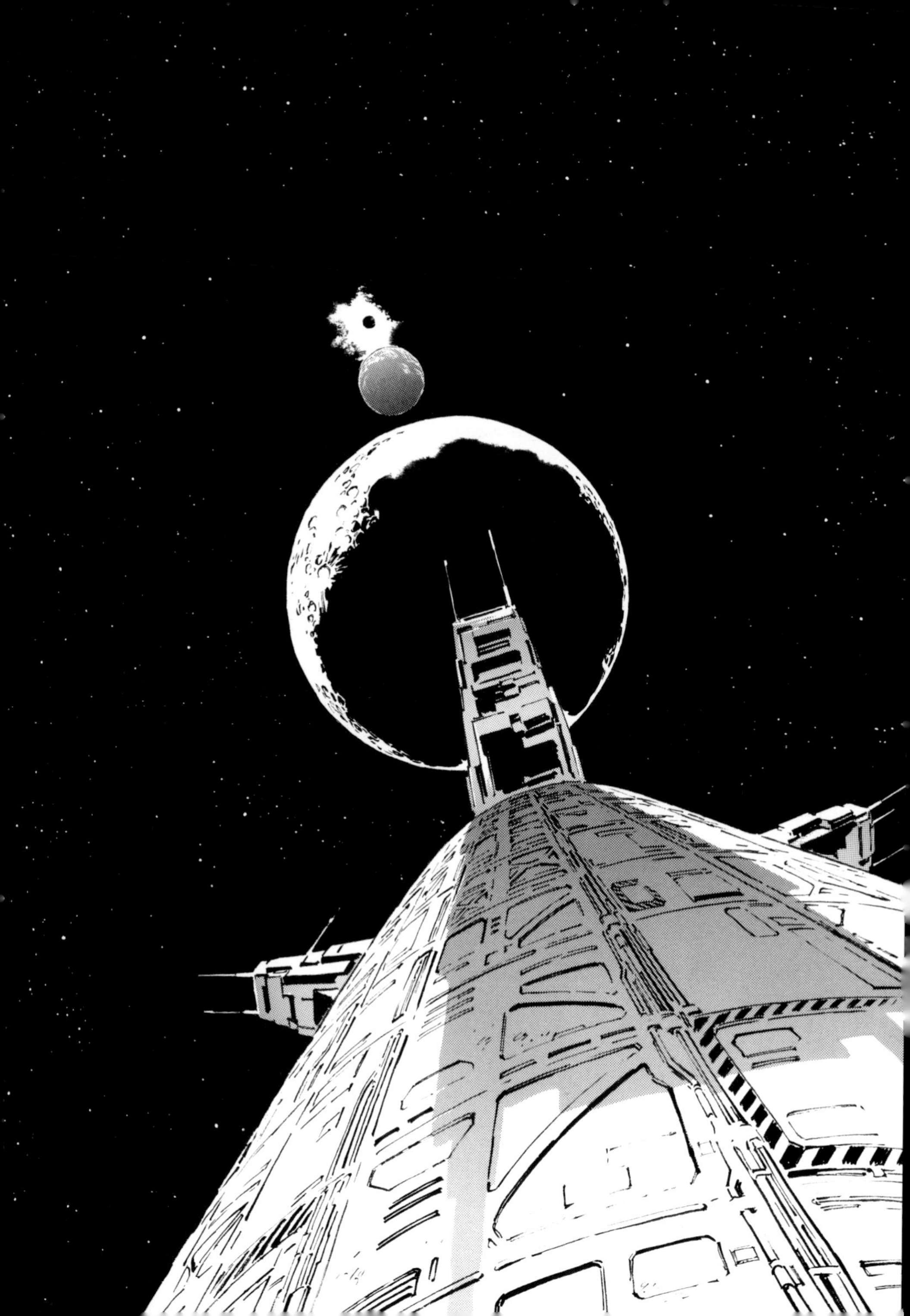

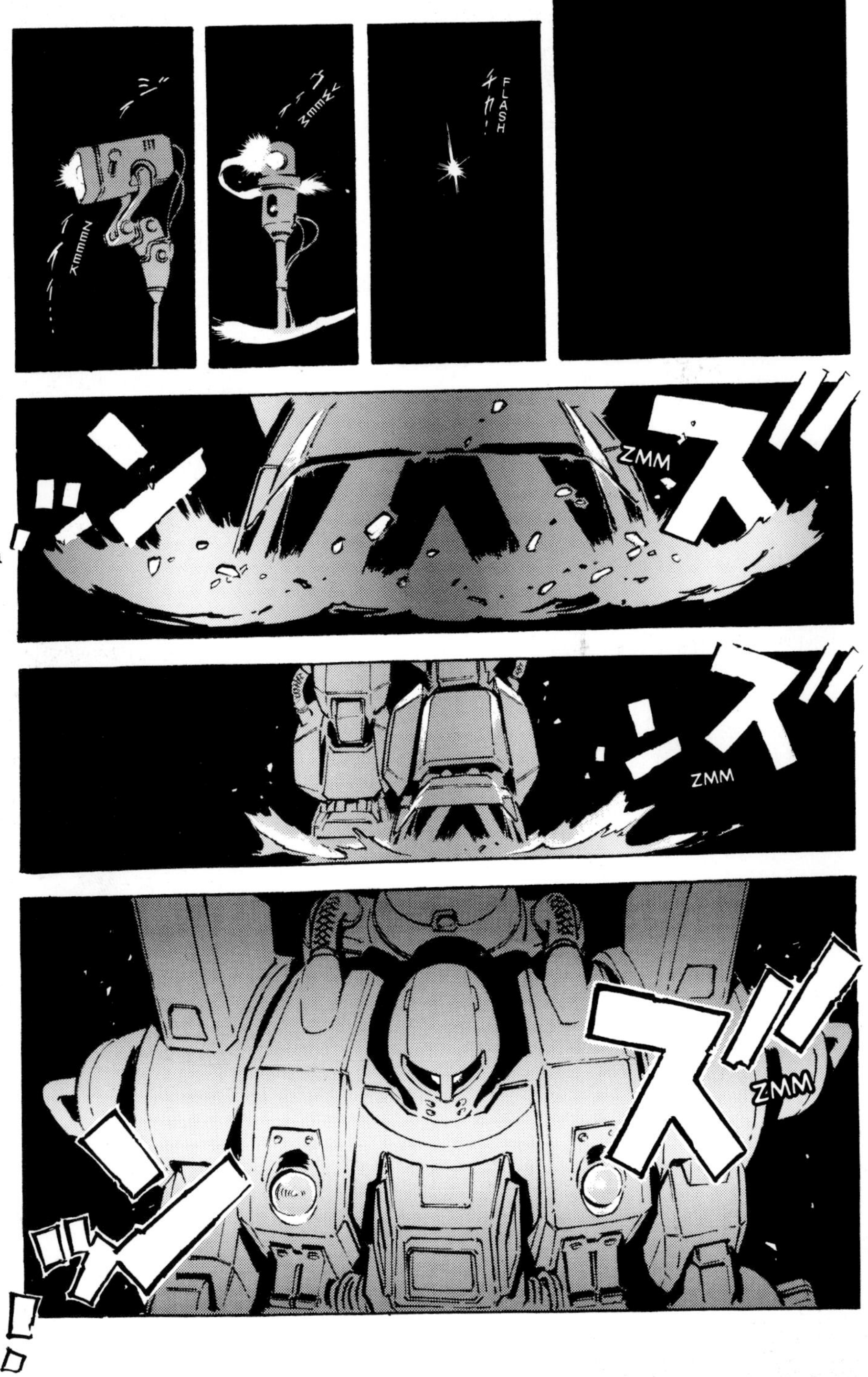

チカ!
FLASH
ウィィ…
ZMMMM
ジィィィィィ…
ZMMMM
ZMM
ZMM
ZMM

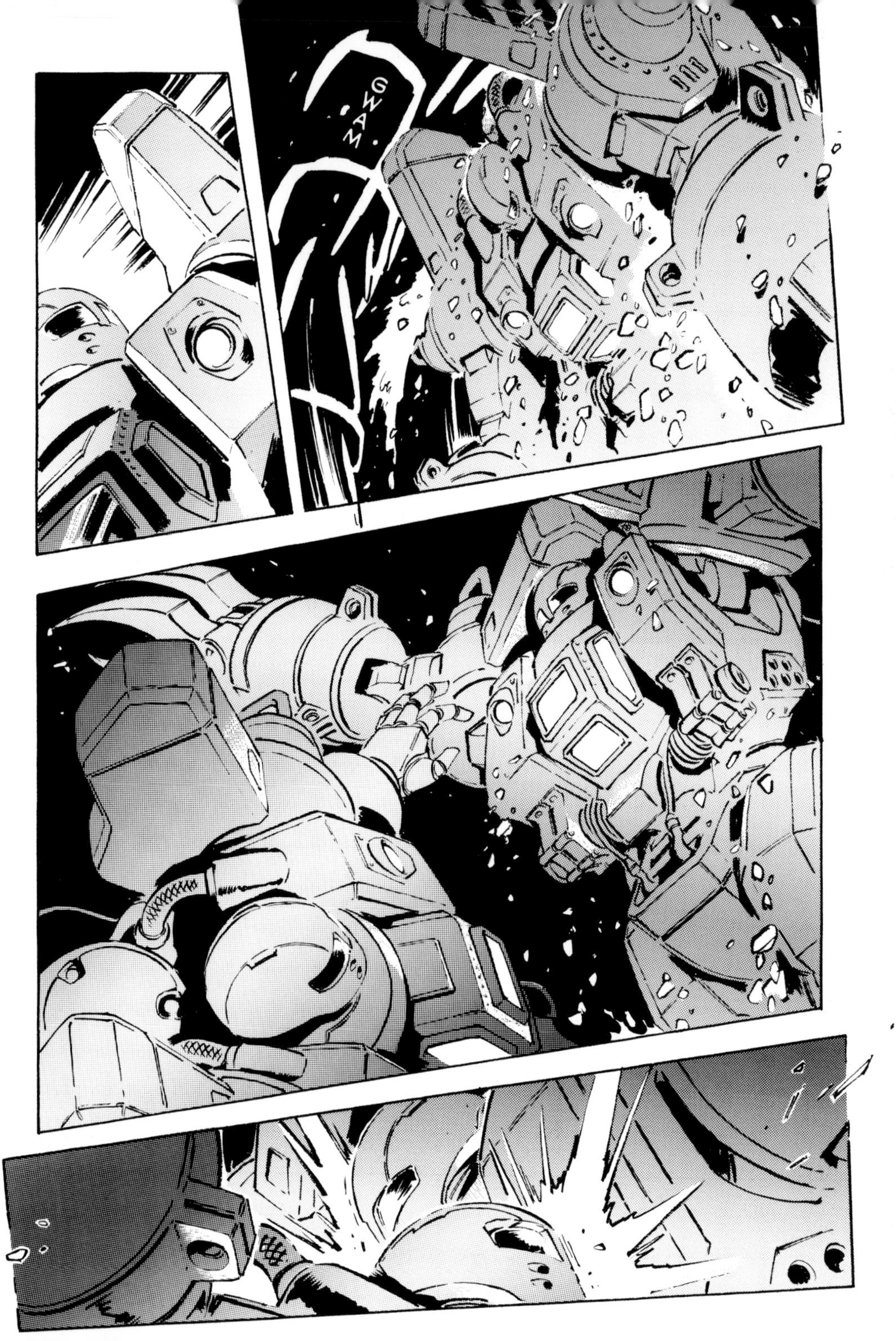
GWAM

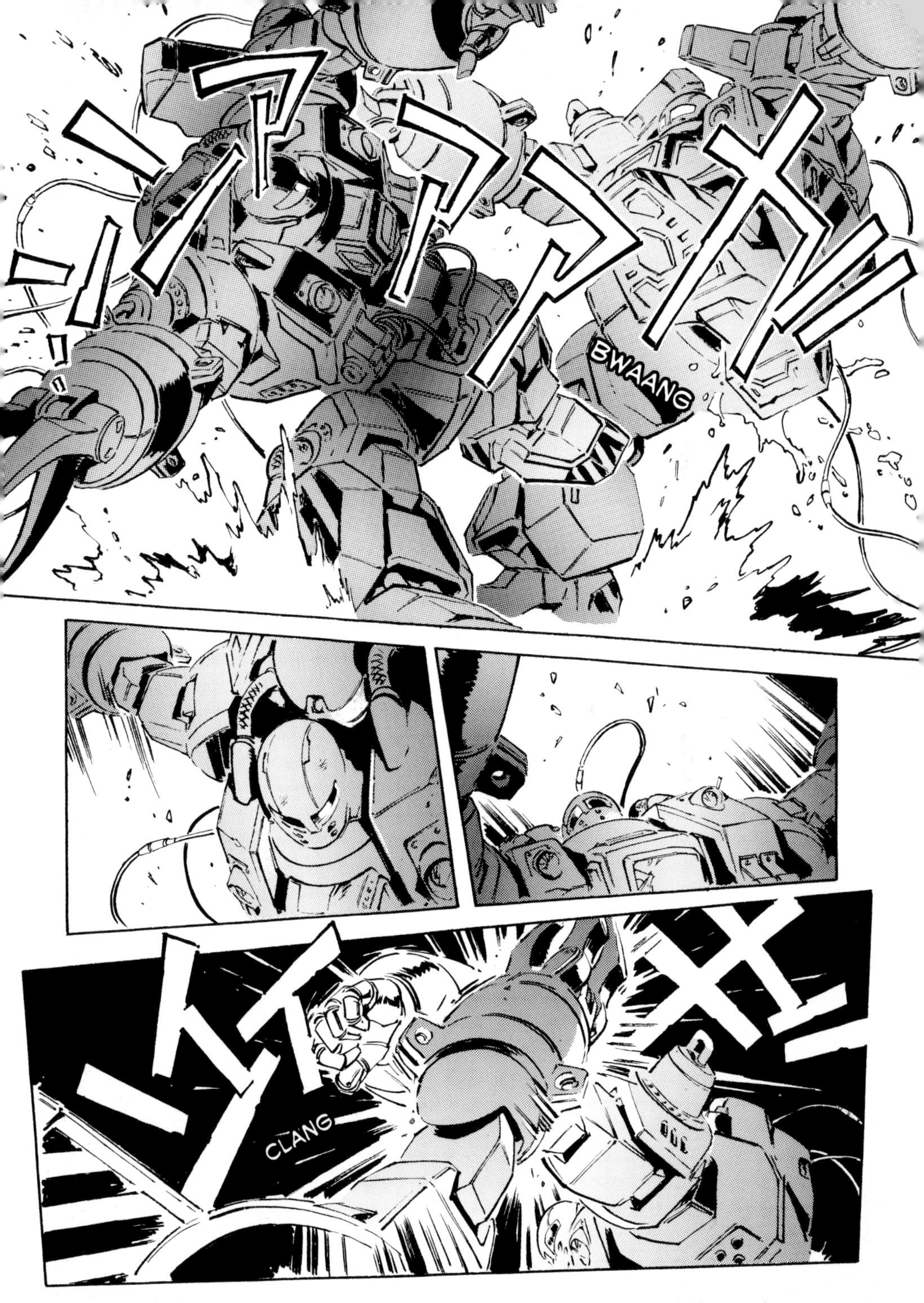
BWAANG
CLANG

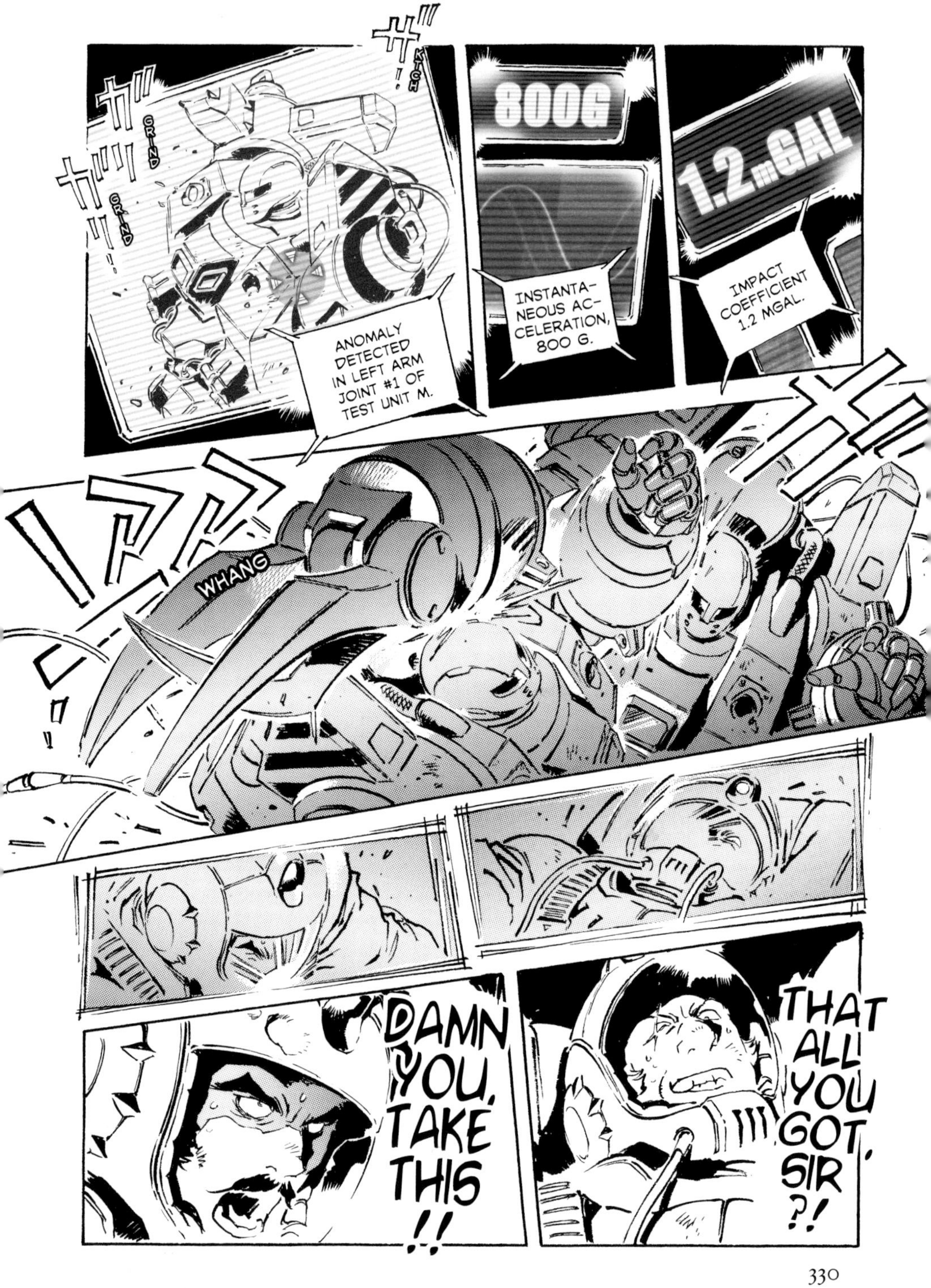
1.2mGAL
IMPACT COEFFICIENT 1.2 MGAL.
800G
INSTANTANEOUS ACCELERATION, 800 G.
KICH
GRIND
GRIND
ANOMALY DETECTED IN LEFT ARM JOINT #1 OF TEST UNIT M.
WHANG
THAT ALL YOU GOT, SIR?!
DAMN YOU, TAKE THIS!!

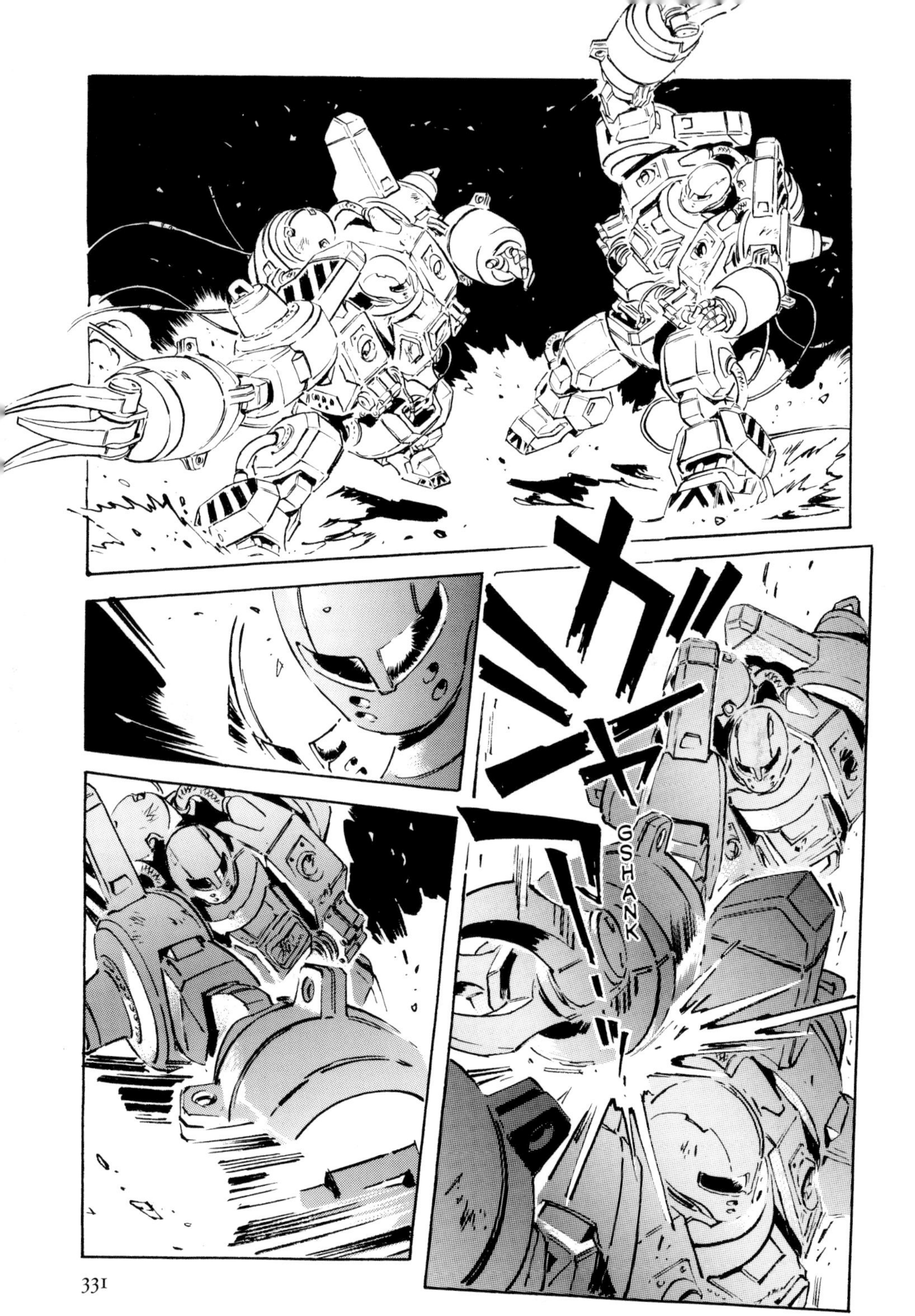
GSHANK

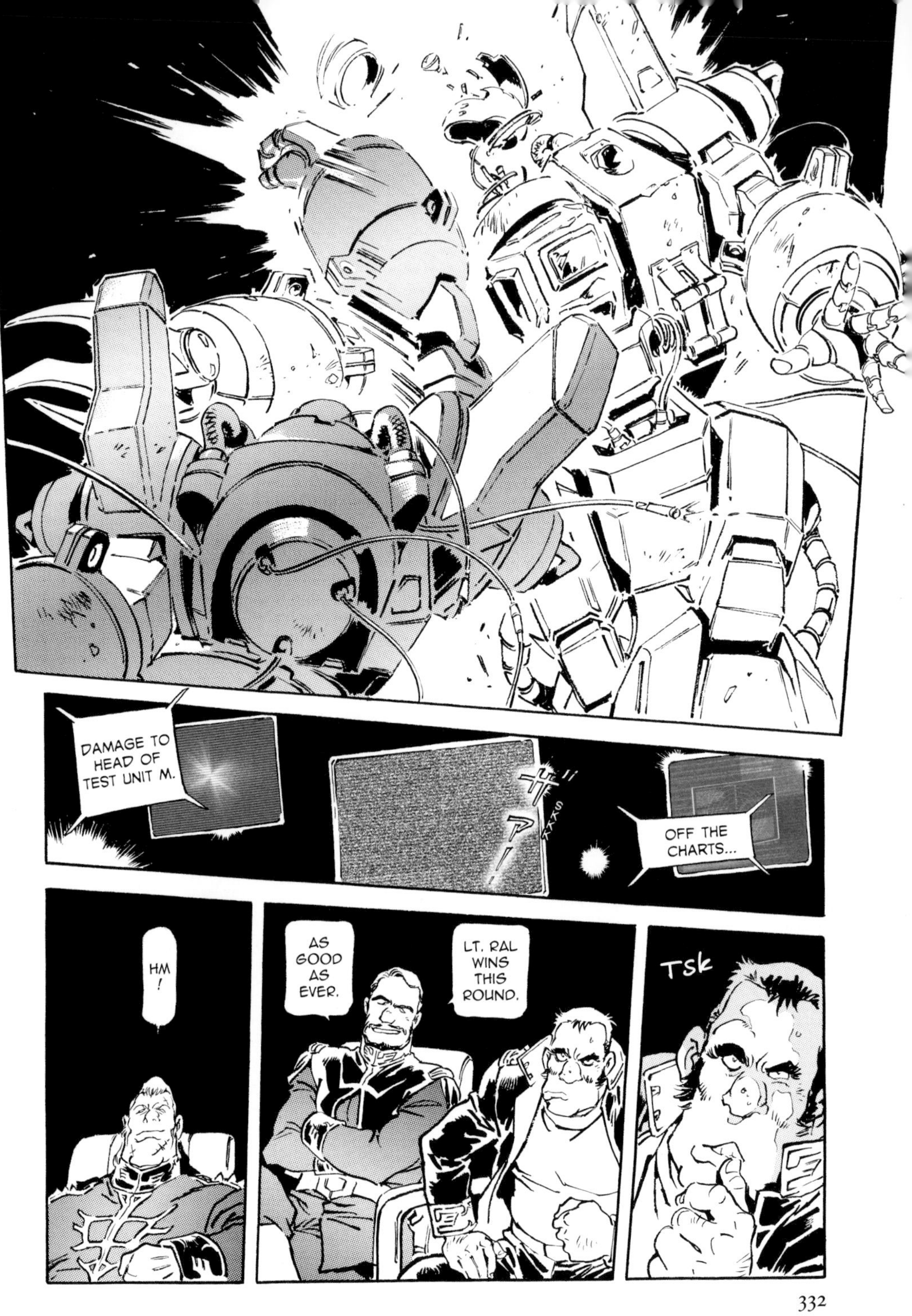
OFF THE CHARTS...
ザァー!
SKKT
DAMAGE TO HEAD OF TEST UNIT M.
TSK
LT. RAL WINS THIS ROUND.
AS GOOD AS EVER.
HM!

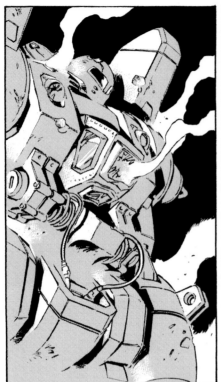

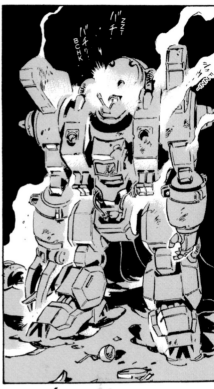

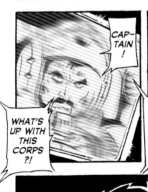

ZZT
BCHK
GET THEM ON THE LINE.
CAN YOU TALK?
WHY DID WE STOP?!
I CAN FIGHT WITHOUT THE HEAD!
CAPTAIN!
WHAT'S UP WITH THIS CORPS?!
SERGEANT MASH JUST TRIED TO KILL ME!
NO, YOU DID, SIR!

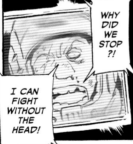

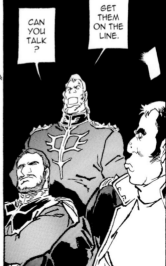

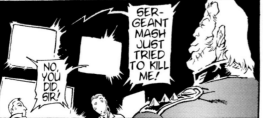

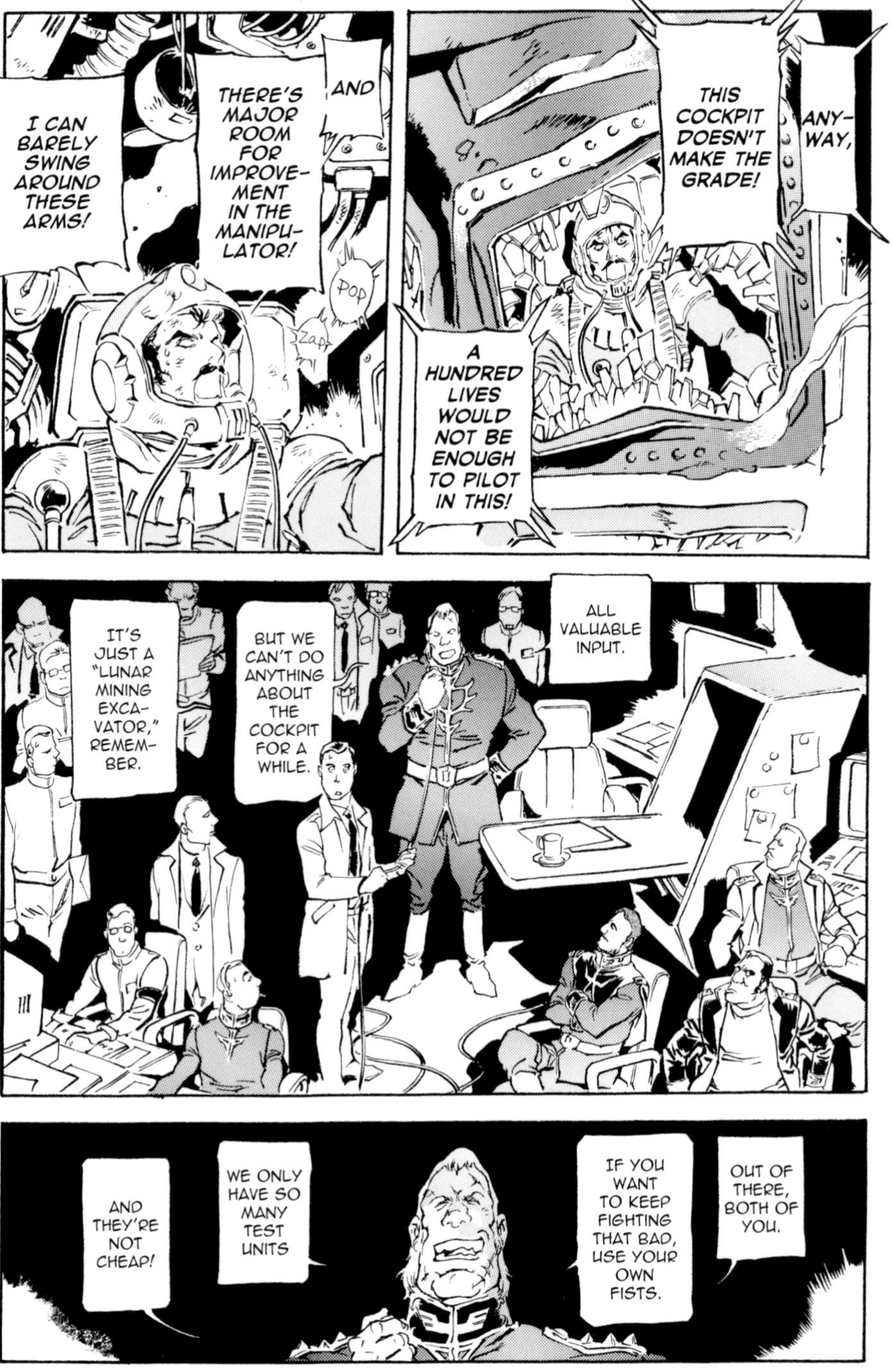
ANY-WAY,
THIS COCKPIT DOESN'T MAKE THE GRADE!
A HUNDRED LIVES WOULD NOT BE ENOUGH TO PILOT IN THIS!
AND
THERE'S MAJOR ROOM FOR IMPROVEMENT IN THE MANIPULATOR!
I CAN BARELY SWING AROUND THESE ARMS!
POP
ZAP
ALL VALUABLE INPUT.
BUT WE CAN'T DO ANYTHING ABOUT THE COCKPIT FOR A WHILE.
IT'S JUST A "LUNAR MINING EXCAVATOR," REMEMBER.
OUT OF THERE, BOTH OF YOU.
IF YOU WANT TO KEEP FIGHTING THAT BAD, USE YOUR OWN FISTS.
WE ONLY HAVE SO MANY TEST UNITS
AND THEY'RE NOT CHEAP!

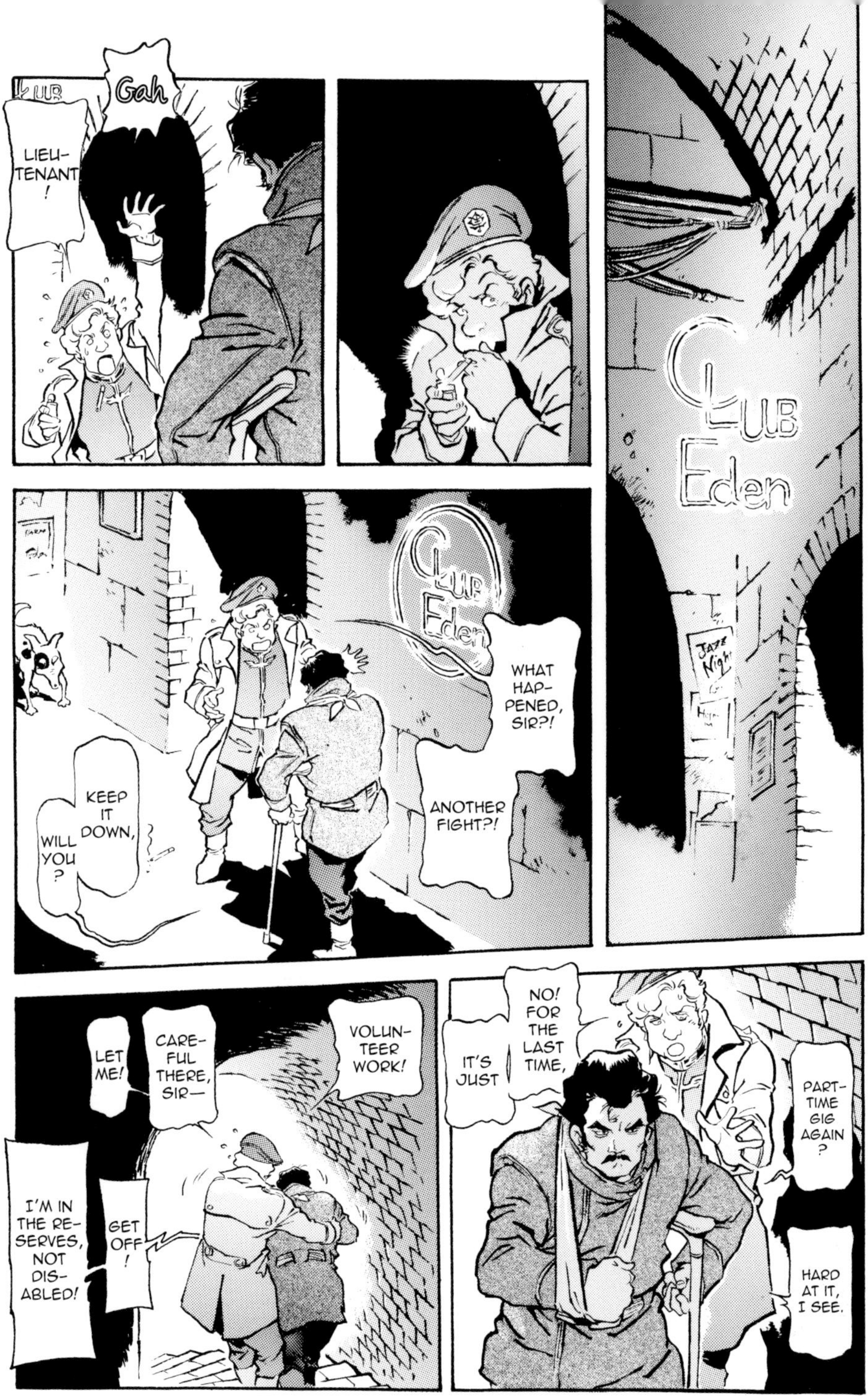
CLUB Eden
JAZZ Night
Gah
LIEUTENANT!
CLUB Eden
WHAT HAPPENED, SIR?!
ANOTHER FIGHT?!
KEEP IT DOWN, WILL YOU?
HARD AT IT, I SEE.
PART-TIME GIG AGAIN?
NO! FOR THE LAST TIME,
IT'S JUST
VOLUNTEER WORK!
CAREFUL THERE, SIR—
LET ME!
GET OFF!
I'M IN THE RESERVES, NOT DISABLED!

I? MAY

HELLO.

WHY
...

IF IT'S THAT DANGEROUS,

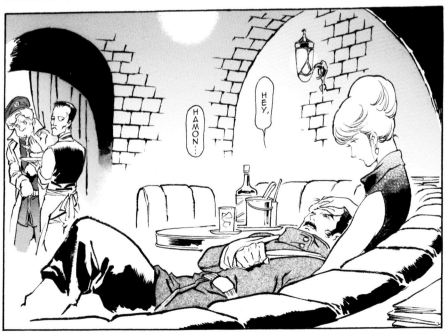

HEY,

HAMON...

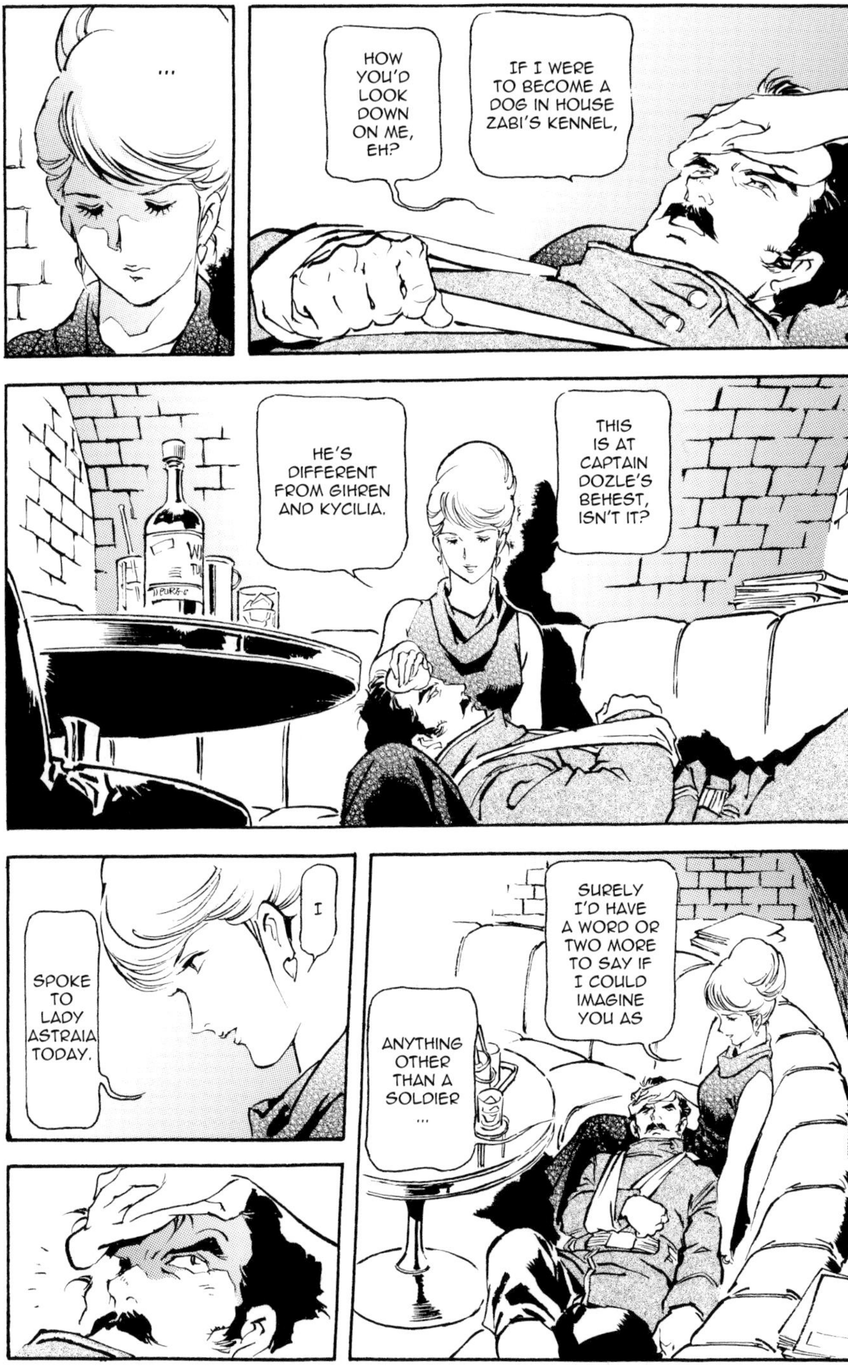
IF I WERE TO BECOME A DOG IN HOUSE ZABI'S KENNEL,
HOW YOU'D LOOK DOWN ON ME, EH?
...
THIS IS AT CAPTAIN DOZLE'S BEHEST, ISN'T IT?
HE'S DIFFERENT FROM GIHREN AND KYCILIA.
SURELY I'D HAVE A WORD OR TWO MORE TO SAY IF I COULD IMAGINE YOU AS
ANYTHING OTHER THAN A SOLDIER ...
I
SPOKE TO LADY ASTRAIA TODAY.

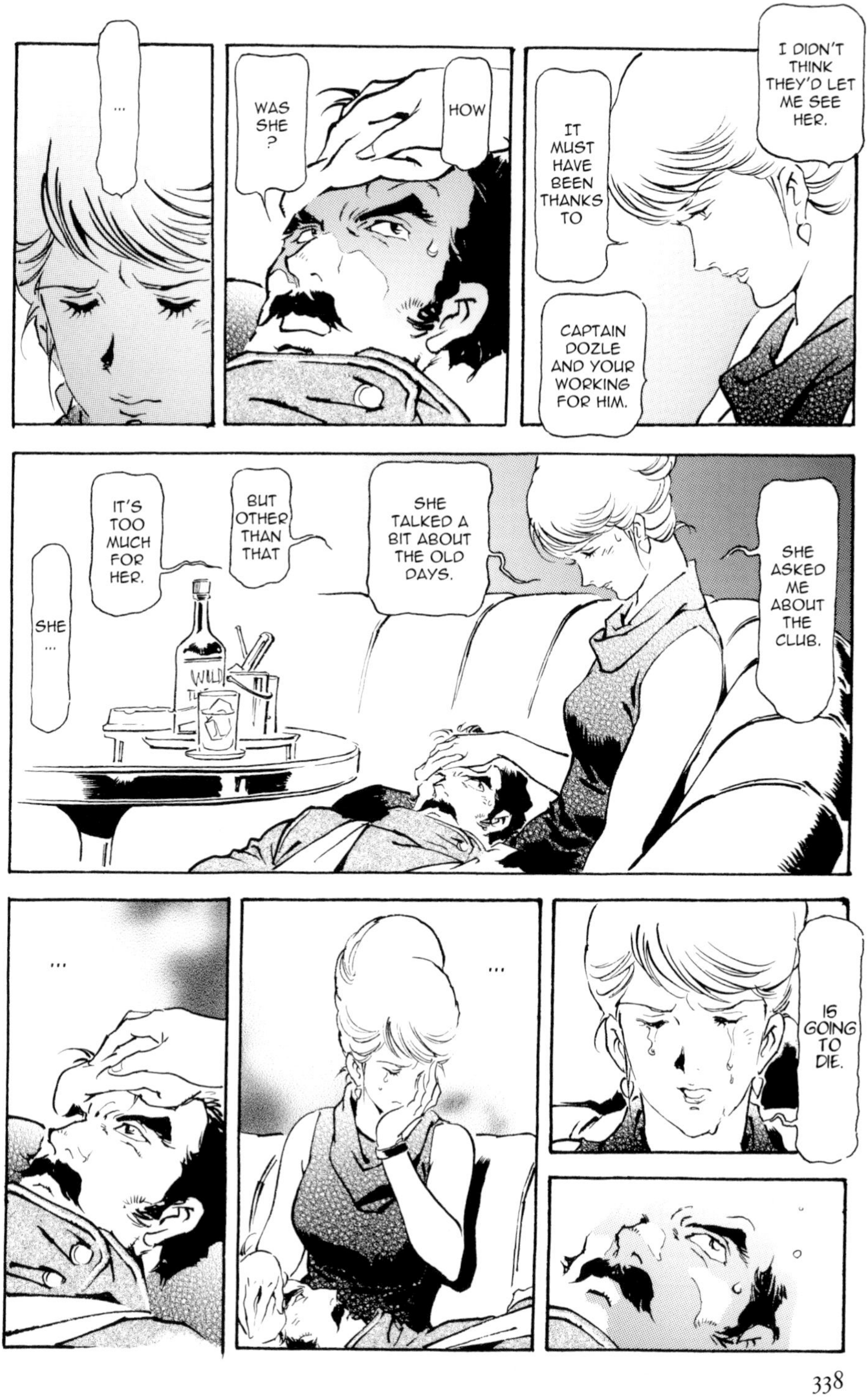
I DIDN'T THINK THEY'D LET ME SEE HER.
IT MUST HAVE BEEN THANKS TO
CAPTAIN DOZLE AND YOUR WORKING FOR HIM.
HOW
WAS SHE ?
...
SHE ASKED ME ABOUT THE CLUB.
SHE TALKED A BIT ABOUT THE OLD DAYS.
BUT OTHER THAN THAT
IT'S TOO MUCH FOR HER.
SHE ...
IS GOING TO DIE.
...
...

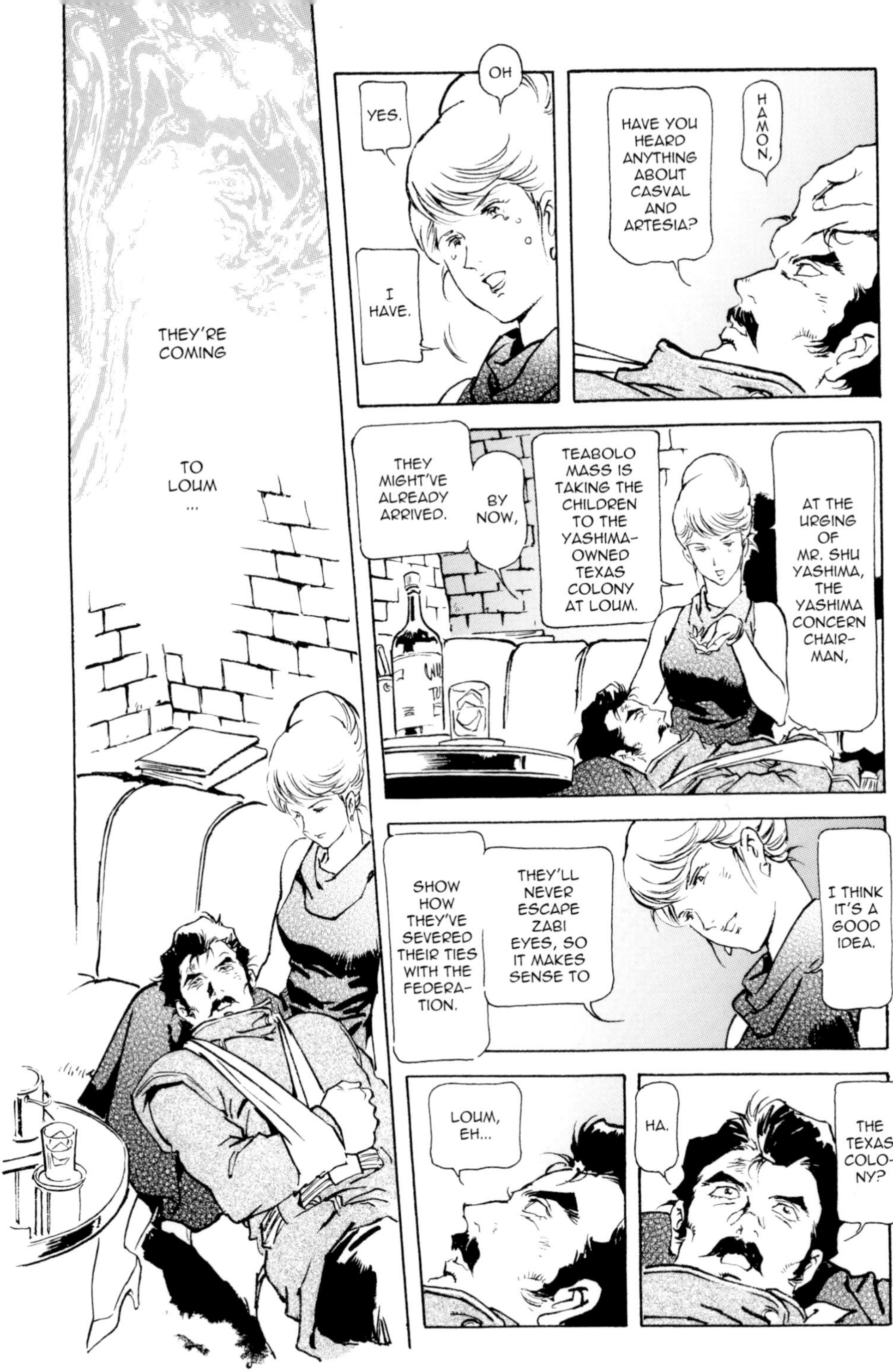
HAMON,
HAVE YOU HEARD ANYTHING ABOUT CASVAL AND ARTESIA?
OH
YES.
I HAVE.
AT THE URGING OF MR. SHU YASHIMA, THE YASHIMA CONCERN CHAIR-MAN,
TEABOLO MASS IS TAKING THE CHILDREN TO THE YASHIMA-OWNED TEXAS COLONY AT LOUM.
BY NOW,
THEY MIGHT'VE ALREADY ARRIVED.
I THINK IT'S A GOOD IDEA.
THEY'LL NEVER ESCAPE ZABI EYES, SO IT MAKES SENSE TO
SHOW HOW THEY'VE SEVERED THEIR TIES WITH THE FEDERA-TION.
THE TEXAS COLO-NY?
HA.
LOUM, EH...
THEY'RE COMING
TO LOUM ...

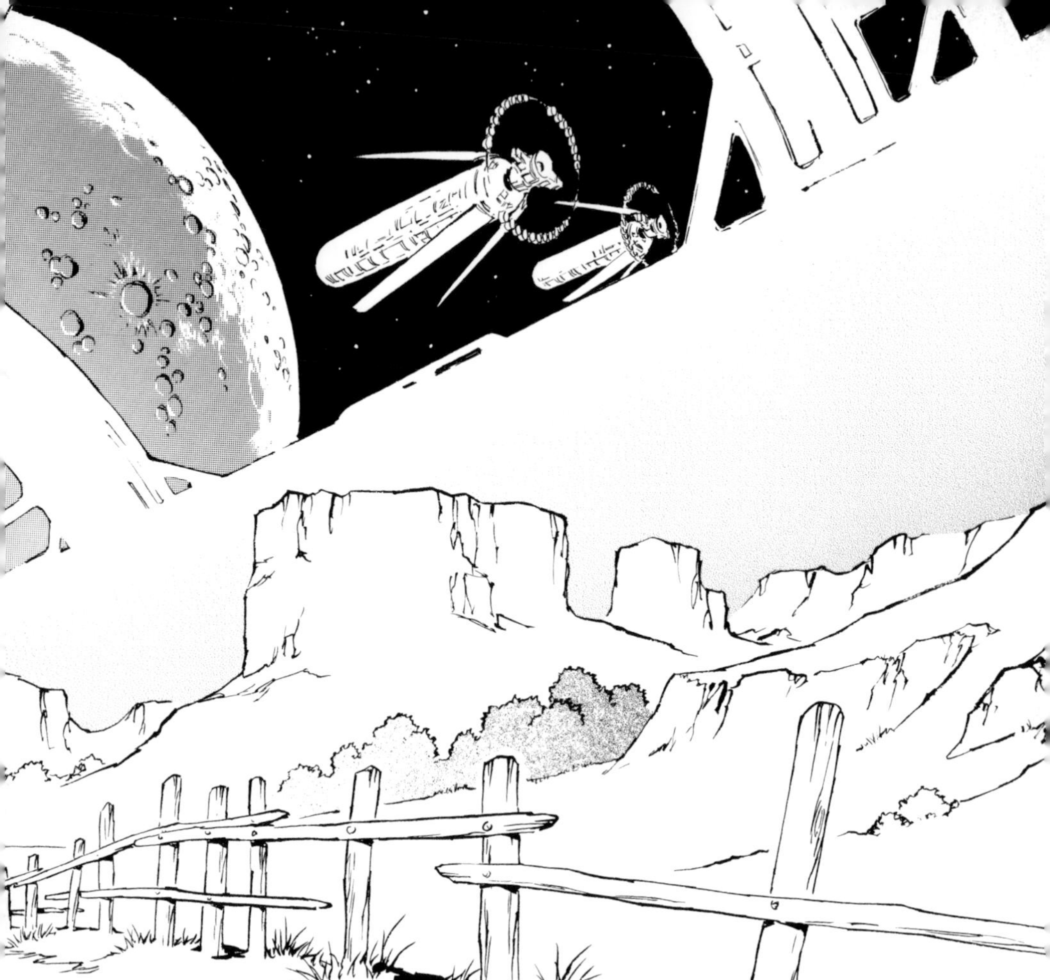

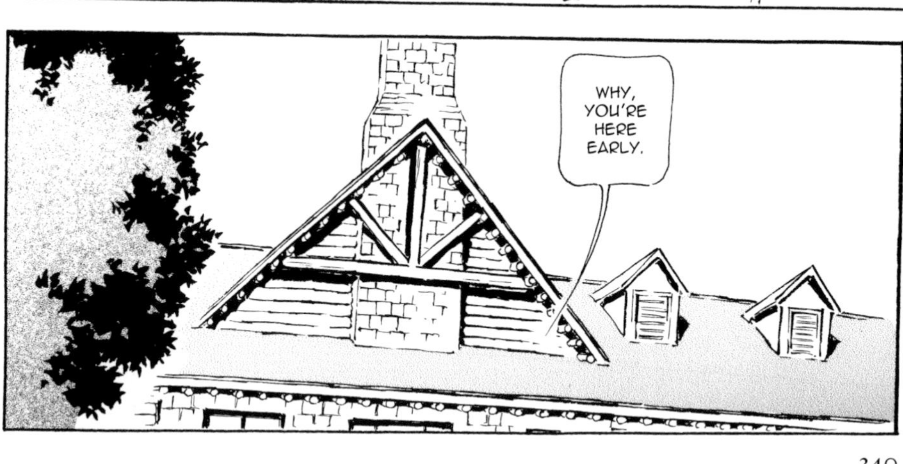
WHY, YOU'RE HERE EARLY.

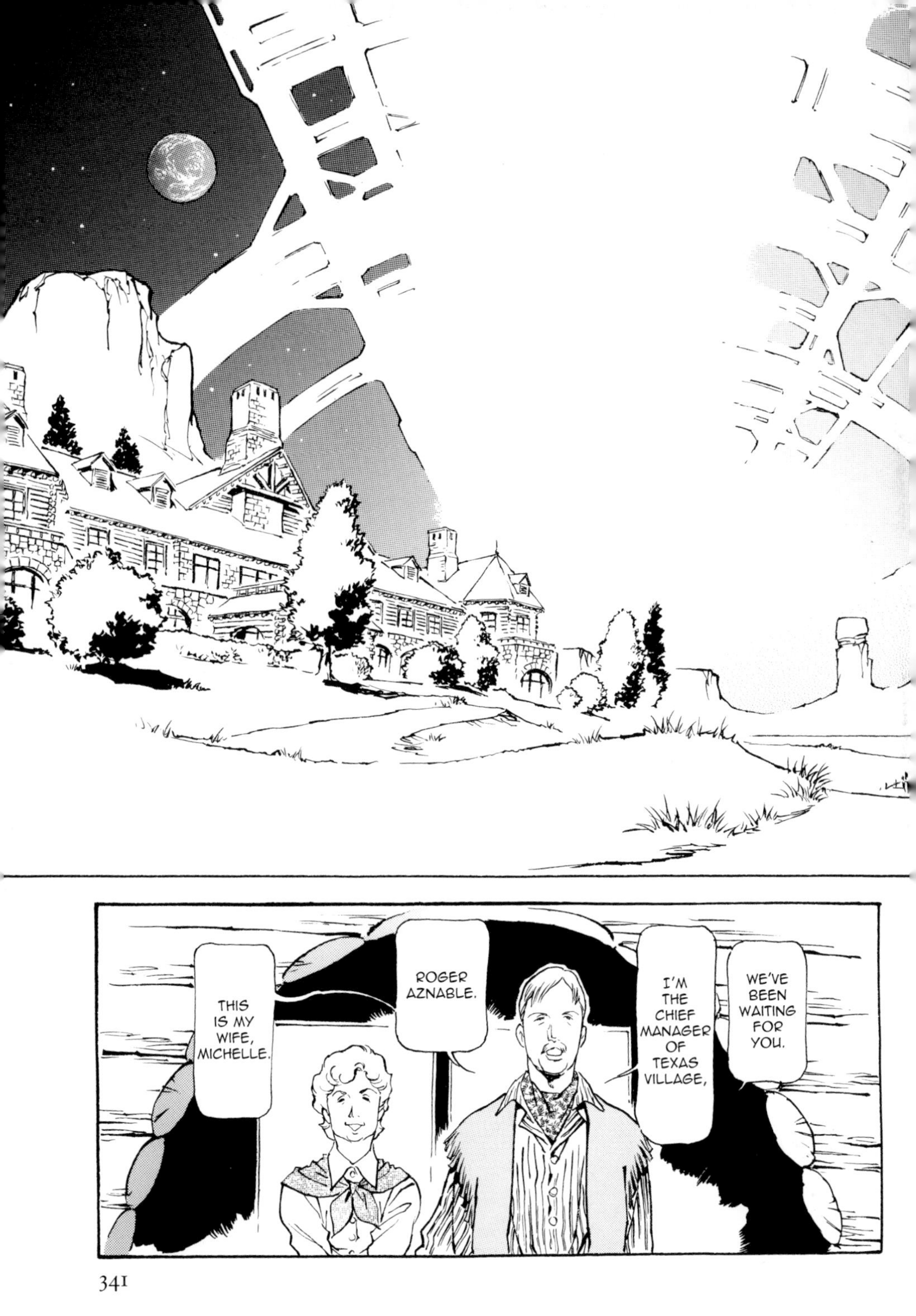
WE'VE BEEN WAITING FOR YOU.
I'M THE CHIEF MANAGER OF TEXAS VILLAGE,
ROGER AZNABLE.
THIS IS MY WIFE, MICHELLE.

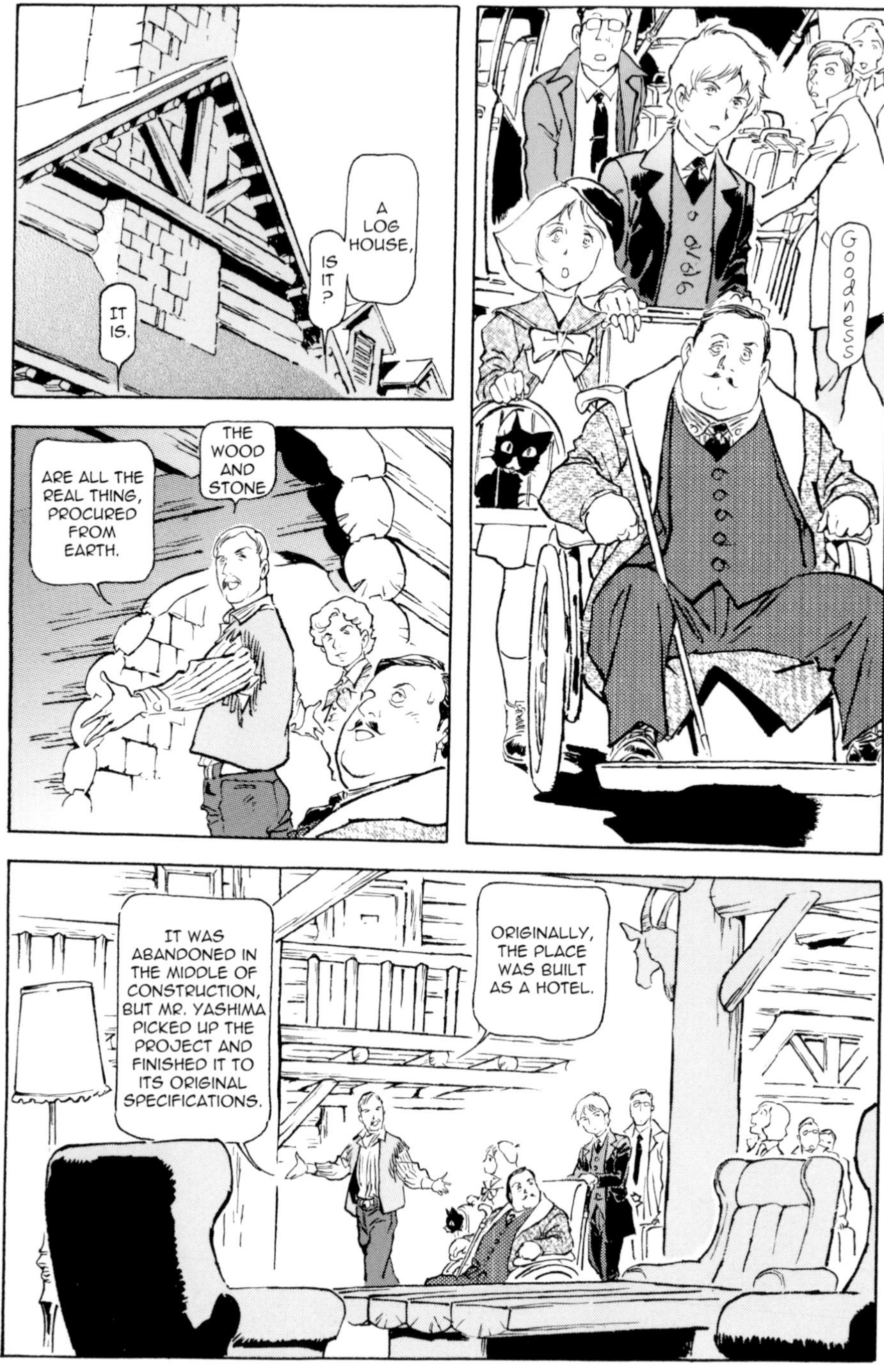
Goodness
A LOG HOUSE,
IS IT?
IT IS.
THE WOOD AND STONE
ARE ALL THE REAL THING, PROCURED FROM EARTH.
ORIGINALLY, THE PLACE WAS BUILT AS A HOTEL.
IT WAS ABANDONED IN THE MIDDLE OF CONSTRUCTION, BUT MR. YASHIMA PICKED UP THE PROJECT AND FINISHED IT TO ITS ORIGINAL SPECIFICATIONS.

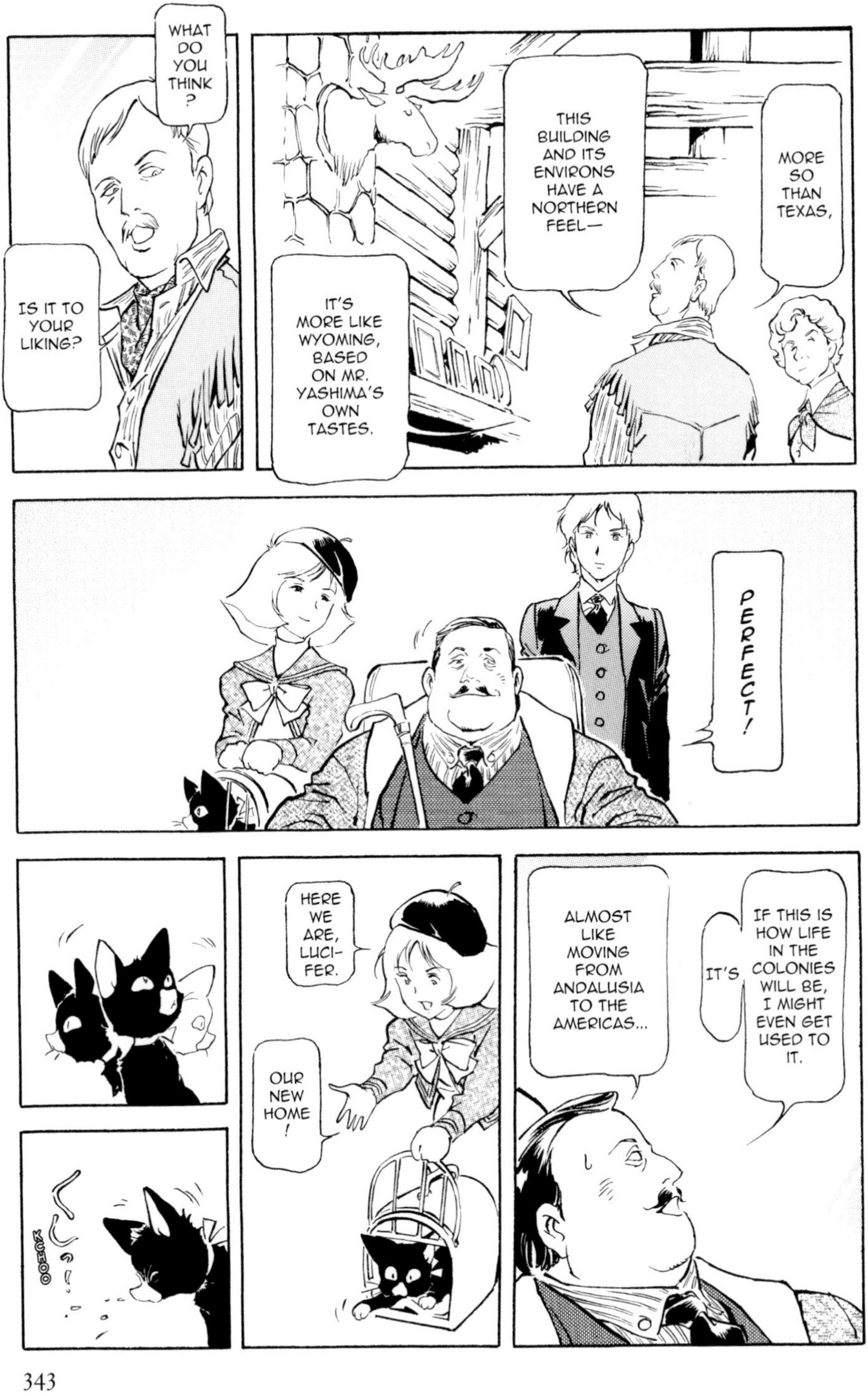
MORE SO THAN TEXAS,
THIS BUILDING AND ITS ENVIRONS HAVE A NORTHERN FEEL—
IT'S MORE LIKE WYOMING, BASED ON MR. YASHIMA'S OWN TASTES.
WHAT DO YOU THINK?
IS IT TO YOUR LIKING?
PERFECT!
IF THIS IS HOW LIFE IN THE COLONIES WILL BE, I MIGHT EVEN GET USED TO IT.
IT'S
ALMOST LIKE MOVING FROM ANDALUSIA TO THE AMERICAS...
HERE WE ARE, LUCIFER.
OUR NEW HOME!
KUHOO

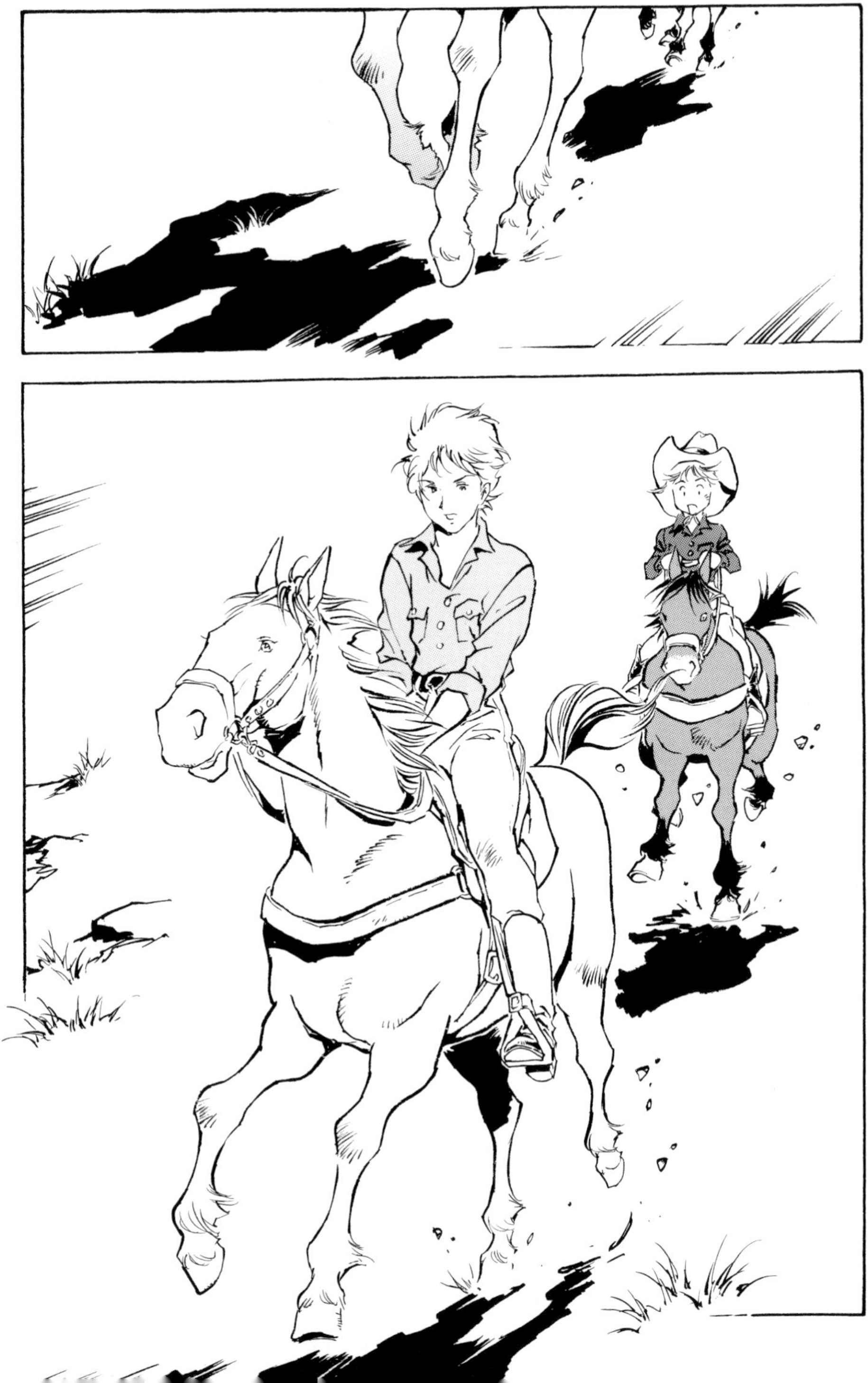

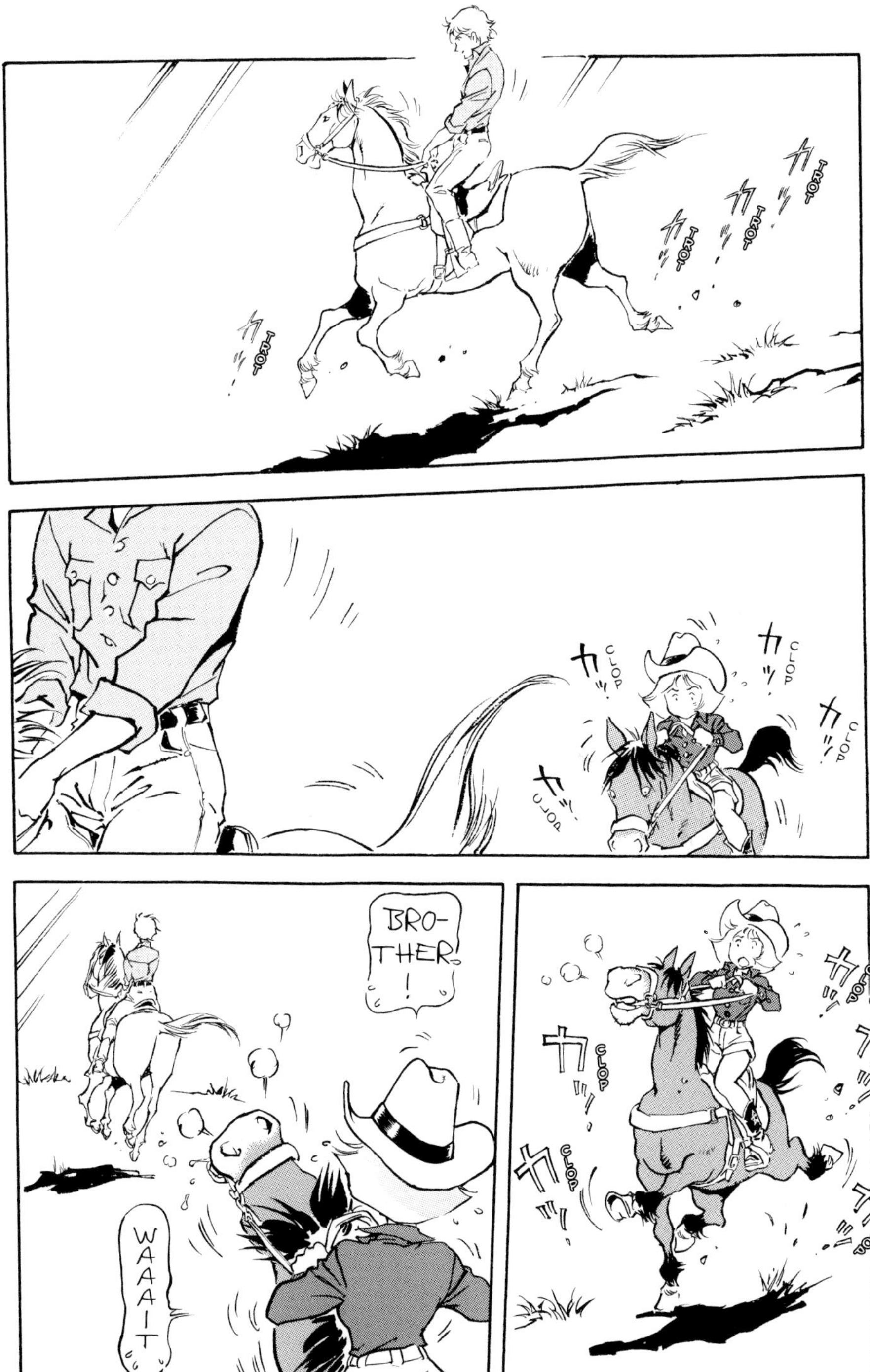
カッ TROT
カッ TROT
カッ TROT
カッ TROT
カッ CLOP
カッ CLOP
カッ CLOP
カッ CLOP
カッ CLOP
カッ CLOP
カッ CLOP
カッ CLOP
BRO-THER!
WAAAIT

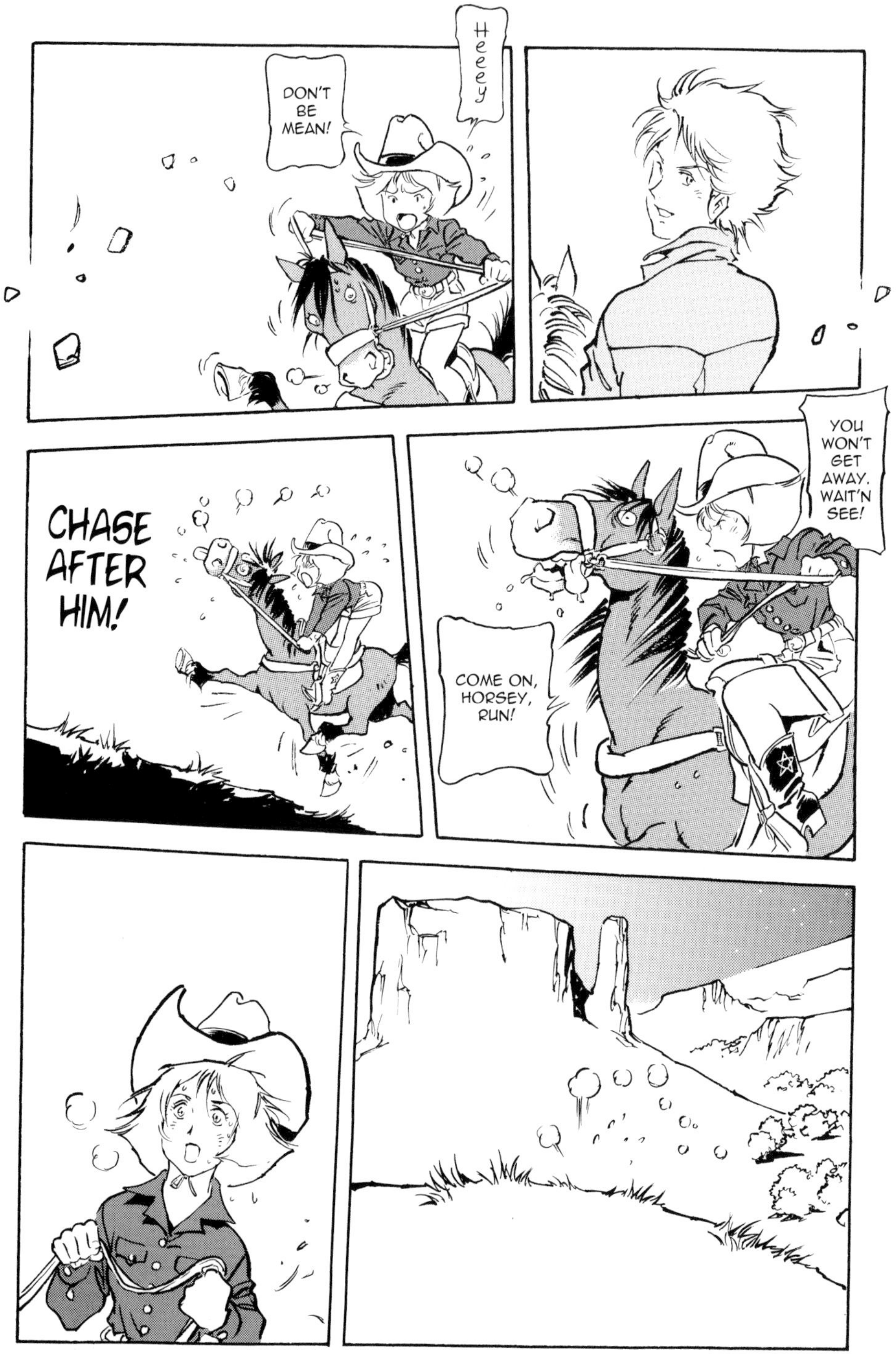
Heeey
DON'T BE MEAN!
YOU WON'T GET AWAY. WAIT'N SEE!
COME ON, HORSEY, RUN!
CHASE AFTER HIM!

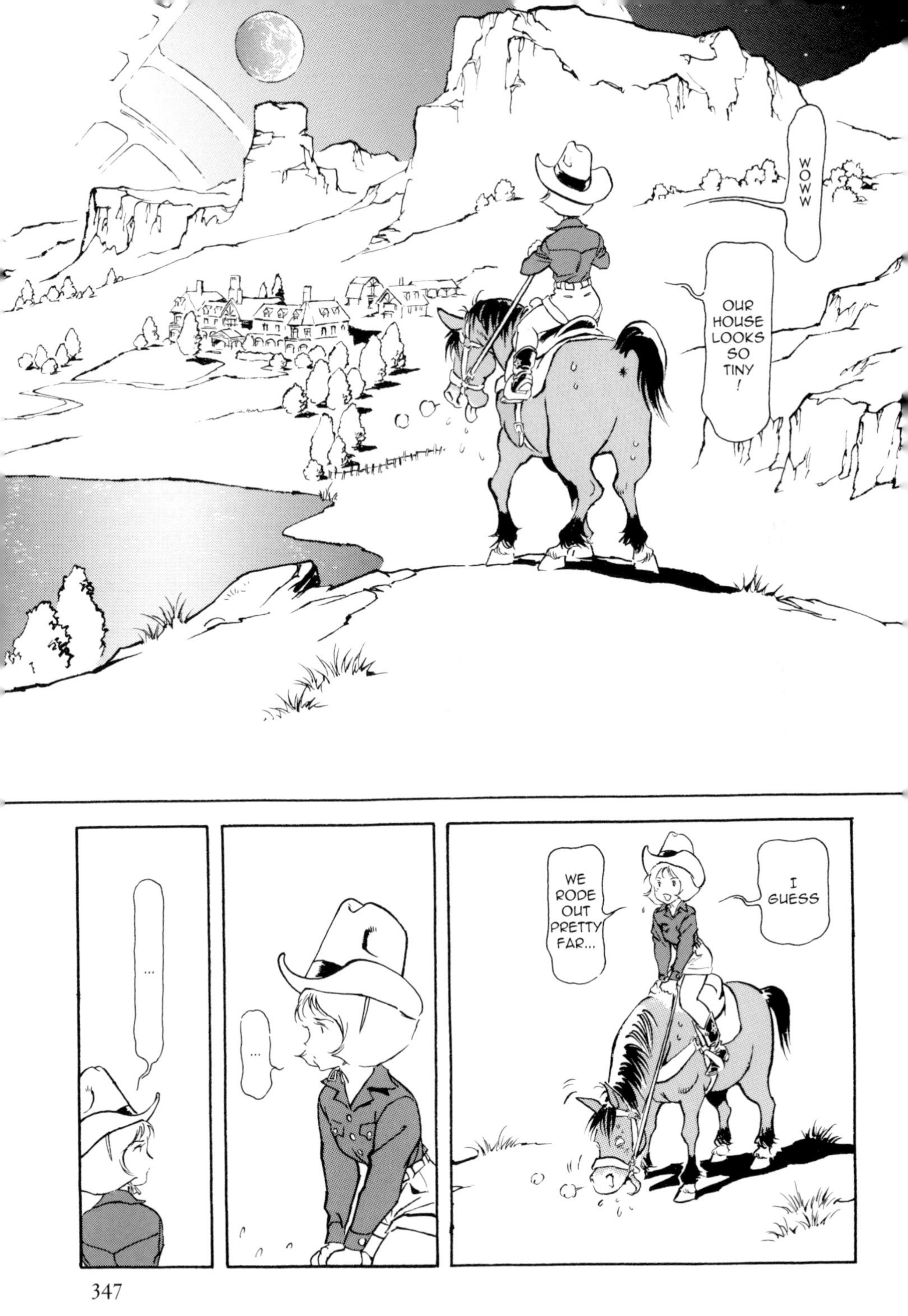
WOWW
OUR HOUSE LOOKS SO TINY!
I GUESS
WE RODE OUT PRETTY FAR...
...
...

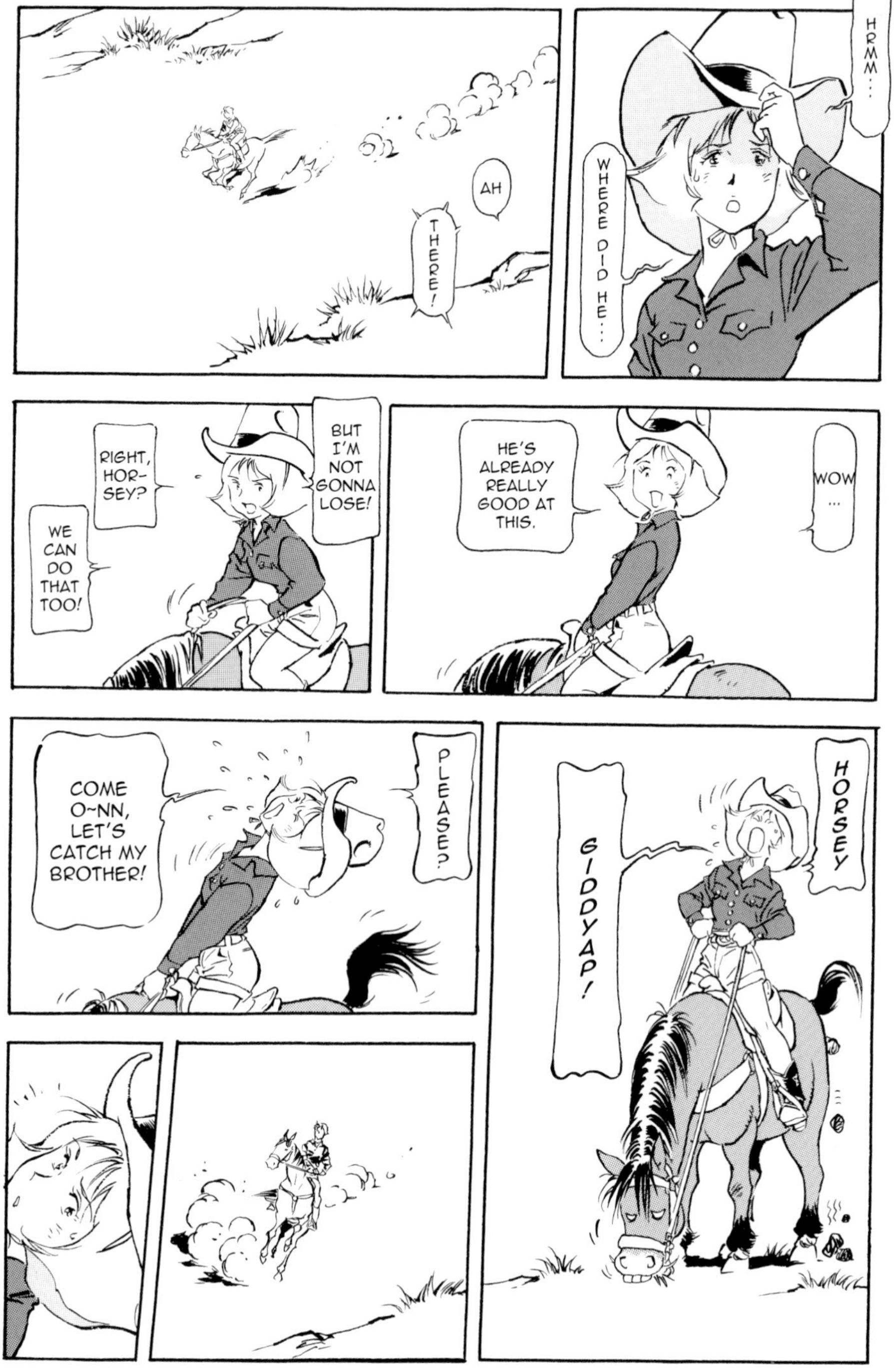
HRMM...
WHERE DID HE...
AH
THERE!
WOW...
HE'S ALREADY REALLY GOOD AT THIS.
BUT I'M NOT GONNA LOSE!
RIGHT, HORSEY?
WE CAN DO THAT TOO!
HORSEY
GIDDYAP!
PLEASE?
COME O~NN, LET'S CATCH MY BROTHER!

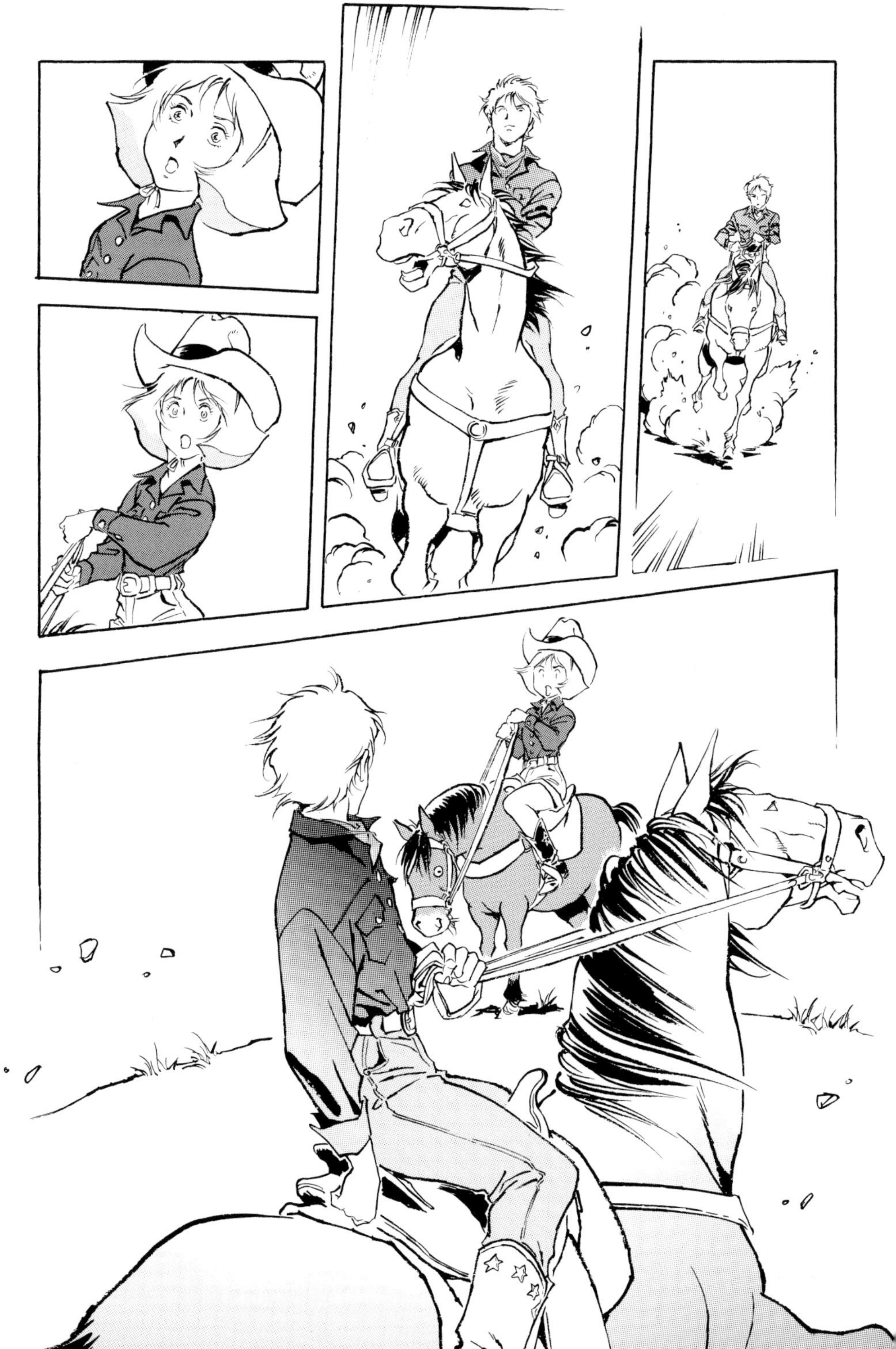

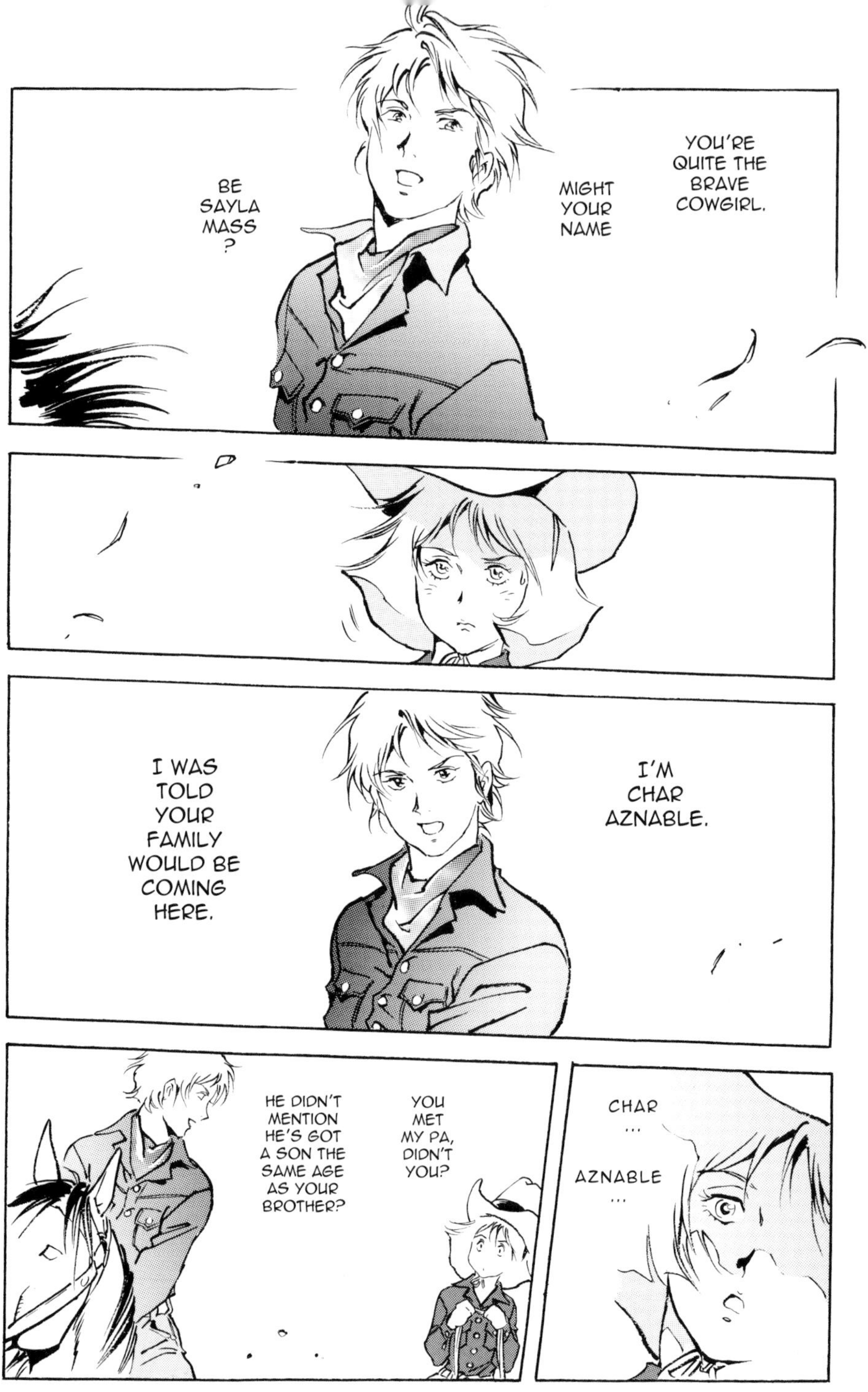
YOU'RE QUITE THE BRAVE COWGIRL.
MIGHT YOUR NAME
BE SAYLA MASS ?
I'M CHAR AZNABLE.
I WAS TOLD YOUR FAMILY WOULD BE COMING HERE.
CHAR ...
AZNABLE ...
YOU MET MY PA, DIDN'T YOU?
HE DIDN'T MENTION HE'S GOT A SON THE SAME AGE AS YOUR BROTHER?

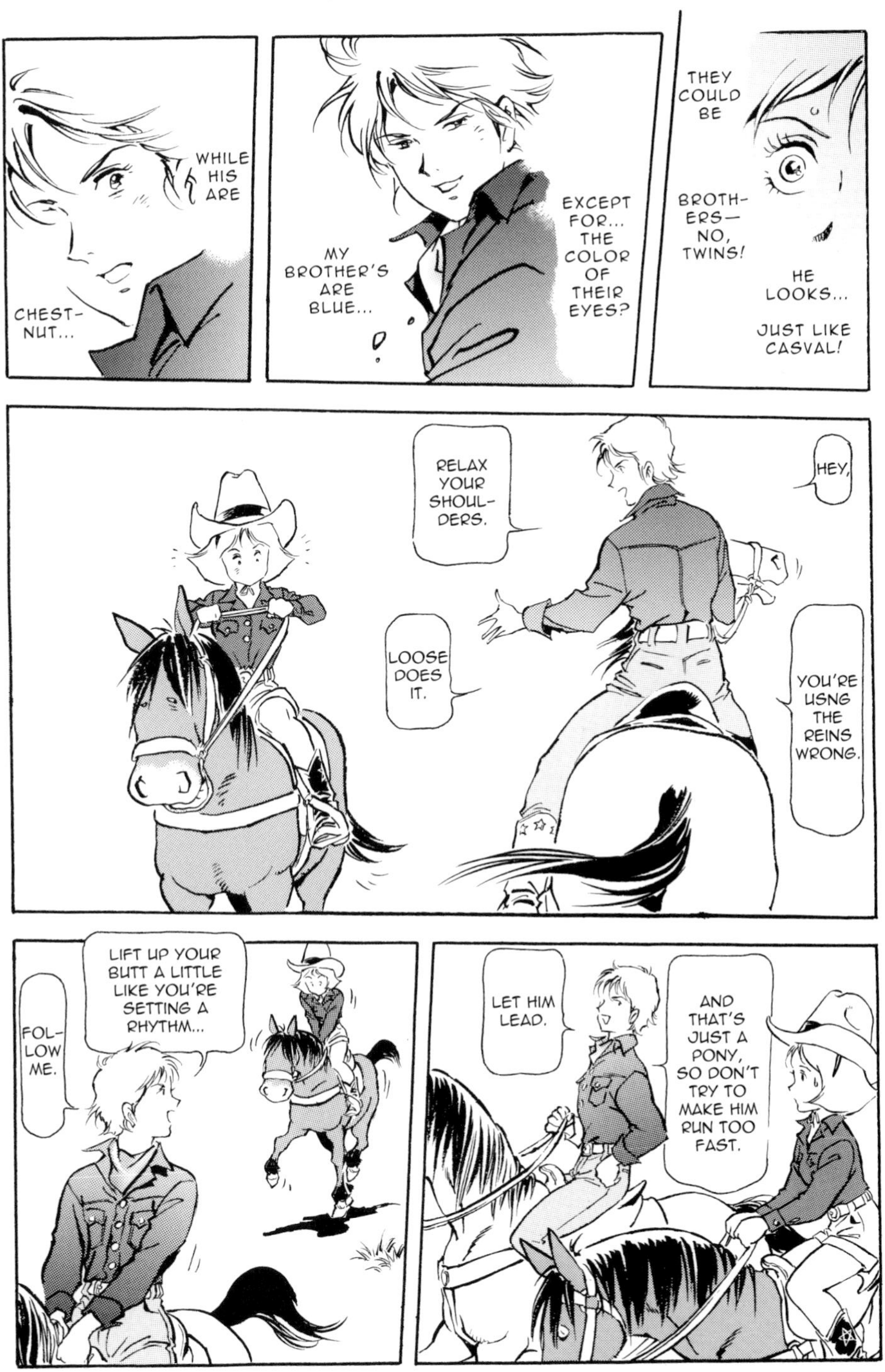
THEY COULD BE
BROTHERS— NO, TWINS!
HE LOOKS... JUST LIKE CASVAL!
EXCEPT FOR... THE COLOR OF THEIR EYES?
MY BROTHER'S ARE BLUE...
WHILE HIS ARE
CHESTNUT...
HEY,
YOU'RE USNG THE REINS WRONG.
RELAX YOUR SHOULDERS.
LOOSE DOES IT.
AND THAT'S JUST A PONY, SO DON'T TRY TO MAKE HIM RUN TOO FAST.
LET HIM LEAD.
LIFT UP YOUR BUTT A LITTLE LIKE YOU'RE SETTING A RHYTHM...
FOLLOW ME.

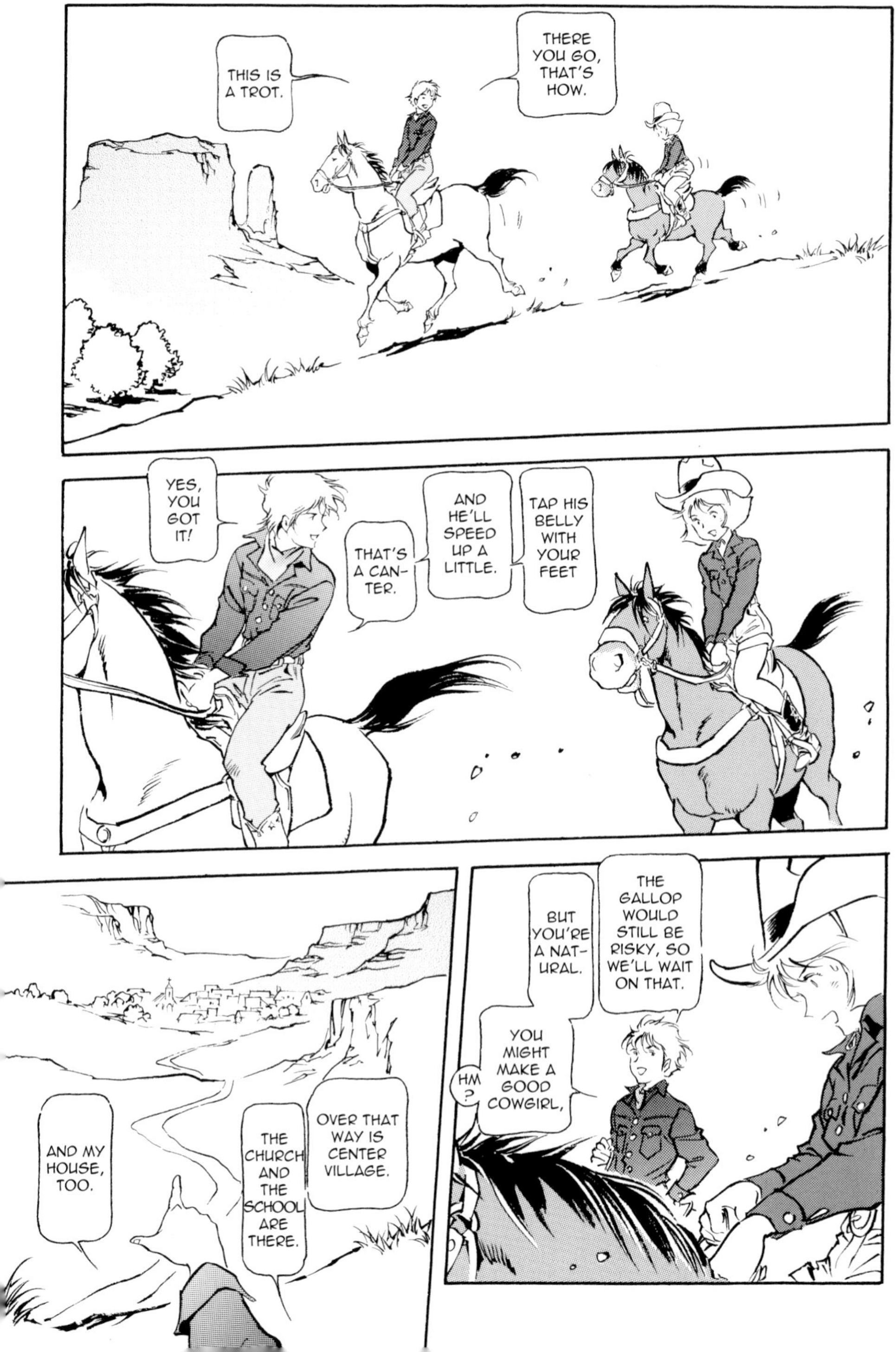
THERE YOU GO, THAT'S HOW.
THIS IS A TROT.
TAP HIS BELLY WITH YOUR FEET
AND HE'LL SPEED UP A LITTLE.
THAT'S A CAN-TER.
YES, YOU GOT IT!
THE GALLOP WOULD STILL BE RISKY, SO WE'LL WAIT ON THAT.
BUT YOU'RE A NAT-URAL.
YOU MIGHT MAKE A GOOD COWGIRL,
HM?
OVER THAT WAY IS CENTER VILLAGE.
THE CHURCH AND THE SCHOOL ARE THERE.
AND MY HOUSE, TOO.

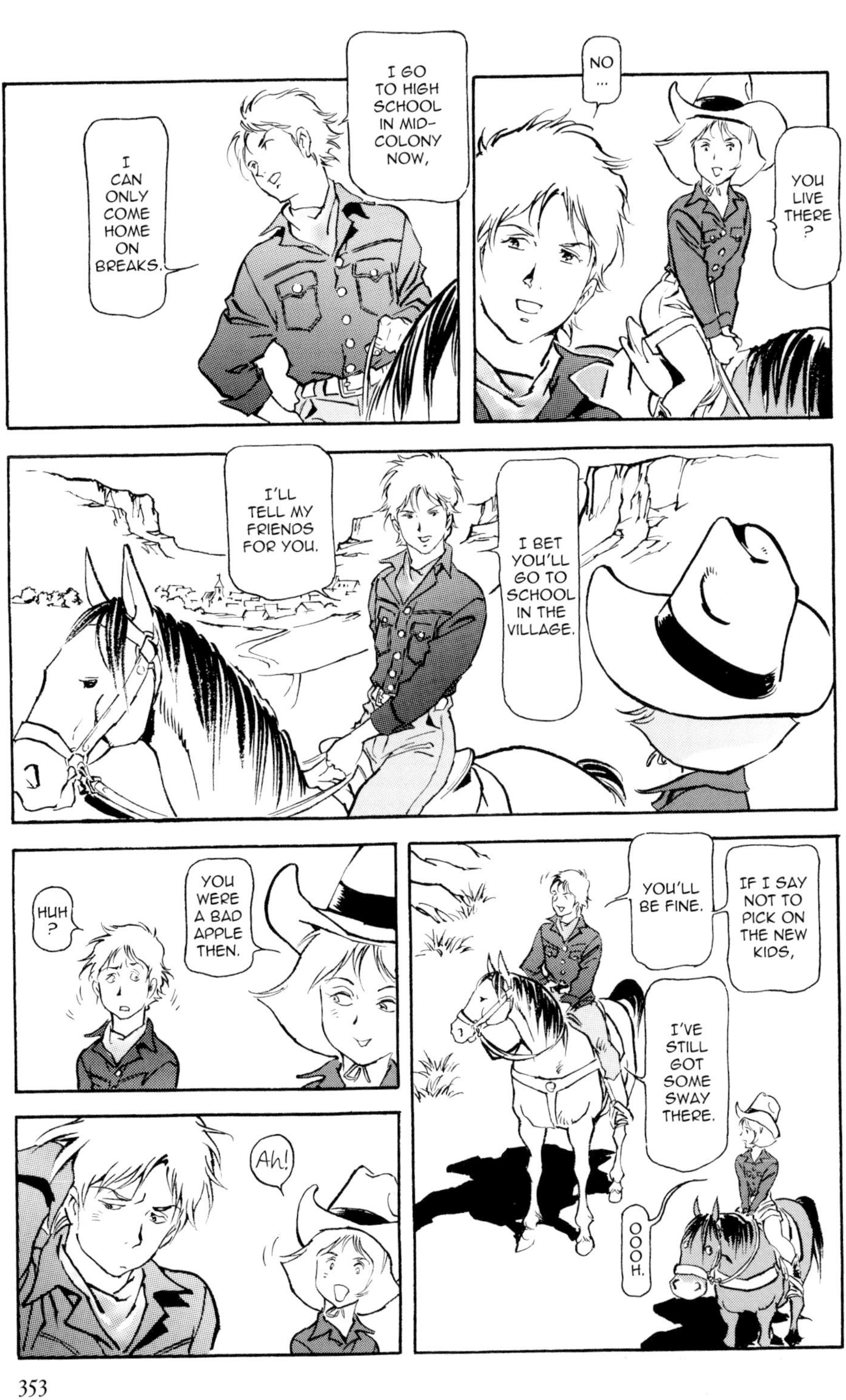
YOU LIVE THERE ?
NO ...
I GO TO HIGH SCHOOL IN MID-COLONY NOW,
I CAN ONLY COME HOME ON BREAKS.
I BET YOU'LL GO TO SCHOOL IN THE VILLAGE.
I'LL TELL MY FRIENDS FOR YOU.
IF I SAY NOT TO PICK ON THE NEW KIDS,
I'VE STILL GOT SOME SWAY THERE.
YOU'LL BE FINE.
OOOH.
YOU WERE A BAD APPLE THEN.
HUH ?
Ah!

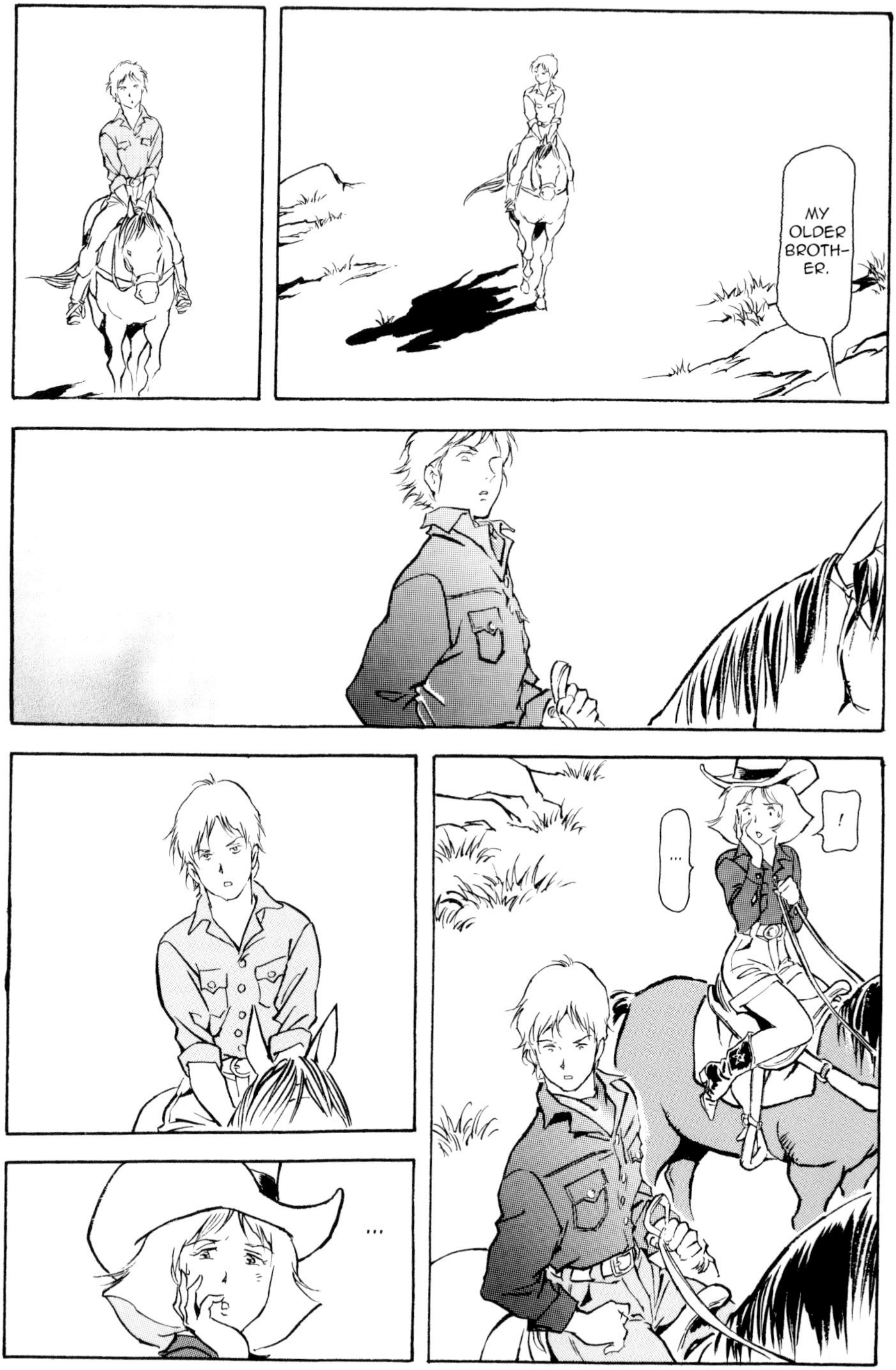
MY OLDER BROTH-ER.
!
...
...

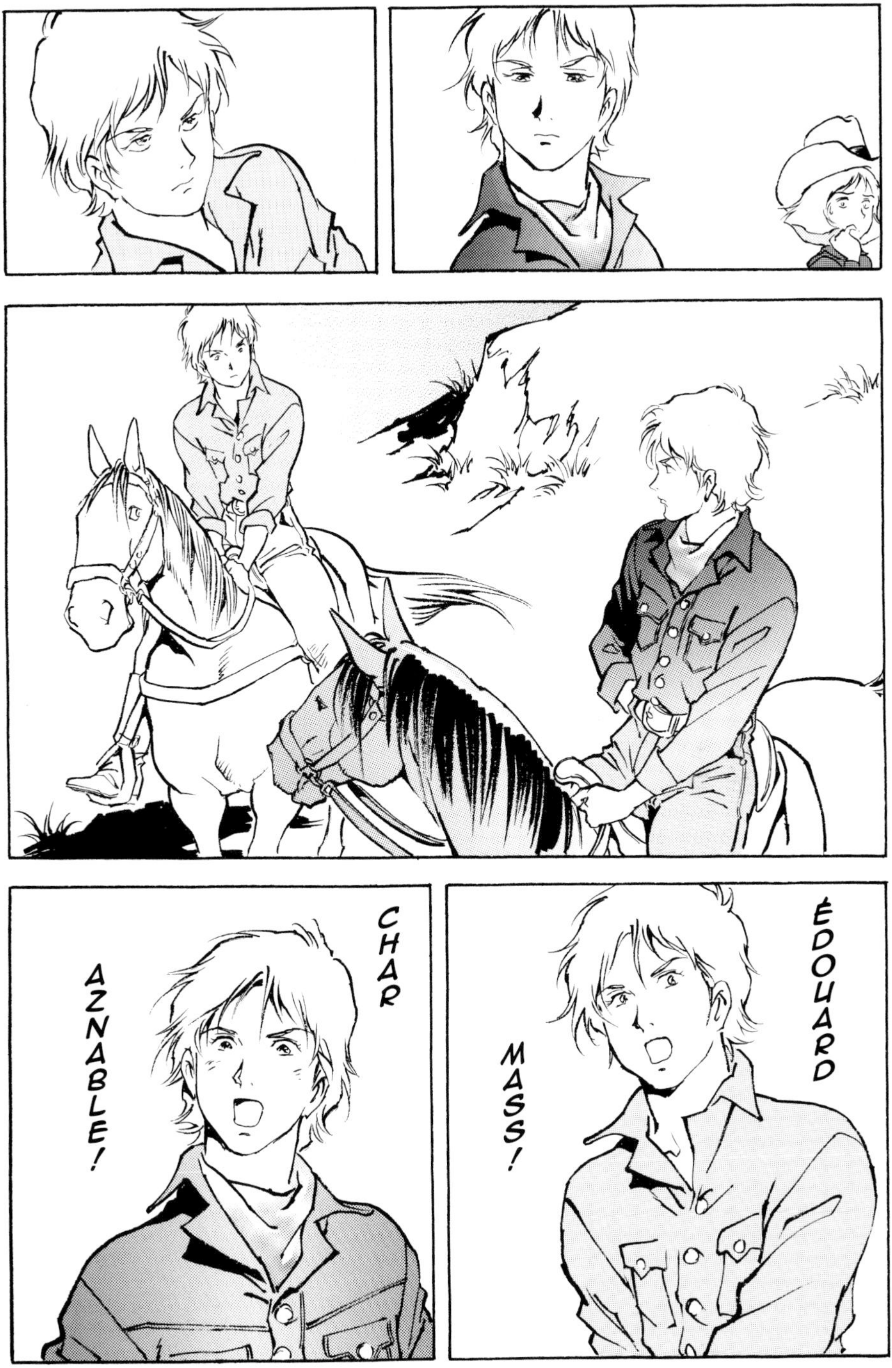
ÉDOUARD MASS!
CHAR AZNABLE!

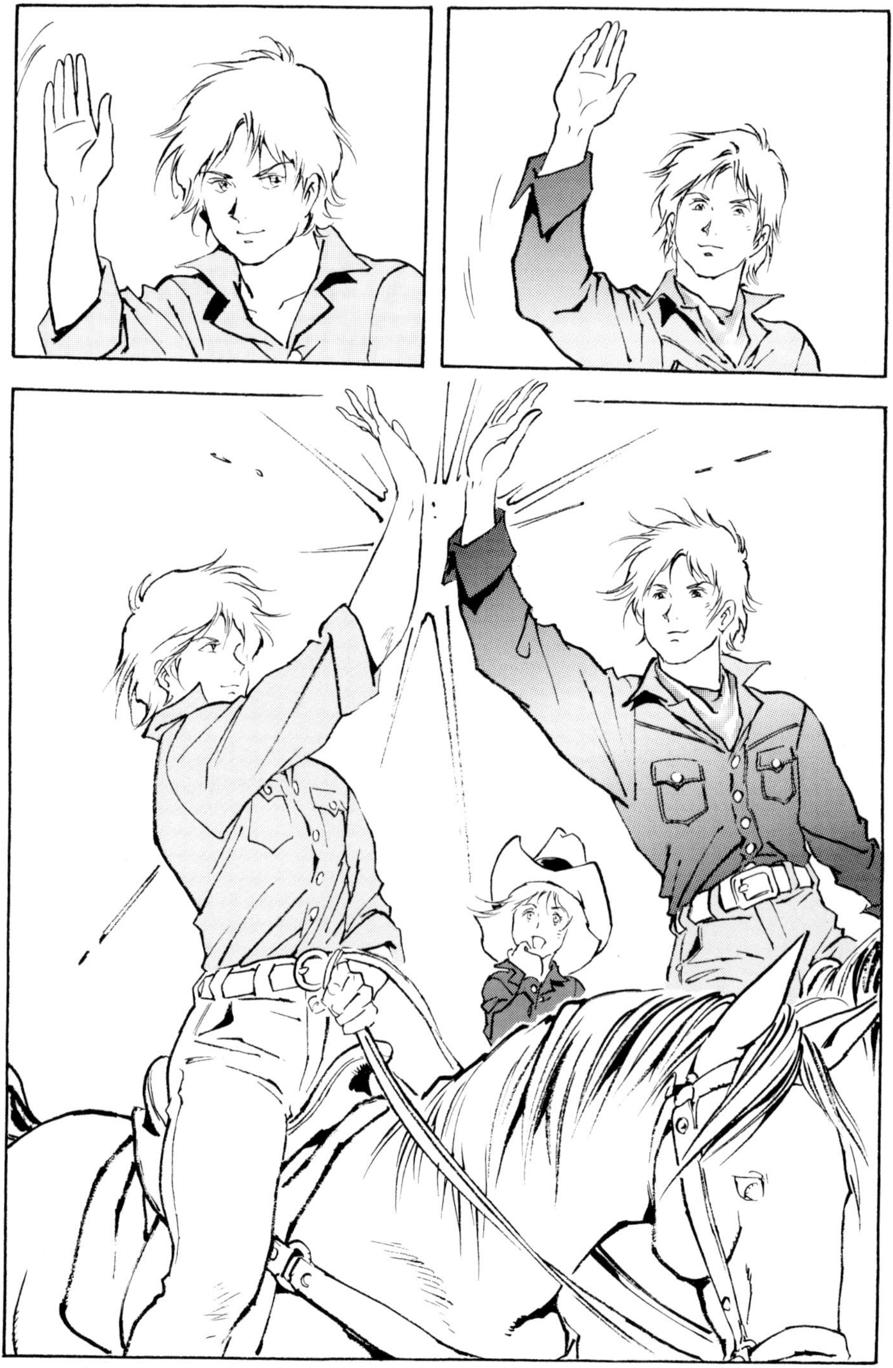

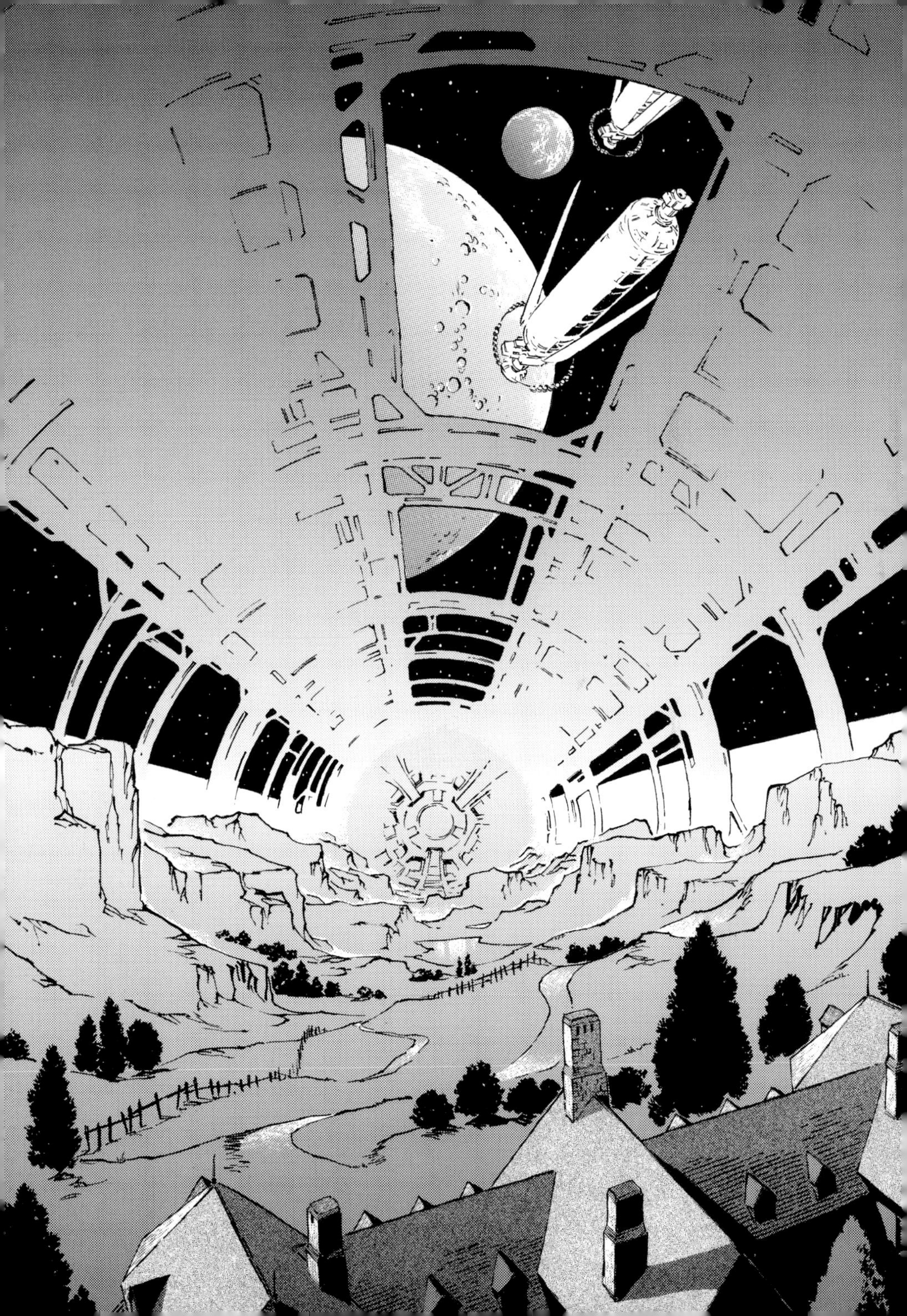

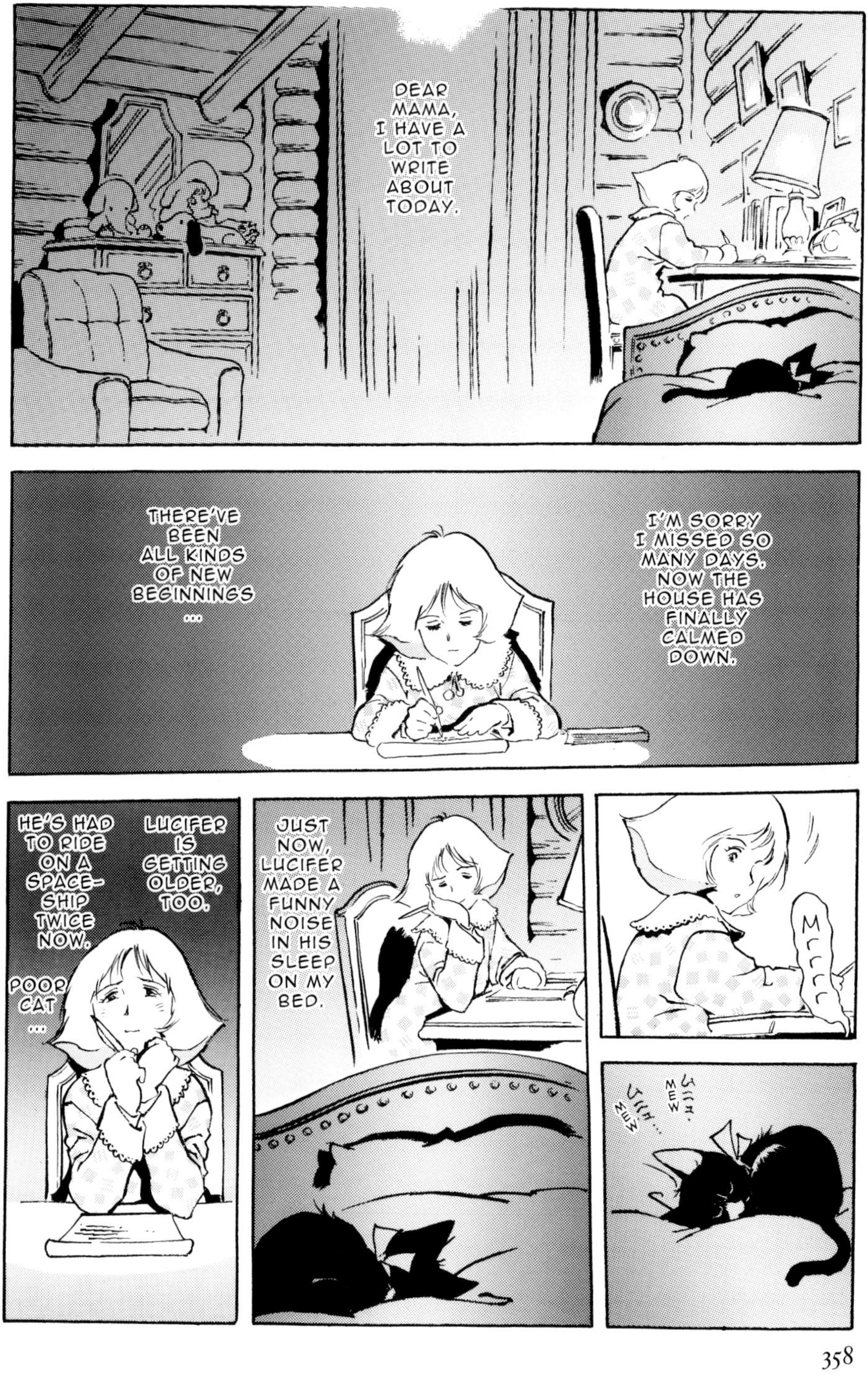
DEAR MAMA, I HAVE A LOT TO WRITE ABOUT TODAY.
I'M SORRY I MISSED SO MANY DAYS. NOW THE HOUSE HAS FINALLY CALMED DOWN.
THERE'VE BEEN ALL KINDS OF NEW BEGINNINGS ...
Mrrrr
MEW
MEW
JUST NOW, LUCIFER MADE A FUNNY NOISE IN HIS SLEEP ON MY BED.
LUCIFER IS GETTING OLDER, TOO.
HE'S HAD TO RIDE ON A SPACE-SHIP TWICE NOW.
POOR CAT ...

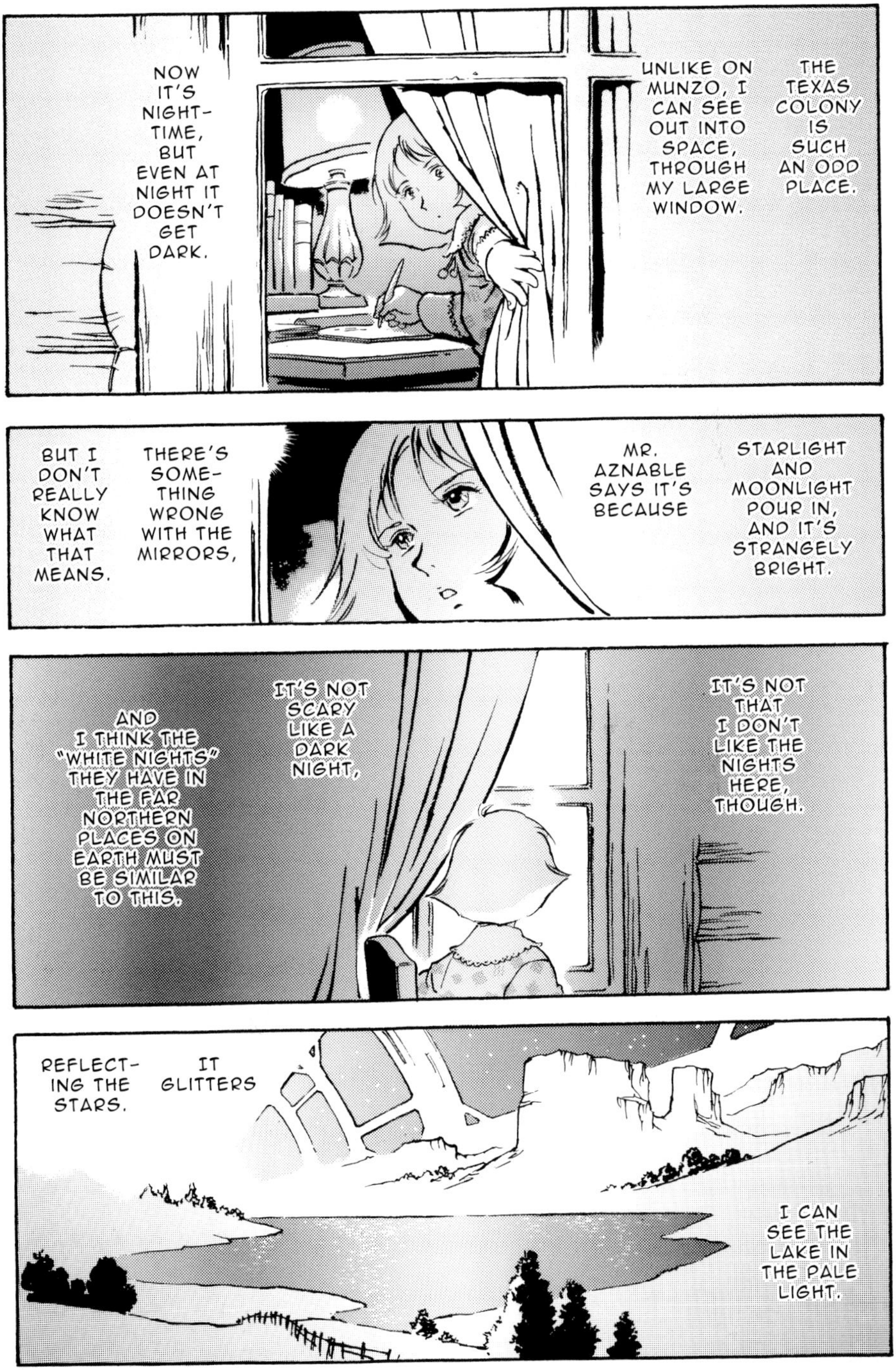
THE TEXAS COLONY IS SUCH AN ODD PLACE.
UNLIKE ON MUNZO, I CAN SEE OUT INTO SPACE, THROUGH MY LARGE WINDOW.
NOW IT'S NIGHT-TIME, BUT EVEN AT NIGHT IT DOESN'T GET DARK.
STARLIGHT AND MOONLIGHT POUR IN, AND IT'S STRANGELY BRIGHT.
MR. AZNABLE SAYS IT'S BECAUSE
THERE'S SOME-THING WRONG WITH THE MIRRORS,
BUT I DON'T REALLY KNOW WHAT THAT MEANS.
IT'S NOT THAT I DON'T LIKE THE NIGHTS HERE, THOUGH.
IT'S NOT SCARY LIKE A DARK NIGHT,
AND I THINK THE "WHITE NIGHTS" THEY HAVE IN THE FAR NORTHERN PLACES ON EARTH MUST BE SIMILAR TO THIS.
I CAN SEE THE LAKE IN THE PALE LIGHT.
IT GLITTERS
REFLECT-ING THE STARS.

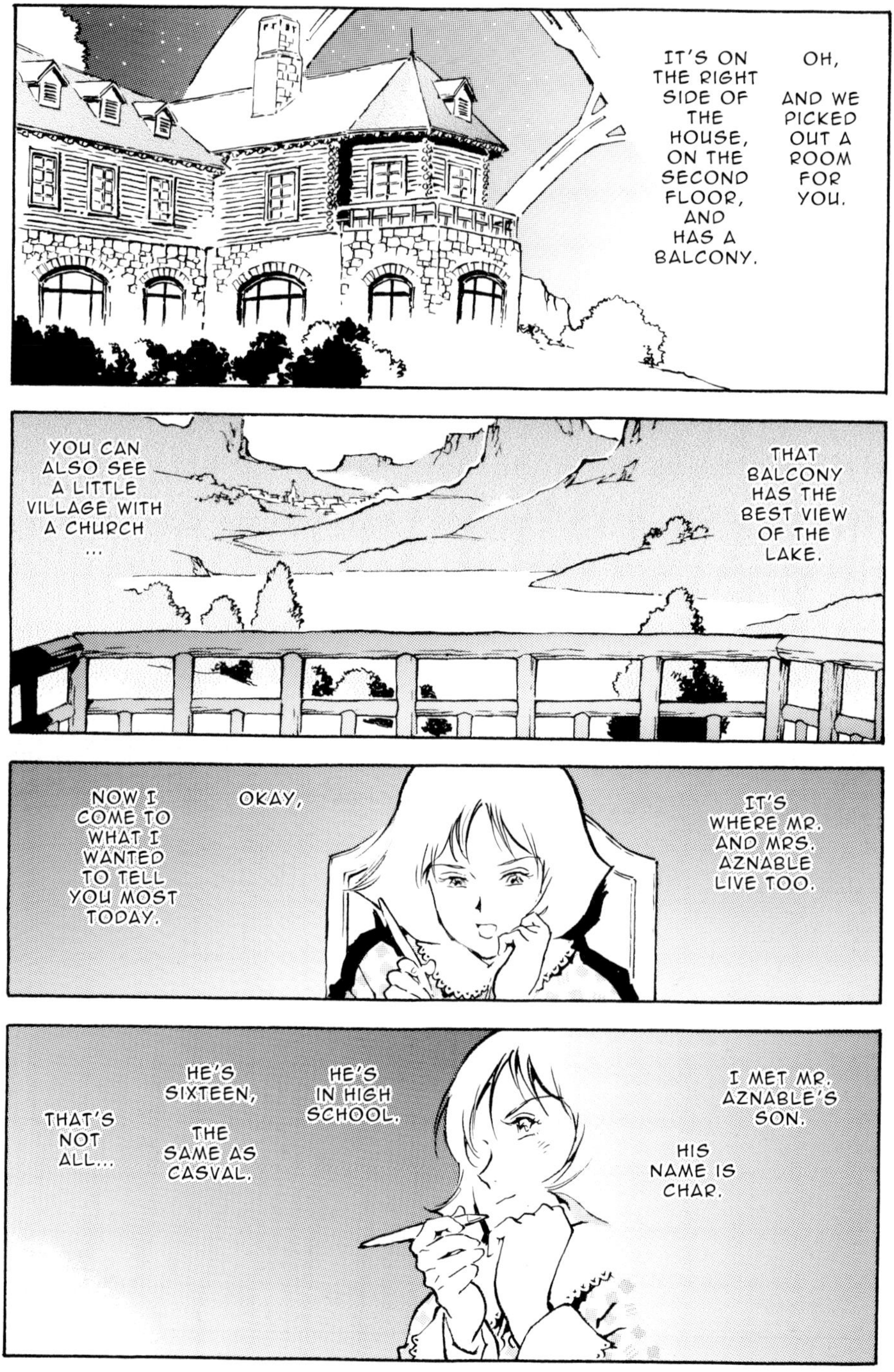
OH,
AND WE PICKED OUT A ROOM FOR YOU.
IT'S ON THE RIGHT SIDE OF THE HOUSE, ON THE SECOND FLOOR, AND HAS A BALCONY.
THAT BALCONY HAS THE BEST VIEW OF THE LAKE.
YOU CAN ALSO SEE A LITTLE VILLAGE WITH A CHURCH ...
IT'S WHERE MR. AND MRS. AZNABLE LIVE TOO.
OKAY,
NOW I COME TO WHAT I WANTED TO TELL YOU MOST TODAY.
I MET MR. AZNABLE'S SON.
HIS NAME IS CHAR.
HE'S IN HIGH SCHOOL.
HE'S SIXTEEN,
THE SAME AS CASVAL.
THAT'S NOT ALL...

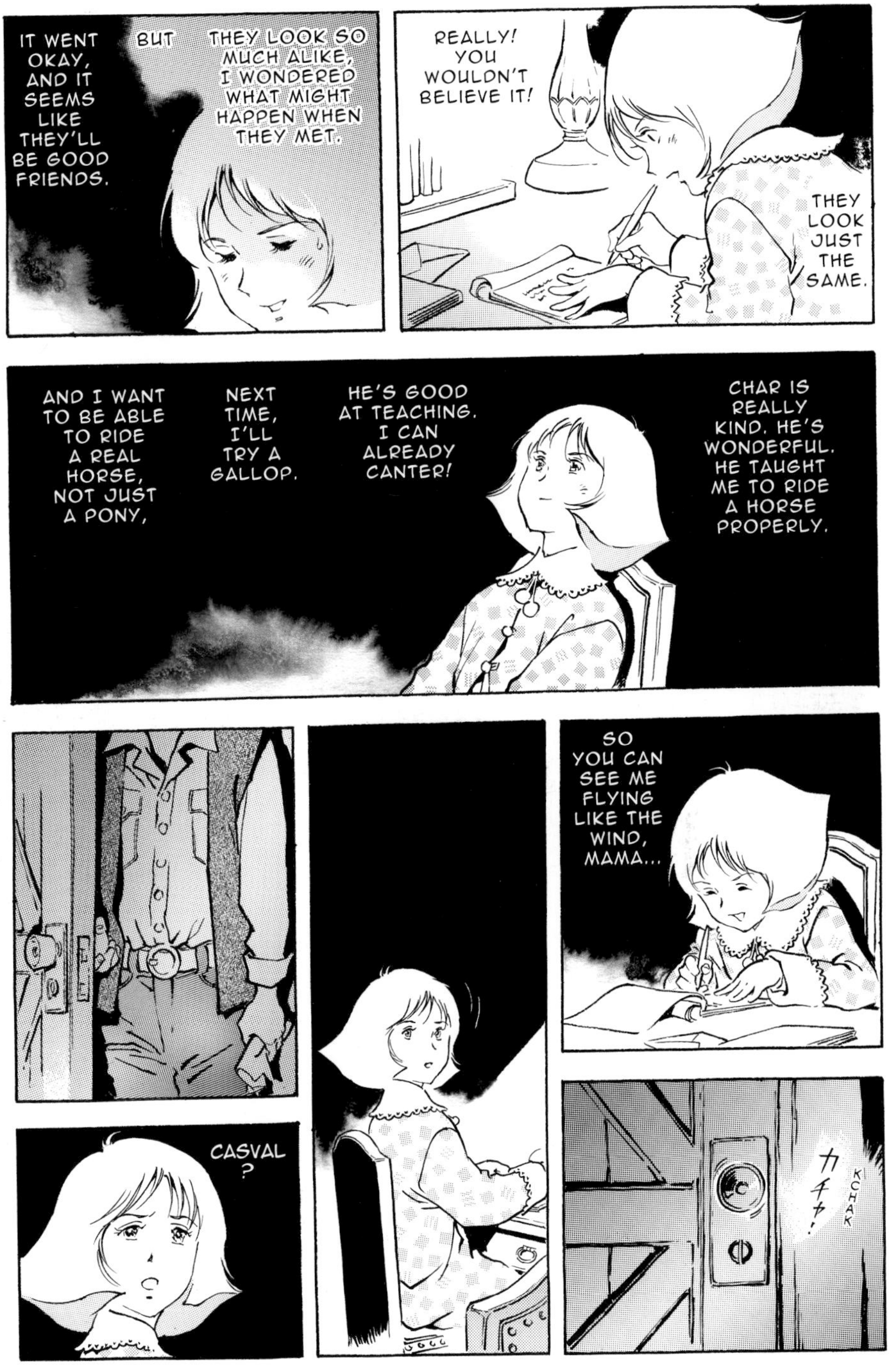
REALLY! YOU WOULDN'T BELIEVE IT!
THEY LOOK JUST THE SAME.
THEY LOOK SO MUCH ALIKE, I WONDERED WHAT MIGHT HAPPEN WHEN THEY MET.
BUT
IT WENT OKAY, AND IT SEEMS LIKE THEY'LL BE GOOD FRIENDS.
CHAR IS REALLY KIND. HE'S WONDERFUL. HE TAUGHT ME TO RIDE A HORSE PROPERLY.
HE'S GOOD AT TEACHING. I CAN ALREADY CANTER!
NEXT TIME, I'LL TRY A GALLOP.
AND I WANT TO BE ABLE TO RIDE A REAL HORSE, NOT JUST A PONY,
SO YOU CAN SEE ME FLYING LIKE THE WIND, MAMA...
カチャ!
KCHAK
CASVAL?

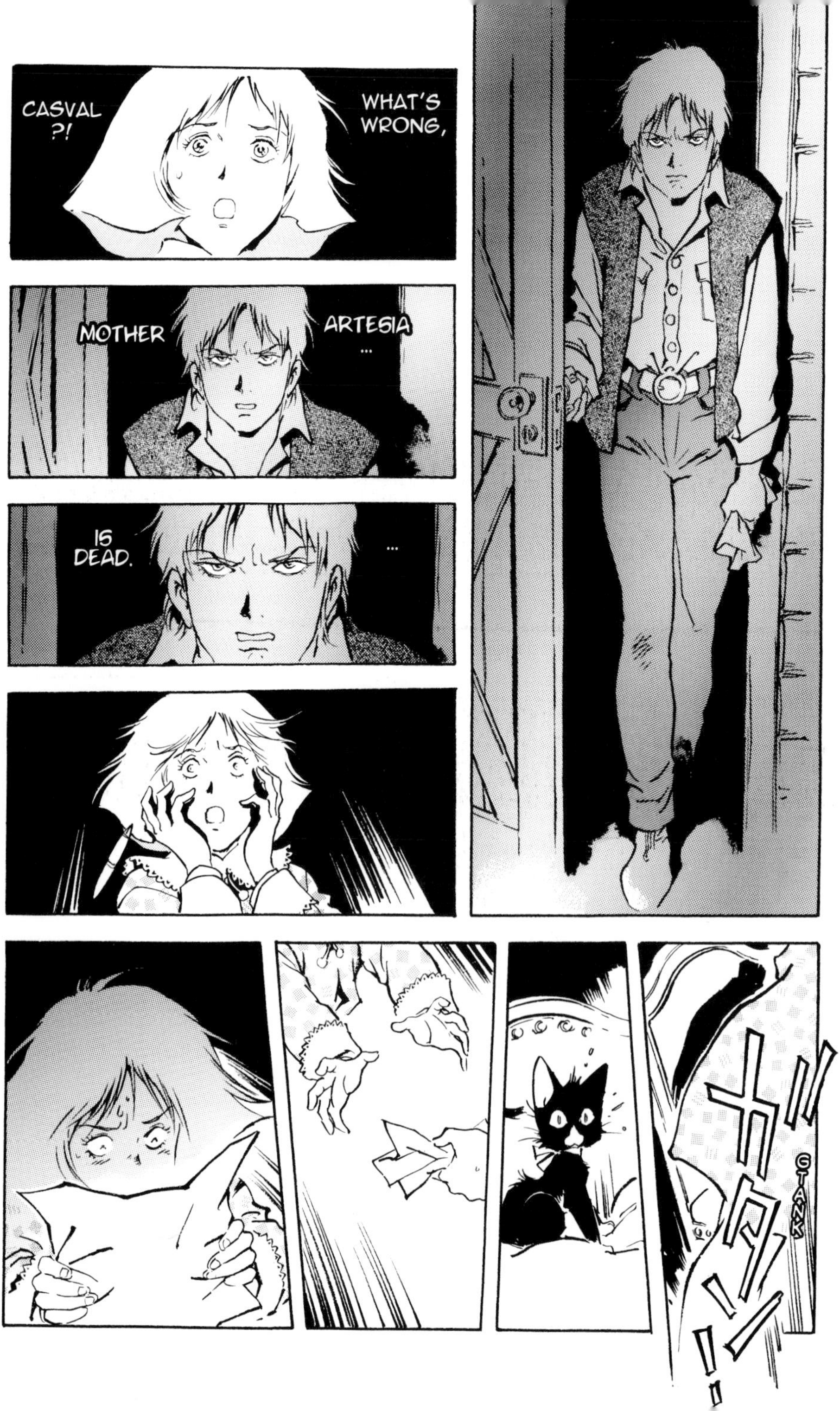

WHAT'S WRONG,
CASVAL ?!
ARTESIA ...
MOTHER
...
IS DEAD.
GTANK

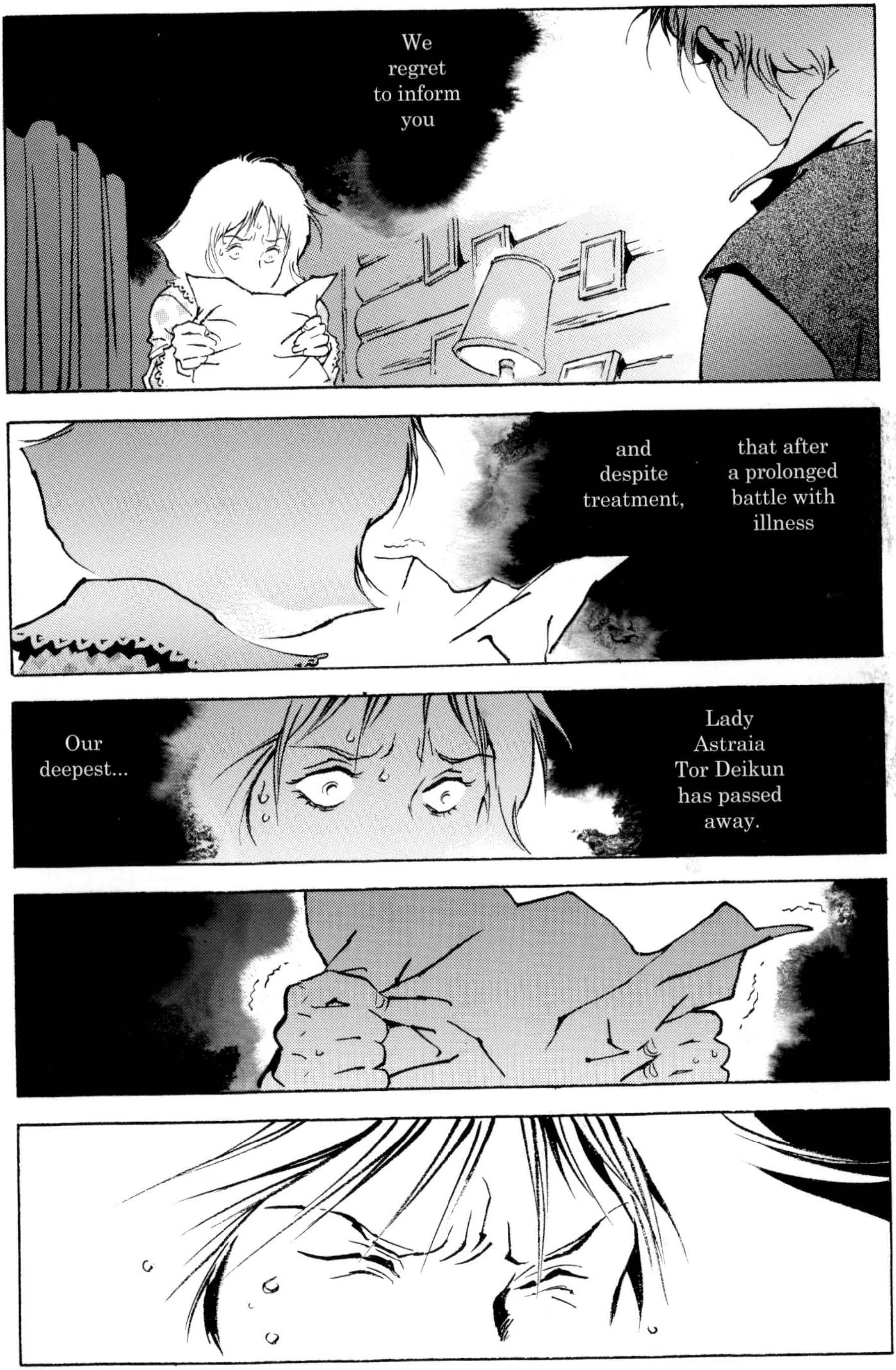
We regret to inform you
that after a prolonged battle with illness
and despite treatment,
Lady Astraia Tor Deikun has passed away.
Our deepest...

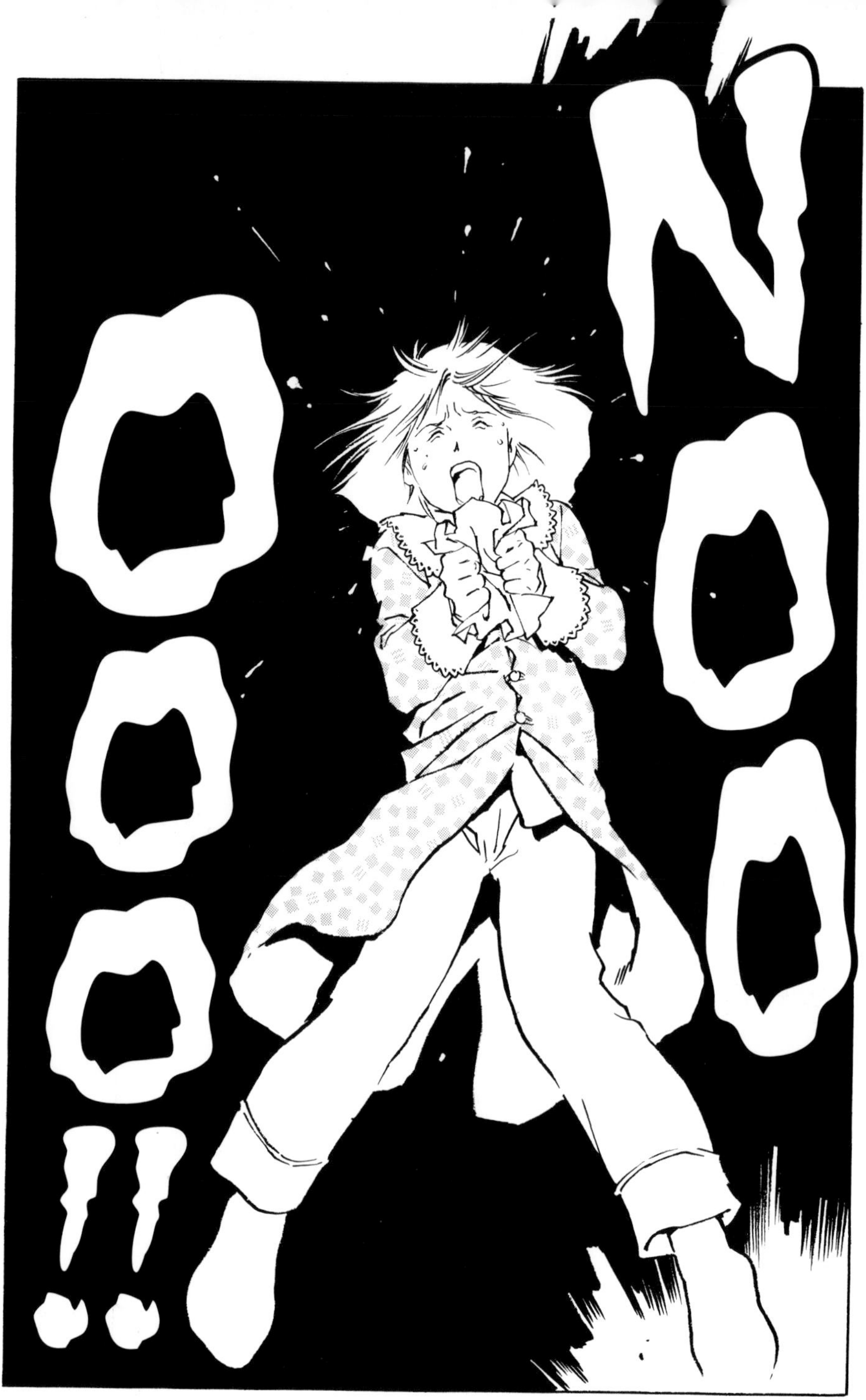
NOOOOO!!

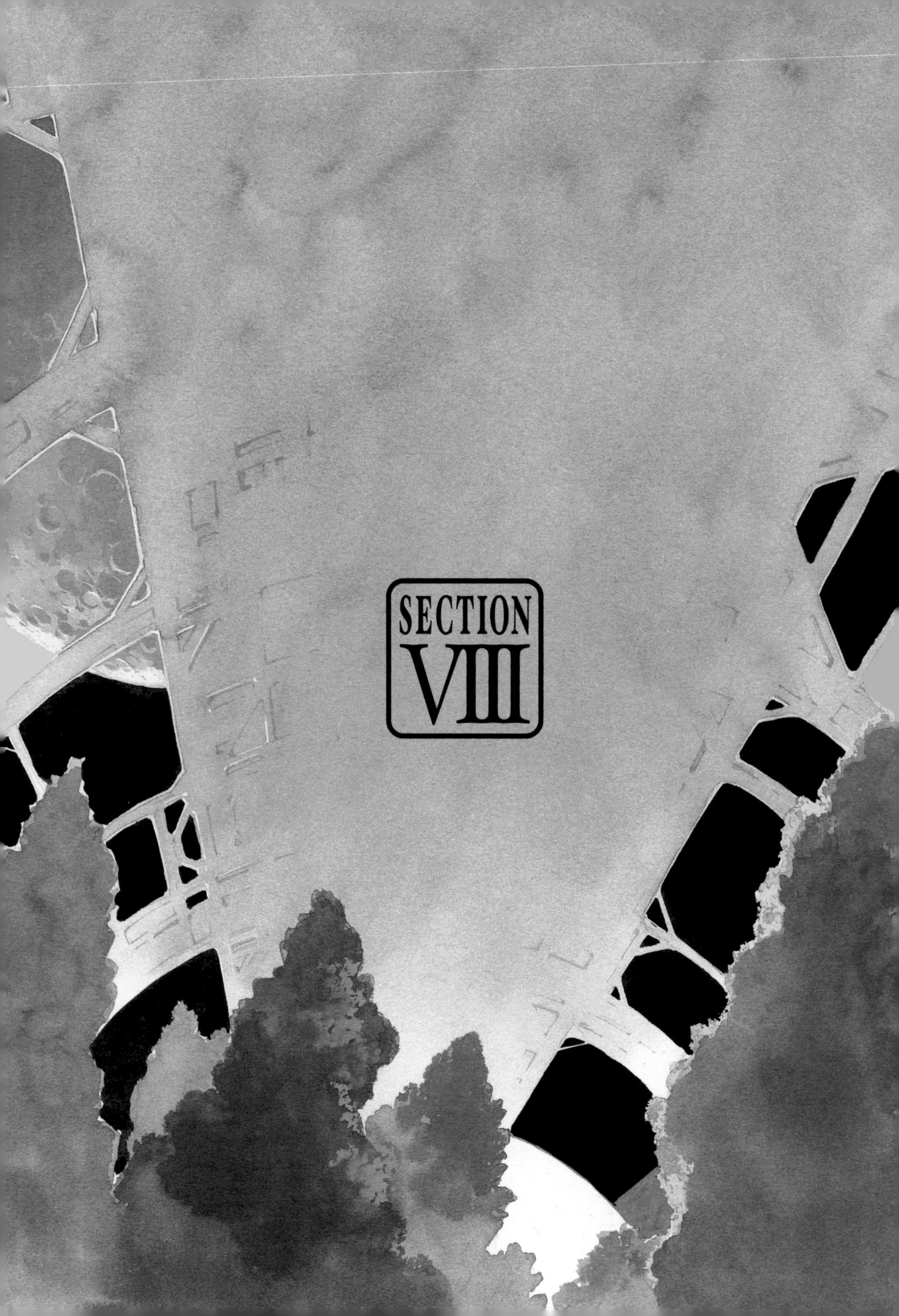
SECTION
VIII

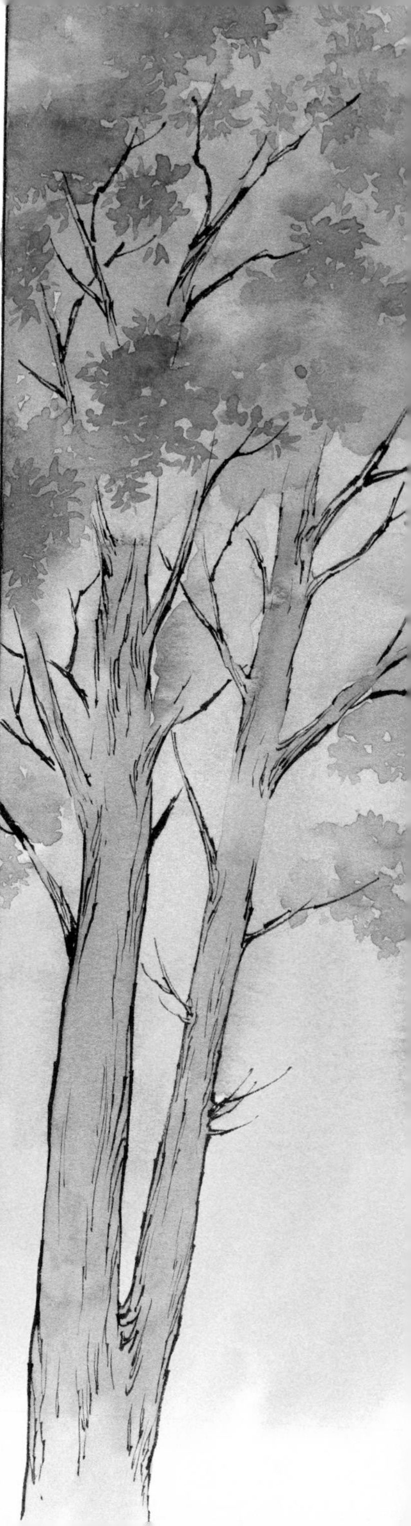

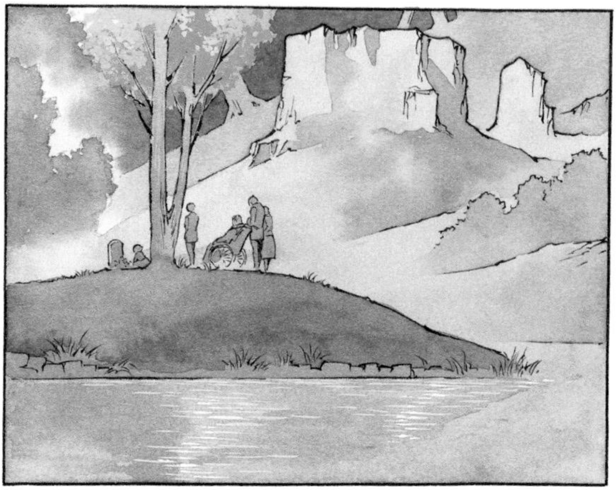

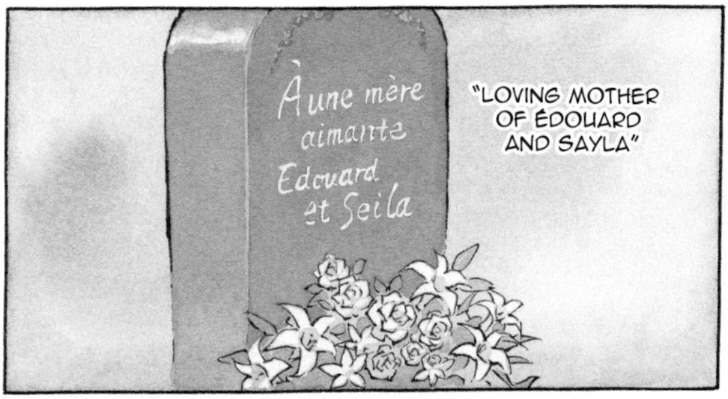
À une mère
aimante
Edouard
et Seila
"LOVING MOTHER OF ÉDOUARD AND SAYLA"

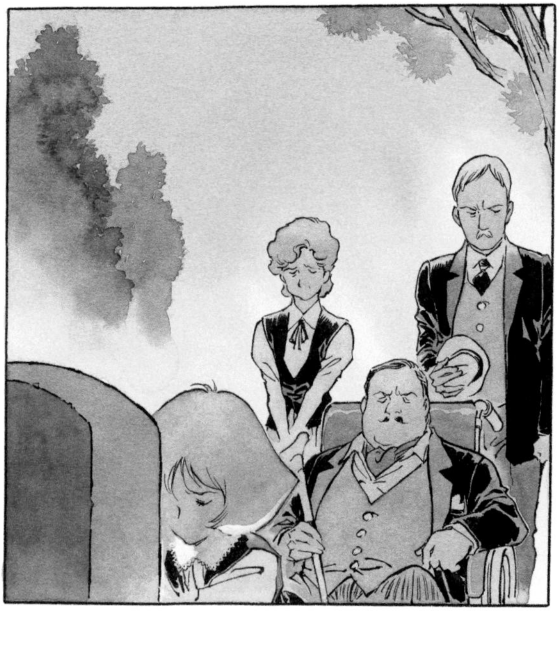

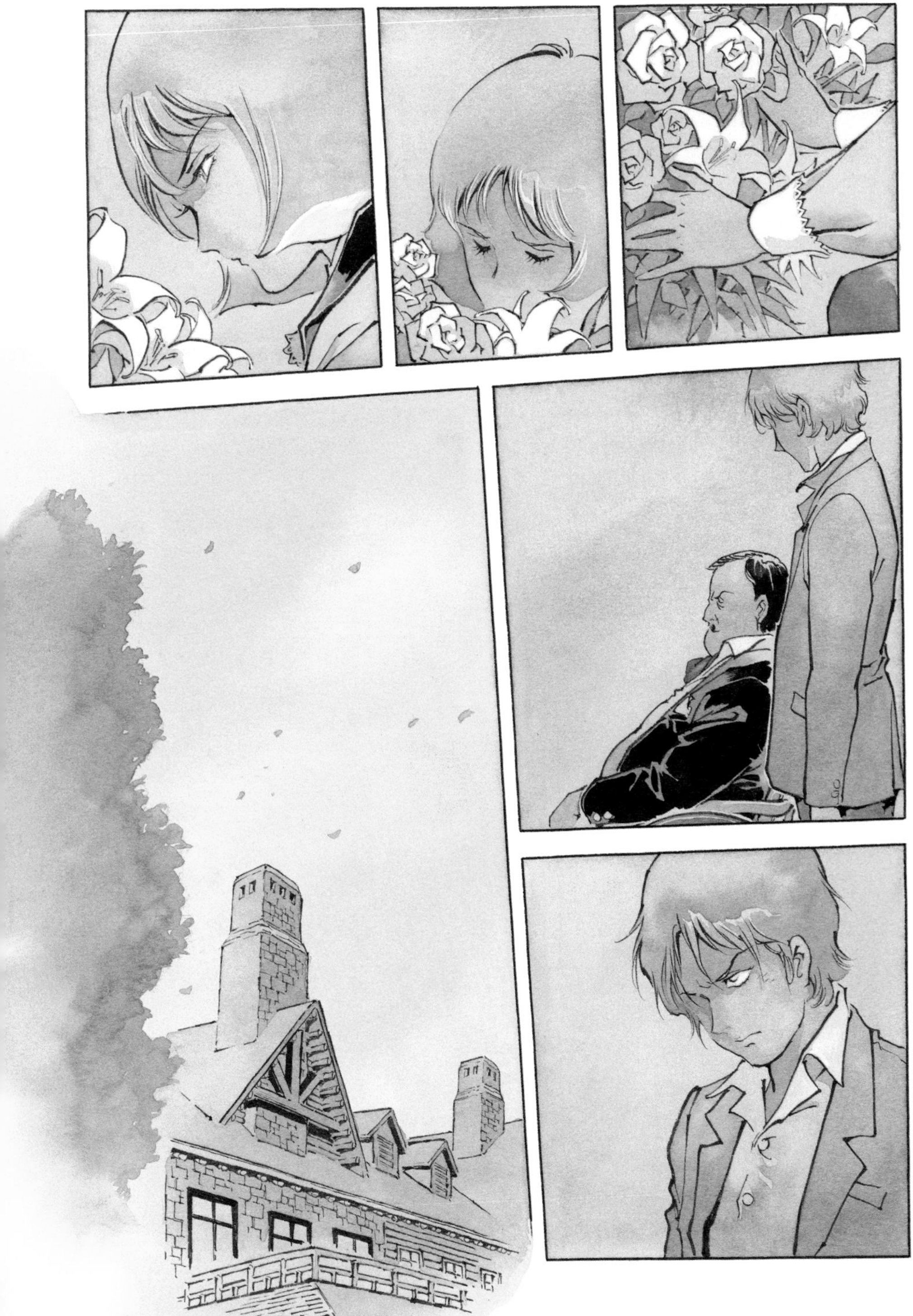

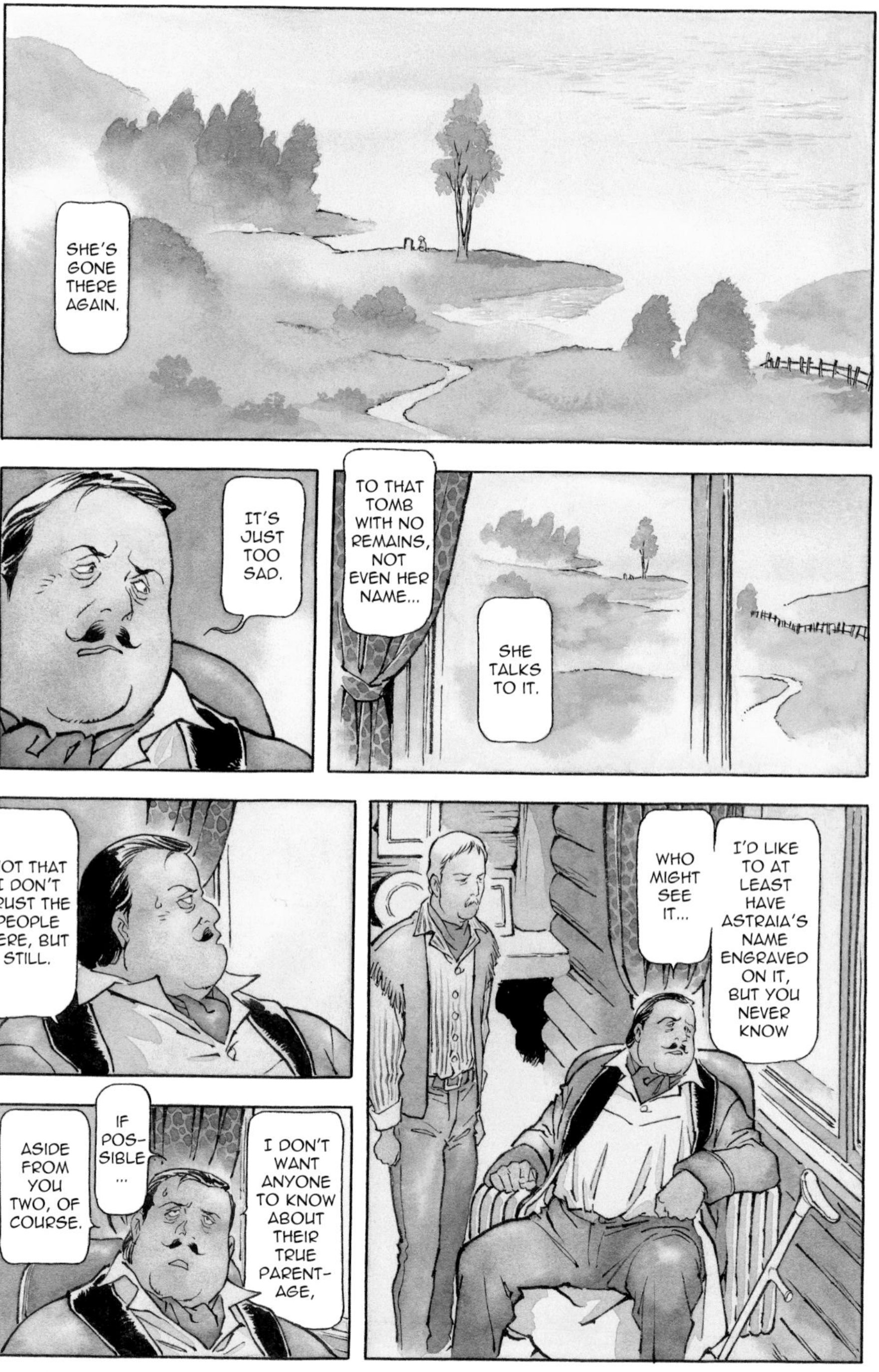
SHE'S GONE THERE AGAIN.
TO THAT TOMB WITH NO REMAINS, NOT EVEN HER NAME...
SHE TALKS TO IT.
IT'S JUST TOO SAD.
I'D LIKE TO AT LEAST HAVE ASTRAIA'S NAME ENGRAVED ON IT, BUT YOU NEVER KNOW
WHO MIGHT SEE IT...
NOT THAT I DON'T TRUST THE PEOPLE HERE, BUT STILL.
I DON'T WANT ANYONE TO KNOW ABOUT THEIR TRUE PARENT-AGE,
IF POS-SIBLE...
ASIDE FROM YOU TWO, OF COURSE.

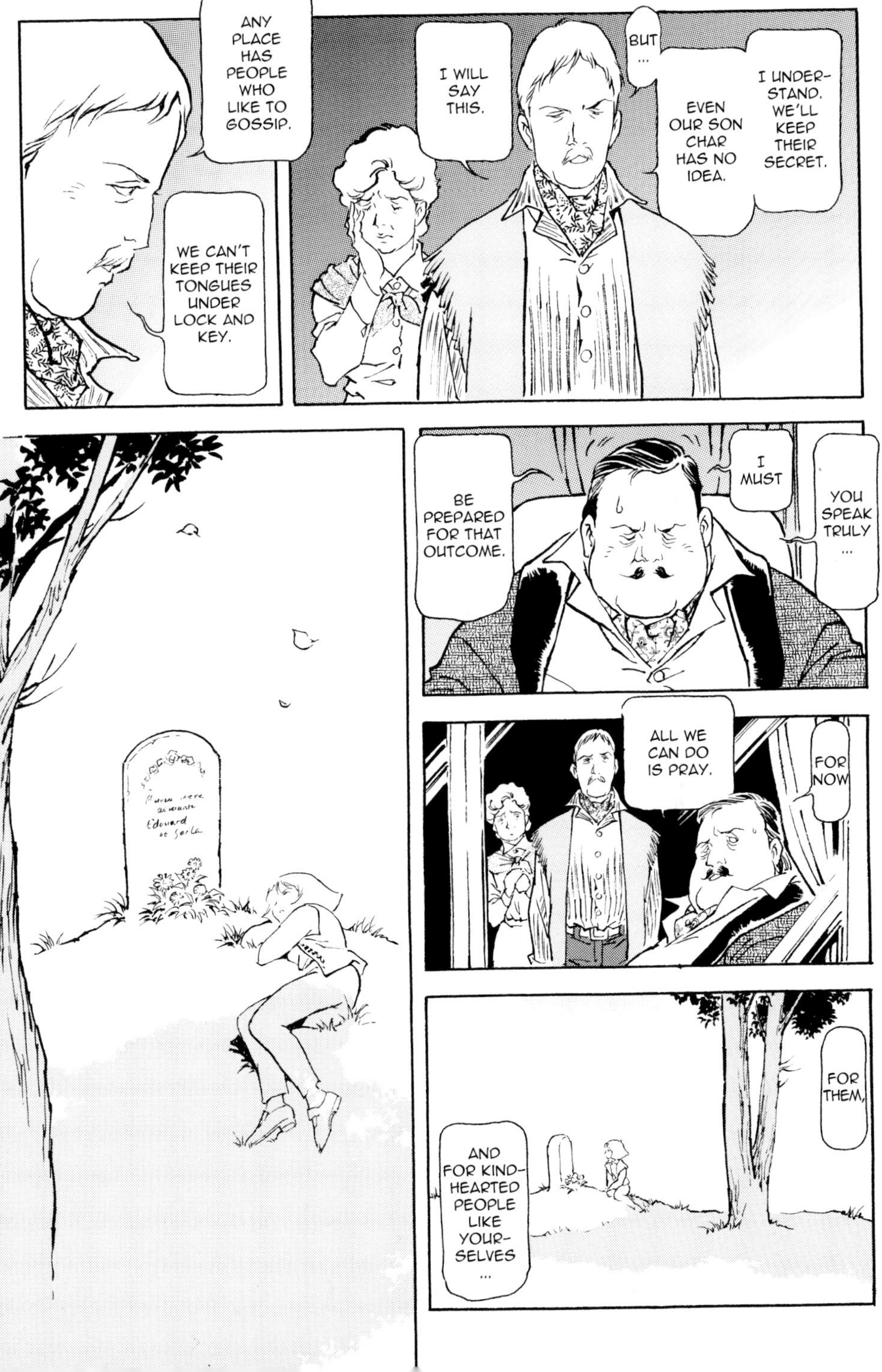
I UNDER-STAND. WE'LL KEEP THEIR SECRET.
BUT ...
EVEN OUR SON CHAR HAS NO IDEA.
I WILL SAY THIS.
ANY PLACE HAS PEOPLE WHO LIKE TO GOSSIP.
WE CAN'T KEEP THEIR TONGUES UNDER LOCK AND KEY.
YOU SPEAK TRULY ...
I MUST
BE PREPARED FOR THAT OUTCOME.
FOR NOW
ALL WE CAN DO IS PRAY.
FOR THEM,
AND FOR KIND-HEARTED PEOPLE LIKE YOUR-SELVES ...

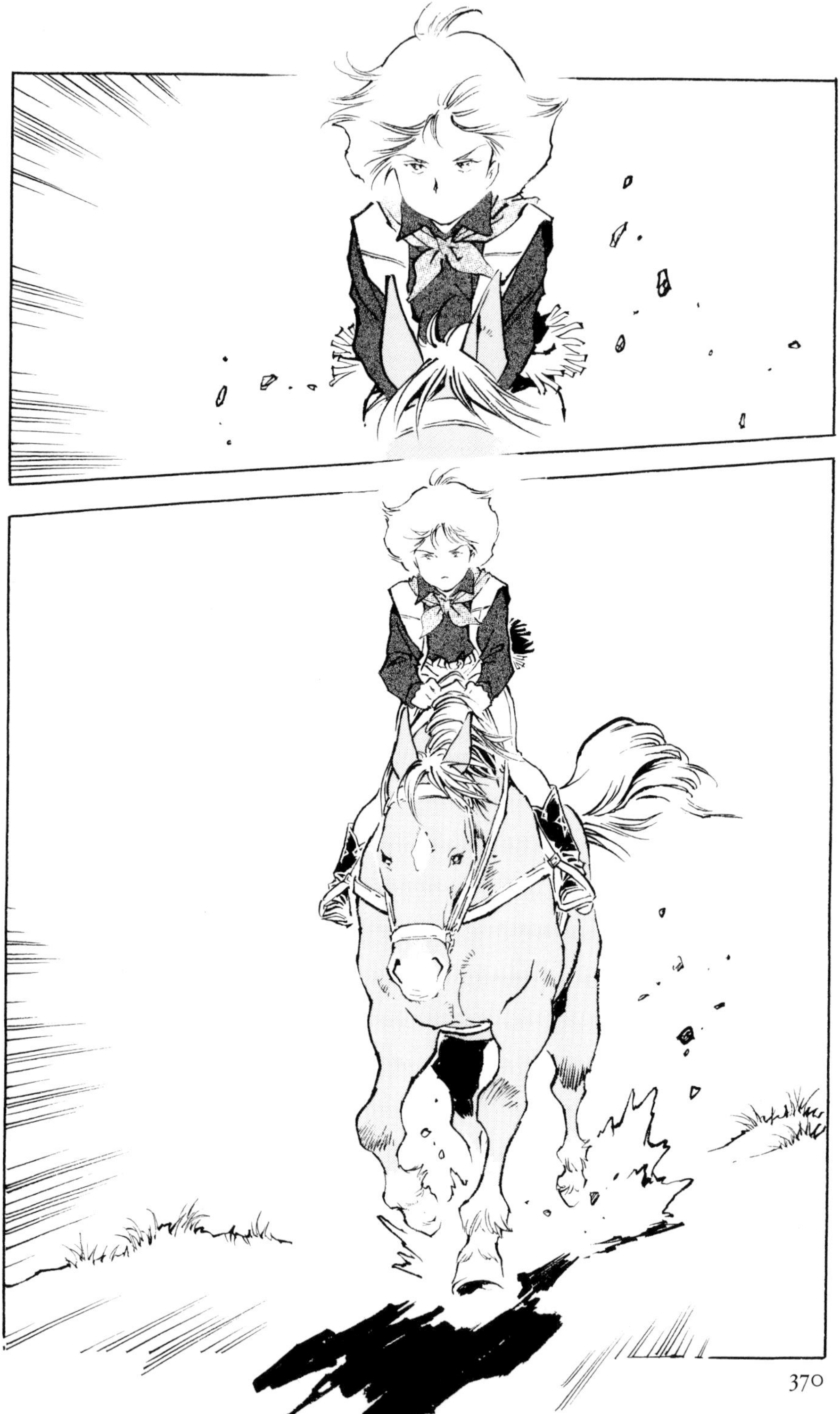

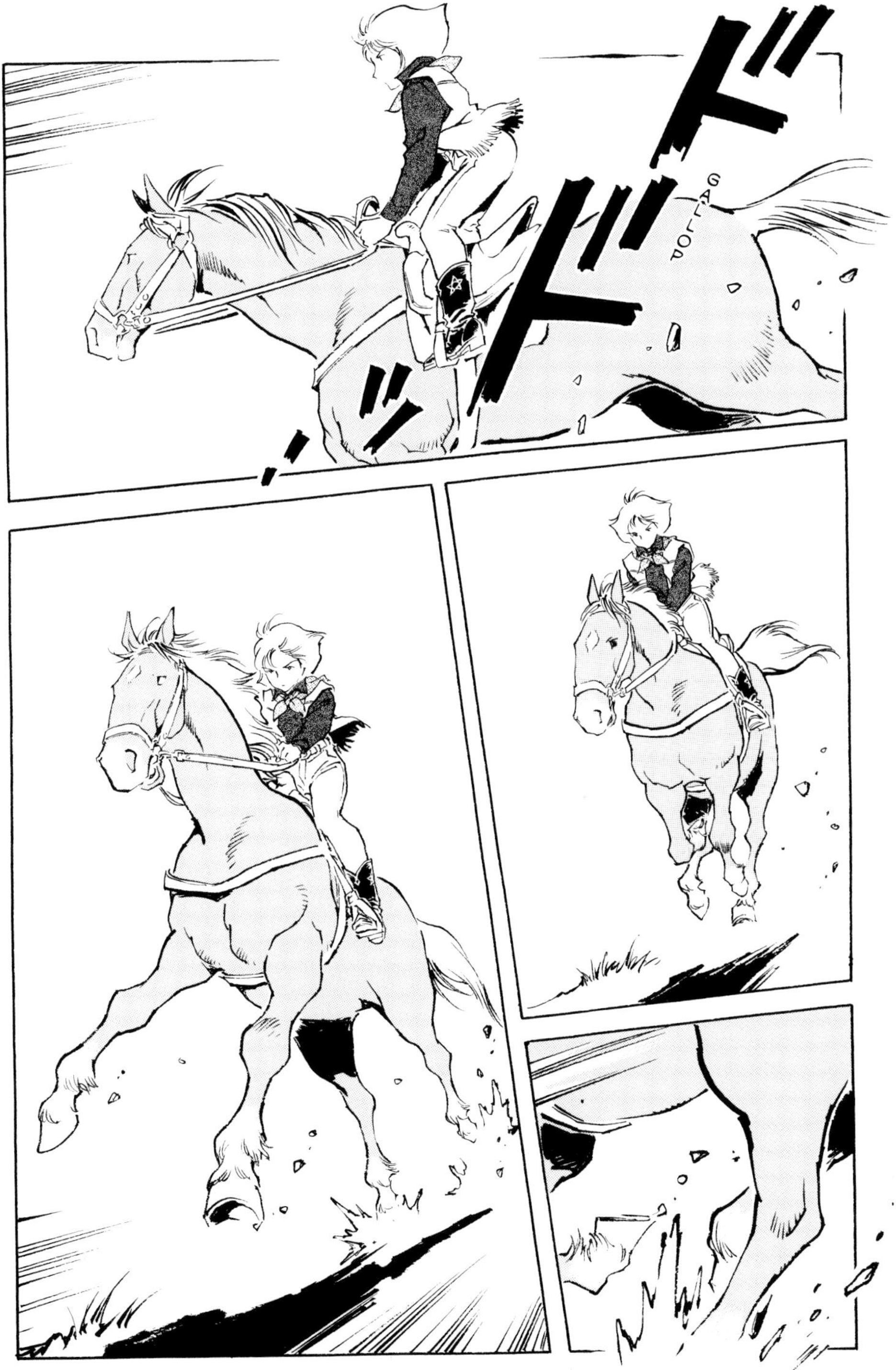
ドドドッ
GALLOP

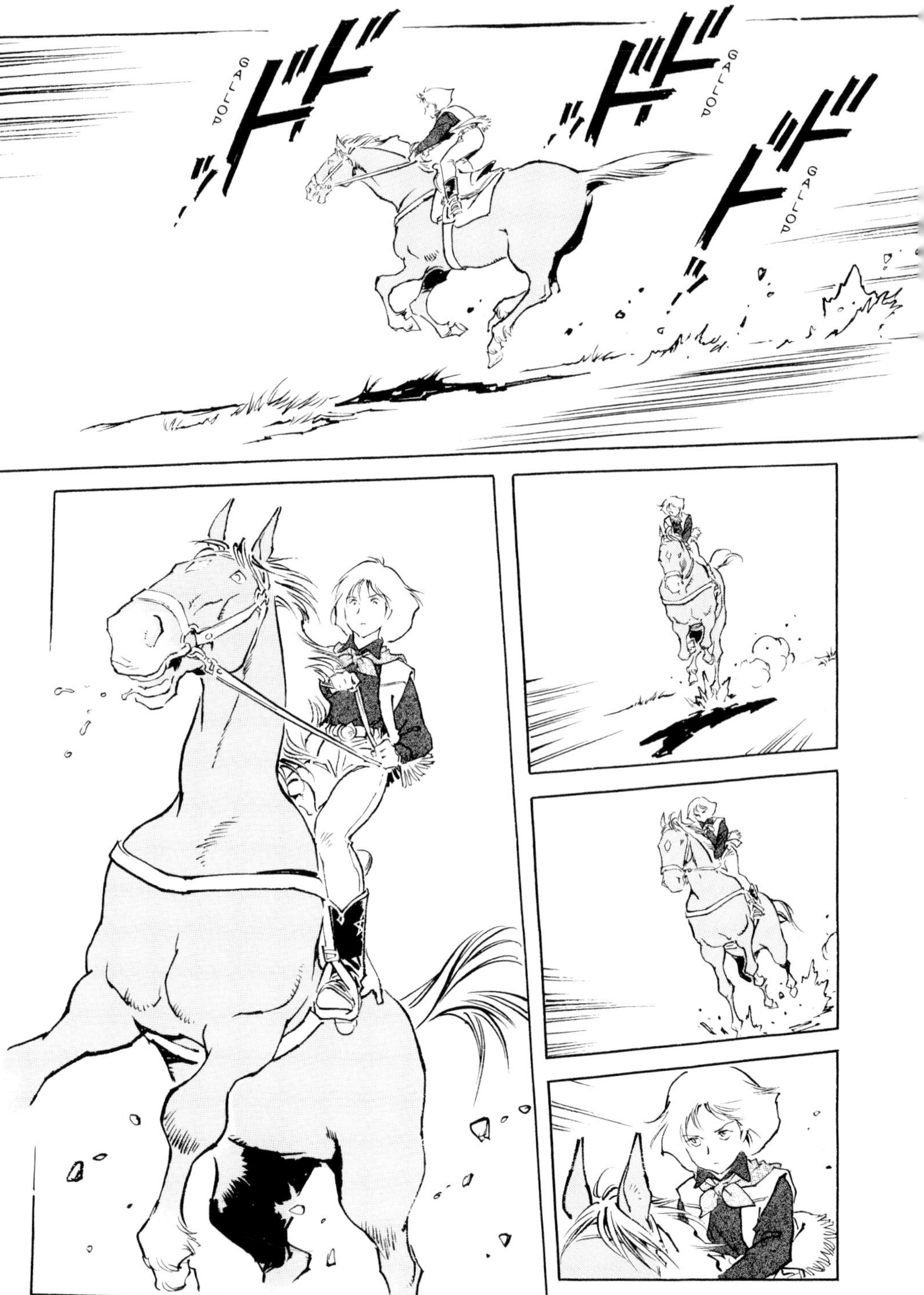
ドドッ
GALLOP
ドドッ
GALLOP
ドドッ
GALLOP

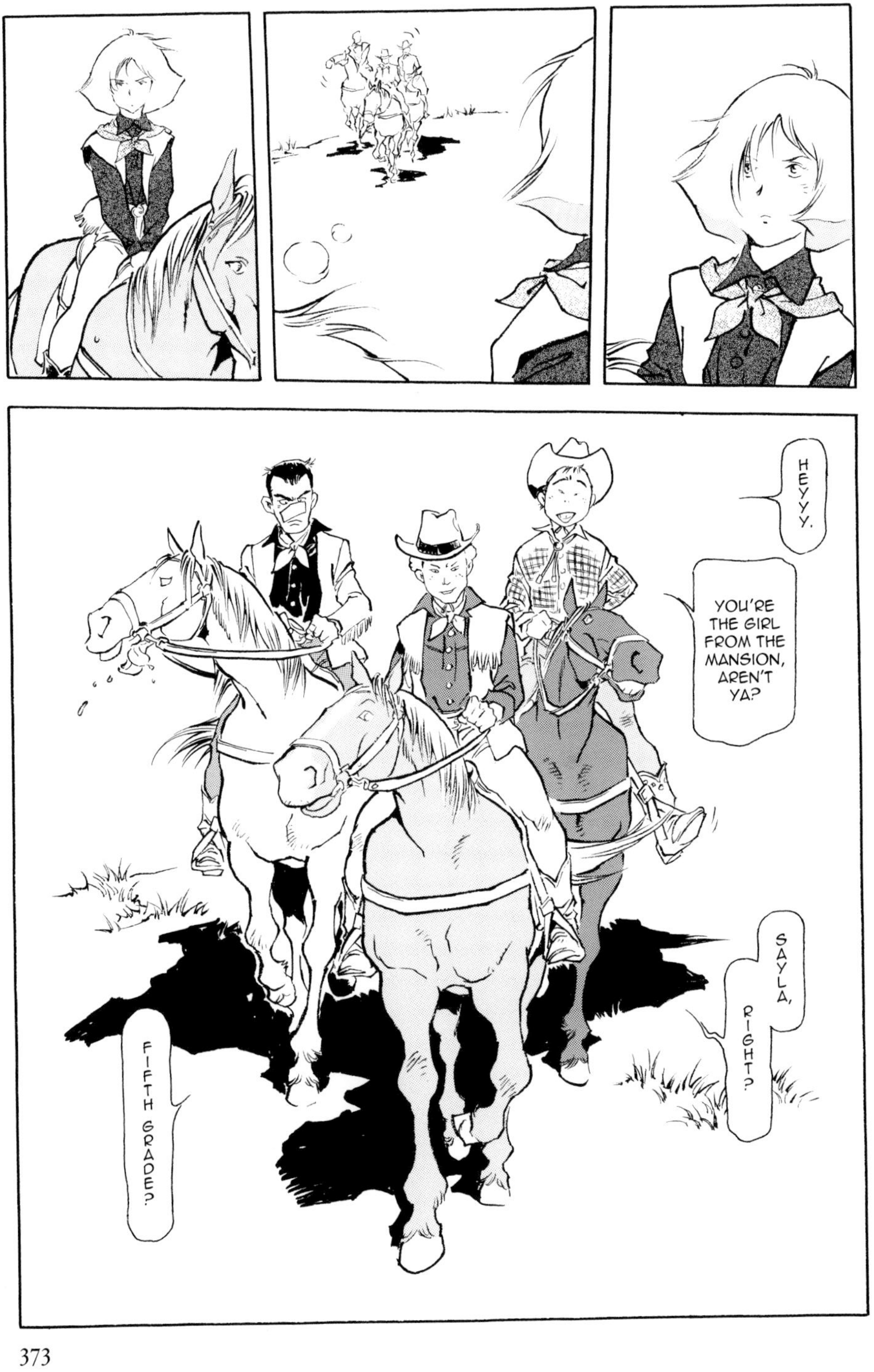
HEYYY.
YOU'RE THE GIRL FROM THE MANSION, AREN'T YA?
SAYLA, RIGHT?
FIFTH GRADE?

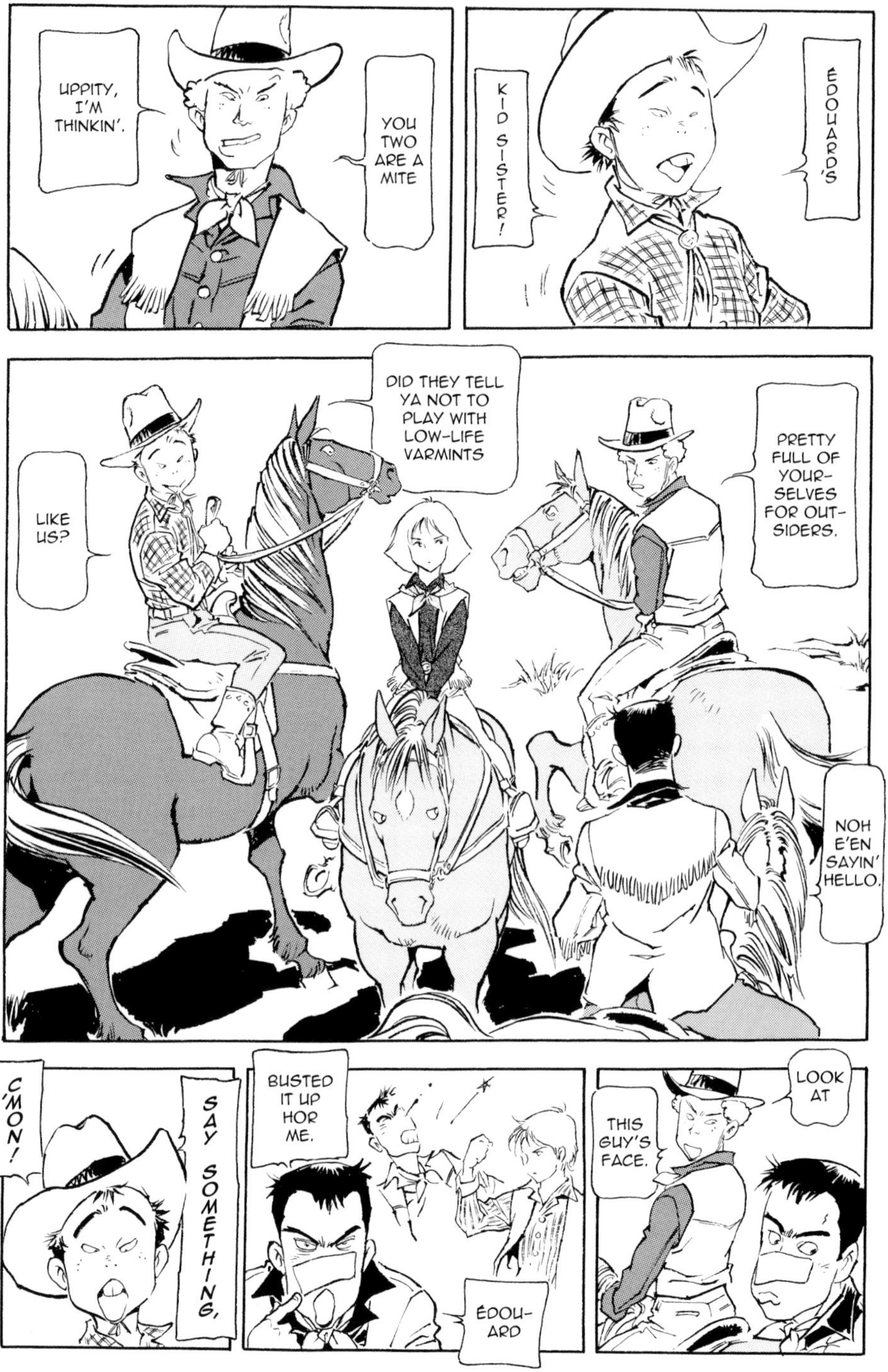
ÉDOUARD'S
KID SISTER!
YOU TWO ARE A MITE
UPPITY, I'M THINKIN'.
PRETTY FULL OF YOUR-SELVES FOR OUT-SIDERS.
NOH E'EN SAYIN' HELLO.
DID THEY TELL YA NOT TO PLAY WITH LOW-LIFE VARMINTS
LIKE US?
LOOK AT
THIS GUY'S FACE.
BUSTED IT UP HOR ME.
ÉDOU-ARD
SAY SOMETHING,
C'MON!

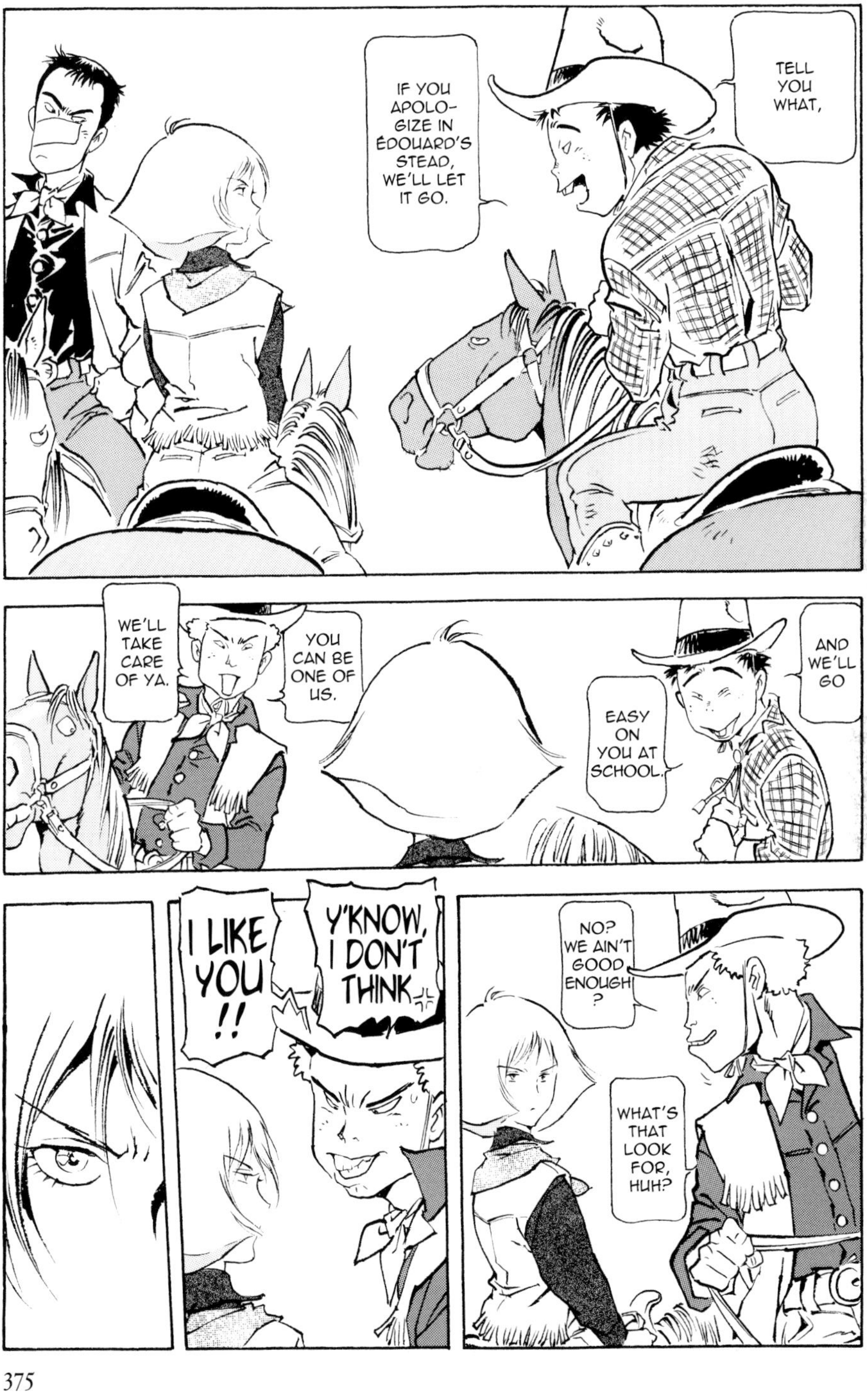
TELL YOU WHAT,
IF YOU APOLOGIZE IN ÉDOUARD'S STEAD, WE'LL LET IT GO.
AND WE'LL GO
EASY ON YOU AT SCHOOL.
YOU CAN BE ONE OF US.
WE'LL TAKE CARE OF YA.
NO? WE AIN'T GOOD ENOUGH?
WHAT'S THAT LOOK FOR, HUH?
Y'KNOW, I DON'T THINK
I LIKE YOU!!

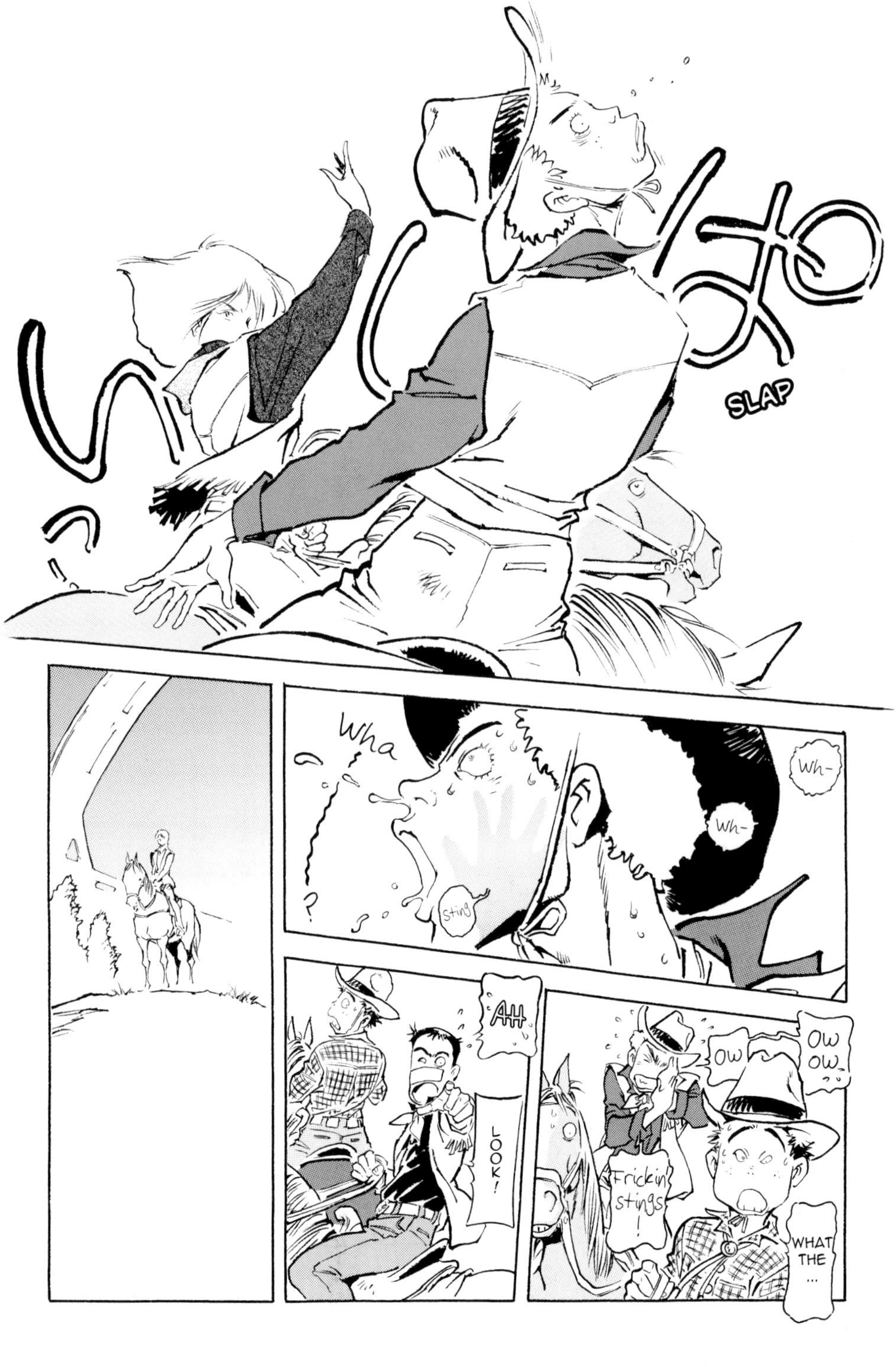
SLAP
Wh-
Wh-
Wha
sting
OW OW
OW
WHAT THE ...
Frickin' stings!
AH
LOOK!

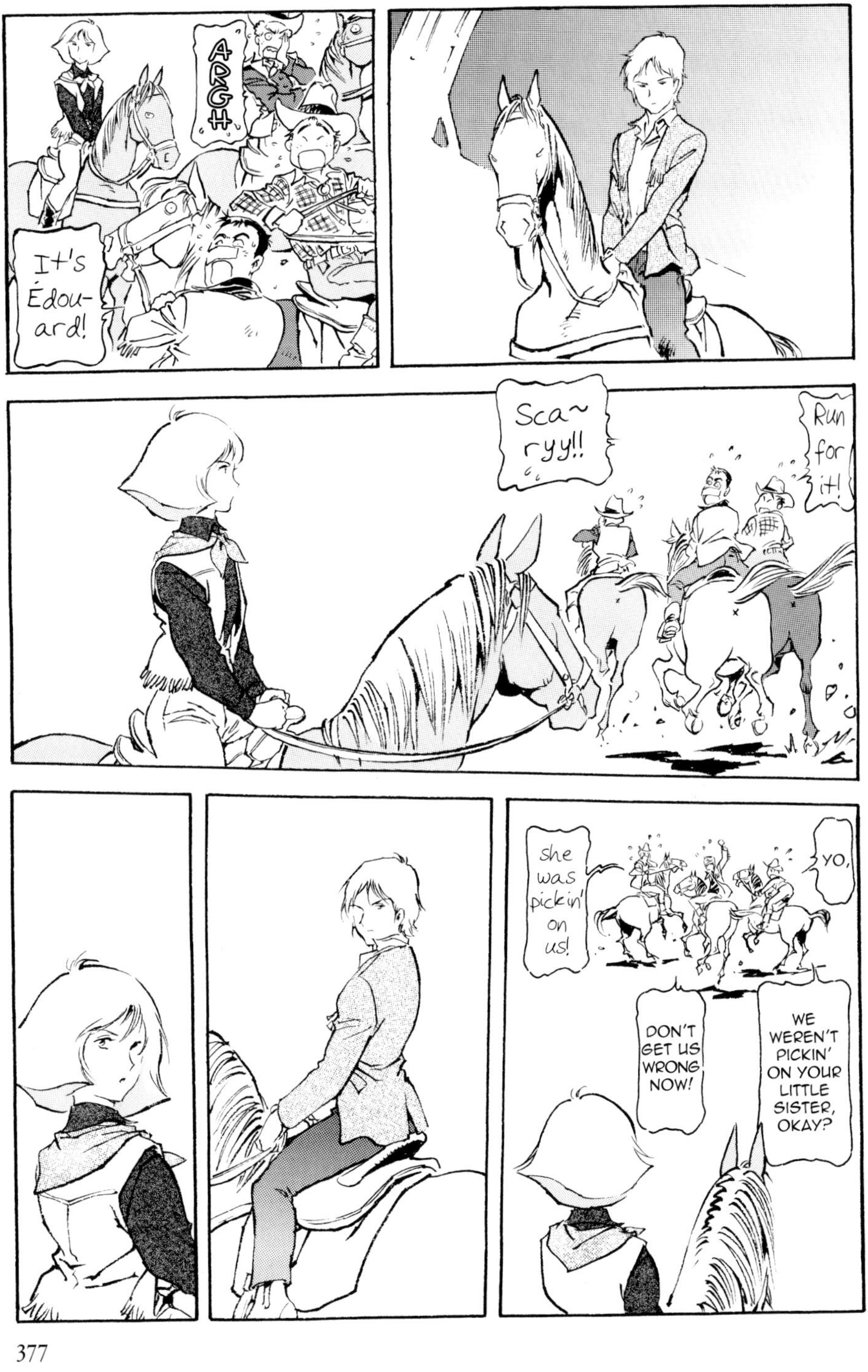
ARGH
It's Édouard!
Run for it!
Sca~ryy!!
YO,
she was pickin' on us!
WE WEREN'T PICKIN' ON YOUR LITTLE SISTER, OKAY?
DON'T GET US WRONG NOW!

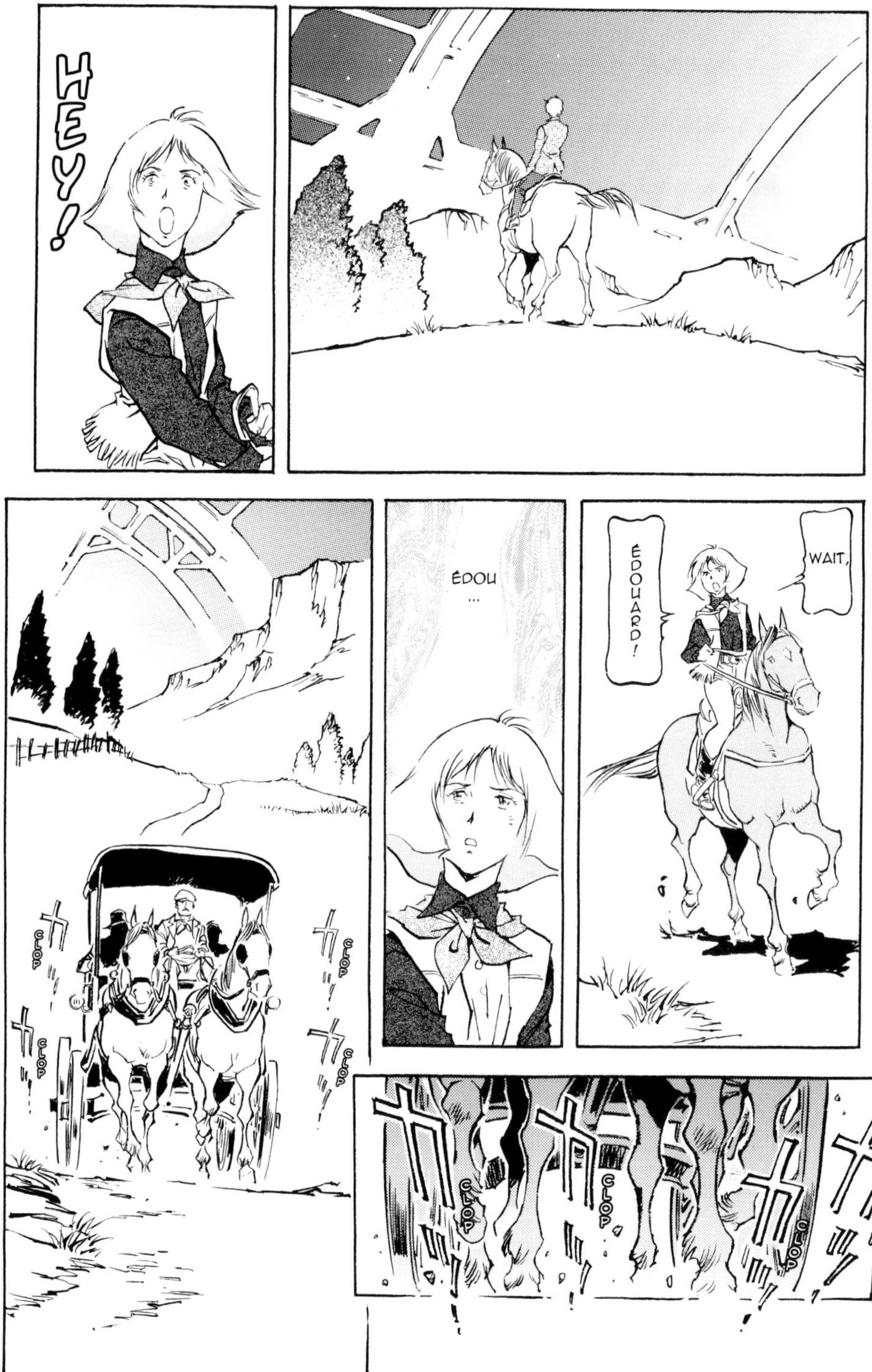
HEY!
WAIT,
ÉDOUARD!
ÉDOU...
CLOP
CLOP
CLOP
CLOP
CLOP
CLOP
CLOP
CLOP

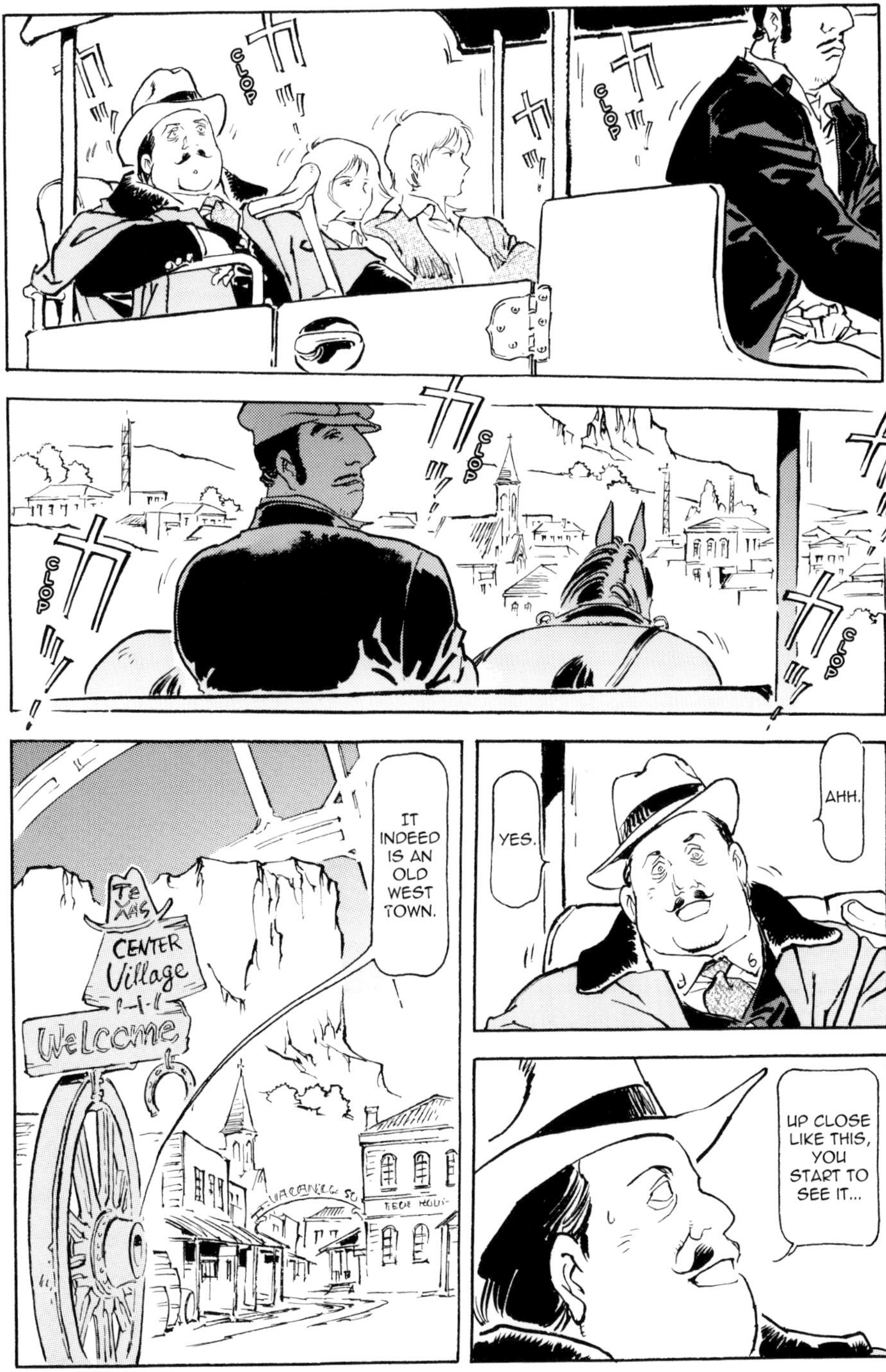
CLOP
CLOP
CLOP
CLOP
CLOP
CLOP
AHH.
YES.
UP CLOSE LIKE THIS, YOU START TO SEE IT...
IT INDEED IS AN OLD WEST TOWN.
TeXAS
CENTER
Village
Welcome

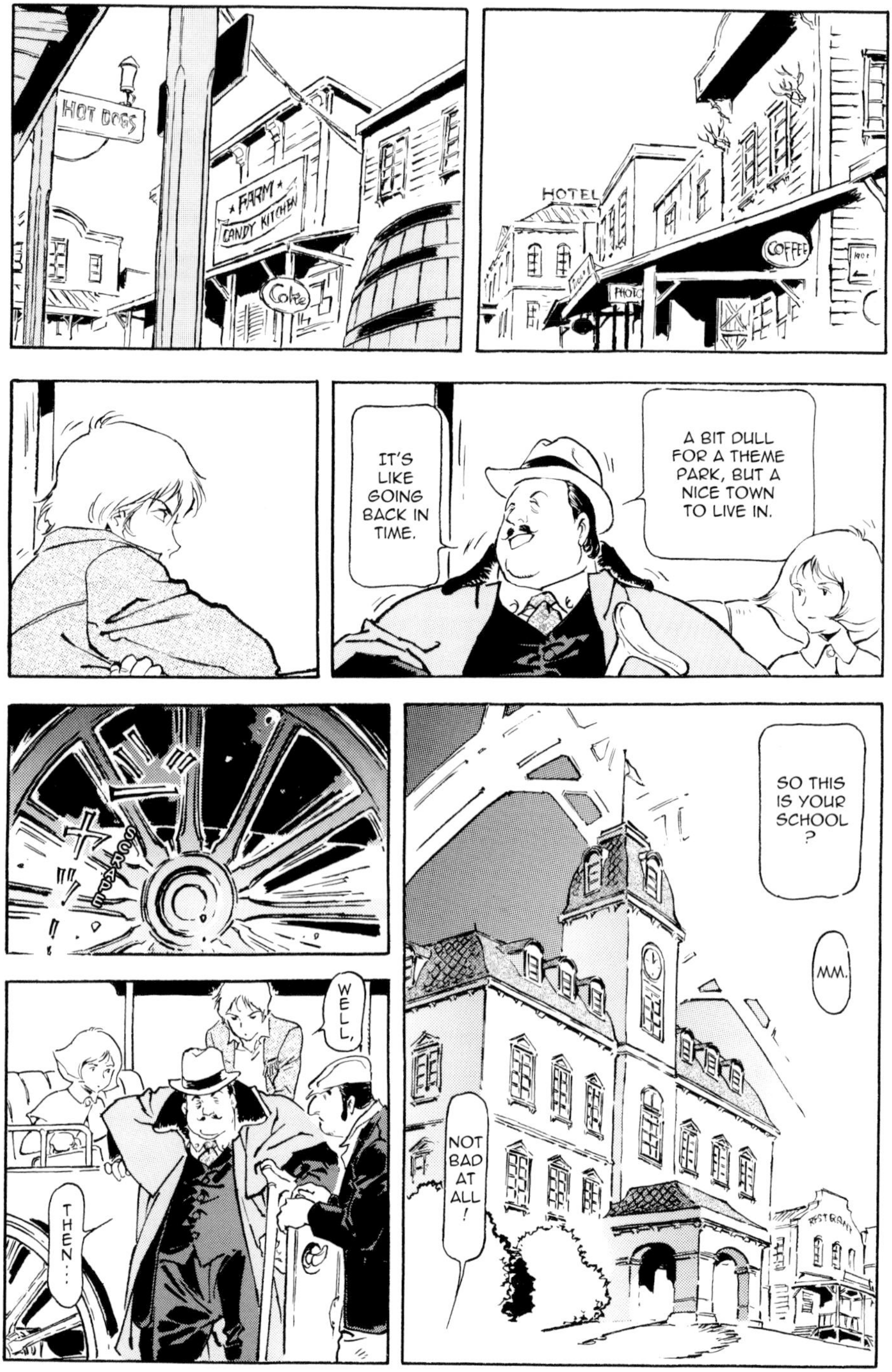
HOTEL
COFFEE
PHOTO
HOT DOGS
FARM
CANDY KITCHEN
A BIT DULL FOR A THEME PARK, BUT A NICE TOWN TO LIVE IN.
IT'S LIKE GOING BACK IN TIME.
SO THIS IS YOUR SCHOOL?
MM.
NOT BAD AT ALL!
SCRAPE
WELL,
THEN...

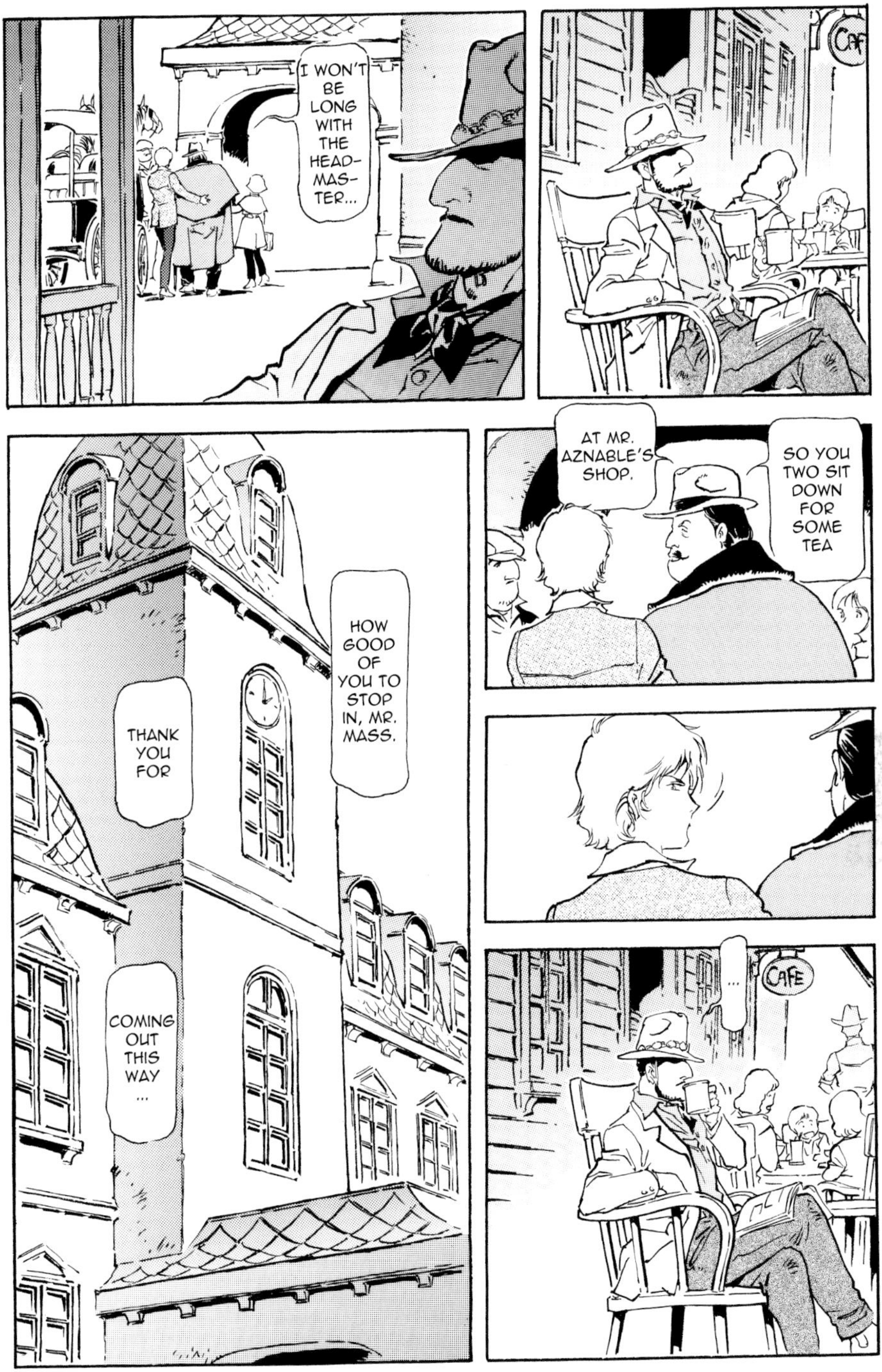
I WON'T BE LONG WITH THE HEAD-MASTER...
SO YOU TWO SIT DOWN FOR SOME TEA
AT MR. AZNABLE'S SHOP.
...
HOW GOOD OF YOU TO STOP IN, MR. MASS.
THANK YOU FOR
COMING OUT THIS WAY ...

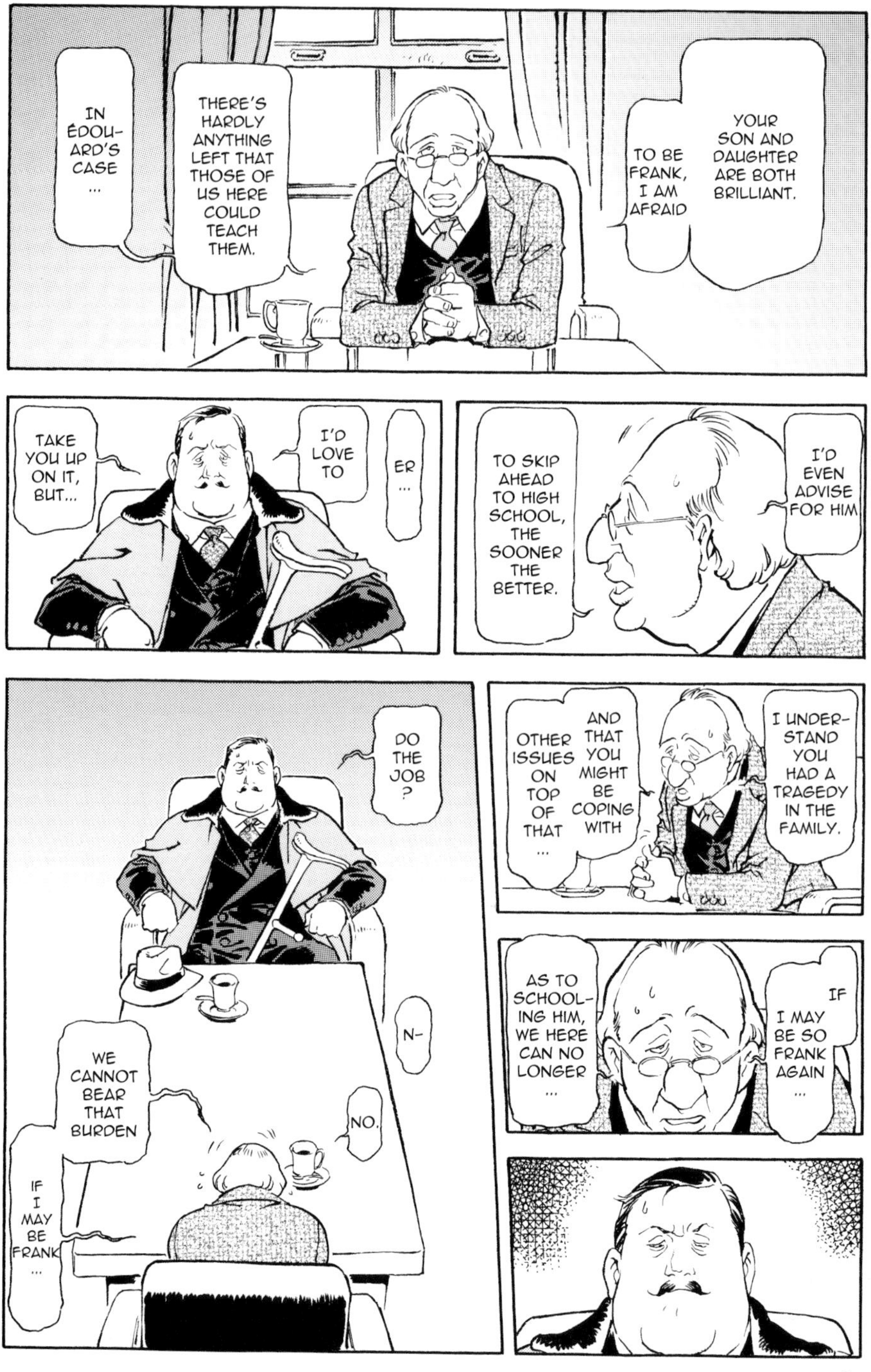
YOUR SON AND DAUGHTER ARE BOTH BRILLIANT.
TO BE FRANK, I AM AFRAID
THERE'S HARDLY ANYTHING LEFT THAT THOSE OF US HERE COULD TEACH THEM.
IN ÉDOUARD'S CASE ...
I'D EVEN ADVISE FOR HIM
TO SKIP AHEAD TO HIGH SCHOOL, THE SOONER THE BETTER.
ER ...
I'D LOVE TO
TAKE YOU UP ON IT, BUT...
I UNDERSTAND YOU HAD A TRAGEDY IN THE FAMILY.
AND THAT YOU MIGHT BE COPING WITH
OTHER ISSUES ON TOP OF THAT ...
IF I MAY BE SO FRANK AGAIN ...
AS TO SCHOOLING HIM, WE HERE CAN NO LONGER ...
DO THE JOB ?
N-
NO.
WE CANNOT BEAR THAT BURDEN
IF I MAY BE FRANK ...

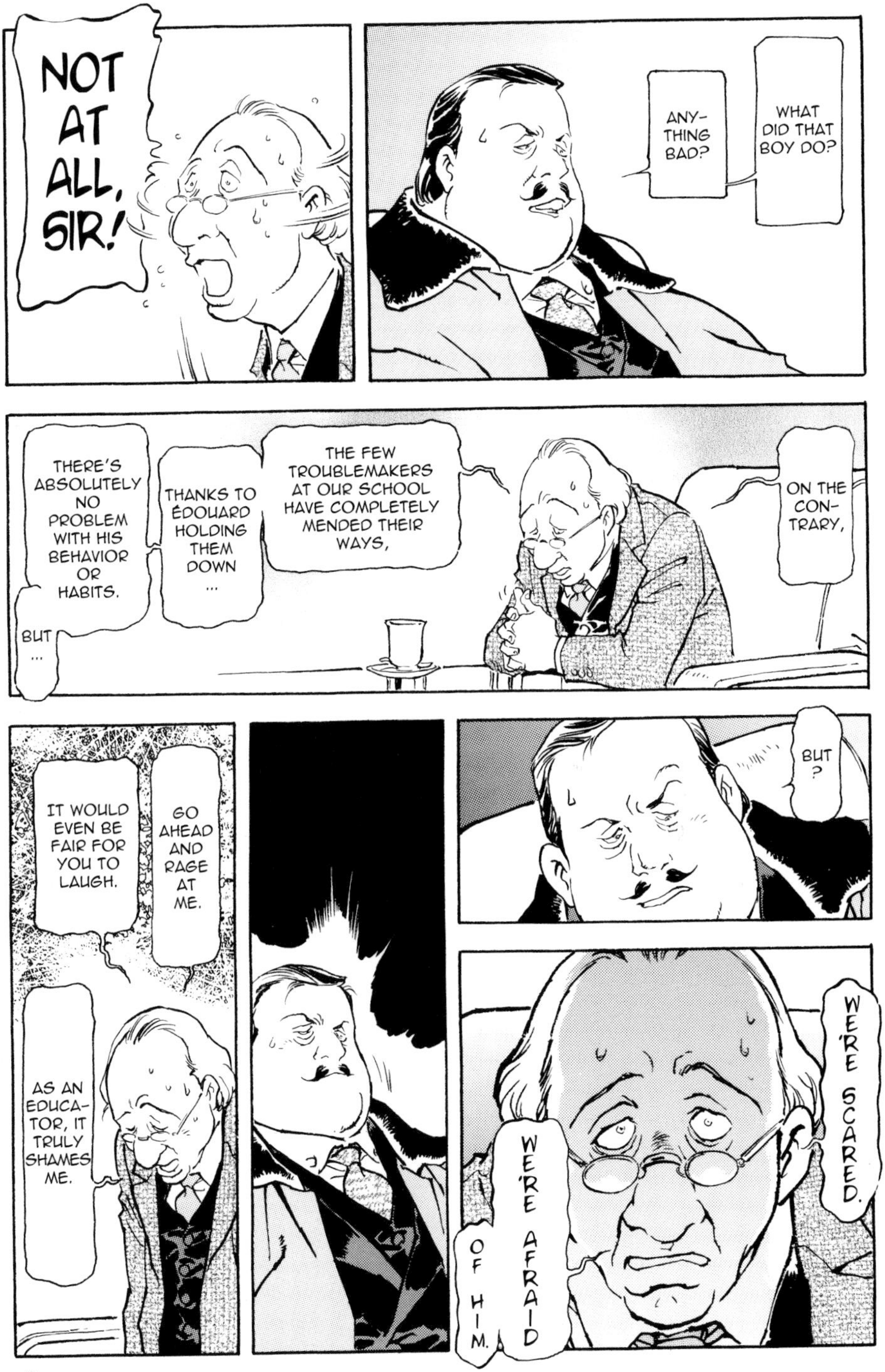
WHAT DID THAT BOY DO?
ANY-THING BAD?
NOT AT ALL, SIR!
ON THE CON-TRARY,
THE FEW TROUBLEMAKERS AT OUR SCHOOL HAVE COMPLETELY MENDED THEIR WAYS,
THANKS TO ÉDOUARD HOLDING THEM DOWN ...
THERE'S ABSOLUTELY NO PROBLEM WITH HIS BEHAVIOR OR HABITS.
BUT ...
BUT ?
WE'RE SCARED.
WE'RE AFRAID OF HIM.
GO AHEAD AND RAGE AT ME.
IT WOULD EVEN BE FAIR FOR YOU TO LAUGH.
AS AN EDUCA-TOR, IT TRULY SHAMES ME.

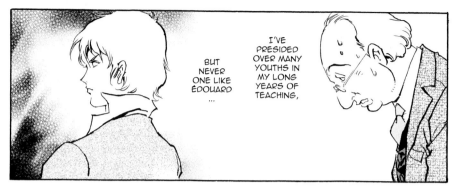

I'VE PRESIDED OVER MANY YOUTHS IN MY LONG YEARS OF TEACHING,

BUT NEVER ONE LIKE ÉDOUARD...

INTELLIGENT,

PERCEPTIVE...

THE BOY IS UNIQUELY AND EXCEEDINGLY GIFTED.

AND YET

HE IS TOO SHARP— COLD— AS IF

HE WERE

A DRAWN KNIFE!

I PRAY THAT HE

DOES NOT BECOME A CAUSE OF GREAT WOES.

ばん？

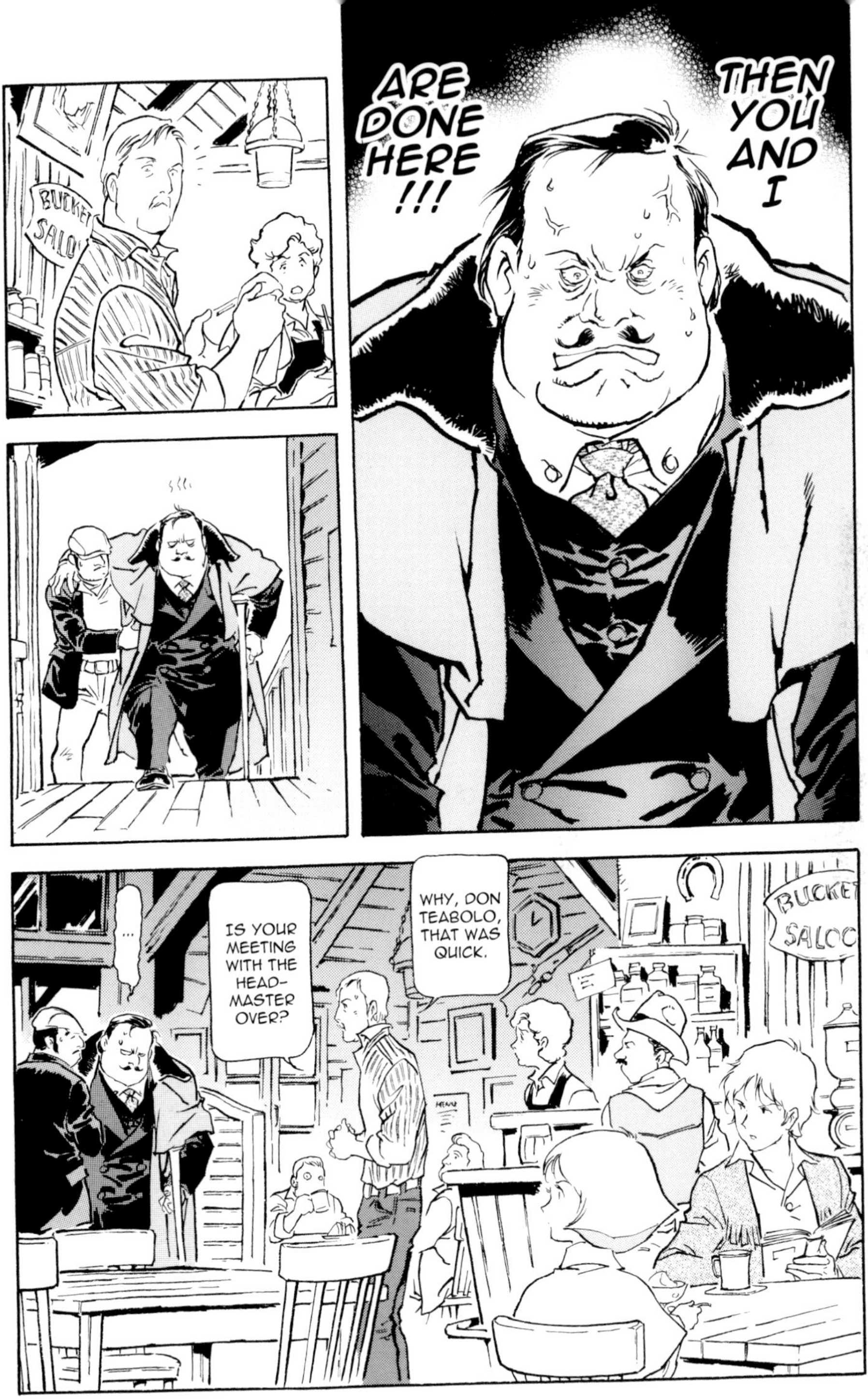
THEN YOU AND I
ARE DONE HERE!!!
WHY, DON TEABOLO, THAT WAS QUICK.
IS YOUR MEETING WITH THE HEAD-MASTER OVER?
...

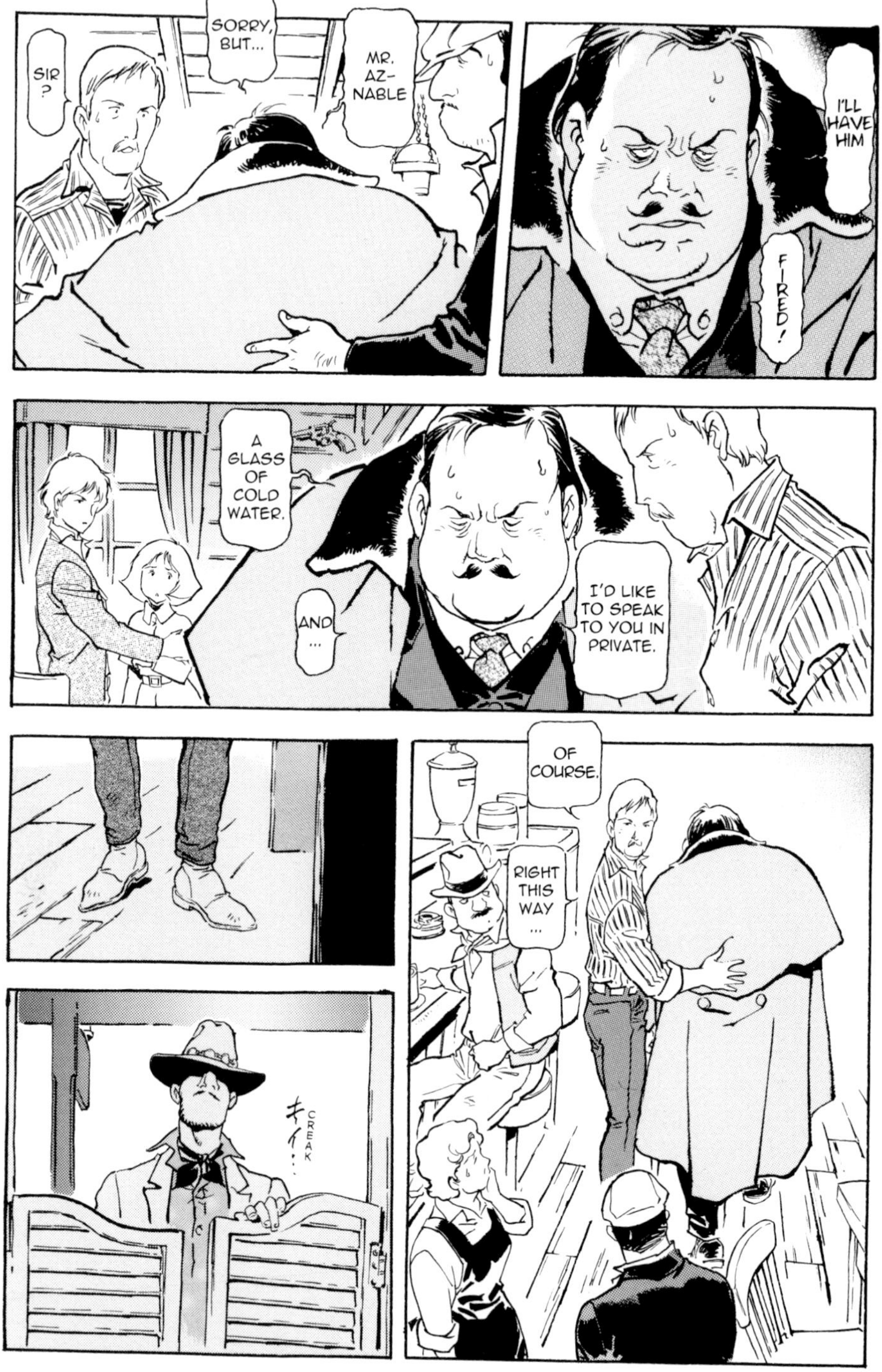
I'LL HAVE HIM
FIRED!
MR. AZNABLE
SORRY, BUT...
SIR?
A GLASS OF COLD WATER.
AND...
I'D LIKE TO SPEAK TO YOU IN PRIVATE.
OF COURSE.
RIGHT THIS WAY...
キイ…
CREAK

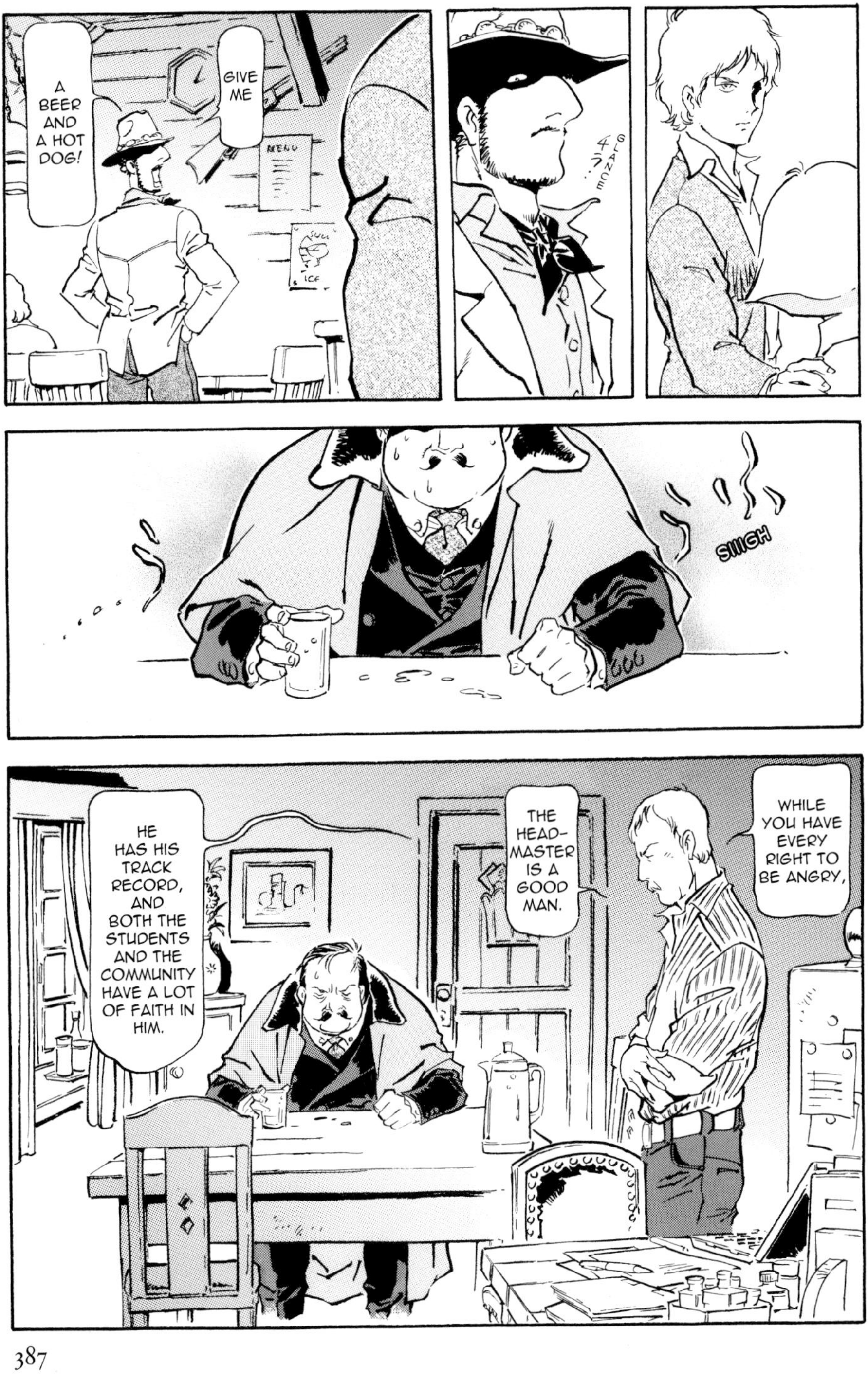
GLANCE
GIVE ME
A BEER AND A HOT DOG!
SIIIGH
WHILE YOU HAVE EVERY RIGHT TO BE ANGRY,
THE HEAD-MASTER IS A GOOD MAN.
HE HAS HIS TRACK RECORD, AND BOTH THE STUDENTS AND THE COMMUNITY HAVE A LOT OF FAITH IN HIM.

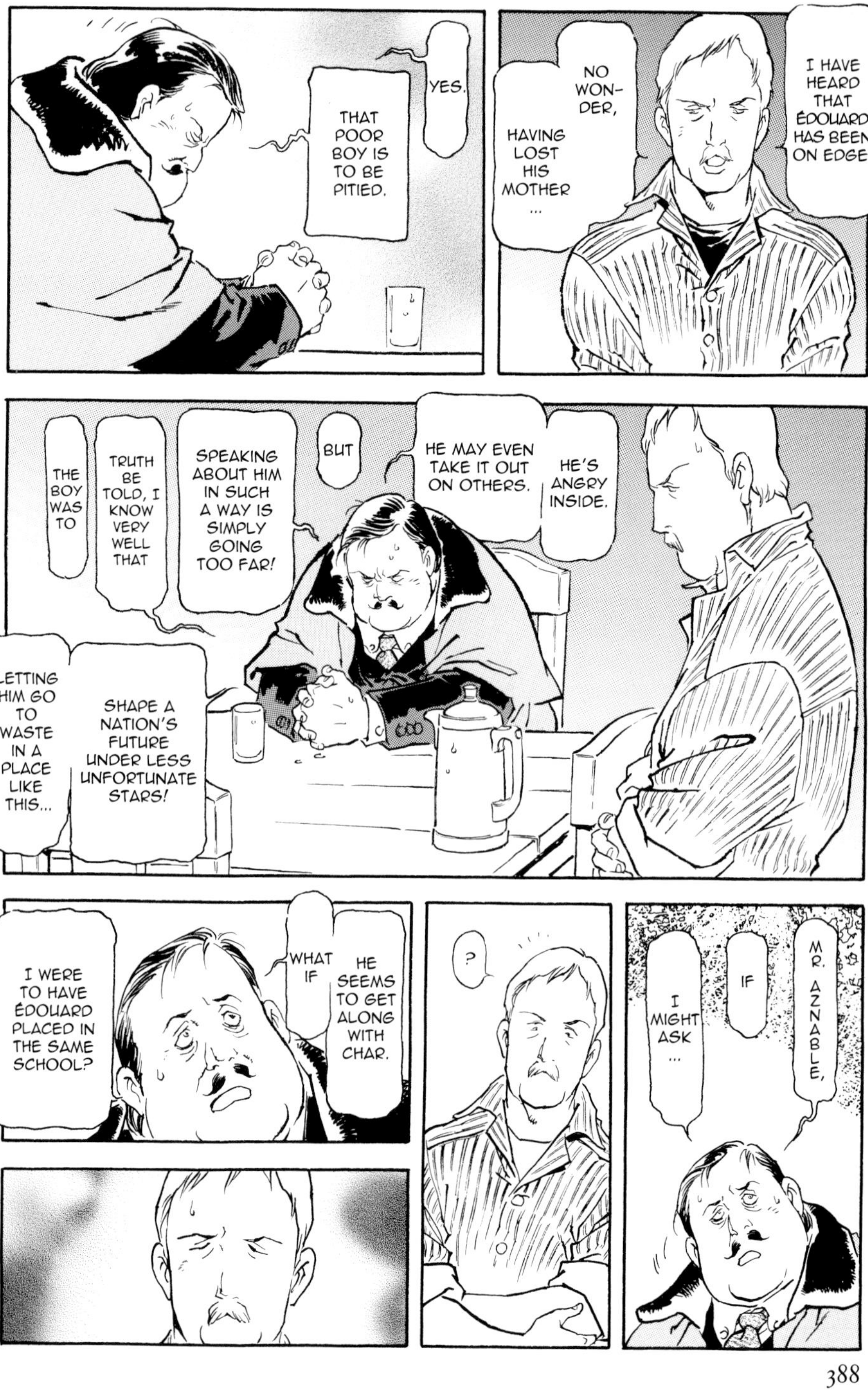
I HAVE HEARD THAT ÉDOUARD HAS BEEN ON EDGE.
NO WONDER,
HAVING LOST HIS MOTHER ...
YES.
THAT POOR BOY IS TO BE PITIED.
HE'S ANGRY INSIDE.
HE MAY EVEN TAKE IT OUT ON OTHERS.
BUT
SPEAKING ABOUT HIM IN SUCH A WAY IS SIMPLY GOING TOO FAR!
TRUTH BE TOLD, I KNOW VERY WELL THAT
THE BOY WAS TO
SHAPE A NATION'S FUTURE UNDER LESS UNFORTUNATE STARS!
LETTING HIM GO TO WASTE IN A PLACE LIKE THIS...
MR. AZNABLE,
IF
I MIGHT ASK ...
?
HE SEEMS TO GET ALONG WITH CHAR.
WHAT IF
I WERE TO HAVE ÉDOUARD PLACED IN THE SAME SCHOOL?

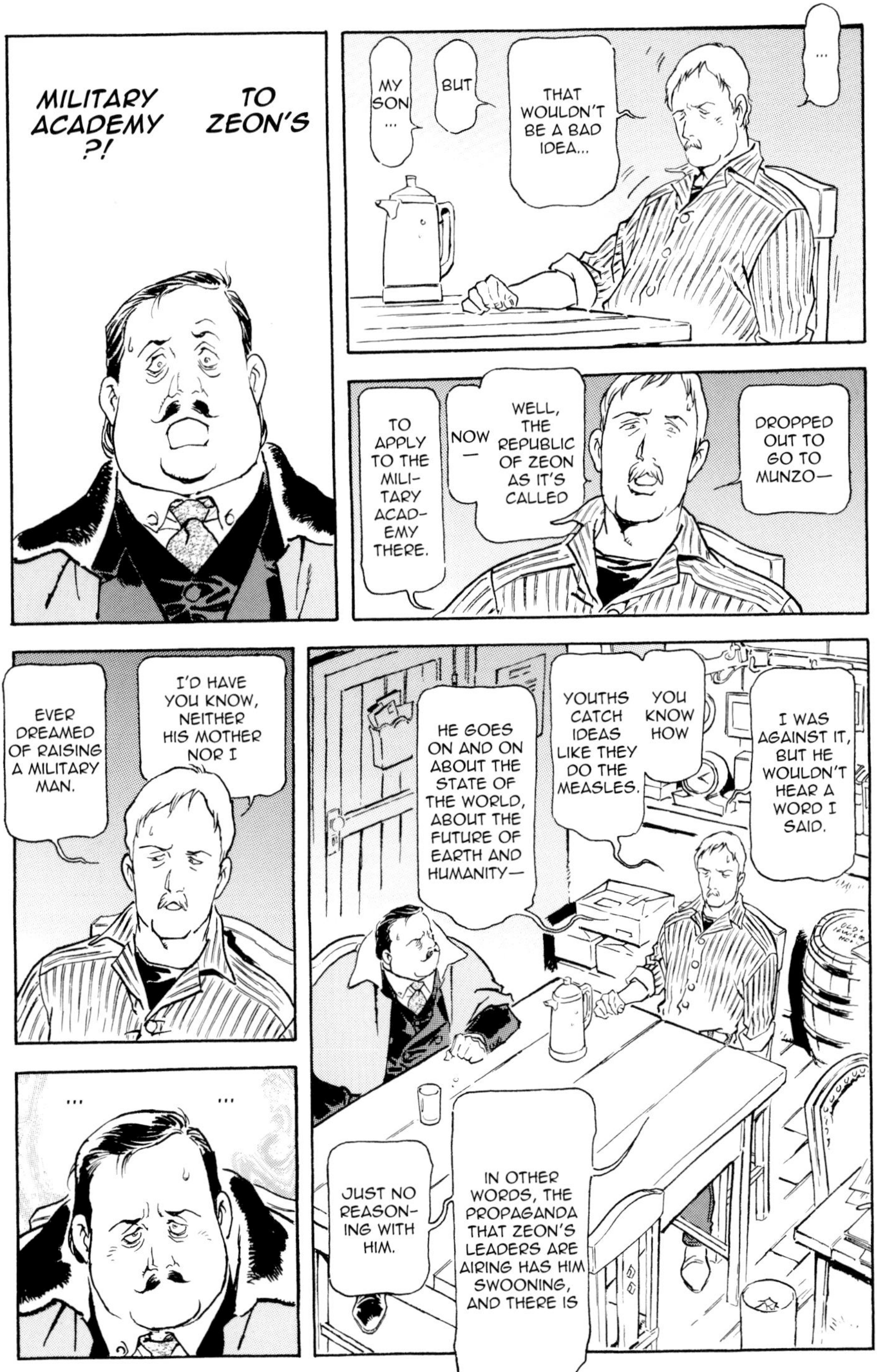
...
THAT WOULDN'T BE A BAD IDEA...
BUT
MY SON ...
DROPPED OUT TO GO TO MUNZO—
WELL, THE REPUBLIC OF ZEON AS IT'S CALLED
NOW —
TO APPLY TO THE MILITARY ACADEMY THERE.
TO ZEON'S
MILITARY ACADEMY ?!
I WAS AGAINST IT, BUT HE WOULDN'T HEAR A WORD I SAID.
YOU KNOW HOW
YOUTHS CATCH IDEAS LIKE THEY DO THE MEASLES.
HE GOES ON AND ON ABOUT THE STATE OF THE WORLD, ABOUT THE FUTURE OF EARTH AND HUMANITY—
IN OTHER WORDS, THE PROPAGANDA THAT ZEON'S LEADERS ARE AIRING HAS HIM SWOONING, AND THERE IS
JUST NO REASONING WITH HIM.
I'D HAVE YOU KNOW, NEITHER HIS MOTHER NOR I
EVER DREAMED OF RAISING A MILITARY MAN.
...
...

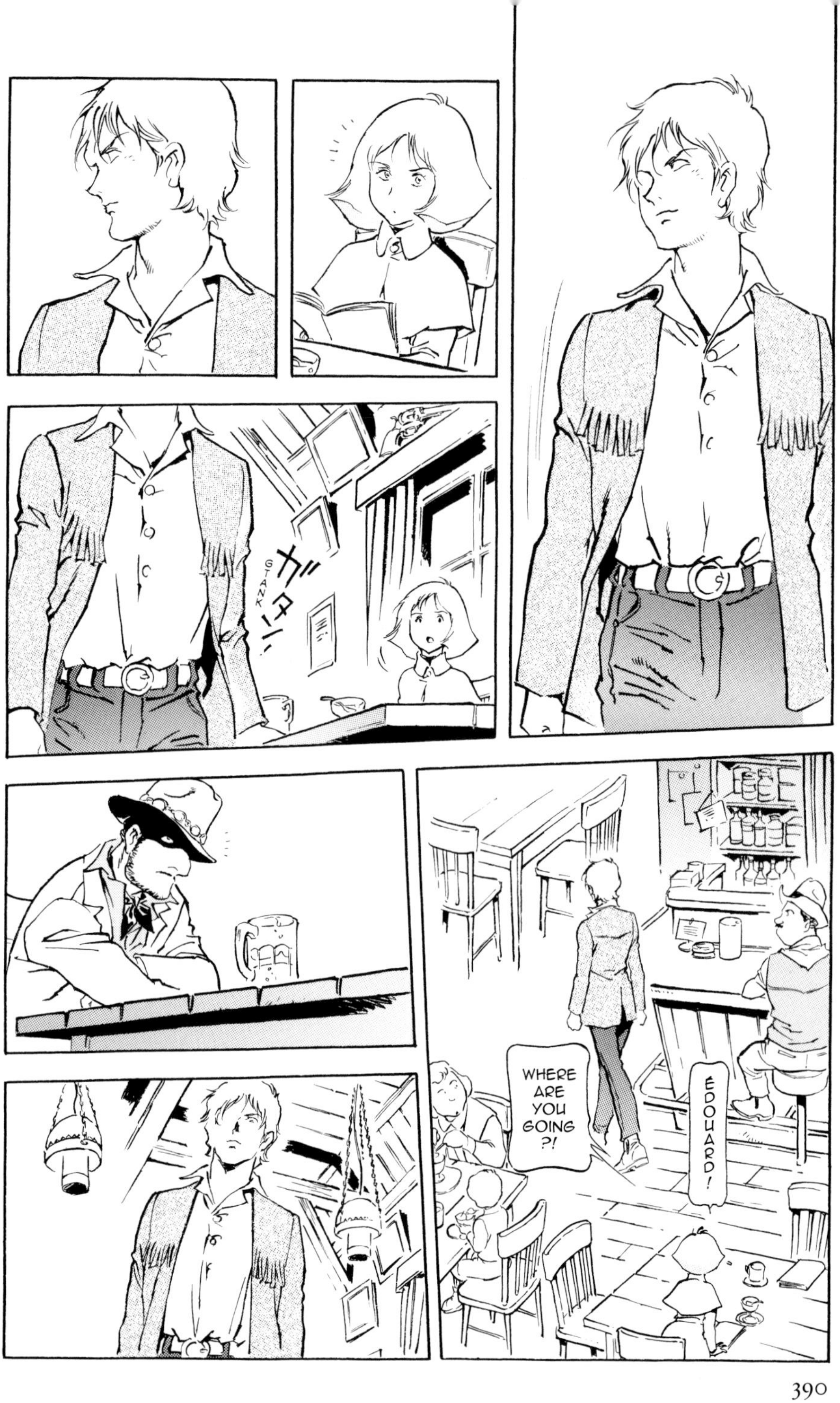
ガタン!
GTANK
ÉDOUARD!
WHERE ARE YOU GOING?!

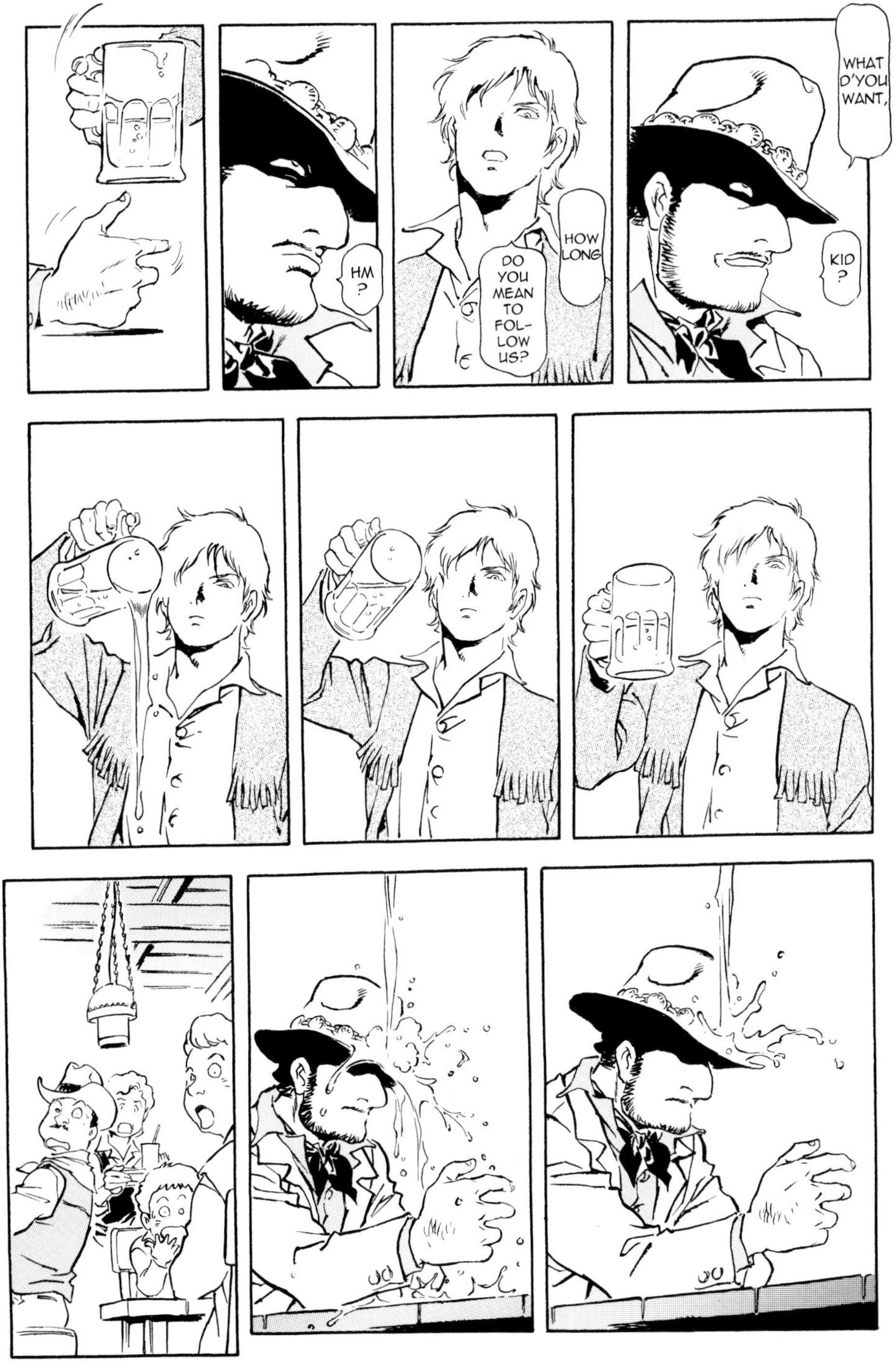
WHAT D'YOU WANT,
KID ?
HOW LONG
DO YOU MEAN TO FOL-LOW US?
HM ?

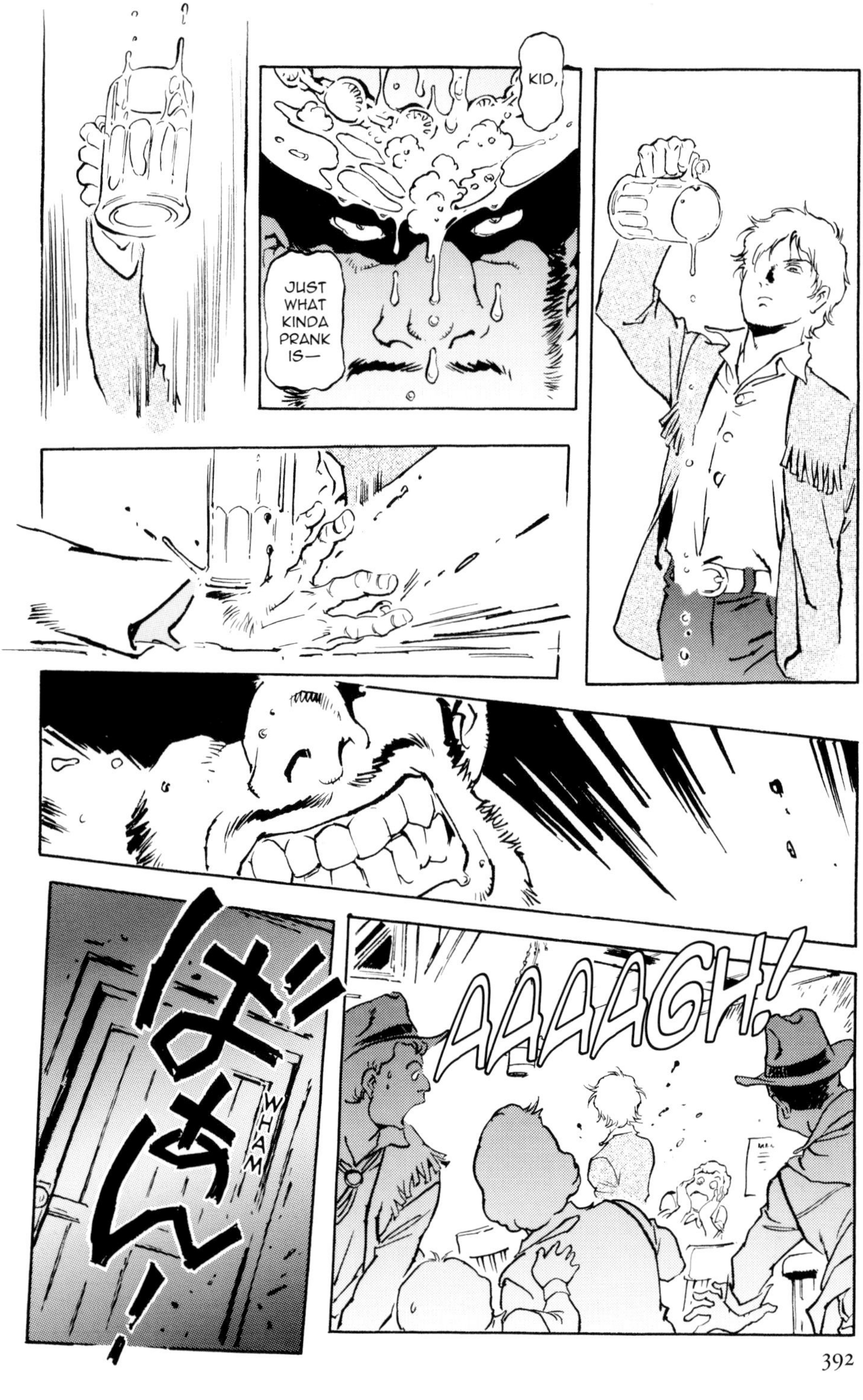
KID,
JUST WHAT KINDA PRANK IS—
AAAAAGH!
ばあん!
WHAM

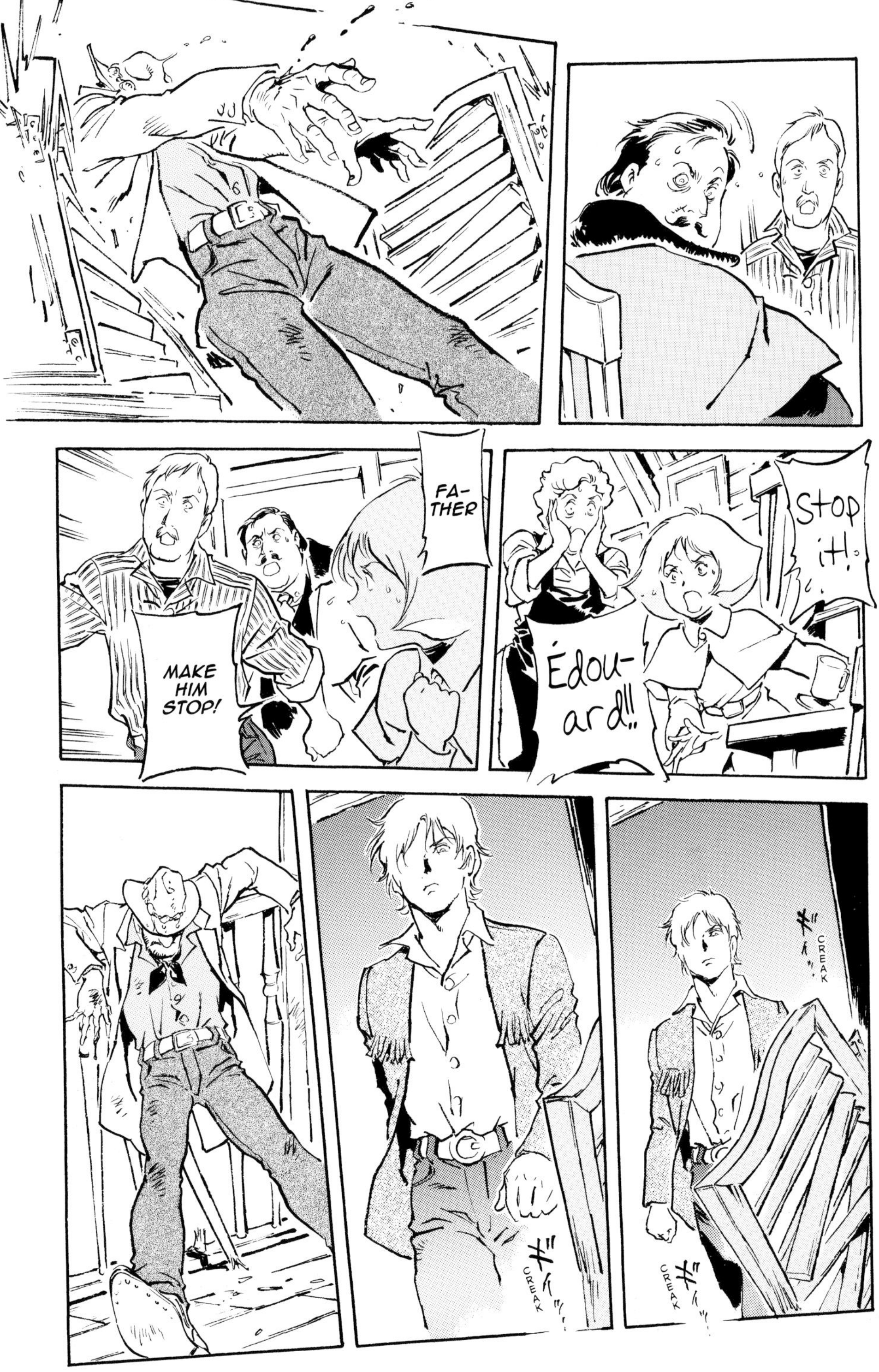
Stop it!
Édou-ard!!
FA-THER
MAKE HIM STOP!
CREAK
CREAK
CREAK

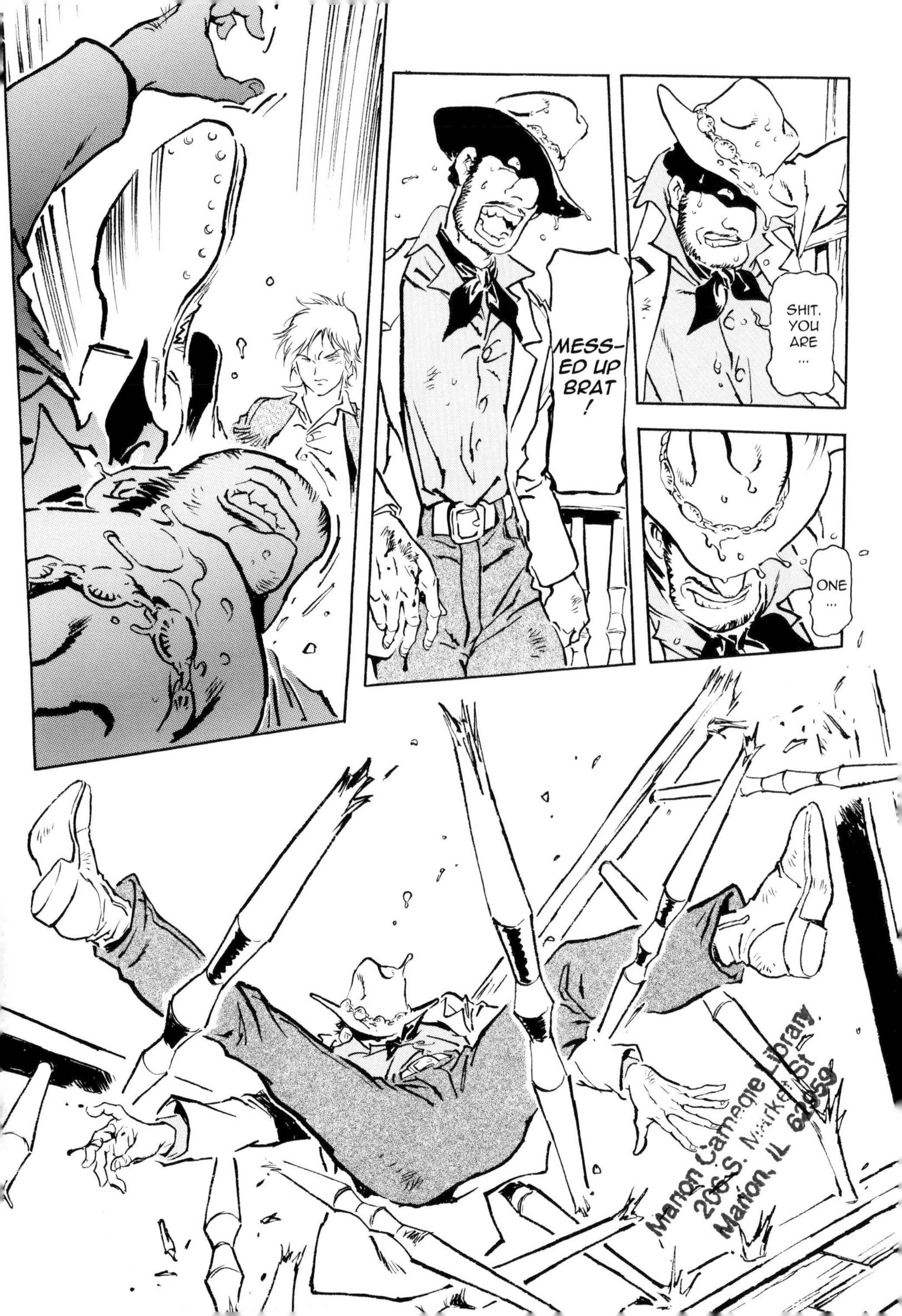
SHIT. YOU ARE ...
ONE ...
MESS-ED UP BRAT!

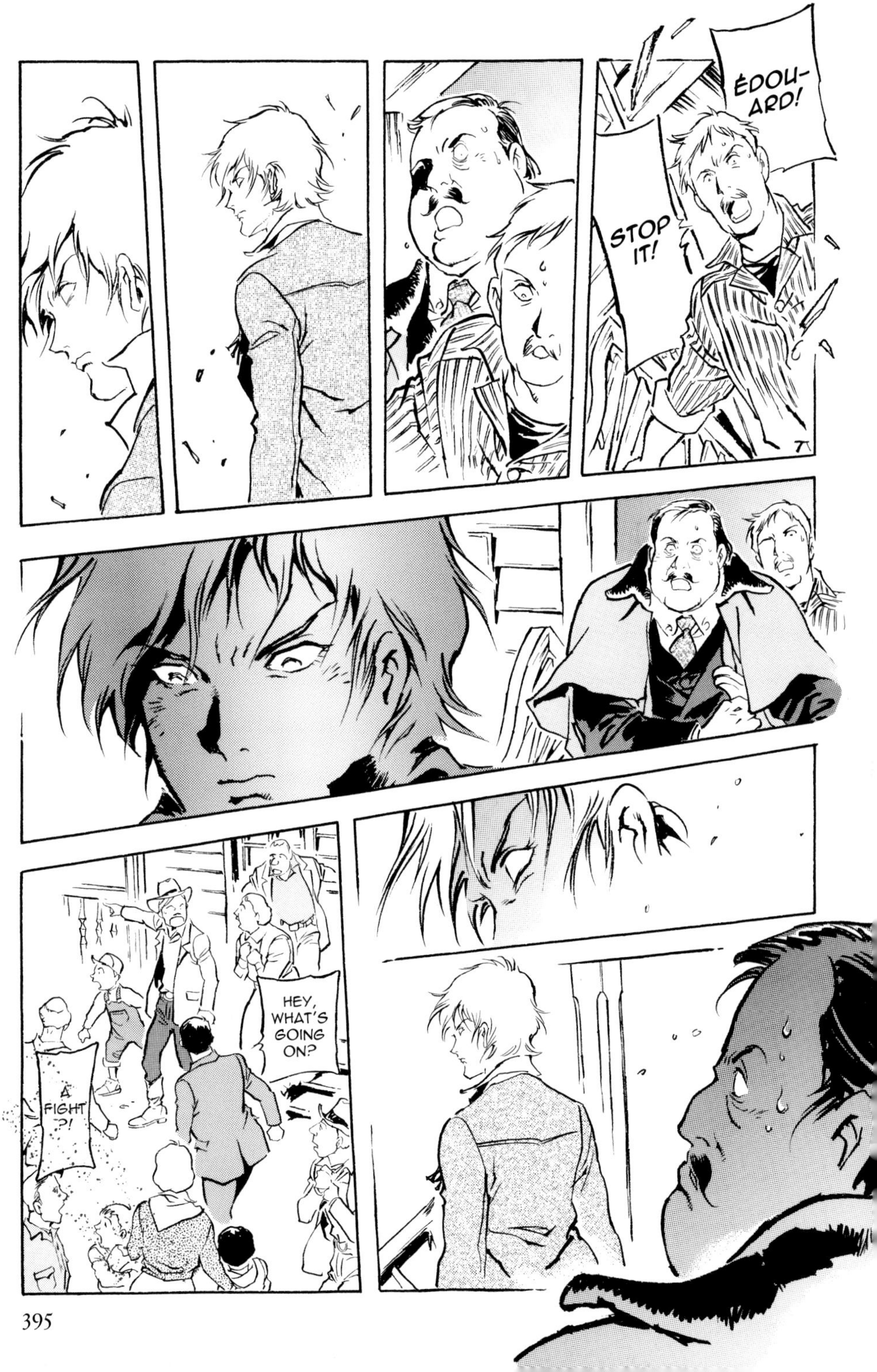
ÉDOU-ARD!
STOP IT!
HEY, WHAT'S GOING ON?
A FIGHT?!

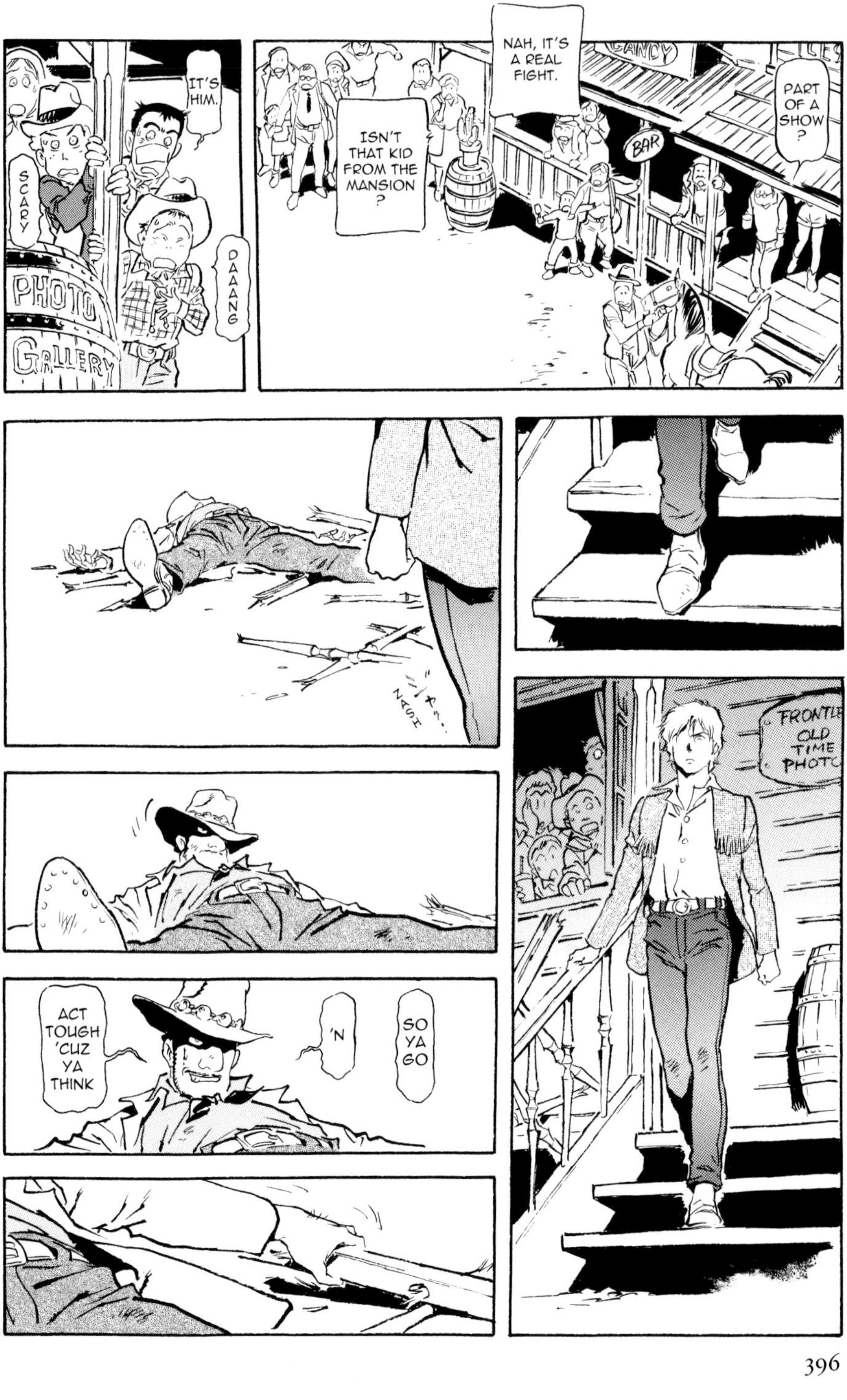
CANDY
PART OF A SHOW?
NAH, IT'S A REAL FIGHT.
BAR
ISN'T THAT KID FROM THE MANSION?
IT'S HIM.
DAAAANG
SCARY
PHOTO GALLERY
NASH
OLD TIME
SO YA GO
'N
ACT TOUGH 'CUZ YA THINK

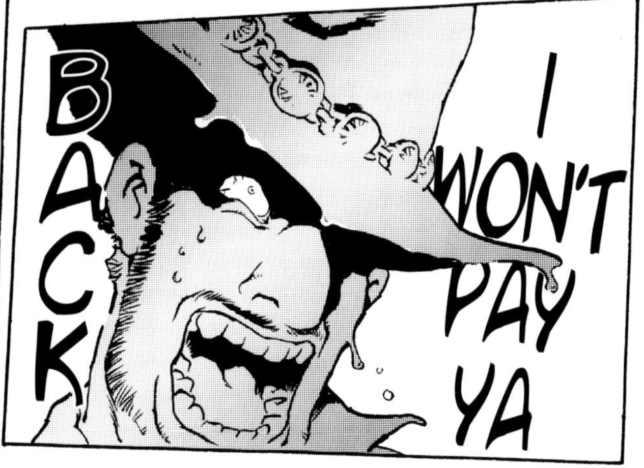
I WON'T PAY YA BACK
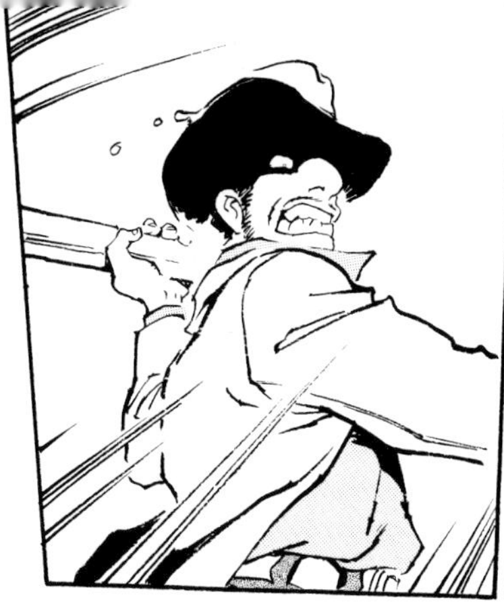
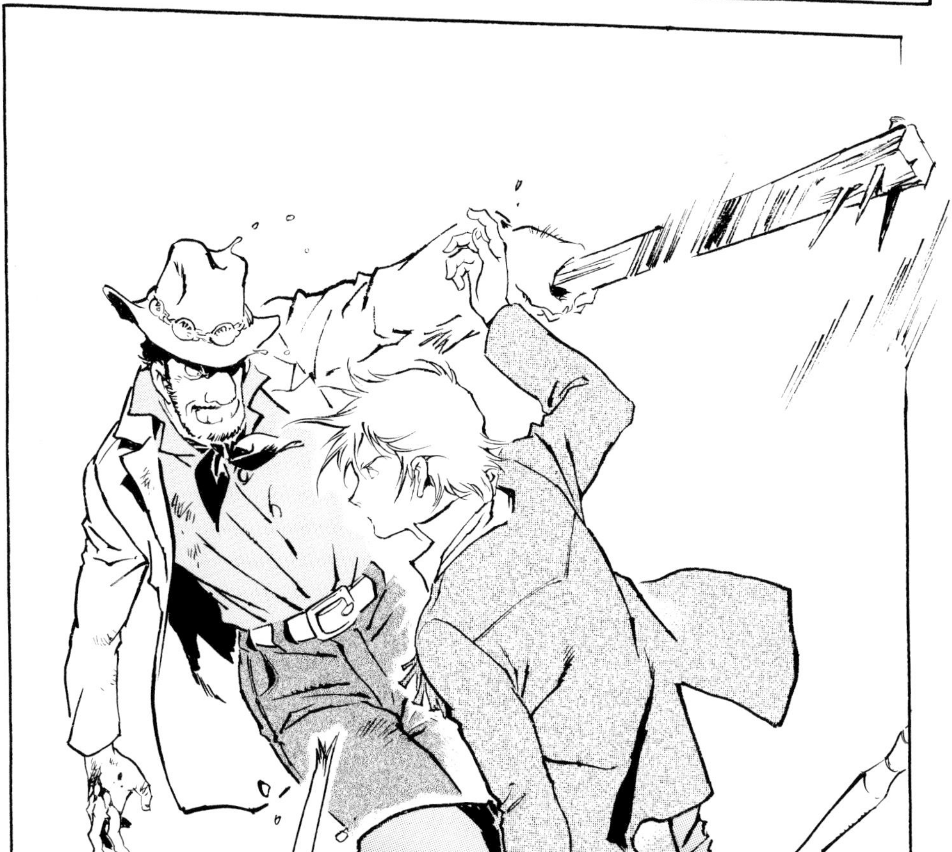

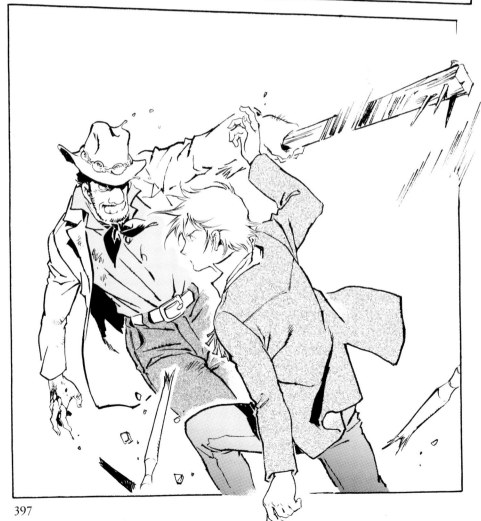

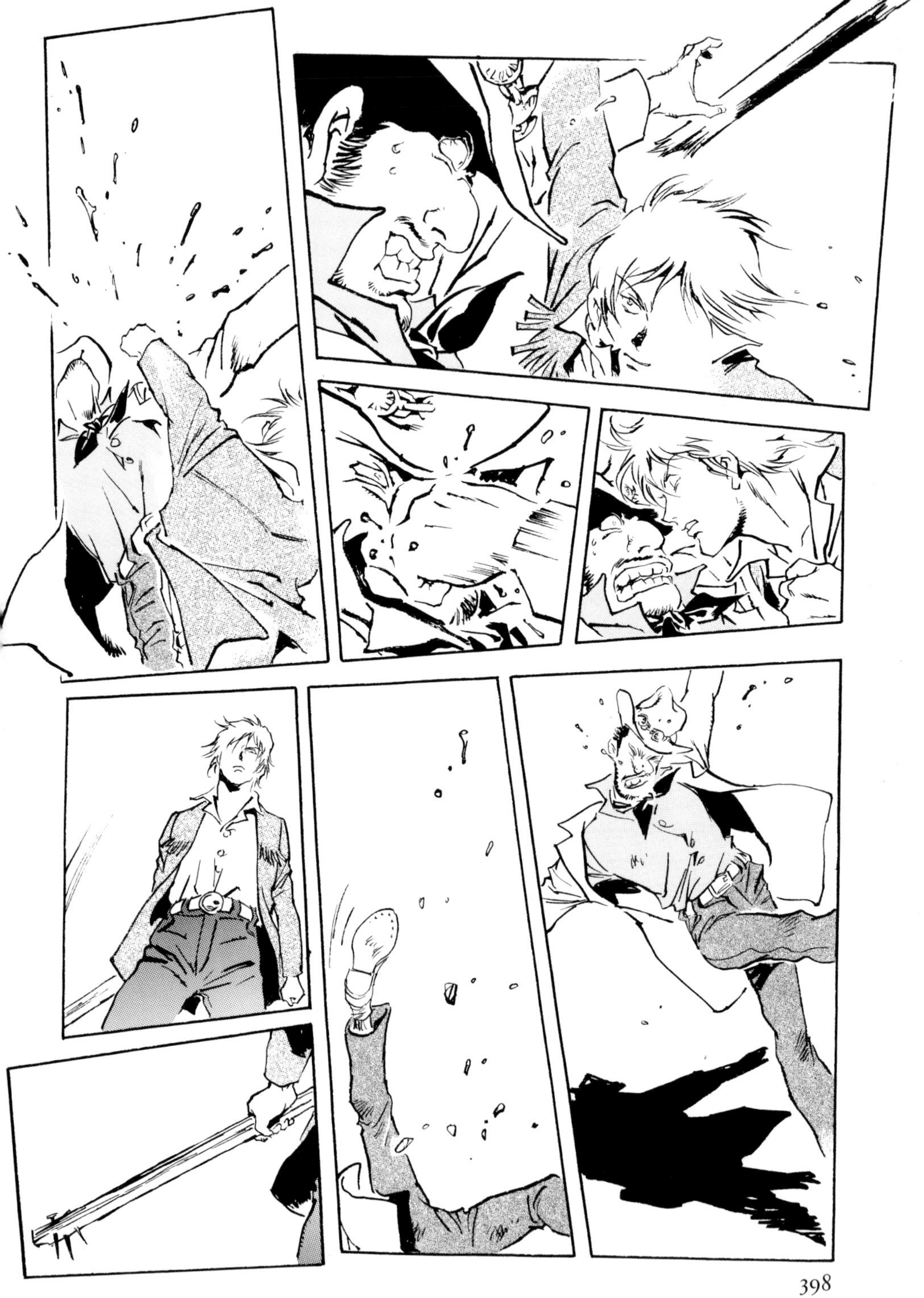

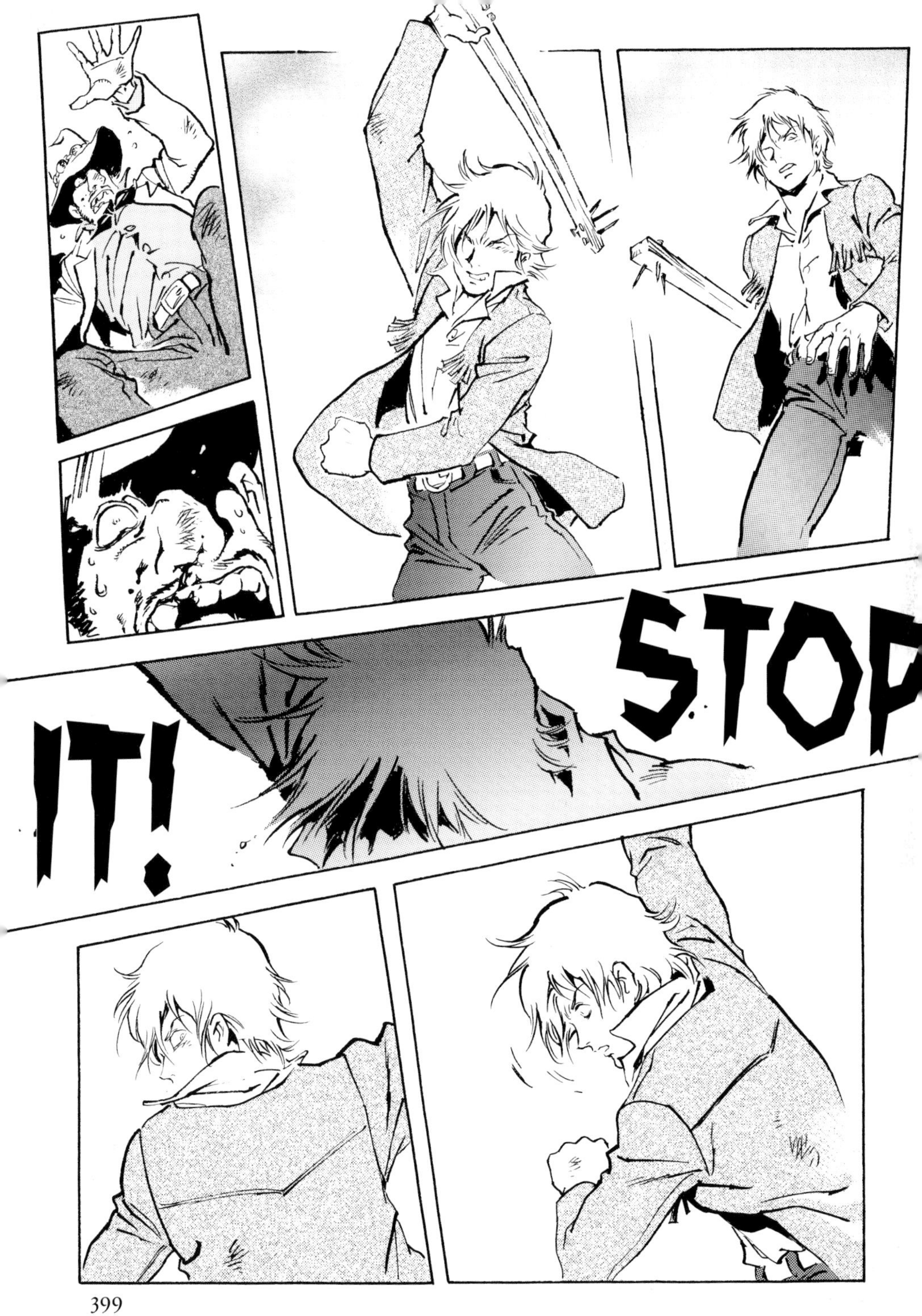
STOP IT!

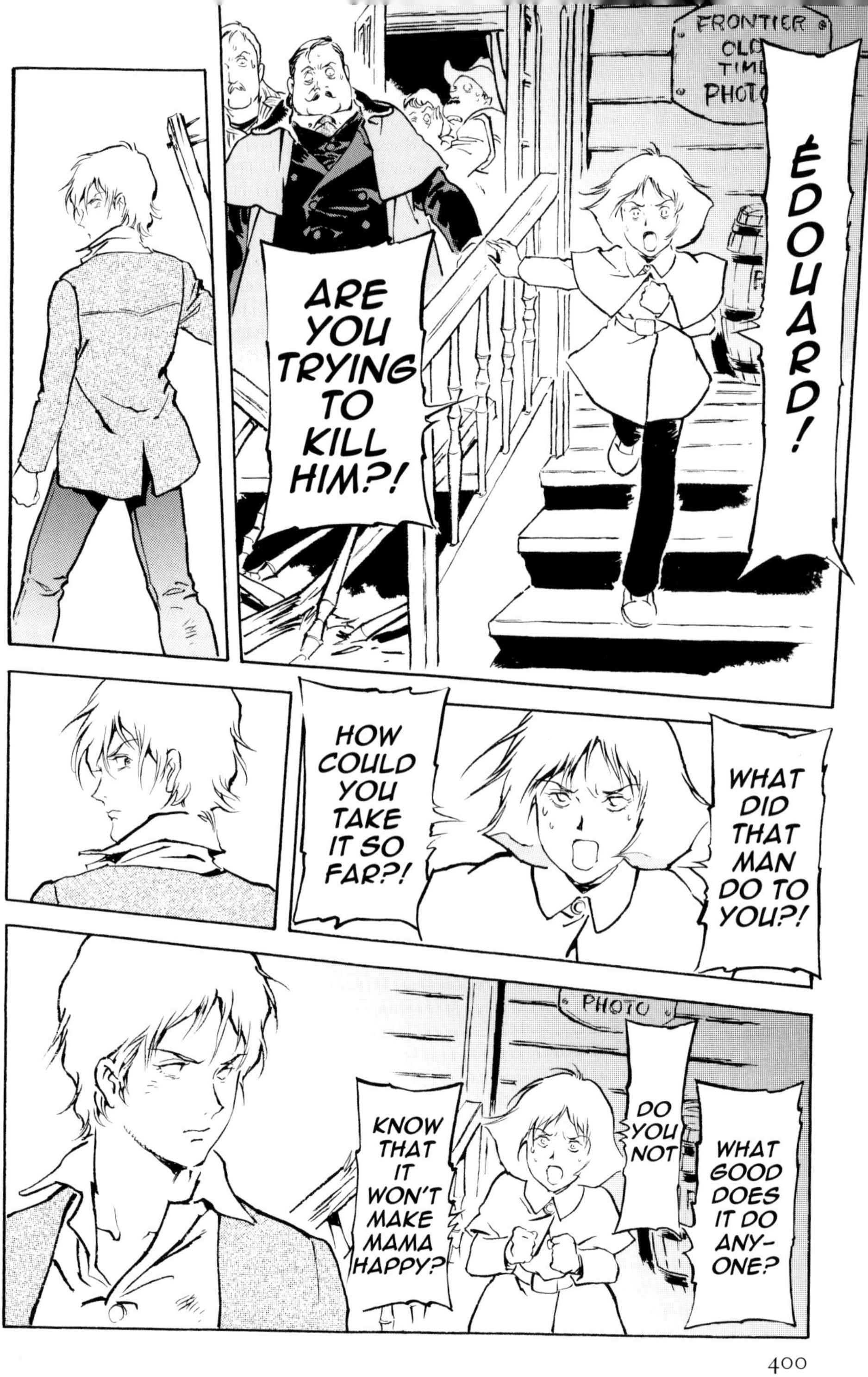
FRONTIER
ÉDOUARD!
ARE YOU TRYING TO KILL HIM?!
WHAT DID THAT MAN DO TO YOU?!
HOW COULD YOU TAKE IT SO FAR?!
PHOTO
WHAT GOOD DOES IT DO ANY-ONE?
DO YOU NOT
KNOW THAT IT WON'T MAKE MAMA HAPPY?

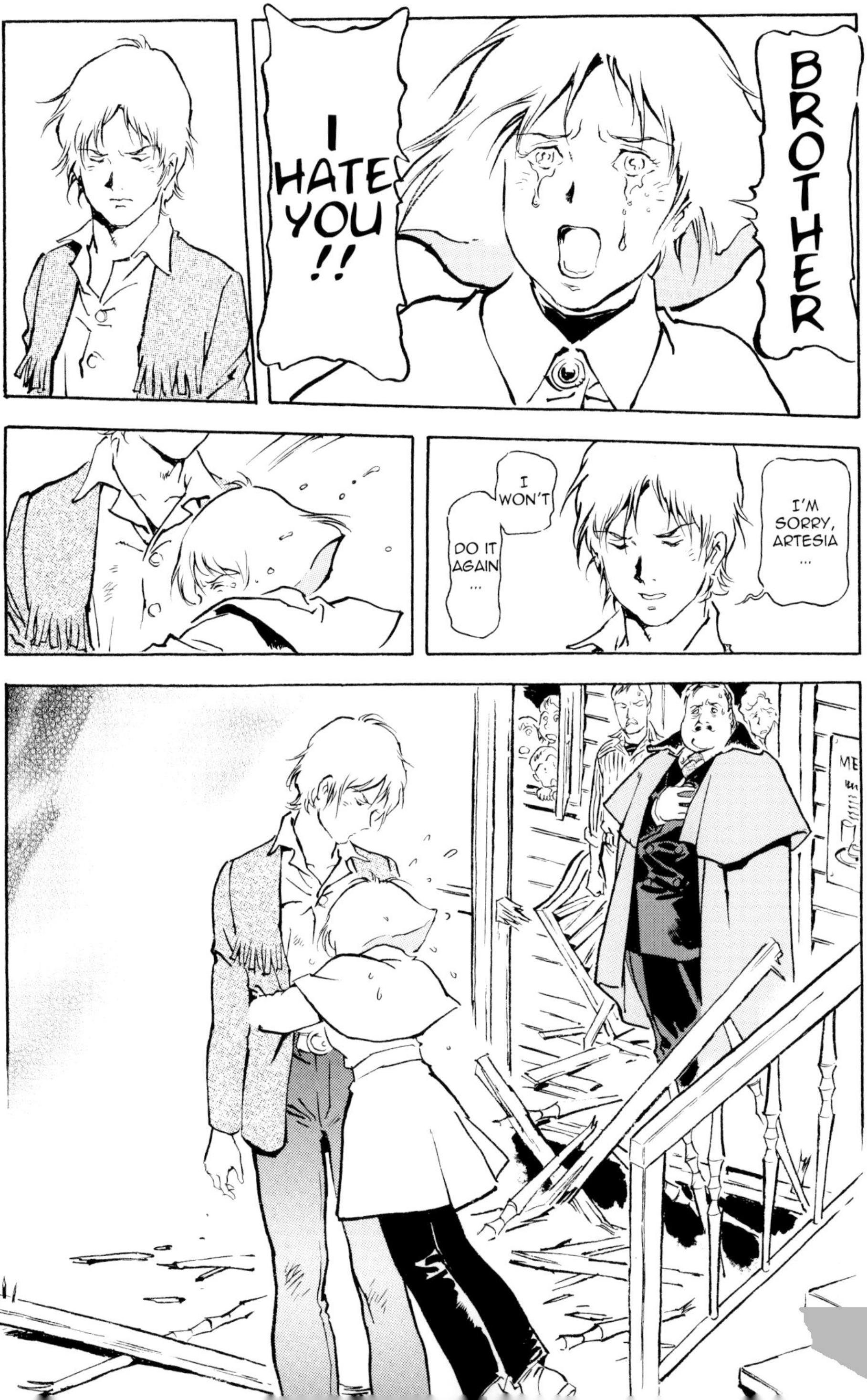
BROTHER
I HATE YOU!!
I'M SORRY, ARTESIA...
I WON'T DO IT AGAIN...

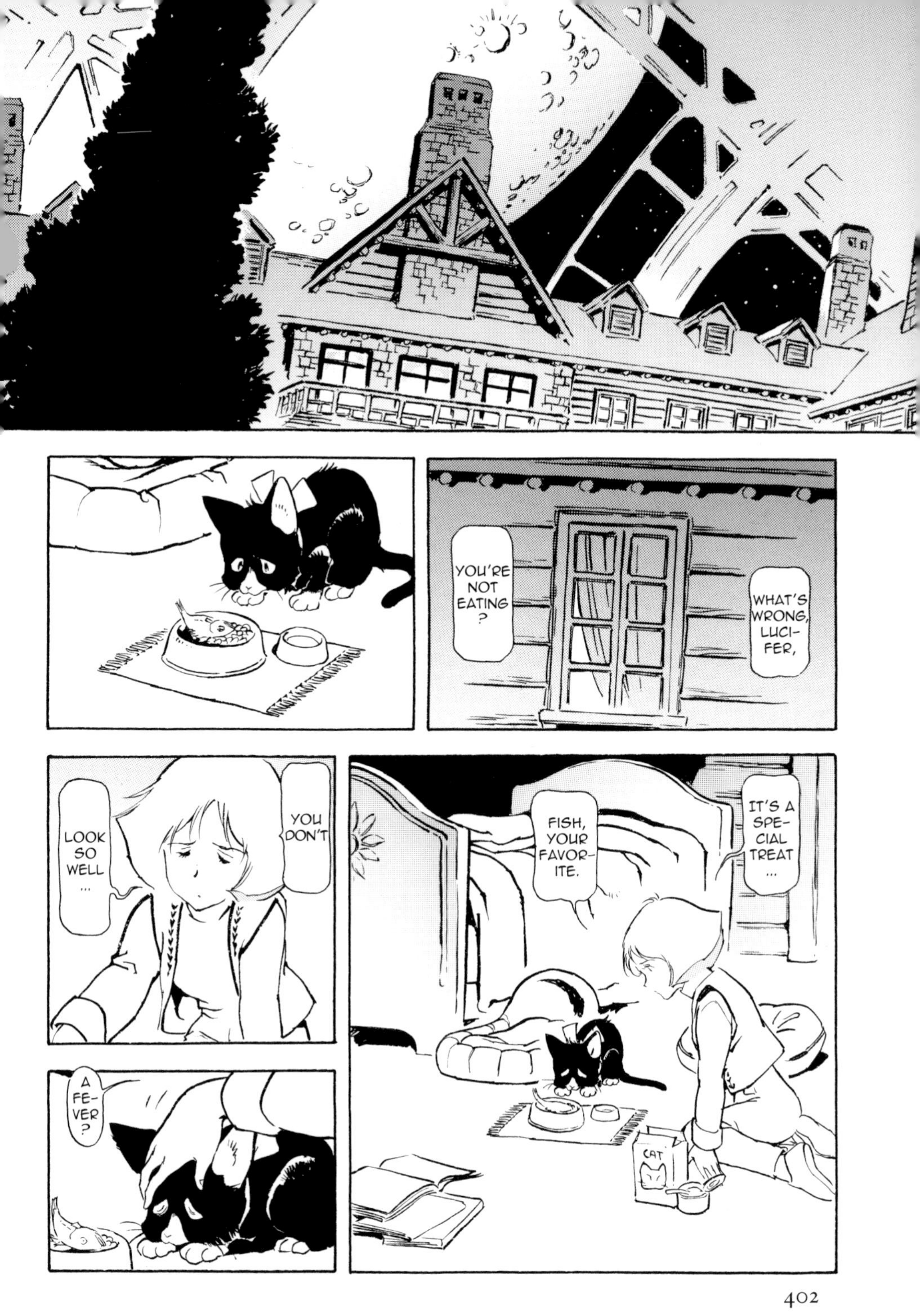
WHAT'S WRONG, LUCI-FER,
YOU'RE NOT EATING ?
IT'S A SPE-CIAL TREAT ...
FISH, YOUR FAVOR-ITE.
YOU DON'T
LOOK SO WELL ...
A FE-VER ?

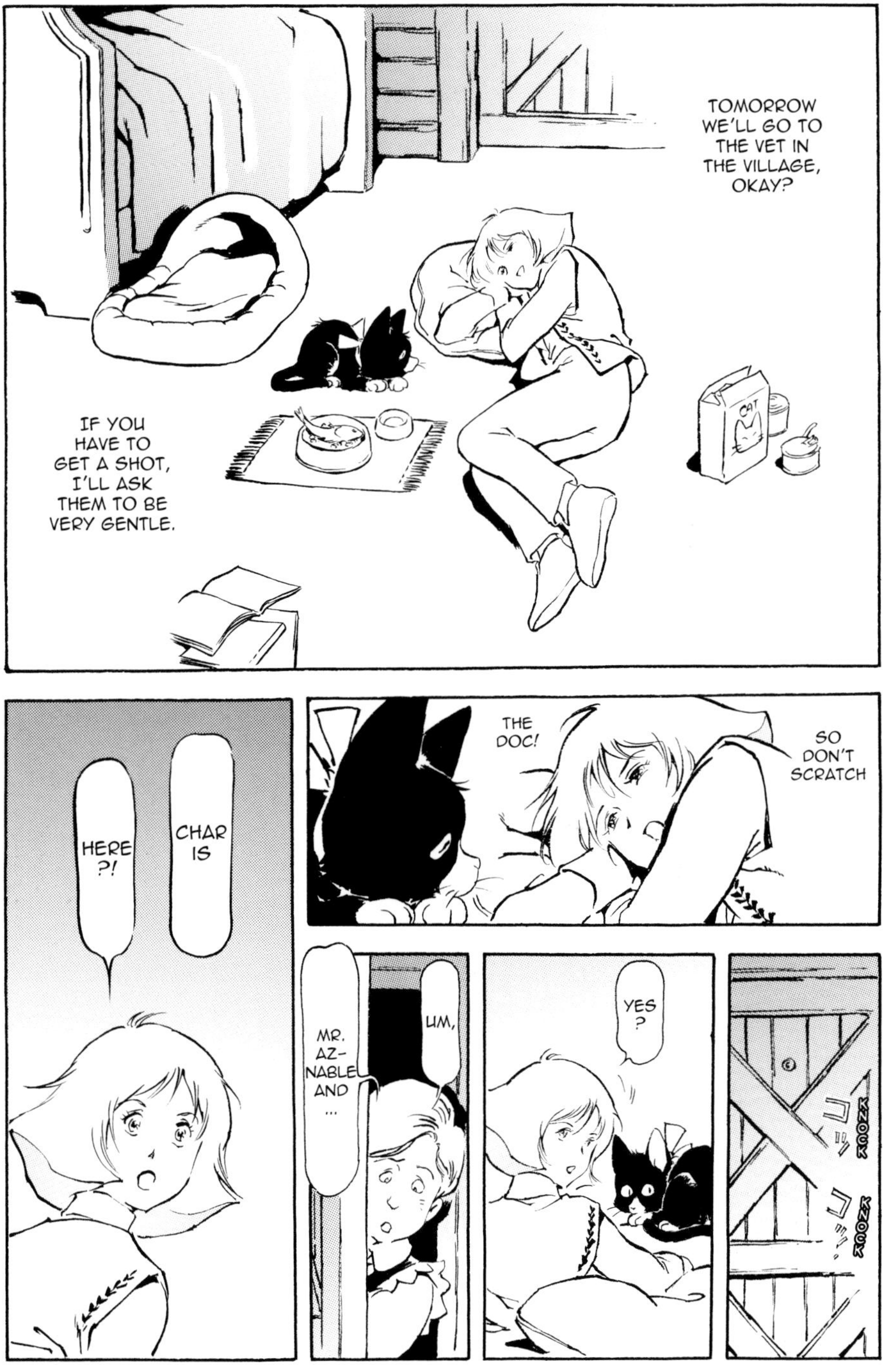
TOMORROW WE'LL GO TO THE VET IN THE VILLAGE, OKAY?
IF YOU HAVE TO GET A SHOT, I'LL ASK THEM TO BE VERY GENTLE.
SO DON'T SCRATCH
THE DOC!
KNOCK
KNOCK
YES?
UM,
MR. AZ-NABLE AND ...
CHAR IS
HERE?!

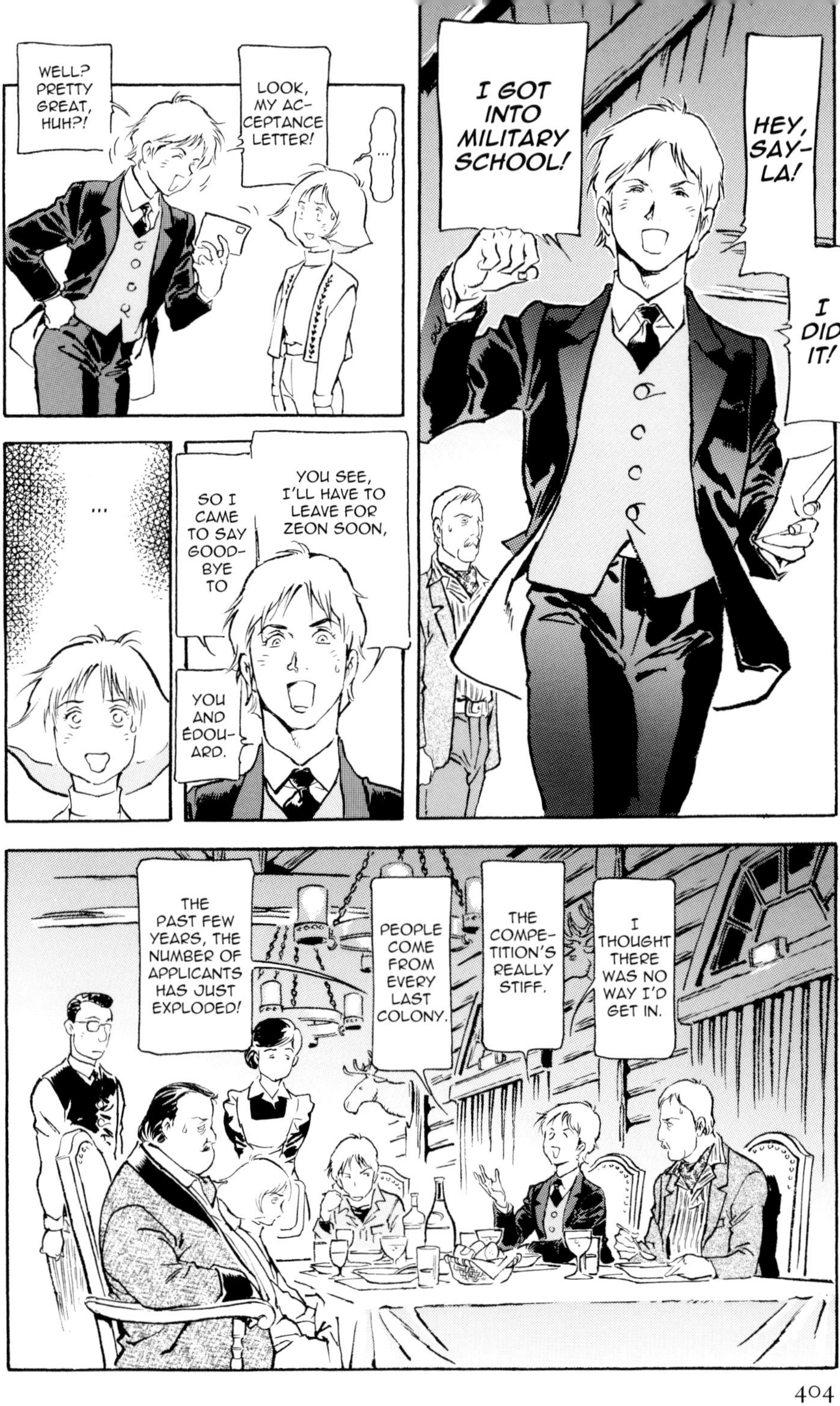
HEY, SAYLA!
I GOT INTO MILITARY SCHOOL!
I DID IT!
LOOK, MY ACCEPTANCE LETTER!
WELL? PRETTY GREAT, HUH?!
...
YOU SEE, I'LL HAVE TO LEAVE FOR ZEON SOON,
SO I CAME TO SAY GOODBYE TO
YOU AND ÉDOUARD.
...
I THOUGHT THERE WAS NO WAY I'D GET IN.
THE COMPETITION'S REALLY STIFF.
PEOPLE COME FROM EVERY LAST COLONY.
THE PAST FEW YEARS, THE NUMBER OF APPLICANTS HAS JUST EXPLODED!

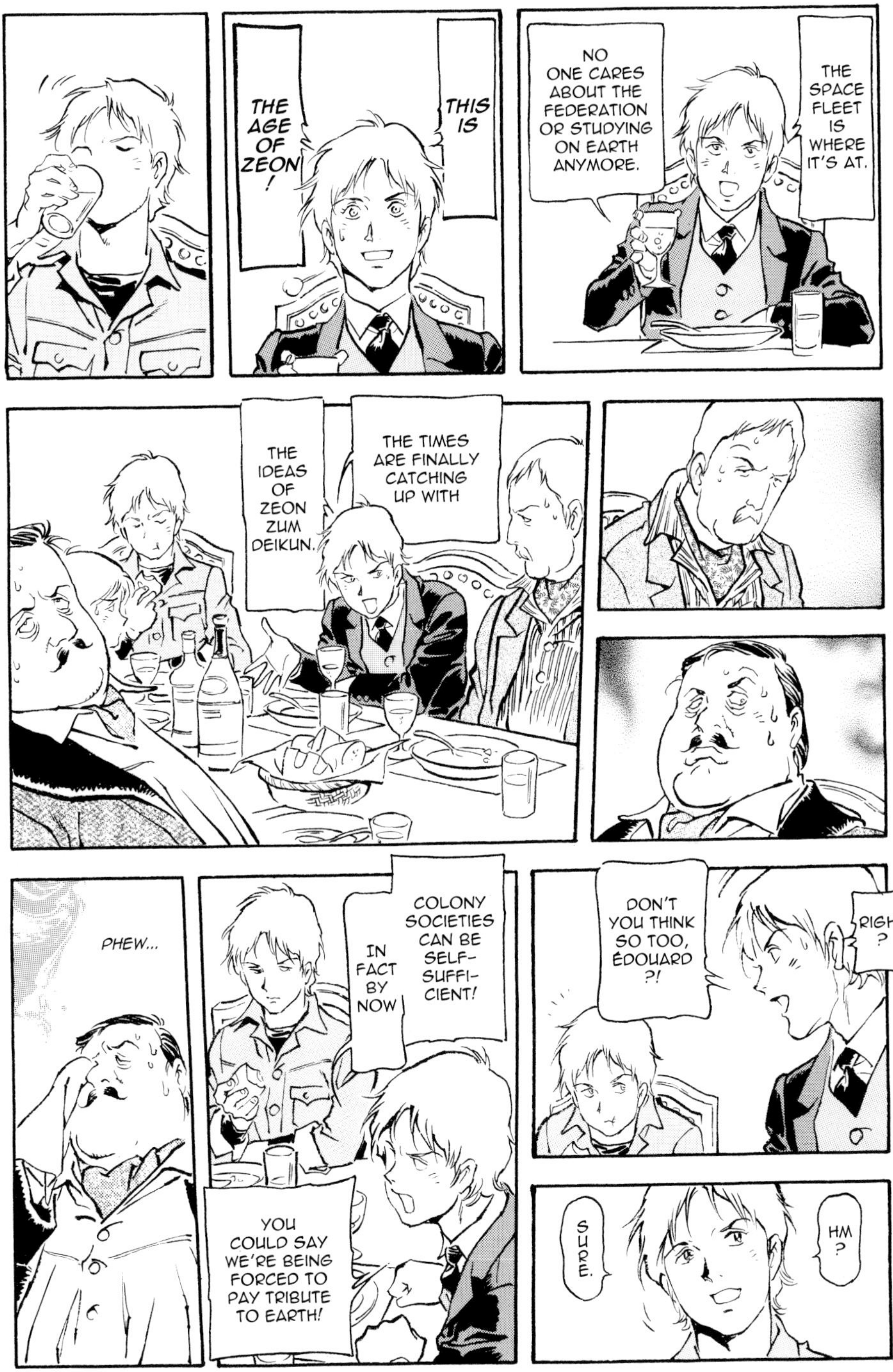
THE SPACE FLEET IS WHERE IT'S AT.
NO ONE CARES ABOUT THE FEDERATION OR STUDYING ON EARTH ANYMORE.
THIS IS
THE AGE OF ZEON!
THE TIMES ARE FINALLY CATCHING UP WITH
THE IDEAS OF ZEON ZUM DEIKUN.
RIGHT?
DON'T YOU THINK SO TOO, ÉDOUARD?!
HM?
SURE.
COLONY SOCIETIES CAN BE SELF-SUFFICIENT!
IN FACT BY NOW
YOU COULD SAY WE'RE BEING FORCED TO PAY TRIBUTE TO EARTH!
PHEW...

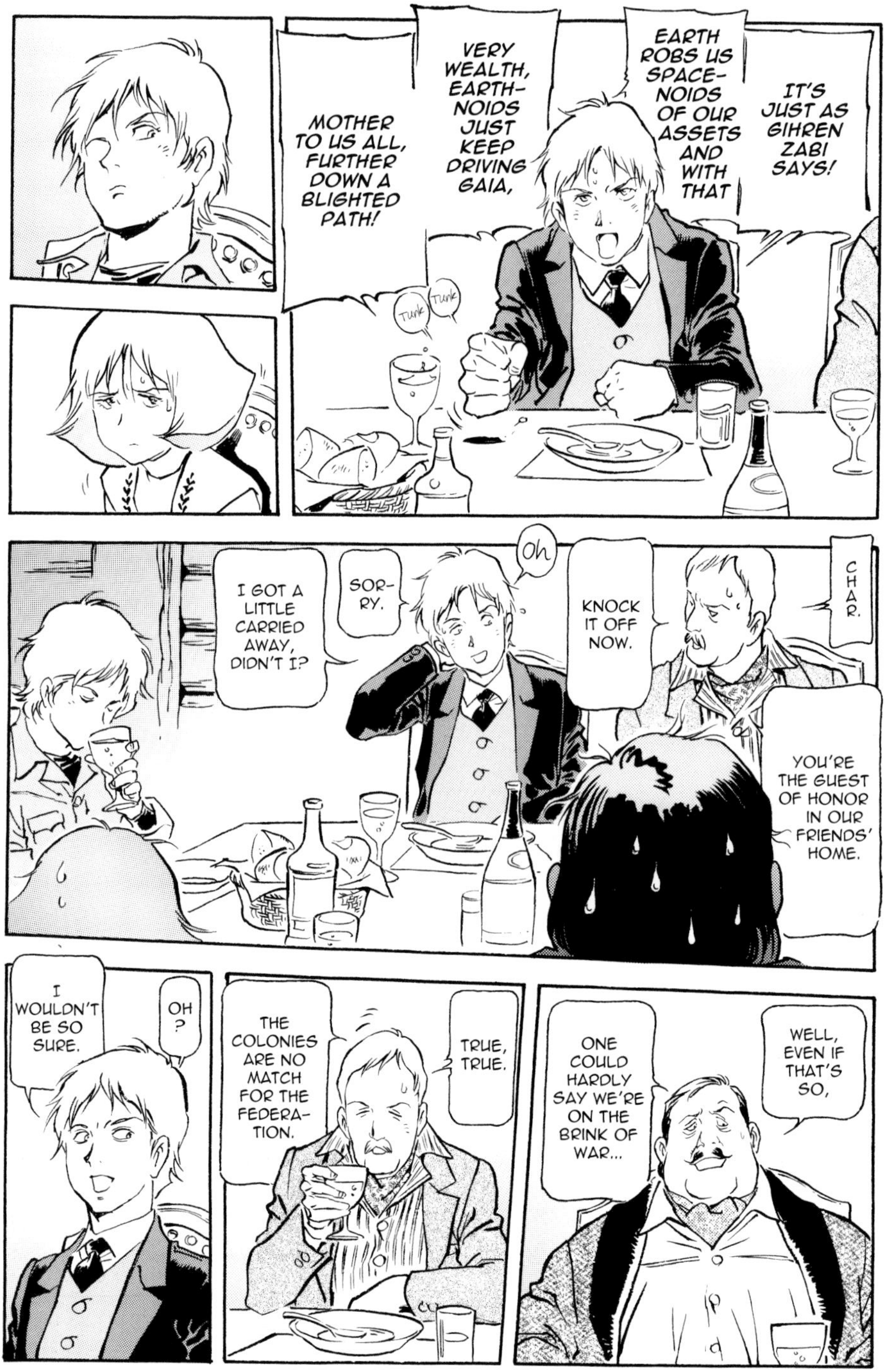
IT'S JUST AS GIHREN ZABI SAYS!
EARTH ROBS US SPACENOIDS OF OUR ASSETS AND WITH THAT
VERY WEALTH, EARTHNOIDS JUST KEEP DRIVING GAIA,
MOTHER TO US ALL, FURTHER DOWN A BLIGHTED PATH!
Tunk
Tunk
CHAR.
KNOCK IT OFF NOW.
YOU'RE THE GUEST OF HONOR IN OUR FRIENDS' HOME.
Oh
SORRY.
I GOT A LITTLE CARRIED AWAY, DIDN'T I?
WELL, EVEN IF THAT'S SO,
ONE COULD HARDLY SAY WE'RE ON THE BRINK OF WAR...
TRUE, TRUE.
THE COLONIES ARE NO MATCH FOR THE FEDERATION.
OH?
I WOULDN'T BE SO SURE.

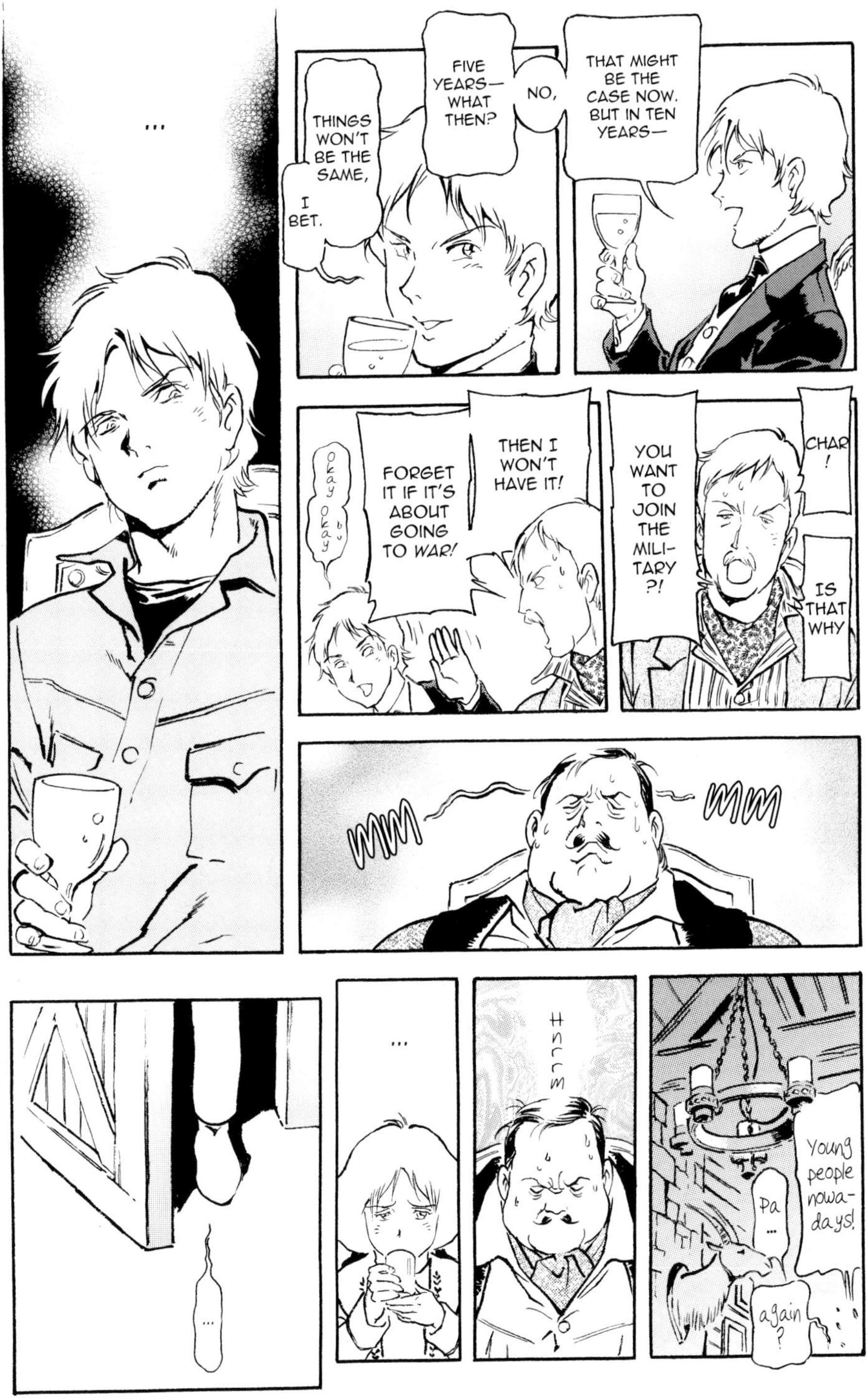
THAT MIGHT BE THE CASE NOW. BUT IN TEN YEARS—
NO,
FIVE YEARS— WHAT THEN?
THINGS WON'T BE THE SAME,
I BET.
CHAR!
IS THAT WHY
YOU WANT TO JOIN THE MILITARY?!
THEN I WON'T HAVE IT!
FORGET IT IF IT'S ABOUT GOING TO *WAR*!
Okay okay bu
MMM
MMM
...
Young people nowa-days!
Pa...
again?
Hnrrm
...
...

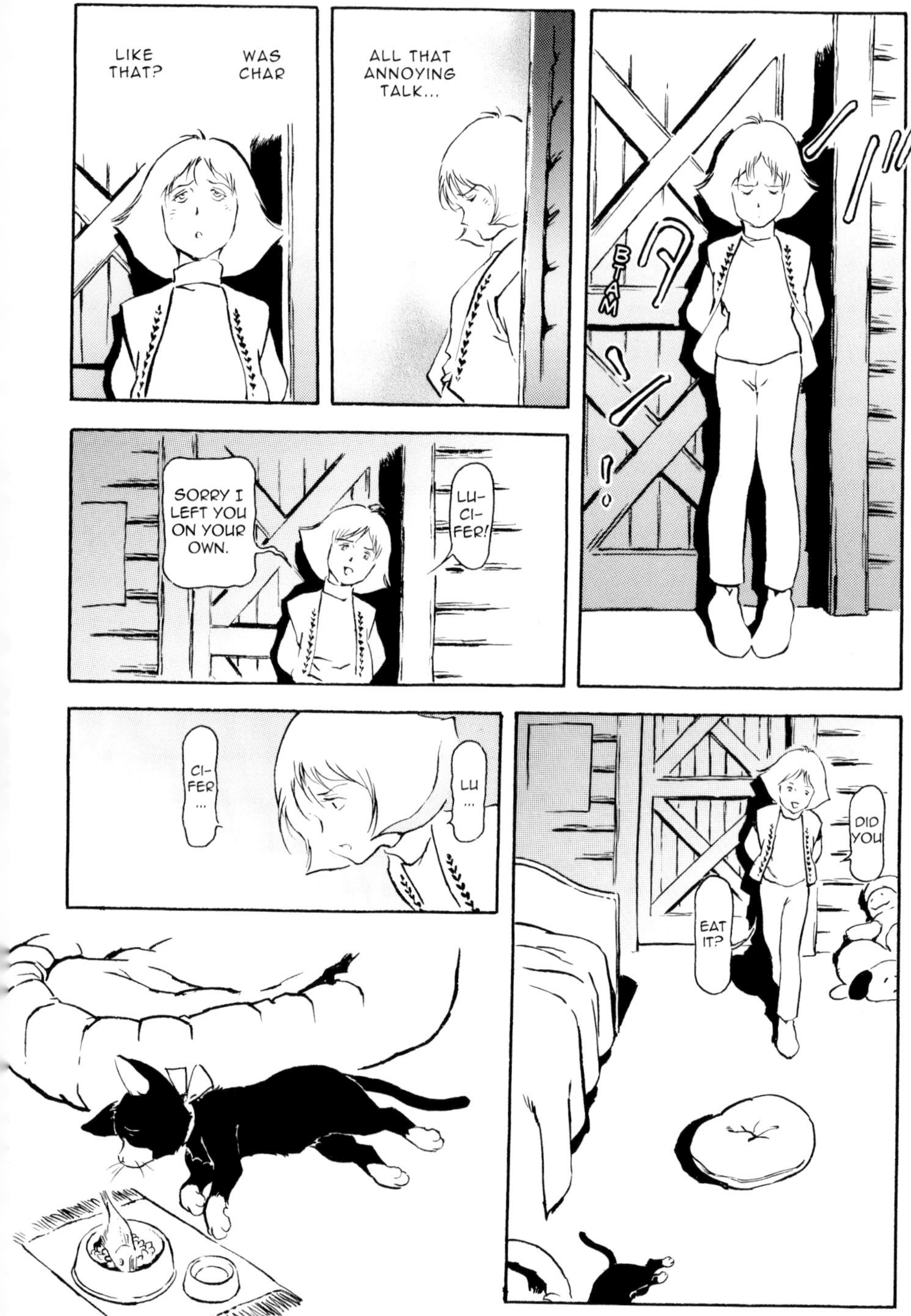
BTAM
ALL THAT ANNOYING TALK...
WAS CHAR
LIKE THAT?
LU-CI-FER!
SORRY I LEFT YOU ON YOUR OWN.
DID YOU
EAT IT?
LU...
CI-FER...

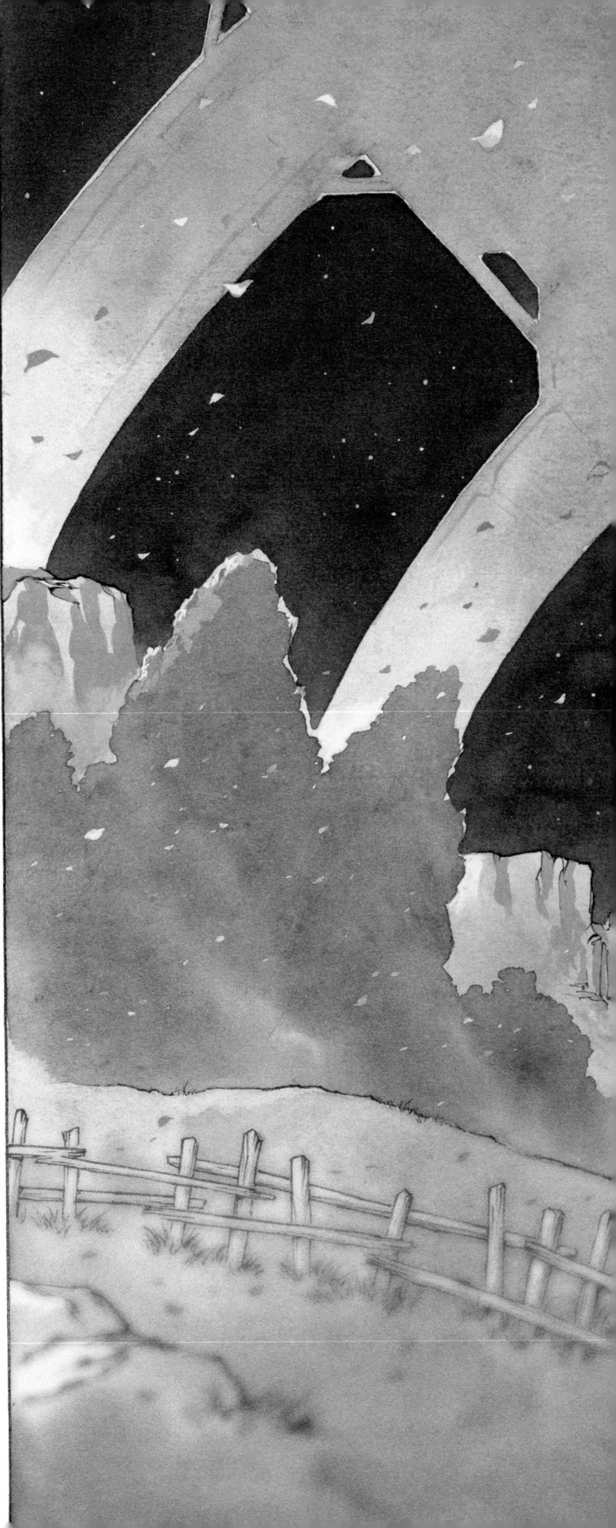

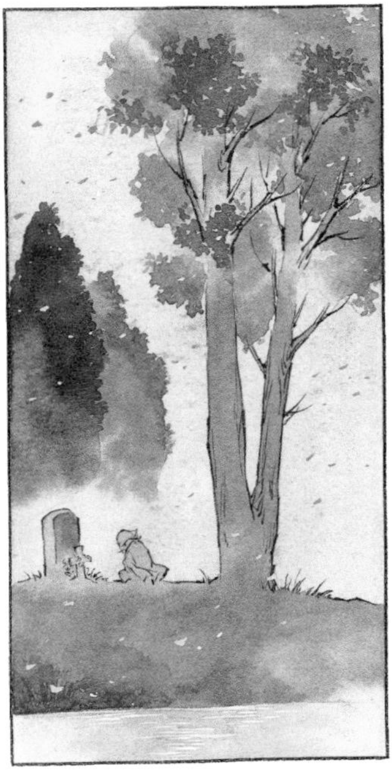

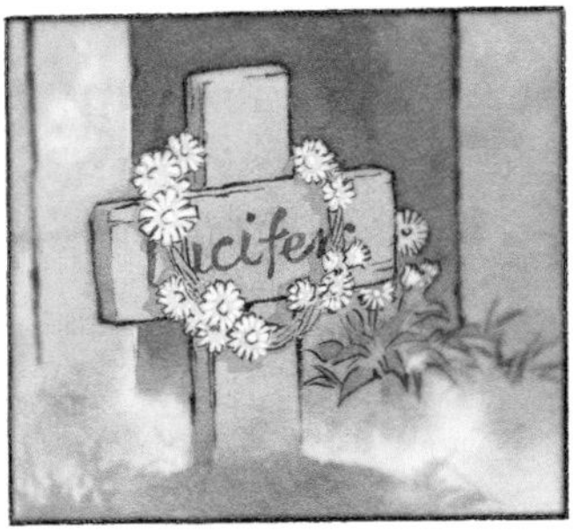

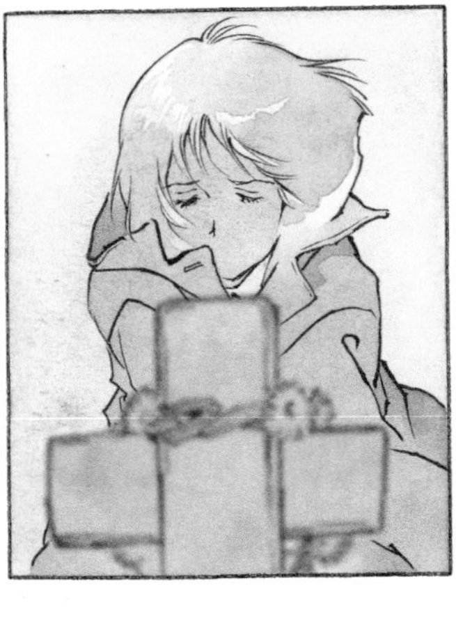

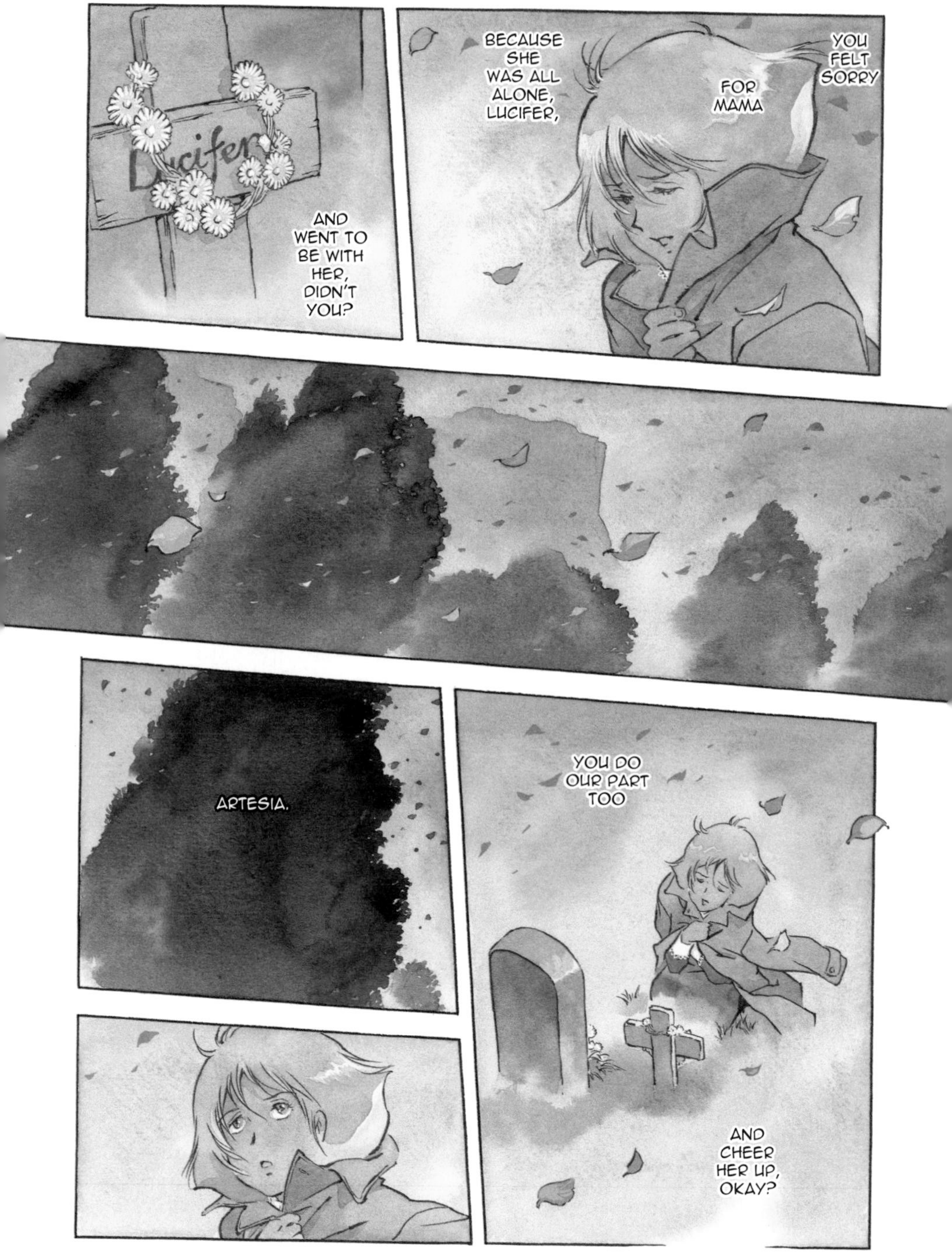
YOU FELT SORRY
FOR MAMA
BECAUSE SHE WAS ALL ALONE, LUCIFER,
Lucifer
AND WENT TO BE WITH HER, DIDN'T YOU?
YOU DO OUR PART TOO
AND CHEER HER UP, OKAY?
ARTESIA.

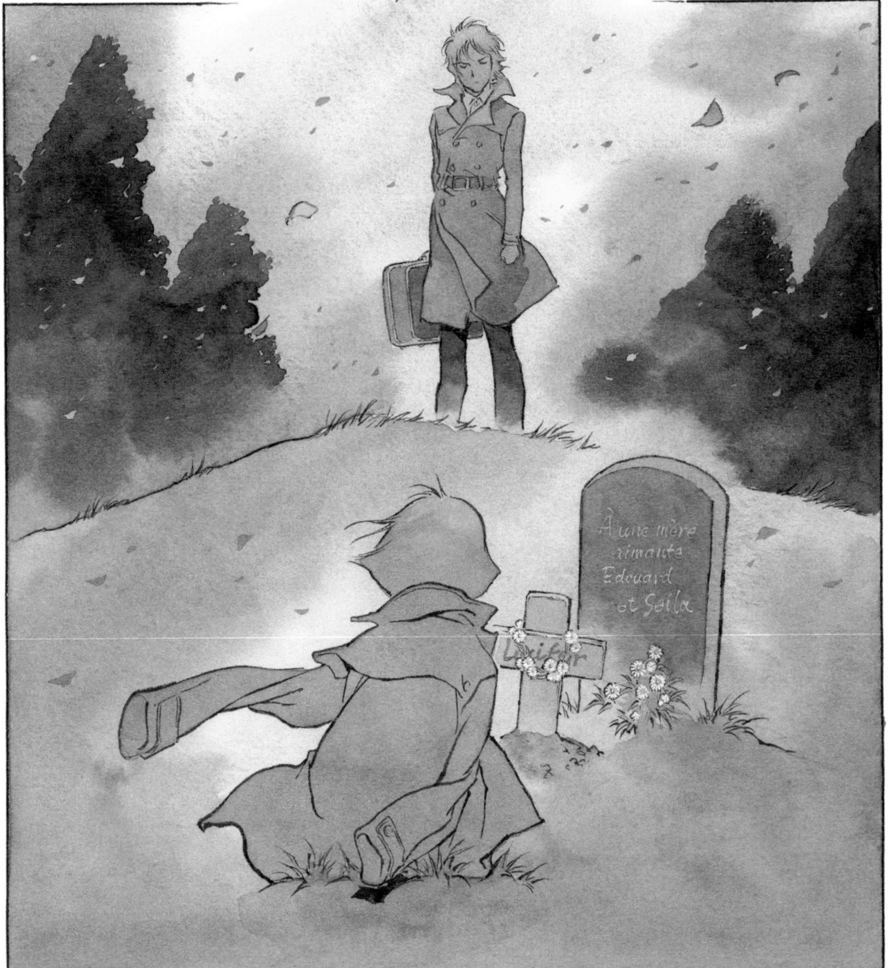
À une mère
aimante
Edouard
et Seila

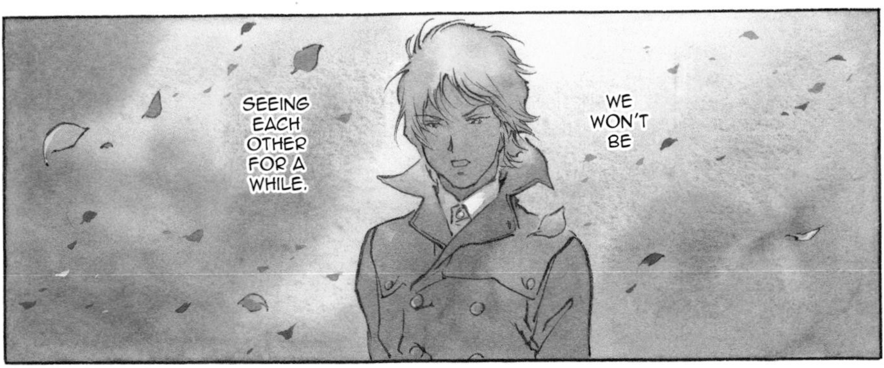
WE WON'T BE
SEEING EACH OTHER FOR A WHILE.

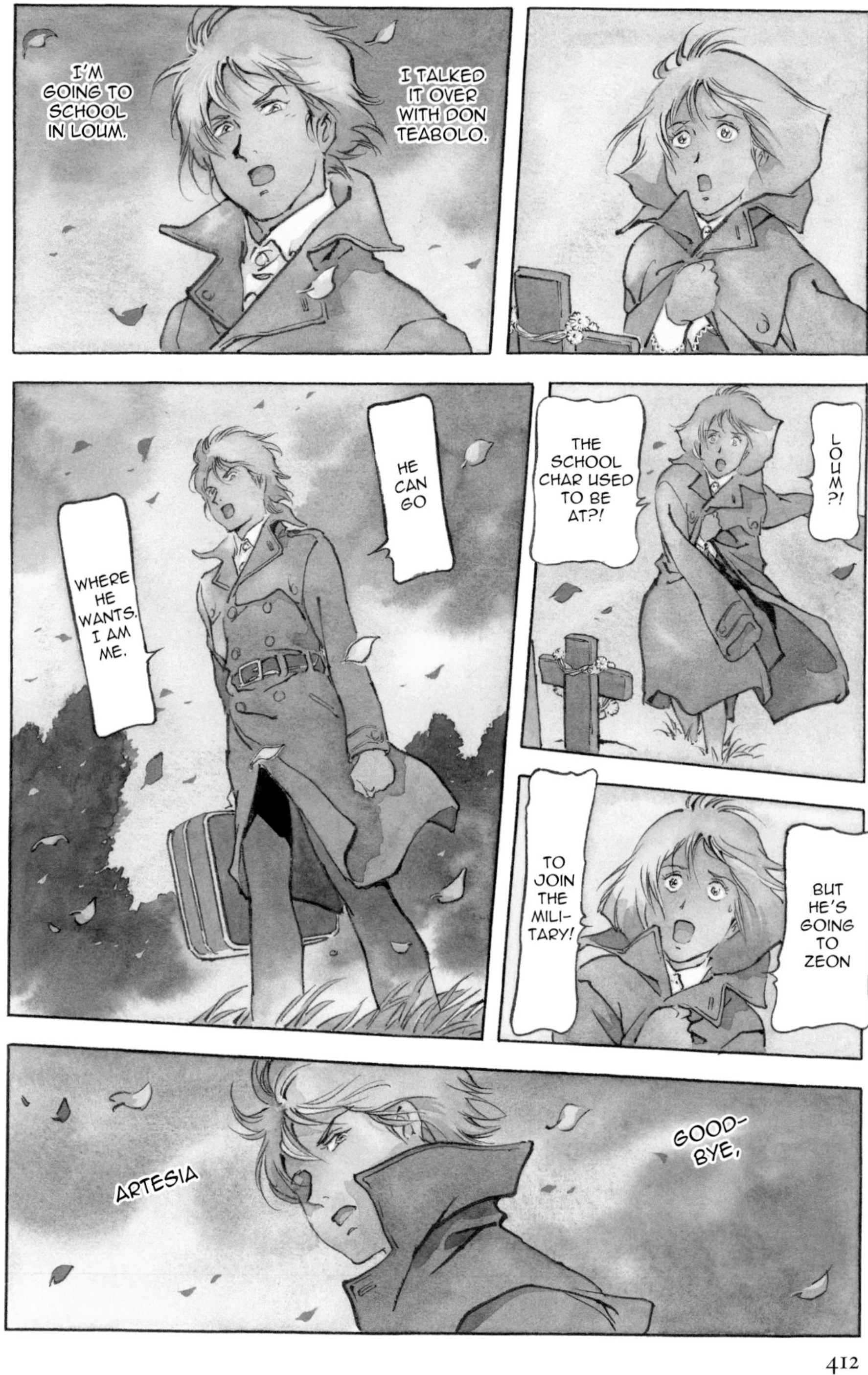
I TALKED IT OVER WITH DON TEABOLO.
I'M GOING TO SCHOOL IN LOUM.
LOUM?!
THE SCHOOL CHAR USED TO BE AT?!
BUT HE'S GOING TO ZEON
TO JOIN THE MILI-TARY!
HE CAN GO
WHERE HE WANTS. I AM ME.
GOOD-BYE,
ARTESIA

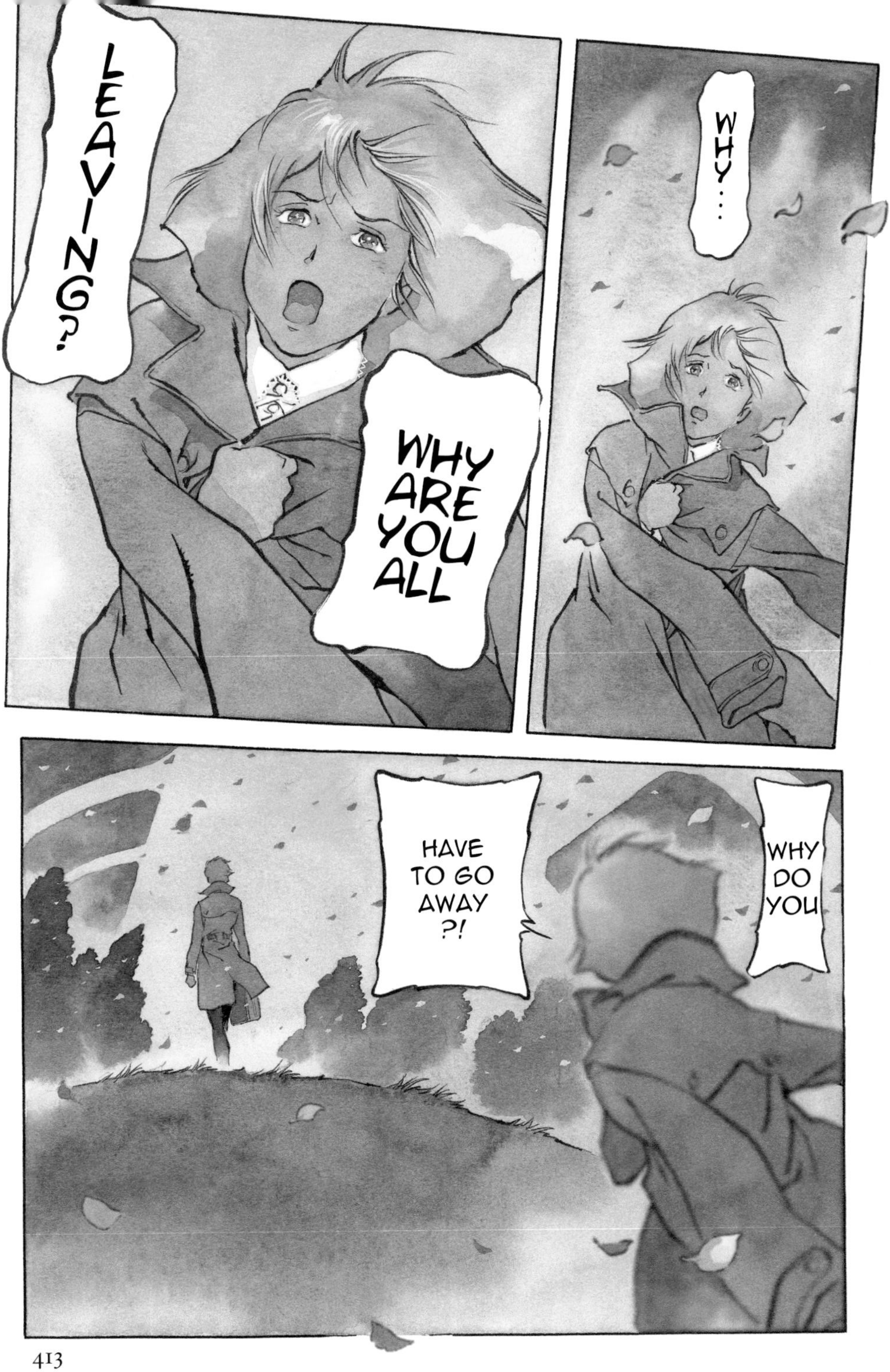

WHY...
WHY ARE YOU ALL
LEAVING?!
WHY DO YOU
HAVE TO GO AWAY ?!

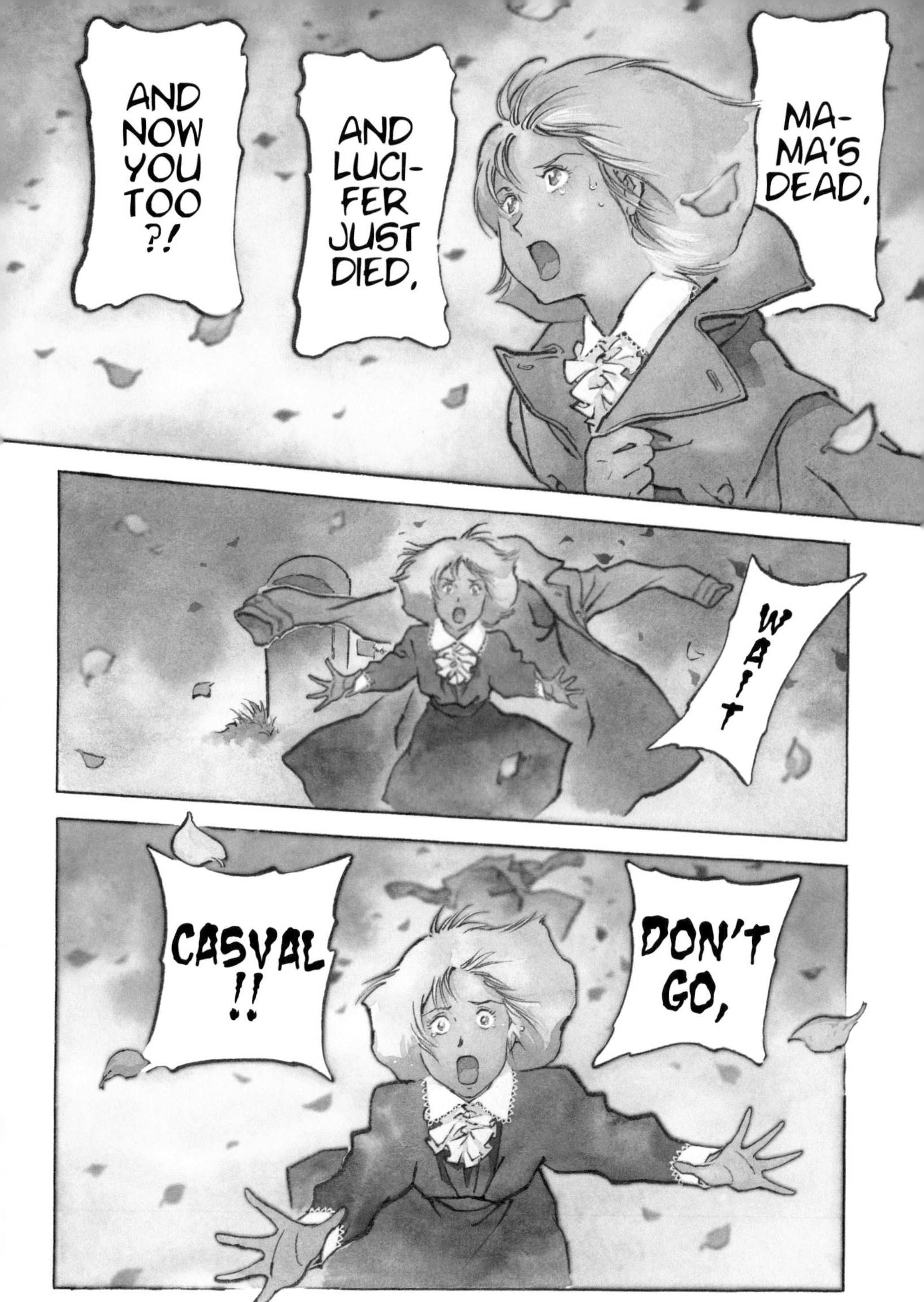
MAMA'S DEAD,
AND LUCIFER JUST DIED,
AND NOW YOU TOO?!
WAIT
DON'T GO,
CASVAL!!

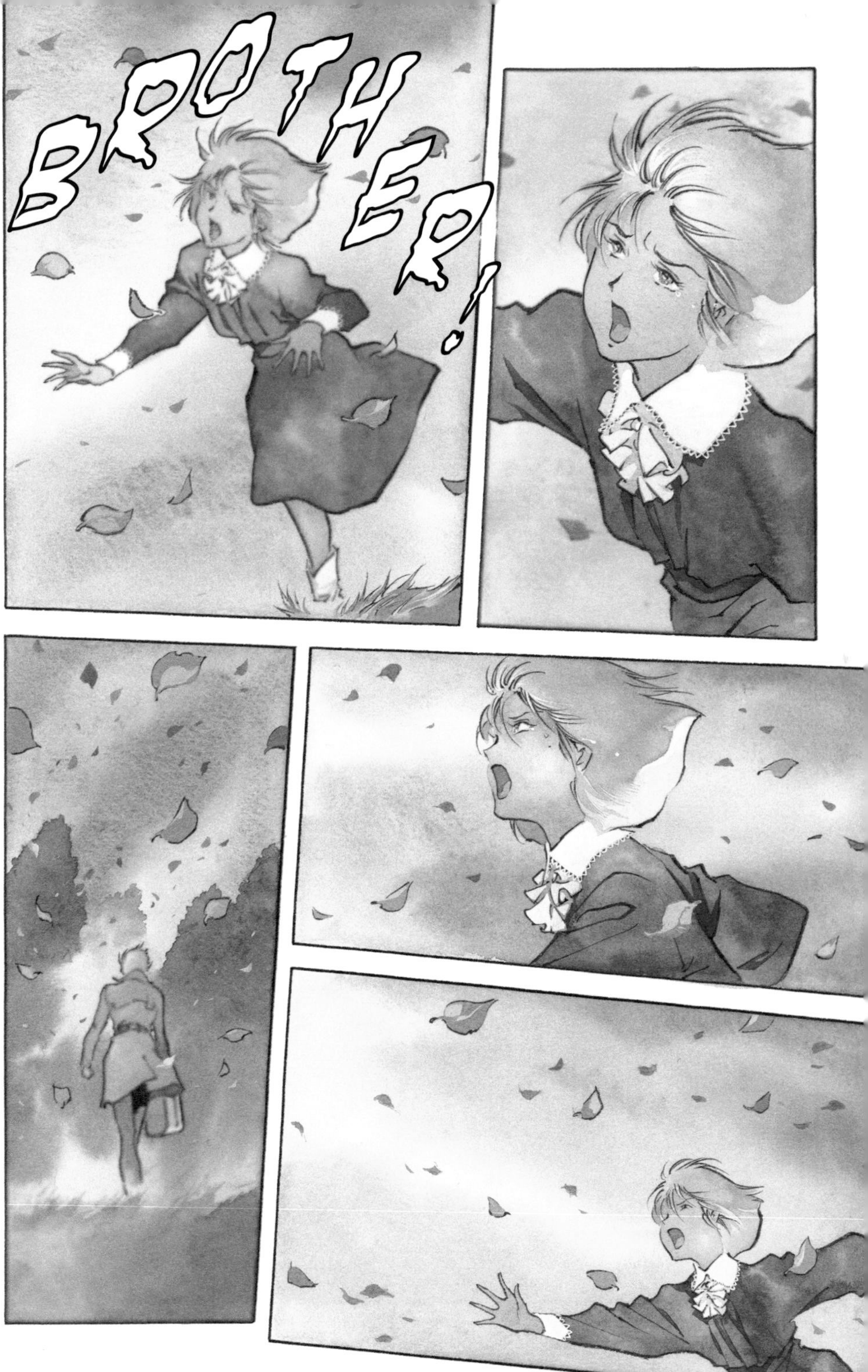
BROTHER!

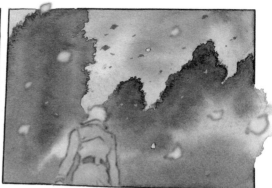

SECTION IX

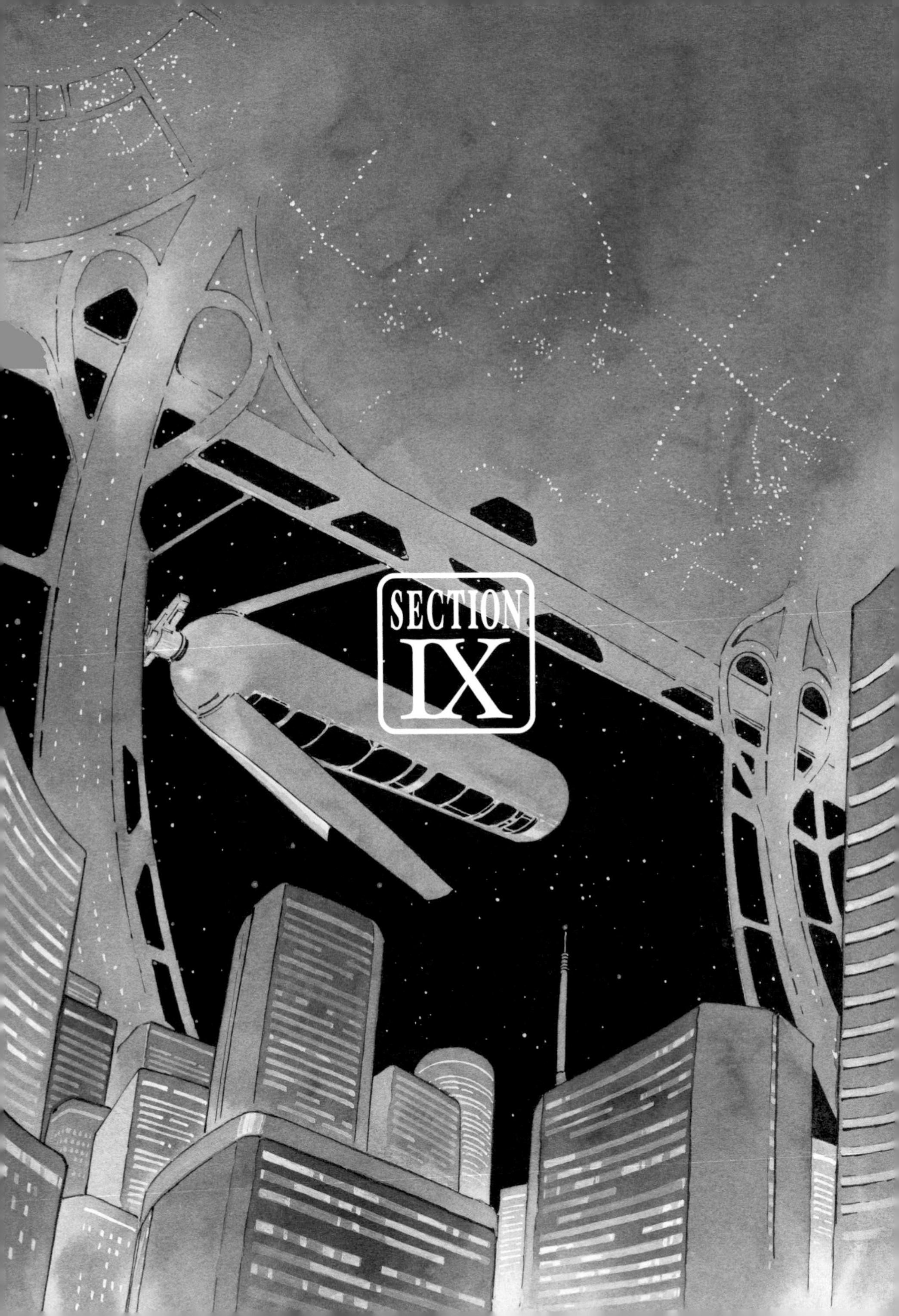

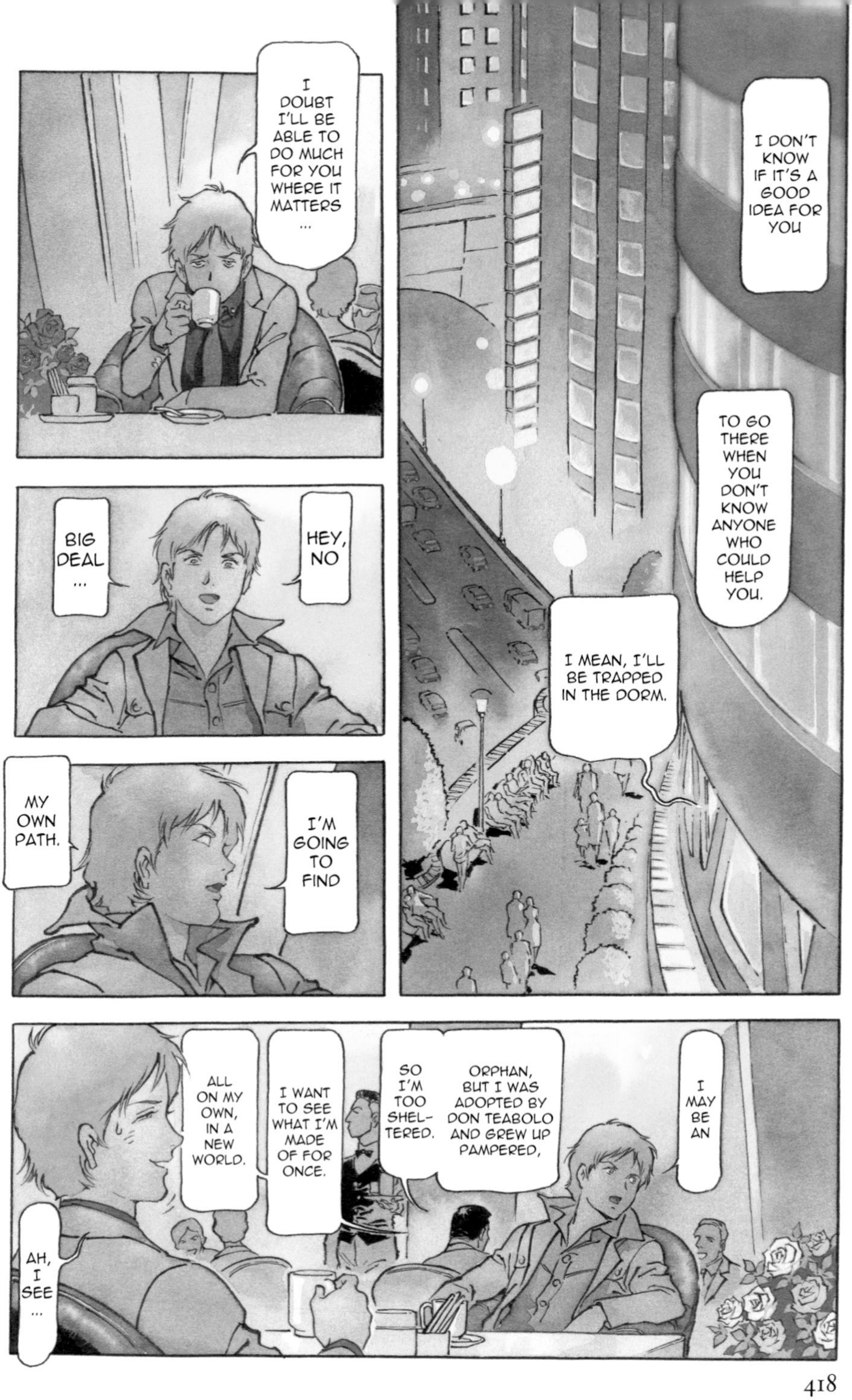
I DON'T KNOW IF IT'S A GOOD IDEA FOR YOU
TO GO THERE WHEN YOU DON'T KNOW ANYONE WHO COULD HELP YOU.
I MEAN, I'LL BE TRAPPED IN THE DORM.
I DOUBT I'LL BE ABLE TO DO MUCH FOR YOU WHERE IT MATTERS ...
HEY, NO
BIG DEAL ...
I'M GOING TO FIND
MY OWN PATH.
I MAY BE AN
ORPHAN, BUT I WAS ADOPTED BY DON TEABOLO AND GREW UP PAMPERED,
SO I'M TOO SHEL- TERED.
I WANT TO SEE WHAT I'M MADE OF FOR ONCE.
ALL ON MY OWN, IN A NEW WORLD.
AH, I SEE ...

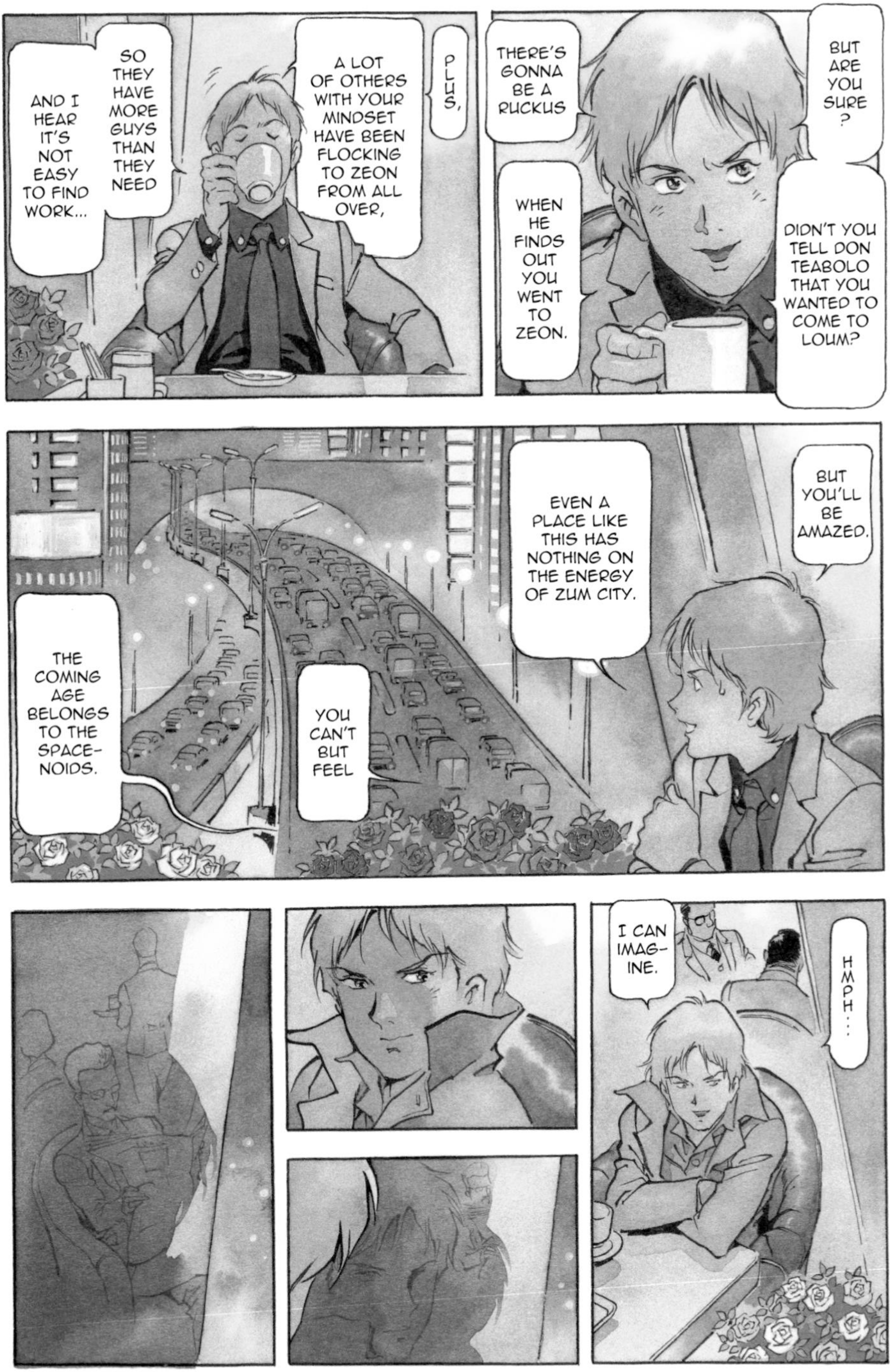
BUT ARE YOU SURE?
DIDN'T YOU TELL DON TEABOLO THAT YOU WANTED TO COME TO LOUM?
THERE'S GONNA BE A RUCKUS
WHEN HE FINDS OUT YOU WENT TO ZEON.
PLUS,
A LOT OF OTHERS WITH YOUR MINDSET HAVE BEEN FLOCKING TO ZEON FROM ALL OVER,
SO THEY HAVE MORE GUYS THAN THEY NEED
AND I HEAR IT'S NOT EASY TO FIND WORK...
BUT YOU'LL BE AMAZED.
EVEN A PLACE LIKE THIS HAS NOTHING ON THE ENERGY OF ZUM CITY.
YOU CAN'T BUT FEEL
THE COMING AGE BELONGS TO THE SPACE-NOIDS.
HMPH...
I CAN IMAGINE.

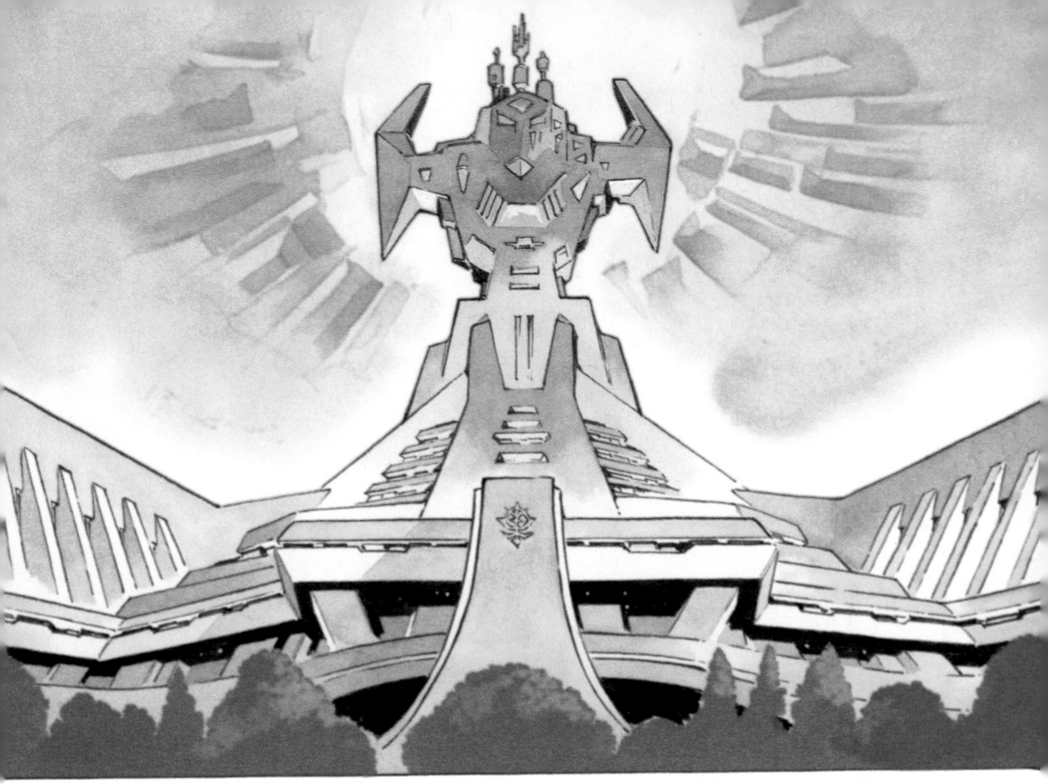

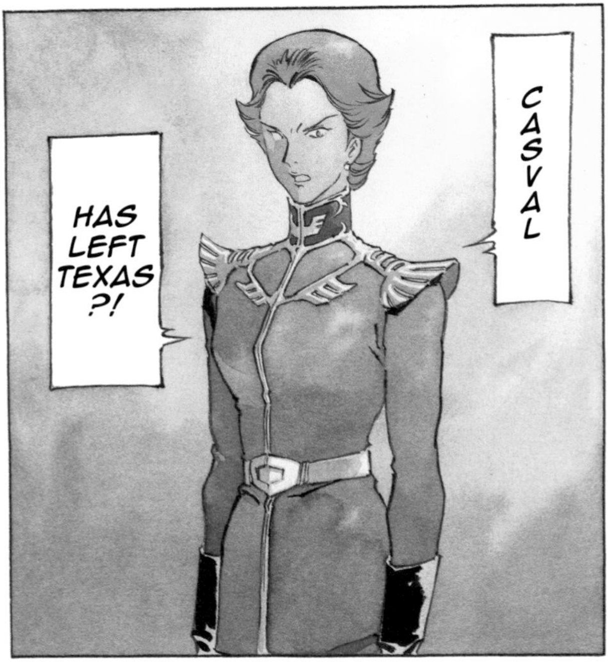
CASVAL
HAS LEFT TEXAS ?!

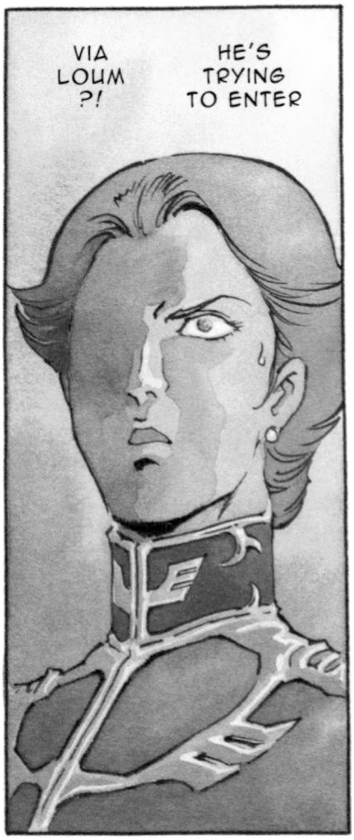
HE'S TRYING TO ENTER
VIA LOUM ?!

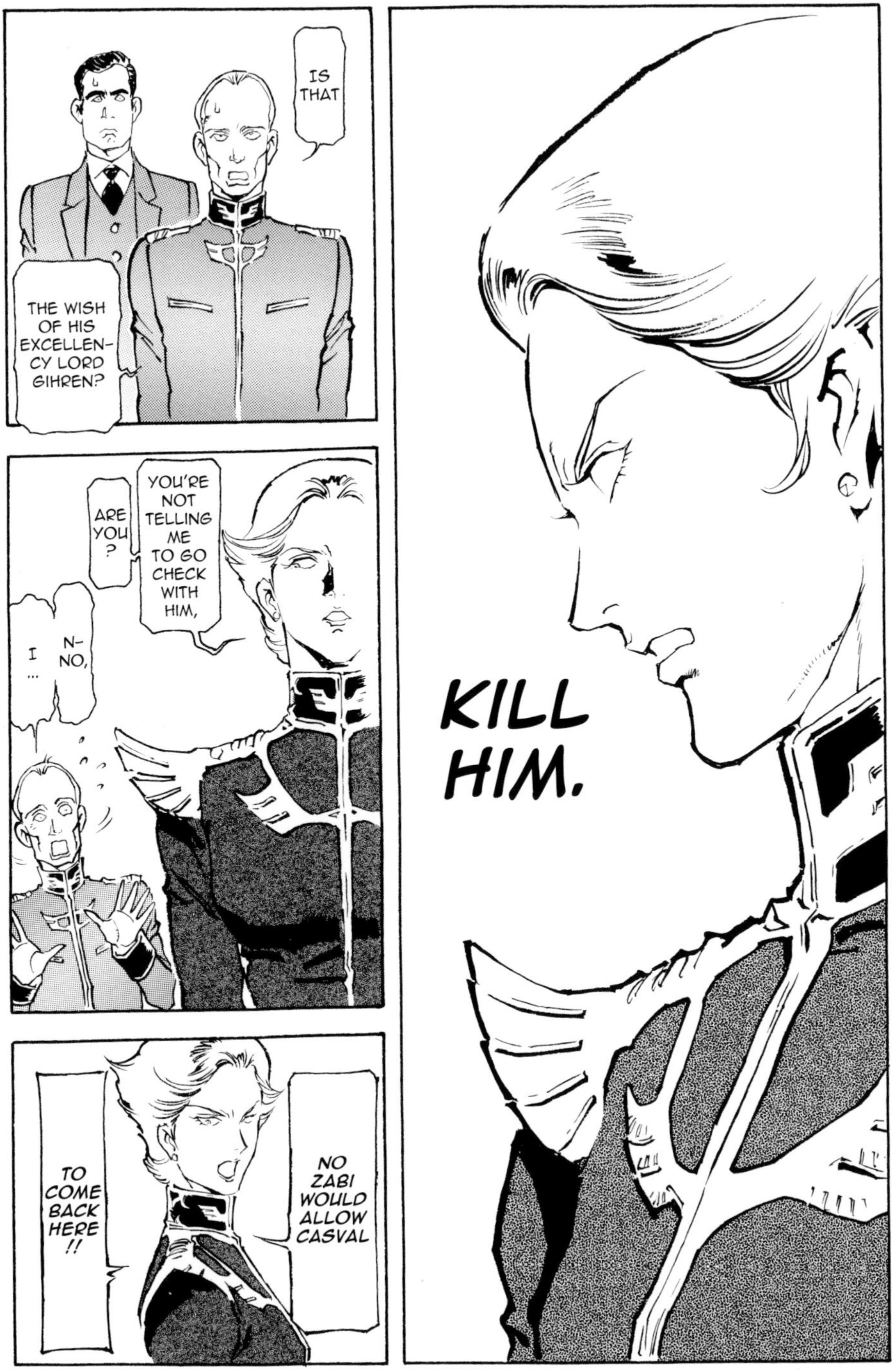
KILL HIM.
IS THAT
THE WISH OF HIS EXCELLENCY LORD GIHREN?
YOU'RE NOT TELLING ME TO GO CHECK WITH HIM,
ARE YOU?
N-NO,
I ...
NO ZABI WOULD ALLOW CASVAL
TO COME BACK HERE!!

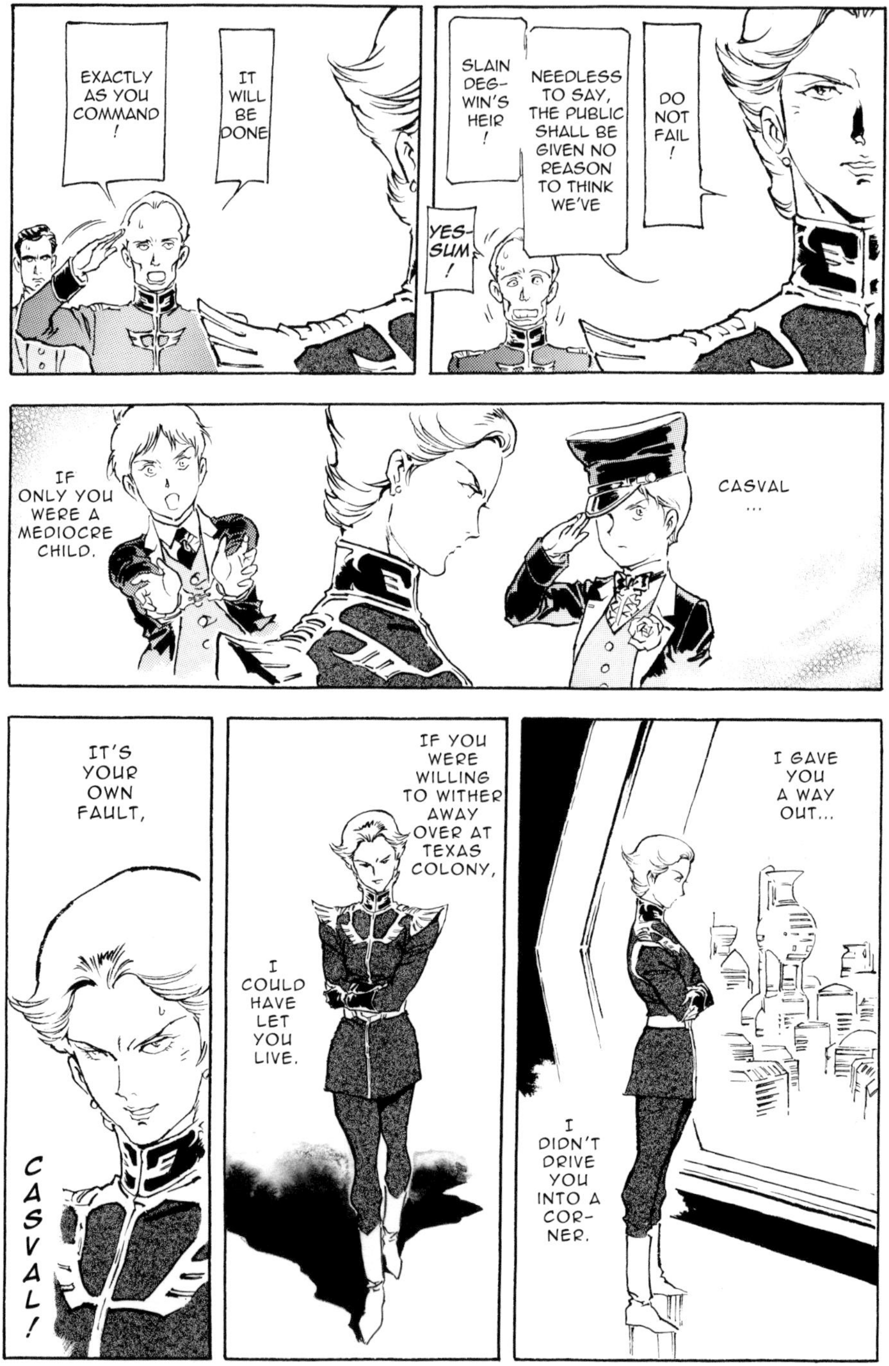
DO NOT FAIL!
NEEDLESS TO SAY, THE PUBLIC SHALL BE GIVEN NO REASON TO THINK WE'VE
SLAIN DEGWIN'S HEIR!
YES-SUM!
IT WILL BE DONE
EXACTLY AS YOU COMMAND!
CASVAL...
IF ONLY YOU WERE A MEDIOCRE CHILD.
I GAVE YOU A WAY OUT...
I DIDN'T DRIVE YOU INTO A CORNER.
IF YOU WERE WILLING TO WITHER AWAY OVER AT TEXAS COLONY,
I COULD HAVE LET YOU LIVE.
IT'S YOUR OWN FAULT,
CASVAL!

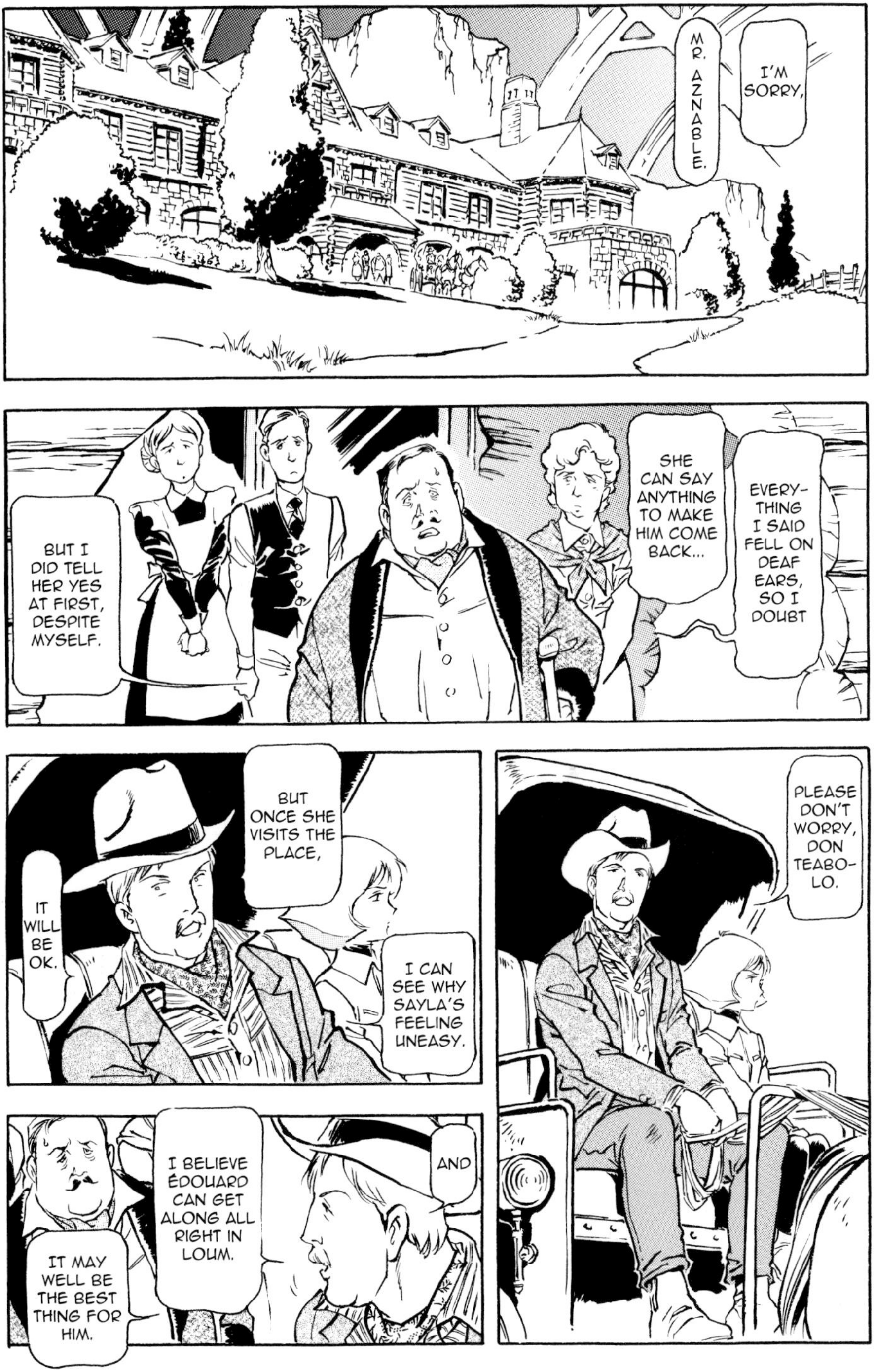
I'M SORRY,
MR. AZNABLE.
EVERY-THING I SAID FELL ON DEAF EARS, SO I DOUBT
SHE CAN SAY ANYTHING TO MAKE HIM COME BACK...
BUT I DID TELL HER YES AT FIRST, DESPITE MYSELF.
PLEASE DON'T WORRY, DON TEABO-LO.
BUT ONCE SHE VISITS THE PLACE,
IT WILL BE OK.
I CAN SEE WHY SAYLA'S FEELING UNEASY.
AND
I BELIEVE ÉDOUARD CAN GET ALONG ALL RIGHT IN LOUM.
IT MAY WELL BE THE BEST THING FOR HIM.

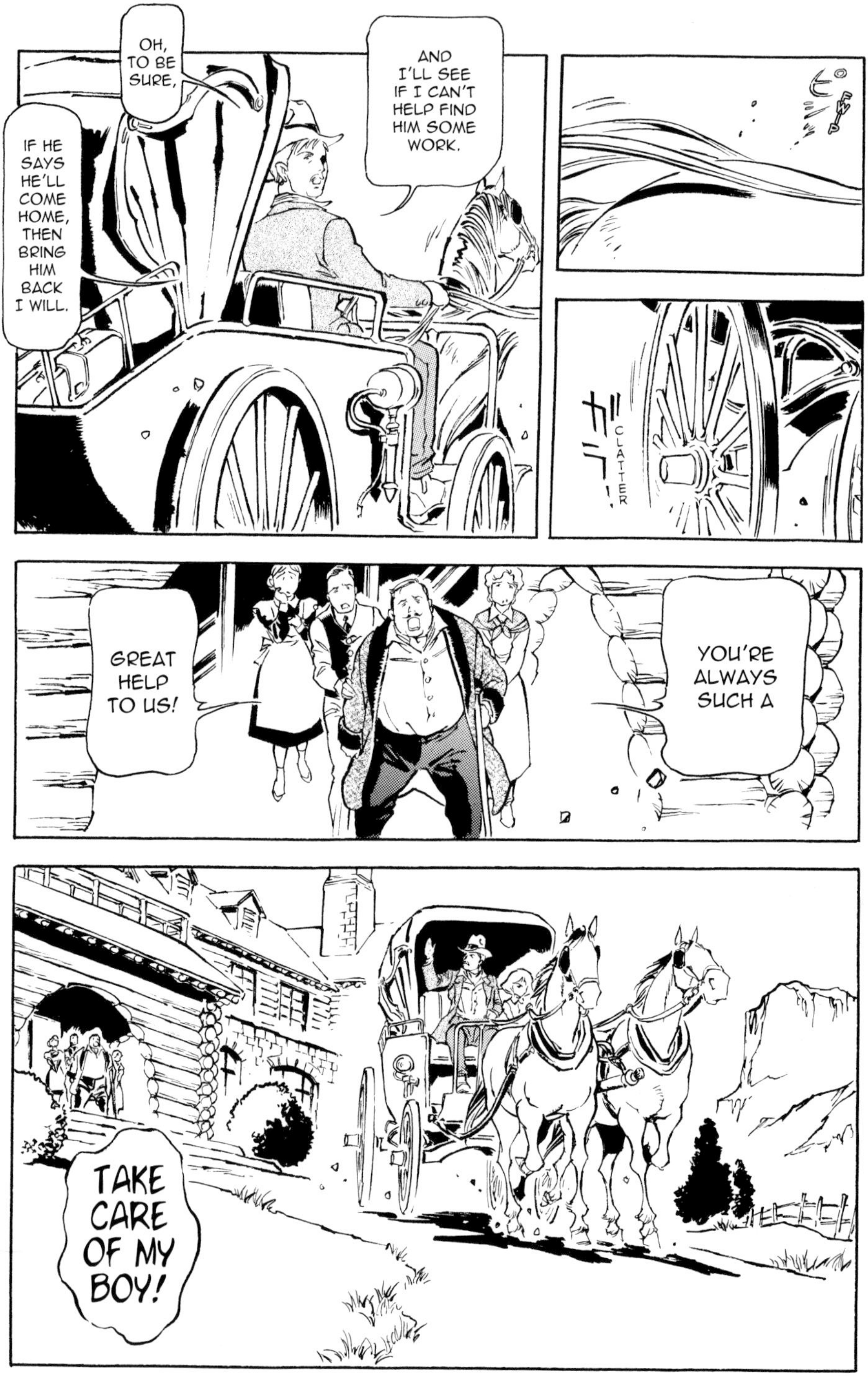
FWP
CLATTER
OH, TO BE SURE,
IF HE SAYS HE'LL COME HOME, THEN BRING HIM BACK I WILL.
AND I'LL SEE IF I CAN'T HELP FIND HIM SOME WORK.
YOU'RE ALWAYS SUCH A
GREAT HELP TO US!
TAKE CARE OF MY BOY!

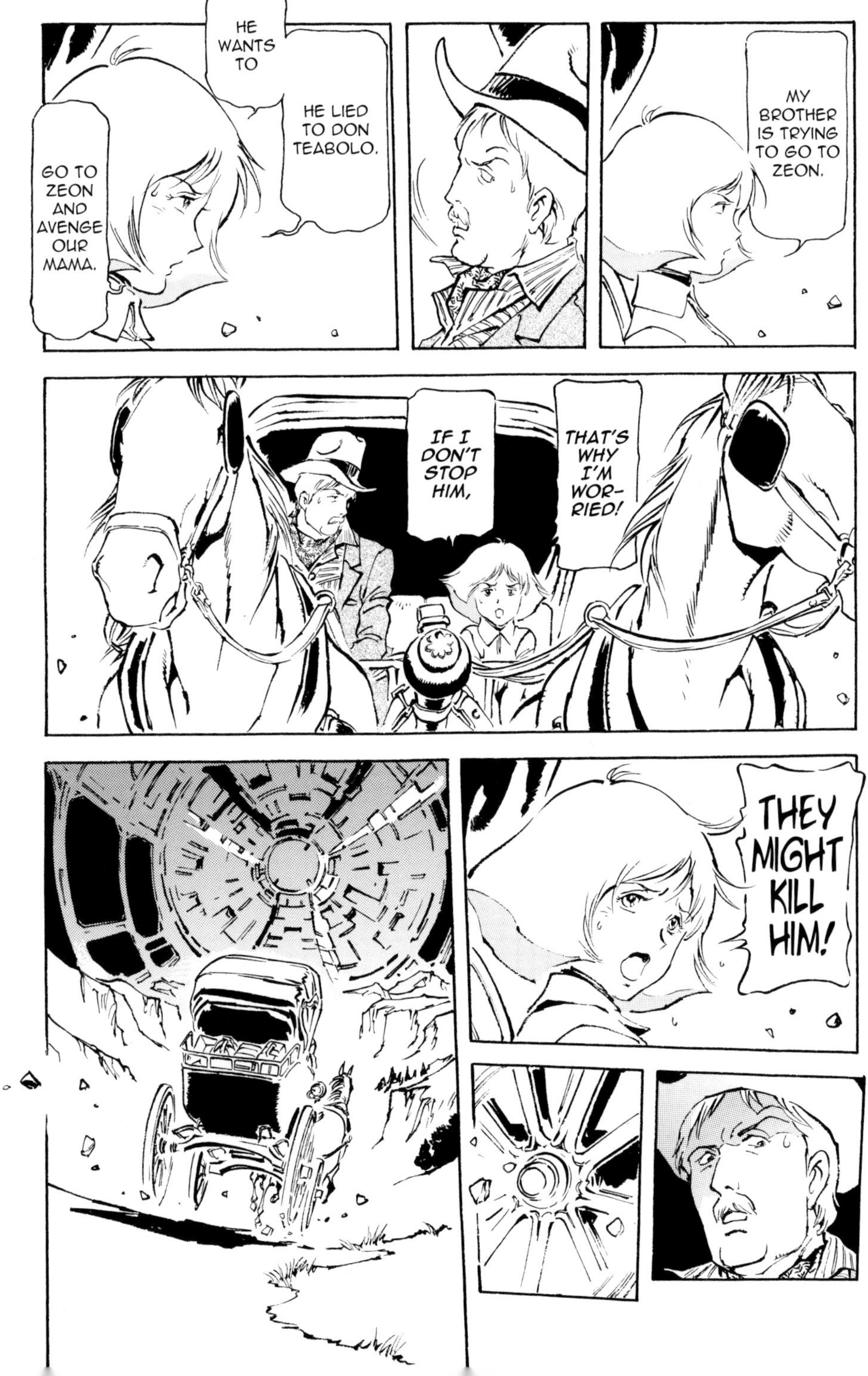
MY BROTHER IS TRYING TO GO TO ZEON.
HE LIED TO DON TEABOLO.
HE WANTS TO
GO TO ZEON AND AVENGE OUR MAMA.
THAT'S WHY I'M WOR-RIED!
IF I DON'T STOP HIM,
THEY MIGHT KILL HIM!

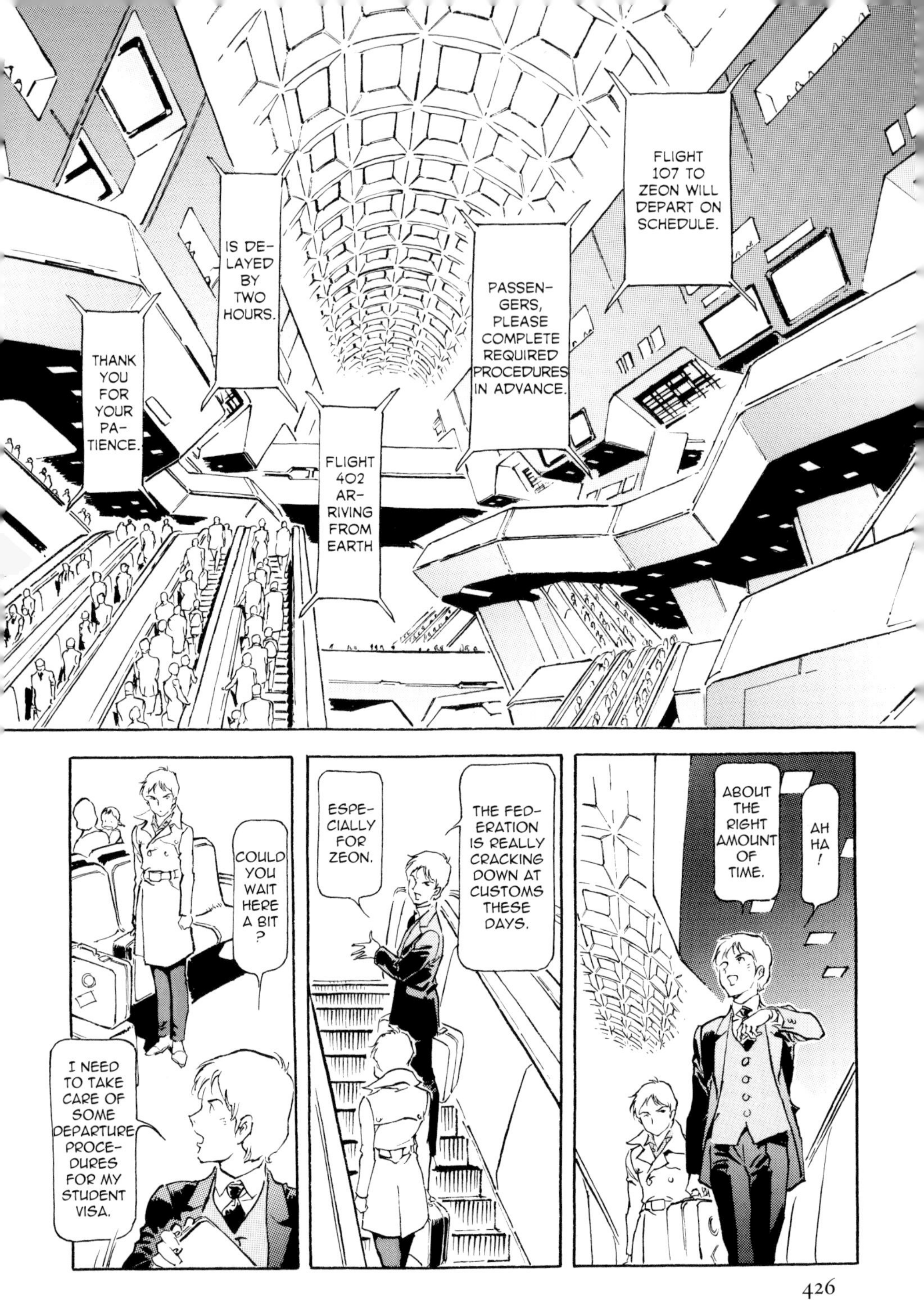

FLIGHT 107 TO ZEON WILL DEPART ON SCHEDULE.
PASSENGERS, PLEASE COMPLETE REQUIRED PROCEDURES IN ADVANCE.
FLIGHT 402 ARRIVING FROM EARTH
IS DELAYED BY TWO HOURS.
THANK YOU FOR YOUR PATIENCE.
AH HA!
ABOUT THE RIGHT AMOUNT OF TIME.
THE FEDERATION IS REALLY CRACKING DOWN AT CUSTOMS THESE DAYS.
ESPECIALLY FOR ZEON.
COULD YOU WAIT HERE A BIT?
I NEED TO TAKE CARE OF SOME DEPARTURE PROCEDURES FOR MY STUDENT VISA.

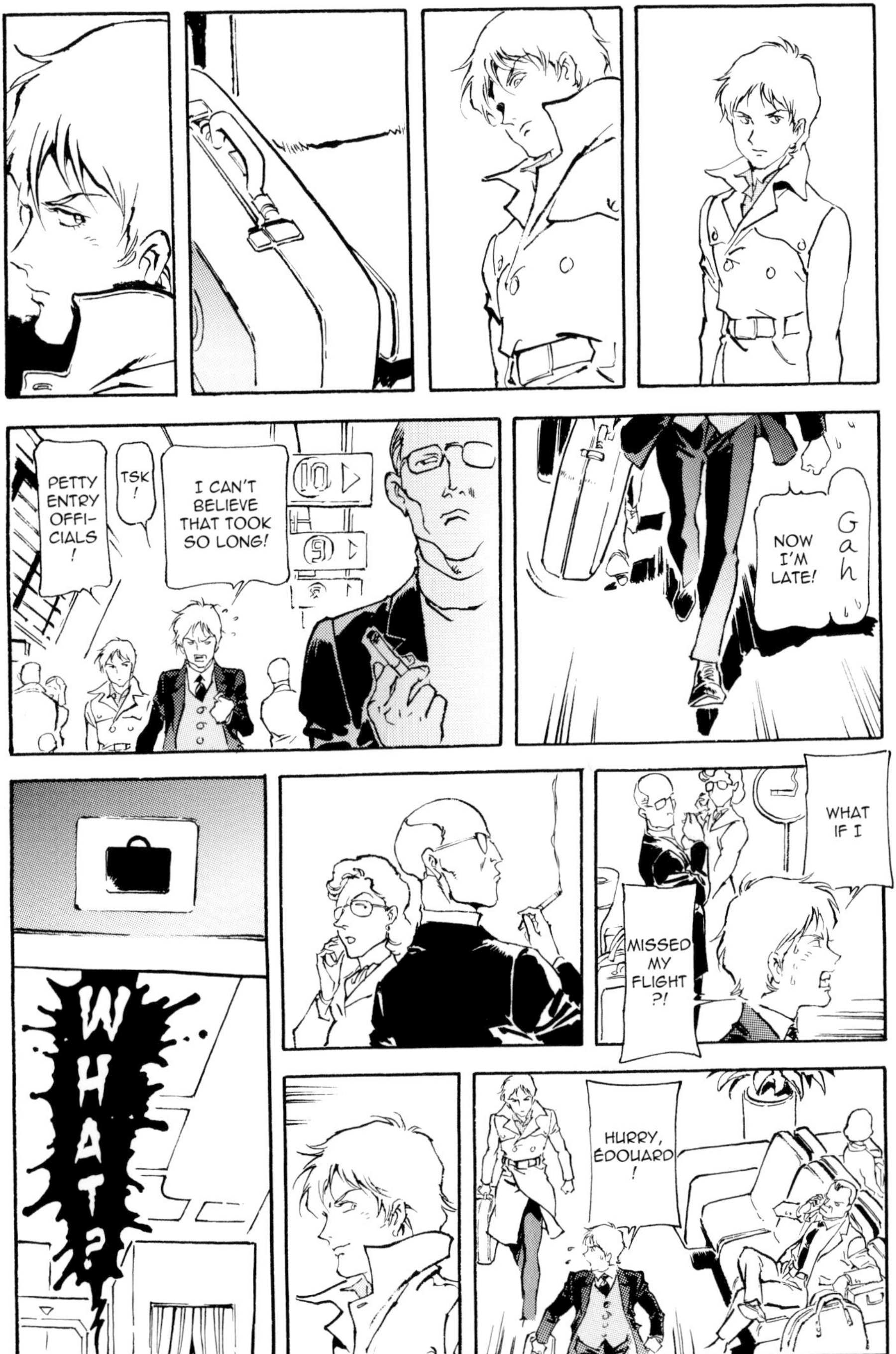
NOW I'M LATE!
Gah
I CAN'T BELIEVE THAT TOOK SO LONG!
TSK!
PETTY ENTRY OFFICIALS!
WHAT IF I
MISSED MY FLIGHT?!
HURRY, ÉDOUARD!
WHAT?

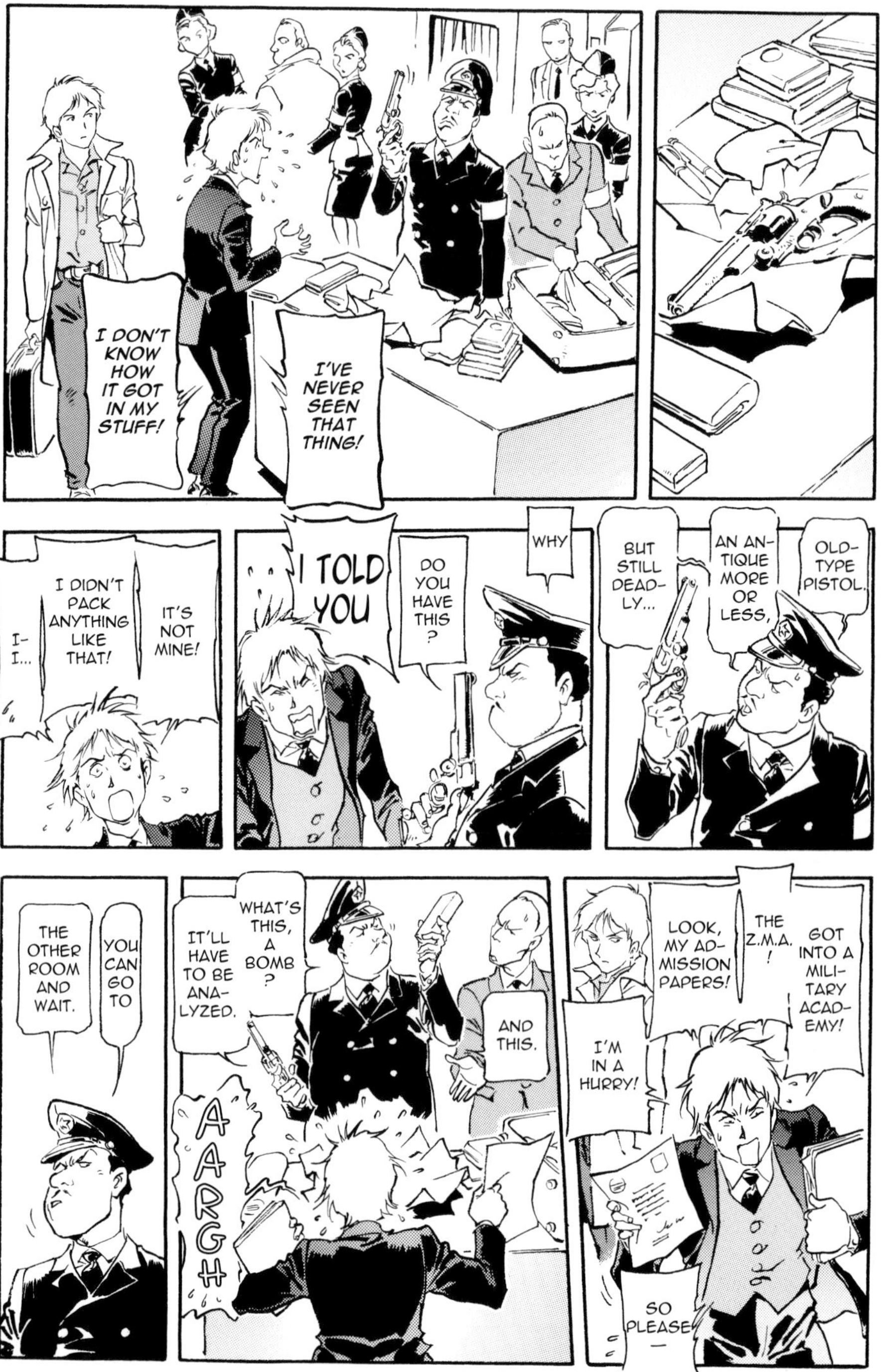
I'VE NEVER SEEN THAT THING!
I DON'T KNOW HOW IT GOT IN MY STUFF!
OLD-TYPE PISTOL.
AN ANTIQUE MORE OR LESS,
BUT STILL DEADLY...
WHY
DO YOU HAVE THIS?
I TOLD YOU
IT'S NOT MINE!
I DIDN'T PACK ANYTHING LIKE THAT!
I- I...
GOT INTO A MILITARY ACADEMY!
THE Z.M.A.!
LOOK, MY ADMISSION PAPERS!
I'M IN A HURRY!
SO PLEASE—
WHAT'S THIS, A BOMB?
IT'LL HAVE TO BE ANALYZED.
AND THIS.
AARGH
YOU CAN GO TO
THE OTHER ROOM AND WAIT.

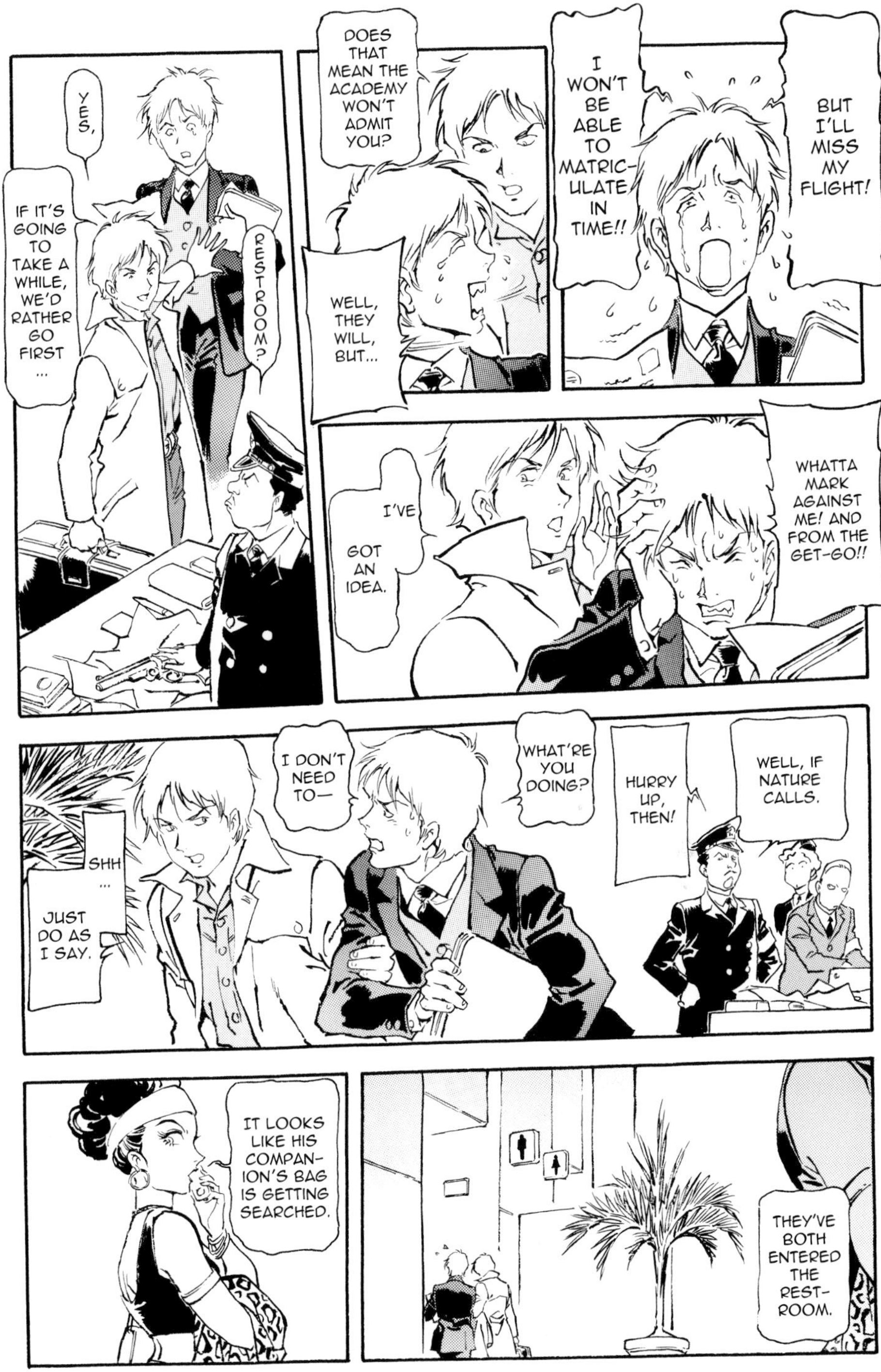
BUT I'LL MISS MY FLIGHT!
I WON'T BE ABLE TO MATRIC-ULATE IN TIME!!
DOES THAT MEAN THE ACADEMY WON'T ADMIT YOU?
WELL, THEY WILL, BUT...
WHATTA MARK AGAINST ME! AND FROM THE GET-GO!!
I'VE GOT AN IDEA.
IF IT'S GOING TO TAKE A WHILE, WE'D RATHER GO FIRST ...
RESTROOM?
YES,
WELL, IF NATURE CALLS.
HURRY UP, THEN!
WHAT'RE YOU DOING?
I DON'T NEED TO—
SHH ...
JUST DO AS I SAY.
THEY'VE BOTH ENTERED THE REST-ROOM.
IT LOOKS LIKE HIS COMPAN-ION'S BAG IS GETTING SEARCHED.

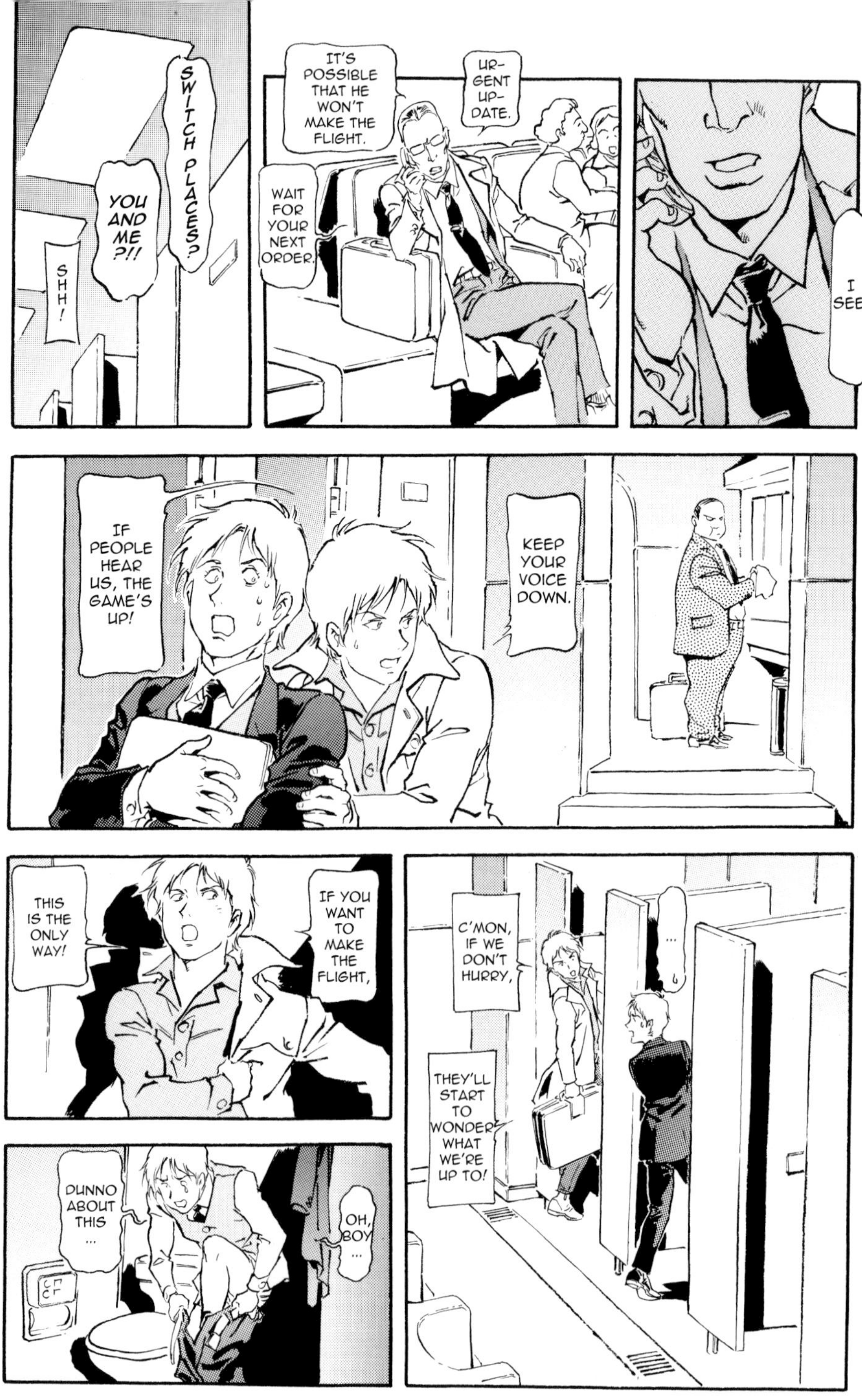
I SEE.
URGENT UPDATE.
IT'S POSSIBLE THAT HE WON'T MAKE THE FLIGHT.
WAIT FOR YOUR NEXT ORDER.
SWITCH PLACES?
YOU AND ME?!!
SHH!
KEEP YOUR VOICE DOWN.
IF PEOPLE HEAR US, THE GAME'S UP!
...
C'MON, IF WE DON'T HURRY,
THEY'LL START TO WONDER WHAT WE'RE UP TO!
IF YOU WANT TO MAKE THE FLIGHT,
THIS IS THE ONLY WAY!
OH, BOY ...
DUNNO ABOUT THIS ...

FOLDER BAG IN THIS SUITCASE.

I'LL PUT THE

GOT IT.

HERE.

OH!

Y YUP!

KCHAK

CREAK

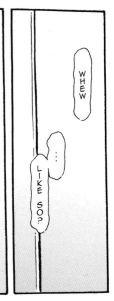

WHEW

...

LIKE SO?

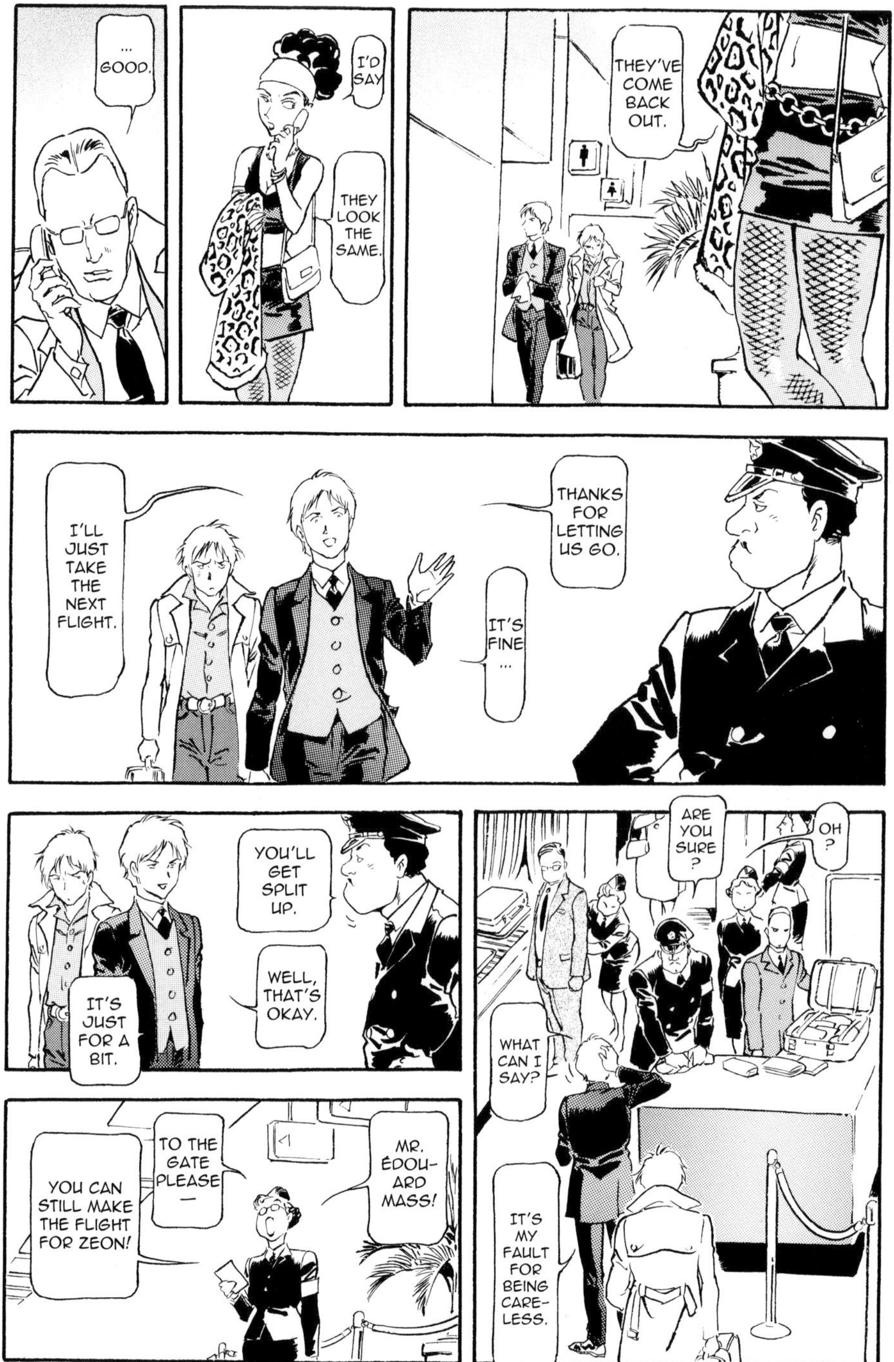
THEY'VE COME BACK OUT.
I'D SAY
THEY LOOK THE SAME.
... GOOD.
THANKS FOR LETTING US GO.
IT'S FINE ...
I'LL JUST TAKE THE NEXT FLIGHT.
OH?
ARE YOU SURE?
WHAT CAN I SAY?
IT'S MY FAULT FOR BEING CARE-LESS.
YOU'LL GET SPLIT UP.
WELL, THAT'S OKAY.
IT'S JUST FOR A BIT.
MR. ÉDOU-ARD MASS!
TO THE GATE PLEASE—
YOU CAN STILL MAKE THE FLIGHT FOR ZEON!

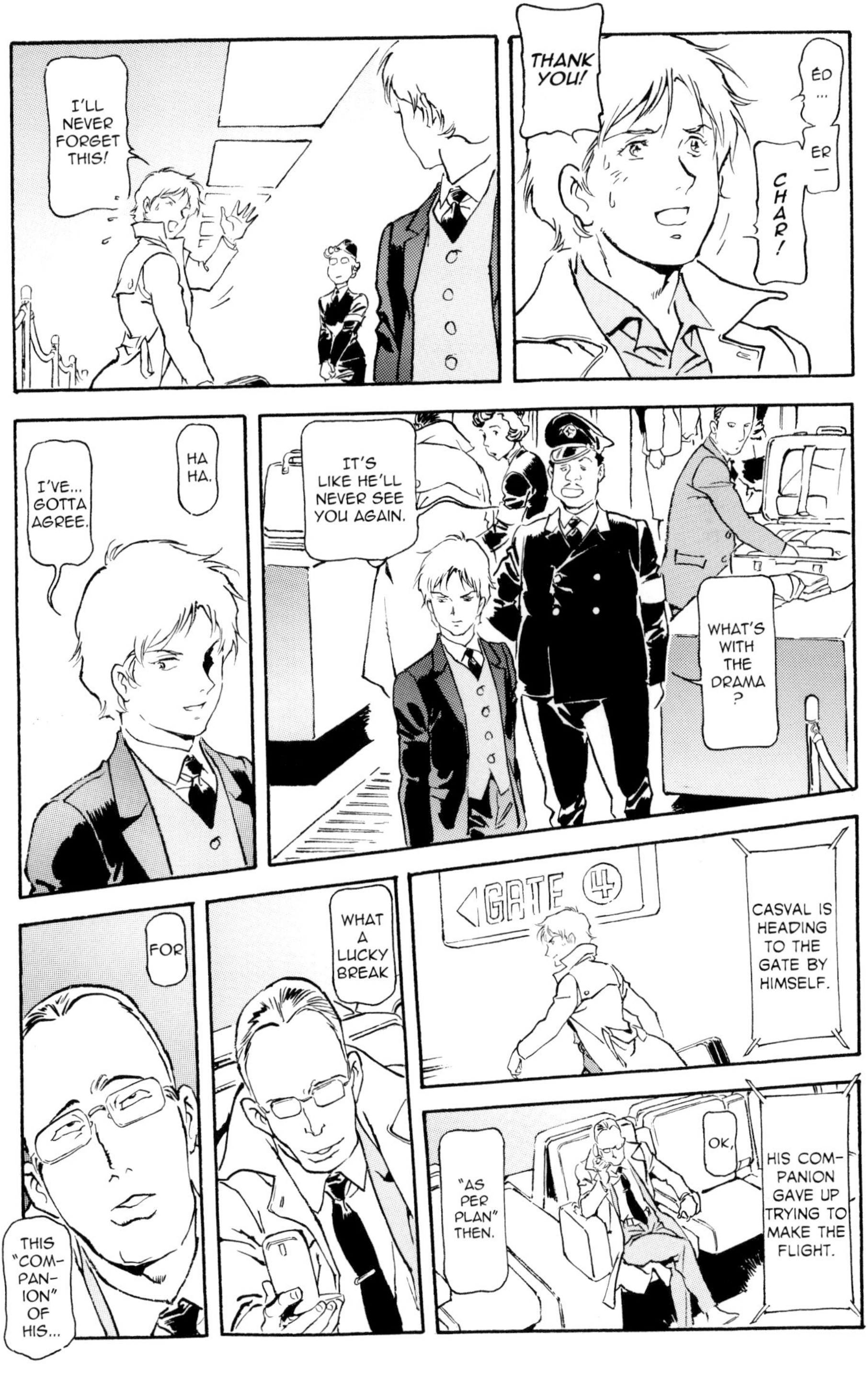
ÉD... ER— CHAR!
THANK YOU!
I'LL NEVER FORGET THIS!
WHAT'S WITH THE DRAMA?
IT'S LIKE HE'LL NEVER SEE YOU AGAIN.
HA HA.
I'VE... GOTTA AGREE.
GATE 4
CASVAL IS HEADING TO THE GATE BY HIMSELF.
HIS COMPANION GAVE UP TRYING TO MAKE THE FLIGHT.
OK,
"AS PER PLAN" THEN.
WHAT A LUCKY BREAK
FOR
THIS "COMPANION" OF HIS...

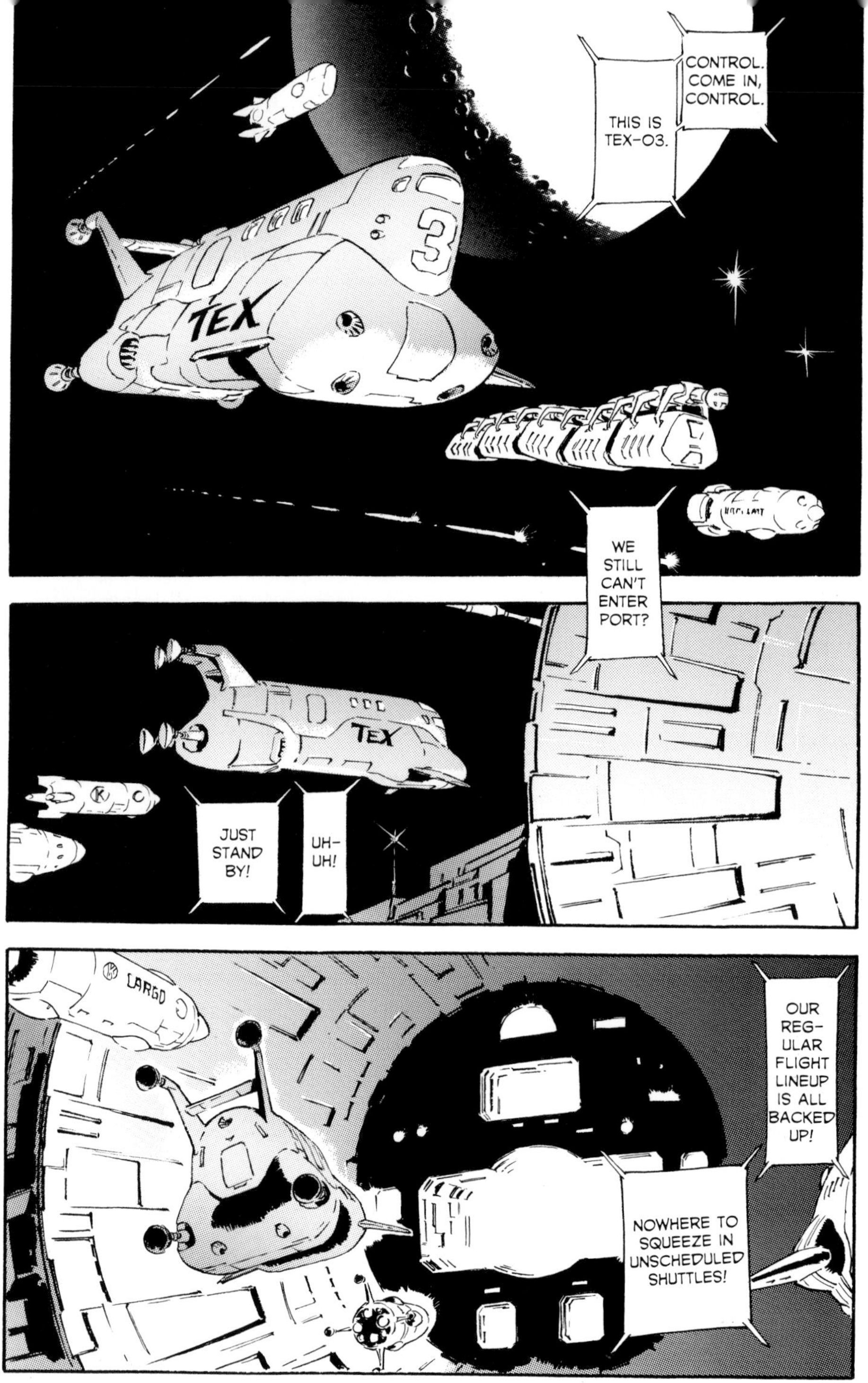
CONTROL. COME IN, CONTROL.
THIS IS TEX-03.
WE STILL CAN'T ENTER PORT?
UH-UH!
JUST STAND BY!
OUR REG-ULAR FLIGHT LINEUP IS ALL BACKED UP!
NOWHERE TO SQUEEZE IN UNSCHEDULED SHUTTLES!

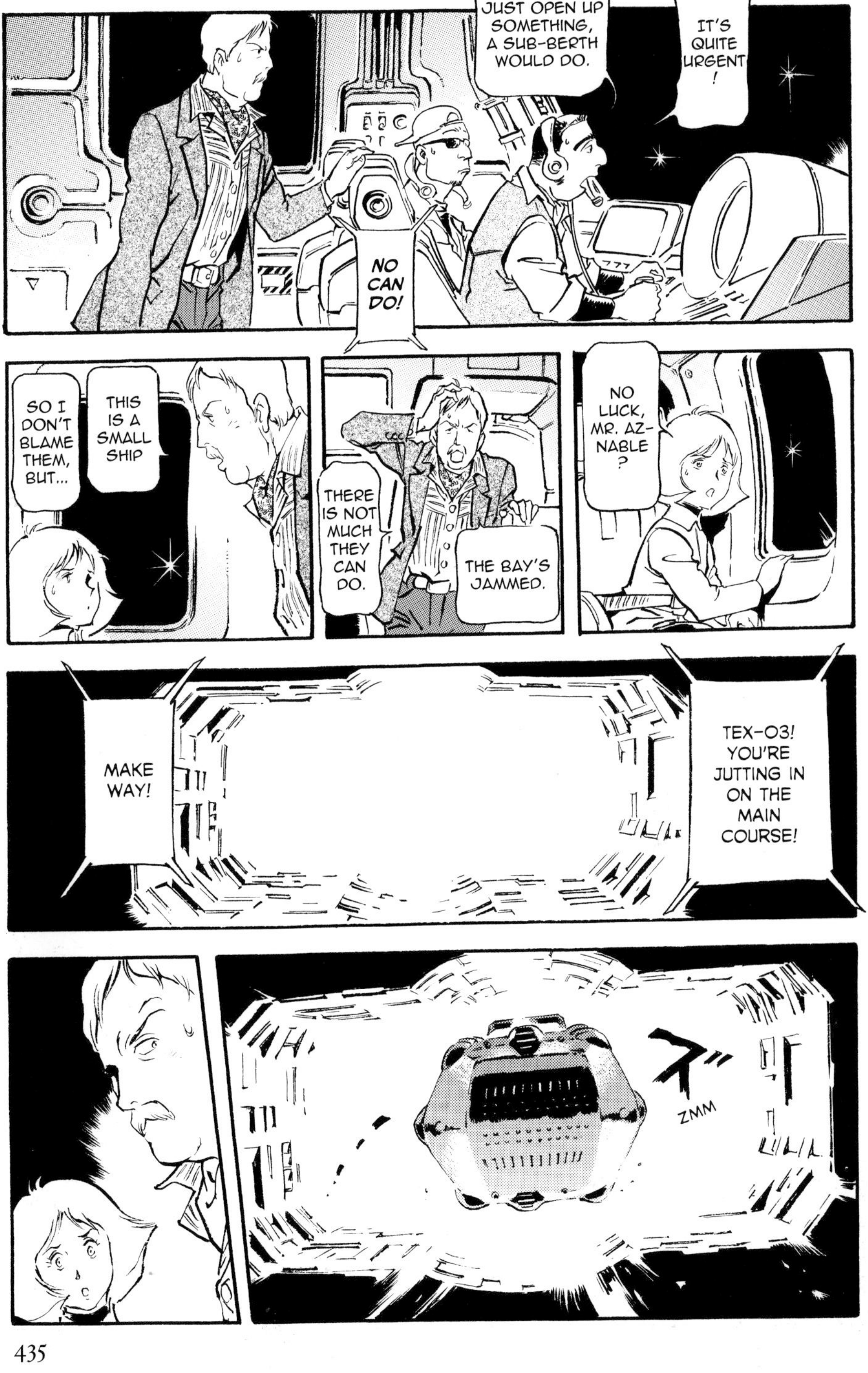
IT'S QUITE URGENT!
JUST OPEN UP SOMETHING, A SUB-BERTH WOULD DO.
NO CAN DO!
NO LUCK, MR. AZNABLE?
THE BAY'S JAMMED.
THERE IS NOT MUCH THEY CAN DO.
THIS IS A SMALL SHIP
SO I DON'T BLAME THEM, BUT...
TEX-03! YOU'RE JUTTING IN ON THE MAIN COURSE!
MAKE WAY!
ズ
ZMM

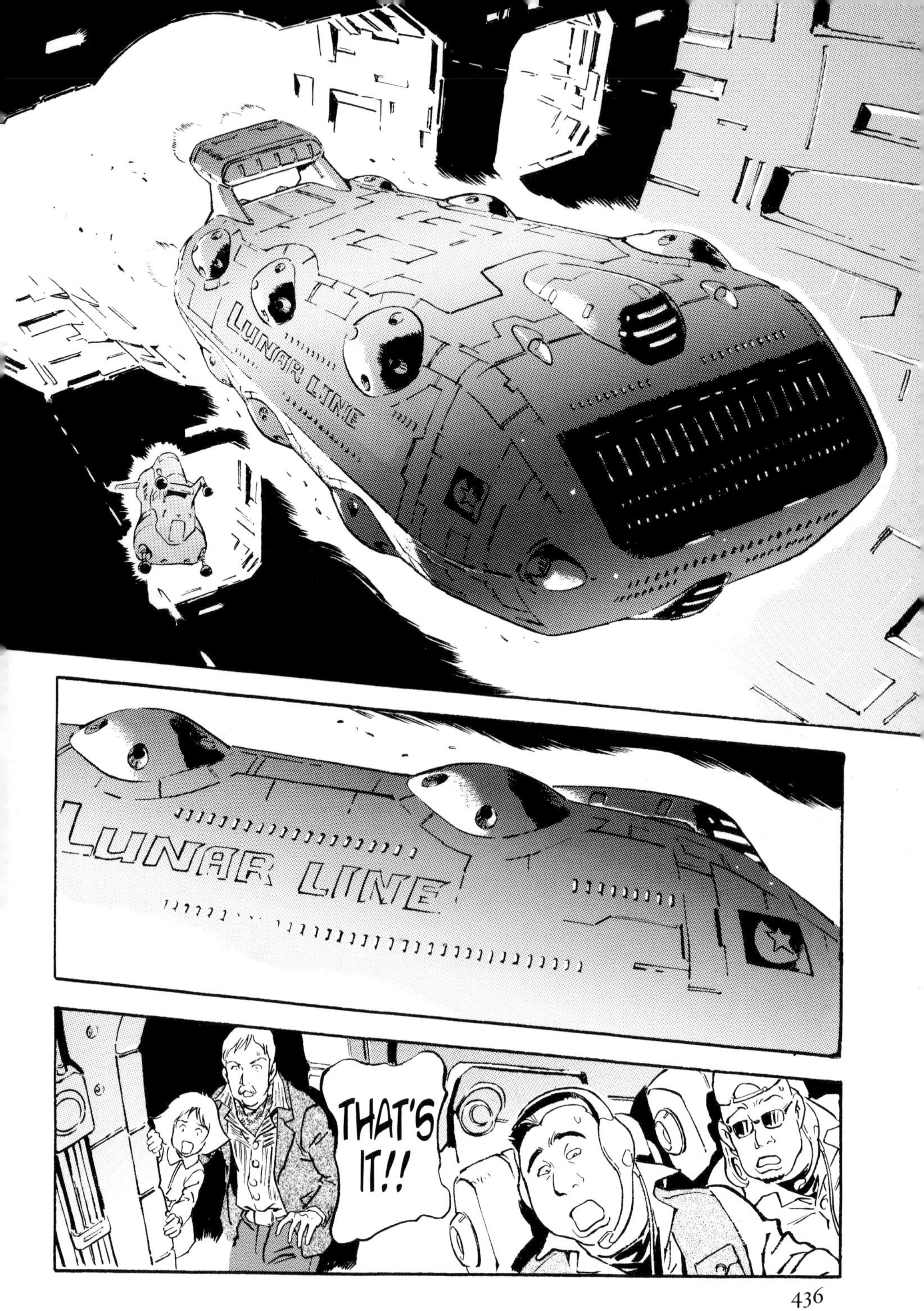
LUNAR LINE
LUNAR LINE
THAT'S IT!!

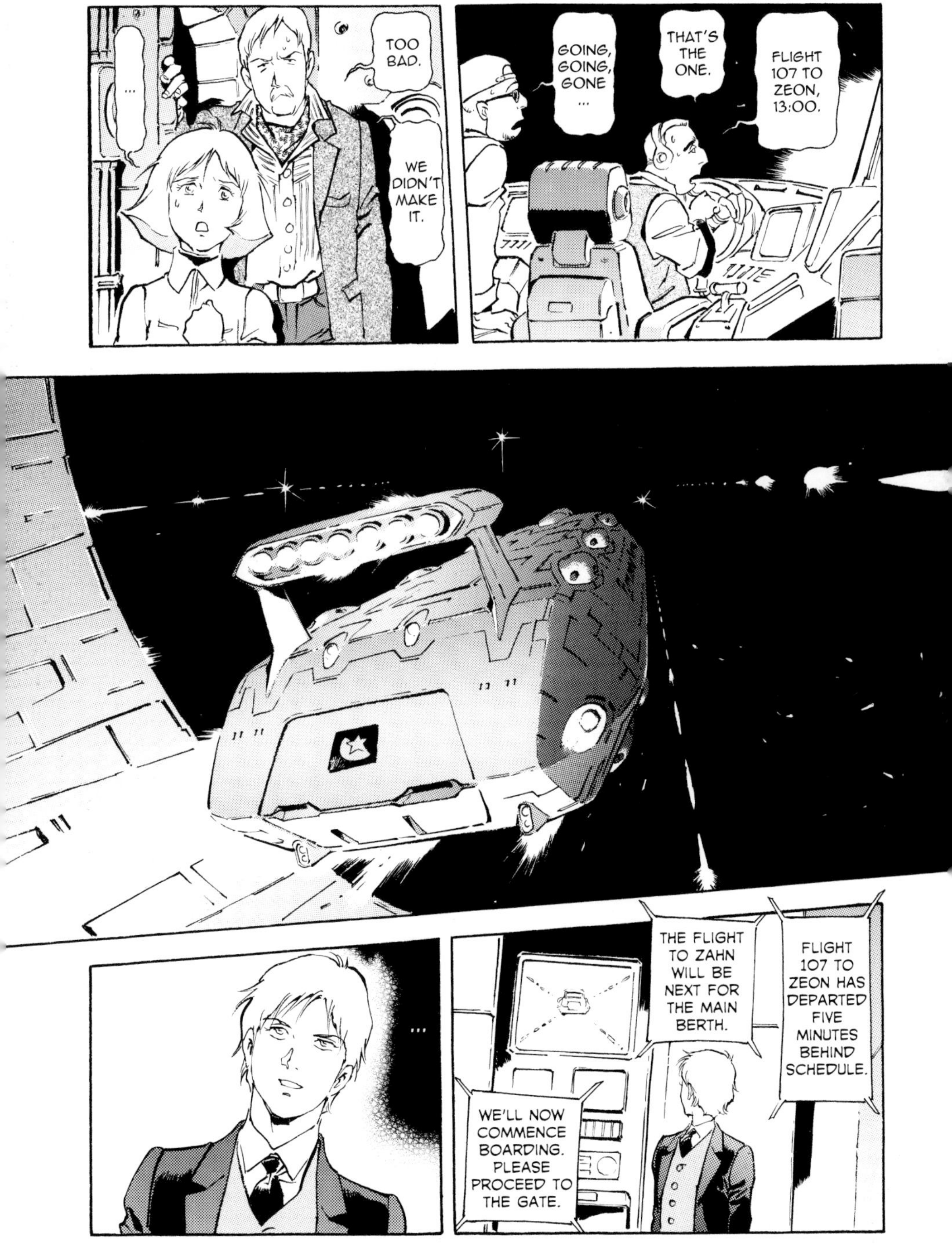
FLIGHT 107 TO ZEON, 13:00.
THAT'S THE ONE.
GOING, GOING, GONE ...
TOO BAD.
WE DIDN'T MAKE IT.
...
FLIGHT 107 TO ZEON HAS DEPARTED FIVE MINUTES BEHIND SCHEDULE.
THE FLIGHT TO ZAHN WILL BE NEXT FOR THE MAIN BERTH.
WE'LL NOW COMMENCE BOARDING. PLEASE PROCEED TO THE GATE.
...

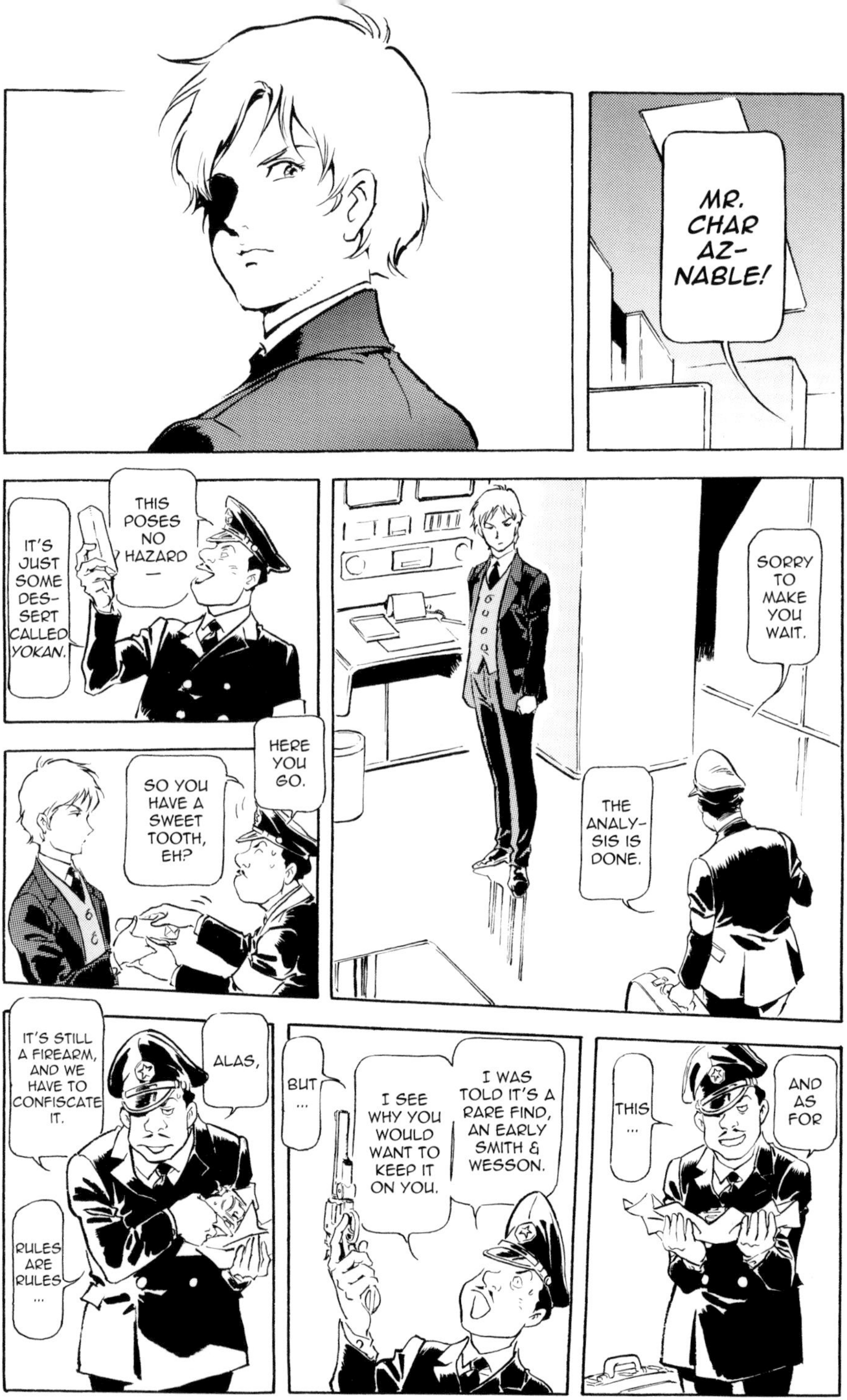

MR. CHAR AZ-NABLE!
SORRY TO MAKE YOU WAIT.
THE ANALYSIS IS DONE.
THIS POSES NO HAZARD —
IT'S JUST SOME DESSERT CALLED *YOKAN*.
HERE YOU GO.
SO YOU HAVE A SWEET TOOTH, EH?
AND AS FOR
THIS ...
I WAS TOLD IT'S A RARE FIND, AN EARLY SMITH & WESSON.
I SEE WHY YOU WOULD WANT TO KEEP IT ON YOU.
BUT ...
ALAS,
IT'S STILL A FIREARM, AND WE HAVE TO CONFISCATE IT.
RULES ARE RULES ...

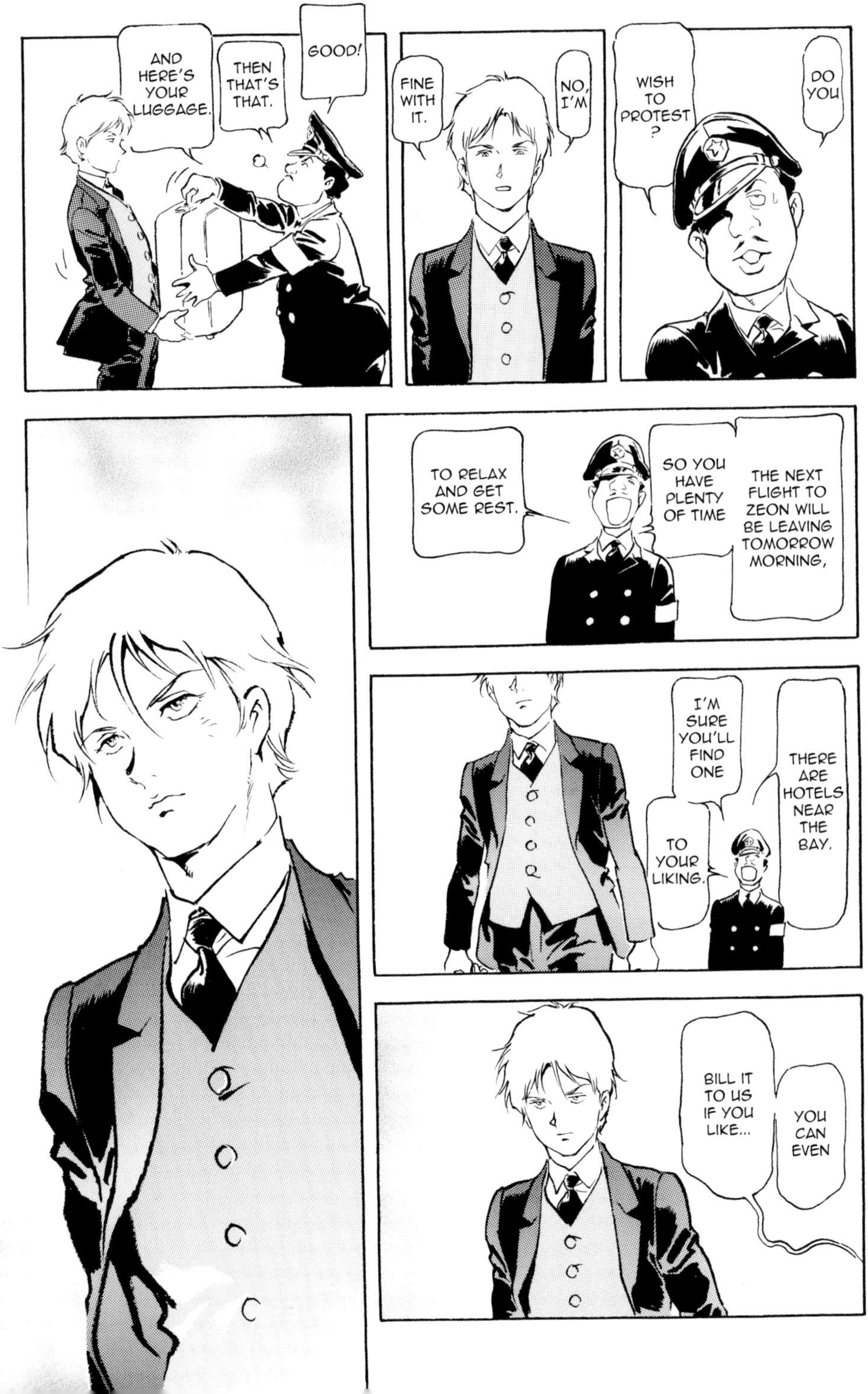
DO YOU
WISH TO PROTEST?
NO, I'M
FINE WITH IT.
GOOD!
THEN THAT'S THAT.
AND HERE'S YOUR LUGGAGE.
THE NEXT FLIGHT TO ZEON WILL BE LEAVING TOMORROW MORNING,
SO YOU HAVE PLENTY OF TIME
TO RELAX AND GET SOME REST.
THERE ARE HOTELS NEAR THE BAY.
I'M SURE YOU'LL FIND ONE
TO YOUR LIKING.
YOU CAN EVEN
BILL IT TO US IF YOU LIKE...

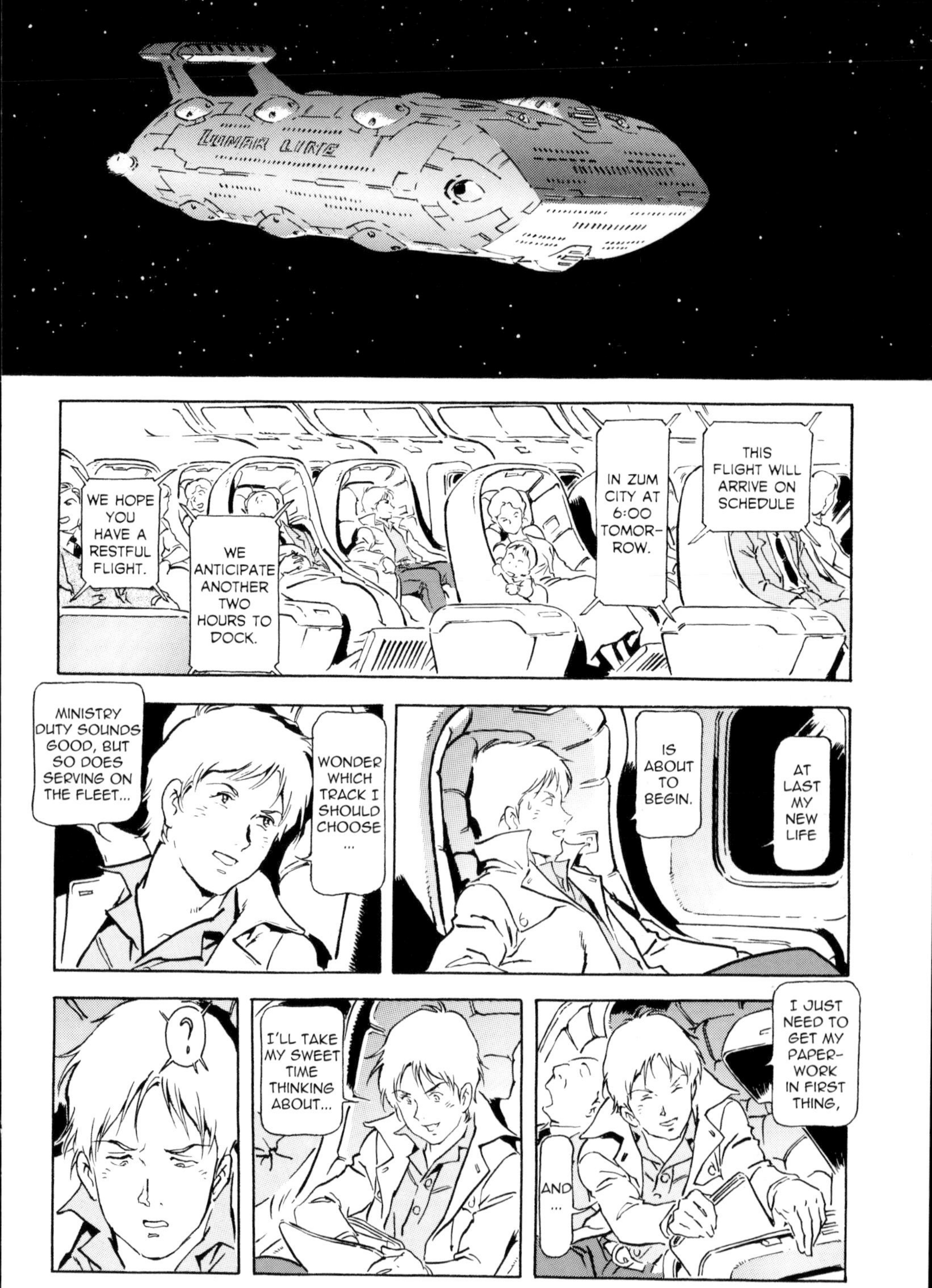
LUNAR LINE
THIS FLIGHT WILL ARRIVE ON SCHEDULE
IN ZUM CITY AT 6:00 TOMORROW.
WE ANTICIPATE ANOTHER TWO HOURS TO DOCK.
WE HOPE YOU HAVE A RESTFUL FLIGHT.
AT LAST MY NEW LIFE
IS ABOUT TO BEGIN.
MINISTRY DUTY SOUNDS GOOD, BUT SO DOES SERVING ON THE FLEET...
WONDER WHICH TRACK I SHOULD CHOOSE ...
I JUST NEED TO GET MY PAPERWORK IN FIRST THING,
AND ...
I'LL TAKE MY SWEET TIME THINKING ABOUT...
?

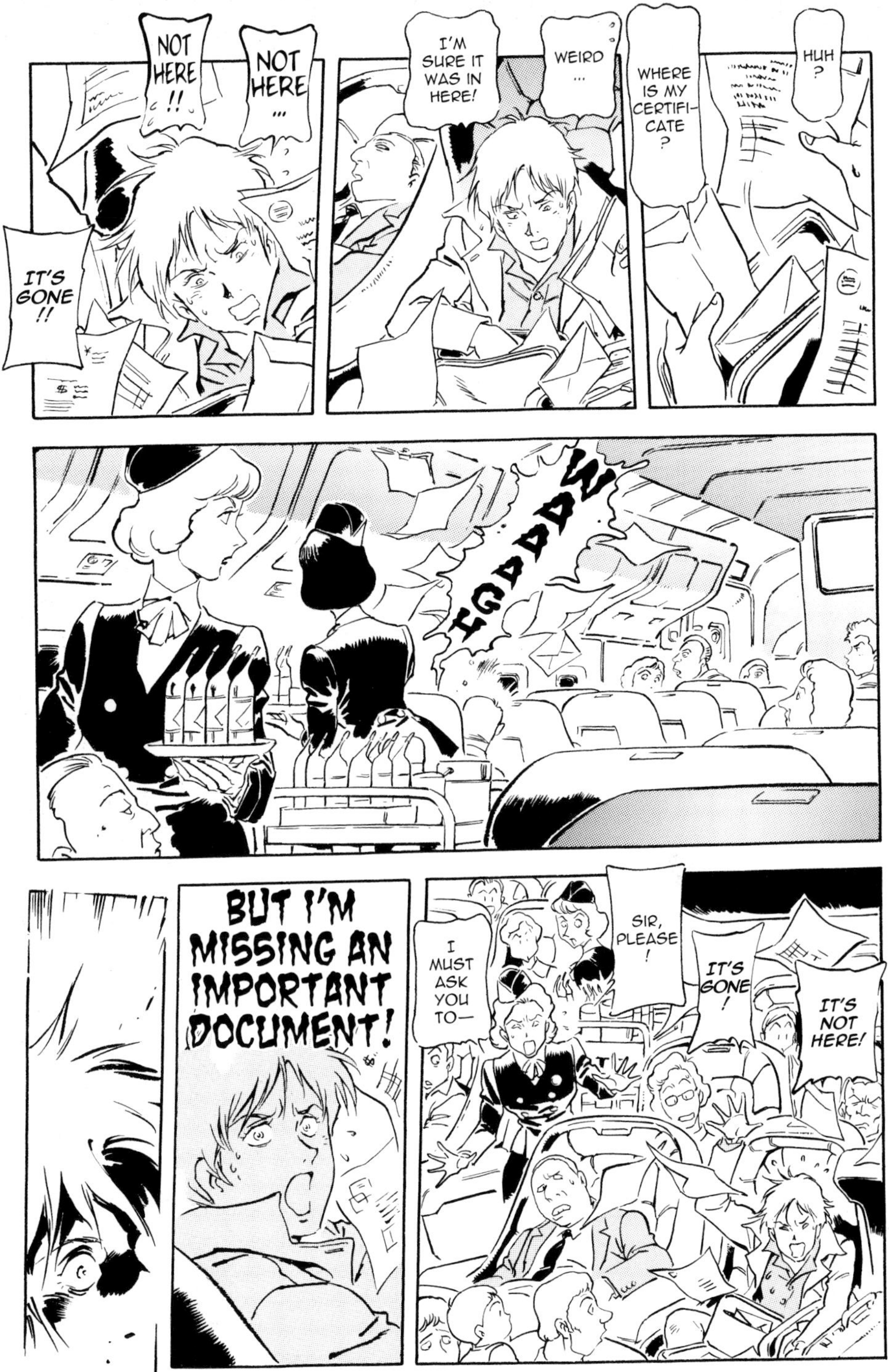
HUH?
WHERE IS MY CERTIFICATE?
WEIRD...
I'M SURE IT WAS IN HERE!
NOT HERE...
NOT HERE!!
IT'S GONE!!
WAAAGH
IT'S NOT HERE!
IT'S GONE!
SIR, PLEASE!
I MUST ASK YOU TO—
BUT I'M MISSING AN IMPORTANT DOCUMENT!

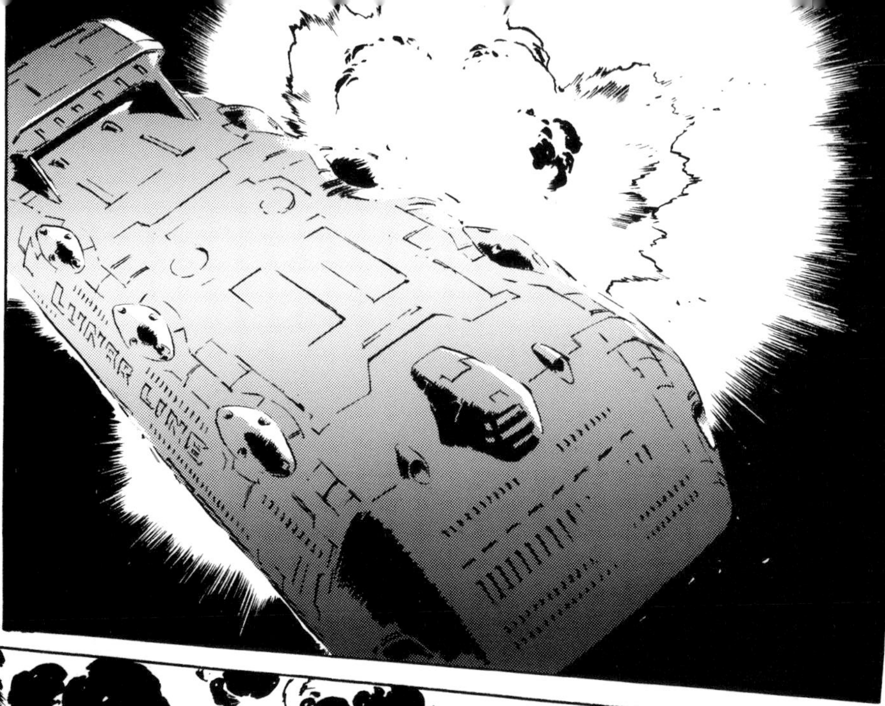
LUNAR CORE
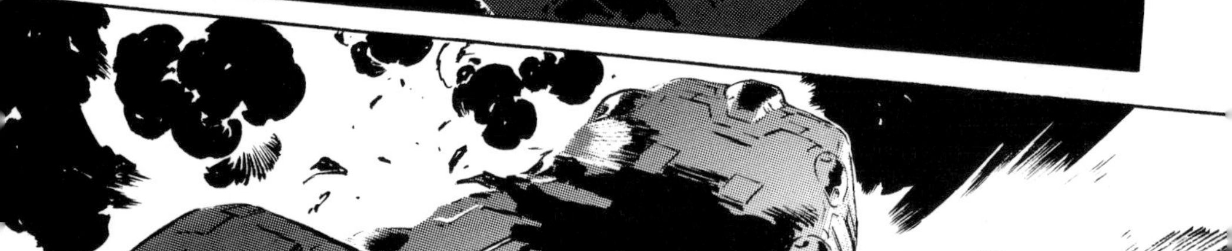
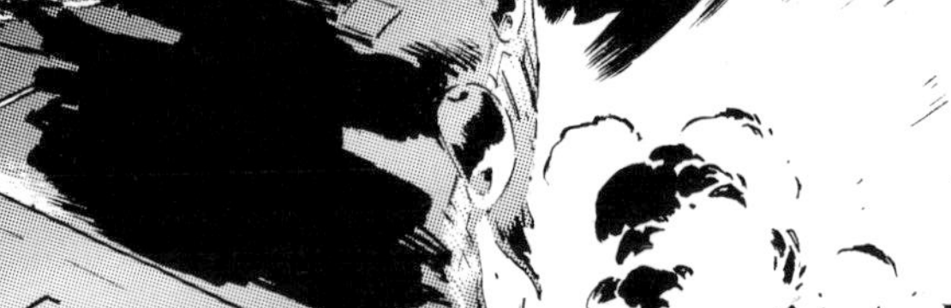
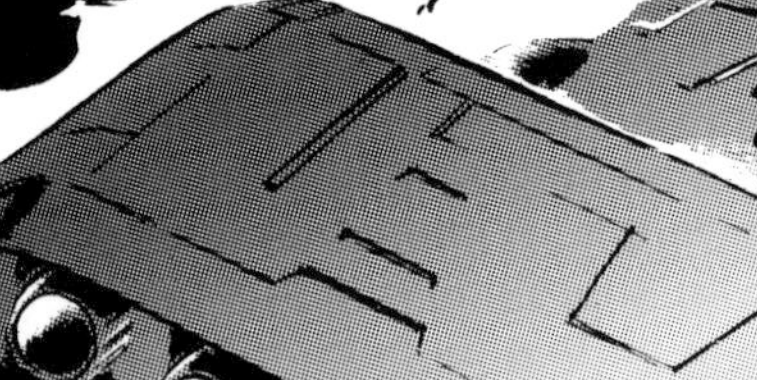

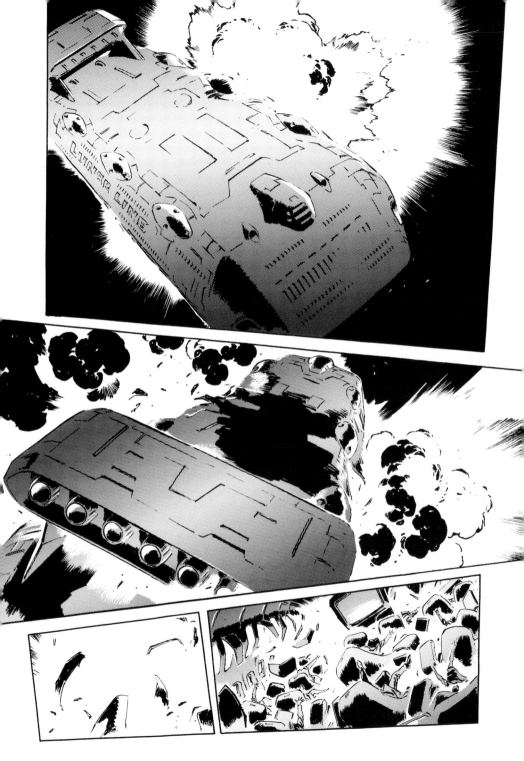

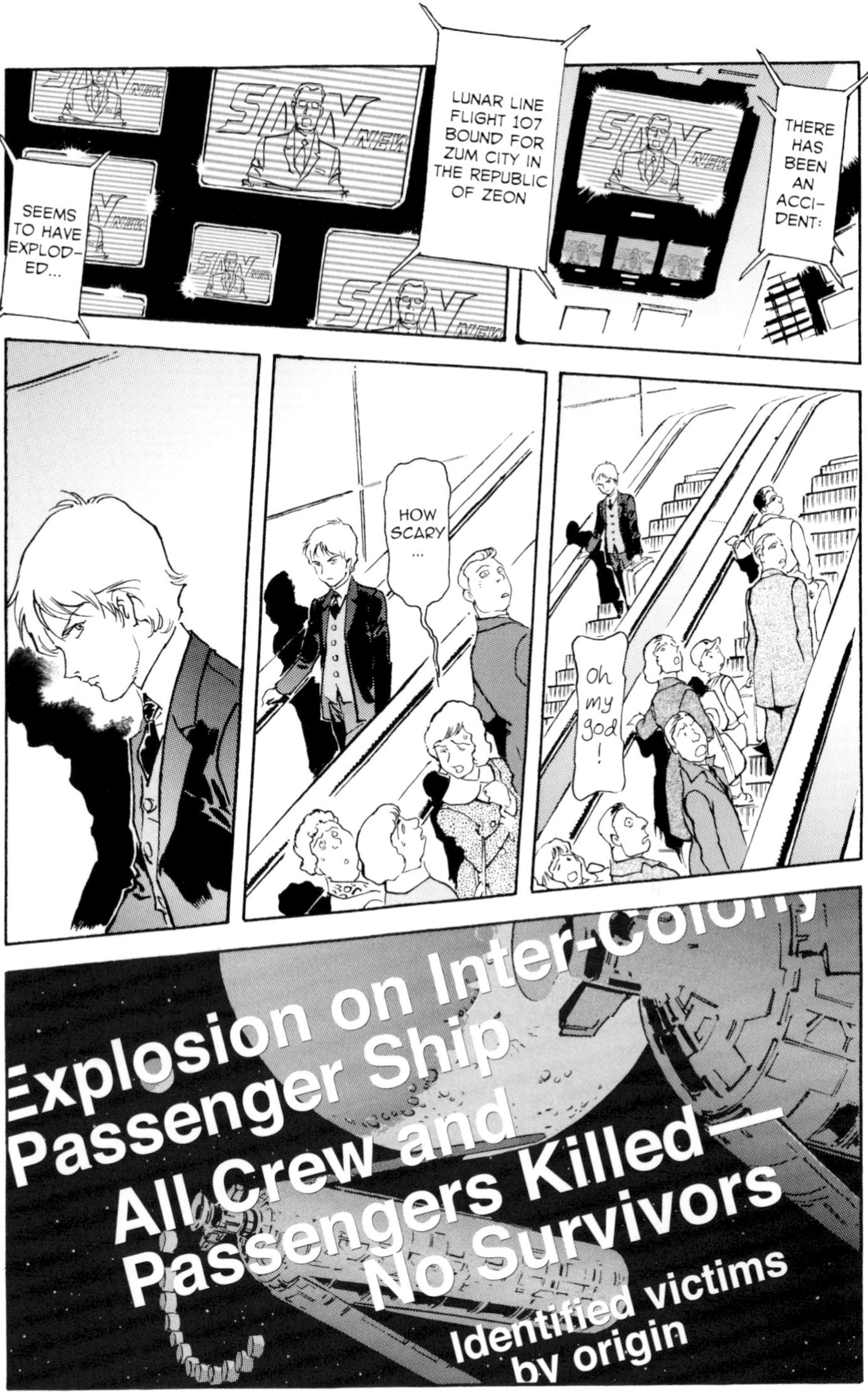
THERE HAS BEEN AN ACCIDENT:
LUNAR LINE FLIGHT 107 BOUND FOR ZUM CITY IN THE REPUBLIC OF ZEON
SEEMS TO HAVE EXPLODED...
Oh my god!
HOW SCARY ...
Explosion on Inter-Colony Passenger Ship
All Crew and Passengers Killed—No Survivors
Identified victims by origin

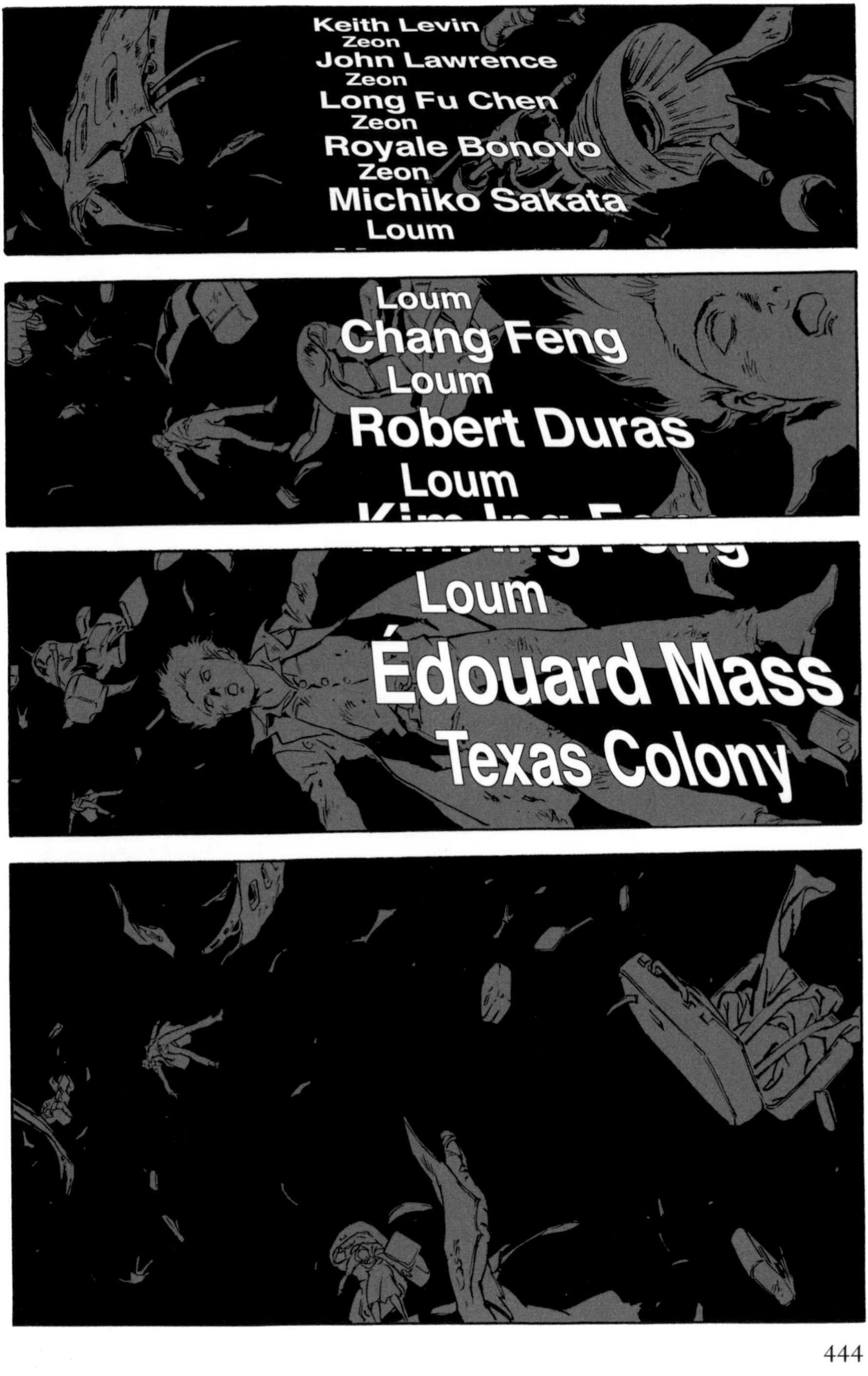
Keith Levin
Zeon
John Lawrence
Zeon
Long Fu Chen
Zeon
Royale Bonovo
Zeon
Michiko Sakata
Loum
Loum
Chang Feng
Loum
Robert Duras
Loum
Loum
Édouard Mass
Texas Colony

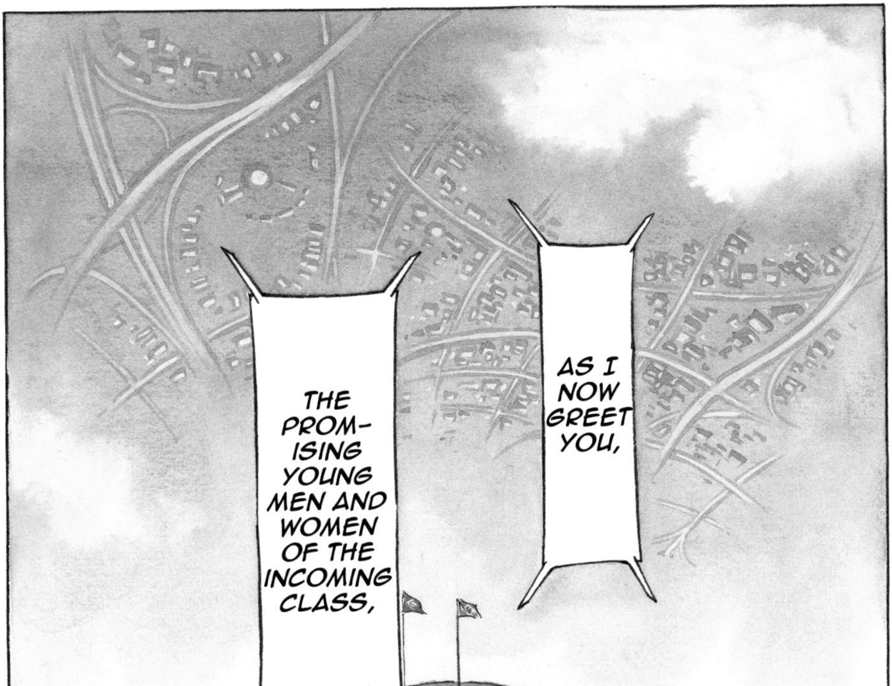
AS I NOW GREET YOU,
THE PROMISING YOUNG MEN AND WOMEN OF THE INCOMING CLASS,

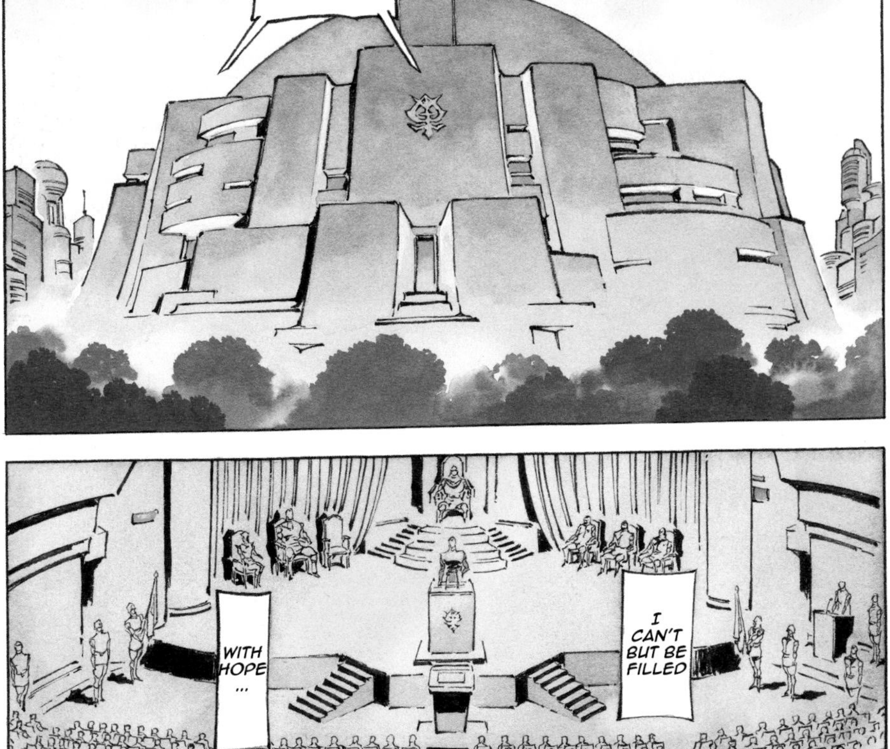
I CAN'T BUT BE FILLED
WITH HOPE ...

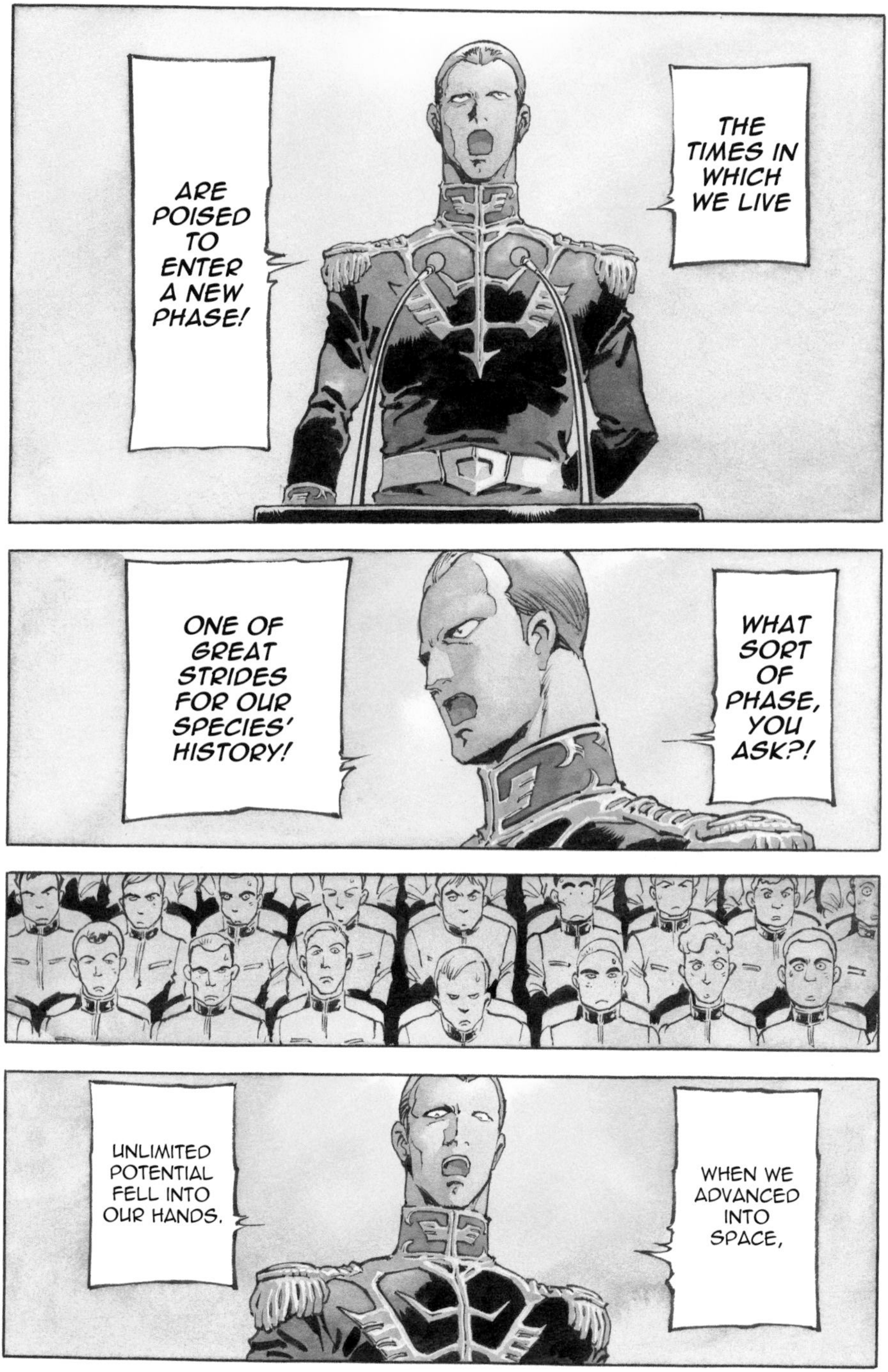
THE TIMES IN WHICH WE LIVE
ARE POISED TO ENTER A NEW PHASE!
WHAT SORT OF PHASE, YOU ASK?!
ONE OF GREAT STRIDES FOR OUR SPECIES' HISTORY!
WHEN WE ADVANCED INTO SPACE,
UNLIMITED POTENTIAL FELL INTO OUR HANDS.

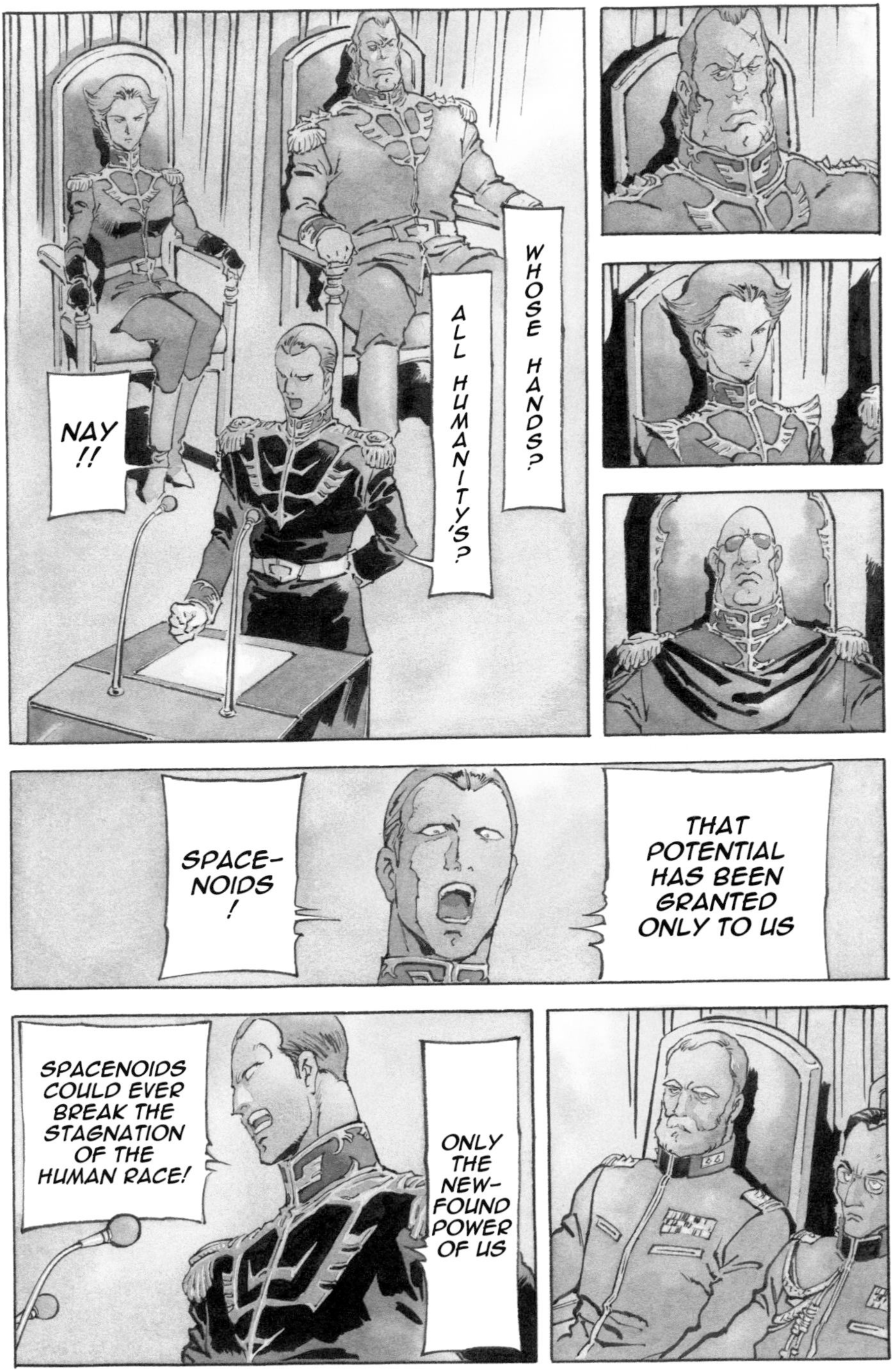
WHOSE HANDS?
ALL HUMANITY'S?
NAY!!
THAT POTENTIAL HAS BEEN GRANTED ONLY TO US
SPACE-NOIDS!
ONLY THE NEW-FOUND POWER OF US
SPACENOIDS COULD EVER BREAK THE STAGNATION OF THE HUMAN RACE!

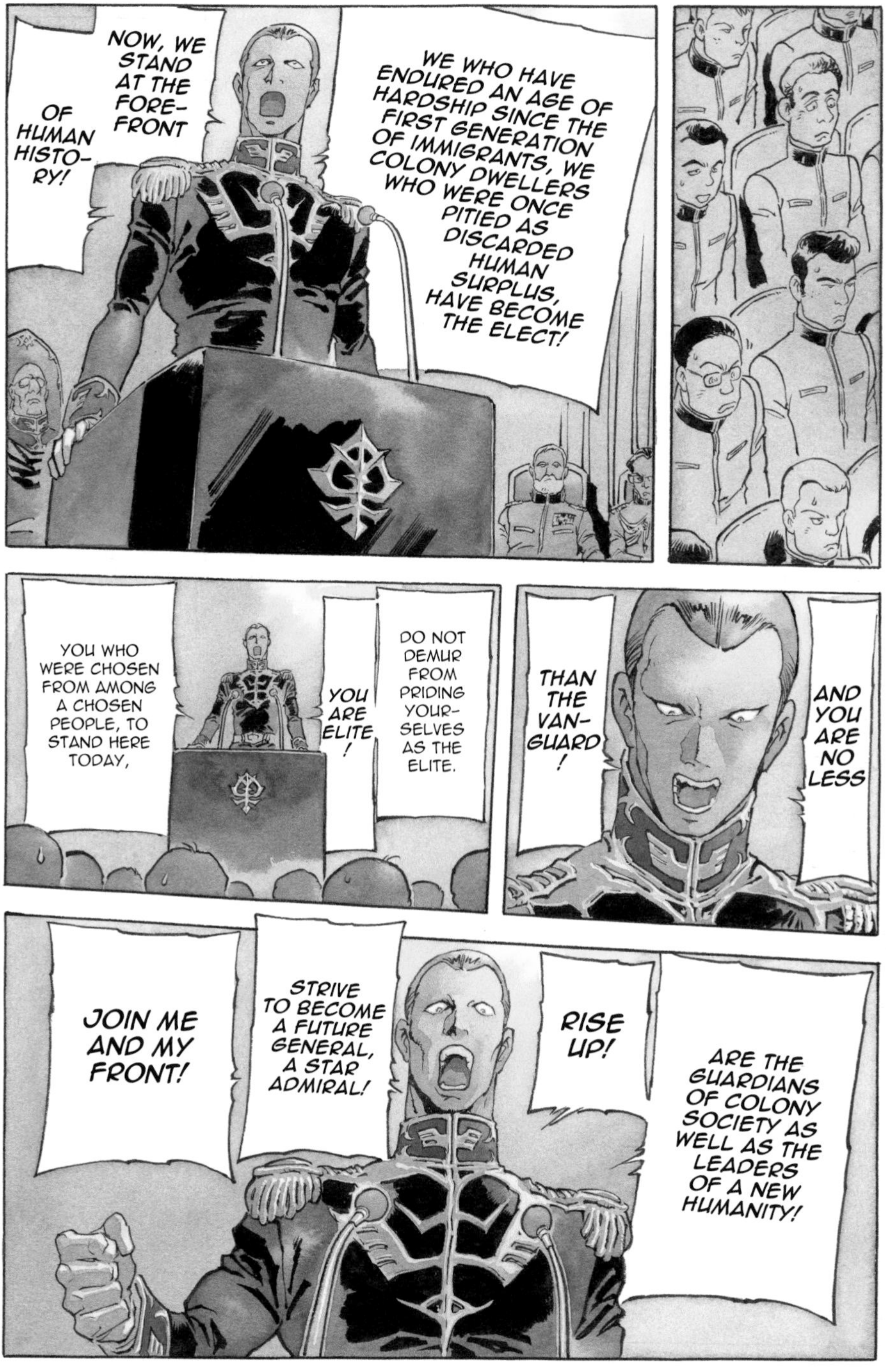
WE WHO HAVE ENDURED AN AGE OF HARDSHIP SINCE THE FIRST GENERATION OF IMMIGRANTS, WE COLONY DWELLERS WHO WERE ONCE PITIED AS DISCARDED HUMAN SURPLUS, HAVE BECOME THE ELECT!
NOW, WE STAND AT THE FORE-FRONT
OF HUMAN HISTO-RY!
AND YOU ARE NO LESS
THAN THE VAN-GUARD!
DO NOT DEMUR FROM PRIDING YOUR-SELVES AS THE ELITE.
YOU ARE ELITE!
YOU WHO WERE CHOSEN FROM AMONG A CHOSEN PEOPLE, TO STAND HERE TODAY,
ARE THE GUARDIANS OF COLONY SOCIETY AS WELL AS THE LEADERS OF A NEW HUMANITY!
RISE UP!
STRIVE TO BECOME A FUTURE GENERAL, A STAR ADMIRAL!
JOIN ME AND MY FRONT!

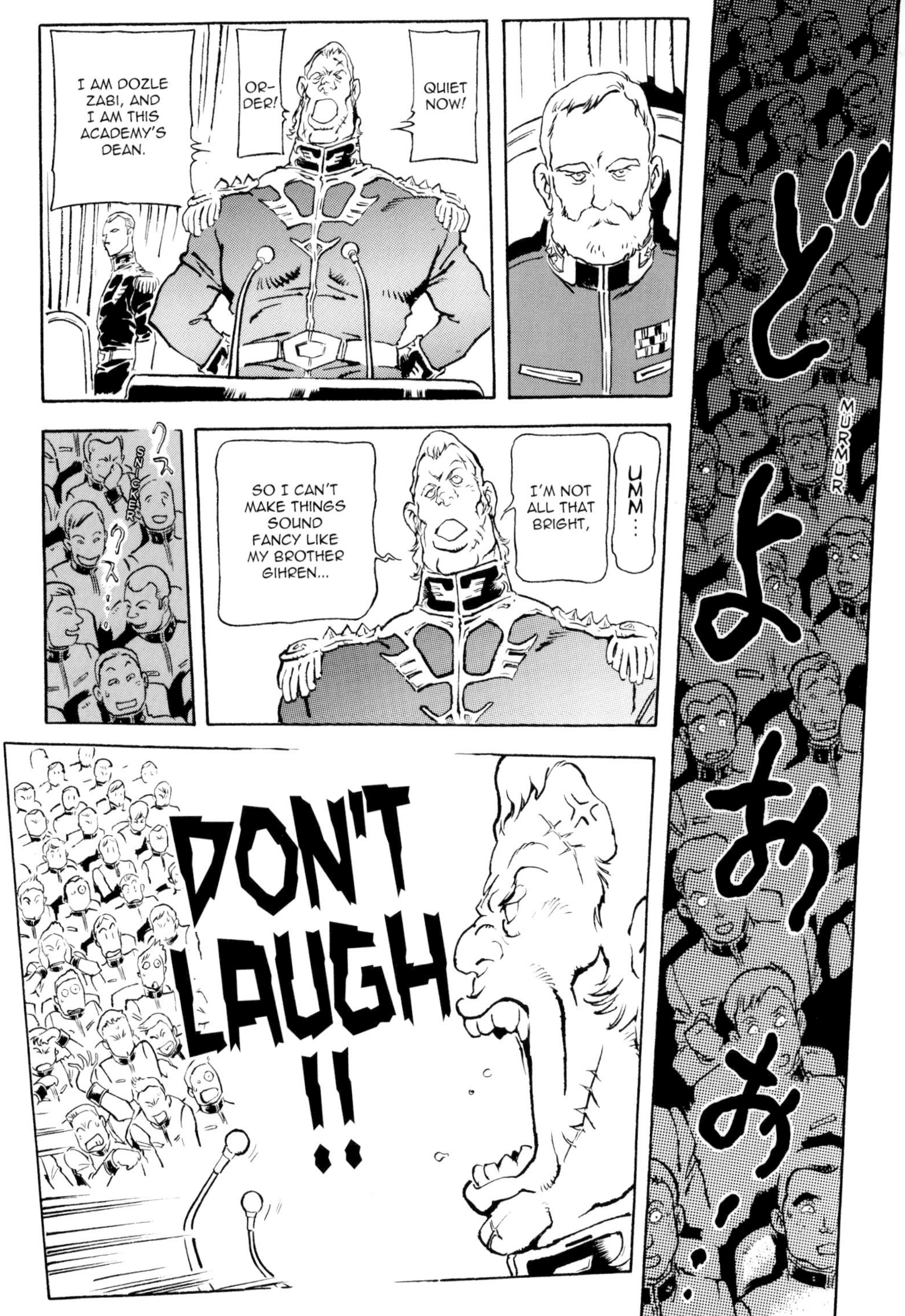
どよよあお…
MURMUR
QUIET NOW!
OR-DER!
I AM DOZLE ZABI, AND I AM THIS ACADEMY'S DEAN.
UMM...
I'M NOT ALL THAT BRIGHT,
SO I CAN'T MAKE THINGS SOUND FANCY LIKE MY BROTHER GIHREN...
クス
SNICKER
クス!!
DON'T LAUGH!!

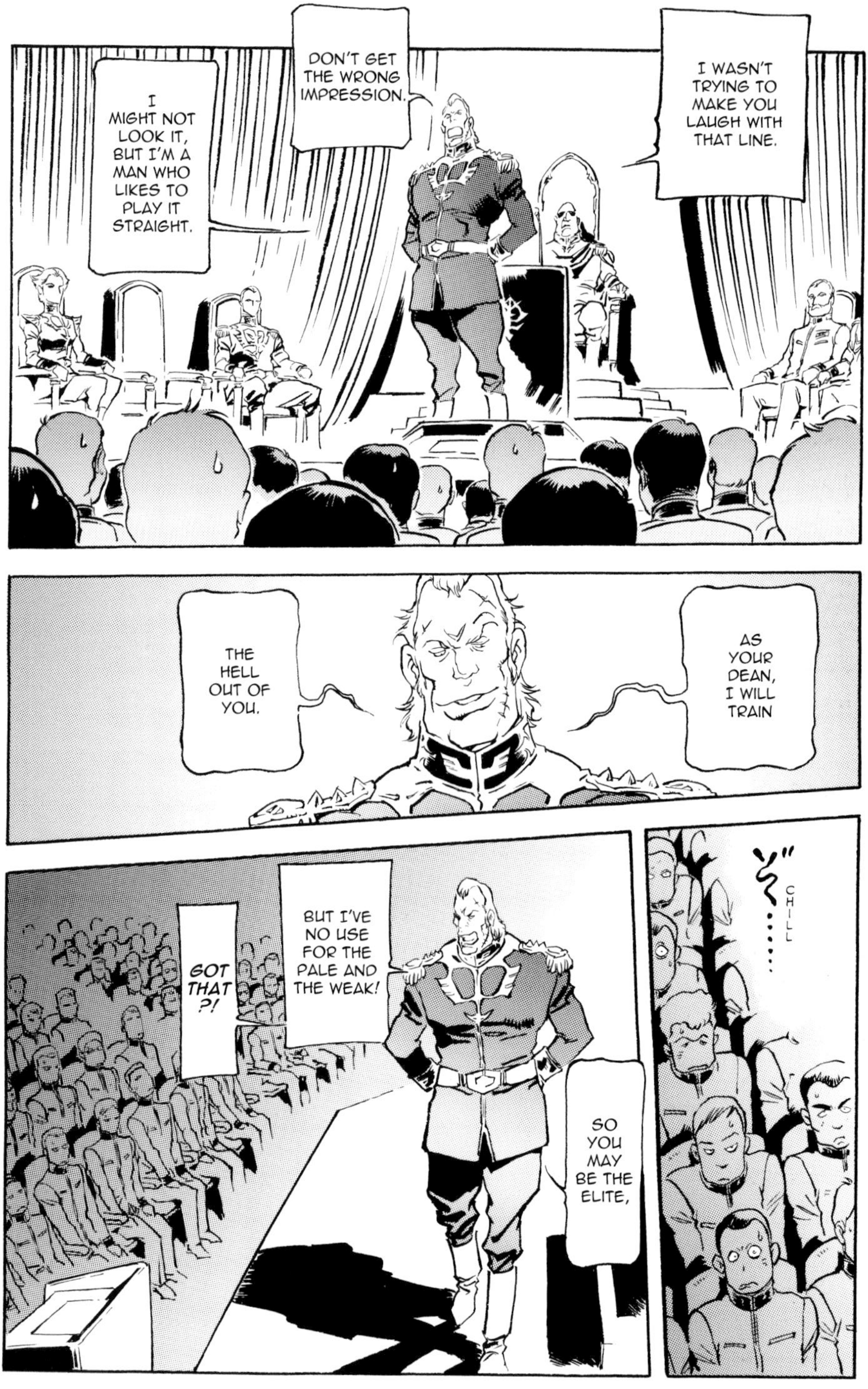
I WASN'T TRYING TO MAKE YOU LAUGH WITH THAT LINE.
DON'T GET THE WRONG IMPRESSION.
I MIGHT NOT LOOK IT, BUT I'M A MAN WHO LIKES TO PLAY IT STRAIGHT.
AS YOUR DEAN, I WILL TRAIN
THE HELL OUT OF YOU.
CHILL
SO YOU MAY BE THE ELITE,
BUT I'VE NO USE FOR THE PALE AND THE WEAK!
GOT THAT?!

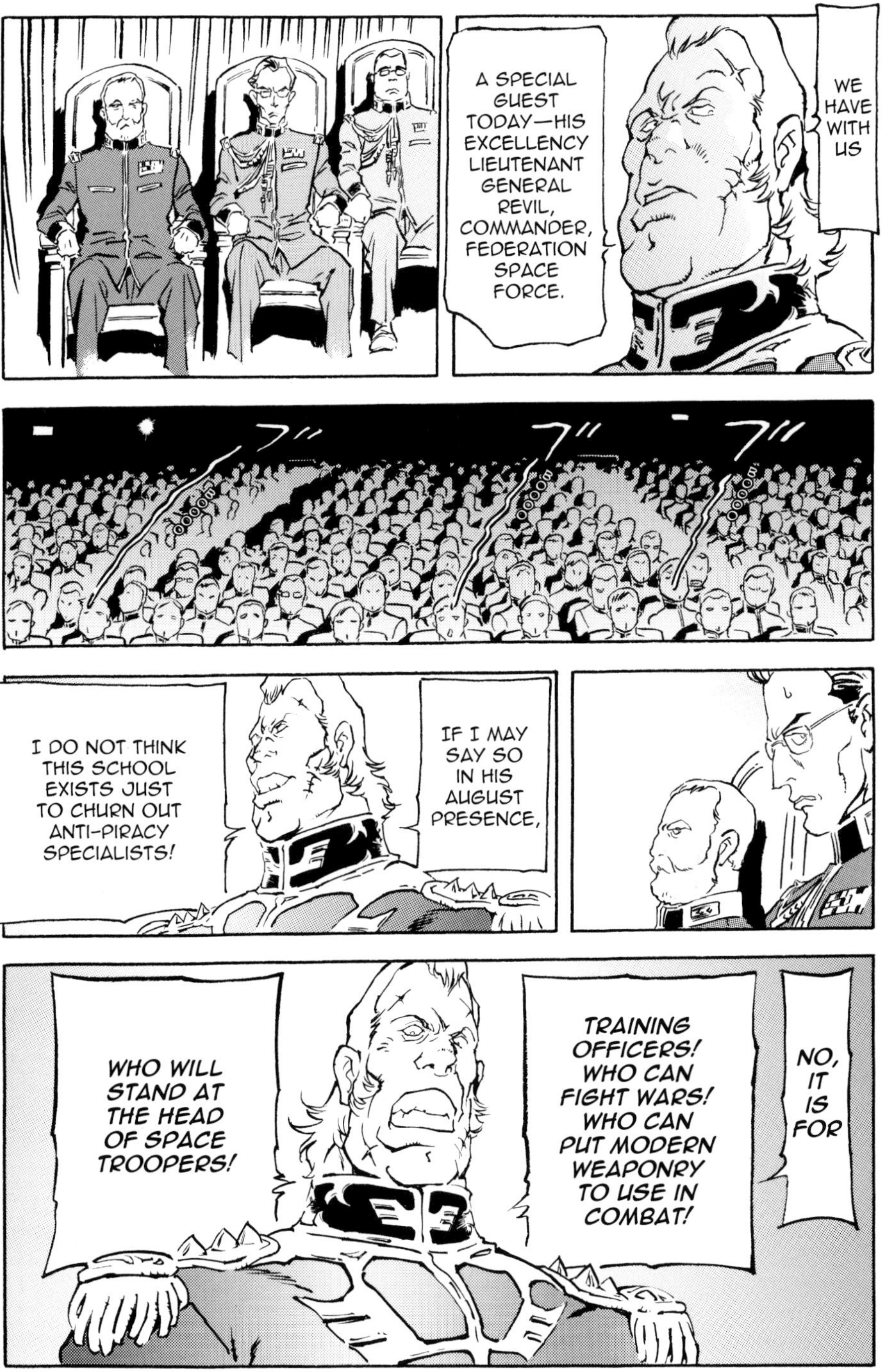
WE HAVE WITH US
A SPECIAL GUEST TODAY—HIS EXCELLENCY LIEUTENANT GENERAL REVIL, COMMANDER, FEDERATION SPACE FORCE.
WOOOOO
WOOOOO
WOOOOO
IF I MAY SAY SO IN HIS AUGUST PRESENCE,
I DO NOT THINK THIS SCHOOL EXISTS JUST TO CHURN OUT ANTI-PIRACY SPECIALISTS!
NO, IT IS FOR
TRAINING OFFICERS! WHO CAN FIGHT WARS! WHO CAN PUT MODERN WEAPONRY TO USE IN COMBAT!
WHO WILL STAND AT THE HEAD OF SPACE TROOPERS!

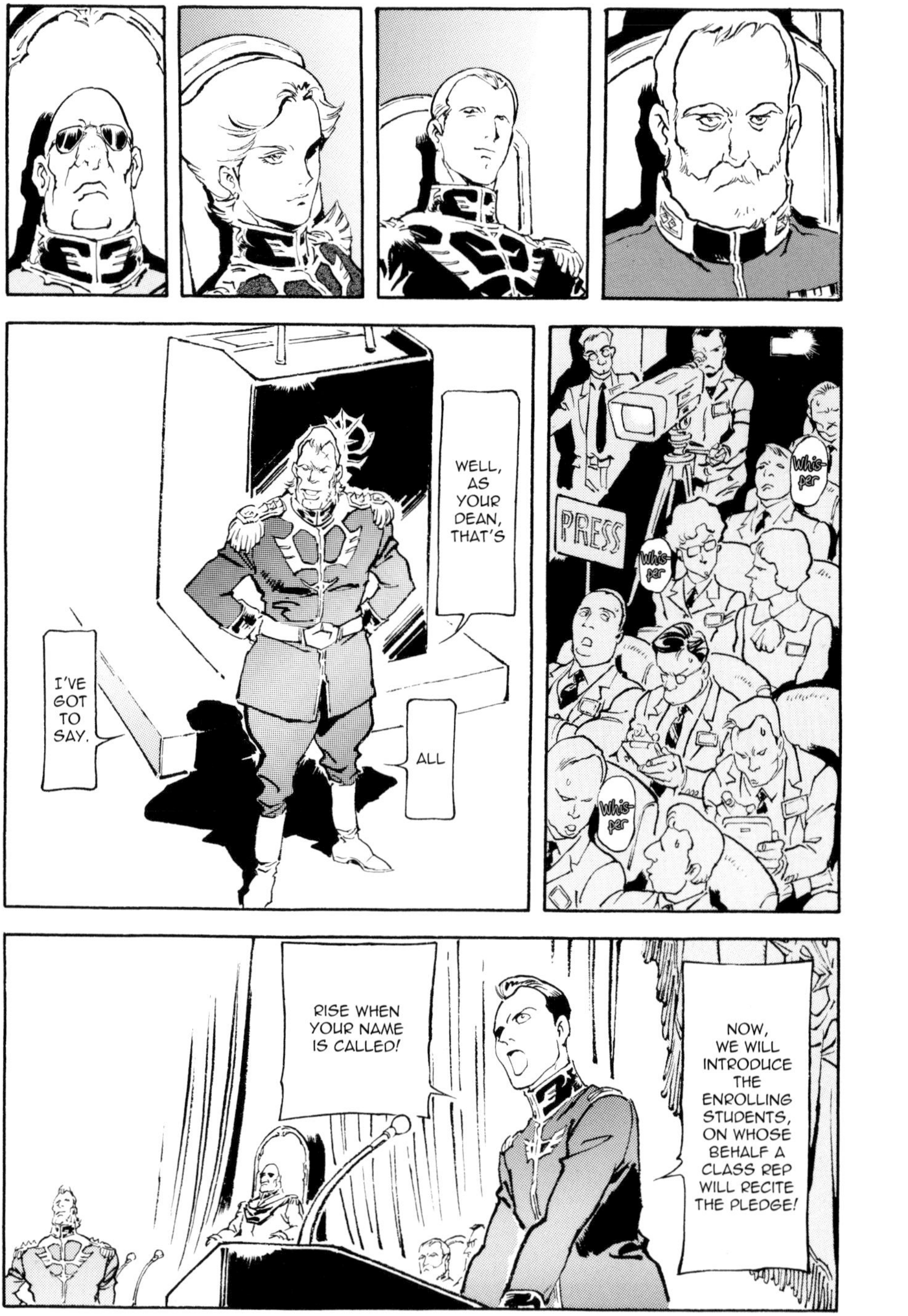
Whis-per
Whis-per
Whis-per
WELL, AS YOUR DEAN, THAT'S
ALL
I'VE GOT TO SAY.
NOW, WE WILL INTRODUCE THE ENROLLING STUDENTS, ON WHOSE BEHALF A CLASS REP WILL RECITE THE PLEDGE!
RISE WHEN YOUR NAME IS CALLED!

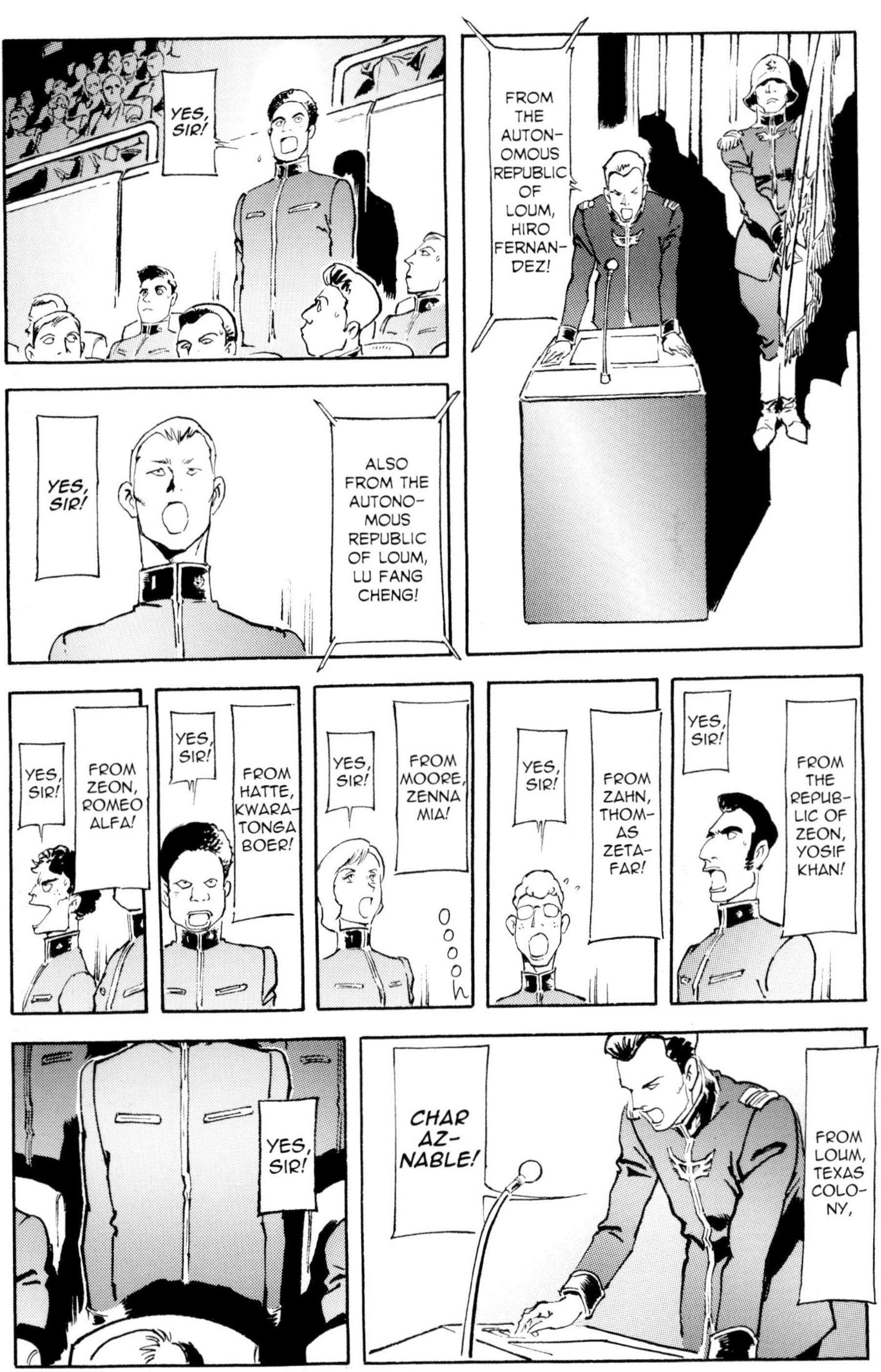
FROM THE AUTONOMOUS REPUBLIC OF LOUM, HIRO FERNANDEZ!
YES, SIR!
ALSO FROM THE AUTONOMOUS REPUBLIC OF LOUM, LU FANG CHENG!
YES, SIR!
FROM THE REPUBLIC OF ZEON, YOSIF KHAN!
YES, SIR!
FROM ZAHN, THOMAS ZETAFAR!
YES, SIR!
FROM MOORE, ZENNA MIA!
YES, SIR!
OOOOh
FROM HATTE, KWARATONGA BOER!
YES, SIR!
FROM ZEON, ROMEO ALFA!
YES, SIR!
FROM LOUM, TEXAS COLONY,
CHAR AZNABLE!
YES, SIR!

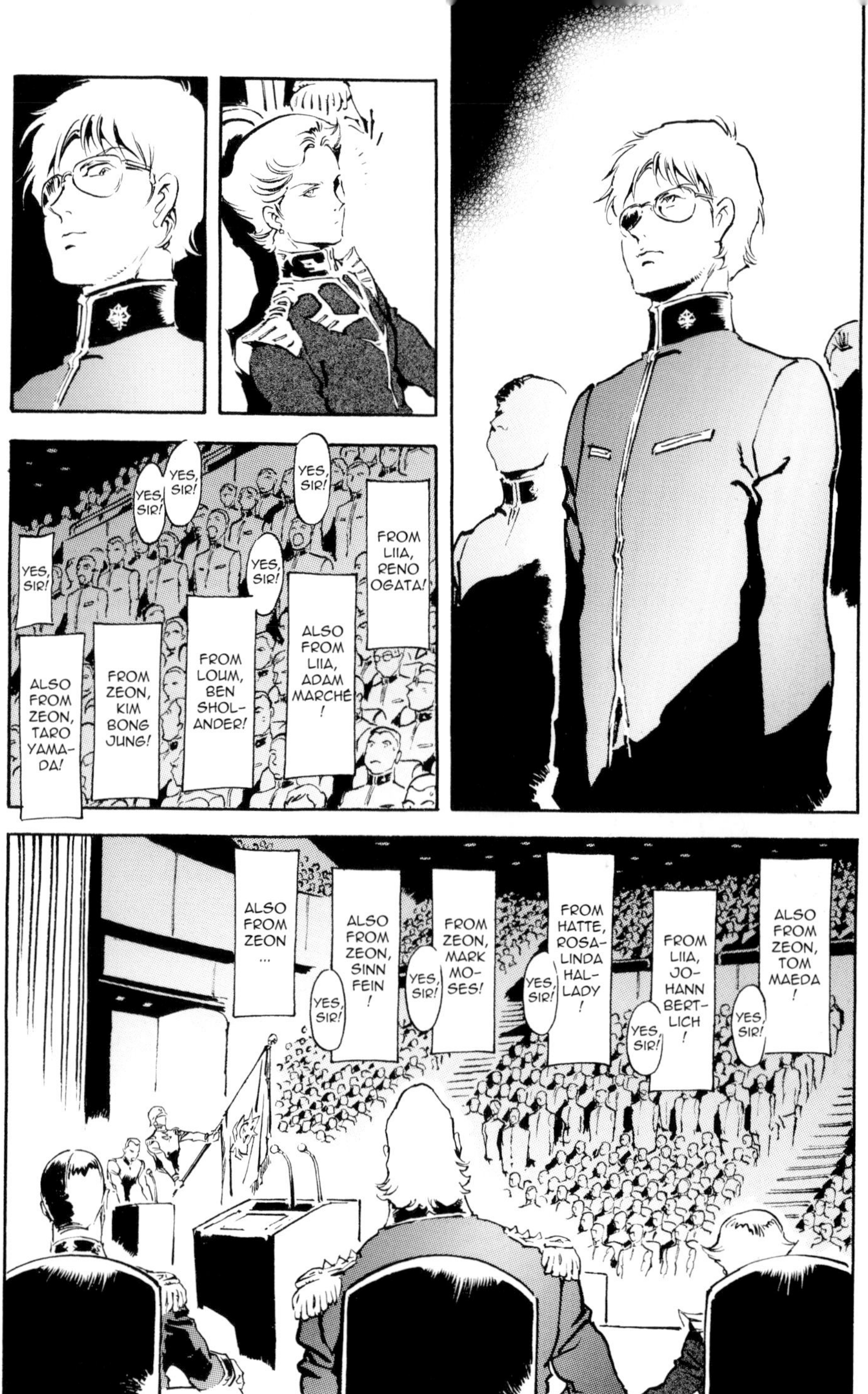
FROM LIIA, RENO OGATA!
YES, SIR!
ALSO FROM LIIA, ADAM MARCHÉ!
YES, SIR!
FROM LOUM, BEN SHOLANDER!
YES, SIR!
FROM ZEON, KIM BONG JUNG!
YES, SIR!
ALSO FROM ZEON, TARO YAMADA!
YES, SIR!
ALSO FROM ZEON, TOM MAEDA!
YES, SIR!
FROM LIIA, JOHANN BERTLICH!
YES, SIR!
FROM HATTE, ROSALINDA HALLADY!
YES, SIR!
FROM ZEON, MARK MOSES!
YES, SIR!
ALSO FROM ZEON, SINN FEIN!
YES, SIR!
ALSO FROM ZEON ...

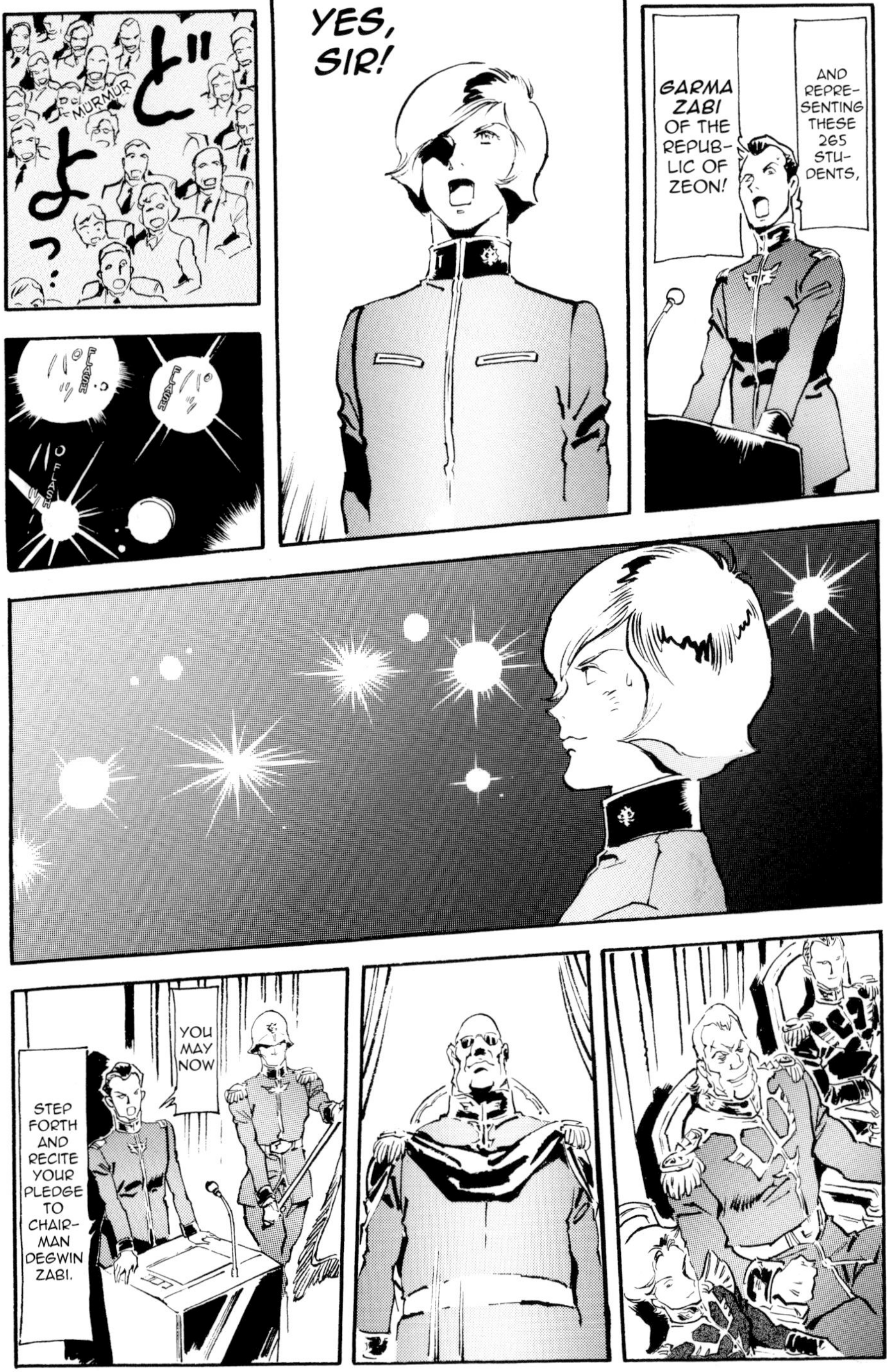
AND REPRESENTING THESE 265 STUDENTS,
GARMA ZABI OF THE REPUBLIC OF ZEON!
YES, SIR!
どよっ
MURMUR
FLASH
FLASH
FLASH
YOU MAY NOW
STEP FORTH AND RECITE YOUR PLEDGE TO CHAIRMAN DEGWIN ZABI.

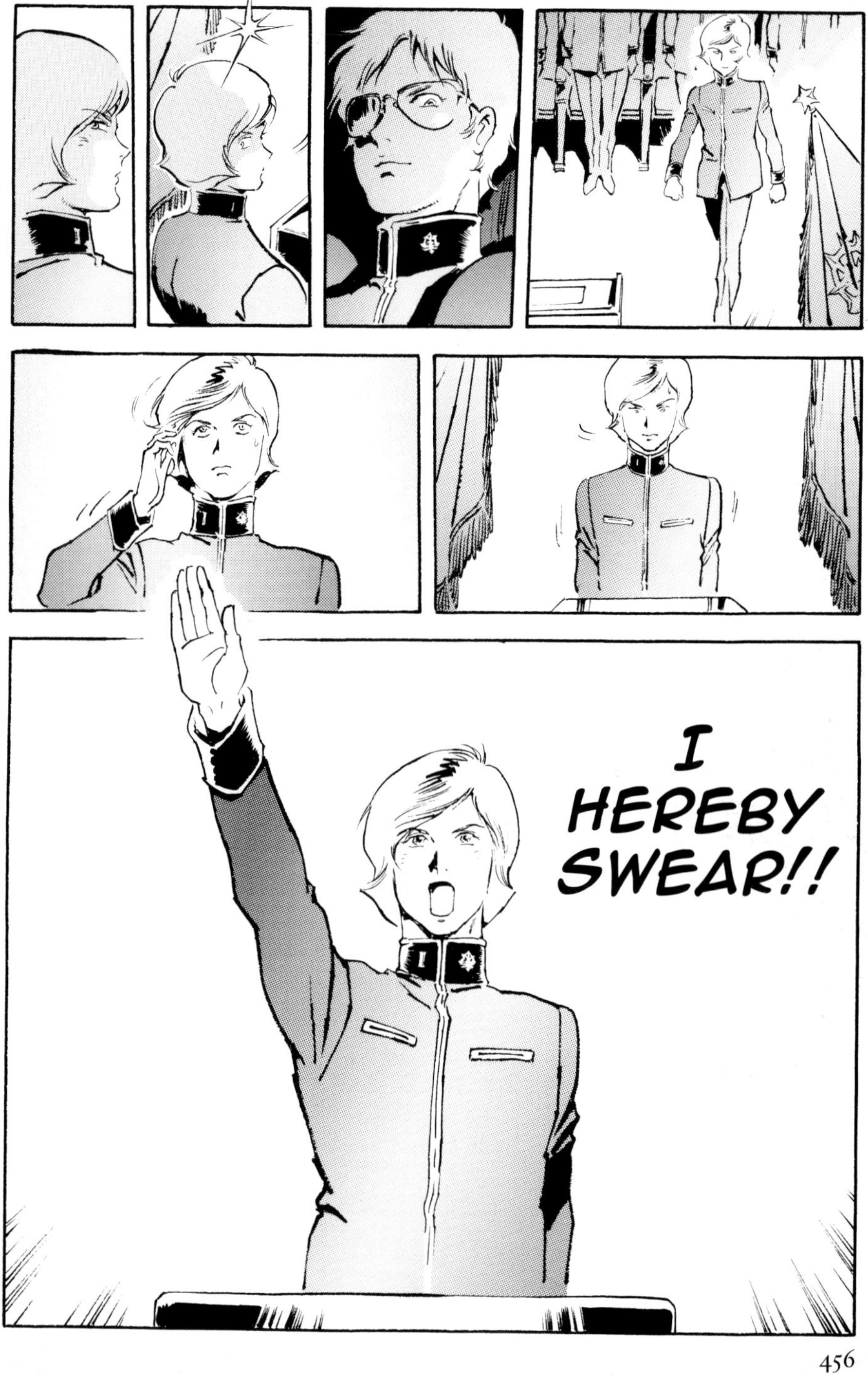
I HEREBY SWEAR!!

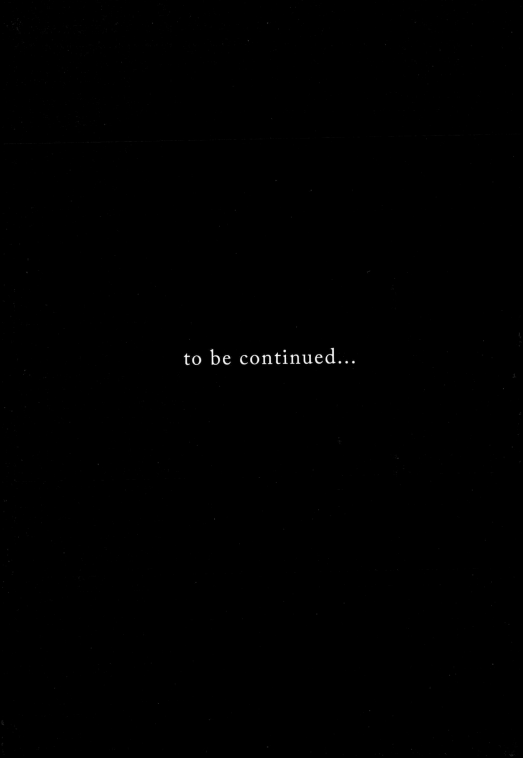

to be continued...

When this volume hits the shelves in June 2009, the serialization in *Gundam Ace* will be reaching the climax of the ferocious battle between the Gundam and Dozle's Big Zam. The telling in *The Origin* delineates Kycilia's calculations and, further in the shadows, Char's machinations behind the isolation of Solomon. Defeating the Gundam with his Gelgoog, revealing his intentions to Sayla upon seeing her again on Texas Colony, Char is a far more intense character than he was when the serialization launched. After having delved into the past subsequent to the Jaburo chapter, *The Origin* has gained an even richer fictional world.

But why were the three "Past" chapters beginning with *Char & Sayla* penned?

We'll let Mr. Yasuhiko answer that question in his own words.

—*Gundam Ace* Editorial Department

On the "Past" Arc

I'm not sure exactly when it first occurred to me that I wanted to write a "Past" arc for *Gundam*. I felt like doing so since "I don't know exactly when" is really the best answer I can manage. While that may be so, searching my mind I do concede that a few elements, though nothing decisive, served as catalysts. For one, there was the episode of the young officer Tachi.

He's unimpressive in the original story. After the manly Ramba Ral dies a warrior's death, Tachi appears at the widowed (?) Hamon's side and suggests that they take revenge, but he accomplishes little and meets an almost comically meaningless end by

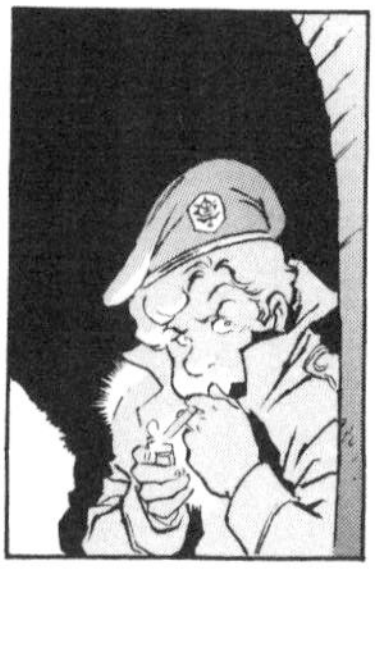

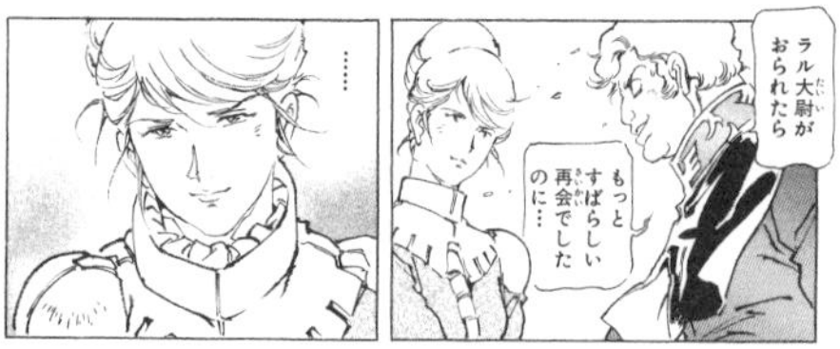
ラル大尉がおられたら
もっとすばらしい再会でしたのに…
……

way of friendly fire or something like that. Bearing a high-toned title ("Deep the Hatred of a Fierce Fight"), Episode 21 of the series is devoted to Hamon's demise and to the unique casualty among regular crew, Ryu Jose, so the fate of some side character among side characters called "Tachi" was "nobody's concern" at the time.

I still remember how, shortly before the episode took shape, Director Tomino said to me with a terribly serious look, "Yasuhiko. Sorry but I'm killing Ryu."

My reply: "Go ahead."

An unsettling exchange for any unsuspecting stranger overhearing us.

Of course, Director Tomino would come to perpetrate countless massacres in story, but at the time he was still approaching me gingerly about killing off a single character. Indeed, he worked on the storyboards for that episode himself, filling the last scene with the crew's laments over Ryu's passing…

When the time came to retell this in *The Origin*, something about the mourning scene bothered me. I decided to take a fresh look at the Tomino-edited cinematic release, and what do you know, we get a fistfight between Amuro and Hayato instead. This is correct as Ryu's death is not the episode's true focus.

Then what is? Hamon's death, of course. It can't be anything else (apologies to Ryu).

When Ramba Ral gets the short straw of having to avenge Garma, Hamon follows him, ready to share any fate that might befall her lover, but she understands better than anyone the foolishness of the mission. Rushing to avenge Ral after losing him to a foolish battle is like doubling down on folly; it's a self-destructive, headlong charge that will wipe the slate clean via death. From the outset she has absolutely no desire to win and live on.

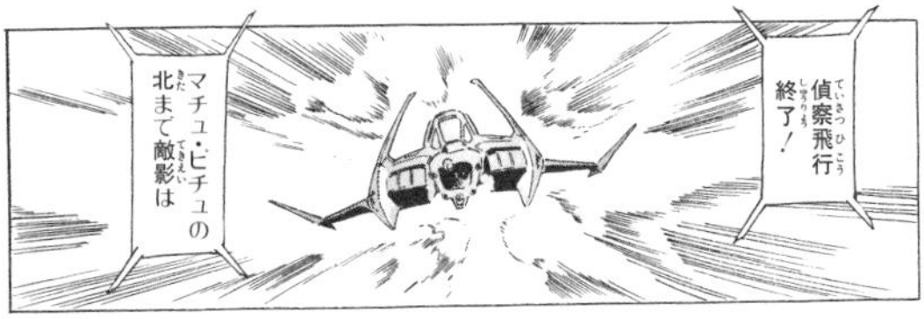
偵察飛行終了！
マチュ・ピチュの北まで敵影は

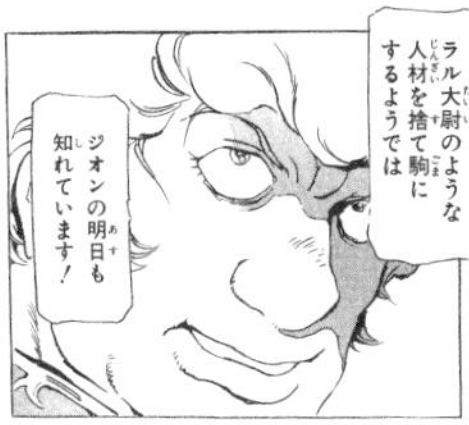
ラル大尉のような人材を捨て駒にするようでは
ジオンの明日も知れています！

Humbly offering her suicide mission what little aid he can render, the epitome of folly, is "Lieutenant (Junior Grade) Tachi."

What is with this guy? I had to ask myself about the bit player who'd failed to snag my attention during the original anime production. No way he was just a guest character, there and gone in one episode. To Ral and Hamon, he was no mere stranger. He couldn't be.

A man in a love triangle who stands no chance against the other fellow but who won't stop burning with unreciprocated adulation is not that rare of a creature. That sort of man tends to know his place to a curious degree and might keep on gazing at his unattainable muse from a distance. It must be painful. Yet, perhaps because he's able to accept that pain as though it were something sweet, he actually weathers the long haul that is unrequited love fairly well.

For the lady's true love, this other man is often nothing but an unwanted presence. The guy almost seems like a stalker, and besides, it's just annoying. The beau might tell the lady to do something about the loser, but being woman enough, which is why several men are falling for her, she won't coldly tell off the fellow, not quite.

Hamon is exactly that type of woman. Large-hearted ladies like her frequently go for foolishly upright men precisely because the men are foolishly upright. Thus Hamon and Ral end up as a couple as a matter of course.

Upon hearing of Ral's violent end, Tachi must have leapt with joy. How, wasting no time (taking with him shabby secondhand armaments), he must have chased after Hamon. Not to seize the opportunity to become her true love, but rather, as a luckless lonely-hearted male living out his unrequited love by dying for dear Hamon…

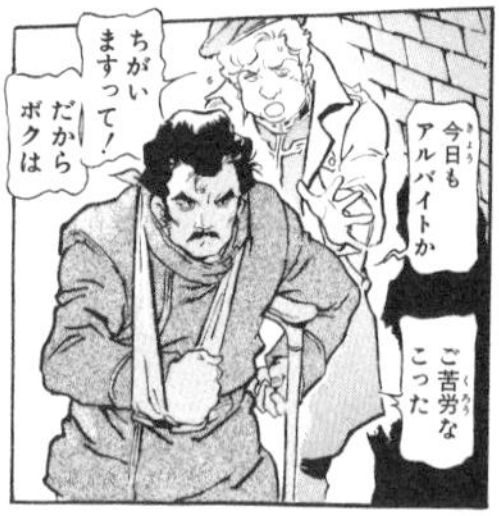
今日もアルバイトか
ちがいますって！
だからボクは
ご苦労なこった

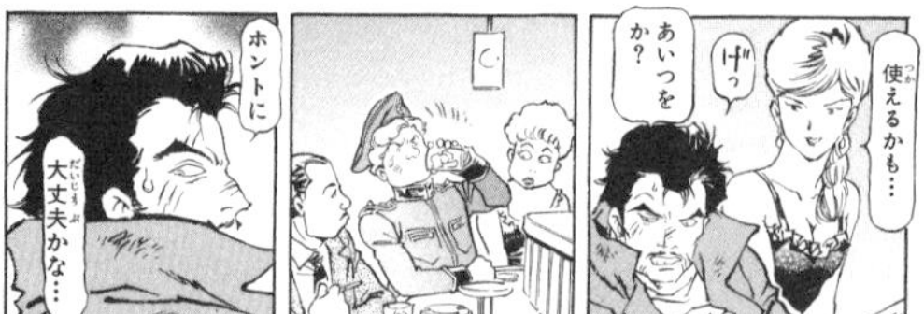
使えるかも…
げっ
あいつをか？
ホントに
大丈夫かな…

The characterizations in *Gundam* are full of little bits that entice the imagination. Many had already pointed out that facet as being indicative of the depth of "First *Gundam*," but I began to think more and more strongly that a large part of its "depth" belongs to its "pre-story." Tachi's presence, unremarkable at first sight, was no doubt one of the factors that stirred me to wade into that pre-story.

I'll bring up another.

Aiming the Magella Top's cannon squarely at the Gundam's back, Hamon pronounces a famous line: "I… really did like you, kid."

It's a fine line as befits a mature woman, but it's not uttered in triumph, because as I mentioned, Hamon has no wish to go on living in a world without Ral.

She must roughly mean, "Be a good boy and die with me." But I didn't want Hamon, with all her life experience, to be embracing death as Amuro's equal. I therefore inserted some new text before the line to showcase her pride as a woman who has lived and loved:

"You have no idea, do you?! You've only lived for fifteen years or so!"

"The life Ral and I had was so much richer than yours! And the one who ended it, kid, was you!"

Perhaps when she says this, she also has a fleeting thought for the unrequited love that Tachi, killed moments before, continued to bear for her. I do believe that by the time I wrote those lines, my desire to pen a "Past" arc was quite strong.

Yoshikazu Yasuhiko

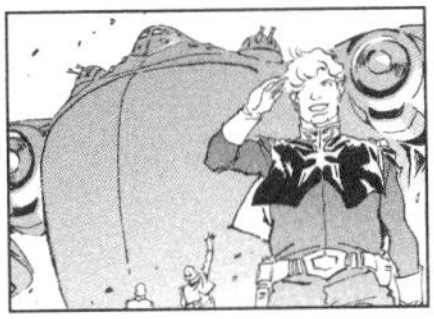

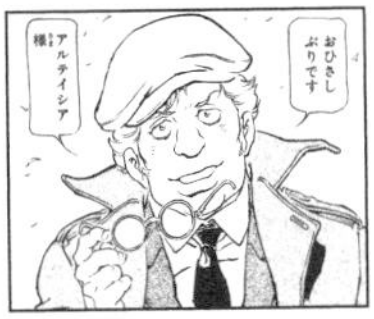
おひさしぶりです
アルテイシア様

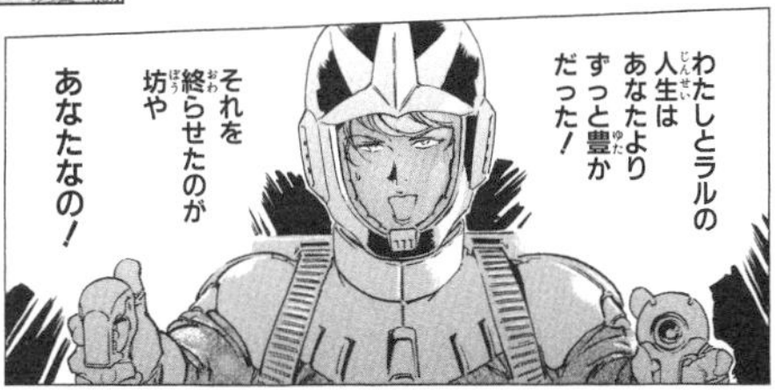
わたしとラルの人生はあなたよりずっと豊かだった！
それを終らせたのが坊やあなたなの！

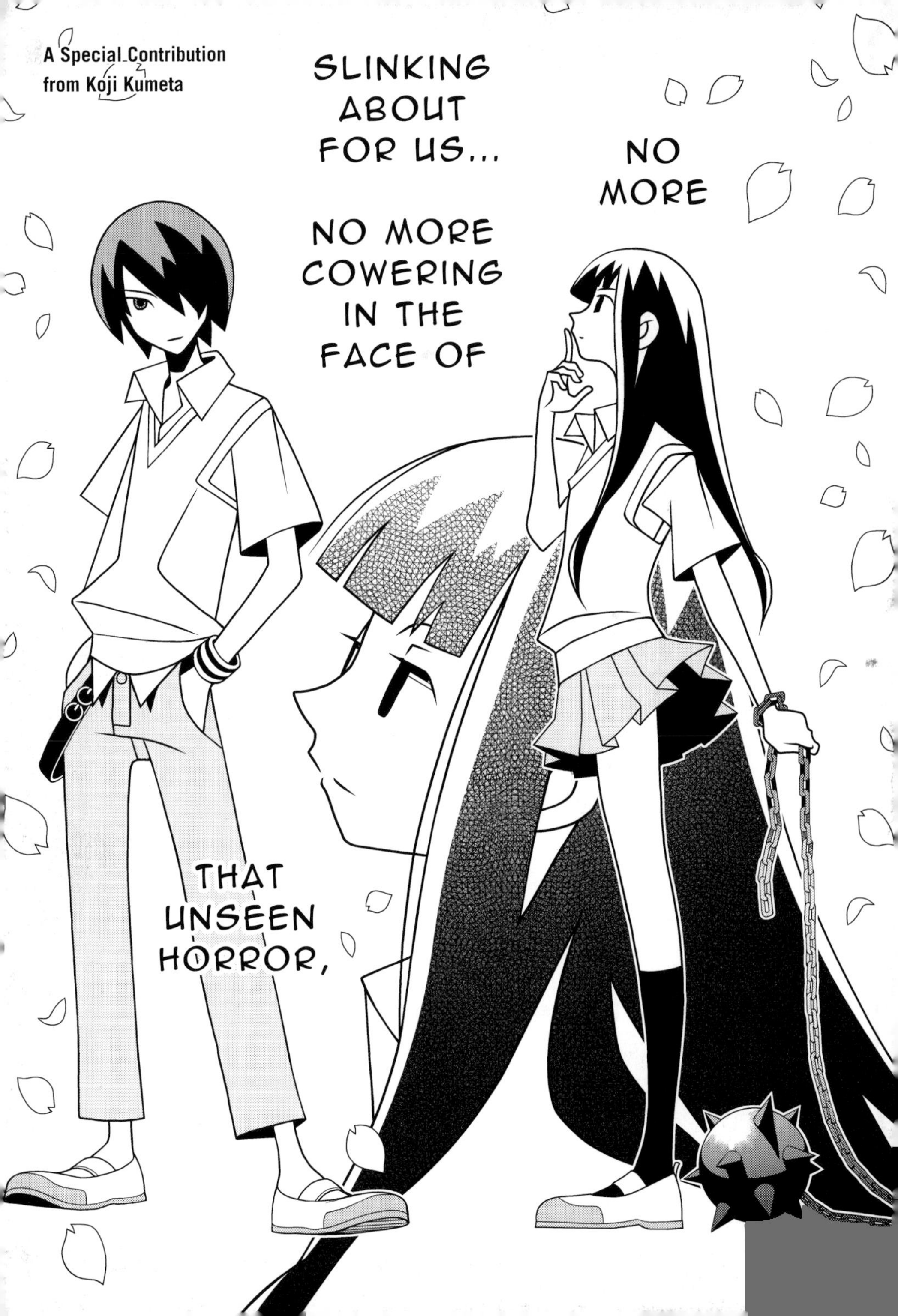
A Special Contribution from Koji Kumeta
NO MORE
SLINKING ABOUT FOR US...
NO MORE COWERING IN THE FACE OF
THAT UNSEEN HORROR,

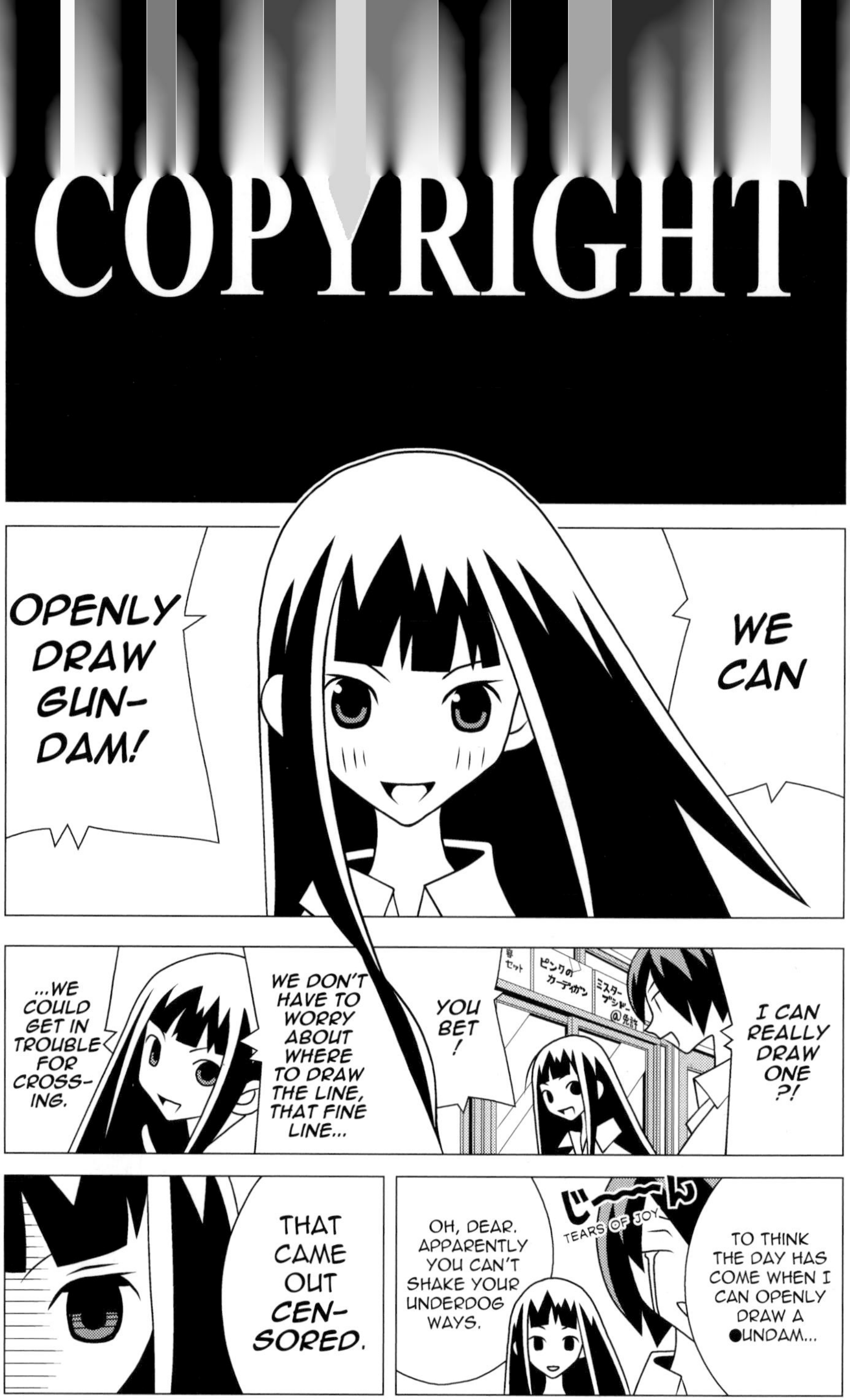

COPYRIGHT
WE CAN
OPENLY DRAW GUN-DAM!
I CAN REALLY DRAW ONE ?!
YOU BET!
WE DON'T HAVE TO WORRY ABOUT WHERE TO DRAW THE LINE, THAT FINE LINE...
...WE COULD GET IN TROUBLE FOR CROSSING.
TO THINK THE DAY HAS COME WHEN I CAN OPENLY DRAW A ●UNDAM...
じーーん
TEARS OF JOY
OH, DEAR. APPARENTLY YOU CAN'T SHAKE YOUR UNDERDOG WAYS.
THAT CAME OUT CEN-SORED.

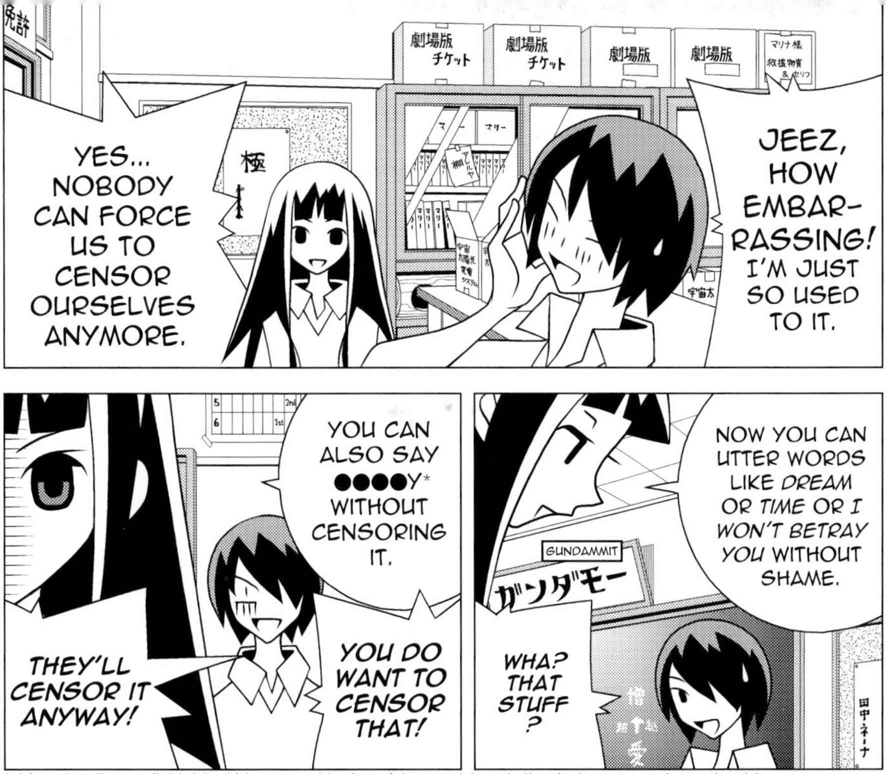

JEEZ, HOW EMBARRASSING! I'M JUST SO USED TO IT.
YES... NOBODY CAN FORCE US TO CENSOR OURSELVES ANYMORE.
NOW YOU CAN UTTER WORDS LIKE *DREAM* OR *TIME* OR *I WON'T BETRAY YOU* WITHOUT SHAME.
GUNDAMMIT
ガンダモー
WHA? THAT STUFF?
YOU CAN ALSO SAY ●●●●Y* WITHOUT CENSORING IT.
YOU DO WANT TO CENSOR THAT!
THEY'LL CENSOR IT ANYWAY!

* Meaning "crazy," *kichigai* (rhymes with *Aggai*) is considered discriminatory and unprintable.

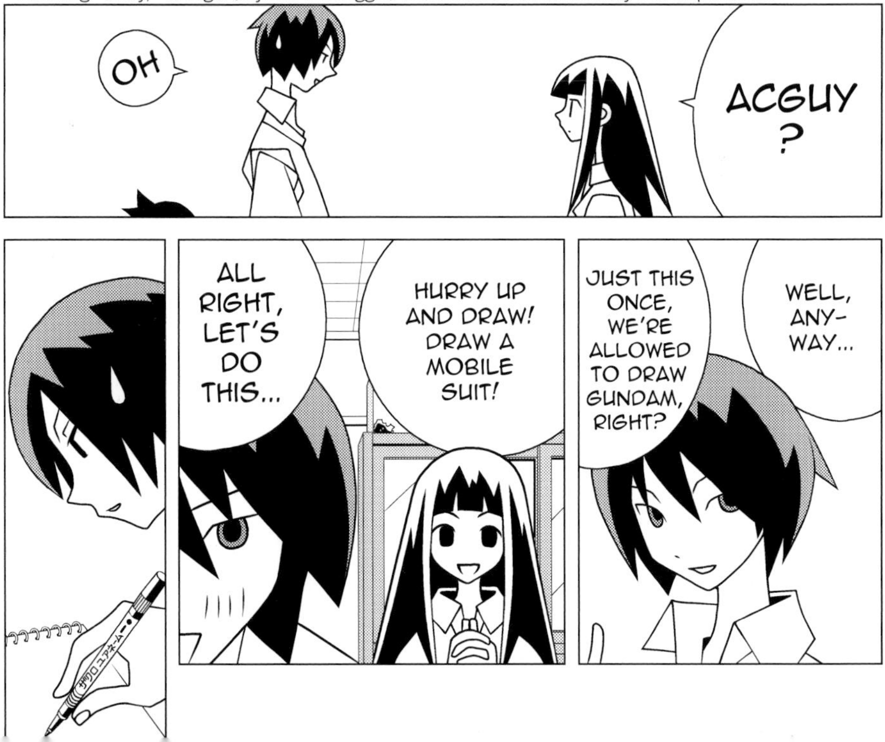

ACGUY?
OH
WELL, ANYWAY...
JUST THIS ONCE, WE'RE ALLOWED TO DRAW GUNDAM, RIGHT?
HURRY UP AND DRAW! DRAW A MOBILE SUIT!
ALL RIGHT, LET'S DO THIS...

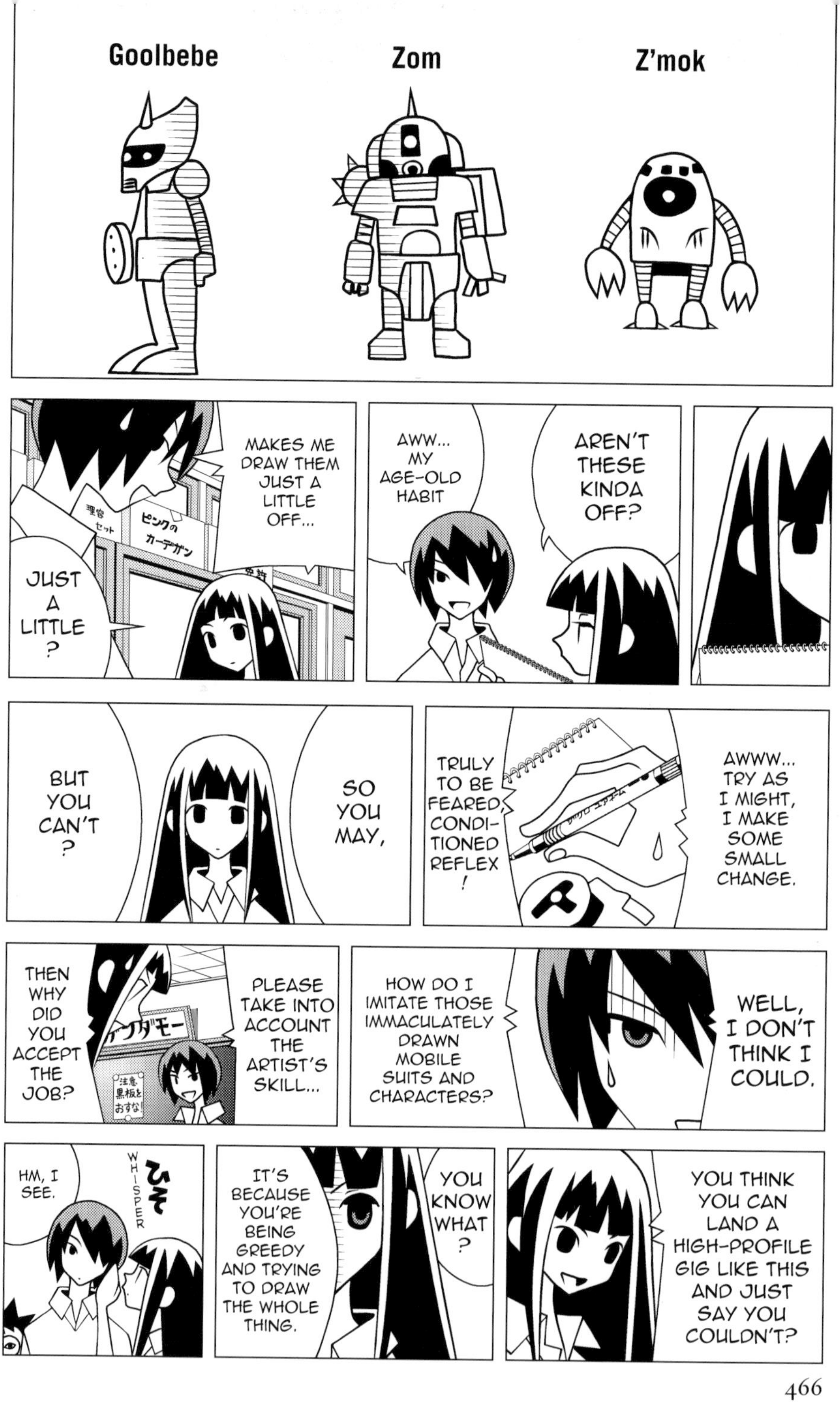
Goolbebe
Zom
Z'mok
AREN'T THESE KINDA OFF?
AWW... MY AGE-OLD HABIT
MAKES ME DRAW THEM JUST A LITTLE OFF...
理容セット
ピンクのカーデガン
JUST A LITTLE ?
AWWW... TRY AS I MIGHT, I MAKE SOME SMALL CHANGE.
TRULY TO BE FEARED, CONDITIONED REFLEX !
SO YOU MAY,
BUT YOU CAN'T ?
WELL, I DON'T THINK I COULD.
HOW DO I IMITATE THOSE IMMACULATELY DRAWN MOBILE SUITS AND CHARACTERS?
PLEASE TAKE INTO ACCOUNT THE ARTIST'S SKILL...
THEN WHY DID YOU ACCEPT THE JOB?
注意 黒板をおすな!
YOU THINK YOU CAN LAND A HIGH-PROFILE GIG LIKE THIS AND JUST SAY YOU COULDN'T?
YOU KNOW WHAT ?
IT'S BECAUSE YOU'RE BEING GREEDY AND TRYING TO DRAW THE WHOLE THING.
ひそ
WHISPER
HM, I SEE.

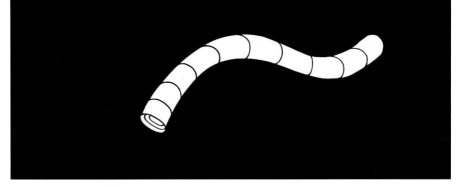

A ZAKU!
THAT IS A ZAKU.
RIGHT, THE WHOLE THING IS TOO MUCH FOR YOU,
BUT YOU CAN DRAW PARTS, CAN'T YOU?
WE'LL JUST HAVE TO DO IT THIS WAY.
IT'S LIKE SPECIAL EFFECTS ON A LOW BUDGET.
LIKE NOT SHOWING THE ENTIRE MONSTER BECAUSE IT'LL LOOK SO CHEAP.
THIS WAY, I CAN EVEN DRAW CHARACTERS!
IT'S LIKE SOME KIND OF QUIZ AT THIS POINT.
①
②
③
AND NOW, HERE'S A QUESTION FOR YOU!
BASED ON WHAT YOU SEE, CAN YOU NAME THE CHARACTER?!

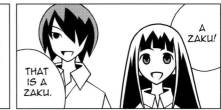

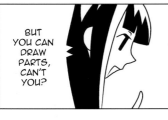

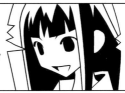

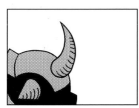

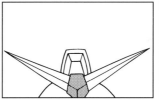

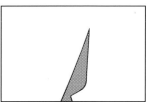

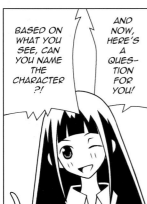

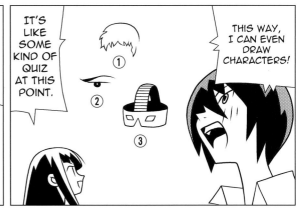

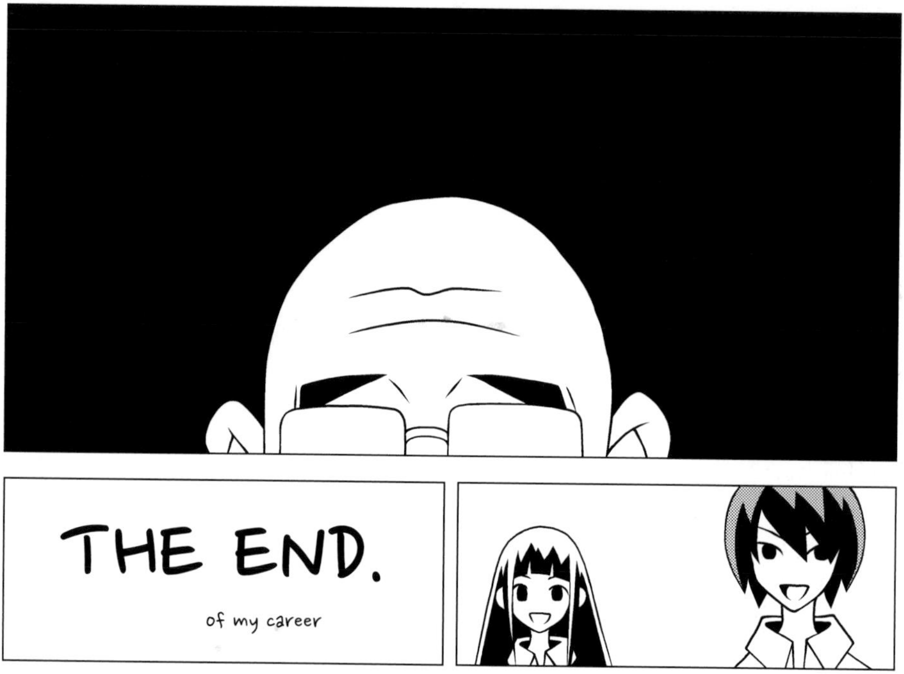
THE END.
of my career

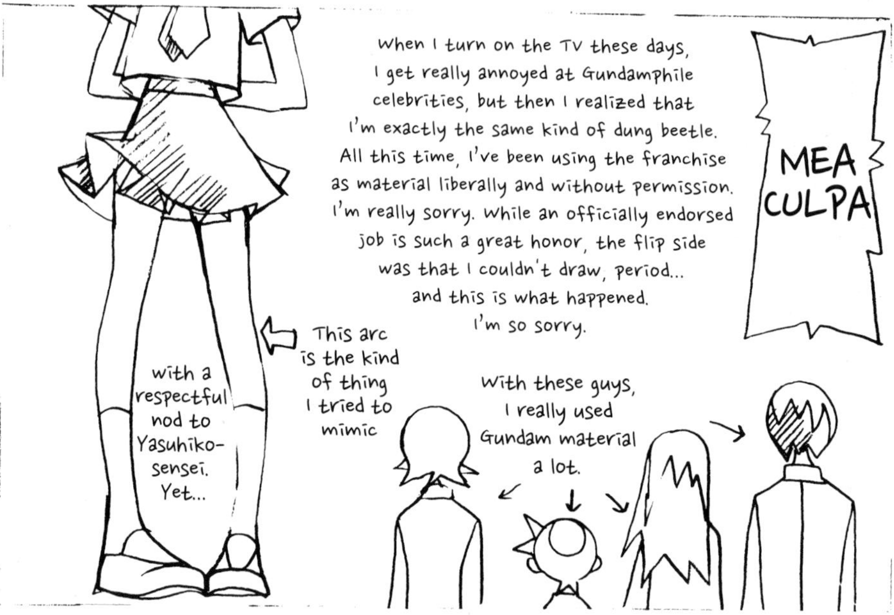
MEA CULPA
When I turn on the TV these days, I get really annoyed at Gundamphile celebrities, but then I realized that I'm exactly the same kind of dung beetle. All this time, I've been using the franchise as material liberally and without permission. I'm really sorry. While an officially endorsed job is such a great honor, the flip side was that I couldn't draw, period... and this is what happened. I'm so sorry.
With these guys, I really used Gundam material a lot.
This arc is the kind of thing I tried to mimic
with a respectful nod to Yasuhiko-sensei. Yet...

Koji Kumeta

A manga artist popular for his unique drawing style and
individual perspective, he counts *Katte ni Kaizo* and
Sayonara Zetsubo-Sensei among a bevy of signature works.
Yasuhiko and Kumeta are hardly strangers—for instance,
Kumeta contributed an illustrated recommendation for
Yasuhiko's *Odo no Inu* (Hakusensha edition), and
Yasuhiko drew an original end card for the anime *Zoku
Sayonara Zetsubo-Sensei*.

CASVAL, LIVING AS CHAR

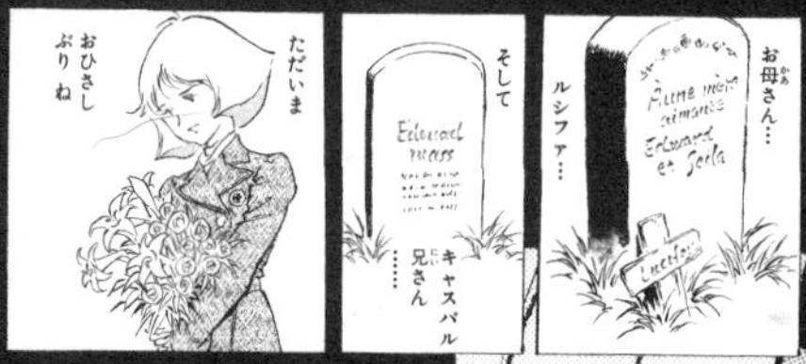
お母さん…
ルシファ…
そして
キャスバル兄さん……
ただいま
おひさしぶりね

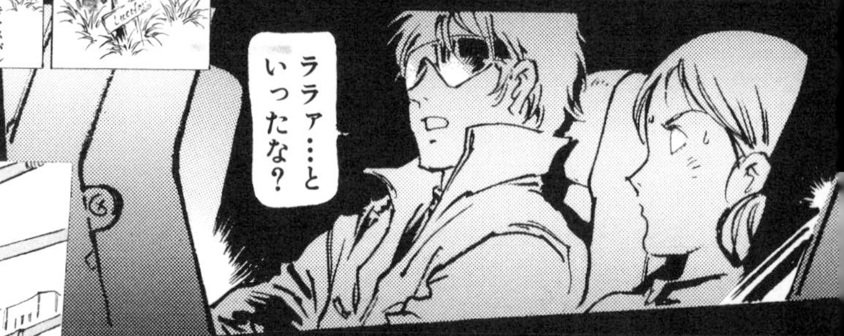
ララァ…といったな？

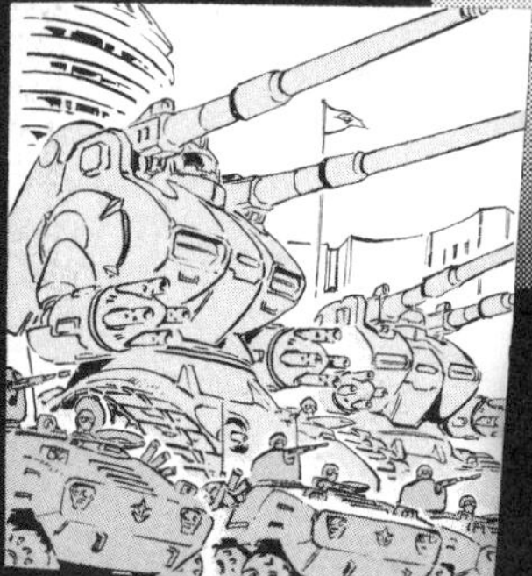

SHARPENING CONFLICT

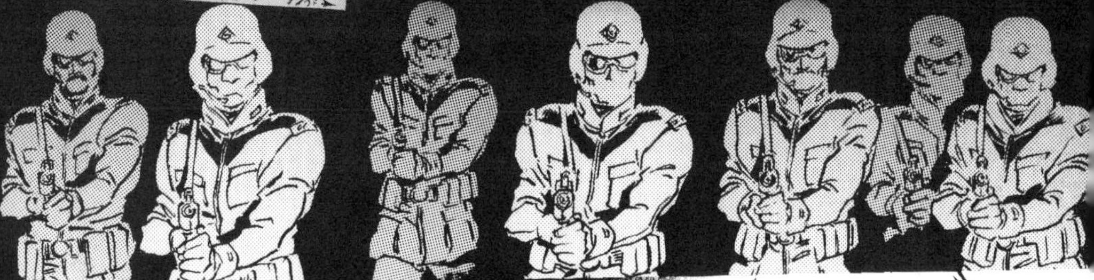

ENTWINED FATES

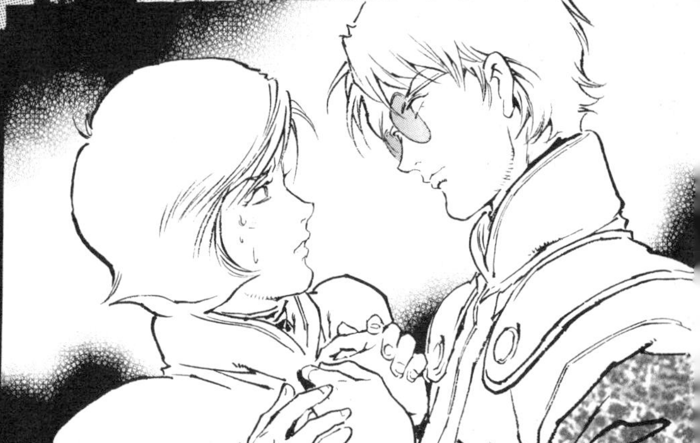

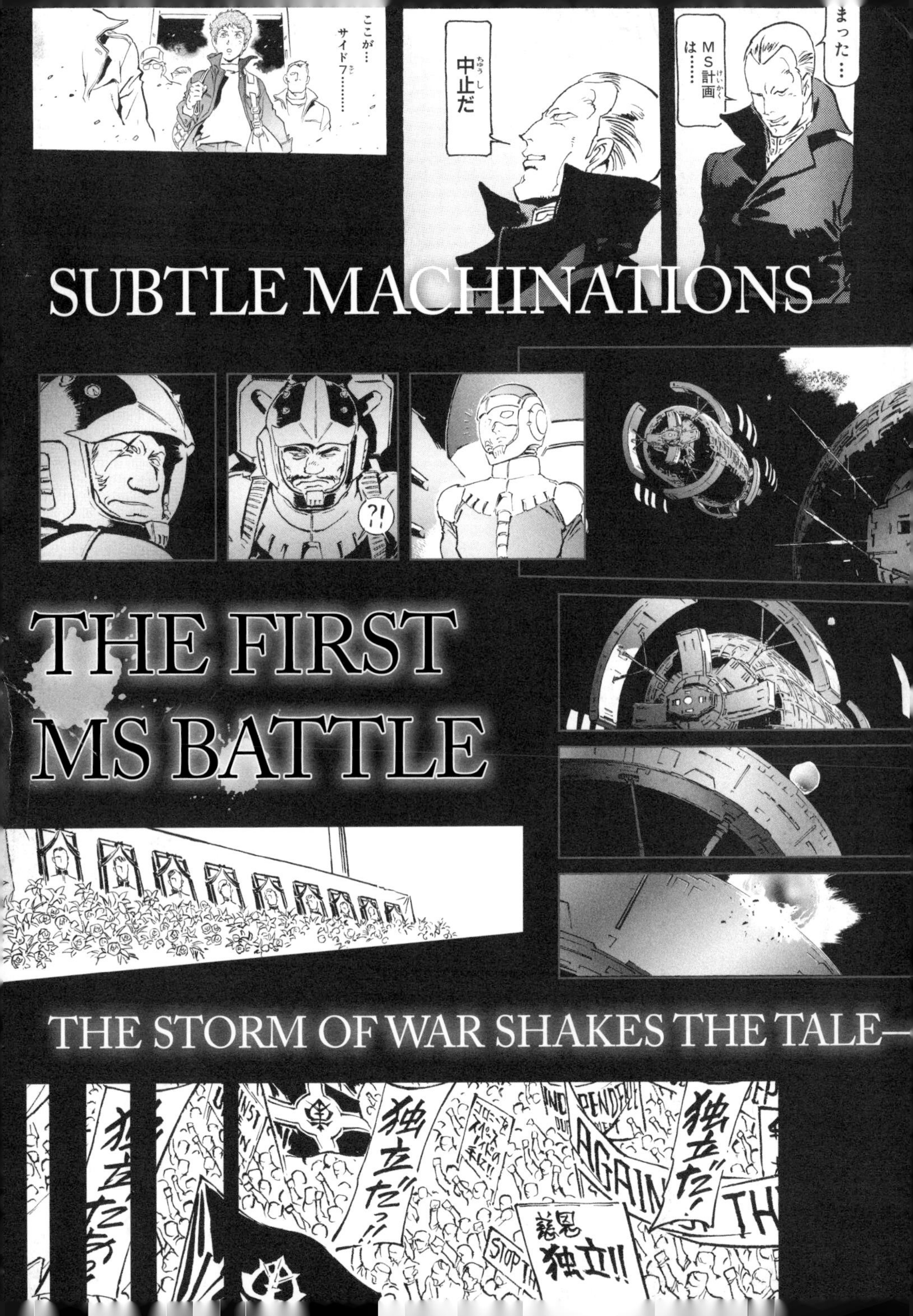

まった…
MS計画は……
中止だ
ここが…
サイド7………
SUBTLE MACHINATIONS
?!
THE FIRST MS BATTLE
THE STORM OF WAR SHAKES THE TALE—
独立だ!
AGAIN
独立だっ!!
独立!!

AIZOUBAN MOBILE SUIT GUNDAM THE ORIGIN vol. 5

Translation: Melissa Tanaka

Production: Grace Lu
Hiroko Mizuno
Anthony Quintessenza

© Yoshikazu YASUHIKO 2009, 2012

© SOTSU • SUNRISE

Edited by KADOKAWA SHOTEN
First published in Japan in 2009, 2012 by KADOKAWA CORPORATION, Tokyo

English translation rights arranged with KADOKAWA CORPORATION,
through Tuttle-Mori Agency, Inc., Tokyo

Translation copyright © 2014 Vertical, Inc.

Published by Vertical, Inc., New York

Originally published in Japanese as *Kidou Senshi Gundam THE ORIGIN*
volumes 9 and 10 in 2005 and re-issued in hardcover as *Aizouban Kidou Senshi Gundam
THE ORIGIN V -Shaa • Seira-* in 2009, by Kadokawa Shoten, Co., Ltd.

Kidou Senshi Gundam THE ORIGIN first serialized in *Gundam Ace,*
Kadokawa Shoten, Co., Ltd., 2001-2011

Tears Of Joy
Words and Music by Michael Jerome Powell, Terry Lewis,
James Harris III, Karyn White and Vernon Fails
Copyright © 1991 EMI Virgin Songs, Inc., EMI April Music Inc., Crystal Rose Music,
Flyte Tyme Tunes Inc., King's Kid Music and Del Von Music Inc.
All Rights on behalf of EMI Virgin Songs, Inc., EMI April Music Inc., Crystal Rose Music
and Flyte Time Tunes Inc. Administered by Sony/ATV Music Publishing LLC,
8 Music Square West, Nashville, TN 37203
International Copyright Secured All Rights Reserved
Reprinted by Permission of Hal Leonard Corporation

ISBN: 978-1-939130-19-8

Manufactured in the United States of America

First Edition

Vertical, Inc.
451 Park Avenue South
7th Floor
New York, NY 10016
www.vertical-inc.com